ENCYCLOPEDIA OF JAPANESE MARTIAL ARTS

Photograph by Pat Lineberger

ENCYCLOPEDIA OF JAPANESE MARTIAL ARTS

David A. Hall

KODANSHA USA

Special thanks to Irie Kōhei, Omiya Shirō and Koike Masaru for their assistance in reviewing the original manuscript.

Edited in cooperation with Musashi Editorial Ltd., and Katherine S. Heins.
Designed by Point & Line Co.,Ltd.

Published by Kodansha USA, Inc.
451 Park Avenue South
New York, NY 10016

Distributed in the United Kingdom and continental Europe by Kodansha Europe, Ltd.

Printed in China.
Toppan Printing Co., Ltd.
ISBN: 978-1-56836-410-0
First edition, 2012
19 18 17 16 15 14 13 10 9 8 7 6 5 4 3 2 1

www.kodanshausa.com

Library of Congress Cataloging-in-Publication Data

Hall, David A.
Encyclopedia of Japanese martial arts/David A. Hall.
p. cm.

Summary: "This authoritative and comprehensive encyclopedia is an invaluable resource for martial artists of all levels, scholars, researchers, institutions, and anyone interested In Japanese history and culture"— Provided by publisher.

ISBN 978-1-56836-410-0 (hardback)
1. Martial arts–Japan–Encyclopedias. I. Title.

GV1100.77.A2H34 2012
796.815–dc23 2012028991

To Margie
who has supported my efforts in this endeavor
for over 25 years

In memory of

Donn F. Draeger (1922–1982)

CONTENTS

Foreword

The *Encyclopedia of Japanese Martial Arts* (武道事典) is the first work of its kind to explore the vast subject of Japanese martial culture. Dr. David A. Hall bases his extensive insight into Japanese language, history, culture and religion on more than four decades of research into Japanese religious and military practices, and his own training in classical Japanese martial arts (*koryū bujutsu*) and modern martial disciplines (*budō*).

The *Encyclopedia of Japanese Martial Arts* provides in-depth insight into the arms, armor, ethos, and fighting systems developed by the classical Japanese warrior. This work will be invaluable to students and practitioners of classical and modern martial systems, researchers, scholars, and anyone with a serious interest in Japanese and Asian martial culture.

It is my great personal honor to have known Dr. Hall for many years. The *Encyclopedia of Japanese Martial Arts* will undoubtedly set the standard for research in this field. We welcome the publication of this outstanding work.

John F. Quinn
Director
Masaki Ryū Bujutsu Kenkyūkai

ACKNOWLEDGMENTS

There are many people to whom I am indebted for providing invaluable information and assistance over the past forty-five years for this publication. In chronological order these include: Ōdo Seikichi, Ben Fusaro, Donn F. Draeger, Hu Shih-chong, Shimamoto Katsuyuki, Rev. Masao Ichishima, Dr. Michael Saso, Quintin Chambers, John F. Quinn, Damaris Kirchhofer, Lynne Riggs-Minamitami, Ōtake Risuke, Pat Lineberger, Kobayashi Ichirō, Shimizu Takaji, Aizawa Kamataro, Meik Skoss, Bruce Brown, Mariko Brown, Larry Bieri, Kaminoda Tsunemori, Phil Relnick, Kuroda Ichitarō, Steve Bellamy, Nishioka Tsuneo, Namiki Yasushi, Itō Masayuki, Katō Tsuneharu and other members of the Jiki Shinkage Ryū in Tokyo, Ellis Amdur, Karunakaran s/o R. Chindan, Jeff Acopian, John Driscoll, Hatakeyama Chiyoko and other members of the Rembukan Dōjō, Ōtsubo Shihō, Higuchi Sadahiro, Hunter Armstrong, Roald Knutsen, Dr. Michel Strickmann, Dr. Bruce Williams, Steve Healey, William Jensen, Ian Frey, Richard Hayes, Yagyū Nobuharu and members of the Yagyūkai, Katō Isao, Imai Masayuki, Tōgō Shigemasa, Mutō Masao, Irie Kōhei, Watanabe Ichirō and other members of the Kinyobikai, Saitō Satoshi, Sasama Yoshihiko, Stanley Pranin, Mike Ashworth, Kurt Schmuker, Robert Deppe, Bradley Duker, Connie Noguchi, John Buckley, Scott Beard, Matt Lawrence, Michael Davenport, George Rogers, Jeff Jones, Arman Partamian, Chris Covington, Brian Wagner, Mike Heiler, David Sims, David Styles, Donald J. McHoul, Mark Schreiber, Ōtsuka Yasuyuki, and Charles Goodin.

I would also like to thank the individuals and organizations who have allowed me to use their photographs and illustrations. These are noted in the text.

Lastly, a special thanks to Kuramochi Tetsuo, who has shepherded the enclopedia through several edits and publishing negotiations, and to Katherine Heins, whose meticulous editing and eloquent prose have made this volume much more accessible.

AUTHOR'S PREFACE

The purpose of this *Encyclopedia* is to provide an introduction to classical Japanese combative terminology and provide a foundation for more advanced study of Japan's classical martial culture. Some entries herein can be found in basic books on this topic and are mentioned only summarily. However, there are many entries in this *Encyclopedia* that are difficult, if not impossible, to locate in Japanese–English and standard Japanese dictionaries. Within the limitations of this *Encyclopedia*, I have attempted to include as many of these as possible.

I originally began compiling Japanese martial glosses for history and Asian Studies classes in which I was lecturing during the 1970s and 1980s. More recently I edited some of those earlier glosses and articles I had written into one volume for the members of my martial arts training group, the Hōbyōkai/Hōbyōkan, in order to help them understand Japanese martial terminology and culture. This *Encyclopedia* is an expansion of that earlier effort.

While many of the terms found in this *Encyclopedia* are straightforward, a number of them include multiple definitions. These are not exhaustive; in several cases, they are introductory-level only. If you are a member of one of the classical traditions listed herein, as you train you will find more depth in these terms and definitions.

Japan's warrior culture contains such a rich tapestry of historical, social, religious, and martial elements that it would take a multi-volume work to do it justice. This *Encyclopedia* barely scratches the surface.

David A. Hall
Rockville, MD
2 June 2012

Quick Guide to Weapons and Systems

Most of these items have entries within the body of this publication. This is simply a quick guide for some of the more common weapons and systems mentioned in this *Encyclopedia*

Weapon (w) or Combative System (s)			Translation
aikidō	(s)	合気道	spirit-development system of grappling
aikijūjutsu	(s)	合気柔術	combative grappling arts
bajutsu	(s)	馬術	horsemanship
bō	(w)	棒	long hardwood staff (5 feet/1.5 m or longer)
bōjutsu	(s)	棒術	long hardwood staff arts
chūdachi	(w)	中太刀	medium-length sword (around 2 feet/70 cm long)
hobaku	(s)	捕縛	capturing arts; arresting arts
hojōjutsu	(s)	捕縄術	arresting-rope arts
hōjutsu	(s)	砲術	matchlock musketry
iaidō	(s)	居合道	spirit-development system of quick-draw swordsmanship
iaijutsu	(s)	居合術	combative quick-draw swordsmanship
jō	(w)	杖	stick, rod, medium-length staff (4 feet/1.2 m)
jōdō	(s)	杖道	spirit-development path of medium-length staff
jōjutsu	(s)	杖術	combative medium-length staff arts
jūdō	(s)	柔道	spirit-development/sportive system of grappling
jūjutsu	(s)	柔術	generic term for combative grappling arts
jūkendo	(s)	銃剣道	spirit-development/sportive bayonet arts
jūkenjutsu	(s)	銃剣術	combative bayonet arts
jutte	(w)	十手	single-tined truncheon
juttejutsu	(s)	十手術	combative truncheon arts
kachimi	(s)	勝身	striking vital points
katana	(w)	刀	longsword (worn cutting-edge up)
ken	(w)	剣	longsword
kenjutsu	(s)	剣術	combative swordsmanship

Weapon (w) or Combative System (s)			Translation
kendō	(s)	剣道	spirit-development path of swordsmanship
kodachi	(w)	小太刀	short sword
kusarigama	(w)	鎖鎌	sickle and chain
kusarigamajutsu	(s)	鎖鎌術	combative sickle-and-chain arts
kyūdō	(s)	弓道	spirit-development system of archery
kyūjutsu	(s)	弓術	combative archery
manrikigusari	(w)	万力鎖	weighted chain
nagae no kama	(w)	長柄之鎌	polearm sickle and chain
naginatajutsu	(s)	長刀術	combative glaive/halberd arts
nawa	(w)	縄	arresting rope
ōdachi	(w)	大太刀	great sword (over 5 feet/1.5 m long)
tachi	(w)	太刀	sword (worn cutting-edge down)
tanjō	(w)	短杖	short stick, cane
tessen	(w)	鉄扇	iron fan
shuriken	(w)	手裏剣	throwing blades and small knives
shurikenjutsu	(s)	手裏剣術	combative art of throwing darts, small knives
sōjutsu	(s)	槍術	combative spear arts
sumō	(s)	相撲	sportive, agonistic grappling system
sutteki	(w)	ステッキ	short stick, cane
suttekijutsu	(s)	ステッキ術	combative stick/cane arts
tachi	(w)	太刀	longsword (worn with the cutting edge down)
tanjōjutsu	(s)	短杖術	combative stick/cane arts
torinawa	(s)	捕縄	arresting-rope arts (same as *hojōjutsu*)
toritejutsu	(s)	捕手術	police/arresting arts

Historical Eras

NOTE: There is often disagreement among scholars on the exact beginning and ending dates of some of these periods. (See also: Nelson, 1966: 1016–1018). All dates below are C.E.

Kofun Jidai 古墳時代 (Tumulus period) c. 250–645

Yamato period	大和時代	(c. 300–c. 550)			

Kosei Jidai 古世時代 (Ancient period) 645–c. 1185

Asuka period	飛鳥時代	(552–646)	Suiko period	推古時代	(552–646)
Nara period	奈良時代	(710–794)	Hakuhō period	白鳳時代	(646–710)
			Tempyō period	天平時代	(710–794)
Heian period	平安時代	(794–1185)	Kōnin period	弘仁時代	(794–897)
			Fujiwara period	藤原時代	(898–1185)

Chūsei Jidai 中世時代 (Medieval period) c. 1185–1558

Kamakura period	鎌倉時代	(1185–1333)			
Nambokuchō period	南北朝時代	(1336–1392)			
Muromachi period	室町時代	(1392–1573)	Ashikaga period	足利時代	(1392–1573)
Sengoku (Warring States) period	戦国時代	(1482–1558)			

Kinsei Jidai 近世時代 (Pre-modern period) c. 1558–1867

Azuchi-Momoyama period	安土桃山時代	(1573–1598)			
Edo period	江戸時代	(1603–1868)	Tokugawa period	徳川時代	(1603–1868)
			Bakumatsu period	幕末	(1853–1868)

Kindai 近代 / Gendai 現代 (Modern period) 1868–present

Meiji era	明治時代	(1868–1912)
Taishō era	大正時代	(1912–1925)
Shōwa era	昭和時代	(1926–1989)
Heisei era	平成時代	(1989–present)

Guide to Entries

Entries appear as follows:

Characters (modern)

Dannō Gennoshin Yoshitaka 団野 源之進義高 【團野源之進義高】 (1761–1849). Jiki Shinkage Ryū—Recognized as twelfth headmaster and successor to eleventh headmaster Akaishi Chikayoshi by the Jiki Shinkage Ryū 直心影流. Dannō's most famous students were Odani Nobutomo (who became thirteenth headmaster) and Katsu Kokichi (father of Katsu Kaishū). The Dannō Ha family line of Jiki Shinkage Ryū descends from Gennoshin through his son, Dannō Matashirō.

Further readings in English:

• Craig, 1988.

Brackets 【】 indicate characters written in the style used before 1946

Brackets 「」 indicate short, unpublished, or scroll documents

Heihō yonjūni ka jō 「兵法四十二ヶ条」 (Forty-two sections on strategy). This document is a text on martial strategy derived from the *Genke kin'etsushū*. A document with the same title, but a slightly different pronunciation, the *Hyōhō shijūni ka jō* 「兵法四十二ヶ条」, was written later by Miyamoto Musashi.

Brackets 『』 indicate a large, well-known, or published document

Heiji monogatari 『平治物語』 (Tale of the Heiji). A Japanese war tale relating the events of the Heiji no Ran, a civil war that took place in the Heiji era (1159). While Hamuro Tokinaga is often credited with writing the document, its actual authorship is in doubt.

See also: *Gikeiki; Heike monogatari; Hōgan monogatari; Shōmonki; Taiheiki.*

Further reading in English:

• Varley, 1994: 66–77.

Numbers indicate multiple entries with similar romanization

Iizasa Ryū 2. 飯篠流. Branch tradition of the Shinkage Ryū (5) 真影流 transmitted in Iyo Yoshida domain (the present-day city of Uwajima in Ehime prefecture, on the island of Shikoku).

Guide to Lineage Charts

Lineage charts may appear in columns or in full page width depending on their size and breadth. As the relationship between some antecedent traditions and the illustrated tradition may be unclear, these are normally indicated by gray boxes. Dashed lines of transmission indicated "accepted but unclear" transmission lineage. For example:

Emmei Ryū (1)
円明流
(abbreviated lineage)

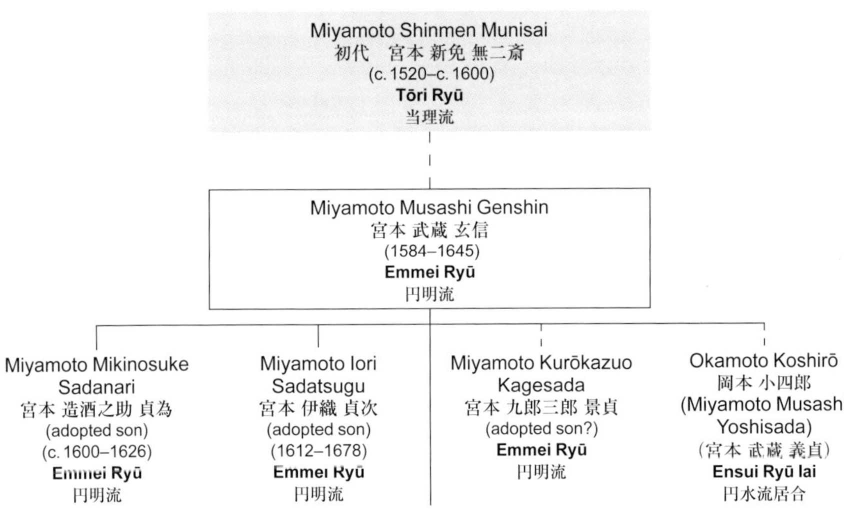

A Note on the Japanese Language and Communication Style

The Japanese use a high-context communication style. The essential meaning of a particular term depends on the context in which that term is used: who is speaking to whom, the relative status of the speaker and listener (senior vs. junior), group membership, the physical location in which the information is passed, who else is listening to the conversation, etc. Consequently, Japanese terms have multiple meanings. In teacher-student relationships within the martial arts, additional factors come into play: the student's level of training, the need for a student to be aware and experienced enough to intuit additional meaning, and, in the classical period, the security of the group.

For example, in classical Japanese martial schools, pre-arranged combative forms (scenarios referred to as *kata*) were and are, with few exceptions, the primary training method. Intensive repetition of these forms is intended to teach the student on several planes: body, speech, and mind; that is, on the physical, respiratory, and psychological level. Through repetitive practice of these forms, the student develops an intuitive understanding of the meaning and purpose of each *kata*, and one's understanding of a particular *kata*, and of the meaning of the name of that *kata*, therefore changes over time. Consequently, a "dictionary definition" of a particular *kata* name will often be inadequate. For this reason, I have avoided including many of these in this *Encyclopedia*.

Romanization

Japanese—For romanization of Japanese terms, the modified Hepburn system found in Kenkyusha's *New Japanese-English Dictionary*, Fourth Edition, 1974, has been used. However, I have included some alterations of the letter *n* when it changes to an *m* before consonants (e.g., *kenpō* can be pronounced and written as *kempō*) as these frequently appear in various books and documents written in European languages. The modified Hepburn system also uses a macron for long vowels instead of doubling the vowel (e.g., ō instead of oo) or blending a final u with a preceding o (e.g., and *sumō* instead of *sumou*). An exception to this is when a final vowel written with a separate character follows immediately after a similar vowel (e.g., *myōō*).

Chinese—For romanization of Chinese terms, the Pinyin system (Mandarin pronunciation) used currently in mainland China, Hong Kong, Malaysia, Singapore, and Taiwan, has been used. However, as trends in Chinese romanization have varied over the years, many publications use older systems such as Wade-Giles and Postal Map. I have included indices for conversion to these alternates. Some exceptions are made in the text in order to show the transliteration of non-Mandarin terms into Japanese.

Sanskrit—For romanization of Sanskrit terms, the International Alphabet of Sanskrit Transliteration (IAST) system, the most commonly used academic standard, has been applied.

Japanese names written in Chinese characters (*kanji*)

As P. G. O'Neil noted in his 1971 work, *Japanese Names: A Comprehensive Index by Characters and Readings*, "There is no final or complete solution to the problems of reading Japanese names written in Chinese characters." (O'Neill, 1971: vii).

When the Japanese borrowed the Chinese writing system, they also imported new technological and cultural items, including vocabulary. Some concepts were already shared by both cultures, while others were new to the Japanese. When the Japanese imported the Chinese writing system and its thousands of ideograms, they also incorporated their Chinese pronunciation. To these characters they also applied Japanese sounds. Today these sounds, or readings, are delineated as *on* readings (for Chinese sounds) and *kun* readings (for Japanese sounds). However, this dual-layer system has been complicated by several factors.

First, while the nature of the Chinese writing systems and the form of its characters have remained relatively fixed over the past two millennia, the borrowing of Chinese characters took place over many hundreds of years, beginning perhaps as early as the first century. By the sixth century, Chinese-language documents written in Japan were sophisticated, showing an infiltration of Japanese-language terms. And the process continued for many more centuries. During that long period China experienced many migrations, invasions, and other demographic changes. This caused the Chinese language to shift its sounds in different geographical areas as people mixed or moved. Today, Chinese linguists and philologists recognize that Chinese characters were pronounced differently in different eras. For example, the character 梵 is today pronounced *fan* in Mandarin Chinese, but was pronounced *buan* in Middle Chinese. ("Middle Chinese" refers to the generally official Chinese spoken language during the Southern and Northern dynasties, and the Sui, Tang, and Song dynasties—roughly the sixth through tenth centuries). The *on* reading (Japanese-borrowed "Chinese" pronunciation) for this charater is *bon*.

Second, there was extensive communication between Japan, China, and Korea (another influence) during these periods. Consequently geographical as well as temporal variances in pronunciation were often preserved for a single character, resulting in the Japanese having multiple pronunciations for a single ideogram. Additionally, variations in Japanese location and dialects led to even more divergence in pronunciation of the borrowed characters.

Third, Chinese is a tonal language. This means that any particular sound—e.g., *ma*—may have different meanings depending on the tone, and may thus be written with a different character. Modern Mandarin Chinese recognizes four tones; modern Cantonese recognizes nine. Other dialects recognize other numbers. In modern Mandarin the sound *ma* may be pronounced in four ways: *mā* (high tone), *má* (rising tone), *mă* (low-dipping tone), and *mà* (sharp falling tone). Each has a different meaning in Chinese and can be written with a variety of characters: *mā* 媽 = an old woman, *má* 麻 = hemp, *mă* 馬 = horse, and *mà* 糢 = blurred or indistinct. As Japanese is not a tonal language, however, such distinctions in pronunciation are lost. The effect of this can be seen in Andrew N. Nelson's *Modern Reader's Japanese-English Character Dictionary*, in which the single borrowed Chinese sound *kai* is used for seventy different characters.

Fourth, the grammar of the Japanese language is very different from Chinese.

Consequently, when the Japanese borrowed the Chinese writing system, it was not an ideal fit. Eventually the Japanese created two phonetic syllabaries. However, since these "alphabets" have a relatively fixed pronunciation, they do not severely hinder the rendering of Japanese using the English alphabet.

Because of all these factors, there are several pronunciations, both of Chinese and Japanese origin, for each Chinese character; many characters have identical pronunciations. For example, the character 成 can be read as follows:

成

(Borrowed Sino-Japanese pronunciations)	(Native Japanese pronunciations)
SEI, JŌ	*na(ru), na(su), ona(ri)*

Fifth, since each character carries meaning as well as sound, the Japanese would often apply additional sounds they liked to characters with meanings they wished to convey in a personal name. Thus, additional sounds have been added to each character over the centuries.

成 **(Additional sounds for names)**

(Borrowed Sino-Japanese reading)	(Native Japanese reading)
Stand-alone names:	
	Shigeru, Minoru, Sadamu, Osamu, Hakaru, Akira
As part of compounds for names:	
SEI, JŌ	nari, shige, fusa, hira, yoshi, naru, sada, masa, aki, nori, michi

As can be seen above, any Chinese character or combination thereof representing a Japanese name has a variety of possible readings. Which is correct? The Japanese themselves are often unsure of the pronunciation unless the person is well known. When Japanese martial historians and researchers print out school and family lineages, they simply list the characters that have been recorded in documents without always being certain of how they are read. Guesses on family names are usually better informed, but personal names are almost impossible to read with total confidence.

Sixth, regional dialects also came into play when readings were assigned to Chinese characters. Sometimes a warrior—e.g.,上泉—is known by both current, "standard" pronunciation of his family name (in this case, "Kamiizumi") and by the local dialectic pronunciation from his geographical area of origin ("Kōizumi"). In other cases—such as 柳生利厳—the warrior in question is referred to both as "Yagyū Yoshitoshi" (the current, "standard" pronunciation of his personal name) and as "Yagyū Toshitoshi" (the colloquial pronunciation primarily used in the family martial arts tradition of the Yagyū).

Finally, members of the warrior class (as well as other classes) commonly changed their names, or the reading of the characters used for their names, several times during a lifetime.

Since this *Encyclopedia* is arranged alphabetically, I have tried to select the best choice from a number of possible readings for obscure names. If any readers would like to provide a substantiated reading for the names listed in this work, I invite them to email it to me: BudoGuidebook@gmail.com.

ENCYCLOPEDIA

A

Abe Gorōtayū Yoritō 安部 五郎太夫 頼任 (c. 1624–c. 1693). Founded Abe Ryū around 1667. Gorōtayū was evidently the first swordsman to use the term *kendō* 剣道 for his art, although the term *ken no michi* 剣の道 had been used earlier.

Abe Ryū 安部流 [Var. ***Abe Ryū*** 安部立]. This system, founded by Abe Gorōtayū around 1667, concentrated on swordsmanship and was one of the earliest martial traditions to begin modifying swordsmanship away from combative *kenjutsu* and toward *kendō*. In doing this in the seventeenth century, the founder of Abe Ryū changed the goal of swordsmanship training from battle effectiveness and group protection to a spiritual discipline aimed at self-perfection.

Abe Shichizaemon Michikore 阿部 七左衛門 道是 (c. 1605–c. 1670). Senior disciple (*deshi*) of Matsubayashi Samanosuke, founder of Gan Ryū (3) 願立. Abe's most notable successor was Wada Jūrōzaemon Masashige, who founded the Kankyoku Ryū.

Abe Tate Ryū 安部立流. See: Abe Ryū.

abumi 鐙. A stirrup.

adauchi 仇討. A vendetta. See: *katakiuchi*

adauchi mono 仇討物 [A.k.a. ***adauchi monogatari*** 仇討物語]. A story of a vendetta, often the theme of Japanese "period plays" (*jidaigeki*), "sword-rattler" movies (*chambara*), traditional *kabuki* theater plays, ballad dramas (*jōruri*), etc.

AGEMAKI ON HEIAN-PERIOD *ŌYOROI*
Festival at Katori Jingū, 1978
(Photograph by Pat Lineberger)

adaya 仇矢 [Var. 徒矢・英矢]. An arrow that missed its target; a futile shot.

agemaki 総角. A decorative knot, often a part of a tassel on various martial accoutrements.

agemakitsuke no kan 総角付の鐶. A decorative device with a ring, found on armor and accoutrements, to which tassels and cords can be attached.

AGEMAKITSUKE NO KAN ON HEIAN-PERIOD *ŌYOROI*
Festival at Katori Grand Shrine, 1978
(Photograph by Pat Lineberger)

ago 顎 [Var. 腮【顋】]. Jaw. ¶ *ago ate* 顎当て, a strike to the jaw. ¶ *agogeri* 顎蹴り, a kick to the jaw. ¶ *ago uchi* 顎打ち, a strike to the jaw.

agura 胡座【胡坐】. A cross-legged sitting posture. *Agura* was the basic posture for sitting favored up through the Warring States period (Sengoku Jidai) by warriors (and most everyone else). (Keeley, 1999: 125–126). See also: *iaidō; iaigoshi; seiza; tatehiza.*

Asahina Mudō Nuklyasu 朝比奈 夢道 貫泰. Fourth-generation successor of the Tamiya Ryū 田宮流, a school of quick-draw swordsmanship (*iaijutsu*). It was under Asahina that Wada Heisuke Masakatsu mastered Tamiya Ryū. Wada later founded the Shin Tamiya Ryū 新田宮流 ("revised" Tamiya Ryū).

aihanmi 合半身. A situation in which two opponents are facing each other in a lateral stance (*hanmi*), standing with the same foot forward. Contrast with *gyaku hanmi*.

aiki 合気【合氣】. 1. *Aiki* essentially means harmony (or unity) of spirit and/or energy. However, this term has developed many shades of meaning over the years. In the area of combative behavior and performance, the Japanese martial concept of *aiki* is synchronicity of physical movement, breath, and/or spirit. This is categorized as one of the eight innate combative traits. (Hayes, 1991:62).

Although proponents of the early martial traditions did not dwell on *aiki*, they were certainly familiar with it. Due to the popularity of *jūjutsu* and *jūdō* at the beginning of the twentieth century, the concepts of *aiki, ki,* and *kiai* took on a new vogue, and their "mystery" was greatly inflated in the popular Japanese press. (This in turn influenced the Western press; see E. J. Harrison's *The Fighting Spirit of Japan,* section on "The Esoteric Aspects of Bujutsu.") One of the earliest texts to appear on *aiki*, published in 1899, was entitled *Budō hiketsu—aiki no jutsu* (Secrets of *budō*: the art of *aiki*). This early text claimed that *aiki* was the most mysterious, profound art in the world, and that one who mastered this secret principle would be a martial genius.

The most illustrative definition from that period is probably that found in a work entitled *Jūjutsu kyōjū sho ryū no maki* (*Jūjutsu* textbook—dragon scroll):

> *Aiki* is a passive state of mind without a blind side, slackness, evil intention, or fear. There is no difference between *aiki* and *kiai*; however, if compared, when expressed dynamically *aiki* is called *kiai* and when expressed statically, it is *aiki*. (Draeger, trans., 1974: 142).

See also: *aiki no ri; kiai; kiaijutsu.*

2. DAITŌ RYŪ—Takeda Tokimune defined *aiki* thusly:

> The *ki* in *aiki* is *go no sen*, meaning to respond to an attack...The Jiki Shinkage Ryū, which (my father) Sokaku practiced, is *sen sen*, which means to initiate the attack. That is winning with *kiai*...*Aiki* is different from the victory of *sen sen*, and is applied in situations of *go no sen*, such as when an opponent thrusts at you. (Pranin, 1996: 54).

Consequently, according to the Takeda Tokimune/Daitō Ryū definition, *aiki=go no sen*=defensive initiative=defense. This contrasts with *kiai=sen no sen*=offensive initiative=attack.

This particular approach is similar to that found in several modern disciplines, such as that of Sasaki Kazusuke, who notes that *kiai* is dynamic or active, whereas *aiki* is static or passive. (Sasaki, 1991:98).

3. AIKIDŌ—Ueshiba Morihei, founder of *aikidō,* greatly refined the concept of *aiki* he studied in the Daitō Ryū. To him *aiki* indicated a "creative life-force," the nature of which was "all-embracing love." In application this can mean completely controlling an aggressive opponent without harming him.

aikibō 合気棒【合氣棒】. This term refers to a variety of techniques that are practiced with a long hardwood staff in modern *aikidō*. Designed primarily as an adjunct to and as reinforcement for standard *aikidō* movement patterns, most are unproven as "combative" technique.

As with the *aikijō* and *aikiken*, there is no standard set of combative forms (*kata*) established which is practiced by all *aikidō* groups. Consequently the *aikibō* practiced by Tōhei Kōichi in the early 1970s was already significantly different from the styles of *aikibō* practiced by, e.g., Saitō Morihiro or Saotome Mitsugi. This is the result of Ueshiba's emphasis on the practitioner's development of *aiki* in lieu of mastery of specific combative *kata*.

aikibudō 合気武道【合氣武道】. 1. DAITŌ RYŪ—One of several names used during the lifetime of Takeda Sōkaku for the teachings of Daitō Ryū. 2. DAITŌ RYŪ—Daitō Ryū *jūjutsu*/*aikijūjutsu* as taught under Takeda Tokimune. 3. ***Aiki Budō***—Abbreviation for both Tenshin Aiki Budō and Takemusu Aiki Budō, which are early terms used by Ueshiba Morihei for the art he modified from Daitō

TYPICAL *AIKIDŌ* TECHNIQUE
Executed by Shimamoto Katsuyuki Sensei (left), Sōsenji Dōjō, 1973
(Photograph courtesy Shimamoto Katsuyuki)

Ryū *aikijūjutsu* into *aikidō*. 4. **Aiki Budō**—Term used by Inoue Noriaki, nephew and disciple of Ueshiba Morihei, for a grappling system he founded after splitting with his uncle. He renamed the system Shinwa Taidō in 1956.

aikidō 合気道 【合氣道】. A modern martial/spiritual way (*shin budō*) system which concentrates on empty-hand grappling techniques. The system also includes training in some weaponry such as the four-foot staff (*jō*), six-foot staff (*bō*), hardwood sword (*bokken*), and wooden dagger (*tantō*), but these weapons are seen only as adjunct exercises to the empty-hand system. Created by Ueshiba Morihei during the 1930s and 1940s, *aikidō* finds its main technical origins in Daitō Ryū *aikijutsu/aikijūjutsu*. Ueshiba also trained in Yagyū Shingan Ryū *taijutsu*, Kashima Shintō Ryū *kenjutsu*, and the Ōmoto religion which, to some extent, influenced his development of his system.

Aikidō, however, is a highly variegated grappling system. Ueshiba constantly modified it over the years, and the lines that have come down via his students—Tomiki Kenji, Shioda Gōzō, Ueshiba Kisshōmaru, Tōhei Kōichi, Saitō Morihiro, and others—are divergent in empty-hand technique, use of weaponry, and philosophy. See: *Ueshiba Ryū Aikidō.*

aikihō 合気法 【合氣法】. Lit. "*aiki*-method." YAGYŪ SHINKAGE RYŪ—A technique by which an enemy's attack can be stopped by gaining initiative over him.

aiki inyōhō 合気陰陽法【合氣陰陽法】. DAITŌ RYŪ—The application of the principles of *yin* and *yang* to breathing and throwing in Daitō Ryū *aikijūjutsu*.

aikijō 合気杖 【合氣杖】. This term refers to a variety of techniques that are practiced with a medium-length staff in modern *aikidō*. Designed primarily as an adjunct to and as reinforcement for standard *aikidō* movement patterns, most are unproven as "combative" technique.

Probably the best-known exponent of *aikijō* was Saitō Morihiro, who spent many years training directly under Ueshiba Morihei in the Iwama *dōjō*. Saitō produced several volumes in the 1970s, with text in both English and Japanese, in a series called *Traditional Aikido*. These volumes covered a good deal of the *aikijō* curriculum. See also: *aikibō.*

aikijūjutsu 合気柔術【合氣柔術】. DAITŌ RYŪ—The term *aikijūjutsu* refers to the portion of the Daitō Ryū grappling system that founder Takeda Sōkaku derived from *oshikiuchi*.

aikijutsu 合気術【合氣術】. See: *aikijūjutsu; Daitō Ryū.*

Aikikai 合気会【合氣會】. The Aikikai Foundation (Aikido World Headquarters). This organization is the central group of the world-wide *aikidō* federation under the Ueshiba family.

aikiken 合気剣【合氣劍】. This term refers to a variety of wooden sword (*bokken*) techniques that are practiced in modern *aikidō*. Designed primarily as an adjunct to and as reinforcement of standard *aikidō* movement patterns, most are unproven as "combative" technique. Since *aikidō* founder Ueshiba Morihei trained in Kashima Shintō Ryū at one time, he may have loosely based these techniques on those of Kashima. However, analysis of the actual techniques of *aikiken* and Kashima Shintō Ryū *kenjutsu* indicates a relationship that is tentative at best.

Probably the best-known exponent of *aikiken* was Saitō Morihiro, who spent many years training directly under Ueshiba in the Iwama *dōjō*. Saitō produced several volumes in the 1970s (text in both English and Japanese) in a series called *Traditional Aikido*. These volumes covered a good deal of the curriculum on *aikiken*. Other followers of Ueshiba have devised numerous systems under this name. See also: *aikibō.*

Aiki no jutsu 1.「合気術」【合氣術】[Abbr. for **Daitō Ryū aiki no jutsu**「大東流合気術」]. The name of a Daitō Ryū transmission scroll (*densho*) which is the second of several awarded in that tradition. It requires mastery of fifty-three techniques.

aiki no jutsu 2. 合気の術. Manifestation of the *aiki no ri* combative adaptive trait. See: *aiki no ri.*

aiki no ri 合気の理. As a combative adaptive trait, *aiki no ri* indicates the innate potentiality of synchronicity. Synchronicity (*aiki*) then is seen as the capability of using the musculoskeletal system in movement patterns in which space and time are brought into play in neutralizing an opponent's kinetic energy and, in fact, using that energy to redirect his attack. The synchronicity trait is described by Hayes (1984a: 10) as the eighth of the eight innate combative adaptive traits. See: *bu no ri.*

Further reading in English:
- Hayes, 1992: 27–29.

aikuchi 合口 [Var. ***kusungobu*** 九寸五分]. A short dagger—around a foot (30 cm) in length—in a mounting with no hand guard (*tsuba*). Since there is no *tsuba*, the opening in the scabbard (*saya*)—which in Japanese is called the "mouth" (*kuchi*)—and the edges of the hilt (*tsuka*) meet smoothly. A weapon thus mounted is called an *aikuchi*, which literally means "matches the mouth."

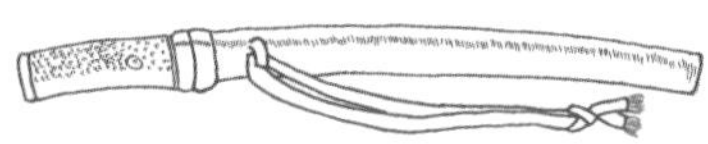

AIKUCHI MOUNTING

Aikuchi Roppō 合口六法. Fifth set of combative scenarios (*kata*) listed by the Hyōhō Niten Ichi Ryū 兵法二天一流 under the general category of Tachi Seihō. This set is made up of six short sword scenarios executed with *aikuchi*. This set is composed of advanced scenarios described only via oral transmission (*kuden*). See: *Hyōhō Niten Ichi Ryū.*

Ainu アイヌ. The aboriginal inhabitants of Hokkaidō, the Kuril Islands (Chishima Rettō 千島列島), and Sakhalin (Karafuto 樺太/Saharin サハリン). They are thought to have been related to the Emishi, who once inhabited Northern Honshu, and with whom the Japanese were often engaged in combat. See: *Emishi.*

ainuke 相抜. Within swordsmanship, *ainuke* is the philosophy of "mutual escape," in contrast to *aiuchi*, which usually means "mutual killing." It was originally used in reference to a style of swordsmanship was promoted by the swordsman Odagiri Ichiun of the Mujū Shinken Ryū 無住心剣流 in the late seventeenth century. In *ainuke*, the Mujū Shinken Ryū practitioner strikes the enemy's sword simultaneously in such a way that neither combatant is injured. Ichiun claimed his master, Harigaya Sekiun, had defeated him several times with this technique. (Sakai, 2010: 320–321).

Further reading in English:
- Suzuki, 1958: 170–180.

Aioi Ryū 相生流. Lit. "Mutual Life School," Aioi Ryū is one of the early (c. 1928) terms used by Ueshiba Morihei for the grappling system he modified from Daitō Ryū *aikijūjutsu* into *aikidō*.

Aisu Hyūga no Kami Ikōsai Hisatada 愛洲日向守 移香斎 久忠. See: *Aisu Ikōsai.*

Aisu Ikō Ryū 愛洲 移香流. Listed by Watatani and Yamada (1978: 9) as a school of espionage (*shinobijutsu*), this is actually the Aisu Kage Ryū.

Aisu Ikōsai 愛洲 移香斎【愛洲移香齋】[A.k.a. ***Hyūga no Kami*** 日向之守; ***Hisatada*** 久忠] (1452–1538). Founder of the Aisu Kage Ryū 愛洲陰流 (also called Kage no Ryū 陰之流 and Kage Ryū 陰流); his most famous student was Kamiizumi Ise no Kami Hidetsuna (a.k.a. Nobutsuna).

The Aisu family, who resided in Ise during the fifteenth century, was a clan of pirates (*wakō*). As they had the protection of several lords (*daimyō*) in western Japan and preyed on commercial traffic between Japan, Korea, China, and the Ryūkyū archipelago, they seem to have been more privateers than pirates. Ikōsai himself had ventured as far as the Chinese mainland several times; this apparently greatly influenced his style of swordsmanship, which he later developed as Kage no Ryū (lit. "Shadow Tradition"). Unusual in the Japanese scheme of things martial is the central prearranged combative form (*kata*) of the Kage no Ryū called Empi (lit. "Twirling Monkey"). The use of combative movements based on those of animals, while not uncommon in Chinese systems, is rare in Japanese classical martial arts (*koryū bujutsu*). This seems to support the case for significant Chinese influence in the original conceptualizations of Ikōsai's system.

In 1487, at the age of thirty-six, Ikōsai was shipwrecked during a storm off the island of Kyūshū. The only survivor, he was barely able to make it to the rocky shore below the Udo Daigongen Shrine.

Due to his miraculous escape, he renounced his life as a pirate and, according to his student Kamiizumi Ise no Kami, entered into a thirty-seven-day spiritual and physical ordeal (*shugyō*) at the shrine. During this spiritual retreat he received an inspiration which became the core of his new Kage no Ryū. He evidently also received a command from the deity Udo Daigongen to duel with a local warrior named Sumiyoshi, which he did. Defeating Sumiyoshi, Ikōsai gained a reputation in Kyūshū as a formidable swordsman. He then set out on a martial pilgrimage (*musha shugyō*) in order to perfect his swordsmanship and his character. In pursuing this path he developed methods of disarming an opponent without the use of a sword. This method he christened *mutōdori*; its techniques have been preserved in various lines of the Shinkage Ryū. Ikōsai also took on a number of students in various locations, and from that point his Kage no Ryū became well known.

In his later years Ikōsai—and his son, Koshichirō—became the martial arts instructors for Satake Yoshiatsu, *daimyō* of Hitachi domain. The Satake clan had a close relationship with the Kamiizumi clan, and it was through this connection that Kamiizumi Hidetsuna came to seek out Ikōsai, from whom he learned the Aisu Kage Ryū. See also: *Aisu Koshichirō Genkōsai; Kage ryū no mokuroku.*

Further reading in English:

- Knutsen, 2004: 200–208.

Aisu In Ryū 愛洲院流. Variant name for the Aisu Kage Ryū.

Aisu Kage no Ryū 愛洲陰流. See: *Aisu Kage Ryu.*

Aisu Kage Ryū 愛洲陰流 [A.k.a. ***Aisu In Ryū*** 愛洲院流; ***Aisu Ryū*** 隼鴨流; ***Aisu Ryū*** 早鴨流; ***Kage Ryū*** 陰流; ***Kage no Ryū*** 陰之流; ***Aisu Kage no Ryū*** 愛洲陰流]. The Aisu Kage Ryū—lit. "Aisu's Shadow Tradition"—of swordsmanship and strategy (also simply called Kage Ryū) was founded by Aisu Ikōsai Hisatada in 1488. It was a comprehensive field-combat system (*sōgo bujutsu*) best known for its swordsmanship (*kenjutsu*) and spearmanship (*sōjutsu*).

Based in principles of *kage* 陰,[1] this tradition proliferated in Japan during the late 1400s and early 1500s under its founder, Hisatada, and his son, Genkōsai. Transmission scrolls indicating its spread to China date from the late 1500s. Oddly, there are few known original Kage Ryū documents available today. Because of this, little detail is known about the original weapon systems or the curriculum of the Kage Ryū. Aisu Koshichirō Genkōsai—second headmaster of the Kage Ryū—took the family name of Hirasawa when he was adopted into that clan. For ten generations the Kage Ryū was transmitted by the Hirasawa family. According to the Hirasawa Records (*Hirasawa monjo* 「平沢文書」)—a collection of documents dating back to 1700—the curriculum of the Kage Ryū was commonly known at that time. The Hirasawa collection lists seventeen *hidensho* (secret transmission documents) of the Kage Ryū. Unfortunately, today the actual contents of most of these documents are unknown.

[Note: In the rough translations that follow, the term *no maki* means "scroll" or "volume."]

Kage Ryū *densho*

- *Mokuroku jūyū shichijiku shoi* 目禄十有七軸所謂 (List [of techniques] including illustrations)
- *Jō no maki* 序之巻 (Prelude/introduction)
- *Sangaku no maki* 参学巻 (The three teachings)
- *Yonka no maki* 四箇巻 (The four)
- *Omote no maki* 表之巻 (Outer techniques)
- *Ura no maki* 裏之巻 (Inner techniques)
- *Chū no maki* 中之巻 (Middle-level techniques)

---

1 The character *kage* 陰, which can also be read as *in*, represents the dark side of *in-yō* (Ch. *yin-yang*) dualism. It has many nuances. For more detail see entry for *Shinkage Ryū* (1).

- *Yurushi no maki* 免之巻 (License)
- *Kurai no maki* 位之巻 (Engagement stance)
- *Todome no maki* 留之巻 (Strategy)
- *On-yō no maki* 陰陽巻 (Yin-yang)
- *Kesshō Sanjin no maki* 決勝三神巻 (The Three Deities of Decision [in contest or battle])
- *Kyūkyoku no maki* 究極巻 (Eventualities/desperate situations)
- *Kirigasumi no maki* 霧霞巻 (Mist)
- *Tora no maki* 虎之巻 (Tiger strategy)
- *Hisoka no maki* 私之巻 (Transmission authority)

These rough translations are just that; they are all guesses based on other similar materials and may be completely off the mark. For example, *Sangaku no maki* may refer to a set of *kata* similar to that passed from Kamiizumi Nobutsuna to Yagyū Muneyoshi. Certainly Kamiizumi was familiar with the Kage Ryū's "Sangaku," as he had mastered that tradition under its founder, Aisu Ikōsai. Other terms such as *omote* and *ura* are fairly common in martial documents. The titles of some documents—e.g., *Tora no maki*—display familiar terminology most likely derived from the *Genke kin'etsushū*. At this point, however, their content is a mystery.

Interestingly, there is one widely available document describing a portion of the Kage Ryū's curriculum. Entitled the *Kage Ryū no mokuroku*, it comes to us from a sixteenth-century Chinese compendium of martial culture known as the *Wubeizhi* (Jp. *Bubishi*). See: *Kage ryū no mokuroku; Bubishi (1).*

Aisu Koshichirō 愛洲 小七郎 [A.k.a. ***Genkōsai*** 元香斎【元香齋】; ***Korenobu*** 惟修] (1518–1590). It is speculated that Aisu Koshichirō, son of Aisu Ikōsai and second headmaster of the Kage Ryū, was also an instructor of Kamiizumi Ise no Kami Hidetsuna. At the time of Aisu Hisatada's death at the age of eighty-seven, Kamiizumi was thirty-one years old, and Koshichirō was only twenty.

Koshichirō took the family name of Hirasawa, and for the next ten generations the Kage Ryū was transmitted in the Hirasawa family.

Aisu Ryū 1. 愛洲流. An abbreviation for Aisu Kage Ryū. See: *Aisu Kage Ryū.*

Aisu Ryū 2. 隼鴨流 [Var. 早鴨流]. Refers to the Aisu Kage Ryū 愛洲陰流. This unusual, variant way of writing Aisu Ryū (1) is found in one of the extant *densho* written by Odani Nobutomo, thirteenth-generation headmaster of the Jiki Shinkage Ryū 直心影流. Odani notes that Okuyama Kyūkasai (third headmaster of that line of Shinkage Ryū) used these characters to indicate the Aisu Ryū line of Shinkage Ryū. See: *Aisu Kage Ryū.*

Aisu Shinkage Ryū 愛洲神陰流. This was a branch of the Hikita Kage Ryū 疋田陰流 that was transmitted in the Yanagawa domain in Chikugo (present-day Fukuoka prefecture in Kyūshū) and the Bōshū domain in Suō (present-day Yamaguchi prefecture in western Honshu). See also: *Ōishi Shinkage Ryū.*

aite 相手. Training partner.

aiuchi 相打(ち) [Var. 相撃(ち); 相討(ち)]. 1. Mutual/simultaneous strike. (This usually resulted in mutual killing or injury.) 2. Mutual defeat; mutual killing. Contrast to *ainuke.*

aiuchi no kachi 相打の勝. JIKI SHINKAGE RYŪ—Winning via a mutual/simultaneous strike.

Aizen Myōō 愛染明王<Ch. Airan Mingwang <Skt. Rāgavidyārāja. 1. The Buddhist Magical King of Passion. A tantric deity, Aizen represents the state at which sexual passion becomes enlightenment and love becomes compassion for all living things. Representing *yin* as a complement to *yang*, or female with male, the female form of Aizen is often found in combination with the male Fudō Myōō. These two forms were a popular motif of the Japanese Tachikawa Ryū, a left-handed[2] tantric Buddhist sect that flourished in the Kamakura and Ashikaga periods. 2. In the warrior context, Aizen represents battle

2 The term "Left-handed tantricism" (Jp. *sadō mikkyō* 左道密教 < Skt. *vāmācāra*) tends to be applied to those Buddhist texts, cults, and practices centering on sexual mysticism and other heterodox practices, including combat applications of spells and rituals. The original Sanskrit term *vāmācāra* literally means "sinister." See, for example, Bharati, 1965; van Gulik, 1961: 339–359; Hall, 1978: 19–29; Sanford, 1991: 1–20.

AIZEN MYŌŌ 愛染 明王 (RĀGA-VIDYĀRĀJA) From a Taizokai Mandala; this is one of several medieval Japanese representations

passion. That passion, however, must be tempered by imperturbability so that intuition and clear thought can come into play in the heat of battle. These two powerful forces, along with the goddess Marishiten, are known as the Sansenjin (three war gods); they appeared on the battle banners of several warriors, including Uesugi Kenshin. See also: *Marishiten; myōō; Sansenjin.*

Aizu Go Ryū 会津五流【會津五流】[Also read ***Aizu Itsutsu no Ryū***]. Lit. the "Five Traditions of Aizu." This term refers to five classical *ryū* developed in Aizu domain:

1. Ittō Ryū Mizoguchi Ha 一刀流溝口派—*kenjutsu*
2. Shinten Ryū 真天流—*kenjutsu*
3. Shintō Seibu Ryū 神道精武流—*kenjutsu, jūjutsu, shurikenjutsu*
4. Taishi Ryū 太子流—*gumpō, kenjutsu*
5. Yasumitsu Ryū 安光流—*kenjutsu*

Aizu Han 会津藩【會津藩】. The feudal domain of Aizu, now part of the modern-day Japanese prefecture of Fukushima. The warriors of Aizu have always been known for their high-spirited and warlike character. During the Bakumatsu era, the warriors of Aizu were some of the most strident in their defense of the Tokugawa shogunate. A number of classical martial traditions originated or were developed in Aizu, including Daidō Ryū 大道流, Daitō Ryū 大東流, Tennen Rishin Ryū 天然理心流, and others. See also: *Aizu Go Ryū; Aizu Kotengu; oshikiuchi; Shinsengumi; Takeda Sōkaku; Tennen Rishin Ryū.*

Aizu Ikōsai 愛洲 移香斎. See: *Aisu Ikōsai.*

Aizu Itsutsu no Ryū 会津五流【會津五流】. See: *Aizu Go Ryū.*

Aizu Ittō Ryū 会津一刀流【會津一刀流】. Founded by Kamiizumi Mondo no Kami Norimoto, second son of Kamiizumi Nobutsuna, this system apparently was not connected to the famous Ittō Ryū of Itō Ittōsai Kagehisa. Its content was that of the Shinkage Ryū (1).

Aizu Kage Ryū 会津陰流【會津陰流】. See: *Aisu Kage Ryū.*

Aizu Kimoto Ha 会津木本派【會津木本派】. A tradition of military tactics and strategy (*gumpō*) founded by an Aizu retainer named Kimoto Kurōzaemon Shigemasa. Having studied the *gumpō* of the Naganuma Ryū (2) 長沼流 with Okada Jinuemon Masakatsu, he received a license (*menkyo*) in 1727 and founded his own school. The system was transmitted through seven generations, disappearing with the end of the feudal period around 1868. Its last known headmaster was Saigō Tanomu Chikanori, the same man who taught the grappling art of *oshikiuchi* to Saigō Shirō and Takeda Sōkaku.

Aizu Kotengu 会津小天狗【會津小天狗】. Lit. "Little Mountain Demon of Aizu." A nickname for Takeda Sōkaku, founder of the Daitō Ryū.

Aizu Oshikiuchi 会津御式内【會津御式内】. See: *oshikiuchi.*

Aizu Shinkage Ryū 会津新影流【會津新影流】. A miscellaneous branch of Shinkage Ryū *kenjutsu* which was transmitted in Chōshū domain (長州藩). See: *Aisu Kage Ryū.*

ajari 阿闍梨 <Ch. *asheli* <Skt. *ācārya*. BUDDHISM—Rank of master teacher, usually found in the Tendai and Shingon schools.

Aji Ittō Ryū 阿字一刀流 [A.k.a. ***Issei Ryū*** 一勢流]. This school of swordsmanship was founded during the Jōkyō era (1684–1688) by Yamakumo Enshin, a samurai who hailed from Edo. "Aji Ittō Ryū" is apparently an alternate name for the Issei Ryū. The Aji Ittō Ryū concentrated on several combative systems, including quick-draw sword arts (*iaijutsu*), long hardwood staff techniques (*bōjutsu*), and arresting-cord arts (*torinawa-jutsu*).

It is unclear why the Buddhist term *aji* is used in the name. However, it may indicate an emphasis placed on Aji Kan, a type of Buddhist *mikkyō* meditation. This also ties in with the founder's name, Enshin 円心, which means "mind circle" or "perfect mind." See: *Aji Kan; Gachirin Kan; Issei Ryū.*

Aji Kan 阿字観【阿字觀】. A type of Buddhist esoteric meditation in which the practitioner concentrates on the Sanskrit letter *a* which is inscribed in a moon-disk (*gachirin*). See: *gachirin kan.*

TYPICAL AJI KAN MEDITATIONAL DEVICE

akagashi 赤樫. Red evergreen oak, often used for weapons. Tougher than white evergreen oak (*shirogashi,* or simply *kashi*), *akagashi* is generally preferred for the shafts of polearms. See also: *kashi; shirogashi.*

Akamatsu Jisan 赤松 慈三 [A.k.a. ***~Mishuza*** 三首座] (fl. late 1300s). One of fourteen students of Nen Ami Jion to receive the full transmission of Nen Ryū 念流. Progenitor of the Akamatsu line of Nen Ryū known as the Nen Shuza Ryū 念首座流.

akitsu 蜻蛉 [Also read ***seirei***]. A dragonfly. Warriors waxing poetic often used the term *akitsu* or its variant reading *seirei* in writing, because the dragonfly is considered a courageous fighter. The dragonfly often appears in decorative sword fittings or on armor. See also: *Akitsu Shima.*

Akitsu Shima 蜻蛉洲 [Var. 秋津洲]. An early name for Japan, now considered poetic. The first set of characters means "land of the dragonfly."

Akiyama Shirobei Yoshitoki 秋山 四郎兵衛 義時 (fl. 1600s). Generally regarded as the founder of the Yōshin Ryū school of *jūjutsu*, Yoshitoki made his living as a physician in the city of Nagasaki. Nagasaki being a busy trade port, Akiyama was able to take one or more trips to mainland China, where he trained in medicine and related combative techniques. However, he was able to pick up only three *jūjutsu*-like techniques—some sources note "striking" techniques—from a Chinese man named Bakuden,[3] as well as three restraining techniques and twenty-eight resuscitation techniques from a teacher named Mukan.[4] (Watatani and Yamada, 1978: 894.) After returning to Japan to practice medicine, he found that few potential students were interested in practicing his limited combative curriculum. Consequently, he made a pilgrimage to Dazaifu Tenmangu Shrine in Kyūshū, where he engaged in prayer (*sanrō*) and self-training. While at the shrine, he noticed how a willow tree covered with new snow was able to shed its load without breaking its branches. With this enlightening experience, he emerged from the shrine with an additional 303 techniques; he named his system Yōshin Ryū 楊心流: Willow (楊) Essence (心) Tradition (流).

Akō gishi 『赤穂義士』(The loyal retainers of Akō). An alternate title for the story of the forty-seven *rōnin*. See: *Akō rōshi.*

Akō rōshi 『赤穂浪士』(The wandering samurai of Akō). An alternate title for the story of the forty-seven *rōnin*. [Var. ***Akō gishi*** 赤穂義士; ***Chūshingura*** 忠臣蔵; ***Genroku akō jiken*** 元禄赤穂事件]. In brief, this story concerns a group of samurai—retainers of Lord Asano Naganori, *daimyō* of Akō—who were suddenly cast adrift when their lord was given a death sentence by the Tokugawa shogunate. Asano had been required to commit ritual suicide (*seppuku*) for assaulting a court official named Kira Yoshinaka with a naked blade in Edo Castle. After pa-

3 Ch. Bozhuan 博轉. Some sources refer to this striking system as *hakuda* 白打, however, Watatani and Yamada make no use of this term.

4 Ch. Wuguan 武官.

tiently waiting and planning for over a year, forty-seven of Asano's retainers took their revenge by killing Kira. During that time they all appeared to become debauched drifters in order to hide their intent from the authorities. After eliminating Kira, they were themselves compelled to commit *seppuku* for the murder they had committed. In fact, they knew they would be required to commit suicide at the end of their vendetta (*adauchi*). However, the accomplishment of avenging their revered lord was a most important value to those Tokugawa-period samurai.

Thought by many Japanese to be the definitive tale of warrior loyalty, the story has been criticized over the years by several authorities on *bushidō*. For example, Yamamoto Tsunetomo, the author of *Hagakure*, notes that if Kira had died before the *rōnin* carried out their vendetta, they would have been remembered as debauched cowards. Yamamoto also thought the *rōnin* leader, Ōishi Yoshio 大石良雄, was more interested in "success" than in demonstrating loyalty in the proper manner of *bushidō*, and maintained that they should have made an immediate, all-out attack on Kira without being concerned with its success.

akuma 悪魔【悪魔】. A demon or evil spirit.

akumabarai 悪魔払【悪魔拂】. An exorcism.

Akumi Kohō 渥美 虎峰. Akumi was a direct disciple of Hakkō Ryū 八光流 founder Okuyama Yoshiji (1901–1987). He subsequently founded his own school of grappling, which he referred to as Shinden Ryū 心伝流.

akurei 悪霊【悪靈】. See: *akuryō.*

akuriyo 悪霊【悪靈】. Archaic romanization of *akuryō.*

akuryō 悪霊【悪靈】[Var. ***akurei; akuriyo***]. 1. An evil demon; an evil spirit. 2. An abbreviation for *akuryō menpō.*

akuryō menpō 悪霊面頬【悪靈面頬】[Abbr. ***akuryō*** 悪霊]. An armored face guard designed to look like a demon.

akusho 悪所【悪所】. Rough terrain. ¶ *akusho otoshi* 悪所落, riding (a horse) over rough terrain.

akusō 悪僧【悪僧】. Lit. "evil monk(s)," "rowdy monk(s)." One of many terms used over the centuries for Japanese warrior monks. See: *sōhei.*

akutō 悪党【悪党】. A medieval (late Kamakura to early Muromachi period) term referring to rowdy or lawless bands of armed men. It can be translated as "brigand," "outlaw," or "swashbuckler." During that era the majority of combatants were not of the *bushi* class; many were referred to by a new term, *nobushi.* Most *akutō* incidents took place in central and western Japan. See also: *nobushi.*

Further reading in English:

- Harrington, 1982.

ama 尼. A Buddhist nun.

amagoi ken 雨乞い剣【雨乞い劍】[Var. 雨請剣【雨請劍】; 雩剣【雩劍】; also read ***amagoi no tsurugi***]. A Japanese temple sword. A votive sword, the *amagoi ken* has a straight, double-cutting-edged blade like a *tsurugi.* Approximately a foot (33 cm) long, the blade is decorated with a dragon curving around it; the hilt is in the form of a three-pronged *vajra* (*sanko*). The design on the blade represents Ama Kurikara, a rain dragon. The *amagoi ken* is often depicted held in the hand of various Buddhist deities such as Fudō Myōō. See also: *Kurikara Fudō; Kurikara Ryū-ō; sankotsuka ken.*

amagoi no tsurugi 雨乞い劍. See: *amagoi ken.*

Ama Kurikara 雨倶梨伽羅 [Var. 雨倶利伽羅]. Ama Kurikara is the rain dragon found wound around sword blades. The term has evolved from the name of the Buddhist "Black Dragon King," Kurikara Ryūō. See: *Kurikara Fudō; Kurikara Myōō; Kurikara Ryūō.*

Amakusa Izunokami 天草 伊豆守. A master of the field-combat system known as Chūjō Ryū 中条流 who lived in the mid-1500s. His best-known student was Marume Kurandonosuke Tessai, whom he taught in 1556.

Amano Ichirōemon Naohisa 海野 一郎右衛門 尚久. Second-generation successor of the Asayama Ichiden Ryū 浅山一伝流. One of his most prominent disciples was Kaneda Gembei Masatoshi (c. 1610–c. 1680), founder of the Kaneda Ichiden Ryū 金田一伝流.

Ama no Murakumo no Tsurugi 天叢雲剣【天叢雲劍】. See: *Ame no Murakumo no Tsurugi.*

Ama Shōgun 尼将軍【尼將軍】. Lit. the "Nun General." This was an unofficial title given to Masako, widow of Minamoto no Yoritomo, after she became a Buddhist nun (*ama*). In this capacity she governed the nation in the name of her sons Yoriie and Sanetomo, who held the title of *shōgun*.

Amaterasu Ōmikami 天照大御神. The Shintō sun goddess.

Amau Ryū 天羽流. See: *Amō Ryū.*

Ame no Murakumo no Tsurugi 天叢雲剣【天叢雲劍】[Also read ***Ama no Murakumo no Tsurugi***]; [Var. 天の雲の剣]; var. ***Kusanagi no Tsurugi*** 草薙の剣【草薙劍】]. A sword of myth and history, said to have been drawn by Susano-o no Mikoto (brother of the sun goddess Amaterasu Ōmikami) from the tail of Yamata no Orochi, the eight-headed snake (or dragon). When the god pulled out the sword, clouds rose up around the dragon, thus the name "pile of clouds" (*murakumo*). Later, when the sword was used by Yamato Dake (a legendary Japanese prince of the Yamato period) to cut a path through burning grass—a trap which had been set by his enemies—the name was changed to Kusanagi no Tsurugi, "Grass-mowing Sword." The blade subsequently became one of the three divine treasures (Sanshu no Jingi) held by the imperial family. The original sword is thought to have been lost in the sea at the battle of Dan-no-ura in 1185. See: *Sanshu no Jingi.*

Ameya Kakuemon 雨夜 覚右衛門【雨夜覺右衛門】. Fourth headmaster of Nagao Ryū 長尾流. According to Serge Mol (2001: 164), Ameya may have significantly modified that school away from its concentration on battlefield combat grappling (*kumiuchi*) and into a civilian self-defense system (*goshinjutsu*).

Amida Butsu 阿弥陀仏【阿彌陀佛】<Ch. Amituofo <Skt. Amitābha (infinite light)/ Amitāyus (infinite life) [Abbr. as ***Amida*** 阿弥陀【阿彌陀】; a.k.a. ***Amida Nyorai*** 阿弥陀如来【阿彌陀如來】<Ch. Amituo Rulai <Skt. Amitābha Tathāgata]. Primary buddha venerated by both the Buddhist Pure Land (Jōdo Shū) and True Pure Land schools (Jōdo Shin Shū/Ikkō Shū) in Japan. Amida was the central buddha focused upon by the revolts of the Ikkō Ikki (single-minded military organization of the Honganji) in the fifteenth and sixteenth centuries. These organizations often carried banners praising Amida. See also: *Ikkō Ikki.*

Amida Nyorai 阿弥陀如来【阿彌陀如來】<Ch. Amituo Rulai <Skt. Amitābha Tathāgata. See: *Amida Butsu.*

Amida Ryū 阿弥陀流【阿彌陀流】. A system of swordsmanship (*kenjutsu*) transmitted in Tsugaru domain (present-day Aomori and Iwate prefectures). Little is known about it, including the founder's reason for using the name of the Buddhist deity Amida in the name of the school. It may indicate that the founder had some connection with one of the Buddhist True Pure Land schools (Jōdo Shin Shū or Ikkō Shū).

Amō Kageyu Nakahide 天羽 勘解由 仲英. [A.k.a. ***Shigehide*** 重英]. Founder of a school of combative arts known as Amō Ryū in the mid-1600s.

Amō Nukiai Ryū 天羽抜合流【天羽拔合流】. A variant name for Amō Ryū.

Amō Ryū 天羽流 [Also read ***Amau Ryū***] [A.k.a. ***Amō Nukiai Ryū*** 天羽抜合流【天羽拔合流】; ***Shinshinkansō Ryū*** 新心貫相流]. Founded by Amō Kageyu Nakahide in the mid-1600s, this branch tradition of the Sekiguchi Ryū focused on quick-draw sword arts (*iaijutsu*), combative swordsmanship (*kenjutsu*), and grappling arts (*jūjutsu*). After traveling about Japan as a masterless samurai (*rōnin*), Amō opened a *dōjō* in Ōsaka. He taught a mixture of Sekiguchi Ryū 関口流, Tamiya Ryū 田宮流, and Yagyū Ryū 柳生流 in one combined system he christened Amō Ryū.

Amō Shigehide 天羽 重英. See: *Amō Kageyu Nakahide.*

Anazawa Uneme 穴沢 采女【穴澤采女】. Direct disciple of Anazawa Tonomonosuke Morihide. Uneme transmitted Anazawa Ryū long-hafted glaive arts (*naginatajutsu*) in Saitama domain.

Anazawa Ichiya Shinobu 穴沢 市弥 信武【穴澤市彌信武】. Son and disciple of Anazawa Tonomonosuke Morihide. Shinobu transmitted Anazawa Ryū longsword (*nagadachi*) and the comprehensive combative arts of Shintō Ryū (6) 新当流 in Takata domain.

Anazawa Jōken Hidetaka 穴沢 浄見 秀俊【穴澤淨見秀俊】. 1. Pseudonym under which Anazawa Tonomonosuke Morihide transmitted the Shintō Ryū (5) 新当流 longsword (*nagadachi*) system in Fukuoka domain. His direct disciple in that line was Yagyū Matsuemon Ienobu. 2. Pseudonym under which Anazawa Tonomonosuke Morihide transmitted the Shintō Ryū (5) longsword (*nagadachi*) system in Satsuma domain. His direct disciple in that line was his son, Anazawa Sakon Genshin.

Anazawa Nyokin 穴沢 如緊【穴澤如緊】. Pseudonym under which Anazawa Tonomonosuke Morihide transmitted Anazawa Ryū long-hafted glaive arts (*naginatajutsu*) in Shinjō domain. His direct disciple in that endeavor was Umeda Mokunoshō 梅田 杢之丞.

Anazawa Ryū 穴沢流【穴澤流】[A.k.a. **Shintō Ryū** 神道流 and **Shinto Ryu** 新当流]. This was primarily a comprehensive field-combat system (*sōgo bujutsu*) founded by Anazawa Tonomonosuke Morihide around 1580. Morihide was a disciple of Iizasa Moritsuna, fourth headmaster of the Katori Shintō Ryū.[5] In forming the Anazawa Ryū he concentrated on long glaive arts (*naginatajutsu*), longsword (*nagadachi*), and long hardwood staff methods (*bōjutsu*).

Iizasa Moritsuna was well known for his expertise with the *nagadachi* and was famous for a posture/technique known as *sen-nagashi* 扇流し (lit. "revolving fan"). After mastering Moritsuna's Katori Shintō Ryū, Anazawa Morihide also trained in the *bōjutsu* of Isshin Ryū 一心流.

Anazawa Morihide, under various pseudonyms, taught his combative systems in a number of locations to produce independent, lasting martial traditions as follows:

Domain (*han* 藩)	Tradition	Weapons system
Fukuoka 福岡	Shintō Ryū (5) 神道流	*nagadachi* 長太刀
Mito 水戸	Anazawa Ryū 穴沢流	*nagadachi* 長太刀
Owari 尾張	Ōshin Ryū 応心流	*naginata* 薙刀
Satsuma 薩摩	Shintō Ryū (5, 7) 神当流	*nagadachi* 長太刀
	Shinjin Ryū 神人流	*naginata* 薙刀
Sendai 仙台	Anazawa Ryū 穴沢流	*nagadachi* 長太刀
Shinjō 新庄	Anazawa Ryū 穴沢流	*naginata* 薙刀
Takata 高田	Anazawa Ryū 穴沢流	*nagadachi* 長太刀
	Shintō Ryū (6) 神道流	(various)
Tsu 津	Chishin Ryū 知新流	*naginata* 薙刀
Yonezawa 米沢	Isshin Ryū 一心流	*bōjutsu* 棒術
	Shinten Ryū 真天流	*kenjutsu* 剣術
[Various]	Shintō Ryū 神道流	*sōjutsu* 槍術

Over its long history Anazawa Ryū has been the antecedent tradition for several other combative schools.

Anazawa Sakon Genshin 穴沢 左近 元真【穴澤左近元真】(c. 1560–c. 1620). Disciple of Anazawa Tonomonosuke Morihide who transmitted the Shintō Ryū (6) 新当流 *nagadachi* system in Satsuma.

Anazawa Sessai 穴沢 雪斎【穴澤雪齋】. Pseudonym under which Anazawa Tonomonosuke Morihide transmitted Tenshinsho-den Katori Shintō Ryū 天真正伝香取神道流 spear arts (*sōjutsu*) in various locations.

[5] Note: Watatani and Yamada (1978: 433) list Moritsuna as the fifth headmaster, but Ōtake (2007: 17) lists him as fourth headmaster.

Anazawa Tonomonosuke Morihide 穴沢主殿助 盛秀【穴澤主殿助盛秀】[A.k.a. ***~Kiyomi Hidetaka*** 浄見秀俊【淨見秀俊】; ***Nobuyuki*** 信之; 如緊; ***Sessai*** 雪斎【雪齋】; ***Tonomonosuke*** 主殿介; etc.]. Founder of Anazawa Ryū, c.1580. Morihide was a disciple of Iizasa Moritsuna, fourth headmaster of the Katori Shintō Ryū.[6] In forming the Anazawa Ryū he concentrated on long glaive arts (*naginatajutsu*), longsword (*nagadachi*), and long hardwood staff methods (*bōjutsu*). Under various pseudonyms he spread variations of Anazawa Ryū throughout Japan. See: *Anazawa Ryū.*

Anazawa Tonomonosuke Nobuyuki 穴沢主殿助 信之【穴澤主殿助信之】. Pseudonym under which Anazawa Tonomonosuke Morihide transmitted Anazawa Ryū longsword (*nagadachi*) and the comprehensive combative arts of Shintō Ryū (6) 新当流 in Takata domain. His direct disciple in this endeavor was his son, Anazawa Ichimi Shinobu.

Anegawa Katsuyoshi 姉川 勝義. Anegawa was a direct disciple of Hakkō Ryū 八光流 founder, Okuyama Yoshiji. He was also a successor of Tenshin Koryū 天心古流 which concentrated on pugilistic fighting techniques (*kempō* [2]) and self-defense arts (*goshinjutsu*).

anji 按司 [Also read ***aji*** or ***anzu***]. OKINAWAN KARATE—An Okinawan title of nobility indicating a descendant of an Okinawan prince. Some Okinawan fighting arts masters were of this social class. See Kerr (1958: 188–189ff.) for more complete information on Okinawan titles. See also: *pēchin.*

Further reading in English:

• Kerr, 1958.

Anji kata no Mekata 按司方の舞方 (Oki.) [Read in Jp. as ***Anji kata no Maikata***]. OKINAWAN KARATE—Primary prearranged combative scenario (*kata*) of the original Motobu Udundī 本部御殿手 school. This form was evidently lost with the death of Motobu Chōyū in 1927.

Anjin 按針. See: *Miura Anjin.*

Anrakuji 安楽寺【安樂寺】. Buddhist temple located in Tsukushi, Kyūshū where Nen Ami Jion performed martial/religious austerities. There, in an oracular dream state (*musō*), he received from the Buddhist goddess Marishiten the innermost secrets of what would become the Nen Ryū.

Aoki Budayū Yasutomo 青木 武太夫 保知 [A.k.a. ***~Takuemon*** 宅右衛門]. Founder of the Aoki Ryū pipe spear (*kudayari*) tradition. Aoki first trained in the Owari Kan Ryū 尾張貫流 pipe spear tradition founded by Tsuda Nobuyuki. According to Watatani and Yamada (1978: 12), Aoki had evidently taken on disciples (*deshi*) while he was still considered a student of the Owari Kan Ryū, and was punished with expulsion (*hamon*) by the headmaster. Aoki then became a masterless samurai (*rōnin*) and moved to Edo, where he named his system Hiden Ryū 飛電流.

Aoki Ha Hiden Ryū 青木派飛電流. Variant name for Aoki Ryū.

Aoki Ryū 青木流 [A.k.a. ***Aoki Ha Hiden Ryū*** 青木派飛電流; ***Hiden Ryū*** 飛電流]. Tradition centering on the pipe spear (*kudayari*) founded by Aoki Budayū Yasutomo. In Bishū, the Aoki Ryū became incorporated into the Ikkan Ryū (3) 一貫流. However, Aoki Yasutomo taught his system in Edo under the title of Hiden Ryū 飛電流.

Aoki Owari no Kami Nobutatsu 青木 尾張守 信辰 (c. 1560–c. 1620). Direct disciple (*deshi*) of Anazawa Tonomonosuke Morihide. Nobutatsu transmitted Ōshin Ryū 応心流 long-hafted glaive arts (*naginatajutsu*) in Owari domain.

Aoyagi Ryū 青柳流. A classical *jūjutsu* system. See: *Iga Ryū (5).*

aragyō 荒行. Ascetic practices; religious austerities.

Arakaki Ryū 新垣流. OKINAWAN KARATE—Okinawan *karate* system transmitted by Arakaki Ankichi (c. 1899–1966). This tradition concentrated on boxing technique (*karate*), the use of the long tapered Okinawan hard-

6 Note: Watatani and Yamada (1978: 433) list Moritsuna as the fifth headmaster, but Ōtake (2007: 17) lists him as fourth headmaster.

wood staff (*bōjutsu*), and skills associated with the combat trident (*sai*).

Arakawa Magosaburō Tokimune 荒川 孫三郎 時宗. Founder of the Arakawa Nen Ryū. According to Nen Ryū archives, Arakawa trained with Tomomatsu Seizo Fujiwara no Ujimune (Gian)—seventh headmaster of the Nen Shuza Ryū 念首座流—sometime during the last decade of the sixteenth century. This was around the same time as Higuchi Sadatsugu. Arakawa subsequently founded the Arakawa Nen Ryū. It is recorded that during the Genna era (1615–1624), Arakawa had a match with Miyamoto Musashi.[7] One of Arakawa's disciples, Atsumi Heihachirō, further modified the Nen Ryū curriculum and subsequently founded the Atsumi Nen Ryū 渥美念流. Arakawa's son, Hachizaemon no Jō 八左衛門尉, evidently passed on the "family line" of Arakawa Nen Ryū.

Arakawa Nen Ryū 荒川念流. Derivative tradition of the Nen Shuza Ryū 念首座流. According to Maniwa Nen Ryū records held by the Higuchi family, the founder of the Arakawa Nen Ryū was a samurai named Arakawa Magosaburō Tokimune. Although concentrating on combative swordsmanship, this system was essentially the same as that passed on to Higuchi Sadatsugu by the seventh headmaster of Nen Shuza Ryū, Tomomatsu Seizo Fujiwara no Ujimune (Gian). Consequently it was a comprehensive field-combat system (*sōgo bujutsu*) which included combative swordsmanship (*kenjutsu*), long-hafted glaive (*naginatajutsu*), and spear (*sōjutsu*). See lineage chart under *Nen Shuza Ryū*.

Araki Mataemon Yasukazu 荒木 又右衛門 保和 [A.k.a. ***Ushinosuke*** 丑之助; ***Minosuke*** 巳之助; ***Yoshimura*** 吉村; ***Yoshitada*** 吉忠; ***Nobukuni*** 信国【信國】; ***Hattori*** 服部; ***Kikuyama*** 菊山; ***Yasutomo*** 保知; etc.]. Having mastered several sword systems—Edo Yagyū Shinkage Ryū 江戸柳生新陰流 under Yagyū Munenori; Chūjō Ryū 中条流; and Shintō Ryū 神道流—Yasukazu founded his own school, the Araki Ryū, in the early 1620s. He is also recognized by Yagyū Shingan Ryū (1) Taijutsu 柳生心眼流体術 as the progenitor of that system.

Araki Mujinsai 荒木 夢仁斎【荒木夢仁齋】[Var. 夢人斎; 無仁斎; a.k.a. ***~Minamoto no Hidetsuna*** 源秀縄] (c.1584–1638). Founder of Araki Ryū Kempō/Kogusoku. Mujinsai had previously trained extensively in the Takenouchi Ryū 竹内流 under Takenouchi Kaganosuke Hisayoshi, third successor of that tradition.

Araki Mujinsai Ryū 荒木夢仁斎流【荒木夢仁齋流】. See: *Araki Ryū Kempo Kogusoku.*

Araki Ryū. Watatani and Yamada (1978: 30–36) list several systems with this same name (荒木流) although one uses alternate characters (荒義流). The various Araki Ryū specialized in a variety of dissimilar combative arts such as swordsmanship (*kenjutsu*), quick-draw sword arts (*iaijutsu*), horsemanship (*bajutsu*), swimming (*suieijutsu*), arresting arts (*torite*), etc.

Araki Ryū 1. 荒木流. This was primarily a system of swordsmanship founded by Araki Mataemon Yasukazu in the early 1620s. Yasukazu was a senior student of Edo Yagyū Shinkage Ryū 江戸柳生新陰流 progenitor Yagyū Munenori. However, Araki had also trained extensively in Chūjō Ryū 中条流 and Shintō Ryū 神道流, based on which Watatani and Yamada (1978: 31) comment that his system was Shinkage Ryū "flavored" by those two other systems. Originally a swordsmanship (*kenjutsu*) school, Araki Ryū weapons systems have come to include the long hardwood staff (*bō*), composite chained staff (*chigiriki*), and composite sickle and chain (*kusarigama*).

Further reading in English:

- Amdur, 2002b: 145–194.

Araki Ryū 2. 荒木流. See: *Araki Ryū Kempo Kogusoku.*

Araki Ryū gunyō kogusoku 荒木流軍用小具足. Lit. "Araki Ryū military system of grappling in light armor."

Araki Ryū Kempō/Kogusoku 荒木流拳法・

[7] This information comes from the *Kenjutsu keizu* 『剣術系図』.

小具足 [A.k.a. ***Araki Ryu (2)*** 荒木流, ***Araki Mujinsai Ryū*** 荒木無人斎流【荒木無人齋流】, ***Moro Kobudō Araki Ryū Kempō*** 茂呂古武道荒木流拳法]. This is primarily a comprehensive field-combat system (*sōgo bujutsu*) which also includes some arresting/restraining arts intended for capturing enemy combatants. This martial tradition was founded by Araki Mujinsai of the Matsudaira family from Echizen province. According to Watatani and Yamada (1978: 32), its combative systems originally included striking arts (*kempō* [2]), combative grappling (*kumitsuku*), grappling in light armor (*kogusoku*), capturing arts (*torite*), hardwood staff (*bō*), glaive arts (*nagamaki*), small throwing blades and darts (*shuriken*), pole with weighted chain (*chigiriki*), sickle and chain (*kusarigama*), quick-draw sword art (*iaijutsu*), tying-cord (*torinawa*), and the striking of vital points (*kachimi*).

aramitama 荒魂 [Var. 荒御魂]. SHINTŌ—According to Shintō belief, an *aramitama* is a rough spirit. See: *mitama.*

aramusha 荒武者. A "wild warrior"; a "rough warrior"; a "berserker." The *aramusha*—which, as Varley (1994: 57) notes, is often compared to the *arauma* (wild, untamed horse)—was an archetype admired by the Heian period warrior. This *aramusha* type, in fact, was also esteemed in later periods, as can be seen in legends of famous warriors such as the youthful Miyamoto Musashi.

arauma 荒馬. A wild, untamed horse. This type of mount was popular among the warriors of the tenth and eleventh centuries. (Varley, 1994: 16).

ariake no metsuke 有明の目付. A method of sighting the target in Japanese archery (*kyūjutsu* and *kyūdō*) in which the bull's-eye of the target is fully exposed just to the left of the bow. Thus the target appears like the moon at dawn (*ariake*) just above the horizon (the bow). See also: *hangetsu no metsuke; yami no metsuke.*

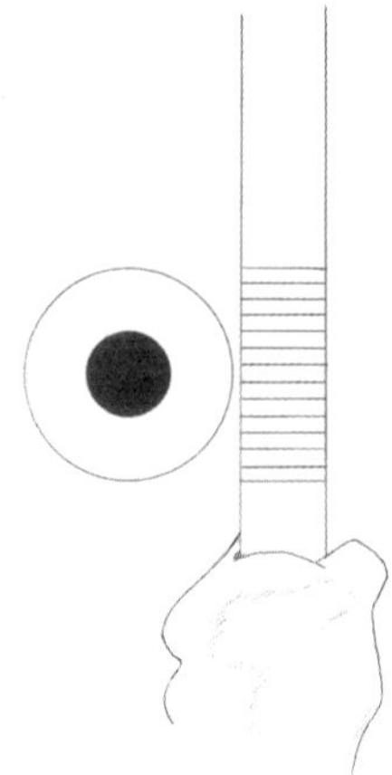

ARIAKE NO METSUKE

Arichi Shinkage Ryū 有地真陰流. Branch tradition of the Yagyū Shinkage Ryū transmitted in Fukuoka domain. This line passed directly from school founder Yagyū Muneyoshi Sekishūsai to his adopted son, Yagyū Matsuemon Munenobu. After Munenobu, the Yagyū school split into two lines in Fukuoka domain: one led by his son Yagyū Hyōsuke (Yagyū Shinkage Ryū), and one stemming from Munenobu's top student, Arichi Kuranosuke Motokatsu (Arichi Shinkage Ryū).

The Arichi line later spread to Hagi domain (present-day town of Hagi in Yamaguchi prefecture) where, several generations later, yet another branch—the Miyake Ha Shinkage Ryū 三宅派新陰流—split off from the Arichi family line.

Arichi Shinkage Ryū
有地真陰流
(abbreviated lineage)

Yagyū Muneyoshi
柳生宗厳
Yagyū Shinkage Ryū
柳生新陰流

Yagyū Matsuemon Munenobu
柳生松右衛門宗信
(a.k.a. Matsuno/Ōno)
(松野/大野)
Yagyū Shinkage Ryū
柳生新陰流

Yagyū Hyōsuke
柳生兵助
Yagyū Shinkage Ryū
柳生新陰流

Arichi Motokatsu
有地元勝
Arichi Shinkage Ryū
有地真陰流

Arichi Kura-no-suke Motokatsu 有地 内蔵丞元勝 [A.k.a. **Tsunenaka** 常掌]. Direct disciple (*deshi*) of Yagyū Matsuemon Munenobu. Mokatsu founded the Arichi Shinkage Ryū.

Ariji Shinkage Ryū 有地真陰流. See: *Arichi Shinkage Ryū.*

aruki kata 歩き方. Way of walking, pace. Many classical combative systems emphasized *aruki kata*; some trained in highly specialized methods.

Asahi Ryū 朝日流. Early (c. 1933–1936) term used for the grappling system Ueshiba Morihei modified from Daitō Ryū *aikijūjutsu* into *aikidō*. This was not an official term but one used for convenience[8] by his trainees when Ueshiba was teaching at the *Asahi News* office in Ōsaka.

Asai Ryū 浅井流【淺井流】. A classical *jūjutsu* system. See: *Iga Ryū (5).*

Asaka Ryū Iai—Koshi no mawari 浅賀流居合腰廻【淺賀流居合腰廻】. This system of swordsmanship (*kenjutsu*) and quick-draw sword art (*iaijutsu*), a branch tradition of Katayama Hōki Ryū, was founded by Asaka Yazaemon Katsuchika sometime during the first half of the seventeenth century. See: *Katayama Hōki Ryū.*

Asaka Yazaemon Katsuchika 浅賀弥左衛門勝周【淺賀彌弥左衛門 勝周】(c. 1600–c. 1675). Founder of Asaka Ryu Iai—Koshi no Mawari.

Asaoka Heibei Shigemasa 浅岡 平兵衛 重政【淺岡平兵衛重政】. Famous archer and warrior who, in 1606, won an archery contest at the Sanjūsangendō temple in Kyōto. He accomplished this by successfully shooting fifty-one arrows at a target located at the end of a 120-meter corridor within the temple building. This contest became a yearly affair at the temple. See: *kyūdō; kyūjutsu; Sanjūsangendō; tōshiya.*

Asari Matashichirō Yoshiaki (Gimei) 浅利又七郎 義明【淺浅利又七郎義明】(c. 1790–c. 1850). Yoshiaki, the foster son of Asari Matashichirō Yoshinobu, was actually the second son of Nakanishi Chūbei Tanemasa, his foster father's *kenjutsu* instructor in the Nakanishi Ha Ittō Ryū 中西派一刀流. Yoshiaki, like his foster father Yoshinobu, was physically small, but—also like his foster father—was able to produce a powerful *kiai*. His most famous student was Yamaoka Tesshū, founder of the Ittō Shōden Mutō Ryū 一刀正伝無刀流.

Asari Matashichirō Yoshinobu 浅利 又七郎義信【淺浅利又七郎義信】(1777–1853). Yoshinobu founded the Asari Ryū, a derivative tradition of the Nakanishi Ha Ittō Ryū 中西派一刀流. Yoshinobu was originally a swordsman of the Nakanishi Ha Ittō Ryū who had trained with both Nakanishi Chūbei Tanemasa and Nakanishi Itarō Tsugumichi 中西 猪太郎 子路. He was well known for his powerful *kiai,* and was said to be able to knock his opponents off balance with it before finishing them with his powerful thrusting technique. (Draeger, 1974: 108). Yoshinobu's most famous students were his foster son Asari Matashichirō Yoshiaki (Gimei), and Chiba Shūsaku, founder of the Hokushin Ittō Ryū 北辰一刀流. See the entry on Ono Ha Ittō Ryū 小野派一刀流 for lineage. See also: *kiaijutsu.*

Further reading in English:

- Hurst, 1998: 88–89, 95, 96.

Asari Ryū 浅利流【淺利流】. As a branch tradition of the Nakanishi Ha Ittō Ryū 中西派一刀流 founded by Asari Matashichirō Yoshinobu, this system focused on *kenjutsu.*

Asato Ankō 安里 安恒 (Oki.). See: *Azato Ankō.*

Asato Yasutsune 安里 安恒. See: *Azato Ankō.*

Asayama Ichiden Koryū 浅山一伝古流【淺山一傳古流】. Branch tradition of Asayama Ichiden Ryū founded by Kobayashi Moemon. This system specialized in *jūjutsu* derived from its parent tradition.

Asayama Ichiden Ryū 浅山一伝流【淺山一傳流】[A.k.a. **Asayama Ichiden Ryū Heihō** ～兵法; **Asayama Ichiden Ryū Taijutsu** ～体術]. Classical, comprehensive field-combat school (*sōgo bujutsu*) developed between 1573 and 1615 by Asayama Ichiden Shigeaki.

[8] As stated by Ueshiba's student Takuma Hisa in an interview with Stanley A. Pranin in 1979. See Pranin, 1996: 110.

Its combative curriculum currently includes long hardwood staff arts (*bōjutsu*), quick-draw sword arts (*iaijutsu*), sickle arts (*kamajutsu*), swordsmanship (*kenjutsu*), and grappling (*taijutsu*). Originally it also included an unspecified form of grappling, arresting techniques (*torite*), small throwing blades and darts (*shurikenjutsu*), combative spear (*sōjutsu*), sickle techniques (*kama*), the use of poisons (*dokugai*), espionage (*shinobi no jutsu*), etc.

The system traces its origins to Marume Mondonoshō, a rural samurai (*goshi*) from Jōshū (present-day Gunma prefecture). Marume's student Kuniie Yashiemon founded the Kageyama Shintō Ryū. After training with Kuniie, a talented warrior named Asayama Ichidensai placed his own stamp on the tradition by combining it with other systems he had mastered and naming it Asayama Ichiden Ryū. However, Asayama was a somewhat enigmatic figure; some versions of his personal history indicate that he also trained with Kamiizumi Nobutsuna of the Shinkage Ryū (1) 新陰流 and/or other disciples of the Shinkage tradition, such as Okuyama Zaemon, disciple of Marume Kurando (Taisha Shinkage Ryū タイ捨新陰流); and Nakamura Senjūrō, direct disciple of Kamiizumi Nobutsuna.

Over its long history, Asayama Ichiden Ryū has been the antecedent tradition for several other combative schools, including the Kaneda Ichiden Ryū 金田一伝流, Fuden Ryū 不伝流, Tsuda Ichiden Ryū 津田一伝流, Sakura Ichiden Ryū 佐倉一伝流, Asayama Ichiden Koryū 浅山一伝古流, Asayama Ichiden Shin Ryū 浅山一伝新流, Ōhen Ryū 応変流, Jishin Ryū 自心流, and others. One of its *kenjutsu kata* known as A-Un 阿吽 was chosen by the Japanese police commission of 1886 for inclusion in their early attempt to standardize *kendō kata*.

Further reading in English:

• D. Skoss, 1997: 63.

Asayama Ichiden Ryū
浅山一伝流
(abbreviated lineage)

Marume Mondonoshō Noriyoshi
丸目主水正則吉

|

Kuniie Yaemon
国家弥右衛門
Kageyama Shintō Ryū
景山真刀流

|

1. Asayama Ichidensai Shigeaki
浅山一伝斎重晨
Asayama Ichiden Ryū
浅山一伝流

Asayama Ichiden Ryū Heihō 浅山一伝流兵法【淺山一傳流兵法】. See: *Asayama Ichiden Ryū.*

Asayama Ichidensai Shigeaki (Sangorō) 朝山 一伝斎 重晨（三五郎）【朝山一傳齋三五郎】. Nineteenth-century samurai who founded the Asayama Ryū.

Asayama Ichidensai Shigeaki 浅山一伝斎重晨【淺山一傳齋重晨】. Warrior who founded the Asayama Ichiden Ryū sometime between 1573 and 1615.

Asayama Ichiden Shin Ryū 浅山 一伝 新流【淺山一傳新流】. Branch tradition of Asayama Ichiden Ryū that was founded by Moriyama Shimizuemon Motoshige and transmitted in Mito domain. This system specialized in *jūjutsu* derived from its parent tradition, but in designating it "Shinryū" (revised tradition) in contrast to Kobayashi Moemon's "Koryū," (classical tradition) Moriyama was apparently emphasizing his support for technique modified from the original system. Both lines were transmitted in the Mito domain. See also: *Asayama Ichiden Koryū.*

Asayama Ryū 朝山流. A martial school created in the nineteenth century by Asayama Ichiden sai Sangorō. It specialized in sword-fighting (*kenjutsu*), grappling (*jūjutsu*), quick-draw sword art (*iaijutsu*), and long hardwood staff techniques (*bōjutsu*). Its transmission seems to have been restricted to Satsuma domain during the feudal period.

ashi 足. A leg, a foot; step, pace. ¶ *ashidome*足留め, a foot block; a foot-check.

ashibumi 足踏み. Lit. "stepping" *ashibumi* is a *kyūdō* term indicating the first of eight stages in firing an arrow, in which the archer turns his body 90 degrees to the right, away from the target, and plants his feet for the shot. See also: *hassetsu*.

ashigarami 足搦. 1. Classical system for grappling in water. 2. KENDŌ—A leg-entanglement technique used when opponents are in close with their hand guards (*tsuba*) locked. 3. JŪDŌ/SUMŌ—A leg-entanglement or leg-scissors technique.

Ashigarazaka 足柄坂. A pass which came to define the border between eastern and western Japanese geographical areas. The early term for eastern Japan, "Bandō," (坂東) literally means "east of the pass." During the reign of Emperor Daigō[9] a gate (*kan*) was erected at Ashigarazaka in order to screen travelers. Subsequently areas east of the pass came to be referred to as "east of the gate" (Kantō 関東), and areas to the west came to be called "west of the gate" (Kansai 関西).

ashigaru 足軽【足輕】. Lit. "light-footed"; a soldier; light infantry. The *ashigaru* were low-ranking, lightly armored foot soldiers not of the *bushi* class. This type of combatant proliferated during the Ōnin War (1467–1477) and the subsequent Warring States period (Sengoku Jidai). The *ashigaru* were especially notorious for their destructive participation in the street-fighting in Kyōto during the Ōnin War.

Further reading in English:

• Turnbull, 2005: 82–141.

ashige 足蹴. A kick. ¶ *ashige ni suru* 足蹴にする, to kick.

Ashihara Hideyuki 芦原 英幸【蘆原英幸】(1944–1995). Founded Ashihara Karatedō 芦原空手道 in 1980. Having begun training in *kendō* at the age of eight, Ashihara became something of a combative arts prodigy after he entered a *karate dōjō* run by a naturalized Korean man by the name of Ōyama Masutatsu in 1961. After intensive training in Ōyama's system, he was awarded the rank of first degree (*shodan*) in 1964. In the same year, Ōyama established the Kyokushinkai 極真会. Ashihara, considered the most proficient fighter in the *dōjō* at that time, was made an instructor at the main training hall of Ōyama's school (Kyokushinkai Hombu Dōjō) in 1966. He was scheduled to travel to Brazil to spread Ōyama's Kyokushinkai Karatedō, but his involvement in a street fight caused Ōyama to banish him to the island of Shikoku to reflect on his wayward behavior. Ashihara developed a following during his exile, and soon began to move away from the Kyokushinkai. Over the next decade he developed his own variation of Ōyama's teachings. Ashihara's system, which he called *sabaki*, was based on circular movement, careful timing, and sensitivity to combative engagement distance (*maai*) and stance. By the late 1970s Ashihara had developed a large following in western Japan; he split completely with the Kyokushinkai in 1980, naming his new system "Ashihara Karatedō." He published three books on his system, which are available in English: *Fighting Karate*, Kodansha International, 1985; *More Fighting Karate,* Kodansha International, 1985; *The Word of Life: For Those Who Love Karate,* Tsuba Books, 1997 (posthumous).

Ashikaga 足利. Minamoto branch family that produced fifteen *shōgun* during the Ashikaga Jidai (1338–1573). The name was first used by Ashikaga Yoshiyasu 足利 義康 (1126–1157) who took the place-name of the village where his father established residence in 1150.

Further reading in English:

• Papinot, 1910: 27–39.

Ashikaga Bakufu 足利幕府. The Ashikaga military government which lasted from 1338 to 1573. See: *Ashikaga Jidai.*

Ashikaga Jidai 足利時代. The Ashikaga period (1392–1573) is so named for the era in which the title of *shōgun* was held by the Ashikaga family. The fifteen Ashikaga *shōgun* descended from Ashikaga Takauji, the first of that family to hold that title. This parallels the Muromachi period (1392–1573), when

---

[9] Daigo Tennō 醍醐天皇 (885–930; r. 897–930), sixtieth emperor of Japan.

the Ashikaga shogunate was located in the Muromachi section of the capital city of Kyōto.

Ashikaga Takauji 足利 尊氏 (1305–1358). Takauji was the first Ashikaga *shōgun*, reigning from 1331 to 1358.

Ashikaga Yoshimasa 足利 義政 (1435–1490). The eighth Ashikaga *shōgun*. Yoshimasa reigned from 1449 to 1472. See: *cha no yu*.

Ashikaga Yoshiteru 足利 義輝 (1535–1565). The thirteenth Ashikaga *shōgun*. Yoshiteru reigned in 1545 and again from 1553 to 1565.

Yoshiteru ascended to the shogunate at a time when the Ashikaga were losing their grip on the country. Yoshiteru was, in fact, under the thumb of the warlord Miyoshi Chōkei 三好長慶 and his powerful vassal, Matsunaga Hisahide 松永久秀. In despair, Yoshiteru committed suicide by *seppuku* in 1565. He was only thirty years old at the time.

Yoshiteru had such a great interest in martial arts that he opened a martial arts hall called the Heihōsho 兵法所 in the Imadegawa area of Kyōto, and hosted the best swordsmen of the day including Tsukahara Bokuden, Kamiizumi Ise no Kami, and many others.

It was in the presence of Yoshiteru that Kamiizumi Ise no Kami and Marume Kurandonosuke Tessai demonstrated the Shinkage Ryū (1) 新陰流. The young *shōgun* was so impressed by this demonstration that he later hired Kamiizumi's top student, Jingo Izu no Kami Muneharu, to instruct him in the Shinkage Ryū. Yoshiteru evidently trained regularly in *kenjutsu* and other combative systems with the top swordsmen of his day, and came to be known as the Kengō Shōgun (Swordsman General).

ashi sabaki 足捌. 1. Footwork; use of the feet. 2. To pivot or turn the body by reversing the positions of the forward and rear foot.

ashi waza 足技. KŌDŌKAN JŪDŌ—Leg-throwing techniques which are a subset of Nage no Kata.

ashura 阿修羅 [Var. 阿素羅·阿須倫; sometimes abbreviated as *shura* 修羅 <Ch. *axiuluo* <Skt. *asura*]. 1. In Brahmanism and Hinduism, an *asura* was a demon who fought with the gods headed by Indra. 2. BUDDHISM—In Buddhism the term *ashura* originally indicated a demon whose nature was to fight. However, the origin of the Sanskrit term *asura* is unclear. It may have meant "not (*a*) divine (*sura*)"; i.e., a demon or devil. Later Sanskrit texts interpret the term as "not (*a*) drinking Vedic liquor (*surā*)"; the term is sometimes translated into Chinese as *wujiu* 無酒 (not consuming alcohol). In most cases, however, the *ashura* is considered a powerful, supernatural being associated with fighting and violence. 3. The *ashuras* are "fighting beings" condemned to an existence of conflict and warfare in the "Realm of Demigods," the fourth of the Six Realms (Rokudō) into which beings are subject to rebirth.

Atagosan Daigongen 愛宕山大権現【愛宕山大權現】. RYŌBU SHINTŌ—A mountain god also known as Shōgun Jizō, whose main shrine is located on Mount Atago just north of Kyōto. Pilgrims journey to this shrine to seek protection from the "destructive power of fire." The cult itself represents the fusion of Buddhism and Shintō via the mountain priests (*yamabushi*) of Shugendō. Images of the deity, or simply its name, are sometimes found as talismans on martial accoutrements and weapons. See also: *gongen; Kanemaki Jisai Michiie; Ryōbu Shintō; Shōgun Jizō Bosatsu; Shōgun Jizōhō.*

Further reading in English:

• Bouchy, 1987: 255–277.

TALISMAN FOR ATAGOSAN DAIGONGEN
Small plaque affixed to Edo-period scabbard (*saya*)
(Private collection)

atarashii naginata 新しいなぎなた [A.k.a. ***keiko naginata*** 稽古薙刀; ***shiai naginata*** 試合薙刀]. The "modern" art of *naginata* generally practiced in *shiai* form much like *kendō*. It is most popular among women trainees, although some men take part in the sport as well.

~atari 当たり【當たり】. A strike, a hit. ¶ *tai-atari* 体当, a body strike; a body check.

atemi 当身【當身】[***atemijutsu*** 当身術【當身術】]. 1. Lit. "body strike," this term commonly denotes a methodology for striking an enemy's vital areas, either with fists, feet, or weapons. 2. The martial art of striking specific vital points (*kyūsho*) on an opponent's body. See also: *genkotsu; kassatsujutsu.*

atemijutsu 当身術【當身術】. See: *atemi.*

atemi waza 当身技【當身技】. See: *ate waza.*

ate waza 当技【當技】. Striking techniques found in certain *jūjutsu* systems. See also: *atemi; Kanō Jigorō; Kōdōkan Jūdō; Tenshin Shin'yō Ryū.*

Atsumi Heihachirō 渥美 平八郎 (?–1701). Retainer of the Hikone domain who founded the Atsumi Nen Ryū 渥美念流.

Having mastered the Nen Ryū teachings of Arakawa Magosaburō Tokimune, Atsumi further modified the Nen Ryū curriculum and founded his own system which he christened the Atsumi Nen Ryū. In contrast to his teacher Arakawa, Atsumi instituted the use of padded bamboo swords (*shinai*) and dropped the use of iron-reinforced headbands (*hitaikane*) and wooden swords (*bokken*) for match practice (*shiai*). This became one of the early schools of *gekken* in the 1690s.

Atsumi Nen Ryū 渥美念流. Branch tradition of the Arakawa Nen Ryū 荒川念流 founded by Atsumi Heihachirō in the 1690s. This system began moving away from the classical swordsmanship (*kenjutsu*) of its parent Arakawa Nen Ryū and emphasized an early, severe form of *kendō* known as *gekken.* See lineage chart under *Nen Shuza Ryū.*

Atsuta Daijingū 熱田大神宮. Atsuta Grand Shrine, established in Owari (present-day Nagoya), which contains the treasure sword known as Ame no Murakumo no Tsurugi.

auhyōshi 合拍子. Lit. "synchronous beat." YAGYŪ SHINKAGE RYŪ—An attack in which both opponents strike at the same instant. See: *hyōshi.*

a-un 1. 阿吽 <Ch. *a-hong* <Skt. *a-hūṁ*. A Japanese transliteration of the Sanskrit term *a-hūṁ.* A parallel to "alpha and omega" (beginning and end), this term is found in many "mystic" references in martial *densho.*

a-un 2. 阿吽 [Var. 阿吽]. a. Name of a variety of classical combative forms (*kata*) developed by various martial schools. b. ASAYAMA ICHIDEN RYŪ—A-Un is one of a number of classical pre-arranged combative forms (*kata*) developed by this school. It was also one of ten classical *kata* adapted by the Japanese Police Commission of 1886 for their Keishichō Ryū 警視庁流 system.

a-un no kokyū 阿吽の呼吸. 1. Synchronicity in breathing. 2. JIKI SHINKAGE RYŪ—Term used to describe a type of breathing/breath control. In this case *a* refers to inhalation and *un* refers to compression. The proponent's breath is synchronized with that of the enemy. The Jiki Shinkage Ryū also equates *a-un no kokyū* with the Ni-ō temple guards, which are normally depicted intoning the sacred syllables *a* and *un.* 3. SHINDŌ MUSŌ RYŪ—Term used to describe a type of breathing/breath control. In this case *a* refers to exhalation and *un* refers to inhalation. The proponent's breath is synchronized with that of the enemy. See also: *Ni-ō.*

Awaji Ryū 淡路流. See: *Awaji Shizu Suigun.*

Awaji Shizu Suigun 淡路倭文水軍 [Var. ***Awaji Suigun*** 淡路水軍; ***Awaji Ryū*** 淡路流]. School of naval tactics (*suigun*) founded by Murakami Moronobu 村上師信 during the mid-seventeenth century.

Awaji Suigun 淡路水軍. See: *Awaji Shizu Suigun.*

Awa Kenzō 阿波 研三 (1880–1939). Japanese archery master featured in Eugen Herrigel's famous book *Zen and the Art of Archery.*

Awa began studying classical Japanese archery (*kyūjutsu*) in a tradition known as the Heki Ryū Sekka Ha 日置流雪荷派 around

1900. He proved to be a prodigy, mastering the curriculum in only two years. He was given a full license (*menkyo kaiden*) around 1902, and subsequently opened his own archery training hall (*kyūdōjō* 弓道場). By this time Awa was capable of "hitting the mark nearly one hundred times for every one hundred shots" (*hyappatsu hyakuchū*).

During the early Taishō era (1912–1926), Awa began moving away from classical *kyūjutsu*. According to traditional Heiki Ryū Sekka Ha doctrine, while a beginner necessarily must learn a good deal of archery technique, the advanced archer must reach a point where he no longer thinks of any technique. This point was referred to by master archer Yoshida Toyokazu as "nothing is needed" (*nani mo iranu*). Awa, however, expanded this concept into a belief that no technique at all was needed, even from the beginning. He then proceeded to teach his own "way of shooting" (*shadō*), the purpose of which was, again according to Yamada (2001: 8), "austere training in which one masters the study of humanity" (*ningengaku o osameru shugyō*). This was a radical departure from traditional *kyūjutsu*, and Awa was ridiculed by many in the classical archery community.

He persevered, however, seeing his evolution of *kyūjutsu* into *shadō* as a parallel of Kanō Jigorō's modification of various *jūjutsu* schools into *jūdō*. Then, in 1920, Awa experienced a mystical awakening. From this he emerged with two critical philosophical concepts that became the core of his *shadō*. First was to "put one's entire life—even unto death—into each shot" (*issha zetsumei*); second was to "see true nature in the shot" (*shari kenshō*).

He transmitted these concepts to Eugen Herrigel, who was his student in the 1920s. In 1936, after returning to Germany, Herrigel published an article on *kyūdō* which later became the core of his book *Zen and the Art of Archery* (published in English in 1953). Herrigel does not mention Awa's name in the book, but refers to him only as "the master." Although Awa did not associate the teachings of his *shadō* with Zen, Herrigel evidently decided the teachings he had learned from Awa were derived from Zen. See: *kyūdō*.

Further reading in English:

- Herrigel, 1953.
- Stevens, 2007.
- Yamada, 2001.

awanu kataki 合わぬ敵. Medieval term meaning "unworthy foe." Contrast to *yoki kataki* (worthy foe).

Further reading in English:

- Varley, 1994: 62–63.

aware 哀れ. See: *mono no aware*.

awase 合わせ. 1. A posture in which both parties cross their weapons in *seigan no kamae*. This position may vary somewhat from tradition to tradition, but it is used in some form by most classical Japanese martial schools in which weapons are employed. 2. The performance of a prearranged combative scenario (*kata*) without lethal content or intent.

AWASE
Donn F. Draeger (left) and Ōtake Risuke (right) move through *awase* while demonstrating Katori Shintō Ryū at Katori Grand Shrine in 1978
(Photograph by Pat Lineberger)

Ayō Hikita Ryū 阿陽疋田流. Branch tradition of the Hikita Kage Ryū concentrating on combative spear (*sōjutsu*). The lineage follows the Shinkage line from Kamiizumi through his nephew Hikita Bungorō.

The founder of this school, Nagao Katsushi, was a retainer of Awa domain (present-day Tokushima prefecture). His original surname was Murakami 村上, so at some point he was adopted by the Nagao family. Nagao was one of Inoda Shigekichi's primary disciples (*deshi*) and may have even trained with Inoda's master, Hikita Denbei. Having received the Hikita

Ryū from Inoda, Nagao transmitted it in Awa domain as Ayō Hikita Ryū.

Ayō Hikita Ryū
阿陽疋田流
(abbreviated lineage)

Aisu Ikō
愛洲 移香
Aisu Kage Ryū
愛洲陰流

|

Kamiizumi Ise no Kami Nobutsuna
上泉 伊勢守 信綱
Shinkage Ryū
新陰流

|

Hikita Bungorō Kagekane
疋田 豊五郎 景兼
Hikita Kage Ryū
疋田(新)陰流

|

Hikita Denbei Kageyoshi
疋田 伝兵衛 景吉
Hikita Kage Ryū
疋田(新)陰流

|

Inoda Iori Shigekichi
猪多 伊織 重吉
Inoda Ryū *sōjutsu*
猪多流 槍術

|

Nagao Ichizaemon Katsuyuki
中尾 市左衛門 勝之
Ayō Hikita Ryū *sōjutsu*
阿陽疋田流 槍術

ayumiashi 歩み足. A normal walking step. See also: *fumikomiashi; okuriashi; suriashi.*

Azato Ankō 安里 安恒 <Oki. Asato Ankō [Var. ***Asato Yasutsune***] (1827–1906). OKINAWAN KARATE—One of the key developers of Okinawan *karate* and teacher of Funakoshi Gichin. Azato was a child prodigy who excelled in both classical learning (Confucianism) and martial endeavors such as Western horsemanship, archery (*shagei*), and Jigen Ryū 示現流 swordsmanship (*kenjutsu*). He trained in Okinawan fighting arts with Matsumura Sōkon. According to Funakoshi, Azato came from a noble background of landed gentry and was in a high political office when the Ryūkyū archipelago was absorbed by Japan in 1879. Martin (2007: 4), notes that Azato was a foreign-affairs advisor to the Okinawan king.

The popular legends concerning Azato are many. One interesting tale notes that in a duel he was able use empty-hand *karate* technique to disarm fellow Jigen Ryū swordsman Yorin Kanna. Azato was a contemporary and close friend of Itosu Ankō, who also studied *karate* under Matsumura Sōkon and led the movement to have *karate* entered into the public school system.

Azato's best-known student was Funakoshi Gichin, who was primarily responsible for popularizing *karate* in Japan in the 1920s. See also: *Funakoshi Gichin; Itosu Ankō; Matsumura Sōkon; Sakugawa Tōde.*

Azato Ha karate 安里派 空手. Within the general Shōrin (少林・小林) *karate* styles of Okinawa, the Azato Ha (Azato branch line) is a classification made by the Japanese encompassing the traditions of Okinawan *karate* that descended from Matsumura Sōkon via his student Azato Ankō.

Azato Yasutsune 安里安恒. See: *Azato Ankō.*

Azechi Ken Chinju Shōgun 按察使兼鎮守将軍【按察使兼鎮守將軍】. See: *Chinjufu Shōgun.*

Azuchi-Momoyama Jidai 安土桃山時代. The Azuchi-Momoyama period (1573–1598). This era encompasses the time at the end of the Warring States period (Sengoku Jidai) when Japan was brought under control by the warlord Oda Nobunaga and his successor, Toyotomi Hideyoshi. The name of the period is taken from the residences of the two warlords: Azuchi was a lavish palace Nobunaga had built on the shore of Lake Biwa in 1576, and Momoyama was a magnificent castle built by Hideyoshi in Kyōto in 1593. (Both were ultimately destroyed.) The period is sometimes measured from the date of Nobunaga's entry into Kyōto in 1568 (at which time he installed Ashikaga Yoshiaki as the fifteenth and final Ashikaga *shōgun*), ending with the defeat of the Toyotomi forces by Tokugawa Ieyasu at Sekigahara in 1600. However, the dates more commonly accepted by Japanese scholars span from the fall of the last Ashikaga *shōgun* (at the hand of Oda Nobunaga) in 1573 to the death of Toyotomi Hideyoshi in 1598.

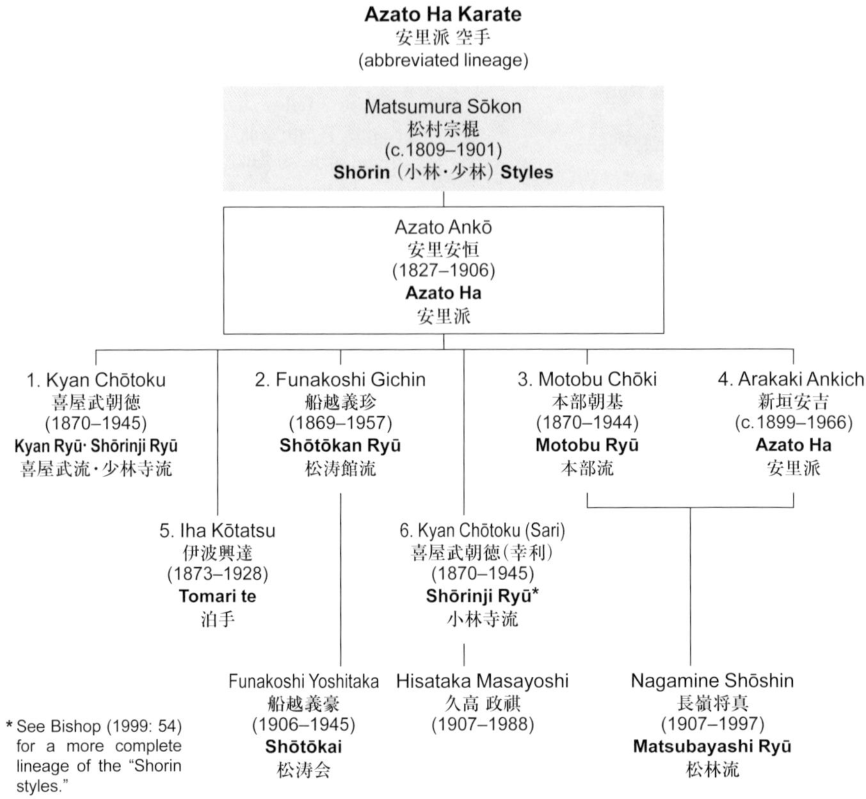

Azuma 吾妻. An ancient name for the eastern and northern provinces of the island of Honshu.

Azuma kagami 『吾妻鏡』 [Var. 東鑑]. Lit. "The lessons of the East." The *Azuma kagami* is a chronicle of the Kamakura shogunate compiled some time after 1266. It covers the period from 1180 to 1266.

Azuma Ryū 1. A school of espionage (*ninjutsu*) that was apparently still preserved during the Taishō era (1912–1925). The only practitioner from that time known today is Azuma Tarō Uemon. 2. A school specializing in swordsmanship (*kenjutsu*) with the standard sword (*katana*) and dagger (*tantō*) in the area of Fukuoka domain in Kyūshū. The only known practitioner is Suyama Ichiemon. 3. A school specializing in arresting-cord arts (*torinawa*) that was a splinter tradition of the Namba Ippo Ryū 難波一甫流.

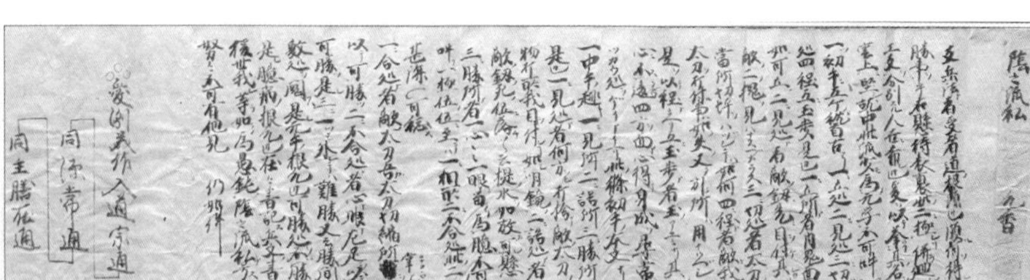

Aisu Kage no Ryū scroll entitled *Hisoka no Maki*
(Hirasawa Family Archives)
(*Kendō Nihon*, 1977, no. 8, used with permission)

B

baben 馬鞭. Lit. "horse whip," the *baben* is a short stick of about three feet (90 cm) in length, to which is attached a weighted chain. The length of the stick and chain together is about 6 feet (1.8 m).

bagu 馬具. Horse accoutrements and trappings such as harnesses, etc.

baishin 陪臣. During the Kamakura and Muromachi shogunates, this term indicated warriors who were indirect vassals of the *shōgun*, in contrast to *jikisan* 直参, direct vassals. Consequently, the direct vassals (*jikisan*) of a lord (*daimyō*) were the indirect vassals (*baishin*) of the *shōgun*. See also: *jikisan; hatamoto.*

bajutsu 馬術. Lit. "horse art." 1. Horse-mounted fighting men were an important factor in the development of Japanese culture as early as the third century C.E. By the sixth century, families and clans specializing in martial endeavors and horsemanship were being mentioned in the earliest written histories. However, it was also at this time that the Japanese began seriously experimenting with Chinese methods of government and warfare under the Ritsuryō Kyakushiki system. This included a reliance on conscript infantry.

With the decline of the Ritsuryō-style government and its dependency on conscript foot soldiers in the eighth century, the rise of the horse-mounted warrior class began. This had a dramatic effect on the way warfare was carried out and led to a shift in weaponry away from the infantry cut-and-thrust straight sword (*ken*) and toward the curved, slashing saber-like sword (*tachi*) of the mounted warrior. This was a gradual process, however, and we do not find the professional, horse-mounted warrior well established until the tenth or eleventh century. This trend may have been accelerated in eastern Japan. The war tales of the tenth through fourteenth centuries, from the *Shōmoki* through the *Taiheiki*, often mention the superiority of the horsemen of the Bandō (the Kantō plain area of eastern Japan).

For the *bushi*, or classical warrior, horsemanship was an indispensable part of the martial curriculum. Consequently he had to be well versed in the handling of various equestrian equipment—saddles, stirrups, bits, etc., as well as appropriate riding gear. From horseback, the *bushi* wielded a number of weapons, including the bow and arrow, sword, spear, long- and short-hafted glaives, and staffs made of hardwood or iron. While mounted swordsmanship led to a revolution in sword design, the primary weapon of the mounted warrior was the bow and arrow. In fact, the term for warriorship that arose in the subsequent Kamakura period (1185–1333) was "the way of the bow and horse" (*kyūba no michi*). The skills of mounted archery are still practiced today in the form of *yabusame*, a regulated competition involving target shooting while riding at full gallop.

With the rise of the classical *ryū* during the Muromachi period, it was not long before the horsemanship of the classical warrior started becoming systematized. The first documented classical school to organize *bajutsu* was the Ōtsubo Ryū in the fifteenth century. Fujita (1960:2) notes 153 *ryū* specializing in *bajutsu*. See also: *kiba musha; kisha (1); uma (1).*

bakken 抜剣【拔劍】. Lit. "striking sword." *Bakken* is one of several alternate terms for quick-draw sword art (*iaijutsu*). See also: *battōjutsu.*

bakufu 幕府. Sometimes translated as "tent government," the term *bakufu* actually refers to the curtains or screens that were used to create the headquarters precincts in the encampment of a commander in the field. The term originally meant "field headquarters," but came to refer to the permanent military government first established by Minamoto no Yoritomo in 1192. Since the commanding generals (*shōgun*) prior to that time were appointed for particular campaigns and had no fixed residence while on the move, they essentially administered from an encampment. With the establishment of a permanent *shōgun* in the person of Yoritomo, the tent government became a fixed institution, and the post became hereditary for the Minamoto family.

Although all subsequent *bakufu* leaders (that is, *shōgun*) still had to be nominated by the emperor, the shogunates themselves would recommend the next general.

Three shogunates controlled Japan over the next seven hundred years: the Kamakura *bakufu* (1192–1333) founded by Minamoto no Yoritomo; the Muromachi *bakufu* (1336–1573), run by the Minamoto branch family called the Ashikaga; and the Edo *bakufu* (1603–1868), run by the Minamoto branch family called the Tokugawa. See also: *Sei-i-taishōgun.*

Bakufu Jidai 幕府時代. The period of Japanese history in which political and military authority was held by a *shōgun*; i.e., 1192–1867.

bakugun 幕軍. The army of the shogunate.

bakuhei 幕兵. A soldier of the shogunate.

bakumatsu 幕末. Lit. the "end of the shogunate (tent government)," *bakumatsu* refers to the period from around 1853 through 1867. This short span of time began with the opening of Japan to the West by Admiral Perry (1853) and ended with the collapse of the Tokugawa shogunate (1867). Not only did this period see the end of the Tokugawa shogunate begun in 1603, it saw the end of the Bakufu Jidai (or Buke Jidai), the nearly seven hundred years during which warriors had ruled the country through the shogunate in lieu of the emperor. The year 1868 saw the Meiji Restoration, in which "official" political power returned to the office of the emperor.

Bakumatsu Edo Sandai Dōjō 幕末江戸三大道場. Lit. the "Three Great Training Halls of Bakumatsu-era Edo." During the final years of the Edo period, these *dōjō* stood out due to their large memberships and the skill of their headmasters. These metropolitan centers —known as *machi dōjō* (city training halls) in that they were not attached to the Tokugawa shogunate or specific domains—included the Gembukan, under swordsman Chiba Shūsaku of the Hokushin Ittō Ryū; the Rempeikan, under swordsman Saitō Yakurō of the Shindō Munen Ryū; and the Shigakkan, under swordsman Momonoi Shunzō of the Kyōshin Meichi Ryū.

Bakumatsu no Sanshū 幕末の三舟. Lit. the "Three *Shū* of the Bakumatsu." This term refers to three important swordsmen/statesmen who figured prominently in Japan's transition from a feudal society into a modern nation in the mid-1800s. The three were Katsu Kaishū 勝海舟, Yamaoka Tesshū 山岡鉄舟, and Takahashi Deishū 高橋泥舟. As can be seen, all have names that end with the character *shū* 舟.

bakuryō 幕僚. A shogunate staff officer or advisor.

bakushō 幕将【幕將】. A shogunate general.

bakushin 幕臣. A term used for direct vassals of the Tokugawa shogunate.

bampei 番兵. A sentry; a guard.

Bandō 坂東. A term used for the eight provinces east of Ashigara Pass (Ashigarazaka) that now make up the Kantō area of Japan. These eastern provinces were Awa, Hitachi, Kazusa, Kōzuke, Musashi, Sagami, Shimōsa, and Shimotsuke. According to Farris (1992: 90) this term for "eastern Japan" came into use around the year 750 in order to distinguish it from the provinces of northeast Japan (Tōhoku).

Bandō musha 坂東武者. Term used in the Heian, Kamakura, and Muromachi periods to denote warriors from the Kantō area of eastern Japan. The Bandō *musha* were well known for their élan, martial prowess, and superb horsemanship.

bangusoku 番具足. A type of armor worn by low-level retainers.

bankokuchōki 蛮国諜器 【蠻國諜器】. Lit. "weapon (or tool) used by barbarian spies." This device was a metal ring (a concealed weapon much like brass knuckles) used in *jūjutsu*-type arts. See also: *tekkan (1).*

banpei 番兵. See: *bampei.*

banrui 伴類. A term for the common foot soldier or fighting man in the tenth to twelfth centuries. The *banrui* evidently had only loose ties of interdependency with local warriors/lords, and were often criticized for fleeing the battlefield if things began to turn against them.

Referring to their participation in the army of Taira no Masakado, Farris (1992) translates *banrui* as "ally," but this definition—as with his translations of *innen* as "relative" and *jūrui* as "dependent"—obscures the combative function of these fighting men. The *banrui* were part-time soldiers who were not completely economically dependent on the warriors (*tsuwamono*) whom they accompanied in battle. (They differed from the *innen* and *jūrui* in this respect.) The *banrui* tended to be infantrymen who carried hand-held weapons into battle; they probably made up the majority of the troops in any particular conflict. See Farris (1992: 150–159) for a description of Taira no Masakado's combat force. See: *ikusa (1).*

Bansen shūkai 『万川集海』【萬川集海】. See: *Mansen shūkai.*

Banzai! 万歳!【萬歳】<Ch. *Wansui!* Lit. "10,000 ages," "forever," "infinity." 1. "Long live the king (emperor)!" 2. "Hooray!" "Hurrah!" (This victory shout is usually given with both arms held high.)

~barai (〜払い)【拂い】. From the verb *harau* 払う, to sweep. ¶ *ashibarai* 足払い, a foot sweep. ¶ *dōbarai* 胴払い, a sweep to or from the trunk of the body.

bashin 馬針 [Also read ***umabari***]. Lit. "horse needle." One of the "three tools of the stable" (*umagoya sangu*), this was a small knife used to bleed horses. This secondary weapon could also be used as a throwing blade (*shuriken*), either for throwing or held in the hand. Its use is still seen today in some branches of the Yagyū Shingan Ryū.

The *bashin* was usually a small, double cutting-edged blade with a decorated hilt (*tsuka*). The decorations tended to be martial and/or religious symbols such as a boar's eye (*i no me*) or *vajra* (*kongō*).

Bassai 抜塞【拔塞】<Oki. Passai. See: *karate kata; Passai.*

Batō Kannon 馬頭観音【馬頭觀音】<Ch. Matou Guanshiyin 馬頭觀世音 <Skt. Hayagrīva Avalokiteśvara [Var. ***Batō (Dai) Myōō*** 馬頭(大)明王 <Ch. Matou (Da) Mingwang <Skt. Hayagrīva Mahāvidyarāja; var. ***Kayak'rība*** 何耶掲二合利引婆 <Ch. Heyej'lipo <Skt. Hayagrīva].

In popular religious beliefs in Japan, especially among the horse-riding warrior class (*bushi*), Batō Kannon is a Buddhist deity considered to be a protector of horses. He was (and is) identified by the Tendai and Shingon sects as the Shishi Mui Kanzeon 獅子無畏観世音 (Fearless Lion Kanzeon), one of a group of deities known as the Six Kannon. There were statues and temples devoted to him around the country. According to van Gulik (1935: 80), races were run in honor of the deity every year in September at a temple known as Entsūji 円通寺, which is located at the foot of Mt. Fuji.

Further reading in English:

• van Gulik, 1935.

BATŌ KANNON
From the *Taizōkai Mandara*

battō 抜刀【拔刀】. Lit. "striking sword." Abbreviation for *battō iai, battōjutsu,* etc.

battō iai 抜刀居合【拔刀居合】. A term for combative, quick-draw sword arts (*iaijutsu*) used by the Takenouchi Ryū 竹内流.

battōjutsu 抜刀術【拔刀術】. Lit. "striking sword skill." *Battōjutsu* is one of several alternate terms for combative, quick-draw sword art (*iaijutsu*). In some systems (*ryū*) the term is used for both kneeling and standing techniques; in others it specifically indicates standing techniques. See also: *iai; iaidō; iaijutsu.*

battō shugyō 抜刀修行【拔刀修行】. Austere training in quick-draw swordsmanship. Mima Yoichizaemon Kagenobu, the founder of the Suiō Ryū 水鴎流, is said to have engaged in this training for about twenty years before establishing his own school. See: *Mima Yoichizaemon Kagenobu; Suiō Ryū.*

Battōtai 抜刀隊【拔刀隊】. Lit. "Sword Unit." A special Japanese police unit established in the early to mid 1870s. These samurai-turned-policemen were an important element in controlling the Satsuma warriors of the Jigen Ryū during the Satsuma Rebellion in 1877. Their feat led the Japanese police, newly formed in 1879, to accept the study of swordsmanship as an important police discipline.

bei 鞞 <Ch. *bing* <Skt. *vai* 𑖪𑖹. *Bei* is the seed syllable (*shuji*) for the Buddhist warrior deity Bishamonten. The character was often written as a talisman on war flags, weapons, armor and other accessories.

Benkei 弁慶【辨慶】[A.k.a. ***Saitō Musashibō Benkei*** 西塔 武蔵坊 弁慶【西塔武藏坊辨慶】] (1155–1189). Benkei was a Japanese warrior monk (*sōhei*) whose life story is complicated by a multiplicity of legends. As a young man he joined an order of Buddhist monks and traveled widely among the monasteries of Japan. During this period, Buddhist monasteries were centers of political, economic, and military power. They often aligned themselves with factions at the imperial court, and joined in violent demonstrations and out-and-out warfare. Benkei was probably trained in a variety of martial arts from an early age. According to legend he was over 6 feet (2 m) tall when, at the age of seventeen, he left the Buddhist order and joined an organization of mountain monks, the *yamabushi*, who belonged to an agonistic religious tradition known as Shugendō.

It was around this time that Benkei is said to have taken his signature long-hafted glaive (*naginata*) and posted himself at Gojō

BENKEI DEFEATED BY YOSHITSUNE
(Print by Totoya Hokkei, 1780–850)

Bridge in Kyōto, where he began threatening every passing swordsman. The price for crossing "his" bridge was the customer's sword. Supposedly he had collected 999 swords (he intended to collect 1000) when he met his match in Minamoto no Yoshitsune. After his defeat by the young warrior, Benkei became Yoshitsune's retainer, and fought with him in the Genpei War against the Taira clan. Yoshitsune, one of Japan's best-known generals, was responsible for several of the Minamoto clan's victories over the Taira, especially the final naval battle of Dannoura.

Unfortunately, Yoshitsune's popularity as the general who defeated the Taira made him an enemy of his brother, Minamoto no Yoritomo. Yoshitsune spent the next two years evading his brother's forces, with Benkei accompanying him during his flight. In the end they were encircled in the castle of Takadachi. Legend has it that Benkei, pierced by arrows, fought to the end, and died standing on his feet with dozens of arrows pinning him to a wall.

Benzaiten 弁財天【辯才天】<Ch. Biancaitian <Skt. Sarasvatī. Buddhist goddess of good fortune, music, and the fine arts. Benzaiten is a warrior protectress when grouped with Marishiten and Daikokuten in the Yumiya Santen.

betsuden 別伝【別傳】. Abbreviation of *kyōge betsuden*, a term used for oral or written transmissions containing information which is sometimes separate from, or an addition to, that transmitted in a school's normal curriculum. This information is often considered secret and may not be transmitted to all trainees. See: *kyōge betsuden*.

bettō 別当【別當】. A chief administrator or director of an organization. See: *Mandokoro Bettō; Samurai-dokoro Bettō*.

bikuni 比丘尼 <Ch. *biqiuni* <Skt. *bhikṣuṇī*. 1. A Buddhist nun. 2. Until the beginning of the modern era in 1868, this term was sometimes used pejoratively to indicate a prostitute who shaved her head and dressed up like a nun.

binjo 便女. Ancient to medieval-period term for a female servant or assistant.

Birushana Butsu 毘盧舎那佛 [A.k.a. ***Rushana (Roshana)*** 盧舎那]. Buddha described as Lord of the Lotus Realm[1] depicted in a sacred text called the *Kegon-kyō*.[2] This buddha is represented by the gigantic bronze figure (*daibutsu*) housed in Tōdaiji in Nara. See: *Dainichi Nyorai*.

bisentō 眉尖刀. OKINAWAN KOBUDŌ—A Chinese glaive used in some schools of Okinawan *kobudō*. See: *Okinawa kobudō; Ryūei Ryū (2)*.

Bishamon 毘沙門. 1. Abbreviation for Bishamonten, a Buddhist deity and protector of warriors. See *Bishamonten*. 2. A type of armored sleeve (*kote*) which takes its name from the Buddhist deity.

Bishamon suneate 毘沙門 脛当【毘沙門 脛當】. Lower-leg protectors (greaves) comprising three metal slats, one of which is longer than the others in order to protect the knee. See: *suneate*.

Bishamonten 毘沙門天 <Ch. Pishamentian <Skt. Vaiśravaṇa [A.k.a. ***Tamonten*** 多聞天]. One of several important Buddhist deities adopted as a protector by the Japanese warrior class, Bishamonten is king of *yassha* (Skt. *yakṣas*) and is often depicted wearing armor and holding a long glaive. Among the martial traditions which hold him in particular esteem is the Katori Shintō Ryū. Bishamonten is also one of a group of twelve guardian deities adopted from Brahmanism by Buddhism. See also: *bei; Bishamon; Jūniten; Tamonten*.

BISHAMONTEN (TAMONTEN)
Thirteenth-century image at
Tamonin, Chiba prefecture
(Photograph by author)

Further reading in English:

- Getty, 1962.
- Matsunaga, 1969.

biwa 枇杷. A loquat; a Japanese medlar. Though not nearly as popular as evergreen white oak (*kashi*), this wood is also used to make training weapons. It is lighter, tougher, and more splinter-resistant than *kasha*. Weapons made from *biwa* are usually avoided by the Japanese, however, as it is thought that the impact from a weapon made of *biwa* is likely to cause bone cancer in the recipient. This comes from the belief that the wood has somewhat sinister magical properties. Japanese tradition holds that planting a *biwa* tree near one's house invited bad fortune and sickness.

biwa hōshi 琵琶法師. Itinerant blind Buddhist priests who traveled around Japan reciting war tales (*gunkimono*) while accompanying themselves on the lute (*biwa*). These bards first appeared in the late thirteenth century. Their subjects were usually the Hōgen, Heiji, and/or Heike *monogatari*.

Bizen den 備前伝【備前傳】. See: *Gokaden*.

bō 1. 棒. A hardwood staff. The length of the Japanese *bō* is not set, but the most common

---

1 Rengezō-sekai 蓮華蔵世界 <Ch. Lianhuacang shijie < Skt. Kusuma-tala-garbha-vyūhālaṁ-kāra-locadhātu-samudra.

2 *Kegon-kyō* 『華嚴經』 < Ch. *Huayan jing* < Skt. *Avataṁsaka-sūtra*).

length today is about 6 feet (1.8 m). However, depending on the martial tradition, lengths range from 4 feet to over 6 feet (1.2 to 1.8 m). See also: *ichiizue; konsaibō; rokushaku bō; tetsubō; yoribō.*

bō 2. 卯. See: *u.*

Bō Ai Bō Seihō 棒合棒勢法. Second set of combative scenarios (*kata*) listed by the Hyōhō Niten Ichi Ryū under the general category of Bōjutsu. This set is made up of thirteen staff vs. staff techniques. See: *Hyōhō Niten Ichi Ryū.*

bōbiya 棒火矢. Lit. "flaming arrow staff," this was an early term for the matchlock musket.[3] See also: *hiyatō; Miki Ryū.*

bodai 菩提 <Ch. *puti* <Skt. *bodhi.* BUDDHISM—Supreme Enlightenment; wisdom; buddhahood.

bodaisatta 菩提薩埵 <Ch. *putisatuo* <Skt. *bodhisattva.* See: *bosatsu.*

Bō Gengi 茅 元儀 [Also read ***Mō Gengi***] <Ch. Mao Yuanyi (1594–1640). Ming-dynasty Chinese editor of the *Wubeizhi* (Jp. *Bubishi*), a large compendium on military matters.

bōgu 防具. Protective equipment. See also: *dōgu.*

bōjin 房人. Lit. "resident." Adolphson (2007: 66) translates this term as "residential people." *Bōjin* is a late Heian-period term used in connection with militant monks at Enryakuji, the Tendai temple complex on Mount Hiei (Hieizan), Kongōbuji on Mount Kōya (Kōyasan), and other locations. Incidents are recorded in which *bōjin* were involved in violent acts on temple grounds (vandalism, armed conflicts, etc.). It is evident that the *bōjin* were not ordained priests, for they are not referred to as such, although they were "residential people" at those temple compounds. See also: *sōhei (1).*

3 See illustration on page 61, which is taken from the 1610 text *Inatomi Ryū Hidensho.* According to the National Museum of Japanese History, the man firing the gun is depicted wearing only a loincloth (*fundoshi*) so that his posture and the location of his hands on the weapon can be clearly seen.

bōjutsu 棒術. 1. A generic term for "long hardwood staff arts," martial disciplines concentrating on a staff approximately 4 to 6 feet (1.2 to 1.8 m) in length. While the *bō* was not normally considered a primary weapon by the *bushi,* it was widely used by combatants of other social classes, such as warrior monks (*sōhei*), part-time soldiers (*ashigaru* and *jisamurai*), mendicants (monks and other commoners), and, in later times, arresting officers (*torimono*). The *bushi* had to be familiar with its use and, consequently, more than three hundred classical *ryū* included *bōjutsu* in their curriculum. See also: *bō; jō (1); jōdō; jōjutsu; rokushaku bō; tetsubō; yoribō.* 2. **Bōjutsu** 棒術. Second of two major categories of combative scenarios (*kata*) taught in Hyōhō Niten Ichi Ryū 兵法二天一流. The first category is entitled Tachi Seihō. See: *Hyōhō Niten Ichi Ryū.*

bokken 木剣. 1. A hardwood sword. 2. A hardwood sword with a "boat-shaped" point (*funazaki*). Some systems differentiate between *bokken* and *bokutō* by the shape of the point (*kensaki*).

BOKKEN WITH BOAT-SHAPED TIP (*FUNAZAKI*)

Bokuden 卜伝【卜傳】. See: *Tsukahara Bokuden.*

Bokuden Ryū 卜伝流【卜傳流】. Purported to be a branch tradition of the Kashima Shintō Ryū 鹿島新当流, this school preserves a number of classical combative arts, including swordsmanship (*kenjutsu*) with long and short swords, sickle-spear arts (*kamayari*), medium-length staff techniques (*jōjutsu*), lightly armored grappling (*koshi no mawari*), arresting arts (*torite*), and composite sickle and chain arts (*kusarigama-jutsu*). The system is extant today.

bokujū 僕従. A tenth-century term indicating warrior followers of Kyōto aristocrats.

bokutō 木刀. 1. A hardwood sword. 2. A hardwood sword with a "clamshell-shaped" point (*hamagurizaki*). Some systems differentiate between *bokken* and *bokutō* by the shape of the point (*kensaki*).

BOKUTŌ WITH CLAMSHELL-SHAPED TIP (*HAMAGURIZAKI*)

bokutō kendō 木刀剣道. An intense training practice found in Ryūshinkan Budō 柳心館武道. *Bokutō kendō* is performed much like a *kendō* match. However, wooden swords (*bokutō*) are used instead of bamboo *shinai*, and the participants wear no armor.

bōkyū 鉾弓 [Also read **hokoyumi**]. See: *hazuyari.*

Bon 梵 <Ch. Fan <Skt. Brahmā. An abbreviation (and common compound word element) for Bonma 梵摩 <Ch. Fanmo <Middle Chinese Buan-ma <Skt. Brahmā (masc.) and Brahman (neut.). (Note that the Middle Chinese pronunciation is much closer to both the original Sanskrit and Japanese than to modern Mandarin Chinese.)[4] 1. As a transliteration of "Brahman," the term *bon* refers to the ultimate reality of all things or the Absolute as found in non-Buddhist texts such as the *Upaniṣads* and the *Vedānta.* 2. As an abbreviated transliteration of "Brahmā," Bon refers to the supreme Hindu deity. However, that term is usually written as Bonten 梵天 in Japanese. 3. An abbreviation (and common compound word element) for Bondo 梵土, the land of India; lit. "Brahman-land."

Bon Chū Wa 梵中和. This term—often encountered in Buddhist texts and Japanese martial transmission scrolls (*densho*)—indicates the three countries/cultures of India (Bon), China (Chū), and Japan (Wa).

bonden 梵天 [Also read **bonten**]. SHUGENDŌ —A long pole about 6 feet (1.8 m) in length, with paper streamers attached to one end. It is often erected outside the home of a *yamabushi* who is undergoing strict religious austerities.

Bondo 梵土. India. See: *Bon (3).*

bonge 凡下. A commoner (in contrast to a noble).

Bongo 梵語. 1. The Sanskrit language. Sanskrit is the parent language of all Indo-Aryan languages, and has many similarities to Indo-Iranian, Avestan, ancient Latin, and Greek. In fact, the study of Sanskrit in Europe that began in the nineteenth century led to the development of modern linguistics. The term Sanskrit (Skt. *saṁskṛta*) means "perfect language," which stands in contrast to Prakrit (Skt. *prākṛta*), or "common language." The earliest known form of Sanskrit (called Vedic, as it is found in the *Rig Veda*) dates back to about 1000 B.C.E.; this was the language of the Aryan invaders who entered India through the Khyber Pass around 1800 B.C.E. While the common language devolved into various Prakrits, Sanskrit was preserved as the holy language of Vedic priests and the Indo-Aryan–speaking ruling class. In fact, in the early centuries of the first millennium C.E., Sanskrit became something of an international diplomatic language between the governments of South and Southeast Asia.

Furthermore, around the beginning of the first millennium C.E., Buddhist texts (which had previously been composed in a hybrid Prakrit language called Pāli) began to appear in Sanskrit in north and northwest India.[5] In general, it was these Buddhist texts, written in Sanskrit language and using *shittan* (Skt. *siddhaṁ*) script, that began to be carried to China. There they were translated into Chinese and eventually made their way to Korea and Japan. As Buddhism evolved into its later tantric form, many of the spells (*mantra* and *dhāraṇī*) of that tradition were

[4] There are many transliterations: 梵磨; 梵覧摩; etc. See Soothill, 1935: 353.

[5] In many cases, Buddhist texts originally composed in Prakrit languages were Sanskritized or poorly translated into proper Sanskrit. This process created a variant referred to today as "hybrid Sanskrit."

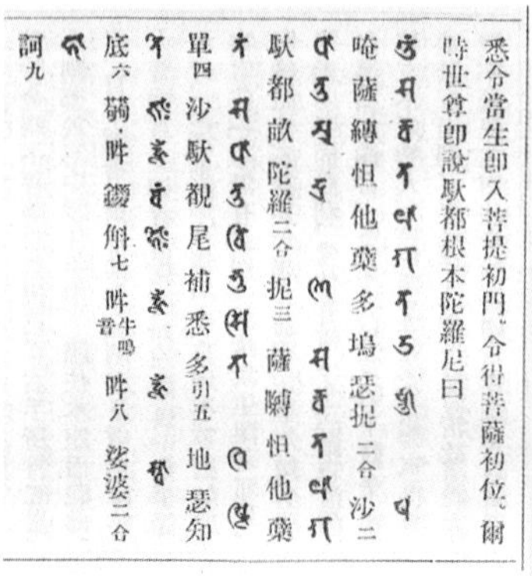

BONGO (SANSKRIT) MIXED WITH CHINESE IN A CHINESE BUDDHIST TEXT
(Detail from Taishō Canon, Vol. 19, p. 336)

preserved both in Chinese translation and original Sanskrit. (See illustration above.) In China, and later in Japan, these spells were used as talismans, and are often found decorating armor, weapons, and other martial equipment. 2. Any early Indian language.

bonji 梵字. Lit. "Sanskrit writing," "Sanskrit script." The *bonji* found in Japan are primarily that of a script used for writing Sanskrit known as *siddhaṁ* (*shittan* 悉曇). *Siddhaṁ* originated in North India, where it evolved around the seventh century C.E. from an earlier alphabet known as Gupta. (A later evolution of Gupta script in South India became its cousin Devanāgarī script, which is still used in India today for writing a variety of modern dialects in addition to the original ancient Sanskrit.)

As Buddhism moved into Central and East Asia, *siddhaṁ* script—which came to be called *fanzi* 梵字 in Chinese (*buan-tzu* 梵字 in Middle Chinese, pronounced *bonji* in Japanese)—was used primarily for the writing of magic spells (Skt. *dhāraṇī* and *mantra*), and magic syllables. These magic syllables are sometimes referred to as "seed syllables" (Jp. *shuji* <Skt. *bījākṣara*). The Chinese who translated Buddhist texts into their own language revered the written form of the *dhāraṇī* and *mantra* as much as the sound, so they often preserved the original script for magical spells. These mystical letters were used primarily by esoteric Buddhist sects in China and Japan.

Such spells and magic syllables are often found written in *bonji* as talismans on martial accessories such as weapons, armor, helmets, war fans, flags, and variety of other items. In the photo above, a spear blade is engraved with the *bonji* "*Ka Kirīku Sa*" (read *Ha Hrīḥ Sa* in Sanskrit). These magical "seed syllables" represent the Buddhist deities Jizō Bosatsu, Amida Nyorai, and Kannon Bosatsu. See also: *shuji*.

Further reading in English:

- van Gulik, 1956.
- Stevens, 1981: 1–69.

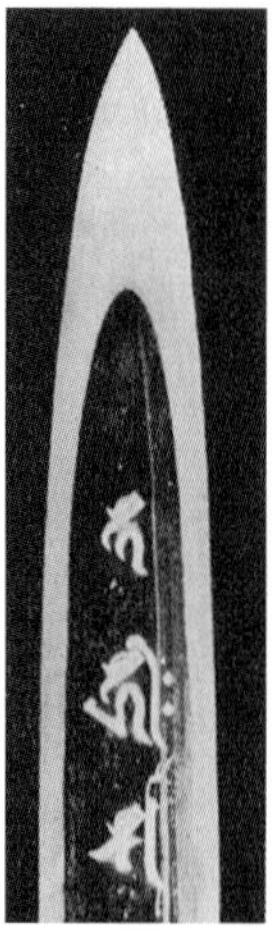

SPEAR BLADE ENGRAVED WITH THREE *BONJI* LETTERS: *Ka Kirīku Sa* (Skt. *Ha Hrīḥ Sa*)
Spear named "Mayfly Cutter" (*Kagerōgiri* 蜻蛉切) carried into battle by Honda Tadakatsu in the late 1500s
(Yabe Collection, Numazu; photograph courtesy Roald Knutsen)

Bonma 梵摩. See: *Bon*.

bonnō 煩悩【煩惱】<Ch. *fannao* <Skt. *kleśa*. 1. In Buddhism, the term *bonnō* refers to defiling passions. There are various lists of these; several of the more important are covetousness, anger, ignorance, arrogance, doubt, and false views. 2. In a martial context, the warrior sometimes equated *bonnō* with those mental distractions which can cause the combatant to lose steadfast/imperturbable-mind (*fudōshin*), thus presenting an opening (*suki*) to an enemy.

bonshō 梵鐘. The bell or gong of a Buddhist temple. See also: *kane (1)*; *kane (2)*; *shikigu*.

bonsō 梵僧 < Ch. *fanseng* (Mid.Ch. *buan seng*). This term refers to a Buddhist monk. *Bon* 梵 refers to India, while the term *sō* 僧 is a transliteration of the Sanskrit term *saṁghaḥ*, which indicated the brotherhood of monks. The Portuguese adopted the term *bonsō* and wrote it as *bonzo*, from which it migrated to French and then English as *bonze*.

Bonten 梵天. 1. Bonten is the Hindu deity Brahmā, given the title of *ten* 天 (Skt. *deva*) in the Buddhist pantheon. In East Asian Buddhism he is classified as one of the Six Heavenly Warriors (Roku Buten). Bonten is also one of a group of twelve guardian deities adopted from Brahmanism by Buddhism. See also: *Jūniten; ten.* 2. SHUGENDŌ—See: *bonden.*

boroboro 梵論梵論. See: *boronji.*

boronji 梵論字 [A.k.a. ***boroboro*** 梵論梵論]. A fourteenth- to fifteenth-century term for ruffians who posed as lay monks (*ubasoku*). Armed with swords, the *boronji* were more often brigands than priests. They are first mentioned in the *Tsurezuregusa*, a poetic work written by Yoshida Kenkō in the fourteenth century. Although from an earlier period, they are sometimes confused with the *komusō* of the Tokugawa period.

Further reading in English:

• Keene, 1967: 98–99.

bōsan 坊様 [Also read ***bōsama***]. A Buddhist monk.

bosatsu 菩薩 [Abbr. of ***bodaisatta*** 菩提薩埵] <Ch. *pusa* <Skt. *bodhisattva*. A future buddha; a being who has reached awakening (enlightenment) but postponed attainment of final *nirvāṇa* (*nehan*), and has vowed to first assist all sentient beings in attaining enlightenment.

Boshin no Eki 戊辰役. This civil war, which took place in 1868, resulted in the fall of the Tokugawa shogunate and the establishment of the Meiji government.

bōzu 坊主. A Buddhist monk.

bu 1. 分. A measurement equal to .12 inches (3 mm).

bu 2. 武. Martial; military. The ideogram is composed of two elements: 戈 (pronounced *ka* or *hoko*), which is a pictogram of an ancient Chinese halberd; and the element 正, which, according to Chinese sources, originally indicated a human foot in the compound character 武.[6] This character element, then, originally indicated a foot soldier carrying the weapon. Later, the Japanese interpreted this differently, especially with the rise of less combatively oriented *budō* systems, and even more so with the development of post–World War II systems. The Japanese now interpret the second character element 止 as the verb "to stop" or "discontinue" (pronounced *shi* or *tomeru*). The shades of meaning for this interpretation drift between "quelling war" and "preventing conflict."

bubi no ie 武備之家. A "warrior house" or "military family." This eleventh-century term, found in war tales such as the *Hōgen monogatari*, is roughly equivalent to *tsuwamono no ie* and *yumi-ya no ie*.

BUBISHI (*WUBEIZHI*) DETAIL
(Volume 90, chapter 92)

Bubishi 1.『武備志』<Ch. *Wubeizhi* (Records of armaments). A Chinese compendium on warfare compiled by Mao Yuanyi[7] in the late Ming dynasty period, and completed in 1621. This massive work consists of 240

---

6 Thus the compound element 正 is derived from the character 足.

7 Jp. Bō Gengi <Ch. Mao Yuanyi 茅元儀.

chapters in five parts and ninety-one volumes. For more information on Mao, see Goodrich (1976: 1051–1054).

Bubishi 2.『武備志』. See: *Okinawaden Bubishi.*

budō 武道. 1. Martial (spiritual) way. 2. Generic term for martial arts. 3. ***Budō***『武道』. Title of a film produced in the 1930s by Hisa Takuma. Hisa's film featured Ueshiba Morihei demonstrating Daitō Ryū *aikibudō* techniques. 4. ***Budō***『武道』. Title of a film produced in the 1980s featuring several Japanese combative arts. See also: *budō/bugei/bujutsu.*

budō/bugei/bujutsu 武道・武芸・武術. There are numerous views on the evolution of Japanese "martial arts" into "martial ways." Furthermore, the fact that Japanese today often use the various terms interchangeably to describe these skills and systems does not help clear up the issue. This author tends to agree with the analytical process of martial historian and hoplologist Donn F. Draeger[8] (1973a; 1973b; 1974a; 1974b; 1974c; 1974d) in evaluating combative systems. That said, however, Draeger's restrictive definitions of the terms *bujutsu* (martial technique), *bugei* (martial art), and *budō* (martial/spiritual way) are simply not observed by the Japanese.

Historically, these terms can be assigned to various periods in which they describe the type of martial activity being carried out by the warrior class (and others). For example, although *bujutsu* (lit. "martial technique") has always had a spiritual element, its primary purpose was success in battle or dueling. Its historical context (though not the actual use of the term) dates from the tenth century, when the warrior class began to assert its political independence. It continued through the sixteenth century, when, during the late Warring States period (Sengoku Jidai) the country became unified politically. During this period, the intense warfare drove some warriors to achieve extremely high levels of combative skill, as well as the psychological development needed to survive the stress of protracted combat. This psycho-physical element both harkened back to and reinforced the spiritual element innate to *bujutsu*.

At the beginning of the Edo period (1603–1867), the Tokugawa shogunate was faced with the problem of thousands of underemployed armed men, a cessation of general warfare, and a number of feudal domains which were only somewhat loyal to the central government. The military government consequently promoted a policy of *bunbu ryōdō*, which encouraged the warrior class to practice civilian "arts" (literature, calligraphy, etc.) on a par with martial "arts." In this process, the psychological/spiritual achievements of famous warriors of the recent past were looked upon as ideals toward which the peacetime warrior should advance. This, along with other Tokugawa policies and restrictions, generally redirected the warrior class toward reforming *bujutsu* into *bugei* (martial art). Thus, martial training itself became a peacetime art aimed at both preserving martial skills and funneling warrior practitioners toward a more peaceful goal of self-development. The political intent, of course, was to prevent rebellion, vendetta, and any type of unregulated combat that might disturb the political balance.

By the late seventeenth century (c. 1668) systems such as the Abe Ryū 安部流 were shifting their training even further toward spiritual (in contrast to purely combative) goals with the introduction of the term *kendō*. Consequently, the earliest *budō* (martial/spiritual way) began to appear. This trend has continued to the modern day.

Not all schools followed this trend. Some rejected it entirely, some accepted it partially, and others embraced it fully. By the late seventeenth century, some competent swordsmen were decrying the fact that many schools had drifted so far toward non-combative goals that they had lost touch with combative reality. Their severe training in prearranged combative forms (*kata*) had degenerated into an artistic dance referred to with the pejorative term *kahō kempō* 華法剣法 (lit. "flowery sword methods"), and their martial élan had evaporated. This motivated swordsmen of the times such as Yamada Ippūsai, headmaster of the Jiki Shinkage Ryū

[8] See Bibliography.

直心影流, to institute severe training with bamboo swords (*shinai*) and the use of protective armor (*bōgu*) in a practice called *uchikomigeiko*. In some systems, this became a primary method of training, supplementing older *kata*. In other systems, training had begun to drift into sportive competition by the late eighteenth century. Thus a new element —sport-like competition—also became part and parcel of the *budō*. However, the Japanese have never used a standardized naming convention—whether *bujutsu*, *bugei*, *budō*, or some other term—to categorize these combative systems.

Budō hiketsu—aiki no jutsu 『武道秘訣・合氣之術』 (The secret of martial arts—the art of *aiki*). One of the earliest books to concentrate on the concept of *aiki*. The text was published in 1899 by an anonymous author. See: *aiki*.

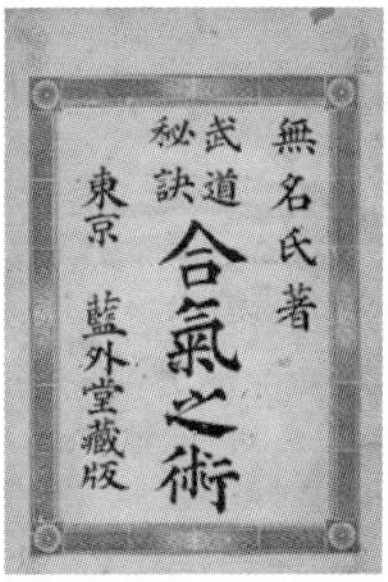

BUDŌ HIKETSU—AIKI NO JUTSU (COVER) c. 1899

budōka 武道家. 1. A proficient practitioner of premodern and contemporary spiritual, sportive combative systems (*budō*). 2. Generic term for a combative arts practitioner. 3. Generic term for a martial artist.

Budōkan 武道館 [Abbrev. of ***Nippon Budōkan*** 日本武道館, also read ***Nihon Budōkan***]. The "Martial Ways Hall." The Budōkan—more officially the Nippon Budōkan—was built in Tōkyō's Kudanshita ward (not far from Yasukuni Shrine) in 1962 for the *jūdō* competition in the 1964 Summer Olympics. From the 1970s onward, the coliseum-sized structure was also frequently used for rock concerts, with several international musical artists recording live albums there. However, the Nihon Budōkan—like the newer Tōkyō Budōkan, built in Ayase in 1989—is primarily used as a training and demonstration hall for a number of classical and modern martial arts and ways. See also: *Nihon Kobudō Kyōkai*.

budō seishin 武道精神. A modern term meaning, literally, "the spirit of *budō*." For example, in 1967 Kimura Tokutarō, then president of the Zen Nihon Kendō Renmei, used this term in a speech in order to emphasize his view of the purpose of Japanese martial training; that is, martial training with a focus on promoting a spirit of world peace and prosperity.

Budō shoshinshū 『武道初心集』 (The martial ways primer). This text, an introductory work on martial arts and Bushidō, was written for the warrior class by Daidōji Yūzan (1639–1730). It comprises forty-four chapters on subjects such as education, filial piety, dignity, and how to deal with death.

Further reading in English:

• Wilson, 1984.

Budō Zendendō 武道全伝道 【武道全傳道】. Name of a *dōjō* awarded by Tokugawa Yoshimichi 徳川吉通 to Chikamatsu Hikonoshin Shigenori in 1713. It was there that Chikamatsu taught his Ichizen Ryū 一全流 combative arts, which were collectively known as Zenryū Rempeiden 全流練兵伝. See: *Ichizen Ryū*.

bugei 武芸 【武藝】. Lit. "martial arts." This term generally refers to classical warrior arts; however, the seventeenth-century Confucian scholar Kaibara Ekken 貝原益軒 (1630–1714) used *bugei* in a specific way to indicate the Edo-period evolution of things martial from a goal of battlefield combat to one of art and redirection toward spiritual pursuit. (Irie, 2005: 159). Yagyū Nobuharu, late headmaster of the Yagyū Shinkage Ryū 柳生新陰流, described this redirection of martial pursuits into building character and instilling a certain values in the warrior class as a change from "swordsmanship which conquered the country to swordsmanship which ruled the country." See also: *budō/bugei/bujutsu*.

bugei jūhappan 武芸十八般【武藝十八般】. Lit. the "eighteen martial arts," this is a list of martial arts originally created in China. The actual list varies depending on the era and the location where the list was compiled.

In Japan today the "eighteen" are usually enumerated as follows:

Japanese	Character	Combative Art
1. *Yumi*	弓	Archery
2. *Uma*	馬	Horsemanship
3. *Yari*	槍	Spearmanship
4. *Ken*	剣	Swordsmanship
5. *Sui'ei*	水泳	Swimming
6. *Battō*	抜刀	Sword drawing
7. *Tantō*	短刀	Dagger
8. *Jutte*	十手	Tined truncheon
9. *Shuriken*	手裏剣	Throwing blades
10. *Fukibari*	含針	Blowing needles
11. *Naginata*	薙刀	Long-hafted glaive
12. *Hō*	砲	Musketry
13. Torite	捕手	Seizing/arresting
14. *Yawara*	柔	Grappling
15. *Bō*	棒	Hardwood staff
16. *Kusarigama*	鎖鎌	Sickle and chain
17. *Mojiri*	錑	Tangler
18. *Shinobi*	忍	Espionage

However, earlier lists by such Edo-period personages as Hirayama Koryū 平山子竜 give alternate entries:

Japanese	Character	Combative Art
1. *Yumi*	弓	Archery
2. *Kisha*	騎射	Equestrian archery
3. *Yari*	槍	Spearmanship
4. *Kusarigama*	鎖鎌	Sickle and chain
5. *Konaginata*	小薙刀	Small glaive
5. *Tachi-nagamaki*	太刀長巻	Long-bladed glaive
6. *Iai*	居合	Sword drawing
7. *Hōjutsu*	砲術	Musketry
8. *Daikyū*	大弓	Large bow
9. *Hankyū*	半弓	Small bow
10. *Kenjutsu*	剣術	Swordsmanship
11. *Ōnaginata*	大薙刀	Large long-hafted glaive
12. *Jūmonji kusarigama*	十文字鎖鎌	Crosspiece sickle and chain
13. *Kagiyari*	鍵槍	Crosspiece spear
14. *Nageyari*	投槍	Javelin
15. *Bōjutsu*	棒術	Hardwood staff arts
16. *Jūjutsu*	柔術	Grappling

Etc.

The original Chinese list is somewhat different:

Chinese (Jp)	Character	Combative Art
1. *Mou* (Bō)	矛	Lance or spear
2. *Chui* (Tsui)	鎚	Horsemanship
3. *Gong* (Kyū)	弓	Archery
4. *Nu* (Do)	弩	Crossbow
5. *Chong* (Jū)	銃	Firearms
6. *Bien* (Ben)	鞭	Whip
7. *Jian* (Kan)	簡	Dagger
8. *Jian* (Ken)	劍	Double-edged sword
9. *Lian* (Ren)	鏈	Chain
10. *Kua* (Ka)	楇	Knuckle-duster

11. *Fu* (Fu)	斧	Axe
12. *Yue* (Etsu)	鉞	Halberd/ battle-axe
13. *Ge* (Geki)	戈	Halberd
14. *Ji* (Geki)	戟	Crescent-blade halberd
15. *Pai* (Hai)	牌	Shield
16. *Bang* (Bō)	棒	Hardwood staff
17. *Qiang* (Sō)	鎗	Spear
18. *Ba* (Hachi)	朳	Rake without teeth

Like the Japanese lists, the Chinese lists vary greatly over different time periods. Other entries included the following:

Dao	刀	Single-edged saber
Cha	叉	Fork
Buna	捕拿	Arresting arts
Ba	騎	Martial horseback riding
Huojian	火箭	Fire arrows/ firearms
Badao	拔刀	Sword drawing
Meijiandao	眉尖刀	Glaive; eyebrow-shaped saber
Lian	鎌	Sickle
Bashe	騎射	Equestrian archery
Shuiyong	水泳	Swimming

bugeisha 武芸者【武藝者】. A warrior; a practitioner of martial arts (*bugei*).

Bugei zufu tsūshi 『武藝圖譜通志』 <Ko. *Muye dobo tongji* (Illustrated record of martial arts). This text is a Korean work ordered by King Jungjo and written by three scholars —Yi Duk-moo, Pak Je-ga, and Pak Dong-soo—in 1790. Interestingly, among the many combative arts detailed in the text are several Japanese sword traditions, which the Korean authors collect in a chapter entitled "A Complete Manual of Japanese Swordsmanship" (Waken Sōfu 倭劍總譜 <Ko. Wae Gum Chong Bo).

BUGEI ZUFU TSŪSHI, C. 1790
Korean text illustrating Japanese swordsmanship of the Ryūbi Ryū 柳彼流

Many, if not all, of these systems were probably transported to Korea either by Japanese pirates (*wakō*) or warriors during Hideyoshi's Korean invasions during the fifteenth and sixteenth centuries. Several of the systems listed in the "Waken Sōfu" chapter are familiar and even exist today in Japan, while others are obscure and are not mentioned in standard Japanese historical records. Included here is a partial list of those systems well known in Japan:

Korean	Characters	Japanese
Shindo Ryu	神道流	Shintō Ryū
Um Ryu	陰流	Kage Ryū
Shinum Ryu	新陰流	Shinkage Ryū

Other systems mentioned in the "Waken Sōfu" are more obscure. For example, the first uncommon system detailed is Toyu Ryū 土由流 <Ko. Toyu Ryu. However, the closest equivalent located by this author is an obscure system—written with similar, but not identical, characters—known as Tsuchida Ryū 土田流. This was a *kenjutsu* school attributed to Tsuchida Jūrōbei Shigetsuna 土田十郎兵衛尉重綱 by Watatani and Yamada (1978: 586). However, as Tsuchida apparently flourished after 1600, it is doubtful that this is the same system.

The subsequent systems listed—Unkō Ryū 運光流 <Ko. Woonkwang Ryu; Senryū Ryū 千柳流 <Ko. Chunryu Ryu; and Ryūbi Ryū 柳彼流 <Ko. Ryupee Ryu—seem to have no known equivalent in Japan. Consequently they were most likely small, obscure schools that flourished on the periphery of

the Japanese home islands.

Further readings in English:

• Kim, 2001.

bugu 武具. Arms and armor.

Bugu Bugyō 武具奉行. This title, created in 1863 by the Tokugawa shogunate, essentially meant "chief master-at-arms." It combined functions previously held by several agencies:

Gusoku Bugyō	具足奉行	Armor
Yari Bugyō	槍奉行	Spears
Yumi-ya Bugyō	弓矢奉行	Bows and arrows

bugugura 武具倉. An arsenal.

bugyō 奉行. Originally this term referred to a "chief of administration." Appended as a suffix, it can be found in a number of terms such as *machi bugyō* (chief of city administration), *jisha bugyō* (chief of temple administration), etc. During the Tokugawa period the *machi bugyō* were normally samurai who were vassals of the shogunate (*hatamoto*). See: Bugu Bugyō; *Machi Bugyō*.

buji 武事. Martial arts; military affairs.

Bujinkan 武神館. Modern combative arts school founded by Hatsumi Masaaki. Based primarily on the teachings Hatsumi received from Takamatsu Toshishigu, the school encompasses the curricula of nine classical traditions (*koryū*):

Koryū	System	Skill Set
Togakure Ryū 戸隠流	*ninpō* 忍法	espionage
	taijutsu 体術	grappling, pressure points, striking
Gyokko Ryū 玉虎流	*kosshijutsu* 骨指術	grappling, pressure points, striking
Kuki Shinden Ryū 九鬼神伝流	*happō biken-jutsu* 八法秘剣術	swordsman-ship, spear, staff
Kotō Ryū 虎倒流	*koppōjutsu* 骨法術	bone-breaking, -setting
Shinden Fudō Ryū 神伝不動流	*dakentaijutsu* 打拳体術	striking
Takagi Yōshin Ryū 高木揚心流	*jūtaijutsu* 柔体術	grappling, striking
Gikan Ryū 義鑑流	*koppōjutsu* 骨法術	skeletal-structure attacks
Gyokushin Ryū[9] 玉心流	*ninpō* 忍法	espionage
Kumogakure Ryū[9] 雲隠流	*ninpō* 忍法	espionage

Like severel modern *budō* schools, Hatsumi's Bujinkan is an eclectic system which combines classical skills with a modern approach appealing to would-be martial artists. For example, a *kyū-dan* grading system has replaced the classical *mokuroku-menkyo* licensing system. In addition, selected skills of various classical *ryū* have been incorporated into a hybrid mix in order to make it more appealing to modern *budō* students. This process actually began with Hatsumi's teacher, Takamatsu Toshishigu. (See Watatani and Yamada, 1969: 537.)

Further reading in English:

• Hatsumi, 2008.

bujutsu 武術. Martial skills; martial techniques. See also: *budō/bugei/bujutsu*.

bujutsuka 武術家. 1. A term used from the late Tokugawa period through the Meiji era to indicate someone well versed in traditional martial disciplines. 2. A modern term indicating a proficient practitioner of premodern and contemporary combative systems (*bujutsu*). 3. Generic term for a combative arts practitioner. 4. Generic term for a martial artist.

Bujutsu ryūso roku 『武術流祖録』(A directory of the founders of classical martial schools). This publication is a work on martial schools

[9] Evidently Takamatsu did not pass an official *menkyo* in these traditions to Hatsumi, and no documentation of their actual contents has been preserved. Watatani and Yamada (1978) list Takamatsu and Hatsumi in the lineages of Gikan Ryū (p. 214) and Kumogakure Ryū (p. 247), but not in any of the lines of the various Gyokushin Ryū (pp. 230–231). In fact, Watatani and Yamada do not list a Gyokushin Ryū that specialized in *ninpō* or *ninjutsu*.

and founders. It was published in 1843 (late Edo period), but its author is unknown. The work covers about fifty classical martial systems and is divided into seven sections according to type of martial art: 1. strategy and tactics (*heihō*); 2. archery (*shajutsu*); 3. horsemanship (*bajutsu*); 4. swordsmanship (*kenjutsu*); 5. spear arts (*sōjutsu*); 6. grappling (*jūjutsu*); and 7. gunnery (*hōjutsu*).

buke 武家. 1. Lit. "warrior family." A generic term for *bushi* families.

Buke Jidai 武家時代 [equivalent to ***Bakufu Jidai*** 幕府時代]. An approximately 700-year period during which various military shogunates and warrior families ruled Japan. The period began with Minamoto no Yoritomo's shogunate in 1192, and ended with the fall of the Tokugawa in 1867.

buke seiji 武家政治. Lit. "government by the warrior clans." This term denoted the government of military feudalism as established by Minamoto no Yoritomo. See: *Buke Jidai*.

Buke shohatto 『武家諸法度』 (Rules for military houses). A set of laws in thirteen chapters set up initially by retired shōgun Tokugawa Ieyasu in 1615 relating to feudal lords (*daimyō*) and the warrior class (*bushi*). Emphasizing that the warrior should pursue both the study of martial and civil arts, the code was revised several times over the length of the Tokugawa period. See also: *bunbu ryōdō*.

Further reading in English:

• Sansom, 1961: 401, 404–406; 1963: 7–8 ff.

buki 武器【武噐】. Generic term for weapons.

bukigura 武器倉【武噐倉】. An arsenal.

buki waza 武器業. Techniques using weapons. This term tends to be used more by *jūjutsu* schools that concentrate on unarmed techniques. Since most classical martial traditions were primarily weapons systems, there was little need to designate a technique as being a "weapons technique."

Bukkō Kokushi 仏光国師【佛光國師】[A.k.a. Bukkō Zenji 仏光禅師【佛光禪師】; Mugaku Sogen 無学祖元 【無學祖元】 <Ch. Wuxue Zuyuan] (1226–1286). Chinese *chan* (Jp. *zen*) priest who came to Japan in 1279 at the invitation of Hōjō Tokimune to head Kenchōji, a temple in Kamakura. Bukkō founded Engakuji, a leading Zen temple in Japan, in 1282,[10] and was one of three key figures in the development of what came to be known as "warrior Zen" or "Kamakura Zen."

The nineteenth-century swordsman Yamaoka Tesshū was so affected by an inspirational poem composed by Bukkō referring to the spring wind (*shunpū* 春風) that he named his training hall the Shunpūkan 春風館. See also: *Kamakura Zen*.

Further reading in English:

• Leggett, 1985.

• Collcutt, 1981.

Bukkyō 仏教 【佛教】[A.k.a. ***Butsudō*** 仏道]. Buddhism; the Buddhist religion. The history and nature of Buddhism in Japan has been well documented since its introduction in the sixth century. As noted elsewhere,[11] Buddhism's long association with combat and warriors is ironic, since Buddhism is both a religion and a philosophy aimed at ending suffering, whereas combat is essentially a manifestation of violent behavior. However, neither Buddhist philosophy nor combative psychology is one-dimensional. Buddhism has been able to accommodate combatants in its fold in order to lead them toward its highest ideals, and combatants have benefited greatly from Buddhist practices, philosophy, and psychology. See also: *mikkyō; Shingon Shū; Tendai Shū*.

Further readings in English:

• Hall, 1990: 190–363; 1997.

• Matsunaga, 1969.

• Matsunaga and Matsunaga, 1974; 1976.

• McMullin, 1985.

• Suzuki, 1958.

• Tsang, 2007.

---

10 Interestingly, one of his primary students was a well-educated woman from the Hōjō family named Mugai. Named as Bukkō's successor, Mugai was the first Japanese woman to qualify not just as a nun, but as a Zen priest (*Zen sō* 禅僧). (Yamamura, 1990: 504–505).

11 See Hall, 1997: 87.

Bukō Ryū 武甲流. See: Toda Ha Bukō Ryū.

bukyō 武侠. Chivalry; heroism. See also: *Yamaga Sokō*.

bunbu ryōdō 文武両道【文武兩道】. A social concept and political philosophy which was emphasized by the shogunate (military government) during the Tokugawa period (1603–1867). It can be interpreted as "traveling both the path of cultural learning and the path of martial arts." *Bunbu ryōdō* was a concept that strongly encouraged the Tokugawa-period warrior class to emphasize and engage in cultural learning—literature, the arts, etc.—on an equal level with martial training. On the one hand, this policy was aimed at controlling the thousands of men-at-arms on the streets of Japan in the post–Warring States period for the sake of stability. On the other hand, it redirected the combativeness of the samurai into more peaceful, spiritual pursuits, guiding them toward civility and away from a militaristic mindset.

Bun'ei no Eki 文永役. The Bun'ei no Eki was the first war to repel the Mongols. It occurred in 1274, during the Bun'ei imperial period. See: *Genkō no eki*.

bunkai 分解. Analysis; decomposition. This term is sometimes used when deconstructing a combative form (*kata*).

bu no ri 武の理. Lit. "martial/military principles." Hayes (1984a: 10) interprets this hoplologically as "innate combative adaptive traits." These innate traits are seen as static principles in contrast to their active counterparts, the "manifest adaptive traits" (*bu no jutsu*). Hayes postulates eight such innate combative traits derived from Japanese culture and their corresponding manifestations:

1. Steadfast/imperturbable mind trait—*Fudōshin no ri* 不動心の理
2. Cognition/intuition trait—*Kangae/kan no ri* 考え・感の理
3. Volition trait—*Sen no ri* 先の理
4. Omnipoise trait—*Mukamae no ri* 無構の理
5. Abdominal trait—*Hara no ri* 腹の理
6. Respiratory/vocality trait—*Kiai no ri* 気合の理
7. Force/yield trait—*Gōjū no ri* 剛柔の理
8. Synchronous trait—*Aiki no ri* 合気の理

Each of these traits has a corresponding manifestation in which "~ *no ri*" is replaced with "~ *no jutsu*."

Further reading in English:

- Hayes, 1984a; 1984b; 1985; 1986; 1987a; 1987b; 1988a; 1988b; 1989; 1990; 1992; 1994.
- Hall, 1990; 1997.

bu no jutsu 武の術. 1. Lit. "martial/military means/skills" (equivalent to *bujutsu*). 2. Hayes (1984a: 10) interprets this hoplologically as "manifest combative adaptive traits." See: *bu no ri*.

bunsho 文書. A record, document, or archive.

Buntō 文韜. See: *Rikutō*.

burakumin 部落民. An outcast minority during the Tokugawa period and up through the early Meiji era. They were officially liberated in 1871. Members of the *burakumin* caste were not considered part of the official four social classes (*shi-nō-kō-shō*), and were restricted to occupations regarded by Buddhism and Shintō as being tainted by death. These included jobs as executioners, undertakers, leather tanners, etc. Today *burakumin* is considered a pejorative term, as is *eta*, a synonym literally meaning "filthy."

Buryaku shichi sho 武略七書 <Ch. *Wujing qi shu* 武經七書 (The seven military classics). A collection of seven military texts canonized under this (Chinese) title during the Song dynasty (960–1279). Japanese strategists have made use of these works since the tenth century. The seven Chinese texts are as follows:

1. Tai Gong Liutao (Jp. Taikō rikutō) 太公六韜 (Tao Gong's Six Strategies)
2. Sima fa (Jp. Shibahō) 司馬法 (Sima's Methods)
3. Sunzi bingfa (Jp. Sonshi no heihō) 孫子兵法 (Sunzi's Art of War)
4. Wuzi (Jp. Goshi) 呉子 (Wuzi)
5. Wei Liaozi (Jp. Utsuryōshi) 尉繚子 (Wei Liaozi)
6. Huang Shigong sanlue (Jp. Kōsekikō sanryaku)

黄石公三略 (Huang Shigong's Three Briefs on Strategy)

7. Tang Taizong • Li Tō Weigong wendui (Jp. Taishū Ri Eikō montai) 唐太宗李衛公問對 (Questions and Answers between Tang Taizong and Weigong)

There are a number of English translations of *Sunzi bingfa* (*Sun Tzu's Art of War*). However, the only translation to date including all seven works is that by Sawyer and Sawyer in 1993.

Further reading in English:

- Sawyer, 1993.

bushakei 歩射型. Archery (*kyūjutsu*) shooting style developed for and by foot soldiers. Contrast to *kishakei*.

bushi 武士. Medieval (and later) term for warrior. The term refers to the semi-aristocratic Japanese warrior who flourished from the twelfth century through the 1800s. The characters 武士, which can also be read as *mononofu*, first appeared in the *Manyōshū*, a collection of poems compiled in the mid-700s. The word *bushi* has, over the centuries, become a generic term for warrior. See also: *bugeisha; heihōka; heihōsha; ikusa (1); kondei; kuni no miyatsuko; musha; tsuwamono.*

Further reading in English:

- Draeger, 1973a: 24–51 ff; 1973b; 1974.
- Farris, 1992.
- Friday, 1992.

bushi dan 武士团【武士團】. A term from the twelfth and thirteenth centuries used for a (private, feudal) warrior band attached to a local land-owning strongman. These warrior bands, led by a warrior chieftain (*bushi no chōja*), were often responsible for opening new lands, or reopening lands which had lain fallow after the terrible plagues of smallpox and famine in the twelfth century. As members of the band often took their surname from these lands, the land parcels were consequently called "name-fields" (*myōden*). See also: *kaihatsu ryōshu.*

bushidō 武士道. Lit. "the way of the warrior." This "warrior's code" was a restrictive view of warriorship (ethics, behavior, attitudes, etc.) which developed during Japan's Edo period (1603–1868). The concept of *bushidō* was greatly influenced by such early Edo-period works as *Hagakure*. See also: *kyūba no michi.*

Further readings in English:

- Draeger and Smith, 1969: 85–90.
- Draeger, 1973a; 1973b; 1974.
- Nitobe, 2002.
- Wilson (Trans.), 1984.
- Yamamoto, 2002.

bushidō seishin 武士道精神. The spirit of the warrior; samurai spirit.

bushi kaikyū 武士階級. The warrior class.

bushi katagi 武士気質【武士氣質】. Warrior spirit.

Bushi Matsumora 武士松茂良. See: *Matsumora Kōsaku.*

Bushi Matsumura 武士松村. See: *Matsumura Sōkon.*

bushi no chōja 武士の長者. A twelfth-century term for a warrior chief; warrior commander.

bushi no konjō 武士の根性. Lit. "the essential nature/spirit of the warrior." This *Encyclopedia* lists a number of characteristics termed the "Classical Warrior Ideal." For many classical warriors (*bushi*), this ethical/spiritual ideal was as important as perfection in combative capability; in fact, it was thought that the latter could not be achieved without the former. However, the view of what constituted the ideal warrior type changed from period to period in Japanese history, and there are a number of varying lists concerning what the classical warrior should be. Certainly thousands of warriors and other combatants never lived up these ideals, just as most never obtained the highest level of swordsmanship.[12] However, many warriors took these ideals as a benchmark against which to measure their achievements. According to accounts of the martial pilgrimages (*musha shugyō*) carried out in the sixteenth and early seventeenth centuries and again in the nineteenth century, the goal of the pilgrimage was to improve ethical/spiritual charac-

[12] See Hall (1997: 110–116).

ter as well as to perfect combative capability.

The following is an amalgam from a number of sources. Most are described in greater detail under separate entries in this *Encyclopedia*:

CLASSICAL WARRIOR IDEAL		
buyū	武勇	valor; bravery
enryo	遠慮	restraint
gi	義	integrity
jin	仁	courtesy and benevolence
kansha	感謝	thanks; grace
kenshin	献身	self-sacrifice
kokoro	心	a sincere, humble spirit
kotodama	言霊	correct use of words
meiyo	名誉	honor
muyoku	無欲	freedom from avarice
on	恩	a sense of obligation
shinsetsu	臣節	loyalty; integrity
shingi	信義	fidelity, trust
wa	和	peace and harmony
yūga	優雅	elegance, refinement

See also: *kyūba no michi; tsumi; tsuwamono no michi; Yamaga Sokō.*

bushō 武将【武將】. A general, commander, or warlord.

Bushū 武州. Chinese name for Musashi province. This area comprised the border of modern-day Saitama and Kanagawa prefectures and the Tōkyō metropolitan area.

busō 武装【武裝】. Armaments.

Butō 武韜. See: *Rikutō.*

Butokuden 武徳殿. Lit. "Hall of Martial Virtue." Built adjacent to the Heian Shrine in Kyōto in 1899, the Butokuden is a large martial training and meeting hall (*dōjō*) for the classical martial disciplines. The building was constructed under the auspices of the Dai Nippon Butokukai and has been utilized by leading practitioners of both classical and modern martial arts and ways.

Butokukai 武徳会【武德會】. See: *Dai Nippon Butokukai.*

Butokukai Aiki Budō 武徳会合気武道【武德會合氣武道】. Term used for *aikidō* when Ueshiba Morihei was teaching under the Dai Nippon Butokukai (c. 1942) with Hirai Minoru. Watatani and Yamada (1978:730) equate Butokukai Aiki Budō with Hirai's Kōrindō Aikidō. See: *Hirai Minoru; Kōrindō; Ueshiba Morihei; Ueshiba Ryū Aikidō.*

butsudan 仏壇【佛壇】. A family or household Buddhist altar. These home altars normally contain Buddhist religious items—bells, candles, etc.—along with a small statue of the Buddha (often gilded) and memorial tablets (*ihai*) on which are written the posthumous Buddhist names (*kaimyō*) of deceased family members. Small offerings of food and drink for deceased ancestors are also placed in the altar. It should be noted that *butsudan* are not Shintō shrines (*kamidana*), and are not placed in martial training halls (*dōjō*).

Butsudō 仏道【佛道】[Var. ***Bukkyō*** 仏教]. Lit. "Path of the Buddha." The Buddhist religion.

buyū 武勇. CLASSICAL WARRIOR IDEAL—Valor; bravery; martial prowess. *Buyū* as valor was considered one of the essential characteristics of the classical warrior (*bushi*). See: *bushi no konjō.*

buyūden 武勇伝【武勇傳】. A martial story or tale.

Buzenbō 豊前坊【豐前坊】. A mountain demon

THE *TENGU* BUZENBŌ ADDRESSING THE WARRIOR KOBAYAKAWA TAKAKAGE
(Print by Tsukioka Yoshitoshi, 1780–1850)

(*tengu*) king with whom the *daimyō* Kobayakawa Takakage (1532–1590) is supposed to have had several dialogues while on Mount Hiko 彦山.

Byakkotai 白虎隊. Lit. the "White Tiger Corps." This was a reserve unit of around three hundred samurai-class young men from Aizu domain. During the Japanese civil war of 1868 (Boshin no Eki) one subunit of about twenty boys became separated from their comrades and, believing they saw their castle burning, committed suicide rather than be captured by the enemy. Unfortunately, their lord's castle had not fallen, and their sacrifice was in vain. (One boy survived the suicide attempt.) A memorial was later dedicated to this group of young warriors.

Byakurenmon ken 白蓮門拳 <Ch. *Bailianmen quan*, lit. "White Lotus Sect boxing." This term was used by Shōrinji Kempō founder Sō Dōshin to designate a form of Chinese boxing he claimed to have mastered during his long stays in China during the 1930s and 1940s. However, this art is generally referred to in Chinese as *Bailian quan* 白蓮拳 (Jp. *Byakurenken*). See: *Sō Dōshin.*

Byakurenken 白蓮拳 <Ch. *Bailian quan*. Lit. "White Lotus boxing" or the "boxing arts of the White Lotus society." See: *Sō Dōshin.*

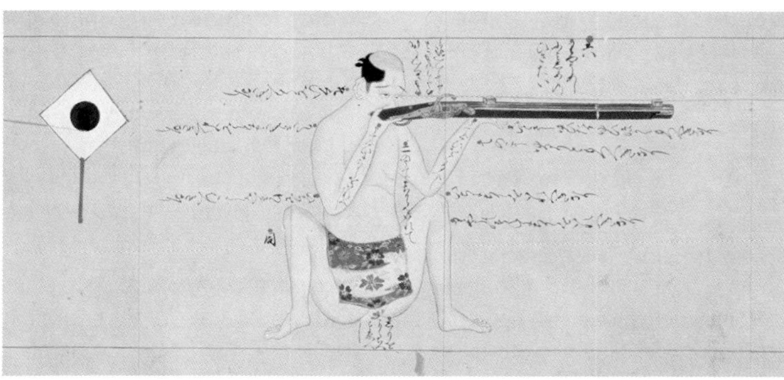

Early illustration from a text on the matchlock musket (*bōbiya*).
Illustration from the *Inatomi Ryū Hidensho*『稲富流秘伝書』, dated 1610.
(Courtesy of the National Museum of Japanese History)

C

chakushi 嫡子. A principal heir; a legitimate heir. A *chakushi*, usually the oldest son, became the inheritor of property. During the Tokugawa period the term also denoted the inheritor of a family-line martial tradition who was not necessarily the eldest in the family.

chambara チャンバラ. A modern term meaning "sword-rattlers"; that is, Japanese films filled with samurai fight scenes. These films usually fall within a genre known as "period dramas" (*jidaigeki*) which most often, but not always, depict the Edo period (1603–1867). These films are also referred to as *rantōgeki* (melee dramas) and *kengeki* (sword dramas). See also: *jidaigeki; shuraba; tate (2).*

chanbara チャンバラ. See *chambara.*

chadō 茶道 [Also read ***sadō***]. See: *cha no yu.*

cha no yu 茶の湯. Lit. "hot water for tea." This term refers to the Japanese tea ceremony first attributed to Murata Shukō[1] in the fifteenth century. Murata, a former priest, apparently developed a close relationship with the renowned Zen priest Ikkyū.[2] Ikkyū, being familiar with tea practices in China and Korea, suggested that a combination of tea practices and the Zen Buddhist practice of sitting meditation (*zazen*) might be useful for the Japanese. Murata spent the rest of his life perfecting this art.

In the sixteenth century the ceremonial drinking of tea spread to all levels of society, and a number of schools arose. Probably the best known was that founded by Sen no Rikyū, who made many groundbreaking innovations regarding the way the tea ceremony was carried out and the implements used in its performance. He also emphasized the native Japanese aesthetic of appreciating beauty in the natural, imperfect, and impermanent (*wabi-sabi*). Consequently, Sen no Rikyū's form of *cha no yu* was sometimes called *wabi cha* 侘び茶 ("aesthetic" or "subdued" tea) in contrast to *kaisho* 会所 (lit. "banquet chamber" tea), which was then current among the elite classes. See also: *Sen no Rikyū.*

Further reading in English:

- Anderson, 1991.
- Fisher, 2010.
- Okakura, 1964.

chasengami 茶筅髪. Lit. "tea-whisk coiffure." This was a method used by some warriors (*bushi*) for winding string around their hair to form it into an upright pigtail. The resulting hairdo resembled the whisk used in the tea ceremony.

chi 血. Blood.

Chiba Kichinojō Tsuneshige 千葉 吉之丞 常成 (c. 1745–c. 1810). Founded the Hokushin Musō Ryū 北辰夢想流 around 1772; that school became the family martial arts tradition of the Chiba family for several generations. Kichinojō was the grandfather of the renowned swordsman Chiba Shūsaku Narimasa.

Chibana Chōshin 知花 朝信 (1885–1969). OKINAWAN KARATE—Chibana founded the Kobayashi Ryū 小林流, (actually a variant pronunciation for Shōrin Ryū 小林流) system of *karate.* At age fifteen he began training with Itosu Ankō, and remained with this teacher for thirteen years. After his master's death in 1915, Chibana opened a training hall (*dōjō*) in the town of Shuri in 1918.

World War II was very destructive to Okinawa; many *dōjō* and documents were destroyed and many practitioners—masters as well as students—were killed. In an effort to revive the practice of *karate*, the Okinawa Kobayashi Ryū Karatedō Kyōkai was formed in 1948, with Chibana as its president. Chibana's legendary skill is exemplified by the fact that he was hired as the chief *karatedō* instructor (*karatedō shihan*) at the Shuri Police Station in 1954 when he was sixty-nine years old, a post he retained until 1958. He became president of the Okinawa Karatedō Renmei in 1956, and was instrumental in the development and spread of

[1] Murata Shukō 村田 珠光, also read Murata Jukō, 1423–1502.

[2] Ikkyū Sōjun 一休 宗純 (1394–1481).

karate until his death in 1969. Chibana emphasized the Passai (Dai) Kata and often performed it in yearly demonstrations held by the Okinawa Shōrin Ryū Karatedō Kyōkai. For lineage, see: *Itosu Ryū.*

Chiba Shūsaku Narimasa 千葉 周作 成正 (1794–1855). Swordsman of the late Edo period who founded Hokushin Ittō Ryū 北辰一刀流. Chiba, an expert swordsman, was highly proficient in the *kendō* of the times. He put together a unique blend of *kendō* (as a spiritual discipline) and sport. Being first grounded in his family's own martial tradition—Hokushin Musō Ryū 北辰夢想流—he later studied Nakanishi Ha Ittō Ryū 中西派一刀流 with Nakanishi Chūbei Tsugumasa, and with Nakanishi's disciple Asari Matashichirō Yoshinobu. In founding the Hokushin Ittō Ryū, Chiba created a style of swordsmanship he called *kumitachi.*

Chiba was a close friend of Odani Nobutomo, thirteenth headmaster of the Jiki Shinkage Ryū 直心影流. Although Chiba could not match Odani's caliber as a swordsman, Odani introduced him to Mito domain officials who subsequently made *kumitachi* their official style of swordsmanship.

A formidable technician with a bamboo sword (*shinai*), Chiba promoted competitive matches as a part of his school's training regimen. These bouts were often extended to include challengers armed with lightweight *naginata*; occasionally these opponents were female. The matches were public events, and spectators were charged admission.

One of Chiba's most important disciples (*deshi*) was Sakamoto Ryōma, who at the time they met was a masterless samurai (*rōnin*) from Tosa domain. Ryōma later became a key figure in the movement to topple the Tokugawa shogunate.

Further reading in English:

- Draeger, 1974: 98, 99, 175.
- Hurst, 1998: 88–90.
- Sugawara, 1985: 207–209.

chibō 智謀. Resourcefulness.

chiburi 血振り. Lit. "shaking/flinging off blood"; blood removal. In quick-draw sword arts (*battōjutsu, iaijutsu, iaidō,* etc.) *chiburi* is the practice of shaking the imagined blood from a blade after a prearranged combative form (*kata*) has been completed. This is performed before replacing the sword in the scabbard (*notō*). In the context of *kata* training, *chiburi* is part of *zanshin*, the focused, extended vigilance aimed at keeping the practitioner's awareness at a high level before, during, and after an opponent has been downed. It should be noted, however, that in the context of real battle or duel, the *chiburi*, if used at all, would not be followed by *notō.* Since blood is a very good adhesive, the unclean sword would stick to the inside of the scabbard. Blood also causes rust, so if it adheres to the blade it must be wiped away completely before the weapon is replaced in the scabbard.

chidori ashi 千鳥足. Lit. "walking like a plover." This term is used in some combative systems to indicate moving with a zig-zag, crossover step.

chie 智慧 <Ch. *zhihui* <Skt. *prajñā*. BUDDHISM—wisdom; one of the three types of learning (*sangaku*).

chigiriki 乳切木. A polearm consisting of a staff of 3 to 4 feet (1–1.2 m) with a chain of about the same length attached to a metal weight (*fundo*). The *chigiriki* is similar in size and function to a *furijō.* Likely a Korean import in the late 1500s, this weapon was used by only a few traditions in Japan. See: *Araki Ryū.*

Further reading in English:

- Amdur, 2002: 128–147.
- Mol, 2001: passim.

CHIGIRIKI

chigirikijutsu 乳切木術. The combative art of the *chigiriki.* Fujita (1960: 2) notes only ten *ryū* specializing in *chigirikijutsu.*

chikaken 智火剣. BUDDHISM—The flaming wisdom-sword held by the Buddhist deity Fudō Myōō. Lit. "wisdom-flame sword," the *chikaken* is so called because it represents the ability of wisdom to cut through ignorance. The Black Dragon King, Kurikara (also known as Ama Kurikara, the Rain Dragon) is often pictured coiled around the sword blade. The *chikaken* is also used as a meditational symbol/device. See: *Kurikara Fudō; sammayagyō.*

chikama 近間. This term, an abbreviation of *chikamaai*, indicates a "close" combative engagement distance/temporal interval between opponents. Although interpreted with different shades of meaning in the classical traditions, *chikama* is generally the interval obtained at the point where the protagonists can attack one another without taking a full step. According to some classical systems, *chikama* is any combative engagement distance/interval closer than the length of a standard sword. See: *maai.*

Chikamatsu Hikonoshin Shigenori 近松彦之進 茂矩 (1695–1778). Founder of the Ichizen Ryū 一全流. Chikamatsu was passionate about martial arts from a very young age, and became an expert in several systems including the quick-draw sword techniques (*iaijutsu*) of Katayama Ryū 片山流 and the combative swordsmanship (*kenjutsu*) of Takanao Ryū 貴直流. He also developed a system of long hardwood staff arts (*bōjutsu*) he christened Shinnen Ryū 心念流.

In 1715[3] the lord of Owari domain, Tokugawa Yoshimichi, awarded Chikamatsu a training hall called the Budō Zendendō, where all of these systems were taught under the rubric of Zenryū Rempeiden 全流練兵伝, lit. "transmission of the military drills of all the schools." Among these, Chikamatsu included swordsmanship (*kenjutsu*), spear techniques (*sōjutsu*), martial drills (*renpeihō*), use of armor (*katchūden*), swimming (*suieijutsu*), fast cross-country riding (*sōjōsōchi*), military horsemanship (*gunba*), equestrian archery (*kisha* 騎射 [2]) derived from Ogasawara Ryū 小笠原流, military strategy and tactics (*gunra*), and both Iga Ryū 伊賀流 and Kōga Ryū 甲賀流 espionage (*shinobi no jutsu*).

Along with the systems mentioned above, Chikamatsu continued to add to the curriculum taught at the Budō Zendendō, eventually mastering and including both Imagawa Ryū 今川流 and Ōno Ryū 大野流 gunnery (*hōjutsu*), which he reformatted into his own system called Jitoku Ryū 自得流. In addition, he also founded the Taiseigai Ryū 大星外流 system of martial divination (*gumbai*).

chikkyo 蟄居. The third-most severe of the five grades of penalties applied to samurai during the Tokugawa period. *Chikkyo*, which literally means "cooping up insects," refers to solitary confinement; it was a form of house arrest a bit more severe than *hissoku*. *Chikkyo* could be applied in three grades: single-room confinement; temporary retirement; and permanent retirement, which indicated a life sentence. See also: *heimon; hissoku; kaieki; seppuku.*

Further reading in English:

- Brinkley and Kikuchi, 1915: 641–642ff.
- Schreiber, 2001.
- Seward, 1968.

Chikubujima Ryū 竹生島流 [A.k.a. Chikubujima Ryū Bōjutsu 竹生島流棒術]. This school, founded by Namba Heiji Mitsunori, encompasses a classical system of long hardwood staff techniques (*bōjutsu*) that is still practiced today. Its powerful *kiai* resembles that of the Tatsumi Ryū 立身流.

Namba had earlier founded a glaive system (*naginatajutsu*) known as Namba Ryū. However, after receiving a vision from the oracle of Chikubujima Benten[4] he created the combative staff system he called Chikubujima Ryū. The tradition was passed down in several domains.

chikujōjutsu 築城術. The art of planning and constructing field fortifications, including the determination of proper directions via divination; i.e., geomancy/*feng shui* (Jp. *fūsui*).

Chikurin Ryū 竹林流 [A.k.a. ***Chikurin Ha***

[3] This is an approximate date. Watatani and Yamada (1978: 56) give the year as 1715. However, Tokugawa Yoshimichi 徳川吉通 died in September 1713. If the dōjō was opened in 1715, it would have been awarded by Tokugawa Tsugutomo 徳川継友, who was daimyō of Owari domain that year.

[4] Chikubushima, an island on the northern side of Lake Biwa, is known as the "Island of the Gods."

竹林派; ***Heki Ryū Izumo Ha*** 日置流出雲派]. School of archery founded by Ishidō Chikurinbō Sukenari, a Shingon priest residing on Mount Kōya (Kōyasan). As a monk, Chikurinbō had a special association with the Yoshida clan as their *kigan sō* 祈願僧, a priest who prayed and performed rituals especially for the benefit of the clan. (This might indicate that Chikurinbō or his family was already closely aligned with the Yoshida clan when he entered the priesthood.) Other versions of Chikurinbō's life report that he was a Tendai monk from Mount Hiei who served the Yoshida clan as *kigan sō*. In any case, he later left the priesthood.

Chikurinbō trained in both Heki Ryū 日置流 archery and the martial arts of the Yoshida clan before developing his own system. His school of archery proliferated and divided into many branches during the Edo period. See also: *Heki Ryū*.

chikushi 竹士. A swordsman who is an expert at using a bamboo practice sword (*shinai*; *chikutō*) in contrast to a sharpened blade (*shinken*) or wooden sword (*bokutō*; *bokken*). See also: *kenshi (1), mokushi.*

Chikushō 畜生 <Ch. *chusheng* <Skt. *triyagyoni*. 1. BUDDHISM—One of the six realms (Rokudō) into which beings are subject to rebirth. Chikushō includes all sub-human animals: birds, beasts, fish, insects, worms, etc. 2. ***Chikushō!*** An expletive meaning "You beast!" or "You brute!" Like the English "Damn you!" the term relegates the addressee to the realm of Chikushō.

chikushō heihō 畜生兵法. Lit. "beastly martial arts" or "brute strategy," *chikushō heihō* was a term used by seventeenth-century swordsman Odagiri Ichiun to describe many of the swordsmen of the mid-1600s. Professor Irie Kōhei quotes from Odagiri's *Sekiun ryū kenjutsusho* 『夕雲流剣術書』:

> ...many warriors fight not differently than beasts. They defeat those who are weaker than they, are beaten by those who are stronger, and both are killed when their skill level is the same. This situation is hopeless...The warrior must understand that the way to absolute victory is contained within their very being. (Irie, 2005: 168, note 2)

chikutō 竹刀 [Also read ***shinai***]. A bamboo sword. This variant reading of the characters used for *shinai* was most commonly used in pre–World War II *kendō*.

Chin Genpin 陳 元贇 <Ch. Chen Yuanbing (1587–1672). A Chinese architect and martial artist who arrived in Japan in 1628 after fleeing the turbulent situation on the Chinese mainland. According to some sources, Chin attached himself to the Owari branch of the Tokugawa family. He was, in fact, commissioned by Tokugawa Yoshinao[5] to design and build Yoshinao's mausoleum at Jōkōji 定光寺, a Rinzai Zen temple on Mount Ōmu.

CHIN GEMPIN

During the more than forty years he lived in Owari, Chin is thought to have taught a Chinese combative system that influenced the development of the Kitō Ryū 起倒流 (under Fukuno Shichirōuemon Masakatsu). Chin died in Nagoya at the age of eighty-five.

chinjufu 鎮守府. Headquarters of the military government/expeditionary forces in Tōhoku in the late eighth and early ninth centuries.

chinjufu shōgun 鎮守府将軍【鎮守府將軍】. This title referred to the commanding general of the "pacification headquarters"; i.e., the head of the military government/expeditionary forces in Tōhoku in the late eighth and early ninth centuries.

Prior to the ninth century, when the imperial army was first sent out against the aboriginal Emishi (Ebisu) people in the north, its commander was designated a *chintō shōgun* 鎮東将軍 (eastern-area military government general), *chinteki shōgun* 鎮狄将軍 (barbarian-area

[5] Tokugawa Yoshinao 德川義直 (1601–1650).

military government general), or *sei Ezo shōgun* 征蝦夷将軍 (Ezo-conquering general). These were temporary expeditionary titles; the *shōgun* on the campaign had no permanent residence.

Then, in the ninth century, Ōno Azumabito was given the title *azechiken chinju shōgun* 按察使兼鎮守将軍 (inspector-general for the northeast [Tōhoku]); he took up residence at Taga Castle in Mutsu, the far northeast of Honshu. Later, in the tenth century, the castle of Izawa in Mutsu became assigned to the commander of the area, along with the titles *chinjufu shōgun* and *chinjufu gunken* 鎮守府軍監 (pacification headquarters inspector-general). In the twelfth century, when Minamoto no Yoritomo became the permanent *seii taishōgun*, the awarding of the title of *shōgun* was suppressed. Later, under the Ashikaga shogunate, it was finally abolished. See also: *seii taishōgun.*

Chi no Maki 「地乃巻」. KASHIMA SHINTŌ RYŪ—Scroll listing a set of five advanced quick-draw sword forms (*battōjutsu*). See: *Kashima Shintō Ryū.*

chinpei 鎮兵. Permanent troops of the Tōhoku (northeastern Japan) expeditionary forces in the eighth and ninth centuries. The term also applies to Tōhoku garrison soldiers—fortress soldiers—of the same period.

chinsho 鎮所. An eighth-century term for fortifications.

chinteki shōgun 鎮狄将軍【鎮狄將軍】. See: *chinjufu shōgun.*

Chintō 鎮闘. OKINAWAN KARATE—One of eighteen Matsubayashi Ryū 松林流 *kata* practiced in Shōrin Ryū 少林流. Chintō was transmitted by Matsumura Sōkon, who, according to legend, learned it from a shipwrecked sailor. See also: *Kūshin Ryū.*

chintō shōgun 鎮東将軍【鎮東將軍】. See: *chinjufu shōgun.*

Chishin Ryū 知新流. Branch tradition of Anazawa Ryū 穴沢流 taught in Tsu domain (the present-day city of Tsu in Mie prefecture). This line, which specialized in combative, long-hafted glaive arts (*naginatajutsu*), attributed its origin to Anazawa Moriyoshi and his direct disciple (*deshi*) Hōzōin Inei.

Chitō Ryū 千唐流. JAPANESE KARATE—System of *karatedō* founded by Chitose Tsuyoshi in 1946. Chitose evidently gave his system the name "Chitō" to indicate that it was a thousand- (*chi* 千) year-old tradition of Chinese (*tō* 唐) boxing. The name indicates a connection to older Okinawan traditions of Chinese boxing known as *tōde* 唐手, and is also a homophone for part of his family name. Although Chitose formulated Chitō Ryū while residing in Japan, the system's content is technically based in Okinawan *tōde*, and includes various Okinawan weapons systems (Okinawan *kobudō*). However, authoritative sources on Okinawan *karate* schools and systems, such as Takamiyagi et al. (2008) and Bishop (1999), do not list Chitō Ryū as an Okinawan system.

The following are the primary fighting forms of Chitō Ryū:

- Shihōhai 四方拝
- Niseishi 二十四歩
- Seisan 正整
- Bassai 抜塞
- Chintō 鎮東
- Sōchin 荘鎮
- Tenshin 転身
- Kusanku 公相君
- Ryūsan 龍山
- Sanchin 三戦

These *kata*, which tend to be eclectic, resemble various lines of Okinawan *karate*, including Naha *te*, Shuri *te*, Shōrin Ryū, and others.

Chitose Tsuyoshi 千歳剛直 (1898–1984). Founder of Chitō Ryū karate. Chitose began his study of karate at the age of seven under Arakaki Seishō 新垣世璋, a martial arts teacher who had trained in China during the 1870s. After Arakaki passed away in 1918, Chitose moved on to other instructors who gave him an eclectic knowledge of Okinawan fighting arts. In 1921 Chitose moved to Japan to study medicine, and for the next few years had little time to devote to *karate*. However, according to information from the

Chito-Ryu Karate Sohonbu office, Chitose assisted Gichin Funakoshi in establishing a dojo in Tokyo, and also helped Funakoshi's students establish and promote Shotokan *karate* in Japan. Chitose is credited with founding his own style of *karate*, which he called Chitō Ryū, in 1946. He taught U.S. soldiers in the post–World War II years, and later traveled to the Americas to demonstrate and spread his system.

Further reading in English:
- Chito-Ryu Karate (Sohonbu office) website

Chiten 地天. <Ch. Ditian <Skt. Pṛthīvī. In Indian mythology, Pṛthīvī is the earth god, an elemental spirit. In East Asia and Japan, Pṛthīvī was one of a group of twelve guardian deities adopted from Brahmanism by Buddhism. See: *Jūniten.*

chitsuki hata 乳付旗. A battlefield "banner with loops." The loops (*chitsuki*) facilitate the attachment of the banner to bamboo rods or poles. This first use of this type of banner is attributed to Hatakeyama Masanaga in 1456. See: *noboribata.*

chō 諜. Variant term for an espionage agent, somewhat equivalent to a secret agent (*mawashi-mono*) or spy (*ukagau-mono*). It also indicates "one who colludes" or "one who conspires." See: *ninjutsu.*

chōbukuro 調伏爐 [Also read ***jōbukuro***]. <Ch. *diaofulu* <Skt. *abhicāraka.* A fire ritual for causing enemies to surrender. This is one of the more "martial" Esoteric Buddhist fire rituals, aimed at defeating demons, heretics, and enemies. This term is equivalent to *gōbukuro* (exorcism fire ritual), one of the five purposes for which ritual fires (*goma*) are conducted. See: *gōbukuro; goma.*

chōdachi 長太刀. A longsword similar to an *ōdachi*. See: *Anazawa Ryū; ōdachi (3).*

chōdai 帳内. An eighth-century term for quasi-military royalty. According to Farris (1992: 57) the *chōdai* were nobility who held military posts and titles but were not actual warriors.

chōdokake 調度掛. A stand for bows and arrows. The term is derived from *chōdo*, which originally referred to "(a warrior's) utensils"; i.e., bows and arrows.

chōegama 長柄鎌. See: *nagae no kama.*

chōichiryū kenshi 超一流剣士. A superior swordsman; a top swordsman.

chōja 諜者. Variant term for espionage agent. See: *ninjutsu.*

chōjiyū 丁子油. Clove oil. *Chōjiyū* is used for protecting and lubricating swords and other bladed weapons.

chōken 長剣【長劍】. A longsword.

chokuritsu seigan (no kamae) 直立青眼(の構). A combative engagement posture (*kamae*, *kurai*) found in a number of *ryū*, in which the proponent's sword is pointed directly at the eyes of the enemy (*teki*); both feet are together with both legs straight.

chokuritsu shisei 直立姿勢. An upright posture with feet together and legs straight.

chokusō 直槍 [Sometimes read ***choku yari***]. A straight-bladed spear. See: *suyari.*

chokutō 直刀. Straight swords with a single cutting edge. These blades, which date from around the fifth century, are similar in appearance to the *kubutsuchi no tachi*. For Illustration, see: *kubutsuchi no tachi.*

Chokuyūshin Ryū 直猶心流 [A.k.a. ***Chokuyushin Ryū Kusarigama-jutsu*** ～鎖鎌術【～鏁鎌術】]. This sickle-and-chain weapon system founded by Inoue Yūshinsai 井上猶心斎 is essentially an collateral martial art (*fuzoku bugei*) of Jiki Shinkage Ryū Naginatajutsu 直心影流薙刀術. After Inoue, the lineage passed to Sonobe Hide, from which point it is identical to that of Jiki Shinkage Ryū Naginatajutsu.

chōnin 町人 [Also read ***machibito***]. During the Edo period this term referred to townsmen and the merchant class. Contrast to *machikata* (senior town officials).

chonmage 丁髷. A topknot hairstyle commonly worn in the Edo period. One version is still worn today by professional *sumō* wrestlers in Japan.

chōren 調練. Military drill.

chōshi 調子. Rhythm; beat. See: *hyōshi.*

Chōshū han 長州藩. Chōshū domain; present-day Yamaguchi prefecture, at the extreme southwest end of the island of Honshu. Chōshū *han* was one of the primary domains involved in the overthrow of the Tokugawa shogunate in the 1860s.

chōteki 朝敵. 1. Lit. "enemies of the court," *chōteki* is a fourteenth-century term used in the *Taiheiki* (a multivolume account of the wars of that age) to indicate the Kamakura *bakufu*. Contrast to *kangun*. See: *Taiheiki.* 2. In later years this term was used to refer to a traitor, rebel, or any enemy of the emperor.

chū 1. 忠. Loyalty; devotion; fidelity.

chū 2. 丑. See: *ushi.*

chūdachi 中太刀. YAGYŪ SHINKAGE RYŪ—A medium-length sword around 2.5 feet (80 cm) long—slightly larger than a *chisakatana*. The *chūdachi* was used specifically for training in a set of *kata* known as Ōmarobashi 大転.

Chūdan 中段. Lit. "intermediate level." 1. SHINDŌ MUSŌ RYŪ—The second series of *waza* consisting of twelve standard *kata* and one variation. 2. YAGYŪ SHINKAGE RYŪ—Second set of Shiai Seihō (match dueling techniques using bamboo swords), which comprises twenty-one match scenarios—i.e., dueling forms—containing one hundred eight *kata*.

chūdan chokusei (no kurai) 中段直勢(の位). YAGYŪ SHINKAGE RYŪ—An engagement posture in which the weapon/hands are held midway up the body in the trunk area with the sword tip (*kensaki*) pointed toward the enemy (*teki*). The right foot is slightly forward, pointing toward the opponent.

chūdan no kamae 中段の構え. An engagement posture in which the weapon/hands are held midway up the body in the trunk area with the sword tip (*kensaki*) pointed toward the enemy (*teki*).

chūdan no kurai 中段の位. YAGYŪ SHINKAGE RYŪ—Any middle-level engagement posture in which the hands are held at or above waist level and at or below shoulder level.

Chūdan Yari no Shidai 中段槍之次第. KASHIMA SHINTŌ RYŪ—Mid-level combative spear forms (*sōjutsu kata*). See: *Kashima Shintō Ryū.*

Chūefu 中衛府. A section of the Imperial Palace Guards (Efu) added in the year 728 to the original five Efu that were created by the Taihō Code (Taihō Ritsuryō) in 702. According to Farris (1992: 71), the Chūefu were primarily responsible for the security of the Fujiwara family. See: *Efu.*

chūgen 中間. A low-level samurai attendant; a samurai's lackey.

chūgibara 忠義腹. Suicide (*seppuku*) performed to show support and loyalty to a superior; this term covered both *seppuku* performed as an act of remonstration (*kanshi*) or in order to follow one's master into death (*junshi*). See: *seppuku.*

Chūgoku 中国【中國】. 1. Modern term for China. 2. Abbreviation for the Chūgoku Chihō district of western Honshū.

Chū Gokui 中極意. KASHIMA SHINTŌ RYŪ—Mid-level combative swordsmanship forms (*kata*) encompassing three subsets. See: *Kashima Shintō Ryū.*

Chūjō Hyōgo no Kami Nagahide 中条兵庫頭 長秀. A sixth-generation warrior/leader of the Chūjō clan's martial system. Nagahide extensively modified and systematized the martial arts of the Chūjō family into a classical *ryū*. He is thought to have made these modifications subsequent to his training, in 1368, with Nen Ami Jion, a monk from Jufukuji temple in Kamakura who founded Nen Ryū 念流. See also: *Nen Ryū.*

Chūjō Ryū 中条流 [Var. 中将流 【中將流】] [A.k.a. ***Chūjō Ryū Heihō*** 中条流平法; ***Hōgan Ryū*** 判官流]. A comprehensive field-combat system (*sōgo bujutsu*) founded some time during the mid to late thirteenth century, originally passed down within a single family. Its main emphasis was on the sword and spear. However, it appears that its curriculum was extensively modified after 1368, when headmaster Chūjō Hyōgo no Kami Nagahide trained with Nen Ami Jion, a monk from Jufukuji temple in Kamakura. Nagahide's revised Chūjō Ryū was sought after by numerous warriors, and many later systems trace their origins to this school:

- Toda Ryū (1) 戸田流
  founded by Toda Seigen
- Ittō Ryū (1) 一刀流
  founded by Itō Ittōsai Kagehisa
- Tomita Ryū 富田流
- Gan Ryū (1) 厳流
  founded by Sasaki Kojirō

Chūjō Ryū Heihō 中条流平法. See: *Chūjō Ryū.*

Chūkō Shinkan Ryū 忠孝真貫流. This school was primarily a system of swordsmanship (*kenjutsu*) which gained popularity in the late 1700s. Its founder, Hirayama Kōzō, also taught military strategy to Odani Nobutomo, thirteenth headmaster of the Jiki Shinkage Ryū 直心影流.

chūma 中間. Abbreviated from *chū maai*, this term indicated a "medium" combative engagement distance/temporal interval between opponents. This term is interpreted with different shades of meaning in the classical traditions; some do not use it at all. See: *maai.*

chūnin 中忍. The term *chūnin* is often used to indicate non-warrior sub-leaders of espionage groups. It should be noted that this designation is anecdotal, and should not be taken to apply to all espionage operations during the classical period. See: *jōnin—chūnin—genin; ninjutsu.*

Chūsei 中世. Japan's medieval age, an era that lasted roughly from 1185 to 1568.

chūshin 忠臣. A loyal retainer.

Chūshingura 『忠臣蔵』 (The storehouse of loyal retainers). A play based on the Akō *rōshi* vendetta. Written some fifty years after the incident, this is a retelling of the story of the forty-seven *rōnin*. See: *Akō rōshi.*

chūshin yūshi 中臣勇士. A loyal subject; a brave warrior. This term was used by Kusunoki Masashige in one version of the *Taiheiki*. Varley (1994: 195) quotes: "To cherish honor (*gi*) and ignore death is the way of the brave warrior (*chūshin yūshi*)."

CHIBA SHŪSAKU
Tōjō Kaikan Collection
(*Kendō Nihon*, 1978, no. 3, used with permission)

D

Daiba 提婆 <Ch. *tipo* <Skt. *devas* [A.k.a. ***ten*** 天]. BUDDHISM—The Realm of Gods and Goddesses. Daiba is one of six realms (Rokudō) into which beings are subject to rebirth. *Daiba* are in the dimension above human beings; that is, the realm of gods and goddesses.

daibutsu 大仏【大佛】. BUDDHISM—A great image of the Buddha made of metal, wood, or stone. In Japan these images are usually depicted in sitting posture with crossed legs. There are several of these images: for example, at Tōdaiji in Nara is housed a great image of the Buddha Vairocana (Rushana or Birushana); and in Kamakura there is a large image of Amida Buddha (Amida Butsu).

Daidōji Yūzan 大道寺 友山 [A.k.a. ***Shigesuke*** 重祐; ***Magokurō*** 孫九郎] (1639–1730). Warrior (*bushi*) of the early Edo period who authored several works, including *Budō shoshinshū* 『武道初心集』 (The warrior's primer), *Iwabuchi yawa* 『岩淵夜話』 (Iwabuchi's evening talks), and *Ochiboshū* 『落穂集』 (Collected gleanings).

Daidō Ryū 大道流. Comprehensive school of martial arts (*sōgō bujutsu*) founded by Gotō Tamauemon Tadayoshi (1644–1736), a retainer of Aizu domain. Gotō taught swordsmanship (*tōjutsu*), mounted bow-and-arrow combat (*kyūba*), spearmanship (*sōjutsu*), and the art of explosives and gunnery (*kajutsu*). Having a practical, eclectic approach to martial arts, Gotō combined the secret teachings of nine systems into his Daidō Ryū.

Daigō Kiyomatsu 大剛 清松. Samurai of Shibata domain in the mid-1800s who was a licensed master (*menkyo kaiden*) practitioner of Ien Ryū 威遠流 gunnery (*hōjutsu*) and infantry training (*gumpō chōren*). Daigō's teacher, Shimosone Kanesaburō Nobuatsu, had changed the name of the school from Seiyō Ryū 西洋流 (lit. "Western Tradition") to Ien Ryū after the founder of the system, Takashima Shūhan, had been imprisoned in 1842 for his use of "Western" gunnery and the taint of associating with Westerners. Both Shimosone and Daigō changed the name of the system back to Seiyō Ryū in 1854 after Takashima Shūhan was pardoned and released from prison. Kiyomatsu appears to have taught the system only in Shibata domain. See: *Ien Ryū.*

Daihannya-haramita-kyō 『大般若波羅蜜多經』 <Ch. *Da banjo boluomiduo jing* <Skt. *Mahāprajñāpāramitā-sūtra*. BUDDHISM—A large (600 fascicles and 200,000 verses) text detailing the perfection of wisdom (Skt. *prajñāpāramitā*). It was translated into Chinese by Xuanzang[1] in 659 and into English by Edward Conze in 1975. See also: *Hannya-shin-gyō.*

Further reading in English:

- Conze, 1975 (translation).

Daihonzan Chōzenji 大本山超禅寺. Zen temple founded by Ōmori Sōgen, located in Hawaii.

Dai Jingū 大神宮. Abbreviation for Ise Dai Jingū, the Grand Shrine at Ise devoted to the sun goddess, Amaterasu Ōmikami.

Daikaku 大覚【大覺】<Ch. Dajue. Chinese *chan* (Jp. *zen*) priest who came to Japan in 1246, ultimately residing at a temple called Kenchōji. Due to language problems—Daikaku spoke Song-dynasty Chinese and little Japanese—he soon had to modify his Chinese-style Zen practices to fit the needs of the warriors of Kamakura. This modified style came to be called "on-the-spot Zen" (*shikin Zen*). Discarding the use of classical Chinese Buddhist riddles (*kōan*) and their long explanations, Daikaku began making up *kōan* instantly "on the spot" to fit the needs of the local warriors. See: *Kamakura Zen; kōan; shikin Zen.*

daiki 大毅. TAIHŌ MILITARY SYSTEM—The *daiki* was the leader of an assembly of six *tai* (platoons) for a total of about 600 conscript soldiers in the Chinese-style eighth-century provincial militia unit (*gundan*). As a commander of 600 men, the *daiki* was somewhat equivalent to a modern army or Marine Corps colonel who commands a battalion. In the

[1] Jp. Genjō 玄奘 <Ch. Xuanzang (603–664).

chain of command he was in charge of a *shōki* (lieutenant colonel or executive officer) and assisted by a *shuchō* (clerk). See: *gundan.*

Daikokuten 大黒天 (Great Black Deva) <Ch. Daheitian <Skt. Mahākāla. BUDDHISM—Originally Daikokuten was a deity in esoteric Buddhism whose purpose was to conquer evil. The god was usually represented in "heroic" or violent form, with three heads. In this form, known as the "Three-Headed Great Black Deva" (Sanmen Daikokuten), he has six arms and black skin, wears snakes as bracelets and a necklace of skulls, and typically carries a sword. In this manifestation he is one of the three Yumi-ya Santen, Japan's warrior-protecting deities.

SANMEN DAIKOKUTEN
Image from the *Taizōkai Mandara*

After the seventeenth century Daikokuten came to be recognized as a god of wealth; in that manifestation he is normally represented as a small, chubby, gnome-like man standing on two bales of rice. This form also has many phallic associations.

daikyū 大弓. Lit. "large bow." A term used to designate a standard war bow in contrast to smaller weapons such as the votive bow (*yōkyū*) and the half-bow (*hankyū*).

daimyō 大名. The term *daimyō* was originally an abbreviation for *daimyōden* 大名田 (large [holdings in] name fields). *Myōden* (name fields) were thus called because their owners took the geographical names of their land holdings as their surnames. An early medieval landowner who had large income-producing holdings could afford to support vassals, and thus was able to bring a large entourage of warriors and support troops to battle. Many of these men became known as skilled commanders because of the acts of their vassals. Consequently, an early meaning of *daimyō* came to be "commander." However, large land holdings were not the sole criteria for the title *daimyō*. Other references in the war tales note that a warrior chieftain (*daimyō*) had to command at least five hundred horsemen.

Under Minamoto no Yoritomo and during the Kamakura period, provincial-level constables who acted as liaisons between the Kamakura *bakufu* and its provincial vassals were called *shugo* 守護. Some of these constables who also held large areas of land came to be called *shugo daimyō* during the late Kamakura and early Muromachi periods.

During the protracted combat of the Warring States period (Sengoku Jidai), the nature of the *daimyō* began to shift. As the Ashikaga *bakufu* began to lose control of these provincial *daimyō* during the mid to late 1400s, they either evolved into or were replaced by independent regional warlords. In fact, Davis (1974: 234) notes that "During the sixteenth century, nearly all families that had been prominent during the previous hundred years either disappeared or changed beyond recognition." These independent warlords were later referred to as *sengoku daimyō* 戦国大名. *Daimyō* in that period were also divided into three categories: *kokushu* 国主 (essentially "governors" who controlled one or more provinces), *ryōshu* 領主 (lords of smaller territories) and *jōshu* 城主 (castle commanders). According to Papinot (1910:66), prior to Tokugawa Ieyasu, there were "18 *kokushu*, 32 *ryōshu*, and 212 *jōshu*."

With the ascent of the Tokugawa family after the battle of Sekigahara in 1600, Shōgun Tokugawa Ieyasu declared all commanders who had an income above 10,000 *koku* (a value measured in bushels of rice) to be *daimyō*. He then divided the *daimyō* into three categories, depending on their loyalty to the Tokugawa. These were:

1. *Shimpan daimyō* 親藩大名 The twenty-three

lords who were directly related to the Tokugawa or from collateral related families.

2. *Fudai daimyō* 譜代大名 The 176 lords who sided with Ieyasu before the battle of Sekigahara in 1600.

3. *Tozama daimyō* 外様大名 The eighty-six lords who submitted to Ieyasu only after having been defeated at Sekigahara.

There were about 270 *daimyō* in 1800. See also: *gokenin; hatamoto; jitō; kōke; myōden; shōmyō shugo.*

Dainichi-kyō 『大日経』【大日經】<Ch. *Dari jing* <Skt. *Mahā-vairocana-sūtra*. BUDDHISM—One of three central texts in the tantric practices of the Tendai and Shingon schools of Buddhism in Japan. This text is closely associated with the *Taizōkai Mandara*. Many of the Buddhist "deities" listed in the *Dainichi-kyō* and depicted in the *Taizōkai Mandara* have been used as talismans on martial equipment and weaponry. See also: *Kongōchō-kyō; Soshijjikara-kyō; Taizōkai Mandara; Taizōkai shiki.*

Dainichi Nyorai 大日如来 <Ch. Dari Rulai <Skt. Mahāvairocana Tathāgata. 1. BUDDHISM—Dainichi Nyorai, the Great Sun Buddha or Great Shining Buddha, is the primary buddha venerated by the major Tantric Buddhist traditions in East Asia. In Japan his cult is centered in the Tendai and Shingon traditions. His image is displayed as the central figure in both of the *ryōbu mandara*. Many other buddhas and bodhisattvas are seen to be a manifestation of Dainichi Nyorai. The gigantic buddha image located in Tōdaiji in Nara is an early version of Dainichi referred to as Rushana (also Birushana <Skt. Vairocana). 2. RYŌBU SHINTŌ—The primary deity of the Shintō pantheon, the sun goddess Amaterasu Ōmikami, is identified with Dainichi Nyorai. See: *Ryōbu Shintō.*

Dai Nippon Budō 大日本武道. One of the early (c. 1937) terms used by Ueshiba Morihei for the grappling system he modified from Daitō Ryū *aikijūjutsu* into *aikidō*.

Dai Nippon Butokukai 大日本武徳会【大日本武德會】(Great Japanese Martial Virtue Society). Founded in Kyōto in 1895, this organization aimed at preserving those classical martial traditions which had not disappeared after the Meiji Restoration in 1868. In 1899, the group built the Butokuden (Hall of Martial Virtue) next to the Heian shrine in Kyōto. In addition to providing training and lectures in classical and modern disciplines, the Butokukai was instrumental in having *kendō* and *jūdō* made part of compulsory education by 1911. One of the major aims of this paramilitary school was to toughen up future soldiers and prepare them for war. Branch *dōjō* of the Butokukai were created around Japan; instructors of both modern and classical disciplines gave seminars and held training sessions at these diverse locations over the next thirty years.

As the Pacific War intensified in 1942, Lieutenant General Tanaka Ryūkichi ordered the Butokukai to subordinate its martial arts instruction to the war effort. Many instructors resisted, but they were quickly silenced. The teachers and trainees in these arts were soon funneled into a program that the military considered necessary for the war effort. As Svinth (2002) notes:

> ...tournament judo came to be described as a waste of time, kendo was derided as dancing with bamboo rods, and kyudo was ridiculed for being hopelessly out of date. Consequently, by 1945, martial arts ("budo") had come to mean training in hand-to-hand fighting rather than kendo, judo, and kyudo.

With the Allied occupation of Japan in 1945, the Butokukai was disbanded. However, it has been replaced by various postwar organizations such as the Zen Nihon Kendō Renmei and the Nihon Kobudō Shinkokai. Martial-arts demonstrations (*embu*) and examinations for high *dan* ranks (sixth degree and above) are still held at the Butokuden each year.

Dai Nippon Kempō 大日本拳法. See: *Nihon Kempō.*

Dai Nippon Teikoku Kai 大日本帝国会【大日本帝國會】(Great Imperial Japan Society; Imperial Japan Society). Pre–World War II name for the martial system founded by Nakajima Shōhitsu. The system was renamed Ryūshinkan Budō after the war.

Dai Nippon Teikoku Kendō Kata 大日本帝国剣道形. See: *Nihon Kendō Kata.*

Dai Nippon Yamato Yagyū Kai 大日本大和柳生会. See: *Edo Yagyū Shinkage Ryū Yamane Ha.*

daisan 大三. KYŪDŌ—Lit. "great" (*dai* 大) "three" (*san* 三), *daisan* is part of drawing the bow (*hikiwake*), the fifth stage in firing an arrow (*hassetsu*) in the modern martial way of archery (*kyūdō*). According to the late *kyūdō* master Onuma Hideharu, *daisan* is the first element of *hikiwake*: the archer pushes the bow toward the target with the left arm as his right arm folds at the elbow. This must be performed in coordination with proper breathing and mental and spiritual focus. Thus, according to Onuma, the archer must "push big (*dai*) and pull one-third (*san*)" Onuma (1993: 76–77). See also: *daisan no tsuriai.*

daisan no tsuriai 大三の釣合い. KYŪDŌ—Lit. the "balance of the *daisan*." As related to *daisan*, the term *tsuriai* (balance, being in harmony) means that the bow hand (left hand), the drawing hand on the string (right hand), and the right elbow must be in correct juxtaposition to each other. It also indicates that the body posture, breath, and total physical composure must be in harmony prior to the release of the arrow. (Onuma 1993: 77).

daishō 大小. This term refers to the large (*dai* 大) and small (*shō* 小) swords which became the badge of samurai status during the Edo period. During those centuries, only those of samurai status were allowed to wear two swords, especially the longer sword (*tachi* or *katana*).

daishō no soroimono 大小の揃い物. A complete set of sword fittings for the set of two swords (*daisho*) typically worn by samurai during the Edo period. See: *soroimono.*

daishu 大衆. 1. A medieval term for general Buddhist clergy. 2. Term used erroneously by some scholars to indicate warrior monks (*sōhei*).

daitō 大刀. A long sword; a great sword; a blade of *katana* or *tachi* length (23.5 in. [60 cm] or greater).

Daitōkan 大東館. Located in Abashiri, Hokkaidō, the Daitōkan was the headquarters of Daitō Ryū Aikibudō under second headmaster Takeda Tokimune. Opened in 1953, the *dōjō* closed in 1994, about a year after Tokimune passed away.

Daitō Ryū 大東流 [A.k.a. ***Aikibudō*** 合気武道; ***Daitō Ryū Aikibudō*** 大東流合気武道; ***Sōkaku Ryū*** 惣角流; ***Takeda Ryū Jūjutsu*** 武田流柔術; ***Takeda Ryū Aikijūjutsu*** 武田流合気柔術]. A school of *jūjutsu/aikijūjutsu* developed by Takeda Sōkaku around 1895–1905. Sōkaku, a skilled and experienced swordsman of the Ono Ha Ittō Ryū 小野派一刀流 and Jiki Shinkage Ryū 直心影流, hailed from the feudal domain of Aizu. Sometime during the 1890s Sōkaku formulated his own school of *jūjutsu/aikijujutsu*, combining the Takeda clan's native field-combat *jūjutsu* system with a sophisticated civilian self-defense system known as *oshikiuchi*. This second system had been transmitted by the Matsudaira and Hoshina lines of Shintō priests in Aizu domain. Prior to that time, *oshikiuchi* (a *jūjutsu*-like art intended for use in the palace of the *daimyō*) had only been transmitted to a limited group of upper-class Aizu samurai. To this synthesis Sōkaku added his practical experience of more than ten years of warrior pilgrimage (*musha shūgyō*). According to Inoue Yusuke (successor to Horikawa Kōdō, a direct student of Takeda Sōkaku), techniques derived from the Takeda clan's field-combat *jūjutsu* were referred to as Daitō Ryū *jūjutsu*; those derived from *oshikiuchi* were referred to as Daitō Ryū *aikijūjutsu* (Pranin, 1996: 101). The *aikijūjutsu* portion of the system is evidently much more difficult to master.

Although the system traces its origins to the emperor Seiwa[2] via the Takeda and Minamoto family lines, there are no *densho* that predate Takeda Sōkaku.

Under Sōkaku, the Daitō Ryū curriculum consisted of *taijutsu* (empty-handed techniques), the use of small throwing blades and darts (*shurikenjutsu*), and, for some of his senior students, the *kenjutsu* of the Ono Ha Ittō Ryū.

[2] Seiwa Tennō 清和天皇 (850–880; r.859–876), fifty-sixth emperor of Japan.

As practiced by Sōkaku, this renowned sword school had a great influence on the empty-handed techniques he added to and modified from *oshikiuchi.* According to Sōkaku's son, the late Takeda Tokumune:

When I teach, I teach the sword and *taijutsu* [empty-handed techniques] separately. Our sword is Ono Ha Ittō Ryū. I explain as I teach that such and such a technique comes from the sword of [Jiki] Shinkage Ryū or Ono Ha Ryū. Since it is too much work for me to teach all of them, I teach the Ono Ha Ittō Ryū techniques only to leading members of the

Daitō Ryū
大東流
(abbreviated lineage)

Hoshina Chikanori
保科 近悳
Aizu *oshikiuchi*
会津 御式内

Takeda Sōkichi
武田 惣吉
Takeda *jūjutsu*
武田 柔術

Sakakibara Kenkichi
保科 近悳
Jiki Shinkage Ryū *kenjutsu*
直心影流 剣術

Takeda Sōkaku
Minamoto no Masayoshi
武田 惣角 源正義
Daitō Ryū *jūjutsu* • *aikijūjutsu*
大東流(柔術・合気柔術)

(1) Satō Hirotsune
佐藤 完実
Kyōju Dairi 教授代理,
1902

(2) Shimoe Shūtarō
下江 秀太郎
Kyōju Dairi 教授代理,
1903

(3) Harada Nobuzō
原田 信蔵
Kyōju Dairi 教授代理,
1903

(4) Mikami Tomiji
三上 富治
Kyōju Dairi 教授代理,
1907

(5) Horikawa Taisō
堀川 泰宗
Kyōju Dairi 教授代理,
1913

(7) Yoshida Kotarō
吉田 幸太郎
Kyōju Dairi 教授代理,
1903

(8) Ueshiba Morihei
植芝 盛平
Kyōju Dairi 教授代理,
1922
Ueshiba Ryū Aikidō,
1939
植芝流合気道

(10) Sagawa Yukiyoshi
佐川 幸義
Kyōju Dairi 教授代理,
1924

(11) Matsuda, Hōsaku
Toshimi
松田 豊作 敏美
Kyōju Dairi 教授代理,
1928

Okuyama Ryūhō
Yoshiji
奥山 龍峰 吉治
Hakkō Ryū, 1939
八光流

(14) Horikawa Kōdō
堀川 幸道
Kyōju Dairi 教授代理,
1931
Daitō Ryū Aikijūjutsu
Kōdōkai
大東流合気柔術幸道会

Okamoto Seigō
岡本 正剛
Kyōju Dairi 教授代理,
1931
Daitō Ryū Aikijūjutsu
Roppokai
大東流合気柔術六方会

(16) Satō Keisuke
佐藤 啓輔
Kyōju Dairi 教授代理,
1935

(20) Hisa Takuma
久 琢磨
Menkyo Kaiden
免許皆伝, 1939
Nipponden Aikijūjutsu
日本伝合気柔術

(29) Yamamoto Kakuyoshi
山本 角義
Kyōju Dairi 教授代理, 1941
Nipponden Aikijūjutsu
無限神刀流 躰道

Takeda Tokimune
武田 時宗
Sōke 宗家, 1941
Daitō Ryū Aikibudō

dōjō. As you know, there are sixty techniques in this school alone. You are not practicing the art properly unless you practice both sword and *jūjutsu*, that is to say, unless you practice both Daitō Ryū and Ono Ha Ittō Ryū. (Pranin,1996: 75)

Under Takeda Tokimune, the *taijutsu* was passed on as *aikibudō*. And, today, under Takeda Tokimune's successor, Kondo Katsuyuki, the *taijutsu* is passed on as Daitō Ryū *aikijūjutsu*.

Curriculum

The curriculum of the school is composed of techniques listed in traditional *densho* and transmitted orally.

Transmission scrolls/licenses (*densho*)

Jūjutsu/Aikijūjutsu Curriculum

1. *Hiden mokuroku*「秘伝目録」(118 techniques)
2. *Aiki no jutsu*「合気術」(53 techniques, *omote* 表 and *ura* 裏)
3. *Hiden ōgi mokuroku*「秘伝奥義目録」(36 techniques, *omote* 表 and *ura* 裏)
4. *Daitō Ryū aiki nitōryū*「大東流合気二刀流」(20 dual-sword techniques created by Takeda Sōkaku)
5. *Goshinyō no te*「御信用の手」(84 self-defense techniques categorized by type of attack: *jō* 上, *chū* 中, *ge* 下)
6. *Kyōju dairi*「教授代理」(Teaching license; no additional techniques included)
7. *Kaishaku sōden*「解釈総伝」(Selected summary of 477 of the previous techniques)

   NOTE: *Kaishaku sōden* was the "highest level" *densho* Sōkaku awarded until he taught at the *Asahi News* office in Osaka, where he awarded the first *menkyo kaiden* to Takuma Hisa in 1939.
8. *Menkyo kaiden*「免許皆伝」(88 techniques)

Kondo Katsuyuki notes that in addition to the technical teachings of the *Daitō Ryū kaishaku sōden* and *Daitō Ryū menkyo kaiden*, there is

> …another important body of knowledge in Daitō Ryū—all of the Daitō Ryū oral teachings and secrets. I can't express these in a few words, but they are something fundamentally important to Daitō Ryū. In my case, it took fourteen years to go the two steps from Goshinyo to Kaiden. (Pranin,1996: 101)

As of this writing, the only award of the following designations has been from Takeda Tokimune to Kondō Katsuyuki:

9. *Sōke kyōju dairi*「宗家教授代理」
10. *Sōke dairi*「宗家代理」

Kenjutsu Curriculum

[NOTE: Not all students were taught the *kenjutsu* curriculum]

Ittō Ryū kenjutsu「一刀流剣術」(60 techniques)

Several other documents are extant in Daitō Ryū; however, they were not awarded as part of the ranking system and are very rare. According to a student of Kondo Katsuyuki, The first of these documents is the *Sōden*『総伝』of the Takumakai (an organization formed by students of Hisa Takuma and Nakatsu Heizaburo). The full name of this document is *Daitō Ryū aiki budō densho zen jūikkan mokuroku*『大東流会気武道伝書全十一巻目録』. It is in the form of eleven volumes of technical descriptions and photographs taken just after classes taught by Ueshiba (1933–1936) and Sōkaku (1936–1939). The eleven volumes are divided into three sections: *ten* 天, *chi* 地, and *jin* 人. Kondo Katsuyuki has a copy of the eleven books (reserved for high-ranking members of the Takumakai) as well as copies of all of the photographic negatives.

Additional Daitō Ryū scrolls were awarded to Sagawa Yukiyoshi, who received at least one, perhaps two of these additional documents. The first scroll is called *Aiki no tachi*「合気太刀」(The longsword of *aiki*). Sagawa is the only person known to have received it, and little is known about it. There is also a possible second scroll whose title is unknown; its contents are said to include descriptions of techniques for spear, sword, long staff and other weapons.[3]

Takeda Tokimune changed the *densho* system to *dan* ranks.

Lineage

Sōkaku and Tokimune had, literally, thousands of students. However, the headmastership has passed as outlined above.

See also: *Genji no heihō; oshikiuchi; Saigō Shirō; Saigō Tanomo Chikanori; Sōkaku Ryū; Takeda Ryū (2); Takeda Sōkaku.*

Daitō Ryū Aikibudō 大東流合気武道. The

[3] Special thanks to Chris Covington for this information.

term used for Daitō Ryū teachings under Takeda Tokimune, second headmaster. See: *Daitō Ryū.*

Daitō Ryū Aikibudō densho zenjūikkan mokuroku 『大東流合気武道伝書全十一巻目録』【大東流合氣武道傳書全十一巻目録】[A.k.a. ***Sōden*** 『相伝』【相傳】]. An eleven-volume set of notebooks with photographs detailing techniques taught by Ueshiba Morihei and Takeda Sōkaku at the Asahi Budō Dōjō in the 1930s. These notebooks are still held by the Takumakai organization and are available to members only. However, Kondo Katsuyuki, Takeda Tokimune's successor in Daitō Ryū, also has copies.

Daitō Ryū Aikijūjutsu Kōdōkai 大東流合気柔術幸道会. A Daitō Ryū organization founded by Horikawa Kōdō in 1950.

Daitō Ryū Aikijūjutsu Roppōkai 大東流合気柔術六方会. A Daitō Ryū organization founded by Okamoto Seigō in 1980.

Daitō Ryū aiki nitōryū 「大東流合気二刀流」【大東流合氣二刀流】. A Daitō Ryū transmission scroll (*densho*), the fourth of several awarded in that tradition (although few students of the system have ever received it). It requires mastery of twenty dual-sword techniques created by Takeda Sōkaku. See: *Daitō Ryū.*

Daitō Ryū Kōdōkai 大東流幸道会. See: *Daitō Ryū Aikijūjutsu Kōdōkai.*

Daitō Sonbei Hidesada 台島 孫兵衛 英貞【臺島孫兵衛英貞】. Founder of a *jūjutsu* system during the Kyōhō era (1716–1736) which he christened the Ōhen Ryū 応変流, lit. "quick-response tradition." The school was based on the Asayama Ichiden Ryū 浅山一伝流, which Daitō had mastered.

Daiwadō 大和道. A martial school founded by Satō Kinbei in 1966. This system is a mixture of grappling techniques (*aikijutsu* and *jūjutsu*), fist attacks (*kempo [2]*), and the use of weapons, including sword (*kenjutsu*), long hardwood staff (*bōjutsu*), and medium-length hardwood staff (*jōjutsu*). In appearance Daiwadō is very similar to the *aiki* systems Satō studied: Daitō Ryū 大東流, Hakkō Ryū 八光流, Ueshiba Ryū Aikidō 植芝流合気道, etc.

Daizen Daifu Moritada 大膳 大夫 盛忠. Famous spearman who is thought to have taught the sickle spear (*kama yari*) to Hōzōin Inei around 1565–1570.

daken taijutsu 打拳体術. A primarily pugilistic (boxing/striking) system derived from the Shinden Fudō Ryū 神伝不動流 and Kuki Shin Ryū 九鬼神流 that was incorporated into the Bujinkan via Hatsumi Masaaki. The system contains elements defined as attacks against the skeletal structure (*koppōjutsu*) and attacks against musculature (*koshijutsu*).

Further reading in English:

- Hatsumi, 2008: 144–167; 168–207.

dakkō 奪口. Variant term for an espionage agent, evidently used in the Kusunoki Ryū 楠流. This term indicated an agent who was intimately familiar with a target area's language, local dialects, and customs. With this knowledge, intelligence information from the target area could be properly evaluated and analyzed. See: *Kusunoki Ryū; ninjutsu.*

Dampatsurei 断髪令【斷髮令】. A law issued in 1871 by the Meiji government requiring samurai to cut off their topknots (a traditional symbol of the warrior class) and wear their hair in the Western style.

dan 段. 1. Lit. "step," "level," or "grade." See: *dan-kyū.* 2. A term for the division of *kata* sets in the Jigen Ryū 示現流.

dangyō 男業. SHINDŌ MUSŌ RYŪ—*Dangyō* (lit. "men's arts") was a colloquial term used within the Kuroda domain in Kyūshū. According to Matsui Kenji (1991a: 35), it appears in an old Bakumatsu-period text of the Kuroda clan, and refers to the martial arts of the *ashigaru* (low-ranking samurai). The *dangyō* evidently included the medium-length staff (*jō*), police arresting arts (*torite*), and tying-cord arts (*torinawa*). *See also: Ikkaku Ryū; Ittatsu Ryū; Shindō Musō Ryū.*

Further reading in English:

- Matsui, 1993.

dan'i 段位. Lit. "grade level." A modern term referring to modern *budō* grading systems; one's *dan* level. See: *dan–kyū*.

danjiki 断食【斷食】. Fasting. 1. BUDDHISM—The custom of going without food and water has long been a standard practice found in various Buddhist schools. 2. SHUGENDŌ—Among the *yamabushi*, the aim of fasting (then as now) was to develop spiritual power for performing exorcisms and healing, and to achieve heightened states of consciousness.

dan–kyū 段級. *Dan*=grade, degree; *kyū*=class. *Dan–kyū* refers to the grading system used in modern *budō* since the Meiji era (1868–1912). More recently, some classical *ryū* and classical disciplines in transition to modern *budō* have replaced their traditional licensing system (*mokuroku menkyo*) with *dan–kyū* ranks.

The *dan–kyū* system was evidently originated by Kanō Jigorō, founder of Kōdōkan Judō, when he established the designations of *mudansha* (non-graded) and *yudansha* (graded) in 1883.[4] The terminology is based in Neo-Confucian/Chu Hsi dualism. Chu Hsi's philosophy categorizes phenomena as either "having form" (*yūkei* 有形) or "without form" (*mukei* 無形). Consequently, *budō* practitioners holding *dan* (grade) rank are referred to as *yūdansha* 有段者 (one having grade rank) while those having no *dan* are referred to as *mudansha* 無段者 (one without grade rank).

Today class ranks (*kyū*) are normally numbered in descending order from five (sometimes higher) to one, while grade ranks (*dan*) are normally numbered in an ascending sequence from one through five, or nine, or ten, etc., depending on the system or discipline:

CLASS (*KYŪ*) RANKS

gokyū	五級	fifth class
yonkyū	四級	fourth class
sankyū	三級	third class
nikyū	二級	second class
ikkyū	一級	first class

GRADE (*DAN*) RANKS

shodan	初段	first grade
nidan	二段	second grade
sandan	三段	third grade
yondan	四段	fourth grade
godan	五段	fifth grade
rokudan	六段	sixth grade
nanadan	七段	seventh grade
hachidan	八段	eighth grade
kyūdan	九段	ninth grade
jūdan	十段	tenth grade
jūichidan	十一段	eleventh grade
jūnidan	十二段	twelfth grade

Requirements for each of these ranks vary greatly from system to system.

Kanō may have also been the first, around 1886, to institute the use of black and white belts to denote *yudansha* and *mudansha* respectively. However, the origin of the use of other colors for various *dan* and *kyū* ranks is more difficult to determine. Lowry (2006) attributes this development to Kawaishi Mikonosuke, a Japanese *jūdō* instructor who spent many years teaching in Paris.

Further reading in English:

• Lowry, 2006: 49–58.

Dannō Gennoshin Yoshitaka 団野 源之進 義高【團野源之進義高】(1761–1849). JIKI SHINKAGE RYŪ—Recognized as twelfth headmaster and successor to eleventh headmaster Akaishi Chikayoshi by the Jiki Shinkage Ryū 直心影流. Dannō's most famous students were Odani Nobutomo (who became thirteenth headmaster) and Katsu Kokichi (father of Katsu Kaishū). The Dannō Ha family line of Jiki Shinkage Ryū descends from Gennoshin through his son, Dannō Matashirō.

Further reading in English:

• Craig, 1988.

Dan no Kata (Gokui) 段の型 (極意). JIGEN

[4] A recent article speculates that Funakoshi Gichin's Shōtōkan Karatedō obtained its *dan* ranking system due to the influence of Jigen Ryū on Okinawan *karate*. This is an interesting claim, as several sequential levels of kata training in Jigen Ryū are denoted as *shodan*, *nidan*, *sandan*, and *yondan*. However, it is presumptuous to accept this claim at face value. Funakoshi introduced *karate* to Japanese government officials in 1917 and promoted it publicly from 1922. Kanō's Kōdōkan Jūdō had been using *dan* ranks at least as early as 1883.

RYŪ—Advanced-level combative swordsmanship forms used by the Jigen Ryū. There are four levels of Dan no Kata, each containing three scenarios and beginning with different postures (*kamae*). The practice of these advanced forms is intended to reveal the hidden meanings of an earlier combative scenario (*kata*) called Empi. See: *Jigen Ryū.*

Dan-no-Ura no Tatakai 壇ノ浦の戦い. Decisive sea battle fought in 1185 in the bay near Shimonoseki in which the Minamoto forces under Yoshitsune destroyed the Taira. It was also during this battle that the seven-year-old former emperor Antoku[5] and his grandmother, Nii-no-ama (Taira Kiyomori's widow, who had headed the Taira), perished.

darani 陀羅尼 <Ch. *tuoluoni* <Skt. *dhāraṇī*. Among both Hindus and Buddhists in India, *dhāraṇī* are magical formulae which, when uttered properly, allow devotees to obtain religious merit from the texts from which they are taken. They help improve memory and are thought to give the user special magical powers. A *dhāraṇī* may contain a shorter utterance called a *mantra* (*shingon*). In East Asia both *dhāraṇī* and *shingon* were commonly used among Buddhists and martial artists alike. See also: *shingon; shuji.*

Further reading in English:

- Bharati, 1965: 101–163.
- Hall, 1990: 30–44.
- Winternitz, 1933.

Daruma 達磨 [Abbreviation of ***Bodai Daruma*** 菩提 達磨 <Ch. Puti Damo <Skt. Bodhidharma. Daruma is the legendary monk recognized as first patriarch of Chinese Chan Buddhism and thought to have journeyed from India to China in the sixth century. Legend tells us he was the son of the king of "Kōshi," a country located in South India. He arrived in China in 520, and after settling at the Shaolin temple in Honan province, is said to have sat in meditation for nine years. He later became recognized as the founder of both Chan (Jp. Zen) Buddhism and a physical training regimen which evolved into the martial system practiced by the monks of the temple.

date 立. A common misreading, in Western books on Japanese armor and related subjects, of the term for "helmet crest." See: maedate; tatemono.

Dazaifu 大宰府. A regional government office which had jurisdiction over the islands of Kyūshū, Iki, and Tsushima. This was a critical area during the seventh and eighth centuries, when the Japanese feared an invasion from the continent.

Dazaifu Tenmangu 大宰府天満宮. Shintō shrine located in Chikuzen (present-day Fukuoka) in Kyūshū, where Akiyama Shirobei Yoshitoki had the enlightening experience on which he based his Yōshin Ryū school of *jūjutsu* in the late 1600s. See also: *Akiyama Shirobei Yoshitoki.*

de-ai 出会【出會】. Lit. an "encounter," or "meeting." This term is sometimes used in martial arts training to indicate the first "clash of blades" in a particular prearranged combative form (*kata*).

Deguchi Onisaburō 出口 王仁三郎 [Also read ***Deguchi Wanisaburō***; originally his name was ***Ueda Kisaburō*** 上田喜三郎] (1871–1948). Developer of the Ōmoto Kyō religion and spiritual guide of Ueshiba Morihei. In 1898, at the age of twenty-seven, Onisaburō met a Japanese woman named Deguchi Nao, founder of the new Ōmoto Kyō religious movement. Quickly becoming not only a convert but an enthusiastic advocate of Ōmoto Kyō, Onisaburō married Nao's daughter Sumiko in 1900 and was subsequently adopted by Nao into the Deguchi family. At that time he changed his name from Ueda Kisaburō to Deguchi Onisaburō. With Nao's death in 1918, Onisaburō took over the leadership of Ōmoto Kyō. By that time his appealing, flamboyant personality had already brought many members into the new religion.

Onisaburō was also a prolific writer. He published an omnibus, eighty-one-volume work entitled *Reikai monogatari*『霊界物語』(Tales of the spiritual realm) which not only illustrated many Ōmoto Kyō tenets but also

5 Antoku Tennō 安徳天皇 (1178–1185, r. 1180–1185). Eighty-first emperor of Japan.

elaborated on his personal treks into various spiritual worlds.

In 1919 he met Ueshiba Morihei, the talented personal disciple (*deshi*) of Takeda Sōkaku, founder of Daitō Ryū. Ueshiba quickly became an ardent follower of Onisaburō, and in 1924 accompanied him on a pilgrimage to Mongolia.

In the 1920s Onisaburō considered himself to be an incarnation of Miroku Bosatsu (Skt. Maitreya Bodhisattva). His vision was to create a spiritual kingdom in Mongolia which would then unite Xinjiang,[6] Tibet, India, and China, creating an East Asian Spiritual Union. Evidently he also wanted to spread this religious influence to Russia, Europe, America, and eventually Jerusalem, where he would be able to enter that city as the Second Coming of Christ. (Kanemoto, 1990: 63.)

A pacifist—as were other Ōmoto Kyō members—Onisaburō was very talented at handling people and was able to move fluidly between the anti-government religious movement, government officials, and even ultra-righest groups such as the Kokuryūkai.[7] In doing this he intended to subvert policies he found amoral. He did not always succeed in this practice, however, and on two occasions the Ōmoto Kyō compounds were raided by the Japanese police. In one of the incidents, many of the pacifist members were imprisoned and tortured. Notably, Deguchi's disciple Ueshiba was warned and "spirited away" by friends in the Japanese police just before the razing of the compound. Onisaburō's charisma is legendary, and even under government pressure Ueshiba always remained loyal to him.

denchū iaijutsu 殿中居合術 【殿中居合術】. Lit. "quick-draw sword techniques for use inside the palace." This term is used in some current schools to refer to late-period *iaidō* techniques thought to have been originally designed for use inside a building. However, the only *denchū iaijutsu* observed by this author is that practiced by Saigō Ha Daitō Ryū Aikibujutsu. Since this group focuses on using the long sword (*katana*) from the *seiza* kneeling posture, the historical authenticity of these techniques is questionable. Historically, the *katana* was left at the door when samurai entered a palace; only the shorter *wakizashi* would have been worn.[8] See: *iaidō*.

Dengyō Daishi 伝教大師 【傳教大師】. See: *Saichō*.

Denkibō Ryū 伝鬼坊流 【傳鬼坊流】. See: *Tendō Ryū*.

densho 伝書 【傳書】. A transmission scroll. Although usually in scroll form, *densho* are occasionally bound as books. Contents vary greatly from *ryū* to *ryū*; some contain only text, others have illustrations along with text. A general term for scrolls containing illustrations is *emaki* (lit. "picture scroll"). A restricted or "secret" transmission scroll is called a *hidensho*.

Densho vary greatly, as they can contain anything a tradition wishes to transmit. These scrolls tend to fall into several broad categories:

Ranking or Certifications of Proficiency

These documents are normally presented to recipients as an indication of rank or skill level.

- *inka* 印可 [also written 允可]—Lit. "seal of mastery." This term finds its origins in Chinese Buddhist texts and indicates the recipient has mastered the contents of the tradition—or at least the contents of the scroll itself.
- *kirigami* 切紙—Lit. "cut paper." In some traditions this is an official name for a first certificate, in others it is a generic term for a short document not of scroll length. A typical *kirigami* document might simply be a commitment from the headmaster to teach the student the intricacies of the tradition. It may or may not contain a list of techniques.
- *mokuroku* 目録—Lit. "list." This term, singularly or in combination with other descriptive terms, usually indicates a list of combative

[6] Xinjiang is the westernmost province of China; it borders both Mongolia and Tibet.

[7] See photograph under the entry on Tōyama Mitsuru.

[8] During the seventeenth century, the Tokugawa shogunate allowed *daimyō* to arm themselves with *chisa katana* when in the *shōgun*'s presence.

DENSHO
Densho entitled *Kōgen Ittō Ryū mokuroku* (List [of techniques and concepts] of the Kōgen Ittō School [of swordsmanship]).
(Densho from the archives of Nitta Suzuyo)

forms (*kata*) or concepts in which the recipient has attained proficiency.

- *menjō* 免状—Lit. "certificate." This term may be used for any document short of a full license in a tradition. It may simply certify that the recipient has achieved proficiency in a certain set of *kata*, or it may indicate a level of proficiency required for teaching.
- *menkyo* 免許—Lit. "license." This document may indicate that the recipient has a limited or full license in a tradition.
- *menkyo kaiden* 免許皆伝—Lit. "license of complete transmission."

There are many others.

Historical, Philosophical, and/or Ritual Directions

These documents are not necessarily presented to recipients as an indication of rank or proficiency (although in some cases they may be). They generally contain other elements important to the tradition in historical or

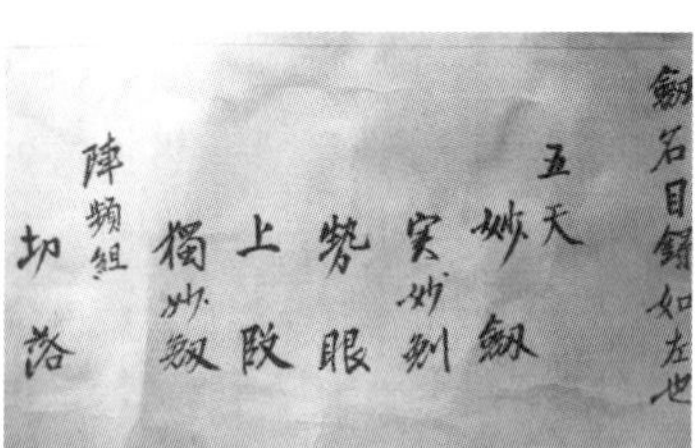

TYPICAL LIST OF TECHNIQUES IN A *MOKUROKU*-TYPE *DENSHO*
From *Kōgen Ittō Ryū mokuroku*
(Densho from the archives of Nitta Suzuyo)

philosophical context; or they may contain important information on ritual or other practices of the tradition. Only a few examples are included here.

- ***Maniwa Nen Ryū:*** *Marishiten setsu shōgun kyō*「魔利支天説勝軍經」(The Marishiten discourse on defeating armies)
- ***Shinkage Ryū: Dōjō sōgon gishiki***「道場荘厳儀式」(Ritual for adorning the dōjō); *Kanjō gokui no maki*「灌頂極意之巻」(Initiation ritual into the deepest mysteries)
- ***Tenshin Shōden Katori Shintō Ryū:*** *Katori shinryo shintōryū kongenshō*「香取神慮神刀流根元鈔」(The divine origin of the Katori Shintō Ryū)

denshō 伝承【傳承】. A transmission; a tradition.

deshi 弟子. A disciple.

dō 1. 胴. a. Trunk; torso. b. Trunk-protecting armor; the Japanese corselet. Within the two main classes there are a variety of types of each. The first class, known as *dōmaru*, opens at the side; the second, called *haramakidō*, opens at the back. c. KENDŌ—The armor worn to protect the *kendō* practitioner's torso. This term comes from earlier body-protecting armor called *dōmaru* (lit. "around the trunk").

dō 2. 動. Movement, action.

~dō 3. ~道 [Also read **michi**]. Lit. "way," "path," "road." When used in combination with other words, this character indicates training with a goal of spiritual development; e.g., the term *kyūdō* refers to archery (*kyū*) for spiritual development (*dō*).

dōbarai uchi 胴払打【胴拂打】. Lit. "sweep away from the torso and strike," "sweeping strike to the torso." SHINDŌ MUSŌ RYŪ—A technique in which the medium-length staff (*jō*) is used to sweep the weapon of the opponent away from the trunk/body. This is the eleventh of the twelve basic techniques (*kihon*) extrapolated from the classical forms of Shindō Musō Ryū by Shimizu Takaji.

dōbōshū 同朋衆. Lit. "companions." This was an early fourteenth-century term referring to a certain type of Buddhist layman (*tonseisha*) who came to serve the Ashikaga shogunate and some *daimyō* as "arbiters of taste and practitioners of the arts." All of the *dōbōshū* came from lowly backgrounds, and all had taken names that ended in the term *ami* 阿弥, a common abbreviation for the Buddhist deity Amida Butsu. Originally, the appellation also indicated a connection with the Jishū branch of the Buddhist Pure Land School (Jōdo Shū), whose members also followed the practice of using *ami* in their adopted names. However, by the mid-1300s this usage had become formulaic, and no longer indicated a direct connection with the Jishū branch.

By the 1300s *dōbōshū* were often accompanying armies onto the battlefield, where they assisted the wounded and attended to the dead and dying. Varley (1977: 189) notes that approximately 200 of these priests accompanied the Kamakura forces when they assaulted Kusunoki Masashige's fortification at Chihaya in 1333.

Varley goes on to note that their status as Buddhist lay priests gave them some social mobility, and by the latter half of the fourteenth century many had achieved special positions in society. Employed by the shogunate or various warrior houses, they came to perform a variety of miscellaneous cultural services, including arranging and participating in poem reading, tea competitions, banquets, the handling of art pieces, etc.

Further reading in English:
- Varley, 1977.

dodan 土壇. A mound of earth on which a corpse was mounted as a target for the purpose of testing swords (*tameshigiri*). The corpse was usually held in place by bamboo or wooden stakes and ropes.

Dōgaku 道学【道學】. 1. Confucian philosophy or ethics. 2. Daoism.

Dōgashira 動頭. One of several prearranged combative forms of the Kagemasa Ryū 陰政流.

Dōgen Zenji 道元禅師 【道元禪師】 [A.k.a. Dōgen Kigen 道元 希玄; Eihei Dōgen 永平道元] (1200–1253). Buddhist priest who founded the Sōtō school of Zen (Sōtō Shū 曹洞宗) in Japan in the thirteenth century.

do-geza 土下座. Essentially the same as *zarei*, *do-geza* is a prostration or bow from a kneeling posture such as *seiza*. ¶ *Do-geza shite mukaeru* 土下座して迎える, to salute or welcome (one's lord) with a prostration.

dōgi 道着. Lit. "apparel for practicing the 'way.'" The term *dōgi* refers to the upper portion (jacket) of the training outfit worn by modern practitioners of martial arts and ways. Most are blue, black, or white in color. Texture and thickness vary depending on the rigors of the discipline. See also: *karategi; jūdōgi; uwagi.*

dōgu 道具. Paraphernalia, tools, or instruments used by someone in a profession or art. The *dōgu* of a *kendō* practitioner might consist of protective gear (*bōgu*) such as a head protector (*men*), trunk protector (*dō*), padded gloves (*kote*), etc., while the *dōgu* of a priest might consist of ritual instruments such as a *vajra* scepter (*gokosho*), bell (*kane*), and other implements.

dōgusuri 胴薬. Gunpowder.

dōgusuriiri 胴薬入. A gunpowder flask. Also called an *enshōiri*.

dōhai 同輩. An equal; a person who entered training around the same time as oneself. (Compare to *kohai*, *sempai*.)

dohyō 土俵. 1. Sandbags. 2. SUMŌ—The *sumō* wrestling ring.

dohyō-iri 土俵入り. SUMŌ—The ceremonial entrance of *sumō* wrestlers into the ring at the beginning of a tournament.

doikki 土一揆. See: *tsuchi ikki.*

dōjō 道場 <Ch. *daochang* <Skt. *bodhimaṇḍa*. Lit. "the place of the 'way.'" 1. BUDDHISM—This term originally referred to the ground under the *bodhi* tree where the Buddha was seated at the time of attaining enlightenment. It later came to mean a holy place of learning and practicing the way. See: *mandara*. 2. A training hall (for both martial and Buddhist training.) Martial *dōjō* began to proliferate during the Edo period. Before that time most training took place outside.

dōjō arashi 道場荒し [A.k.a. ***dōjō yaburi*** 道場破]. 1. Lit. "*dōjō*-storming." This term usually refers to the practice (in Japan) of traveling around the country to various *kendō* training halls (*kendōjō*) or *jūdō* training halls (*jūdōjō*) and forcing the best students or headmaster into a match. See also: *dōjō yaburi.*

Further reading in English:

- Draeger, 1974: 99.

dōjōchō 道場長. The head of a *dōjō* (who may or may not be the head instructor). Such a person may hold the title of *kanchō* 館長, which means essentially the same thing.

dōjō kun 道場訓. The maxims or rules of a training hall (*dōjō*).

dōjō yaburi 道場破 [Var. ***yaburi dōjō*** 破り道場]. Lit. "to break a *dōjō*" or "to destroy a *dōjō*." Similar to *dōjō arashi*, this term indicates the act of visiting a *dōjō* in order to try and defeat the members in match contests. See also: *dōjō arashi.*

dōka 道歌. Didactic poems sometimes included in transmission documents of modern *budō*. However, the term *dōka* is most often used to describe the transmission poems of Morihei Ueshiba, founder of *aikidō*. While didactic verse is often found in classical martial transmission scrolls (*densho*), it is usually referred to simply as *koka* 古歌 (old verse).

dokko 独鈷【獨鈷】. See: *tokkosho* (3).

Dokkōdō 『独行道』【獨行道】(The path of self-reliance; the path walked alone). A short list of twenty-one precepts on swordsmanship attributed to Miyamoto Musashi and supposedly written just before his death in 1645. In the original text, as reprinted in Imamura (1966, Vol. 1: 492–493), the text is addressed to Musashi's disciple, Terao Magonojo.

Further reading in English:

- Tokitsu, translation. 2004: 216–226.

dokkogata shuriken 独鈷形手裏剣【獨鈷形手裏劍】[Var. ***dokko shuriken***]. Lit. "*tokko*-shaped *shuriken*." As the name indicates, this is a hand-held throwing blade shaped like a Buddhist *tokkosho* (single-pointed *vajra* scepter). This term can also denote a Buddhist *tokkosho* used as a *shuriken.*

dokko shuriken 独鈷手裏剣【獨鈷手裏劍】. See: *dokkogata shuriken.*

dokuya 毒矢. A poisoned arrow.

Dōkyō 道教 <Ch. *daojiao*. Daoism.

dokyū 弩弓. A crossbow. Although crossbows were highly valued by the imperial court in the eighth century, little if any archeological evidence of the weapon has been found in Japan. However, the court did appoint crossbowmen (*doshi* 弩師) in a number of provinces in northern Kyūshū, western Honshu, and northern Honshu, evidently because the crossbow was considered the weapon of choice for fighting "barbarians" and external enemies. (Farris, 1992: 113). The crossbow probably fell out of use because the government support of production that its relative complexity and high manufacturing cost required would have disappeared with the weakening of the central government after 900 C.E. Furthermore, crossbows were manned by common foot soldiers, and the trend from 900 C.E. was away from common conscript foot soldiers and toward horse-mounted elite warriors armed with the Japanese longbow.

Further reading in English:

- Farris, 1992: 113–116.

dōmaru 胴丸. A type of *dō* 胴 (trunk-protecting armor) which opens at the right side. See also: *dō* (1).

dōmawari 胴廻. Lit. "around the trunk." Term used for grappling in light armor in the Namba Ippo Ryū 難波一甫流. As the Namba Ippo Ryū was a branch tradition of the Takenouchi Ryū, this grappling system was very likely similar to *koshi no mawari*, a term used for grappling in light armor by the original school.

dono 殿. An honorific used for someone of high rank or deserving high respect. ¶ *Shimizu dono* 清水殿, the Honorable Mr. Shimizu. See: *tono.*

dontō 鈍刀. A dull-bladed sword. This term is

DAI NIPPON BUTOKUKAI
(Kyōto, 1906)
Members of the committee for establishing *jūdō kata*

Represented classical *jūjutsu ryū* are as follows:

Front row, left to right

System (ryū)		Representative	
Miura Ryū	三浦流	Inazu Masamitsu	稲津 政光
Kyūshin Ryū	扱心流	Eguchi Yazō (*kyōshi*)	江口 彌三(教士)
Yōshin Ryū	揚心流	Katayama Takayoshi	片山 高義
Shiten Ryū	四天流	Hoshino Kumon (*hanshi*)	星野 九門(範士)
Kōdōkan	講道館	Kanō Jigorō (*hanshi*)	嘉納 治五郎(範士)
Yōshin Ryū	揚心流	Totsuka Hideyoshi (*kyōshi*)	戸塚 英美(教士)
Sekiguchi Ryū	関口流	Sekiguchi Jūshin	関口 柔心
Takenouchi Santō Ryū	竹内三統流	Yano Hirotsugu (*kyōshi*)	矢野 廣次(教士)
Yōshin Ryū	揚心流	Hiratsuka Katsuta	平塚 葛太

Back row, left to right

System (ryū)		Representative	
Sōsuishitsu Ryū	双水執流	Aoyagi Kihei (*kyōshi*)	青柳 喜平(教士)
Sekiguchi Ryū	関口流	Tsumizu Mokichi	津水 茂吉
Takenouchi Ryū	竹内流	Ōshima Hikosaburō (*kyōshi*)	大島 彦三郎(教士)
Kōdōkan	講道館	Satō Hōken (*kyōshi*)	佐藤 法賢(教士)
Takenouchi Ryū	竹内流	Imai Kōtarō (*kyōshi*)	今井 行太郎(教士)
Fusen Ryū	不遷流	Tanabe Matauemon (*kyōshi*)	田辺 又右衛門(教士)
Takenouchi Ryū	竹内流	Takeno Shikatarō	竹野 鹿太郎
Kōdōkan	講道館	Nagaoka Hideichi (*kyōshi*)	永岡 秀一(教士)
Kōdōkan	講道館	Yokoyama Sakujirō (*kyōshi*)	横山 作次郎(教士)
Kōdōkan	講道館	Isogai Hajime (*kyōshi*)	磯貝 一(教士)
Kōdōkan	講道館	Yamashita Yoshitsugu (*kyōshi*)	山下 義韶(教士)

sometimes written/read *namakura gatana* 鈍ら刀. See also: *iaitō.*

dora 銅鑼. A hand-held gong sometimes used by battle commanders for signaling. See: *shikigu.*

dōsa 動作. 1. An action or movement; carriage; manner; deportment. 2. An exercise.

dōsha 堂射. Lit. "temple archery." An archery contest held annually at Sanjūsangendō temple in Kyōto. See: *tōshiya.*

doshi 弩師. A crossbowman; a crossbow expert. See: *dokyū.*

dōshi 道士. A Daoist; a Daoist practitioner.

dōshin 同心. A term referring to Edo-period policemen. It literally means "same heart" or "like spirit." *Dōshin* is an abbreviation of *machikata dōshin torimono* 町方同心捕者. The *dōshin* were in many ways the Edo-period equivalent of police constables, the cops on the beat. They were relatively low-level members of the samurai class, but often inherited their jobs, and, in the city of Edo, lived in a communal neighborhood along the Hatchōbori canal. In addition to police work the *dōshin* and their commanders—the *yoriki*—had additional responsibilities involving fire watch and local administration. They were also responsible for a number of ceremonial duties. See also: *Edo Machikata Jutte Torinawa Atsukaiyō; Machi Bugyō; Machikata; yoriki.*

Further reading in English:

• Schreiber, 2001: 27–33.

dōshu 1. 堂衆. Low-ranking monks assigned to various duties in medieval Buddhist temples. The *dōshu* were often a major component of the warrior monk (*sōhei*) units at those temples.

Dōshu 2. 道主. Lit. "lord of the 'way' "; "master of the spiritual path." AIKIDŌ—*Dōshu* is a title given by the Aikikai (World Aikidō Headquarters) to the leader of the system. Thus far there have only been three people who have held this title: Ueshiba Morihei, founder of *aikidō*; his son/successor, Ueshiba Kisshomaru; and his grandson/successor, Ueshiba Moriteru.

dōzukuri 胴造り. KYŪDŌ—Lit. "fixing the torso." *Dōzukuri* is the second of eight stages in firing an arrow in the modern martial way of archery (*kyūdō*). In *dōzukuri* the archer straightens his body and fixes his concentration through abdominal breathing. See also: *hassetsu.*

E

ebira 箙. KYUDŌ—A quiver which hangs over the right hip. Essentially a large, open box for holding arrows, this is sometimes equipped with a drawer for extra bow strings and other items.

Ebisu 夷 [Also written 戎 or 狄]. See: *Emishi.*

Echigo 越後. Old provincial name for modern-day Niigata prefecture. The area came under the control of Uesugi Kenshin and his relatives during the Warring States period (Sengoku Jidai). During the Edo period the region was controlled by the Matsudaira family.

Echigo Kaden 越後家伝【越後家傳】. See: *Echigo Ryū.*

Echigo Kenshin Ryū 越後謙信流. See: *Echigo Ryū.*

Echigo Ryū 越後流 [A.k.a. ***Echigo Kaden*** 越後家伝【越後家傳】; ***Echigo Kenshin Ryū*** 越後謙信流; ***Kenshin Ryū*** 謙信流]. A major school of combative strategy and tactics (*gungaku*) including espionage (*shinobijutsu*) thought to have been founded by the famous Sengoku-period warlord Uesugi Kenshin around 1560. Three branches descend from direct successors of Uesugi: Usamiden Echigo Ryū 宇佐美伝越後流 founded by Usami Sadayuki; Kajiden Echigo Ryū 加治伝越後流 founded by Kaji Tōtōmi no Kami Kagehide; and Nipponden Echigo Ryū 日本伝越後流 founded by Uesugi Minbu Daisuke Yoshiharu.

Eleven transmission documents of this school and its descendent branches have been reprinted in Ishioka and Arima (1969): *Echigo Ryū heihō—Kenshin Ryū heihō* 『越後流兵法—謙信流兵法』. See also: *Uesugi Ryū.*

Echizen Unchū Ryū 越前運籌流. See: *Itō Ryū (1); Unchū Ryū (1).*

Edo 江戸. Old name for Tokyo. Originally an obscure fishing village, the city appears to have had no impact on Japanese history until a fort was built there in 1456. The Hōjō family lost possession of the village to Tokugawa Ieyasu in 1590. Ieyasu selected it as his residence, and built an impressive castle which became the seat of the Tokugawa shogunate. Edo was the center of the Tokugawa government from 1603 until 1868. Following the Meiji Restoration of 1868, the town was renamed Tōkyō, meaning "Eastern Capital."

Edo Jidai 江戸時代. The period from 1603 through 1867 when the city of Edo was the seat of the Tokugawa shogunate. Also referred to as the "Tokugawa Jidai."

Edo Machikata Jutte Torinawa Atsukaiyō 江戸町方十手捕縄扱い様【江戸町方十手捕縄扱い様】[Also read ***Edo Machikata Jutte Hojō Atsukaiyō***] (Compilation of arresting-cord and truncheon techniques for Edo city police). A comprehensive system of police arts (*hobakujutsu*) that came to be taught as a separate but collateral system of the Masaki Ryū by eighth headmaster Nawa Yoshimasa. According to John Quinn, a *menkyo/shihan* practitioner of this system:

> This system is a compilation of arresting methods researched and modified by one Kamei Magoroku Shigemura of the Sanshu Yoshida *han* at the order of the eighth Tokugawa *shōgun*, Yoshimune.[1] According to tradition, Kamei researched the *hobakujutsu* of thirty-some *ryū*. The result was a somewhat standardized system for Edo-period arresting officers.
>
> Kamei was a renowned master of the *mitsudōgu* [the three arresting implements used by the Edo police], and this may have influenced Yoshimune's decision. From the thirty systems he investigated, Kamei produced a compendium which became known as *Edomachikata Jutte Hojō Atsukaiyō* (A treatise on the methods of *jutte* and *hojō*). Because the system was based on a compilation of existing martial *ryū* it was referred to as *atsukaiyō* (lit. a "compilation") rather than a separate *ryū*.

Nawa Yumio, the chief successor of Edo Machikata Jutte Torinawa Atsukaiyō, also founded of the Masakikai, its training organization in Tōkyō. However, he taught this system as a collateral art (*fuzoku bugei*) to Masaki Ryū 正木流.

[1] Tokugawa Yoshimune 徳川 吉宗 (1684–1751), r. 1716–1745.

D E

Curriculum of the Edo Machikata Jutte Torinawa Atsukaiyō

Arts		Number of Techniques
Juttejutsu 十手術 [police truncheon (*jutte* 十手) and police baton (*hananeji* 鼻捻)]		
Kamae no Kata	構型	6
Jutte Kumikata	十手組型	12
Sōkaku no Kata	双角型	4
Hojōjutsu 捕縄術 [police arresting-cord art]		
Hayanawa	早縄	11
Okuden	奥伝	5

Edo Machikata Jutte Torinawa Atsukaiyō
江戸町方十手捕縄扱い様
(abbreviated lineage)

1. Yagyū Hida no Kami Munefuyu
柳生 飛騨守 宗冬[2]

2. Yagyū Tajima no Kami Hidekatsu
柳生 但馬守 秀勝

3. Morimoto Unai Sadataka
森本 宇内 貞高

4. Kamei Magoroku Shigemura
亀井 孫六 重村
(c. 1745)

5. Kamei Rokuzaemon Shigemasa
亀井 六左門 重正

6. Okada Umezo Shigenaga
岡田 梅蔵 重長

7. Nawa Toyotoshi Yoshizane
名和 豊年 美眞

8. Nawa Yumio Shōan
名和 弓雄 柾庵
(1912–2006)

Shihanke
師範家
(2006–present)

When Nawa retired from active teaching, he decided there would be no single successor to carry on these two systems. Instead, he instituted a *shihanke* system (much like that in other classical traditions like the Jiki Shinkage Ryū) in which any member awarded the rank of *shihan* may continue the tradition. See also: *Masaki Ryū; Nawa Yumio.*

Edo murasaki 江戸紫. Lit. "Edo purple." IKKAKU RYŪ—A color of *jutte* cord indicating that the practitioner is a master of Ikkaku Ryū *juttejutsu*.

Edo Yagyū Shinkage Ryū 江戸柳生新陰流 [A.k.a. Yagyū Ryū 柳生流]. The line of the Yagyū Shinkage Ryū and associated combative arts that began with Yagyū Munenori. After the battle of Sekigahara in 1600, Tokugawa Ieyasu controlled the country from the town of Edo, and Yagyū Munenori accompanied him. The Edo Yagyū Shinkage Ryū dates from that time.

This school produced a number of expert swordsmen during its early years. However, toward the end of the Tokugawa era it went into a decline and had essentially disappeared as a significant martial arts school by 1868. Some of its combative forms are preserved today within the several Owari Yagyū Shinkage Ryū lines.

The curriculum parallels that of the Owari Yagyū, with some variances.

Edo Yagyū Shinkage Ryū Curriculum

Set of Sword Forms		Number of *Kata*
Empi 燕飛		8
1. Empi	燕飛	
2. Enkai	猿廻	
3. Tsukikage	月影	
4. Yamakage	山陰	
5. Uranami	浦波	
6. Ukifune	浮舟	
7. Sekkō	折甲	
8. Juppō	十方	
Sangaku En no Tachi 三学圓太刀		5
1. Ittō Ryōdan	一刀 両段	
2. Zantei Settetsu	斬釘 截鉄	
3. Hankai Hankō	半開 半向	
4. Usen Saten	右旋 左転	
5. Chōtan Ichimi	長短 一味	
Kuka no Tachi 九箇之太刀		9
1. Hisshō	必勝	
2. Gyakufū	逆風	

[2] Although Nawa (1996: 86) lists the founder of this system as Yagyū Tajima no Kami Munefuyu 柳生但馬守宗厳, he appears to be in error. Yagyū Munefuyu, fourth headmaster of the Edo Yagyū Shinkage Ryū, is listed by that family as Yagyū Hida no Kami Munefuyu 柳生 飛騨守 宗冬.

3. Jūdachi	十太刀	
4. Kaboku	和卜	
5. Shōkei	睫徑	
6. Kozume	小詰	
7.Ōzume	大詰	
8. Yaegaki	八重垣	
9. Murakumo	村雲	
Tengushō 天狗抄		8
1. Kōrinbō 高林坊	(Kasha 花車)	
2. Fūgenbō 風眼房	(Akemi 明身)	
3. Tarōbō 太郎房	(Zentai 善待)	
4. Eiibō 栄意坊	(Tebiki 手引)	
5. Chiraten 智羅天	(Nitō 二刀)	
6. Karanbō 火乱房	(Uchimono 打物 /Jō序)	
7. Shutokubō 修徳房	(Ranken 乱剣 /Ha 破)	
8. Konpirabō 金比羅房	(Ninin Gakkari 二人懸/Kyū 急)	
Hakka no Hisshō 八箇必勝		8
Okugi no Tachi 奥儀太刀		6
1. Tensetsu Ransetsu	添截乱截	
2. Muniken	無二剣	
3. Katsunintō	活人刀	
4. Kōjō	高上	
5. Gokui	極意	
6. Shinmyōken	神妙劍	
Nijūnana-ka-jō Kiriai 廿七箇条截相		27
• Jo 序—*jōdan* 上段 (3) *chūdan* 中段 (3) *gedan* 下段 (3)		
• Ha 破—*sekkō* 折甲 (2) *tōbō* 刀棒 (3) *uchiai* 打合 (4)		
• Kyū 急—*jōdan* 上段 (3) *chūdan* 中段 (3) *gedan* 下段 (3)		

Other

Various sets of empty-handed and armored grappling, small weapons, etc. are found in Edo Yagyū derivative lines. The lists vary widely, and include such categories as Kogusoku 小具足 (armored grappling, close combat with short sword or other weapons) and Mutōdori 無刀取 (empty-handed techniques against an armed opponent).

See also: *Edo Yagyū Shinkage Ryū Yamane Ha; Owari Shinkage Ryū; Shinkage Ryū.*

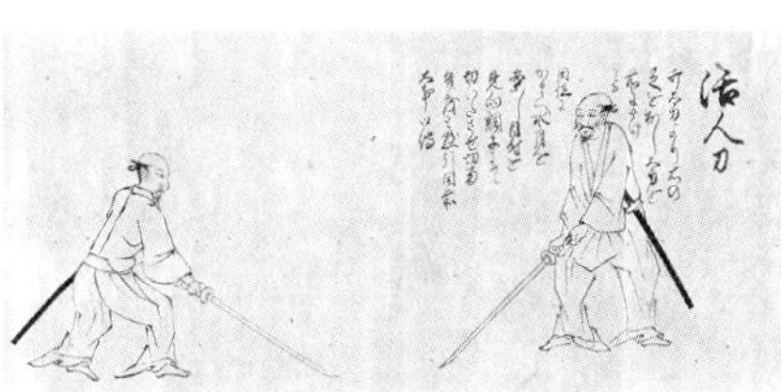

DENSHO OF THE EDO YAGYŪ SHINKAGE RYŪ
Excerpt text and illustration from an Edo Yagyū Shinkage Ryū picture scroll entitled *Shinkage ryū heihō mokuroku*
(*Densho* from the archives of Hōzanji temple in Nara)

Edo Yagyū Shinkage Ryū Yamane Ha 江戸柳生新陰流山根派 [A.k.a. ***Dai Nippon Yamato Yagyū Kai*** 大日本大和柳生会; ***Yamato Yagyū Kai*** 大和柳生会]. There is a general consensus that by the fourteenth generation, the family line of the Edo Yagyū Shinkage Ryū was no longer a viable combative tradition. The Edo family line is in fact still extant, although they no longer practice swordsmanship. However, in Ōsaka, Japan, there is at least one line claiming descent from the venerated sword tradition outside the family line. It is referred to in this *Encyclopedia* as the "Edo Yagyū Shinkage Ryū Yamane Ha," as it traces its lineage to two men who were purportedly disciples of Yagyū Toshihisa: Yamane Muneichirō and Saitō Jisaburō. At least two splinter groups have developed in this line. One, under Sono Seigō, calls itself the Yamato Yagyū Kai; another, under Ueki Yasuyuki, is called the Dai Nippon Yamato Yagyū Kai.

The swordsmanship of the Yamane Ha line is reminiscent of that performed by the various extant lines of Owari Shinkage Ryū. However, it differs significantly in its movement and execution of Edo Yagyū Shinkage Ryū techniques as preserved in the Owari lines. Consequently, if it is historically authentic, the Yamane Ha appears to have drifted significantly from its origins. This is even more evident in the collateral arts that were probably added to the tradition at a later time, such as practice cutting (*tameshigiri*) and quick-draw sword techniques (*iaijutsu*).[3]

[3] Although current members of the Owari Yagyū Shinkage Ryū also practice quick-draw sword arts (*battō*), these forms are seen as supplemental to the central Shinkage Ryū tradition, and are designated "Yagyū Seigō Ryū." While they reflect the influence of Yagyū Shinkage Ryū in their format, they are not originally part of that tradition and are not classified as such. No known documents indicate that Kamiizumi ever included quick-draw sword arts in his Shinkage Ryū.

Edo Yagyū Shinkage Ryū・Yagyū Ryū

江戸柳生新陰流・柳生流

(abbreviated lineage)

Kamiizumi Ise no Kami Nobutsuna
上泉 伊勢守 信綱
Shinkage Ryū (1)
新陰流

Yagyū Sekishūsai Tajima no Kami Muneyoshi
初代 柳生 石舟斎 但馬守 宗厳
(1827–1906)
Yagyū Shinkage Ryū
江戸柳生新陰流

1. Yagyū Tajima no Kami Munenori
初代 柳生 但馬守 宗矩
(1571–1646)
Edo Yagyū Shinkage Ryū
江戸柳生新陰流

Note: Watatani and Yamada (1978: 856–859) list fifty known disciples of Yagyū Munenori who mastered the Edo Yagyū Shinkage Ryū.

Nabeshima Shinano no Kami Katsushige
鍋島 信濃守 勝茂
Nabejima Goryūgi
鍋島御流儀

Shōda Kazaemon Noritaka
荘田 嘉左衛門 教高
Shōda Shin Ryū
荘田心流

- Tokizawa Yahei
時沢 弥平
Tenshin Ryū
天心流

- Kotaki Yoemon
小滝 与右衛門
Kagami Ryū
鏡見流

- Ishikawa Kurando Masaharu
石川 蔵人 政春
Shin no Shin Ishikawa Ryū
真之真石川流

2. Yagyū Jūbei Mitsuyoshi
二代 柳生 十兵衛 三厳
Edo Yagyū Shinkage Ryū
江戸柳生新陰流

Kimura Sukekurō Noritaka
木村 助九郎 矩孝
Shinkage Ryū
新陰流
Unchū Ryū (2)
運籌流

- Takenaga Hayato Naoiri
竹永 隼人 直入
Yagyū Shingan Ryū
柳生心眼流

Araki Mataemon Yasukazu
荒木 又右衛門 保和
Araki Ryū
荒木流

- Matsudaira Etchū no Kami Sadatsuna
松平 越中守 定綱
Kōotsu Ryū
甲乙流

3. Yagyū Hida no Kami Munefuyu
三代 柳生 飛騨守 宗冬
Edo Yagyū Shinkage Ryū
江戸柳生新陰流

4. Yagyū Tsushima no Kami Muneari
四代 柳生 対馬守 宗在

5. Yagyū Bizen no Kami Toshikata
五代 柳生 備前守 俊方

6. Yagyū Hida no Kami Toshihira
六代 柳生 飛騨守 俊平

7. Yagyū Bizen no Kami Toshimine
七代 柳生 備前守 俊峯

8. Yagyū Tajima no Kami Toshinori
八代 柳生 但馬守 俊則

9. Yagyū Naizen Toshimori
九代 柳生 内膳 俊豊

10. Yagyū Tajima no Kami Toshiakira
十代 柳生 但馬守 俊章

11. Yagyū Hida no Kami Toshiyoshi
十一代 柳生 飛騨守 俊能

12. Yagyū Tsushima no Kami Toshimune
十二代 柳生 対馬守 俊順

13. Yagyū Tajima no Kami Toshirō
十三代 柳生 但馬守 俊郎

14. Yagyū Toshihisa
十四代 柳生 俊久

The fourteenth generation of the Edo Yagyū family line (late 1800s) was the last to engage in swordsmanship. The family itself still exists.

Edo Yagyū Shinkage Ryū Yamane Ha
江戸柳生新陰流山根派
(abbreviated lineage)

14. Yagyū Toshihisa
十四代　柳生 俊久
Edo Yagyū Shinkage Ryū
江戸柳生新陰流

15. Yamane Muneichirō & Saitō Jisaburō
山根 宗一郎・斉藤 治三郎
Edo Yagyū Shinkage Ryū Yamane Ha
江戸柳生新陰流山根派

16. Ōtani Seigen Genshū
大谷 精源 玄州
Dai Nippon Yamato Yagyū Kai
大日本大和柳生会

17. Sono Seigō
曽野 正鴻
Yamato Yagyū Kai
大和柳生会

17. Ueki Yasuyuki
植木 康行
Dai Nippon Yamato Yagyū Kai
大日本大和柳生会

That being said, the Yamane Ha lists an interesting array of original Shinkage Ryū forms (*kata*) categorized as modern quick-sword draw forms (*iaidō kata*). They also practice an unusual arrangement of Shinkage Ryū forms (considered *kenjutsu kata*).

Efu 衛府 [Later ***Ejifu*** 衛士府]. TAIHŌ MILITARY SYSTEM—The Efu were imperial guard units authorized by the Taihō Code (Taihō Ritsuryō) in 702. Five units were originally authorized, but the system went through several modifications over the years. The imperial guards also had many permutations, including the Roku Efu 六衛府 (six imperial guard units) and the Shie Nifu 四衛二府.

1. Emonfu 衛門府 Gate Guards
2. Sa Ejifu 左衛士府 Guards of the Left
3. U Ejifu 右衛士府 Guards of the Right
4. Sa Hyōefu 左兵衛府 Noble Guards of the Left
5. U Hyōefu 右兵衛府 Noble Guards of the Right

Additional units were created in the years indicated:

6. Chū Efu 中衛府 Center Guards (728)
7. Jutō Efu 授刀衛府 Sword Guards (759)
8. Kono Efu 近衛府 Close-in Guards (775)[4]
9. Gai Efu 外衛府 Outer Guards (765)[5]

The guard units were reorganized in 807:

1. Sa Konoe 左近衛 Imperial Attendants of the Left
2. U Konoe 右近衛 Imperial Attendants of the Right
3. Sa Eji 左衛士 Guards of the Left
4. U Eji 右衛士 Guards of the Right
5. Sa Hyōe 左兵衛 Noble Guards of the Left
6. U Hyōe 右兵衛 Noble Guards of the Right

In 811, the units were reorganized yet again:

1. Sa Konoe 左近衛 Guards of the Left
2. U Konoe 右近衛 Guards of the Right
3. Sa Emon 左衛門 Gate Guards of the Left
4. U Emon 右衛門 Gate Guards of the Right
5. Sa Hyōe 左兵衛 Noble Guards of the Left
6. U Hyōe 右兵衛 Noble Guards of the Right

The actual guardsmen, called *eji*, were drawn from provincial militia on one-year tours of duty. The corps of about 800 men was divided into two units: Sa Ejifu (Left Capitol Guard Unit) and U Ejifu (Right Capitol Guard Unit). According to Farris (1992: 55–56) the men trained in mounted archery, swordsmanship, spear handling, crossbow marksmanship, and the use of catapults. In addition to performing security services for the imperial palace, they also escorted the emperor's carriage and worked in cooperation with the imperial palace guards (Hyōefu). Whereas the Hyōefu was a native Japanese institution comprising members of the rural warrior elite, however, the Efu/Ejifu included conscripted commoners in accordance with the Chinese-based Taiho Code.

In 808, the Ejifu took over the duties of the Emonfu. However, the practice of placing commoners in these sensitive positions became untenable. By the ninth century most *eji* were working as common laborers around the capital in the positions of messengers, porters, and even gardeners.

In the tenth and eleventh centuries the Ejifu shared guard, police, and military duties in the capital of Kyōto with the public investigators (*kebiishi*) and the private-sector semi-aristocratic warriors (*shoka no heishi*). Gradually, however, these functions were taken over by the office of the imperial capital police (Kebiishi Chō). See also: *Emonfu*.

[4] Created from the Jutō Efu.
[5] Var. for Emon and Hyōe.

Egami Shigeru 江上 茂 (1912–1981). One of the earliest students of Funakoshi Gichin. Many consider Egami to be the disciple who followed Funakoshi's style and principles most closely. Egami began training with Funakoshi around 1930 at the age of eighteen, when he was a student at Waseda University. He also helped found the university's Karatedō Club. At that time Egami was already experienced in *jūdō*, Ueshiba's evolving version of *aikijutsu/aikidō*, and *kendō*. He subsequently travelled around Japan, demonstrating and promoting *karatedō*, with Funakoshi, Funakoshi's son Yoshitaka, and Takeshi Shimoda. Soon after that he was appointed a member of the evaluator committee, the youngest practitioner to be accorded that honor in those days, and was soon teaching *karatedō* at several universities. Egami and Funakoshi Yoshitaka co-founded the Shōtōkai 松濤会 in 1936. With the death of Funakoshi Gichin in 1957, Egami moved in a more traditional direction with the Shōtōkai while Nakayama Masatoshi split away to form the more sport-oriented Nihon Karate Kyōkai 日本空手協会 (Japan Karate Association, or JKA). Following the principles of Funakoshi Gichin, Egami spent the rest of his life trying to change the image of *karate* from that of a killing art to that of true "*dō*"; a combatively based spiritual "way" aimed at self-perfection and self-defense. At least two of his books on *karate* have been published in English: *The Way of Karate: Beyond Technique* (Kodansha International, 1976) and *The Heart of Karate-Do* (Kodansha International, rev. ed., 2000).

egashira 柄頭. See: *heitō.*

Ehata Mukoemon Manshin 江畑 杢右衛門 満真. Ehata founded the Iga Ryū (5) 為我流, a *jūjutsu* system he derived from extensive training in several other grappling schools.

Ei! Ei! Oh! えい! えい! お! During the Warring States and early Tokugawa periods, *Ei! Ei! Oh!* was a cheer used just before troops set off for battle.

Eihei Dōgen 永平 道元. See: *Dōgen Zenji.*

eiji happō 永字八法. 1. Lit. "the eight laws of [the ideogram] 'eternal.'" In Sino-Japanese calligraphy (*shodō*), this phrase indicates that the eight brush strokes used to write the character 永 provide the patterns of movement from which all other characters can be written. 2. NAKAMURA RYŪ—Nakamura Taisaburō drew upon the term *eiji happō* and its historically associated Buddhist meaning of "eight" (=myriad) and "eternal." Nakamura applied this to his modern practical system of quick-draw swordsmanship (*battōjutsu*) as "the myriad sword trajectories" (*happōgiri no tōsen* 八方斬りの刀線). Note here that Nakamura used the homophone *happō* 八方 (eight directions) for *happō* 八法 (eight laws).

Eisai 栄西【榮西】[Var. ***Myōan Eisai*** 明庵 栄西【明菴榮西】; ***Eisai Zenji*** 栄西 禅師【榮西禪師】(Zen Master Eisai)] (1141–1215). Founder of the Rinzai School of Zen Buddhism in Japan, Eisai is also credited with being the first to import the *matcha* 抹茶 style of green tea preparation into Japan. (*Matcha* is the finely powdered green tea used in the tea ceremony.)

Like the founders of most Kamakura-period Buddhist schools in Japan, Eisai first studied Tendai Buddhism. However, dissatisfied with the Tendai practices he found in Japan, in 1168 he traveled to Mount Tiantai (the original home of Tendai Buddhism) in China, where he first encountered Chan 禪 (pronounced *zen* in Japanese) Buddhism. He initially trained there for only six months, but returned in 1187 to stay for about four years. Returning to Japan in 1191, he began to propagate his new school but ran into opposition from many of the established schools such as Tendai, Shingon, and Pure Land Buddhism. Eisai subsequently moved to Kamakura in 1199 and established Jufukuji, the first Zen temple in that city. Kamakura was the center of the new shogunate; in order to appeal to its warriors, Eisai included a good deal of Tendai *mikkyō* (Esoteric/tantric Buddhism) in his own version of Zen: Rinzai, or "Kamakura Zen" as it came to be called. See also: *Jufukuji; Shingon Shū; Tendai Shū; and Zen Shū.*

Further reading in English:
- Collcutt, 1981.
- Matsunaga and Matsunaga, 1976.

Eishin 英信. Buddhist name for Hasegawa Chikaranosuke Eishin (Hidenobu), founder of the Musō Jikiden Eishin Ryū 無双直伝英信流 school of swordsmanship.

Eishin Ryū 英信流. See: *Musō Jikiden Eishin Ryū.*

Eishōji 永昌寺. Temple in the Shitaya area of Tōkyō where Kanō Jigorō first established Kōdōkan Jūdō in 1882.

Ei! Ya! Tō! 永! 弥! 遠!【永彌遠】. *Ei, ya*, and *tō* are three verbal *kiai* commonly used by the Katori Shintō Ryū, Toda Ha Bukō Ryū 戸田派武甲流, and other martial traditions. These ideograms, as well as the unusual way of reading them, are set forth in the *Marishiten Oharai*『摩利支天御拔』, an esoteric text on the spiritual and cosmological origins of the Tenshinshō-den Katori Shintō Ryū 天真正伝香取神道流 (Ōtake, 1989).

Eiyū 栄祐【榮祐】. Buddhist priest at Jufukuji in Kamakura who is supposed to have transmitted the secrets of combative arts to Nen Ami Jion in the mid-fourteenth century.

eji 衛士. Troops serving in the Efu (Ejifu) or Emonfu imperial guard units. The *eji* were conscript soldiers serving as guards before the rise of the warrior class. See: *Efu.*

Ejifu 衛士府. See: *Efu.*

ēku 櫂 (Oki.). OKINAWAN KOBUDŌ—An oar or paddle used as a weapon in some schools of Okinawan *kobudō*. Often referred to in Japanese as a *kai*. See: *ēkujutsu; kai (4); Okinawa kobudō.*

ēku fa 櫂法 (Oki.). OKINAWAN KOBUDŌ—Combative scenarios for the *ēku*. See: *Kai no hō.*

ēkujutsu 櫂術 [Var. *ēku tī* 櫂手] (Oki.). OKINAWAN KOBUDŌ—The combative art of using an oar or paddle (Oki. *ēku*, Jp. *kai*).

ēku tī 櫂手 (Oki.). See: *ēkujutsu.*

emaki 絵巻【繪巻】[A.k.a. ***emakimono*** 絵巻物【繪巻物】]. A picture scroll. A number of martial *densho*, being illustrated, are classified as *emaki*.

embu 演武. A martial exhibition. See: *hōnnō embu.*

embujō 演武場. A place where a martial exhibition is held. For example, a temporary stage is often erected in a central location in Kashima shrine in order to create an *embujō*. *Embujō* located within Shinto shrines (*jinja, jingū*) are often bounded by *shimenawa*, a straw rope from which are hung narrow strips of zigzag-shaped white paper (*gohei*).

EMBUJŌ
Young members of Kashima Shintō Ryū demonstrate *kenjutsu* within the *shimenawa*-boundary of a temporary *embujō* at Kashima Jingū, 1979
(Photograph by author)

Emishi 蝦夷 [Var. 毛人] [Also read ***Ezo***; a.k.a. ***Ebisu*** 夷; (var. 戎)]. Old Japanese term for the aboriginal inhabitants of northeastern Honshu, whom the Japanese fought for control of the land for many centuries. The ethnonym for this group is "Ainu" although the reference is somewhat controversial. See: *Ainu.*

Emmaō 閻魔王 <Ch. Yanmowang <Skt. Yamarāja. See: *Emmaten.*

Emmaten 焔摩天【燄摩天】[Var. 炎摩天] <Ch. Yanmotian <Skt. Yama. One of a group of twelve guardian deities adopted from Brahmanism by Buddhism. In Indian mythology, Yama was known as the king of the underworld. In East Asia and Japan, he is also known as Emmaō 閻魔王 <Ch. Yanmowang <Skt. Yamarāja, lit. "King Yama." It was Yama's duty to judge the dead upon their arrival in his domain. See: *Jūniten.*

Emmei Ryū 1. 円明流【圓明流】[Also read ***Enmei Ryū***]. Lit. "Shining Circle School" or "Brilliant Circle School"; also "Wisdom Circle School." School of swordsmanship which traces its origins to Miyamoto Musashi (c. 1584–1645). Watanabe and Yamada (1978: 115) state that it originated with Musashi's father, Minamoto Munisai. However, it is unclear how much of Munisai's school was passed on to his son.

Musashi used the term Emmei Ryū with his students during his early to middle-aged years. It first appeared in his earliest work on strategy, the *Hyōdōkyō* (A mirror on the way of strategy), in 1605. One transmission document (*densho*) from this tradition, entitled

Emmei Ryū (1)
円明流
(abbreviated lineage)

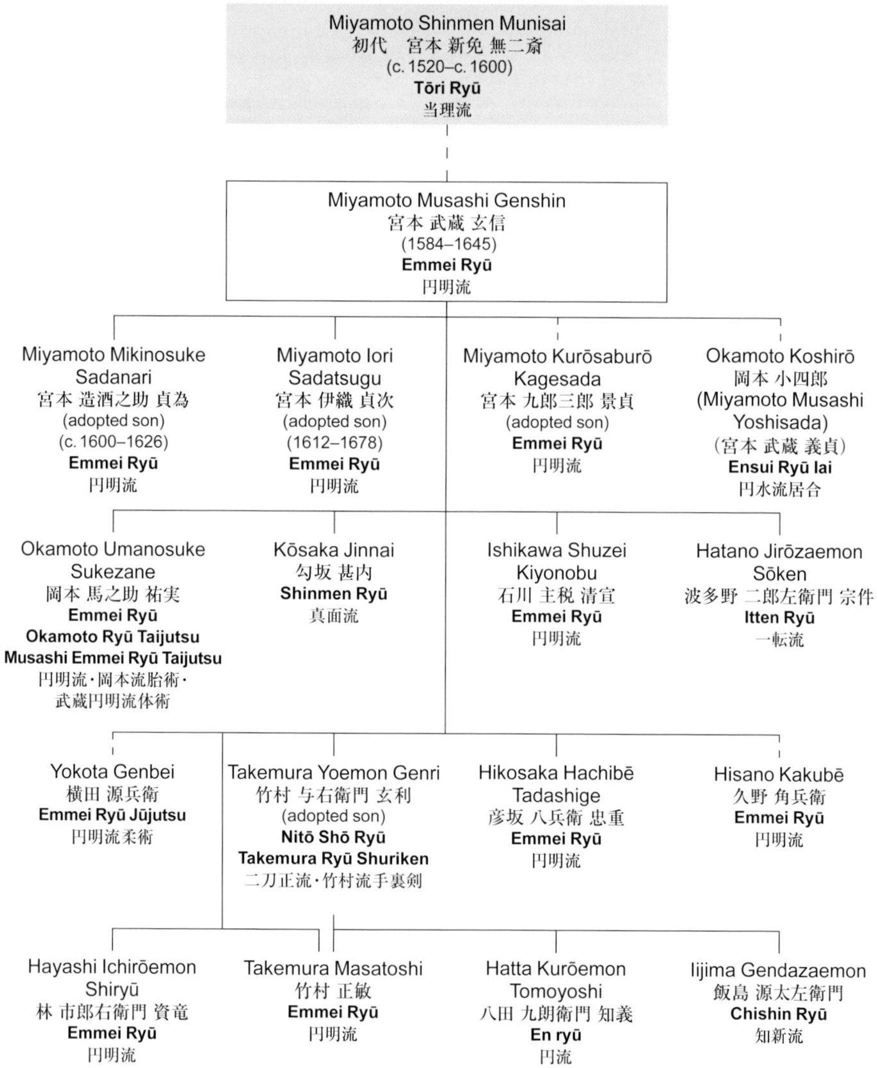

Emmei ryū kempōsho『円明流劍法書』, was published in Imamura (1966, Vol. 1: 514–524). See also: *emmyō; Miyamoto Musashi.*

Emmei Ryū 2. 円明流【圓明流】[Also read ***Enmei Ryū***]. A branch tradition of the Seigō Ryū, founded by Igaya Chūzō Genna.

emmyō 円明【圓明】. BUDDHISM—Term derived from *emmyō hi* 円明日 (equated with *nyorai hi* 如来日) which means the "day of the perfectly awakened one," i.e., timelessness unbounded by past, present, or future. Consequently the term *emmyō* came to be used to indicate "perfect wisdom." In the secular vernacular in Japan, it was often pronounced *emmei* or *enmei.*

Emonfu 衛門府. Gate-guard unit in the imperial palace. The Emonfu were originally established in 643 by Empress Kōgyoku. At that time, the guard members were drawn from the Ōtomo and Kumebe families. However, after the Kumebe were wiped out, the Saiki took their place. Later, members of the Kadobe, Mononobe, Eji, and Hayato families served in the Emonfu. The approximately 200 members of the gate-guard unit were normally drawn from aristocratic warrior families which, like those in the Hyōefu, (imperial guards drawn from the rural elite) had had military status (*yugei* 靫負) prior to 645 C.E. The Emonfu were one of the five imperial guard units authorized by the Taihō Code (Taihō Ritsuryo) in 702. By the mid-ninth century the members of the Emonfu had generally lost their status as military men; their functions were replaced by a new organization. See: *Efu.*

emono 得物. A sharp weapon.

Empi 1. 猿飛. Lit. "Flying Monkey." HIKITA KAGE RYŪ/SHINKAGE RYŪ—Variant term used for both a specific *kata* and the continuous "set" of *kata* in Kamiizumi's Shinkage Ryū.

Empi 2. 燕飛. Lit. "Flying Swallow." SHINKAGE RYŪ—Term used for both a specific *kata* and the continuous "set" of *kata* in Kamiizumi's Shinkage Ryū. These *kata* were modified by Kamiizumi from the curriculum he studied in the Kage Ryū. It appears that Kamiizumi commonly used the characters for "flying monkey" (猿飛) in the early development of Shinkage Ryū; the same term was used in the Kage Ryū. While traveling on a *musha shūgyō* (warrior pilgrimage), Kamiizumi changed the characters to "flying swallow" (燕飛). YAGYŪ SHINKAGE RYŪ—Abbreviation for Empi no Tachi. JIGEN RYŪ—The first primary *kata* in the Jigen Ryū curriculum. This set was inherited by founder Tōgō Tōbei Shigetaka from the Taisha (Kage) Ryū. See also: *Bubishi; Kage Ryū no mokuroku; Shinkage Ryū; Taisha Ryū.*

Empi 3. 圓飛. Lit. "flying circle." a. KATORI SHINTŌ RYŪ—Name of a prearranged combative form (*kata*) included in the curriculum of the Tenshinshō-den Katori Shintō Ryū. b. SHIN NO SHINKAGE RYŪ—Name of a set of *kata*, probably equivalent to Empi no Tachi, included in the curriculum of the Shin no Shinkage Ryū 真心陰流.

empi 4. 猿臂. A long arm. May also indicate the elbow (more commonly referred to as *hiji*). ¶ *empi uchi* 猿臂打ち, an elbow strike (as may be used in *karate*).

Empi no Kodachi 猿飛之小太刀. Lit. "Flying Monkey Short Sword." HIKITA KAGE RYŪ—The six *kata* of Empi performed with *kodachi* in lieu of *tachi*. Generations ago, this set came into the Owari Yagyū line from the Hikita Kage Ryū. Although no longer practiced in the Owari Yagyū Shinkage Ryū family line, the forms are preserved in other branch lines of the Owari Yagyū Shinkage Ryū and Hikita Kage Ryū traditions.

Empi no maki「燕飛之巻」(Flying swallow scroll). YAGYŪ SHINKAGE RYŪ—Name of the first illustrated scroll (*emaki*) presented to Yagyū Muneyoshi by Kamiizumi Ise no Kami Nobutsuna (founder of the Shinkage Ryū) in 1566. This scroll contains drawings of the set of *kata* now called Empi no Tachi 燕飛之太刀.

Empi no Naginata 猿飛之薙刀 [A.k.a.: Shinto Ryū Naginata no Empi 神道流薙刀之猿飛]. HIKITA KAGE RYŪ—Empi performed with

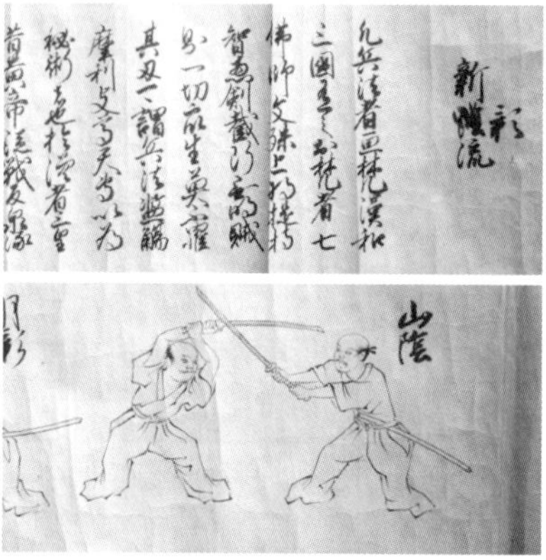

EMPI (NO MAKI)
Excerpt text and illustration from the Empi *emaki*
(From the Yagyū family archives)

naginata in lieu of *tachi*. Generations ago this set came into the Owari Yagyū line from the Hikita Kage Ryū. Although no longer practiced in the main Owari Yagyū Shinkage Ryū line it is preserved in other branch lines of the Owari Yagyū and Hikita Kage Ryū lines.

Empi no Ōdachi 猿飛之大太刀. Lit. "Flying Monkey Great Sword". HIKITA KAGE RYŪ—The six kata of Empi performed with *ōdachi* in lieu of *tachi*. Generations ago, this set came into the Owari Yagyū line from the Hikita Kage Ryū. Although no longer practiced in the Owari Yagyū Shinkage Ryū family line, the forms are preserved in other branch lines of the Owari Yagyū and Hikita Kage Ryū lines.

Empi no Tachi 燕飛之太刀/猿飛之太刀. YAGYŪ SHINKAGE RYŪ/HIKITA KAGE RYŪ—The six *kata* (practiced as one fluid set) from the Empi「燕飛」*densho* include Empi 燕飛, Enkai 猿廻, Yamakage 山陰, Tsukikage 月影, Uranami 浦波, and Ukifune 浮舟. This key set in the Yagyū Shinkage Ryū was modified from an earlier version created by Aisu Ikōsai, founder of the Kage Ryū. Various lines of Shinkage Ryū have differing versions of this, probably due to Kamiizumi's ongoing modification of the set as he travelled around Japan engaged in *musha shugyō* (not to mention modifications made over the years in other lines).

Enanji 『淮南子』<Ch. *Huainanzi*. A classic Chinese philosophical text of the Han dynasty. It mixes Taoist, Confucian and Legalist concepts and contains detailed theories on yin-yang (*on'yō*) and the five elemental movers (*gogyō*). Composed under the patronage of Liu An, king of Huainan. See also: *gogyō; on'yō*

FUDŌ MYŌŌ
Image carved by Enkū.

Enkū 円空 【圓空】 (1632–1695). Japanese Buddhist monk who, during the mid to late seventeenth century, wandered around Japan helping the poor. He is best known for the approximately 120,000 wooden Buddhist statues he carved during his travels. Most of these were crudely made from scraps of wood he encountered along the way. Enkū usually gave away these statues to assuage the grief of people who had lost loved ones or to the dying to help ease their journey into the afterlife. No two of these images are alike, although many of them depict the warrior protector, Fudō Myōō. The figures are now classed as a genre in themselves: the "Enkū Buddhas."

Further reading in English:
- Alphen, 1999.

Enmei Ryū 円明流. See: *Emmei Ryū.*

Enmyō Ryū 円明流. See: *Emmei Ryū.*

Enryakuji 延暦寺. Home temple of the Tendai School of Buddhism in Japan. See: *Hieizan.*

enryo 遠慮. 1. Reserve; restraint; keeping one's distance; standing on ceremony. 2. CLASSICAL WARRIOR IDEAL—Prudence; forethought. *Enryo* was considered a warrior virtue.

En Ryū 円流 【圓流】. School of combative

swordsmanship (*kenjutsu*) founded by Hatta Kurōemon Tomoyoshi during the Kan'ei era (1624–1644). It was a branch tradition of the Emmei Ryū. See: *Emmei Ryū.*

Enshin Ryū 円心流【圓心流】[A.k.a. Enshin Ryū Iaidō 円心流居合道]. The Enshin Ryū began as a martial school concentrating on quick-draw swordsmanship (*iai*) and combative swordsmanship (*shiken*). It was founded in the early part of the nineteenth century by a samurai named Kobashi Shōbei 小橋庄兵衛 who created an eclectic school by combining an earlier Enshin Ryū 円心流 with Shindō Munen Ryū 神道無念流. Later, in 1877, second-generation successor Fujimoto Ringorō added teachings from four additional schools to this tradition: from Takamatsu Oryūgi 高松御流儀, swordsmanship (*kenjutsu*);[6] from Kyūshinryu 扱心流 and Sekiguchi Ryū 関口流, grappling (*jūjutsu*) and quick-draw swordsmanship (*iai*); and from the Takenouchi Ryū 竹内流, armed grappling (*kumiuchi*) and quick-draw swordsmanship (*iai*).

The third headmaster, Kobashi Nikkan, later became a direct disciple of Hakkō Ryū 八光流 founder Okuyama Yoshiji. In a similar fashion to his predecessors, Nikkan incorporated the grappling system of the Hakko Ryu into the eclectic system of Enshin Ryu. The fourth (and current) headmaster of Enshin Ryū is Tanaka Fumon 田中普門.

Enshin Ryū Iaidō 円心流居合道. See: *Enshin Ryū.*

enshō-ire 焔硝入【煖硝入】. A gunpowder flask for a matchlock musket. Also called a *hayago*.

enshū 演習. Mock warfare; maneuvers. See also: *kidō enshū.*

ensō 円相【圓相】. 1. An area encompassed by a simple circle. 2. ZEN BUDDHISM—The *ensō* is a symbol of enlightenment or the potential enlightenment of the human mind. 3. In some classical martial arts schools, such as the Jiki Shinkage Ryū, the *ensō* appears on the transmission scrolls (*densho*) conferring full mastery of the tradition (*menkyo kaiden*). 4. ESOTERIC BUDDHISM—In the Tantric schools the *ensō* often appears as a ring which encompasses the divinities in a mandala (*mandara*). In these cases it represents the moon circle (*gachirin*), signifying wisdom; and the round shape of the lotus (*renge*), signifying reason.

Enwa 円和【圓和】. See: *Hirai Minoru.*

eta 穢多. A pejorative term for outcasts in Tokugawa and post-Tokugawa Japanese society. See: burakumin.

Ezo 蝦夷. 1. Equivalent to Emishi. See also: *Ainu.* 2. Abbreviation of Ezochi, an old term for the island of Hokkaidō.

Ezochi 蝦夷地. Edo-period term for the island of Hokkaidō; it literally means "land of the Ezo."

[6] Takamatsu Oryūgi was known for a number of combative arts in addition to kenjutsu: quick-draw swordsmanship (*iai*), unarmed grappling (*jūjutsu*), arresting arts (*torite*), spear (*sōjutsu*), and several others. It is not known exactly which ones Fujimoto actually included in his mix.

F

fu 歩. See: *fuhyō.*

fuchi 縁. An ornamental ring around the mouth of the hilt (*tsuka*) of a sword. This was often made by the same artisan in a matching design with the pommel cap (*kashira*).

fudai daimyō 譜代大名. Hereditary vassals under the Tokugawa shogunate. The *fudai daimyō* had aligned themselves with Tokugawa Ieyasu before the battle of Sekigahara in 1600, in contrast to the *tozama daimyō*, who pledged their allegiance after the battle was over. See: *daimyō; hatamoto; gokenin.*

fudai zu 譜代図【譜代圖】. Lineage charts used by provincial authorities in the tenth and eleventh centuries in order to select military overseers (*ōryōshi*) and arresting officers (*tsuibushi*). The charts certified a candidate's martial heritage.

FUDŌ MYŌŌ IMAGE ON SWORD BLADE
Inscribed above Fudō is
the Sanskrit *shittan* letter *Hāṁ* (*Kan*)
(*Chūdachi* from a private collection)

Fuden Ryū 不伝流【不傳流】. Branch tradition of Asayama Ichiden Ryū 浅山一伝流 that was founded by Itō Chōdayū Tsugiharu Fuden during the Empō era (1673–1681). The system concentrated on quick-draw sword techniques (*iaijutsu*).

fudōchi 不動智. Wisdom and understanding of the state of imperturbability.

Fudōchi shinmyō roku 『不動智神妙録』 (Record of the miraculous wisdom of imperturbability). 1. A treatise on swordsmanship written by the Rinzai Zen priest Takuan Sōhō around 1832. The text was authored by Takuan at the request of Yagyū Munenori, founder of the Edo Yagyū Shinkage Ryū and personal martial arts instructor of the *shōgun*. The text itself concentrates on the application of the spirit of Zen Buddhism to martial arts. It soon became a classic which greatly influenced the evolution of martial strategies and techniques (*bujutsu*) into martial arts (*bugei*) and, subsequently, martial/spiritual "ways" (*budō*) during the Edo period (1603–1868). 2. KATORI SHINTŌ RYŪ—A treatise on swordsmanship written in the mid-1400s by Iizasa Chōisai Ienao, founder of the Tenshinshōden Katori Shintō Ryū. (Ōtake, 1986–1990).

Further reading in English:

- Wilson, 2003.

Fudō Myōō 不動明王 <Ch. Budong Mingwang <Skt. Acalāgra-vidyārāja or Acalanātha-vidyārāja. BUDDHISM—Fudō is the commander of the five (sometimes eight) great *vidyārāja* (*myōō*). His origins are in the Indian god Śiva, and by the order of the Buddha Dainichi Nyorai, he manifests anger.

A minor Buddhist deity in India, his cult grew in China and became widespread in Japan. Fudō became especially popular with the warrior class during Japan's Middle Ages (Chūsei Jidai). His martial bearing and connection with *fudōshin* (imperturbable mind), a key psychological trait for warriors, made for a natural association between Fudō Myōō and the *bushi*. See also: *Aizen Myōō; Kurikara Fudō; Myōō; Ni-ō.*

Further reading in English:

- Oda, (1963): 155–161.

fudō no seishin 不動の精神. Lit. "the spirit of the steadfast/imperturbable mind," this was a term emphasized by the famous swordsman Tsukahara Bokuden. See: *fudōshin.*

FUDŌ MYŌŌ
From the *Taizōkai Mandara*

fudōshin 不動心. 1. Lit. "immovable mind." The psychological state of steadfast/imperturbable mind, in which the exponent is able to avoid panic due to fear of death, has been seen as a key element in classical Japanese combatives since at least the Middle Ages (1185–1573). From the Warring States era through the early Edo period, famous swordsmen used similar terms to indicate this mental state of accepting the inevitability of, and transcending concerns over, life and death (*seishi o chōetsu*); e.g., Kamiizumi's *fumetsu no kokoro*, Musashi's *iwao no mi*, Harigaya's *mujūshin*, Kamiya's *jikishin*, etc. 2. HOPLOLOGY—In the area of combative behavior and performance, the Japanese martial concept of *fudōshin*—steadfast, imperturbable mind—is one of the three key psychological combative adaptive traits; the other two being intuition (*kan*) and volition (*sen*). The human system normally responds to the threat of danger with an alarm reaction, which in turn gives rise to the "fight, flight, or freeze" reaction. However, some individuals are able to control or completely stop the alarm reaction, resulting in states that are referred to respectively as "steadfast mind" and "imperturbable mind." Inability to block the alarm reaction results in such energy-wasting reactions as anxiety, fear, panic, and mindless rage. Japanese warriors who could achieve *fudōshin*—blocking the alarm reaction—held up much better during protracted periods of combat and could stay collected and cool in the heat of battle. The ability to block the alarm reaction is not unique to Japanese culture, as evidenced, for example, by the German term *kaltblütig* and the French *sangfroid*, as well as the English "cold-blooded" or "cool."

While *fudōshin* was considered a key psychological element in hand-to-hand combat for the Japanese warrior, the classical Japanese *ryū* did not concentrate on cultivating "coolness" alone. It was usually tied to several other capabilities including those psychological traits mentioned above—*kan* (cognition/intuition) and *sen* (initiative)—as well as several physical traits: omnipoise trait (*shizen no kamae*), abdominal trait (*haragei*), respiratory/vocal trait (*ki-ai*), force/yield trait (*gōjū*), and synchronicity (*aiki*).

The ability of a warrior to achieve a state of *fudōshin*—especially in the early *ryū*—was often attributed to Buddhist warrior deities such as Fudō Myōō, Bishamonten, Marishiten and others. See also: *bu no ri; iwao no mi; kan (1); sen.*

Further reading in English:
- Hall, 1997.
- Hayes, 1988b:7–12.
- Hayes, 1994.

fugō no tomogara 富豪の輩. An eighth- and ninth-century term used to refer indirectly to local martial strongmen (*kuni no miyatsuko*) and wealthy commoners. At that time, aristocrats in the capital began creating political and economic ties with *fugō no tomogara*, which resulted in the development of early tax-free estates (*shōen*).

fuhyō 歩兵 [Abbr. as ***fu*** 歩]. SHŌGI—Lit. "foot soldier." In the chess-like Japanese game of *shōgi*, the *fuhyō* is somewhat equivalent to the pawn in Western chess.

Fujibayashi Ryu 1. 藤林流. School of espionage (*ninjutsu/shinobi-no-jutsu*) founded by Fujibayashi Nagato no Kami 藤林長門守, a resident of Iga. 2. School of military strategy and tactics (*gunkai*) which branched off from the Migumo Ryū 三雲流 in the mid-1700s. It was passed down by the Hattori family in the Tosa domain.

Fuji Issuishi Masatake 藤一水子正武. See: *Fuji Masatake.*

Fujikawa Ha 藤川派. See: *Jiki Shinkage Ryū Fujikawa Ha.*

Fujikawa Ha Jiki Shinkage Ryū 藤川派直心影流. Alternate term for Jiki Shinkage Ryū Fujikawa Ha.

Fujikawa Ryū 藤川流. Alternate term for Jiki Shinkage Ryū Fujikawa Ha. See also: *Fujikawa Yashirōemon Chikayoshi.*

Fujikawa Yahachirō Chikatsune 藤川 弥八郎 近常【藤川彌八郎近常】(c. 1788–c. 1860). After being adopted and trained by Akaishi Takasuke of the Jiki Shinkage Ryū, Chikatsune headed the Fujikawa Ha Jiki Shinkage Ryū.

Fujikawa Yashirōemon Chikayoshi 藤川弥司郎右衛門 近義 【藤川彌司郎右衛門近義】(1726–1798). JIKI SHINKAGE RYŪ—Recognized as tenth headmaster by the Jiki Shinkage Ryū 直心影流, Chikayoshi also established the Jiki Shinkage Ryū Fujikawa Ha in 1772.

Chikayoshi began as a student of Naganuma Shirōzaemon Kunisato (eighth headmaster of the Jiki Shinkage Ryū and son of Yamada Ippūsai), completing his training under ninth headmaster Naganuma Shōbei Tsunasato Katsuzensai. Naganuma recognized Chikayoshi's outstanding performance and understanding of the system by naming him as the tenth-generation headmaster of the Jiki Shinkage Ryū.

In 1756, Chikayoshi opened a training hall (*dōjō*) in Shitaya Chōjamachi, an area in Edo. After Naganuma passed away in 1772, the term Fujikawa Ha began to be applied to Chikayoshi's school. Several trainees obtained licenses of full mastery (*menkyo kaiden*). His named successors were Akaishi Chikayoshi (Jiki Shinkage Ryū main line) and his son, Fujikawa Kintoku (Jiki Shinkage Ryū Fujikawa Ha).

Fuji Masatake 藤 正武 [A.k.a. ***Issuishi*** 一水子; ***Natori Sanjūrō*** 名取三十郎]. Fuji, a strategist (*heihōsha*) attached to the Tokugawa family, is credited with the authorship of the *Shōninki*『正忍記』, a text on the espionage tactics (*shinobi no jutsu*) of the Kishū Ryū 紀州流, written around 1681.

Fujimoto Ringorō 藤本 林五郎. Second-generation successor of Enshin Ryū 円心流. See: *Enshin Ryū.*

Fujisan 富士山. Lit. "Mount Fuji." SHINDŌ MUSŌ RYŪ—Commonly used term for the beginning etiquette (*reihō*) for a training match (*shiaikuchi*). It takes its name from the position in which the sword (*tachi*) and staff (*jō*) are placed, which recalls the shape of the iconic mountain. See also: *kazari; reihō.*

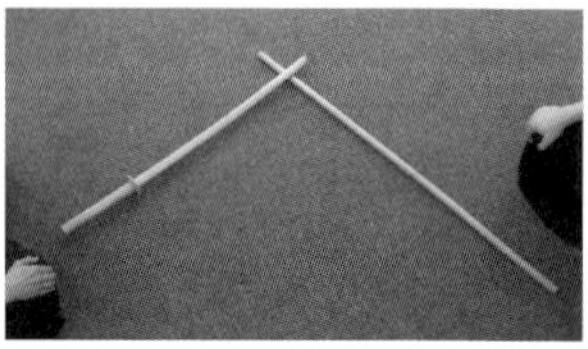

FUJISAN
Beginning etiquette (*reihō*) in Shindō Musō Ryū.

Fujita Fumoto Norisada 藤田 麓 憲貞. A master of Ryōi Shintō Ryū 良移心当流 in the Kuroda domain in Kyūshū. Fujita founded the Isei Jitoku Tenshin Ryū 為勢自得天真流 sometime during the first half of the eighteenth century.

Fujita Seiko 藤田 西湖 (1899–1966). Considered by many to be the "last *ninja*" Fujita Seiko is listed by Watatani and Yamada (1978: 272, 921) as the inheritor of the Kōga Ryū Wada Ha 甲賀流和田派 espionage tradition. Fujita received training in Kōga Ryū *shinobi no jutsu* under the tutelage of his grandfather (thirteenth inheritor of the Kōga School) and he listed himself as the "fourteenth headmas-

FUJITA SEIKO, C.1925

ter of Kōga Ryū Ninjutsu" on the cover of his 1958 book on *ninjutsu* entitled *Doronron*.

Fujita was certainly respected for his knowledge of the various aspects of the classical arts of espionage (*shinobi no jutsu*). During World War II he was charged by the Imperial Japanese Army to teach these systems to military espionage agents at an army school in Tōkyō called the Rikugun Nakano. It is not known how many of the traditional arts of the Kōga Ryū were passed on to these young military intelligence specialists. According to one of them—Saitō Satoshi of the Negishi Ryū 根岸流—he and his colleagues were very interested in the tactics of espionage but there was little interest in some of the more esoteric teachings such as methods for mixing various types of poisons, etc. (Saitō, 1985–1990).

In addition to his "family line" Kōga Ryū, Fujita also studied a variety of Japanese classical martial systems (*koryū*) and modern cognate arts (*budō*), including *karate*, Shindō Musō Ryū *jōjutsu*, and various types of *shurikenjutsu*, among others. He published several books on these arts, some of which contained detailed illustrations of weapons and technique. A partial list is included here.

Bujutsu kenkyū shōbō 『武術研究所報』 (Research report on martial arts). Bujutsu kenkyūjo, no date. (c. 1960)

Doronron 『どろんろん』. Tōkyō, 1958. (Reprinted by Shinpūsha Bunko, 2004.)

Kempō gokui atemi setsu-kappō meikai 『拳法極意當身殺活法明解』 (Secrets of boxing methods: A clear explanation of body strikes for killing and healing). Tōkyō: Meicho Kankōkai (reprint), 1985.

Shindō Musō Ryū jōjutsu zukai 『神道夢想流杖術図解』 (The illustrated Shindō Musō Ryū). Bujutsu kenkyūjo, 1953; (Reprinted: Tōkyō: Meicho Kankōkai, 1985.)

Zukai Hojōjutsu 『図解捕縄術』 (Illustrated combative arresting-rope technique). Tōkyō: Meicho Kankōkai (reprint), 1985.

Zukai Shurikenjutsu 『図解手裏剣術』 (Illustrated throwing-dart technique). Tōkyō: Meicho Kankōkai (reprint), 1985.

Further reading in English:

- Hevener, 2008.

Fujita Shichizaemon no jō Mitsushige 藤田 七左衛門尉 光成. Founder of Nikaidō Ryū (2) 二階道流. See: *Nikaidō Ryū (2)*.

Fujiwara 藤原. A powerful noble family known as the Nakatomi until 699. The clan included ministers, statesmen, poets, and warriors; in addition, especially during the Fujiwara period (898–1185), the Fujiwara family was the primary source of wives for the Japanese imperial family, which allowed them to maintain strong political and fiscal bonds with the emperors.

Many *bushi* families, such as the Kamiizumi branch family, are descended from the Fujiwara. The affiliation is often included with family names listed in official documents such as martial *densho*. For example, in the *densho* showing the lineage of the Shinkage Ryū, the name of Kamiizumi Nobutsuna might be listed as "Kamiizumi Isenokami Fujiwara no Nobutsuna 上泉 伊勢守 藤原信綱."

Further reading in English:

- Papinot, 1910: 88–106.

Fujiwara Genshin 藤原 玄信. See: *Miyamoto Musashi*.

Fujiwara Hidesato 藤原 秀郷. A tenth-century warlord. Hidesato was governor of Shimotsuke when the rebellion of Taira no Masakado began in 939. Hidesato united his forces with those of Taira no Sadamori, the governor of Hitachi, and defeated Masakado. When Masakado was wounded and fell from his horse, Hidesato beheaded him. Many legends evolved about the life of Hidesato; in such stories he was called "Tawara no Toda."

Fujiwara no Yasumasa 藤原 安正 (958–1036). A Heian-period courtier who became legendary due to his mastery of swordsmanship and combative dominance. Legend states that Yasumasa was pursued by an infamous brigand on a windswept, desolate moor. Yasumasa, completely relaxed and fearless, began playing his bamboo flute as he walked, apparently ignoring the thief's approach. This so frustrated the bandit that he purposely made noise in order to startle his target. However, Yasumasa, imperturbable, kept playing. The incident is depicted in a nineteenth-century triptych by Yoshitoshi (see below). Hoplologist Richard Hayes (1994: 25) describes the incident:

> ...Yasumasa, with relaxed comportment, devoid of the slightest feather of ego, pride, or hubris that the footpad's aggressive intent can snag upon, grasp, and cling to, walks on. The interval between them opens, deepens, step by step, and the footpad's initiative (volition) is proportionately sapped and drained. Yasumasa walks on.

Fujiwara Sumitomo 藤原 純友 (d. 941). A tenth-century warlord who was notorious for his pirate activities. Sumitomo evidently had an agreement with Taira no Masakado; when the latter escalated his revolt in Shimōsa, Sumitomo invaded Harima, Bizen, and Sanyō. After his defeat at Hakata, he fled to Iyo, where he was apprehended and executed. See also: *keigoshi.*

Further reading in English:

- Farris, 1992: 142–149.
- Friday, 2007: *passim.*

Fujiyama Ryū 藤山流. Edo-period *jūjutsu* tradition. See: *Iga Ryū (5).*

Fuji Zuio Kiyonobu 富士 隋翁 清信 (1675–1762). After mastering the comprehensive combative school (*sōgō bujutsu*) of Zuihen Ryū 随変流, Fuji founded the Zuihen Tō Ryū 随変当流, a more limited martial school concentrating on swordsmanship (*kenjutsu*) and grappling (*jūjutsu*).

Fukao Kakuma Shigeyoshi 深尾 角馬 重義 [A.k.a. ***Seia*** 井蛙] (1630–1682). A landed warrior (*goshi*) of Tottori domain who founded the Seia Ryū 雖井蛙流 around 1670. This martial school concentrated on combative swordsmanship (*kenjutsu*) with either the longsword (*katana*) or short sword (*kodachi*); spearmanship (*sōjutsu*); and armored grappling (*kumiuchi*).

An eclectic martial artist, Fukao learned Tanseki Ryū 丹石流 from his father; he then proceeded to train in a number of systems, including Bokuden Ryū 卜伝流, Gan Ryū 岩流, Kadoi Ryū 門井流, Kyosui Ryū 去水流, Matsumoto Ryū 松本流, Nen Ami Ryū 念阿弥流, Shinkage Ryū 新陰流, Shintō Ryū 神道流, Taisha Ryū タイ捨流, Toda Ryū 戸田流, and Tōgun Ryū 東軍流. With this experience, Fukao proceeded to modify the armored swordsmanship of the Tanseki Ryū into an efficient system adaptable to unarmored situations. Fukao categorized these revised, unarmored forms as *heihō*, but used the characters 平法 (methods of peace) in lieu of 兵法 (combative strategies). Due to some misfortune, Fukao was ordered to commit seppuku in 1682, at the age of fifty-two.

Fuke Shū 普化宗 [A.k.a. ***Komusō*** 虚無僧]. BUDDHISM—Traditionally considered a subsect of Rinzai Zen, the Fuke Shū is thought to have been founded in the mid-thirteenth century by the Japanese priest Kakushin. The sect is also referred to as Komusō, a term also applied to the flute-playing, mendicant monks who are its devotees. (Komusō 虚無僧 [lit. "monk of emptiness"] was the name of one of the founder's successors.)

Considerable misunderstanding surrounds the origins and nature of the Fuke Shū. From the popular history of the sect, it seems its members' most obvious characteristics were their violent behavior and their practice of playing the *shakuhachi* flute. As itinerant flute players, the Komusō were supposedly attempting to express a Zen type of enlightenment via their haunting music. However, according to Sanford (1977: 412), the sect actually dates from the late 1500s, and has little connection with Zen. He postulates that the actual antecedent of the *komusō* (emptiness monks) were the *komosō* 弧僧, a term meaning "mat monks." The mat monks apparently date from the late Ashikaga period (mid-1500s) and were itinerant "semi-religious beggars" who attracted alms-givers by playing the flute. The *komosō* mat monks were, in general, not fully ordained priests, but simply lay-brothers (*ubasoku*), a religious status a step below that of the Buddhist lay priest (*zaike hōshi*) which was popular among the warrior class.

It is popularly believed that espionage agents (*shinobi no mono*) often traveled disguised as members of the Komusō; this is not unlikely, as wearing a basket-like hat over one's head would aid in obscuring one's identity. (It should be noted here that the size and shape of the typical Komusō headgear evolved over time in the Tokugawa period, going from a straw hat similar to that worn by Zen monks to the basket-like hat that appeared in the early to mid 1700s.) In the late 1500s through the 1600s the Komusō monks wore a variety of headgear and clothing, including light armor and helmets.

The wearing of light armor gives another clue as to the origins of many Komusō. Yamashita (1972:27–35) notes that around the beginning of the Tokugawa period a number of masterless samurai (*rōnin*), who were essentially experienced combatants —out of work men-at-arms—flooded into the Komusō. It was a convenient way to make a living, especially if one was a criminal or avoiding the law for some other reason.

The great efforts made by the Fuke Shū to become recognized as a legitimate Buddhist sect met a modicum of success as the Tokugawa period progressed. However, the group never really escaped its rough origins during this time. Sanford (1977:418) notes that the Komusō monks were known to have occasionally been employed as spies by the Tokugawa Bakufu. In fact, during the Tokugawa period the monks of the Fuke Shū were granted the privilege of unrestricted travel around the country and the right to wear a single sword.

Consequently, whether they were espionage agents disguised as Komusō adherents, or Komusō monks acting as operatives for the Tokugawa, the members of the Fuke Shū were often as close to their combative origins as they were to the life of a religious ascetic or renunciant. See: *boronji, komusō, ubasoku.*

Further reading in English:

- Sanford, 1977.

fukibarijutsu 吹針術 [A.k.a. *fukumibarijutsu* 含針術]. Lit. the "skill of blowing needles" *fukibarijutsu* refers to the combative art of blowing small needles from the mouth. Fujita (1960:2) notes only one *ryū* specializing in this art.

fukikaeshi 吹返し. The winglets on a Japanese helmet (*kabuto*). *Fukikaeshi* were designed to deflect cutting blows to the lacings of the overlapping strips of metal forming the neck guard which hung from the sides and rear of the helmet.

Fūkoshi 風湖子 <Ch. Feng Huzi. A legendary sword appraiser in ancient China. Legend tells us that during the Chinese "Spring and Autumn" period (c. 771–c. 403 B.C.E.) he commissioned three wonderful swords from the renowned swordsmith Ou Yezi (Jp. Ōyashi). The three swords were given the names Gongfu (Jp. Kōfu), Longyuan (Jp. Ryūen), and Taia (Jp. Taia). The Taia sword became well known in the legends of Japan in the seventeenth century, due in part to a letter called the *Taiaki*, which was written to swordsman Yagyū Munenori by Rinzai Zen priest Takuan. See also: *Kōfu no ken; Ōyashi; Ryūen no ken; Taiaki; Taia no ken.*

Fukuda Hachinosuke 福田 八之助 (Also read ***Fukuda Yanosuke***) (c. 1828–1880). Fukuda was Kanō Jigorō's first teacher in the *jūjutsu* of the Tenshin Shin'yō Ryū. Fukuda had been a direct disciple of Iso Mataemon, founder of that system.

Fukuhara Ha 福原派. See: *Fukuhara Shinzaemon; Masaki Ryū Fukuhara Ha Kusarigama-jutsu.*

Fukuhara Shinzaemon 福原 新左衛門. Ninth headmaster of Suiō Ryū 水鷗流 during the early to mid-1800s. Fukuhara added sixteen sickle-and-chain scenarios (*kata*) to the curriculum of the Suiō Ryū. This weapons system was adopted from Masaki Ryū *kusarigama-jutsu*. It subsequently became a collateral system of the Suiō Ryū under the name of Masaki Ryū Fukuhara Ha Kusarigama-jutsu 正木流 福原派 鎖鎌術 (a.k.a. Heiden Masaki Ryū Kusarigama-jutsu 併伝正木流鎖鎌術). See also: *Masaki Ryū; Suiō Ryū.*

Fukui Harunosuke 福井 治之助. A disciple of Ueshiba Morihei. Fukui established the Yaei Ryū 弥栄流, through which he taught his own version of *aikidō*. See: *Ueshiba Ryū aikidō.*

Fukuji Seikō 福地清幸. Considered the first headmaster of Gōhaku Ryū 剛泊流, Fukuji founded the Okinawa Karate Gōjū Ryū Senbukai 沖縄空手剛柔流専武会 in 1967. Second headmaster Tokashiki Iken evidently reformulated the system and renamed it the Gōhaku Ryū in 1982.

fukumibarijutsu 含針術. See: *fukibarijutsu.*

Fukuoka Sekiryūkan Dōjō 福岡隻流館道場. Current home training hall (*hombu dōjō*) of the Sōsuishitsu Ryū, a school focusing on grappling (*taijutsu*) and swordsmanship (*kenjutsu*).

fukurohoyari 袋穂槍. See: *fukuro yari.*

fukuro naginata 袋薙刀 [A.k.a. ***makura naginata*** 枕薙刀]. A short glaive (*naginata*) blade made with a socket or sleeve that could be fitted over the end of a shaft. (Standard *naginata* have the tang mounted inside the shaft.) The tube-like sleeve of the *fukuro naginata* allowed the detached blade to be wielded like a short sword. This made it convenient to keep by the bedside; thus the alternate name, *makura* (pillow) *naginata.*

fukuro shinai 袋撓 [Var. 袋竹刀; 韜]. Originally a practice sword made of a rod of bamboo that was split into eighths or sixteenths at the distal end and encased in a lacquered leather sleeve. Over the years many versions of *fukuro shinai* have evolved, some made from separate strips of bamboo bound together and encased in a leather sleeve. The original model, created by Kamiizumi Ise no Kami Nobutsuna, was called a *hikihada shinai*, or, more simply, *hikihada.* See also: *chikutō (2); shinai.*

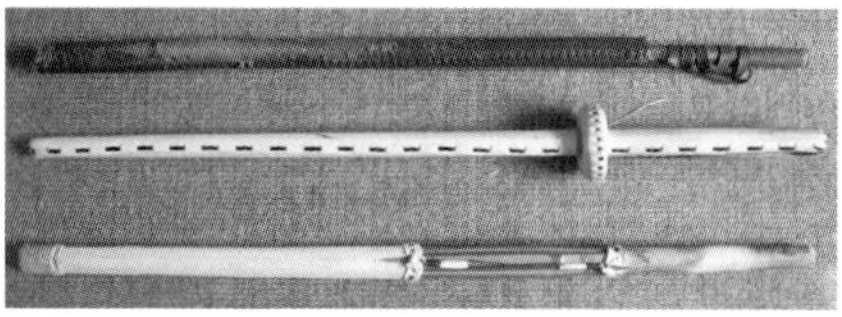

FUKURO SHINAI
Top: Yagyū Shinkage Ryū *hikihada shinai*
Center: Maniwa Nen Ryū *fukuro shinai*
Bottom: Jiki Shinkage Ryū *fukuro shinai*

fukuro yari 袋槍 [Also called ***fukurohoyari*** 袋穂槍]. A socket-mounted spearhead similar to a *hoko* (1) 矛. Instead of being forged with a tang, the *fukuro yari* had a socket that slid over the end of a shaft. Several types are known to have been used. See also: *sōjutsu; yari.*

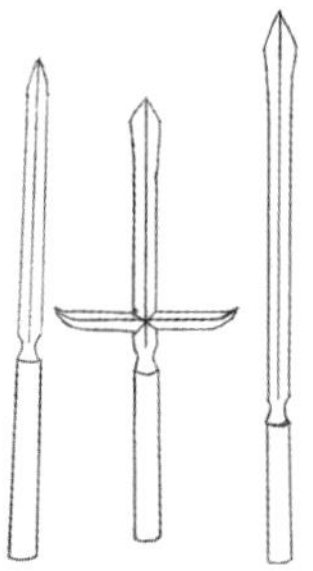

TYPES OF *FUKURO YARI*

fumetsu no kokoro 不滅の心. Lit. imperishable mind; indestructible spirit; eternal mind. A term used by Kamiizumi Ise no Kami of the Shinkage Ryū (1) 新陰流 which both denotes an acceptance of the inevitability of life and death and the mental state transcending them. Similar in meaning to *fudōshin.*

fumiashi 踏足. Treading water. Not surprisingly, this is one of the fundamentals of combative swimming arts (*suieijutsu*).

fumikomi 踏み込み. An attack; a strike or thrust. ¶ *fumikomu* 踏み込む, to step in (to attack; to strike). See also: *uchikomi.*

fumikomiashi 踏み込み足. A stamping step made with the forward foot. This type of step is common in the practice of *kendō* and usually occurs after a "springing forward" step known as *okuriashi.* See also: *ayumiashi; okuriashi; suriashi.*

funa ikusa 船軍 [Also read *sengun* 船軍]. 1. A sea battle. 2. Abbreviation for *funa-ikusa no hō.*

funa-ikusa no hō 船軍法. Naval strategy and tactics (in contrast to military/martial strategy and tactics, or *gumpō*).

Funajima 船島. See: *Ganryūjima.*

Funakoshi Gichin 船越 義珍 [Also written 富名腰 義珍] <Oki. Tominakoshi Gichin (1869–1957). Funakoshi, an Okinawan *karate* master, was an expert in Shuri *te* and a disciple of Azato Ankō. He was credited with introducing *karate* into Japan in 1922. It should be noted that Funakoshi demonstrated *karate* in 1917 at the Butokuden in Kyōto, but that demonstration was held for govern-

ment officials; it was not open to the public. Even as he proceeded to introduce *karate* into Japan, Funakoshi limited his public appearances to audiences of intellectuals—mostly artists and lawyers. His rationale was that professionals with sharp minds tended to be physically underdeveloped. As his popularity increased in the 1920s, Funakoshi expanded his demonstrations to include universities and Kanō Jigorō's Kōdōkan *Jūdō* school. By the mid-1920s a number of universities had created *karatejutsu* clubs under Funakoshi's influence.

Several of his disciples became important innovators and leaders in the development of *karatedō* in Japan, including Nakayama Masatoshi, Ōtsuka Hironori, and many others.

Funakoshi Gichin, c.1923

Though many practitioners contributed to the development of a truly Japanese style of *karatedo*, Funakoshi is recognized as the central figure in this process. In 1933 he changed the ideograms of the name of the art from *karatejutsu* 唐手術 (China-hand skill) to *karatejutsu* 空手術 (empty-hand skill).[1] Again, in 1935, he changed the term from *karatejutsu* to *karatedō* 空手道 (spiritual path of the empty hand) indicating his emphasis on spiritual forging through *karate*.

Funakoshi is credited with creating the Taikyoku Kata and Ten no Kata, both of which are simplified forms of Pinan (Heian), although some sources attribute these to Gichin's son Yoshitaka.

In 1936 Funakoshi established a main *dōjō* in Tōkyō which he named the Shōtōkan. It should be noted that, like Kanō, Funakoshi never intended for his system to be of the same nature as the feudal-period classical *ryū*. Hence, he never referred to it as Shōtōkan Ryū, though this began happening after his death. With the help of his son Yoshitaka, Funakoshi formed the Nihon Karatedō Shōtōkai in 1936. Soon after World War II, with the help of his students, he went on to found the Nihon Karate Kyōkai (Japan Karate Association) in 1948. See also: *Azato Ankō; Itosu Ankō; Matsumura Sōkon; Sakugawa Tōde.*

Further reading in English:

- Bishop, 1999: *passim.*
- Draeger, 1974: *passim.*
- Funakoshi, 1973; 1975; 2001.
- Nagamine, 2000: 69–80.

Funakoshi Yoshitaka 船越 義豪 (1906–1945). Son of Funakoshi Gichin. Yoshitaka led Shōtōkan Karatedō, and is credited with making many dramatic changes to the Shōtōkan system.

funazaki 船先. A "boat-shaped point" on a wooden sword (*bokken*). See: *bokken.*

fundō 分銅. 1. A weight attached to the end of a rope or chain. 2. ISSHIN RYŪ—A weight attached to the end of the chain fitted to the composite sickle and chain (*kusarigama*), which is the primary weapon of the Isshin Ryū.

fundōgusari 分銅鎖. A weighted chain. See: *kusarigama; manrikigusari.*

fundoshi 褌. Traditional Japanese men's undergarment, similar to a loincloth. Samurai wore *fundoshi* under their armor.

fundōzuke jutte 分銅付十手. A *jutte* with an attached weighted chain, such as the one used in Ikkaku Ryū.

funshi 憤死. The act of committing suicide by self-disembowelment (*seppuku*) due to indignation. *Funshi* was the equivalent of *munenbara*. See: *seppuku.*

[1] This may have been partly due to the rise of right-wing nationalism in Japan in the 1930s. That trend included a de-emphasis on "things foreign" and the expurgation of foreign terms from pure Japanese. For example, Horace Wilson's *besu bōru* (romanized Japanese for English "baseball") became *yakyū* 野球 (lit. "field ball").

F

furibō 振棒. 1. A heavily weighted staff used as a bludgeon. 2. JIKI SHINKAGE RYŪ—Oversized, end-heavy *bō* used for training proper sword movement.

FURIBŌ
A Jiki Shinkage Ryū trainee practices with *furibō* at the Chūō-ku Taikukan, Tōkyō, 1978
(Photograph by author)

Furigakari 振掛. The eighth set of primary sword forms (*kata*) used by the Jigen Ryū.

furijō 振杖. 1. A medium-length weighted staff. 2. A medium-length staff to which a chain and iron weight are attached. This weapon essentially has the same function as a *chigiriki*.

FURIJŌ

fūrinkazan 風林火山. Lit. "wind, forest, fire, mountain." *Fūrinkazan* was a battle slogan used by warlord Takeda Shingen in the Warring States period (Sengoku Jidai). Shingen took the phrase from the Chinese classic *Art of War* (*Sonshi no heihō* 孫子兵法).

The original text[2] in the *Art of War* states:

> When campaigning, be swift as the wind; in leisurely march, majestic as the forest; in raiding and plundering, like fire; in standing, firm as the mountains. As unfathomable as the clouds, move like a thunderbolt.
>
> Griffith, 1963: 106

Shingen had this motto placed on the battle flags (*noboribata*) carried by his troops.

furisode 振袖. A woman's kimono with long (hanging) sleeves. See: *Yoshin Ryū*.

furui nyōbō 古い女房. Lit. "old wife." A warrior slang term used as early as the Warring States period (Sengoku Jidai) to indicate a commander's right-hand man. It indicates that, like an old wife, the right-hand man is a completely trusted companion who takes care to make sure everything gets done. Kurosawa incorporated this term into his film *Seven Samurai* (*Shichinin no samurai* 七人の侍).

furyūmonji 不立文字. BUDDHISM—A Zen term indicating "intuition," this phrase refers to a transmission of knowledge that takes place "without the use of words or letters." See also: *ishin denshin*.

fuse 布施 <Ch. *bushi* <Skt. *dāna*. The act of giving; charity. See *hodokoshi* for the martial application of this concept.

fusegu 防ぐ. To defend.

Fusen Ryū 不遷流 [Also known as ***Motsugai Ryū*** 物外流]. A martial school specializing in *jūjutsu* and a variety of weapons arts including swordsmanship (*kenjutsu*), long hardwood staff techniques (*bōjutsu*), and sickle-and-chain techniques (*kusarigama-jutsu*), among others. The Fusen Ryū *jūjutsu* system was based on a pugilistic art known as "Buddhist priest fist" (*genkotsu oshō*). It was founded around 1840 by Takeda Motsugai, a ninth-generation descendant of Takeda Shingen, a famous *daimyō* from the Warring States period.

Fusen Ryū was heavily influenced by Buddhism; the term *fusen* 不遷, as Watatani and Yamada note (1978: 726), is a synonym for *shukke* 出家 (a monk; one who has left his home and family).

fūsui 風水 <Ch. *fengshui*. Geomancy; the Chinese-derived practice of combining astrology and geography in order to select locations for structures which would provide the most positive energies for the occupants. *Fūsui* was applied to the building of forts and castles, as well as for designing and constructing field fortifications (*chikujōjutsu*) and in battle planning/divination (*gumbai heihō*).

[2] 故其疾如風、其徐如林、侵掠如火、不動如山、難知如陰、動如雷霆 (Murayama, 1965: 78).

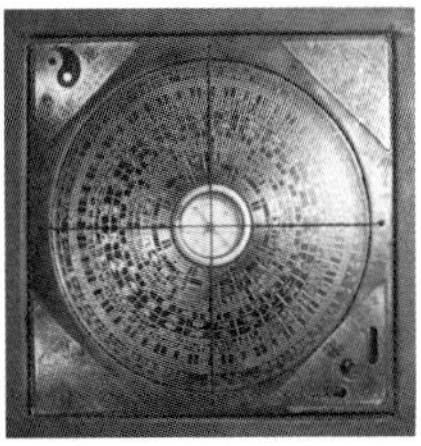

FENGSHUI (*FUSUI*) COMPASS FROM HONG KONG
Fengshui/*fūsui* compass known in Japanese as a *rōhan* (Ch. *luopan*)
(Private collection)

Futagami Hannosuke 二神 半之助 [A.k.a. ***~Masaaki*** 正聴]. Founder of Futagami Ryū and Sōsuishitsu Ryū 双水執流. Having mastered the swordsmanship (*kenjutsu*) and combative grappling (*koshin no mawari*) of the Takenouchi Ryū 竹内流 in the 1640s, Futagami founded his own system, which he christened "Futagami Ryū." However, he was not satisfied with his creation, so he set out on a warrior pilgrimage (*musha shugyō*). Around 1650, after completing his journey, he revised his system and renamed it "Sōsuishitsu Ryū." This system focuses on combative grappling and quick-draw swordsmanship, collectively referred to as *kumiuchi koshi no mawari* or *taijutsu*. See: Sōsuishitsu Ryū.

Futagami Ryū 二神流. See: *Sōsuishitsu Ryū.*

futari iaidō 二人居合道. A practice found in Shin Shin Musō Ryū 神心無想流 in which quick-draw swordsmanship is practiced with a partner (in standard *iaidō*, by contrast, the proponent practices solo forms). See: *kumi iai; Ryūshinkan Budō; sannin iaidō.*

Fūten 風天 <Ch. Fengtian <Skt. Vāyu. In Indian mythology, Vāyu is the god of wind; essentially an elemental. In East Asia and Japan, Vāyu became one of a group of twelve guardian deities adopted from Brahmanism by Buddhism. See: *Jūniten.*

Futsunushi no Kami 経津主神【經津主神】. See: *Futsunushi no Ōkami.*

Futsunushi no Mikoto 経津主命【經津主命】. See: *Futsunushi no Ōkami.*

Futsunushi no Ōkami 経津主大神【經津主大神】[Var. Futsunushi no Kami 経津主神; Futsunushi no Mikoto 経津主命]. 1. The main deity (*kami*) enshrined in Katori Jingū in Chiba prefecture; he is considered a deity of the sword. According to Japanese mythology, Futsunushi no Ōkami was one of two warrior deities called upon by the Sun Goddess, Amaterasu Ōmikami, to pacify the earth by subduing a number of trouble-causing spirits (*kami*). 2. KATORI SHINTŌ RYŪ—The warrior deity (*kami*) who transmitted, via the Buddhist goddess Marishiten, the most secret teachings of combative tactics and strategy (*heihō*) to Iizasa Chōisai Ienao, the founder of the Tenshinshō-den Katori Shintō Ryū. See also: *Takemikazuchi no Mikoto.*

Further reading in English:

- Ōtake, 1977a; 2007.

fuzoku bugei 付属武芸【付屬武藝】. Lit. "attached martial arts," "collateral martial arts." This term refers to martial systems—sometimes entire *ryū*—that have been subsumed and adapted to another tradition. For example, Ikkaku Ryū *juttejutsu* became a *fuzuko bugei* of Shindō Musō Ryū; Seigō Ryū *battōjutsu* (under the title "Yagyū Seigō Ryū") became a *fuzuko bugei* of Yagyū Shinkage Ryū; etc.

FUJIWARA NO YASUMASA
Triptych by Tsukioka Yoshitoshi (1839–1892)

G

Gachirin Kan 月輪観【月輪觀】. BUDDHISM—A type of Buddhist esoteric meditation in which the practitioner concentrates on an empty moon-form circle (*gachirin*). See also: *Aji Kan.*

TYPICAL GACHIRIN KAN MEDITATIONAL DEVICE

~gaeshi (～返し). Lit. "to return" or "to reverse"; "to counter." This form of the term *kaeshi* is used in some compound words. ¶ *kotegaeshi* 小手返し, a technique in which the opponent's wrist (*kote*) is turned back on itself. See: *kaeshi.*

gaiden 外伝【外傳】. Lit. "outside tradition" or "outside of the tradition." This term indicates later additions to a training curriculum not passed down in the original tradition. For example, see the entry for *shiai seihō.*

Gaiden Shiai Seihō 外伝試合勢法【外傳試合勢法】. See: *shiai seihō.*

Gaiefu 外衛府. An imperial guard unit established in 765 by Empress Kōken.[1] The unit was abolished in 772. See: *efu.*

gaki 餓鬼 <Ch. *wogui* <Skt. *preta*. BUDDHISM—A spirit that inhabits the "Realm of Hungry Ghosts" (Gakidō).

Gakidō 餓鬼道. BUDDHISM—The "Realm of Hungry Ghosts." This is the fifth of the six realms (Rokudō) into which beings are subject to rebirth. The hungry ghosts are condemned to an existence of hunger and thirst which can never be sated.

[1] Kōken Tennō 孝謙天皇 (718–770, r. 749–758). Empress Kōken was both the forty-sixth and forty-eighth imperial ruler of Japan. She reigned as Kōken Tennō, 749–758, and Shōtoku Tennō 称徳天皇, 764–770.

Ganritsu Ryū 願立流. See: *Gan Ryū (3).*

Gan Ryū 1. 巌流【巖流】. This system, primarily a *kenjutsu* school limited to swordsmanship, was founded by Sasaki Kojirō, who was also known by the name "Ganryū." Kojirō mastered Chūjō Ryū 中条流 and, after engaging in many duels while on a martial pilgrimage (*musha shūgyō*), founded his own school. He was well known for his expertise with a *tachi* so long that it approached *ōdachi* size, and for his gentlemanly manner. He was killed in 1612 in a duel with Miyamoto Musashi.

Gan Ryū 2. 眼流. System of swordsmanship (*kenjutsu*) attributed to Matsu Uemon, a.k.a. Yagyū Matsuemon Ienobu.

Gan Ryū 3. 願立 [Var. 願流・眼流; a.k.a. ***Ganritsu Ryū*** 願立流; ***Muun Ryū*** 無雲流]. Founded by Shōrin Samanosuke around 1625, this school included the study of combative swordsmanship (*kenjutsu*), quick-draw sword arts (*iaijutsu*), small throwing blades and darts (*shurikenjutsu*), spear techniques (*sōjutsu*), long hardwood staff (*bōjutsu*), long-hafted glaive (*naginatajutsu*), and grappling (*jūjutsu*).

Ganryūjima 巌流島【巖流島】[A.k.a. ***Funajima*** 船島; ***Mukōjima*** 向島 (also read ***Mukaijima***)]. Name of the island where Miyamoto Musashi fought his famous duel against Sasaki Kojirō in 1612.

gantsubushi 眼潰 [Also called *metsubushi* 目潰]. Lit. "demolishing the eyes." 1. A small weapon used by Japanese police (*torimono*), especially during the Edo period (1603–1867). The *gantsubushi* was a very small lacquered box used for blowing dust or pepper into the eyes of a suspect resisting arrest. Such devices have a mouthpiece on one side and a pipe or hole on the other for directing the pepper. 2. The name for a number of techniques in a variety of *ryū* which were used to temporarily or permanently blind an enemy.

Gassan Ryū 月山流. School concentrating on three weapons systems—long-hafted glaive (*naginata*), spear (*yari*), and long-hafted sickle (*nagae no kama*)—which traced its origins back to Iizasa Chōisai Ienao, founder of the Katori Shintō Ryū. However, according to Watatani and Yamada, this school only became differentiated from the Katori Shintō Ryū with its sixth headmaster, Yorino Gohei Tadatsugu 頼野五兵衛尉忠次. It was Yorino who named the school Gassan Ryū.

gasshō 合掌. BUDDHISM—Lit. "palms together." A Buddhist hand seal (*in*) in which the hands are placed together, palm to palm. Various exoteric and esoteric meanings are assigned to the gesture.

gasshō gamae 合掌構. The basic salutation posture used in Nippon Shōrinji Kempō. The exponent stands straight up, feet together, arms horizontal, with the hands held palms-together (in *gasshō*) with the fingers pointing vertically. This *kamae* is performed before and after every Shōrinji Kempō practice, but it has no precedent in Chinese Shaolin *quanfa* (*kempō* [2] 拳法). In fact, by holding the hands directly in front of the face and partially obscuring the eyes, the defensive capability of the stance is weakened.

gasshuku 合宿. A training camp or seminar. In the context of modern *budō*, a *gasshuku* is an occasion for various individuals and groups to get together for training and socializing. See also: *kangeiko; shochūgeiko.*

Gatten 月天 <Ch. Yuetian <Skt. Candra. [A.k.a. ***Gattenson*** 月天尊 <Ch. Yuetianzun]. In Indian mythology, Candra is the moon god. Gatten is one of a group of twelve guardian deities adopted from Brahmanism by Buddhism. See: *Jūniten; suigetsu.*

Gedan Hasseihō 下段 八勢法. See: *shiai seihō.*

gedan no kamae 下段(の構). A lower-level engagement posture in which the point of the sword (*kensakii*) is held about 6 inches (15 cm.) above the ground and pointed toward the opponent.

gedan no kurai 下段の位. YAGYŪ SHINKAGE RYŪ—any lower-level engagement posture in which the hands are held around or below waist level.

Gedan no Tsuki 下段の突. HOKUSHIN ITTŌ RYŪ—One of a number of classical prearranged combative forms (*kata*) developed by the Hokushin Ittō Ryū. Gedan no Tsuki was also one of ten classical *kata* adapted by the Japanese Police Commission of 1886 for their Keishichō Ryū 警視庁流 system.

gehanen 下半円【下半圓】. Lit. "lower half-circle." JIKI SHINKAGE RYŪ—The half-circle inscribed by the hands at the end of each of the *kata* in Hōjō. See also: *jōhanen; Jiki Shinkage Ryū.*

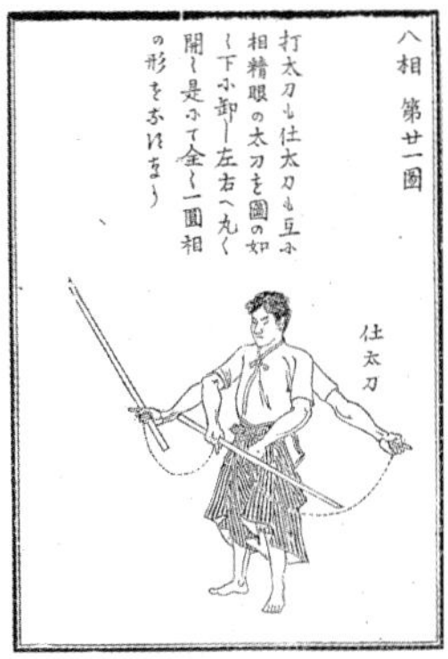

JIKI SHINKAGE RYŪ *GEHANEN*
Illustration from *Jiki Shinkage Ryū kenjutsu* by Saitō Akinobu, 1901

Geijutsu bukōron 『芸術武功論』【藝術武功論】 (Discourses on martial arts exploits). This text, published in five volumes in 1768, is an in-depth description of the combative arts taught by eighteenth-century swordsman Masaki Toshimitsu. The now-rare text was written and illustrated by Masaki's student Kashiwabuchi Yūgi. Kashiwabuchi was careful to delineate which weapons arts were derived from Kotōda Ha Ittō Ryū, which were from Sen'i Ryū, and so on, but all the techniques he described contain elements of the warrior arts (*bugei*) taught to samurai of the Tōda domain.

The first volume (*Jiri kokumon* 事理或問) concentrates on Masaki's personal history and teachings. The second (*Kemyō shiranami no ki* 假名白波之記) is a description of training weapons and techniques such as basic cuts; the third (*Chuntō shiranamisei no zu* 杶刀白波勢之図) contains illustrations of training weapons and armor and *naginata* techniques. The fourth volume (*Sokuhō zufu* 足法図譜) contains illustrations of footwork; and the fifth (*Kemyō jiri kokumon* 假名事理或問) comprises an afterword.

gekiken 撃剣. See: *gekken.*

Gekikenkai 撃剣会【撃劍會】. An organization formed in 1873 by Sakakibara Kenkichi, fourteenth headmaster of the Jiki Shinkage Ryū. The aim of the group was to promote traditional Japanese martial arts. To accomplish this, the Gekikenkai sponsored events known as *gekken kōgyō*, which featured matches between swordsmen and other combatants armed with bamboo swords (*shinai*), wooden glaives (*naginata*), and wooden-bladed sickle-and-chain composite weapons (*kusarigama*). Patterning his *gekken kōgyō* matches after the popular *sumō* tournaments of his day, Sakakibara developed a stable of contenders divided into "eastern" and "western" groups. Some of the swordsmen, such as Takeda Sōkaku, were from his own school, the Jiki Shinkage Ryū.

gekken 撃剣【撃劍】[Also read ***gekiken***]. Lit. "aggressive sword" or "severe sword." Evolving in the mid- to late-Edo period, *gekken* was a form of dueling with protective gear and bamboo swords. During the Meiji era it evolved into the harsh style of *shinai-geiko* developed under the Dai Nippon Butokukai after its establishment in 1895. (Apparently, however, universities in the Meiji era preferred to refer to their training as *kendō* rather than *gekken.*) *Gekken* was used by militarists to help develop a sense of nationalism among the populace in preparation for war. Until the formation of the Zen Nippon Kendō Remmei (All-Japan Kendo Federation) in 1927, there was no national standardization of *gekken*/*kendō.*

gekken kōgyō 撃剣興行【撃劍興行】. Public martial arts shows in which matches with non-lethal weapons—bamboo swords (*shinai*), etc.—were held. These shows proliferated during the 1870s and 1880s. See: *Gekikenkai; Sakakibara Kinkichi.*

Gekken sōdan 『撃剣叢談』【撃劍叢談】. A compilation of history, stories, legends, and tales about famous swordsmen. The book was put together by Minamoto Tokushu in 1844.

gekkira 隙棄羅. See: *shakujō.*

gekokujō 下剋上. A type of political upheaval indicating the overthrow of social superiors (those above) by their inferiors (those below). This term is commonly used to describe the political upheavals of the Warring States period (Sengoku Jidai).

Gembukan 玄武館. 1. *Dōjō* located in the Nihonbashi area of Edo (modern-day Tokyo) where Chiba Shūsaku taught his Hokushin Ittō Ryū during the mid-1800s. Established in 1822, the *dōjō* is still considered one of the three great Edo *dōjō* of the late Tokugawa period (the other two being the Rempeikan and the Shigakkan). See: *Bakumatsu Edo Sandai Dōjō; Chiba Shūsaku; Hokushin Ittō Ryū; Rempeikan; Shigkkan.* 2. Abbreviation for Gembukan Ninpō Bugei.

Gembukan Ninpō Bugei 玄武館忍法武芸. Modern combative arts organization founded by Tanemura Shōtō in 1984. Tanemura's Gembukan is similar in content and purpose to that of Hatsumi Masaaki's Bujinkan. See: *Bujinkan.*

gembuku 元服 [Also read ***gempuku***; also called ***kakan*** 加冠]. A coming-of-age ceremony. In the case of the warrior class (*bushi*), a young samurai received his first adult haircut, a sword, armor, and an adult name between the ages of twelve and sixteen. The equivalent ceremony for a young woman—held sometime between the ages of twelve and fourteen—was called *mogi* 裳着.

Gempei Gassen 源平合戦【源平合戰】[Also read ***Gempei Kassen***; var. ***Gempei no Tatakai*** 源平の戦い, etc.]. The war between the Minamoto and the Taira which took place from 1180 to 1185. Although the conflict was known as the "Gempei" war (Gem 源=Genji; Pei 平=Heike), it was much more complex than a mere rivalry between the Minamoto and the Taira families. Some of the Taira fought alongside the Minamoto, and some Minamoto fought against other Minamoto branch families. Although many warrior families were involved, some remained neutral. The Minamoto chiefs who led in taking up arms against the Taira of Ise included Yoritomo of the Kawachi Minamoto, Yoshinaka of the Shinano Minamoto, and the Kai Minamoto. Yoritomo, the most famous of these and the eventual supreme Minamoto leader, spent most of his time solidifying his control of the Kantō plain. He eventually took control of all domains in the east, including vassals of many warrior families. Some of these (such as the Chiba and Miura) were from the Taira line; others, like the Nitta and Ashikaga, were related to the Minamoto.

Further reading in English:

- Farris, 1992: 289–307.
- Kitagawa and Tsuchida, 1975 (translation of *Heike monogatari*).
- McCullough, 1988 (translation of *Heike monogatari*).
- Varley, 1994: 78–115 *ff.*

Gempei Kassen 源平合戦【源平合戰】. See: *Gempei Gassen.*

Gempei no Tatakai 源平の戦い【源平の戰い】. See: *Gempei Gassen.*

Gempei seisuiki 『源平盛衰記』 (Chronicle of the rise and fall of the Minamoto and the Taira). This is a large historical work (forty-eight volumes) covering the period from 1160 to 1185 and the various conflicts between the Minamoto and the Taira families. It dates from the thirteenth century, but its authorship is obscure.

Further reading in English:

- Varley, 1994, *passim*.

gempuku 元服. See: *gembuku.*

Genbukan 玄武館. See: *Gembukan.*

gendai budō 現代武道. Modern, spiritual/sportive combative self-defense systems for civilians. See also: *budō/bugei/bujutsu.*

gendaitō 現代刀. Lit. "modern swords." This term refers to blades made after the 1876 prohibition against the wearing of swords. Many of these were mass-produced for the military before and during World War II; such blades are generally referred to as Showatō. Some, however, were fine traditionally forged weapons. In the latter category are the Yasukunitō, swords made in the traditional manner by smiths at Yasukuni Shrine in Tōkyō. See also: *guntō; kaiguntō; kotō; kyūguntō; Nippontō; shinguntō; shinshintō; shintō (2); Shōwatō; Yasukunitō.*

gendatsuba 乾闥婆 [Also read *gendabba*; *kendatsuba*] <Ch. *qiantapo* <Skt. *gandharva*. One of the eight types of beings who are considered protectors of Buddhism. See: *Hachibu Shū.*

genin 1. 下人. A twelfth-century term for a groom or attendant. See: *shojū.*

genin 2. 下忍. A term commonly used by the popular press to indicate non-warrior espionage group agents (*ninja*). The *genin* was at the bottom of the espionage hierarchy, and was therefore subservient to the "middleman" assignment officer (*chūnin*) and organizational headman (*jōnin*). It should be noted that these designations are anecdotal and should not be taken to apply to all espionage operations during the classical period. See: *jōnin–chūnin–genin; ninjutsu.*

Genji 源氏. The Minamoto family. See also: *Gempei Gassen.*

Genji monogatari 『源氏物語』 (Tale of Genji). Sometimes called the world's first novel, the *Genji monogatari* is attributed to Murasaki Shikibu, a noblewoman of early eleventh-century Japan. The novel presents an intimate description of court life and politics at the height of the Heian period, just prior to the time when political control shifted to the warrior class.

Further reading in English:

- Seidensticker (translation), 1976.
- Tyler (translation), 2001.

Genji no Chōja 源氏長者. Title used by the Tokugawa *shōgun* to refer to the chief of the Minamoto clan. See also: *uji no kami.*

Genji no heihō 『源氏兵法』 (Strategy and tactics of the Minamoto family). According to Daitō Ryū 大東流 tradition, the *Genji no heihō* was a text on combative strategy from

G

the time of the Gempei war (1180–1185) that was supposed to contain information on strategy, swordsmanship (*kenjutsu*), and grappling (*jūjutsu*). This compendium supposedly became the guide to combative strategy for the Takeda family, who were related to the Minamoto clan. Daitō Ryū tradition holds that the combative weapons systems and grappling described in the text (which came to be called the *Takeda heihō*) somehow were the antecedent for Takeda Sōkaku's Daitō Ryū. However, most references to the *Takeda heihō* seem to trace back to Takeda Sōkaku himself.

There are a number of problems with this tradition. There was, in fact, a compendium on strategy used by the Minamoto family and its later branch lines, called the *Genke kin'etsushū*. This text, which was by the Ogasawara (another Minamoto branch family), may very well date back even earlier than the Gempei war. However, the Ogasawara text contains only a few descriptions of armed combat[2]—certainly not unarmed *jūjutsu*-like arts, which did not really proliferate until the much later Edo period (1603–1867). Also, even if the use of the sword had been described in the text of the *Genke kin'etsushū* or *Genji no heihō*, the use of the *tachi* in the late twelfth century was much different than the effective *kenjutsu* that evolved from the fourteenth to the sixteenth centuries.

If the *Genji no heihō*-cum-*Takeda heihō* actually dated from Japan's middle ages, one would expect it to have been much like the *Genke kin'etsushū* of the Ogasawara family: a text concentrating on a mixture of strategy, religious esoterica, and military divination. Even so, the earliest written copy of the *Genke kin'etsushū* dates only from the late 1500s.

The Minamoto may well have had a common pool of "secret, strategic teachings" that gave rise to the Ogasawara branch *Genke kin'etsushū*, the Takeda branch *Genji no heihō*, and possibly other Minamoto traditions. However, while strategic principles and divination procedures may have remained the same as they were passed down over the centuries, weapons and tactics changed significantly from the twelfth century to the sixteenth century to the nineteenth century. Consequently, the claim that ancient sets of secret swordsmanship (*kenjutsu*) and grappling (*jūjutsu*) techniques derived from the *Genji no heihō*-cum-*Takeda heihō* are now preserved in the Daitō Ryū is most likely an attempt to assign early historical connection between the famous figures of the Gempei war and Takeda Sōkaku's modern *jūjutsu* system. See also: *Genke kin'etsushū; Kiichi Hōgan; Kiichi Hōgan Ryū; Ōe Koretoki; Rikutō; Sanryaku.*

Genke kin'etsushū 『源家訓閲集』 [Var. ***Kin'etsushū*** 訓閲集] (The Minamoto family's collected examinations of military matters). This is a large compendium on martial/military matters and strategy attributed to Minamoto Yoshiie (1041–1108). The text was created from a combination of Chinese works on military science and a mixture of Buddhist and Daoist esoterica. It became the family-transmitted martial tradition of the powerful Minamoto warrior clan. Its existence was a well-guarded secret and, consequently, it did not emerge in written form until the late 1500s, at which time it appeared within the Ogasawara family (a Minamoto branch family) under the title of *Genke kin'etsushū*.[3]

In addition to Tantric Buddhist, Daoist, and Shugendō esoterica, the work contains recipes for military divination (*gumbai heihō*) and rituals related to the Buddhist goddess Marishiten.

From the Nambokuchō period (1336–1392) through the end of the Muromachi period (1392–1573) a number of texts on martial strategy (*heihō*) based on the *Genke kin'etsushū* appeared within the developing classical

[2] Sections 37–39 concentrate on archery with some minimal reference to swordsmanship. See Manabe, 1938: 40–43.

[3] Manabe Takejirō, editor of the *Genke kin'etsushū*, dates his copy of the text to around 1564–1565, but notes the language used in the text appears to be from the mid-Muromachi period (c. 1470–1480). See Manabe, 1938: 1. Several other editions under this title are available, all dated after Manabe's text. See Ishioka and Arima, 1967 (Vol. 6): 18–19.

martial traditions (*koryū*). These texts and excerpts were given titles such as *Heihōjutsu ryūko sanryaku no maki* (Dragon-tiger stratagem briefs on tactics and war methods), *Heihō hijutsu ikkan no sho* (One-scroll text on the secret methods of strategy), *Heihō reizuisho* (Strategy based on miraculous signs), *Heihō yonjūni ka jō* (Forty-two sections on strategy), [*Heihō*] *Tora no maki* (Tiger scroll [on strategy]), and [*Heihō*] *Ryū no maki* (Dragon scroll [on strategy]). See also: *Genji no heihō; Kiichi Hōgan; Kiichi Hōgan Ryū; Minamoto Yoshiie; Ōe Koretoki; Ōe Ryū; Rikutō; Sanryaku.*

Further reading in English:

• Hall, 1990: 248–261.

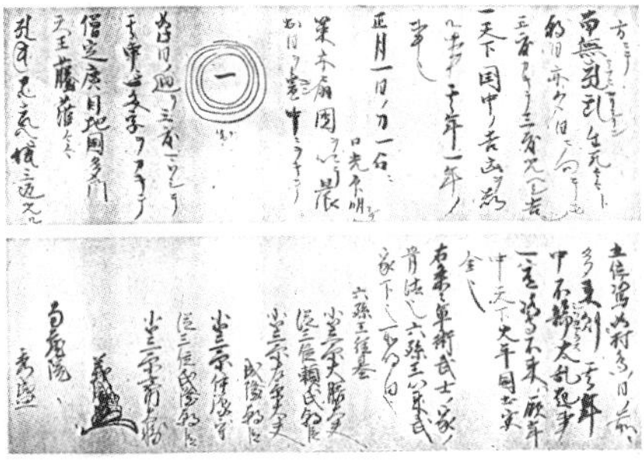

GENKE KIN'ETSUSHŪ
Excerpt from the Ogasawara family-transmitted *Genke kin'etsushū*
(From the archives of Mutō Masao)

Genkō no Eki 元寇役. Lit. the "campaign (役) against the Yuan dynasty (元) invasion (寇)." This refers to the battles against the Mongol invasions of Japan that took place in 1274 and 1281. These incursions, which were undertaken by Mongol leader Kublai Khan (1215–1294), were major operations aimed at invading Japan after the Mongol conquest of Korea.

The terms *Bun'ei no Eki* and *Kōan no Eki* are also used for these battles, as they took place during the Bun'ei era (1264–1275) and during the Kōan era (1278–1288).

Further reading in English:

• Conlan, 2001.

• Turnbull, 1977: 84–94.

genkotsu 拳骨. Lit. "fists and knuckles." This term refers to methods for assaulting vital points. Watatani (1967:30) notes that

MONGOL ARCHERS FIRING AT A JAPANESE WARRIOR
Depiction from the *Moko Shurai Ekotoba*, c. 1293

genkotsu is the equivalent of both *atemi* and *kassatsujutsu*.

genkotsu oshō 拳骨和尚. This term, which literally means "combative fist art (*genkotsu*) of Buddhist priests (*oshō*)" was used by the Fusen Ryū 不遷流, a martial school specializing in *jūjutsu* and weapons arts. It apparently referred to a pugilistic art with Buddhist origins. (The term *oshō* normally indicated a Zen priest.)

Genpei Gassen 源平合戦 【源平合戰】. See: *Gempei Gassen.*

Genpei Kassen 源平合戦 【源平合戰】. See: *Gempei Gassen.*

genpuku 元服. See: *gembuku.*

Genroku Akō jiken 『元禄赤穂事件』 (The Genroku [-era] Akō Incident). An alternate title for the story of the Forty-seven Rōnin. See: *Akō rōshi.*

Gen'yōsha 玄洋社 (Genkai Nada Society; Dark Ocean Society; Black Ocean Society). An extreme right-wing nationalist society and political pressure group formed in 1881 by Hiraoka Kōtarō, a wealthy former samurai (*shizoku*) who was also a mine owner, along with Tōyama Mitsuru (also a *shizoku*) and several other men from the Fukuoka area of Kyūshū. Most of the group's early members were, in fact, *shizoku* from Fukuoka (formerly part of Chikuzen domain under the Tokugawa); they eventually began working in secret with the Japanese army to further its goals of expansion on the Asian mainland.

While not restricted to men of former samurai lineage from Fukuoka, the Gen'yōsha was never a very large organization. In its early years its membership rarely exceeded fifty, and at its largest during World War II, it only expanded to about three hundred. Membership was highly selective: potential affiliates were required to participate in *jūjutsu* training sessions with members at the Gen'yōsha *dōjō* in Fukuoka called the Meidōkan (the Hall of the Shining Path) where, according to Sabey (1973: 76), characteristics such as "…their composure, mental alertness and ability to withstand physical strain and crisis…" were observed.[4]

Further reading in English:

- Matsui (Trans.), 1993.
- Sabey, 1973.

geppo 齧哺 [Also read ***getsuho***]. Lit. "crunching maw." A combative system created by Mizuno Tomojūrō Toshitada (c. 1835) that included swordsmanship with long sword (*ōdachi*), short sword (*kodachi*), and a combination of both (*nitō*), along with grappling (*kumiuchi*). Mizuno taught his system at first under the name of Ishō Ryū 猪嘯流 (Wild Boar's Roar Tradition) but later changed the name to Mizuno Shinpō Ichiden Ryū 水野真法一伝流.

getsuin 月陰. See: *tsuki kage (2).*

gi 1. 義. CLASSICAL WARRIOR IDEAL—Moral obligation, honor, integrity, chivalry, devotion. In his *Shuyo Shosei Ron* (Treatise on the meaning of life), Yamada Jirōkichi, fifteenth headmaster of the Jiki Shinkage Ryū, referred to *gi* as one of the qualities a good swordsman must not forget. See: *bushi no konjō.*

~gi 2. 着. This ideogram can be used as both a prefix and a suffix indicating wearing apparel. However, as a prefix, it is pronounced "*ki*." For example, it is found as a prefix in the term *kimono* 着物. As a suffix[5] it is found in a number of terms referring to the upper portion (i.e., the jacket) of the training outfit worn by modern practitioners of martial arts and ways: ¶ *karategi* 空手着, a training jacket for *karate*. ¶ *jūdōgi* 柔道着, a training jacket for *jūdō*. ¶ *keikogi* 稽古着, a training jacket for use in martial training (*keiko*). ¶ *uwagi* 上着, the "upper" portion of a training outfit. ¶ *dōgi* 道着, apparel for training in (martial) ways. Most of these jackets used in martial training are blue, black, or white in color. Texture and thickness may vary depending on the rigors of the discipline. Outside Japan, the abbreviation "*gi*" is commonly used to refer to a training outfit, but Japanese practitioners do not use the word in this way.

Further reading in English:

- Lowry, 2006: 35–61.

gihō 技法. Technique.

gijutsu 技術. Technique.

Gikeiki 『義経記』【義經記】(The chronicle of Yoshitsune). This fifteenth-century war tale traces the rise and fall of Minamoto no Yoshitsune, half-brother of Minamoto no Yoritomo (the first permanent *shōgun*). Yoshitsune's generalship was a large factor in the victory of the Minamoto over the Taira in the Gempei war of 1180–1185. There are a number of similar texts on Yoshitsune—*Hōgan monogatari*, *Yoshitsune monogatari*, etc.—but, according to McCullough (1966: *v*), the content is largely the same.

Further reading in English:

- McCullough, 1966.

Gikei Ryū 義経流【義經流】. See: *Yoshitsune Ryū.*

giki 義気【義氣】. Chivalry, heroism.

gimu 義務. Duty, obligation.

gin 銀. See: *ginshō.*

ginshō 銀将【銀將】[Abbr. as ***gin*** 銀]. SHŌGI—Lit. "silver general." In the chess-like Japanese game of *shōgi*, the *ginshō* is somewhat like a bodyguard for the "jeweled king" (*gyokushō* 玉将).

girei 儀礼【儀禮】. Formal etiquette.

giri 義理. A sense of duty or obligation.

[4] Although Sabey (1973: 76) refers to these training sessions as "*jūdō*," Matsui (1991: 78) indicates that Jigō Tenshin Ryū *jūjutsu* 自剛天真流柔術 was taught at the Meidōkan.

[5] This character is only pronounced *gi* when in a compound as a suffix following a voiced prefix such as *keikogi* 稽古着or *uwagi* 上着.

~giri ～切り. Lit. "cutting." This compound form of the term *kiri* is used following a voiced syllable. When used as a suffix in a compound it indicates the type of cut; e.g., *kotegiri* literally means "wrist (*kote*) cutting (*giri*)." See: *kiri.*

gisen 擬戦【擬戰】. A sham battle; battle maneuvers. Synonym for *kidō enshū.*

gishi 義士. A loyal retainer.

gishiki 儀式. Ceremonies, rites.

gitō 儀刀. A ceremonial sword.

Giwadan 義和団【義和團】<Ch. Yihetuan. The revolutionary martial cult known as the "Boxers" that fomented the Chinese Boxer Rebellion of 1899–1901. See: *Giwaken.*

Giwadan no Ran 義和団の乱【義和團の亂】[A.k.a. ***Kempi (no) ran*** 拳匪乱【拳匪亂】<Ch. Quanfei Luan]. The Boxer Rebellion in China, which lasted from 1899 to 1901.

Further reading in English:

- Chesneaux, 1971: 115–125 *ff*; 1973: 51–52 *ff*.
- Davis, 1971: *passim*.
- Esherick, 1987.
- Purcell,1963.

Giwaken 義和拳 <Ch. Yihe quan [A.k.a., ***Giwamonken*** 義和門拳 <Ch. Yihemen quan]. Lit. "Righteous, Harmonious Fist." 1. The Boxers. 2. The fighting arts of the Boxers.

The origins of the terms Giwaken and Giwamonken are convoluted; they were used by various groups during several historical periods. This includes, but is not limited to, the school which is generally considered to be the origin of the combative fighting style of the Boxers, i.e., the "Plum Flower Boxing" (Ch. Meihua quan 梅花拳; Jp. Mekaken). It should further be noted that one of these groups, the Yihemen Quan-bang 義和門拳棒 (Righteous, Harmonious Boxing and Cudgel Society), was known for its use of stick and staff weaponry. The Yihemen Quan was descended from an eighteenth-century martial organization known as the Li Trigram sect. However, Esherick makes a convincing case for *not* associating the Yihe Quan (or Yihemen Quan) boxers of the mid-Qing with those who formulated the Boxer Rebellion of 1899–1901. The group associated with the Boxers was an organization which seems to have been active from the early 1800s in the Qingzhou area south of Tianjin. (Esherick, 1987: 336).

Sō Dōshin, founder of Nippon Shōrinji Kempō, claimed to have founded his Japanese fighting system based on his training in the Yihemen Quan in China in the 1930s and 1940s.

Further reading in English:

- Esherick, 1987, 153–154; 333–340 *ff.*

Giwamonken 義和門拳. See: *Giwaken.*

go 1. 後. Lit. "the rear," "the latter." SHINDŌ MŪSŌ RYŪ—The second technique (as opposed to the first) in a set of two; i.e., Ushirozue (*zen*) and Ushirozue (*go*). Contrast to *zen* 前.

go 2. 碁 [Abbr. of ***igo*** 囲碁【圍碁】]. A strategic board game often referred to as the national game of Japan. The term *igo* means "(the game of) surrounding/besieging (*i* 囲) game pieces (*go* 碁)." See also: *shōgi.*

go 3. 伍. TAIHŌ MILITARY SYSTEM—A five-man combat team established by the Taihō Codes (Taihō Ritsuryō) in 701 C.E. Two *go* formed a ten-man *ka* (squad), which was the basic military formation unit of the eighth-century provincial militia (*gundan*). A *go* was led by a *gochō*, the equivalent of a modern corporal. The modern equivalent of a *go* might be a "combat team." See: *gundan.*

goban 碁盤. The wooden board on which the game of *go* is played.

gobanshū 御番衆 Lit. "banner group" (also 五番衆, five-banner group). Personal bodyguard established by *shōgun* Ashikaga Yoshimitsu. Under the Ashikaga, this unit became more military and less ceremonial as time went by.

gōbuku 降伏. See: *gōbukuhō.*

gōbukuhō 降伏法. <Ch. *jiangfufa* <Skt. *abhicāraka* [A.k.a. **gōbukuro** 降伏爐; **chōbukuro** 調伏爐]. BUDDHISM—Essentially an exorcism by fire, the *gōbukuhō* is an aggressive form of fire ritual (*goma*). The aim of this fire rite is to subjugate enemies

and drive out demons, heretics, etc. The rite was sometimes used as a weapon: the Esoteric Buddhist Tendai and Shingon schools performed the *gōbukuhō* in hopes of driving the invading Mongols out of Japan in 1274 and 1281. It was also used against the Allied Seventh Fleet in 1945.

The *gōbukuhō* fire ritual was employed as a weapon in other cases, as well. For example, during Japan's medieval period a Buddhist priest named Monkan 文観 (1278–1357), a member of the heterodox Tachikawa sect of the Shingon school, burned ritual fires in order to attack Hōjō Takatoki, the last Kamakura *shikken* (first minister to the *shōgun*). Monkan, an ally of Emperor Go-Daigo,[6] had initiated the emperor into the Tachikawa sect. He supported Go-Daigo's attempt to regain control of the country and rid himself of the domination of the Kamakura shogunate, which had been run by the Hōjō family since the early thirteenth century. Unfortunately for Monkan, Go-Daigo's faction was defeated, and the emperor was exiled to Chiburi island. Monkan was exiled to Iōtō in 1331. However, Go-Daigo escaped his exile in 1333, joining his champions Ashikaga Takauji, who had just taken Kyōto; and Nitta Yoshisada, who had defeated Hōjō Takatoki in Kamakura. Go-Daigo again took the throne, and Monkan was returned to Kyōto with his position and titles restored; no further mention is made of the *gōbukuhō*. However, when Go-Daigo fled Kyōto in 1335, Monkan was again exiled, supposedly due to "his practice of 'heterodox (tantric) doctrine.'" The real reason, however, was most likely his political association with Go-Daigo and his use of esoteric rituals against Go-Daigo's enemies. (Hall, 1982: 21). See: *goma*.

gōbukuro 降伏爐 <Ch. *jiangfulu* [A.k.a. **chōbukuro** 調伏爐]. See: *gōbukuhō*.

gochō 伍長. TAIHŌ MILITARY SYSTEM—Leader of a five-man squad (*go* [3] 伍); somewhat equivalent to a modern corporal.

gochū (kyōiku) 郷中(教育). District youth organizations located in the Satsuma area of Kyūshū during the mid-1800s. The *gochū* taught Zhu Xi[7] (neo-Confucian) values, emphasizing honesty, self-reliance, and "manliness," to young samurai. A number of Satsuma samurai youth, including Ōkubo Toshimichi—one of the three great nobles who led the revolution against the Tokugawa shogunate in 1868—attended the *gochū* as young men.

gofu 護符. A wooden talisman. See: *ofuda*.

gogyō 五行 <Ch. *wuxing*. 1. DAOISM—The five elemental forces of Chinese Daoist cosmology: wood, fire, earth, metal, and water. The literal translation of *gogyō* is the "five movers," as these elements are seen as dynamic forces in contrast to static entities. In Daoist cosmology, they are seen to be derived from the interaction of positive and negative forces; e.g., *yin* and *yang* (Jp. *in-yō* or *on-yō*). The interaction of the *gogyō* is seen as the source of all other phenomena.

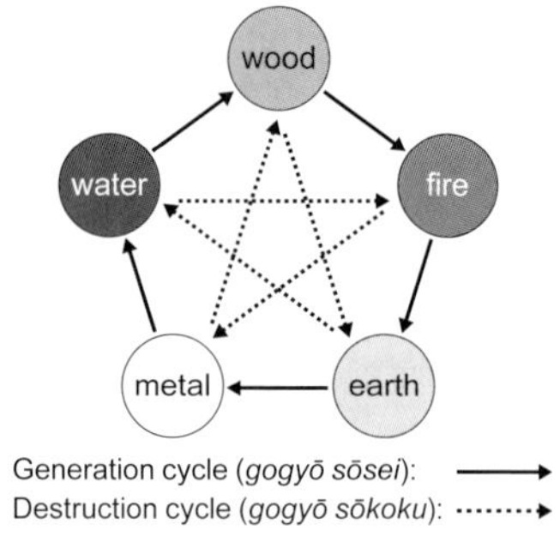

These five elemental movers interact in two ways: one is a cycle of generation (*gogyō sōsei* 五行相生); the other is a cycle of destruction (*gogyō sōkoku* 五行相剋). In the generation cycle, each element generates the next: wood generates fire, fire generates earth, earth generates metal, metal generates water, and water generates wood. In the destruction cycle, each element counters or destroys the next: wood breaks up earth, earth dams up water, water quenches fire, fire melts metal, and metal cuts wood.

As with various other symbols in Chinese Daoist cosmology, the *gogyō* have a variety

6 Go-Daigo Tennō 後醍醐天皇 (1288–1339; r. 1318–1339) was the ninety-sixth emperor of Japan.

7 Ch. Zhu Xi 朱熹 > Jp. Shuki.

Element	Wood	Fire	Earth	Metal	Water
Ideogram	木	火	地	金	水
Direction	East	South	Center	West	North
Color	Blue/Green	Red	Yellow	White	Black

of equivalencies:

There are many more. A detailed explanation of these phenomena is found in the *Huainan Zi* 『淮南子』 (Jp. *Enanji*), a Han-dynasty text from the second century B.C.E.

The use of Chinese symbolism such as *yin* and *yang* (*in-yō*) and the five elements is common in various Japanese classical martial traditions (*koryū*). *In* and *yō* are often used in combination with the *gogyō* to describe the tactical advantage or disadvantage of a combative engagement posture (*kamae*). The basic idea is that no element or equivalent posture (*kamae*) is ultimately superior; each has its advantages and disadvantages. This is illustrated in the diagram above showing the two types of interaction between the five. In the destruction cycle, wood overcomes earth, but wood can be overcome by metal, which in turn can be overcome by fire, which can be overcome by water, which can be overcome by earth. Some traditions interpret this as follows: If an opponent's posture (*kamae*)—e.g., *jōdan no kamae*, in which a sword is held overhead ready to strike—is equated to fire, it may be advantageous to take a water element posture such as *gedan no kamae*, in which a sword is held below the waist with the tip pointed down. The lower *gedan no kamae* (water) may be used to overcome the seemingly more powerful, higher *jōdan kamae* (fire).[8] 2. KATORI SHINTŌ RYŪ—An abbreviation for Gogyō no Tachi. See also: *Gogyō no Tachi; gorin; Gorin no sho; gorin no tō; Enanji.*

Gogyō no Bō 五行之棒. KATORI SHINTŌ RYŪ—Second set of long hardwood staff forms taught in the Tenshinshō-den Katori Shintō Ryū 天真正伝香取神道流. There are six forms (*kata*) included in this set.

Gogyō no Shuriken 五行之手裏剣. KATORI SHINTŌ RYŪ—Second set of combative throwing blade/dart forms taught in the Tenshinshō-den Katori Shintō Ryū 天真正伝香取神道流. There are eight forms (*kata*) included in this set.

Gogyō no Tachi 五行之太刀. KATORI SHINTŌ RYŪ—Second set of sword forms (*kenjutsu kata*) traditionally taught in the Tenshinshō-den Katori Shintō Ryū 天真正伝香取神道流. The inner meaning of these forms, which are taught in the context of unarmored *kenjutsu*, is given in an oral explanation relating them to the Chinese Daoist five elemental movers (*gogyō*). There are five forms (*kata*) included in this set. See also: *gogyō; Tenshinshō-den Katori Shintō Ryū.*

gogyō sōkoku 五行相剋. "Destruction cycle" of the Daoist five elemental movers. See: *gogyō.*

gogyō sōsei 五行相生 [also read ***gogyō sōshō***]. "Creation cycle" of the Daoist five elemental movers. See: *gogyō.*

Gōhaku Ryū 剛泊流 [A.k.a. Gōhakukai Karatedō 剛泊会空手道]. OKINAWAN KARATE—A derivative of both Gōjū Ryū (Naha *te*) and Tomari *te*, this *karate* tradition was developed by Fukuji Seikō. It was, however, given its name and current form by second headmaster Tokashiki Iken in 1982.

The basic Gōhaku Ryū *kata* tend to be typical of most *gōjū* systems:

Basic forms (Kihon kata 基本型):

- Sanchin 三戦
- Saifā 砕破
- Sēpai 十八手
- Tenshō 転掌
- Naihanchi (Shodan–Sandan) 内歩進(初段～三段)

Additional *kata* are derived from Tomari *te* systems:

- Wankan 王冠
- Wansū 汪輯 (Dai 大 and Shō 小)
- Rōhai 鷺碑
- Passai 抜塞

[8] Excerpted from Hall, (1979b): 4–5.

gohei 御幣. Zigzag paper strips used in Shintō shrines; also, a sacred staff with zigzag paper attached. Early *gohei*, which represented offerings to the *kami*, were originally made of flax yarn. However, around the ninth century the yarn began to be replaced by paper dyed in five colors and shaped in a zigzag form, probably representing lightning. This was evidently due to influence from Buddhism.[9] As these strips are also hung on hemp rope to designate a sanctified area—such as that used for a martial exhibition—the relationship to the thunderbolt circles of *vajra* (*kongō*) protecting various mandala seems clear. Over time, the use of white strips became preferred; these are used today. See also: *shimenawa.*

gōhō 業報. The effects of *karma.*

Gohon no Midare 五本の乱. SHINDŌ MŪSŌ RYŪ—The sixth series of Shindō Mūsō Ryū *waza*. This set, consisting of five *kata*, was created by Shimizu Takaji Sensei in the twentieth century.

Gohōten 護方天 [A.k.a. ***Goseten*** 護世天; ***Jūniten*** 十二天]. Lit. the "Direction-Protecting Devas." These deities are found in groups of four, eight, and twelve. Their images sometimes appear in martial scrolls (*densho*) or on military accoutrements as talismans. See: *Jūniten.*

go ishi 碁石. *Go* stones; playing pieces for the game of *go.*

gōjū 剛柔. Lit. "force-yield" or "hard-soft." *Gōjū* is an important concept in a number of *jūjutsu* and *karate* systems. See: *gōjū no ri.*

Gōjūkai 剛柔会. JAPANESE KARATE—Gōjū Ryū *karate* organization founded by Yamaguchi Gōgen in 1950.

Gōjū no Kata 剛柔の形. See: *Gō no Kata.*

gōjū no ri 剛柔の理. HOPLOLOGY—As a combative trait, *gōjū no ri* is the capability to discern the correct time and situation in which to apply force or yield to force in order to gain advantage in a combative encounter. The force/yield trait is described by Hayes (1984a: 10) as the seventh of the eight innate combative adaptive traits. See also: *bu no ri.*

Further reading in English:

• Hayes, 1992: 27–29.

Gōjū Ryū 剛柔流. OKINAWAN KARATE—The term *gōjū* 剛柔 can be translated as "hard-soft" or "force-yield" and refers both to the technical and psychological nature of this widespread *karate* tradition. Named by its founder, Miyagi Chōjun, in 1937,[10] Gōjū Ryū finds its antecedents in the Shōrei Ryū/Naha *te* system of Higaonna Kanryō and the Chinese combative systems (Ch. *wushu* 武術) he studied in Fuzhou.

During the mid to late 1800s, a thriving trade developed between the Okinawan city of Naha and the Chinese maritime city of Fuzhou. Consequently, a number of Okinawans had the opportunity to learn Chinese combatives both in Naha and on the Chinese mainland. One of those young men, Higaonna Kanryō, journeyed to China, perhaps more than once, between the years of 1867 and 1882. The dates of his actual visit(s) are uncertain, as are the names of his teachers.[11] However, he apparently devoted a number of years to training in the southern Shaolin systems of the Fuzhou area. One current Gōjū Ryū teacher, Miyazato Eiichi, has confidently claimed that Higaonna trained with a Chinese combative arts master called Rū-rū Kō[12] and his colleague Wai Shinzan[13] (Bishop, 1999: 25).[14]

Upon his return to Okinawa, Higaonna found it difficult to establish himself. He persisted, however, and around 1890 named his

[9] Both the Buddhist mandala, in which the sacred inner area is surrounded by thunderbolts (*vajra*), and the five-tiered stupa (*gorin no tō*) use the same five colors indicating direction.

[10] Some sources give this date as 1928.

[11] Research by McCarthy (2008: 72) specifies March 1873 as the year Higaonna departed for Fuzhou and 1882 as the year of his return to Okinawa. McCarthy also specifies 1877 as the year Hiagonna began training with Rū-rū Kō. See also McCarthy (2008: 92, note 11).

[12] See entry on Rū-rū Kō 如如哥.

[13] Ch. Huai Zhenshan 淮振山.

[14] Karate master Nagamine Takayoshi notes that Higaonna also learned Chinese combative arts (*xingyi quan* 形意拳) from Wan (Bishop, 1999: 25).

system Shōrei Ryū 昭霊流 (Bright Spirit Tradition).[15] This came to be known locally as Naha *te* 那覇手, a term used to distinguish it from the *karate* of the towns of Shuri and Tomari.

The real developer of the Gōjū system, however, was Miyagi Chōjun. In 1902, at the age of fourteen, Miyagi began studying with Higaonna. In 1915 he and a friend named Nakamoto Eishō traveled to Fuzhou in order to study with Higaonna's teacher, Rū-rū Kō. Although the venerable master was unavailable,[16] it is thought that they were able to locate the mountain temple where Rū-rū Kō had taught Higaonna in the 1870s. They also purchased a secret document on White Crane boxing[17] called the *Bubishi*.[18] They returned to Okinawa that year. In 1917 Miyagi again journeyed to Fuzhou, this time with a Chinese colleague named Go Kenki, in order to further research some of the details of the *Bubishi* and its White Crane combative arts. (Higaonna, *et al*, 2008: 531). Go Kenki, who became a specialist in Shaolin White Crane combative arts, had great influence on Miyagi's *karate*.[19]

Miyagi introduced Gōjū Ryū *karate* to Japan via the Kyōto Imperial University Club in 1928. He brought it to Hawaii in 1934, registering the term Gōjū Ryū Karate 剛柔流唐手 with the Nippon Butokukai Hombu in Japan that same year. (Higaonna, *et al*, 2008: 532). In Japan, Gōjū Ryū was later promoted by Yamaguchi Gōgen, a student of Miyagi.

Miyagi established twelve *kata* as the basis for his Gōjū Ryū. These remain the core of the school today:

Closed-hand forms (*heite* 閉手):

- Sanchin 三戦
- Tenshō 転掌

Open-hand forms (*hirakite* 開手):

- Gekisai Daiichi (I) 撃砕第一
- Gekisai Daini (II) 撃砕第二
- Saifā 砕破
- Seiyunchin 制引戦
- Shisōchin 四向戦
- Sanserū 三十六手
- Sēpai 十八手
- Kururunfā 久留頓破
- Sēsan 十三
- Sūpārinpē 壱百零八手

Some branch traditions have added other *kata*. See also: *Gōjū karatedō; Shitō Ryū; Shōtōkan.*

Further reading in English:

- Bishop, 1999: 24–38.

Gokaden 五箇傳. The "Five Traditions" of Japanese sword-making. The schools are named after the geographical areas in which they flourished: Bizen *den* 備前伝, Yamato *den* 大和伝, Yamashiro *den* 山城伝, Sōshū *den* 相模伝, and Seki *den* 関伝 (Mino *den* 美濃伝).

Further readings in English:

- Nakagama, 1998: 116–123.
- Robinson, 1971: 43–44.

gokai 五戒. BUDDHISM—The "five precepts" for laymen and -women:

1. *fusesshō* 不殺生 Not to kill
2. *fuchūtō* 不偸盗 Not to steal
3. *fujain* 不邪淫 Not to commit adultery
4. *fumōgo* 不妄語 Not to tell lies
5. *fuonju* 不飲酒 Not to drink intoxicants

Gokajō 五箇條. See: *Yagyū Seigō Ryū.*

gokan 五間. The five types of secret agents (*shinobi no mono; ninja*) mentioned in Sun Tzu's *Art of War* (*Sonshi no heihō*). See: *kanja; Sonshi no heihō; ninjutsu.*

gōkan 郷間 <Ch. *xiangjian*. The first of the five types of secret agents (*shinobi no mono; ninja*) mentioned in Sun Tzu's *Art of War* (*Sonshi no heihō*). The term *gōkan* refers to native agents who are spies employed from the local population. See: *kanja; kyōdan (1); ninjutsu; Sonshi no heihō.*

---

15 According to Miyagi Chōjun, this system, although not by the same name, may have been brought to Naha as early as the 1820s. (McCarthy, 2008: 73)

16 Bishop (1999: 27) speculates, probably accurately, that the school had disappeared due to the chaos caused by the Boxer Rebellion of 1899–1901.

17 Jp. *hakkakuken* or *hakutsuruken* 白鶴拳 <Ch. *bai hao quan*.

18 This document is one of several similar texts that came to be known as the *Okinawaden bubishi* 『沖縄伝武備志』.

19 Matayoshi Shinpo, late headmaster of Matayoshi Kobudō, also began training in White Crane boxing with Go in 1935. (Bishop, 1999: 127).

G

goken 護拳. Isshin Ryū—Iron hand-guard for the Isshin Ryū *kusarigama*.

gokenin 御家人. Lit. "housemen." During the Minamoto and Ashikaga shogunates, this term referred to high-ranking direct vassals of the *shōgun*. This included vassals of the rank of *shugo* (heads of provinces) and *jitō* (estate stewards). Contrast to *higokenin*.

Under the Tokugawa, the *gokenin* were ranked below the elite *hatamoto*. They received small stipends of 100 *koku* or less, did not have the right of audience with the *shōgun*, and were only eligible for low-ranking posts. There were about 20,000 *gokenin* in 1800. See also: *kenin*.

Go Kenki 呉賢貴 <Ch. Wu Xiangui (1886–1940). Okinawan Karate—Go Kenki was a Chinese national who became a naturalized Japanese citizen in the early part of the twentieth century. Some researchers believe that he strongly influenced Miyagi Chōjun's development of Gōjū Ryū *karatedō*. See also: *Gōjū Ryū*.

gōketsu 豪傑. 1. Medieval term for a warrior mogul. 2. A hero or great warrior.

goko 五鈷. See: *gokosho*.

gokosho 五鈷杵. A five-pointed Buddhist *vajra* scepter. The *gokosho*, or simply *goko*, is a ritual instrument around 5 to 8 inches (12–25 cm) long, generally made of brass. It is used in various rituals performed by the Esoteric Buddhist Tendai and Shingon sects and Shugendō practitioners.

The *gokosho* is sometimes found as a talismanic engraving on sword blades and various other weapons. In addition, it occasionally forms the hilt of a sword in Buddhist paintings and statues. However, this is much less common than the three-pointed sword hilt (*sankotsuka-ken*). Some versions of the *gokosho* are made with the five points turned outward instead of inward, making it a more formidable weapon. For illustration, see: kongōsho. See also: tokkosho; sankosho.

gokuhi 極秘. Lit. "most secret," "top secret." Special techniques, principles, and/or interpretations of martial subjects which are taught by master teachers to their closest or most gifted students. Variant terms may be used in different traditions: *gokui* (mystery, most important concepts and principles), *hiden* (secret transmission), *hiden gokui* (secret transmission of the most important concepts and principles), *hijutsu* (hidden or secret techniques), *hihō* (hidden or secret methods), *okugi* (mystery, secret, hidden), etc.

gokui 極意. Lit. "most meaningful," "most significant," or "mystery." 1. The mysteries or secrets (in the sense of the innermost knowledge) of an intuitive art. 2. Yagyū Seigō Ryū—The seventh series of *battō waza* in the Yagyū Seigō Ryū. 3. Shindō Musō Ryū—See: *Go Musō no Jō*.

Gokuiden 「極意伝」【極意傳】(Transmission of Secrets). Jiki Shinkage Ryū—The fifth *densho* (teaching license) in the Jiki Shinkage Ryū.

Gokui no Iai 極意之居合. Katori Shintō Ryū—Third set of combative quick-draw swordsmanship forms taught in the Tenshinshō-den Katori Shintō Ryū 天真正伝香取神道流. There are five forms (*kata*) included in this set.

Gokui no Kodachi 極意之小太刀. Katori Shintō Ryū—Fourth set of *kenjutsu kata* traditionally taught in the Tenshinshō-den Katori Shintō Ryū. In these forms, the Katori proponent (*shidachi*) uses a short sword (*kodachi*) against an opponent armed with a longsword (*katana*). There are three forms (*kata*) included in this set.

Gokui Shichijo no Naginata 極意七条之長刀. Katori Shintō Ryū—Second set of *naginatajutsu kata* traditionally taught in the Tenshinshō-den Katori Shintō Ryū. There are three forms (*kata*) included in this set.

Gokui no Shuriken 極意之手裏剣. Katori Shintō Ryū—Third set of forms using combative throwing blades or darts taught in the Tenshinshō-den Katori Shintō Ryū 天真正伝香取神道流. There are nine forms (*kata*) included in this set.

goma 護摩 <Ch. *humo* <Skt. *homa*. 1. Buddhism—The *goma* is a fire ritual adapted

from Brahmanism by the tantric (esoteric) Buddhists of India. It was transported along with later Buddhism to China and then Japan. Basically, the fire in Buddhism represents wisdom which burns away karmic defilements as well as the effects of demons and other evil entities. The *goma* is one of four basic exoteric/tantric rituals that must be mastered by members of the Tendai and Shingon schools of Japanese Buddhism.

The *goma* consists of three main elements: the deity (a buddha or other pure and powerful entity from the Buddhist pantheon which is visualized in the fire); the hearth or fire-pot located in the center of a mandala (*mandara*); and the worshipper (the priest performing the fire ritual). In the ritual matrix there are actually two *goma* being performed: an external ritual (*gegoma* 外護摩) in which evil influences in the physical world are swept away by the ritual performed with the fire if the empowered practitioner's body-speech-mind are pure; and an internal ritual (*naigoma* 内護摩) in which the practitioner's body-speech-mind merges with the plane of awakening.

KŌCHŌRO GOMA
Goma dedicated to the warrior goddess Marishiten at Tairinji in Oyama, Japan, 1988
(Photograph by author; previously published in Hall, 1990)

In addition to these two aspects of the *goma*, several types of fire rituals were developed within East Asian esoteric Buddhism, including *sokusairo* 息災爐 (calamity-stopping fire); *zōyakuro* 増益爐 (merit-increasing fire); *keiairo* 敬愛爐 (pacification by bewitchment fire); *gōbukuro* 降伏爐 (subjugation of enemies and demons fire); and *kōchōro* 鉤召爐 (summoning fire). 2. SHUGENDŌ—The aim of the *goma* practice among the *yamabushi* (in the past as now) is to develop spiritual power for performing exorcism and healing and to achieve heightened states of consciousness. See also: *gōbukuhō.*

Further reading in English:

- Strickmann, 1981; 1983.

Goma shiki 『護摩私記』. BUDDHISM—A text containing directions for performing the esoteric fire ritual (*goma*). Composed in Japan, the *Goma shiki* was originally derived from ritual instructions included in various Buddhist texts (*o-kyō*) and associated Chinese manuals. Several variations of this text may be found in both the Tendai and Shingon schools. See: *goma; Jūhachidō shiki; Kongōchō-kyō; Kongōkai shiki; Shido kegyō; Taizōkai shiki.*

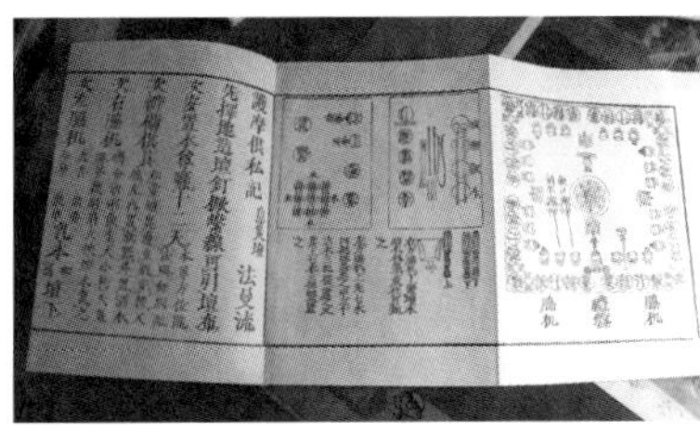

GOMA SHIKI
Detail from text used to perform *goma* rituals
(Private collection)

Gomeiken 五名剣【五名劍】. The five most famous Japanese swords. These include:

1. Onimaru Kunitsuna
鬼丸国綱【鬼丸國綱】
2. Ōdenta Mitsuya (Ōdentai Mitsuyo)
大典太光世
3. Dōjigiri Yasutsuna
童子切安綱
4. Mikazuki Munechika
三日月宗近
5. Juzumaru Tsunetsugu
数珠丸恒次【數珠丸恆次】

Gomokuroku 「後目録」. Lit. "Latter list." SHINDŌ MŪSŌ RYŪ—Third teaching license (*densho*) given in the Shindō Mūsō Ryū. See: *Shindō Musō Ryū Gomokuroku.*

Go Musō no Jō 五夢想の杖 [A.k.a. ***Hiden Gokui*** 秘伝極意【秘傳極意】]. SHINDŌ MŪSŌ RYŪ—Lit. the "five revealed staff techniques" or "five oracular staff techniques." This is the eighth set of techniques taught in Shindō Musō Ryū; it consists of five combative forms (*kata*).

These five *kata* were supposedly transmitted to Musō Gonnosuke during his *musō* (spiritual revelation) and are considered the seminal techniques of the *ryū*. Their distribution is restricted to members of Shindō Musō Ryū who attain the status of *menkyo* or *menkyo kaiden*; that is, the inheritors or successors of the *ryū*. These five *kata* are known today as:

1. Yamiuchi 闇打
2. Yumemakura 夢枕
3. Murakumo 村雲
4. Inazuma 稲妻
5. Dōbo 導母

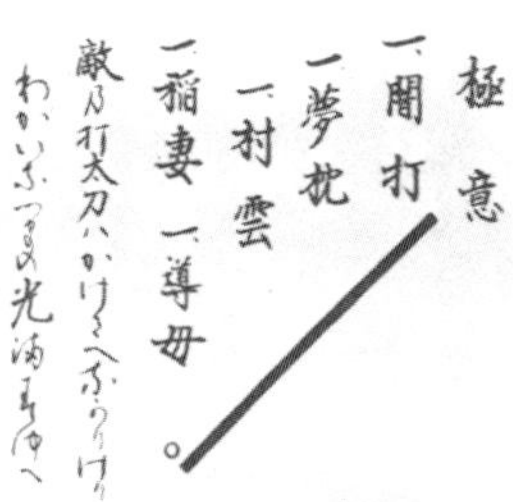

SHINDŌ MUSŌ RYŪ *GOKUI* DATED 1972
Shindō Musō Ryū *menkyō* showing five *kata* in a contemporary *densho*
(Kaminoda and Nakajima, ©1976, with permission)

According to Shindō Musō Ryū oral tradition, Gonnosuke may not have had formal names for the *gokui kata*, but he had certainly created these forms, along with fifteen or sixteen additional functional techniques, by the time of his arrival in Fukuoka in 1607. Kuroda Ichitaro (Shindō Musō Ryū *menkyo kaiden* under Shimizu Takaji) assumed the five *gokui kata* were named around that time. The late Kuroda's archives included an early transmission document (*densho*) passed from Okubi Magozaemon (second headmaster of Shindō Musō Ryū) to Matsuzaki Kin'emon (third headmaster of the school and founder of Ikkaku Ryū). That document includes the names of all five *gokui*.[20]

[20] Special thanks to Steve Bellamy for providing information on Shindō Musō Ryū oral tradition derived from Kuroda Ichitarō.

gongen 権現【權現】. A Ryōbu Shintō term often used to identify Shintō *kami* (deities and personages) as a temporary manifestation of a buddha; e.g., the term "Udo Daigongen" identifies a native Japanese deity enshrined in Kyūshū as a temporary Shintō manifestation of a Buddhist deity. Tōshō Daigongen, meanwhile, is a posthumous title used in reference to Tokugawa Ieyasu. Images or names of various Daigongen were sometimes used as talismans on weapons or accoutrements. See also: *Atagosan Daigongen*.

Gō no Kata 剛の形. KŌDŌKAN JŪDŌ—Lit. "forms of strength" or "forms of force"—in contrast to forms of flexibility (Jū no Kata). These *kata* were originally referred to as "forms of strength and flexibility" (Gōjū no Kata 剛柔の形). These ten forms, developed in 1887 from antecedent *jūjutsu kata*, were evidently dropped from Kanō's syllabus, and for many decades were not taught as part of Kōdōkan Jūdō. However, it now appears that the Gō no Kata may be seeing a revival, as they were demonstrated at the Kōdōkan for the first time in over half a century in 1998.

Further reading in English:

- Cundy, 1999.
- Ohlenkamp, 2006.

go no saki 後の先. One of three categories of initiative (*sen*) recognized in modern Japanese police tactics (*taihōjutsu*). *Go no saki* is akin to the older concept of *go no sen*; that is, an arresting officer is able to receive an assailant's surprise attack and still be able to counter it. In *taihōjutsu* this is considered the third level of three types of initiative (*sen*). The other two are *saki* and *sensen no saki*. See also: *bu no ri; go no sen; saki; sen; sen no sen; sensen no saki; sensen no sen.*

go no sen 後の先 [Var. ***machi no sen*** 待の先]. Response action (indicating the seizing of initiative and launching a counterattack at the moment of an opponent's attack); luring/forcing an enemy (*teki*) into an attack so that a counterattack may be used; counterattack initiative. See also: *bu no ri; go no saki; go no sen; saki; sen; sen no sen; sensen no saki; sensen no sen.*

gonyū 悟入. 1. BUDDHISM—To become enlightened or awakened in the Buddhist sense. 2. MARTIAL ARTS—To realize, or awaken to a realization of, the deepest mysteries of a martial school; to intuit the innermost secrets of a martial system. This state is considered similar to a Buddhist awakening experience or the vision of a Shintō oracle (*musō*).

gorin 五輪 <Ch. *wulun* <Skt. *pañcacakra*. Lit. the "five circles." BUDDHISM—1. The five yogic chakras (Skt. *cakras*) corresponding to the root, navel, heart, throat, and crown. 2. The five great elements, which correspond to those making up the stupa in esoteric Buddhism: Earth, Water, Fire, Wind, and *Śūnyatā*. 3. An abbreviation for the *gorin no tō*, or five-tiered stupa. 4. The five fingers of the Buddha. 5. The five extensions of the human body: both arms, both legs, and the head.

Gorin no sho 『五輪書』. Normally translated as the *Book of Five Rings*, this work might be more accurately called the *Book of the Five Elements*. This is a text—actually a set of five transmission scrolls (*densho*)—concerned with the underlying principles and applications of martial strategy (*heihō*) as defined by Miyamoto Musashi. Although attributed to Musashi—in which case it was probably completed around 1643—its authorship is in doubt. It may have been composed by Musashi's disciples.

Each of the five scrolls has a title corresponding to one of the five Buddhist elements.

Scroll	Title	Translation
5	*Kū* 空	*Śūnyatā*
4	*Fū* 風	Wind (Air)
3	*Ka* 火	Fire
2	*Sui* 水	Water
1	*Chi* 地	Earth

In keeping with the methodology of the stupa of Esoteric Buddhism (see *gorin no tō*) or mandala, each chapter of Musashi's *Book of Five Elements* presents strategic concepts which are progressively more subtle than those in the previous chapter. This work is considered a classic among martial arts texts.

gorin no tō 五輪塔. The five-tiered stupa of Esoteric (Tantric) Buddhism, which is a graphic representation of a variety of concepts: the five elements of existence, the human body, the five *cakras*, etc.

GORIN NO TŌ
Detail from Seigō Ryū *densho* dated 1801
(From the collection of Mutō Masao)

In contrast to the five elemental movers (*gogyō*) of Daoism—earth, metal, water, air, wood—the Esoteric Buddhist five elements represent the Indo-European concept of the elements of physical existence (earth, water, fire, air, and aether) but replace the fifth element with *śūnyatā*, a concept particular to Mahāyāna Buddhism. *Śūnyatā* is a philosophical concept referring to the non-substantiality of all phenomena. Moving from bottom to top in this simple, five-tiered matrix, the nature of each element appears more subtle than the previous. As this five-element matrix symbolizes human existence and its underpinning in *śūnyatā*, the five-tiered esoteric stupa can also represent the human body and five of the yogic *cakras*.

Jp. word	Character	Element	Chakra
5. *Kū*	空	*Śūnyatā*	Crown
4. *Fū*	風	Wind (Air)	Throat
3. *Ka*	火	Fire	Heart
2. *Sui*	水	Water	Navel
1. *Chi*	地	Earth	Root

Many classical martial systems (*bujutsu ryū*) elaborate on these basic associations in order to pass on subtle concepts in their curriculum.

gorin sotoba 五輪卒塔婆 [Var. 五輪率都婆] <Ch. *wulun shuaidupo* <Skt. *pañcacakra-stūpa.* A tombstone made in the shape of the *gorin no tō* of Esoteric Buddhism.

Gosannen no Eki 後三年役. The Later Three-Years' War (1086–1089) chronicled in the *Ōshū gosannen ki*. The conflict is sometimes called "Yoshiie's War" because its star general, Minamoto no Yoshiie, never received the sanction of the imperial court for his actions, even though he defeated the rebel forces.

Goseibai shikimoku 『御成敗式目』 [Also called the ***Jōei shikomoku*** 『貞永式目』 (Feudal law code of the Jōei era)]. Title of the Jōei Code of 1232. Called the "Jōei Formulary" by Jeffrey Mass, an authority on Japanese history, this feudal law code became the model for Japanese military law in later centuries.

Further reading in English:
- Mass, 1979: 103–110 *ff.*

Goseten 護世天. See: *Gohōten.*

Goshi 『呉子』 <Ch. *Wuzi*. One of the seven Chinese classics on military strategy. See: *Buryaku shichi sho.*

gōshi 郷士. A *samurai* who held and maintained or administered farmland; a "landed" *bushi*.

goshimbō 護身法. See: *goshimhō.*

goshin 護身. System of self-defense. *Goshin* is a modern term used by Senmoto Akiteru and Watanabe Akiteru for the combative discipline they used to form the core of Uchūdō 宇宙道. Senmoto and Watanabe were both direct disciples of Okuyama Yoshiji, the founder of Hakkō Ryū 八光流.

goshinjutsu 護身術. A modern term usually used to refer to grappling systems focused on civilian self-defense, in contrast to battlefield grappling systems such as *kumiuchi.*

goshinhō 護身法 [often pronounced ***goshinbō***]. Lit. "body protection method" or "self-defense method." BUDDHISM—A Buddhist ritual series of mudra (*in* [2]) and mantra (*shingon*) aimed at spiritually protecting the practitioner from evil influences and attacks. This ritual is performed at the beginning of many East Asian tantric rituals, and is often found used in combination with the performance of the Kujihō.

goshin rentan 護身練胆. Lit. "development of a self-defense capability." This is one of the primary aims espoused by practitioners of Nippon Shōrinji Kempō.

go-shintai 御神体【御神體】[A.k.a. ***shintai*** 神体]. SHINTŌ—An object of worship within a Shintō shrine. The spirit of the enshrined deity (*kami*) is thought to inhabit the object. Also called *mitama shiro*.

Goshin'yō no te 「御信用之手」 [Abbr. for ***Daitō Ryū Goshin'yō no te*** 「大東流御信用之手」]. DAITŌ RYŪ—The fifth of several transmission scrolls (*densho*) awarded in the Daitō Ryū tradition. Earning it requires mastery of eighty-four self-defense techniques categorized by attack to the upper, middle, and lower levels (*jō-chū-ge* 上中下).

gōso 強訴 [Var. 嗷訴]. Lit. "strong petition"; var. "noisy petition." *Gōso* were incidents in which thousands of warrior monks (*sōhei*) of some of the large Buddhist temples would march into Kyōto to forcefully petition the imperial court by threatening violence. These incidents were generally limited to Japan's medieval period, (1185–1558). However, research by Adolphson (2007) points out that the actual identity of the so-called "*sōhei*" participating in the *gōso* is unclear. They may not even have been ordained monks, or, if armed, perhaps were hired warriors supporting a particular temple. Adolphson goes on to note that many of the *gōso* may have been more peaceful than depicted by later accounts. See also: *sōhei.*

Further reading in English:
- Adolphson, 2007.
- McMullin, 1985.

gosō nawa 護送縄 [A.k.a. ***inchi nawa*** 引致縄]. Lit. "escort rope." This alternate term for *inchi nawa* refers to a set of police tying-cord techniques (*hojōjutsu*) in which the aggressor is bound up for escort or transport.

Goten 五天. A variation of the Goten no Shidai

used by the Kōgen Ittō Ryū 甲源一刀流. See: *Goten no Shidai.*

gotende 御殿手 <Oki. *udundī.* See: *Motobu Udundī.*

gotenjutsu 御殿術. See: *Motobu Udundī.*

Goten no Shidai 五点之次第【五點之次第】[A.k.a. ***Goten*** 五天]. ITTŌ RYŪ (1)—A set of five special, sure-win techniques (*kata*) found within the most privileged, secret transmission (Kōjō Gokui 高上極意) of the Ittō Ryū (1). These *kata* are listed in the *Ittō Ryū heihō shidai*[21] as follows:

1. Myō Ken 妙剣
2. Zetsumyō Ken 絶妙剣
3. Makoto no Ken (Shin Ken) 真剣
4. Kinshichōō Ken 金翅鳥王剣
5. Dokumyō Ken 独妙剣

Sasamori (1986: 503–528), who lists these techniques under the title of "Shin no Goten 真之五点," presents several interpretations of all five *kata* in detail. However, little is written about them in English, the one exception being Tokitsu (2004:72), who translates a small portion of Sasamori's text. See also: *Ittō Ryū (1), Kinshichōō Ken; Ono Ha Ittō Ryū.*

gōtō 強盗. 1. Burglar, robber. 2. A Warring States–period term for brigands. See also: *suppa.*

Gotō Tamauemon Tadayoshi 後藤 玉右衛門 忠栄【後藤玉右衛門忠榮】(1644–1736). Retainer of Aizu Han who founded the Daidō Ryū 大道流. A master swordsman, Gotō studied and trained widely, combining the secret teachings of nine *ryū* to found the Daidō Ryū.

Goyō 御用. Lit. "official business." The exclamation "*Goyō!*" was shouted by Edo-period law enforcement officers to move pedestrians and vehicles out of the way. The ideograms were often painted on flags and lanterns used by the police of that era when carrying out a raid. The use of the lantern and exclamation was somewhat equivalent to modern-day police using lights and sirens.

gozan 五山 [Also read *gosan*]. The five Rinzai Zen temples of Kamakura which flourished during Japan's middle ages. In addition to being popular centers of Buddhist learning among the Kamakura-period warrior class, the *gozan* were also active as part of a state bureaucracy used for political and administrative purposes by the Ashikaga shogunate.[22]

The five Kamakura temples were Kenchōji 建長寺, Enkakuji (Engakuji) 円覚寺, Jufukuji 寿福寺, Jōchiji 浄智寺, and Jōmyōji 浄妙寺. These five temples were central in the development of "warrior Zen" (*nyūdō* Zen), sometimes referred to as "Kamakura Zen" by scholars. During the Kamakura period, several Buddhist monks who were central in the development of warrior Zen taught at these temples, including Eisai at Jufukuji, Daikaku at Kenchōji, and Bukkō at Enkakuji. See: *Kamakura Zen; kōan.*

Further reading in English:

• Collcutt, 1981.

gōzoku 豪族. A Muromachi-period term for a powerful locally based warrior clan.

gūji 宮司. A chief priest at a Shintō shrine.

gumba 軍馬 [Also read ***gunba***]. 1. A war horse. 2. A term used for the combative horsemanship of the Ichizen Ryū 一全流. See also: *bajutsu.*

gumbai 軍配 [Var. 軍敗; also read ***gunbai***; variant/archaic romanization: ***gumbei***]. The ideograms 軍配 mean "allocation of armies," while the variant characters 軍敗 mean "defeating armies." 1. The use of astrology, divination techniques, and geomancy (*fūsui*) for deciding the selection of direction, date, and hour of battle. 2. Although it may be considered a division of strategy, *gumbai* is sometimes used as a synonym for *heihō* 兵法 and related terms. 3. Abbreviation used for *gumbai heihō*, *gumbai uchiwa*, etc.

gumbai heihō 軍配兵法 [Also read ***gunbai***

[21] An example of this *densho*, dated 1689, was published in Imamura, 1966, vol. 2: 45–50. A variation on the list, called the Goten, was used by the Kōgen Ittō Ryū branch tradition; an illustration of this can be found in the entry on *densho* in this *Encyclopedia.*

[22] This policy was based on an earlier Chinese model.

heihō]. Martial/military divination. 1. During the Kamakura and Muromachi periods, the military science of the Japanese warrior clans centered on a smattering of ancient Chinese military strategies and a large portion of Tantric Buddhist, Daoist, and Shugendō esoterica. By the mid to late Muromachi period, these practices came to be called *gumbai heihō.* Many of them find their origins in a text called the *Genke kin'etsushū.* 2. Synonym for *heihō* 兵法 and related terms.

gumbaisha 軍配者 [Also read ***gunbaisha***]. A practitioner of battlefield divination (*gumbai heihō*).

gumbai uchiwa 軍配団扇 【軍配團扇】[Also read ***gunbai uchiwa***]. 1. A war fan on which was inscribed a *gumbai* divination chart. These charts, which vary in content, were used for divining the date and time of battle. They usually featured diagrams in which the Sanskrit letter *vaṁ* (Jp. *ban*)[23] was surrounded by a circle of stars. The numbers vary, but the stars are usually found in specific groupings that represent, for example, the "twelve branches" (*jūnishi*—the twelve Chinese characters used in the cyclic computation of time); the "twenty-eight constellations" (*nijūhasshuku*) of the Chinese zodiac; the

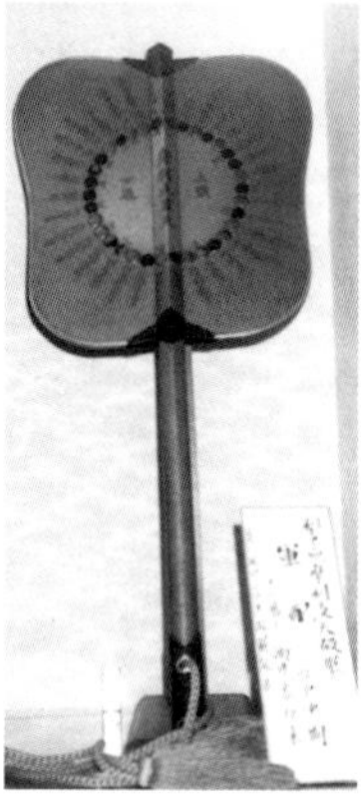

GUMBAI UCHIWA
The circle of moons surrounds the name of the goddess Marishiten
(Fan located at the Kyōto Arashiyama Museum)

[23] The Sanskrit letter *vaṁ* (*ban*) represents the central buddha, Dainichi Nyorai, in the Diamond Matrix Mandala (Kongōkai).

seven stars of the Big Dipper, etc. According to Ōtake (2007: 274–275), the Katori Shintō Ryū version of this diagram is referred to as the "army-destroying stars" (*hagunsei*). A *gumbai uchiwa* would enable a commander or trusted retainer who knew the divining process to determine the proper date, time, and direction of battle. Many of these fans are also adorned with references to Marishiten and/or other important warrior deities. See: Appendix 1. 2. SUMŌ—The *gumbai uchiwa* also plays a prominent role in *sumō*, where it has been traditionally used by referees (*gyōji*) to signal instructions to wrestlers (*sumotori*).

Further reading in English:

- Ōtake, 2007: 267–275.

gumbei 軍配. Archaic romanization of *gumbai*.

Gumbō-ryō 『軍防令』 [Also read ***gunbō-ryō***]. TAIHŌ MILITARY SYSTEM—A section of the Taihō Code (Taihō Ritsuryō) which the Japanese borrowed from the Chinese in the early eighth century. The *Gunbōryō* dealt with military organization and maintenance, and reflected the Chinese style of military organization prominent in the period from 500 to 800 C.E.

Further reading in English:

- Farris (1992: 47–57) for a description of the Chinese system and its application and implications for the eighth-century Japanese.

gumpō 軍法 [Also read ***gunpō***]. 1. Military strategy and tactics. 2. Synonym for *heihō* 兵法 and related terms. Like *heihō*, the term *gumpō* is normally used in the generic sense and may refer to a wide range of activities including, but not limited to, battlefield strategy and tactics, guerrilla warfare, espionage, astrology and battlefield divination, weapons handling, and a variety of other skills. See: *heihō (1).*

gumpō chōren 軍法調練 [Also read ***gunpō chōren***]. A system of Western-style gunnery exercises and infantry drills developed by Takashima Shūhan during the first half of the nineteenth century.

gun 軍. TAIHŌ MILITARY SYSTEM—A provincial army corps created by joining together several provincial military garrisons (*gundan*). This organization was implemented under the eighth-century Chinese-style military system defined in the Taihō Codes (Taihō Ritsuryō). A *gun* was commanded by a general (*shōgun*). If three army corps joined together, they were commanded by a "great general" (*taishōgun*).

Further reading in English:

- Farris, 1992.
- Friday, 1992: 25-26.

gunba 軍馬. See: *gumba.*

gunbai 軍配. See: *gumbai.*

gunbai heihō 軍配兵法. See: *gumbai heihō.*

gunbaisha 軍配者. See: *gumbaisha.*

gunbai uchiwa 軍配団扇 【軍配團扇】. See: *gumbai uchiwa.*

Gunbōryō 『軍防令』. See: Gumbō-ryō.

gundan 軍団【軍團】. TAIHŌ MILITARY SYSTEM—A provincial militia garrison of about a thousand men made up of foot soldiers, who were conscripts under the labor tax equal-fields system, and elite mounted warriors from the rural gentry (*kuni no miyatsuko*). The *gundan* were originally created by the Taika Reform (Taika no Kaishin) of 645 and were reorganized under the Tang military model by the Taiho Codes (Taihō Ritsuryō) of 702.

These soldiers were sometimes posted as border guards (*sakimori*) in Kyūshū and as imperial guards (Efu and Hyōefu) in the capitol. The number of conscripts in any particular *gundan* varied; most were composed of soldiers from five or six rural districts. Each conscript was required to bring his own equipment including weaponry; i.e., a bow and bowstrings, a sword, and a knife. (See Farris [1992:50] quoting from the *Gumbōryō no gige* and the *Bijūgu no jō.*) In battle, several *gundan* might join together to form a corps (*gun*). This system turned out to be untenable, and was abolished under Emperor Kammu[24] in 792.

Further reading in English:

- Farris, 1992: 47–57.
- Friday, 1992: 17–20.
- Varley, 1994: 2–5, 214.

gungaku 軍学 【軍學】. 1. Military science, strategy, tactics. 2. Synonym for *heihō* 兵法 and related terms.

gungaku heihō 軍学兵法【軍學兵法】. Military science, strategy, tactics.

gunji shizoku 軍事氏族. Ancient noble families of the Yamato court that specialized in martial pursuits. Two of the best known were the Mononobe and the Ōtomo no Muraji. According to Farris (1992: 27) the Mononobe were originally Shintō priests who accompanied military expeditions as far as Korea in order to provide prayers for victory. They gradually evolved into a clan specializing in military pursuits. The Ōtomo were in charge of an archery guard unit assigned to the Yamato palace.

gunkai 軍貝. Lit. "military (conch) shell." 1. Military strategy and tactics. 2. Synonym for *heihō* 兵法 and related terms. See also: *gunra; jingai.*

Gunkan Bugyō 軍艦奉行. Office of the Chief of Naval Forces. The position was created by the Tokugawa shogunate in 1829.

gunki 1. 軍気【軍氣】. Martial heart, spirit, essence, or inspiration; the "heart" of the army. Equivalent to *shiki* 士気 and *heiki* 兵気.

gunki 2. 軍記. A war chronicle. See also: *gunkimono.*

gunki 3. 軍器【軍噐】. Weapons of war; armaments. Equivalent to *heiki* 兵器.

gunki 4. 軍毅. TAIHŌ MILITARY SYSTEM—A regimental commander in the eighth-century provincial militia (*gundan*). There were apparently two levels of *gunki*: the commander (*daiki* 大毅), and the assistant commander (*shōki* 小毅).

gunkimono 軍記物 [Var. ***gunki monogatari*** 軍記物語; ***senkimono (gatari)*** 戦記物(語)]. War tales. This genre of Japanese literature centered on war and warriors. The stories are partly historical and partly fiction, and are

[24] Kammu Tennō 桓武天皇 (737–806; r. 781–806), fiftieth emperor of Japan.

somewhat moralistic in their emphasis on the warrior ethos and warrior ideal.

Gunkimono first appeared in the tenth century, when the rural warrior elite began to emerge as a dominant force in Japanese society; and continued to the beginning of the Edo period in the seventeenth century. Many *gunkimono* have been translated into English—some more than once:

Shōmonki	Rabinovitch, 1986
Heike Monogatari	Kitagawa & Tsuchida, 1975
Taiheiki	McCullough, 1959
Gikeiki	McCullough, 1959
Hōgen monogatari	Wilson, 1971

Varley summarizes a number of these tales in his detailed 1994 work, *Warriors of Japan as Portrayed in the War Tales*.

gunki monogatari 軍記物語. See: *gunkimono.*

gunpō 軍法. See: *gumpō.*

gunpō chōren 軍法調練. See: *gumpō chōren.*

gunpyō 軍兵. Foot soldiers; troops.

gunra 軍螺. Lit. "military conch," "military shell." 1. A conch shell (*horagai*) used for signaling troops, much as a bugle was used in the West. 2. Military strategy and tactics. 3. Synonym for *heihō* 兵法 and related terms.

gunryaku 軍略. Military strategy and tactics.

gunsen 軍扇. A commander's war fan. These were usually folding fans with talismanic designs including sun, moon, stars, Sanskrit letters, etc. Unlike the *gumbai uchiwa*, however, *gunsen* were not used for divination. There are many varieties. See also: *uchiwa.*

裏 Reverse

GUNSEN
Reverse—Crescent moon and seven dipper stars

表 Obverse

GUNSEN
Obverse—Sun in red sky with clouds
(After an illustration in the *Gunjin kikigaki*『軍陣聞書』)

gunshi 軍使 [Var. ***tsukaiban*** 使番]. Messengers whose job it was to transport messages between commanding generals and troops during battle.

guntō 軍刀. Swords carried in military mountings by most Japanese officers during World War II. Some of these were cheap, mass-produced, factory-made swords; others were traditionally forged blades. Yumoto (1958: 49) notes that during wartime most members of the imperial army and navy carried Japanese-style blades, rather than the Western sabers which had come into vogue after the Meiji Restoration of 1868.

Guntō swords and their mountings were of several types:

1) *Kyūguntō* 旧軍刀—"old military sword" mountings. These were designed in the same fashion as the English naval cutlass. Army scabbards were chromed metal, while navy scabbards were of blue or black colored wood or leather. Japanese police also used this saber-type mounting.
2) *Shinguntō* 新軍刀—"new military sword" mountings. This type of mounting was adopted by the Japanese army in 1937. Swords used by the army were generally mounted in brown-colored metal scabbards; according to Yumoto (1958: 50), this scabbard could be covered with brown leather. Many of the swords in *shinguntō* mountings were factory-made and of poor quality; they may have serial numbers stamped into the blade. A variant of this type, carried by non-commissioned officers, had a hilt made of brown-colored cast iron.
3) *Kaiguntō* 海軍刀—"naval sword" mountings. Naval sword mountings were of three styles: short swords around 15 inches (40 cm) long; longswords worn with the cutting edge down, like the earlier *tachi*; and longswords worn in saber-style mountings, much like the *kyūguntō*.

See also: *gendaitō; kotō; Nippontō; shinshintō; shintō (2); Shōwatō; Yasukunitō.*

Further reading in English:

• Yumoto, 1958.

guntō sohō 軍刀操法. A method of sword use

created at the Rikugun Toyama Gakkō Bujutsu Kyōkan (often simply called the Toyama Gakkō) in 1925. This system, which was specifically designed for the Japanese army, originally included seven quick-draw sword and cutting techniques (*battōhō*) extrapolated from classical traditions (*koryū*). The Toyama Gakkō was closed by the Allied powers at the end of World War II in 1945. However, after the ban on martial arts was lifted, several of the *guntō sohō* teachers resumed teaching the system on their own. The best known of these was Nakamura Taisaburō, who initially taught the system as Toyama Ryū *guntō sohō*. However, as he began to modify the system he changed the name first to Toyama Ryū *battōjutsu* and later to Toyama Ryū *iaidō/battōdō*. See *Nakamura Taisaburō; Toyama Gakkō.*

gunyō 軍用. Military techniques and tactics.

gunyō enka 軍用煙火. Military use of rockets and fireworks for signaling.

gunyō kanchōjutsu 軍用間諜術. Military intelligence strategies and techniques. See: *Hōjō Ryū.*

gusoku 具足. Light armor normally worn by low-ranking foot soldiers (*ashigaru*).

Gusoku Bugyō 具足奉行. This title was created in 1641 for officials acting as chief armorer of the Tokugawa shogunate. The Gusoku Bugyō was responsible for the production and maintenance of armor, helmets, and related accoutrements for the army of the *shōgun*. The office was folded into the Bugu Bugyō in 1863.

gyaku 逆. 1. Reverse, opposite. 2. YAGYŪ SHINKAGE RYŪ—Abbreviation of *gyaku no kurai.*

gyaku hanmi 逆半身. A position in which two opponents face each other in a lateral, mirrored stance (*hanmi*), standing with opposite feet forward. Contrast to *aihanmi*.

gyaku no kurai 逆の位. YAGYŪ SHINKAGE RYŪ—Middle level (*chūdan*) sword posture (*kurai*) which is the reverse of *jun seigan*. In this posture, the sword is held to the front with the *kissaki* at about mouth level, just over the big toe of the left foot, which is pointed directly at the enemy. The *tsuka* is at the level of the right hip.

gyakute 逆手. 1. Reverse hand. 2. A hand-reversal/wrist joint technique in which an opponent's hand is reversed toward the joint.

gyakute no kamae 逆手の構え. SHINDŌ MŪSŌ RYŪ—Posture in which the body is positioned very slightly in *hanmi*. The *jō* is held to the front in *seigan no kamae*, but with the forward hand in a reverse grip (thumb side toward the body). *Gyakute no kamae* can be taken with either the right foot forward (*migi* 右 *gyakute no kamae*) or the left foot forward (*hidari* 左 *gyakute no kamae*).

GYAKUTE NO KAMAE
Jōjutsu practitioner (L) engages the swordsman (R) with *gyakute no kamae*
(Photograph by author, 1978)

gyakute tsuki 逆手突. See: *gyakutezuki.*

gyakute uchi 逆手打. Lit. "reverse-hand strike." SHINDŌ MŪSŌ RYŪ—Reverse-hand strike accomplished from *gyakute no kamae*. This is the second of the twelve basic techniques (*kihon*) extrapolated from the classical forms of Shindō Musō Ryū by Shimizu Takaji.

gyakutezuki 逆手突. [Also read **gyakute tsuki**] Lit. "Reverse-hand thrust." SHINDŌ MŪSŌ RYŪ—A technique in which the staff (*jō*) is reversed and thrust (with the hands in *gyakute* position) at the opponent's vital areas. This is the fifth of the twelve basic techniques (*kihon*) extrapolated from the classical forms of Shindō Musō Ryū by Shimizu Takaji.

gyō 行 [Abbr. of **shugyō** 修行, 修業]. In both Buddhism and Japanese martial culture, the

G

term *gyō* refers to austere practice. Literally, it means "to go" or "to walk," indicating a relationship with the practice of pilgrimage. In combative arts, the "walker" is the one who moves toward spiritual and physical perfection. In Buddhism, the "walker" is "one who does not reside anywhere, who abides in emptiness." (Grapard, 1995: 39). In addition, the term indicates that the journey—i.e., the going—is also the goal.

In classical warrior culture, the purpose of *gyō* was purification of the spirit (*mitama* 御魂). Consequently, in addition to perfecting combative technique through *gyō*, the warrior also sought to achieve wisdom and tranquility, develop compassion, become purified, and achieve joy and honesty. (Draeger, 1995: 3.4) *Gyō* could be performed in a variety of places—a training hall (*dōjō*), a Shintō shrine (*jinja*/*jingū*), a mountain retreat, etc. Influenced by Esoteric Buddhist and Shugendō practices, the rituals of *gyō* normally included purification with cold water, a vegetarian diet, sitting in meditation, possibly with a mentor, and practicing over an extended period of time, such as seven days, thirty-seven days, or ninety days.

gyōja 行者 <Ch. *xingzhe* <Skt. *ācārin*. 1. A religious ascetic. 2. A religious pilgrim. 3. TENDAI BUDDHISM—A monk who diligently practices the Shidō Kegyō and other rituals. 4. BUDDHISM—An itinerant monk. 5. SHUGENDŌ—A mountain ascetic.

gyoji 行司. SUMŌ—A *sumō* referee.

gyoku 玉. See: *gyokushō*.

gyokushō 玉将【玉將】[Abbr. as ***gyoku*** 玉]. Lit. "jeweled general." SHŌGI—In the chess-like game of *shōgi*, the *gyokushō* is the challenging general and is equivalent to the "black" king in chess, although there are no black or white colored pieces in *shōgi*.

gyo-umamawarishū 御馬廻衆. See: *umamawari*.

H

ha 1. 刃. The cutting edge of a blade.

ha 2. 破. See: *shu-ha-ri*.

habaki 鎺. The "blade collar" on a Japanese sword or other bladed weapon. The *habaki* is a metal collar or ferrule that fits around a sword blade next to the handguard (*tsuba*). It may be in one or two pieces. Older *habaki* are usually made of gold or are heavily gold plated, while more recent ones are made of gilded bronze or brass. Many are decorated with family crests or other symbols. They may be separated from the handguard by metal washers or spacers called *seppa*.

HABAKI ON A FOURTEENTH-CENTURY SHORT SWORD (*KODACHI*)
(*Kodachi* from a private collection)

habakimoto 鎺元. The part of a Japanese sword blade that is covered by the *habaki*. Also called the *temoto*.

habatsu 派閥. A clique; a political division; a branch of a martial tradition which has politically separated itself from the main line tradition.

haba zanken 羽々斬剣【羽々斬劍】. A sword technique of the Kageyama Ryū 影山流.

habiki 1. 刃引. A training sword made of metal, in contrast to one made of wood (*bokutō*, *bokken*) or bamboo (*chikutō*; *shinai*; *fukuro shinai*). Also used to refer to a sword without a sharpened cutting edge.

Habiki 2. 刃挽. JIKI SHINKAGE RYŪ—The fourth series of *waza* of the Jiki Shinkage Ryū. Consisting of four *kata*, the Habiki are the *urawaza* of Hōjō. In them, live swords (or unsharpened blades) are used by both the person executing the technique (*shidachi*) and the one receiving it (*uchidachi*). For photo, see: *Jiki Shinkage Ryū*.

hachi 鉢 [Abbrev. of ***hattara*** 鉢多羅 <Ch. *boduoluo* <Skt. *pātram*; a.k.a. ***jihatsu*** 持鉢]. 1. BUDDHISM—A Buddhist priest's begging bowl; an alms bowl. 2. MARTIAL ARTS—The bowl of a Japanese helmet.

Hachibu Shū 八部衆. The eight types of beings who are considered protectors of Buddhism:

Japanese		Chinese	Sanskrit
1. *ten*	天	*tian*	*deva*
2. *ryū*	龍	*long*	*nāga*
3. *yasha*	夜叉	*yecha*	*yakṣa*
4. *gendatsuba*	乾闥婆	*qiantapo*	*gandharva*
5. *ashura*	阿修羅	*axiuluo*	*asura*
6. *karura*	迦樓羅	*jialouluo*	*garuḍa*
7. *kinnara*	緊那羅	*jinnaluo*	*kinnara*
8. *magoraga*	摩睺羅伽	*mohouluojia*	*mahoraga*

In the martial arts, a number of these turn up as warrior-protecting tutelary deities; talismans are made from their seed syllables (*shuji*) and images.

hachimaki 鉢巻. A band of white cotton cloth, sometimes adorned with symbolic designs, worn around the head. The use of a *hachimaki* is not restricted to martial traditions, but wearing it is always a symbol of great physical and mental exertion and determination. The members of some martial traditions—more often than not those attached to Kashima Jingū—may wear a *hachimaki* during special training sessions; others wear them only at martial exhibitions (*embu*). Dur-

HACHIMAKI WORN IN A MARTIAL DEMONSTRATION
Kajitsuka Yasushi (L) and Mutō Masao (R) demonstrate Yagyū Shingan Ryū at Katori Grand Shrine in 1978
(Photograph by Pat Lineberger)

ing the periods when armor and helmets were in use, a *hachimaki* was often worn under the helmet to pad the user's head. This method of using a *hachimaki* persists today in modern *kendō*. See also: *hitaigane*.

Hachiman 八幡 [Also read ***Yawata***]. Hachiman is the posthumous name for Emperor Ōjin.[1] Honored as the god of war, he became the tutelary deity of the Minamoto family.

Hachiman Daibosatsu 八幡大菩薩. RYŌBU SHINTŌ—The Great Bodhisattva Hachiman. Under the process of assimilation of Shintō deities and the Buddhist pantheon,[2] the Shintō war god Hachiman was accorded Buddhist *bodhisattva* (*bosatsu*) status. See: *Ryōbu Shintō*.

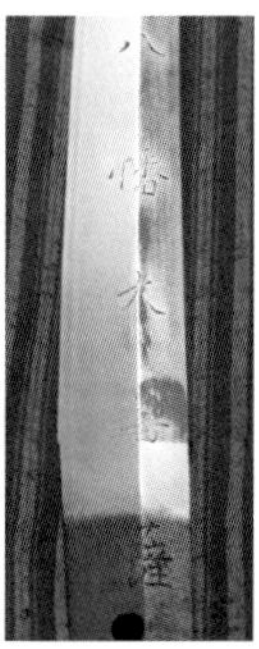

IDEOGRAMS FOR
HACHIMAN DAIBOSATSU 八幡大菩薩
Carved as a talisman on a sword blade
(Private collection.)

Hachimangū 八幡宮. See: *Tsurugaoka Hachimangū*.

Hachimanza (no ana) 八幡座(の孔) [Var. ***tehen no ana*** 天辺の孔; ***tenkū ikidashi*** 天空息出]. Lit. "(the opening for) Hachiman's seat." According to Sasama (1982: 488) this term for the *tehen no ana* (a ring around the opening in the top of a Japanese warrior's helmet) came into use during the early Edo period. For illustration, see: *tehen no za*.

hachiwari 鉢割 [Var. ***kabutowari*** 兜割]. 1. Lit. "helmet breaker." This weapon is often about the size and shape of a short sword (*kodachi*). However, it has no cutting edge and may sometimes have a single tine. It is thought to be an early antecedent of the *jutte*. *Hachiwari* come in many varieties and sizes.

HACHIWARI (TOP) WITH SCABBARD
(Private collection)

hada 肌. Lit. "grain," "texture," "skin." This term refers to the pattern on the surface of a Japanese sword blade. There are several varieties, including *masame hada* 真肌 (straight grain), *matsu hada* 松肌 (pine bark; ragged like pine tree bark), *nashi hada* 梨肌 (fine-grained like pear flesh), etc.

hadashi 裸足. Bare feet.

hadome 歯止【齒止】. A crosspiece on a spear (*yari*) or glaive (*naginata*) used as a parrying bar. See: *kagi (1); kagi (2)*.

Hagai Asaemon Yoshihisa Isshinsai 羽賀井 浅右衛門 義久 一心斎. Direct disciple of Kamiizumi Ise no Kami in the Shinkage Ryū (1) 新陰流. Hagai founded a branch tradition known as the Hagai Ryū 羽賀井流 in the mid-1500s.

hafuribe 祝部. Shintō shrine officials whose duties included acting as security detachment personnel for the shrine to which they were associated. During the Muromachi period (1392–1573), the *hafuribe* were warriors selected from *bushi* clans (*kanbe*) who were attached to various shrines. In addition to their official duties, these groups were responsible for developing and passing on the particular system of martial arts developed for protection of those sacred grounds. Some of these shrine-attached martial traditions evolved into classical *ryū*. This transition was often accomplished by an expert warrior who, after undergoing some kind of revelatory experience, modified the system; e.g., Tsukahara Bokuden's modification of Kashima no Tachi 鹿島之太刀 into Kashima Shintō Ryū 鹿島新当流, or Iizasa Chōisai Ienao's revision of Katori no Ken

---

1 Ōjin Tennō 応神天皇 (c. 201–c. 312). Legendary emperor whose actual dates are unknown.
2 See *Ryōbu Shintō*.

香取之剣 into Tenshinshō-den Katori Shintō Ryū 天真正伝香取神道流.

Hagakure 『葉隠』【葉隱】(Hidden by the leaves). *Hagakure* is an early eighteenth-century text on the martial spirit of *bushidō* by Yamamoto Tsunetomo. The book, which exalted the idea of self-sacrifice in the service of one's lord, is often (if erroneously) held up as the be-all and end-all of Japanese warrior philosophy. While service and loyalty were encouraged by the culture of the times, *Hagakure* was aimed at a specific geographical group—the warriors of the Nabeshima family of Hizen. In fact, a variety of similar treatises espousing the values of disparate warrior groups were produced before and during the Edo period. See also: *Budō shoshinshū.*

Further reading in English:

• Wilson, 2002 (translation).

hagane 鋼. *Hagane* is steel with a high carbon content. Sword-quality steel such as this is required in order to form the extremely hard surface and sharp edge of traditionally forged Japanese blades

hagunsei 破軍星. Lit. "army-destroying stars." The *hagunsei* is a diagram of stars used for military divination (*gumbai heihō*) and inscribed on a commander's war fan (*gumbai uchiwa*). See: *gumbai uchiwa.*

haidate 佩楯. Lit. "shield clothing" or "a shield that is worn." *Haidate* are apron-like thigh guards made of cloth with overlapping pieces of metal armor sewn on. The upper portion may be made of brocade or leather while the lower part is covered with metal plates or mail.

haisen 敗戦【敗戰】. A defeat; a lost battle.

Haitōrei 廃刀令. Edict against wearing swords promulgated on 28 April 1876. The decree restricted sword-wearing to soldiers in uniform, and military and police officers. This ban, which generally eliminated the wearing of swords by former samurai (*shizoku*), precipitated several revolts, the best known of which was the Satsuma Rebellion (Seinan Sensō).

haja kenshō 破邪顕正【破邪顯正】<Ch. *poxie xianzheng*. Lit. "to destroy evil and spread the truth." BUDDHISM—The refutation (*haja*) of heterodox views and the elucidation (*kenshō*) of orthodox views; the destruction of the sinister and the establishment of the noble or benevolent. During the seventh-century reign of Chinese emperor Gaozu[3] of the Tang dynasty, the priest Falin 法琳 wrote a treatise entitled the *Poxielun* 『破邪論』(Jp. *Haja-ron*) in order to refute the anti-Buddhist views of the early Tang government. Later, in Japan, *haja kenshō* became an important dogmatic catchphrase for some of the aggressively political, populist Buddhist sects such as Jōdo Shin Shū and Nichiren Shū. In some Japanese martial traditions, especially those of the Edo period, *haja kenshō* became a central philosophical concept; the phrase was sometimes ritually recited as a martial technique was executed. For example, in the first teaching of the combative police truncheon system (*juttejutsu*) incorporated within the Edo-machikata Jutte Torinawa Atsukaiyō school, this catchphrase is expressed as a verbal incantation signifying authority in coordination with the physical movements of the first *kata*.

haji 恥. Shame; loss of face. Literature as early as the tenth century war tale entitled the *Shōmonki* makes it clear that what the warrior—at least the idealized warrior—feared most was the shame of defeat. In fact, it almost seems that as a victorious warrior's fame (*na*) rose, his defeated opponent's shame (*haji*) rose proportionately. This shame often led to a bloody vendetta by the defeated warrior or, if he had been killed, by his family and/or vassals.

Hajime! 始め! A command: "Begin!"

hakama 袴. The divided skirt-like trousers or pantaloons worn by practitioners of *kendō* and of most classical martial traditions (*koryū bugei*), and by *yūdansha* in various schools of *aikidō*. *Hakama* were originally worn by the Japanese warrior class. There were several types and lengths. The standard samurai outdoor *hakama* in earlier times, the *kukuri-bakama*, were more like loose pants

[3] Gaozu 高祖 (566–635; r. 618–626).

H

or European pantaloons.[4] Inside, during formal events, the samurai might be required to wear the long *naga-bakama*, which covered the feet and restricted movement. When worn with a formal kimono top and stiff vest (*kataginu*), the whole outfit was referred to as a *naga-kamishimo.* For wear around the home, the *hanbakama*, which did not cover the feet and allowed free movement, was normally chosen.[5] This is the type of *hakama* normally worn today in martial practice. When the *hanbakama* was worn with the *kataginu* vest, the outfit was referred to as a *kataginu-bakama.*

Further reading in English:

- Lowry, 2006: 62–79.

Hakkō Ryū 八光流. The "Eight Lights Tradition" or the "Infinite Light Tradition." Hakkō Ryū is a school of *jūjutsu/aikijūjutsu/goshinjutsu* created in 1938 by Okuyama Yoshiji (also known as Okuyama Ryūhō). Originally referred to as Meishidō 名士道, the system was renamed Hakkō Ryū in 1941. Okuyama trained extensively in Daitō Ryū under Matsuda Hōsaku, and for a short time under Daitō Ryū headmaster Takeda Sōkaku. One of Okuyama's students, Nakano Michiomi (better known as Sō Dōshin), was the founder of Nippon Shōrinji Kempō.

Further reading in English:

- http://www.hakkoryu.com/
- Palumbo, 1987, 1988, 1993.

hakuda 白打 [Var. 伯打] <Ch. *baida*. 1. A primarily pugilistic fighting art imported from China to Japan in the early 1600s. Some Japanese sources claim this term (which literally means "white strike" or "pure strike") has Buddhist origins. In these explanations, *hakuda* was a boxing art practiced by Chinese Buddhist monks, who used the art for self-defense and learned to strike without malice (hence the term "pure strike"). See: *Akiyama Shirobei Yoshitoki.* 2. A variant term for *jūjutsu*-like grappling and striking arts.

hakugeki 迫撃. An attack at close quarters; a looming attack.

hakujin 白刃 [Also read ***shiraha***]. Lit. "white blade" or "pure blade." A naked blade.

hakutsuruken 白鶴拳 [Also read ***hakkakuken***] <Ch. *baihao quan*. Japanese term for Chinese White Crane boxing. This art was imported from Fujian province in China to Okinawa during the early twentieth century. See also: *Gōjū Ryū.*

Haku-un Ryū 白雲流. Lit. "White Cloud Tradition." The Haku-un Ryū is a legendary school/tradition of espionage (*shinobi no jutsu*). It is attributed to a Daoist (*dōshi*) named Haku-un who flourished sometime around the Yōwa era (1181–1182). There is no original documentation from that period confirming the historical authenticity of this legend.

hamagurizaki 蛤先. A "clam-shaped point" on a wooden sword (*bokutō*). For illustration, see: *bokutō.*

hamayumi 破魔弓. Lit. "demon-crushing bow." A bow used for exorcisms; usually used in ridgepole-raising ceremonies.

hamidashi 喰出 [Var. 食出]. Lit. "to strike a blow." A short blade or dagger, generally longer than an *aikuchi* but shorter than a *kodachi* (i.e., ranging from 8 to 14 inches/20–35 cm) with a guard (*tsuba*) only slightly larger than the hilt (*tsuka*).

hamon 1. 刃文. The border of the hardened steel area (*yakiba*) along the cutting edge of a Japanese sword; sometimes referred to as the temper line. The *hamon* appears as a whitish line, sometimes with a repeating pattern.

hamon 2. 破門. Formal excommunication or expulsion from a classical *ryū.*

hampei 藩兵. A *daimyō's* troops; his soldiers.

Hamuro Tokinaga 葉室 時長. A nobleman (*kuge*) of the imperial court in the thirteenth century who held the office of Second Assistant to the Minister of Taxation (Minbunoshō 民部少輔). Hamuro is credited with the authorship of several war tales, including the

---

4 See the illustration of *Kyōjaku no maki* in the entry for Hikita Kage Ryū; the spearman on the left is wearing *kukuri-bakama*

5 See illustration in the entry for *hanbakama.*

Hakkō Ryū
八光流
(abbreviated lineage)

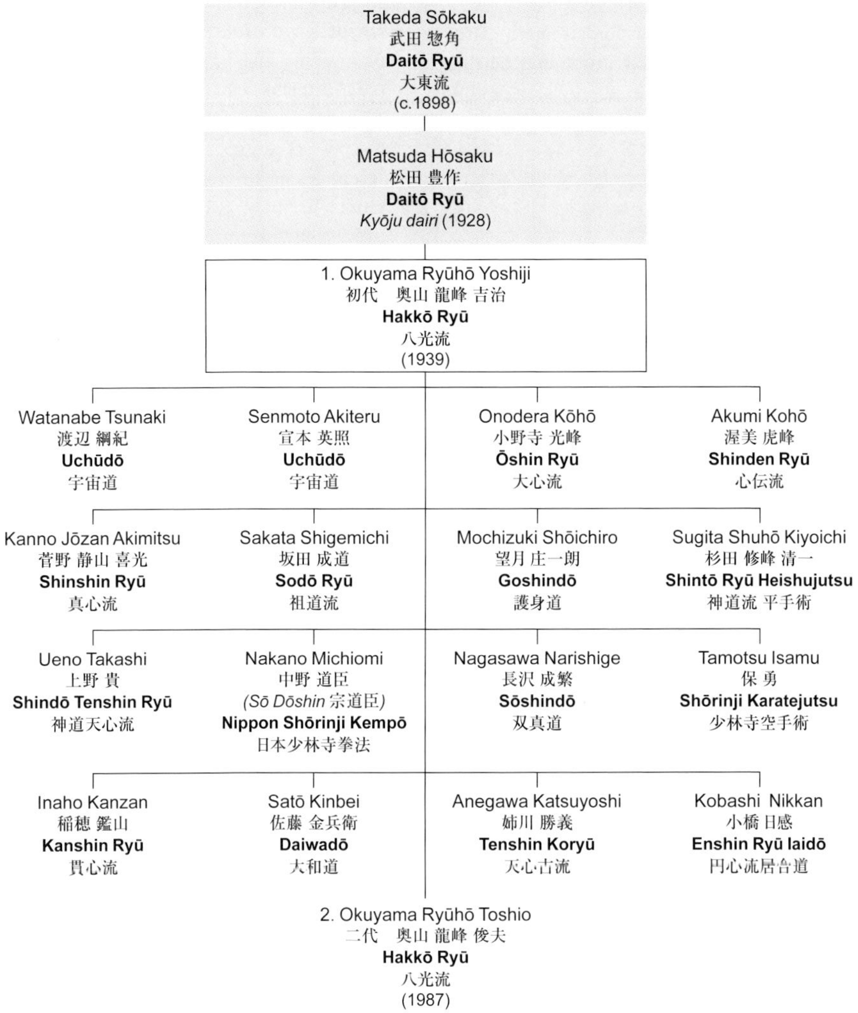

Hōgen monogatari, *Heiji monogatari*, and others. However, there is little proof that he is responsible for such works.

han 藩. A *daimyō* domain during the Tokugawa period.

hanamusubi 花結. Lit. "flower knot." A knot commonly used in tying armor corselets.

hananeji 鼻捻 [Var. 鼻捩子; abbr. of ***hananejiri bō***]. See: *hananejiri bō.*

hananejiri bō 鼻捻り棒 [Var. 鼻捩り棒; var. ***hananeji*** 鼻捻]. Lit. "nose-twisting (manipulating) staff." The *hananejiri bō* was one of the "three tools of the stable" (*umagoya sangu*). It was a baton used to control horses, but could also be used to control armored or unarmored opponents. Its use is still seen today in the Yagyū Shingan Ryū, Edo Machikata Jutte Torinawa Atsukaiyō, and other systems.

hanare 離れ. KYŪDŌ—Seventh of the eight formal stages (*hassetsu*) in firing an arrow in the modern martial way of archery (*kyūdō*). *Hanare* is the process of releasing the arrow. See also: *hassetsu.*

hanbakama 半袴. Semi-formal dress pants for samurai intended for inside and outside use. The term is usually abbreviated simply as "*hakama.*" See: *hakama.*

HANBAKAMA

hanbō 半棒. A short staff or cane around 25 to 30 inches (60–75 cm) in length. See also: *tanjō.*

hanbōjutsu 半棒術. Techniques for using the cane or short staff (*hanbō*). See also: *tanjōjutsu; sutekki-jutsu.*

handachi 半太刀. Lit. "half-*tachi*." This term refers to swords which had a combination of *tachi* and *katana* mountings. They were generally carried like *katana*—that is, with the cutting edge up and the scabbard thrust through the sash (*obi*).

hangaku 藩学【藩學】. A school for samurai children; a domain school.

Hangaku Gozen 坂額 御前. Lit. "Lady Hangaku." Hangaku, the daughter of Jō Sukekuni 城資国, became famous as a woman warrior in the early thirteenth century. She was a member of the Jō clan, a *daimyō* family from Echigo province. Her fame was due to her display of archery skills in the defense of Torisaka castle (Torisakajō 鳥坂城) in 1201; she also commanded over three thousand troops against the Hōjō. After the fall of the castle, she was taken, wounded by arrows, to Kamakura. There she met and married Asari Yoshitō, a warrior of the Kai Genji. See also: *Jō (2).*

Further reading in English:
• Ellis, 2002a: 182.

hangeki 反撃. Counterattack.

hangetsu no metsuke 半月の目付. A method of sighting the target in Japanese archery (*kyūjutsu* and *kyūdō*) in which the bull's-eye of the target is partially obscured (*yami*) by the bow. The exposed half of the bull's-eye resembles a half-moon (*hangetsu*), just to the left of the bow. See also: *ariake no metsuke; yami no metsuke.*

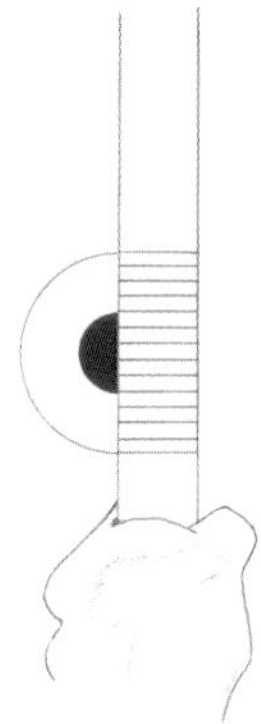

HANGETSU NO METSUKE

hangusoku 半具足. Lit. "half-armor." In times of emergency when the classical warrior (*bushi*) did not have time to don a full set of armor, he might wear only a combination of helmet (*kabuto*) and body armor (*dōmaru*) or gauntlets (*kote*) and body armor. Either of these protective combinations was referred to as *hangusoku*, "half-armor."

haniwa 埴輪. Ceramic figures found in the great burial tombs (*kofun*) of the Kofun period (third to fourth centuries). Many of the figures are martial in nature.

hankan 反間 <Ch. *fanjian*. The third of the five types of secret agents (*ninja*; *shinobi*) mentioned in Sun Tzu's *Art of War* (*Sonshi no heihō*). The term *hankan* refers to double agents who are employed from the enemy's spies. See: *kanja; kyōdan (1); ninjutsu; Sonshi no heihō.*

Hankōnan Ryū 半硬軟流 [Also read ***Pangainū(n) Ryū*** パンガイヌー流]. See: *Kōnan Ryū; Uechi Ryū.*

Hankō Ryū 半剛流 (also read ***Hangō Ryū***). OKINAWAN KARATE—An early name for the Shitō Ryū founded by Mabuni Kenwa. See: *Mabuni Kenwa; Shitō Ryū.*

hankyō 藩境. The boundary of a feudal domain.

hankyū 半弓. Lit. "half-bow." A term generally used for bows of foreign design, whether made inside or outside Japan. These were generally smaller than the standard Japanese war bow (*daikyū*).

hanmi 半身. Lit. "half-body." A lateral stance with hips turned to the side so that the opponent can see only half the body.

hanmyō 藩命. Official documents/directives produced by a feudal domain.

Hannya-shin-gyō 『般若心経』【般若心經】[Var. ***Hannya-haramitta-shin-gyō*** 『般若波羅蜜多心経』【般若波羅蜜多心經】] <Ch. *Boruoboluomiduo Xin Jing* <Skt. *Prajñāpāramitā-hṛdaya-sūtra*. BUDDHISM—The *Hannya-shin-gyō*, or Heart Sutra, is a short (one page, thirty lines) summary of the perfection of wisdom (Skt. *prajñāpāramitā*) literature. Its title means the "essence of the perfection of wisdom." The sutra is a key text in East Asian Buddhism, especially in the Tendai and Zen schools. It is often recited at the beginning or end of a variety of rituals. See also: *Daihannya-haramitta-kyō.*

hanpei 藩兵. See: *hampei.*

hanrō 藩老. The chief retainer of a *daimyō*.

hanseki 藩籍. A fief.

hanshi 範士 [Var. 範師]. A master teacher of swordsmanship. Compare to *shihan*; contrast to *kyōshi* and *renshi*. In modern martial arts and ways systems (*budō*) the title of *hanshi* is usually accorded (or awarded) to practitioners who have attained the level of eighth or ninth dan in the ranking system. However, there is no direct relationship between, for example, eighth dan and the title of *hanshi*. An eighth-dan practitioner might be titled a *kyōshi*. The titles of *hanshi* (and *renshi* and *kyoshi*, for that matter) may be awarded by an organization outside the recipient's ranking organization.

han no shihan 藩師範. The chief instructor of martial arts within a domain during the Edo period.

hanshin 半身. See: *han sonkyo (no shisei).*

hanshōgote 半鐘小手. Short armored sleeves (*kote*) covering only the hands and forearms. These were generally composed of mail and/or three strips of longitudinal plates made of metal or lacquered leather, which were mounted on padded cloth.

hanshu 藩主. A *daimyō*; a feudal lord.

hansō 半槍. Lit. "half-spear." A short spear. See: *Shinbu Ryū.*

han sonkyo no shisei 半蹲踞の姿勢. A lowered posture like *sonkyo*, but with one knee on the ground. Also referred to as *hanshin* and *iaigoshi* in some classical schools. See: *sonkyo.*

happō 八方. Eight directions; all directions.

happōgiri no tōsen 八方斬りの刀線. NAKAMURA RYŪ—A term used for sword trajectories in Nakamura Ryū. See: *eiji happō; Nakamura Ryū.*

hara 腹 [Var. 肚]. Lit. "belly"; "the lower abdomen." The term *hara* in Japanese culture has numerous shades of meaning. It denotes the lower abdomen, which also contains the center-of-balance point for body, breath, and mind. This point is referred to as the *tanden*. ¶ *hara ga tatsu* 腹が立つ, to be angry. ¶ *hara o kimeru* 腹を決める, to make up one's mind; to be resolved to do something. See: *haragei.*

Further reading in English:

- Dürckheim, 1962.

hara-ate 腹当【腹當】. 1. A corselet, usually made of leather, worn by low-status fighting men. It resembled a fireman's jacket. 2. Armor worn under ceremonial dress, that only covered the front of the body from neck to knee.

hara-ate-gawa 腹当革【腹當革】. A *hara-ate* made of leather.

haragei 腹芸【腹藝】[Var. 肚芸【肚藝】]. The cultivation of *hara* through rigorous mar-

H

tial austerities. *Haragei* is said to enable the trainee to bear not only emotional discomfort but also physical pain, danger, and adversity. Perfection of *hara* is tantamount to achieving the egoless state of "not-I" (*muga*), and indicates a seamless union of body, speech, and mind; i.e., a balanced human being.

Further reading in English:

- Dürckheim, 1962.
- Harrison, 1956, *passim.*

harai 1. 払い【拂い】(often part of a compound as the suffix ***~barai***). Lit. "sweeping," this term is used in many technical combinations; e.g., *ashibarai* (foot-sweep).

harai 2. 祓. To purify or exorcise; to drive out demons. SHINTŌ—This exorcism, which is part of the purification process, usually begins with prayers that are read or recited in the form of ritual prayer (*norito*). See: *norito.*

hara kiri 腹切. See: *seppuku.*

Hara Kiuemon Masanori 原 喜右衛門 政軌. One of several fifth-generation inheritors of Ōno Ryū 大野流 gunnery (*hōjutsu*) in the early 1700s.

haramaki 腹巻. Lit. "wrapped around the abdomen." An abbreviation of *haramakidō*.

haramakidō 腹巻胴. A type of *dō* (1) 胴 (trunk-protecting armor) made of mail or plate and lined with silk. The vest-shaped *haramakidō* opens at the back and is fastened with cords. See also: *dō (1).*

Harazawa Saemon 原沢 左衛門【原澤左衛門】. Direct disciple of Kamiizumi Ise no Kami in the Shinkage Ryū (1) 新陰流. Harazawa founded a branch tradition known as the Noda Shinkage Ryū 野田新陰流 in the late 1500s.

hari 針. A needle. Some combative schools teach the art of blowing needles from the mouth (*fukibarijutsu*).

Harigaya Sekiun 針ヶ谷 夕雲 (1592–1662). Founder of Mujū Shinken Ryū 無住心剣流. This swordsman's name is listed in D. T. Suzuki's *Zen and Japanese Culture* as "Hariya Sekiun," an error that has subsequently found its way into many other publications. Harigaya was a Japanese sword master reputed to have emerged undefeated from fifty-two duels. Himself a disciple of Ogasawara Genshin Nagaharu, he subsequently founded the Mujū Shinken Ryū. His best known disciple was Odagiri Ichiun. See: *ainuke; Mujū Shinken Ryū.*

Further reading in English:

- Suzuki, 1958: 170–173; 201.

hari ishime 針石目. Lit. "needle-grained." *Hari ishime* refers to a background decoration on the surface of sword fittings. Surfaces decorated in this way look as though they have been pricked with a needle.

harinuki 張り抜き. The Japanese version of papier-mâché. *Harinuki* was used for making armor cases because it would not split or warp.

Haritsuke kei 磔刑 [Also read ***takkei***]. Crucifixion (*haritsuke kei*) was one of the four prescribed forms of execution for Tokugawa-period commoners. The victim was placed on a cross and quickly dispatched by spearmen, ensuring that—unlike the earlier Middle Eastern version of crucifixion—the victim would not suffer for days on end. It should be noted, however, that *haritsuke kei* was considered one of the most horrible and painful ways to be executed. See: *shikei.*

Hariya Sekiun 針屋 夕雲. An erroneous reading for the name "Harigaya Sekiun" that appears in D. T. Suzuki's *Zen and Japanese Culture.* See: *Harigaya Sekiun.*

hasaki 刃先. The cutting edge of a blade.

Hasedō Kōgeki 長谷堂攻撃 [The offensive of Hasedō]. Hasedō was a village in Uzen (present-day Yamagata prefecture) where, in 1600, the forces of the army of Date Masamune and Mogami Yoshiaki defeated the troops of Uesugi Kagekatsu. It was in this offensive that Kamiizumi Nobutsuna's second son Norimoto, who had fought alongside the Uesugi forces, was killed in battle. See: *Kamiizumi Mondō no Kami Norimoto.*

Hasegawa Chikaranosuke Eishin (***Hidenobu***) 長谷川 主税助 英信 (c. 1700–c. 1775). Seventh headmaster of the Shimmei Musō

Ryū 神明夢想流 (=Shin Musō Hayashizaki Ryū 神夢想林崎流); founder of the Musō Jikiden Eishin Ryū 無双直伝英信流.

The Shimmei Musō Ryū was founded by Hayashizaki Jinsuke Shigenobu in the early seventeenth century. However, in the first half of the eighteenth century, Hasegawa Eishin evidently surpassed even Jinsuke in his mastery of the art of the quick-draw sword. The system he taught came to be called Hasegawa Eishin Ryū 長谷川英信流.[6] Eishin, an inspired martial artist, at some point renamed his system Musō Jikiden Eishin Ryū.

Hasegawa Eishin Ryū 長谷川英信流. Alternate name for Musō Jikiden Eishin Ryū. See also: *Musō Shinden Ryū.*

Hasetsu 破折. 1. Name of a variety of classical combative forms (*kata*) developed by various martial schools. 2. YAGYŪ RYŪ—Hasetsu is one of a number of classical prearranged combative forms (*kata*) developed by this school. It was also one of ten classical *kata* adapted by the Japanese Police Commission of 1886 for their Keishichō Ryū 警視庁流 system.

hashi 箸. Chopsticks. See: *wari kōgai.*

hashigo 梯子. A ladder (such as those used in firefighting) often used in the art of *hobaku* (police restraining methods) to entrap swordsmen. See illustration entitled "Hobaku from the early 1800s" at the end of this section.

hashiri nawa 走縄【走繩】. SHUGENDŌ—One of the "sixteen accoutrements of the *yamabushi*" (*yamabushi jūroku dōgu*) used during the medieval period. The *hashiri nawa* was a rope used for rituals and climbing; it could also be deployed as a weapon to subdue and bind opponents. See: *hojōjutsu; torinawa; yamabushi; yamabushi jūroku dōgu.*

ha sode 羽袖. An unusual type of armored shoulder guard (*sode*) shaped like a wing (*ha*). This fashon seems to have become popular during the Edo period.

[6] One line of this system was pared down into the Musō Shinden Ryū 夢想神伝流 by Nakayama Hakudō in 1932.

Hasō Ryū 破想流. See: *Mujū Shinken Ryū.*

hassetsu 八節. KYŪDŌ—The eight formal stages or movements leading up to, including, and following the release of an arrow. The stages are: 1. stepping (*ashibumi* 足踏み); 2. fixing the torso (*dōzukuri* 胴造り); 3. readying the bow (*yugamae* 弓構え); 4. addressing the target (*uchiokoshi* 打起し); 5. drawing the bow (*hikiwake* 引分け); 6. the "joining" or "completion of the draw" (*kai* 会); 7. releasing the arrow (*hanare* 離れ); and 8. focused, extended vigilance (*zanshin* 残心). See also: bushakei.

Hassō 八相 [Var. 撥草]. Lit. "facing eight directions," "facing all directions" [var. 撥草 "to strike out or force away the grass," perhaps an allusion to the "Grass-cutting Sword," Ame no Murakumo no Tsurugi]. 1. BUDDHISM—The eight important events in the life of the Buddha; the eight stages of becoming a buddha. In martial schools these two variations (八相 and 撥草) are often used interchangeably. *Hassō* is also the name of prearranged combative forms (*kata*) used in several martial traditions. 2. JIKI SHINKAGE RYŪ—Hassō (Happa) 八相 (発破), the first pre-arranged combative form (*kata*) taught to Jiki Shinkage Ryū trainees, is the first *kata* of the set known as Hōjō. It was one of ten classical *kata* adapted by the Japanese Police Commission of 1886 for their Keishichō Ryū 警視庁流 system. 3. An abbreviation for *hassō no kamae* 八相構.

hassō no kamae 撥草構 [Var. 八相構]. 1. Sword posture of which there are many variations. In general, the sword is held on the right side with the tip (*kensaki*) pointed up or to the rear. According to Nawa Yumio, this posture evolved from warriors in battle simply resting the sword on their right shoulder due to fatigue. This "resting" posture can still be seen in some traditions, such as Muhi Muteki Ryū, today. 2. YAGYŪ SHINKAGE RYŪ—Middle-level (*chūdan*) sword posture in which the sword is held almost vertically in front of the right side with the *tsuba* close to and about the level of the right breast. This version of *hassō* is used primarily in the armored (*koden/katchū kempō*) versions of Yagyū Shinkage Ryū *kata.* 3. YAGYŪ SHINKAGE RYŪ—Abbreviation for *takahassō no kamae* 高八相構. 4. SHINDŌ MUSŌ RYŪ—Sword posture (*kamae*) similar to (1), but with the *tsuba* closer to and about the level of the chin; left foot forward, right foot to the rear.

JIKI SHINKAGE RYŪ *HASSŌ NO KAMAE*
(Photograph by author)

hasuji 刃筋. The trajectory of a blade through a target.

hata age 旗揚げ. Lit. "to raise a (battle) flag"; to raise an army.

hatabugyō 旗奉行. Lit. "flag magistrate" or "flag officer." A warrior in charge of ensuring all flags were displayed in battle according to plan.

hata iro 旗色. The tide of battle; tide of war.

hatajirushi 旗標 [Var. 旗印; var. ***kishi*** 旗幟; also called ***nobori*** 幟]. Lit. "flag mark" or "flag with a design." 1. The design on a battle standard. 2. A slogan (written on a flag). 3. A battle flag with dimensions of about 2 feet wide by 10 feet long (.6 × 3.7 m) in size, the *hatajirushi* was normally attached vertically to a long pole; the short side of the banner supported along the top by either a swinging arm or a fixed arm. For illustration, see: *noboribata. See also: sashimono (hata).*

Hatakeyama Masanaga 畠山 政長 (?–1493). Hatakeyama is credited with the creation of the *chitsuki hata*—a battlefield "banner with loops"—in 1456. He also invented a special arrow-protecting device called a *horo* during the Ōnin era (1467–1468). He was made prime minister to the Ashikaga *shōgun* (Kyōto *kanryō* 管領) in 1464.

hatamoto 旗本. Lit. "at the foot of the flag"; a bannerman. 1. During the Warring States period (Sengoku Jidai, 1482–1558), this term referred to a commander of a military group (*kumi*). 2. During the Tokugawa period, the term *hatamoto* referred to the direct vassals of the *shōgun* who ranked below the *daimyō* and above the *gokenin*. *Hatamoto* had fiefs, and received stipends of less than 10,000 but more than 100 *koku* (one *koku* was the amount of rice that would feed a person for a year). They served in the middle- to upper-level posts of the shogunate, and were considered elite among the samurai; higher-ranking *hatamoto* could have vassals of their own. There were about 6,000 *hatamoto* in 1800.

hatamoto yakko 旗本奴. The *hatamoto yakko* were vagrant, masterless samurai (*rōnin*) who proliferated in the early years of the Edo period. Some of these may not have been samurai at all, but low-ranking armed men who sometimes formed into groups for nefarious purposes. Such men dressed in colorful, often outlandish *kimono* of the type referred to as *kabukimono*, which were normally worn by young women. *Hatamoto yakko* became such a problem that the Tokugawa *bakufu* tightened its regulations and banned all *yakko* gangs in 1686. Contrast to *machi yakko*.

Further reading in English:
- Seigle, 1993: 56–58.

hatasashi 旗指. A standard-bearer. Warrior chiefs in the medieval war tales often designated vassals to serve as their *hatasashi*.

hatashijō 果し状. A fighter's letter of challenge; a letter of challenge to a duel.

Hatchōbori 八丁堀. Lit. the "Hatchō canal"; the "Hatchō moat." This was the name of a canal along which the Edo police sergeants (*yoriki*) and constables (*dōshin*) lived with their families. The area's function as a police enclave had an impact on Edo history and culture. For example, the constabulary were called *Hatchōbori no danna* ("master" or "gentleman" of the Hatchōbori); and a particularly tenacious or fearsome officer who literally never gave up the chase was referred to as a *Hatchōbori no oni* (demon of Hatchōbori).

The area has long made appearances in fiction; in modern times a *manga* comic-book series called *Hatchōbori*, portraying the lives of the *yoriki* and *dōshin*, has become popular. Koike Kazuo and Kojima Goseki, in their graphic novel series entitled *Kubikiri Asa* (*Samurai Executioner* in its English translation edition), make frequent reference to Hatchōbori. Television shows often portray the police of the district swaggering around the area or running full tilt from the Machi Bugyōsho office after receiving their orders. A current popular series, *Hatchōbori Seven*, features the adventures of a *yoriki* and six *dōshin*.

Hatchōbori no danna 八丁堀の旦那. See: *Hatchōbori.*

Hatchōbori no oni 八丁堀の鬼. See: *Hatchōbori.*

hatomunedō 鳩胸胴. Lit. "pigeon-breasted corselet." This term referred to corselets (*dō*) which copied the European style and looked much like those of the Spanish Conquistadors. They were one of the varieties of "foreigner's corselet" (*nambandō* 南蛮胴).

hato-o no ita 鳩尾之板. Variant reading of the characters for *kyūbi no ita.*

Hattengiri 八天切. TSUTSUMI HŌZAN RYŪ—*Hattengiri* is one of a number of classical prearranged combative forms (*kata*) developed by this school. It was also one of ten classical *kata* adapted by the Japanese Police Commission of 1886 for their Keishichō Ryū 警視庁流 system.

Hattori Buzaemon Masanobu 服部 武左衛門正信. Founder of Iga Ryū (2) 伊賀流, a martial school specializing in espionage (*shinobi no jutsu*).

Hattori Hanzō 服部 半蔵 [A.k.a. ***Hattori Masashige (Masanari)*** 服部正成] (1541–1596). Recognized progenitor of Iga Ryū (1) (a branch of the clan espionage tradition which evolved in Iga province) after his assignment by Tokugawa Ieyasu. Hanzō was a member of a clan of *suppa* (low-ranking retainers, much like *nobushi*) from Iga province who became a retainer of Tokugawa Ieyasu. Since he hailed from an area close to Iga, Ieyasu had a long and continuing relationship with the *suppa* of Iga, and had even sheltered survivors from Nobunaga's invasion of Iga in 1580. Hanzō fought alongside Ieyasu in several battles, including Anegawa (1570) and Mikatagahara (1572). He performed his greatest service to Ieyasu, however, right after the assassination of Oda Nobunaga in 1582. Ieyasu's forces, camped near Ōsaka at the time of the assassination, were almost surrounded by the troops of Akechi Mitsuhide. Hanzō suggested Ieyasu and his troops travel via Iga province to reach their stronghold at Mikawa. One of Ieyasu's generals, Honda Tadakatsu, sent Hanzō on ahead so that he could arrange not only safe passage but also an escort for Ieyasu. The trip through Iga was evidently one of the most perilous of Ieyasu's career, and the powerful leader was greatly indebted to Hanzō and the Iga *suppa*.

HATTORI HANZŌ
Seventeenth-century portrait

In 1590, Hanzō received the rank of *yoriki* 与力. He was placed in command of 200 troops that would later become the Edo Castle guard under his son, Hattori Masanari.

Artifacts of Hanzō's legacy remain to this day. For example, the imperial palace (formerly Tokugawa Ieyasu's Edo castle) has a gate named after him (Hanzōmon 半蔵門). The legendary Hanzō is also a popular motif in Japanese comics (*manga*) and fiction.

Hattori Kanetsugu Masaji 服部 包次 正次. Founder of Fujibayashi Ryū 藤林流, a school of strategy and tactics (*gunkai*).

Hattori Mino no Kami Yasukiyo 服部 美濃守 保清. Yasukiyo, a descendant of Hattori Hanzō, is credited with compiling the teachings of Hanzō's Iga Ryū *nimpō* into a four-volume collection entitled the *Ninpiden* in 1653.

haya 甲矢. The first of two arrows fired in the practice of Japanese archery (*kyūdō*). (The second arrow is called the *otoya*.) Japanese arrows are fletched with feathers that curve left or right, depending on which wing of the bird they are from. The *haya* has fletching which curves to the left, causing the arrow to rotate clockwise in flight.

hayagake 早駆. Techniques used to improve speed in walking and running. Watatani and Yamada (1978:30) note that this term is the equivalent of both *hayamichi* and *michidatsusha*.

hayagakejutsu 早駆術. See: *hayagake*.

hayago 早合. A gunpowder flask; a speed-loader for a matchlock musket. See also: *enshō-ire*.

hayamichi 早道. See: *hayagake*.

Hayanawa 早縄 【早繩】. Initial set of four restraining cord ties that are taught in the Ittatsu Ryū 一達流.

Hayasha 早捨. Sixth set of primary swordsmanship forms (*kata*) used by the Jigen Ryū 示現流.

Hayashi Yazaemon Iekiyo 林 弥左衛門 家清 【林彌左衛門家清】 (1882–1964). Master teacher (*shihan*) and head instructor of the Katori Shintō Ryū during the mid-twentieth century. Hayashi joined the Tenshinshō-den Katori Shintō Ryū 天真正伝香取神道流 in 1897 at the age of fifteen. As a disciple (*deshi*) of the eighteenth headmaster, Iizasa Morisada, he trained vigorously and became one of the top students in the system. Consequently, in 1916 he was given the privilege of demonstrating Shintō Ryū for Emperor Taishō.[7] In his heyday Hayashi attracted over 200 students to the school; it was due to his efforts that Katori Shintō Ryū became the first sword school to be officially designated as an "intangible cultural asset" (*mukei bunkazai*). Hayashi's successor as chief instructor of the *ryū* is Ōtake Risuke.

Hayashizaki Jinsuke Shigenobu 林崎 甚助 重信 [A.k.a. ***Hōjō Jinsuke Shigenobu*** 北条 甚助 重信] (c.1546–1621). Founder of Shin Musō Hayashizaki Ryū 神夢想林崎流 (=Shimmei Musō Ryū 神明夢想流). According to Japanese tradition, Jinsuke founded the art of the quick-draw sword (*iaijutsu*) when he established the Shimmei Musō Ryū. However, it is a matter of record that the art of *iaijutsu* was being practiced by members of the Tenshinshō-den Katori Shintō Ryū a hundred years prior to Jinsuke's time.

In any case, little is actually known about Jinsuke. It is believed he was born around 1546 and probably had combat experience. An Edo-period work entitled *Bujutsu taihaku seiden* 『武術太白成伝』 notes that he spent the years from 1595 to 1601 "studying swordsmanship." He christened his technique of sword drawing "the art of the striking sword" (*battōjutsu*), toured the country on a *musha shūgyō* (martial pilgrimage), and gained many disciples who then passed on his teachings. Around the year 1616, at the age of seventy, he again set off on a martial pilgrimage and subsequently disappeared. During the remaining Edo period, over 200 *ryū* evolved which traced their roots to his inspiration.

Not long after Jinsuke's disappearance, his successors named his system Shin Musō (Hayashizaki) Ryū 神夢想[林崎]流. In the mid-1700s this system was renamed Hasegawa Eishin Ryū 長谷英信流 by the seventh headmaster. During the peaceful times of the Edo period the combative effectiveness of the *ryū* declined as emphasis was shifted to non-combative postures such as *seiza* and *tatehiza* and the wearing of a single sword instead of the *daishō*.

After the eleventh headmaster, a split developed in the main line of the tradition. One of these branches has been in dispute since the death of the sixteenth headmaster, the

[7] Taisho Tennō 大正天皇 (1879–1926; r. 1912–1926), 123rd emperor of Japan.

famous Meiji/Taisho-era swordsman Nakayama Hakudō. The second branch claimed continuity down through the nineteenth headmaster, Kono Momonori, but has been in dispute since the death of seventeenth headmaster Ōe Masamichi. (See Shin Musō Hayashizaki Ryū for lineage.)

Hayashizaki Musō Ryū 林崎夢想流 [A.k.a. ***Musō Ryū (3)*** 夢想流]. Alternate name for the Hayashizaki Musō Ryū line, which flourished in Akita domain and Nihonmatsu domain from the mid to late 1700s.

Hayashizaki Ryū 林崎流. Variant name for Shimmei Musō Ryū. See also: *Hasegawa Chikaranosuke Eishin (Hidenobu); Hayashizaki Jinsuke Shigenobu; Shin Musō Hayashizaki Ryū.*

hazu 筈. The notch of an arrow.

hazushi 外し. *Hazushi* is a form of the verb *hazusu* (to avoid; to escape) found in compounds indicating techniques of avoidance or escape, e.g. *tsuki-hazushi* 突外 (avoiding a thrust).

hazuyari 弭槍 [A.k.a. ***hokoyumi*** 鉾弓]. A socketed spearhead attached to the upper end of a bow (*yumi*). Spear-head bows were often used by units of low-ranking foot archers (*yumigumi ashigaru*). If the bowstring broke and no replacement was available, the bow itself could be used as a spear. This dual-purpose weapon proliferated among *yumigumi ashigaru* around the end of the Momoyama period (c. 1600).

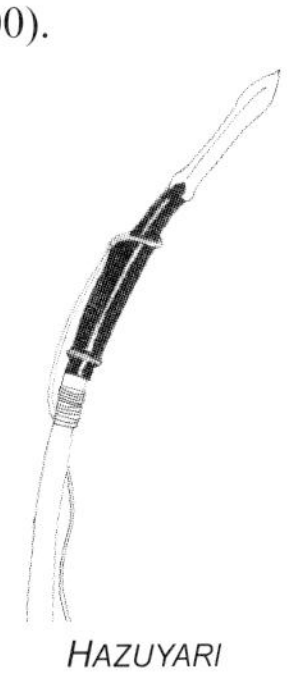

HAZUYARI

hei 塀. Wooden walls (as might be used for a fortification).

Heianchō 平安朝. The period (794–1185) when the seat of political power in Japan was located in the city of Heian (Heiankyō). See: *Kyōto.*

Heian Kata 平安型 <Oki. *Pinan Kata.* JAPANESE KARATE—Japanese pronunciation for Pinan Kata. See: *karate kata; Pinan Kata.*

Hei An Kō 平安行. *Sandan*-level combative forms taught by the Jigen Ryū 示現流. See: *Jigen Ryū; Sandan (1).*

Heiankyō 平安京 [A.k.a. ***Kyōto*** 京都]. The city that served as the Japanese imperial capital from 794 to 1868. The Heian period (794–1185) takes it name from the time when actual governmental power resided in Heiankyō. See: *Kyōto.*

heichōzan 平頂山. Lit. "flat-topped mountain." A type of helmet with a flat top.

heiden 併伝【併傳】. Nineteenth-century term used by the Suiō Ryū 水鴎流 to indicate a collateral combative system.

Heiden Masaki Ryū Kusarigama-jutsu 併伝正木流鎖鎌術【併傳正木流鏁鎌術】. See: *Masaki Ryū Fukuhara Ha Kusarigama-jutsu.*

Heidō no kagami『兵道鏡』. See: *Hyōdōkyō.*

Heigakkō 兵学校【兵學校】. Lit. "Military School." The Heigakkō was an early name for the institution that became the Toyama Gakkō.

heigaku 兵学【兵學】. Martial science, military science, strategy, tactics, and ethics. See: *heihō.*

heigo 兵語. Military terminology; martial jargon. This term includes, but is not limited to, "martial arts" terminology.

heihō 1. 兵法 [Also read ***hyōhō***] <Ch. *bingfa.* Lit. "war methods; war arts." Many classical martial schools (*koryū*) included some form of *heihō* in their teachings. Consequently, since the mid-1500s the term *heihō* has become synonymous with skill in swordsmanship. The earliest usage of *heihō*, however, refers to military/martial strategy. The term can include strategy, tactics, espionage, astrology and battlefield divination, and a variety of other related arts such as directing troops in battle by

bugling with a conch shell (*horagai*).

Depending on the historical period, geographical location, and particular school of combat (*ryū*), the term *heihō* may include, and occasionally be used interchangeably with, *gumbai* 軍配 (combat divination), *gungaku* 軍学 (tactics and strategy), *gunkai* 軍貝 (tactics and strategy including specific operational techniques such as espionage), *gumpō* 軍法 (synonymous with *gungaku*), *gunra* 軍螺 (synonymous with *gunkai*), *jingai* 陣貝 (synonymous with *gunkai*), *sōren* 繰練 (tactics and strategy), *senryaku* 戦略 (battle tactics), *senjutsu* 戦術 (battle skills/arts), *sentōhō* 戦闘 (battle strategy/combat strategy), and others.

Ishioka (1972: 17) lists the names of fifty-six *ryū* which concentrated on military *heihō*, and notes that there were about sixty that dealt with naval strategy and tactics (*suigun* 水軍). This information, Ishioka notes, was taken from a work entitled *Heika keizu*『兵家系図』(A genealogical study of strategists) published in 1808. Fujita (1960: 2) notes 272 *ryū* specializing in *heihōjutsu*.

heihō 2. 平法 [Also read ***hyōhō***]. Lit. "peace methods"; "arts of peace." Sometimes contrasted with *heihō* 兵法 "arts of war."

Heihō hijutsu ikkan no sho「兵法秘術一巻書」(One-scroll text on the secret methods of strategy). This document, dating from 1354, is a text on martial strategy which was derived from the *Genke kin'etsushū*.

heihōjutsu 兵法術. See: *heihō (1)*.

Heihōjutsu ryūko sanryaku no maki「兵法術龍虎三略巻」(Dragon-tiger stratagem—three briefs on tactics and war methods). A text on martial strategy which was derived from the *Genke Kin'etsushū*.

heihōka 兵法家. 1. From around the early to mid-1500s, this term came to mean a warrior (*bushi*). 2. A strategist; a tactician.

Heihō kadensho『兵法家伝書』【兵法家傳書】(The family transmission of martial strategy). The (Yagyū) family-transmitted treatise (*kadensho*) on Shinkage Ryū martial strategy (*heihō*). Written by Yagyū Munenori in the early seventeenth century, this is an insightful presentation of the Edo Yagyū Shinkage Ryū as practiced at that time. There are two English versions, neither of which was translated by a practitioner of Shinkage Ryū.

Further reading in English:

- Sato, 1986 (Trans.).
- Wilson, 2004 (Trans.).

Heihō kuji no daiji『兵法九字の大事』(Critical points of the martial strategy of the nine [mystical] letters). SHUGENDŌ—The *Heihō kuji no daiji* is a text on martial strategy and the use of the "Ritual Method of the Nine Seals" (Kujihō). See: *Kujihō*.

Heihō Niten Ichi Ryū 兵法二天一流. See: *Hyōhō Niten Ichi Ryū*.

Heihō reizuisho「兵法霊瑞書」【兵法靈瑞書】(Strategy based on miraculous signs). A text on martial strategy, dating from 1359, which was derived from the *Genke Kin'etsushū*.

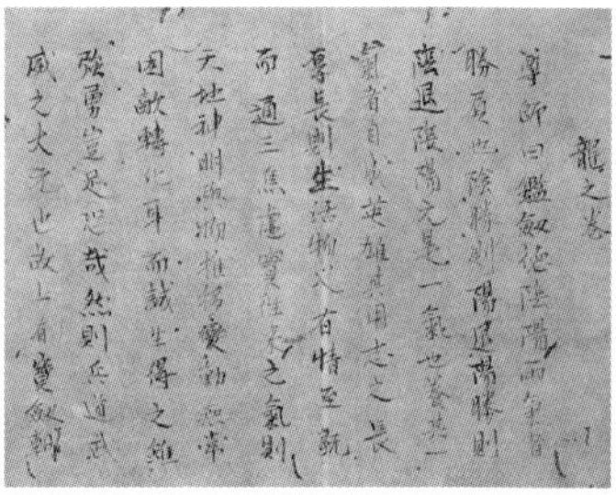

RYŪ NO MAKI (DETAIL)
From the Jiki Shinkage Ryū *Kyūri no maki*, 1823
(*Densho* from a private collection)

Heihō ryū no maki「兵法龍之巻」(Dragon scroll on strategy) [Var. ***Ryū no maki*** 龍(之)巻]. A text on martial strategy which was derived from the *Genke Kin'etsushū*.

Heihō sanjūgo ka jō『兵法三十五ヶ条』. See: *Hyōhō sanjūgo ka jō*.

heihōsha 兵法者. 1. From around the early to mid-1500s, this term came to mean a warrior (*bushi*). 2. A strategist; a tactician.

Heihōsho 兵法所. Martial arts hall (*dōjō*) built in the Imadegawa area of Kyōto by Shōgun Ashikage Yoshiteru during the mid-1500s. Many famous swordsmen of that era demonstrated their art there. See: *Ashikaga Yoshiteru*.

Heihō tora no maki「兵法虎之巻」(Tiger

scroll on strategy) [Var. ***Tora no maki*** 虎(之)巻]. A text on martial strategy derived from the *Genke kin'etsushū*.

Heihō wa heihō nari 兵法は平法なり. Well-known phrase meaning "The arts of war are arts of peace." Often attributed to the Tenshinshō-den Katori Shintō Ryū, this concept is actually found throughout Japanese martial culture in various places and times. For example, martial historian and hoplologist Donn F. Draeger[8] sometimes noted that the Masamune family, famous for their sword-making for several centuries, created their weapons in the spirit of *nukazu ni sumu* 抜かずにすむ. This phrase means to do things or settle issues without drawing the sword. In fact, from the ninth century—the earliest era in which the classical warrior became a powerful force in Japanese culture—until the dissolution of the warrior class in the early Meiji period (1870s), this ideal was esteemed as the ultimate in swordsmanship. Legends as well as historical accounts of swordsmen living this ideal are found in Japanese history all the way from Fujiwara Yasumasa (958–1036) to Yamaoka Tesshū (1836–1888).

Heihō yonjūni ka jō 「兵法四十二ヶ条」 (Forty-two sections on strategy). This document is a text on martial strategy derived from the *Genke kin'etsushū*. A document with the same title, but a slightly different pronunciation, the *Hyōhō shijūni ka jō* 「兵法四十二ケ条」, was written later by Miyamoto Musashi.

Heiji monogatari 『平治物語』 (Tale of the Heiji). A Japanese war tale relating the events of the Heiji no Ran, a civil war that took place in the Heiji era (1159). While Hamuro Tokinaga is often credited with writing the document, its actual authorship is in doubt. See also: *Gikeiki; Heike monogatari; Hōgan monogatari; Shōmonki; Taiheiki.*

Further reading in English:

- Varley, 1994: 66–77.

heijin 兵刃. A military sword.

Heiji no Ran 平治乱【平治亂】. This war, which took place during the Heiji era (1159), brought the Minamoto and the Taira, the two most important warrior families of the period, into direct conflict for the second time. In 1159, Fujiwara Nobuyori and Minamoto Yoshitomo revolted against the rule of the Taira, who were led by Taira Kiyomori and Fujiwara Tadamichi. Both Nobuyori and Yoshitomo were defeated and killed. As a result of this, Yoshitomo's third son, Minamoto no Yoritomo, who was thirteen years old, was exiled to Hiruga-oshima in Izu. His youngest son, Minamoto no Yoshitsune, was sent to the Tendai temple called Kuramadera to be raised as a Buddhist monk at the age of one. The events of this war are recorded in the *Heiji monogatari*.

Further reading in English:

- Farris, 1992: 270–273.

heijō 兵杖. Combative art of the medium-length staff, as developed by Sasaki Tessai Tokuhisa in the first two decades of the seventeenth century.

heijōshin 平常心. 1. BUDDHISM—An impartial mind and, by extension, a tranquil mind. Literally, a "normal" mind. 2. MARTIAL ARTS—The normal or tranquil state of mind which must be maintained when one is under attack. In other words, one must remain relaxed and self-confident. See also: *fudōshin; sanchin kokyūhō.*

heijutsu 兵術. A generic term referring to strategy and hand-to-hand combative arts. The specific meaning varies, as it was often defined within the specific group or school which used it.

Heike 平家. See: *Taira.*

Heike monogatari 『平家物語』 (Tale of the Heike). Probably the most famous Japanese war tale, this text relates the events of the Gempei War (Gempei Gassen) between the Minamoto (Gen 源) and Taira (Pei 平) families. See also: *Heiji monogatari; Hōgen monogatari; Shōmonki; Taiheiki; Yoshitsune monogatari.*

Further reading in English:

- Kitagawa and Tsuchida (translation), 1975.
- McCullough (translation), 1988.
- Varley, 1994: 78–125.

[8] See Bibliography.

H

heiki 兵気【兵氣】. Martial heart or spirit. See: *gunki (1).*

heimin 平民. Lit. "commoner," "plebeian." *Heimin* was an early Meiji-era term denoting citizens who were descendents of non-samurai families, in contrast to descendents of warrior families (*shizoku*). The term *heimin* is also found in compounds such as *heiminshugi* 平民主義, "democracy."

heimon 閉門. Fourth-most severe of the five grades of legal penalties applied to the samurai during the Tokugawa period. *Heimon*, which literally means "closing the gate," refers to house arrest. *Heimon* could be applied for fifty or one hundred days. See also: *chikkyo; hissoku; kaieki; seppuku.*

Further reading in English:
- Brinkley and Kikuchi, 1915: 641–642 *ff.*
- Schreiber, 2001.
- Seward, 1968.

heishi 1. 兵士. TAIHŌ MILITARY SYSTEM—A conscript soldier in a provincial regiment (*gundan*) formed under the Taihō Codes (Taihō Ritsuryō) of 702. As a soldier at the bottom of the chain of command, the *heishi* was somewhat equivalent to a modern army private. See: *gundan.*

Heishi 2. 平氏. See: *Taira.*

heishiya 兵士屋. Medieval term for military barracks.

heishujutsu 平手術. Grappling system developed by Sugita Shuhō Kiyoichi in the mid-twentieth century. Sugita was a direct disciple of Hakkō Ryū founder Okuyama Yoshiji.

heitō 柄頭. See: *tsukagashira.*

Heki Danjō Masatsugu 日置 弾正 正次【日置彈正正次】(c.1443–1502). Heki Masatsugu founded the Heki Ryū around 1480. Due to the later spread of his particular system of archery (*kyūjutsu*), he is sometimes known as the progenitor of modern archery (*kinsei kyūjutsu no so* 近世弓術の祖). Various documents assign different names to Masatsugu, but little is known about him or his life. Oral tradition tells us that, at around the age of forty, he experienced an oracle revelation (*musō*) in which three elements that would become the secret core of his new system were bestowed upon him: *hi* 飛 (fly), *kan* 貫 (pierce), and *chū* 中 (center). These enigmatic terms evidently enabled Heki to revolutionize his archery technique. As his system spread among later generations, it revolutionized the art of Japanese archery. During the succeeding centuries, offshoots of the Heki Ryū were the most prominent and widespread of any archery school in Japan.

Hekiganroku 『碧巌録』【碧巖錄】<Ch. *Biyan Lu* (Blue Cliff records). *Hekiganroku* is the title of a collection of a hundred *kōan* (riddles) originally compiled, with appreciatory verses, by Xuedou Zhongxian[9] (980–1052). Yuanwu Keqin[10] (1063–1135) later added commentaries, pointers, and notes to the text.

Kamiizumi Nobutsuna based some of the *kata* and concept names for his Shinkage Ryū (1) 新陰流 on the *Hekiganroku*. See also: *kōan.*

Further reading in English:
- Clery and Clery (trans.). (1977).
- Clery (trans.). (2002).

Heki Ryū 日置流. School of archery (*kyūjutsu*) founded around 1480 by Heki Danjō Masatsugu. One of the most popular schools of *kyūjutsu*, the Heki Ryū proliferated widely during the Warring States and Edo periods. It is considered the basis for most currently practiced schools and methods of modern Japanese archery (*kyūdō*).

Further reading in English:
- Hurst, 1998: 121–135 *ff.*
- Onuma, 1993.

Henmi Ryū 逸見流. School of combative archery (*kyūjutsu*) founded by Henmi Seikō.

Henmi Seikō 逸見清光. Founder of the Henmi Ryū, a system of combative archery (*kyūjutsu*).

Henmi Shōgen Yoshimine 逸見 将監 義峰. Founder of the Iga Ryū (5) 伊賀流, an empty-handed striking system (*kempō* 拳法) which became prominent during the Tempō era (1830–1844).

---

9 Ch. Xuedou Zhongxian 雪竇重顯 > Jp. Setchō Juken.

10 Ch. Yuanwu Keqin 圜悟克勤 > Jp. Engo Kokugon.

Heki Ryū
日置流
(abbreviated lineage)

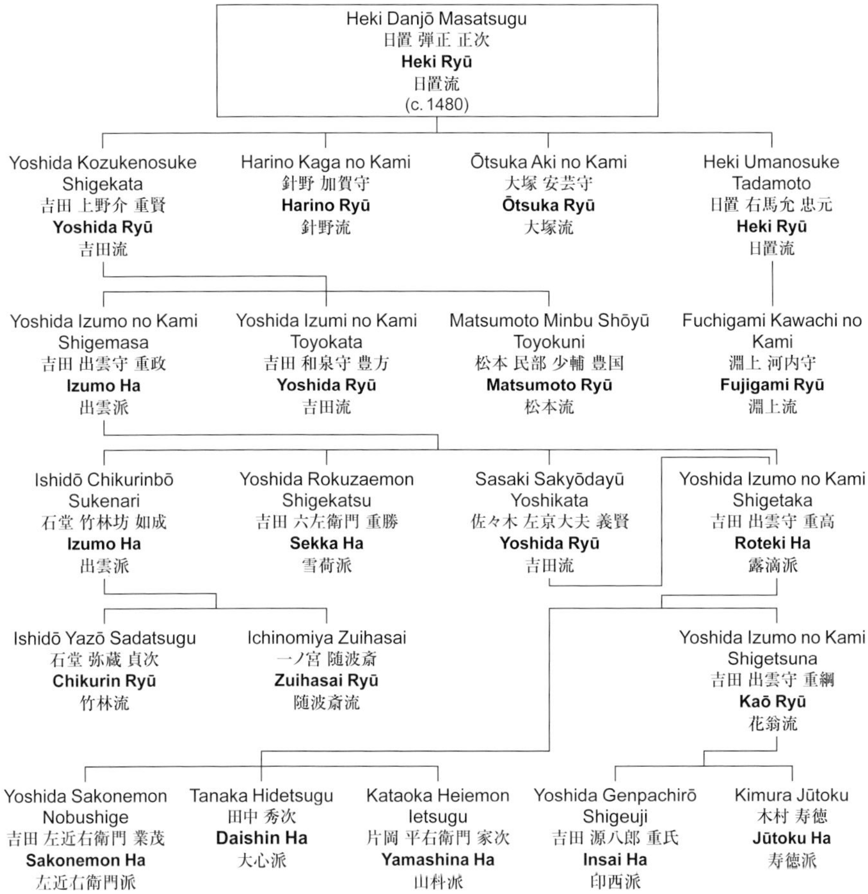

henka 変化【變化】. Lit. a "variation." 1. MARTIAL ARTS—A variation on a standard combative form (*kata*) or technique. 2. KURAMA RYŪ—*Henka* was one of ten classical *kata* adapted by the Japanese Police Commission of 1886 for their Keishichō Ryū 警視庁流 system.

Henmi Tashirō Yoshitoshi 逸見 太四郎 義年 (1746–1828). Swordsman who founded Kōgen Ittō Ryū 甲源一刀流 around 1780. See: *Kōgen Ittō Ryū.*

henshu 変手【變手】. OKINAWAN KARATE—In *karate*, *henshu* is the practice of suddenly using the forward hand to attack an opponent (in contrast to the normal practice of using the rear hand). See also: *kisei; shinte.*

heō 経鷲【經鷲】[Also read ***oō***]. A falcon's leash. A *heō* was normally made of red silk, but a falcon that had killed a crane was given one of purple silk. Falconry was a popular practice among warriors during various historical periods. Varieties of purple, such as Edo *murasaki* (which is almost red in color), were often used among the warriors and noble classes to denote rank or mastery in an art; the custom was extended to eagles or falcons that were especially skillful. See: *takagari; washi (1).*

heyazashi 部屋差. 1. Lit. "carried inside a room (in the home)." A short sword or dagger designed to be wielded in the home.

hi 樋 [Also referred to as ***kessō*** 血相]. Lit. "gutter," "trough." *Hi* refers to a groove in a blade. There are a variety of types, such as *bōhi* (wide grooves), *koshihi* (short grooves), etc.

Further reading in English:

- Yumoto, 1958: 57–59.

hi 飛. SHŌGI—An abbreviation or notation for *hisha* 飛車. See: *hisha.*

hi aburi 火炙 [Var. 火焙]. Burning at the stake was one of the four prescribed forms of execution for Tokugawa-period commoners. This form of punishment was generally applied to arsonists. See also: *shikei.*

Further reading in English:

- Schriber, 2001: 46; 75–77.

hibasami 火鋏. The match-holder (serpentine) of a matchlock musket.

hibuta 火蓋. A matchlock pan cover.

hidari 左 [Also read ***sa***]. Left. ¶ *hidari ni* 左に, to the left.

hiden 秘伝【秘傳】. Lit. "secret transmission"; "privileged transmission." See also: *gokuhi; gokui; gokuiden; hiden gokui; okugi; okuden.*

hiden gokui 秘伝極意【秘傳極意】. 1. Secretly transmitted principles/mysteries of an art such as swordsmanship. 2. SHINDŌ MUSŌ RYŪ—*Hiden Gokui.* See: *Go Musō no Jō.*

Hiden mokuroku 「秘伝目録」【秘傳目録】 [Abbr. of ***Daitō Ryū hiden mokuroku***]. The first of several Daitō Ryū transmission scrolls (*densho*) awarded in that tradition. Mastery of 118 techniques is required to earn the scroll.

Hiden ōgi mokuroku 「秘伝奥義目録」【秘傳奥義目録】 [Abbr. of ***Daitō Ryū ōgi mokuroku***]. The third of several Daitō Ryū transmission scrolls (*densho*) awarded in that tradition. Mastery of thirty-six techniques is required to earn the scroll.

Hiden Ryū 飛電流 [A.k.a. ***Aoki Ha Hiden Ryū*** 青木派飛電流]. Hiden Ryū was a tradition centering on the pipe spear (*kudayari*) of the Aoki Ryū 青木流. Hiden Ryū was founded by Aoki Budayū Hochi. See: *Aoki Budayū Hochi.*

hidensho 秘伝書【秘傳書】. A restricted or secret transmission document. See: *densho.*

Hideyoshi 秀吉. See: *Toyotomi Hideyoshi.*

Hieizan 比叡山. Mount Hiei. In 788 the monk Saichō, founder of the Tendai school of Buddhism, established a temple called Enryakuji on top of this mountain, which is located northeast of Kyōto. The school flourished; however, as it grew in power and influence, it also produced an army of warrior monks (*sōhei*) to protect its extensive property holdings. For this reason, Oda Nobunaga razed Enryakuji in 1571, putting many monks to the sword. The temple was rebuilt and remains the headquarters of the Tendai school today. See also: *Tendai Shū; sōhei.*

Higaonna Kanryō 東恩納 寛裕 [Var. 寛量; a.k.a. ***Higashionna Kanryō***] (1853–1916). An Okinawa *te* master, Higaonna was the progenitor of the school of Okinawan *karate* which later came to be formulated into Gōjū Ryū. According to Miyazato Eiichi, a disciple of Miyagi Chōjun, Higaonna journeyed to Fuzhou, China around 1873 in order to study Chinese boxing. However, Mura Kamikatsuni's *Karatedō to Ryūkyū kobudō* states that Higaonna travelled to Fuchou several times as a boy aide to Yoshimura Udun (Bishop, 1999: 24–25). While in Fuchou, Higaonna evidently trained in various empty hand and weapons styles, including *hsing-i*. However, his primary instructor in Chinese boxing was a master boxer commonly referred to as Rū-rū Kō.[11] Returning to Okinawa around 1882, Higaonna began to teach what he had learned. Although he called his school Shōrei Ryū 昭霊流, it became known locally as Naha *te* 那覇手 after the city in which it was practiced. In addition, research by McCarthy (2008: 73) has indicated that a Naha *te*/Shōrei Ryū/Gōjū Ryū "style" had been practiced in Naha since the 1820s.

Watatani and Yamada (1978: 279–280) list eight senior students of Higaonna, among

[11] Ju-ju Ko and other variations in Chinese. See entry under *Rū-rū Kō.*

whom the foremost were Miyagi Chōjun, Koki Shiroma, and Jūhatsu Kyuoda.[12] See also: *Gōjū Ryū; Rū-rū Kō.*

Further reading in English:

- Bishop, 1999: 24–27 *ff.*
- McCarthy, 2008: 70–74 *ff.*
- Nagamine, 2000: 60–68.

Higashionna Kanryō 東恩納寛裕. See: *Higaonna Kanryō.*

Hiki Yoshio 比企良雄. Founder of Jikishin Ryū (4) 直心流. Hiki was a *shugenja* (practitioner of Shugendō) of the Raigakuin temple on Mount Horai (Hōraisan 蓬莱山). In addition to being a *yamabushi*, Hiki was an accomplished martial artist who had trained in the Gassan Ryū 月山流 of Sawara Minamoto no Nisaburō Sukemitsu. After mastering the three polearms of that system—glaive (*naginata*), spear (*yari*), and pole sickle (*nagae no kama*)—Hiki succeeded Sawara to become the tenth headmaster of the system around 1625. In addition, Hiki also trained in Hisshō Muni Ryū 必勝無二流 swordsmanship (*kenjutsu*), Shintō Katori Ryū 真当揖取流, Emmei Ryū 円明流, Itō Ryū (1) 伊東流, and others.

higokenin 非御家人. 1. A Kamakura-period term referring to those warriors who had not sworn loyalty to the Kamakura shogunate, in contrast to the Kamakura housemen (*gokenin*). 2. A Muromachi-period term referring to warriors who were not direct retainers (*gokenin*) of the Ashikaga shogunate.

higuchi 火口. The touchhole in a matchlock firearm.

Higuchi 樋口. 1. A warrior family descended from the Minamoto clan. 2. A noble family (*kuge*) descended from the Fujiwara clan.

Higuchi Kaneshige 樋口 兼重 [A.k.a. ***Higuchi Tarō Minamoto no Kaneshige*** 樋口 太郎 源兼重] (fl. mid-1300s). Recognized second-generation headmaster (*sei* 世) of the Nen Ryū and progenitor of the Higuchi Nen Ryū. Kaneshige was a tenth-generation descendant of Higuchi Kanemitsu (?–1184), one of the Shitennō (four great retainers) of Minamoto Yoshinaka (1154–1184).

As one of the fourteen disciples of Nen Ami Jion, Kaneshige received the most secret teaching of the Nen Ryū 念流, and became the progenitor of the Higuchi Nen Ryū.

Higuchi Matashichirō Minamoto no Sadatsugu 樋口 又七郎 源定次. See: *Higuchi Sadatsugu.*

Higuchi Nen Ryū 樋口念流. The early Higuchi line of the Nen Ryū 念流 beginning with Higuchi Tarō Kaneshige (c. 1370) and ending with his grandson, Higuchi Takashige (1425–1513), around 1500.

Higuchi Sadahiro 樋口 定広 (d. 1998) [A.k.a. ***Higuchi Minamoto no Sadahiro*** 樋口 源定広]. Recognized as twenty-fourth-generation headmaster (*sei* 世) of the Nen Ryū.

HIGUCHI SADAHIRO
The late twenty-fourth headmaster of the Nen Ryū demonstrating *yadomejutsu* (arrow deflection with a short sword)
(©1991, *Hiden Koryū Bujutsu Quarterly* 6; used with permission)

Higuchi Sadatsugu 樋口 定次 [A.k.a. ***Higuchi Matashichirō Minamoto no Sadatsugu*** 樋口 又七郎 源定次] (fl. mid-1500s–mid-1600s). Progenitor of the Maniwa Nen Ryū. Sadatsugu, having mastered the local Shintō Ryū system, decided to return the Higuchi family martial arts to the tradition of his ancestors. (The Higuchi family had dropped the Nen Ryū in the late 1400s when they moved to Maniwa.) He sought out Tomomatsu Seizo Fujiwara no Ujimune (Gian), the seventh headmaster of the Akamatsu line of the Nen Ryū (known then as Nen Shuza Ryū). After several years of arduous training, Higuchi succeeded Tomomatsu as eighth-generation headmaster of the

[12] Jūhatsu noted that Higaonna also taught several weapons arts. (McCarthy, 2008: 74). However, these were not learned by Miyagi and, consequently, were not carried over into Gōjū Ryū.

Nen Shuza Ryū. Since Higuchi was a *gōshi* (a "landed" warrior who resided on his estate) living in Maniwa, the tradition has been called Maniwa Nen Ryū since that time.

Further reading in English:

- Hurst, 1998: 63–64.

hihō 秘法. Hidden or secret methods. See also: *gokuhi.*

hiji 肘. Elbow; also referred to as *empi (4)*. ¶ *hiji ate* 肘当て, an elbow strike. ¶ *hijijime* 肘締め [肘絞め], an elbow lock.

Hijikata Toshizō 土方 歳三 (1835–1869). Tennen Rishin Ryū 天然理心流 swordsman and member of the Shinsengumi (a special corps of *samurai* and armed peasants sent by the shogunate to restore order to Kyoto in the early 1860s). Hijikata was a deputy leader in the Shinsengumi in the 1860s. See: *Shinsengumi.*

hijutsu 秘術. Lit. "secret techniques." See also: *gokuhi; gokui.*

hikan 被官. 1. Muromachi-period term indicating warriors (*bushi*) who were retainers of the provincial *bakufu*-appointed military governors (*shugo daimyō*). 2. Muromachi-period term indicating personal subordinates of *kokujin* lords. (Hall and Toyoda, 1977: 360). 3. According to Mass (1982: 288), the term *hikan* was used in the Muromachi period to indicate followers or retainers of low rank, as well as low-ranking personal retainers of the Ashikaga *bakufu*. See also: *hōkōshū.*

Hikida Bungorō 疋田豊五郎. See: *Hikita Bungorō.*

Hikida (Shin) Kage Ryū 疋田(新)陰流. See: *Hikita Kage Ryū.*

hikigane 引金. A matchlock trigger.

hikihada 1. 蟇肌. Lit. "toadskin." An abbreviation for *hikihada shinai.*

hikihada 2. 比伎波駄. Joly and Inada (1913: 30) say this term refers to "scabbard covers which were used when traveling."

Further reading in English:

- Joly and Inada (1913; repr. 1979).

hikihada kawa shinai 蟇肌革竹刀【蟆肌革竹刀】. See: *hikihada shinai.*

hikihada shinai 蟇肌竹刀【蟆肌竹刀】[Var. 引膚竹刀; 袋撓; also called the ***hikihada kawa shinai*** 皺文革竹刀]. Lit. "toadskin-covered bamboo sword." Original model of the *fukuro shinai* designed by Kamiizumi Ise no Kami Nobutsuna. This may, as the name indicates, have been a shaft of split bamboo covered in tough toadskin (*hikihada*). On the other hand, the lacquered leather used today resembles toadskin, so the original may have also been made of leather.

hikime 蟇目 [Var. 引目; 挽目; 曳目]. An arrow with a perforated head.

hikiotoshi no kamae 引落の構え. SHINDŌ MUSŌ RYŪ—Posture in which the body is positioned in *hanmi* with the *jō* held diagonally along the front of the body. Both right foot forward with *jō* held to the left, across the front of the body (*hidari* 左 *hikiotoshi no kamae*), and left foot forward with *jō* held to the right, across the front of the body (*migi* 右 *hikiotoshi no kamae*) postures are used.

hikiotoshi uchi 引落打ち. Lit. "pull and strike down." SHINDŌ MUSŌ RYŪ—Technique in which the enemy or his weapon is struck from *hikiotoshi no kamae.* This is the third of the twelve basic techniques (*kihon*) extrapolated from the classical forms of Shindō Musō Ryū by Shimizu Takaji.

Hikita Bungorō 疋田 豊五郎 [A.k.a. ***Hikita Bungorō Kagetomo*** 疋田 豊五郎 景兼; ***Denbei*** 伝兵衛【傳兵衛】] (1537–1606). Founder of the Hikita Kage Ryū; nephew and student of Kamiizumi Ise no Kami Nobutsuna. With his uncle and the swordsman Jingo Muneharu, perhaps accompanied by one of Nobutsuna's sons, Bungorō traveled around Japan on a martial pilgrimage (*musha shūgyō*) during the 1560s. At Hōzōin temple, it was Bungorō who, using only a bamboo sword (*fukuro shinai*) against an opponent with a hardwood sword (*bokken*), defeated Yagyū Muneyoshi in a duel. Bungorō is sometimes credited with the invention of the *fukuro-shinai* 袋竹刀, which was at that time called the *hikiha-*

da shinai 蟇肌竹刀—lit. "toadskin-covered bamboo sword"—but it was actually most likely invented by Kamiizumi. Bungorō later founded his own school of swordsmanship known as the Hikita Kage Ryū 疋田陰流 (var. Hikita Shinkage Ryū 疋田新陰流). He served as a retainer and swordsmanship instructor for several notable figures, including Hosokawa Fujitaka and Tokugawa Ieyasu.

HIKITA SHINKAGE RYŪ *DENSHO* ENTITLED *EMPI NO MAKI*
Illustration of Enkai from the Hikita Shinkage Ryū *densho* entitled *Empi no maki*, dated 1619
(Irie, 1990, used with permission)

Hikita Kage Ryū 疋田陰流 [***Hikita Ryū*** 疋田流; ***Hikita Shinkage Ryū*** 疋田新陰流]. 1. Combative tradition founded by Hikita Bungorō, nephew of Shinkage Ryū founder Kamiizumi Ise no Kami Nobutsuna. Watatani and Yamada (1978: 704) note that this tradition incorporated combative spear (*sōjutsu*), long-hafted glaive (*naginatajutsu*), swordsmanship (*kenjutsu*), and composite sickle-and-chain weaponry (*kusarigama-jutsu*). Many of the *densho* that have survived are dedicated to spear arts. The swordsmanship of the Hikita Kage Ryū closely resembles that transmitted via the Yagyū family; many of the *mokuroku densho* (catalogs of techniques) such as *Sangaku*, *Kūka*, *Tengushō*, and *Empi* are identical, both in name and content, to those of the Yagyū. In addition, however, a number of

HIKITA RYŪ *DENSHO* ENTITLED *KYŌJAKU NO MAKI*
Dated 1746
(Irie, 1990, used with permission)

Hikita Kage Ryū
疋田陰流
(abbreviated lineage)

Kamiizumi Ise no Kami Nobutsuna
上泉 伊勢守 信綱
Shinkage Ryū
新陰流

Hikita Bungorō
疋田 豊五郎
Hikita Kage Ryū
疋田(新)陰流

- Hikita Sōhōsai Keikichi 疋田 宗保斎 景吉
- Yamada Fugetsusai 山田 浮月斎 — **Hikita Kage Ryū** 疋田陰流
- Ida Ionosuke Shigenori 猪多 伊織佐 重能 — **Ida Ryū (*sōjutsu*)** 猪多流(槍術)
- Ueno Sayū Manosuke Kagemochi 上野 左右馬助 景用 — **Ueno Shinkage Ryū** 上野新陰流
- Katori Heizaemon Tadamune 香取 兵左衛門 忠宗 — **Katori Ryū** 香取流
- Nakae Shinpachi Tsuguyoshi 中江 新八 二義 — **Nakae Ryū · Battō Ryū** 中江流·抜討流
- Sakai Hansuke Shigeie 阪井 半助 茂家
  - Saitō Hirosuke 斉藤 啓助 — **Kanewa Ryū (*kusarigama*)** 金輪流(鎖鎌)
  - **Shinkage Ryū** 真陰流

other documents exist which are not included in the Yagyū tradition, such as *Kyōjaku no maki*「強弱之巻」(Power scroll), *Kōjō gokui no maki*「向上極意之巻」(Highest mysteries scroll), and *Kanjō no maki* 「灌頂之巻」(*Abhiṣeka* [Esoteric consecration] scroll), to name a few. At some point, part of the curriculum of the Hikita Kage Ryū was incorporated into the Yagyū Shinkage Ryū, where it has been preserved to this day.

Hikita Ryū 疋田流. See: *Hikita Kage Ryū.*

Hikita Shinkage Ryū 疋田新陰流. See: *Hikita Kage Ryū.*

hikitate oyobi 引立及び. Methods for bringing a resisting detainee to his feet. These techniques are a subdivision of a variety of arresting techniques taught by the modern Japanese police force under the rubric *taiho-jutsu*.

hikitategeiko 引立稽古. A training method used to improve a partner's technical skill. The senior literally used the training session (*keiko*) to "pull up" (*hikitate*) the skill level of the junior.

hikiwake 引分け. Lit. "pull and separate." KYŪDŌ—Fourth of the eight formal stages (*hassetsu*) in firing an arrow in the modern martial way of archery (*kyūdō*). *Hikiwake* is the process of drawing the arrow. In this stage the bow and arrow, which have been held above the head in *uchiokoshi* (stage 3) are slowly lowered until the archer's left arm is horizontal to the ground, the target is sighted over the fully extended left arm and hand, and the right hand has pulled the arrow back past the right side of the head.

himogatana 紐刀. A one-piece (i.e., the hilt and blade are one) stiletto. *Himogatana* are usually about 6 inches (15 cm) long.

hinawa 火縄【火繩】. The match cord for a matchlock firearm.

hinawajū 火縄銃【火繩銃】. Lit. "fuse gun." 1. A matchlock musket; an arquebus. 2. Matchlock musketry. Some of the main components for a Japanese matchlock are: match cord (*hinawa*); pan (*hizara*); pan cover (*hibuta*); projectile (*hiya*); match holder or "serpentine" (*hibasami* or *uchigane*); touchhole (*higuchi*); and trigger (*hikigane*).

hinawa sashi 火縄差【火繩差】. A type of reel for carrying a match cord.

hineri 捻り [Var. ***neji*** 捻子]. A polearm similar to a *tsukubō* which was used to entangle and entrap swordsmen.

hineri tsuki 捻り突き. An attack characterized by thrusting the weapon with a twist.

hinin 非人. Lit. "non-human." *Hinin* was a pejorative Tokugawa-period term used for ex-convicts, drifters, vagrants, and entertainers.

hinoki 檜. A Japanese cypress. The wood of the *hinoki* is often used for storage scabbards (*shirasaya*).

Hinomaru 日の丸. The Japanese national flag. The Hinomaru is often found in the *shōmen* position at the head of a *dōjō,* especially at training halls located in public sports centers.

HINOMARU
The Japanese national flag displayed below a Shintō shrine in the Rembukan Dōjō, Tōkyō, in 1977
(Photograph by author)

hiōgi 檜扇 [Var. 火扇]. SHUGENDŌ—Lit. "cypress fan" [var. "fire fan"]. The *hiōgi* is used in the Shugendō fire ritual (*saitō goma*) to fan the fire in order to burn away evil passions. As one of the "sixteen accoutrements of the *yamabushi*" (*yamabushi jūroku dōgu*), it can be used as a weapon in a similar manner to the way the warrior's iron fan (*tessen*) is manipulated. See: *yamabushi; yamabushi jūroku dōgu.*

Hirai Minoru 平井 稔 [A.k.a. ***Enwa*** 円和【圓和】] (1903–1998). A licensed practitioner of

Tōgun Ryū 東軍流, Hirai was a senior *aikidō* disciple of Ueshiba Morihei who founded his own combative system called Kōrindō 光輪洞. While training with Ueshiba in the early 1940s, Hirai acted as general director of Morihei Ueshiba's Kōbukan Dōjō. At that time Ueshiba was teaching his *aiki* system —which included grappling and the use of the hardwood sword (*bokken*) and medium-length staff (*jō*)—under the Butokukai; in order to avoid political conflicts with the *jūdō* and *kendō* groups, Hirai suggested the art be called *aikidō* (in contrast to *aiki-jūjutsu*). This term, he reasoned, was vaguer in meaning and would allow for training in armed and unarmed techniques without conflicting with the already established groups. Hirai was therefore instrumental in renaming Ueshiba's art *aikidō*. See also: *Kōrindō*.

Further reading in English:

- Pranin, 1994: 10–15.

Hiraiwa Chikayoshi 平岩 親吉 (1542–1611). Hiraiwa, a samurai of Mikawa, grew up with Tokugawa Ieyasu. As a retainer of Ieyasu, Hiraiwa was subsequently entrusted with the education of Ieyasu's oldest son, Nobuyasu. He was later appointed governor of Owari, but died without an heir.

hiraki 開き. *Hiraki* is a form of the verb *hiraku* (to open) often found in compounds indicating postures/stances that are "open," e.g., *hiraki-gamae* 開構 (open posture).

hirane 平根. A flat arrowhead.

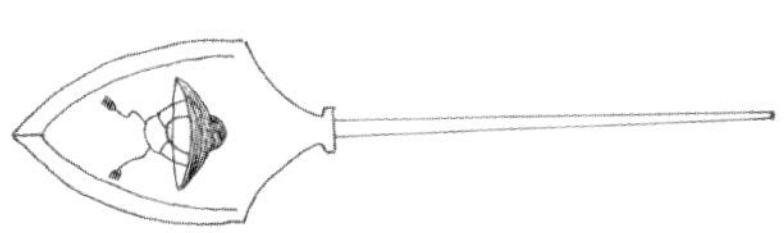

HIRANE WITH TANG
The arrowhead features the Yagyūgasa crest

Hirano Kuniomi 平野 国臣【平野國臣】(1828–1864). Rebel against the Tokugawa *bakufu* and hero of the Meiji Revolution. Kuniomi was a well-known practitioner of Shindō Musō Ryū in Kyūshū during the mid-1800s. He was the son of Hirano Kichizō, a Kuroda-domain martial arts (*dangyō*) instructor and *menkyo kaiden* holder in Shindō Musō Ryū. Kuniomi trained in the *dangyō* martial arts of the Kuroda domain and received a license (*mokuroku*) in Shindō Musō Ryū. By 1855 he had become a political activist and admirer of Saigō Takamori, and subsequently took part in the uprising at Ikuno (Hyōgo prefecture); he was later recognized as a patriot for his efforts.

In 1862 Kuniomi was on the losing side of the battle of Giken in Tajima no Ikuno. He was captured and, along with thirty-three other *bushi*, was executed by the Shinsengumi in Kyōto Prison in July 1864. According to Matsui Kenji:

> It is said that the *bushi* of the Shinsengumi executed the prisoners by thrusting spears from outside the jail—a scene of mayhem with screams and cries of agony. Thereupon, Kuniomi recited his death poem from his jail window, clapping in reverence toward the Imperial Palace. Then, composed, he offered his bared chest at the window opening, declaring, "*Koko-ja!*" (Here!) and died from two spear thrusts. (Matsui, 1993: 16)

After the Imperial Restoration in 1868, many of the Kyūshū *shizoku* (disenfranchised *samurai* families) felt a strong attachment to Hirano Kuniomi and his efforts on behalf of the country. Due to Kuniomi's Kuroda-domain origins and his stature as a patriot, a close, mutually supportive relationship developed between ultra-rightist groups in Kyūshū (such as the Gen'yōsha) and the Shindō Musō Ryū.

Hirayama Kōzō 平山 行蔵【平山行藏】(1750–1827). Hirayama was fourth headmaster of Kōbu Jitsuyō Ryū 講武実用流, a school of strategy (*gumpō*), swordsmanship (*kenjutsu*), and a variety of other combative arts. He also founded the Chūkō Shinkan Ryū 忠孝真貫流 system of swordsmanship (*kenjutsu*). Hirayama taught military strategy to Odani Nobutomo, thirteenth headmaster of the Jiki Shinkage Ryū.

Hiroi Tsunetsugu 広井 常次 (c.1925–). Shindō Musō Ryū *menkyo kaiden* under Shimizu Takaji. Hiroi was a police *jōjutsu* instructor for the Tōkyō Kidōtai (riot police). He has co-authored two books with Yoneno Kōtarō: *Jōdō kyōten*『杖道教典』(A *jōdō* teaching guide), 1982, and *Jōdō*『杖道』in 2004.

HIROI TSUNETSUGU (L) DEMONSTRATES IKKAKU RYŪ *JUTTEJUTSU* WITH YONENO KŌTARŌ (R)
In the rear at far left is martial arts scholar Watanabe Ichirō; second from left is Shimizu Takaji, headmaster of the Shindō Musō Ryū
(Photograph courtesy Nishioka Tsuneo)

hisage no kamae 引下の構(引サゲの構). SHINDŌ MUSŌ RYŪ—Posture in which the body is held in full *hanmi*, left foot forward pointing about 45° to the right front and right foot pointing about 45° to the right rear. The stance is rather like an archer's, with the staff (*jō*) held vertically in the right hand so that it is hidden behind the body. The left hand is along the left thigh; the eyes and head are turned straight ahead toward the enemy.

Hisa Takuma 久 琢磨 (1895–1980). Daitō Ryū *menkyo kaiden* under Takeda Sōkaku (1939), and founder of Nipponden Aikijūjutsu. Hisa went to work for the *Asahi Shinbun* (Asahi News) in Tōkyō in the 1920s. Having a love for *sumō* and related fighting arts, he was placed in charge of security for the Office of General Affairs. (The paper at that time was under attack by right-wing activists.) Hisa performed well in that position, and was promoted and moved to the Ōsaka office in 1932. In 1933 he was introduced to Ueshiba Morihei, from whom he and his staff began to learn *aikijūjutsu*. Ueshiba did not inform Hisa or other *Asahi Shinbun* trainees that he was a student of Takeda Sōkaku's Daitō Ryū. Consequently, the trainees began to refer to the system they were learning as Asahi Ryū 朝日流. The training sessions continued until 1936 when, suddenly, Takeda himself appeared at the Asahi Budō Dōjō. Just as suddenly, Ueshiba disappeared. Takeda continued training Hisa and the Asahi crew until 1939, at which time Hisa was awarded one of the only two full licenses (*menkyo kaiden*) Sōkaku ever granted in Daitō Ryū.

During the Ueshiba and Takeda years, Hisa and his fellow trainees made a series of photographs of the techniques they were being taught. These photos, which numbered more than 1500, were later collected into a set of notebooks (eleven volumes in all) under the title *Daitō ryū aiki budō densho zen jūikkan mokuroku* 『大東流合気武道伝書全十一巻目録』, normally abbreviated as *Sōden* 『相伝』. Earlier, in 1935, Hisa also produced and directed a film called *Budō* 『武道』 featuring Ueshiba demonstrating his technique.

Further reading in English:
• Pranin, 1996: 106–135.

HISAGE NO KAMAE
Shindō Musō Ryū combative engagement posture
(Author's collection)

hisha 飛車 [Abbr. as ***hi*** 飛]. SHŌGI—Lit. "flying chariot." In the strategic game of *shōgi*, the *hisha* is comparable to the rook in Western chess.

Hisshō Heijutsu 必勝兵術. Lit. "sure victory martial strategy," Hisshō Heijutsu was a variant name for Ichidō Ryū 一道流. The school was a branch tradition of Itō Ittōsai Kagehisa's Ittō Ryū (1) 一刀流 passed down in Saitama domain.

Hisshō Muni Ryū 必勝無二流. System of combative swordsmanship (*kenjutsu*) practiced in Bishu domain during the early to mid-1600s. See also: *Hiki Yoshio*.

hissoku 逼塞. Lit. "To be locked up." This was the least severe of the five grades of penalties applied to the samurai during the Tokugawa period. *Hissoku*, essentially a light form of house arrest, could be subdivided into three grades depending on the severity of the crime.

See also: *chikkyo; heimon; kaieki; seppuku.*

Further reading in English:

- Brinkley and Kikuchi, 1915: 641–642 *ff.*
- Schreiber, 2001.
- Seward, 1968.

hitai 額. The forehead; the brow.

hitaiate 額当【額當】. See: *hitaigane.*

HITAIGANE
The late Donn F. Draeger wearing *hitaigane* headgear for a celebration at Katori Jingū in 1978
(Photograph by Pat Lineberger)

hitaigane 額金 [Also read ***hitai kane***; var. ***hitai ate*** 額当【額當】]. A piece of headgear—similar to a *hachimaki* headband—to which an iron or steel plate has been attached, providing light protection in lieu of a helmet. The *hitaigane* was worn by *jisamurai, ashigaru,* and other low-ranking fighting men during the Warring States period. It was also used extensively for *kenjutsu* training by the Maniwa Nen Ryū until the development of the padded *men* and adoption of the bamboo *shinai* in the early 1700s.

Hitotsu no Tachi 一太刀 [Also read ***hitotsu tachi***]. See: *Ichi no Tachi.*

Hitotsu Tachi 一太刀 [Also read ***hitotsu no tachi***]. See: *Ichi no Tachi.*

hitsuji 未 [Also read ***mi***]. A ram. 1. The hour of the Ram is the eighth duodenary hour of Chinese Twelve Branches (Jūnishi): 1 to 3 p.m. 2. KYŪSHO—In certain Sino-Japanese boxing texts, the Ram character indicates the optimal time of day for striking the corresponding vital point (*kyūsho*). See also: *kyūsho;* Appendix 1.

hiwatari 火渡. The ritual practice of fire walking as performed by the *yamabushi*. The aim of this practice (then as now) was to develop spiritual power for performing exorcism and healing, and to achieve heightened states of consciousness.

hiya 火矢. 1. A flaming arrow fired by a bow. 2. An early term for a "fire arrow" or other projectile fired by a matchlock musket or cannon.

hiyatō 火矢筒. 1. Lit. "fire-arrow tube." A musket-like weapon, used during the Warring States and early Edo periods, whose projectile resembled an arrow. 2. Variant term for *bōbiya.*

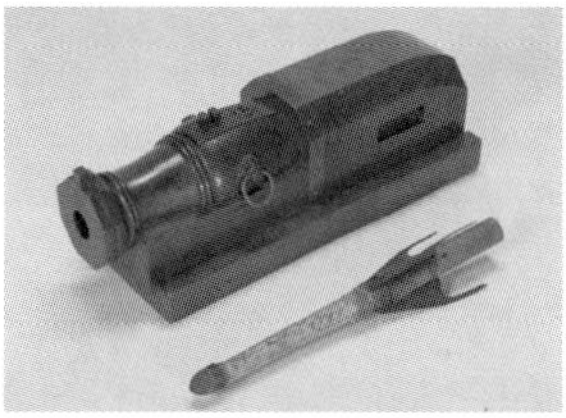

HIYATŌ
Fire-arrow tube from the early Edo period
(Courtesy of the National Museum of Japanese History)

hiza 膝. Knee; the knees.

hizara 火皿. The pan of a gunlock on a matchlock firearm.

hō 鋒. A sword point; a spear point; the tip of a blade. See also: *kissaki.*

hōate 頬当【頬當】. Lit. "cheek protector." A type of protective mask (*menpō*) that covers only the lower half of the face.

hobaku 捕縛. This term is generally associated with older capturing arts, including empty-handed grappling (*jūjutsu/yawara*) and several small weapons such as tined truncheon (*juttejutsu*), tying-cord (*hojōjutsu*), and baton (*hananeji*). However, a number of weapons and implements at the disposal of constables during the Edo period fall under the general use rubric of *hobakujutsu*. These include the "three implements" (*mitsudōgu*); medium-length staff (*jō*); long hardwood staff (*bō*); hook-rope (*kaginawa*); pole-noose (*uchikomi*), etc. According to the late authority Nawa Yumio, the term *hobaku* dates back to the Muromachi period and was used up through the Edo period. See also: *tode; taihojutsu; torimono; torinawa; torite.*

hobakujutsu 捕縛術. See: *hobaku.*

Hōbokushi 『抱朴子』【抱樸子】<Ch. *Baopuzi.* Fourth-century Chinese Daoist text by Katsukō (Ch. Ge Hong 葛洪, a minor Jin Dynasty official), in which the origins of the *Kujihō* are found. It refers to the *Kujihō* as the Secret Spell of the Six Martial Spirits (Rokkō hijū; <Ch. Liujiamizhu 六甲秘祝). The *Kujihō* became a key talismanic ritual text incorporated into many works on strategy (*heihō*) during Japan's medieval period. See also: *Rokkō hijū; Kujihō.*

hōbyōin 宝瓶印【寶瓶印】<Ch. *baoping yin.* An abbreviation for Marishiten *hōbyōin.* See: *ongyōin (2).*

hodokoshi 施. 1. A "tanking" training method. In the context of combative *kata* training, a senior practitioner will assume a prearranged posture (*kamae*) in order for the junior to learn a specific technique. The senior will "tank" for the junior—that is, take the fall or receive the technique without countering—so the junior can learn to perform the technique properly. The term is borrowed from Buddhism. 2. BUDDHISM—In a Buddhist context, the meaning of the character 施 is "giving" or "to give in to"; it is pronounced *se.* See: *fuse.*

hōgan 判官 [Often read as ***hangan*** when used in someone's name]. During the twelfth century this was a term for a lieutenancy in the Kebiishi Chō. The title was one of two[13] conferred upon Minamoto no Yoshitsune by Retired Emperor Go-Shirakawa[14] in 1184; the promotion was apparently partly responsible for the rift between Yoshitsune and his brother Yoritomo. *Hōgan* later became associated with Minamoto no Yoshitsune, and was sometimes used as a variant name for him.

Hōganbiiki 判官贔屓. Lit. "sympathy for the lieutenant (Minamoto no Yoshitsune)." This term has come to mean "sympathy for the loser" or "sympathy for the underdog." Morris (1975: 468) notes its relationship in poetry "in which the beauty of defeat is exemplified by the scattering of blossoms."

[13] The second title was *saemon no shōjō.*

[14] Go-Shirakawa Tennō 後白河天皇 (1127–1192; r. 1155–1158), seventy-seventh emperor of Japan.

Hōgan monogatari 『判官物語』. See: *Gikeiki.*

Hōgan Ryū 判官流. See: *Kiichi Hōgan Ryū.*

Hōgen monogatari 『保元物語』. The earliest of the medieval Japanese war tales. The *Hōgen monogatari*, written around the end of the twelfth century, was concerned with the Hōgen no Ran, a civil war that took place in the Hōgen era (1156). This war was the first to bring the Minamoto and the Taira, two important warrior families of the period, into direct conflict. The text is attributed to Hamuro Tokinaga; the tale forms a trio with the *Heiji monogatari* and the *Heike monogatari.* See also: *Gikeiki; Heiji monogatari; Heike monogatari; Shōmonki; Taiheiki.*

Further reading in English:

- Varley, 1994: 46–66
- Wilson. (Trans.) (1971).

Hōgen no Ran 保元の乱【保元の亂】. A war over an imperial succession dispute that took place during the Hōgen era (1156). It brought two important warrior families of the period, the Minamoto and the Taira, into direct conflict, and resulted in the ascent of the Taira family and its head man, Taira Kiyomori. Just three years later, however, the Minamoto would rise to challenge the Taira again in the Heiji no Ran of 1159. The events of the Hōgen no Ran are chronicled in the *Hōgen monogatari.*

Further reading in English:

- Farris, 1992: 263–270.
- Varley, 1994: 46-66

hōgō 法号【法號】. See: *hōmyō.*

hojō 捕縄【捕繩】. 1.Rope or cord binding. 2. An abbreviation for *hojōjutsu.*

Hōjō 1. 北条. A warrior family descended from Taira no Sadamori. A woman of the family, Hōjō Masako (1157–1225), became the wife of Minamoto no Yoritomo in 1180. In that same year the Minamoto, under Yoritomo, again rose up against the Taira. By 1185 Yoritomo had defeated the Taira; after his death in 1199, Masako shaved her head, becoming a nun, and ruled in her son's name. Under the title of *shikken* 執権 (regent), the Hōjō family ran the Kamakura shogunate from 1200 to 1333.

Hōjō 2. 北条. A warrior family descended from Taira no Sadamori. In contrast to the Kamakura Hōjō Shikken line, this branch resided in Odawara. The Odawara Hōjō became very powerful in the Kantō area during the sixteenth century.

Hōjō 3. 法定. JIKI SHINKAGE RYŪ—An introductory series of sword techniques consisting of four combative scenarios (*kata*). All are performed with *bokken*. Hōjō practice is a key element in the development of Jiki Shinkage Ryū swordsmen. Because it is the tradition's *omote waza*, it contains many gross and subtle elements necessary for the basic training of swordsmen. Emphasis is placed on development of *kiai*, positive/aggressive swordsmanship, balance and walking, and proper manipulation of the sword. An extra-thick and heavy wooden sword (*bokken*) is used specifically for Hōjō training.

Hōjō is also tied in to subsequent sets of *kata* through *kiai*. Each of the four *kata* of Hōjō is assigned a different type of *kiai* corresponding to one of the four seasons:

Hōjō *kata*		**Season/*kiai***	
Hassō (Happa)	八相(発破)	spring	(*haru* 春)
Ittō Ryōdan	一刀両断	summer	(*natsu* 夏)
Uten Saten	右転左転	fall	(*aki* 秋)
Tōtan Ichimi[15]	長短一味	winter	(*fuyu* 冬)

Spring *kiai* is also associated with Tō no Kata (a set of combative forms for the long sword), summer *kiai* with Kodachi no Kata (a set of combative forms for the short sword), fall *kiai* with Habiki (a set of combative forms with unsharpened metal swords), and winter *kiai* with Marobashi (a set of combative forms which reveal the inner secrets of the school). See: *Jiki Shinkage Ryū*.

Hōjō Awanokami Ujinaga 北条 安房守 氏長 [A.k.a. ***Ujinaga*** 氏永; ***Naofusa*** 正房] (1608–1670). A warrior of the Odawara Hōjō family who founded the Hōjō Ryū system of tactics and strategy (*gumpō*). Ujinaga was a retainer of *hatamoto* rank under both Tokugawa Ieyasu and Tokugawa Hidetada.

Hōjō (Hayashizaki) Jinsuke Shigenobu 北条(林崎)甚助 重信. See: *Hayashizaki Jinsuke Shigenobu.*

hojōjutsu 捕縄術 【捕繩術】 [Also read ***torinawajutsu***; abbr. as ***hojō***]. A term for combative tying-cord arts. The primary purpose of *hojōjutsu* is the arresting and binding of prisoners. These systems can also be referred to as *torinawa*. Fujita (1960:2) notes approximately eighty-four *ryū* specializing in *hojōjutsu*. See also: *Araki Ryū; Ittatsu Ryū; kakutō bugei; Masaki Ryū.*

Hōjō Ryū 北条流. Tradition of military strategy and tactics founded by Hōjō Awanokami Ujinaga. This system focused on military intelligence practices (*gunyō kanchōjutsu*). Information on the Hōjō Ryū has been published in Ishioka and Arima (1967, vol. 3). Ten transmission documents (*densho*) are reprinted there, along with an overview of the tradition and extensive lineage charts. See: *Ketsuyō shikan.*

hōjutsu 砲術. A term for combative gunnery using the matchlock musket. Various schools refer to these systems as *bōbiya*, *hōtō*, and *kajutsu* (this last is most common, especially if the handling of various types of explosives is included). Fujita (1960: 2) notes 455 *ryū* that specialized in *hōjutsu*. See also: *Tanegashima.*

hōken 宝剣 【寶劍】. Lit. "treasure sword." A temple sword of the *tsurugi* type. It has a straight blade with a double cutting edge. See also: *Ama Kurikara; Ame no Murakumo no Tsurugi.*

Hōki Ryū 伯耆流 [A.k.a. ***Hōki Ryū Iaijutsu*** ~居合術]. System of swordsmanship (*kenjutsu*) and quick-draw sword arts (*iaijutsu*) founded by Katayama Hōki no Kami Hisayasu (Kuan). There are many variant names. See: *Katayama Hōki Ryū.*

Hokkaidō 北海道. The second-largest island

H

[15] Yagyū Shinkage Ryū groups tend to pronounce this as "Chōtan Ichimi."

of Japan, located north of Honshū. In the past, Hokkaidō was also referred to as "Ezo" and "Ezochi."

Hokke Shū 法華宗 <Ch. Fahua zong <Skt. *Saddharma-puṇḍrīka*. Lit. "Lotus School." BUDDHISM—An East Asian school of Buddhism that concentrates on the *Lotus Sutra*. This school was subsumed in China and Japan under the Tendai (Ch. Tiantai) school.

hoko 1. 矛【鉾】[Var. 鋒]. a. A spear with a socketed head which fits like a glove over the end of the spear shaft. This is in contrast to a *yari*-type head which fits into the spear shaft with a long tang. The *hoko* was in common use until the mid- to late-Heian period, at which time the *yari*-type spear became more popular. See also: *sōjutsu*. b. A halberd. c. OKINAWAN KOBUDŌ—A socketed spear used in the Okinawan *kobudō* system called *tinbē*. See: *Okinawa kobudō; tinbē.*

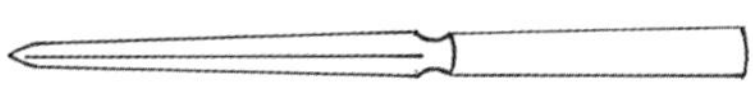

HOKO-TYPE SOCKETED SPEARHEAD

hoko 2. 戈【戟】. An early type of Chinese halberd or glaive.

hoko ore 戟折. Lit. "broken spear (art)." This was a term used by the Kawakami Ryū 川上流 for an art in which a spear shaft was used in the manner of a long hardwood staff (*bō*) if the spearhead or blade was broken off.

hokosaki 鋒先 [Also read ***hōsaki***; var. 矛先]. A sword point; a spearhead.

hōkōshū 奉公衆. A Muromachi-period term referring to the personal military guard of the Ashikaga *shōgun*. This was in contrast to the *hikan* 被官 guards, who were attached to provincial lords or local warrior proprietors. The *hōkōshū* acted as personal army of the Ashikaga shogunate, whereas the *hikan* were the retainers of the Ashikaga-period *shugo daimyō*. See also: *kinjū; gobanshū.*

Further reading in English:

• Grossberg, 1981: 105–112.

hokoyumi 鉾弓 [Also read ***bōkyū***]. See: *hazuyari.*

Hokumen no Bushi 北面の武士. Lit. "Warriors of the Northern Sector." Established in 1087 by Emperor Shirakawa,[16] the Hokumen no Bushi was a military guard unit manned primarily by the Ise Taira. They guarded the retired emperor Shirakawa, and "...were either fighters with small bases in the capital region or Shirakawa's favorite governors" (Farris, 1994: 260). Normally the unit numbered about a hundred men, but that could be expanded in times of need: in 1118, a Hokumen no Bushi unit of 1000 went up against the Tendai warrior monks (*sōhei*) of Enrakuji. The unit was supplemented by the Saimen no Bushi in 1206.

Hokushin Bosatsu 北辰菩薩 <Ch. Beichen Pusa. Lit. the "Bodhisattva of the Pole Star" (Polaris). A variant name for Myōken Bosatsu.

Hokushin Ittō Ryū 北辰一刀流. Lit. "Pole Star" Ittō Ryū. Hokushin Ittō Ryū was founded by Chiba Shūsaku Narimasa. Hokushin Ittō Ryū was a well-rounded system which originally included combative swordsmanship (*kenjutsu*), long-hafted glaive (*naginatajutsu*), spear (*sōjutsu*), and quick-draw swordsmanship (*iaijutsu*). It was well known for its influence on the development of *kendō*.

Shūsaku originally trained in his family's own combative tradition, Hokushin Musō Ryū 北辰夢想流. He subsequently travelled around Japan on a warrior pilgrimage and

HOKUSHIN ITTŌ RYŪ *DENSHO* FROM THE ARCHIVES OF IWASAKI KENZŌ 岩崎兼三
Open—*Kajō mokuroku* 箇条目録
Left—*Heihō Ōmokuroku Kaiden* 兵法大目録皆傳
Right—*Heihō Jun Menkyo* 兵法順免許
(*Kendō Nihon* 1978: 3, used with permission)

[16] Shirakawa Tennō 白河天皇 (1053–1129; r.1073–1129), seventy-second emperor of Japan.

trained in Nakanishi Ha Ittō Ryū 中西派一刀流 with Asari Matashichirō Yoshinobu, and later with Asari's teacher, Nakanishi Chūbei Tsugumasa. After many years he created his own style, which he christened Hokushin Ittō Ryū. In assigning this name to the new school, Shūsaku recognized the technical contributions to his system from Ittō Ryū and the inner secrets from his original family tradition, Hokushin Musō Ryū. Shūsaku originally divided his curriculum into eight levels:

1. Kodachi	小太刀
2. Habiki	刃引
3. Busshatō	仏捨刀
4. Mokuroku	目録
5. Kanaji	かな字
6. Toritate Menjō	取立免状
7. Honmokuroku Kaiden	本目録皆伝
8. Shinan Menjō	指南免状

These levels were tied to three licenses: *Shomokuroku* 「初目録」(Initial List), *Chūmokuroku* 「中目録」(Intermediate List), and *Daimokuroku Kaiden* 「大目録皆伝」(Great List of Complete Transmission). However, there is an additional level, the Okuden ("inner" or "secret" transmission) which is represented as *kuden* (unwritten or "oral" transmission). This ultimate, oral transmission level was concerned with the concept of *seiōken* 星王剣 (lit. "star lord sword"). The term *seiō* 星王 refers to Polaris, the North Star. It is also related to the term Sonjōō 尊星王, an alternate name for Myōken Bosatsu, the deity from whom Chiba Kichinosuke Tsuneshige received the oracle of the secrets of the antecedent Hokushin Musō Ryū. Consequently, the ultimate teachings of Hokushin Ittō Ryū were connected with Shūsaku's original family tradition, Hokushin Musō Ryū.

In founding the Hokushin Ittō Ryū, Shūsaku created a style of swordsmanship he called *kumitachi*. *Kumitachi* was based on four points:

1. Silence: practitioners were to move efficiently, but silently.
2. Walking: in moving in any direction, a practitioner's steps were to be natural.
3. Protective gloves (*uchikote* or *onikode*) were used in order to enable one's training partner to perfect their cutting ability.
4. Straight *bokken* were used in lieu of curved ones.

As Skoss (2002: 116) notes, Shūsaku's Gembukan Dōjō was one of the largest training halls in nineteenth-century Edo; it reputedly had over 5,000 students. Due to Shūsaku's close relationship with Odani Nobutomo, thirteenth headmaster of the Jiki Shinkage Ryū, Hokushin Ittō Ryū and its *kumitachi* were chosen as the official style of swordsmanship in Mito domain, one of the Tokugawa family territories. See also: *Chiba Shūsaku Narimasa; Hokushin Musō Ryū.*

Hokushin Musō Ryū 北辰夢想流. Lit. "Pole Star Oracle School." A school of combative swordsmanship (*kenjutsu*) founded around 1772 by Chiba Kichinosuke Tsuneshige. At about the age of thirty, Chiba engaged in a religious retreat at Hokushinji Myōkengū北辰寺妙見宮 (a sacred shrine associated with the Myōkenji temple 妙見寺) in Sōma (present-day Chiba prefecture). There he performed religious austerities (*shugyō*) and prayer in which he appealed to the Buddhist deity Myōken Bosatsu, the Bodhisattva of the Pole Star.[17] He then received an oracle or revelation which became the basis for the Hokushin Musō Ryū. This school subsequently became the family swordsmanship tradition of the Chiba clan until the end of the feudal period in 1868. See also: *Hokushin Ittō Ryū; Myōken Bosatsu.*

Hokuto 北斗 <Ch. Beidou (the "Northern Dipper") [Var. ***To*** 斗 (the "Dipper"); ***Hokutosei*** 北斗星 (the "stars of the Northern Dipper"); ***Hokuto Shichisei*** 北斗七星 (the "seven stars of the Northern Dipper"); ***Hokkyoku Shichisei*** 北極七星 (the "seven stars of the North Pole")]. All these terms refer to the constellation of the Great Bear, Ursa Major. In Sino-Japanese Esoteric Buddhism, these terms are often used interchangeably with Hokushin 北辰 and Hokkyokusei 北極星 (both refer to Polaris, the North Star).

Notably, the constellation of Ursa Major has been associated with warrior cults in Indo-

[17] This *bosatsu* is venerated by the Esoteric Buddhist sects (Tendai and Shingon) and the Nichiren sect.

IMAGE OF MARISHITEN ASTRIDE A WILD BOAR
The seven stars of the Dipper are represented by the five fingers of the outstretched left hand and the index and middle fingers of the right "sword" hand
(Copy of *honzon* [primary image] at Tokudaiji [Marishiten-san], a Nichiren temple in the Ameyokochō area of Tōkyō)

European cultures since ancient times. These influences also reached East Asia via Buddhism and other religious and magical traditions. The military Daoist of the Pole Star Sect referred to the Buddhist warrior goddess, Marishiten, as Doumu 斗母 (the Mother of the Dipper). These Daoist practitioners of thunder magic also revered the Buddhist *bodhisattva* (*bosatsu*) Myōken 妙見, whose name means "beautiful sight" or "beautiful vision," a euphemism for Ursa Major, the constellation of the Great Bear.

Lt. Col. J. G. O. Whitehead, in a 1961 article describing Pole Star–oriented Indo-European warrior cults, noted some held the bear (Celtic *arc*) as their totem, while others revered the wild boar (Celtic *orc*). He also noted that each of the seven stars of the dipper represented a secret social principle (the first five also being associated with the fingers of the left hand, the final two with the fingers of the right hand). This symbolism is also carried over to the various East Asian warrior groups that venerated the Dipper and its associated deities, as can be seen in the image above of Marishiten standing astride a wild boar, the left hand stretched toward the front with fingers extended, the right hand holding a sword in a low guard position. (The index and middle fingers of the right hand are often used to represent a sword.)

See also: *Hokushin Ittō Ryū; Hokushin Musō Ryū; inoshishi; Marishiten; Myōken Bosatsu.*

Further reading in English:

- Hall, 1990: 102–104 *ff.*
- Whitehead, 1961.

Hokuto Daishin 北斗大晨. Lit. "Great Shining One in the Northern Dipper." An epithet for Marishiten (tutelary goddess of war) found in the *Genke kin'etsushū.* See also: *Hokuto.*

Hokutosei 北斗星 <Ch. Beidouxing. Lit. the "Stars of the Northern Dipper"; the constellation of the Great Bear, Ursa Major. See: *Hokuto.*

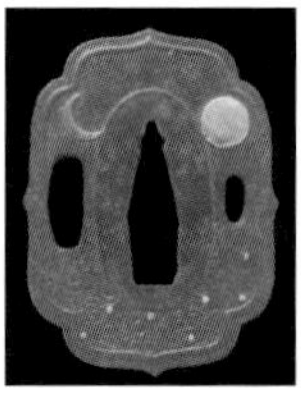

TSUBA INLAID WITH THE MOON, THE SUN, AND THE NORTHERN DIPPER (HOKUTO)
(©2009, Aoi Art, Tōkyō)

Hokuto Shichisei 北斗七星 <Ch. Beidou Qixing. Lit. the "Seven Stars of the Northern Dipper"; the constellation of the Great Bear, Ursa Major. See: *Hokuto.*

hombu dōjō 本部道場. The main, central, or "home" training hall of a modern martial way. For example, the *hombu dōjō* for the original Ueshiba line of *aikidō* is the Tōkyō Aikikai located in Shinjuku Ward, Tōkyō; the *hombu dōjō* for *jūdō* is the Kōdōkan; etc. This is in contrast to a branch training hall, which may be called a *shibu dōjō.* Some classical martial systems (*koryū*) have begun to adopt these designations as their membership and training halls expand. Contrast with *shibu dōjō.*

hōmyō 法名 [Var. ***hōgō*** 法号]. BUDDHISM—Lit. a "*dharma* name." 1. A Buddhist name given to a person being initiated into the priesthood. 2. A posthumous Buddhist name. See also: *kaimyō.*

honagayari 穂長槍 [Also called ***ōmi no yari*** 大身の槍 or ***nagamiyari*** 長身槍]. A spear with a straight blade of around 12 inches (30 cm) or more in length. See also: *suyari.*

Honchō bugei shōden 『本朝武芸小伝』【本朝武藝小傳】(Biographical sketches in Japanese martial arts) [A.k.a. ***Kanjō shōden*** 『干城小伝』【干城小傳】(Biographical sketches of Japanese warriors)]. Text on Japanese martial arts and legends composed by Hinatsu Shigetaka 日夏繁高 and published in 1716. A warrior himself, Hinatsu was a well-known practitioner of Tendō Ryū 天道流. The book describes many combative arts of those times and includes biographies of many practitioners. It comprises ten volumes: The first is on strategy and tactics (*heihō*); the second on warrior etiquette (*shorei*); the third, archery (*shajutsu*); the fourth, horsemanship (*bajutsu*); the fifth and sixth, swordsmanship (*tōjutsu*); the seventh, spearmanship (*sōjutsu*); the eighth, firearms and explosives (*hōjutsu*). The final two volumes deal with armored grappling and related arts (*kogusoku*).

Further reading in English:
- Rogers, 1990a; 1990b; 1991a.
- Shine, 1994.

Honda Hyōsuke 本田 兵助 (c.1560–1627). Disciple of Anazawa Tonomonosuke Moriyoshi who transmitted the Shinjin Ryū 神人流 *naginata* system in Satsuma.

Honda Toshizane 本多 利実【本多利實】. Founder of the Honda Ryū 本多流 tradition of spiritually oriented archery (*kyūdō*) in the early twentieth century. Honda created a new, hybrid version of *kyūdō* from traditional ceremonial and warrior styles. See: *kyūdō*.

honden 本伝【本傳】. Lit. "original tradition," "original transmission." This term is used in some classical martial schools to distinguish between techniques (*waza*) and prearranged combative forms (*kata*) that were created or transmitted by the system's founder and those added by later generations. It may also be used to distinguish between original or traditional forms and variations (*henka*) derived from the originals.

honekudaki 骨砕 [also read ***honekudaki***]. Lit. "bone crushing." A *jūjutsu*-like fighting art of the early Seigō Ryū 制剛流.

honjo ichien shoryō 本所一円所領【本所一圓所領】. A Muromachi-period term indicating lands controlled by religious institutions. No shogunal officer was appointed to oversee these lands.

honke 本家. A Muromachi-period term for the patron/protector of a private estate (*shōen*).

Honnawa 本縄【本繩】[Sometimes read ***moto no nawa***]. Advanced set of twenty restraining-cord ties taught in the Ikkaku Ryū (1) 一角流.

honne 本音. The true intent or underlying motive. Simple on the surface, the term *honne*—along with *omote*, *ura*, and *tatemae*—is a key concept in understanding any facet of Japanese culture, including martial culture. Contrast with *tatemae*. See also: *omote; ura.*

Further reading in English:
- Doi, 1985.
- Hall, Edward, 1973; 1976; 1983
- Lebra, 1976.

hōnō embu 奉納演武. A votive martial exhibition held at a Shintō shrine. Shrines where *hōnō embu* are commonly held include Katori Jingū, Kashima Jingū, Hachimangū (in Kamakura), Meiji Jingū (in Tōkyō), Yasukuni Jinja (in Tōkyō), and Ise Jingū. There are many others. See: *Shintō (1).*

Honshū 本州. The largest of the Japanese islands. Honshū is situated between the Sea of Japan and the Pacific Ocean.

honte no kamae 本手の構え. SHINDŌ MŪSŌ RYŪ—Posture in which the body is turned very slightly in *hanmi*, with the *jō* held to the front in *seigan no kamae.* Both right-foot-forward postures (*migi* 右 *honte no kamae*) and left-foot-forward postures (*hidari* 左 *honte no kamae*) are used.

honte uchi 本手打ち. Lit. "strike from basic hand position." SHINDŌ MŪSŌ RYŪ—Technique in which the opponent is struck from *honte no kamae.* This is the first of the twelve basic techniques (*kihon*) extrapolated from the classical forms of Shindō Musō Ryu by Shimizu Takaji.

honzon 本尊. Principal object of worship; the main image in a Buddhist temple.

hōō 鳳凰 [Also read **zuichō**] <Ch. Fenghuang. The mythical Chinese phoenix or "firebird," which became regarded in Japan as a bird of good luck. The *hōō* was said to be pure; it neither ate insects nor walked upon grass. A well-known Buddhist temple in Uji (near Kyōto) called the Byōdōin 平等院 is also called the *Hōōdō* 鳳凰堂 (Phoenix Hall), as it was designed to look like a phoenix descending toward the ground. The *hōō* was often used as a decorative motif on weapons and armor.

hora 法螺 [Var. 宝螺【寶螺】]. SHUGENDŌ—An abbreviation for *horagai*, a large conch shell commonly carried by followers of Shugendō (*yamabushi*). In Shugendō the *hora* is used for signaling; it is also part of the sacred fire ritual (*saitō goma*). See: *horagai; yamabushi; yamabushi jūroku dōgu.*

horagai 法螺貝 [Var. 宝螺貝【寶螺貝】; abbr. **hora** 法螺 or simply **kai** 貝(螺)]. A large conch shell that the classical *bushi* used much like a bugle to direct troops in battle. The *horagai* was part of a battle commander's standard accoutrements. See: *jingaijutsu; shikigu; yamabushi.*

Hōraisan 蓬莱山. Mount Horai, a mountain close to Lake Biwa on which Raigakuin, a Shugendō temple, was located during the early Tokugawa period. The site is associated with the Jikishin Ryū (4) 直心流.

hori 堀. A moat; a canal.

Horikawa Kōdō 堀川幸道 (1894–1980). Horikawa began training under his own father and Takeda Sōkaku in 1914, and was awarded the Daitō Ryū *hiden mokuroku*, Daitō Ryū *hiden ogi mokuroku*, and Daitō Ryū *kyōju dairi* in 1931. In 1950, he founded the Daitō Ryū Aikijūjutsu Kōdōkai in Hokkaidō.

Further reading in English:

- Pranin, 1996: 89–105.

HŌRIN
Illustration from *Besson zakki*, c.1180

horimono 彫り物. An engraving on a sword blade.

hōrin 法輪. Lit. "wheel of the law," or "the wheel of the *dharma*." This Buddhist symbol is made up of eight spokes, each of which is a single-point *vajra* (*tokkosho*). The *hōrin* occasionally adorned the hand guard (*tsuba*) on both votive temple swords and warrior weapons.

horo 母衣. A large hood sometimes worn with armor by mounted warriors during battle. The *horo* would fill with wind and billow out from the rider's back, evidently to protect the wearer's back from arrows, and later, matchlock fire. *Horo* appeared in a variety of types and sizes, and were sometimes supported by a wicker framework. Some were decorated with votive symbols, including Sanskrit *siddhaṁ* (*shittan*) letters and the names of Buddhist deities such as Bishamonten, Marishiten, Batō Kannon, etc.

The invention of this device is sometimes attributed to the warrior Hatakeyama Masanaga, a well-known general of the Ōnin era (1467–1468). However, use of the *horo* is mentioned at least as early as the twelfth-century *Hōgen monogatari*.[18]

HORO INSCRIBED WITH THE *MANTRA* "NANMU NICHIRIN MARISHITEN"
(Nineteenth-century Japanese illustration)

hōsaki 鋒先 [Var. 矛先]. See: *hokosaki.*

hosha 歩射 [Also read **busha**; a.k.a. **kachiyumi** 徒射]. Infantry archers who shot their bows while on foot (in contrast to shooting from horseback).

hoshi 星. 1. A star. 2. The bull's-eye on a target. 3. **Hoshi** 星. A Japanese family name.

---

[18] Nagazumi and Shimada, 1961: 101. Apparently, not all editions of the *Hōgen monogatari* mention the *horo* in this passage. The text as translated by Wilson (1971: 38) does not include this reference.

hōshi 法師 [Also read ***hosshi***]. A Buddhist priest; a Buddhist monk.

hoshi kabuto 星兜. Lit. "star helmet." A helmet constructed with many rivets visible on the outside, resembling stars. Sometimes the rivets were painted with silver to decorate them.

Hoshi Kunio 星 国雄. Current (fourteenth) headmaster of Yagyū Shingan Ryū Katchū Heihō. See also: *Yagyū Shingan Ryū.*

hōshi musha 法師武者. Lit. "priest-warrior." A generic term for Japanese Buddhist warrior monks. See: *sōhei.*

Hoshina Chikanori 保科近悳. See: *Saigō Tanomo Chikanori.*

hoshinjutsu 保身術. Self-defense. See: *goshinjutsu.*

hosori 細り. Variant term for an espionage agent. *Hosori* is a term taken from the adjective for "thin" (*hosoi* 細い) meaning someone who can slip in "between the cracks" and steal information. Related to the term *saisaku*. See: *ninjutsu; saisaku.*

Hossō Shū 法相宗 <Ch. Faxiang zong. A literal translation of the Sanskrit term *dharmalakṣaṇa* (the characteristics of things). This term refers to the Yogācāra (a.k.a. Vijñānavāda) school of Buddhist philosophy. The school is often called the "mind-only" school, as it emphasized that consciousness (*vijñāna*) is the basis from which the appearance of the phenomenal world arises. The Hossō Shū flourished in Japan during the Nara period.

hōtō 1. 宝刀【寶刀】. A treasure sword; a sacred sword; a votive sword.

hōtō 2. 抱筒. Term used for matchlock musketry in some branches of the Yō Ryū 陽流. See: *hōjutsu.*

Hotoke 仏【佛】. A buddha. Also may refer to the historical Buddha.

Hotta Sagoemon Yoriyasu 堀田 佐五衛門 頼康 [A.k.a. ***Hotta Yorinagi*** 自諾] (c.1650–c.1730). Fourth headmaster of the Kito Midare Ryū 起倒乱流, according to Watatani and Yamada (1978: 218). Hotta's successor in that system was Takino Yūken.

Hōzan Ryū 宝山流【寶山流】[Var. 法讃流]. Comprehensive martial system (*sōgō bujutsu*) which included combative swordsmanship (*kenjutsu*), unarmored grappling (*jūjutsu*), grappling in light armor (*kogusoku*), sickle-and-chain arts (*kusarigama-jutsu*), long hardwood staff (*bōjutsu*), heavy medium-length staff (*furijō*), small throwing blades and darts (*shurikenjutsu*), and tying-cord arts (*torinawa*). See: *Tsutsumi Hōzan Ryū (1).*

Hōzōin 宝蔵院【寶藏院】. A sub-temple of Kōfukuji in Nara. By the late Heian period (twelfth century), many of the large temple complexes—such as the Tendai sect's Enryakuji and Kuramadera, north of Kyōto, and the Kegon sect's Kōfukuji in Nara—had a large number of monks in residence; there were as many as 4,000 in Kōfukuji alone. These temples also maintained large forces of priest-warriors (*sōhei*). These martial monks were frequently involved in combative "incidents" with other temples, and occasionally thousands of them were sent into Kyōto to forcefully petition the imperial court. Due to persistent warfare in the sixteenth century, Kōfukuji was partially destroyed in 1532. However, a Kōfukuji sub-temple called the Hōzōin became known for its spear-wielding monks in the mid- to late 1500s. In fact, it appears the Hōzōin became something of a pilgrimage site for warriors and monks engaged in *musha shūgyō* pilgrimages.

In 1562 a monk named Hōzōin In'ei had become head priest of the temple and arranged for the famous duel between Kamiizumi Nobutsuna and Yagyū Muneyoshi to take place within the temple precincts. Both In'ei and Muneyoshi were greatly impressed by Kamiizumi and his entourage, and for the next few years they became martial disciples (*deshi*) of Kamiizumi. In'ei subsequently founded a spear-centered tradition called Hōzōin Ryū.

By 1604 Kōfukuji had banned its priests from engaging in duels.[19] Consequently,

[19] This did not mean that the Hōzōin Ryū was no longer practiced at the temple. In fact, the Hōzōin Ryū's lineage indicates that at least six generations of Hōzōin priests practiced *sōjutsu* at the temple.

H

HŌZŌIN (KAKUZENBŌ HŌIN) IN'EI
In'ei pictured here holding his famous *kamayari* and wearing a *kesa* around his head in the style used by *sōhei* (warrior monks) of that era
(From the *Honchō bugei shōden* c. 1716)

when Miyamoto Musashi showed up in the hopes of matching his sword style against the famous Hōzōin Ryū, the monks were unable to comply. However, a Hōzōin Ryū practitioner from the neighboring Ōzoin temple was available. The "Nichiren Ōzoin" priest engaged in a non-lethal duel with Miyamoto Musashi, matching his Hōzōin Ryū *kamayari* against Musashi's sword. Musashi beat the monk in two matches. In spite of this, the Hōzōin monks evidently felt no animosity toward Musashi, and even invited him to dinner. They engaged in a discussion of martial concerns which lasted all night, and Musashi departed the next day. See also: *Hōzōin In'ei; Hōzōin Inshu; Hōzōin Ryū; sōhei.*

Hōzōin In'ei 宝蔵院 胤栄【寶藏院 胤榮】[A.k.a. ***Kakuzenbō*** 覚禅房 【覺禪房】, ***Hōin*** 法印] (1521–1607). Head priest (*inshu* 院主) of the Hōzōin, a sub-temple of the Kōfukuji temple complex in Nara. In'ei was also the famous monk and spearman who founded the Hōzōin Ryū. He was a member of the elite Nakamikado family.[20] In addition to developing his own style of spearmanship, In'ei was also an adept politician, and had a close, friendly relationship with both Kitabatake Tomonori, the governor of Ise province in the early 1560s, and Yagyū Muneyoshi of Yagyū village. Muneyoshi was known at that time to be the best swordsman in the Kinki district (Ōsaka–Nara–Kyōto). When Kamiizumi Nobutsuna was engaged in *musha shūgyō* (martial pilgrimage) in 1562, Kitabatake wrote an introduction to Hōzōin In'ei on his behalf. In'ei was greatly impressed by Kamiizumi's Shinkage style and invited his friend Yagyū Muneyoshi to meet with him. On the precincts of the Hōzōin a duel was held between Yagyū Muneyoshi and Hikita Bungorō, Kamiizumi Nobutsuna's disciple. Muneyoshi was quickly and soundly defeated by both Bungorō and Kamiizumi. Muneyoshi and In'ei requested to be taught by Kamiizumi, and three years later they had both mastered Kamiizumi's Shinkage Ryū.

The tales regarding these duels do not normally mention any transmission of spear technique *per se* to Hōzōin In'ei. However, both Kamiizumi Nobutsuna and his travelling-companion disciples were experienced spearmen, having recently been members of an assault group at Minowa Castle known as the Nagano Jūrokunin no Yari, the "Sixteen Spears of Nagano." It is certainly within the realm of possibility that Kamiizumi, perhaps along with his disciples Hikita Bungorō and Jingo Muneharu, instructed In'ei in Shinkage Ryū *sōjutsu*. In fact, some of the Shinkage Ryū *sōjutsu kata* are preserved in some lines of the Yagyū Shinkage Ryū today.

Following his mastery of the Shinkage style, In'ei traveled the country in *musha shūgyō*, training with various experts such as Daizen Daifu Moritada, whose *kamayari* (sickle-bladed spear) techniques he evidently learned and improved upon. From these experiences he created the Hōzōin Ryū of *sōjutsu* (spearmanship), which he brought back to the Hōzōin.

In'ei transmitted his teachings to many students—Buddhist monks, warriors, and *shugenja* (Shugendō priests)—including Hōzōin Inshun (who may have been his son), Nakamura Naomasa, Takada Matabei Yoshitsugu, and others. Inshun became the next headmaster at the Hōzōin temple. See also: *sōhei.*

Hōzōin Inshun 宝蔵院 胤舜【寶藏院 胤舜】[A.k.a. ***Zen'eibō*** 禅栄房 【禪榮房】] (1588–

[20] The Nakamikado 中御門 were a noble family (*kuge*) who had descended from the Fujiwara. The Kōfukuji itself had close ties with the Fujiwara.

Hōzōin Ryū
宝蔵院流
(abbreviated lineage)

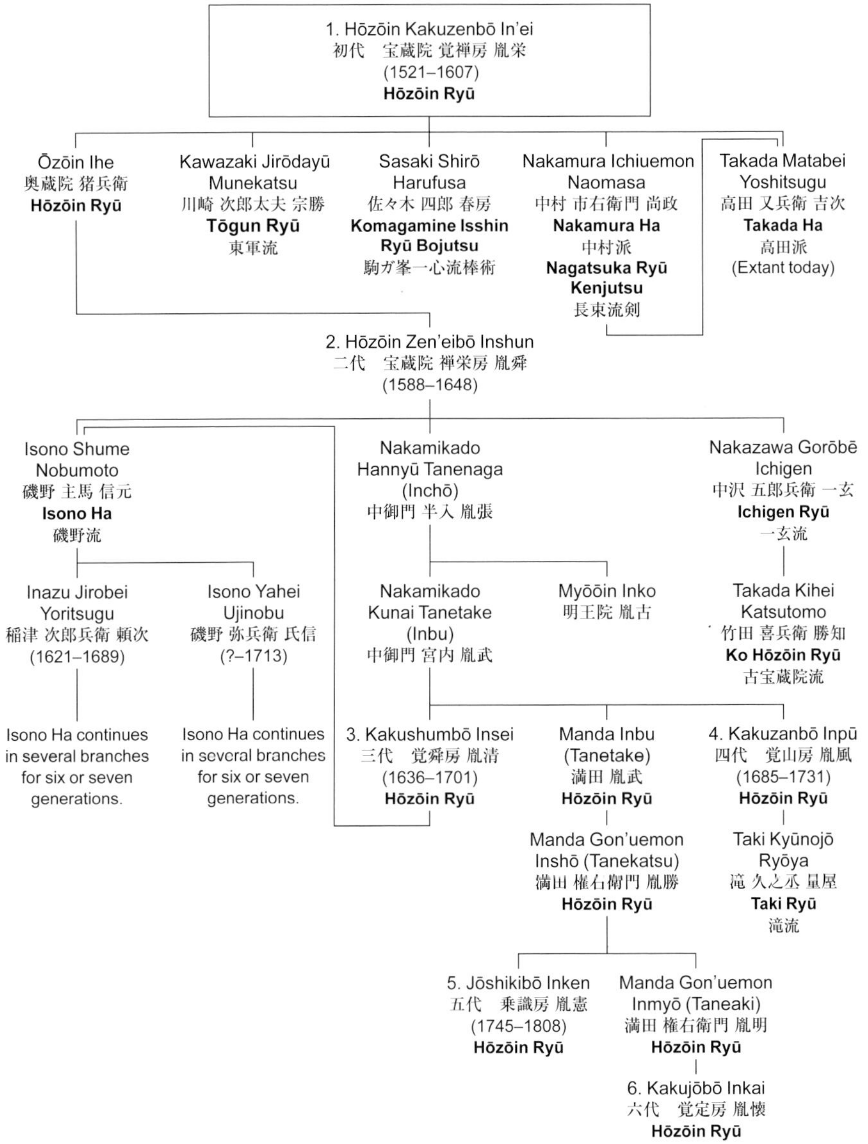

1648). Second headmaster of the Hōzōin Ryū. In addition to his fame both as a spearman and as In'ei's successor, Inshun was also rumored to be Hōzōin In'ei's son. Inshun studied Hōzōin Ryū under In'ei and, after the latter's death in 1607, under a Nichiren priest from neighboring Ōzōin temple who had also studied under In'ei. Some sources say the name of this priest is unknown, but Watatani and Yamada (1978: 751) give his name as Ōzōin Ihei 奥蔵院 猪兵衛. See also: *Hōzōin; sōhei.*

Hōzōin Kakuzenbō Hōin In'ei 宝蔵院 覚禅房 法印 胤栄. See: *Hōzōin In'ei.*

Hōzōin Ryū 宝蔵院流【寶藏院流】[Var. Hōzōin Ryū Sōjutsu 宝蔵院流槍術【寶藏院流槍術】]. A tradition of spearmanship (*sōjutsu*), swordsmanship (*kenjutsu*), and glaive arts (*naginatajutsu*) developed by Hōzōin (Kakuzenbō Hōin) In'ei between 1565 and 1570. Renowned for its deadly spear technique, the lineage at the Hōzōin continued through at least six generations. In addition, one of In'ei's direct students was the progenitor of a line of Hōzōin Ryū that has survived into the present, the Hōzōin Ryū Takada Ha. See also: *Hōzōin In'ei; Hōzōin Inshu; Hōzōin Ryū Takada Ha; Ōzōin Ihei; sōhei.*

Hōzōin Ryū Takada Ha 宝蔵院流高田派【寶藏院流高田派】[A.k.a. ***Hōzōin Ryū Takada Ha Sōjutsu*** ～槍術]. Branch tradition of the Hōzōin Ryū. One of Hōzōin In'ei's students, Nakamura Naomasa, founded the Nakamura Ha (Nakamura branch) of the Hōzōin Ryū and passed it on to Takada Matabei Yoshitsugu. Takada founded his own branch line, the Takada Ha, which survives into the present. Today the weapons systems of the Hōzōin Ryū Takada Ha center on *sōjutsu* with the straight-bladed spear (*suyari*) and sickle-bladed spear (*kamayari*). Any Shinkage Ryū elements, if indeed they were passed on from In'ei, are apparently obscure or no longer extant. See: Hōzōin Ryū.

hyakuhachi 百八. One hundred eight is a special number in Buddhism as it represents the 108 illusions (*hyakuhachi bonnō* 百八煩悩) and the 108 meditative states (*sanmaji* <Skt. *samādhi*) mentioned in the *Mahā-prajñāpāramitā-sūtra* (*Daihannyaharamita-kyō*). Consequently, temple bells and gongs are rung 108 times on New Year's Eve. In the context of martial arts, the number 108 is associated with movements in combative forms (*kata*), *kata* names, the number of rivets on helmets, etc.

hyakuhon geiko 百本稽古 (Also read ***hyappon geiko***). JIKI SHINKAGE RYŪ—A special training ordeal (*shūgyō*) in which two training partners (*shidachi* and *uchidachi*) perform the Hōjō *kata* sequence a hundred times a day for a period of a week. As in normal Jiki Shinkage Ryū training, both participants must strive to maintain complete, continual dominance over each other—manifesting *kiai, zanshin,* eye contact, etc.—even while exchanging roles within the *kata.* About ten sets can be completed in one hour.

ARMORED HYAKUNINCHŌ TEPPŌTAI MEMBERS WITH MATCHLOCKS
(Photograph courtesy John F. Quinn)

Hyakuninchō Teppōtai 百人町 鉄砲隊. Lit. the "Hyakuninchō Matchlock Company." Hyakuninchō is the name of an area in Tōkyō's Shinjuku Ward. During the Tokugawa period a group of matchlock-armed low-ranking samurai were part of the security guard company for the area. In the post–World War II era, a group of matchlock enthusiasts, trained in such classical firearms traditions as the Ikka Ryū 一火流, have adopted the name for their organization.

hyakushō 百姓. Peasant.

hyakushō ikki 百姓一揆. An Edo-period term for peasant uprisings. See: *ikki.*

hyappatsu hyakuchū 百発百中【百發百中】. Target-shooting term meaning "hitting the mark nearly one hundred times for every one hundred shots." See: *Awa Kenzō.*

hyappon geiko 百本稽古. See: *hyakuhon geiko.*

Hyōbushō 兵部省. Originally also read "Tsuwamono no Tsukasa," this was an ancient imperial office somewhat equivalent to a Ministry of War. Prior to 683 C.E., military affairs were handled by the Ōtomo and Monononobe families. However, in 683

Emperor Temmu[21] created the Hyōseikan 兵制官. This name later changed to Tsuwamono no Tsukasa, also read as Hyōbushō 兵部省.

Hyōdōkyō 『兵道鏡』 [Also read ***Heidō no kagami***] (A mirror on the way of strategy). This is the first text on swordsmanship and strategy known to have been produced by Miyamoto Musashi; one copy is dated 1605. There are two versions written by Musashi at different times, one containing twenty-one articles and the other containing twenty-eight. See also: *Hyōhō sanjūgo ka jō; Hyōhō shijūni ka jō.*

Further reading in English:

• Tokitsu, translation, 2004: 197–199.

hyōe 兵衛. The troops who made up the Hyōefu imperial guard units. Friday (1992: 222) notes they were "drawn from the provincial and lower central nobility." See: *Hyōefu.*

Hyōefu 兵衛府. Ancient term for some of the imperial guard units in charge of the gate of the imperial palace. The Hyōefu of the eighth century were the same class of soldiers as the *toneri* of the sixth century. However, they were reorganized by the Taihō Code (Taihō Ritsuryō) in 702 C.E. and officially called the Hyōefu. The units were divided into two sections: the Left Imperial Palace Guard Unit (Sa Hyōefu 左兵衛府) and the Right Imperial Palace Guard Unit (U Hyōefu 右兵衛府)—and also took charge of escorting the emperor and other important personages. In the eighth century, they worked in close cooperation with the capital guards (Ejifu) established by the Taihō Code. Whereas the Hyōefu were members of the rural warrior elite, however, the Ejifu were commoners conscripted under the Chinese-style system of the Taihō Code. Even so, by the mid-ninth century the members of the Imperial Palace Guard Unit had lost their status as military men, and their functions were replaced by a new organization. In later centuries this and similar titles were sometimes awarded by the court for special services performed by warriors of high, noble lineage. The *Taiheiki* tells us that Kusunoki Masashige held the title of Hyōe when he was recruited by Emperor Go-Daigo in the early fourteenth century.

hyōhō 兵法. See: *heihō.*

Hyōhō Niten Ichi Ryū 兵法二天一流 [Also read ***Heihō Niten Ichi Ryū***; var. ***Niten Ichi Ryū*** 二天一流]. One of several martial traditions that trace their origins to the famous swordsman Miyamoto Musashi.

Curriculum	**Number of *kata***
Tachi Seihō 太刀勢法 (Sword Forms)	
Tachi Seihō 太刀勢法 Single longsword techniques	(12)
Kodachi Seihō 小太刀勢法 Single short-sword techniques	(7)
Nitō Seihō 二刀勢法 (Gohō Seihō 五法勢法) Techniques with long and short swords	(5)
Okugi Tachi Seihō 奥義太刀勢法 Secret sword techniques	(4)
Aikuchi Roppō 合口六法 (Kuden 口伝) Short-sword (*aikuchi*) techniques	(6)
Bōjutsu 棒術 (Staff Arts)	
Tachiawase Bō Seihō 太刀合棒勢法 Longsword vs. staff techniques	(7)
Bō Ai Bō Seihō 棒合棒勢法 Staff vs. staff techniques	(13)
Jutte Tōjutsu 十手刀術 Truncheon vs. sword techniques	(5)

Several lines of the Hyōhō Niten Ichi Ryū

PRACTITIONERS OF HYŌHŌ NITEN ICHI RYŪ
Demonstration at Meiji Shrine, 1978
(Photograph by author)

[21] Temmu Tennō 天武天皇 (631–686; r.672–686), fortieth emperor of Japan.

Hyōhō Niten Ichi Ryū
兵法二天一流
(abbreviated lineage)

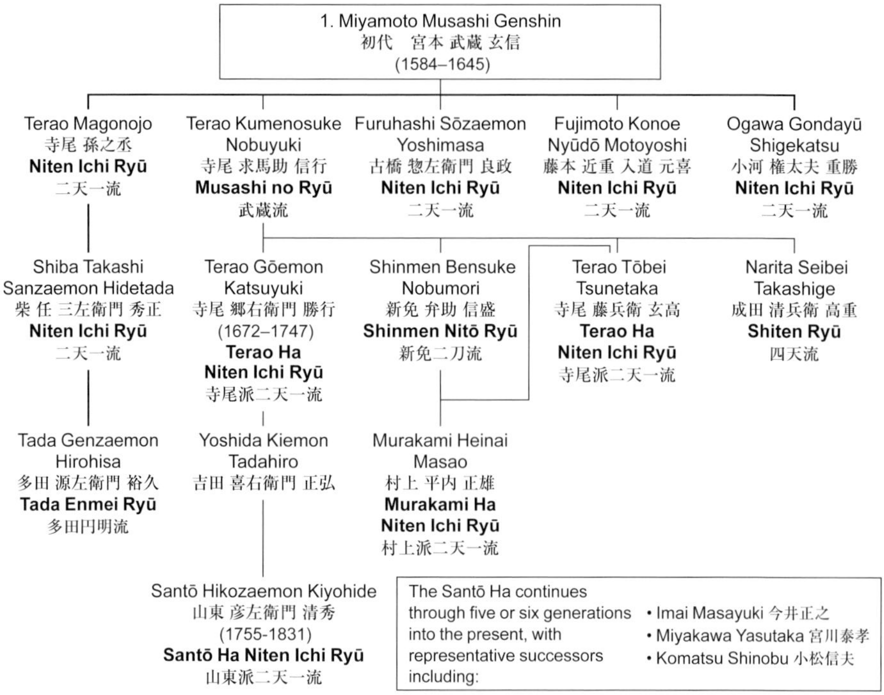

exist in Japan today. See also: *Noda Ha Niten Ichi Ryū.*

Further reading in English:

- Draeger, 1981.
- Tokitsu, 2004.
- Wilson, 2004a.

Hyōhō sanjūgo ka jō 『兵法三十五ケ条』 [Also read ***Heihō sanjūgo ka jō***] (Thirty-five articles on strategy). Late (c. 1641) text on swordsmanship by Miyamoto Musashi, evidently produced for Hosokawa Tadatoshi. This work is thought to be the outline for what later became the *Book of Five Rings* (*Gorin no sho*). The original text may have been passed to Musashi's disciple, Terao Kumenosuke. It has been reprinted in Imamura (1966, vol. 1: 437–445).

Further reading in English:

- Tokitsu, translation. 2004: 199–208.

Hyōhō shijūni ka jō 『兵法四十二ケ条』 [Also read ***Heihō shijūni ka jō***] (Forty-two articles on strategy). A late text on swordsmanship by Miyamoto Musashi. This work is essentially the *Thirty-five Articles on Strategy* (*Hyōhō sanjūgo ka jō*) with several additional maxims.

Further reading in English:

- Tokitsu, translation. 2004: 209–216.

hyōshi 拍子 [Var. ***chōshi*** 調子]. The term *hyōshi* literally means rhythm, musical measure, or beat. It is a concept closely intertwined with that of initiative (*sen*). In a combative context, it refers to the beat of the movement of the body, respiration, and mind of a martial practitioner. Like many classical Japanese terms dealing with human behavior, *hyōshi* refers to both physical and mental activity, and might therefore be viewed as a psycho-physical phenomenon.

There are many types of *hyōshi*, for different people have their own rhythms; and in combative situations, the beat is constantly changing. Sensing and utilizing the *hyōshi* of an enemy without having one's own rhythm used against one requires a high degree of training and sensitivity. The swordsmen of the Shinkage Ryū, for example, codified several general types of *hyōshi*, including *ōbyōshi* (large beat; a large, relatively slow attack) and *kobyōshi* (small beat; a small, relatively swift and incisive attack). Both of these are used in combative swordsmanship and, depending on who holds the initiative (*sen*), each may be used to defeat the other.

One of the most important warriors to write about *hyōshi* was Yagyū Jūbei Mitsuyoshi (1607–1650), the second headmaster of the Edo Yagyū line of the Shinkage Ryū (Mutō, 1985–1990). Jūbei delineated three beats he used to disrupt an opponent's rhythm: *auhyōshi* (synchronous beat) in which both opponents strike at the same instant; *tsurebyōshi* (following or shadowing the opponent's beat), in which the proponent strikes the enemy as the latter prepares to strike; and *kosuhyōshi* (passing by the opponent's beat) in which the proponent avoids the enemy's attack and strikes him just at the moment his attack is expended. Obviously Jūbei's three *hyōshi* are closely related to various types of *sen*, for in all three the initiative must be held in order to take advantage of the enemy's beat. The importance of the taking of *sen* and manipulation of *hyōshi* becomes clear when a practitioner reaches a level where he can experiment with the *kata* for combative effect. Of course, in actual combat they are vital factors.

Further reading in English:

• Hall, 1992, 1993.

hyōshigi 拍子木. Wooden clappers tied together at one end. These were sometimes used by battle commanders for signaling. See: *shikigu*.

Hyōtō 豹韜. See: *Rikutō*.

HOBAKU FROM THE EARLY 1800S
Note the use of firemen's ladders (*hashigo*) and the *mitsudogu*: the *sodegarami*, the *sasumata*, and the *tsukubō*
(From the nineteenth-century text *Tokugawa bakufu keiji zufu honpen*, collection of the Meiji University Museum; used with permission)

I

i 亥 [Also read as ***gai]***. The *kanji* character for "boar." 1. The Boar corresponds to the twelfth duodenary hour of the Chinese Twelve Branches (Jūnishi); that is, between 9 and 11 p.m. 2. KYŪSHO—In certain Sino-Japanese boxing texts, this character indicates the optimal time of day for striking the corresponding vital point (*kyūsho*). See also: *kyūsho;* Appendix 1.

iai 居合 [Var. 居相; 囲合【圍合】]. 1. An abbreviation for *iaidō*. 2. An abbreviation for *iaijutsu.*

iaidō 居合道. The self-discipline–oriented art of quick-draw swordsmanship, a modern *budō.* The term *iaidō* is relatively new; it was first used in 1932 and subsequently became popularized by Nakayama Hakudō. Because the basic *iaido* forms are generally performed with a long sword (*katana*) from the kneeling *seiza* posture, their relevance to actual combat situations is questionable.

Concerning the use of *seiza* in *iaidō,* Keeley (1999: 125–126) notes the following in his essay on Tatsumi Ryū:

> Most modern Japanese historians believe that seiza was confined to women and priests in the Sengoku period...Dramas shown on NHK TV are always careful to show men of that era sitting in the cross-legged *agura* position. The occasional exception is a character such as Sen no Rikyu, founder of the Japanese tea ceremony, and the tea ceremony may indeed have played a role in the spread of seiza among men of the upper classes after the establishment of the Tokugawa shogunate...

In addition, as hoplologist and martial historian Donn F. Draeger[1] often noted—giving Musō Shinden Ryū (a system specializing in *iaidō*) as an example—a number of classical systems (especially those specializing in *iai-* or *battō-jutsu*) moved away from combative reality by adopting the practice of drawing a *katana* from *seiza.* In limiting the practitioner of *iaidō* to the longsword (*katana*), rather than the short sword (*kodachi*) which would normally be kept by one's side while sitting inside a room, these systems evolved away from the cultural and combative realities of the Edo period.

In any case, many schools of quick-draw sword technique today make use of the longsword (*katana*) from the *seiza* position, and refer to their art as *iaidō.* One of the most popular versions of this is the Musō Shinden Ryū 夢想神伝流, a system created by Nakayama Hakudō in the 1930s by combining elements of the earlier Ōmori Ryū 大森流 and Hasegawa Eishin Ryū 長谷川英信流. Other schools of *iaidō*, notably Toyama Ryū 戸山流, Nakamura Ryū 中村流, and Mugai Ryū無外流, are also very active in the US and outside Japan. Hasegawa Eishin Ryū is still widely practiced both within and outside Japan. See also: *battō; battōjutsu; iaijutsu.*

Further reading in English:

- The *Iaido Journal* at http://ejmas.com/tin/
- Warner and Draeger, 1982.
- Shimabukuro and Pellman, 1995.
- Suino, 1994.
- Yamatsuta, 2005.

iaigoshi 居合腰. IAIJUTSU—Any of several kneeling postures from which a sword can quickly be drawn from its scabbard in such arts as *iaijutsu* or *battō* (*jutsu*). See also: *agura, han sonkyo (no shisei); iaidō, iaijutsu, seiza, tatehiza.*

IAIGOSHI
Ōtake Risuke demonstrating Katori Shintō Ryū *iaijutsu* at Kashima Jingū, 1979
(Photograph courtesy John Driscoll)

Iai Hyōhō Izumo no Tachi 威愛兵法出雲太刀. A family-transmitted martial tradition which was formulated into the Kageyama Ryū by Kageyama Zenga Nyūdō Kiyoshige during the Keichō era (1596–1615). Kageyama claimed to have been a direct descendant of Susano-o no Mikoto, a Shintō deity who had fought

[1] See Bibliography.

and defeated the eight-headed dragon Yamata no Orochi in Izumo, in mythical, prehistoric times.

iai irimi ken 居合入身剣【居合入身劍】. Lit. "instant-entering-sword attack." This term was used by the Iizaka Ryū for their quick-draw sword art (*iaijutsu*).

iaijutsu 居合術 [Var. 居相術; 囲合術【圍合術】]. Combative quick-draw sword techniques. In contrast to the better-known and more popular *iaidō* systems which place an emphasis on aesthetic form and spiritual development, *iaijutsu* systems emphasize efficient, lethal attacks on an opponent. Their scenarios (*kata*) also tend to more accurately reproduce battlefield situations and, when reflecting civilian combative situations, more clearly reenact premodern Japanese society than do *iaidō* systems. This art is both offensive and defensive in that the sword is quickly drawn from its resting place in the scabbard in order to deal with an enemy. (Over the centuries it has been known by a variety of names: *battō, battōjutsu*, *nukiai*, *bakken*, etc.) Like *iaidō*, *iaijutsu* is normally performed as a solo exercise[2] (in contrast to partnered *kenjutsu*) and may be executed from a variety of positions such as standing, kneeling, and crouching. As with the historically later derivative systems of *iaidō*, most (but not all) *kata* are performed in four stages:

1. *nukitsuke* 抜付 drawing the sword
2. *kiritsuke* 切付 cutting
3. *chiburi* 血振 flinging off blood
4. *nōtō* 納刀 replacing the blade in the scabbard

Since the appearance of the classical *ryū* in the fourteenth century, approximately 400 traditions have included *iaijutsu* within their curriculum. One of the earliest to do so was the Katori Shintō Ryū.[3]

The first standardized set of *iaijutsu kata* for *kendō* practitioners was developed by the Japanese police during the Meiji era (1868–1912). Many skillful swordsmen had been hired as police instructors in the 1870s; this first standard was an attempt to accommodate some of the most prominent *ryū* incorporated in their training program. Formulated by the police commission of 1886, these *kenjutsu kata* were drawn from ten different schools. (See entry on *Nihon Kendō Kata*.) In addition, according to Yamada (1925: 360), the police also adopted five *iaijutsu kata*, one each from Asayama Ichiden Ryū 浅山一伝流, Shindō Munen Ryū 神道無念流, Tamiya Ryū 田宮流, Kyōshin Meichi Ryū 鏡心明智流, and Tatsumi Ryū 立身流. See also: *iaidō; Keishichō Ryū.*

iai kempō 居合剣法【居合劍法】[A.k.a. ***kempō iai*** 剣法居合【劍法居合】]. General term for swordsmanship (*kenjutsu*, *iai*, etc.) in Suiō Ryū. Within that school *iai kempō* is practiced in several distinct sets. See: *Suiō Ryū.*

iainuki 居合抜. See: *iaijutsu.*

Iai Omote 居合表. YAGYŪ SEIGŌ RYŪ—The first series of *battō waza* consisting of seven *kata* and two additions, making a total of nine.

iaitō 居合刀. A modern metal practice sword, usually without a cutting edge, used primarily for practicing *iaidō*.

Iai Ura 居合裏. YAGYŪ SEIGŌ RYŪ—The second series of *battō waza* in the Yagyū Seigō Ryū, consisting of seven *kata*.

iau 射合. An exchange shooting of arrows, usually taking place at the beginning of a battle.

Iba Zesuiken Hideaki 伊庭 是水軒 秀明 [A.k.a. ***Jōginshi*** 常吟子] (1648–1713). Founder of Shingyōtō Ryū 心形刀流.

icchō kama 一丁鎌. OKINAWAN KOBUDŌ—Single hand-held farmer's sickle used in some schools of Okinawan *kobudō*. See: *nichō kama; ōkama; Okinawa kobudō.*

ichiban no yari 一番の槍. A phrase from the Warring States period (Sengoku Jidai) that refers to an assault group or an individual

2 There are exceptions. See entries in this *Encyclopedia* on Shin Shin Musō Ryū and Ryūshinkan Budō.

3 It is often claimed that Hayashizaki Jinsuke Shigenobu (b. 1549) was the first practitioner of *iaijutsu*. However, the Katori Shintō Ryū was including *iaijutsu* in its curriculum by the mid-1400s.

who creates an opening in the enemy's line.

Ichiden Ryū 一伝流【一傳流】. 1. Abbreviation for Asayama Ichiden Ryū 浅山一伝流 (also written as Ichiden Ryū 一転流). 2. A branch tradition of the Asayama Ichiden Ryū 浅山一伝流 founded by Marume Mondonoshō Noriyoshi .

Note: Several other "Ichiden Ryū" are mentioned by Watatani and Yamada (1978: 57), but little is known about them.

Ichidō Ryū 一道流 [Also read ***Ittō Ryū***]. A branch tradition of Itō Ittōsai Kagehisa's Ittō Ryū (1) 一刀流 passed down in Saitama domain. This school was also called Hisshō Heijutsu 必勝兵術 (lit. "certain-victory martial tactics").

Ichien Ryū 一円流【一圓流】. A branch tradition of the Shin Shinkage Ichien Ryū 新神陰一円流. Founded by Makino Kazuhiro (d. 1729), who was known for not wearing a protective mask (*men*) during training. For this reason this system was also called Sumen Ryū 素面流 (No-mask School). The Ichien Ryū was primarily concerned with combative swordsmanship (*kenjutsu*). Watatani and Yamada (1978: 54) list some of the curriculum; upon seeing this, its relationship to other "Shinkage" schools immediately becomes apparent. (Compare to the curriculum found in the entry for *Shinkage Ryū [1]*):

Sangaku	三学
Ittō	一党
Ryōdan	両段
Sentei	先程
Enka	延可
Kō	甲
Hankai	判廻
Usen	右穿
Sasen	左穿
Chōtan Ichimi	長短一味
Goka Kuka Gohon	五加九加五本
Chōhisshū	丁必周
Gyakuhō	逆方
Ryūdachi	流太刀
Kaboku	和睦
Shōkei	勝警
Ōshime	大閉
Koshime	小閉
Yaegaki	八重垣
Kyūgumo	急雲
Ishin-Denshin Gyaku	以心伝心逆

Ichihara Ha 市原派. See: *Seia Ryū lineage.*

ichiizue 櫧木杖. Lit. an "evergreen oak staff," the *ichiizue* was a hardwood staff made from a weapon-quality wood called *kashi* 樫. According to Watatani and Yamada (1978: 184) the weapon itself was around 10 feet (3.05 m) in length with a circumference of about 8 inches (20 cm). In cross-section, the shape was not round, but was planed into six sides; it was also festooned with iron rivets (*tetsubyō*). The *ichiizue* was evidently a primary weapon of the Kasumi Shintō Ryū 霞神道流.

ichiko 市子. A sorceress. Such a character occasionally appeared in war tales (*gunkimono*). See also: *miko* (3).

ichimon 一門. An extended family or clan.

ichimonji no kamae 一文字の構え. 1. Any of a variety of postures in which a straight weapon is held horizontally resembling the Chinese character for the number "1" which is written as a single horizontal stroke (一). 2. SHINDŌ MUSŌ RYŪ—Posture in which the medium-length staff (*jō*) is held horizontally and perpendicular to the line toward the enemy. See also: *tate ichimonji no kamae.*

ICHIMONJI NO KAMAE
Illustration of the Shindō Musō Ryū posture
(Author's collection)

Ichimu Ryū 1. 一夢流. Variant name for the Inatomi Ryū 稲富流, a school concentrating on firearms (*hōjutsu*). See: *Inatomi Iganokami Naoie; Inatomi Ryū.*

Ichimu Ryū 2. 一夢流. Branch tradition of the Henmi Ryū 逸見流 founded by Kumagaya Ichimu. This was a school concentrating on combative archery (*kyūjutsu*).

ichinen 一念. 1. Lit. "wholeheartedly" or "intently." Equivalent to *isshin* and *isshin furan*. 2. BUDDHISM—A temporal term meaning the time required for a single thought; a very short period of time. 3. BUDDHISM—Intense meditation. 4. BUDDHISM—A single moment of true faith.

Ichini no Tachi 一二の太刀. JIGEN RYŪ—Ichini no Tachi is one of a number of classical prearranged combative forms (*kata*) developed by this school. It was also one of ten classical *kata* adapted by the Japanese Police Commission of 1886 for their Keishichō Ryū 警視庁流 system.

ichinin tōsen no tsuwamono 一人当千の兵【一人當千之兵】. Lit. "a warrior equal to a thousand." This accolade was commonly used in the medieval war tales (*gunkimono*). It is similar in meaning to *narabinaki tsuwamono* (a warrior without peer).

Ichinomiya Ryū 一宮流. Watatani and Yamada (1978: 58-59) list seven "Ichinomiya Ryū," most of which specialized in *kenjutsu* and/or *iaijutsu* systems.

Ichi no Tachi 一太刀 [Also read ***Hitotsu Tachi***, ***Hitotsu no Tachi***] [A.k.a. ***Shinmyōken*** 神妙剣]. As a pivotal swordsmanship strategy of Kashima no Tachi, the Ichi no Tachi strategy is attributed to a revelation received by Kuninazu no Mahito in the seventh century. As a key element in the seven lines of Kashima no Tachi (Kashima Shichi Ryū 鹿島七流), Ichi no Tachi was later incorporated into Kashima Shin Ryū 鹿島神流 by Matsumoto Bizen no Kami (1468–1524) and into the Kashima Shintō Ryū 鹿島新当流 by Tsukahara Bokuden (1489–1571). From these two Kashima lines, Ichi no Tachi is thought to have been transmitted to later descendant traditions such as the Jiki Shinkage Ryū 直心影流.

Ichinotani no Tatakai 一の谷の戦【一の谷の戰】. Battle in 1184 where Minamoto no Yoshitsune had his first great victory over the Taira. In one of the most famous scrimmages in Japanese history, Yoshitsune led a small force of mounted warriors down Hiyodorigoe Cliff to attack the Taira forces from the rear.

Further reading in English:

- Kitagawa and Tsuchida, 1975: 551–553 *ff.*
- Varley, 1994: 129–131 *ff.*

i-chirasu 射散. To scatter the enemy with a volley of arrows.

ichiryō gusoku 一両具足【一兩具足】. A colloquial term used during the Warring States period (Sengoku Jidai) for a low-ranking foot soldier (*ashigaru*) who owned only one suit of armor. See also: *okashi gusoku*.

Ichizen Ryū 一全流. A comprehensive martial school (*sōgō bujutsu*) founded in 1715 by Chikamatsu Hikonoshin Shigenori. The school included a variety of combative arts: swordsmanship (*kenjutsu*), spear techniques (*sōjutsu*), martial drill (*rempeihō*), use of armor (*katchūden*), swimming (*suieijutsu*), fast cross-country riding (*sōjōsōchi*), military horsemanship (*gunba*), equestrian archery (*kisha [2]*) derived from Ogasawara Ryū, military strategy and tactics (*gunra*), and both Iga Ryū and Koga Ryū espionage (*shinobi no jutsu*).

In 1715[4] Tokugawa Yoshimichi, the fourth Tokugawa lord of Owari domain, awarded Chikamatsu a training hall called the Budō Zendendō, where several systems Chikamatsu had mastered were taught under the rubric Zenryū Rempeiden 全流練兵伝, lit. "transmission of the military drills of all the schools."

ichizoku 一族. A lineage, including subbranches.

Ida Iorinosuke Shigeyoshi 猪多 伊織佐 重能 [A.k.a. ***Shigekichi*** 重吉] (c.1558–1633). Founder of the Ida Ryū, a school of combative spear arts (*sōjutsu*).

Ida Ryū 猪多流. School of combative spear arts (*sōjutsu*) founded by Ida Iorinosuke Shigenori. Inoda was a senior student of Hikita Bungorō. See: *Hikita Kage Ryū*.

idori 居取. 1. Part of the modern police self-defense system (*taihojutsu*) developed in the

---

[4] This is an approximate date. See the footnote under the entry for *Chikamatsu Hikonoshin Shigenori* in this *Encyclopedia*.

I

1920s. *Idori* refers to a set of eight techniques dealing with situations involving sitting postures. 2. A subset of Kōdōkan Jūdō's Kime no Kata, these *waza* are performed from a kneeling position.

idori 3. 居捕. Term used for a specific set of grappling techniques in the Shinkage Ryu (8) 真蔭流, a late Edo-period *jūjutsu* school.

Idori no Bu 居取之部. KATORI SHINTŌ RYŪ —First set of *jūjutsu* forms taught in the Tenshinshō-den Katori Shintō Ryū 天真正伝香取神道流. The thirteen forms (*kata*) included in this set all begin from a kneeling posture.

iemoto 家元. See: *sōke.*

Ien Ryū 威遠流. Branch line of the Takashima school of gunnery (*hōjutsu*) and tactical training (*gumpō chōren*). This offshoot was founded by Shimosone Kanesaburō Nobuatsu, who had received a full license (*menkyo kaiden*) in the *hōjutsu* of the Takashima Ryū 高島流 (also called Seiyō Ryū 西洋流, "Western School") from Takashima Shūhan. However, in 1842 Takashima was imprisoned and disgraced (due to anti-Western factions at the *shōgun*'s court), and those close to him had to separate themselves politically from that heritage and its "taint" of Western influence. Shimosone consequently revised the Seiyō Ryū, apparently removing the Dutch-language commands used in drilling and gunnery tactics and eliminating the use of Dutch clothing and accoutrements. He also changed the name of the tradition to Ien Ryū. After Takashima was pardoned in 1853, two masters of the system who had received *menkyo kaiden* in 1854, Mori Ichima of Nagaoka domain and Daigō Kiyomatsu of Shibata domain, changed the name back to Seiyō Ryū. In Tosa domain it was renamed Shingan Ryū (2) 震感流, while in Uwajima domain it was referred to as Shinki Ien Ryū 神奇威遠流.

Iga 伊賀. Abbreviation for Iga no Kuni.

Iga Hakuyūsai Norihiro 伊賀 白祐斎 範弘. See: *Iga Ryū (3).*

Iga mono 伊賀者. 1. Variant term for espionage agent. 2. An espionage agent from Iga. See: *ninjutsu.*

Iga no Kuni 伊賀国【伊賀國】. The name for the old province in Japan which today is in western Mie prefecture. Iga has become known as one of the principal areas in which *ninjutsu* developed as a tradition apart from the warrior-class *ryū.*

Iga Norishige 伊賀 乗重. A land-owning samurai (*goshi*) from Iga domain who founded the Iga Ryū (4) sometime during the Genroku era (1688–1704).

Iga Ryū 1. 伊賀流. Clan system of espionage (*shinobi no jutsu*) transmitted by the Hattori family in Iga domain. Appropriately obscure in its origins and activities, the earliest concrete evidence of the Iga Ryū appears with the historical evidence of the relationship between Hattori Hanzō and the warlord Tokugawa Ieyasu in 1582. At that time Hattori Hanzō aided Tokugawa in escaping the turmoil caused by the assassination of Oda Nobunaga. In 1590, Hattori Hanzō was placed in command of 200 troops that would later become

Iga Ryū (2)
伊賀流
(abbreviated lineage)

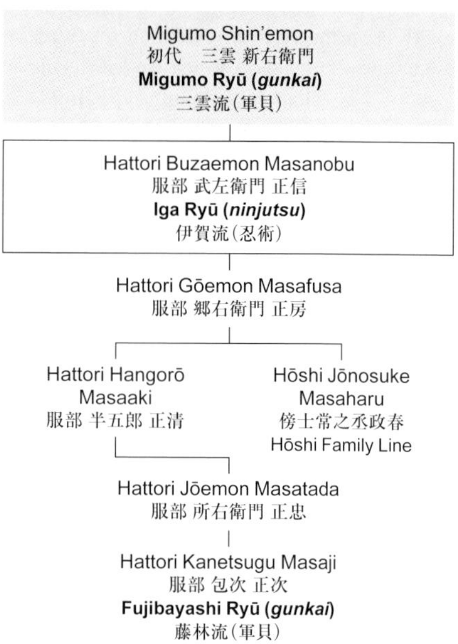

the Edo Castle guard under his son, Hattori Masanari. This castle guard was essentially made up of Iga Ryū *suppa* (low-ranking retainers/espionage agents). See: Hattori Hanzō.

Iga Ryū 2. 伊賀流. System of espionage (*shinobi no jutsu*) transmitted by the Hattori family in Tosa domain. The tradition was related to the Migumo Ryū, which specialized in martial strategy and tactics (*gunkai*) including espionage.

Iga Ryū 3. 伊賀流. Purportedly an espionage (*ninjutsu*) system. In the early twentieth century, a practitioner named Iga Shirayūsai Norihiro claimed to be the seventeenth headmaster of this tradition. However, according to Watatani and Yamada (1978: 43) the only arts he practiced were a variety of *kiaijutsu* demonstrated for popular entertainment, and *anzan* (mental arithmetic), the ability to do large calculations without resorting to an abacus (*soroban*). Compare to Kōga Ryū.

Iga Ryū 4. 伊賀流. Classical school of swordsmanship (*kenjutsu*), quick-draw sword technique (*iaijutsu*), and test cutting (*tameshigiri*). The system was founded sometime during the Genroku era (1688–1704) by Iga Norishige, a landed samurai (*goshi*) from Iga domain, and was passed down in Kaga domain (present-day Ishikawa prefecture).

Iga Ryū 5. 伊賀流. This "Iga Ryū" was an empty-handed striking system (*kempō [2]* 拳法) which was prominent during the Tempō era (1830–1844). At that time it was being taught by Henmi Shōgen Yoshimine in Shirayama. This system may have been a branch family-line derivative of the Seigō Ryū descending from Henmi Shichirōzaemon Nobusato, as Nobusato's line specialized in grappling (*taijutsu*) and a striking system relying on fists, elbows, knees, etc. (*kempō [2]*). Unfortunately, however, no documentation is available to support or disprove this speculation.

Iga Ryū 6. 為我流【爲我流】. System of grappling (*jūjutsu*) founded by Ehata Mukoemon Manshin. A student of Fukuzawa Mataichi Taneji in Yoshioka Ryū 吉岡流 *jūjutsu*, Ehata also trained in other *jūjutsu* systems such as Aoyagi Ryū 青柳流, Fujiyama Ryū 藤山流, and Asai Ryū 浅井流. Several branch *jūjutsu* traditions, including the Kasshin Ryū 勝新流, descended from Ehata's system.

Iga Ryū Ha Katsu Shin Ryū 為我流派勝新流【爲我流派勝新流】. Variant name for Katsu Shin Ryū.

igo 囲碁【圍碁】. See: *go (2)*.

igote 射籠手. See: *yugote*.

ihai 位牌. A Buddhist memorial tablet on which the posthumous Buddhist name (*kaimyō*) of a deceased family member is inscribed. The *ihai* are normally kept in a family Buddhist altar (*butsudan*) in the home.

Iikubō Kuwayoshi Tsunetoshi 飯久保 鍬吉 恒年. Iikubō was Kanō Jigorō's first instructor in Kitō Ryū 起倒流 *jūjutsu*, around 1881. Although lacking the combativeness of the Kitō Ryū of the early Edo period, Iikubō's teaching of *ran* 乱—an emphasis on "freedom of action" that stood in contrast to the *kata* in contemporary *jūjutsu* schools—intrigued Kanō. Kanō's interpretation of *ran* became a key element in his development of Kōdōkan Jūdō.

Iita Ryū 飯板流. Common miswriting for Iizaka Ryū 飯坂流.

Iizaka Ryū 飯坂流. A branch system of Shotoku Taishi Ryu 聖徳太子流. The Iizaka Ryū was a combative system of quick-draw swordsmanship which referred to its art as *iai irimi ken* 居合入身剣 (instant-entering sword attack). Founded by a samurai named Iizaka Shōbei Kagehisa in the early to mid-1600s, it was transmitted mainly in the Sendai domain during the Edo period.

Iizaka Shōbei Kagehisa 飯坂 正兵衛 景久. Founder of the Iizaka Ryū, a martial tradition specializing in *iaijutsu*, in the early Edo period. Having mastered Shōtoku Taishi Ryū, Iizaka created his own system, specializing in what he referred to as *iai irimi ken*. His system proliferated in Sendai domain.

Iizasa Chōisai Ienao 飯篠 長威斉 家直 [A.k.a.

I

Iga no Kami 伊賀守; ***Nyūdō Chōi*** 入道 長威] (1386–1488). Founder of the Tenshinshō-den Katori Shintō Ryū 天真正伝香取神道流. A seasoned warrior at the age of sixty, Ienao organized Katori no Ken (clan-based martial arts in the Katori Jingū geographical area) into the Tenshinshō-den Katori Shintō Ryū, around 1446.

Further reading in English:

- De Lange, (2006): 1–121.
- Ōtake, (1977a): 16–17; (2007): 1–15.

Iizasa Ryū 1. 飯篠流. A branch system of Tenshinshō-den Katori Shintō Ryū. This school attributed its founding to Iizasa Chōisai Ienao, who also established the Tenshinshō-den Katori Shintō Ryū. The tradition evidently retained many of the original Katori Shintō Ryū combative weapons systems, including swordsmanship (*nagadachi*) and long-hafted glaive arts (*naginatajutsu*), but specialized in the long spear (*ōmi no yari*).

The lineage of this branch line follows the standard Katori Shintō Ryū lineage up through the sixth headmaster, but lists a different seventh headmaster from the standard Katori line: Iizasa Gorōemon Nyūdō Shōshin. Shōshin's inheritor, Ajioka Saburōemon Nagasumi, evidently taught the system to a man named Yoshida Heidayū Masatsugu in 1619, after which the Yoshida family transmitted the system in Usuki domain (the present-day town of Usuki in Ōita prefecture) for several generations.

Iizasa Ryū (1)
飯篠流
(abbreviated lineage)

1. Iizasa Iganokami Nyūdō Chōi
初代 飯篠 伊賀守 入道 長威
Tenshinshō-den Katori Shintō Ryū
天真正伝香取神道流
(1446)

|

Abbreviation: Katori Headmasters 2–6
(See Tenshinshō-den Katori Shintō Ryū)

|

7. Iizasa Gorōemon Nyūdō Shōshin (Masanobu)
七代 飯篠 五郎右衛門 入道 正信
Iizasa Ryū
飯篠流
(c. 1580)

|

8. Ajioka Saburōemon Nagasumi
八代 味岡 三郎右衛門 長澄

|

9. Yoshida Heidayū Masatsugu
九代 吉田 平太夫 正次
(c. 1619)

Iizasa Ryū 2. 飯篠流. Branch tradition of the Shinkage Ryū (5) 真影流 transmitted in Iyo Yoshida domain (the present-day city of Uwajima in Ehime prefecture, on the island of Shikoku).

Iizuka Garyūsai Okiyoshi 飯塚 臥竜斎 興義【飯塚臥龍齋興義】(1780–1840). Iizuka formulated Kiraku Ryu 気楽流, a comprehensive field-combat system (*sōgo bujutsu*), in the early part of the nineteenth century. See: *Kiraku Ryū.*

Ijiri Buzaemon Harutsune 井尻 武左衛門 孟雅 [A.k.a. ***Ijiri Budayū*** 井尻 武太夫] (c.1720–c.1800). A master spear- and swordsman of the Hikita Kage Ryū 疋田陰流. Ijiri's best-known successors were his son, Ijiri Masachika, and Ōno Matabei Ikkan, founder of Ikkan Ryū (2) 一貫流.

Ijiri Masachika 井尻 雅局 (c.1745–c.1820). Well-known practitioner of the Hikita Kage Ryū in the late 1700s.

Ijuin Mondo Hisaaki 伊集院 問答 久明 (1632–1713). Founder of Ko Jigen Ryū (1) 小示現流. Ijuin, a warrior of the Satsuma domain, was a disciple of Tōgō Hizen no Kami Shigemasa, second headmaster of the Jigen Ryū 示現流. See also: *Jigen Ryū; Ko Jigen Ryū (1); Nodachi Jigen Ryū.*

Ikaku Ryū 一角流. See: *Ikkaku Ryū.*

ikamonozukuri no tachi 厳物造の太刀【嚴物造の太刀】. See: *jindachi.*

Ikeda Kenmotsu Yoshimasa 池田 監物 吉政. Founded Kakusan Ryū 覚三流, a school focusing on the pipe spear (*kudayari*), sometime during the middle of the Edo period.

Ikeibō Chōhen 意慶坊 長遍. Buddhist monk who was the legendary founder of Musō Jikiden Ryū 無双直伝流. The lineage listed in Musō Jikiden Ryū documents indicates that Ikeibō may have lived in the early fourteenth century. However, there is no collaborative information to support this claim.

iki 息. Breath; respiration.

Iki Ryū 伊岐流. See: *Iki Tōtōmi no Kami Ryū.*

ikite 活手 [A.k.a. ***ote*** 雄手; ***yōte*** 陽手]. OKINAWAN KARATE—Lit. "live hand" or "living hand," this term refers to the hand that is ready for use in attacking or blocking. The equivalent terms *ote* 雄手 (male hand) and *yō te* 陽手 (*yang* hand) both relate to Chinese *yin-yang* theory in which energy waxes and wanes in a cyclical fashion. Funakoshi (2001: 36–37) elaborates on this, noting that the relative movements and principles of *yin* and *yang* are the "cardinal principles of our *karatejutsu*." See also: *kisei; shinte.*

Iki Tōtōmi no Kami Masatoshi (Shinri) 伊岐 遠江守 真利 [A.k.a. ***Kyūzaemon*** 久左衛門]. Founder of Iki Tōtōmi no Kami Ryū. Masatoshi was a descendant of Kōno Michinao 河野通直 (d. 1587), a famous lord (*daimyō*) during the turbulent Warring States period (Sengoku Jidai). Because of this family connection, Masatoshi resided for many years in Yamato Yagyū Tani (the Yagyū valley).

During his early years Masatoshi trained extensively in swordsmanship with Yagyū Muneyoshi, founder of the Yagyū Shinkage Ryū. Upon his mentor's death in 1606, he continued training with Muneyoshi's son, Munenori, in Edo. Masatoshi was passionate about the spear and trained with a number of expert instructors, mastering the deepest esoteric meanings of each tradition he pursued. He went on to found his own school, the Iki Tōtōmi no Kami Ryū..

Iki Tōtōmi no Kami Ryū 伊岐遠江守流 [Var. ***Iki Ryū*** 伊岐流]. A school of combative spear arts founded in the seventeenth century by Iki Tōtōmi no Kami Masatoshi. This tradition, which was centered on a type of spear with a handguard (*tsuba yari*) and a length of 9 *shaku* (about 9 feet, or 2.7 m), was passed down within the Kuroda clan.

Ikka Ryū 一火流. School of gunnery (*hōjutsu*) founded by Tomari Hyōbu Shōsuke Fujiwara no Ikka around 1585, during the seven-year period when he was residing on the island of Tanegashima. The school survived the end of the feudal era and is still extant today. In fact, Nawa Yumio, the late headmaster of Masaki Ryū, was also a member of the Ikka Ryū; he and other members participated in an annual demonstration with the Hyakunin-chō Teppōtai (a group of matchlock musket enthusiasts) in the Shinjuku/Okubo area of Tōkyō.

Ikka Ryū
一火流
(abbreviated lineage)

Tsuda Jiyūsai Sanshō
津田 自由斎 算正
|
Oku Yahei
奥 弥兵衛
|
Oku Yahei Taketada
奥 弥兵衛 猛雅
|
Tomari Hyōbu Shōyū Fujiwara no Ikka
泊 兵部 少輔 藤原一火
Ikka Ryū
一火流

Okada Sukeyuki Shigekatsu
岡田 助之重勝 長澄
Ikka Ryū
一火流
(continues over more than eleven generations into the present)

Aoyama Daizennosuke Sachiyoshi
青山 大膳亮 幸能
Ikka Ryū
一火流
Inatomi Ryū
稲富流

Ikkaku Ryū 1. 一角流. SHINDŌ MUSŌ RYŪ—The Ikkaku Ryū was originally a police-type

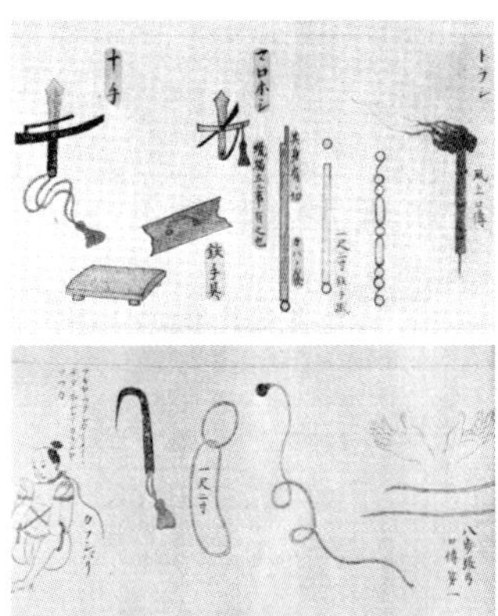

IKKAKU RYŪ *DENSHO*
Excerpt from Ikkaku Ryū *densho* presented to Uchida Ryōgorō in 1867
(Courtesy Nawa Yumio)

arresting-arts system (*hobakujutsu*) which utilized a variety of small weapons and tools, including police truncheon (*jutte*) and iron fan (*tessen*), tying cord (*nawa*), etc. It became a collateral tradition (*fuzoku bujutsu*) first within the martial repertoire (*dangyō*) of the Kuroda clan. After the 1868 Meiji Restoration, it was subsumed under the Shindō Musō Ryū 神道夢想流, retaining as its primary weapons the single-tined truncheon (*jutte*), iron fan (*tessen*), truncheon with an attached weighted chain (*fundō no tsuite jutte*), and the tying cord (*nawa*) used in an art known as *hojōjutsu*. Its founding in the early 1600s is attributed to Matsuzaki Kin'emon, a student of Musō Gonnosuke. As currently practiced under the Shindō Musō Ryū Ikkaku Ryū, the truncheon and iron fan arts consist of two sets of *kata*: Omote (twelve *kata*) and Ura (twelve *kata*).

As late as the early nineteenth century there was an *oku* transmission consisting of thirty *jutte kata*, but according to Kaminoda Tsunemori (interviews, 1985–1990), these have been lost. This tradition is closely related to the Ittatsu Ryū, also founded by Matsuzaki.

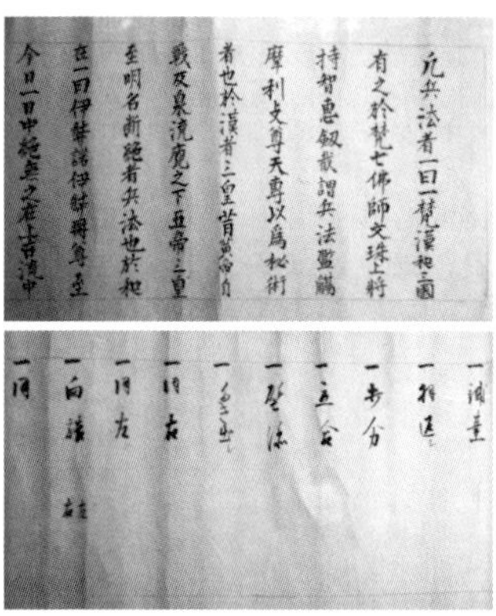

[*IKKAKU RYŪ TORITE MOKUROKU NO KOTO*]
Excerpts from two sections of an Ikkaku Ryū *densho* dated 1812 that lists *oku*-level techniques
(From the collection of Kaminoda Tsunemori)

Ikkaku Ryū 2. 一覚流【一覺流】. A comprehensive martial tradition (*sōgō bujutsu*) founded in 1585 by Satō Ikkaku. The tradition, which evolved over the span of the Edo period, eventually included unarmored striking techniques (*kempō [2]* 拳法), *jūjutsu*-like grappling and striking arts (*taijutsu*), arresting techniques (*torite*), grappling in light armor (*koshi no mawari*), short-sword swordsmanship (*tanken*), arresting rope (*nawa*), long hardwood staff (*bōjutsu*), and medium-length hardwood staff (*jōjutsu*). The school was transmitted primarily in the Matsue, Hirose, Niwase, and Tottori domains. Interestingly, in Matsue domain the system was transmitted by Kawase Heizō 川瀬兵蔵, a disciple of Saitō Denkibo in the Ten Ryū.

Ikkaku Ryū jutte 一角流十手. A single-tined truncheon specifically designed for the techniques of the Ikkaku Ryū (1).

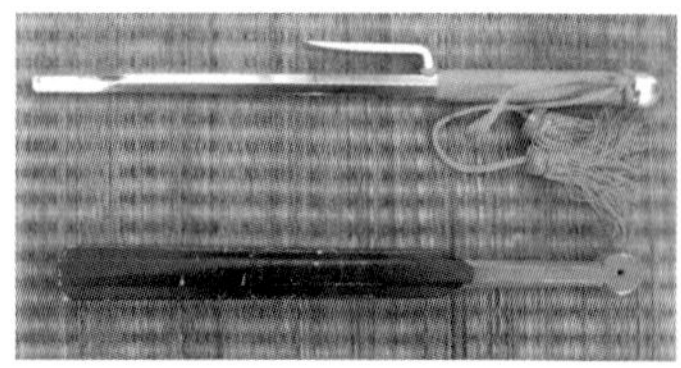

IKKAKU RYŪ (1) *JUTTE* (TOP)
AND MOCK *TESSEN* IRON FAN (BOTTOM)
These weapons are used in combination in the techniques of the Ikkaku Ryū (1)
(Private collection)

Ikkaku Ryū juttejutsu 一角流十手術. The combative truncheon arts of the Ikkaku Ryu (1).

IKKAKU RYŪ (1) *JUTTEJUTSU*
An Ikkaku Ryū exponent (right) manipulates his opponent's sword using a *jutte* and iron fan (*tessen*)
(Photograph by author)

Ikkandō 一貫道 <Ch. Yiguandao. [Unity Sect; Way of Unity (Society)]. The Yiguandao was an eclectic twentieth-century Chinese martial and religio-political organization that incorporated elements of Neo-Confucianism, Daoism, and Chinese Buddhism. Operating as a Chinese secret society even in Japanese-occupied

areas of northern China during World War II, its members were militant Boxers, much like those who had disrupted Beijing in 1900.

Nakano Michiomi (a.k.a. Sō Dōshin), who later founded Nippon Shōrinji Kempō in Japan, was an undercover operative for the Amur River Society (Kokuryūkai) in areas of North China where the Yiguandao was active. He claimed to have been heavily influenced by the Yiguandao's methods of Chinese boxing (Ch. *quanfa* 拳法) during that period, and incorporated that system in his development of Nippon Shōrinji Kempō (Sō, 1970).

Ikkan Ryū 1. 一貫流. System of swordsmanship (*kenjutsu*) and quick-draw sword art (*iaijutsu*) founded by Katayama Hōki no Kami Fujiwara no Hisayasu in 1596. There are many variant names. See: *Katayama Hōki Ryū*.

Ikkan Ryū 2. 一貫流. System of swordsmanship (*kenjutsu*), quick-draw sword art (*iaijutsu*), spear (*sōjutsu*) and archery (*yumi*) founded by Ōno Matabei Ikkan sometime during the Kansei era (1789–1801).

Ikkan Ryū 3. 一貫流 [A.k.a. ***Ikkan Ryū Heijutsu*** 一貫流兵術]. A system that includes swordsmanship (*kenjutsu*), quick-draw sword art (*iaijutsu*), spear techniques (*sōjutsu*), long hardwood staff arts (*bōjutsu*), grappling (*jūjutsu*), and combat sickle techniques (*kamajutsu*). The tradition was founded by a samurai of Bishu whose surname is unknown. However, his eclectic system combines elements of Hiden Ryū 飛電流 pipe spear (*kudayari*), Kagemasa Ryū 陰政流, Kawakami Ryū 川上流 broken-spear art (*hoko ore* 戟折), Ryōrin Sōshin Ryū 両輪相心流 quick-draw swordsmanship (*iaijutsu*), Seigō Ryū 制剛流 grappling (*yawara*), Shin Shin Sekiguchi Ryū 新心関口流 quick-draw sword (*iai* 居相), Shintō Ryū (1) 神道流 straight-bladed spear (*suyari*), Shirai Ryū 白井流 quick-draw sword art (*iaijutsu*), Shiraiwa Ryū 白岩流 long hardwood staff system (*bōjutsu*), Shishin Ryū 止心流 armored grappling (*kumiuchi*), Sunpō Ryū 寸法流 pole-arm sickle (*tegama*), Takenouchi Ryū 竹内流 grappling in light armor (*koshi no mawari*), and Tōgun Ryū 東軍流.

Ikkan Ryū 4. 一貫流. A derivative tradition of the Inatomi Ryū 稲富流. The Ikkan Ryū was a school of gunnery (*hōjutsu*) founded by Oku Yahei Takemasa in the early 1600s. Having first mastered both Inatomi Ryū *hōjutsu* under that school's founder, Inatomi Iganokami Naoie (Ichimusai), and Tsuda Ryū 津田流 *hōjutsu* under third headmaster Tsuda Jiyūsai Masakatsu, Oku established his own system.

ikki 一揆. This term essentially means "single-minded group" or "focus group." Originally, during the fourteenth century, *ikki* indicated a military organization; a band of warriors whose bonds were based on agreement (in contrast to blood ties or vassalage). However, since the *ikki* stood in contrast to contemporary feudal government organizations and were often in conflict with them, they came to be associated with rebellion. In the Warring States period (Sengoku Jidai) the term was used to refer to a rebellion or uprising by low-ranking warriors and peasants. Still later, during the Edo period, a number of peasant revolts referred to as *hyakushō ikki* were later interpreted (although incorrectly) as being modeled on the medieval *ikki*.

In his detailed essay on the topic, David L. Davis (1974) elaborates on two primary types of medieval *ikki*. The first were widespread but locally centered, single-minded groups (*tsuchi ikki* 土一揆). These tended to be peasant organizations that came together to rebel against the economic demands of regional, civil, or military authorities; e.g., the proprietors of private, untaxed estates (*shōen*). The second type was a provincial single-minded group (*kuni ikki* 国一揆), generally made up of upper-level warrior gentry (*kokujin*) who formed self-interest bands as the political system began to crumble in the 1400s. The infamous Ikkō Ikki was a particular *kuni ikki* in Kaga province which became aligned with the Honganji branch of the Buddhist True Pure Land school (Jōdo Shinshū) in 1474.

Further reading in English:

- Davis, 1974.
- Tsang, 2008.

I

ikki uchi 一騎打. Combat in single, mounted warrior style, this tenth-century term refers to a duel-like battle between two mounted archers.

Ikkō Ikki 一向一揆. Lit. "single-minded military organization." The Ikkō Ikki comprised armed provincial groups (*kuni ikki* 国一揆) made up of peasant farmers, low- to middle-ranking warriors, and monks associated with the Honganji (a subsect of the Jōdo Shinshū school of Buddhism that taught that all believers were equally saved by Amida Buddha). The Ikkō Ikki formed in Kaga province in 1474, and was a powerful force there between 1488 and 1580. See also: *Ikkōto no Ran.*

Further reading in English:

- Davis, 1974: 237–247.
- McMullin, 1985, passim.
- Tsang, 2008.

Ikkōto no Ran 一向徒乱【一向徒亂】. General term for the Ikkō Ikki uprisings. See: *Ikki; Ikkō Ikki; sōhei.*

Ikkyoku Mubetsu Ryū 一極無別流. This was a school of swordsmanship (*kenjutsu/kendō*) founded during the 1780s by a samurai named Matsuo Iyonosuke Yoshikazu who hailed from the Tatsuno domain in Harima. It is significant in that it was one of the early schools to espouse the concept of *ken zen ichi* (swordsmanship and *zen* are one).

ikusa 1. 軍. a. A tenth-century term for "army" mentioned in the war tales of that period, such as the *Shōmonki*. These armies were generally made up of armored, mounted warrior-archers (*tsuwamono*) and common foot soldiers (*banrui*). Varley (1994: 12) speculates this arrangement indicates a continuation of the earlier Chinese-style military organization adapted by the Japanese under the seventh-century Taika Reforms. b. A tenth-century term for a warrior band. c. A tenth-century term for battle.

ikusa 2. 戦【戰】. A battle.

Imagawa Godayū 今川 五太夫. Imagawa was a masterless samurai (*rōshi*) hailing from Bushū. In the early 1600s he became an expert at gunnery practices (*hōjutsu*), specializing in the matchlock pistol (*tanjū*), and went on to found the Imagawa Ryū.

Imagawa Ryū 今川流. A school of gunnery (*hōjutsu*) founded by Imagawa Godayū and transmitted in the Owari domain in the seventeenth century. During the early to mid-1700s Chikamatsu Hikonoshin Shigenori, the fifth-generation inheritor of the tradition, reformulated both Imagawa Ryū and Ōno Ryū *hōjutsu* into a revised school of firearms called the Jitoku Ryū.

Imagawa Ujiyori 今川 氏頼 [A.k.a. ***Sakyō-daibu*** 左京大夫]. An advisor to the third Ashikaga *shōgun* Yoshimitsu.[5] Imagawa, along with his colleagues Ogasawara Nagahide and Ise Mitsutada, composed a code of etiquette and ceremonies for the warrior class that was set down in a work called the *Sangi ittō*『三議一統』(Three considerations in one). These codes came to be one of the three central teachings of the Ogasawara Ryū; the other two were horsemanship and mounted archery.

Imaizumi Hachirō Tomoaki 今泉 八郎 智明. Founder of Shinkage Ryū (9) 真蔭流, a martial school concentrating on grappling techniques (*jūjutsu*).

immitsu 隠密【隱密】. See: *onmitsu.*

in 1. 影 [Also read ***kage***]. Lit. "reflection, shadow, silhouette, image."

in 2. 印. a. A Buddhist *mudrā*; a ritual hand seal (gesture). b. An identification seal.

in 3. 院 <Ch. *yuan*. a. A grove or garden; a building within an enclosure. b. BUDDHISM—A Buddhist temple. In China, the term *yuan* was used as a translation for Sanskrit *āramā* (grove) or *paryāṇa* (an encircling structure; a circuit; an enclosure). By the end of the Tang dynasty[6] the term had come to be used as the final character in temple names. This custom was also followed in Japan, where the names of many temple buildings such as Tamonin 多門院 and Hōzōin 宝蔵院 contain this suffix. Later the term *ji* 寺 (also read *tera*

[5] Ashikaga Yoshimitsu 足利義満 (1358–1408; r.1368–1394).

[6] Jp. Tō 唐; 618–907 C.E.

or *dera*) came to be used for a temple compound, while *in* 院 generally referred to a specific building. The term *jiin* 寺院 also came into use as a generic term for temples. c. A title for a retired Japanese emperor. Originally the term *in* referred to the residence of the retired Japanese emperor; in time, however, the retired emperor himself began to be called the *in*. During the ancient and early medieval periods, retired emperors were often heavily involved in intrigues and manipulation of governmental power. Later on, the term *in* was also used for a prince, regent, *shōgun*, or other personage of high status who had retired.

in 4. 寅. See: *tora*.

Inabayama 稲葉山【稻葉山】. A medieval castle built in Mino in 1203 by a warrior named Nikaidō 二階堂, an officer of the Kamakura shogunate. Over the centuries, several *daimyō* resided there. Oda Nobunaga took the castle in 1564, renaming it "Gifu." The place changed hands several times during the late 1500s, and was besieged and razed in 1600. It was not rebuilt; no *daimyō* lived there in the Tokugawa period.

Inagaki Jūrōzaemon Takanao 稲垣 十郎左衛門 貴直【稻垣十郎左衛門貴直】[A.k.a. ***Jūrōbei*** 十郎兵衛]. Founder of the Takanao Ryū 貴直流, a school specializing in military strategy (*gungaku*), combative swordsmanship (*kenjutsu*), long-hafted glaive arts (*naginatajutsu*), and long hardwood staff arts (*bōjutsu*). Inagaki, who was a warrior from Kii, spread the system in the provinces of Bishū and Bungo.

inagashi 射流. Lit. "shower shooting." A combat tactic in which unmounted archers released continual volleys of arrows for hours in order to prevent the enemy from moving into position.

Inaho Kanzan 稲穂 鑑山. A direct disciple of Hakkō Ryū 八光流 founder Okuyama Yoshiji. In the mid-twentieth century, Inaho started a school he called Kanshin Ryū 貫心流, which concentrated on *jūjutsu/aikijutsu*-type combative arts.

inatobi 鰡飛. See: *shihi*.

Inatomi Ichimu Ryū 稲富一夢流. See: *Inatomi Ryū*.

Inatomi Iganokami Naoie 稲富 伊賀守 直家 [A.k.a. ***Ichimusai*** 一夢斎] (1550–1611). Founder of Inatomi Ryū 稲富流 (sometimes referred to as Ichimu Ryū 一夢流). After joining the service of Tokugawa Ieyasu in 1604, Inatomi was appointed a troop commander in Ōsaka. As the officer in charge of national firearms production (Kunitomo Teppō Kaji 国友鉄炮鍛冶), he controlled the mass production of firearms; he was also in charge of arms production for the Tokugawa family.

Inatomi was an instructor in the use and strategy of firearms for many of the feudal lords (*daimyō*), beginning with Tokugawa Ieyasu and his son, the second *shōgun* Hidetada. In 1610 Inatomi was made a vassal (*bakushin*) of the *shōgun* and was granted the name Ōkubo Tōsaburō 大久保藤三郎. Around the same time he published his *Inatomi Ryū Hidensho*『稲富流秘伝書』(Secrets of the Inatomi Tradition), establishing the Inatomi Ryū school of matchlock musketry (*hōjutsu*).

Inatomi Ryū 稲富流【稻富流】[A.k.a. ***Ichimu Ryū*** 一夢流; ***Inatomi Ichimu Ryū*** 稲富一夢流]. A school of matchlock musketry (*hōjutsu*) founded by Inatomi Iganokami Naoie in the early 1600s. See: *Inatomi Iganokami Naoie*.

inazuma 稲妻【稻妻】. Lit. "(flash of) lightning"; "(as quick as) lightning." 1. SHINDŌ MUSŌ RYŪ—Designates two vital points (*kyūsho*) located on the left and right sides of the body over the liver and spleen. 2. ***Inazuma*** 稲妻. SHINDŌ MUSŌ RYŪ—The name of the fourth technique (out of five) in the set known as Hiden Gokui, or Gomusō no Jō.

inchi 引致. 1. Arrest; custody. 2. A prisoner.

inchi nawa 引致縄【引致繩】[A.k.a. ***gosō nawa***]. Within modern Japanese police arresting tactics (*taihojutsu*), *inchi nawa* is a set of tying-cord techniques (*hojōjutsu*) in which the aggressor is bound from the rear.

Inei 胤栄【胤榮】. See: *Hōzōin Inei*.

inga 因果. BUDDHISM—*Karma* as retribution.

I

The popularity of the concept of *inga* among the medieval Japanese is reflected in war tales such as the *Heike monogatari* and the *Taiheiki*.

inka 1. 印可. a. BUDDHISM—Lit. "seal of approval" [also written 允可 meaning "seal of permission"]. The *inka* became a seal of certification by Zen masters that their disciples had gained enlightenment. It should be noted that this term also appears in Chinese Tantric Buddhist texts devoted to Marishiten as early as the eighth century. b. A license of full mastery in a martial tradition. c. **Inka**「印可」. The name of the transmission scroll (*densho*) presented to Yagyū Muneyoshi by Kamiizumi Ise no Kami Nobutsuna (founder of the Shinkage Ryū) in 1565. The title of this scroll indicates Muneyoshi's complete mastery of Kamiizumi's Shinkage Ryū. d. An abbreviation for *Nen Ryū Inka*, the fifth of five licenses awarded by Maniwa Nen Ryū. Evidently *Inka* is awarded only to the succeeding headmaster.

inka 2. 隠花【隱花】. A homophone of *inka* (1), this term literally means "hidden flower." Draeger (1995, 6: 16) used these characters to mean "secret transmission" and as a synonym for the terms *kuden* 口伝 (oral transmission) or *okuden* 奥伝 (inner- or secret-transmission). This may reflect Draeger's training in the esoteric core of Tenshinshō-den Katori Shintō Ryū. However, the Japanese Buddhist traditions associated with the warrior class, such as the Tendai, Shingon, and Rinzai Zen schools, from which the warrior class drew much of its vocabulary for esoteric matters, did not use these characters in this way.[7]

inkajō 印可状. A certificate of full mastery; a license to pass on a classical martial tradition.

inmitsu 隠密. See: *onmitsu*.

innen 因縁. Tenth-century term found in the *Shōmonki* referring to warrior retainers. The *innen*, one of three categories of combatants in Taira no Masakado's army, were high-status warriors; probably horse-mounted archers. They were also of noble lineage, being related by blood to Masakado. See Farris (1992: 150–159) for a description of this combat force.

inninjutsu 陰忍術. See: *innin no jutsu*.

innin no jutsu 陰忍術 [Also read **inninjutsu**, **onnin no jutsu**, and **on-ninjutsu**].The skill of stealth; the skill of being able to conceal one's form; the skill of becoming unnoticeable or "invisible." An ability that allowed espionage agents to carry out operations and obtain intelligence information by appearing and disappearing at will within the enemy's camp. See also: *ninjutsu; yōnin no jutsu*.

i no me 猪目. Lit. "boar's eye." A heart-shaped representation of a boar's eye, used as a sword decoration. The *i no me* can also be found on other weapons, including the axe (*masakari* or *ono*) used by *yamabushi*.

HEART-SHAPED *I NO ME*
Boar's-eye symbol on a scabbard (*saya*)
(Private collection)

i no me horitaru masakari 猪目彫りたる鉞. Lit. an "axe engraved with a boar's eye." The *bushi* and other combatants used small war axes during the Nara and Heian periods and up through at least the Minamoto/Heike war (Gempei Gassen, 1180–1185) for breaking into forts and for attacking men and horses. During the Namboku period the axe heads tended to be larger, and often had a heart-shaped hole cut all the way through the metal of the axe head. This hole, which reduced the weight of the axe head, was called a boar's eye (*i no me*). See also: *masakari; ono*.

I NO ME HORITARU MASAKARI
Boar's-eye symbol on a war axe

[7] No reference to this term is found in *Bukkyō daijiten* (1963), *Mikkyō daijiten* (1969), or *Mikkyō jiten* (1975). The term does occur in *Dai Kan-Wa jiten* (1959: vol. 11: 971), but it is a botanical reference.

inoshishi 猪. A wild boar. As a warrior totem, the wild boar has appeared in many ages and cultures, usually as a symbol of furor and berserker-like behavior. In Indo-European warrior cultures, the connection went much deeper. There warriors often assimilated themselves into the "state of a wild beast," becoming more formidable in battle as a result.

TWO *INOSHISHI* FACING THE GODDESS MARISHITEN
Maedate on a sixteenth-century helmet
(Illustration courtesy Sasama Yoshihiko, 1990)

Among the warriors of tenth- and eleventh-century Japan, a comparison to an *inoshishi* was considered an insult, implying barbaric, mindless rage and a lack of proper demeanor. However, with the spread of the cult of Marishiten and her boar-mounted images among the warriors of the early medieval period, the *inoshishi* came to be seen as a symbol of volition and dominance over an enemy. In fact, the boar image then began to show up as a talisman on arms and armor. See: *Hokuto; Marishiten.*

inoshishi no yari 猪の槍. A boar spear. Normally constructed with a leaf-shaped blade, the *inoshishi no yari* also has a special crosspiece intended to keep the boar from running up the shaft and attacking the person wielding the weapon.

Inoue Dōjō 井上道場. A Tenshin Shin'yō Ryū *jūjutsu* training hall, located in Tōkyō, in which thirteen-year-old Shida Shirō enrolled in 1881. Shida was a student of *oshikiuchi* (the family-based martial system of the Takeda clan) under Saigō Tanomo Chikanori. It was at the Inoue Dōjō that Shida met Kanō Jigorō in 1883. Kanō invited Shida to become an instructor at the Kōdōkan *jūdōjō* where, under the name of Saigō Shirō, he became an important figure in the early development of *jūdō*.

Inoue Dembei 井上 伝兵衛 【井上傳兵衛】 (c.1800–c.1870). As a Fujikawa Ryū[8] 藤川流 swordsman who trained under Fujikawa Yahachirō Chikatsune,[9] Inoue became known as one of the three famous retainers (*sambagarasu*) of the Fujikawa branch of the Jiki Shinkage Ryū. In fact, Inoue may also have been an assistant to Akaishi Gunjibei, the eleventh-generation headmaster of the Jiki Shinkage Ryū main line tradition.

Officially a foot-soldier/retainer (*gokachi*) of the Tokugawa shogunate (Inagaki, 1982: 214), Inoue is known today mainly due to his famous duel with itinerant swordsman Shimada Toranosuke in 1838. After being soundly defeated by Inoue, Shimada requested permission to become his student. Inoue declined, but offered to write a letter of introduction for Shimada to the man he considered to be the most accomplished swordsman in Edo at that time, Odani Seiichirō Nobutomo. This surprised Shimada, because he had visited Odani's training hall (*dōjō*) on the previous day and had only been barely defeated by the small swordsman. Inoue told Shimada that Odani usually allowed an "unknown" challenger to score one point (out of three) in a match so as not to embarrass the stranger. He then wrote a letter of introduction to Odani for Shimada in order to obtain for him a rematch as a "known" and properly introduced challenger. See: *Jiki Shinkage Ryū Fujikawa Ha; Odani Nobutomo; Shimada Toranosuke.*

Inoue Denbei 井上 伝兵衛. See: *Inoue Dembei.*

Inoue Genzaburō 井上 源三郎 (1829–1868). A Tennen Rishin Ryū 天然理心流 swordsman who was a captain of one of the units of the Shinsengumi in the 1860s. See: *Shinsengumi.*

---

8 A.k.a. Jiki Shinkage Ryū Fujikawa Ha 直心影流藤川派.

9 Watatani and Yamada (1978: 724) list Inoue as a disciple of Fujikawa Yashirōemon Chikayoshi, tenth-generation headmaster of the Jiki Shinkage Ryū. However, this seems anachronistic as Inoue was a contemporary of Odani Nobutomo (1789–1864), the thirteenth-generation headmaster. Other sources list Inoue as a disciple of Fujikawa Yahachirō Chikatsune, the twelfth headmaster.

Inoue Hōken (Noriaki) 井上 方軒(鑑昭) (1902–1994). A nephew of Ueshiba Morihei, Inoue helped his uncle spread *aikidō* in the 1930s and 1940s. He later broke with his uncle's system and founded a similar school he first called Aiki Budō. In 1956 he changed the name to Shinwa Taidō 親和体道, and later to Shinei Taidō 親英体道.

inpō 隠法【隱法】. A method used by espionage agents (*ninja/shinobi*) for disappearing by "melting away." This is in contrast to disappearing by "escape" (*tonpō*). See also: *ninjutsu; ongyōjutsu.*

inu 戌 [Also read as ***jutsu***]. 1. This character, the symbol for Dog, indicates the eleventh duodenary hour of Chinese Twelve Branches (Jūnishi), lasting from 7 to 9 p.m. 2. KYŪSHO —In certain Sino-Japanese boxing texts, this character indicates the optimal time of day for striking the corresponding vital point (*kyūsho*). See also: *kyūsho*; Appendix 1.

inu i gote 犬射籠手. A type of gauntlet or armored sleeve worn by mounted archers engaging in the sport of dog hunting. See: *inu ou mono.*

inu i hikime 犬射蟇目. An arrow with a perforated head (*hikime*) used in the sport of dog hunting during the early Kamakura period. The use of such arrows was later prohibited, and the archers began using blunted arrows so as not to harm the dogs. See: *inu ou mono.*

inu i suou 犬射素襖. Special costumes worn during the sport of dog hunting. See: *inu ou mono.*

Inukami Ryū 犬上流. Variant name for Kyūshin Ryū 汲心流.

Inukami Sakonnoshō Nagakatsu 犬上左近将 永勝. Founder of the Inukami Ryū, better known as the Kyūshin Ryū 汲心流. This was a system of grappling (*jūjutsu*) and quick-draw swordsmanship (*iaijutsu*) that proliferated in Kyūshū during the Eroku era (1558–1570).

inu oi 犬追い. See: inu ou mono.

inu ou mono 犬追物. Dog hunting. This was a samurai sport which originated under the Kamakura shogunate. Similar in some respects to fox hunting in England, *inu ou mono* was a contest in which dogs were released into a large area enclosed by bamboo fences and subsequently hunted by archers on horseback. Evidently, under pressure from Buddhist monasteries, blunted arrows later replaced hunting arrows so that the dogs would not be harmed. During Japan's Middle Ages (Chūsei Jidai), *inu ou mono* was one of the "three equestrian archery contests" (*san kisha*) which had both a training and sportive purpose. See: *san kisha.*

in'yō 陰陽 [Also read ***on'yō***] <Ch. *yin yang*. 1. According to Chinese cosmology, *in* and *yō* are the dual forces of nature: negative and positive; female and male; dark and light; moon and sun; etc. From *in* and *yō* arise the five elemental movers (*gogyō*) which give birth to all phenomena. A detailed explanation of these phenomena is found in the *Huainan Zi*『淮南子』(Jp. *Enanji*), a Han-dynasty text from the second century B.C.E. See Saso (1972: 8–16). See also: *gogyō; Enanji.* 2. ***In'yō!*** 陰陽 A distinctive *kiai* used by practitioners of *yabusame* (mounted archery) of the Ogasawara Ryū.

In'yōdō 陰陽道 See: *On'yōdō.*

ippon 一本. In matches such as those in *jūdō* and other modern Japanese combative arts, the term *ippon* indicates scoring a point. In this sense, *ippon* indicates a decisive attack.

ippongachi 一本勝ち. JŪDŌ—To win a match by *ippon.*

ippon make 一本負け. JŪDŌ—To lose a match by *ippon.*

ippō no taishō 一方の大将【一方大將】. Ancient to medieval-period term for a leader or commander.

ippon shōbu 一本勝負. In modern spiritual/sports-oriented *budō* systems, *ippon shōbu* refers to a "sudden death" match, in which the first competitor to make a decisive attack from which the opponent cannot recover is the winner.

Ippūsai 一風斎【一風齋】. Buddhist name for Yamada Heizaemon Mitsunori, the seventh headmaster of the Shinkage Ryū lineage. He renamed the tradition the Jiki Shinkage Ryū 直心影流. See: *Jiki Shinkage Ryū; Shinkage Ryū (1); Yamada Heizaemon Mitsunori.*

irataka no juzu 最多角の数珠 (Var. 刺高の数珠) [A.k.a. ***irataka nenju*** 最多角念珠 (var. 刺高念珠); ***nenju*** 念珠]. SHUGENDŌ—A rosary peculiar to the *yamabushi* made of rough stone beads, bones, or hard berries strung together. As one of the "sixteen accoutrements of the *yamabushi*" (*yamabushi jūroku dōgu*), it can be manipulated in a whip-like fashion for use as a weapon. See: *yamabushi; yamabushi jūroku dōgu.*

irimi 入身. Lit. "entering body." 1. Generic term used by many martial arts traditions indicating techniques in which a proponent enters directly into an opponent's attack. 2. Term used by the Shōtoku Taishi Ryū 聖徳太子流 to refer to their grappling curriculum.

isagiyoki 潔き. A "clean, righteous, brave (death)." *Isagiyoki* was a warrior ideal espoused by Katō Kiyomasa, Hideyoshi's "devil general" (Kishōkan), in Korea in the 1590s. See also: *bushi no konjō.*

Isei Jitoku Tenshin Ryū 為勢自得天真流【爲勢自得天真流】. A school of grappling (*jūjutsu*), swordsmanship (*kenjutsu*), and quick-draw sword arts (*iaijutsu*) founded by Fujita Fumoto Norisada, a master of Ryōi Shintō Ryū 良移心当流 in the Kuroda domain in Kyūshū. Evidently either Fujita's successor, a warrior named Shōbayashi Fujiwara no Michikazu, or Michikazu's successor Shōbayashi Matashichirō combined Fujita's teachings with the parent system (Ryōi Shintō Ryū) to create the Jigō Tenshin Ryū 自剛天真流. However, the lineage is unclear.

Ise Noritada 伊勢 憲忠 [A.k.a. ***Musashi no Kami*** 武蔵守]. Founder of the Ise Ryū and an advisor to the third Ashikaga *shōgun*, Yoshimitsu.[10] Ise, along with colleagues Ogasawara Nagahide and Imagawa Ujiyori, composed a code of etiquette and ceremonies for the warrior class that was set down in a work called the *Sangi ittō* 『三議一統』 (Three considerations in one). These codes came to be one of the three central teachings of the Ogasawara Ryū, the other two being horsemanship and mounted archery.

Ise Ryū 伊勢流. A system of warrior etiquette (*shorei*), archery (*yumi*), and horsemanship (*bajutsu*) founded by Ise Noritada. Its teachings were evidently very close to those of the Ogasawara Ryū, which eventually eclipsed the Ise Ryū as time went on.

Ise Taira 伊勢平 [A.k.a. ***Ise Heishi*** 伊勢平氏; ***Heike*** 平家]. Branch line of the warrior clan known as the Taira. The Ise Taira descended from Taira no Korehira, who moved to Ise in the early eleventh century to take over the governorship. From there his descendants extended their power base into Iga, eventually rising to challenge the powerful Minamoto clan in the twelfth century.

Further reading in English:

- Varley, 1994: 24, 44–45 *ff.*

Ishanaten 伊舎那天 <Ch. Yishenatian <Skt. Iśāna. 1. In Indian mythology, Iśāna is one of the names of Śiva-Rudra. 2. BUDDHISM—One of a group of twelve guardian deities adopted from Brahmanism by Buddhism. See: *Jūniten.*

Ishibashi Takagi Ryū 石橋高木流. A branch tradition of the Takagi Ryū 高木流 that concentrated on *jūjutsu*. It was founded by a man now only known by his surname, Ishibashi, a *sake*-shop owner from the Akashi domain in Banshū province (present-day Hyōgo prefecture). Ishibashi was a direct student of Yagi Ikugorō Hisayashi, thirteenth headmaster of the Takagi Yōshin Ryū 高木揚心流. After mastering Yagi's system, Ishibashi founded his own, naming it Ishibashi Takagi Ryū, around 1850. It is not known who his students were.

Ishidō Chikurinbō Sukenari 石堂 竹林坊 如成. A Buddhist monk who founded the Chikurin Ryū 竹林流 school of archery. See: *Chikurin Ryū.*

[10] Ashikaga Yoshimitsu 足利義満 (1358–1408; r.1368–1394).

Ishigaki Yasuzō 石垣 安造. Recognized by the Jiki Shinkage Ryū Nomi Ha as an eighteenth-generation successor of the Shinkage Ryū through Sakakibara Kenkichi's line. Ishigaki published *Kashima Shinden Jiki Shinkage Ryū gokui denkai* 『鹿島神傳直心影流極意伝開』 (An explanation of the secret teachings of the Kashima Shinden Jiki Shinkage Ryū) in 1992. See: *Jiki Shinkage Ryū; Jiki Shinkage Ryū Nomi Ha.*

Ishiguro Ryū 石黒流. Alternate name for Tenshin Shin'yō Ryū Ishiguro Ha 天神真楊流石黒派.

Ishikawa Hōzan Ryū 石川宝山流 [A.k.a. ***Ishikawa Ryū***]. This system, a branch lineage of the Hōzan Ryū, specialized in a type of *jūjutsu* which concentrated on pinning techniques and hold-downs (*katamewaza [2]* 固術). The branch was founded by a warrior of Himeji domain (present-day Himeji City) named Ishikawa Senjirō.

Ishikawa Kurando Masaharu 石川 蔵人 政春 (c.1600–c.1675). A direct student of Yagyū Munenori who founded the Shin no Shin Ishikawa Ryū 真之真石川流. After mastering Edo Yagyū Shinkage Ryū, Ishikawa traveled around the country on a warrior pilgrimage (*musha shugyō*). The system he created was primarily passed down in the area of old Musashi province (Bushū).

Ishikawa Ryū 1. 石川流. Alternate name for Shin no Shin Ishikawa Ryū 真之真石川流, a tradition centered on swordsmanship (*kenjutsu*). See also: *Ishikawa Kurando Masaharu.*

Ishikawa Ryū 2. 石川流. Alternate name for Ishikawa Hōzan Ryū, a tradition that specialized in grappling arts (*jūjutsu*). Later, one of its branches was named Shintō Goshin Ryū 神道五心流.

Ishikawa Senjirō 石川 仙次郎. A samurai of Himeji domain who founded Ishikawa Hōzan Ryū.

Ishiko Ha 石河派. See: *Seia Ryū Ishiko Ha.*

Ishimine Ō 石嶺 翁 [lit., "Old Man Ishimine"] (c.1830–c.1910). An enigmatic Okinawan combative arts practitioner who was most likely an aristocrat named Ishmine Pēchin 石嶺親雲上 (Bishop, 1999: 62). According to interviews held by Mark Bishop with various Okinawan *karate* practitioners and historians, Ishimine Ō may have been a student of Matsumura Sōkon, the progenitor of the various Shōrin styles of *karate* in Okinawa. However, this is unconfirmed. After World War II, *karate* practitioner Kaneshima Shin'ei named his *karate* school "Ishimine Ryū" in honor of Ishimine, who had taught Kaneshima's father around 1883.

Ishimine Ryū 石嶺流. OKINAWAN KARATE—School of *karate* founded around 1946 by Kaneshima Shin'ei. At age seven, Shin'ei began training under his father, Kaneshima Shinbi 兼島信備. Shinbi had himself begun his own *karate* training in 1883, at the age of fifteen, with a man he later referred to only as Ishimine Ō, "Old Man Ishimine."

At the age of nineteen Shin'ei journeyed to Tōkyō, where he became a policeman, continuing his *karate* training under Funakoshi Gichin and Motobu Chōki. In the 1930s he also travelled around the country demonstrating *karate* with Oyadomari Kanken 親泊寛賢. Shinei returned to Okinawa after World War II and established a school that he named Ishimine Ryū in honor of his father's teacher. He never took on many students, however, and has been referred to as a "hidden warrior" (*kakure bushi* 隠れ武士).

Ishimine Ryū encompasses only three kata:

- Sanchin 三戦
- Naihanchi 内半進
- Passai 抜塞

Ishimine Ryū is unique among Shuri *te* systems in that it contains a type of Sanchin *kata* based on a technique called "bear paw" (*kumade* 熊手 <Oki. *kumadī*). In this unusual variation of Sanchin, a number of the movements are actually patterned after the movements of a bear.

Further reading in English:

- Bishop, 1999: 62–64.

ishin denshin 以心伝心【以心傳心】. Lit. "mind-to-mind transmission." BUDDHISM—A Zen term meaning a "simple, direct transmission of knowledge from mind to mind," which is strongly related to intuition. This emphasis on intuition, a characteristic of the Zen schools, was very appealing to the Japanese warrior psyche. A closely related Zen term indicates a transmission "without the use of words" (*furyūmonji* 不立文字). In a martial context, *ishin denshin*, a term indicating intuition, is commonly used to refer to the transmission of the subtleties and secrets of martial traditions from masters to disciples.

Ishin no Sanketsu 維新の三傑. This moniker, which means the "Three Heroes of the (Meiji) Restoration," was used to refer to three samurai who became key figures in overthrowing the Tokugawa shogunate in 1867: Saigō Takamori and Ōkubo Toshimichi, both of Satsuma domain in Kyūshū, and Kido Takayoshi of Chōshū domain on Honshū. Saigō, probably the most famous of the three, died in 1877 in a revolt against the very government he had helped establish. Ōkubo was assassinated by samurai loyal to Saigō in 1878, and Kido died of natural causes during Saigō's rebellion in 1877.

Ishin Ryū 以心流. A martial system concentrating on combative spear (*sōjutsu*), sword (*kenjutsu*), and glaive (*naginatajutsu*) techniques.

Ishin Sūden 以心崇伝【以心崇傳】. See: *Sūden*.

ishiyumi 石弓. A stone-throwing bow; a pellet bow.

ishizuki 石突. A ferrule on the butt end of a polearm; a metal cap covering the end of a sword hilt (*tsuka*). There are numerous types and shapes of *ishizuki*.

Ishō Ryū 猪嘯流. Lit. "Wild Boar's Roar School." This was the original name for the Mizuno Shinpō Ichiden Ryū 水野真法一伝流.

Isogai Hajime 磯貝 一. A well-known *jūdō* practitioner. When the Butokuden was established in 1899, Isogai was appointed as the first head instructor/lecturer for Kōdōkan Jūdō. (See photograph entitled "Dai Nippon Butokukai" on page 83.)

Isogai Ryū 磯貝流. A school of *jūjutsu* founded by Isogai Jirōzaemon in the first half of the seventeenth century. The grappling system around which this school evolved is thought to have been taught to him by Chin Gempin. Several sources claim that Isogai was actually Mizuhaya Chōzaemon Nobumasa, founder of the Seigō Ryū, but this is unclear.

Iso Masatomo 磯 正智. Son of the founder of Tenshin Shin'yō Ryū 天神真楊流 *jūjutsu*. Masatomo was Kanō Jigorō's teacher in that system for a short while during the late 1870s.

Iso Mataemon 磯 又衛門 [A.k.a. ***~Masatari*** 正足; ***~Ryūkansai*** 柳関斎] (1787–1863). Founder of Tenshin Shin'yō Ryū 天神真楊流 *jūjutsu*. Iso's best-known disciples were his son, Iso Masatomo, and Fukuda Hachinosuke, both of whom taught the system to Kanō Jigorō (founder of Kōdōkan Jūdō).

Isoyama Ryū 磯山流. A branch tradition of Katayama Hōki Ryū 片山伯耆流. This system of swordsmanship (*kenjutsu*) and quick-draw sword arts (*iaijutsu*) was founded by Isoyama Shirōzaemon Chikamasa in the late 1600s. See: *Katayama Hōki Ryū*.

Isoyama Shirōzaemon Chikamasa 磯山四郎左衛門 周正. Founder of Isoyama Ryū.

Issai Chozan (shi) 佚斉 樗山(子)【佚齊樗山子】. Pen name of Niwa Jūrōzaemon Tadaaki 丹羽 十郎左衛門 忠明 (1659–1741). A samurai of the Sekiyado domain, Issai authored several texts on swordsmanship in the eighteenth century, including the *Tengu geijutsu ron* (The *tengu's* discourse on the martial arts) and *Neko no myōjutsu* (The cat's miraculous skill), among others. Issai is much better known for his writing than his abilities as a warrior, although he was apparently a very capable swordsman. He was a scholar of several disciplines, including military science (*gungaku*), Confucianism, Buddhism, Daoism, and Shintō.

Issa Ryū 一佐流 [Var. 壱佐流【壹佐流】]. A comprehensive martial school (*sōgō bujutsu*) founded in 1736 by Sasaki Saburobei Moritsuna. It contained a variety of combative systems, including several weapon-oriented arts—long hardwood staff (*bōjutsu*), half-

I

length hardwood staff (*hanbōjutsu*), and truncheon (*jutte*); lightly armed and unarmed restraint and lethal systems—grappling (*jūjutsu*), arresting (*torite*), slaying (*tōsatsu*), and vital-point striking (*atemi*); and espionage. Sasaki claimed his espionage art, which he referred to as *majutsu* (invisibility art), was derived from Chinese sources. According to Watatani and Yamada (1978: 63–64), the system is known to have been practiced by only three families: the Sasaki 佐々木, the Kanafusa 金房, and the Kuromi 黒見. The last known practitioner, around 1864, was Kuromi Shōgorō.

Issei Ryū 一勢流. A combative school founded by Yamakumo Enshin sometime around the Jōkyō era (1684–1688). The term "Issei Ryū" was apparently an alternate name for the Aji Ittō Ryū 阿字一刀流. The school concentrated on quick-draw sword arts (*iaijutsu*), long hardwood staff techniques (*bōjutsu*), and arresting-cord arts (*torinawajutsu*). Yamakumo was from Edo, but the main line of his Issei Ryū was transmitted in Komezawa domain. It apparently disappeared with the end of the feudal period in 1867. See also: *Aji Kan; Gachirin Kan.*

issha zetsumei 一射絶命. This maxim, one of two key concepts used in the archery system founded by Awa Kenzō in the early twentieth century, means "Put your entire life—even unto death—into each shot."

isshin 一心. Lit. "single-minded," or "unified spirit." ¶ *isshin ni* 一心に, to do something with complete commitment; to be undistracted. Equivalent to *ichinen* and *isshin furan.*

isshin denshin 一心伝心 【一心傳心】. See: *ishin denshin.*

isshin furan 一心不乱【一心不亂】. Complete, wholehearted, intent concentration; undistracted action. ¶ *Isshin furan ni* 一心不乱に, to do something wholeheartedly. Equivalent to *isshin* or *ichinen.*

isshin ittai 一進一退. Advancing and retreating; fluctuating.

isshin ittō 一心一刀. Lit. "single-minded, one-strike swordsmanship" or "complete concentration in one strike." ITTŌ RYŪ—The concept of *isshin ittō* was seen by Itō Ittōsai, founder of Ittō Ryū, as the height of spiritual maturity obtainable via swordsmanship. In this sense, the term implies placing one's whole being into the sword strike. By extension, a person capable of doing this is not distracted by fear of death. Consequently, the concept of *isshin ittō* is closely related to that of imperturbable mind (*fudōshin*) and similar states. See also: *fudōshin; iwa no mi; and shingi ittai.*

Isshin Ryū. A number of martial schools called "Isshin Ryū" use the same ideograms. Watatani and Yamada (1978: 65–67) list eighteen different schools, the names of which are written in three ways: 一心流; 一真流; and 神流. These diverse traditions were known for a variety of combative weapons arts, including spearmanship (*sōjutsu*), swordsmanship (*kenjutsu*), long-hafted glaive arts (*naginatajutsu*), long hardwood staff techniques (*bōjutsu*), quick-draw sword arts (*iaijutsu*), grappling (*jūjutsu*), armored grappling (*koshi no mawari*), and gunnery (*hiya*).

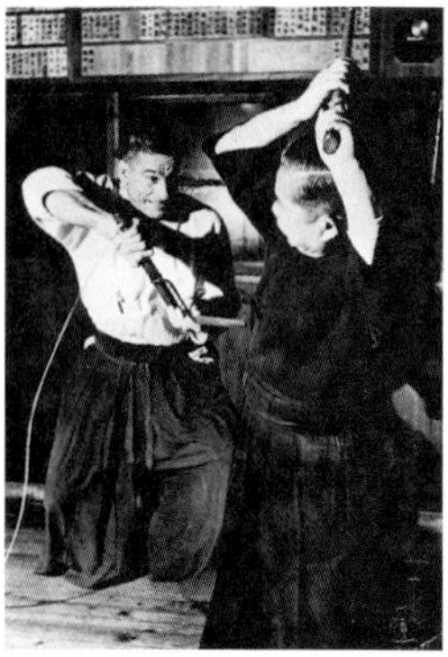

ISSHIN RYŪ *KUSARIGAMAJUTSU*
Donn F. Draeger (L) and Shimizu Takaji (R) demonstrate Isshin Ryū *kusarigamajutsu* in 1968
(Photograph courtesy Nishioka Tsuneo)

Isshin Ryū 1. 一心流. This was originally a comprehensive field-combat school (*sōgo bujutsu*) which included several combative weapons systems: long hardwood staff (*bōjutsu*), sickle and chain (*kusarigamajutsu*), polearm sickle and chain (*nagae *no kama*), and small throwing blades and darts (*shurikenjutsu*), as well as arresting techniques (*hobakujutsu*). Okuyama Nen Ami Jion, who established the Nen Ryū, is often credited with founding the Isshin Ryū (1) in approximately 1368. However, Watatani and Yamada (1978: 66) attribute its founding to Tan Isshin. Although Krieger (1989: 419) indicates Tan was a direct disciple of Nen Ami Jion, Watatani and Yamada (1978: 66) do not make this connection.

One line of this system became a collateral tradition within the Shindō Musō Ryū in the late 1800s; unfortunately, not all of these weapons systems were passed on to the present day. The primary weapons retained within the Shindō Musō Ryū are the sickle and chain and the polearm sickle and chain.

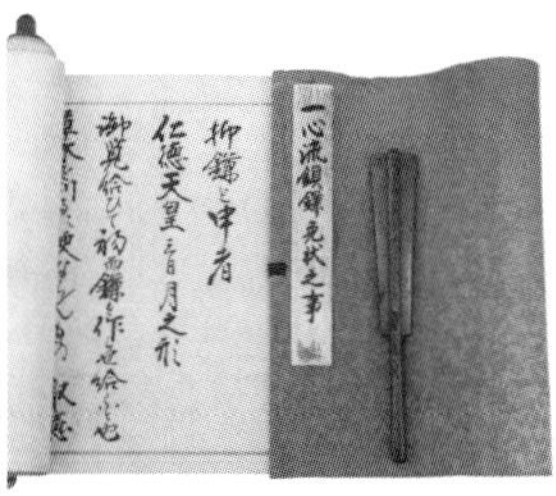

ISSHIN RYŪ *DENSHO*
Excerpt from Isshin Ryū *densho* entitled *Isshin ryū kusarigama menjō no koto*, presented to Kaminoda Tsunemori by Shimizu Takaji in 1978
(Photograph courtesy Kaminoda Tsunemori)

As practiced within Shindō Musō Ryū, the Isshin Ryū consists of four sets of *kata*. The first three sets, in which the *kusarigama* is used, comprise Omote (twelve *kata*); Ura (twelve *kata* plus one variation); and Oku (six *kata*). The fourth and final set, Gokui, consists of eight *kata* in which the *nagae no kama* is used. See also: *nagae no kama*.

The following lineage is, for the most part, taken from the *densho* presented to Kaminoda Tsunemori illustrated above and is repeated in Kaminoda (2002: 7). It should be noted, however, that even if all of the headmasters listed before Shiraishi Hanjirō had lived to be eighty years old, there are simply not enough generations listed here to date back to Nen Ami Jion (1350–c.1410). Watatani and Yamada (1978: 66) note a

Isshin Ryū (1)
一心流
(abbreviated lineage)

Nen Ami Jion
念阿弥 慈恩
(c. 1350–c. 1410)
Nen Ryū
念流

Tsutsumi Yamashiro no Kami Hōzan
堤 山城守 宝山
Tsutsumi Hōzan Ryū
堤宝山流

Yoshioka Munisai
吉岡 無二斎

Yamada Shinryūken
山田 心竜軒

Yui Shōsetsu
由比 正雪

Tan Isshin
丹 一心
Isshin Ryū
一心流

Takagi Jirō
高木 仁郎

Ashita Rinpei
芦田 林平

Morikata Furusaku
森方 両作

Shiraishi Hanjirō
白石 範次郎
(1842–1927)

Takayama Kiroku Takekatsu
高山 喜六 武勝

Otofuji Ichizō
乙藤 市蔵

Takayama Shigeki
高山 重喜

Takayama Shōzō
松田 省三

Shimizu Takaji
清水 隆次
(1896–1978)

Eguchi Tadae
江口 忠衛

Nakajima Asayoshi
中島 浅吉
(1917–1976)

Hamachi Kōichi
浜地 光一

Hiroi Tsunetsugu
広井 常次

Kaminoda Tsunemori
神之田 常盛
(b.1927)

missing section of the lineage after Tan Isshin; this is indicated here by a broken line.

Isshin Ryū 2. 一心流. A composite tradition of Isshin Ryū and Anazawa Ryū 穴沢流 that was taught in Yonezawa domain (the present-day city of Yonezawa in Yamagata prefecture) during the Edo period. This line, which specialized in the long-hafted glaive (*naginatajutsu*) and long hardwood staff arts (*bōjutsu*), attributed its origin to Anazawa Moriyoshi's Anazawa Ryū and to the modifications made to that system by Anazawa's direct disciple, Oyama Tashōgen Sadamasa, and his son, Oyama Tamon Hyōei.

Isshin Ryū 3. 一心流. OKINAWAN KARATE—A school of *karate* founded by Shimabukuro Tatsuo. In 1919, at the age of thirteen, Shimabukuro began training in *karate* with Gōjū Ryū 剛柔流 formulator Miyagi Chōjun. Later he also studied with Kyan Chōtoku, founder of Shōrinji Ryū 少林寺流. In 1956 Shimabukuro combined what he considered to be the best points of both systems into his own school, which he called the Isshin Ryū Karatedō Kyōkai. Due to these antecedents, Isshin Ryū *karate* resembles both the Gōjū Ryū of Miyagi Chōjun and the Shōrin Ryū of Kyan Chōtoku. In 2008 the international division of this *karate* school, the Isshin Ryū Kokusai Karatedō Renmei 一心流国際空手道連盟, encompassed more than 376 branches worldwide.

As an emblem for the school, Shimabukuro Tatsuo chose a depiction of a goddess he had seen in a vision (much as some earlier classical Japanese martial traditions had done), whom he called Mizugami 水神. Being half sea-snake and half woman, she represents the essence of this school: the "strength of the sea snake and the gentleness of a woman" (Bishop, 1999: 84).

Further reading in English:

- Bishop, 1999: 83–84.

Isshin Ryū Karatedō Kyōkai 一心流空手道協会. See: *Isshin Ryū (3).*

Isshin Ryū Kokusai Karatedō Renmei 一心流国際空手道連盟. The international arm of the Okinawan Isshin Ryū *karate* organization. See: *Isshin Ryū (3).*

Isshin Ryū kusarigama 一心流鎖鎌. Primary weapon of the Isshin Ryū (1). The *kusarigama* used in this school is not an adaptation of a farming sickle; its blade has no concave curve for cutting grain. It is, in fact, a modified sword blade, sharpened on both edges, and mounted at a slight angle to the haft. It has always been intended for use as a weapon for close combat and dueling, as its size and shape reveal. Its longer companion weapon, a polearm known as the *nagae no kama*, is more suited for use on the battlefield or in skirmishes. For illustration, See: *nagae no kama.*

ISSHIN RYŪ *KUSARIGAMA*
Weapon intended for use in combat
(Photograph courtesy Kaminoda Tsunemori)

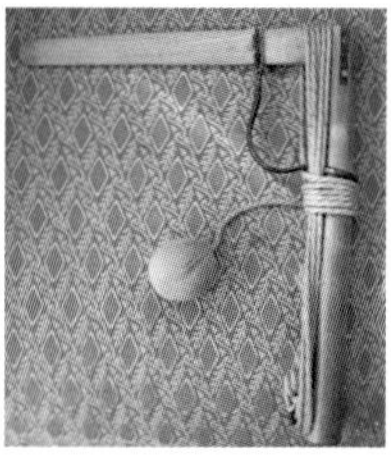

ISSHIN RYŪ *KUSARIGAMA*
Weapon intended for use in practice
(Private collection)

Isshi Ryū 一指流 [Also written 一旨流; 一枝流; 一志流]. Classical martial school concentrating on polearms such as the pipe spear (*kudayari*) and long-hafted glaive (*naginata*). The tradition was founded by Matsumoto Nagato Sadayoshi around 1630. It became very influential, and many branches specializing in the pipe spear have descended from Matsumoto's original school.

isshi-sōden 一子相伝【一子相傳】. A transmission from father to son; a transmission through the eldest son.

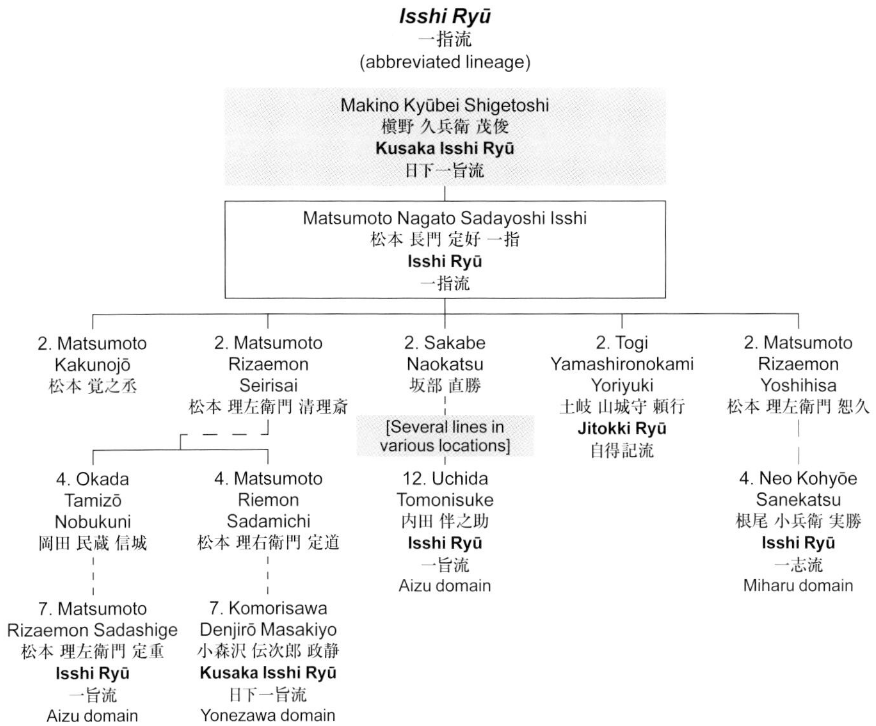

issoku ittō no maai 一足一刀の間合. Lit. "one step, one strike interval." This term refers to an optimal distance for pressing an opponent—neither too near nor too far. See also: *maai; suigetsu* (3).

itatsuki 平箭 [Also read ***itazuki***]. Blunt arrows used for target practice. These are also referred to as *matoya.*

ite 射手 [Also read ***shashu***]. A general term for archers. The word has been in use since the Heian period.

itebune 射手船. An archer's boat used in battle.

itegusoku 射手具足. Accoutrements used in the combative archery (*shagei*) of the Heian, Kamakura, and Muromachi periods. These might include a bow (*yumi*), arrows (*ya*), a quiver (*ebira*), a hat (*kasa*), and so on.

ite no tatōgami 射手畳紙. A type of heavy paper used for a special kind of archery target.

ite suō 射手素袍. A short-sleeved jacket worn by archers engaged in the sport of dog hunting. See: *inu ou mono.*

Itō Chōdayū Tsugiharu Fuden 伊藤 長太夫 次春 不伝 (c.1640–c.1700). A direct disciple of Asayama Ichiden. Itō founded the Fuden Ryū 不伝流 sometime during the Empō era (1673–1681). This system concentrated on quick-draw sword skills (*iaijutsu*).

Itō Ittōsai Kagehisa 伊藤 一刀斎 景久【伊藤一刀齋景久】(1560–1653). Founder of the Ittō Ryū. Ittōsai disdained the use of the term *kenjutsu*, preferring to call his system a "strategy" (*heihō*). He also felt that all sword techniques were actually derived from a single, simple "cutting down" (*kiri-otoshi*). From this principle he gave himself the name Ittōsai 一刀斎 (One-strike man), and named his system Ittō Ryū 一刀流 (One-strike school).

Ittōsai's system influenced several great men of the sixteenth and seventeenth centuries, including Oda Nobunaga, Tokugawa Hidetada, and Tokugawa Iemitsu. Several branches of the Ittō Ryū proliferated during the Tokugawa period, and consequently had great influence on the later development of *kendō*. In addition, Ittōsai's stress on moral behavior and the equal emphasis he placed on literary and martial art (*bunbu ryōdō*) were factors that meshed well with the Tokugawa government's plans for controlling the many *bushi* who were men-under-arms in early Tokugawa Japan.

Further reading in English:

- M. Skoss, 2002: 109–127.
- Sugawara, 1985: 161–182.

Itō Kagehisa 伊藤 景久. See: *Itō Ittōsai Kagehisa*.

Itō Kii no Kami Suketada 伊東 紀伊守 祐忠. See: *Itō Suketada*.

Itō Masayuki 伊藤 雅之 (c.1930–2001). Recognized as the nineteenth-generation inheritor of the Jiki Shinkage Ryū 直心影流 through Yamada Jirokichi's line.

Itō Ryū 1. 伊東流 [Var. ***Itō Ryū*** 伊藤流; ***Kenkō Ryū*** 建孝流; ***Unchū Ryū*** 運籌流]. A martial school centering on the pipe spear (*kudayari*) founded by Itō Suketada sometime during the late Muromachi period, c.1560–1573. In addition to the *kudayari*, Itō's school also taught cross-bladed spear (*jūmonji yari*), long-hafted glaive (*naginata*), and the use of small throwing blades and darts (*shurikenjutsu*). Itō's

Itō Ryū (1)
伊東流
(abbreviated lineage)

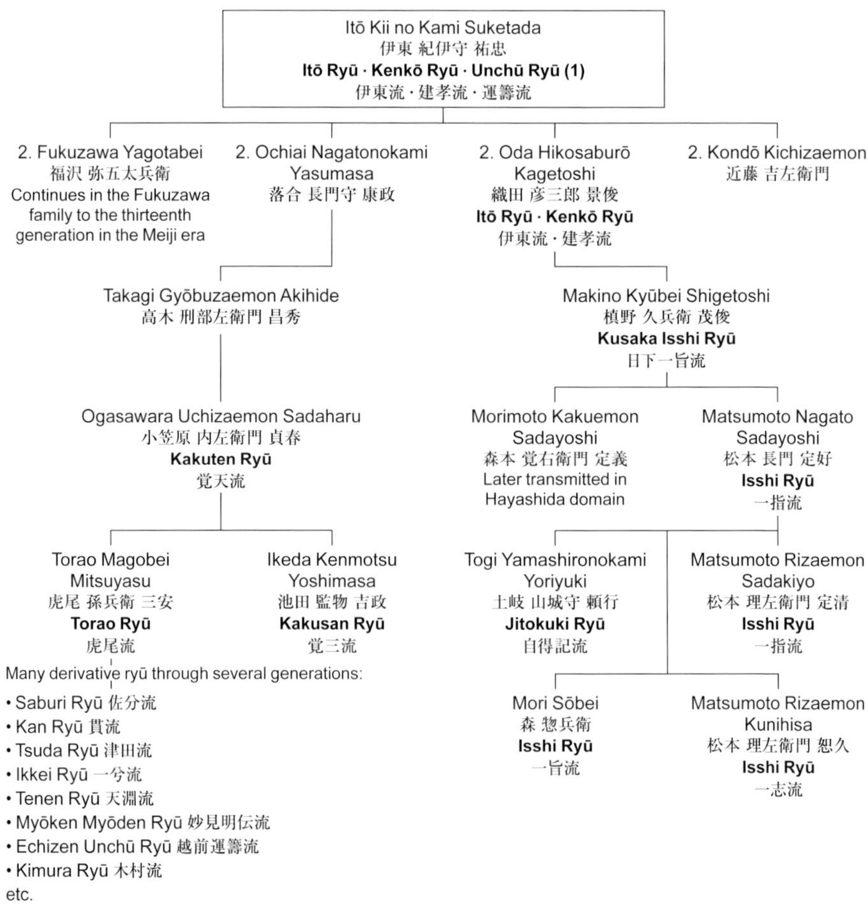

school was very popular, and many later traditions descended from it, including Kan Ryū, Saburi Ryū, Kakuten Ryū, Kakusan Ryū, Torao Ryū, and others.

Itō Ryū 2. 伊籐流. A martial school centering on warrior etiquette (*reihō*) and mounted archery (*kisha*) founded by Itō Sachiuji sometime between 1716 and1746.

Itō Sachiuji 伊藤 幸氏. Founder of Itō Ryū (2).

Itosu Ankō 糸洲 安恒 [Also read ***Itosu Yasutsune***] (1831–1915). Okinawan teacher of Shuri *te karate*. His best-known students were Funakoshi Gichin, Mabuni Kenwa, and Kyan Chōtoku.

Like his close friend Azato Ankō, Itosu had a classical Confucian education. As an adult, he worked as an official in the Okinawan government at the same time as both Azato and Matsumura Sōkon. According to Martin (2007: 4), Itosu was a "secretary and translator for the Okinawan king," Shō Tai.[11]

Itosu began his study of *karate* (then referred to as *tōde* or, simply, *te*) under Nagahama Chikudon Peichin, but later became a student of Matsumura Sōkon. He subsequently trained with Sōkon for thirty years. Funakoshi Gichin highly praised Itosu's strength and physical stamina, likening his body to a "cast-iron torso." (Funakoshi, [trans.] 1973: 240.)

ITOSU ANKŌ
c. 1910

Itosu was the first teacher to introduce *karate* as physical education into the public school system. In 1901 he introduced *tōde* at Jinjo elementary school in the town of Shuri. In 1905, he took the position of the first *tōde* instructor at the Okinawa First Junior Prefectural High School. (Nagamine, 2000: 52–53). Then, in 1908, he wrote a letter outlining ten precepts of *tōde* and emphasizing the values of *karate*. He sent this letter to the Prefectural Ministry of Education, petitioning ministry officials to introduce *karate* throughout the whole Okinawa school system. He succeeded, making *karate* available to the masses for the first time.

Along with Azato Ankō, Itosu was an important innovator in the development of the Okinawan *karate* we see today. He is credited with the creation of the five levels of the Pinan *kata*, a training form based on the earlier Chanan *kata* and Kanku *kata* attributed to Sakugawa Tōde. Pinan subsequently became a cornerstone of the Shuri *te* style of Okinawan *karate*. See also: Azato Ankō; Funakoshi Gichin; Matsumura Sōkon; and Sakugawa Tōde.

Further reading in English:

- Nagamine, 2000: 45–59.

Itō Suketada 伊東 祐忠 [***Itō Kii no Kami Suketada*** 伊東 紀伊守 祐忠; ***Kii Nyūdō*** 紀伊入道]. The founder of Itō Ryū (1) spearmanship (*sōjutsu*). Itō trained in and mastered the sixty-four sword and spear techniques required for a full license (*menkyo kaiden*) in the Shintō Ryū. After a period spent performing austerities at Kashima Jingū, he is said to have received an oracle (*musō*) from the Shintō deity Kashima Myōjin, via the Buddhist warrior goddess Marishiten, in which he received the "secret methods" of the pipe spear (*kudayari* 管槍). The pipe allowed the spear to be thrust and withdrawn very fast in comparison to other methods of the time. According to Watatani and Yamada (1978: 254) Itō's *kudayari* technique was sometimes written as 早槍 (still read as *kudayari*), which means "quick spear." After his vision, he founded the Itō Ryū (1) 伊東流 which, in addition to the *kudayari*, included the use of the long-hafted glaive (*naginata*) and cross-bladed spear (*jumonji yari*).

Itosu Ryū karate 糸州流空手. OKINAWAN KARATE—Within the general Shōrin (小林; 少林) *karate* styles of Okinawa, "Itosu Ryū" (the Itosu School) is a term used by the Japanese to encompass the traditions of Okinawan

[11] Shō Tai 尚泰 (1843–1901, r.1848–1879). Last Okinawan king.

I

Itosu Ryū Karate*
糸州流空手
(abbreviated lineage)

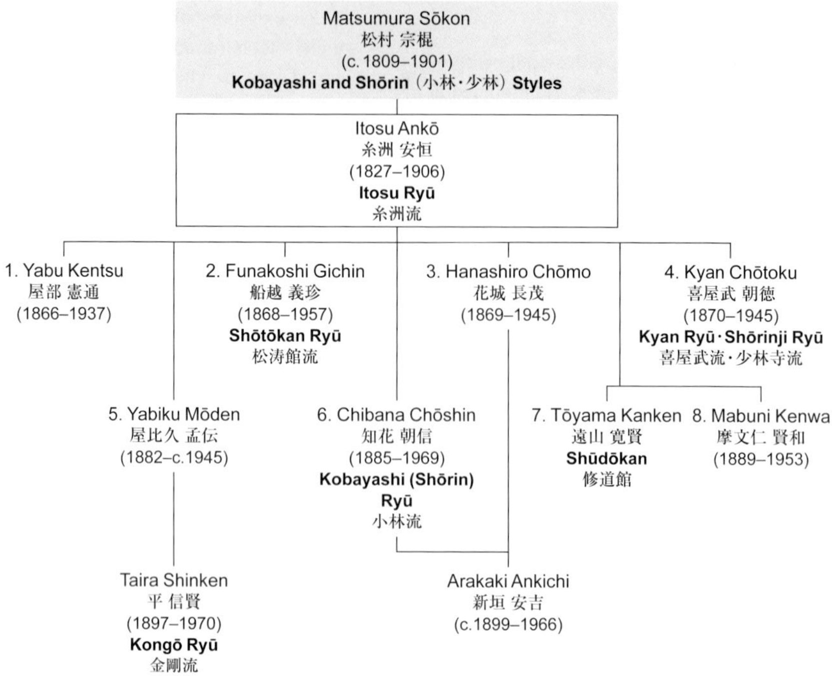

* See Bishop, 1999: 88–103 for a more information on Itosu Ankō and the "Kobayashi" Shorin styles.

karate which descend from Matsumura Sōkon via his student Itosu Ankō. The term here is used as a lineage convenience, not a formal entity in the way of Japanese classical martial schools. See: *Itosu Ankō.*

Itosu Yasusune 糸洲 安恒. See: *Itosu Ankō.*

Itsusai Chozanshi 佚斉 樗山(子). Common misreading of Issai Chozan(shi).

Itsutsu no Kata 五の形. Lit. the "five forms." JŪDŌ—These *kata* are an unusual set in Kōdōkan's curriculum. The first two of the five are closely akin to *jūjutsu* techniques, but the last three are strange, flowing, graceful movements resembling natural forces such as water, the movement of heavenly bodies, etc. They are considered "unfinished."

Ittatsu Ryū 一達流. SHINDŌ MUSŌ RYŪ—Like Ikkaku Ryū (1) 一角流, Ittatsu Ryū was originally a police-type arresting arts system (*hobakujutsu*) which became a collateral tradition within the Shindō Musō Ryū. The primary weapon retained under this status is the cord/rope (*nawa*) used in a restraint and tying art known as *hojōjutsu*. Its founding in the early 1600s is attributed to Matsuzaki Kane'emon, a student of Musō Gonnosuke. The Ittatsu Ryū, as practiced within Shindō Musō Ryū, consists of two sets of *kata* in which the cord is used (sometimes along with other weapons such as the *jutte*): Hayanawa 早縄 (four *kata*) and Honnawa 本縄 (also read "Motonawa") (twenty *kata*). Closely related to Ikkaku Ryū, the lineage parallels that of Shindō Musō Ryū.

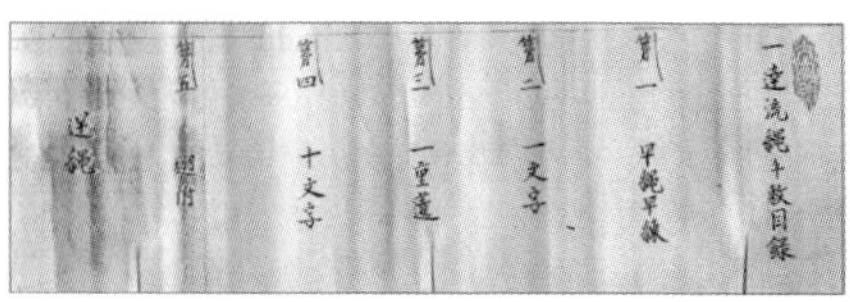

ITTATSU RYŪ MOKUROKU
Excerpt from *hojōjutsu densho* dated 1813
(Photograph courtesy Kaminoda Tsunemori)

Ittatsu Ryū hojōjutsu 一達流捕縄術【一達流捕縄術】. The police tying-cord arts of the Ittatsu Ryū. See: *Ittatsu Ryū; Kaminoda Tsunemori.*

Ittō Ryū. There were, and are, several martial schools called Ittō Ryū, often using the same ideograms. Watatani and Yamada (1978: 71–73) list three written with the characters 一刀流, and one written as 一統流. In addition, there have been a number of branch traditions of various "Ittō Ryū." Watatani and Yamada (1978: 74–75) list thirteen of these, including Ittō Ryū Kawada Ha 一刀流河田派, Ittō Ryū Kotōda Ha 一刀流古藤田派, Ittō Ryū Sugiura Ha 一刀流杉浦派, Ittō Ryū Takayanagi Ha 一刀流高柳派, Ittō Ryū Chūya Ha 一刀流忠也派, Ittō Ryū Nakanishi Ha 一刀流中西派, Ittō Ryū Heihō Myōshin Kumagai Ha 一刀流兵法妙信熊谷派, Ittō Ryū Betsu Ha 一刀流別派, Ittō Ryū Masaki Ha 一刀流正木派, Ittō Ryū Mamiya Ha 一刀流間宮派, Ittō Ryū Mizoguchi Ha 一刀流溝口派, and Ittō Ryū Mito Ha 一刀流水戸派. There are also many lines which place the branch name before "Ittō Ryū"; e.g., Ono Ha Ittō Ryū 小野派一刀流. Most of the branch schools apparently concentrated on swordsmanship (*kenjutsu*).

Further reading in English:

• Skoss, 2002: 109–127.

Ittō Ryū 1. 一刀流. The "One-strike School" created by Itō Ittōsai Kagehisa. In both its technical and spiritual aspects, Kagehisa's system had a significant influence on the Tokugawa shogunate (via Kagehisa's successor Ono Tadaaki) and on the development of *kendō* during the Edo period. However, this was accomplished through the many, variegated and evolved branches (*ha*) of the original Ittō Ryū (1). For the curriculum of Ittō Ryū, see Ono Ha Ittō Ryū. See also: *Hokushin Ittō Ryū; Ittō Shōden Muto Ryū; Kogen Ittō Ryū;*

Ittō Ryū (1)
一刀流
(abbreviated lineage)

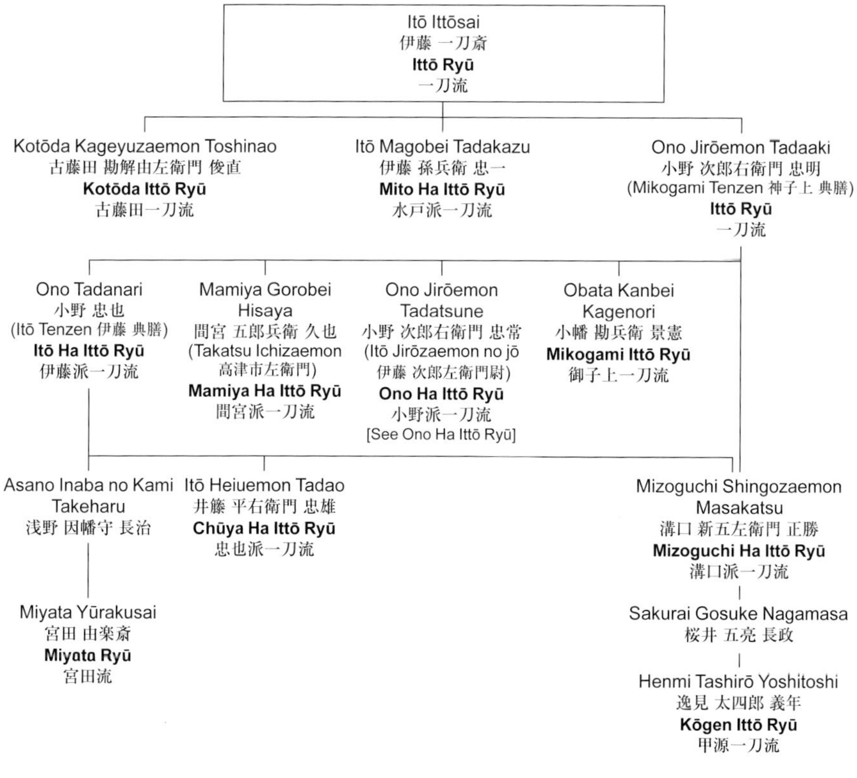

Nakanishi Ha Ittō Ryū; and Ono Ha Ittō Ryū.

Further reading in English:

- Skoss, 2002: 109–127.
- Sugawara, 1985: 161–182.

Ittō Ryū 2. 一刀流. Variant name for Ittatsu Ryū.

Ittō Ryū 3. 一道流. See: *Ichidō Ryū.*

Ittō Ryū Nakanishi Ha 一刀流中西派. See: *Nakanishi Ha Ittō Ryū.*

Ittō Shōden Mutō Ryū 一刀正伝無刀流【一刀正傳無刀流】. A system of *kenjutsu*/*kendō* founded during the Meiji era by Yamaoka Tesshū. Yamaoka required his trainees to exert themselves in attack training (*kakarigeiko*), using *shinai* which approximated the length of a real sword instead of the longer bamboo swords popular in the *kendō* (*gekken*) of that time. He also restricted his trainees from engaging in "free practice" (*jiyū renshū*) until they had at least three years' experience, as he felt it tended to break proper form. See also: *isshin ittō; shingi ittai.*

Iwanaga Gennojō Masamitsu 岩永 源之丞正光. Iwanaga was a landed samurai (*gōshi*) from the old province of Hizen. Born in 1725, he trained in "Yagyū Ryū"[12] *jūjutsu* and *kenjutsu*. By the age of seventeen he had received a full license (*mokuroku menkyo* 目録免許) in Yōshin Ryū 揚心流 *jūjutsu* and Ogino Ryū 荻野流 gunnery (*kajutsu*) from Koga Shigedayū 古賀重太夫. At the age of twenty[13] he set out on a martial pilgrimage (*musha shugyō*), subsequently obtaining licenses in Takagi Ryū 高木流 *jūjutsu* and Kukishin Ryū 九鬼神流 *bōjutsu*. Upon completing his pilgrimage he returned home in 1752.

In the following year he founded a new school he named Shingetsu Musō Yanagi Ryū 心月無想柳流. This school was a comprehensive martial system (*sōgō bujutsu*) that included a number of weapons arts. Several years later, in 1768, he shortened the name of the *jūjutsu* system to Yanagi Ryū. See: *Shingetsu Musō Yanagi Ryū; Yanagi Ryū.*

[12] Sources are unclear as to whether this was Yagyū Shinkage Ryū 柳生新陰流 or Yagyū Shingan Ryū 柳生心眼流.

[13] Watatani and Yamada (1978: 869) note this date as "Enkyō 14 (延享十四年)." However, as the Enkyō era was only ten years long, this is probably a typo for Enkyō 4 (c.1745).

iwa no mi 岩の身. See: *iwao no mi.*

iwao no mi 巌の身【巖身】(also 岩の身, read *iwa no mi*). Lit. "rock body"; or "a body like a rock." EMMEI RYŪ—The concept of *iwao no mi* was seen by Miyamoto Musashi, founder of Emmei Ryū, as an essential spiritual/psychological element of swordsmanship. In this sense, the meaning of the term is much like that of the steadfast/imperturbable mind (*fudōshin*). See also: *fudōshin; isshin ittō; shingi ittai.*

Iwasa Masaru 岩佐 勝 (b.1945). Recognized as an eighteenth-generation successor of the Shinkage Ryū through Hayakawa Kōichi's line and the Hyakurenkai. In 2002, Iwasa published a book in Japanese entitled『鹿島神傳直心影流』(*Kashima Shinden-Jikishinkage-Ryu: The origin of samuraihood—swordsmanship from Kashima Shrine, the god of bushido Kashima—a symbol of justice by the sword*). He also released a set of two Japanese-language DVDs on the system in 2007 entitled *Kashima Shinden Jiki Shinkage Ryū*. See also: *Jiki Shinkage Ryū.*

Iyasaka Ryū 弥栄流. [Also read ***Yaei Ryū***, ***Yasaka Ryū***]. A branch tradition of Ueshiba Aikidō founded by Fukui Harunosuke, a direct disciple of Ueshiba Morihei.

Izawa Gentazaemon Ryōeki 伊沢 源太左衛門 良益 (c.1640–c.1720). Founder of the Izawa Ryū. Izawa was a passionate martial artist who developed an eclectic system of combative arts (*sōgō bujutsu*) after training in many other schools. The systems he studied included:

School	System	Instructor
Hayashizaki Ryū 林崎流	*iaijutsu*	Sakai Butayū 酒井 武太夫
Ittō Ryū 一刀流	*kempō (1)*	Okada Saiemon 岡田 才右衛門
Katayama Ryū 片山流	*iaijutsu*	Katayama Hōki 片山 伯耆
Shinkage Ryū 新影流	*kempō (1)*	Kenmotsu Jūzaemon 剣持 十左衛門

Shintō Ryū 新当流	*kempō (1)*	Yoshida Mataemon 吉田 又右衛門
Tamiya Ryū 田宮流	*iaijutsu*	Tamiya Heibei 田宮 平兵衛
Tanseki Ryū 丹石流	*iaijutsu*	Nasu Okinori 那須 意的
Ten Ryū 天流	*kempō (1)*	Saitō Ichimu 斎藤 一夢
Toda Ryū 戸田流	*kempō (1)*	Matsuyama Gonbei 松山権兵衛
Tōgun Ryū 東軍流	*kenjutsu*	Kawasaki Jirōdayū 川崎次郎太夫

Izawa was employed in the service of the lord Inaba Tamba no Kami 稲葉丹波守. His school of martial arts apparently disappeared sometime around the end of the feudal period in the late nineteenth century.

Izawa Ryū 伊沢流. System founded by Izawa Genta Zaemon Ryōeki during the Kambun era (1661–1673). Izawa Ryū centered on combative swordsmanship (*kenjutsu*) and quick-draw sword arts (*iaijutsu*).

Izubuchi Ha Yagyū Ryū 出淵派柳生流. See: *Izubuchi Ryū.*

Izubuchi Heibei Moritsugu 出淵 平兵衛 盛次. Founder of the Izubuchi Ryū, a school of combative swordsmanship (*kenjutsu*). Izubuchi was a student of Yagyū Munenori and Munenori's disciple Kimura Noriyasu.

Izubuchi Ryū 出淵流 [A.k.a. ***Izubuchi Ha Yagyū Ryū*** 出淵派柳生流]. A system of combative swordsmanship (*kenjutsu*) founded by Izubuchi Heibei during the early Edo period (c.1620). Izubuchi studied under both Yagyū Munenori and Munenori's disciple Kimura Noriyasu. His system was transmitted as an Izubuchi family system in Fukui domain (present-day Fukui prefecture) until the end of the Edo period. At least two other traditions branched from it: the Unchū Ryū (2) 運籌流 and the Yashima Ryū 八島流.

Izumo Ha 出雲派 [A.k.a. ***Heki Ryū Izumo Ha*** 日置流出雲派]. Combative archery (*kyūjutsu*) school founded around 1520 by Yoshida Izumo no Kami Shigemasa. It was a branch of the Heki Ryū. See: *Heki Ryū.*

Izumo Kanja Minamoto no Yoshiteru 出雲冠者 源義照. Founder of Kuki Shinden Happō Hikenjutsu 九鬼神伝八法秘剣術. See: *Kuki Shin Ryū.*

TRIPTYCH BY UTAGAWA KUNIYOSHI (1798–1861)
Minamoto no Yoshitsune and his entourage observe as warrior Nittan no Shiro Tadatsune kills a wild boar (*inoshishi*)

J

jidaigeki 時代劇. Lit. "period play"; "period drama." A period play or film, usually (but not always) depicting the Edo period. These films are also referred to as *chambara* (sword-rattlers) as they are often filled with samurai fight scenes. See also: *chambara; kengeki; shuraba; tate (2).*

jīfā 簪 (Oki.) [Read ***kanzashi*** in Jp.]. OKINAWAN KOBUDŌ—A lady's ornamental hairpin. Techniques involving this weapon-useable object are included in the curriculum of some schools of Okinawan *kobudō*. See: *kanzashi; Okinawa kobudō.*

jigai 自害. A type of ceremonial suicide (*seppuku*) in which the veins of the left side of the neck are cut. This type of suicide was normally performed by samurai-class women in contrast to the ritual *harakiri* of samurai men, in which a blade was driven into the abdomen.

Jigen Ryū 示現流. A comprehensive field-combat system (*sōgo bujutsu*) founded by Tōgō Tōbei Shigekata (1561–1643), a samurai from the Satsuma domain in Kyūshū. The

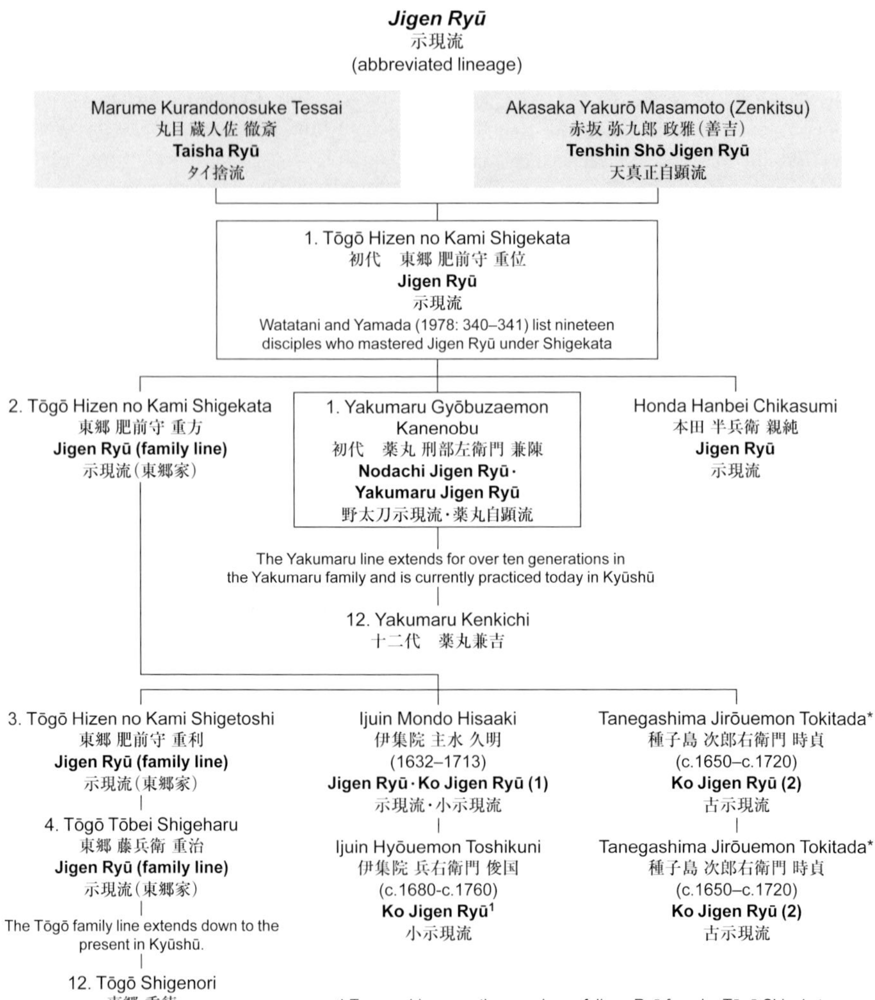

Jigen Ryū falls into the category of "positive" swordsmanship in that it emphasizes taking the initiative and closing with the enemy. Basic training concentrates on the development of powerful *kiai*—both in the sense of breath control and mental/physical domination of an opponent—as well as correct movement and attitude. A practice known as *tategi uchi* is used early in the training regimen to help the novice learn to cut and breathe properly. According to Tōgō Shigemasa (1981–1983), the eleventh headmaster of the Jigen Ryū, in the early days of the *ryū* the new trainee was required to practice 3,000 cuts in the morning and 8,000 cuts in the evening every day for a period of three years before being allowed to move on to the next stage of training. Today a trainee can advance after about two or three months of *tategi uchi*, although this practice is still heavily emphasized.

Once grounded in *tategi uchi*, a trainee learns a relatively long prearranged combative form (*kata*) called Empi, which in the Jigen Ryū was derived from the Taisha Ryū. According to Tōgō Shigemasa, Empi contains the twelve "secret" *gokui* strikes/attacks that are central to this tradition.

JIGEN RYŪ *KODACHI*
Demonstrated at the Tōkyō Budōkan in 1979 by eleventh headmaster Tōgō Shigemasa (L) and Tōgō Shigesada (R)
(Photo courtesy Tōgō Shigemasa)

After Empi, the trainee moves on through several levels of *kata* training using a variety of weapons such as the short sword (*kodachi*), great sword (*nodachi*), long hardwood staff (*bō*), and spear (*yari*). The next stage of training is the Dan no Kata, a series of twelve combative forms equally divided into four stages called *dan*. Each of these *dan* has psychological as well as physical and combative significance. However, the main combative purpose of the Dan no Kata is to refine the swordsman's skills and bring out the "secret" (*gokui*) techniques to which the trainee was introduced in Empi.

JIGEN RYŪ *INKA MOKUROKU*
(From the Jigen Ryū archives of Tōgō Shigemasa)

Current certificate (*menjō*) or license (*menkyo*):

Jigen Ryū Shodan	示現流初段
Jigen Ryū Nidan	示現流二段
Jigen Ryū Sandan	示現流三段
Jigen Ryū Yondan	示現流四段
Inka mokuroku	印可目録
Menkyo kaiden	免許皆伝

Sword (*kenjutsu*) curriculum:

Basics

- Tonbo 蜻蛉
- Okitonbo 置蜻蛉
- Tategiuchi 立木打ち

Primary sword *kata*		**Number of *kata* (if known)**
These *kata* are separated into two levels, Shodo 初度 and Ryōdo 両度		
1. Empi	燕飛	1
2. Kodachi (Zen/Go)	小太刀(前/後)	2
3. Saiki	再起	
4. Mitsutachi	三太刀	
5. Mochigakari	持掛	1
6. Hayasha	早捨	
7. Nagabokutō	長木刀	3
8. Furigakari	振掛	

Dan no Kata (Gokui) 段の型(極意)

1. Shodan	初段	Ryū Sō Etsu	立双越	3
2. Nidan	二段	Sun Man Sen	寸満煎	3
3. Sandan	三段	Hei An Kō	平安行	3
4. Yondan	四段	Kei Dō Shin	軽道真	3

Spear deflection:

Yaridome 鎗留

See also: *Ko Jigen Ryū; Nodachi Jigen Ryū; Tenshinshō Jigen Ryū; Zenkitsu.*

jigoku 地獄. BUDDHISM—The "hell realm." *Jigoku* is one of the six realms (Rokudō) into which beings are subject to rebirth. According to early Buddhist texts, there are eight hot hells, eight cold hells, and three isolated hells.

Jigō Tenshin Ryū 自剛天真流 [Var. 自剛天神流]. The Jigō Tenshin Ryū was primarily a grappling (*jūjutsu*) and vital point-striking (*atemijutsu*) system based in Fukuoka which brought together two earlier schools, the Ryōi Shintō Ryū 良移心当流 and the Isei Jitoku Tenshin Ryū 為勢自得天真流. The combative system was called *gōjutsu* 剛術 (power art) in contrast to *jūjutsu* (flexible art). This union was apparently accomplished by a warrior in the Kuroda domain named Shōbayashi Fujiwara no Michikazu sometime during the early 1800s. Like its parent system, the Jigō Tenshin Ryū also included quick-draw sword arts (*iaijutsu*) and a specialized system for striking vital points on the body called *kempō* (2) 拳法.

The school was taught at the Meidōkan training hall (*dōjō*) during the late 1800s. The Meidōkan belonged to the Gen'yōsha, an ultra-right-wing activist group; the severe training in Jigō Tenshin Ryū *jūjutsu* was used to select candidates for membership in the society. The school survives today in Fukuoka.

jihatsu 持鉢 [Also read ***jihachi***]. See: *hachi.*

jihei 寺兵. BUDDHISM—Late Heian-period term meaning "temple warriors." See: *sōhei (1).*

jihi 慈悲. BUDDHISM—Compassion. In East Asian Buddhism the term *jihi* is thought to be a translation of two Sanskrit terms: *ji* 慈 <Skt. *matrī* (=to give happiness) and *hi* 悲 <Skt. *karuṇā* (=compassion; to save sentient beings by alleviating suffering). A similar Japanese term for compassion, *nasake*, was considered a special characteristic of the classical warrior (*bushi*). In the warrior context, "compassion" referred to the ability to perceive the suffering inherent in the human condition and the ability to "sympathize with the weak and helpless." See also: *nasake.*

jijin 自刃 [Var. 自尽【自盡】]. Suicide via one's own sword.

jika gyōji 寺家行事. A practice developed by the Hōjō family in the late thirteenth and early fourteenth century whereby warrior officials were assigned to manage Rinzai Zen monasteries.

Further reading in English:

- Collcutt, 1981.
- Mass, 1982.

jikideshi 直弟子. A direct disciple; one who trains directly under a master and receives the secrets of a tradition from the teacher.

jikisan 直参. During the Kamakura and Muromachi shogunates, this term indicated direct vassals of the *shōgun*. It was used in contrast to *baishin* 陪臣, indirect vassals. See also: *hatamoto; jikisan hatamoto.*

jikisan hatamoto 直参旗本. An alternate term for *hatamoto* during the Tokugawa period. *Hatamoto* were mid-level direct vassals of the Tokugawa *shōgun*.

jikishin 直心. BUDDHISM—*Jikishin* refers to a mind restored to its original nature; a simple, correct mind; a calm, awakened mind. Nakamura Hajime, a well-known Buddhist scholar, notes that the term means a clear, genuine frame of mind without impurities, a mind that is compliant and obedient. (*Bukkyōgo daijiten*: 1975: vol. 1, p. 580). In this way it is analogous to the term *bodaishin* 菩提心, awakened mind. The term *jikishin* became well known in the context of martial arts due to its use by swordsman Kamiya Denshinsai, who founded the Shinkage Jikishin Ryū 新陰直心流 around 1630. For Kamiya, *jikishin* was a mental state transcending concerns over the inevitability of life and death; it was somewhat equivalent to *fudōshin.* It is also used in maxims such as, "*Jikishin kore dōjō*" 直心是道場, i.e., "The (real) training hall (*dōjō*; 'place of the Way') is the mind restored to its original nature (*jikishin*)."

Jikishin Dōjō 直心道場. A martial-arts *dōjō* founded by Ōmori Sōgen in the Koshikawa area of Tōkyō on 1 January 1934. Ostensibly a Jiki Shinkage Ryū training hall, it was, according to Brian Daizen Victoria (2003: 50), an institute where Ōmori established a curriculum of the arts he wished to practice: Zen, *kendō, jūdō,* and calligraphy. The actual practice of Jiki Shinkage Ryū at the *dōjō* was apparently included along with the *kendō* training. However, the purpose of this practice was to prepare trainees for "the realization of the Shōwa Restoration." (The Shōwa Restoration was to be a new era of direct rule by the emperor supported by various right-wing extremist groups.)

Further reading in English:

- Hosokawa, 1999: *passim*.
- Victoria, 2003: 50–53.

jikishi ninshin kenshō jōbutsu 直指人心見性成佛. BUDDHISM—A Zen Buddhist aphorism. The thrust of it is that by directly pointing to one's mind (*jikishi ninshin*) and seeing one's own nature (*kenshō*), one becomes a buddha (*jōbutsu*).

Jiki Shinkage Ryū 直心影流 [More formally ***Kashima Shinden Jiki Shinkage Ryū*** 鹿島真傳直心影流; a.k.a. ***Jiki Shinkage Ryū Seitō Ha*** 直心影流正統派]. JIKI SHINKAGE RYŪ—This was originally a comprehensive field-combat system (*sōgo bujutsu*), but in its current form, its curriculum is restricted to *kenjutsu.* The name of the system, Jiki Shinkage Ryū, has a number of possible translations, such as "True Shinkage Ryū," and "Correct-mind Kage Ryū." The name was first used by Yamada Heizaemon Ippūsai Mitsunori (1638–1716) to clarify the status of his transmission line of the Shinkage Ryū (in contrast to the Edo Yagyū line), and has been kept by the tradition since his time.[1]

Although the Jiki Shinkage Ryū traces its roots to sixteenth-century swordsmen Matsumoto Bizen no Kami and Kamiizumi Ise no Kami, the technical and spiritual essence of the tradition as it has come down to the present day most likely derives from the fourth headmaster, Ogasawara Genshin Nagaharu (1574–1644), and the seventh headmaster, Yamada Heizaemon Mitsunori (Ippūsai) (1638–1716).

The Jiki Shinkage Ryū falls into the category of "positive" swordsmanship, in that it emphasizes taking the initiative and closing with the enemy. Basic training concentrates on the development of powerful *kiai*—both in the sense of breath control and mental/physical domination of an opponent—as well as correct movement and attitude. A *furibō* is used early in the training regimen to help the trainee learn to move and breathe properly. This is followed by extensive training in the first set of prearranged combative forms (*kata*), known as Hōjō. Once the trainee has become grounded in proper *kiai* (four distinctive types are taught in Hōjō), he moves on to other *kata* in order to polish his abilities.

JIKI SHINKAGE RYŪ HŌJŌ
Demonstration at Kashima Shrine in 1980 by eighteenth headmaster Namiki Yasushi
(Photograph by author)

Successive sets of *kata* and their corresponding *kiai* are as follows:

- Spring Kiai—Tō no Kata [forms with *shinai* (bamboo sword)]
- Summer Kiai—Kodachi no Kata—[forms with a heavy wooden *kodachi* (short sword)]
- Fall Kiai—Habiki—[forms with a *shinken* (live sword) or *habiki* (sword with a dulled edge)]
- Winter Kiai—Marubashi—[forms with a *shinken kodachi* (live short sword)]

According to the late Namiki Yasushi, the eighteenth headmaster, Jiki Shinkage Ryū was a true *sōgo bujutsu* (comprehensive combative system) through the time of fourteenth headmaster Sakakibara Kenkichi. Up to that time

[1] The name chosen by Yamada can also be read and interpreted as "Jikishin Kage Ryū"; i.e., the "Kage Ryū line of the awakened mind," along with various other permutations of the term *jikishin*.

J

members of the *ryū* had trained in a variety of weapon systems, including long hardwood staff (*bōjutsu*), combative swordsmanship (*kenjutsu*), spear arts (*sōjutsu*), glaive techniques (*naginatajutsu*), lightly armed and unarmed grappling (*yawara*), and sickle-and-chain techniques (*kusarigama-jutsu*), among others. Since the end of the feudal period in 1867, however, the Jiki Shinkage Ryū has been limited to sword techniques.

Current certificate (*menjō*) / license (*menkyo*):

Shomokuroku	初目録
Jōmokuroku	上目録
Reikenden	霊剣伝
Kyūri no maki	窮理の巻
Menkyo	免許

Sword (*kenjutsu*) curriculum:	**Number of *kata***
Hōjō 法定	4
• Hassō (Happa)	八相(発破)
• Ittō Ryōdan	一刀両断
• Uten Saten	右転左転
• Tōtan Ichimi	長短一味
Tō no Kata 韜之形	14
• Ryūbi (right and left)	龍尾(右左)
• Menkage (right and left)	面影(右左)
• Teppa (advancing, right, and left)	鐵破(進右左)
• Teppa (yielding, right, and left)	鐵破(退右左)
• Matsukaze (right and left)	松風(右左)
• Hayafune (right and left)	早船(右左)
• Kyokushaku	曲尺
• Enren (*tōren tairen*)	圓連(刀連體連)
Kodachi no Kata 小太刀の形	6
• Fūsei	風勢
• Suisei	水勢
• Tsubatori	鍔取
• Kissaki Gaeshi	切先返
• Toppi Oppi	突非押非
Kodachi no Kata (cont.)	
• Enkai 圓快	
Habiki (*urawaza* of Hōjō) 刃挽	4
• Hassō (Happa)	八相(発破)
• Ittō Ryōdan	一刀両断
• Uten Saten	右転左転
• Tōtan Ichimi	長短一味
Marubashi 丸橋	5
• Hassō	八相
• Hissa	提
• Suisha	水車
• Enkai	圓快
• Enbashi	圓橋
Kami no Kata 神之形	4
• Hassō (Happa)	八相(発破)
• Ittō Ryōdan	一刀両断
• Uten Saten	右転左転
• Tōtan Ichimi	長短一味

[Additional combative forms practiced in various other lines are not listed here.]

Unlike, e.g., the Yagyū Shinkage Ryū, which has been passed down by a series of *sei* (a line of headmasters related by blood), the Jiki Shinkage Ryū as it comes to us today was passed down by a series of *dai* (a line of headmasters not related by blood). From an historical or hoplological perspective, this second

JIKI SHINKAGE RYŪ TŌ NO KATA
Demonstration at Yasukuni Shrine, 1979
(Photograph from author's collection)

JIKI SHINKAGE RYŪ KODACHI NO KATA
Demonstration at Kashima Shrine, 1979
(Photograph by author)

JIKI SHINKAGE RYŪ HABIKI
Katō Tsuneharu (L) teaching Habiki in 1979
(Photograph by author)

type of transmission is generally more problematic. As there is no family or geographical nexus to provide stability in the technical and spiritual content of the *ryū*, there tends to be more drift in these areas. On the other hand, sometimes headmasters who are not constrained by blood relations can introduce changes that keep the curriculum and martial spirit of a tradition from becoming stagnant. These modifications may be reflected in the name used for the tradition. According to the Jiki Shinkage Ryū *densho*, the school has had several name changes, as noted in the lineage chart below.

As can be seen, the period of family/geographical stability from the seventh to the ninth headmaster—the Nagunamas were direct descendents of seventh headmaster Yamada Ippūsai, and continued a separate "Nagunuma Line" of Jiki Shinkage Ryū for many generations—seems to have stabilized the name and curriculum of the tradition.

The Jiki Shinkage Ryū saw its heyday during the 1800s under the headmastership of men like Dannō Yoshitaka, Odani Nobutomo, Sakakibara Kenkichi, and Yamada Jirokichi. During the period when Japan had to make a traumatic transition from an isolated feudal country to a modern state, many sword traditions went into decline or disappeared altogether. The Jiki Shinkage Ryū, however, stood out as a bastion of powerful, effective, classical swordsmanship. Many warriors of other traditions, such as Takeda Sōkaku of the Ittō Ryū, as well as warrior-statesmen like Katsu Kaishū and Yamaoka Tesshū, were influenced by their training in this tradition.

Odani Nobutomo and Sakakibara Kenkichi were both advocates of *shinai shiai* (*kendō*-like duels with bamboo swords), and drew in many students by promoting these matches. Yamada Jirokichi, the fifteenth headmaster, was very famous for his ability in *shinai shiai*, but he placed more emphasis on Hōjō *kata* training than his predecessor. Apparently, the emphasis on *shinai shiai* by Sakakibara had caused a good deal of the older *kata* and weaponry to be lost. In addition, some of the *kata* remaining today may have been reformulated by Sakakibara.

Several lines of the Jiki Shinkage Ryū are still extant today; the most prominent are listed below.

- **Jiki Shinkage Ryū main line (Seitō Ha)**—This lineage, listed above, is considered the mainstream tradition by the Kashima Shrine.
- **Hyakuren Kai line**—The current head of this line, Iwasa Masaru, has recently published a book, two videos, and a number of magazine articles on this tradition in Japan. While interesting and admittedly informative, Iwasa's publications tend to make it appear that he is the sole legitimate successor of Jiki Shinkage Ryū. The Kobudō Shinkokai does recognize Iwasa as a legitimate successor of the tradition, but the Kashima Shrine recognizes the Seitō Ha under Yoshida Hajime as the orthodox stream. As the Jiki Shinkage Ryū—at least since the time of Sakakibara Kenkichi—has maintained a *shihan* system instead of a single-successor headmaster system, it appears the person to assume the title of senior

JIKI SHINKAGE RYŪ MARUBASHI
Yoshida Hajime (L) and Namiki Yasushi (R) at Yasukuni Shrine in 1985
(Photograph by author)

J

Jiki Shinkage Ryū
直心影流
(abbreviated lineage)

1. Matsumoto Bizen no Kami
初代 松本 備前守
(c. 1467–c. 1534)
Kashima Shin(kage) Ryū
鹿島神(影)流

2. Kamiizumi Ise no Kami Nobutsuna
二代 上泉 伊勢守 信綱
(1508–1577)
Shinkage Ryū
新陰流/新影流

3. Okuyama Kyūgasai Kimishige
三代 奥山 休賀斎 公重
(1526–1602)
Shinkage Ryū·Okuyama Ryū
神影流·奥山流
(c.1550)

Hikita Bungorō Kagetomo
疋田 豊五郎 景兼
Hikita Kage Ryū
疋田陰流

Jingo Izu no Kami Muneharu
神後 伊豆守 宗治
Jingo Ryū
神後流

Yagyū Sekishūsai Muneyoshi
柳生 石舟斎 宗厳
Yagyū Shinkage Ryū
柳生新陰流
(1565)

Marume Kurando no Suke Tessai
丸目 蔵人佐 徹斎
Taisha Ryū
タイ捨(新陰)流
(1567)

4. Ogasawara Genshin Nagaharu
四代 小笠原 玄信 長治
(1574–1644)
Shin Shinkage Ryū
真新陰流

5. Kamiya Denshinsai Naomitsu
五代 神谷 伝心斎 直光
(1582–1663)
Shinkage Jikishin Ryū
新陰直心流

Harigaya Sekiun
針ヶ谷 夕雲
(1592–1662)
Mujū Shinken Ryū·Sekiun Ryū
無住心剣流·夕雲流

6. Takahashi Danjōzaemon Shigeharu
六代 高橋 弾正左衛門 重治
(1610–1690)
Jikishin Seitō Ichi Ryū
直心正統一流

Odagiri Ichiun
小田切 一雲
(1630–1706)
Mujū Shinken Ryū

Takada Genzaemon
高田 源左衛門
Shinshin Kage Ryū
神信影流

7. Yamada Heizaemon Ippūsai
七代 山田 平左衛門 一風斎
(1638–1716)
Jiki Shinkage Ryū
直心影流

8. Naganuma Shirōzaemon Kunisato
八代 長沼 四郎左衛門 国郷
(1688–1767)
Jiki Shinkage Ryū
直心影流

9. Naganuma Shōbei Tsunasato
九代 長沼 正兵衛 綱郷
(1702–1772)
Jiki Shinkage Ryū
直心影流

10. Fujikawa Yashirōemon Chikayoshi
十代 藤川 弥司郎右衛門 近義
(1726–1798)
Jiki Shinkage Ryū (Seitō Ha)*
直心影流(正統派)
Fujikawa Ryū (Fujikawa Ha)
藤川流(藤川派)

11. Akaishi Chikayoshi
十一代 赤石 近義
(1749–1825)
Jiki Shinkage Ryū (Seitō Ha)*
直心影流(正統派)

12. Dannō Gennoshin Yoshitaka
十二代 団野 源之進 義高
(1761–1849)
Jiki Shinkage Ryū (Seitō Ha)*
·Dannō Ha
(正統派)·団野派

headmaster will always be in question.

- **Daihonzan Chozenji** (Zen Dōjō)—This line was founded by Ōmori Sōgen. The current headmaster is Terayama Katsujo.
- **Jiki Shinkage Ryū Nomi Ha**—The current headmaster of the lineage is Ishigaki Yasuzō. This line has apparently been inactive since the SCAP ban on martial arts practice in Japan after World War II. However, Ishigaki published a book on the tradition in 1992, and evidently claims his line, descending from Sakakibara Kenkichi, is the one true system.

See also: *Jiki Shinkage Ryū Dannō Ha; Jiki Shinkage Ryū Fujikawa Ha; Jiki Shinkage Ryū Shimada Ha; Jikishin Seitō Ichi Ryū; Seigan Jiki Shinkage Ryū.*

Jiki Shinkage Ryū Dannō Ha 直心影流団野派【直心影流團野派】[A.k.a. ***Dannō Ha*** 団野派【團野派】]. An alternate term used for the orthodox line of the Jiki Shinkage Ryū at the time of twelfth headmaster Dannō Gennoshin Yoshitaka (1761–1849). After inheriting the mantle of the Jiki Shinkage Ryū from Akaishi Chikayoshi, Dannō passed the orthodox line (*seitō ha*) on to Odani Nobutomo and eleven other disciples (*deshi*), including his own son, Dannō Matajirō 団野 又次郎.

Jiki Shinkage Ryū Fujikawa Ha 直心影流藤川派 [A.k.a. ***Fujikawa Ryū*** 藤川流]. A branch school of the Jiki Shinkage Ryū. This system of martial arts was a comprehensive combative school (*sōgō bugei*) founded by Fujikawa Yashirōemon Chikayoshi in approximately 1772. Beginning as a student of Naganuma Shirōzaemon Kunisato (eighth headmaster and son of Yamada Ippūsai), Fujikawa completed his training under ninth headmaster Naganuma Shōbei Tsunasato Katsuzensai. Katsuzensai named him as the tenth-generation headmaster of the Jiki Shinkage Ryū due to his outstanding performance and understanding of the system.

When the Fujikawa Ha of the Jiki Shinkage Ryū branched off from the Yamada/Naganuma family line in 1772, it became the source from which most subsequent surviving branches of this school descended.

In 1756, Fujikawa opened a *dōjō* in Shitaya Chōjamachi, an area in Edo. At least seven swordsmen reached the level of full mastery of the system (*menkyo kaiden*) under Fujikawa. The legitimate main line of the school passed to his most skilled student, Akaishi Gunjibei Takayū.

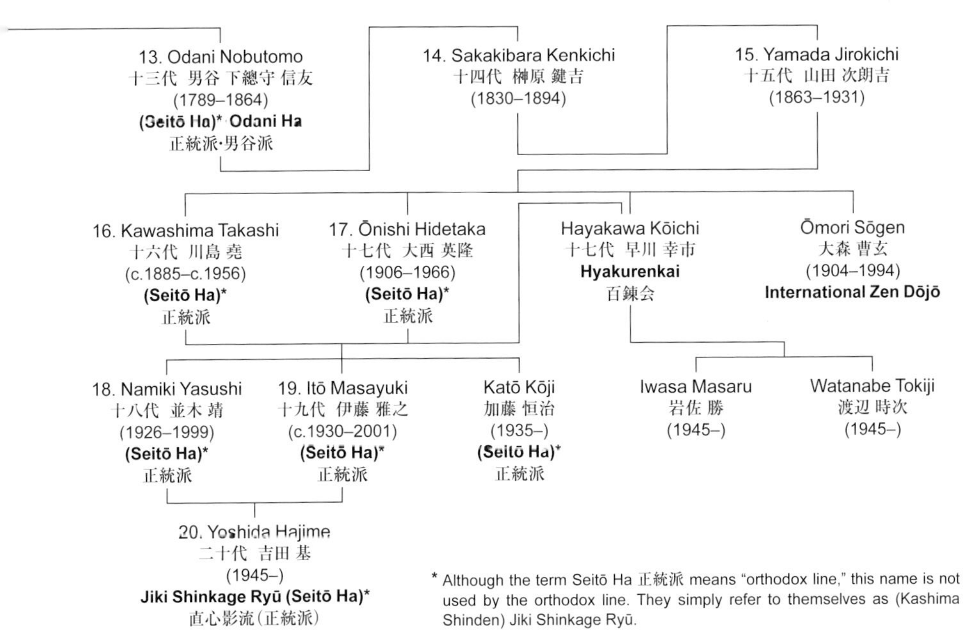

* Although the term Seitō Ha 正統派 means "orthodox line," this name is not used by the orthodox line. They simply refer to themselves as (Kashima Shinden) Jiki Shinkage Ryū.

Fujikawa Chikayoshi passed away in 1798 at the age of 72; soon afterward, his adopted son, Fujikawa Jirōshirō Kintoku, suddenly died as well. This left Kintoku's son, Fujikawa Yahachirō Chikatsune, an orphan. In an impressive show of obligation and honor, Akaishi Gunbei took in Chikatsune, his teacher's grandson, and raised him. Under Akaishi's guidance, Chikatsune developed into an expert, well-known swordsman. The complete teachings of Chikatsune's line were also passed on to six or seven other swordsmen, and Chikatsune's lineage subsequently continued as the Fujikawa line of the Jiki Shinkage Ryū. In addition, as a student of Ise Sadatake 伊勢貞丈, Chikatsune also transmitted the *Buke kojitsu*「武家故実」(Ancient warrior customs and practices) to later generations. Akaishi's line, meanwhile, came to be considered the "main" legitimate Jiki Shinkage Ryū lineage.

Jiki Shinkage Ryū Fujikawa Ha
直心影流 藤川派
(abbreviated lineage)

7. Yamada Ippūsai
七代 山田 一風斎
(1638–1716)
Jiki Shinkage Ryū
鹿島真傳直心影流

8. Naganuma Shirōzaemon Kunisato
八代 長沼 四郎左衛門 国郷
(1688–1767)

9. Naganuma Shōbei Tsunasato Katsuzensai
九代 長沼 正兵衛 綱郷 活然斎
(1702–1772)

10. Fujikawa Yashirōemon Chikayoshi
十代 藤川 弥司郎右衛門 近義
(1726–1798)
Jiki Shinkage Ryū / Fujikawa Ha
直心影流・藤川派

Jiki Shinkage Ryū Naganuma Ha
直心影流 長沼派
(Naganuma Ryū [1])
(長沼流)*

11. Akaishi Gunjibei Takasuke
十一代 赤石 郡司兵衛 孚祐
(1726–1798)
Jiki Shinkage Ryū (main line)
直心影流(正統派)

11. Fujikawa Jirōshirō Kintoku
藤川 次郎四郎 近徳
(c. 1746–c. 1799)
Fujikawa Ha · Fujikawa Ryū
藤川派・藤川流

12. Fujikawa Yahachirō Chikatsune
十二代 藤川 弥八郎 近常
(c. 1795–c. 1860)

The Fujikawa Ryū continued into the post-feudal period in several lines, some as many as nine generations long.

13. Inoue Denbei
十三代 井上 伝兵衛
(c. 1800–c. 1870)

13. Fujikawa Yaemon Sadachika
十四代 藤川 弥右衛門 貞近
(c. 1815–c. 1880)

14. Murata Masaharu
十四代 村田 政陽
(c. 1815–c. 1880)

15. Saitō Seiji Uemon Akenobu
十五代 斉藤 誠次 右衛門 明信
(c. 1835–c. 1910)
Jiki Shinkage Ryū Fujikawa Ha
直心影流 藤川派

* The Naganuma Ha survived for about nine generations until Bakumatsu times.

Jiki Shinkage Ryū Naginatajutsu 直心影流薙刀術. A modern *naginata* tradition which, with respect to technique, is at best only peripherally connected to the Jiki Shinkage Ryū proper. This *naginata* school was evidently begun by either the wife of fourteenth Jiki Shinkage Ryū headmaster Sakakibara Kenkichi, or by Satake Shigeo, the wife of Satake Kanryūsai. (Satake Kanryūsai, a student of Sakakibara Kenkichi, founded the Jikishin Ryūei Ryū 直心柳影流.) The "official" lineage of Jiki Shinkage Ryū Naginatajutsu has evidently been modified over the past thirty years and now there are varying versions of the line of succession.

Aside from the numbers assigned to a particular headmaster, the following seems reasonably accurate as far as can be determined in the present.

14th–Satake Yoshifumi	佐竹義文
Satake Shigeo	佐竹 茂雄 (wife of Yoshifumi)
15th–Sonobe Hideo	園部 秀雄
16th–Sonobe Asano	園部 朝野
17th–Toya Akiko	戸谷 明子

From a technical standpoint, Jiki Shinkage Ryū Naginatajutsu may have been influenced by other weaponry of the mainline Jiki Shinkage Ryū martial tradition that is no longer practiced. Furthermore, it is apparent that the prearranged combative forms (*kata*) practiced today by the Jiki Shinkage Ryū Naginatajutsu organization were developed by Satake Shigeo around 1900, not long after the time that the

Jiki Shinkage sword tradition dropped its other weaponry and began focusing on *shinai shiai*.

While the modern *naginata* system and the weapons used today bear no resemblance to the classical sword system pictured in this *Encyclopedia*, its *kiai* may be a different story. In the late 1970s, Donn F. Draeger[2] said he thought Shimada Teruko, daughter of Sonobe Hide, had one of the most menacing, piercing *kiai* he had ever experienced. See also: *Jiki Shinkage Ryū; Jikishin Ryūei Ryū; Sakakibara Kenkichi; Satake Kanryūsai Yoshifumi; Satake Shigeo.*

Jiki Shinkage Ryū Nomi Ha 直心影流野見派. A branch tradition of the Jiki Shinkage Ryū founded by Nomi Hamao Minamoto no Yasuchika. A direct student of Sakakibara Kenkichi, Nomi was a fifteenth-generation successor of the Jiki Shinkage Ryū tradition. His line continues into the present with Ishigaki Yasuzō, the eighteenth-generation successor, who states that, while his line is the "one, true, successor to Sakakibara Kenkichi," it ceased active training during the SCAP ban on martial arts training in the post–World War II era.

Jiki Shinkage Ryū Nomi Ha
直心影流野見派
(abbreviated lineage)

14. Sakakibara Kenkichi
榊原 鍵吉
(1830–1894)
Jiki Shinkage Ryū
直心影流

15. Nomi Teijirō Minamoto no Yasuhira
十五代 野見 釘次郎 源安平
(1826–1908)
Jiki Shinkage Ryū Nomi Ha
直心影流 野見派

16. Nomi Hamao Minamoto no Yasuchika
十六代 野見 浜雄 源安親
(1854–1932)

17. Ishigaki Kōryusai Minamoto no Yasutsune
十七代 石垣 甲龍斎 源安常
(1896–1950)

18. Ishigaki Yasuzō
十八代 石垣 安造
(c. 1930–)

2 See Bibliography: Interviews, Conversations, Correspondence.

Jiki Shinkage Ryū Shimada Ha 直心影流島田派. A branch tradition of the Jiki Shinkage Ryū founded by Shimada Toranosuke around 1838. See: *Shimada Toranosuke Naochika.*

Jikishin kore dōjō 直心是道場. See: *jikishin.*

Jikishin Ryū 1. 直心流 [Var. 直信流]. A school of *jūjutsu* founded by Terada Kanemon, a low-ranking *bushi* of the Matsue feudal domain, around 1650. Kanemon had studied the Teishin Ryū 貞心流 founded by his grandfather, as well as the Kitō Midare Ryū 起倒乱流 and Ryōi Shintō Ryū 良移心当流, with his father, Terada Yorishige.

Kanemon was a successor to his father in the Kitō Midare Ryū. However, at some point he struck off in a new direction and renamed his school Jikishin Ryū Yawara 直心流柔 (sometimes referred to as Jikishin Ryū Jūjutsu 直心流柔術). As a result, two lines descend from Kanemon: the Kitō Midare Ryū and the Jikishin Ryū.

The Jikishin Ryū line continued in Matsue domain, where in 1724, under fourth headmaster Inoue Masayori, the name (and emphasis) was changed from Jikishin Ryū *jūjutsu* 直心流柔術 to Jikishin Ryū *jūdō* 直信流柔道, indicating a shift in focus to a goal of spiritual perfection. It was not a purely empty-hand system in the 1700s, however; documents dating from that time indicate the use of a variety of sword techniques. (Mol, 2001: 130). For lineage, see: *Kitō Ryū.*

Jikishin Ryū 2. 直心流. A variant name for Shinkage Jikishin Ryū 新陰直心流, a school of swordsmanship (*kenjutsu*) founded by Kamiya Denshinsai Naomitsu around 1630. See also: *Matsuoka Shinkage Ryū.*

Jikishin Ryū 3. 直心流. A school of combative spear (*sōjutsu*) founded by Takino Yūken during the Hōei era (1704–1711). Takino, a warrior who hailed from the Matsue domain (present-day Shimane prefecture), was also a successor of Hotta Jidaku 堀田自諾 of the Kitō Midare Ryū 起倒乱流.

Jikishin Ryū 4. 直心流. A school of combative sword (*kenjutsu*) and long hardwood staff arts (*bōjutsu*). The tradition was founded by Hiki Yoshio, who was a *shugenja* of the Raigakuin, a Shugendō temple on Mount Horai (Hōraisan 蓬莱山). Hiki had previously trained in the Gassan Ryū 月山流 under Sawara Sukemitsu, the ninth lineal headmaster of that system. See: *Hiki Yoshio.*

Jikishin Ryūei Ryū 直心柳影流 [Also read ***Jikishin Yanagi Kage Ryū***; var. **Ryūei Ryū** 柳影流]. Sword (*ken*) and glaive (*naginata*) system founded by Satake Kanryūsai Yoshifumi around 1900. Satake originally called his system the Ryūei Ryū, but after training with Sakakibara Kenkichi, the fourteenth headmaster of the Jiki Shinkage Ryū, he combined the systems and changed the name to Jikishin Ryūei Ryū. Satake's most prominent student was a woman named Sonobe Hideo, who went on to make the system well known. See: *Jiki Shinkage Ryū; Jiki Shinkage Ryū naginatajutsu.*

Jikishin Ryū Jūdō 直信流柔道. See: *Jikishin Ryū (1).*

Jikishin Ryū Jūjutsu 直心流柔術. See: *Jikishin Ryū (1).*

Jikishin Ryū Yawara 直心流柔. See: *Jikishin Ryū (1).*

Jikishin Seitō Ichi Ryū 直心正統一流. This school encompassed a comprehensive field-combat system (*sōgo bujutsu*). "Jikishin Seitō Ichi Ryū" was the name used by Takahashi Danjōzaemon Shigeharu (1610–1690) for what came to be called the Jiki Shinkage Ryū. See also: *Jiki Shinkage Ryū.*

Jikishin Yanagi Kage Ryū 直心柳影流. See: *Jikishin Ryūei Ryū.*

Jikkai 十界. BUDDHISM/SHUGENDŌ—The Ten Realms or Ten Worlds of all living beings. The first six correspond to the Rokudō (the six realms of transmigration through which all beings pass), while the last four correspond to stages of Buddhist enlightenment. The ten realms are:

1. Hells	*jigoku*	地獄
2. Hungry ghosts	*gaki*	餓鬼
3. Animals	*chikushō*	畜生
4. Demons	*ashura*	阿修羅
5. Humans	*ningen*	人間
6. Heavenly beings	*daiba* (*tenjō*	提婆 天上)
7. Śrāvaka[3]	*shōmon*	聲聞
8. Pratyekabuddha[4]	*engaku*	縁覺
9. Bodhisattva	*bosatsu*	菩薩
10. Buddha	*butsu*	佛

Earhart (1970: 29) notes that by the thirteenth century, Shugendō practitioners (*yamabushi*) had formalized their ascetic practices in sacred mountains into ten sequential stages patterned on the Jikkai. The first six of these, also known as the Rokudō, were of special importance to the *yamabushi*:

Stage	Practice	Meaning
Jigoku	*gōhakari*	業秤 weighing *karma*
Gaki	*kokudachi*	穀斷 fasting from grain
Chikushō	*mizudachi*	水斷 fasting from water
Shura	*sumai/sumō*	相撲 wrestling
Ningen	*sange*	懺悔 penitence
Tenjō	*ennen*	延年 dance of longevity

See also: *sumai.*

Jikkan 十干 [A.k.a. ***Tenkan*** 天干]. The Jikkan (lit. Ten Stems) is a base-ten numbering system used in East Asia. This is in contrast to the Jūnishi, a base-twelve system which is also used in East Asia. The Jikkan, as well as the Jūnishi, was used in calculations in military divination (*gumbai heihō*)—including the use of *fengshui* (*fūsui*)—and other calculations related to military matters. See: Appendix 1.

Jikokuten 持国天【持國天】<Ch. Chiguotian <Skt. Dhṛtarāṣṭra. BUDDHISM—One of the Shitennō (Four Deva Kings), Jikokuten is a deity who guards the East. His name means "the *deva* who keeps his kingdom"; his color is white, and he carries a spear or sword.

Jikuten 竺天 [Var. ***Tenjiku*** 天竺; ***Jikudo*** 竺土]. Lit. "Bamboo Heaven"; var. the "Land of

[3] Originally referring to a disciple of the Buddha who listened to the original teachings and became enlightened, the term *śrāvaka* came to represent a stage on the path to enlightenment.

[4] Originally the term *pratyekabuddha* referred to a self-enlightened buddha. In this Shugendō example, the word indicates a stage on the path to enlightenment.

Bamboo." 1. BUDDHISM—A term frequently found in Buddhist texts referring to India. 2. A term occasionally found in martial transmission scrolls (*densho*) referring to India.

Jikudo 竺土. See: *Jikuten.*

jimmaku 陣幕 [Also read as ***jinmaku***; abbr. ***maki*** 幕]. A curtain or hanging bunting used as a war-camp enclosure. There were several types of *maki*, some including tents with or without canvas walls. The more elaborate were divided into several rooms for various purposes. During medieval and warring states times many were decorated with religious symbolism for talismanic purposes.

jin 1. 仁. CLASSICAL WARRIOR IDEAL—A concept indicating courtesy, benevolence, and tolerance. *Jin* was usually expressed through ritual and formal etiquette; as such, it was considered one of the essential characteristics of the classical warrior (*bushi*). See: *bushi no konjō.*

jin 2. 陣. a. A battle formation; a military camp. b. The sixth seal/character of the nine mystic letters (*kuji*), the recitation found in the Kujihō (Ritual Method of the Nine Seals). The term literally means "battle" or "military forces." See: *Kujihō.*

jinchi 陣地. An encampment; a war camp.

jindachi 陣太刀. Lit. "battle sword." In early times these blades were referred to as *ikamono-zukuri no tachi* 厳物造の太刀. The *jindachi* was normally a blade approximately 33 inches (85 cm) long or more. See also: *nodachi; ōdachi.*

jindate 陣立. A battle array; a battle formation.

jindaiko 陣太鼓. 1. A large war drum. 2. The combative skill of signaling with a large war drum. See: *taiko.*

jindori 陣取. A war encampment; a battle array.

jin'ei 陣営【陣營】. A war camp; a barracks.

jin'eigu 陣営具【陣營具】. See: *shikigu.*

jingai 陣貝. Lit. "military conch," "military shell." 1. A conch shell (*horagai*) used for signaling troops, much as a bugle was used in the West. 2. Military strategy and tactics; synonym for *heihō* 兵法 and related terms.

jingaijutsu 陣貝術. 1. The art of using the conch shell (*horagai* or *jingai*) to direct troops in battle; martial bugling. 2. Synonym for *heihō.*

jingama 陣鎌. Lit. "military encampment sickle." This short-bladed sickle was one of the "three tools of the stable" (*umagoya sangu*). As a secondary weapon, it could be used for cutting the reins of a horse or dealing with an armored or unarmored opponent. It is still used today in the Yagyū Shingan Ryū.

jingamajutsu 陣鎌術. The combative art of the camp sickle. See also: *jingama; Kitō Ryū; umagoya sangu; Yagyū Shingan Ryū.*

For a demonstration of jingamajutsu

• Acopian, Hall, and Skoss, 1982. (video)

jingasa 陣笠. An open helmet most often used by foot soldiers such as *ashigaru*. There are many types; they were often made of steel during the Warring States period (Sengoku Jidai), but in later years some were made of lacquered wood or leather and worn by retainers for ceremonial occasions. See also: *kawagasa; kasa.*

Jingo Izu no Kami Muneharu 神後伊豆守宗治 [A.k.a. ***Motoharu*** 元治; ***Korenobu*** 惟宣; ***Jingūji Izu*** 神宮寺伊豆] (c.1530–c.1600). Founder of Jingo Ryū 神後流 (also known as the Shinkage Ryū [6] 神影流). Jingo, a disciple of Kamiizumi Ise no Kami Nobutsuna, was often referred to as Kamiizumi's most skilled student. After the fall of Minowa Castle in 1561, Jingo made a martial pilgrimage (*musha shūgyō*) around Japan with Nobutsuna, Nobutsuna's nephew Hikita Bungorō, and possibly Nobutsuna's son, Kamiizumi Hitachinosuke Hidetane.

Jingo's swordsmanship and understanding of the principles of Shinkage Ryū was of such depth that not only was he awarded a license of full mastery (*kara* 化羅), but his teacher Kamiizumi also passed on to him a Buddhist surplice (*kesa*) and begging bowl (*hachi*). These items had been given to Kamiizumi by a monk during their travels.

Jingo went on to train many well-known officials such as Shōgun Ashikaga Yoshiteru and Kampaku Toyotomi Hidetsugu (nephew and retainer of Toyotomi Hideyoshi). Later he

J

resided with the Owari branch of the Tokugawa family. See also: *Kamiizumi Nobutsuna.*

Jingo Ryū 神後流 [Var. ***Shinkage Ryū (6)*** 神影流]. A derivative tradition of Kamiizumi Ise no Kami Nobutsuna's Shinkage Ryū created by Jingo Izu no Kami Muneharu.

Jingo Ryū·Shinkage Ryū (6)
神後流·神影流
(abbreviated lineage)

Jingo Izu no Kami Muneharu
神後 伊豆守 宗治
Jingo Ryū·Shinkage Ryū
神後流·神影流

Hattori Fujisawa Hyōe Munetada 服部 藤沢 兵衛 宗正 **Jingo Ryū·Shinkage Ryū**	Wada Hyōsai Takamasa 和田 兵斎 隆正 **Shinshin Ryū** 真心流
Tsuchiya Shōgen 土屋 将監 **Shinkage Ryū** 心陰流	Fukuzawa Musai Tokitada 福沢 務斎 時忠 **Jingo Ryū·Shinkage Ryū**

Saitō Hanzaemon Ietsugu
斎藤 半左衛門 家次
Jingo Ryū·Shinkage Ryū

Yanagisawa Jōzaemon Yoshimichi
柳沢 丞左衛門 良道
Jingo Ryū·Shinkage Ryū

5. Suzuki Tazaemon Shigeoki 鈴木 太左衛門 重奥 **(Suzuki Line)** **Shinkage Ryū**	5. Watanabe Mitsunoemon Sadatsuna 渡辺 三之右衛門 貞綱 **(Watanabe Line)** **Shinkage Ryū**
6. Ōshio Yozaemon Shigesada 大塩 与左衛門 茂貞	6. Maruyama Kasaemon Katsue 丸山 加左衛門 勝重
7. Ōshio Yozaemon Shigemichi 大塩 与左衛門 茂充	7. Hirai Monzaemon Masatada 平井 紋左衛門 政直
8. Ōshio Yozaemon Shigetaka 大塩 与左衛門 茂高	8. Nakane Shōbei Masatane 中根 庄兵衛 政種
9. Ishitani Matasuke Tsunenori 石谷 又助 常閑	9. Mitsumura Gihei Kiyomaru 三村 儀兵衛 清丸
10. Yamataka Sawaemon Nobutoshi 山高 沢右衛門 信順	10. Hirai Monzaemon Kōatsu 平井 紋左衛門 幸厚
11. Ishitani Matasuke Jōkan 石谷 又助 常閑	11. Hirai Shinnojō Yukiyoshi 平井 新之丞 幸之

Watatani and Yamada (1978: 402–403) trace only two lines of this school going down to the eleventh-generation successor. However, Nakajima Shōhitsu claimed to be a twenty-fourth generation successor via his father Nakajima Katsu. It is unknown if there is any original documentation to support this claim. (See Shinkage Ryū [6] Nakajima lineage below.) Shōhitsu reformed his line into Shin Shin Musō Ryū in 1942 and, later expanded it into the more comprehensive Ryūshinkan Budō in 1953.

According to the official history of Nakajima's Ryūshinkan Budō,[5] Shinkage Ryū (6) developed and proliferated in western Japan (Kansai) and on the island of Kyūshū during the early and mid-Edo period. Under the leadership of seventeenth headmaster Yoshida Nagajirō, it proliferated and was fully transmitted in what is now Hyōgo prefecture. Around the mid-1800s, the Jingo Ryū/Shinkage Ryū (6) tradition came to be passed down by the Nakajima family. This continued even after the end of the premodern period in 1868 with several successive generations of the Nakajima family covering the Meiji, Taishō, and Shōwa eras. During the Shōwa era, twenty-fourth headmaster Nakajima Shōhitsu taught swordsmanship at the Toyama Gakkō, an imperial martial-arts training school. The Jingo Ryū/Shinkage Ryū (6) today is preserved under the auspices of twenty-fifth headmaster Toyoshima Kazutora.

jingū 神宮. SHINTŌ—A shrine of particularly high status. Meiji Jingū and Ise Jingū are two such shrines, as are the warrior shrines Kashima Jingū and Katori Jingū.

jinja 神社. SHINTŌ—Generic term for a Shintō shrine. See also: *jingū.*

jinkai 陣貝. See: *jingai.*

jinkama 陣鎌. See: *jingama.*

jinkamajutsu 陣鎌術. See: *jingamajutsu.*

[5] http://www.shinkageryu-udoujyo.com/intoro.html

(Shinkage Ryū [6]—Nakajima Lineage)

Note: The Nakajima lineage traces itself back to the Suzuki line, with Ōshio Yoshitaka as ninth headmaster. They begin their count with Kamiizumi Nobutsuna, Jingo's teacher. However, there are some variances with Watatani's representation.

9. Ōshio Yozaemon Shigetaka 大塩 与左衛門 芳高
10. Yamataka Sawaemon Nobutoshi 山高 沢右衛門 信順
11. Yamataka Sawaemon Nobuatsu 山高 沢右衛門 信篤
12. Watanabe Sannoemon Sadatsuna 渡辺 三之右衛門 貞綱
13. Maruyama Kazaemon Katsue 丸山 加左衛門 勝重
14. Maruo Yozaemon Masatada 丸尾 与左衛門 政直
15. Nakane Shōbei Masaaki 中根 庄兵衛 政明
16. Mitsumura Gihei Kiyomaru 三村 儀兵衛 清丸
17. Yoshida Nagajirō Kōei 吉田 長次郎 幸影
18. Yoshida Nagajirō Masakatsu 吉田 長次郎 正勝
19. Yoshida Nagajirō Yoshikatsu 吉田 長次郎 美勝
20. Nakajima Takezō Munekatsu 中島 竹蔵 宗勝
21. Nakajima Iwaki'chi Iwakatsu 中島 岩吉 岩勝
22. Nakajima Katsujirō Tamayoshi 中島 勝次郎 圭祥
23. Nakajima Masaru Yoshikatsu 中島 勝 芳勝
24. Nakajima Shōhitsu Shōun 中島 将弼 勝雲
25. Toyoshima Kazutora Katsumine 豊島 一虎 勝峰 (current headmaster)

jinmaku 陣幕. See: *jimmaku.*

jinsen 陣扇. A type of iron fan (*tessen*). The *jinsen* was a folding war fan generally made with iron ribs. Contrast to *tenarashigata* and *uchiwa*.

JINSEN (IRON-RIBBED FAN)
(Private collection)

Jinsuke Shigenobu 甚助重信. See: *Hayashizaki Jinsuke Shigenobu.*

jintai 人体【人躰】. The human body.

jin'ya 陣屋. A war encampment.

Jion 慈恩. See: *Nen Ami Jion.*

Jion Ryū 慈恩流. See: *Nen Ryū.*

jiriitchi 事理一致 [A.k.a. ***jiriittai*** 事理一体]. 1. BUDDHISM—*Jiri* refers to all things, both phenomena and noumena; *itchi* (or *ittai*), to their underlying unity. 2. MARTIAL ARTS—This often-mentioned term refers to martial training carried out in such a way that truth or realization is facilitated through the combined training of body and mind. The term finds its martial application in the early Edo-period writings of swordsmen, such as Yagyū Jūbei's *Tsuki no sho.*[6]

jiriki 自力. BUDDHISM—Lit. "self-power," this term is used to refer to practices which require the practitioner to seek/work for his own enlightenment and not depend on any "gods" or "Buddhas" or "Bodhisattvas." Contrast to *tariki.*

Jiri Mokuroku 「事理目録」 [Abbr. for ***Nen Ryū Jiri Mokuroku*** 念流事理目録]. Third of five licenses awarded by Maniwa Nen Ryū.

jisei no uta 辞世の歌【辭世の歌】. A seventeen-syllable death poem. Although this term was often used to indicate a warrior's "death song," the *jisei no uta* was not restricted to the warrior class.

jisamurai 地侍 [Also read ***jizamurai***]. 1. Village fighting men who began to appear as a distinct sub-class during the fourteenth century. According to Davis (1974: 234), at that time a number of these low-ranking fighting men began to identify more with their own villages and their own private land interests than with their warrior-superiors—the provincial, land-owning warrior class (*kokujin*) and their immediate vassals. Prior to this, the *kokujin* had been an intermediate level of authority between the peasants and villages on the one hand and the *daimyō* on the other. 2. Field hands who were part-time warriors.

6 For example, see Imamura (1962: 10).

See also: *nobushi.*

Further reading in English:

- Davis, 1974: 233–237.

jisha 寺社. BUDDHISM/SHINTŌ—Buddhist temples and Shintō shrines.

Jisha Bugyō 寺社奉行. BUDDHISM/SHINTŌ—An office created by the Kamakura shogunate in 1293. The Jisha Bugyō had authority over matters concerning priests, temple and shrine property, ceremonies, and so on. The office was reestablished by the Tokugawa shogunate in 1635.

Jishin Ryū 自心流. A branch system of the Asayama Ichiden Ryū 浅山一伝流, specializing in combative swordsmanship (*kenjutsu*). The system was founded by Komine Denshichirō (?–1660) after he had mastered the Asayama Ichiden Ryū under Katō Shigeri Masakatsu.

jissen 実戦【實戰】. Actual combat; combat action.

jita kyōei 自他共栄【自他共榮】. KŌDŌKAN JŪDŌ—Lit. "mutual prosperity for self and others." This term was used by Kanō Jigorō, founder of Kōdōkan Jūdō, to express the concept of harmonizing one's self with others for mutual benefit. *Jita kyōei* was one of two principles which Kanō held as the highest ideals for *jūdō* practitioners; the other was "maximum, efficient use of energy" (*seiryoku zenyō*).

jitō 地頭. An estate (*shōen*) steward during the late Heian, Kamakura, and early Muromachi periods. This was a military position normally appointed by the shogunate. See also: *Jōkyū no Ran; shōen; shugo.*

Further reading in English:

- Mass, 1990: 80–87.

Jitoku Ryū 自得流. A school of gunnery (*hōjutsu*) established by Chikamatsu Hikonoshin Shigenori in the early to mid-1700s. Chikamatsu mastered and included elements of both Imagawa Ryū 今川流 and Ōno Ryū 大野流 *hōjutsu* in his new, reformatted school.

Jitokuki Ryū 自得記流. A branch tradition of Itō Ryū (1) 伊東流, a school concentrating on the pipe spear. It was founded by Toki Yamashiro no Kami Yoriyuki.

jitte 1. 実手【實手】. YAGYŪ SHINGAN RYŪ—a. A police truncheon. b. Police-truncheon arts as incorporated in the early Yagyū Shingan Ryū.

jitte 2. 十手. Archaic romanization for *jutte.*

jiyū kata 自由型. OKINAWAN KARATE—A term used in Kūshin Ryū 空真流 to refer to free-form-style training. See: *Kūshin Ryū.*

jiyū keiko 自由稽古 Lit. "free training." This term refers to free practice in such modern *budō* as *kendō*, *atarashii naginata*, etc.

jiyū kumite 自由組手. KARATE—Lit. "free sparring." This practice began as early as 1936 in Funakoshi Gichin's Shōtōkan tradition. *Jiyū kumite* was one of the major factors in the evolution of Japanese *karate* toward sport.

jiyū renshū 自由練習. Lit. "free training." This term is not specific to any particular combative art; it is used in some systems and schools and not in others.

jizamurai 地侍. See: *jisamurai.*

Jizō Bosatsu 地蔵菩薩【地藏菩薩】<Ch. Dizang Pusa <Skt. Kṣitigarbha-bodhisattva. Lit. "Earth Store" Bodhisattva. Jizō is a bodhisattva (*bosatsu*) venerated by various Buddhist sects in Japan as the protector of travelers and children; he is prominent in many folk tales. His Sanskrit seed syllable *ha* 成 (Jp. *ka*) is occasionally found inscribed on weapons as a talisman. See also: *Shōgun Jizō Bosatsu; Shōgun Jizōhō.*

Further reading in English:

- Matsunaga, 1969: 235–237 *ff.*
- de Visser, 1915.

jō 1. 杖 [Also read **tsue**]. a. A stick; a medium-length staff around 3.5 feet (1–1.5 m) long. b. SHINDŌ MŪSŌ RYŪ—a round, straight stick, usually about 4 feet (1.3 m) long and 1 inch (2.6 cm) in diameter, though dimensions vary. c. SHINDŌ MŪSŌ RYŪ—Pre-modern-era (i.e., pre-1868) term for the combative art of the stick. The terms *jōjutsu* and *jōdō* are later, and have different connotations. d. **Jō** 杖. SHINDŌ MUSŌ RYŪ—The term for the *shidachi*, the person executing the technique (in contrast to "Tachi" for *uchidachi*, the person receiving the technique) in Shindō Musō Ryū *kata*.

Jō 2. 城. A twelfth-century *daimyō* family of Echigo province that was descended from Taira Yoshikane. They were allies of Minamoto no Yoritomo, and revolted against the Hōjō family after Yoritomo's death in 1199. In 1202, however, they were defeated and the family was destroyed. Several Jō warriors are remembered by history for their valiant fighting, but perhaps the most famous member of the clan was Lady Hangaku (Hangaku Gozen). She is remembered for the ability as a commander and the impressive—and deadly—archery skills she exhibited in defending the Jō stronghold at Tossake Castle in 1202.

~jo 3. 城 [Also read ***~shiro***]. Suffix indicating a castle; e.g., Ōsakajō 大阪城, Ōsaka castle.

jō 4. 杖. A measurement of 10 *shaku*; this is equivalent to about 3.5 feet (3 m).

jōba no rōtō 乗馬の郎等【乘馬之郎等】. Tenth-century term found in the *Shōmonki* that means "mounted retainer." The use of this phrase, essentially the equivalent of *tsuwamono*, indicated the combatant was a "full warrior" who fought from horseback.

jōdangamae 上段構. See: *jōdan no kamae.*

jōdan no kamae 上段の構. Lit. "upper-level posture." 1. A combative engagement posture used in many weapons arts in which the weapon is held above the head. 2. SHINDŌ MUSŌ RYŪ—An engagement posture in which the sword is held above the head with the joint of the left thumb lightly touching the center of the forehead and the joint of the right thumb lightly touching the right rear area of the top of the head. 3. JIKI SHINKAGE RYŪ—An engagement posture in which the sword is held above the head with both arms extended directly upward. See also: *raitō.*

Jōdo 浄土【淨土】<Ch. Jingtu <Skt. Sukhāvatī. BUDDHISM—The Pure Land; a Buddhist paradise described in Pure Land Buddhist texts (*o-kyō*). Followers of the various branches of Pure Land Buddhism during Japan's middle ages believed the world was in the grip of the "final period of the influence of the Law of the Buddha" (*mappō*). During *mappō*, which the medieval Japanese calculated began in 1052 C.E., it was thought that the Buddha's teachings were still available, but Buddhist practice could no longer enable sentient beings to become awakened. Consequently, beings had first to be reborn in the Pure Land paradise of Amida Buddha in order to be able to effectively use Buddhist practice to become enlightened. To enable this rebirth, followers of Pure Land Buddhism in Japan chanted the *nembutsu*, a practice which was supposed to guarantee one's rebirth in the Pure Land. This practice is still followed today. See also: *Ikkō Ikki; nembutsu; Jōdo Shin Shū; Jōdo Shū.*

jōdō 杖道. 1. A generic term for medium-length staff arts; those martial disciplines concentrating on a staff of around 3 to 4 feet (1–1.2 m) in length. 2. SHINDŌ MUSŌ RYŪ—A modern *budō* developed in the mid-twentieth century by Shimizu Takaji, twenty-fifth headmaster of the Shindō Musō Ryū.

jōdori 杖取り. See: *jō tori.*

Jōdo Shin Shū 浄土真宗【淨土眞宗】. BUDDHISM—THE Japanese True Pure Land school of Buddhism, which was founded by the monk Shinran 親鸞 in the early thirteenth century. See also: *Ikkō Ikki; nembutsu; Jōdo, Jōdo Shū; mappō.*

Further reading in English:

- Matsunaga and Matsunaga, 1976: 85–127 *ff.*

Jōdo Shū 浄土宗【淨土宗】. BUDDHISM—The Japanese Pure Land school of Buddhism, which was founded by the monk Hōnen 法然 in 1175. See also: *Ikkō Ikki; nembutsu; Jōdo, Jōdo Shin Shū; mappō.*

Further reading in English:

- Matsunaga and Matsunaga, 1976: 58–85 *ff.*

Jōei shikimoku 貞永式目. The Jōei Code. This legal code, established in 1232 (the first year of the Jōei era), became a model for warrior law in later centuries.

jōhanen 上半円【上半圓】[Also read ***kamihanen***]. Lit. "upper half-circle." JIKI SHINKAGE RYŪ—Upper half-circle inscribed by

JIKI SHINKAGE RYŪ *JŌHANEN*
Illustration from *Jiki Shinkage Ryū Kenjutsu* by Saitō Akinobu (1901)

the hands and sword at the beginning of each of the prearranged combative forms (*kata*) in the Hōjō set of forms. See also: *gehanen; Jiki Shinkage Ryū.*

jōhei 精兵. Reading used for 精兵 by Farris (1992). See: *Seihei.*

jōhō 情報. An intelligence report; news, information.

jōhō shūshū 情報蒐集. A collection of intelligence reports.

jōju 成就. Magical or miraculous powers. See: shijji.

jōjutsu 杖術. 1. Combative stick/medium-length staff arts. Since the development of Shindō Musō Ryū 神道夢想流 in the early seventeenth century, approximately seventy traditions have included *jōjutsu* within their curricula. 2. SHINDŌ MUSŌ RYŪ—The more combative antecedent of *jōdō* founded by Musō Gonnosuke Katsukichi during the first decade of the seventeenth century. The term *jōjutsu* has, since around 1990, come back into popularity, and many groups that previously referred to their systems as *jōdō* now refer to them as *jōjutsu*. Groups in Kyūshū have generally always preferred to use the term *jōjutsu* over *jōdō*. The techniques of modern Shindō Musō Ryū *jōjutsu* and *jōdō* are essentially the same.

jōkaku 城郭. 1. In medieval war tales (*gunkimono*), this term refers to a barricade, fortress, or citadel. Though the meaning varies depending on geographical location and context, most *jōkaku* were wooden walls or forts. At the time, siege warfare had become a prominent element of medieval *gunkimono* such as the *Taiheiki*, a development that coincided with the evolution of the war axe (*i no me kizamitaru masakari*) into a heavier weapon which was used against the wooden doors of these fortresses. See also: *kaidate.* 2. YAGYŪ SHINKAGE RYŪ—A middle-level (*chūdan*) sword posture (*kurai*) very similar to *jun seigan*. However, in this posture, the hands are raised to just above shoulder level, while the sword tip (*kissaki*) is lowered to below shoulder level.

jōkamachi 城下町. A castle town.

Jōkyūki 『承久記』. See: *Shōkyūki.*

Jōkyū no Ran 承久乱【承久亂】. See: *Shōkyū no Ran.*

jōnin 上忍. *Jōnin* is a term commonly used by non-academics to indicate non-warrior leaders of espionage groups. See: *jōnin–chūnin–genin; ninjutsu.*

jōnin–chūnin–genin 上忍・中忍・下忍. Often described by non-hoplologists as "*ninja* ranks." In this context, *jōnin* is usually used to refer to *ninja* leaders, *chūnin* to *ninja* sub-leaders, and *genin* to *ninja* operatives. While such categorizations may not be inaccurate, historian Nawa Yumio was somewhat skeptical of them. In his primary work on *ninjutsu*, Nawa (1972: 135) proposes that the terms *yōninjutsu* 陽忍術 and *inninjutsu* 陰忍術 better fit the functions of those traditional espionage agents during the Warring States period (Sengoku Jidai). The term *yōninjutsu*, according to Nawa, indicated strategy used by an agent to openly insert himself among the enemy. In contrast, the term *onninjutsu* indicated using skills of stealth to hide from the enemy. See also: *kanja; ninjutsu.*

jōruri 浄瑠璃. A ballad drama or period play. Such plays were often about warrior vendettas. See: *adauchi mono; chambara.*

jōseki 上席. Lit. "upper seat." This term is

equivalent to *kamiza* (1) 上座.

Jōshikibō Inken 乗識房 胤憲【乘識房胤憲】[Var. ***Hōzōin Inken*** 宝蔵院 胤憲【寶藏院胤憲】] (1745–1808). Fifth headmaster of the Hōzōin Ryū. See: *Hōzōin Ryū* lineage chart.

jōshu 城主. Prior to the Tokugawa period the *jōshu* were commanders of castles. According to Papinot (1910: 66), there were 212 *jōshu* just before the start of the Tokugawa period. See also: *daimyō*.

jotei 助丁. TAIHŌ MILITARY SYSTEM—An assistant (to a commander) in the Chinese-style provincial militia unit (*gundan*) of the eighth century.

jōtei 上丁. TAIHŌ MILITARY SYSTEM—An alternate term for a conscript soldier in the Chinese-style provincial militia unit (*gundan*) in the eighth century. See: *heishi (1)*.

jō tori 杖取り. Techniques, most commonly found in *aikidō*, in which an unarmed practitioner takes a medium-length staff (*jō*) away from an armed attacker. Late *aikidō* master Saitō Morihiro devoted a chapter of his *Traditional Aikidō: Sword・Stick・and Body Arts* (1973: 121–142) to these techniques.

ju 鷲. See: *washi (1)*.

jubaku 呪縛. A magical, binding spell; a binding incantation.

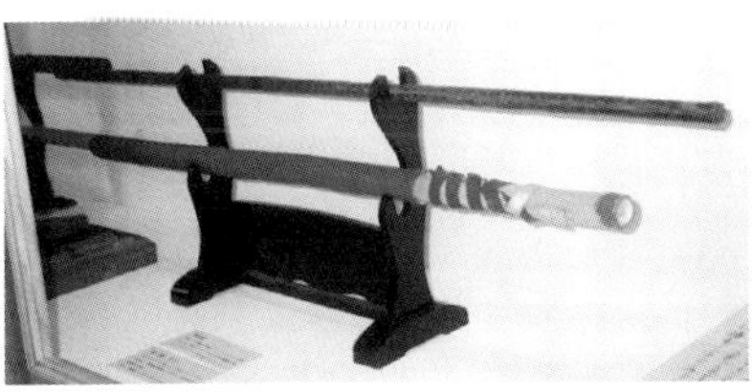

JŪBEI NO JŌ ON DISPLAY IN YAGYŪ VILLAGE
Top: *Jūbei no jō*; bottom: Yagyū *fukuro shinai*
(Photograph courtesy of Michael Davenport)

Jūbei no jō 十兵衛之杖. A staff created by Yagyū Jūbei Mitsuyoshi, second headmaster of the Edo Yagyū Shinkage Ryū. Though the staff, approximately 4 feet (1.2 m) in length, looks like a rod of lacquered bamboo, it is actually a metal rod from which extend three metal flanges placed at 120° to each other and covered with lacquered bamboo (see photograph below).

The term "*Jūbei no jo*" also may indicate the *kata* designed for this weapon. It has been speculated that most such *kata* currently practiced were reconstructed by Yagyū Genchō, but some sets in the non-family lines of Owari Yagyū Shinkage Ryū appear to be much older.

JŪBEI NO JŌ
Cross-section view
(Photograph courtesy Michael Davenport)

jūdō 柔道. 1. This term is most commonly used to indicate Kanō Jigorō's Kōdōkan Jūdō, which was founded in 1882. Like modern *karatedō* and Shōrinji Kempō, its spiritual aims and disdain for weaponry place it outside the realm of Japanese classical martial systems (*koryū bugei*), but firmly within the parameters of modern combative spiritual/sport systems (*gendai budō*). See: *Kōdōkan Jūdō*. 2. A term used by the Jikishin Ryū (1), a classical *jūjutsu* tradition, to categorize its grappling arts.

jūdōgi 柔道着. A heavyweight cotton jacket, similar to a *karategi* or *keikogi*, worn by practitioners of *jūdō* and similar arts. The material is usually thicker and heavier than that used by *karate* practitioners or classical martial arts practitioners. *Jūdōgi* are almost always white. See: *dōgi; karategi; keikogi; karategi; uwagi*.

jūdōjō 柔道場. A *jūdō* training hall.

jūdōka 柔道家. A proficient practitioner of *jūdō*.

Jufukuji 寿福寺【壽福寺】. A temple in Kamakura established by the Zen monk Eisai in 1199. By 1368, just over 170 years later, Jufukuji had become the training center where Nen Ami Jion reputedly received the innermost teachings of swordsmanship and strategy. It is also thought to be where Jion taught a number of pupils in eastern Japan.

Jufukuji burned down in 1247 and again

J

in 1395. As a result many of the original records, including those containing information on "warrior Zen" and combative training, were destroyed.

jūgō awase 柔剛合わせ. A phrase meaning "to combine flexibility with power." In modern *kendō*, this concept is seen as a way to integrate the mind and body of the trainee in order to focus his or her energy as efficiently as possible.

Jūhachidō 十八道. BUDDHISM—1. One of four primary rituals of Japanese Esoteric Buddhism. The Jūhachidō is practiced in both the Tendai and Shingon schools. In performing the ceremony, the practitioner embarks on a psychological journey in which he ritually purifies and empowers himself, and then visualizes an idealized form of enlightenment, which normally takes the form of a selected Buddhist deity such as Fudō Myōō. The practitioner then enters into a psychological union with the object of visualization and experiences the enlightened state of the deity. After separating himself from the object, he finally returns to the mundane world. See also: *Shido kegyō; Soshijjikara-kyō*. 2. ***Jūhachidō*** 『十八道』. Abbreviated title of the *Jūhachidō shiki* 『十八道私記』. See: *Jūhachidō Shiki*.

Further reading in English:

• Ichishima, 1995; 2007.

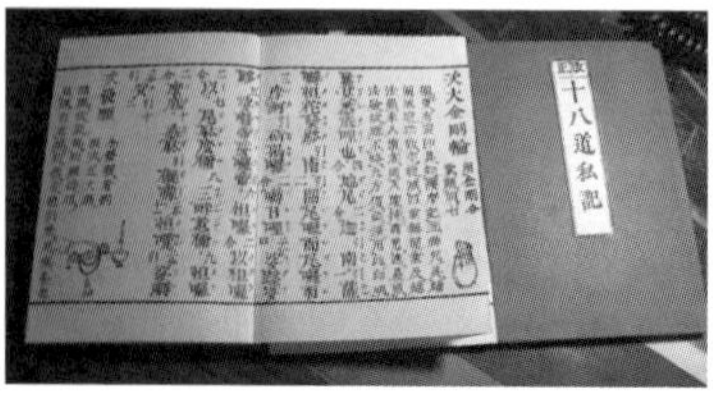

JŪHACHIDŌ SHIKI
Text used in performing the Jūhachidō ritual
(Private collection)

Jūhachidō shiki 『十八道私記』. BUDDHISM—The *Jūhachidō shiki* is a text which contains directions for performing the Jūhachidō, one of four basic exoteric/tantric rituals that must be mastered by members of the Tendai and Shingon schools of Japanese Buddhism. Composed in Japan, the text was originally derived from ritual instructions included in the *Soshijjikara-kyō* and associated Chinese manuals. Several variations of the *Jūhachidō* are found in both the Tendai and Shingon schools. See also: *Goma shiki; Kongōkai shiki; Shido kegyō; Soshijjikara-kyō; Taizōkai shiki.*

Further reading in English:

• Ichishima, 1995; 2007.

jūji 十字. Lit. "tenth letter." This term refers to the tenth character inscribed in the center of the grid made when performing the Ritual Method of the Nine Seals (Kujihō). See also: *kuji; Kujihō*.

jūji dome 十字留 [Var. 十字止]. SHINDŌ MUSŌ RYŪ—An X-shaped blocking technique. *Jūji dome* played an important role in the legendary duels between Musō Gonnosuke and Miyamoto Musashi. See also: *Yoneno Kōtarō* (photograph).

jūji shuriken 十字手裏剣【十字手裏劒】. A star-shaped or cross-shaped *shuriken*; a *shaken*.

jūjitsu 柔術. Archaic romanization of *jūjutsu*.

jujutsu 呪術. Magic; sorcery; a magic spell.

jūjutsu 柔術. 1. Lit. "flexible art"; "yielding technique." 2. A generic term for grappling arts dating generally from the Tokugawa period (1603–1867). *Jūjutsu*-type arts find their early origins in some of the battlefield grappling systems of the late Sengoku through early Edo periods. These include such seminal *ryū* as Takenouchi Ryū 竹内流, Kitō Ryū 起倒流, Sekiguchi Ryū 関口流, and Seigō Ryū 制剛流. These systems tended to emphasize small weapons (for close-in, armored combat) in the early Edo period. However, as the Edo period progressed there was less of a need for armored combat grappling and more of a need for civilian self-defense technique. Thus, unarmored and lightly-armed or unarmed techniques and systems—such as Jikishin Ryū (1) 直心流 *jūjutsu*—began to proliferate. Fujita (1960: 2) notes approximately 504 *ryū* specializing in various *jūjutsu* curricula.

Jūjutsu kyōjūsho ryū no maki 『柔術教授書龍の巻』 (*Jūjutsu* textbook—dragon scroll). A textbook on *jujutsu* published in 1913 which, according to Donn F. Draeger,[7] gives the best

[7] See Bibliography.

definition of the term *aiki* from that period. Draeger (1974: 142) translates:

> *Aiki* is a passive state of mind without a blind side, slackness, evil intention, or fear. There is no difference between *aiki* and *kiai*; however, if compared, when expressed dynamically *aiki* is called *kiai* and when expressed statically, it is *aiki*.

jūken 銃剣【銃劍】. A bayonet.

jūkendō 銃剣道. The modern "sportive" cognate form of *jūkenjutsu*. In *jūkendō* the rifle and bayonet are replaced by a wooden mock-rifle (*mokujū*) with a rubber tip on the end of the barrel to represent the bayonet. Players outfit themselves in armor similar to that used in *kendō*.

jūkenjutsu 銃剣術【銃劍術】. A term for the combative bayonet techniques developed from spear systems (*sōjutsu*) since the beginning of the Meiji era (1868–1912). Fujita (1960: 2) notes only one *ryū* specializing in *jūkenjutsu*.

Jukyō 儒教【儒敎】. Neo-Confucianism. This was the dominant form of Confucianism followed by the Tokugawa government during the Edo period.

Further reading in English:

- Tsunoda, et al, 1958: 344–442.
- Fung, 1953.

jumon 呪文. A magic spell, magical formula, incantation, or curse; a "magical spell text." *Jumon* is a generic term for a magical spell such as a Buddhist *mantra* (*shingon*) or *dhāraṇī* (*darani*). For example, the term is found used in martial and Buddhist documents to indicate the *Kuji ketsu-in goshimbō* (a spell used for protection from enemies and evil demons); the *Ongyō no ju* (a spell used for obtaining invisibility); the *Butsu-bu sammaya no ju* (a spell used as part of the "self-defense method" [*goshinhō*] commonly performed at the beginning of tantric rituals); or the *Hikō goshin no ju* (another spell used as part of the *goshinhō*). Various *jumon* are found in the transmission documents (*densho*) of many martial schools.

jūmonji 十文字. 1. The numeral "10." 2. A name used by many traditions for a pre-arranged combative form (*kata*).

jūmonji kamayari 十文字鎌槍. See: *jūmonji yari.*

jūmonji yari 十文字槍 [A.k.a. ***jūmonji kamayari*** 十文字鎌槍]. A spear with a spearhead shaped like the Chinese character *jū* (十); a type of *kamayari* (a spear with a blade, or blades, at a right angle to the shaft). In some examples the cross-blades tend to curve forward, somewhat like a trident; on others they stand at right angles to the central blade, or curve slightly backward. There are many types. See also: *kamayari; katakama yari; sōjutsu; yari.*

Further reading in English:

- Knutsen, 1963.
- Knutsen and Knutsen, 2004.

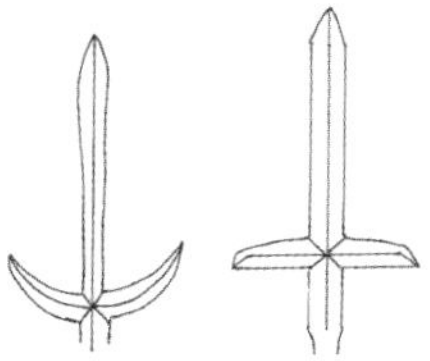

TWO EXAMPLES OF *JŪMONJI YARI*

Jūni Chishi 十二地支. See: *Jūnishi.*

Jūni no Yari Kumi 拾二之槍組. KASHIMA SHINTŌ RYŪ—Twelve combative spear forms (*sōjutsu kata*) taught after a trainee has mastered the mid-level combative spear forms (Chūdan Yari no Shidai) of the Kashima Shintō Ryū. See: *Kashima Shintō Ryū.*

Jūnisha Gongen 十二社権現【十二社權現】. See: *Jūnisō Gongen.*

Jūnishi 十二支 (The Twelve Branches) [Var. ***Jūni Chishi*** 十二地支 (The Twelve Earth Branches) or, simply, ***Chishi*** 地支 (Earth Branches)]. The Jūnishi is a classical system of enumeration using base twelve. (A second system, the Ten Stems or *Jikkan*, uses base ten.) The Jūnishi uses a series of twelve animal symbols which represent the divisions of the Chinese zodiac, the twelve months of the year, the twelve double hours of the day, and the twelve points of the compass.

Up until the time of the Meiji Restoration in 1868 the Japanese used the duodenary cycle, in which each symbol indicates a two-hour period by Western reckoning, to indicate the

J

hours of the day. At that time it was abolished in favor of the Western system of twenty-four numbered hours of the day. Until 1868 people spoke of the "Hour of the Dog" or the "Hour of the Boar" instead of "seven o'clock P.M." or "nine o'clock P.M."

The twelve symbols of the Jūnishi are:

Animal	Symbol		Hour
1. Rat	*ne*	子	11 P.M.– 1 A.M.
2. Ox	*ushi*	丑	1 A.M.– 3 A.M.
3. Tiger	*tora*	寅	3 A.M.– 5 A.M.
4. Hare	*u*	卯	5 A.M.– 7 A.M.
5. Dragon	*tatsu*	辰	7 A.M.– 9 A.M.
6. Serpent	*mi*	巳	9 A.M.–11 A.M.
7. Horse	*uma*	午	11 A.M.– 1 P.M.
8. Ram	*hitsuji*	未	1 P.M.– 3 P.M.
9. Monkey	*saru*	申	3 P.M.– 5 P.M.
10. Cock	*tori*	酉	5 P.M.– 7 P.M.
11. Dog	*inu*	戌	7 P.M.– 9 P.M.
12. Boar	*i*	亥	9 P.M.–11 P.M.

The symbols of the Jūnishi have no specific esoteric meaning in themselves. However, East Asian numerologists, astrologers, and in some cases martial artists have assigned various subtle meanings and associations to each symbol. In the case of Japanese combative culture, various classical traditions have assigned their own special properties to the symbols. See also: *gunbai uchiwa;* Appendix 1.

Jūnisō Gongen 十二社権現 【十二社權現】 [Also read ***Jūnisha Gongen***]. RYŌBU SHINTŌ—Jūnisō Gongen is a Shintō manifestation of the Buddhist deity Fudō Myōō. For many years there was a shrine and waterfall in Edo which bore this name. After the 1868 Meiji Restoration, when Edo became Tokyo, the shrine and waterfall were destroyed by urban development. The shrine was an important element in the life of Mima Yoichizaemon Kagenobu, who founded the Suiō Ryū 水鴎流 around 1600. See: *Mima Yoichizaemon Kagenobu.*

Jūniten 十二天 [A.k.a. ***Goseten*** 護世天; ***Gohōten*** 護方天]. The "Twelve Devas." The Jūniten are a group of Indian deities dating from the Vedic period.[8] Within Buddhism they were grouped in this assembly to guard the twelve directions (in contrast to the Shitennō, who guard the four cardinal directions). This group or its members are occasionally found in martial *densho*, and may also be used as talismans on martial accoutrements.

Deva (*ten*)		Direction	Skt. Name
Taishakuten	帝釈天	East	Indra
Katen	火天	Southeast	Agni
Emmaten	燄摩天	South	Yama
Rasetsuten	羅殺天	Southwest	Rākṣasa /Nirṛti
Suiten	水天	West	Varuṇa
Fūten	風天	Northwest	Vāyu
Bishamonten	毘沙門天	North	Vaiśravaṇa
Ishanaten	伊舎那天	Northeast	Iśāna
Bonten	梵天	Heaven	Brahman
Chiten	地天	Earth	Pṛthīvī
Nitten	日天	Sun	Sūrya /Āditya
Gatten	月天	Moon	Candra

Jū no Kata 柔の形. Kōdōkan Jūdō's "Forms of Flexibility." These fifteen *kata* (consisting of three sets of five *kata* each) concentrate on using strength effectively and handling one's body in an emergency.

Further reading in English:

- Fukuda, 2004.

jū no ri 柔の理. The principle (*ri* 理) of yielding and flexibility (*jū* 柔). The interpretation of this phrase varies among classical systems. However, in the case of execution of technique, many of the classical *jūjutsu ryū*, as well as Kōdōkan Jūdō, interpret it as combining one's own strength with that of an opponent in order to defeat him.

jun seigan no kurai 順青眼の位. YAGYŪ SHINKAGE RYŪ—A middle-level (*chūdan*) sword posture (*kurai*) in which the sword is held pointing toward an enemy to the front, with the hips turned slightly to the left.

junshi 殉死. "To sacrifice (oneself) in death." This was a practice in which a retainer, in order to express his loyalty, would commit ritual suicide (*seppuku*) upon the death of

[8] The Vedic period was the era in India during which the Vedas—the oldest texts of Hinduism—were composed. It is generally considered to span the second and first millennia B.C.E., ending around 600 B.C.E.

JUN SEIGAN
The late Yagyū Nobuharu assumes *jun seigan no kurai* during a training session in 1989
(Photograph by author)

his lord. The most extreme case of *junshi*, as recorded in the *Taiheiki*, occurred in 1333 after the death of Hōjō Takatoki, when over 870 retainers followed Hōjō into death. (McCullough, 1959: 310–311). In 1616 the Tokugawa shogunate outlawed *junshi* with the publication of its House Laws, and it was abolished again by the Meiji government in 1868, but it took several generations to suppress the practice. General Nogi Maresuke 乃木希典 and his wife Shizuko 静子 committed *junshi* (he via *seppuku*, she via *jigai*) shortly after Emperor Meiji's death in 1912.[9] See: *seppuku.*

jūrui 従類. A "warrior follower." This term indicated a lord/retainer (*shū/jū*) relationship. In the tenth century *Shōmonki* period, the term *jūrui* almost always referred to blood or marriage relationships. In later centuries it came to include vassals who were not "kin" to their lord. However, as Varley (1994: 20) notes, the term actually means "superior/inferior"; it indicates a patron/client relationship; and does not necessarily indicate an exclusive relationship between fighting men.

jūshi 戎士. A warrior.

jūshin 1. 銃身. A gun barrel.

jūshin 2. 重臣. A chief retainer; a chief vassal.

jūshin 3. 重心. One's center of gravity.

Jūshin Ryū 重信流. See: *Shin Musō Hayashizaki Ryū.*

jūshoku 住職. The chief priest of a Buddhist temple.

jūtaijutsu 柔体術【柔體術; 柔躰術】. A grappling/striking system taught as part of the traditional Kuki Shin Ryū 九鬼神流.

Jutō Efu 授刀衛府. An imperial guard corps created in 759. Its name was later changed to Kono Efu. See: *efu.*

jutō toneri 授刀舎人. Troops who made up the guard unit known as the Jutō Efu. See: *efu.*

jutsu 戌. See: *inu.*

~jutsu ～術. Suffix indicating a skill or art; a combative skill. For example, skill with a sword (*ken* 剣) is *kenjutsu* 剣術.

jutte 十手 [Also read ***jitte***]. 1. A metal truncheon commonly used by police during the Edo period. There are many varieties and types of this weapon, and numerous different schools (*ryū*) developed their use and configuration. As the Edo period progressed, the *jutte* itself became a symbol of police authority. For illustration, see: *juttejutsu.*

JUTTE BEING USED IN TANDEM WITH IRON FAN (*TESSEN*) AGAINST A SWORD
Ikkaku Ryū *juttejutsu* demonstration at Meiji Shrine, 1980
(Photograph by author)

juttejutsu 十手術. 1. The combative art of the *jutte*. This weapon system often includes auxiliary weapons such as the iron fan (*tessen*), baton (*hananeji*), arresting/tying cord (*torinawa*), and so on. A variety of classical systems (*koryū*) employing the *jutte* exist today. Fujita (1960: 2) notes thirty-seven *ryū* specializing in *juttejutsu*. 2. IKKAKU RYŪ—A

[9] Meiji Tennō 明治天皇 (1852–1912; r.1867–1912), 122nd emperor of Japan.

J

combative art that uses an iron truncheon (*jutte*) and iron fan (*tessen*). See also: *Edo Machikata Jutte Torinawa Atsukaiyō; Ikkaku Ryū.*

Further reading in English:

- Gruzanski, 1968.
- Mol, 2001; 2003.

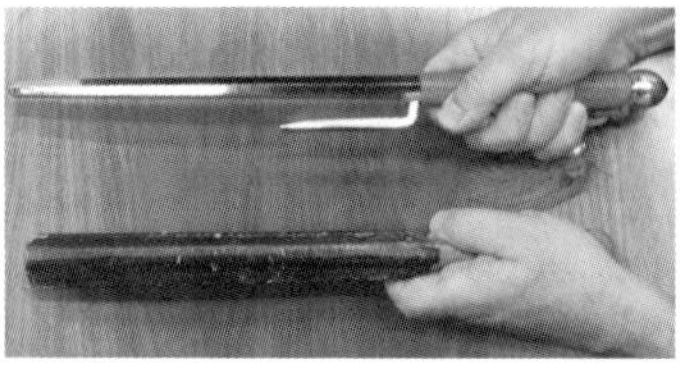

JUTTE AND *TESSEN* (IRON FAN)
Shown to illustrate comparative size
(Private collection)

Jutte Tōjutsu 十手刀術. HYŌHŌ NITEN ICHI RYŪ—The third set of combative scenarios (*kata*) listed by the Hyōhō Niten Ichi Ryū under the general category of Bōjutsu. This set consists of five *kata* in which the truncheon is used against a sword. See: *Hyōhō Niten Ichi Ryū.*

jū yoku gō o seisu 柔能制剛. KŌDŌKAN JŪDŌ—This old *jūjutsu* maxim, which means "flexibility can overcome strength," can be traced back to the *Laozi*. However, as Kanō evidently found that it could not be applied in all combative situations, he added additional principles, such as "maximum, efficient use of energy" (*seiryoku zenyō*), to his Kōdōkan Jūdō.

juzu 数珠【數珠】. BUDDHISM/SHUGENDŌ—A priest's rosary.

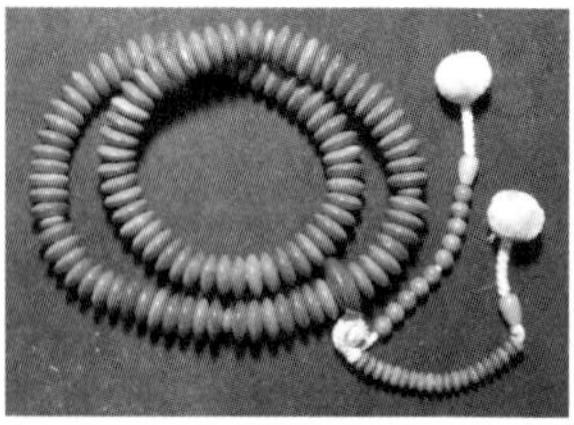

TENDAI-TYPE *JUZU*
(Private collection)

JIKI SHINKAGE RYŪ MEMBERS AT YASUKUNI SHRINE EXHIBITION, 1978

K

ka 1. 火. a. A campfire. b. TAIHŌ MILITARY SYSTEM—A ten-man squad established by the Taiho Codes (Taihō Ritsuryō) in the early eighth century. The *ka*, the basic military formation unit of the eighth-century provincial militia (*gundan*), was composed of conscript soldiers called *heishi* and commanded by a squad leader (*kachō*). The squad could be divided into two smaller groups called *go*. See: *gundan;* Appendix 2.

~ka 2. 家. A suffix denoting a competent practitioner of an art such as a martial art. ¶ *bujutsuka* 武術家, a martial arts practitioner; *kendōka* 剣道家, a *kendō* practitioner; *jūdōka* 柔道家, a *jūdō* practitioner; etc.

kabuki 歌舞伎. A category of traditional Japanese drama which became popular during the seventeenth century. Though the term literally means "singing and dancing skills," it also carries a sense of outlandishness. These often eccentric plays quickly became popular among mixed classes of patrons during the socially stratified Edo period (1603–1867), in contrast to the more restrained Noh musical plays (*nōgaku*) favored by the warrior class. *Kabuki* plays often centered on warrior vendettas. See: *adauchi mono; chambara; nōgaku.*

Further reading in English:
- Ernst, 1974.

kabukimono 歌舞伎者. See: *hatamoto yakko.*

kabura ya 鏑矢. A "humming-bulb" arrow; an arrow with a turnip-shaped head which makes a humming sound in flight. In the Heian and Kamakura periods, *kabura ya* were sometimes used to signal the beginning of battle. This ritual opening was followed by a volley exchange of arrows (*ya awase*) by both sides.

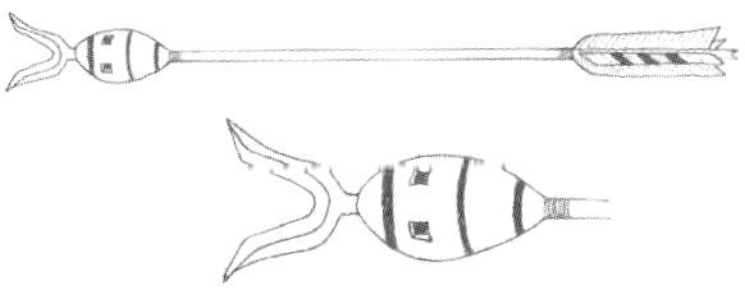

TYPICAL *KABURA YA*

kabuto 冑 [Also 兜] . A helmet.

kabuto kake 冑掛 [A.k.a. ***kabuto tate*** 兜立] . A helmet stand.

kabutowari 兜割 [Var. 冑割]. See: *hachiwari.*

kachi 1. 勝. Victory.

kachi 2. 徒士 [Also read ***kajishi***; ***toshi***]. A foot soldier. See: *okachi.*

kachizamurai 徒士. See: *okachi.*

kachigumi 徒士組. A perimeter security detail. *Kachigumi* was an official designation used during the Edo period for the perimeter guard unit which accompanied the Tokugawa *shōgun* whenever he went out in public.

kachiguri 勝栗. Dried chestnuts, lit. "victory chestnuts." *Kachiguri* were part of the ritual "last meal" sometimes eaten by warriors before battle. Also traditionally consumed were abalone (*awabi* 鮑), kelp (*kombu* 昆布), and rice wine (*sake* 酒).

kachihashiri 徒走. Medieval term for foot soldier. Equivalent of *kachimusha.*

kachimi 勝身. ARAKI RYŪ—The art of striking the vital points; a combination of *atemi* (striking skills using both body parts—elbows, knees, etc.) and *kyūsho* (targeting skills aimed at critical points on the body).

kachimusha 徒武者. A foot soldier. See: *tohosen.*

kachi nanori 勝名乗. Lit. "victory name-announcing." A twelfth-century practice in which a warrior or a member of his entourage would shout out his feats to the enemy. These achievements might be victories in battle or duels, instances where the warrior led a successful attack, etc. See: *nanori.*

Further reading in English:
- Varley, 1994: 59–63.

kachinuki-sen 勝ち抜き戦. An elimination-series tournament such as is often practiced in modern *kendō* or *jūdō*.

kachishū 徒士衆. See: *kachizamurai.*

kachiyumi 徒射 [A.k.a. ***hosha*** 歩射]. Shooting a bow while on foot (in contrast to shooting from horseback).

J K

kachizamurai 徒士侍. An Edo-period term for warriors who walked at the front of processions, acting as the vanguard or guidon.

kachō 火長. TAIHŌ MILITARY SYSTEM—The *kachō* was the leader of the ten-man squads (*ka* [2]) in the Chinese-style provincial militia unit (*gundan*) of the eighth century. His role was somewhat equivalent to that of a modern sergeant. See: *gundan*.

kaden 家伝【家傳】. Family tradition; handed down from father to son. For example, the *Heihō kaden sho*『兵法家伝書』is a text on the strategy of the Yagyū family which was handed down from father to son.

Kadono Den 上遠野伝【上遠野傳】. See: *Kadono Ryū*.

Kadono Ryū 上遠野流 [A.k.a. ***Kadono Den*** 上遠野伝【上遠野傳】]. A school concentrating on small throwing blades and darts (*shurikenjutsu*) that flourished in Sendai domain from around the Meiwa/An'ei era (1764–1780). Its techniques and weapons were influential in the later formation of Shirai Ryū 白井流 and Negishi Ryū 根岸流.

kaerizuno 逆角 [Also read ***kaeshizuno***]. See: *soritsuno*.

kaeshi 返し. 1. Lit. To reverse or turn in the opposite direction; to counterattack. 2. YAGYŪ SHINKAGE RYŪ—a large movement in which the practitioner's sword is swept back to deflect the enemy's sword and immediately brought forward (returned) with a *jun* or *gyaku* strike to the enemy's wrist area (*kote*) or head. Contrast to *nagashi*.

kaeshi waza 返技. A reversing technique; a technique that counters one that is being applied.

kaeshi zuki 返突. Lit. "reverse and thrust." SHINDŌ MŪSŌ RYŪ—A technique in which the medium-length staff (*jō*) is reversed and thrust (with the hands in *honte* position) at an opponent's vital areas. *Kaeshi zuki* is the fourth of the twelve basic techniques (*kihon*) extrapolated from the classical forms of Shindō Musō Ryū by Shimizu Takaji.

kaeshizuno 逆角 [Also read ***kaerizuno***]. See: *soritsuno*.

kagami-biraki 鏡開き. Lit. "breaking the mirror"; a special New Year's ceremony. Although not restricted to martial arts groups, *kagami-biraki* is often held in martial training halls (*dōjō*) as part of the first training session of the new year. In this ceremony, a round rice cake (*kagami-mochi* 鏡餅) is placed on an altar as an offering to the deities (*kami*) of the *dōjō*. The rice cake is traditionally broken on January 20.

Kagami Ryū 鏡見流. A branch school of the Edo Yagyū Shinkage Ryū. The Kagami Ryū specialized in combative swordsmanship (*kenjutsu*). The school was founded sometime during the first three decades of the seventeenth century by Kotaki Yoemon, a direct disciple (*deshi*) of Yagyū Munenori.

kagariya banyaku 篝屋番役. A Muromachi-period term for a security guard service that patrolled the streets of Kyōto. See also: *Kamakura Ōbanyaku; Kyōto Ōbanyaku; ōbanyaku; Shōgun Gosho Naibanyaku.*

kage 1. 陰. a. Shade, back, secret, obscured. The term *kage* is given a variety of meanings by classical martial traditions. It can be used as both a noun meaning "reflection," "shadow," etc. or an adjective meaning "hidden," "obscured," "invisible," etc. b. YAGYŪ SHINKAGE RYŪ—The mind. *Kage* is an essential concept for the Shinkage Ryu (1). See also: *Shinkage Ryū (1); Aisu Kage Ryū.*

kage 2. 影. a. Reflection, shadow, silhouette, image. b. SHINDŌ MŪSŌ RYŪ—Kage is the fourth series, containing twelve *kata* (plus two variations), considered the *urawaza* of Omote. c. SHINKAGE RYŪ—Synchronicity and explosiveness; the mind.

Kagemasa Ryū 陰政流. A martial school founded by Suzuki Saburōemon no Jō Kagemasa sometime in the late seventeenth or early eighteenth century in which a two-sword style of swordsmanship was studied. Watatani and Yamada (1978: 172) list several of the combative forms, such as Kazumichi no Tai 和満の体, Dōgashira 動頭, and Jūmonji 十文字.

(Note: The pronunciation of these names is uncertain.) In Bishū province, the Kagemasa Ryū became incorporated into Ikkan Ryū (3).

kagemusha 影武者. Lit. "shadow warrior." A body-double used to impersonate important generals during battle.

Kage no Ryū 1. 陰流 [Var. 陰之流]. See: *Aisu Kage Ryū.*

Kage no Ryū 2. 景之流. A branch tradition of Katayama Hōki Ryū 片山伯耆流. This system of swordsmanship (*kenjutsu*) and quick-draw sword arts (*iaijutsu*) was founded by Yamamoto Kyūya Masakatsu sometime between 1600 and 1630. According to some sources, after mastering Katayama's system, Yamamoto had a vision of a group of monkeys swinging tree branches like swords. This vision enlightened him to the secrets of swordsmanship "as if out of the darkness a bright moonbeam (*tsuki kage* 月影) shone upon him." See: *Katayama Hōki Ryū.*

kagerō 陽炎. 1. Often translated as "a shimmering in the air," a "heat haze," the martial sense of *kagerō* involves causing a visual distortion or mirage that blinds an opponent. In this sense, it is also related to the concepts of *kasumi* and *samidare* and the powers attributed to the warrior goddess Marishiten. 2. In the twentieth century the Imperial Japanese Navy named a class of destroyers "Kagerō." This was certainly apropos, as one of the main tasks of destroyers was to screen larger craft such as aircraft carriers, cruisers, battleships, and troop carriers by using smoke screens and other tactics. See also: *kasumi, samidare.*

Kage Ryū 陰流. See: *Aisu Kage Ryū.*

Kage ryū no mokuroku 「陰流之目録」<Ch. *Yin Liu zhi mulu*. A unique Kage Ryū list (*mokuroku*) found in a larger Chinese text on warfare known as the *Wubeizhi* 武備志 [Jp. *Bubishi* (Records of armaments)] dating from around 1561. This *mokuroku* lists a set of *kata* known as Empi, which contains six separately named sections:

Kage ryū no mokuroku 『陰流之目録』
(Kage Ryū syllabus)

1. *Empi* 猿飛 (Flying Monkey)
2. *Koryū* 虎龍 (Tiger and Dragon)
3. *Seigan* 青岸 (Blue Coast)
4. *Ingen* 陰見 (Shadow Seer)
5. *Enkai* 猿回 (Twirling Monkey)
6. *Dai-san Yamakage* 第三山陰 (Third Mountain Shadow)

There is a direct linguistic relationship between this document and the Empi no Tachi of the various branches of the Shinkage Ryū in Japan. However, the technical relationship may be more distant, as Kamiizumi continually revised his curriculum and there have been changes since those times.

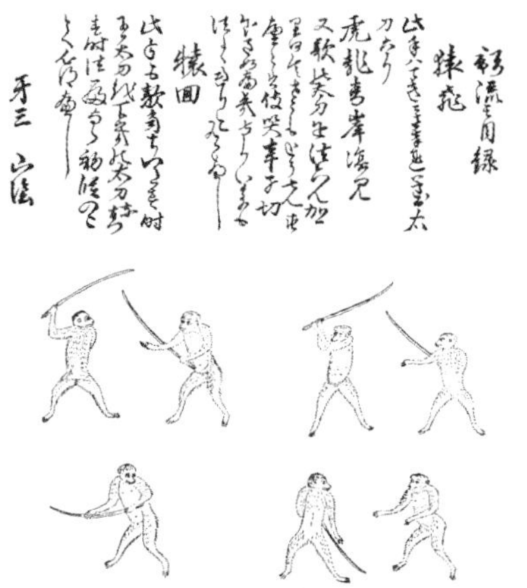

KAGE RYŪ *MOKUROKU*
Text describing Kage Ryū Empi forms
Reprinted from Mao Yuanyi's
sixteenth-century *Wubeizhi*

Kageyama Zenga Nyūdō Kiyoshige 影山善賀 入道 清重 [A.k.a. ***Zenga*** 善嘉; ***Kurando Senga Nyūdō*** 蔵人仙賀入道] (c.1580–c.1650). Founder of the Kageyama Ryū.

Kageyama Ryū 影山流. A classical martial system specializing in swordsmanship (*kenjutsu*), quick-draw sword arts (*iaijutsu*), grappling in light armor (*kogusoku*), and arresting arts (*torite*). This system was founded during the Keichō era (1596–1615) by Kageyama Zenga, a warrior (*bushi*) from Yagi-gun in Tamba (the present-day village of Yagi, in the Tamba area near Kyōto). Kageyama was supposedly a descendant of Susano-o no Mikoto, and he based his sword school on a technique called the "serpent-cutting sword" (*haba* *zanken* 羽々斬剣)[1] (a reference to the sword Susano-o used to destroy the great mythical serpent Yamata no Orochi). Whatever his origins, Kageyama was a highly skilled martial artist who mastered the teachings of some twenty-eight *ryū*, including Kashima Shintō Ryū 鹿島新当流 swordsmanship (*kempō* [1]), Shizuka Ryū 静流 glaive (*naginata*), Santoku Tō Ryū's 三徳当流 three arresting implements (*mitsudōgu*), and Shinkyoku Ryū 真極流 *jūjutsu*. There are many descendent branches from Kageyama's original school. See also: *Iai Hyōhō Izumo no Tachi.*

kagi 1. 鍵. a. A crosspiece on a polearm such as a spear or glaive, which is used to parry or suppress an enemy's weapon. This is a relatively rare device on a glaive (*naginata*), and only a few classical *ryū*, such as the Toda Ha Bukō Ryū's *kagitsuki naginata*, incorporate weapons systems that use it. A number of systems, however, use a spear (*yari*) with a *kagi*. b. Abbreviation for *kaginawa.*

kagi 2. 鉤【鈎】. a. A crosspiece or hook on a polearm; a hook on a rope. b. Abbreviation for *kaginawa.*

kagi 3. 嗅. A variant term for an espionage agent that implies the ability to "sniff out" or "ferret out" secret intelligence. The word is derived from the verb *kagidasu* 嗅ぎ出す. See: *mitsumono; ninjutsu.*

kagi-jūji 鉤十字【鈎十字】. Lit. a "hooked cross"; a swastika 卍. See: *manji.*

kagi naginata 鉤薙刀【鈎薙刀】[Var. 鍵長刀]. A glaive with a crosspiece (*kagi*) used for entrapping or parrying an opponent's weapon. See also: *kagi yari; naginata.*

kaginawa 鉤縄【鈎繩】[Var. 鍵縄【鍵繩】]. Lit. "hooked rope." A cord, usually made of silk, about ¼ inch (.5 cm) in diameter and about 18 feet (5.5 m) long with a hook attached to one end. An all-purpose rope used by mounted warriors, it normally hung from a saddle.

kagitsuki naginata 鍵付長刀. A glaive with an iron crosspiece (*kagi*). Only a few *ryū* are known to use this weapon. See: *Toda Ha Bukō Ryū; Shingyōtō Ryū.*

kagi yari 鍵槍 [Var. 鑰鎗; 鍵鑓; 鉤槍【鈎槍】]. A spear with a crosspiece (*kagi*) used for entrapping an opponent's weapon. See also: *sōjutsu; yari.*

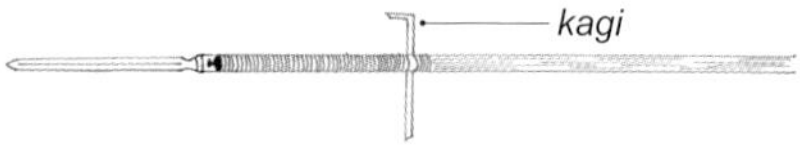

KAGI YARI
Typical design

kago 駕篭【駕籠】. A palanquin: a sedan chair supported by a single beam and carried by two attendants.

kahō 華法【華法】[Var. 花法【花法】]. See: *kahō kempō.*

kahō kempō 華法剣法【華法劍法】[Var. 花法剣法【花法劍法】]. A term dating from the late seventeenth century that was used pejoratively to describe some martial arts training of that time. Literally meaning "flowery swordsmanship," it implies ineffective technique and unrealistic training practices.

Certainly, vigorous martial and police combat training in any culture tends to wane in times of protracted peace. An examination of the classical Japanese martial systems (*koryū bugei*) that survived into and developed during the relatively serene Edo period (1600–1867), shows that some retained martial vigor in their prearranged combative forms (*kata*) while others did not. These systems were referred to as "positive" and "vacant" respectively by martial historian and hoplologist, Donn F. Draeger.[2]

Early Edo critics of "vacant" swordsmanship included such notables as Yagyū Jūbei of the Edo Yagyū Shinkage Ryū and Ono Tadaaki of the Ono Ha Ittō Ryū, both of whom opined that real combat experience was necessary for a swordsman to fully understand the art. In the mid-Edo period, Yamada Heizaemon Ippūsai of the Jiki Shinkage Ryū criticized the vacant, *kahō*-centered schools of swordsmanship. Yamada supplemented *kata* train-

[1] The term *haba* 羽々 (lit. "feathers") is an alternate name for the great mythical serpent, Yamata no Orochi.

[2] See Bibliography: Interviews, Conversations, Correspondence.

ing with vigorous *uchikomigeiko* matches in which protective gear and bamboo swords (*shinai*) were used.

Regardless of whether a school was "positive" or "vacant," the primary training method of almost all the *koryū bugei* still practiced today is the prearranged combative scenario (*kata*). See: *budō/bugei/bujutsu; kata.*

kai 1. 皆. Lit. "all"; "everything." The fifth seal/character of the nine mystic letters (*kuji*) found in the martial Kujihō (Ritual Method of the Nine Seals). See: *Kujihō.*

kai 2. 貝 [Var. 螺]. A conch shell. See: *horagai.*

kai 3. 会【會】. KYŪDŌ—The sixth of eight formal stages (*hassetsu*) in firing an arrow in the modern martial way of archery (*kyūdō*). *Kai*, which literally means "assembly" or "joining," is the process of aiming and concentration. There are three methods of aiming: *ariake no metsuke*, in which the target is sighted, fully exposed, to the left of the bow; *hangetsu no metsuke*, in which the target is half-obscured by the bow; and *yami no metsuke*, in which the target is almost fully obscured by the bow as it is sighted.

While taking aim, the archer concentrates on correct posture and stance; the abdomen must be firm and the legs and hips motionless. This brings about calmness of spirit and a unity of body, breath, and mind which is referred to as *haragei.* See also: *hassetsu.*

kai 4. 櫂 [Read ***ēku*** in Oki.]. OKINAWAN KOBUDŌ—An oar; a paddle. This weapon-usable object has combative applications in some Okinawan *karate*/*kobudō* systems. The combative art using the *kai* (*ēku*) is called either *ēkujutsu* 櫂術 or *ēku tī* 櫂手.

kai 5. 戒 <Ch. *jie* <Skt. *śīla*. BUDDHISM—moral conduct, moral precepts; one of the three types of learning (*sangaku*).

kai 6. 会. A group. In modern Japan, a martial arts training or research group is often referred to as a *kai*. The word may refer to an officially sanctioned classical *ryū* research/training group or an informal, non-sanctioned training group.

kaichō 会長. A group leader. A relatively modern title, *kaichō* indicates the leader of a martial arts training group (*kai*) who may or may not be the head instructor. See also: *dōjōchō; kanchō (2).*

kaidate 垣盾. A shield barrier; a shield wall.

kaiden 皆伝【皆傳】. Lit. "complete transmission." Usually used as a shortened form of *menkyō kaiden*.

kaieki 改易. The second-most severe of the five grades of legal penalties applied to the samurai during the Tokugawa period. *Kaieki* literally means "attainder"; that is, the loss of samurai status and all the rights and privileges that went with it. See also: *chikkyo; heimon; hissoku; monzenbarai; seppuku.*

Further reading in English:

- Brinkley and Kikuchi, 1915: 641–642 *ff.*
- Schreiber, 2001.
- Seward, 1968.

kaiguntō 海軍刀. Lit. "naval swords." The term *kaiguntō* refers to swords intended for use by officers in the post-1867 Japanese navy. Yumoto (1958: 50) notes three styles of *kaiguntō* mountings used by the Japanese Imperial Navy. Two of these were similar to a model used by the Japanese army, except that the color of the naval scabbard was blue. The third type more closely resembled the Japanese police saber. Most of the weapons in these mountings were poor-quality factory-made blades. However, some naval officers—especially those who were descended from samurai families (*shizoku*)—used these fittings for high-quality handmade swords that had been passed down in their own families as heirlooms. See: *guntō.*

kaihatsu ryōshu 開発領主. A fourteenth-century term meaning "land-developer lord" or "land-clearance lord." *Kaihatsu ryōshu* referred to Kamakura-period provincial strongmen—essentially warrior-landowners—who also opened up new field land for cultivation. This concept ties in with *zaichi ryōshu* ("country lord" or "residential lord"), another standard term for such a warrior. Japanese scholars have traditionally associated these men with

K

the organization of followers into bands of loyal warriors (*bushi dan*) who, unlike the foot soldiers (*banrui*) of earlier times, did not flee the field if the tide of battle turned against them. See also: *daimyō and myōden.*

Further reading in English:

• Farris, 1992: 206–222.

kaiken 懐剣 【懷劍】 [Also referred to as a ***kaitō*** 懐刀 【懷刀】 or ***koshigatana*** 腰刀]. A small knife without a guard that was generally regarded as a dagger for self-defense. A *kaiken* has a single or double cutting edge, and is approximately 3 to 6 inches (8–16 cm) long. According to some sources, the *kaiken* was also used by women for ritual suicide (*jigai*).

kaikin 海禁. Lit. "maritime restrictions." The term *kaikin* refers to the Tokugawa shogunate's policy of closing the country. See: *sakoku.*

kaimyō 戒名. BUDDHISM—1. Lit. a "precepts name." The *kaimyō* is given to someone taking the Buddhist precepts, and replaces the secular name. The *kaimyō* of a warrior who did not take all of the precepts was usually preceded by the term *nyūdō* 入道, indicating that he was "entering the path" but was not yet fully committed to the life of a monk. 2. A posthumous Buddhist name given to lay adherents after their death. In Japan *kaimyō* are normally found inscribed on memorial tablets and placed in Buddhist altars (*butsudan*) in one's home. See also: *hōmyō.*

Kai no Hō 櫂の法 <Oki. Ēku Fa 櫂法. OKINAWAN KOBUDŌ—Set of combative scenarios (*kata*) involving the oar which are part of the curriculum of the Ryūei Ryū (2) 劉衛流.

kaisha kempō 介者剣法. Armored swordsmanship. Equivalent to *katchū kempō*.

kaishaku 介錯. To assist in ritual suicide (*seppuku*).

kaishakunin 介錯人. A "second"; the assistant in a ritual suicide (*seppuku*) who stood by ready to behead the warrior performing the self-disembowelment.

Kaishaku Sōden 「解釈相伝」 【解釋相傳】 [Abbr. of ***Daitō Ryū Kaishaku Sōden*** 「大東流〜」]. DAITŌ RYŪ—The seventh of several Daitō Ryū transmission scrolls (*densho*) awarded in that tradition, containing a selected summary of 477 of the techniques previously mastered by the recipient. Kaishaku Sōden was the "highest level" *densho* awarded by Takeda Sōkaku until he taught at the Asahi News office in Ōsaka. There, in 1939, he awarded the first *menkyo kaiden* to Takuma Hisa.

Kaishū 海舟. See: *Katsu Kaishū.*

kaitō 1. 懐刀 【懷刀】. See: *kaiken.*

kaitō 2. 廻刀. YAGYŪ SHINKAGE RYŪ—A technique in which the sword is spun in a circle by one hand—usually vertically—with the wrist as the axis. In the Yagyū Shinkage Ryū this technique occurs in the *kata* sets Empi, Nanatachi, and Kuka. See also: *oni no tachi.*

kaiyaku 貝役. Trumpeting on a conch shell to send messages or signals. *Kaiyaku* was originally practiced by warrior monks (*yamabushi*), but it later became a specialty of the warrior class, much like military bugling in the West. See also: *jingai; jingaijutsu.*

kaizoku 海賊. Pirates. See also: *wakō.*

kaizokusen 海賊船. A pirate ship. See also: *wakō.*

kaji 1. 加持 <Ch. *jiachi* <Skt. *adhiṣṭhāna*. Lit. "to bestow upon and embrace." BUDDHISM—"Empowerment." In esoteric (tantric) Buddhism, the term *kaji* usually indicates a ritual which is responded to by the Buddha. However, the real meaning of the term is closer to "empowerment." In tantric practice a ritual is performed in which the practitioner enters into a temporary union with the target deity of a ritual text. In doing this the practitioner not only "experiences" the enlightened state of the deity but also obtains the marvelous powers (*shijji*) of that deity. This ritual of empowerment was adopted and adapted by the founders of many Japanese martial traditions and is echoed even today in the ritual etiquette associated with training in the martial *dōjō*. See also: *Jūhachidō.*

kaji 2. 鍛冶. a. A blacksmith. b. An abbreviation of *katana kaji* 刀鍛冶 (swordsmith).

Kajiden Echigo Ryū 加治伝越後流【加治傳越後流】. A branch school of combative strategy (*gungaku*) founded around 1560 by Kaji Tōtōmi no Kami Kagehide, a direct disciple of Uesugi Kenshin. See: *Echigo Ryū.*

Kajima Shinbu Ryū 加島神捕流. See: *Shinbu Ryū.*

Kaji Tōtōmi no Kami Kagehide 加治 遠江守 景英. A warrior and disciple of *daimyō* Uesugi Kenshin who founded the Kajiden Echigo Ryū 加治伝越後流. Established around 1560, the Kajiden Echigo Ryū was a school of combative strategy (*gungaku*).

Kajitsuka Yasushi 梶塚 靖司. Successor to Mutō Masao in the Ōtsubō line of the Owari Yagyū Shinkage Ryū. Kajitsuka is therefore a twenty-third-generation successor of the Owari Yagyū Shinkage Ryū. He is also an eleventh-generation successor of Yagyū Shingan Ryū.

kajutsu 火術. Lit. "fire art." General name for the use of firearms and explosives; gunnery. See: Daidō Ryū; *hōjutsu.*

kakan 加冠. A coming-of-age ceremony. See: *gembuku.*

KAJITSUKA YASUSHI
Twenty-third generation successor, Yagyū Shinkage Ryū; third headmaster, Ōtsubo Line of Shinkage Ryū; eleventh headmaster, Yagyū Shingan Ryū
(Photograph by author)

kakarigeiko 懸かり稽古. Lit. "attack training." KENDŌ—In this practice, a junior trainee works with a senior who acts as a target for the junior's strikes without countering or striking back. *Kakarigeiko*, which had become a part of basic *kendō* practice by the Meiji era, is intended to develop a positive attitude in the junior so that s/he learns to attack without falling into the "four evils" of fear, doubt, surprise, or worry.

kake 掛 [Var. 懸]. A rack or stand for weapons such as swords or staves. *Kake* may be freestanding or attached to walls. The type of weapon placed on a *kake* is often included in the term; for example, a rack primarily intended for holding a *katana*-type sword is called a *katana-kake.*

Tachi are placed either vertically, with the pommel at the base; or horizontally with the cutting edge down. Other blades are placed horizontally with the cutting edge up. Functional weapons were usually placed on the rack with the hilt or grip to the right so that the scabbard could be readily grasped with the left hand while the right hand quickly drew the blade. Swords placed on a rack for display purposes were placed with the grip to the left. The reason for this is that the ornamentation is normally on the *omote* side of the weapon; that is, the side that faces outward when the sword is worn.

kakemusha 懸武者 [Also written 駆武者【驅武者】]. "Brave warriors"; i.e., those who, when facing the enemy, advance and attack.

kaku 角. SHŌGI—An abbreviation or notation for *kakugyō* 角行.

kakugyō 角行 [Abbr. as ***kaku*** 角]. SHŌGI—Lit. "angle mover." In the strategic board game of *shōgi*, the *kakugyō* is somewhat analogous to the bishop in Western chess.

Kakujōbō Inkai 覚定房 胤懐【覺定房胤懷】[Var. ***Hōzōin Inkai*** 宝蔵院 胤懐【寶藏院胤懷】]. Sixth headmaster of the Hōzōin Ryū. See: *Hōzōin Ryū* lineage chart.

kakuju [Also read *kakushu*] 角珠. See: *kakute.*

Kakusan Ryū 覚三流【覺三流】. Edo-period branch school of Kakuten Ryū 覚天流 founded by Ikeda Kenmotsu Yoshimasa. The Kakusan Ryū concentrated on the pipe spear (*kudayari*).

kakushi 角指. See: *kakute.*

kakushi buki 隠し武器【隱し武器】. Lit. "con-

K

cealed weapons." A general term given to small weapons such as *shuriken* and *kaiken*. A number of books have been written on the subject in Japanese, some of the best of which are by Nawa Yumio. See also: *Negishi Ryū*.

kakushi metsuke 隠し目付 【隱し目付】. A variant term for an espionage agent. During the Edo period the term *metsukeyaku* 目付役 was used for police censors and their public "watchdog" hirelings. Consequently the term "hidden [*kakushi*] watcher [*metsuke*]" came to be used for espionage agents in some areas. They were somewhat like secret police. See: *metsukeyaku; ninjutsu*.

Kakushin 覚心【覺心】. See: *Kakushin Hōtō Zenji*.

Kakushin Hōtō Zenji 覚心 法灯 禅師【覺心 法灯 禪師】. A Zen Buddhist priest. Kakushin was the legendary founder of a Buddhist sect known as the Fuke Shū (a.k.a. Komusō). See: *Fuke Shū*.

kakushu [Also read ***kakuju***] 角珠. See: *kakute*.

Kakushunbō Insei 覚舜房 胤清【覺舜房胤清】 [Var. ***Hōzōin Insei*** 宝蔵院 胤清]【寶藏院胤清】] (1636–1701). Third headmaster of the Hōzōin Ryū. See: *Hōzōin Ryū* lineage chart.

kakute 角手. Lit. "horned hand." *Kakute* refers to metal finger-rings studded with small spikes. The number and shape of the spikes vary, and there are several designs. These devices have a number of names, including *kakuju* (*kakushu*) 角珠 (horned jewel), *kakushi* 角指 (finger spike), and *kakuwa* 角輪 (horned ring).

Kakuten Ryū 覚天流【覺天流】[A.k.a. ***Nippon Kakuten Ryū*** 日本覚天流]. An Edo-period martial school founded by Ogasawara Uchizaemon Sadaharu. The Kakuten Ryū was a branch tradition of the Itō Ryū (1). The school concentrated on the pipe spear (*kudayari*) and long-hafted glaive (*naginata*). See Itō Ryū (1) for lineage.

kakutō 格闘. 1. A fight; a scuffle; grappling. 2. Hand-to-hand combat.

kakutō bugei 格闘武芸【格鬪武藝】. Lit. "fighting martial arts." *Kakutō bugei* refers to martial arts which actually contain fighting techniques. There has been no set list of these, as the disciplines have changed over the centuries; Fujita Seikō listed a total of thirty-four, whereas Watatani Kiyoshi listed forty-four. Among these are the following arts:

1. bajutsu	馬術	horsemanship
2. kenjutsu	剣術	swordsmanship
3. kumiuchi	組討	grappling
4. kyūjutsu	弓術	archery
5. naginatajutsu	薙刀術	glaive
6. sōjutsu	槍術	spearmanship
7. sumō (sumai)	相撲	wrestling

kakuwa 角輪. See: *kakute*.

Kakuzanbō Inpū 覚山房 胤風【覺山房胤風】 [Var. ***Hōzōin Inpū*** 宝蔵院 胤風【寶藏院胤風】] (1685–1731). Fourth headmaster of the Hōzōin Ryū. See: *Hōzōin Ryū* lineage chart.

Kakuzenbō In'ei 覚禅房 胤栄【覺禪房胤榮】. See: *Hōzōin Inei*.

kama 鎌. A sickle.

kamae 構え. A combative engagement posture. According to Donn F. Draeger,[3] more than 300 *kamae* were developed by the Japanese in their martial arts. See also: *kurai; marobashi; setsunintō katsujinken*.

kamajutsu 鎌術. Combative arts using a sickle. Fujita (1960: 2) notes forty-one *ryū* specializing in *kamajutsu*.

Kamakura 鎌倉. Currently a small city south of Tōkyō, this town became the center of governmental power in 1185, after Minamoto no Yoritomo became *shōgun*. Yoritomo established his shogunate there in order to avoid the "corrupting" influences of locating near the imperial court in the capital city of Kyōto.

Kamakura bakufu 鎌倉幕府. The Kamakura shogunate, which officially ruled from 1192 to 1333.

Kamakura jidai 鎌倉時代. The Kamakura period (1185–1333) was the era in which the country was ruled by the shogunate founded by Minamoto no Yoritomo. While the official government was still located in the imperial

[3] See Bibliography: Interviews, Conversations, Correspondence.

court in Kyōto, the real power had shifted to the *bakufu* located in Kamakura.

Kamakura Nen Ryū 鎌倉念流. See: *Nen Ryū.*

Kamakura Ōbanyaku 鎌倉大番役. A security guard service that was instituted in Kamakura in 1225 to complement the Kyōto guard service (Ōbanyaku). It was composed of warrior vassals of the *bakufu*, and functioned during the Kamakura and Muromachi periods. See also: *kagariya banyaku; Kyōto Ōbanyaku; Ōbanyaku; Shōgun Gosho Naibanyaku.*

Kamakura Zen 鎌倉禅【鎌倉禪】[A.k.a. ***nyūdō sanzen*** 入道参禅【入道參禪】(lit. "warrior Zen practice")]. A term used by some scholars to describe the Rinzai Zen school as taught by the Buddhist monk Eisai to the warriors (*bushi*) of Kamakura during the late twelfth and early thirteenth centuries. This form of *zen* was quite fluid, as Eisai and his successors were very creative in developing training methods for the warriors. Eisai also included a number of esoteric teachings (*mikkyō*) in order to make his new school more appealing to warrior tastes. While the Japanese priest Eisai was a master of "scriptural Zen" and a scholar, the Chinese priests Daikaku[4] and Bukkō[5] who trained warriors and monks were more responsible for actually shaping the Zen training style of Kamakura in the early thirteenth century. This innovative Zen practice style flourished until the end of the sixteenth century and declined quickly during the early decades of the seventeenth century. (Leggett, 1985: 2). See also: *kien Zen; kōan; nyūdō sanzen; Nyūdō sanzenki; shikin Zen.*

Further reading in English:

- Collcutt, 1981.
- Draeger, 1995.
- Leggett, 1985.

kamari 1. かまり. Surprise attack troops; a surprise attack. During the Sengoku and Tokugawa periods, a number of Chinese characters (*kanji*) were used interchangeably for writing the term *kamari*; such as 蟠, 奸, and others. In addition, several other terms were equated to *kamari*, including *kamari monomi* 蟠まり物見; *shibami* 芝見; *kusa* 草; etc. According to Miyazaki (1974: 216–217), such terms were used interchangeably to refer to the practice of covert assault troops hiding in various locations—reed fields, forests, mountain valleys, and even in villages—in order to suddenly form up in order to carry out a surprise attack against enemy forces. Depending on their nature, these combatants were variously referred to as covert assault troops in a hamlet (*sato kamari*), those in a village (*mura kamari*), and those in a large group (*ōkamari*), as well as covert sacrifice assault troops (*sute kamari*), joint assault troops (*aikamari*), and deceptive assault troops (*yae kamari*), among others. While these terms later came to be associated with *ninjutsu*, in the context of the battlefield they are more akin to shock troops lying in ambush.

kamari 2. 蟠. A variant term for an espionage agent. Under this definition, a *kamari* is able to remain completely concealed during reconnaissance missions by lying in grass, crawling on the ground, etc. In this context of a military scout or lookout, *kamari* (2) is related to similar terms: *shinobi monomi* (concealed lookout), *kamari monomi* (lurking scout), *kamari* (3) 奸 (cunning or villainous spy), and *shibami* (bush scout). See: *ninjutsu.*

kamari 3. 奸. A variant term for an espionage agent, indicating a cunning or villainous spy. See: *kamari (2); ninjutsu.*

kamari monomi 蟠まり物見. A variant term for an espionage agent. *Kamari monomi* is used to refer to a lurking scout. See: *kamari (2); ninjutsu.*

kamayari 鎌槍 [A.k.a. ***magari yari*** 曲槍]. Lit. "sickle-spear." A spear with a blade or blades at a right angle to the shaft. The blade is shaped much like a sickle blade; there are many types. The cutting edge of the blade ranged from 6 to 8 inches (15–20 cm) long. There are two major categories of *kamayari*: those with one horizontal blade protruding from one side (*kata-kamayari*), and those with two horizontal blades protruding from

[4] Daikaku 大覚【大覺】<Ch. Dajue.

[5] Bukkō 仏光【佛光】<Ch. Foguang.

two sides (*jūmonji yari*). Large/longer versions were called *ōkamayara*. See *jūmonji yari* for illustration. See also: *Hōzōin Ryū; jūmonji yari; sōjutsu; yari.*

kambe 神戸. See: *kanbe.*

Kambe Kinshichihei Takeyasu 神戸 金七平 武保 (1894–1980). Seventh headmaster of the Owari Kan Ryū, a twenty-first generation successor to the Yagyū Shinkage Ryū, progenitor of the Kambe line of Owari Yagyū Shinkage Ryū, and founder of the Shunpūkan *dōjō*. Kambe mastered the Owari Kan Ryū's pipe-spear (*kudayari*) system and began training under Yagyū Genshū in 1913. After Genshū passed away, Kambe continued training with Genshū's senior students, including Shimojō Kosaburō, Yagyū Toshinaga (Genchō), and others. He consequently received one of the most comprehensive educations in the Shinkage Ryū of anyone in his generation. This entire curriculum has been transmitted by his successors to the current generation.

YAGYŪ GENCHŌ (L) AND KAMBE TAKEYASUI (R) demonstrate Yagyū Shinkage Ryū c. 1955
(Photograph courtesy Mutō Masao)

Kamei Magoroku Shigemura 亀井 孫六 重村【龜井孫六重村】. Though not a *ryū* founder himself, Kamei was the "compiler" of Edo Machikata Jutte Torinawa Atsukaiyō. At the order of the eighth Tokugawa *shōgun*,[6] Kamei researched the police arresting arts (*hobakujutsu*) of thirty-some *ryū*. The result was a somewhat standardized system for Edo-period arresting officers. See also: *Masaki Ryū, Nawa Yumio.*

kami 神. SHINTŌ—1. A manifestation of spiritual power; miraculous power. Anthropologists and linguists have speculated that the Japanese term *kami* is related to the Polynesian terms *kapu* and, by extension, *taboo.* 2. Something or someone superior to the ordinary. 3. A Shintō deity. 4. In the area of combative traditions, *kami* have an intimate relationship with all things martial in Japanese culture. Many of the 9,000 martial traditions (*ryū*) that have appeared in Japan over the centuries were reputedly inspired by a revelation from a particular *kami*, often in combination with a specific Buddhist deity. Martial accoutrements, especially swords and other bladed weapons, are also believed to be permeated with *kami*. Blades for warriors were forged in a spiritual environment, and their making was closely integrated with Shintō ritual. Blades produced in this way were carefully named, and many were thought to have displayed divine attributes. Japanese literature has produced many stories of blades performing magical feats such as appearing and disappearing, fighting alone for their injured masters, punishing profanation with disease or death, healing the sick, and responding to prayer. See also: *mitama; Ryōbu Shintō; Shintō (1).*

kamidana 神棚. SHINTŌ—Lit. "sacred shelf." The *kamidana* is a small Shintō altar located in a home or a training hall (*dōjō*) that serves as an abode for the *kami* (spiritual beings) of the *dōjō*. It is placed above any other items on the wall.

Further reading in English:

- Joya, 1985: 518–519.
- Lowry, 2006: 95–112

KAMIDANA AT REMBUKAN DŌJŌ, 1977
(Photograph by author)

kami hanen 上半円【上半圓】. See: *jōhanen.*

Kamiizumi Hitachinosuke Hidetane 上泉 常陸介 秀胤 [Also read ***Kōizumi Hitachinosuke Hidetane***] (c. 1536–1564). Eldest son of Kamiizumi Ise no Kami, progenitor of

6 Tokugawa Yoshimune 徳川吉宗 (1684–1751; r.1716–1745).

Kamiizumi Ryū Gumpō 上泉流軍法. Hidetane inherited the Shinkage Ryū from his father and transmitted it as the Kamiizumi Ryū school of battlefield tactics (*gumpō*). Soon afterward, Hidetane entered the service of the lord Hōjō Tsunashige. He was killed in battle at Kōnodai in 1564.

Kamiizumi Ise no Kami Nobutsuna 上泉伊勢守 信綱 [A.k.a. ***Kōizumi Ise no Kami Nobutsuna***; ***Musashi no Kami*** 武蔵守; ***Hidetsuna*** 秀綱 in lieu of Nobutsuna] (1508–1577). Founder of the Shinkage Ryū (1); recognized as second headmaster by the Jiki Shinkage Ryū 直心影流. Yagyū Genchō, in his *Shōden Shinkage Ryū*『正傳新陰流』(1957: 14), states that Kamiizumi Hidetsuna (as Nobutsuna was known in his early years) studied the Nen Ryū of Nen Ami Jion in Kamakura during his youth, then journeyed to the Katori Shrine area, where he studied Iizasa's branch of the Shintō Ryū as well as Bokuden's Kashima Shintō Ryū; after this, he began his study of the Aisu Kage Ryū under its founder, Aisu Ikōsai Hisatada. However, other sources give a somewhat different history of his early years.

The Kamiizumi family descended from Fujiwara nobility. The branch that came to reside in the area called Kamiizumi took that geographical identifier as their family name (this practice, called *myōden*, was common at the time). Although Kamiizumi Hidetsuna's father Hidetsugu was only a minor local lord, he was well known for his martial accomplishments. Hidetsugu had trained with Iizasa Chōisai Ienao, founder of the Katori Shintō Ryū and Aisu Ikōsai, founder of the Kage Ryū. Consequently, we can assume that by his early twenties, Kamiizumi had been exposed to Nen Ryū, Shintō Ryū, and Kage Ryū. In addition, according to the Jiki Shinkage Ryū tradition, Kamiizumi also mastered the Kashima Shin(kage) Ryū under Matsumoto Bizen no Kami. He must have accomplished this before 1534, since Matsumoto is thought to have died around that time. In 1530, at the age of twenty-two, Kamiizumi received the title "Ise no Kami" (protector/lord of Ise) and began his military career.

At that time, Aisu Ikōsai was a famous but elderly swordsman around eighty years of age. He and his son Koshichirō were under the employ of Satake Yoshiatsu, lord of Hitachi, and were residing at Ōta Castle on the Pacific coast. Around 1534, carrying a letter of introduction from his father, Kamiizumi traveled to Hitachi to train in the Kage Ryū. As the Satake clan was embroiled in an internal rivalry between two brothers, Yoshiatsu and Yoshimoto, Kamiizumi participated in a fair amount of actual combat during his years of training in the Kage Ryū with Ikōsai and Koshichirō. Ikōsai passed away in 1538, and the Satake rivalry came to an end with the suicide of Yoshimoto in 1540. Around this time, Kamiizumi received a full license in the Kage Ryū, probably from Koshichirō (although he could have received it from Ikōsai earlier). He was probably thirty-two or thirty-three at the time.

Having experienced intensive combat and mastered the Kage Ryū, Kamiizumi entered into a period of self-training and religious austerities (*shugyō*). According to various documents that have come down from Kamiizumi, this *shugyō* centered on esoteric Buddhist practices, including the Marishiten *hihō* (secret ritual methods of the Buddhist goddess). In one of these texts, he states:

> After practicing the *Secret Methods of Marishisonten* day after day for an extended period, and training day and night, I received an inspiration from the deity. Suddenly, from my own heart, the Shinkage Ryū gushed out!
>
> *Empi no maki*, dated 1566

After this insight, Kamiizumi renamed his school of strategy the Shinkage Ryū (Revised Kage Ryū). He would continue to evolve and refine this system for the next thirty years. Around this time he also began to attract disciples. Though there is scant documentation regarding his students, one of his earliest disciples was Okuyama Kyūgasai (1526–1602), who later became a third headmaster of the Shinkage Ryū. It is recorded that Kyūgasai "trained with Kamiizumi as a young man"; this presumably took place around 1545 to 1550, so Kyūgasai would have been between nineteen and twenty-five years old.

Between 1550 and 1560, Kamiizumi began training other disciples, several of whom are known. These included his two sons, Hidetane and Norimoto, his nephew Hikita Bungorō, and Jingo Muneharu, usually considered his most skilled student.

In 1561, Kamiizumi was fighting for Nagano Narimasa as his retainer. Nagano, lord of Minowa Castle in Kōzuke, was loyal to the forces of Uesugi Kenshin in Uesugi's periodic battles against Takeda Shingen. Minowa Castle had become a thorn in the side of Takeda's army, and was under siege at the time. Kamiizumi was the leader of a formidable assault group known as Nagano Jūrokunin no Yari, the "Sixteen Spears of Nagano." After valiantly defending Minowa Castle against repeated attacks by Takeda forces, the siege was ended with the deaths of Nagano and his son. Takeda, greatly impressed (as well as chagrined) by the outstanding performance of the castle defenders, offered to incorporate the best of them into his army.

KAMIIZUME ISE NO KAMI NOBUTSUNA
Wooden statue in Seirin Temple,
Kamiizumi Ward, Maebashi

Kamiizumi declined the offer, as he wished to embark on a martial pilgrimage (*musha shūgyō*) in order to further perfect and spread his Shinkage Ryū. Takeda allowed him to depart, and gave him the gift of one of the characters of his name. Thus, from Shingen (信玄), Kamiizumi Hidetsuna (秀綱) took the character *shin* 信 (also pronounced *nobu*) and became Kamiizumi Nobutsuna (信綱). During the next ten years he traveled throughout Japan transmitting the Shinkage Ryū.

There are many stories concerning Kamiizumi's travels during his *musha shūgyō*. Japanese film director Kurosawa Akira, in fact, incorporated one of these tales into his 1954 production of *Shichinin no samurai* (The Seven Samurai). According to this legend, in the course of his wandering Kamiizumi came upon a village where a brigand was holding a child hostage. As any show of force or frontal assault might cause the child to be killed, no one knew what to do. Kamiizumi approached a Buddhist priest standing in the crowd and asked to borrow the man's robes. He also asked the monk to shave his head so he could disguise himself as a priest—a shocking request. At that period in Japan history, one's hairstyle identified the social class to which one belonged, and only monks had shaved heads. Kamiizumi was essentially removing his high samurai status along with his hair. Nonetheless, his head shaved, Kamiizumi disarmed himself, put on the monk's robes, and approached the house in which the bandit was holding the child. In his guise as a monk, he offered food to the bandit and the child. As the brigand reached for the food, Kamiizumi leaped upon him and subdued him. The monk was so impressed by this that he gave his surplice (*kesa*) and begging bowl (*jihatsu*) to Kamiizumi. Later Kamiizumi passed these articles on to his most skilled student, Jingo Muneharu.

On his spiritual quest, Kamiizumi traveled the country teaching his Shinkage Ryū to the best swordsmen in the land. During this period more than twenty warriors became his disciples and mastered the key technical and psychological teachings of his Shinkage Ryū. Many of his students went on to establish *ryū* of their own. Kamiizumi is believed to have passed away in his home domain in 1577. See also: *hikihada shinai; katsujinken setsunintō; Shinkage Ryū (1).*

KAMIIZUMI FAMILY CREST
Illustration of the Kamiizumi *noboribata*

The following disciples of Kamiizumi have separate entries of their own:

- Hikita Bungorō Kagetomo
- Hōzōin Inei
- Jingo Izu no Kami Muneharu
- Komagawa Tarōzaemon no jō Kuniyoshi
- Marume Kurandonosuke Tessai
- Nishi Itton
- Ogasawara Genshin Nagaharu
- Okuyama Kyūgasai Kimishige
- Yagyū Sekishūsai Muneyoshi

Kamiizumi Mondo no Kami Norimoto 上泉 主水正 憲元 [Also read ***Kōizumi***; a.k.a. ***~Norimura*** 憲村, ***~Michiharu*** 通治] (c.1552–1600). Second son of Kamiizumi Ise no Kami Nobutsuna, inheritor of the Shinkage Ryū 新陰流, and founder of Aizu Ittō Ryū 会津一刀流.

Norimoto, by some accounts, accompanied his father on a warrior pilgrimage (*musha shūgyō*) during the early 1560s, along with his cousin Hikita Bungorō, and Kamiizumi's most talented student, Jingo Izu no Kami Muneharu. Subsequently Norimoto entered the service of Uesugi Kagekatsu, who was then lord of Aizu Wakamatsu castle. Noritomo was a favorite of the lord and was adopted into the Uesugi clan, consequently giving up his surname of Kamiizumi. At Aizu Wakamatsu he founded the Aizu Ittō Ryū. He was evidently killed in battle at the offensive of Hasedō (Hasedō Kōgeki) in 1600.

Kamiizumi Ryū Gumpō 上泉流軍法 [Also read ***Kōizumi Ryū Gumpō***]. School of strategy, tactics, and espionage (*gumpō*) founded by Kamiizumi Hitachinosuke Hidetane around 1560.

Kamiizumi Ryū Heihō 上泉流兵法. See: *Kōizumi Ryū Hyōhō*.

kamikaze 神風 [Also read ***shimpū***, especially when referring to suicide pilots during World War II]. Lit. "divine wind." Though it is best known as a reference for Japanese suicide pilots in the Second World War, this term originally referred to typhoons which destroyed two Mongol invasion fleets in 1274 and 1281. The original *kamikaze* typhoons were supposedly "powered" by the Tendai and Shingon schools of Buddhism. Monks spent days performing fire rituals (*goma*) in order to drive the Mongols away. (Tendai and Shingon monks tried this again in 1945 as the U.S. Seventh Fleet approached, but neither typhoons nor suicide pilots succeeded in deterring the Allies.)[7]

Kaminoda Tsunemori 神之田 常盛 (b.1927). The last disciple to receive the Shindō Musō Ryū *menkyo kaiden* from Shimizu Takaji. Kaminoda was a police *jōjutsu* instructor for the Tōkyō Kidōtai (Riot Police) at the Yonki Dōjō. He is currently the chief instructor at the Zōshūkan in Shibuya Ward, Tōkyō.

Kaminoda was a close friend of Donn F. Draeger,[8] and wrote a posthumous *menkyo kaiden* for Draeger when the latter passed away in 1982.

In the mid-1970s Kaminoda established what was to have been Shimizu Takaji's permanent Shindō Musō Ryū *dōjō* at the Zōshūkan. Until the 1960s Shimizu had taught *jōjutsu* and *jōdō* in a variety of locations. However, as the chief *jōjutsu* instructor for the Tōkyō Riot Police (Kidōtai), most of the *dōjō* he used were police training halls. After retiring from the police force in the 1960s, Shimizu established the Rembukan Dōjō in Shibuya Ward—a non-police *dōjō*, although several of his senior police students taught there. The Rembukan Dōjō, which had been constructed from the disassembled old Imperial Police Dōjō, was

KAMINODA TSUNEMORI (L) AND SHIMIZU TAKAJI (R)
Demonstration of Shindō Musō Ryū Ran'ai
(Photograph courtesy Nishioka Tsuneo)

---

7 Oddly enough, in September 1945, shortly after Japan had signed its surrender document with the Allies, an extremely powerful typhoon struck Okinawa, destroying many U.S. planes and sinking several ships.

8 See Bibliography: Interviews, Conversations, Correspondence.

K

placed on a piece of land next to Shibuya Park that had been temporarily donated by one of Shimizu's students. Upon Shimizu's death in 1978, the Zōshūkan (a new *dōjō* located in a different part of Shibuya, originally intended to replace the Rembukan) became Kaminoda's personal *dōjō* and the home of his Nippon Jōdōkai, where he has continued to teach until the present (2009). The stated purpose of Kaminoda's organization is to return to the earlier teachings of Shimizu Takaji. Consequently, Kaminoda's organization, the Nihon Jōdōkai, echoes the name of the Dai Nippon Jōdō Kai, an organization Shimizu had established in the 1930s. According to Kaminoda, as Shimizu's original group also wore black *uwagi* and *hakama*, that practice is now followed by the Nippon Jōdōkai group. This is unusual, as *jōdō* trainees normally wear standard *kendō* dark blue *uwagi* and *hakama*.

Kaminoda has produced several books on Shindō Musō Ryū and its collateral arts, and has been interviewed for numerous articles on those systems. Several of these are listed here:

Shindō Musō Ryū jōdō kyōhan 『神道夢想流杖道教範』 (Shindō Musō Ryū stick arts—the master text). Japan Publications Trading Company, 1976. Co-authored with Nakajima Asakichi and published under Shimizu Takaji's editorial direction.

Isshin Ryū kusarigama-jutsu 『一心流鎖鎌術』 (Isshin Ryū sickle-and-chain arts). Privately published, 2002.

Ikkaku Ryū jutte-jutsu and Ittatsu Ryū hojō jutsu 『一角流十手術 一達流捕縄術』 (Ikkaku Ryū single-tined truncheon arts and Ittatsu Ryū tying-cord arts). Privately published, 2005.

Kenjutsu—Shintō Kasumi Ryū; Heiki—Uchida Ryū tanjōjutsu, mitsudōgu (tsūshō) sasumatajutsu 『剣術 神道霞流 併記 内田流短杖術 三道具(通称)刺服術』 (Swordsmanship—Shintō Kasumi Ryū; including Uchida Ryū short staff arts and polearm arresting weapons). Privately published, 2006.

kami no otsukai 神のお使 [Abbr. ***otsukai*** お使]. A familiar spirit; a familiar; a spirit servant or supernatural messenger. In several classical martial traditions (*koryū*), it is believed that the secret teachings of the system were transmitted from a deity to the founder of the tradition via a familiar spirit. For example, Ōtake Risuke of the Tenshinshō-den Katori Shintō Ryū 天真正伝香取神道流 has mentioned the belief that the tutelary deity ofthat system, Futsunushi no Mikoto, was the transmitter (*kami no otsukai*) of some of the secret teachings of their school from the Buddhist goddess Marishiten to their founder, Iizasa Chōisai Ienao (Ōtake, 1986 interview). Similarly, Nen Ryū 念流 transmission documents list Shō Tengu as their the *kami no otsukai*. See: *Marishiten setsu shōgun kyō; tengu.*

kamishimo 裃. A formal two-piece costume worn by warriors (*bushi*) during the Edo period. The *kamishimo* consisted of a stiff vest (*kataginu*) worn over a kimono and loose pantaloons (*hakama*). For illustration, see: *hanbakama.*

Kamiya Denshinsai Naomitsu 神谷伝心斎直光【神谷傳心斎直光】(1582–c.1645). Recognized as fifth headmaster by the Jiki Shinkage Ryū 直心影流; successor to Ogasawara Genshin Nagaharu in the Shin Shinkage Ryū 真新陰流. Kamiya became Ogasawara's student around 1624 at the age of forty-two. Upon achieving full mastery of Ogasawara's tradition, he renamed the school the Shinkage Jikishin Ryū 新陰直心流, c.1630. His lineal successor was Takahashi Danjōzaemon Shigeharu. See also: *Takahashi Danjōzaemon Shigeharu; Jiki Shinkage Ryū.*

kamiza 1. 上座. Lit. "senior seat," or "upper seat." The position at the head of a table or the front of the line where the most senior participant sits. Located to the left of the "god seat" (*shinza* 神座), it stands in contrast to the *shimoza*.

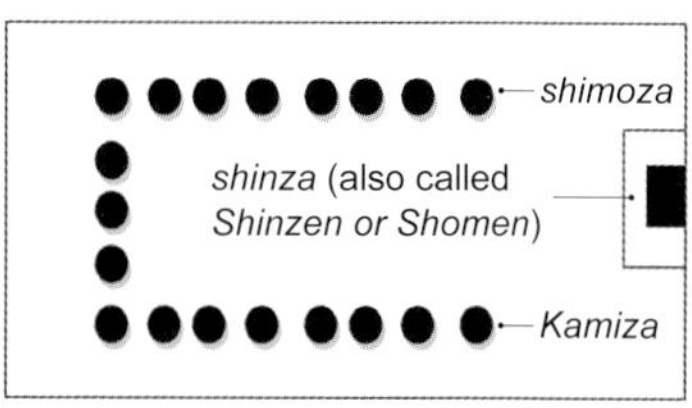

kamiza 2. 神座. Alternate reading for *shinza.* See: *shinza.*

kamon 家紋. A family crest placed on banners, helmets, and armor. The *kamon* identifies a person's family or the family with which they are affiliated. It is also worn in five places on overcoats (*haori*)—in which case they are called *gomonbaori* (lit. "five-crest overcoat")—and on formal kimono known as *mon-tsuki,* also in five places: on the back between the shoulders, on each sleeve, and on each breast. Upper-level *daimyō* were allowed three *mon,* others had two *mon,* and common samurai only one. Some of the most recognizable *mon* include the following:

Tokugawa

Three asarum leaves

Ashikaga/Hosokawa/Oda/Uesugi

Paulownia

Minamoto

Three gentian leaves above five bamboo leaves

Taira/Ikeda

Butterfly

Hōjō

Three triangles

kampaku 関白【關白】. The title of Imperial Regent. From 882 to 1868 this was the highest position at the imperial court. The *kampaku* represented the emperor at court and served as his intermediary. If the holder of this title—usually a member of the Fujiwara family—passed it on to his son while still living, his post-*kampaku* title became *taikō.* The most notable non-Fujiwara holder of this title was Hidetsugi, the adopted son of Toyotomi Hideyoshi, who took office in 1592. See also: *taikō.*

kan 1. 感 [Var. 勘]. Lit. "intuition." a. In the context of Japanese martial culture, the ability to make intuitive "leaps" meant that a warrior trainee had advanced past the stage of taking a plodding, analytical approach to dealing with combative situations, and had advanced to one of instantaneous, intuitive response. Such flashes of intuition or insight experienced by the seasoned Japanese warrior, especially in the early *ryū,* were often seen as divine revelations from Shintō and/or Buddhist martial deities. b. HOPLOLOGY—In the area of combative behavior and performance, the Japanese martial concept of *kan,* or intuition, is one of the three key psychological combative adaptive traits; the other two are steadfast/imperturbable mind (Jp. *fudōshin*) and volition (Jp. *sen*). See also: *yūgen.*

Further reading in English:

- Draeger, 1973b: 11 *ff*; 1974: 59 *ff.*
- Hall, 1997.
- Hayes, 1988a.

Kan 2. 唅 <Ch. *Han* <Skt. *Hāṁ.* The seed syllable (*shuji*) for Fudō Myōō. This is one of the most common Sanskrit syllables appearing in *siddhaṁ* (*shittan*) script inscribed on Japanese sword blades and accoutrements.

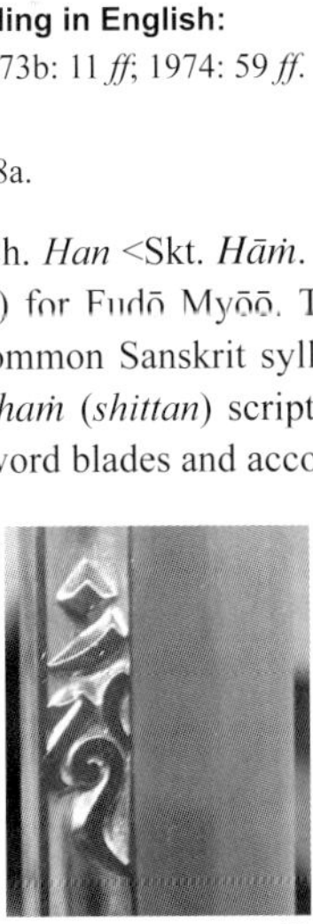

SANSKRIT *SIDDHAM* LETTER *KAN* 唅 (Skt. *Hāṁ*)
Engraving on the blade of a short sword (*kodachi*)
(Private collection)

kan 3. 関【關】. A gate; a checkpoint.

kan 4. 間. See: *kanja.*

kanabō 金棒. An iron staff or wooden staff to which iron strips have been attached.

kanagu 金具. Sword mountings on a *tachi*, not including the guard (*tsuba*). Mountings on other types of swords are called *kodōgu*.

kanamono 金物. Lit. "metal items"; "hardware." Miscellaneous sword or armor fittings.

kambe 神戸. Clans, often of the warrior class (*bushi*), who served as shrine officials, attendants, and security forces. They were supported via a tax system known as *so-yō-chō* 租庸調 (crop, labor, and in-kind taxes). See: *hafuribe*.

kanchō 1. 間諜. A spy or secret agent; espionage (reconnaissance). See: *ninjutsu*.

kanchō 2. 館長. A training-hall leader. As a title, *kanchō* indicates the head of a *dōjō* who may or may not be the head instructor. This title means essentially the same thing as *dōjōchō*. See also: *kaichō*.

kanchōjutsu 間諜術. Espionage.

SMALL BUDDHIST TEMPLE GONG (*KANE [1a]*). (Photograph by author)

kane 1. 鐘 <Ch. *zhong*. a. A temple gong. Battle commanders with a headquarters unit often had available a small temple gong (*kane*) for signaling. See: *shikigu*. b. A Buddhist priest's hand-held bell, often used in ritual along with the five-point *vajra* scepter.

kane 2. 鉦 <Ch. *zheng*. A hand-held gong; also called a *dōra* 銅鑼. Battle commanders sometimes used these for signaling. See: *shikigu*.

Kaneda Gembei Masatoshi 金田 源兵衛 正利 (c.1610–c.1680). Direct disciple of Amano Ichirōemon Hisataka, the second-generation successor of the Asayama Ichiden Ryū 浅山一伝流. Kaneda was a talented warrior who founded the Kaneda Ichiden Ryū.

Kaneda Ichiden Ryū 金田一伝流 【金田一傳流】. Branch tradition of Asayama Ichiden Ryū 浅山一伝流 founded around 1640 by Kaneda Gembei Masatoshi. The system concentrated on swordsmanship (*kenjutsu*) and quick-draw sword arts (*iaijutsu*).

Kaneko Shinkurō Morisada 金子 新九郎 盛貞 (c.1520–c.1585). Second-generation successor of the Tenshinshō Jigen Ryū 天真正自顕流. His best-known student was a warrior named Terasaka Yakurō Masatsune, who later became the monk Zenkitsu. Zenkitsu succeeded Kaneko as third-generation headmaster.

Kanemaki Jisai Michiie 鐘捲 自斎 通家 [***Kanemaki*** is variously written as 鐘巻, 鐘牧, etc.; ***Jisai*** as 自在; a.k.a. surname ***Toda*** 外他; and variously named ***Tarō*** 太郎, ***Michimune*** 通宗] (c.1536–c.1615). Founder of Kanemaki Ryū 鐘捲流. After training under Toda Kagemasa 富田 景政, of the Chūjō Ryū 中条流 and Toda Ryū 富田流 lineage, Kanemaki set out on a warrior pilgrimage which led him to the Atagosan Daigongen temple in Kyōto. After performing ritual austerities and engaging in prayer to the Buddhist worthy Shōgun Jizō, he is said to have awakened to the deepest mysteries of swordsmanship, upon which that he founded the Kanemaki Ryū in 1595. Kanemaki is generally recognized as the teacher of both Sasaki Kojirō, founder of Gan Ryū (1) 厳流, and Itō Ittōsai Kagehisa, founder of the Ittō Ryū 一刀流. However, due to the various ways in which Kanemaki's name has been written, those relationships are difficult to verify. Kanemaki is also credited with the founding of Sanshin Ryū 三心流, a school specializing in sickle-and-chain techniques (*kusarigama-jutsu*).

As noted, it is generally thought that Kanemaki was a disciple of Toda Kagemasa. However, this claim is suspect. Watatani and Yamada (1978: 195) note that other sources[9] indicate Kanemaki was a disciple of Toda Kiyoharu 戸田清元, a master of Toda Ryū 戸田流. The curriculum of Toda Ryū included techniques for the long curved sword (*tachi*), the straight

9 Watatani and Yamada cite two works: *Kenjutsu keizu*『剣術系図』and Bugei denkei『武芸伝系』.

sword (*tsurugi*), and quick-draw swordsmanship (*iaijutsu*), among others.

Kanemaki Ryū 鐘捲流 [A.k.a. ***Kanemaki Ryū Battōjutsu*** ~抜刀術]. Founded by Kanemaki Jisai Michiie, this classical school was originally a system of combative swordsmanship (*kenjutsu*), spear arts (*sōjutsu*), grappling (*jūjutsu*), and quick-draw sword arts (*battōjutsu*). At least one line of this school exists today as Kanemaki Ryū Battōjutsu, a system concentrating on quick-draw sword arts.

Kanemaki Toda Ryū 鐘捲外他流. A branch line of the Kanemaki Ryū that flourished in Maebashi domain during the Edo period.

Kaneshima Shin'ei 兼島 信栄 <Oki. Kaneshima Shinyei (c.1910–c.1990). OKINAWAN KARATE—Founder of Ishimine Ryū 石嶺流 and the Ishimine Ryū Karatedō Preservation Society.

Kaneshima Shinsuke 兼島 信助 (1897–1990). OKINAWAN KARATE—Founder of a *karate* tradition known as the Tozan Ryū 渡山流.

kaneyaku 鐘役. BUDDHISM—A temple gong. *Kaneyaku* are used to signal the hours of the day and night. Since they can be heard at great distances, armed forces also used them for signaling as early as the Heian period.

kangeiko 寒稽古 [A.k.a. ***kanshugyō*** 寒修行]. Special winter practice held in many modern martial-arts training halls (*dōjō*). *Kangeiko* is held during the coldest winter months, and may last for several weeks. The trainees push themselves to the limit of their ability to resist cold and fatigue. At least as early as the Edo period,[10] *kangeiko* was seen as a key mental and spiritual discipline for practitioners of swordsmanship (*kenjutsu*), spearmanship (*sōjutsu*), combative archery (*kyūjutsu*), combative horsemanship (*bajutsu*), and a variety of other martial disciplines. Contrast to *shochūgeiko*. See also: *gasshuku*.

kangun 官軍. In the fourteenth-century war saga *Taiheiki*, the term *kangun* indicates the loyalist imperial forces who fought against the *chōteki*, or Kamakura *bakufu* forces. In later eras, *kangun* was used to refer to government forces or the imperial army. See: *Taiheiki*.

kanja 間者 <Ch. *jianzhe* [Abbr. as ***kan*** 間]. A variant term for espionage agent. The word is taken from a Chinese term found in the Sun Tzu's *Art of War* (*Sonshi no heihō*). The thirteenth and final chapter of this text, which is devoted to espionage agents and their strategies, had a significant influence on the development of Japanese intelligence operations (*shinobi no jutsu/ninjutsu*) during the feudal period. The title of the chapter, *Yōkan* 用間 in Japanese,[11] literally means "to employ (用) the space (間) (between two objects)." *Kanja* consequently indicates someone who "employs" or "slips through" the cracks; i.e., a spy or espionage agent. Miyazaki (1974: 217) elaborates on this, noting that the character for space (*kan* 間) is a pictogram of a gate (門) through which the sun (日) is shining; and comparing the idea of the sunlight penetrating the gate to an espionage agent slipping between walls to obtain information.

Sun Tzu describes five types of agents (*gokan* 五間):

Chinese	(Jp)	Character	Type
1. *Xiangjian*	(Gōkan)	郷間	Native agents
2. *Neijian*	(Naikan)	内間	Inside agents
3. *Fanjian*	(Hankan)	反間	Double agents
4. *Sijian*	(Shikan)	死間	Expendable
5. *Shengjian*	(Seikan)	生間	Living agents

Native agents are spies employed from the local population; inside agents are employed from the enemy's governmental officials; double agents come from the ranks of the enemy's spies; expendable agents (lit. "death-" or "dead-agents") are employed to spread false information among the enemy; and living agents are spies who return with information. See: *ninjutsu*.

Further reading in English:

- Griffith (trans.), 1963: 144–149.

10 Sasama (1982: 229–232) quotes from a passage in the *Edo funai ehon fūzoku ōrai*『江戸府内絵本風俗往来』, an illustrated text on the various customs and fashions of feudal-period Edo, elaborating on the practice of *kangeiko* by warriors and other martial artists during that era.

11 *Yōkan* 用間 <Ch. *yongjian*.

K

kanjō 灌頂 <Ch. *guanding* <Skt. *abhiṣeka*. BUDDHISM—Often referred to as the "Buddhist baptism," the *kanjō* is a ceremony performed by tantric schools such as the Tendai Shū and the Shingon Shū for a candidate who is being consecrated to the most profound truths of the doctrine. In this ceremony, which is patterned after the anointing of kings in the ancient Middle East, a small amount of incense-sweetened water is poured on the head of the adept. *Kanjō* was adopted by many institutions in medieval Japan for the transmission of important texts and knowledge. The *kanjō* ceremony was later imported from tantric Buddhism into some martial traditions; it is performed when a trainee is initiated into the deepest truths and secrets of the school (*ryū*).

Further reading in English:

- Hall, 1990: 125–133; 301–303.
- Rambelli, 2006.

Kanku 公君. See: *Kūsankū.*

Kanku Dai 公君大. See: *Kūsankū (Dai).*

Kanku Shō 公君小. See: *Kūsankū (Dai).*

Kankyoku Ryū 鑑極流 [A.k.a. ***Wada Ryū*** 和田流]. Founded by Wada Jūrōzaemon Masashige Zuishin Zuika, the Kankyoku Ryū was a branch tradition of both the Seigō Ryū/Zuishin Ryū line and the Gan Ryū (3) 願立. Wada's system concentrated on combative swordsmanship (*kenjutsu*). See Zuishin Ryū for lineage.

Kanno Jōzan Yoshimitsu 菅野 静山 喜光. A direct disciple of Hakkō Ryū 八光流 founder Okuyama Yoshiji. Kanno subsequently founded the Shinshin Ryū 真心流, a school which concentrated on grappling (*jūjutsu* and *aikijutsu*).

Kannon Bosatsu 観音菩薩 【觀音菩薩】 <Ch. Guanyin Pusa <Skt. Avalokiteśvara-bodhisattva. The Buddhist goddess of mercy. As a bodhisattva (*bosatsu*) venerated by various Buddhist schools and sub-sects in Japan, Kannon is seen as a manifestation of mercy and compassion.

kannushi 神主. SHINTŌ—A Shintō priest.

Kanō Jigorō 嘉納 治五郎 (1860–1938). Established Kōdōkan Jūdō in 1882. Kanō was physically weak and plagued by bullies as a boy, so he set out on a two-year regimen of gymnastics, hiking, rowing, and baseball to improve his health and strength. In 1877, he began training in Tenshin Shin'yō Ryū 天神真楊流 *jūjutsu* with Fukuda Hachinosuke, a disciple of Iso Mataemon, the system's founder. Tenshin Shin'yō Ryū at that time was a civilian self-defense system specializing in striking techniques (*ate waza*) and grappling techniques (*katame waza*). Upon Fukuda's death Kanō continued training for a while with Iso's son, Masatomo, until he also passed away. Kanō then began training in Kitō Ryū 起倒流 with a teacher named Iikubo Tsunetoshi. Kitō Ryū had also evolved into a civilian self-defense system at that time, but Kanō was interested in Iikubo's emphasis on *ran*, or freestyle training, in contrast to reliance on pre-arranged *kata*. The Kitō Ryū also emphasized throwing techniques (*nage waza*). Kanō began researching other classical *bujutsu* systems, concentrating most of his efforts on the Sekiguchi Ryū 関口流 and Seigō Ryū 制剛流.

Toward the end of the nineteenth century, many Japanese were turning their eyes to the West and discarding many elements of Japanese tradition. Kanō felt *jūjutsu* was an important Japanese cultural asset, and he made great efforts to restore the art to what he felt was its proper place in the cultural hierarchy. In 1882 he founded a synthesized *jūjutsu* system he christened Kōdōkan Jūdō. His first training hall (*dōjō*) was located in a relatively small room in Eishōji, a Buddhist temple in the Shitaya area of Tōkyō. Kano's cultural

KANŌ JIGORŌ, C. 1935

emphasis is clear from the name he chose for his system: Kōdōkan—*kō* 講 (study, practice); *dō* 道 (way, spiritual path, doctrine); *kan* 館 (hall)—the Hall for Studying the Way.

Kanō had eclectic interests and investigated many martial traditions. In fact, in the late 1920s or early 1930s, he befriended Shimizu Takaji of the Shindō Musō Ryū and instituted a policy in which *jūdō* students who had attained the rank of fourth-degree black belt (*yondan*) could also train in Shindō Musō Ryū at the Kōdōkan. He was also on friendly terms with all the well-known martial artists in Tōkyō during the first half of the twentieth century.

Professionally, Kanō was an educator; in his career he served as the director of primary education in the Ministry of Education (Mombushō) and as the president of Tōkyō Higher Normal School. In these positions he was a key figure in getting *kendō* and *jūdō* adopted as part of the physical education program in public schools. He was also among the first Asian members of the International Olympic Committee (IOC), and tried for many years to have *jūdō* included as an Olympic sport. Kanō died at sea in 1938 while returning from an IOC meeting in Cairo, where he had been lobbying for the 1940 Olympics to be held in Tōkyō, and to include *jūdō*. The cataclysmic events of World War II, however, delayed both of these goals until 1964.

Further reading in English:
- http://judoinfo.com/history.htm.

Kanrin Maru 咸臨丸. The ship used for the Tokugawa shogunate's first trans-Pacific diplomatic mission to San Francisco in 1860. The mission was headed by Jiki Shinkage Ryū swordsman Katsu Kaishū.

Kan Ryū 貫流. See: *Owari Kan Ryū.*

Kansai 関西【關西】. Western Japan (in contrast to the Kantō region of eastern Japan). Kansai encompasses the area west of the Ashigarazaka gate on the island of Honshu.

kansashi 簪. See: *kanzashi.*

kansetsu waza 関節技【關節技】. KŌDŌKAN JŪDŌ—A subcategory of *jūdō*'s Katame no Kata (Grappling Forms). *Kansetsu waza* focus on joint techniques.

kansha 感謝. CLASSICAL WARRIOR IDEAL—Thanks; grace. *Kansha* as grace or an attitude of thanks was considered one of the essential characteristics of the classical warrior (*bushi*). See: *bushi no konjō.*

kanshi 諫死. A category of suicide (*seppuku*) performed as a statement of non-support for a superior; i.e., *seppuku* performed as an act of remonstration. See: *seppuku.*

Kanshin Ryū 貫心流. A school of *jūjutsu*/*aikijutsu*-type combative arts founded in the mid-twentieth century by Inaho Kanzan. Inaho had previously mastered Hakkō Ryū 八光流 under founder Okuyama Yoshiji.

kanshugyō 寒修行. See: *kangeiko.*

Kantō 1. 関東【關東】. Eastern Japan; the great plain of eastern Japan; areas on the island of Honshu east of the Ashigarazaka gate.

kantō 2. 関刀【關刀】<Ch. *guandao*. The large glaive named after (and usually pictured with) the Chinese general Kan'u (Ch. Guan Yu). See: *Kan'u; seiryō ken.*

Kantō kanrei 関東管領【關東管領】. The deputy of the Kantō *kubō* (the *kubo* was essentially the governor of Kantō) in the time of the Ashikaga shogunate. The office of Kantō *kanrei* was traditionally held by the Uesugi family.

Kantō kubō 関東公方【關東公方】. The highest-ranking officer of the Ashikaga shogunate in eastern Japan. Based in Kamakura, the Kanto *kubō* was in charge of the eastern domains of the Kyōtō-based Ashikaga shogunate.

Kantō Shichi Ryū 関東七流【關東七流】[A.k.a. ***Kashima Shichi Ryū*** 鹿島七流]. See: *Kashima no Tachi.*

kantō tachi 鐶頭大刀 [Var. 鐶頭太刀]. Swords with a round handgrip (*tsuka*) that were generally imported from China and Korea during the sixth century. See also: *chokutō; kubutsuchi tachi.*

Kan'u 関羽【關羽】<Ch. Guan Yu (often romanized as Kwan-yu). A second-century Chinese

K

general and the hero of the classic tale *Romance of the Three Kingdoms*.[12] In 1594 Kan'u was deified as the god of war, and his image frequently adorns Japanese sword fittings. He is usually represented with a large glaive (*seiryō ken*, or *kantō* [2]) which is sometimes carried by an attendant.

kanzashi 簪. An ornamental hairpin. As a last resort, women who used *kanzashi* to keep their hair in place could utilize this object as a stabbing weapon. See also: *jīfā; Okinawa kobudō.*

kappō 活法 [Var. ***katsu*** 活]. 1. Resuscitation techniques and methods. These were normally included in grappling and striking systems in which the effects of certain training techniques result in shock to the nervous system. 2. KŌDŌKAN JŪDŌ—A formalized set of resuscitation techniques, usually taught to advanced students.

karajishi 唐獅子 (Lit. "Chinese lion") <Ch. *shizi gou* 獅子狗 (lit. "lion dog") [Var. Oki. ***shīsā*** 獅子]. BUDDHISM/SHINTŌ—The open-mouthed *karajishi* is usually found paired with the closed-mouth "Korean dog" (*koma inu*) at the gates of Shintō shrines. These images were probably introduced into Japan around the seventh century. According to Ball (1927: 59), the *koma inu* is a "distinctively Shintō creature," while the *karajishi* was imported from China along with the cult of the Buddhist deity Mañjuśrī-bodhisattva (Monju Bosatsu). Together, the pair represents male and female forces (*yin* and *yang*); due to Buddhist influence, they also represent the Sanskrit syllables *a* and *hūṁ* in a similar fashion to the Buddhist Niō.

KARAJISHI
Shintō shrine entrance at the Fudōin Iwayadō, a Shugendō temple in Wakasa, Japan
(Photograph courtesy Mike Davenport)

At first, the *karajishi* and the *koma inu* were stationed at the gates of Shintō shrines, *karajishi* on the left with mouth open, *koma inu* on the right with mouth closed. However, as time went by, they were placed near the entrances of buildings both "ecclesiastical and secular," and, except for the open and closed mouths, their features became almost identical. The *karajishi* is sometimes referred to in the west as a fu dog, lion dog, or Korean dog. In a martial context, the *karajishi* and the *koma inu* often adorn martial accoutrements as talismans. See also: *koma inu; Niō; shishi (1).*

kara kawa 唐革. Lit. "Chinese leather." A term used in the medieval *Heiji* and *Heike* war tales (*gunkimono*) to describe a famous suit of armor prized by the Taira clan. Made of hardened leather, the armor was so tough that the arrows of the Minamoto were unable to penetrate it.

karasu tengu 烏天狗. A type of mountain demon (*tengu*) with the appearance of a bird, specifically a crow (*karasu*). See also: *ko no ha tengu; tengu.*

karate 空手. Lit. "empty hand" or "empty hand-to-hand combative art"; [Var. ***karate*** 唐手, lit. "China hand" (i.e., Chinese hand-to-hand combat); also read in Jp. as ***tōde*** < Oki. *tōdī*].

The term *karate* may be an abbreviation of *karatedō* or *karatejutsu*, both of which are defined below. In the main, however, it is a modern generic term for a range of primarily pugilistic fighting systems that can trace their current form to Okinawa.

Karate evolved from a mixture of native Okinawan combative arts—referred to in that native tongue as *tī*—and Chinese combative arts known variously as "martial arts" (Ch. *wushu* 武術), "boxing" (Ch. *quanfa* 拳法), and a variety of other generic terms which are often school/tradition specific. Although a number of *karate* styles are now practiced in Okinawa, they have never had the same formality and strict licensing systems used by the classical Japanese warrior system (*koryū*),

[12] *Sangoku shi engi*『三國志演義』<Ch. *Sanguo yanyi*『三國演義』.

a fact that reflects differences in Okinawan and mainland Japanese cultures.

Tī Systems: Okinawan combatives that developed prior to the nineteenth century generally come under the rubric *tī* 手 (Jp. *te*). There is little documentation on the origins and development of the *tī* of those earlier times. Beginning in the eighteenth century, Okinawa's trade with China led to the importation of Chinese *wushu* and *quanfa* systems, which the Okinawans modified and often mixed with their original *tī* systems until the latter nearly disappeared. One or two of these remaining systems have been included in this *Encyclopedia*.[13] However, to date the most comprehensive English reference materials on *tī* have been produced by *karate* historian Mark Bishop (1996; 1999).[14] As Bishop notes in various places, *tī* systems tend to illustrate a relaxed character similar to that of Chinese Wudang Shan 武當山 style "internal" combative systems such as *taiji quan* 太極拳, *bagua zhang* 八卦掌, and *xingyi quan* 形意拳; their actual technical aspects, however, differ from those Chinese systems. *Tī*, notes Bishop (1999: 10), "…is still in existence and has affected the technical and fighting forms of some modern *karate* styles."

Tōdī (Karate) Systems: According to tradition, the earliest use of the term *tōdī* 唐手 (also read *karate*) dates from the late eighteenth or early nineteenth century, when a Chinese national named Kūsankū 公相君 held a public demonstration of Chinese boxing and grappling in the city of Naha. Kūsankū's skills were referred to as *tōdī* 唐手. One of his Okinawan students, in fact, came to be called Sakukawa Tōdī. Although the literal meaning of the term is "Chinese 唐 hand 手," by the eighteenth century the Okinawan term *tī* 手 (Jp. *te*) had come to mean "combative skill" or "hand-to-hand combat."[15]

In the strict sense of the term, *tōdī/tōde* has come to refer to those Okinawan combatives derived from, or influenced by, Chinese combative arts. The heaviest influence occurred during the fifty-year period from around 1870 to about 1920. This roughly parallels the years between the end of the Japanese early modern era (1868) and the end of China's dynastic period (1911).

Generally referred to around that time as Shuri *te*, Naha *te*, and Tomari *te* (based on geographical names where these disciplines were practiced), these three categories are not clearly defined. It is important to note, however, that *te* included both unarmed and armed combat training. Thus, *tōdī* (Chinese combative arts) stood in contrast to *tī*, which indicated native Okinawan combat skills. Under Japanese control and influence during the late nineteenth and early twentieth century, the pronunciation generally shifted to *karate*.[16]

Legends abound regarding the development of *karate*, a number of which have been debunked by the practitioners themselves. For example, the idea that *karate* was developed by Okinawan peasants as a way to defend themselves against Satsuma samurai has long been discredited; Higaonna Morio, a well-known and respected practitioner of Gōjū Ryū 剛柔流 *karate*, stated as much to this author in 1980. In addition, some scholars researching the history of *te* have noted that the pugilistic fighting arts of Okinawa were not the province of peasants, but of the local noble/warrior class (*shizoku*), especially after the Satsuma domain took control of the island in 1609. This restriction apparently did not apply, however, for many of the young Okinawan men who either journeyed to the Chinese mainland to study *wushu* or were able to train with Chinese immigrants in Okinawa ware not of *shizoku* origins. The were, instead, *heimin*; that is, descendants of feudal-era commoners.

After its annexation by Japan in 1879, Okinawa was incorporated into that country's sphere of influence. This included conscription of Okinawans into the new Japanese

13 See, for example, the entry on Motobu Udundī 本部御殿手.

14 Patrick McCarthy's 2008 publication on the Okinawan *Bubishi* is also well done. However, it is not as comprehensive as Bishop's works.

15 This is reflected in some other Okinawan combative terms such as *ēku tī* 櫂手, which refers to combative skill using an oar or boat paddle.

16 However, Bishop (1999: 13, n. 2) notes that some styles were still using the term *tōde* well into the 1960s.

K

Uechi Ryū *
上地流
(17 *kata*)

Kata Transmitted in All Uechi Ryū Lines	
Okinawan *Kata* Name	
Sanchin	三戦
Kanshiwa	完子和
Kanshū	完周
Sēchin	十戦
Sēsan	十三
Sēryū	十六
Kanchin	完戦
Sansēryū	三十六
Ryūko	龍虎
Shōhei	昭平

Kata Transmitted in Single Uechi Ryū Lines			
Okinawan *Kata* Name		**Okinawan School / Organization Name**	
Kōbuken	孝武拳	Kōbu Ryū	孝武流
Taikyoku Shodan	大極初段	Uechi Ryū Karatedō Shinkōkai	上地流空手道振興会
Rokukenkū	禄拳空	Uechi Ryū Karatedō Shinkōkai	上地流空手道振興会
Fūhaochen	虎鶴拳	Kōnan Ryū	硬軟流
Haofū	鶴虎	Kōnan Ryū	硬軟流
Ōdō	王道	Kōnan Ryū	硬軟流
Baiken	南拳	Kōnan Ryū	硬軟流

* Takamiyagi, *et al*, 2008: 224-228.

Gōjū Ryū †
剛柔流
(21 *kata*)

Kata Transmitted in All Gōjū Ryū Lines	
Okinawan *Kata* Name	
(Open Hand)	
Sanchin	三戦
Tenshō	転掌
(Closed Hand)	
Gekisai Daiichi	撃砕第一
Gekisai Daini	撃砕第二
Saifā	砕破
Seiyunchin	制引戦
Shisōchin	四向戦
Sansēryū	三十六手
Sēpai	十八手
Kururunfā	久留頓破
Sēsan	十三手
Sūpārinpē	壱百零八手

Kata Transmitted in Single Gōjū Ryū Lines			
Okinawan *Kata* Name		**Okinawan School / Organization Name**	
Tenchi	天地	Gōjū Ryū Meibukan	剛柔流明武館
Seiryū	青龍	Gōjū Ryū Meibukan	剛柔流明武館
Byakko	白虎	Gōjū Ryū Meibukan	剛柔流明武館
Shujaku	朱雀	Gōjū Ryū Meibukan	剛柔流明武館
Genbu	玄武	Gōjū Ryū Meibukan	剛柔流明武館
Gekiha Daiichi	撃破第一	Gōjū Ryū Shōreikai	剛柔流尚禮会
Gekiha Daini	撃破第二	Gōjū Ryū Shōreikai	剛柔流尚禮会
Kakuha Daiichi	鶴破第一	Gōjū Ryū Shōreikai	剛柔流尚禮会
Kakuha Daini	鶴破第二	Gōjū Ryū Shōreikai	剛柔流尚禮会

† Takamiyagi, *et al*, 2008: 230–234.

Shōrin Ryū ††
少林流
(33 *kata*)

Shōrin (Matsubayashi) Ryū *Kata* 松林流型	
Wankan	王冠
Rōhai	鷺碑
Tomari Passai	泊抜塞
Chintō	鎮闘
Chatan Yara nu Kūsankū	北谷屋良の公相君
Fukyū Kata I	普及型 I
Fukyū Kata II	普及型 II
Pinan Shodan	平安初段
Pinan Nidan	平安二段
Pinan Sandan	平安三段
Pinan Yondan	平安四段
Pinan Godan	平安五段

Shōrin (Kobayashi) Ryū *Kata* 小林流型	
Itosu Passai	糸洲抜塞
Matsumura Passai	松村抜塞
Ūsēshī	五十四歩
Sēsan	十三
Kūsankū (Dai)	公相君(大)
Kūsankū (Shō)	公相君(小)
Chibana Kūsankū	知花公相君
Pinan Shodan	平安初段
Pinan Nidan	平安二段
Pinan Sandan	平安三段
Pinan Yondan	平安四段
Pinan Godan	平安五段

Naihanchi Shodan	内歩進初段
Naihanchi Nidan	内歩進二段
Naihanchi Sandan	内歩進三段
Ānankū	安南空
Wansū	汪輯
Ūsēshī	五十四歩

†† Takamiyagi, *et al*, 2008: 236–244.

Naihanchi Shodan	内歩進初段
Naihanchi Nidan	内歩進二段
Naihanchi Sandan	内歩進三段
Unshu	雲手
Koryū Passai	古流抜塞
Kihon Kata Shodan	基本型初段 (Nakazato Shōrinryu 仲里小林流)
Kihon Kata Nidan	基本型二段 (Nakazato Shōrinryu 仲里小林流)
Kihon Kata Sandan	基本型三段 (Nakazato Shōrinryu 仲里小林流)
Jitte	十手
Chintī	チンテイー
Jion	慈恩
Sōchin	壯鎮

Shitō Ryū §
糸東流
(52 *kata*)

Itosu Ha 糸洲派	
Pinan/Heian Shodan	平安初段
Pinan/Heian Nidan	平安二段
Pinan/Heian Sandan	平安三段
Pinan/Heian Yondan	平安四段
Pinan/Heian Godan	平安五段
Naifanchi Shodan	ナイフアンチ初段
Naifanchi Nidan	ナイフアンチ二段
Naifanchi Sandan	ナイフアンチ三段
Jitte	ジッテ
Jion	ジオン
Jiin	ジイン
Wanshū	ワンシュウ
Passai Dai	パッサイ大
Passai Shō	パッサイ小
Kokusōkun Dai	コクソウクン大
Kokusōkun Shō	コクソウクン小
Shihō Kokusōkun	四方コクソウクン
Chintī	チンテイー
Chintō	チントー
Rōhai Shodan	ローハイ初段
Rōhai Nidan	ローハイ二段
Rōhai Sandan	ローハイ三段
Gojūshiho	五十四歩

Higaonna Ha 東恩納派	
Sanchin	サンチン
Tenshō	テンショウ
Saifa	サイファ
Seienchin	セイエンチン
Sēsan	セーサン
Sēpai	セーパイ
Shisōchin	シソーチン
Sanseru	サンセール
Kururunfa	クルルンファ
Sūpārinpai	スーパーリンパイ

§ Takamiyagi, *et al*, 2008: 246–252.

Matsumura Ha 松村派	
Matsumura Rōhai	松村ローハイ
Matsumura Passai	松村パッサイ

Shingaki Ha 新垣派	
Nīseishi	ニーセイシ
Sōchin	ソーチン
Unshū	ウンシュウ

Go Kenki 呉賢貴	
Nīpaipo	二十八歩
Haofā	ハウファー
Pāpūren	八歩連

Mabuni Kenwa 摩文仁賢和	
Matsukaze	松風
Jūroku	十六
Aoyagi	青柳
Shinpā	シンパー

Mabuni Kenei 摩文仁賢榮	
Yotsu no Kata	四つの形
Shinsei Daiichi	新生第一
Shinsei Daini	新生第二
Myōjō	明星

Sankō Kata 参考形	
Chatan Yara Kōsōkun	北谷屋良コウソウクン
Ishimine Passai	石嶺パッサイ

K

military. The Japanese government subsequently approved the inclusion of *karate* as part of the physical education system in Okinawan schools in 1902. According to Draeger (1974a: 127), this was done because it served the Japanese military's purpose of building a pool of well-conditioned future conscripts. By the late 1920s, several Okinawan *karate* teachers had moved to Japan, where the Okinawan art soon became popular and, like many of the Japanese *budō* schools, began the almost inevitable evolution into a sportive system.

Fujita (1960: 2) lists approximately forty-seven *ryū* specializing in *karate* in Japan (including Okinawa). In contrast, Draeger (1974: 124) gives a total of a hundred, and Takamiyagi *et al* (2008: 157–194) list twenty-four schools in Okinawa alone. See also: *Funakoshi Gichin; karatedō; karatejutsu; Sakukawa Tōde.*

Further reading in English:

- Bishop, 1999; 1996.
- Draeger, 1974a: 124–136.
- Funakoshi, 1973; 1975; 2001.
- Haines, 1968.
- McCarthy, 2008.
- Nagamine, 2000.

karatedō 空手道. *Karatedō* is a modern (twentieth-century) evolution of an Okinawan fighting art known variously as *karatejutsu*, *tōde,* or simply *te.* Many styles and branch systems have evolved in Japan, Okinawa, and other locations around the world since *karatedō* was first introduced publicly into Japan in the 1920s. Like modern *jūdō* and Shōrinji Kempō, its spiritual aims and lack of emphasis on weapons place it outside the realm of classical Japanese martial systems (*koryū bugei*) but firmly within the parameters of modern agonistic spiritual/sport systems (*gendai budō*). See: *Funakoshi Gichin; karate.*

karatedō shihan 空手道師範. A master of *karatedō*; a chief instructor of *karatedō.*

karategi 空手着. Similar to a *jūdōgi* or *keikogi*, the *karategi* is a cotton jacket worn by practitioners of *karate* and similar arts. The weight of the material is usually lighter than that used by *jūdō* practitioners or classical martial arts practitioners, and the color is normally white. See: *dōgi; keikogi; Kūshin Ryū; jūdōgi; uwagi.*

karatejutsu 唐手術 [Var. 空手術]. *Karatejutsu* is a modern (twentieth-century) term used to describe a number of civilian fighting systems (primarily pugilistic) that find their origins in Okinawa. Most of these systems were originally referred to as *tōde* (Oki. *tōdī*), or simply *te* (Oki. *tī*). However, under the influence of Japanese culture in the twentieth century, the practitioners of a number of the original Okinawan and Japanese derivative systems began referring to their practice as *karatejutsu.* See: *Funakoshi Gichin; karate; karatedō; Sakukawa Tōde.*

karateka 空手家. A proficient practitioner of *karate.*

karate kata 空手型. As prearranged combative forms, Okinawan *karate kata* have much more in common with their Chinese *wushu* antecedents than with Japan's classical martial systems. In general, unlike *kata* in classical Japanese martial systems, *karate kata* are normally performed solo, without weapons. A number of the *kata* dating from the nineteenth and twentieth centuries are practiced in divergent schools; consequently, they have evolved in different directions while retaining similar names. Some of these divergences date back to the proliferation of antecedent forms on the Chinese mainland in the eighteenth and nineteenth centuries; other changes were made after the forms entered (or were created in) Okinawa.

This state of affairs complicates any strict categorization of these forms. However, the recently published (2008) *Okinawa karate kobudō jiten* does provide several lists of *karate kata* that are broadly practiced in several of the major Okinawan *karate* lineages:

Karate ni sente nashi. 空手に先手なし. A maxim meaning "In *karate* there is no first attack." The normal explanation of this saying is that *karate* is for defense only. As a trainee progresses through the curriculum of any traditional *karate* school, this maxim may seem to present a contradiction, as the fighting system incorporates attack, defense, and combined tactics. However, as the practitioner becomes more experienced, this phrase can be seen as a riddle—in the sense of a zen *kōan*—with which the advanced trainee must grapple.

kara waza 唐技. Lit. "Chinese techniques." Term used by the Ryūei Ryū (2) 劉衛流 to indicate Chinese weapons forms.

karimata 雁股【鴈股】. See: *karimata ya.*

karimata ya 雁股矢【鴈股矢】[Abbr. ***karimata***]. An arrow with a forked arrowhead. See also: *ya no ne.*

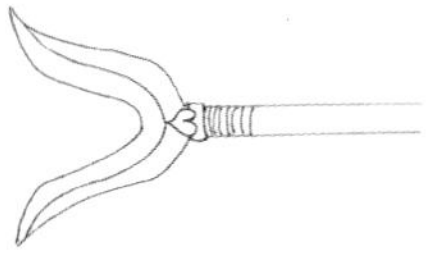

KARIMATA YA

karimusha 駆武者【驅武者】. Temporary warriors. In twelfth-century war tales, the term *karimusha* refers to warriors recruited on a short-term campaign basis. Although the Taira often used *karimusha*, they were apparently unreliable.

karō 家老. A term used from the Muromachi to Tokugawa periods to denote a high-ranking warrior such as a chief retainer or minister to a *daimyō*.

karumijutsu 軽身術 [A.k.a. ***tobikiri no jutsu*** 飛切り術]. Techniques used to "lighten" oneself for increased agility in jumping, dodging, etc.

Karura 迦楼羅 <Ch. Jialouluo <Skt. Garuḍa. 1. Japanese transliteration of the name of the Hindu deity Garuḍa. See: *Kinshichōō.* 2. ***karura*** 迦楼羅. One of the eight types of beings considered to be protectors of Buddhism. See: *Hachibu Shū.*

kasa 笠. A hat. See also: *jingasa; kawagasa.*

kasagake 笠掛 (Also read ***kasa kake***). Lit. "suspended hat." A type of archery contest engaged in by warriors of Japan's medieval period. A hat was suspended from a bamboo pole; mounted archers would try to pierce the hat with an arrow as they galloped by. During that age, *kasagake* was one of the "three equestrian archery contests" (*san kisha*) which had both a training and sportive purpose. See: *san kisha.*

kasajirushi 笠標. A device attached to the back of a helmet or hat to identify a warrior to his colleagues and allies. Commonly used during Japan's medieval period.

kasa kake 笠掛. See: *kasagake.*

kashi 樫. 1. An evergreen oak native to Japan and north central China. *Kashi* is the most popular wood used for training weapons in Japan, as it is very tough, plentiful, and resistant to splintering. The hands can therefore slide along the shaft of a weapon made of *kashi* without danger of picking up splinters. This wood was also used in shafts of weapons intended for battlefield use. The wood is normally seasoned only by the sweat of the handler. See: *akagashi; shirogashi.*

Kashima Chūko Ryū 鹿島中古流. See: *Kashima no Tachi.*

Kashima Jingū 鹿島神宮. Kashima Shrine, located northeast of Tōkyō in Ibaraki prefecture, was probably established sometime in the seventh century. It enshrines Takemikazuchi no Mikoto, a deity of the bow and arrow, and is a primary warrior shrine, being the tutelary shrine of Kashima Shintō Ryū, Jiki Shinkage Ryū, and many others. Classical martial arts demonstrations are held there several times a year. See also: *Kashima no Tachi; Katori Jingū; Tsukahara Bokuden; Tsurugaoka Hachimangū; Yasukuni Jinja.*

Kashima Jōko Ryū 鹿島上古流. See: *Kashima no Tachi.*

Kashima no Tachi 鹿島之太刀. A clan-based martial tradition (weapons systems, strategy, etc.) whose founding is attributed to Kuninazu no Mahito. According to the research into Kashima Shrine archives by the late Yoshikawa Kōichirō, sixty-fourth headmaster of Kashima Shintō Ryū, the Kashima no Tachi combative tradition dates back to the seventh century (Knutsen, 2009). At that time Kuninazu no

K

Mahito,[17] a "senior ritualist,"consecrated a small shrine close to Kashima Jingū. There he received a revelation referred to as both Ichi no Tachi (Hitotsu no Tachi) 一太刀 and Shimmyō Ken 神妙剣. According to Yahagi, legend states that Kuninazu no Mahito journeyed to the "high plane of heaven" (Takamagahara) "where this deep philosophy of 'Heavenly Swordsmanship' was revealed." (Knutsen, 2004: 25). If this is the case, the revelation on which Kashima no Tachi was founded is the earliest known in Japan.

In a 1979 interview with Meik Skoss, Yoshikawa Kōichirō clarified that Kuninazu no Mahito was a swordsman of note who was appointed to the post of lead guardian (*hafuribe*, who essentially functioned as chief of security) for Kashima Jingū. This was an important post, as Kashima Jingū was a major shrine with large land holdings. Mahito used his extensive knowledge of battlefield strategy and hand-to-hand combat, along with his revelation, to develop and organize a large body of combative technique and strategy in which he trained his shrine guards and his descendants, the Yoshikawa Urabe.

Mahito's system was passed on by succeeding generations of the Kashima clan. During the reign of Emperor Sutoku,[18] Kashima no Tachi came to be called Kashima Shichi Ryū 鹿島七流 (a.k.a. Kantō Shichi Ryū 関東七流), lit. the "Seven Traditions of Kashima" or the "Seven Traditions of the Kantō." These seven traditions were actually the seven families closely aligned with Kashima Shrine. Again according to Knutsen (2009), only two of the family names are known: the Yoshikawa (or Urabe) and the Matsumoto. The terms "Kashima Shichi Ryū" and "Kantō Shichi Ryū" are normally contrasted with contemporary combative traditions in the area of the capital in Kyōto, sometimes referred to as the Kyō Hachi Ryū 京八流, the "Eight Traditions of the Capital." See: *Kiichi Hōgan Ryū.*

Sometime between 1200 and 1400, during Japan's middle ages, Kashima no Tachi divided into two "trends": the Kashima Jōko Ryū 鹿島上古流 (the orthodox or "ancient age" trend) and the Kashima Chūko Ryū 鹿島中古流 (the "middle ages" trend). In the early 1500s, a martial genius by the name of Tsukahara Bokuden, hailing from the Yoshikawa/Urabe family, revised the Kashima Chūko Ryū into the Kashima Shintō Ryū 鹿島新当流, a classical martial tradition still practiced today on the grounds of Kashima Shrine.

Further reading in English:

• Knutsen, 2004.

Kashima Ōkami 鹿島大神. See: Takemikazuchi no Mikoto.

Kashima Shichi Ryū 鹿島七流 [A.k.a. ***Kantō Shichi Ryū*** 関東七流]. See: *Kashima no Tachi.*

Kashima Shinkage Ryū 鹿島神影流. See: *Kashima Shin Ryū.*

Kashima Shin Ryū 鹿島神流 [Var. ***Kashima Shinkage Ryū*** 鹿島神影流]. A classical martial tradition attributed to Matsumoto Bizen no Kami (1468–1524). A number of martial traditions trace their origins to this school.

Further reading in English:

• Friday and Seki, 1997.

KASHIMA SHIN RYŪ
Demonstration of spear technique (*sōjutsu*) at Kashima Jingū, 1979.
(Photograph courtesy John Driscoll)

Kashima Shinden Jiki Shinkage Ryū 鹿島神傳直心影流. Formal name for the Jiki Shinkage Ryū.

[17] Various dates are given for Kuninazu, ranging from the mid-fourth century to the mid-Heian period (c.1000 C.E.). From records at Kashima Jingū, Yoshikawa and Yahagi believed the mid-seventh century was the most accurate estimate.

[18] Sutoku Tennō 崇徳天皇 (1119–1164; r.1123–1142), seventy-fifth emperor of Japan.

Kashima Shinden Jiki Shinkage Ryū Reikenden 「鹿島神伝直心影流霊剣伝」【鹿島神傳靈劍傳】. See: *Reikenden.*

Kashima Shintō Ryū 鹿島新当流【鹿島新當流】. Founded by Tsukahara Bokuden in the early sixteenth century, the Kashima Shintō Ryū is one of the oldest surviving comprehensive field combat systems (*sōgo bujutsu*) in Japan. It encompasses several combative weapons systems, including swordsmanship (*kenjutsu*), long hardwood staff techniques (*bōjutsu*), long-hafted glaive arts (*naginatajutsu*), quick-draw sword arts (*iaijutsu*), spear techniques (*sōjutsu*), the use of small throwing blades and darts (*shurikenjutsu*), and others. The Kashima Shintō Ryū falls into the category of "positive" swordsmanship in that it emphasizes taking the initiative and closing with the enemy. It is the primary Shintō Ryū attached to Kashima Jingū in Ibaraki Prefecture (in contrast to the Katori Shintō Ryū, which is attached to Katori Jingū in Chiba Prefecture).

KASHIMA SHINTŌ RYŪ
Members of Kashima Shintō Ryū demonstrate Kuruma no Tachi (one of the Nanajō no Tachi) at Meiji Shrine, (Meiji Jingū), 1979
(Photograph by author)

Bokuden was born a member of the Yoshikawa family, who were the shrine guards and diviners of Kashima Jingū (*hafuribe*). He took the new family name of Tsukahara upon being adopted into that clan. In addition to the Kashima no Tachi of his birth family, he later learned the Tenshinshō-den Katori Shintō Ryū 天真正伝香取神道流 from his adoptive father. While engaging in *musha shugyō* (warrior pilgrimage and ascetic training), he received a vision or spiritual revelation from which he systematized the teaching of the Kashima area's local martial arts into a new system he christened the Kashima Shintō Ryū.[19]

Curriculum		Number of *kata*
Omote no Tachi	面の太刀	12
Chū Gokui	中極意	
• Nanajō no Tachi	七条ノ太刀	7
• Kasumi no Tachi	霞ノ太刀	7
• Ma no Tachi	間ノ太刀	3
Kōjō Okui Jikka no Tachi	高上奥位十箇ノ太刀	10
To no Mono Tachi	外之物太刀	12
Bōjutsu	棒術	8
Sōjutsu	槍術	
• (Basics)		6+
• Chūdan Yari no Shidai	中段槍之次第	9
• Jūni no Yari Kumi	拾二之槍組	12
Kōjō Sanka no Yari	高上三箇乃槍	3
Battōjutsu	抜刀術	
• Ten no Maki	天乃巻	21
• Chi no Maki	地乃巻	5

A number of additional *kata* are listed in the *Kashima shintō ryū heihō jikan shō* 「鹿島新當流兵法自観照」 transmission scroll (*densho*). See also: *Kashima no Tachi.*

Further reading in English:

• Knutsen, 2004: *passim.*

kashin 家臣. A retainer; a vassal.

kashiradate 頭立 [Also read ***zudate***]. An ornament located on the top of a helmet. See: *tatemono.*

kashiragane 頭金 [Var. ***heitō*** 柄頭]. The cap covering the pommel of a sword or knife. Its design often matches that of the metal collar (*fuchi*) on the opposite end of the hilt, and is usually made by the same artist.

Kashiwabuchi Yūgi 柏淵 有義 (c.1750–c.1830). A student of Masaki Toshimitsu, Kashiwabuchi composed and illustrated a five-volume work on the early field-combat arts of the Toda domain. This work, published in 1767, was entitled the *Geijutsu bukōron.* See also: *Kotōda Ha Ittō Ryū; Masaki Toshimitsu; Sen'i Ryū.*

kashiwa-de 拍手 [柏手]. SHINTŌ—The practice

[19] During his lifetime Bokuden evidently engaged in three *musha shugyō*, one lasting more than twenty years. See Knutsen, 2004: 224–229.

of clapping one's hands to gain the *kami's* attention when worshiping at a Shintō shrine. This practice is carried out in some training halls (*dōjō*) prior to training sessions.

kashō 和尚. See: *oshō.*

kassatsujutsu 活殺術 [Also read ***katsusatsujutsu***]. Lit. "techniques of life and death"; the assaulting of vital points. Watatani (1967: 30) notes that this term is the equivalent of both *atemi* and *genkotsu*.

kassei 活生. See: *kappō.*

Kasshin Ryū 勝新流 [Also read ***Katsu Shin Ryū***; a.k.a. ***Iga Ryū Ha Kasshin Ryū*** 為我流派勝新流]. *Jūjutsu* system derived from Iga Ryū (5) 為我流.

kasumi 霞. 1. *Kasumi* literally means a "haze" or "mist," with the implication of blurring or dimming the eyes. In many classical martial traditions (*koryū*), the term *kasumi* is used in the names of combative forms (*kata*) and postures (*kamae*), often indicating a technique which blinds or momentarily confuses the enemy, giving the proponent a moment of "invisibility." Consequently its meaning in martial terms is related to *kagerō* 陽炎 and *samidare* 五月雨.

In the twentieth-century Imperial Japanese Navy, the name *Kasumi* was given to an Asashio-class destroyer—an appropriate name, as one of the main tasks of destroyers was to screen larger craft such as aircraft carriers, cruisers, battleships, and troop carriers from enemy vessels. See also: *kagerō, samidare.* 2. JŪJUTSU—In various *jūjutsu* systems the term *kasumi* refers to a backhand strike or poke to the eyes intended to temporarily blind an opponent. See also: *metsubushi.* 3. MASAKI RYŪ—The term *kasumi* is used in *manrikigusarijutsu* to indicate a snapping strike to the face of an opponent with the weighted chain from the concealed *gohō no kamae* engagement posture. 4. An abbreviation for *kasumi no kamae*, a posture found in a number of classical weapons systems. There is a large variety of these. 5. SHINDŌ MŪSŌ RYŪ—*Kasumi* denotes a vital point on the head at the location of the temple.

kasumi no kamae 霞の構. 1. Many *ryū* use some sort of "*kasumi no kamae*" posture, generally with a weapon tip pointed between the eyes of an opponent. 2. SHINDŌ MŪSŌ RYŪ—an engagement posture in which the weapon and hands are held over the head, elbows bent, thumb joint of the forward hand lightly touching the forehead, the tip of the *jō* (*jōsaki*) pointed at *uto* (the vital point between the eyes).

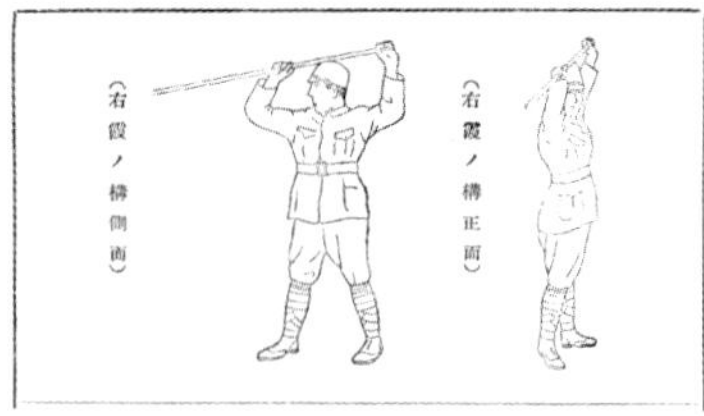

SHINDŌ MŪSŌ RYŪ
RIGHT-SIDE *KASUMI NO KAMAE*
(Illustration from *Jōdō Kyōhan* by Shimizu Takaji, 1940)

Kasumi no Naginata 霞之薙刀. KATORI SHINTŌ RYŪ—Third combative form of Katori Shintō Ryū's Omote no Naginata. See: *Tenshinshō-den Katori Shintō Ryū.*

Kasumi no Tachi 1. 霞ノ太刀. KASHIMA SHINTŌ RYŪ—The third set of combative forms in the Chūgokui *kenjutsu* curriculum.

Kasumi no Tachi 2. 神集之太刀. KATORI SHINTŌ RYŪ—The third combative form of Katori Shintō Ryū's Omote no Tachi. See: *Tenshinshō-den Katori Shintō Ryū.*

Kasumi Ryū 1. 霞流. See: *Kasumi Shintō Ryū.*

Kasumi Ryū 2. 霞流. A school of firearms (*hōjutsu*) founded around 1603 by Maruta Kyūzaemon Moritsugu after he had trained under Katagiri Sakon Shōyū.

Kasumi Shin Ryū 霞新流. Founded by Morikawa Buhei Takamasa, this was a branch line of the Seigō Ryū/Zuishin Ryū tradition. See Zuishin Ryū for lineage chart.

Kasumi Shintō Ryū 霞神道流 [Var. ***Kasumi Ryū*** 霞流; ***Shintō Kasumi Ryū*** 神道霞流]. Kasumi Shintō Ryū was a martial tradition with origins in both the Tenshinshō-den Katori Shintō Ryū and Kashima Shin(kage) Ryū. Founded by Makabe An'yaken Ujimoto, this school was a comprehensive martial system (*sōgō bujutsu*), but its specialty was combative swordsmanship (*kenjutsu*) and long staff arts (*bōjutsu*) which made use of a large polearm called an *ichiizue*.

Musō Gonnosuke, founder of the Shindō Musō Ryū, was a master of the Kasumi Shintō Ryū, having been licensed in it by Sakurai Ōsumi no Kami in the early 1600s. Gonnosuke travelled around Japan in the first decade of the seventeenth century, taking on all comers. He remained undefeated until his famous duel with Miyamoto Musashi. After this loss, Gonnosuke embarked on a period of self-training and spiritual austerities (*shugyō*) on Mount Homan (Homanzan) in Kyūshū. During his *shugyō*, he had a vision, and based upon this insight he created a new system relying on a smaller, more maneuverable weapon called the *jō*. He named his new school the Shindō Musō Ryū.

It is claimed by some that the twelve sword *kata* contained as the "Oku: Yatsu no Tachi Yotsu no Kodachi" in Shindō Musō Ryū today are derived from the Kasumi Shintō Ryū tradition practiced by Musō Gonnosuke. While this historical connection may be valid, the character of the current *kata* bears little resemblance to the antecedent Katori Shintō Ryū or Kashima Shin Ryū.

kata 1. 形 [Var. 型]. As prearranged combative forms, *kata* played a significant role in the training of the classical Japanese warrior. The earliest *kata* began to appear during the late Kamakura to early Muromachi periods, although little about them is known except a few of their names. *Kata*, in fact, are still being created today.

In the classical martial traditions (*koryū*) these combative forms varied greatly among the myriad traditions and, from an historical and hoplological perspective, not all *kata* were equal. Generally speaking, there were at least three categories of *kata* developed in the classical schools. One such category includes forms designed by warriors who, having survived battle and/or personal duels, encoded their successful strategies as prearranged combative scenarios; these were often seen as divinely inspired by a particular deity. The second type includes those created by warriors, most without battle experience, in the peaceful years of the Tokugawa shogunate or later. The third type of *kata* includes those extrapolated from earlier forms in order to teach basic and intermediate combative technique, or to cover variations in earlier combative scenarios. Many classical *ryū* existing today contain *kata* of all three types.

In the case of this first category, some warriors—martial geniuses—were able, in the midst of battle or at locations of spiritual power, to intuit and create highly effective strategies and tactics for combat. The strategies (*heihō*) were not simply techniques in the sense of manipulating a weapon. They were methods requiring psycho-physical perfection; a supreme synergy of body, breath, and mind in a unified whole. This synergy would enable the warrior to defeat an enemy with what might often appear to an observer as the simplest of movements. While these strategies may be analyzed cognitively, they were not designed constructions arrived at through normal cognition. Rather, they were intuited in the heat of battle, or as the culmination of exhaustive, protracted religious austerities. Furthermore, these strategies were neither applied through normal, cognitive consciousness nor taught through normal intellectual-pedagogical means. A master teacher passed them on to a disciple in a way that required the student to use intuition under stressful conditions; in several martial traditions this was accomplished in front of altars indicating a line of direct transmission from the divine.

These subtle strategies were not "taught" in an intellectual sense. Learning them required the disciple to use intuition based on years of experience and training. This teaching approach becomes clear when viewed in light of current studies in psychology. According to current research into intuition, people possess that special ability precisely because they have mastered a relatively narrow field of endeavor. The thousands of hours of effort the warrior devoted to train-

K

ing would have provided him with a large body of experience/knowledge which actually created a change in the way he thought and reasoned, giving him the ability to deal with larger "chunks" of internalized knowledge. The trainee could therefore make intuitive leaps in the midst of combat instead of taking a plodding, analytical approach to dealing with a dangerous enemy. In addition to cultivating intuition, training in these scenarios was aimed at developing a variety of other combative capabilities. (See: *bu no ri.*)

Finally, probably due to the influence of Buddhism—especially Rinzai Zen—many of these early classical *kata* were constructed, both in name and pedagogy, in the form of riddles. The Zen *kōan*, a teaching method popular in Rinzai Zen, was intended to force the student to intuit an answer under stressful situations. Some warriors, such as Kamiizumi Ise no Kami, took phrases directly from collections of Zen *kōan* and applied them as names of *kata*.

The second type of *kata*, which were created by samurai—some headmasters of older schools, some founders of new schools—were intended to have the same purpose as earlier forms. However, with the evolution of the warrior's art and capabilities during the peaceful years of the Tokugawa era, these forms often lack the depth and vigor of their Warring States–period predecessors.

The third type of *kata*, as noted above, often have no pretention of being battlefield-inspired. Many are limited to the repetitive teaching of specific techniques, and, during the mid to late Tokugawa period, were often aimed at success in sportive, competitive matches with other schools (*taryūjiai*). This type of *kata* is still being created today.

Further reading in English:

- Draeger, 1973a, 1973b, 1974.
- Hall, 1990: 344–353; 1997.
- Hayes, 1984a–1994.
- Leggett, 1985.
- Rosenbaum, 2005.

kata 2. 肩. The shoulder.

kataginu 肩衣. A stiff vest with protruding shoulders. When worn with *hakama*, it formed an outfit called a *kamishimo*.

Katagiri Sakon Shōyū 片桐 左近 少輔. Katagiri was a specialist in firearms (*hōjutsu*). His best-known student, Maruta Kyūzaemon Moritsugu, founded the Kasumi Ryū (1) 霞流.

katakama yari 片鎌槍. Lit. "single-sickle spear." The unusual L-shaped spearhead of the *katakama yari* is basically a straight-bladed spear (*suyari*) intersected horizontally by a blade with the point turning back on one side (either toward the tip of the spear or away from it). There may also be a very short blade on the opposite side. See also: *kamayari; sōjutsu; yari.*

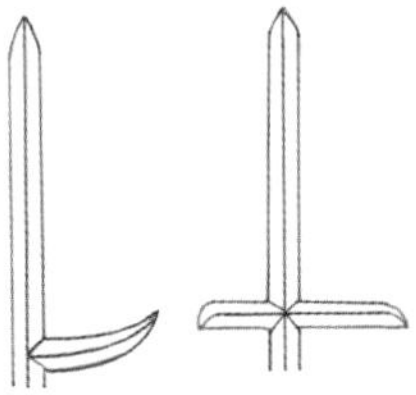

TWO EXAMPLES OF *KATAKAMA YARI*

kataki 敵 [Also read ***teki***; var. 仇]. An opponent; an enemy.

katakiuchi 敵討 [A.k.a. ***adauchi*** 仇討]. A vendetta. A *katakiuchi* was often a violent, formal affair. Its aim was to restore warrior honor (*na* or *menboku*) which had been damaged by a defeat or insult.

Further reading in English:

- Varley, 1994: 33–34.

Katame no Kata 固めの形. KŌDŌKAN JŪDŌ—Lit. "grappling forms." A category of Kōdōkan Jūdō *kata*. See: *Kōdōkan Jūdō; katame waza (1); Randori no Kata.*

katame waza 1. 固め技. a. Grappling techniques as may be found in certain *jūjutsu* systems. b. KŌDŌKAN JŪDŌ—In Kōdōkan Jūdō, *katame waza* are categorized as grappling techniques. These fall into three categories: hold-down or pinning techniques (*osaekomi waza*), strangling techniques (*shime waza*), and joint techniques (*kansetsu waza*). See also: *Kanō Jigorō; Katame no Kata; Kōdōkan Jūdō; Tenshin Shin'yō Ryū.*

katame waza 2. 固術. The hold-down/pinning techniques (*katame waza*) of the Ishikawa Hōzan Ryū 石川宝山流.

katana 刀. A curved longsword with a single cutting edge and less curvature (*sori*) than a *tachi*. In contrast to the *tachi*, the *katana* is usually worn cutting-edge-up. While *tachi* and *katana* have very similar blades, they are normally signed on opposite sides of the tang, so that the swordsmith's signature faces outward when the blade is worn.

During Japan's Muromachi period there was a shift away from cavalry tactics—many of which utilized *tachi*—to infantry tactics. This required a new type of swordsmanship and a new type of sword. Consequently there was also a shift to a new, less curved sword called the *uchigatana* 打刀 (or *katana* 刀).

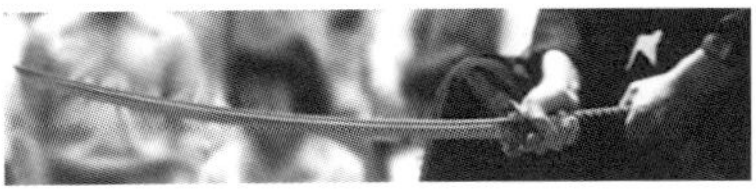

KATANA

Due to its comparatively straight blade, the *katana* was better suited for infantry cut-and-thrust use than the *tachi*. The blades for both *katana* and *tachi* were normally in the range of 25 to 30 inches (60–75 cm) long.

SWORD WORN IN *KATANA* STYLE
Ōtake Risuke at Kashima Jingū, 1979
(Photograph courtesy Jon Driscoll)

katanagari 刀狩 [A.k.a. ***Taikō katanagari*** 太閤刀狩; also read ***Taikō no katanagari***]. A famous "sword hunt" ordered in 1588 by Toyotomi Hideyoshi, who was then the imperial regent (*kampaku*). The purpose of the sword hunt was to disarm peasants, Buddhist monks, and other civilians who had exhibited a propensity toward armed rebellion during the fifteenth and sixteenth centuries. See also: *ikki; Ikkō Ikki; kuni ikki; tsuchi ikki.*

Further reading in English:

- Berry, 1982: 102–106 *ff.*
- Sansom, 1961: 331–333 *ff.*

katana kaji 刀鍛冶 [Abbr. *kaji* 鍛冶]. A swordsmith.

katana kake 刀掛 [Var. 刀懸]. See: *kake.*

katana kizu 刀疵. A sword wound. See also: *tōshō.*

katana togishi 刀研師. A sword polisher, also called a *togimonoshi*. Often abbreviated as *togishi.*

Further reading in English:

- Takaiwa *et al.* (2006).

Katayama Hōki no Kami Fujiwara no Hisayasu 片山 伯耆守 藤原久安 [A.k.a. ***Tōjirō*** 藤次郎; ***Katsujirō*** 勝次郎] (1574–1650 or 1561–1637). Founder of the Katayama Hōki Ryū. Katayama was a disciple (*deshi*) of Hayashizaki Jinsuke Shigenobu, the founder of Shinmusō Hayashizaki Ryū and the legendary creator of the art of the quick-draw sword (*iaijutsu*). However, legend also has it that Katayama first learned a secret family transmission of eighteen quick-draw sword techniques from his uncle, Shōan.[20] New Year's

Day of 1596 found Katayama in prayer at Mount Atago shrine in Kyōto,[21] where he underwent an awakening experience (*meigo*) centered on the ideogram *kan* 貫. At that point he named his combative system Ikkan Ryū 一貫流. However, later generations have referred to the tradition with a variety of terms (see entry on Katayama Hōki Ryū below).

Katayama's system was very influential, and he taught swordsmanship to a number of notable figures of the late sixteenth and early seventeenth centuries. Watatani and Yamada (1978:186–188) list eleven direct disciples of Katayama and numerous lines and branches of his tradition (*ryū*).

20 The name Shōan 松庵 indicates that Katayama's uncle was a warrior who had taken Buddhist vows.

21 This shrine has long been a popular pilgrim destination near Kyōto. See Bouchy, 1987.

K

Katayama Hōki Ryū 片山伯耆流. System of combative swordsmanship (*kenjutsu*) and quick-draw sword arts (*iaijutsu*) founded by Katayama Hōki no Kami Fujiwara no Hisayasu. Originally called Ikkan Ryū 一貫流 by Katayama, later generations have referred to the tradition with a variety of terms including Katayama Hōki Ryū 片山伯耆流, Battō Hōki Ryū 抜刀伯耆流, (abbreviated as both Hōki Ryū 伯耆流 and Katayama Ryū 片山流), and others. The system has also been called Shin Ryū (written both as 神流 and 真流). See also: *Shin Musō Hayashizaki Ryū.*

Katayama Ryū 片山流. System of swordsmanship (*kenjutsu*) and quick-draw sword arts (*iaijutsu*) founded by Katayama Hōki no Kami Fujiwara no Hisayasu. There are many variant names. See: *Katayama Hōki Ryū.*

Katayama Tomotarō 片山 智太郎. See: *Shinkage Ryū (5).*

katchū 甲冑 [Also read ***kōchū***]. Lit. "armor and helmet." 1. Armor. 2. Abbr. for *katchū bujutsu.*

Katayama Hōki Ryū
片山伯耆流
(abbreviated lineage)

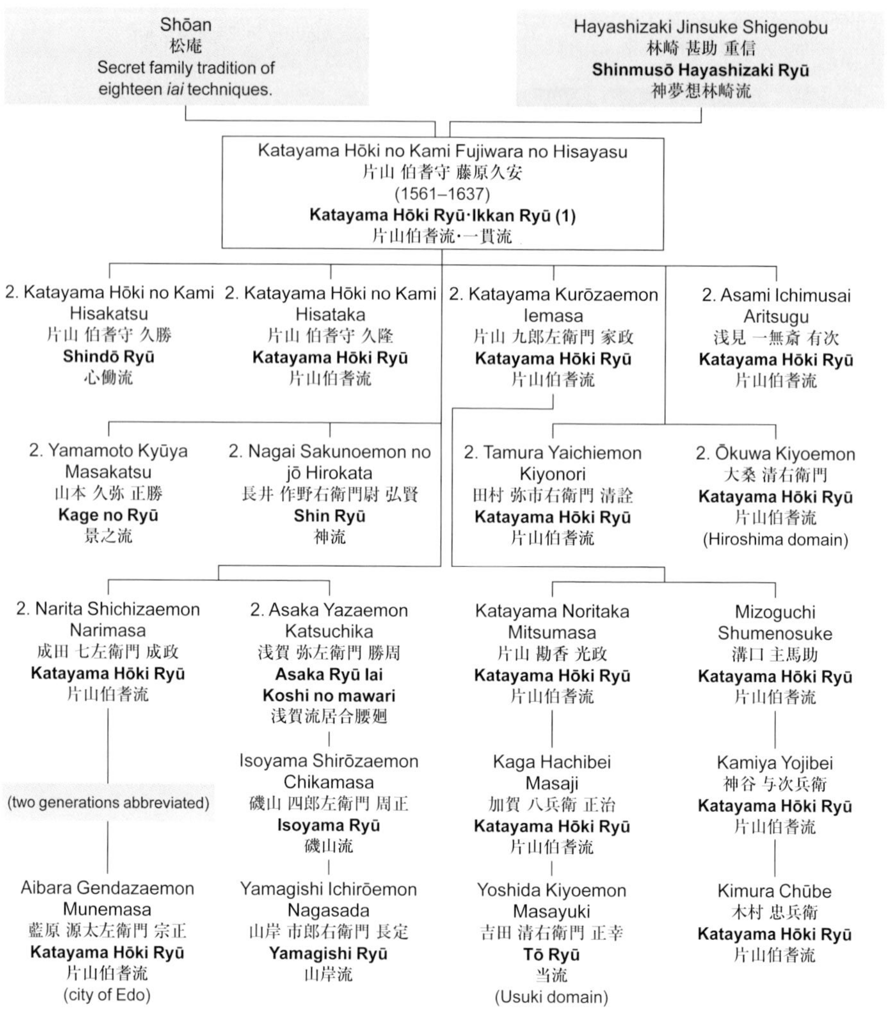

3. Abbr. for *katchūden*. ¶ *Katchū ni shin o katameru* 甲冑に身を固める, to be fully armed; to be armored.

katchū bujutsu 甲冑武術. 1. Martial techniques practiced in armor. 2. Systems in which the exponents are typically dressed in armor. See also: *yoroi kumiuchi.*

katchūden 甲冑伝【甲冑傳】[Also read ***kōchūden***]. Training in the use of armor. See: *Ichizen Ryū.*

katchū kempō 甲冑剣法【甲冑劍法】. Lit. "armored swordsmanship." YAGYŪ SHINKAGE RYŪ—This term is used when referring to the original *kata* of the Shinkage Ryū tradition (*honden*) when practiced in their armored form. In the Yagyū Shinkage Ryū *katchū kempō* is synonymous with "old transmission" (*koden*), and is another term for armored swordsmanship (*kaisha kempō*).

katchūshi 甲冑師. An armorer.

KAMBE TAKEYASU (SEATED) AND KATŌ ISAO
Seventh- and eighth-generation headmaster, respectively, of the Owari Kan Ryū
(Photograph courtesy Hunter Armstrong)

Katen 火天. <Ch. Huotian <Skt. Agni. In Indian mythology Agni is the god of fire, an "elemental" spirit. One of twelve guardian deities adopted from Brahmanism by Buddhism. See: *Jūniten.*

katō 裹頭. Head cowls typically associated with Tendai warrior monks. (See illustration under *sōhei* [1].)

Katō Isao 加藤 伊三男 (b. 1934). Current (eighth-generation) headmaster of the Owari Kan Ryū and the Kambe line of Owari Yagyū Shinkage Ryū.

Katō Kiyomasa 加藤 清正 (1562–1611). A general and *daimyō* under Toyotomi Hideyoshi. Kiyomasa lost his father at the age of three. As his mother was related to Hideyoshi's mother, Kiyomasa was raised and educated by that family. In his twenties he quickly rose in status as a warrior among Toyotomi Hideyoshi's troops. Along with Konishi Yukinaga, he commanded the vanguard of the Korean expedition in 1592, and later returned to Korea when hostilities broke out in 1597. In Korea his aggressiveness and skill caused his enemies to nickname him Kishōkan (Devil General).

Upon returning to Japan after Hideyoshi's death in 1598, he sided with Tokugawa Ieyasu, and was generously rewarded. However, his death in 1611 is suspicious; it may have been orchestrated by Ieyasu, who evidently feared Kiyomasa would side with Toyotomi Hideyori, Hideyoshi's son.

One of Kiyomasa's key retainers, who evidently contributed much to his lord's strategic success in battle, was Migumo Shinemon, founder of the Migumo Ryū 三雲流, a school of strategy and tactics specializing in espionage (*gunkai*).

Further reading in English:
- Wilson, 1982: 127–132.

Katori Jingū 香取神宮. Katori Shrine, located east of Tōkyō in Chiba prefecture, enshrines Futsunushi no Kami, a deity of the sword. Primarily a warrior shrine, Katori Jingū is the tutelary shrine of Tenshinshō-den Katori Shintō Ryū and several other martial traditions. Classical martial arts demonstrations are held there on special occasions. See also: *Iizasa Chōisai Ienao; Kashima Jingū; Katori no Ken; Tsurugaoka Hachimangū; Yasukuni Jinja.*

Katori no Ken 香取之剣【香取之劍】. A clan-based martial culture (comprising weapons systems, strategy, and other disciplines) which originated in the area of Katori Jingū. These various elements were organized into the Tenshinshō-den Katori Shintō Ryū by Iizasa Ienao in 1446.

K

Katori Shintō Ryū 香取神道流. See: *Tenshinshōden Katori Shintō Ryū.*

katsu 活 [Var. ***kappō*** 活法]. Lit. "life." 1. Resuscitation. 2. An abbreviation for *kappō*.

katsujinken 活人剣【活人劍】[Also read ***katsuninken***]. Lit. "life-giving sword." 1. The concept of *katsujinken*, taken from the *Hekigan Roku*, was promoted by Kamiizumi Nobutsuna, founder of the Shinkage Ryū 新陰流. Various sword schools, notably Ittō Ryū, have variant definitions of this term. See: *setsunintō katsujinken.* 2. SHUGENDŌ—The term *katsujinken* is often used for the sword carried by the *yamabushi*.

katsujinken setsunintō 活人剣 殺人刀【活人劍殺人刀】. See: *setsunintō katsujinken.*

Katsu Kaishū 勝 海舟 (1823–1899) [A.k.a. ***Awa Katsu*** 安房勝; ***Kaishū*** 海舟; ***Rintarō*** 麟太郎; ***Yoshikuni*** 義邦]. A Jiki Shinkage Ryū swordsman, philosopher, retainer of the Tokugawa shogunate, Japanese naval officer, and statesman in the Meiji government.

Although he was not designated as a successor to headmastership of the Jiki Shinkage Ryū, Katsu Kaishū was a swordsman of note. He is credited with founding the Japanese navy, and was instrumental in saving thousands of lives by negotiating an end to hostilities in Edo when the Tokugawa shogunate fell in 1868.

Like his father Katsu Kokichi, Kaishū devoted his formative years to rigorous training in the Jiki Shinkage Ryū. He studied under thirteenth headmaster Odani Nobutomo and one of Odani's senior students, Shimada Toranosuke. He also devoted an extensive amount of time to the study of Zen, and later attributed his ability to survive the revolution to this discipline. Kaishū was also very forward-thinking, and cultivated some of the young rebels who would later overthrow the Tokugawa shogunate. He even commanded the first Tokugawa ship, the *Kanrin Maru*, which sailed to San Francisco in 1860. In 1868, as thousands of imperial troops under the command of Saigō Takamori were set to attack Edo Castle, Kaishū put his life at risk in order to negotiate a peaceful resolution. This facilitated the avoidance of a protracted civil war, saved many lives, and helped prevent colonization of Japan by Western powers.

Further reading in English:

- Hillsborough, 1999; 2001.
- Craig, 1988.

KATSU KAISHŪ
c. 1860

Katsu Kokichi 勝 小吉 (1802–1850). A Jiki Shinkage Ryū swordsman and low-ranking retainer (*hatamoto*) of the Tokugawa shogunate. Kokichi was also the father of Katsu Kaishū.

A very skilled swordsman by his late teens, Kokichi trained under Dannō Gennoshin Yoshitaka, twelfth headmaster of the Jiki Shinkage Ryū, and with the top swordsmen in various branches of that system. He apparently trained in strategy and swordsmanship under Hirayama Kōzō, who also taught strategy to Odani Nobutomo. Kokichi traveled throughout Japan on several different martial pilgrimages (*musha shugyō*), defeating most of his opponents. However, he was no paragon of virtue, nor did he exemplify a "balanced mixture of cultural and martial learning" (*bun bu ryōdō*). In fact, as Teruko Craig points out in her translation of his biography, he was "neither a scholar nor an administrator, and certainly not a model of feudal loyalty." He twice ran away from home, had endless troubles finding official employment, and was even placed in a cage for several years by his family in order to control his unbendable spirit.

All of this is recorded by Kokichi himself in an autobiography entitled *Musui dokugen* 『夢酔独言』(A monologue by Musui). "Musui," Kokichi's pen name, literally means "intoxicated by dreams" or "dream-besotted." It is a revealing document of daily life in early nineteenth-century Japan before the arrival of Commodore Perry. See also: *Jiki Shinkage Ryū; Katsu Kaishū; Shimada Toranosuke.*

Further reading in English:

- Craig, 1988.

katsusatsujutsu 活殺術. See: *kassatsujutsu.*

Katsu Shin Ryū 勝新流. See: *Kasshin Ryū.*

KAWAGASA
Early 1800s
(Photo courtesy Cowan's Auctions, Inc.)

kawagasa 革笠. A lacquered leather helmet worn by low-ranking retainers during the Tokugawa period. See also: *jingasa; kasa.*

Kawakami Ryū 川上流. A martial system specializing in the use of the spear (*sōjutsu*) and an art called "broken spear" (*hoko ore* 戟折). *Hoko ore* was evidently used if the spear blade became broken from the shaft. (This was apparently a common occurrence when dueling or battling spear against spear.) Not simply a few last-ditch techniques, the art was apparently so well constructed that Watatani and Yamada (1978: 203) classify it as a long hardwood staff art (*bōjutsu*). In Bishū, the Kawakami Ryū became incorporated into both Seigō Ryū 制剛流 and Ikkan Ryū (3) 一貫流.

Kawanishi Mikonosuke 川西 神子助 (1899–1969). A Japanese *jūjutsu/jūdō* practitioner who taught *jūjutsu* and *aiki-jūjutsu* in the U.S., England, and France. He spent many years in France (1936–1939; c.1950–1969) teaching a modified version of *jūjutsu/jūdō*. Kawanishi is sometimes credited with establishing the colored belt system for identifying rank in *jūdō* that later spread to the whole international *jūdō* establishment. In 1955 he published a book on his system entitled *My Method of Judo*.

Further reading in English:

- Lowry, 2006: 52.
- Papenfuss, 1997.

Kawasaki Jirōdayū Munekatsu 川崎 次郎太夫 宗勝 (c.1620–c.1680). Kawasaki was an eighth-generation successor in Tōgun Ryū 東軍流 who taught the system to Izawa Genta Zaemon Ryōeki. Sometime during the Kanbun era (1661–1673) Izawa adapted the Tōgun Ryū teachings into his own eclectic system he called Izawa Ryū 伊沢流.

Kawashima Takashi 川島 堯 (c.1885–c.1956). JIKI SHINKAGE RYŪ—Recognized as sixteenth headmaster of the Jiki Shinkage Ryū 直心影流 through Yamada Jirokichi's line. See also: *Jiki Shinkage Ryū.*

KAWASHIMA TAKASHI
Sixteenth-generation headmaster of the Jiki Shinkage Ryū
(Photograph courtesy Namiki Yasushi)

kawa tabi 革足袋. Socks (*tabi*) made of tanned leather.

kayaku 火薬【火藥】. Gunpowder.

kazari 飾. Lit. "adornment," "decoration." 1. SHINDŌ MŪSŌ RYŪ—An alternate name for the beginning and ending formalities (*reihō*) in Shindō Musō Ryū training. Although sometimes used in a somewhat pejorative or disdainful sense, its Buddhist origins indicate respect. See also: *Fujisan and Reihō.* 2. SHINKAGE RYŪ—Several *densho* within the various Shinkage Ryū traditions deal with the "adornment" of a *dōjō* for a ritual or votive purposes.[22]

---

[22] See, for example, *Shinkage Ryū dōjō sōgon gishiki kumotsutō no koto*「新陰流道場荘厳儀式供物等之事」in Imamura (1967, vol. 2: 404–405).

Kazumichi no Tai 和満の体. A prearranged combative form (*kata*) of the Kagemasa Ryū 陰政流.

kazunuki 数抜【數拔】. Lit. "counting draws." *Kazunuki* is a special practice followed in the Tatsumi Ryū 立身流 in which the exponents draw their blade 3,000 times in one day, or 10,000 times over a three-day period.

Further reading in English:

• Keely, 1997.

kebiishi 検非違使【檢非違使】. A term meaning "investigator" or "police inspector." Before the thirteenth century, the *kebiishi* were somewhat equivalent in function to capital police. They were organized sometime between 815 and 834 (the actual date is unclear), but only came into full operation in 895. Their duties included criminal arrests, arbitration of disputes, tax collection, guard duty, seizure of property for the government, and "challenging a person for wearing clothing or using a cart improper to his or her station." (Farris, 1992: 167). Most administrators (*jō*) in the *kebiishi* were not of warrior lineage. However, the two levels below administrator—secretary (*sakon*) and clerk (*fushō*)—were sometimes filled from the warrior class. Furthermore, when arresting criminals, *kebiishi* sometimes took along private retainers. In the tenth and eleventh centuries the *kebiishi* shared guard, police, and military duties in the capital of Kyōto with imperial guards (Efu) and the private-sector semi-aristocratic warriors (*shoka no heishi*). During the twelfth century they became stronger due to appointments by the court from the Taira and Minamoto families. However, after Minamoto no Yoritomo became *shōgun* in 1192, he began to assign policing duties to the *daimyō* in their respective domains, and the office of the *kebiishi* (the Kebiishi Chō) began to decline in power and responsibility. In the Ashikaga period, the term came to be used for provincial warrior police officials.

Kebiishi Chō 検非違使庁【檢非違使廳】. The office of the *kebiishi*; the Kyōto Metropolitan Police Office.

kei 桂. See: *keima.*

keibatsu 刑罰. A penalty; a judgment or punishment.

keibō 警棒. A modern wooden police baton.

keibōjutsu 警棒術. See: *keibō sōhō.*

keibō sōhō 警棒操法. The modern art of the police baton. The *keibō* techniques of the Tōkyō Kidōtai (riot police) were originally derived from Ikkaku Ryū *juttejutsu* and Uchida Ryū *suttekijutsu.*

Further reading in English:

• Draeger, 1974: 72–73 *ff.*

Kei Dō Shin 軽道真. Yondan-level combative forms taught by the Jigen Ryū. See: *Jigen Ryū; Yondan (2).*

keigoshi 警固使. A tenth-century term for "watch guards" assigned by the court to the ports of Yamazaki and Kawajiri in 936. Their purpose was to guard against pirates led by the notorious Fujiwara Sumitomo.

keijō 警杖. A medium-length hardwood staff, about 4 feet (1.2 m) long, used primarily for crowd control by the modern Japanese police. It closely resembles the Shindō Musō Ryū *jō*, from which it was derived.

keijōjutsu 警杖術. The combative art of the medium-length hardwood staff used by the modern Japanese police. The *keijōjutsu* techniques of the Tōkyō Kidōtai (riot police) were originally extrapolated from Shindō Musō Ryū *jōjutsu* by Shimizu Takaji in 1931.

Further reading in English:

• Draeger, 1974: 68–69 *ff.*

keiketsu 経穴【經穴】[Also read ***tsubo***; a.k.a. ***maketsu*** 麻穴]. 1. An acupuncture point. 2. TENSHIN SHIN'YO RYŪ—An alternate term for a vital point; a pressure point. (Minouchi, 1982: 15.) See also: *kyūsho.*

keiko 稽古. Lit. "traditional (form) practice." A training session; martial training.

keikō 挂甲. Chainmail armor worn by combatants in the early sixth century.

keikoba 稽古場. A training "place." In contrast to a *dōjō*, a *keikoba* is a place for practicing that is not necessarily a formally prepared location. It can be located inside or outside.

keikogi 稽古着 [Var. ***uwagi*** 上着]. The upper portion (jacket) of the training outfit now worn by practitioners of classical martial traditions and modern *kendō*. The *keikogi* is made of medium-weight cotton and is normally colored dark blue or black. White versions are also common in some traditions. See: *dōgi; karategi; jūdōgi; uwagi.*

Further reading in English:

• Lowry, 2006: 35–61.

keiko naginata 稽古薙刀 [A.k.a. ***shiai naginata*** 試合薙刀]. A training glaive composed of a wooden shaft and a split bamboo blade. It is used in the practice of *atarashii naginata.* See: *atarashii naginata.*

keiko yari 稽古槍 [A.k.a. ***tanpo yari*** たんぽ槍]. A training spear with a padded tip.

keima 桂馬 [Abbr. as ***kei*** 桂]. SHŌGI—Lit. "laurelled horse." In the strategic game of *shōgi*, the *keima* is somewhat equivalent to the knight in Western chess.

Keishichō Ryū 警視庁流【警視廳流】[Abbr. ***Keishi Ryū*** 警視流]. The name given by the police commission of 1886 to a new combative system which included a set of ten paired sword forms (*kumitachi kata*) and five quick-draw sword forms (*iai kata*). Although formulated by the police commission, the *kumitachi* forms were drawn from ten classical *ryū* as follows:

Kata Name	School of Origin
1. Hassō 八相	Jiki Shinkage Ryū 直心影流
2. Henka 変化	Kurama Ryū 鞍馬流
3. Hattengiri 八天切	Tsutsumi Hōzan Ryū 堤宝山流
4. Makiotoshi 巻落	Tatsumi Ryū 立身流
5. Gedan no Tsuki 下段の突	Hokushin Ittō Ryū 北辰一刀流
6. A Un 阿吽	Asayama Ichiden Ryū 浅山一伝流
7. Ichini no Tachi 一二の太刀	Jigen Ryū 示現流
8. Uchiotoshi 打落	Shindō Munen Ryū 神道無念流
9. Hasetsu 破折	Yagyū Ryū 柳生流
10. Kuraizume 位詰	Kyōshin Meichi Ryū 鏡新明智流

This selection also came to be called the Keishichō Ryū Kendō Kata.

The Keishichō Ryū *iai* forms were also taken from classical *ryū*:

Kata Name	School of Origin
1. Zen'etsu 前越	Asayama Ichiden Ryū 浅山一伝流
2. Musōgaeshi 夢相返し	Shindō Munen Ryū 神道無念流
3. Mawarigake 廻り掛	Tamiya Ryū 田宮流
4. Migi no teki 右の敵	Kyōshin Meichi Ryū 鏡新明智流
5. Shihō 四方	Tatsumi Ryū 立身流

Ranking for proficiency was given in an early *kyū–dan* system which paralleled classical licenses, with the first class (*ikkyu*) being most advanced:

First class (*ikkyū* 一級) = Master (*meijin* 名人)
Second class (*nikyū* 二級) = Full license (*menkyo kaiden* 免許皆伝)
Third class (*sankyū* 三級) = List (*mokuroku* 目録)
Fourth class (*yonkyū* 四級) = Certificate (*kirigami* 切紙)
Fifth class (*gokyū* 五級)
Sixth class (*rokkyū* 六級)
Seventh class (*nanakyū* 七級)

See: *iaijutsu; Nihon Kendō Kata.*

Keishichō Ryū Kendō Kata 警視庁流剣道型【警視廳流劍道型】. See: *Keishichō Ryū.*

Keishi Ryū 警視流. An abbreviation of Keishichō Ryū.

kekka fuza 結跏趺坐 <Ch. *jiejia fuzuo* <Skt. *nyaṣīdat paryaṅkam ābhujya*. BUDDHISM—A term for the "lotus" sitting posture, in which the legs are crossed with the each foot on the opposite thigh. In Esoteric Buddhism, this sitting position is called *rengeza* (lotus posture).

kembu 剣舞【劍舞】[Also read ***kenbu***]. A sword dance. Knutsen and Knutsen (2004: 111) note that while these sword and spear dances were "performed by warriors to encourage 'spirit,'" they were originally performed "to entertain the deities."

K

Kempi 拳匪 <Ch. Quanfei. See: *Giwadan; Giwaken.*

Kempi no Ran 拳匪乱【拳匪亂】<Ch. Quanfei Luan. China's Boxer Rebellion, 1898–1901. See: *Giwadan; Giwaken.*

kempō 1. 剣法 【劍法】[Also read ***kenpō***]. Swordsmanship; the art of fencing; combat via swordsmanship.

kempō 2. 拳法 [Also read ***kenpō***] <Ch. *quanfa*. Lit. "fist method." *Kempō* (2) refers to combat, primarily involving the use of fists or other body parts for striking. This Japanese term usually refers to systems based on or thought to have been influenced by Chinese combative arts methods (Ch. *quanfa*). While these Chinese systems concentrate on use of hands, knees, feet, and so on as "weapons," they may also include implements such as sword, spear, and staff.

Kempō Ryū 憲法流. See: *Yoshioka Ryū.*

kempō iai 剣法居合【劍法居合】. See: *iai kempō; Suiō Ryū.*

ken 1. 剣【劍; 劒】<Ch. *jian* [Also read ***tsurugi***]. a. In the latter half of the first millennium C.E., the most common type of sword used in Japan was the straight sword, or *ken*. Two types of these were imported from the Asian mainland: the *tsurugi*, which had a double cutting edge, and the single-edged *tachi*. The oldest swords found in burial mounds and tombs are of the *ken* type. b. A general term for sword. c. A term used in compound words to indicate combative swordsmanship (*kenjutsu*) or sportive fencing (*kendō*). d. A prearranged combative scenario (*kata*) focusing on the sword. e. A counting word for sword-oriented combative scenarios (*kata*); e.g., *jūyon ken* 十四剣 (fourteen sword techniques).

ken 2. 懸. Lit. "attack," "fall upon." a. YAGYŪ SHINKAGE RYŪ—A mental state in which one's mind is in "attack mode," ready to assault the enemy single-mindedly (*isshin*), strongly, and immediately. b. YAGYŪ SHINKAGE RYŪ—A physical state in which one moves toward the enemy for an attack. Contrast to *tai* 待. See: *Kuka no Tachi; Sangakuen no Tachi.*

ken 3. 拳 [Often read ***kem~*** in compound words]. This term, which means "fist," is found in many compounds; e.g., *kempō* 拳法 ("fist method"; boxing).

kenbu 剣舞【劍舞】. See: *kembu.*

kendō 剣道【劍道】. Lit. the "way of the sword," *kendō* was one of the earliest "martial ways" (*budō*) to appear. In the early Edo period, swordsmen such as Miyamoto Musashi began using the term *ken no michi* 剣の道 to indicate the evolution of a spiritual emphasis in their pursuit of perfection via swordsmanship. By the late 1600s schools such as the Abe Ryū were using the term *kendō* 剣道 to indicate a similar shift in emphasis. During the 1700s the movement away from an emphasis on field combat, in combination with the evolution of protective gear, inspired the development of competitive matches called *uchikomigeiko*, and accelerated the trend toward a more popular competitive, sportive version of classical Japanese fencing. Many schools contributed to this evolution, including the Jiki Shinkage Ryū, the Hokushin Ittō Ryū, various branches of the Nen Ryū, and others.

With the end of the Tokugawa period in 1867 and the dissolution of the samurai class, many martial traditions simply disappeared. If not for the promotional efforts of former samurai like Sakakibara Kenkichi (fourteenth headmaster of the Jiki Shinkage Ryū) and others, *kendō* and a number of other classical martial disciplines might have been lost as well. Furthermore, in 1876 the Satsuma Rebellion occurred, in which thousands of samurai revolted, using swords as their primary weapon. This uprising forced the Japanese government—particularly the police and the military—to see the necessity of including swordsmanship training in their curriculum. Consequently the police commission of 1886 created a standardized training curriculum which included *kendō*-like *shinaigeiko* and paired and solo sword forms (*kata*). Paralleling this development, the Butokukai created a commission to form its own system of *kata* and competitive match rules in 1906.This project, which was completed in 1912, resulted in the creation of the Imperial Japanese Kendō Forms (Dai

Nippon Teikoku Kendō Kata 大日本帝国剣道形). (See: *Keishichō Ryū and Nihon Kendō Kata*).

Kendō continued to evolve, and by the early part of the twentieth century had become an intrinsic element of the Japanese school system. Today it is practiced by thousands of enthusiasts all over the world.

Further reading in English:

- Dann, 1978.
- Draeger, 1974: 77–111.
- Sasamori & Warner, 1964.

kendōgi 剣道着【劍道着】. The *kendōgi* is the jacket (a.k.a. *uwagi*) portion of a *kendō* training outfit. It is also called a *keikogi* (training jacket). *Kendōgi* are generally made of medium-weight blue-dyed cotton, but may be also be black, white, or dyed with a simple geometric pattern.

kendōgu 剣道具【劍道具】[Abbr. ***dōgu***]. Protective equipment used in *kendō* training. These items generally include a mask (*men*), chest/abdomen protector (*dō*), waist/hip protector (*tare*), and gauntlets to protect the hands and forearms (*kote*). All of these items have counterparts in classical Japanese armor (*yoroi*).

kendōjō 剣道場【劍道場】. A *kendō* training hall.

kendōka 剣道家【劍道家】. A proficient practitioner of *kendō*.

Kendō Renmei jōdō seiteigata 剣道連盟杖道制定形. See: *Zen Nippon Kendō Renmei jōdō seiteigata*.

ken'en 軒轅. See: *nokizaru*.

kengeki 剣劇【劍劇】. A melee drama; a swordplay movie. See: *chambara; jidaigeki; shuraba; tate (2)*.

kengi 剣技【劍技】. Sword technique.

kengō 剣豪【劍豪】. A strong, skillful swordsman.

Kengō Shōgun 剣豪将軍【劍豪將軍】. Nickname given to *shōgun* Ashikaga Yoshiteru due to his involvement in martial arts training alongside the famous swordsmen of the mid-1500s. See: *Ashikaga Yoshiteru*.

ke'nin 家人. A retainer. This medieval term indicates a retainer of any lord, in contrast to the term *gokenin*, which referred to retainers of the Kamakura shogunate. The literal meaning of both terms is essentially the same; that is, "house man."

kenjō 謙仗. A tenth-century term for "soldier," used in northern Kyūshū.

kenjū 拳銃. Lit. "fist gun," "hand gun." A pistol; a handgun.

kenjutsu 剣術【劍術】. "Combative sword arts." *Kenjutsu* was a central weapons system in over 2,000 classical combative schools (*koryū*). Even those schools that did not specialize in *kenjutsu* often included sword techniques against which to apply their own weapons systems. See also: *tōjutsu*.

kenjutsuka 剣術家【劍術家】. A proficient practitioner of *kenjutsu*.

K

kenjutsu keiko sewayaku 剣術稽古世話役【劍術稽古世話役】. The title "caretaker/chief instructor of swordsmanship training" awarded by Echigo domain in 1847 to two swordsmen trained in the Jiki Shinkage Ryū. See: *Seigan Jiki Shinkage Ryū*.

kenjutsu no tatsujin 剣術の達人【劍術の達人】. A master swordsman.

kenjutsu shinanyaku 剣術指南役【劍術指南役】. Title given when assigned to an official post (*yaku*) as chief instructor (*shinan*) of swordsmanship (*kenjutsu*). See (e.g.): *Ono Jirōemon Tadaaki*.

kenkaku 剣客【劍客】[Also read: ***kenkyaku***]. A swordsman; a master fencer.

Kenkō Ryū 建孝流. A martial school concentrating on the pipe spear (*kudayari*). The Kenkō Ryū was an alternate line of the Itō Ryū 伊東流 founded by Itō Suketada sometime during the late Muromachi period, c.1560–1573.

kenkyaku 剣客【劍客】. See: *kenkaku*.

kenmi 検見【檢見】. An espionage agent. See: *mitsumono; ninja*.

ken no michi 剣の道【劍の道】. A term used

in the late 1500s to early 1600s by some warriors, including Miyamoto Musashi, to denote their spiritual quest via swordsmanship. During the Edo period, the term was modified to *kendō* 剣道.

kenpō 1. 剣法. See: *kempō (1).*

kenpō 2. 拳法. See: *kempō (2).*

Kenpō Ryū 憲法流. See: *Yoshioka Ryū.*

kenshi 1. 剣士【劍士】. a. An expert swordsman. b. An expert swordsman who uses a live blade (*shinken*), in contrast to a wooden sword (*bokutō*; *bokken*) or bamboo training sword (*shinai*; *chikutō*). c. A fencer. *See also: chikushi, mokushi.*

kenshi 2. 拳士. Lit. a "boxer." This term is used to refer to practitioners of modern Nippon Shōrinji Kempō.

kenshin 献身【獻身】. Classical Warrior Ideal—Lit. "self-sacrifice." *Kenshin* was the warrior ethic ideal that required a warrior vassal be utterly committed—even to the point of death by self-sacrifice—to his lord. This term is often found in the war tales (*gunkimono*) but was probably much rarer in the reality of Japan's medieval period. [See Varley (1994) and Draeger (1973a) on loyalty.] However, as Varley (1994: 32) points out, "…the lord/vassal relationship in warrior society was not unilateral, but bilateral: A vassal served his lord as a fighting man for various rewards, including benefits (usually land)." See: *bushi no konjō; junshi.*

Kenshin Ryū 謙信流. See: *Echigo Ryū.*

Kentō 犬韜 <Ch. Quantao. See: *Rikutō.*

kenukigata tachi 毛抜形太刀. Lit. "tachi in the shape of tweezers." An old type of *tachi* in which the blade and hilt are all one piece—that is, the handle is an extension of the blade. The hilt is pierced down the center by an opening in the shape of a pair of hair tweezers (*kenuki*); i.e., the ends of the slot are widened and rounded. This type of sword was mainly used for ceremonial purposes.

ken zen ichinyo 拳禅一如 【拳禪一如】. A philosophical phrase relating *karate* to the Zen school of Buddhism in Japan. It means "boxing and Zen are one."

ken zen itchi 剣禅一致【劍禪一致】. A philosophical phrase related to the Zen school of Buddhism in Japan; it means "swordsmanship and Zen are one." See: *Ikkyoku Mubetsu Ryū; Ōmori Sōgen; Tsuji Gettan Sukemochi.*

kenzoku 眷族. A tenth- and eleventh-century term for a vassal or retainer. This word appears in the *Konjaku monogatari*. See also: *rōdō; ruiban.*

keppan 血判. Lit. "blood seal," "blood stamp." An oath signed with one's own blood. A number of classical *ryū* required *keppan* from new applicants.

kerai 家来【家來】. A vassal; a retainer.

kesa 袈裟 <Ch. *jiasha* <Skt. *kaśāya*. A Buddhist monk's surplice, which is worn draped across the body from the left shoulder.

kesagiri 袈裟切. To cut through the shoulder diagonally. The cut was called *kesagiri* because the trajectory (*hasuji*) of the blade passed through the shoulder at the location over which a monk's *kesa* was draped.

kessō 血相 [A.k.a. ***hi*** 樋]. Lit. "meeting the blood." Lengthwise grooves in the blade of a sword or dagger. Although *kessō* are sometimes referred to as "blood grooves," their real purpose is to strengthen and lighten the structure of the blade.

Further reading in English:

- Yumoto, 1958: 57–59.

Ketsuyō shikan 『結要士鑑』. A text on military strategy (*gumpō*) produced by the Hōjō Ryū. It is reprinted in Ishioka and Arima (1967, vol. 6): 407–446.

ki 気【氣】. In the context of East Asian martial arts, this is a rather enigmatic term referring to breath, intrinsic energy, and life force. That being said, the classical warrior traditions of Japan (*koryū bujutsu*) did not normally concern themselves with the concept of *ki* outside that of *kiai*. See: *aiki; kiai.*

kiai 気合【氣合】. 1. The term *ki* 氣 (Ch. *qi*) refers to "intrinsic energy" and the term *ai* 合

(Ch. *he*) denotes "harmony." In a combative context, *kiai* therefore refers to the harmonization of one's *ki* with that of an opponent in such a way as to obtain some advantage; e.g., by startling the opponent and creating an opening or weakness (*suki*) in his attention, posture, etc. A *kiai* can also be a word or phrase which affects the composure of the enemy.[23] In combative contexts *kiai* is normally accomplished via a shout, a quiet or silent exhalation, or a breath compression synchronized with a cut, strike, or thrust; a threat; or other actions. Each classical martial tradition developed its own set of distinctive *kiai* along with interpretations—both exoteric and esoteric—of their use and significance. The classical warrior traditions of Japan (*koryū bujutsu*) developed over 2000 different *kiai*. (Draeger, 1995: Part 4, p. 34). 2. JIKI SHINKAGE RYŪ—Dominance of an enemy via breath control, body posture, and eye contact; taking the initiative; *sen no sen*. See also: *Shimada Toranosuke*. 3. HOPLOLOGY—See *kiai no ri*. See also: *aiki; a-un no kokyū; kiaijutsu; kiai no jutsu; kokyū; zanshin.*

kiaijutsu 気合術【氣合術】. See: *kiai no jutsu.*

Ki Aikidō 気合気道. See: *Shinshin Tōitsu Aikidō.*

kiai no jutsu 気合の術【氣合術】[A.k.a. ***kiaijutsu*** 気合術【氣合術】; ***tōate no jutsu*** 遠当術]. Lit. "*kiai* arts" or "*kiai* techniques." 1. Beyond some obscure references in E. J. Harrison's *The Fighting Spirit of Japan: A Study of the Esoteric Basis of Judo and Martial Arts in Relation to Japanese Culture and Way of Life*, there are no available sources that mention any classical martial school (*koryū*) that practiced *kiaijutsu* as a separate art. For example, in their comprehensive works on the classical martial schools, neither Fujita (1960) nor Sasama (1982) lists *kiaijutsu* (or *tōate no jutsu*) as a separate martial art. There are, however, many classical *ryū* which cultivate powerful *kiai*, and there are numerous accounts of warriors with forceful *kiai*. Asari Matashichirō Yoshinobu, a swordsman of the Nakanishi Ha Ittō Ryū 中西派一刀流 who taught Chiba Shūsaku and founded the Asari Ryū 浅利流, was said to have been able to knock an opponent off balance with *kiai* alone prior to using his favored thrusting techniques. In more recent times, according to Donn F. Draeger,[24] Shimada Teruko 島田照子, daughter of the fifteenth headmaster of Jiki Shinkage Ryū *naginatajutsu*, had "an extremely deadly, piercing *kiai*."

In the final analysis, however, the practice of *kiaijutsu* in the classical martial systems is not about "making noise" per se. In those classical traditions which emphasize *kiai*, such as the Jiki Shinkage Ryū, the most advanced practitioners use a silent *kiai* to dominate an opponent. See also: *aiki; kiai; seishinryoku.* 2. HOPLOLOGY—In analyzing combative behavior, hoplologist Richard Hayes has classified *kiai no jutsu* as the "combative, manifest respiratory/vocality trait." This refers to the neutralization of opponents through the use of respiration and vocality. See: *bu no ri; kiai no ri.*

Further reading in English:

• Hayes, 1984b: 2–4; 1990: 30–33.

kiai no ri 気合の理【氣合理】. HOPLOLOGY—As a combative trait, *kiai no ri* indicates the innate potentiality of dominating a combative encounter—essentially neutralizing an opponent—through the use of respiration and vocality. The respiration/vocality trait (*kiai no ri*) is described in detail by Hayes (1990: 30–33). See: *kiai no jutsu; kiai.*

kiba musha 騎馬武者. A mounted warrior.

kibasen 騎馬戦【騎馬戰】. Lit. "mounted warfare." This term referred to battle conducted from horseback, as opposed to warfare dominated by infantry tactics (*tohosen*).

Kibi no Makibi 吉備 真備 (693–775). A seventh-century figure credited with importing several aspects of Chinese culture to Japan. In 716, at the age of nineteen, Makibi journeyed to Tang China with Abe no Nakamaro. When he returned in 735, he brought with him the game of *igo*, the four-string lute (*biwa*) and other interesting cultural artifacts, including a number of texts on Chinese arts such as divination,

[23] Hayes (1990: 32) illustrates this with the example of shouting "Fire!" in a crowded theater.

[24] See Bibliography.

brush writing, and various other skills. Makibi is also said to have imported a library of several volumes on military strategy.

kidachi 木太刀. An Edo-period term for a wooden sword. See also: *bokken; bokutō.*

kido 木戸. The outer doors of a fortress or citadel.

kidō enshū 機動演習. (Military) maneuvers. The term is often abbreviated as *enshū*.

Kido Takayoshi 木戸 孝允 (1833–1877). A samurai of Chōshū domain, Kido was one of the "Three Heroes of the (Meiji) Restoration" (Ishin no Sanketsu).

kien Zen 機縁禅【機縁禪】. Lit. "opportunity Zen." *Kien* Zen, a practice in which Zen riddles (*kōan*) are tailored to the needs of the pupil, was first used with warrior and non-warrior students in Kamakura in the thirteenth century. As these pupils lacked the contextual knowledge and Chinese-language skills needed to understand classical Chinese *kōan*, the Chinese Zen masters created *kōan* related to incidents or situations with which the pupils were familiar. Only when the students became comfortable with the process of dealing with test questions (*satsumon* 拶門) and general *kōan* methodology would they be subjected to the more demanding classical Chinese *kōan*. See also: *Kamakura Zen; kōan; shikin Zen; sokon Zen.*

Further reading in English:

- Leggett, 1985.

kihaku 気魄【氣魄】[Var. 気迫【氣迫】]. Mental power; spirit; vigor. In a martial-arts context, *kihaku* refers to the ability to project one's mental power or spirit in such a way as to control an opponent. See also: *kiai no jutsu.*

kihon 基本. The "basics" of an art or practice. In martial arts, *kihon* are basic movement patterns and techniques.

kihon waza 基本技. Basic combative technique. For example, in the case of the modern Japanese police, *kihon waza* (basic arresting techniques) are an introductory subdivision of the various arresting techniques taught by the modern Japanese police force under the rubric *taihojutsu*.

Kiichi Hōgan [Also read ***Kiichi Hōgen***] 鬼一法眼. A legendary, enigmatic Daoist magician and alchemist who is said to have placed the collected texts of the *Genke kin'etsushū* in Kurama temple (Kuramadera) during the reign of Emperor Go-Shirakawa.[25] These texts were supposedly then copied by Minamoto no Yoshitsune, who became one of Japan's greatest tacticians. Much later (in the sixteenth and seventeenth centuries), a number of smaller texts on strategy, divination, and magic, turn up with titles referring to these two famous men; e.g., *Kiichi Hōgan tora no maki* 「鬼一法眼虎之巻」 and *Yoshitsune tora no maki* 「義経虎之巻」. See also: *Genji no heihō; Genke kin'etsushū; Kiichi Hōgan Ryū; Ōe no Koretoki; Rikutō; Sanryaku.*

Kiichi Hōgan Ryū 鬼一法眼流 [Also read ***Kiichi Hōgen Ryū***; a.k.a. ***Kiichi Ryū*** 鬼一流; ***Kurama Hachi Ryū*** 鞍馬八流; ***Kyō Hachi Ryū*** 京八流]. A legendary school of combative strategy and tactics (*gumpō*) and swordsmanship (*kenjutsu*) said to have originated with the enigmatic Daoist magician and alchemist Kiichi Hōgan.

According to the *Honchō bugei shōden*,[26] Ōe no Koretoki, a Japanese ambassador to Tang China, returned to Japan during the reign of Emperor Daigo,[27] bringing to Japan forty-two Chinese texts on various topics of interest, including "military strategy, tactics, and espionage" (*gumpō*) (Watatani, 1961: 27). Among these volumes were the *Rikutō*, the *Sanryaku*, the *Gunshōzu*,[28] and others. These texts were evidently translated into Japanese sometime around the tenth century, after which, along with a mixture of Buddhist and Daoist esoterica, they became part of the family-transmitted martial tradition of the powerful Minamoto warrior clan. This family-transmitted compendium on military strategy was a well-guarded secret, and therefore

25 Goshirakawa Tennō 後白河天皇 (1127–1192; r. 1155–1158), seventy-seventh emperor of Japan.

26 First published during the Kyōhō era (1716–1735), this work was republished in Watatani (1961: 17–382).

27 Daigo Tennō 醍醐天皇 (885–930; r.897–930), sixtieth emperor of Japan.

28 *Gunshōzu*『軍勝図』<Ch. *Junshengtu*『軍勝圖』.

did not appear in full written form until the late 1500s, at which time it emerged within the Ogasawara family under the title of *Genke kin'etsushū*.

There are various tales of how these texts were translated into Japanese. One story states they were translated by Ōe no Masafusa (1041–1111), a descendant of Koretoki; another attributes the translations to either Minamoto Yoriyoshi (995–1082) or Minamoto Yoshiie (1041–1108). Most Japanese historians tend to accept that the Minamoto were involved in this process. The Japanese editions of these documents later became associated with the story of the Daoist Kiichi Hōgan and his sequestering of the texts in Kuramadera, a Tendai temple located about twelve kilometers north of old Kyōto. And it was at Kuramadera where the young Minamoto no Yoshitsune (and later, Nen Ami Jion) were supposed to have copied these texts while being tutored in military strategy and combative arts.

However, the story does not stop there. Accounts from later eras as to who actually received knowledge from Kiichi are inconclusive. For example, a document (*densho*) transmitted from Jingo Izu no Kami of the Shinkage Ryū (6) 神影流 notes that Yoshitsune passed this information on in the form of "Kurama Ryū 鞍馬流" documents which he presented to the Shimogamo shrine (Shimogamosha 下鴨社) in Kyōto. However, that same document also notes that Jingo learned this fact through a divine dream (*reimu* 霊夢) (Watatani and Yamada, 1978: 213). In another version of the story, Yoshitsune received the teachings in the form of a document called the "Tiger Scroll" (*Tora no maki* 『虎の巻』). Many classical martial traditions from the fourteenth through nineteenth centuries passed on a document called the *Tora no maki*. Like the *Genke kin'etsushū*, however, these Tiger Scrolls are not simply copies of the tactics and strategies of the *Rikutō* or *Sanryaku*. Rather, they are filled with methods of divination (e.g., *hachimon tonkō no senjutsu* 八門遁甲の占術) and magical spells and incantations of the type found in the secret teachings of Tendai/Shingon/Shugendō esoterica (*mikkyō*).

The legend goes on to state that a combination of these Tang Chinese strategies, the tactics of the tenth-century Minamoto clan, and the spiritual esoterica of Kiichi were passed on by Kiichi to eight monks of the Tendai Kuramadera temple. This system became known as Kyō no Hachi Ryū[29] 京の八流 (the eight traditions of the capital). Furthermore, Minamoto no Yoshitsune (then known as Ushiwakamaru) was supposedly present at Kuramadera during the same period as the eight monks. In the transmission documents of the Hōgan Ryū 判官流,[30] a tradition whose history is closely aligned with the Chūjō Ryū 中条流, the transmission line of that system is listed as passing from Kiichi Hōgan to Minamoto Hōgan Yoshitsune, and then on to the Eight Monks of Kuramadera (Kurama Hōshi 鞍馬法師). The names of these eight monks are listed as follows: 1. Yūrai 祐頼, 2. Seison 清尊, 3. Chōbon 朝範, 4. Seison 性尊, 5. Ryūson 隆尊, 6. Kōson 光尊, 7. Seiyū 性祐, and 8. Ryōson 了尊. See also: *Genji no heihō; Genke Kin'etsushū; Kashima no Tachi; Kiichi Hōgan; Ōe no Koretoki; Rikutō; Sanryaku.*

Kiichi Hōgen 鬼一法眼. See: *Kiichi Hōgan.*

Kiichi Hōgen Ryū 鬼一法眼流. See: *Kiichi Hōgan Ryū.*

Kikuchi yari 菊地槍. A rare type of spear that took the name of its creators, the Kikuchi family of Higo province. The spearhead is shaped like a straight dagger (*tantō*) with a long tang. See also: *sōjutsu; yari.*

kikusui 菊水. A "floating chrysanthemum" crest (*kamon*). The *kikusui* became famous due to its use by Kusunoki Masashige in the fourteenth century. Much later, in the twentieth century, it became a patriotic symbol in World War II, and was often used by *kamikaze* units. (Morris 1975: 470). See: *Kusunoki Masashige.*

kime 決め. Decision; checking; conclusion.

Kime no Kata 極の形. KŌDŌKAN JŪDŌ—Lit. "forms of decision" or "checking forms." This is a category of Kōdōkan Jūdō *kata* devel-

[29] A.k.a. Kyōhachi Ryū 京八流.

[30] The name of this system, 判官流, can also be read "Hangan Ryū."

K

oped around 1888. These scenarios, which were originally known as Shinken Shōbu no Kata (forms for actual combat), were developed to teach the fundamentals of real combat, and therefore include strikes to vital points (*kyūsho*). Since these techniques are applicable to actual combat (martial or civil) they are banned from *randori* practice. These *kata* are divided into two groups, depending on whether the practitioners are kneeling (*idori*) or standing (*tachiai*). See: *Kōdōkan Jūdō.*

Kimoto Kurōzaemon Shigemasa 木本 九郎左衛門 成理 (1697–1771). A retainer of the Aizu *han*. Kimoto founded the Aizu Kimoto Ha 会津木本派, which specialized in military strategy and tactics (*gumpō*), around 1727.

Kimura Sukekurō Noriyasu 木村 助九郎 矩泰 [A.k.a. ***Tomoshige*** 友重] (1580–1650). A senior disciple of the famous swordsman Yagyū Munenori. Kimura, who founded the Unchū Ryū (2) 運籌流 sometime around 1610, was known for his expertise with the short sword (*kodachi*). He was one of Munenori's top students, and his new school was named by Munenori himself. However, Izubuchi Heibei, one of Kimura's students, founded a branch tradition known as the Izubuchi Ha Yagyū Ryū 出淵派柳生流; Kimura was considered the first headmaster of that school also. His own son, Kimura Sukekurō Tomoyasu, continued the tradition under the title of Yagyū Ryū 柳生流. Kimura Noriyasu had many disciples to whom he taught Yagyū Shinkage Ryū 柳生新陰流, calling it "Unchū Ryū 運籌流."

Kimura Sukekurō Tomoyasu 木村 助九郎 友安 (c.1605–c.1670). As successor to his father Kimura Noriyasu, Tomoyasu carried on the Yagyū Ryū 柳生流, his father's tradition, as a family line.

kin 金. See: *kinshō.*

Kinai 畿内. The geographical area surrounding the ancient capitals of Heijō and Heiankyō. Kinai included the old provinces of Izawa, Kawachi, Settsu, Yamashiro, and Yamato. The term is still used to refer to this area today.

kinji 近侍. A personal samurai attendant; a personal guard.

Kinjō Kensei 金城 兼盛. Founded Kūshin Ryū 空真流 *karate* with the help of Ueshima Sannosuke in 1937.

kinjū 近習. Originally a name for the emperor's bodyguard unit. During the Kamakura period, the term came to refer to the bodyguard group attached to the Kamakura *shōgun*. The Ashikaga later reorganized the *kinjū* into *gobanshū*.

Kinnara 緊那羅 <Ch. *jinnaluo* <Skt. *kinnara* [Var. Skt. *kiṁnara*]. BUDDHISM—Celestial musicians usually depicted as half-human, half-horse (in India) and half-human, half-bird (Southeast Asia). They are one of the eight groups considered protectors of Buddhism. See: *Hachibu Shū.*

Kinsei jidai 近世時代. Japan's Early Modern Age, c.1568–c.1867.

Kinshichōō 金翅鳥王 <Ch. *Jinchi Niaowang* <Skt. Garuḍa [A.k.a. ***Myōshi*** 妙翅; ***Karura*** 迦楼羅]. BUDDHISM—The "king of birds with golden wings," Garuḍa is the companion of the Hindu god Viṣṇu. Kinshichōō (Garuḍa) is also a synonym for the Buddha.

Kinshichōō Ken 金翅鳥王剣【金翅鳥王劍】. Lit. "Garuḍa Sword" or "Buddha Sword." The Kinshichōō Ken is one of a group of five special Ittō Ryū 一刀流 sword techniques called the Goten no Shidai. Kinshichōō Ken, which is found listed in the *densho* entitled *Ittō Ryū heihō shidai*,[31] is often compared with Sasaki Kojirō's famous "Returning Swallow" technique (Tsubamegaeshi 燕返). Sasamori (1986: 503–528) presents several detailed interpretations of all five *kata*.

kinshin 近臣. A trusted vassal; a personal guard.

kinshō 金将【金將】[Abbr. as ***kin*** 金]. SHŌGI—Lit. "gold general." In the Japanese strategic game of *shōgi*, the *kinshō* is somewhat like a bodyguard for the "white king" (*ōshō* 王将). There is no piece corresponding to the *kinshō* in Western chess.

Kiraku Ryū 気楽流【氣樂流】. A comprehensive

[31] An example of this *densho* bearing a date of 1689 was published in Imamura, 1966, vol. 2: 45–50.

field-combat system (*sōgo bujutsu*) claiming Toda Echigo no Kami 戸田越後守 as its founder. (Iijima, 1985). However, research conducted by Mol (2001: 209) points to Watanabe Mokuemon 渡辺杢右衛門 as the founder; Watatani and Yamada (1978: 233), meanwhile, list the progenitor as Iizuka Garyūsai Okiyoshi. The Kiraku Ryū lists Watanabe as its sixth headmaster and Iizuka as its eleventh. (Iijima, 1985).

According to Watatani and Yamada, at the age of fourteen Iizuka Okiyoshi journeyed to Edo, where he trained diligently with his uncle in the grappling (*jūjutsu*) and swordsmanship (*kenjutsu*) of Kinugawa Ryū 絹川流. Following that, he trained extensively in Shinkage Ryū (6) 神影流, Sanka Muteki Ryū 三化無敵流, Hikita Ryū 疋田流, and Toda Ryū 戸田流.[32] After his uncle's death, Okiyoshi received the most secret transmissions of Kinugawa Ryū from Hirugawa Kikuemon Okitada 蛭川菊右衛門興但. The date given for this is 1799, when Okiyoshi was nineteen years old.

Okiyoshi then set out on a warrior pilgrimage (*musha shugyō*). During his travels, he trained in a number of systems, including the Araki Ryū 荒木流, Shindō Munen Ryū 神道無念流, Ryūgō Ryū 柳剛流, Kasumi Shin Ryū 霞新流, Okuyama Nen Ryū 奥山念流, Asayama Ichiden Ryū 浅山一伝流, Yoshitsune Ryū 義経流, Kitō Ryū 起倒流, Tenshin Shin'yo Ryū 天神心揚流, and Yōshin Ryū 楊心流. Okiyoshi added this experience to his system, and is thereby credited with formulating the Kiraku Ryū as it exists today. Okiyoshi died in 1840 at the age of sixty.[33]

KIRAKU RYŪ *KUSARIGAMA-JUTSU*
Kashima Shrine, 1980
(Photograph by author)

kiri~ 切～. Lit. "cut"; from the verb *kiru* (to cut). This form is often used in compounds as a prefix; e.g., *kiriotoshi*, cutting (*kiri*) and taking/knocking down (*otoshi*). See also: ~giri.

kiri-ai 切り合い [Var. 斬り合い]. Fighting with swords; a swordfight.

kirigami 切紙. Abbreviation for *kirigami menjo*.

kirigami menjō 切紙免状 [Abbr. ***kirigami*** 切紙]. A license or certificate written on a simple piece of cut paper, in contrast to one written on a scroll or in book form.

kiriji ni 斬死に. Fighting to the death with swords; falling in battle.

kirin 麒麟 <Ch. *qilin*. A mythical hermaphroditic creature that combines the male animal *ki* 麒 and the female animal *rin* 麟 into one. It has the body of a deer, the tail of an ox or a lion, the legs and hooves of a horse, and a head somewhere between a horse and a dragon. It has one fleshy horn on its head and particolored hair on its back, while its belly is yellow. Some representations illustrate it with scales or protuberances, and it is often surrounded by flames. It eats nothing living and it treads so lightly that it leaves no tracks, even in new-fallen snow. (At some point the Japanese began using this term for a strange new animal imported from Africa—the giraffe.)

The *kirin* was highly respected in China and Japan, as its rare manifestation indicated the imminent appearance of a great sage who would rule the country with compassion and wisdom. The *kirin* is sometimes found as a decoration on sword furniture.

K

---

32 Watatani and Yamada (1978: 233) note that Okiyoshi's training in these four schools was accomplished simultaneously. Sanka Muteki Ryū is a branch of Shinkage Ryū, as is Hikita Ryū. In addition, the lineage of Okiyoshi's system indicates that the "Shinkage Ryū" he trained in was via the Toda line. It is therefore likely that Okiyoshi trained in these four schools under the same master in the same location.

33 An alternate history of this system can be found in Mol, 2001: 209–210.

KIRIN
(Nineteenth-century illustration)

kiriotoshi 切落し. Lit. "Cutting and knocking down." A simultaneous dominating cut.

kirisute gomen 切捨て御免. Essentially "permission to kill and depart," this was a privilege restricted to the warrior class during the mid to late Tokugawa period (c.1780–1867). It allowed the samurai to cut down—without fear of official retaliation—any member of the lower classes who had shown disrespect. However, lower-class individuals who committed murder were severely punished. See: *shikei.*

The Tokugawa-era social system, which was based on modified Neo-Confucianism, set the warrior apart as an ideal of virtue. Consequently, the samurai were allowed *kirisute gomen*, but they were expected to refrain from gambling, frequenting disreputable places, and participating in shameful behavior—unwholesome practices generally permitted for commoners. See also: *tsujigiri.*

kiritsuke 切付. 1. Cutting with the sword. 2. IAIJUTSU/IAIDŌ/BATTŌ—The act of cutting, (as opposed to the other movements such as drawing and *chiburi*) in the quick-draw sword arts. See: *iaijutsu.*

kisei 奇正. OKINAWAN KARATE—The strange and the mundane; the mysterious and normal; the esoteric and the exoteric. *Kisei*, according to Funakoshi (2001: 36–37), indicates the relative movement of the two hands in combative *karate.* Embodying the movement of *yin* and *yang*, it is the "cardinal principle of our *karatejutsu.*" See also: *ikite; shinte.*

kisha 1. 騎者 [Abbr. for ***kiba musha*** 騎馬武者]. Combative horsemanship. See: *Oguri Ryū.*

kisha 2. 騎射. Equestrian archery. See also: *san kisha.*

kishakei 騎射型. A shooting style in classical archery (*kyūjutsu*) developed by horse-mounted warriors. In modern *kyūdō*, *kishakei* is normally referred to as "ceremonial style" (*reishakei*) because of its association with Ogasawara Ryū etiquette and ceremonial archery. Both styles have been influential in the development of the modern *kyūdō* shooting method called *hassetsu.* (Contrast to *bushakei.*)

kishi 旗幟. A battle flag. See: *hatajirushi.*

kishō 起請. BUDDHISM/SHINTŌ—A prayer (or written document of a prayer) requesting divine guidance. This is normally executed when one is making religious vows.

Kishōkan 鬼将官【鬼將官】. Lit. "Demon General." See: *Katō Kiyomasa.*

kishōmon 起請文. A written vow sometimes required on entering a classical martial tradition. See: *kishō.*

Kishū Ryū 紀州流. A school of espionage (*shinobi no jutsu*) attributed to a religious pilgrim from the Kumano Sanzan area. According to a text called the *Togakure Ryū kudensho* 『戸隠流口伝書』, the founder of the Kishū Ryū was also an adept of Hakuun Ryū 白雲流 espionage. However, Watatani and Yamada (1978: 215) are very critical of this document, noting that it is filled with fictional accounts and is highly unreliable. They also consider the *Shōninki* 『正忍記』, a transmission document (*densho*) attributed to the Kishū Ryū, to be unreliable. See: *Kumano Sanzan; ninjutsu; Shōninki.*

kissaki 切先. The tip of a blade. See also: *hō.*

Kita Machi Bugyō 北町奉行. The title of an Edo-period magistrate who presided over the northern half of the city of Edo (Chuo ward, near Kajibashi 鍛冶橋, in modern-day Tōkyō). The samurai who held this position was normally of *hatamoto* rank. See: *Miachi*

Bugyō; Minami Machi Bugyō.

Kitō Midare Ryū 起倒乱流【起倒亂流】. A variant name for the Kitō Ryū.

Kitō Ryū 起倒流 [Originally ***Kitō Midare Ryū*** 起倒乱流【起倒亂流】; var. ***Kitō Ryū Midare*** 起倒流乱【起倒流亂】; later ***Kitō Ryū Heihō Yoroi Kumiuchi*** 起倒流兵法鎧組討]. The Kitō Ryū was originally a comprehensive field-combat system (*sōgo bujutsu*) believed to have been founded around 1637 by Ibaraki Sensai. Like its antecedent, the Edo Yagyū Shinkage Ryū, the Kitō Ryū was a very aggressive system which emphasized taking the initiative and closing with the enemy in an encounter. The tradition evolved into an influential *jūjutsu* system over a period of years under several successive headmasters. However, the actual origins of the Kitō Ryū are not clear.

As noted, the most likely founder of the *ryū* was Ibaraki Sensai. Most sources are in agreement that Ibaraki worked for the Yagyū family in Edo sometime during the 1620s and 1630s. He may even have studied martial arts under Edo Yagyū Shinkage Ryū progenitor Yagyū Munenori, and Zen under Munenori's confidant, Takuan Zenji. However, there are no documents that confirm this.

Another possible founder of the Kitō Ryū is Fukuno Shichirōuemon Masakatsu, who was a student of Munenori's father, Yagyū Muneyoshi. In his extensive work on *jūjutsu*, *Classical Fighting Arts of Japan: A Complete Guide to Koryū Jūjutsu*, Serge Mol (2001: 127) speculates that Ibaraki and Fukuno may have met together and exchanged ideas.

Ibaraki Sensai trained in several systems

Kitō Ryū
起倒流
(abbreviated lineage)

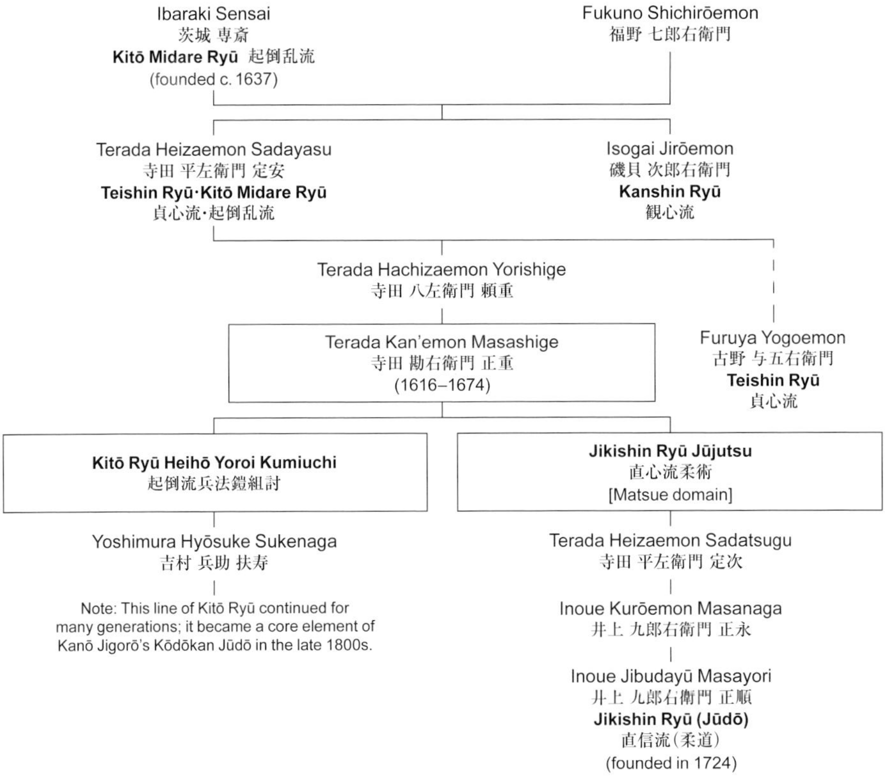

concentrating on combative grappling. He was experienced in unarmored grappling (*yawara*), armored grappling (*yoroi kumiuchi*), quick-draw sword arts (*iaijutsu*), and the combative arts of the "camp sickle" (*jinkamajutsu*) and long hardwood staff (*bōjutsu*). From his background in these arts, Ibaraki established a system he christened Kitō Midare Ryū 起倒乱流 around 1637.

Later, Terada Kan'emon, a practitioner of Teishin Ryū 貞心流 grappling (*yawarajutsu* 和術), modified Kitō Midare Ryū to include a new timing concept called *muhyōshi* 無拍子, meaning "rhythm-less" or "empty timing." Terada then renamed the system Kitō Ryū Heihō Yoroi Kumiuchi and passed it on to Yoshimura Hyōsuke Sukenaga; that line's name was eventually shortened to "Kitō Ryū." However, a second line which descended from Terada later came to be called Jikishin Ryū Yawara 直心流柔 or Jikishin Ryū Jūjutsu 直心流柔術.

The Kitō Ryū contributed greatly to the wide development of *jūjutsu* in later years. Watatani Kiyoshi (1974: 4) includes it as one of the "Big Four" schools of grappling which, because of their technical acumen and wide base of practitioners, most influenced Japanese *jūjutsu*. (The other three noted by Watatani are the Sekiguchi Ryū, Seigō Ryū, and Takenouchi Ryū.)

In the late 1800s Kitō Ryū was one of the grappling systems studied by Kanō Jigorō, and it directly influenced his development of Kōdōkan Jūdō. Kanō preserved twenty-one of the principal Kitō Ryū *kata* in a set of Kōdōkan combative forms he called "Koshiki no Kata" (Classical Forms).

Further reading in English:

• Mol., 2001: 127–129.

Kitō Ryū Heihō Yoroi Kumiuchi 起倒流兵法鎧組討. A variant name for the Kitō Ryū.

Kitō Ryū Midare 起倒流乱. A variant name for Kitō Ryū.

Kitō Ryū no Kata 起倒流の形. See: *Koshiki no Kata.*

Kitsuke shingunden 『橘家神軍伝』【橘家神軍傳】. One of several transmission scrolls (*densho*) which preserve the martial strategies of the Shingun Ryū 神軍流, a system of combative strategy (*gumpō*) founded by a warrior named Inbe Shōsai Sōgorō 忌部正斉宗五郎 around 1625. This text has been published in Ishioka and Arima (1967, vol. 6: 370–382).

kiza 跪座【跪坐】. A kneeling posture in which the toes are turned under so that the ball of the foot is in contact with the floor. As this was a common posture in traditional Japan, many combative systems use it as a position from which to manipulate hand-held weapons.

kizu 1. 疵 [Var. 瑕]. A flaw or crack (as in a sword blade).

kizu 2. 傷 [Var. 創]. A wound.

kōa isshin 興亜一心【興亞一心】. Lit. "Asian development one spirit." The thrust of the phrase appears to be "Complete dedication to the Greater East Asian Co-Prosperity Sphere." This patriotic (expansionist/imperialistic) slogan is found on a number of sword blades forged by Japanese sword-makers in Manchuria during the 1930s.

Further reading in English:

- "KOA ISSHIN MANTETSU." 23 April 2009. http://www.geocities.com/alchemyst/koa.htm
- "The whole aspect of the Kōa-Issin sword." 23 April 2009. http://www.k3.dion.ne.jp/~j-gunto/gunto 149.htm

kōan 公案 <Ch. *gongan.* BUDDHISM—Questions and answers created by Zen masters; Zen riddles. *Kōan* are used in Zen Buddhism as a test of a student's psychological state on the way to enlightenment. According to some sources, there are as many as 1700 codified *kōan*, many of which have been organized into various collections such as the *Hekiganroku.* When the monk Eisai brought the Rinzai Zen tradition to Japan in the late twelfth century, he popularized it outside the classical Chinese monastic setting by teaching the laity, including the Japanese warrior class (*bushi*). However, as the scholar Trevor Leggett (1985: xii) has pointed out, "…the warrior pupils of the early period of Kamakura Zen had no bent for scholarship." In fact, the warriors of the early Kamakura shogunate had difficulty both

with the context of the classical Chinese *kōans* and the alien language of visiting Chinese monks. Consequently, the Japanese Zen teachers of the early thirteenth century began making up *kōans* on the spot to fit the needs of their warrior trainees. This came to be called "this-moment Zen" (*shikin zen*). Over the next few centuries, Rinzai Zen and its *kōan* practice became an established part of Japanese Zen Buddhism.

Koan also had significance in a martial context. Due in part to the association between the Japanese warrior class (*bushi*) and Kamakura Zen *kōan* methods from the late twelfth century onward, a powerful teaching element in the development of the Muromachi-period classical martial schools (*koryū*) became the *kata*-as-*kōan* methodology. Using the *kōan* as a central element, those classical schools were able to transmit combative technique and encourage the development of several psychological combative adaptive traits—steadfast/imperturbable mind (*fudōshin*), volition (*sen*), and especially intuition (*kan*)—via prearranged combative forms (*kata*). This gave the classical *kata* a depth that could only be plumbed by the student in whom the training regimen had developed insight and intuition. See: *Kamakura Zen; kien Zen; shikin Zen.*

Further reading in English:

- Collcutt, 1981: *passim.*
- Leggett, 1978: 239–255.
- Leggett, 1985.
- Miura and Sasaki, 1965.

Kōan no Eki 弘安役. The second war to repel the Mongols. This conflict took place in 1281. See: *Genkō no eki.*

Kobashi Nikkan 小橋 日感. Kobashi was a direct disciple of Hakkō Ryū founder Okuyama Yoshiji. Already the third generation successor of Enshin Ryū Iaidō 円心流居合道, Kobashi combined that eclectic system with the grappling system of Hakkō Ryū 八光流.

Kobashi Shōbei 小橋 庄兵衛. Founder of Enshin Ryū 円心流, an eclectic system of quick-draw swordsmanship (*iai*) and other arts. Kobashi established the school in the early 1800s. See: *Enshin Ryū.*

Kobayakawa Takakage 小早川 隆景 (1532–1590). A *daimyō* who, according to legend, had several dialogues with the *tengu* king Buzenbō while on Mount Hiko (Hikosan 彦山).

Further reading in English:

- Wilson, 2006. (Translation).

Kobayashi Ha Shōrin Ryū 小林派小林流. OKINAWAN KARATE—A nonstandard nomenclature for Kobayashi Ryū 小林流. Traditional works in Japanese do not normally refer to this system as "Kobayashi Ha Shōrin Ryū." See: *Kobayashi Ryū.*

Kobayashi Masao 小林 正郎. Current (2008) headmaster of the Shingyōtō Ryū.

Kobayashi Moemon 小林 茂右衛門. Founder of the Asayama Ichiden Koryū 浅山一伝古流. After mastering the martial systems of the Asayama Ichiden Ryū 一伝流 as taught by seventh lineal successor Nakada Shichizaemon Masatsune, Moemon founded his own system specializing in *jūjutsu*, which he passed on in Mito domain.[34] By changing the name to "Koryū" meaning "classical school," he was apparently indicating he was reviving the original grappling system of the parent tradition.

Kobayashi Ryū 小林流. OKINAWAN KARATE—"Kobayashi" is an alternate pronunciation for the term "Shōrin" in Shōrin Ryū 小林流, a school of *karate* descended from Chibana Chōshin. See: *Chibana Chōshin; Itosu Ryū Karate; karate kata.*

Kobayashi Tōjūrō Tadahide 小林 藤十郎 忠秀. The founder of Sakura Ichiden Ryū 佐倉一伝流. Having mastered Asayama Ichiden Ryū 浅山一伝流 as taught by its thirteenth lineal successor, Morito Sandayū Kanesada, Tadahide reformed it into the Sakura Ichiden Ryū. He transmitted this art in the Sakura domain.

kōbō 攻防. Attack and defense.

Kōbō Daishi 弘法大師. Posthumous title for Kūkai, the founder of the Shingon school of esoteric Buddhism. See: *Kūkai.*

34 Ref. *Mito eikōkan bunsho*『水戸影考館文書』.

K

kōbō itchi 攻防一致. Lit. "attack and defense are one." For the classical Japanese warrior, there was no dichotomy between attack and defense. He saw combat—whether in battlefield or civilian circumstances—to be regulated by *kōbō itchi*; the choice of whether to use an attack or defensive tactic was to be decided upon by the warrior depending on the situation. *Kōbō itchi* was one of the classical warrior concepts on which Kanō Jigorō based his Kōdōkan Jūdō. This principle, which sees offensive and defensive actions as basically the same, ensured that Kanō's *jūdō* was not a narrowly defined defensive system.

kobudō 古武道. 1. Traditional martial ways. 2. A generic term for classical martial arts and ways. 3. Abbreviation for Okinawa *kobudō*.

Kobudō Shinkōkai 古武道振興会. See: *Nihon Kobudō Shinkōkai.*

kobujutsu 古武術. Traditional martial arts.

Kōbukai Aikijutsu 皇武会合気術【皇武會合氣術】. One of the early terms (c. 1932) used by Ueshiba Morihei for the grappling system he modified from Daitō Ryū *aikijūjutsu* into *aikidō*.

Kōbun Jitsuyō Ryū 講武実用流【講武實用流】. The Kōbun Jitsuyō Ryū was a school of strategy (*gumpō*), swordsmanship (*kenjutsu*), and a variety of other combative arts which flourished in the early 1800s. Hirayama Kōzō, its fourth headmaster, taught strategy to Odani Nobutomo, thirteenth headmaster of the Jiki Shinkage Ryū.

kobushi 拳. A fist.

Kōbusho 講武所. A short-lived government training establishment founded in 1856. The purpose of the Kōbusho was to teach fighting arts to Tokugawa retainers. The facility was originally headed by Odani Nobutomo of the Jiki Shinkage Ryū. Training at the Kōbusho included swordsmanship (*kenjutsu*), combative spear (*sōjutsu*), archery (*kyūjutsu*), gunnery (*hojutsu*), and grappling (*jūjutsu*). Although the institution closed in 1866, its faculty and students included some of the most prominent warriors of the period.

kobyōshi 小拍子. A small beat; a small, relatively swift and incisive attack. See: *hyōshi.*

kōchū 甲冑 [Also read ***katchū***]. Lit. "armor and helmet." See: *katchū.*

kōchūden 甲冑伝【甲冑傳】. See: *katchūden.*

kodachi 小太刀. A short sword.

kodachi no kata 小太刀之形. 1. A generic term for combative forms (*kata*) executed with a short sword. 2. ***Kodachi no Kata*** 小太刀之形. JIKI SHINKAGE RYŪ—The third series of *waza* in the Jiki Shinkage Ryū, consisting of six *kata*. All are performed with *kodachi* (for the *shidachi* role) and *tachi* (for the *uchidachi* role).

Kodachi Seihō 小太刀勢法. The second set of combative scenarios (*kata*) listed by the Hyōhō Niten Ichi Ryū under the general category of Tachi Seihō (sword forms). This set consists of seven *kata* performed with a single short sword (*kodachi*) for the *shidachi* role. See: *Hyōhō Niten Ichi Ryū.*

koden 古伝【古傳】. 1. Lit. "old tradition" or "old transmission." 2. YAGYŪ SHINKAGE RYŪ—See: *katchū kempō.*

kodōgu 小道具. The fittings (other than the *tsuba*) of a sword or dagger. For *tachi* fittings, however, the term *kanagu* is used.

Kōdōkai 幸道会. See: *Daitō Ryū Aikijūjutsu Kōdōkai.*

Kōdōkan Goshinjutsu 講道館護身術. KŌDŌKAN JŪDŌ—Kōdōkan Self-Defense Forms. A set of twenty-one *kata* developed around 1958. Twelve of the forms were designed for use against an unarmed assailant. The first seven of these pertain to a scenario in which the practitioner is being held; the second subgroup of five is to be used when the attacker is at a distance. The remaining nine forms were designed to be used against an armed assailant. These are subdivided into three groups, depending on whether the assailant is armed with a knife, stick, or pistol. See also: *Kōdōkan Jūdō.*

Kōdōkan Jūdō 講道館柔道. The system of *jūdō* founded by Kanō Jigorō in 1882. Kanō gave his training hall the name "Kōdōkan" to delineate his system and distinguish it from earlier *ryū*-type *jūjutsu* schools. Kano's use of the term *jūdō* was neither new nor unique; it had been used by the Jikishin Ryū more than 150 years earlier.

Under Kanō, Kōdōkan Jūdō was an eclectic system incorporating elements of sport, fighting arts, spiritual discipline, physical education, and recreation. Kanō was very conscious of the moral quality of the various social classes in the complex hierarchy of Meiji-era Japan, and he admitted only students he judged to have high moral character. As Donn F. Draeger has pointed out, "Kano never intended his system to be taught indiscriminately to any and all people." (Draeger, 1974: 114.)

In developing his own form of *jūdō,* Kanō incorporated the *ran* 乱 system of Kitō Ryū, modifying it into *randori* 乱捕り (free exercise), along with a strong emphasis on classical-style *kata*. According to Kanō, "What is deficient in free exercise (*randori*) must be supplemented by prearranged form (*kata*)" (Draeger, 1974: 121).

In the first decade of the Kōdōkan, Kanō's *jūdō* was essentially a new school of *jūjutsu*, and was seen as such. During this time, Kanō established it as an effective fighting system, as shown in the famous police match of 1886.[35] However, he continued to develop the system and began separating dangerous combative techniques—thenceforth to be practiced only in *kata*—from contest matches, which were more sport-like. Examples of this include Kanō's modifications of *ukemi* techniques from Kitō Ryū 起倒流 and Sekiguchi Ryū 関口流, and his *randori* techniques from Jigō Tenshin Ryū 自剛天真流 (Sakudō, 2005: 188).

Kanō incorporated a number of philosophical/psychological concepts into Kōdōkan Jūdō. Among the most significant of these is *kōbōitchi* (the idea that attack and defense are different aspects of the same thing). Kanō's Kōdōkan Jūdō is a combination of both yielding and resisting techniques; it is not a system restricted to defense. A second important concept is Kanō's interpretation of *jū no ri* (the principle of flexibility). From a physical standpoint, this meant that a person executing *jūdō* technique would combine his own strength with that of the opponent in order to dominate. From a psychological perspective, the *jūdō* practitioner must also have a flexible mind in order to meet and adapt rapidly to dangerous situations.

Up until the end of World War II, the real purpose of Kōdōkan Jūdō was spiritual forging (*seishin tanren*). By this time the art had reached a high level of technical perfection. Along with other combative arts, *jūdō* was banned by postwar occupation forces. On its revival in 1947, Kōdōkan Jūdō emerged with a new emphasis on sport competition. National championships were held for the first time in 1948 and, in 1964, *jūdō* became an Olympic sport. Due to this trend, a number of *jūdō* traditionalists have lamented that it is difficult today to find judoists who train and practice in the manner in which Kanō had originally intended.

Kōdōkan Jūdō *Kata* Curriculum

- *Randori no Kata* 乱取の形 (free exercise forms)
  - *Nage no Kata* 投の形 (throwing forms), 1884–1887.
  - *Katame no Kata* 固の形 (grappling forms), 1884–1887.
- *Kime no Kata* 極の形 (forms of decision), c. 1888.
- *Kōdōkan Goshinjutsu* 講道館護身術 (Kodokan self-defense forms), c. 1958
- *Jū no Kata* 柔の形 (flexible forms), 1887.
- *Gō no Kata* 剛の形 (strength forms), 1887. [These are no longer taught as a standard part of Kōdōkan Jūdō.]
- *Itsutsu no Kata* 五の形 (the five forms), 1887.
- *Koshiki no Kata* 古式の形 (classical forms). [These forms were inherited from Kitō Ryū. Along with the *Gō no kata*, they are among the earliest in Kōdōkan Jūdō.]

---

35 The Tokyo Metropolitan Police hosted a *jūjutsu* tournament in 1886. The main purpose of this meet was to test Kanō Jigorō's new Kodokan Jūdō against Totsuke Hikosuke's more traditional Yoshin Ryū. The Kōdōkan team won thirteen of fifteen matches (the other two ended in a draw) and firmly established Kōdōkan Jūdo as the superior system, at least in the eyes of the police.

- *Seiryoku Zen'yo Kokumin Taiiku no Kata* 精力善用国民体育の形 (maximum-efficiency National Physical Education forms)

The Kōdōkan system also includes training in a number of separate *randori* techniques, as well as resuscitation techniques under a system known as Kappō.

Further reading in English:

- Draeger, 1974: 112–123.
- Fukuda, 2004.
- Kano, 1986.
- Kodokan Judo Institute, 2000.
- Mifune, 2004.
- Otaki and Draeger, 1982.
- Smith, 1958.

kodzuka 小柄. See: *kozuka.*

kofū 古風. Old customs; old traditions; classical manners.

Kōfu no ken 工夫の剣【工夫劍】<Ch. Gongfu *jian*. The "Sword of Kōfu." "Kōfu" is the Japanese pronunciation of "Gongfu," the name of one of the three legendary Chinese swords commissioned by Feng Huzi (Fūkoshi). See also: *Fūkoshi; Ōyashi; Ryūen no ken; Taiaki; Taia no ken.*

kofun 古墳. An ancient burial mound; a tomb; a tumulus. Seen from the air, these tombs usually appear keyhole-shaped. They were constructed by the early Japanese during the Kofun period (c.250–552 C.E.).

kōgai 笄 [Var. 髪掻【髮搔】]. A skewer-like implement often secured to the scabbard of a Japanese short sword or dagger. The earlier ideograms 髪掻 are used to refer to an ornamental hairpin or hair comb.

Kogaku 古学【古學】. A school of Confucian-based learning that appeared in the late 1600s. The Kogaku arose in opposition to the Tokugawa academies that were based in Neo-Confucianism. The greatest proponents of the Kogaku school were the *bushi* Yamaga Sokō (a warrior from Aizu *han*) and a scholar named Ogyū Sorai 荻生徂徠.

Further reading in English:

- Tsunoda et al, 1958: 393–442.

Kōgamono 甲賀者. 1. A variant term for an espionage agent. 2. An espionage agent specifically from Kōga. See: *ninjutsu.*

Kōga Ryū Wada Ha 甲賀流和田派. One of the fifty-three clan lines of the Kōga Ryū, which concentrated on espionage (*shinobi no jutsu*). The Wada Ha (Wada branch) was representative of one of the six Nanzan families (Nanzan Rokke 南山六家). The last known Wada Ha practitioner was Fujita Seiko, who died in 1966.

Further reading in English:

- Hevener, 2008.

kogatana 小刀 [Also read ***katana***; ***ko katana; shōtō***]. Lit. "small sword." 1. A small knife carried in the scabbard of a sword. 2. A sword around 18 to 24 inches (45–60 cm) long. Lighter than a normal sword, the *kogatana* is similar to the *chūdachi* of the Yagyū Shinkage Ryū. This sword was normally worn with court clothing such as the *nagabakama.* During the seventeenth century the Tokugawa shogunate began requiring all *daimyō* attending the *shōgun* to be armed only with a *kogatana.*

Kōgen Ittō Ryū 甲源一刀流. A school of swordsmanship founded around 1780 by Henmi Tashirō Yoshitoshi. Henmi was a student of Sakurai Gosuke Nagamasa, a master of the Mizoguchi Ha Ittō Ryū 溝口派一刀流. However, Henmi was apparently such a prodigy that Sakurai became Henmi's student in the Kōgen Ittō Ryū. While there are now several branches of this tradition, the main line is still within the Henmi family.

Unlike some other Ittō Ryū lines, this school has a repertoire of only twenty-five sword forms (*kata*). (The main parent tradition known as Ono Ha Ittō Ryū 小野派一刀流, for example, contains a curriculum of over 100 *kata*.) The Kōgen Ittō Ryū also contains five long-hafted glaive (*naginata*) forms which originated in the Toda Ha Bukō Ryū 戸田派武甲流. According to M. Skoss (2002: 121), members of the Kōgen Ittō Ryū also used to practice a series of quick-draw swordsmanship techniques. Though these are no longer extant, the names of the forms are preserved in Kōgen Ittō Ryū transmission documents. They apparently follow the names of the nine letters of the Kujihō (Ritual Method of the Nine Seals).

Further reading in English:

- Skoss, Meik, 2002: 114–116; 121–123 *ff.*

Kōgi Onmitsu 公儀隠密【公儀隱密】. An espionage agency in the service of the Tokugawa shogunate. Founded in the early Edo period, it was directed and developed under *shōgun* Tokugawa Ieyasu. It organized various existing espionage groups into a system which served his shogunate. Agents of this organization were known as *onmitsu*. See: *ninjutsu; onmitsu.*

kogusoku 小具足 [A.k.a. ***kogusoku-jutsu*** 小具足術]. Grappling in light armor, either empty-handed or with a variety of short weapons. See: *Araki Ryū; Takenouchi Ryū.*

kogusoku-jutsu 小具足術. See: *kogusoku.*

kōgyō 公業. Lit. "public entertainments." *Kōgyō* were combative matches held in the 1870s. They were sponsored by Sakakibara Kenkichi's Gekikenkai organization, whose purpose was to promote traditional martial arts.

kohai 後輩. A junior; a fellow trainee who entered an organization after oneself. (Compare to *dōhai* and *sempai.*)

kōhaku 紅白. Lit. "red and white." Refers to the respective clan colors of the Taira and Minamoto (Genji and Heike, or Gempei) warrior clans, which were the primary contestants in the great civil war of 1180–1185 (the Gempei Gassen). Today, the colors red and white are often used today to represent contestants in sports matches. A *kōhaku shiai* is a contest or tournament between two groups; the term is not restricted to a martial context.

kōhaku shiai 紅白試合. A contest between two groups. See: *kōhaku.*

kohori 郡 [Also read ***kōri***]. Military districts set up in the late seventh century after the coup of 645. The establishment of these districts was an attempt by Prince Naka and Nakatomi no Kamatari to exert greater control over the arms and warriors of the hinterland while weakening the entrenched power of the local warrior leaders (*kuni no miyatsuko*).

kōi 攻囲. Siege.

koiguchi 鯉口. Lit. "carp's mouth." The opening for the sword at the end of the scabbard (*saya*).

koiguchi o kiru 鯉口を切る. Lit. "to cut the carp's mouth." This phrase actually means to loosen the sword in the scabbard.

Kōizumi Ise no Kami Nobutsuna 上泉 伊勢守 信綱. See: *Kamiizumi Ise no Kami Nobutsuna.*

NOTE: While "Kōizumi" is considered the correct pronunciation in the geographical area where Nobutsuna was born, most English publications use the standard Japanese pronunciation for his family name: *Kamiizumi.*

Kōizumi Ryū Hyōhō 上泉流兵法 [Also read ***Kamiizumi Ryū Heihō***]. Lit. the "military strategy of the Kōizumi clan." A set of texts on military strategies and precepts developed by the Kōizumi (Kamiizumi) family. These rely heavily on the *Genke kin'etsushū* and include a lineage indicating its origin in a divine inspiration from the Buddhist goddess Marishiten. The *Kōizumi Ryū Hyōhō* consists of the following three scrolls:

Kōizumi Ryū Hyōhō *densho*:

- *Kōizumi ryū gumbai seimyaku* 「上泉流軍配正脈」(Correct line of transmission of the Kōizumi tradition of military discipline)
- *Kin'etsushū gunki no maki* 「訓閲集軍気之巻」(Martial "essence" in the *Kin'etsushū*)
- *Kin'etsushū gunki no zu* 「訓閲集軍気之図」(Illustrations of martial "essence" in the *Kin'etsushū*).

These documents have been published in Ishioka and Arima, 1967 (vol. 6): 80–128.

Ko Jigen Ryū 1. 小示現流. Lit. the "Lesser Jigen Ryū." A comprehensive field-combat system (*sōgo bujutsu*) derived from Jigen Ryū by Ijuin Mondo Hisaaki (1632–1713). Having begun training in swordsmanship with Tōgō Shigekata, second headmaster of the Jigen Ryū, Ijuin received a full license (*menkyo kaiden*) in Jigen Ryū from third headmaster Tōgō Shigetoshi. Ijuin was an expert swordsman and was also well known for his expertise with the Jigen Ryū spear (*yari*).

When Tōgō Shigetoshi became an invalid and was unable to continue as headmaster,

K

Ijuin temporarily assumed leadership of the Jigen Ryū. Consequently, he was responsible for passing on the tradition to Tōgō Shigeharu (who later became the fourth headmaster). Ijuin eventually organized his own branch of Jigen Ryū which was then passed down in the Ijuin clan in parallel to the main Tōgō line. See also: *Jigen Ryū; nodachi; Nodachi Jigen Ryū; Tōgō Tōbei Shigetaka.*

Ko Jigen Ryū (1)
小示現流
(abbreviated lineage)*

2. Tōgō Hizen no Kami Shigekata
東郷 肥前守 重方
Jigen Ryū
示現流

3. Tōgō Hizen no Kami Shigetoshi
東郷 肥前守 重利
Jigen Ryū
示現流

1. Ijuin Mondo Hisaaki
伊集院 主水 久明
(1632–1713)
Ko Jigen Ryū
小示現流

2. Ijuin Hyōuemon Toshikuni
伊集院 兵右衛門 俊国
(c. 1680–c. 1760)
Ko Jigen Ryū
小示現流

3. Ijuin Yahachirō Kaneyoshi
伊集院 弥八郎 兼喜
(c. 1730–c. 1810)
Ko Jigen Ryū
小示現流

4. Ijuin Yashichirō (uncertain)
伊集院 弥七郎
(c. 1760–c. 1840)
Ko Jigen Ryū
小示現流

Matsumura Sōkon
松村 宗棍
(1809–1901)
Ko Jigen Ryū
小示現流

* The lineage given by Watatani and Yamada (1978: 340–341) varies somewhat from the one given here. Several Japanese sources (e.g., Takamiya, 2008: 520) note that Okinawan karate master Matsumura Sōkon received a "full license (*menkyo kaiden*) in Jigen Ryū" from Ijuin Yahachirō. However Yahachirō's dates do not match with those of Sōkon. One source (Bishop, 1999: 53) gives the name of Sōkon's master as "Ijuin Yashichirō." However, Watatani and Yamada do not list anyone by this name.

Ko Jigen Ryū 2. 古示現流. Lit. the "Old Jigen Ryū." This was a comprehensive field-combat system (*sōgo bujutsu*) spun off from Jigen Ryū by Tanegashima Jirouemon Tokitada. Tokitada was the grandson of Tōgō Shigetaka, founder of Jigen Ryū. This line continued for about five generations. See also: *Jigen Ryū; nodachi; Nodachi Jigen Ryū; Tōgō Tōbei Shigetaka.*

kojiri 鐺. The chape or tip of a scabbard (*saya*); the closed end of a *saya.*

kōjō 攻城. A siege.

Kōjō Okui Jikka no Tachi 高上奥位十箇ノ太刀. KASHIMA SHINTŌ RYŪ—Advanced-level combative swordsmanship forms (*kenjutsu kata*). See: *Kashima Shintō Ryū.*

Kojō Ryū 湖城流 <Oki. Kugusuku Ryū. OKINAWAN KARATE—A school of *karate* which traces its current combative system to Kojō Isei (1832–1891). Bishop (1999: 44–47), who interviewed the current Kojō Ryū headmaster, notes that Isei learned Shaolin-style boxing from a teacher named "Iwah" during a twenty-year stay in Fujian province (1848–1868). The Kojō family has practiced a variety of fighting arts since establishing itself in Kume, Naha, around 1393, and from the eighteenth through the early twentieth centuries maintained martial training halls (*dōjō*) both on the Chinese mainland in Fuzhou and in Okinawa. However, all documentation of earlier fighting systems was lost during World War II.

According to Shinzato (2008: 170) the current system encompasses three empty-hand *kata* as follows:

Empty-hand forms:

- Ten 天 Heaven (upper level *kamae*)
- Kū 空 Sky (middle level *kamae*)
- Chi 地 Earth (low level *kamae*)

Interestingly, the Ten, Kū, and Chi *kata* contain named combative engagement postures (*kamae*) which are also equated to the Chinese enumeration system known as the Twelve Branches (Jūnishi) and its equivalent animal symbols as follows:[36]

36 Shinzato's list varies somewhat from that of Bishop.

Kamae		Jūnishi		Animal symbol
Ten 天 (upper-level postures):				
shōshin	正真	*ne*	子	rat
fudō	不動	*ushi*	丑	ox
chinfū	陳風	*tora*	寅	tiger
jūmonji	十文字	*u*	卯	hare
Kū 空 (middle-level postures):				
unryū	雲竜	*tatsu*	辰	dragon
aiki	合気	*mi*	巳	serpent
seigan	青眼	*uma*	午	horse
dōkō	動光	*hitsuji*	未	ram
Chi 地 (low-level postures):				
tenchi	天地	*saru*	申	monkey
suika	吹下	*tori*	酉	cock
chiseigan	地青眼	*inu*	戌	dog
ichimonji	一文字	*i*	亥	boar

Bishop (1999: 44–47) lists an additional three empty-hand *kata* and two weapons forms—one for the long staff and one for the baton:

- Hakuryū 白竜 White Dragon
- Hako 白虎 White Tiger
- Hakutsuru 白鶴 White Crane
- Staff form
- Stick form

Further reading in English:

- Bishop, 1999: 44–52.

Kōjō Sanka no Yari 高上三箇乃槍. KASHIMA SHINTŌ RYŪ—Advanced-level combative spear forms (*sōjutsu kata*). See: *Kashima Shintō Ryū.*

koka 古歌. A generic term for didactic verse often found in old transmission scrolls (*densho*). These verses often reveal important, esoteric information concerning the essence of the tradition. See also: *dōka.*

ko katana 小刀. See: *kogatana.*

kōke 高家. Lit. "high family"; "exalted house." During the Edo period, *kōke* was a special title bestowed by the Tokugawa on dispossessed *daimyō* such as the Imagawa, Kira, Ōsawa, Toda, etc. They had no domains (*han*) or castles (*shiro*) and were given a very small yearly stipend of less than 1,000 *koku* by the Tokugawa government. However, they were often given important formal tasks such as carrying the *shōgun*'s messages to the imperial palace in Kyōto, acting as a representative of the *shōgun* at formal ceremonies in Nikkō, and regulating ceremonies in the *shōgun*'s palace. It was, in fact, in his capacity as a *kōke* in 1700 that Kira Kōzuke no Suke Yoshihisa 吉良上野介義央, who held the title of "master of ceremonies" in the *shōgun's* palace, publicly reprimanded the *daimyō* Asano Naganori. This led to a scuffle in which Asano struck Kira with a dagger, an incident which resulted in the famous vendetta of the Forty-seven Rōnin. See also: *Akō rōshi; daimyō.*

kokoro 心. "Heart," "spirit," "mind"; the "essence" of something. CLASSICAL WARRIOR IDEAL—*Kokoro*, referring to a sincere, humble spirit, was considered one of the essential characteristics of the classical warrior (*bushi*). See: *bushi no konjō.*

koku 石. A traditional unit of measure equivalent to 4.96 bushels of rice. From the sixteenth century through the nineteenth century, *daimyō* revenues and salaries of government officials were specified in *koku.* The actual value of a *koku* varied over time. Papinot (1910: 300) notes that in 1787 one *koku* was valued at a little over five *ryō*. (During the Tokugawa period a *ryō* was a gold piece weighing just over half an ounce, about 16.5 g.) One *koku* of rice was a quantity sufficient to feed one person for one year.

kokujin 国人【國人】. A medieval term for semi-independent local warrior-proprietors and provincial warriors during the Ashikaga period. As the fourteenth century progressed, the *kokujin* began to lose control over villages and rural fighting men (*jisamurai*). Consequently, the *daimyō* began bypassing them and dealing directly with the villages. Cut off from their agrarian support, many of the *kokujin* gave up their status as rural gentry and became full-time warriors for the *daimyō*. Others who were located away from agricultural areas resisted this change by forming provincial warrior groups (*kuni ikki*).

Further reading in English:

- Davis, 1974: 233–237.
- Tsang, 2008.

kokujin ikki 国人一揆【國人一揆】. See: *kuni ikki.*

K

Kokuryūkai 黒竜会【黒龍會】. The Amur River Society (often rendered in English as the "Black Dragon Society"). The Kokuryūkai was an ultra-rightist organization formed in 1901 by Uchida Ryōhei, a Shindō Musō Ryū *menkyo kaiden* of samurai lineage (*shizoku*). As an organization closely related to the Gen'yōsha, the major goals of the Kokuryūkai were to promote Dai Ajiashugi[37] and increase the awareness of the Japanese populace regarding the perceived threat of Russia's expansion across the Amur River into China. In order to achieve these goals they carried out intelligence missions and guerilla activities in Korea and Manchuria. They also supported Sun Yat-sen in his attempts to foment an anti-Qing revolution in China.

From its beginning, the name of the society was translated literally by the Western press as "Black Dragon," a misleading interpretation which somehow seemed more sinister than its actual meaning. In Japanese, "Kokuryū" refers to the Chinese name for the Amur River (Ch. Heilong Jiang 黑龍江, lit. "Black Dragon River"), which runs between Manchuria and Russia.

As in the Gen'yōsha, a large number of the Kokuryūkai's early members were men of samurai lineage (*shizoku*) from Fukuoka (formerly part of Chikuzen domain under the Tokugawa). Due to their promotion of Dai Ajiashugi, the members of this organization—particularly its leader, Uchida Ryōhei—have often been painted as dangerous right-wing extremists. However, in his in-depth essay on the Kokuryūkai and Gen'yōsha, John Wayne Sabey (1973: 328–329, 331) notes the similarity between this mission and certain socio-political philosophies in the West (white man's burden, Manifest Destiny, etc.), and points out:

> ...it is perhaps more helpful to view them as misguided idealists who were indifferent to humanistic and democratic values because their samurai training had not inculcated such conceptions and they, unlike some of their fellow *shizoku*, were either unwilling or unable to see things in terms of social values imported from the West. To them, the (Japanese) empire's dignity and autonomy, combined with the preservation of Asian culture, was of much more importance than individual rights and freedoms or a certain amount of human suffering.
>
> ...Although the samurai tradition did not ask men to shrink from war or bloodshed in the defense of higher ideals, neither did it allow for torture, cruelty and rape as ends in themselves, and Tōyama and Uchida were honest and faithful adherents to the samurai ideal.

Like the Gen'yōsha under Tōyama Mitsuru, the Kokuryūkai promoted the preservation of traditional Japanese martial arts. Not surprisingly, a number of twentieth-century martial artists in Tōkyō—Kanō Jigorō (Kōdōkan Jūdō), Ōmori Sōgen (Jiki Shinkage Ryū), Shimizu Takaji (Shindō Musō Ryū), Sō Dōshin (Nippon Shōrinji Kempō), and Ueshiba Morihei (Aikikai Aikidō) among them—were associated with the Kokuryūkai and the Gen'yōsha.

Further reading in English:

• Sabey, 1973.

Kokusai Jōdō Renmei 国際杖道連盟 (the International Jodo Federation). In order to promote the international dissemination of Shindō Musō Ryū *jōdō*, Shimizu Takiji, the twenty-fifth headmaster of the Shindō Musō Ryū, founded the Kokusai Jōdō Renmei in 1966, with the assistance of his students Donn F. Draeger, Phil Relnick, and Donald Buck. After Shimizu's death in 1978, and Draeger's[38] death in 1982, Phil Relnick[39] assumed the presidency of the organization. Later, in order to secure a strong link with Shindō Musō Ryū in Japan, Relnick invited Nishioka Tsuneo, a Shindō Musō Ryū *menkyo kaiden* under Shimizu Takaji, to become the technical authority for the organization. As of 2009, Pascal Krieger (*okuiri* under Shimizu Takaji; *shomokuroku* under Kaminoda Tsunenori; *menkyo kaiden* under Nishioka Tsuneo) is the current president of the IJF.

The IJF today is composed of national federations from several nations. Although it retains ties with Japanese master teachers as technical advisors, this organization operates

[37] Lit., "Greater Asianism"—a vision of Japan expelling European imperialists from Asia after which Japan would lead East Asia to a more enlightened future.

[38] See Bibliography.

[39] See Bibliography.

independently of any Japanese *jōdō* organization.

Kokusai Jūdō Renmei 国際柔道連盟 (the International Judo Federation). Kanō Jigorō, founder of Kōdōkan Jūdō, traveled abroad many times to further his goal of an internationalized *jūdō*. Although he passed away in 1938, his goal came to fruition in 1952 with the formation of the Kokusai Jūdō Renmei. Today the Federation is considered the senior world body for *jūdō*. It is composed of national federations from more than seventy countries.

Kokusai Kendō Renmei 国際剣道連盟 (the International Kendo Federation). The stated purpose of the Kokusai Kendō Renmei, which was founded in 1971, is to promote peace and prosperity through the "spirit of *budō*" (*budō seishin*). Partly due to this organization's efforts, thousands of people around the world practice *kendō* today.

Kokusai Kyūdō Renmei 国際弓道連盟 (the International Kyūdō Federation). The stated purpose of the Kokusai Kyūdō Renmei is "finding peace and harmony through the practice of *kyūdō*." In 2009, the IKF was composed of seventeen nations totaling about 130,000 participants, most of them in Japan.

kokushu 国主【國主】. Prior to the Tokugawa period, the *kokushu* were *daimyō* who ruled over large areas of the country, functioning as "governors" who controlled one or more provinces. According to Papinot (1910: 66), just prior to the Tokugawa period there were eighteen *kokushu*. See also: *daimyō*.

Kōkyō 孔教 [A.k.a. ***Kōmōgaku*** 孔孟学【孔孟學】]. Confucianism.

kokyū 呼吸. Breath, breathing.

kokyūhō 呼吸法. Breathing method. Many martial traditions, both classical and modern, include some type of *kokyūhō* in their training regimen. While some may be theoretically similar, they are often diverse in actual practice.

Komagawa Kaishin Ryū 駒川改心流. A comprehensive school of martial arts (*sōgō bujutsu*) founded by Komagawa Tarōzaemon no jō Kuniyoshi around 1570. The school included combative swordsmanship (*kenjutsu*), with substantial curricula covering both the long (*katana*) and short (*kodachi*) swords, long-hafted glaive arts (*naginatajutsu*), quick-draw swordsmanship (*iaijutsu*), spear arts (*sōjutsu*), composite sickle and chain (*kusarigama*), police-truncheon techniques (*juttejutsu*), the three police arresting polearms (*mitsudōgu*), and other police-type weaponry.

Komagawa, who hailed from the old province of Kai, was one of the later disciples of Kamiizumi Nobutsuna, founder of the Shinkage Ryū (1) 新陰流. Komagawa then proceeded to develop his own system, for which he created close to 140 combative forms. He was succeeded by another warrior from Kai known as Sakurada Jirōzaemon Sadakuni. Sakurada was an avid martial artist who roamed all around the country on a warrior pilgrimage for twenty years from the age of twenty-two. He renamed Kamagawa's school the Sakurada Ryū 桜田流. The school was passed down in various areas for as many as fifteen generations into the twentieth century.

K

Komagawa Tarōzaemon no jō Kuniyoshi 駒川 太郎左衛門尉 国吉 (fl. second half of the sixteenth century). A student of Kamiizumi Nobutsuna who founded the Komagawa Kaishin Ryū around 1570.

KOMA INU
Shintō shrine entrance at the Fudōin Iwayadō, a Shugendō temple in Wakasa, Japan
(Photograph courtesy Mike Davenport)

koma inu 狛犬 [Also written 高麗犬]. Lit. "Korean dog." SHINTŌ—Much like statues of the Buddhist deity Niō, the *koma inu* is usually found paired with the "Chinese lion" (*karajishi*) on martial accoutrements and at the gates of Shintō shrines. Originally the *koma inu* was placed on the right with its mouth closed, representing the Sanskrit sound *hūṁ* (Jp. *un*). The *karajishi* was traditionally placed on the left of entranceways with its mouth open, representing the Sanskrit sound *a*. Originally distinctive, over time the design of the two animals and their relative placement became indistinguishable aside from the open or closed mouth. The *koma inu* is sometimes referred to in the West as a fu dog, lion dog, or Korean dog. In a martial context, the *koma inu* and the *karajishi* are frequently used as talismans on martial accoutrements. See: *karajishi; Niō; shishi (1).*

komarobashi 小転. YAGYŪ SHINKAGE RYŪ—In addition to being a principle of the Shinkage Ryū, *marobashi* is a term used in several sets of Yagyū Shinkage Ryū forms. These forms are used to cultivate/express the concept of *marobashi* within the parameters of combative *kata*. *Komarobashi* is a technique using a large or small sword, and a small movement. The same name is also used for a set of *kata* executed with a short sword used against a long sword. Contrast to *ōmarobashi*.

kombō 棍棒. See: *konbō.*

Komine Denshichirō 小峰 伝七郎【小峰傳七郎】(?–1660). Founder of the Jishin Ryū 自心流, a system specializing in combative swordsmanship (*kenjutsu*). Komine did so after mastering the Asayama Ichiden Ryū 浅山一伝流 as taught by Katō Shigeri Masakatsu.

Kōmokuten 広目天【廣目天】<Ch. Guangmutian <Skt. Virūpākṣa. One of the Four Deva Kings (Shitennō). Kōmokuten guards the western slope of Mount Sumeru (Shumi-sen). His name means "the *deva* of the broad (or ugly) eyes," and his color is red. His accoutrement is the writing brush. See also: *Miru.*

komusō 虚無僧. 1. Lit. "monks of emptiness." Flute-playing mendicant Buddhist priests of the Fuke Shū. 2. ***Komusō*** 虚無僧. An alternate name for the Fuke Shū, a supposed subsect of Rinzai Zen Buddhism. The name is popularly thought to have originated with the Japanese priest Kakushin in the mid-thirteenth century. See: *Fuke Shū.*

Further reading in English:

- Sanford, 1977: 411–440.

KOMUSŌ

kōmyō 高名. A medieval term for fame. *Kōmyō* was obtained by fighting an enemy of proper status; that is, someone of equal or higher rank who had a reputation as a strong warrior.

kon 棍 <Ch. *gun*. OKINAWAN KOBUDŌ—A generic term for the club or staff used in some schools of Okinawan *kobudō*. See: *Okinawa kobudō.*

Kōnan Ryū 硬軟流. OKINAWAN KARATE—A *karate* school which split off from the Uechi Ryū Karate Kyōkai 上地流空手協会 in 1978. It takes its name from Uechi Kambun's original name for his school, Pangainūn Ryū *karatejutsu* 半硬軟流空手術 (also read Hankōnan Ryū *karatejutsu*).

konbō 棍棒 [Also read ***kombō***]. A generic term for a stick or cudgel.

Konchiin Sūden 金地院 崇伝【金地院 崇傳】. See: *Sūden.*

kondei 健児. Lit. "stalwart youth." This term was used in a 792 edict to indicate provincial martial artists who would be selected for duty in the government's forces. The *kondei* were members of the warrior class which had formerly commanded the conscript armies formed under the Taihō Codes (Taihō Ritsuryō). They came from families of the provincial governors and strongmen (*kuni no miyatsuko*). The *kondei* replaced the conscripted troops formerly sent from the capital and, at least officially, fell under the authority of the Ministry of War (Hyōbushō). Farris (1992: 108–109) notes that *kondei* were allowed two grooms, who also probably acted as foot soldiers. This indicates that the *kondei* were mounted warriors with two footsoldier attendants, an arrangement very much like that enjoyed by the twelfth-century *bushi*. See also: *bushi; ikusa; kuni no miyatsuko; musha; tsuwamono.*

Kondei Sho 健児所. An eighth-century governmental department that dealt with the *kondei* (see above), much as the later Kebiishi Chō handled police affairs.

Kondō Isami Masayoshi 近藤 勇 昌宜 [A.k.a. ***Ōkubo Yamato*** 大久保 大和] (1834–1868). Fourth headmaster of the Tennen Rishin Ryū 天然理心流. Born as the third son of Miyakawa Kujiro, Isami began training in the Tennen Rishin Ryū in 1849, at the age of sixteen. Later he became the adopted son of the third headmaster and assumed leadership of the school. At that time he changed his name to Kondō Isami.

Kondō is best known as one of the commanders of the infamous shogunate-sponsored Shinsengumi police force in Kyōto. The Tokugawa shogunate sent the Shinsengumi to Kyōto to quell dissent during the mid-1860s. Their reign of terror ended with the collapse of the shogunate in 1868. Kondō and several other leaders were arrested and executed by the new government.

KONDŌ ISAMI MASAYOSHI
(Image courtesy Ryūgenji temple in Tōkyō)

Kondo Katsuyuki 近藤 勝之 (b.1945). Current successor of the main (Takeda family) line of Daitō Ryū. Kondo began training in Daitō Ryū in 1957 under Hosono Tsunejirō, and later under Yoshida Kōtarō in Tōkyō. He began training with Takeda Tokimune in 1960. In 1974 he was the first, and evidently only, trainee to receive the Daitō Ryū *kyōju dairi* certification from Takeda. Kondo was also the only practitioner to receive the license of Daitō Ryū *sōke dairi* (May 1988) from Takeda.

Further reading in English:
• Pranin, 1996: 152–177.

Kondō Kuranosuke Nagahiro 近藤 内蔵助 長裕. Founder of the Tennen Rishin Ryū 天然理心流. He established the school at some point during the Kansei era (1789–1801).

kon'efu 近衛府. See: *konoefu.*

kongō 金剛 <Ch. *jingang* <Skt. *vajra*]. Lit. "strong/rigid metal." This term normally indicates something that is very hard, adamantine, or diamond-like. In India, the Sanskrit term *vajra* (usually translated as *kongō* in East Asia) could also mean "thunderbolt," a "diamond," a "priest's scepter,"or an Esoteric Buddhist symbol of the absolute (Skt. *śūnyatā*). In ancient India, the god Indra, much like his Indo-European counterparts Zeus and Thor, was depicted using his highly effective thunderbolts (*vajra*) to destroy his enemies. In East Asian Esoteric Buddhism, the term 金剛 (Ch. *jingang*) was used by the Chinese to translate the Sanksrit word *vajra.* Buddhist scholar Edward Conze (1951: 178) noted, "Itself unbreakable, it breaks everything else." See also: *kongōsho; Niō.*

Kongōchō-kyō 『金剛頂経』【金剛頂經】<Ch. *Jingang ding jing* <Skt. *Vajraśekhara-sūtra*). BUDDHISM—One of three central texts in the tantric practices of the Tendai and Shingon schools of Buddhism in Japan. This text is closely associated with the *Kongōkai Mandara.* Many of the Buddhist "deities" depicted in the *Kongōkai Mandara* are used as talismans on martial accoutrements and weaponry. See also: *Dainichi-kyō; Kongōkai Mandara; Kongōkai shiki; Soshijikara-kyō.*

KONGŌKAI MANDARA
Heian-period painting (c. 1000 CE)
Tōji temple (Shingon school) in Kyōto

Kongōkai Mandara 金剛界曼荼羅 <Ch. *Jingangjie mantuluo* <Skt. Vajradhātu-maṇḍāla. BUDDHISM—The Diamond Matrix (mandala). Represented in a matrix of nine sections, the Kongōkai is one of the two great mandalas which are the central ritual focus of the Tendai and Shingon Japanese Tantric Buddhist schools. Representing the spiritual world, the Kongōkai is filled with a pantheon of Buddhas, *bodhisattva*, *deva*, and other beings. The mandala and its ritual texts are based on a major Tantric Buddhist text, the *Kongōchō-kyō* (Skt. *Vajraśekhara-sūtra*); the ritual is an integral part of the training series all Tendai and Shingon monks must master. Many of the Buddhist deities in the Kongōkai which became popular in Japanese culture were seen as protectors, and were associated with talismans for the warrior class. See also: *Kongōkai shiki; Shido kegyō; Taizōkai Mandara.*

KONGŌKAI MANDARA (SECTION DETAIL)
Heian-period painting (c. 1000 CE)
Tōji temple (Shingon school) in Kyōto

Kongōkai shiki 『金剛界私記』. BUDDHISM—The *Kongōkai shiki* is a text, composed in Japan, which contains directions for performing the ritual associated with the Kongōkai Mandara. It is one of four basic exoteric/tantric rituals (*shidō kegyō*) that must be mastered by members of the Tendai and Shingon schools of Japanese Buddhism. Originally derived from ritual instructions included in the *Kongōchō-kyō* and associated Chinese manuals, there are several variations of this text found in both the Tendai and Shingon schools. Many of the Buddhist deities which became popular in Japanese culture are found in the *Kongōkai shiki*. They were seen as protectors, and were associated with talismans for the warrior class. See also: *Goma shiki; Jūhachidō shiki; Kongōchō-kyō; Shido kegyō; Taizōkai shiki.*

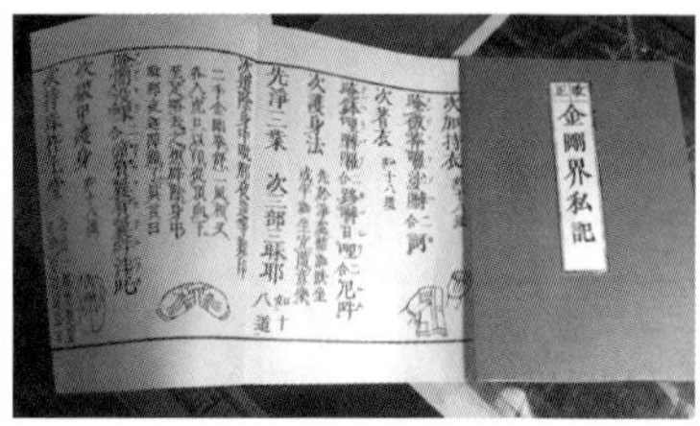

KONGŌKAI SHIKI
Ritual text used in conjunction
with the Kongōkai Mandara
(Private collection)

kongōsho 金剛杵 <Ch. *jingangchu*. 1. BUDDHISM—A votive *vajra* scepter. For the Esoteric Buddhist schools—Tendai, Shingon, etc.—the *vajra* scepter is a variegated symbol to which many powers are assigned: it represents diamond hardness, indestructibility, the Buddhist Law, mystic Truth, Knowledge, the power of knowledge over ignorance, and the thunderbolt flash of enlightenment. As a scepter, it also symbolizes sovereignty.

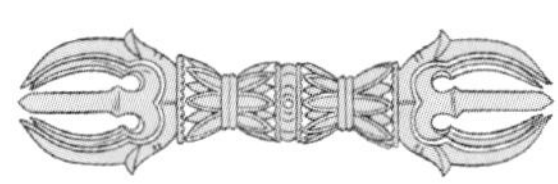

JAPANESE *KONGŌSHO*
Goko (five-point *vajra*) type
(Illustration after a Japanese text)

A variety of *vajra* scepters are found in East Asian Esoteric Buddhism, each having a different number of points: one, two, three, four, five, nine, and a special crossed-three-point version; each symbolizes certain philosophical aspects of Buddhism.

2. *Kongōsho* are not meant to be used as weapons in Esoteric Buddhist rituals. However, there is a variety of *vajra* scepter in India, the *vajramuṣṭi*, which clearly indicates the martial origins of this votive object. *Vajramuṣṭi* are shaped much like brass knuckles, and are used in a popular form of wrestling in India.

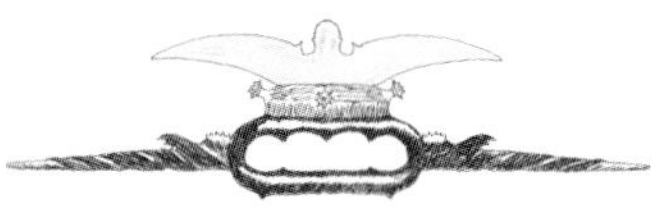

INDIAN *VAJRAMUṢṬI*
Antecedent of the East Asian *kongōsho*
(Illustration of a *vajramuṣṭi* held at the Madras Museum)

In addition, several *vajramuṣṭi* preserved at the Madras Museum have long points and cutting blades, and were clearly intended for combat (Sandesara and Mehta, 1964: 31).

In East Asia the points of the *kongōsho* scepter are normally turned inward to prevent accidental injury. However, occasional examples of *vajra* scepters can be found with their tines turned outward, reminiscent of the Indian *vajramuṣṭi*.

kongō zue 金剛杖. Lit. "*vajra* staff," "diamond staff," "thunderbolt staff." BUDDHISM—A medium-length staff or cane representing a single-point *vajra* scepter (*tokkosho*). This staff was used by religious pilgrims and *yamabushi*.

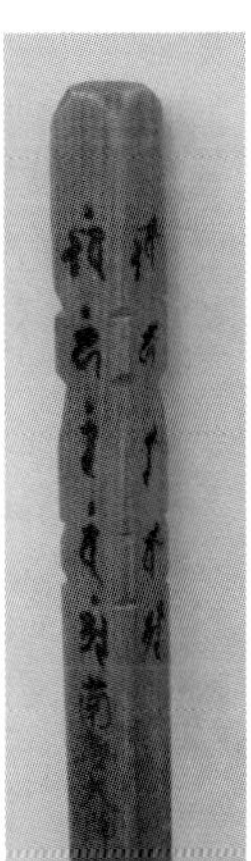

JAPANESE *KONGŌ ZUE*
Kongō zue of the type used by lay pilgrims (*henro*)
(Author's collection)

There are various types: some have a bell attached; some have the symbols of the Esoteric Buddhist stupa (*gorin no tō*) carved into the top end. The *kongō zue* was not necessarily intended as a weapon; however, almost any type of staff (*bō, jō,* etc.) can certainly be used as a weapon. In fact, as one of the "sixteen accoutrements of the *yamabushi*" (*yamabushi jūroku dōgu*), the *kongō zue* is a weapon-usable object that could be utilized as a cane for climbing or as a defense against animals or bandits. See also: *bō; gorin no tō; hanbō; jō; nyoi; shakujō; tokkosho; yamabushi; yamabushi jūroku dōgu.*

Konjaku monogatari 『今昔物語』. An early twelfth-century compilation of "tales from long ago," some of which are war tales (*gunkimono*). See Wilson (1973) for a translation of the war tales within this work.

Further reading in English:

- Varley, 1994: 22–35.
- Wilson, 1973.

Kon no Bu 棍の部. OKINAWAN KOBUDŌ—Curriculum used by the Ryūei Ryū (2) 劉衛流 which contains imported Chinese combative staff scenarios.

Kōnodai Sensō 鴻の台戦争. Two battles between the Hōjō and Satomi clans, the first of which took place in 1538; the second, in 1564. Both battles were won by the Hōjō. Kōnodai (present-day Kokufudai) was a small but strategically located village on the Edo River. Kamiizumi Hidetane, son of the founder of the Shinkage Ryū (1) 新陰流, was killed in the second battle in 1564.

Kono Efu 近衛府 (Also read **Kon'efu**). A ninth-century term for imperial guards. The Kono Efu were divided into two units: the Imperial Guards of the Left (Sa Konoefu 左近衛府), and the Imperial Guards of the Right (U Konoefu 右近衛府). See: *Efu, Hyōefu.*

ko no ha tengu 木の葉天狗. A human-shaped *tengu* with wings and a long nose. See also: *karasu tengu; tengu.*

konsaibō 金砕棒. Lit. "metal-crushing staff."

A hardwood staff reinforced with metal strips. See also: *bō; bōjutsu; rokushaku bō; tetsubō; yoribō.*

konshi 健士 [Also read *kenshi*]. Lit. a "strong warrior." This was a ninth-century term for veterans of several conflicts that took place in Tohoku. According to Farris (1992: 112), because of their combat experience the *konshi* were sent by the imperial court in Kyoto to replace the garrison soldiers (*chinpei*) at Fort Izawa and Tamazukiri Palisade.

Konshin Ryū 今真流. A school of grappling and capturing arts (*jūhojutsu* 柔捕術) founded sometime around 1800. Its last known headmaster was Ueshima Sannosuke who, with the help of an Okinawan *karate* teacher named Kinjō Kensei, combined the system into a hybrid *karate-jūjutsu* school in 1937. The new school was called the Kūshin Ryū 空真流.

Kōotsu Ryū 甲乙流. A branch tradition of the Edo Yagyū Shinkage Ryū that concentrated on swordsmanship (*kenjutsu*) and armored grappling (*kumiuchi* 組討). It was founded in the early 1630s by Matsudaira Sadatsuna, a direct disciple (*deshi*) of Yagyū Munenori.

koppō 骨法. One of several terms for unarmored grappling, all of which are subsumed under the term *jūjutsu.*

koppōjutsu 骨法術. A subsystem of *daken taijutsu* (a boxing/striking fighting system) derived from Shinden Fudō Ryū 神伝不動流. This system, which focuses on attacks against an enemy's skeletal structure, is currently (2012) taught by the Bujinkan under Hatsumi Masaaki. See also: *koshijutsu.*

kōran 撹乱【攪亂】. An agitator; an espionage agent. See: *ninjutsu.*

kōri 郡 See: *kohori.*

kōrin 光輪. BUDDHISM—A halo; the aura of a buddha or *bodhisattva.*

Kōrindō 光輪洞 [Abbr. of ***Nipponden Jūjutsu Kōrindō Aikidō*** 日本伝柔術光輪洞合気道; a.k.a. ***Kōkadō*** 恒河洞]. A branch tradition of Ueshiba Ryū *aikidō* founded by Hirai Minoru in 1945. Kōrindō is a modern, eclectic, martial-ways system (*sōgō budō*). It is based not only on Hirai's study of *aiki budō* under Ueshiba in the early 1940s, but also his own background in other classical martial disciplines such as quick-draw swordsmanship (*iaijutsu*), Tōgun Ryū 東軍流 strategy and tactics (*heihō*), *jūjutsu*, and so on. Training in Kōrindō under Hirai included *jūjutsu*, as well as the use of the sword (*ken*), spear (*yari*), medium-length staff (*jō*), and long hardwood staff (*bō*).

In Buddhist texts, the term *kōrin* refers to a halo (as in an aura around a saint or buddha), with the associated meaning of "spreading light in all directions." This is reflected in the core practice of Kōrindō, eight body displacement forms (*taisabaki*) that are aimed at instilling the ability to handle combative situations via "circular displacement."

Further reading in English:

• Pranin, 1994: 10–15.

koryū 古流. The "old" or "classical" martial traditions. The appearance of the early *koryū* (schools/traditions) of martial arts (*bugei*) in Japan was due to a number of interrelated factors and events. The profession of arms in Japan was primarily dominated by the warrior class (*bushi*) from the eleventh through fourteenth centuries. Throughout that era, becoming a warrior was a hereditary occupation, and the *bugei* were taught privately within family and clan lines. For a number of reasons, however, this custom of familial teaching began to shift. In the political/military arena, the Ashikaga shogunate (the military government of the Muromachi period) was never able to tightly control the country. This paralleled an increase in the strength and number of contending political/military factions, such as warrior families not aligned with the Ashikaga, independent warlords, monasteries with powerful armies of warrior monks (*sōhei*), bands of brigands (*nobushi*), and so forth. After the Ōnin War (1467–1477), the fortunes of these contending factions fluctuated greatly.

This state of uncertainty had several consequences concerning the development of the early *ryū*. For one, civilians became more interested in learning combatives for self-preservation. Further, the number of combatants from non-*bushi* clans expanded greatly to fill the ranks of the numerous contending military forces. In addition, the number of disenfranchised *bushi* who began to hire themselves out as mercenaries or trainers for warriors of other clans expanded greatly, as did bands of rascals and brigands (*nobushi*) and lightly armored foot soldiers (*ashigaru*). In contrast to the traditional clan-oriented instruction of the classical *bushi*, training ever-greater numbers of combatants in a shorter length of time required systemized martial curricula such as Iizasa Chōisai Ienao's modification of Katori no Ken (Katori swordsmanship) into the Tenshinshō-den Katori Shintō Ryū, and Tsukahara Bokuden's transformation of Kashima no Tachi (Kashima swordsmanship) into Kashima Shintō Ryū.

As the number of mercenary *bushi*, *nobushi*, and *ashigaru* increased, the relative percentage of wealthy hereditary warriors decreased proportionally, changing the character of warfare in Japan in a distinct way. Since most of these "common" soldiers and mercenary *bushi* did not have the economic backing enjoyed by a mounted, armored warrior, fewer horses were used. This, in turn, led to an increasing shift in emphasis on the battlefield away from mounted warfare (*kibasen*) tactics to infantry (*tohosen*) tactics.

Infantry tactics required a new type of swordsmanship and a new type of sword. From as early as the eighth century, the preferred sword of the Japanese horse-mounted warriors was at first the *warabite tō*, and later the *tachi*, both curved blades that were used primarily for one-handed slashing from horseback. As early as the turbulent beginnings of the Muromachi period, however, a slightly smaller sword with less curvature, the *uchigatana* (or *katana*), began to appear. This weapon was better suited for infantry cut-and-thrust use than the *tachi*. As combat with the *katana* grew more sophisticated, survivors of the battlefield began to evolve their own "secret techniques" which they felt guaranteed success in combat.

These interrelated elements—an increase in the demand for combative training; the systematization and modification of clan-based warrior arts in order to teach both *bushi* and non-*bushi* combatants; the decrease in the use of the horse; the modification of the sword and attendant increase in the need for infantry-useable swordsmanship with specialized techniques—led to the rise of itinerant master swordsmen (*kensei*). The earliest *ryū* formed around these martial geniuses and their systematization of secret techniques centered on the *katana* and its longer sibling, the *ōdachi*. It should be noted here that a number of weapons systems were taught by these early *ryū* founders. However, their combative arts teachings usually centered either on using the *katana* or on dealing with the *katana* when using other weapons. The martial curricula taught by *kensei* were comprehensive, however, including not only combative weapons-handling, but also strategy and tactics, field fortifications, espionage, etiquette, morals, and Buddhist, Daoist, and Shintō esoterica.

Almost all of these early *ryū* and their secret techniques claimed as their inspiration Shintō spiritual powers (*kami*), often in co-operation with, or manifested as, one or more Buddhist esoteric deities. This spiritual connection between the warrior and esoteric Buddhism goes back at least as early as the Heian period (794–1185).

These earliest traditions included the Nen Ryū (c.1368), the Chūjō Ryū (c.1368), the Tenshinshō-den Katori Shintō Ryū (c.1446), and the Kage no Ryū (c.1488). Many early *ryū* taught such skills as combative swordsmanship (*kenjutsu*), archery (*kyūjutsu*), long-hafted glaive (*naginatajutsu*), and grappling in armor (*yoroi kumiuchi*). Skills not directly related to weapon use were also taught, such as the construction of field fortifications including geomancy (*chikujōjutsu*), espionage (*shinobi no jutsu*), signaling troops in battle with the conch shell (*jingaijutsu*), and so on. The *ryū* also taught various forms of strategy, and imbued their members with a warrior ethos. These martial traditions were transmitted from one generation to another through a series of consanguineous (*sei*) and non-consanguineous (*dai*) headmasters. Martial creativity flourished in Japan, and by the late Edo period about 9,000 *ryū* had been catalogued.[40] With the opening of Japan to the West and the establishment of a Western-style military in the late 1800s, these earlier warrior traditions became referred to as the *koryū* (old traditions).

Further reading in English:

- Bennett, 2005.
- Draeger, 1973a.
- Hall, 1990: 243–304.
- Farris, 1992.
- Friday, 1988 and 1992.
- Skoss, D., 1997; 1999; 2002.

Kōsaka Masanobu 高坂 昌信 (d.1578). One of the Takeda Nijūyon Shō (Takeda's twenty-four generals), Masanobu was considered one of the most loyal vassals of warlord Takeda Shingen. He began compiling records of the exploits and tactics of the Takeda; these were later edited into a larger work, the *Kōyō gunkan*, by a samurai named Obata Kagenori.

Kosei jidai 古世時代. Japan's Ancient Age, roughly 645 to 1185 C.E.

Ko Sekiguchi Ryū 小関口流. A school of quick-draw sword arts (*iaijutsu*) founded by Mizuno Sakubei Tadakatsu. Mizuno first mastered the Sekiguchi Ryū under Suzuki Kozaemon Masashige, who was a headmaster in the line from Sekiguchi Yazaemon Yorinobu. Up until that time there had been two theories of quick-draw sword arts in Yorinobu's line: one preferring to use a longsword and one preferring a short sword. Mizuno favored the short-sword approach; his line, which came to be called the Ko Sekiguchi Ryū (Small [blade] Sekiguchi Ryū), stood in contrast to others in the Yorinobu line, which came to be called the Ō Sekiguchi Ryū (Large [blade] Sekiguchi Ryū). See also: *Sekiguchi Ryū*.

Kōsekikō sanryaku 『黄石公三略』<Ch. *Huang Shigong sanlue*. One of the seven Chinese classics on military strategy. See: *Sanryaku*.

[40] The number of *koryū* that have existed in Japan is unknown. Nine thousand was the estimate made by Watatani Kiyoshi in the 1970s. However, other sources vary. Fujita Seiko (1960: 3), for example, estimated 4,425. The nature of the *koryū* makes it impossible to determine an exact count.

Kose Yosazaemon Osamune 小瀬 与三左衛門 長宗. See: *Tose Yosazaemon Osamune*.

koshi 腰. Lower back; hip(s).

Kōshi 孔子. Confucius.

koshigatana 腰刀. Lit. "hip sword." See: *kaiken*.

Koshiki no Kata 古式の形. KŌDŌKAN JŪDŌ—Lit. "classical forms." The Koshiki no Kata are *jūjutsu* forms from Kitō Ryū 起倒流 that were incorporated into Kōdōkan Jūdō by Kanō Jigorō. They are also known as the Kitō Ryū no Kata. Kanō noted, "These techniques are of a high order and highly refined, and their practice brings insight into *jūdō* theory." The set of twenty-one *kata* is divided into two sections: Omote, which contains fourteen forms; and Ura, which contains seven. See also: *Kōdōkan Jūdō*.

Further reading in English:

- Kano, 1986.
- Mifune, 2004.

koshinawa 腰縄【腰繩】. A rope about 5 feet (1.5 m) long with a ring or loop affixed to one end; it was carried by mounted warriors (*bushi*). The *koshinawa* was affixed to the belt (*obi*) or fastened to the saddle (*kura*). It could be used as a spare girth, a rope for binding prisoners (*torinawa*), a horse tether, etc.

koshi no mawari 腰回 [Also written 腰廻]. Lit. "around the hips." 1. TAKENOUCHI RYŪ—A small-weapon grappling system created by Takenouchi Hisamori, founder of the Takenouchi Ryū. This system makes use of a short sword (*kodachi*) and a length of rope called a *koshi no mawari* wound around one's hips. Successive headmasters elaborated on this system, creating a number of related fighting arts. *Koshi no mawari* is apparently equivalent to the term *dōmawari* used in Namba Ippo Ryū. 2. SŌSUISHITSU RYŪ—A term used to refer to quick-draw sword arts.

koshirae 拵え. Lit. "make" or "workmanship." In the case of Japanese swords (*nihontō*), the term *koshirae* refers to the sword's fittings or "furniture" apart from the blade.

koshitate 腰楯. A standing shield. *Koshitate* were used to protect soldiers from arrows;

they were also used on Japanese skiffs during the Mongol invasions (Genkō no Eki) of the late thirteenth century.

koshi waza 腰技. KŌDŌKAN JŪDŌ—Hip-throwing techniques. *Koshi waza* represent a subset of Nage no Kata.

Kosokun 公相君. See: *Kūsankū.*

kosshijutsu 骨指術. A subsystem of *daken taijutsu* (a boxing/striking fighting system) which concentrates on attacks against an enemy's musculature. Derived from Shinden Fudō Ryū 神伝不動流, this system is currently taught by the Bujinkan under Hatsumi Masaaki. See: *koppōjutsu.*

kosuhyōshi 越拍子. Lit. "to pass by the opponent's beat." YAGYŪ SHINKAGE RYŪ—An attack in which the proponent avoids the enemy's attack and strikes him just at the moment his attack is expended. See: *hyōshi.*

Kotaki Yoemon 小滝 与右衛門【小瀧 與右衛門】. Seventeenth-century founder of a school of combative swordsmanship known as the Kagami Ryū 鏡見流. Kotaki was a direct disciple (*deshi*) of Yagyū Muneynori, the leader of the Edo Yagyū Shinkage Ryū.

kote 小手 [Var. 籠手]. 1. The hand/wrist/forearm target area. 2. A gauntlet; an armored sleeve. There are many types and designs of *kote* (2). 3. Thick protective gloves or mitts worn in the practice of *kendō*.

kotō 1. 古刀. Lit. "old swords." A Japanese sword made prior to the seventeenth century.[41] *Kotō* are further divided into those made before the tenth century and those made after. See also: *gendaitō; guntō; kaiguntō; kyūguntō; Nippontō; shinguntō; shinshintō; shintō (2); Shōwatō; Yasukunitō.*

Kotō 2. 虎韜. See: *Rikutō.*

Kotōda Ha Ittō Ryū 古藤田派一刀流. A system of combative swordsmanship (*kenjutsu*) and spear arts (*sōjutsu*) practiced in Tōda domain during the eighteenth and nineteenth centuries. Kashiwabuchi Yugi, a student of Masaki Toshimitsu, illustrated a number of the techniques of this *ryū* in his late eighteenth-century work *Geijutsu bukoron*. See also: *Edo Machikata Jutte Torinawa Atsukaiyō; Masaki Ryū; Sen'i Ryū.*

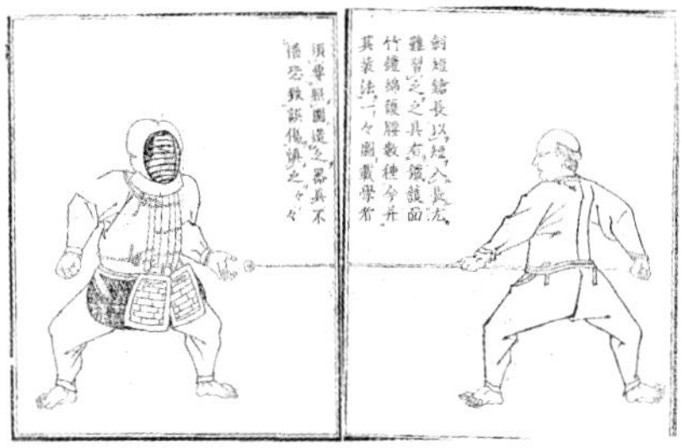

ILLUSTRATION OF KOTODA HA ITTŌ RYŪ *SŌJUTSU*
Detail from the *Geijutsu bukoron* (1768)

kotodama 言霊【言靈】. 1. *Kotodama* refers to the soul/spirit/power of language; the magical power of words or sacred sounds. 2. CLASSICAL WARRIOR IDEAL—Correct use of words. In this sense, *kotodama* was considered one of the essential characteristics of the classical warrior (*bushi*). See: *bushi no konjō.*

kotsukudaki 骨砕. See: *honekudaki.*

ko umajirushi 小馬印. A small battle standard. See: *umajirushi.*

kowami 剛身. A variant term for *jūjutsu.*

Koyama Takako 小山 孝子. The current (thirteenth) headmaster of the Yōshin Ryū. Koyama teaches Yōshin Ryū *naginatajutsu* (glaive arts) in Hiroshima.

Kōyō gunkan 『甲陽軍鑑』【甲陽軍鑒】(The Military chronicles of the Takeda clan of Kai). Although largely compiled by Kōsaka Danjō Masanobu, a vassal of Takeda Shingen, the *Kōyō gunkan* was completed in 1616 by Obata Kagenori. The text is a twenty-volume work divided into fifty-nine chapters. Essentially concerned with the strategy, tactics, customs, and history of the Takeda clan of Kai during the Sengoku Jidai (1482–1558) this omnibus work greatly influenced the warrior class (*bushi*) of the peaceful Edo period (1603–1867).

Although frequently referenced as a sort of "bible of the *samurai*" for its information on the history and military strategy of the Warring States period, it was perhaps most prominent in its use as an ethics textbook for the

[41] Technically, *kotō* are swords made before 1596.

Edo-period warrior. In fact, in his detailed essay on this text Alexander C. Bennett notes that an "ethics" section of the work dealing with four types of foolish lords was the "most often-quoted portion of the *Kōyō gunkan*."

Further reading in English:

- Bennett, 1999.

kozuka 小柄. A small, narrow knife kept in a slot on the inside of a scabbard and used for throwing at enemies; the targets were usually the forehead, throat, and wrists. Samurai youth were expected to be able to accurately throw the *kozuka* before being allowed to don the *daishō*, the two swords symbolizing samurai status.

KOZUKA
Above: secured in scabbard; below: full image
(Private collection)

Kozukahara 小塚原. See: *Kozukappara.*

Kozukappara 小塚原. One of two infamous execution grounds during the Tokugawa period. Kozukappara was located in the northern section of Edo. See also: *shikei; shikeijjo; Suzagamori.*

kū 空 <Ch. *kong* <Skt. *śūnyatā*. BUDDHISM—Non-substantiality, emptiness; void. *Śūnyatā* is a concept derived from the Buddhist Mahāyāna "perfection of wisdom" literature (*prajñāpāramitā*) and the teachings of the Buddhist philosopher Nāgārjuna. Though it indicates the emptiness of the self-nature of all phenomena, it does not mean that there are no substances in our conventional world. Consequently, it is not a nihilistic concept. When the Chinese translated *śūnyatā* as *kong*, the word took on new shades of meaning colored by Chinese culture and concepts.

Further reading in English:

- Inada, 1970.
- Robinson, 1976.

kubi 首. Head, neck.

kubibukuro 首袋. Lit. "head bag." A net or bag with shoulder straps attached, in which the severed head of an enemy could be carried. When on foot a warrior hung it from his waist; when mounted it was hung from the saddle.

kubijikken 首実験 【首實驗・首實驗】. Inspection of heads. The war tales (*gunkimono*) of the early medieval period often mention a review of every head taken after battle. This was done in order to determine the rewards to be doled out to battle participants.

kubikiri 首切. A "decapitator." 1. A short sword or knife with an incurved, chisel-edged blade used to decapitate a dead enemy. 2. A type of dagger (*tantō*).

Kubikiri Asaemon 首切り朝衛門. Lit. "Asaemon the Decapitator." See: *Yamada Asaemon.*

kubioki 首置. Lit. "head bucket." A shallow wooden bucket with a wooden spike in the center and a tall cover. The *kubioki* was used for sending the head of a samurai sentenced to commit *seppuku* to the local governor for identification. After identification the head and *kubioki* were returned to the family for burial or cremation.

kubitori 首取り. The act of taking heads from fallen opponents.

Kubota Ryōzaburō 窪田 鐐三郎. A samurai from the Shibata domain in Echigo province. Both Kubota and another warrior, Mizoguchi Shūta, trained with Odani Seiichirō in the Jiki Shinkage Ryū from 1843 through 1847. Both were awarded the title of "caretaker of swordsmanship training" (*kenjutsu keiko seiwayaku*) by their domain. Their lines came to be called Seigan Jiki Shinkage Ryū.

kubutsuchi no tachi 頭槌大刀. A sixth-century straight sword generally found in eastern Japan (Kantō). See also: *chokutō; kantō tachi.*

KUBUTSUCHI TACHI

kuchigusuri 口薬【口藥】. Priming powder for a matchlock.

kuchigusuri ire 口薬入【口藥入】. A priming flask used with a matchlock.

kuda 管. 1. Pipe; tube. 2. A sleeve or tube used with a *kudayari.*

kudaki 砕き. Lit. "crushing." The term is sometimes found in the names of prearranged combative forms (*kata*); e.g., *sune kudaki*—shin (*sune*) crusher (*kudaki*).

kudaya 管矢. A tube device for firing arrows.

kudayajutsu 管矢術. A weapons system for the use of the *kudaya*. Fujita (1960: 2) lists only one *ryū* specializing in *kudayajutsu*. See: *Ogasawara Ryū.*

kudayari 管槍 [Var. 早槍; this second term also read *hayayari* meaning "quick spear"]. 1. A pipe spear; a sleeved spear. The sleeve (*kuda*) is normally a short iron pipe, occasionally with a round flange on one end acting as a handguard (*tsuba*). The spear was thrust and retrieved by quickly sliding it back and forth through the pipe; the pipe allowed for more rapid action than using a spear in the hands alone. See also: *Owari Kan Ryū; sōjutsu; yari.* 2. A spear pipe. See: *Itō Suketada; kuda.*

kuden 口伝【口傳】. 1. Oral transmission; oral teaching. 2. Secret transmission.

kuge 公家. A noble of the imperial court. In order to be considered nobility, one had to be awarded the fifth court rank or lower. (The lower the number of the court rank, the higher the status.) Holders of the fifth or fourth court rank were "gentlemen" or "high stewards" (*taifu*). Above them, in the third through first court ranks, were the "high nobles" (*kugyō*). Warriors who had some official capacity or post with the court were usually accorded the sixth court rank and the status of "servant" (*samurai*).

Further reading in English:
- McCullough and McCullough, 1980a.

kuge no tachi 公家之太刀 [A.k.a. **kugyō no tachi** 公卿之太刀]. Lit. "noble's sword." A special form of sword (*tachi*) reserved for use by the princes and nobles of the imperial court.

Kugusuku Ryū 湖城流 (Oki.). See: *Kojō Ryū.*

kugyō 公卿. A noble holding court rank between the third and first level. *Kugyō* means "high noble." See also: *kuge; pēchin; samurai; taifu.*

kugyō no tachi 公卿之太刀. Lit. "high noble's sword." See: *kuge no tachi.*

KUJAKU MYŌŌ
The "Peacock Wisdom Queen" is a deification of a magical formula used against snakebite
(From the Taizōkai Mandara)

Kujaku Myōō 孔雀明王 <Ch. Kongque Ming Wang <Skt. Mahāmāyūrī-vidyārājñī. BUDDHISM—The Peacock Wisdom Queen, a deification of a magical formula used to cure snakebite. Kujaku was one of the first Myōō to appear. Her image is sometimes found on martial accoutrements.

kuji 九字. 1. An abbreviation of Kujihō 九字法 (the Ritual Method of the Nine Seals), which is a Daoist-*cum*-Buddhist ritual of protection

KUJI SYMBOLS ENGRAVED ON THE TANG OF A MUROMACHI-PERIOD *KATANA*
(Private collection)

associated with Marishiten and often found in martial *densho*. 2. The nine mystic letters used in the Kujihō. These symbols are often used as talismans on weapons and accoutrements.

Kujihō 九字法. The Ritual Method of the Nine Seals. In Japan the Kujihō has acquired many talismanic uses during its long history. The earliest of these appear to have been for protection while traveling in the mountains and as a talisman for the battlefield. One researcher into the Chinese origins of the ritual, H. Byron Earhart, noted that the nine characters of the Kujihō can be translated literally as "the armed forces are arrayed against the powers of evil." (Earhart, 1970: 133, fn. 60) The ritual was originally known to Chinese Daoist as the "Secret Spell of the Six Armoring (Martial Spirits)" 六甲秘祝 (Liujia Mizhu). It first appears in a fourth-century Chinese work entitled the *Baopuzi* 『抱朴子』 (J. *Hōbokushi*). Its use among Daoists and soldiers is well known (Watatani, 1964: 103; Earhart, 1970: fn. 60), but it remains especially important to the *shugenja* or *yamabushi* (practitioners of Shugendō) going into the mountains to perform austerities.

The Kujihō is found in many Shugendō texts and martial *densho*. There are several versions. It is unknown when the spell entered Shugendō; it is also unclear when the nine *mudra* (ritual hand gestures or "seals") were added. However, it is possible that the nine-character grid used in the Kujihō ritual was influenced by the Chinese Esoteric Buddhist (Ch. *Mi zong*) development of the nine-section adamantine-realm mandala (Kongōkai). The Chinese arrangement, which dates from the eighth century, was most likely based on an earlier Daoist model. (Saso, conversations, 1974–1977).

The practitioner normally performs the Buddhist Goshinhō (Self-defense ritual) prior to the Kujihō. In executing the Kujihō, the practitioner recites nine single-character sounds: "*rin pyō tō sha kai jin retsu zai zen*." There are several varieties of corresponding *mudra*; the following should be considered only one example:

As the nine sounds are uttered, the practitioner simultaneously gestures to form the appropriate seal. Each of these sounds and seals also corresponds to a particular Buddhist deity, although the list may vary.

At the end of this performance, the practitioner places his left fist against his left hip (representing a scabbard) which encloses the index and middle fingers of his right hand (representing a sword). He then draws out the two-fingered sword and, holding his left hand out in front of his face (like a writing tablet) he inscribes the *kuji* grid on his hand, again repeating the nine sounds.

Completing this, he uses the "sword" hand to inscribe a tenth *kanji* (Chinese character)

THE *KUJI* GRID
EXCERPT FROM AN OLD MANUAL ON *KUJI*

Character		Mudra		Seal Name
rin	臨	*kongō shin-in*	金剛針印	*vajra* needle
pyō	兵	*daikongōrin-in*	大金剛輪印	great *vajra* wheel
tō	闘	*gejishi-in*	外獅子印	outer lion
sha	者	*naijishi-in*	内獅子印	inner lion
kai	皆	*gebaku-in*	外縛印	outer binding
jin	陣	*naibaku-in*	内縛印	inner binding
retsu	列	*chiken-in*	智拳印	wisdom-fist
zai	在	*nichirin hōkō in*	日輪放光印	light-emitting sun disk
zen	前	*hōbyō-in*	宝瓶印	precious receptacle

in the palm of his hand. This character may vary, depending on the purpose for which the *Kujihō* is being performed.

As there are several versions of the Kujihō, the corresponding Chinese characters, seals, and deities vary. The version closest to the variation used in some of the martial *ryū* is the Shugendō *Heihō kuji no daiji* (Miyake, 1985: 402).

Further reading in English:
- Hall, 1990: 231–239.
- Knutsen, 2004: 230–238.
- Ōtake, 2007: 247–255.

Kuji ketsu-in goshinhō 九字結印護身法 [A.k.a. ***jumon*** 呪文]. A method of using the Kujihō and Goshinhō as a ritual meditation for strengthening and focusing one's spirit. This version of the Kujihō was especially popular among warriors (*bushi*), practitioners of Shugendō (*shugenja/yamabushi*), and (by some accounts) espionage specialists. The spell was used for empowering and protecting one's self and scattering or exorcising evil spirits (*akuma*) or malicious enemies (*onteki*).

In the warrior version of the ritual, several lines are added after the ninth seal (the *ongyō-in* or *hōbyō-in*) is completed:

Aku ma gō buku 悪魔降伏
Evil demons are subjugated.
On teki tai san 怨敵退散
Malicious enemies are dispersed.
Shichi nan soku metsu 七難速滅
The seven calamities are
quickly extinguished.
Shichi fuku soku seihi 七福速生秘
The mystery of the seven blessings is
quickly produced.

See also: *Kujihō; Marishiten; ongyōin.*

Further reading in English:
- Hall, 1990: 231–239.
- Otake, 2007: 247–255.

kuji kiri 九字切. Lit. "cutting the nine seals"; the "nine symbolic cuts." *Kuji kiri* means to perform the Kujihō ritual. Specifically, this refers to the practice of drawing the *kuji* grid on the palm of the left hand using the right hand as a sword/pen (see illustration of the *kuji* grid above). In some variants the "cutting" is executed in the air in front of the practitioner with the right hand or, in some cases in specific martial *ryū*, a weapon such as a truncheon (*jutte*).

Kūkai 空海. [A.k.a. ***Kōbō Daishi*** 弘法大師 (posthumous title)] (774–835). Kūkai was the monk who founded the Shingon school (Shingon Shū) of Buddhism. Shingon is one of the primary schools of Tantric Buddhism (*mikkyō*) in Japan. Kūkai was one of several monks who journeyed to Tang China in the early ninth century. There, in the capital city of Chang'an, he trained with the Chinese monk Huiguo[42] at the Green Dragon temple.[43] Kūkai returned to Japan in 806 with a large number of tantric scriptures, ritual manuals and implements. From these beginnings he founded the Shingon school, which was eventually headquartered on Mount Koya (Kōyasan 高野山).

Kuka (no maki) 「九箇(之巻)」(The scroll of the nine). YAGYŪ SHINKAGE RYŪ—The fourth picture scroll (*emaki*) presented to Yagyū Muneyoshi by Kamiizumi Ise no Kami Nobutsuna (founder of the Shinkage Ryū) in 1566. This scroll lists the contents

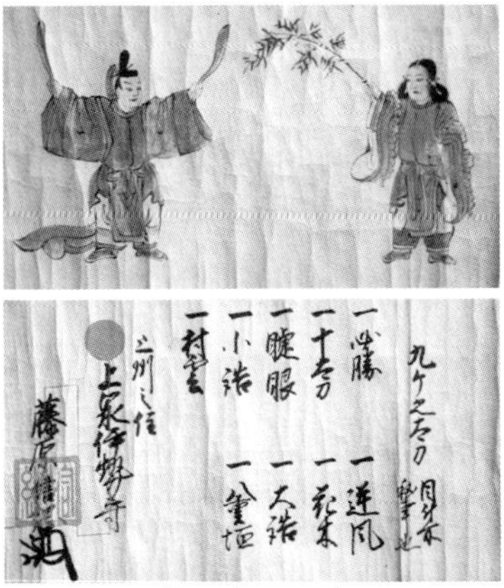

KUKA (*NO MAKI*)
Excerpt text and illustration from the original *densho* presented to Yagyū Muneyoshi in 1566
(From the archives of Yagyū Nobuharu)

---

[42] Jp. Keika <Ch. Huiguo 慧果.

[43] Jp. Seiryūji <Ch. Qinglongsi 青龍寺. The Green Dragon temple was one of two primary centers of Esoteric Buddhism in Chang'an (modern-day Xi'an 西安) in the eighth century (Chou, 1945: 331).

K

of the set of *kata* called Kuka no Tachi 九箇之太刀. Several versions of this document have been passed down in the variant lines of Shinkage Ryū.

Kuka no Tachi 九箇之太刀. YAGYŪ SHINKAGE RYŪ—The second series of *kata* taught to trainees in some lines of the Yagyū Shinkage Ryū. In contrast to Sangakuen no Tachi, the emphasis in these nine *kata* places the mind of the practitioner in *tai* 待 (waiting mode) and the body in *ken* (2) 懸 (attack mode) as he advances on the enemy. See also: *Empi no Tachi; Sangakuen no Tachi; Shinkage Ryū.*

kuki 茎【莖】. The tang of a blade. Also referred to as the *nakago*.

Kuki Shinden Happō Hikenjutsu 九鬼神伝八法秘剣術. See: *Kuki Shin Ryū.*

Kuki Shin Ryū 九鬼神流 [A.k.a. ***Kuki Shinden Happō Hikenjutsu*** 九鬼神伝八法秘剣術]. A tradition believed to have originally been a comprehensive combative system (*sōgō bujutsu*). The history of the Kuki Shin Ryū is variegated and, at the same time, somewhat obscure. Watatani and Yamada (1978: 240–241) list several branches, each which was known for variant weapons systems, including combative swordsmanship (*kenjutsu*), long hardwood staff techniques (*bōjutsu*), medium-length staff techniques (*jōjutsu*), grappling (*yawara*), long-hafted glaive arts (*naginatajutsu*), spear arts (*sōjutsu*), throwing-blade techniques (*shurikenjutsu*), sickle-and-chain techniques (*kusarigama-jutsu*), and naval tactics (*suigun*), as well as a smattering of healing arts such as bone-setting (*seikotsu*). Historically, the Kuki Shin Ryū is closely related to the Takagi Yōshin Ryū 高木揚心流, a school concentrating on *jūtaijutsu* (grappling); and the Chōsui Ryū 澄水流, a system specializing in *daken taijutsu* (a boxing/striking fighting system). The two major Kuki Shin Ryū lines have overlapping lineages, one founded by Kuki Yakushimaru Kurando Ryūshin, the other by Izumo Kanja Minamoto no Yoshiteru. The best-known line is the one practiced by Takamatsu Toshitsugu in the mid-twentieth century and passed on to Hatsumi Masaaki. See: *Bujinkan.*

Further reading in English:
- Hatsumi and Chambers, 1971.
- Hatsumi, 2008: 168–207.
- Kiba (translation), 2002.

Kuki Yakushimaru Kurando Ryūshin 九鬼薬師丸 蔵人 隆真【九鬼藥師丸藏人隆真】. The man believed to have founded the main line of the Kuki Shin Ryū 九鬼神流, probably during the fifteenth century. The family line of this tradition extends twenty-four generations from Kuki Yakushimaru.

kukuribakama 括袴. Pantaloons. This type of *hakama* could be bound up to facilitate walking and riding outside (much as modern military trousers may be bloused for field use).

kumade 熊手. 1. Lit. "bear claw." A common term for a rake (the gardening tool). 2. In the combative sense, a *kumade* is a grappling hook with two or three prongs, and sometimes a spike, attached to a pole about 5 to 6 feet (1.5–1.8 m) long. 3. ***Kumade*** 熊手 <Oki. *kumadī*. OKINAWAN KARATE—*Kumade* is a variation of *sanchin kata* practiced in Ishimine Ryū 石嶺流. It contains several techniques which are patterned after the movements of a bear.

kumadī 熊手 (Oki.). See: ***kumade (3).***

Kumagaya Ichimu 熊谷 一夢. Founder of the Ichimu Ryū (2) 一夢流, a branch tradition of Henmi Ryū archery (*kyūjutsu*).

Kumano Sanzan 熊野三山. RYŌBU SHINTŌ—Kumano Sanzan is a sacred area in the southeastern part of the Kii mountain range in Japan. As a spiritual center dating back to pre-historical times, it consists of three shrines: Kumano Hongu Taisha 熊野本宮大社, Kumano Hayatama Taisha 熊野速玉大社, and Kumano Nachi Taisha 熊野那智大社. As Ryōbu Shintō developed, the original Shintō deities of the three shrines became identified with their Buddhist counterparts: Amida Nyorai, Yakushi Nyorai, and Senju Kannon. Consequently, since ancient times Kumano Sanzan has been considered an area of great spiritual power and has attracted pilgrims and practitioners of religious austerities (*gyōja*). It is also associated with martial asceticism; for example, the founding of the Kishū Ryū 紀州流 is attributed to a *gyōja* from Kumano Sanzan. See: *Kishū Ryū; Shōninki.*

Kumebe 久米部. An ancient noble family that specialized in martial arts and flourished during the Yamato period (c.300–550 C.E.). The Kumebe were thought to have been brothers-in-arms with the first emperor, Jimmu Tennō; according to legend, he commissioned them to guard the gates of the imperial palace. Later, the clan was destroyed, and the Saiki family took their place.

kumi 組. During the Warring States period (1482–1558), a *kumi* was a subdivision of a rural warrior group (*kuni ikki*).

kumiai 組合. 1. An association; a society. 2. In a martial context, *kumiai* may refer to grappling or hand-to-hand combat.

kumiiai 組居合. 1. A practice found in some systems of quick-draw swordsmanship, in which techniques are done against one or more live partners (in contrast to standard *iaidō* in which the proponent practices in solo form). 2. The name of a category of partner training sets used in Mugai Ryū 無外流 and Suiō Ryū 水鴎流. See: *futari iaidō; sannin iaidō.*

kumitachi 組太刀. A style of fencing created in the early to-mid-1800s by Chiba Shūsaku, founder of the Hokushin Ittō Ryū 北辰一刀流. Chiba's *kumitachi*, which emphasized spiritual forging over combative technique, was based on four points:

1. Silence: one's should move efficiently, but silently.
2. Walking: when moving in any direction, one's steps should be natural.
3. Protective gloves (*uchikote* 打小手 or *onikode* 鬼小手) were used in order to perfect cutting ability.
4. Straight *bokken*, rather than curved ones, were used.

Chiba promoted competitive matches as a part of training. These bouts were often extended to include opponents armed with lightweight glaives (*naginata*), sometimes wielded by women. The matches were public events and spectators paid admission.

Through Chiba's association with Odani Nobutomo of the Jiki Shinkage Ryū, *kumitachi* became the official style of swordsmanship in Mito domain. It was also an important force in the development of *kendō* in late Tokugawa-period Japan.

kumite 組手. KARATE—An abbreviation for *jiyūkumite*. This term refers to free sparring in modern *karatedō.*

kumitsuku 組付. Combat via grappling. See: *Araki Ryū.*

kumiuchi 組打 [Var. 組討]. A form of battlefield-oriented armored grappling. See also: *Oguri Ryū; yoroi kumiuchi.*

kumiuchi koshi no mawari 組討腰之廻. An eclectic, synthesized combat system used in the Sōsuishitsu Ryū. It was originally based on the battlefield-oriented armored grappling (*kumiuchi*) and quick-draw sword techniques (*koshi no mawari*) of the Takenouchi Ryū.[44] See: *Sosuishitsu Ryū.*

K

kumoashi manji ken 蜘蛛足万字剣【蜘蛛足萬字劍】. Lit. the "sword technique of the spider-legged swastika." See: *Ōyama Tamon Sadashige.*

Kumogakure Ryū 雲隠流【雲隱流】. A school of espionage (*shinobi no jutsu*) which traced its origins to the Toda family.

kun'i 勲位. A merit rank awarded to outstanding combatants during campaigns. The *kun'i* ranks were part of the military organization copied almost entirely from the Chinese in the eighth century. According to Friday (1992: 223), *kun'i* ranks paralleled court ranks, but were based on combative performance in battle instead of heritage and court politics.

kuniguni no heishi 国々の兵士【國々の兵士】. A twelfth-century term for rural fighting men.

kuni ikki 国一揆【國一揆】[Var. ***kokujin ikki*** 国人一揆]. Organizations formed by semi-independent local warrior-proprietors (*kokujin*) and

[44] Within the Takenouchi Ryū, *koshi no mawari* does not refer specifically to quick-draw sword technique. See: *koshi no mawari; Takenouchi Ryū.*

provincial warriors in the fourteenth century. Some *kokujin* gave up their status as rural gentry and became full-time warriors for the *daimyō* after being cut off from their agrarian support. However, many who were located away from agricultural areas resisted this change by forming provincial warrior groups (*kuni ikki*). See: *ikki; Ikkō Ikki; tsuchi ikki.*

Further reading in English:

• Davis, 1974: 233–237.

Kuninazu no Mahito 国摩 真人【國摩眞人】(fl. seventh century). A senior "ritualist" and swordsman from the precincts of Kashima shrine. Mahito is generally recognized as the founder of an early sword system known as Kashima no Tachi 鹿島之太刀. He is also credited with the first revelation of divinely inspired swordsmanship known as Ichi no Tachi 一太刀 (also read Hitotsu no Tachi) or Shinmyōken 神妙剣. See: *Kashima no Tachi.*

kuni no miyatsuko 国造【國造】. Often translated as "governors of provinces." The *kuni no miyatsuko* were local strongmen—warrior-leaders—who, during the Yamato Court centuries (c.300–550 C.E.) had established themselves in the hinterland by pacifying the local areas. Once established, their position was hereditary as long as they acknowledged the authority of the Yamato court. Considered noble, they had ties to the imperial family that in some cases went back to the days of the first emperor, Jimmu Tennō. Whatever their origins, by the early sixth century there were about 144 *kuni no miyatsuko* on the mainland (strongmen who governed islands were called *shima no miyatsuko*). There was an attempt to suppress these local lords by the Taika Reform of 645, but with mixed results. Farris (1992: 34) speculates that they were probably mounted archers who commanded peasant foot soldiers. See also: *bushi; ikusa; kondei; musha; tsuwamono.*

kuni no musha 国の武士【國の武士】. A twelfth-century term for warriors of the provinces (as opposed to warriors of the capital, *miyako no musha*).

kuni no tsuwamono 国の兵【國の兵】. An eleventh-century term for rural warriors.

Kunishige Nobuyuki 国重 信行【國重信行】(fl. 1910). A master teacher of Shinden Isshin Ryū *jūjutsu* 神伝一心流柔術 who is quoted extensively in E. J. Harrison's *Fighting Spirit of Japan*. Kunishige's comments on *jūdō, jūjutsu, taijutsu,* and *haragei* are well worth reading today.

Further reading in English:

• Harrison, 1956: 108–126.

kunoichi くノ一 [Var. 九ノ一; 九能一] . A female espionage agent. Although the term *kunoichi* is commonly understood in popular literature to mean a "female ninja," the actual writing of the term varies, and most etymologies are speculative at best.[45] Japanese scholars on the subject such as Nawa Yumio and Fujita Seiko do not list either of the variations above in their in-depth essays on *ninjutsu*.

In the first example given here, the three characters *ku* く, *no* ノ, and *ichi* 一 can be put together into a single character, resulting in the ideogram for "woman" 女. The third rendering (九能一) can be interpreted as "nine skills in one person" or "nine capabilities in one person." It may also relate to the ritual of the nine mystic letters (Kujihō). However, esoteric explanations would have been restricted to the espionage traditions (if any) that actually used these terms.

kura 鞍. A saddle.

kurai 位. YAGYŪ SHINKAGE RYŪ—A combative engagement posture. Within the Yagyū Shinkage Ryū, this term is preferred over the term *kamae*. In the Yagyū view, *kamae* is static, whereas *kurai* (which conveys the sense of "almost," "as," or "thereabouts"; as well as "dignity," "nobility") is considered more flexible. See also: *kamae; marobashi; setsunintō katsujinken.*

Kuraizume 位詰. 1. A name used for a range of classical combative forms (*kata*) developed by various martial schools. 2. Kurai-

[45] One English source points to two Japanese literary works that supposedly support these etymologies: *Enshū Senkuzuke Narabi Nihyaku In*『遠舟千句附并百韵』c.1680, and, *Maekuzukeshū*『前句付集』c.1716. However, exact references are not given.

zume is one of a number of classical prearranged combative forms (*kata*) developed by the Kyōshin Meichi Ryū 鏡新明智流. It was also one of ten classical *kata* adapted by the Japanese Police Commission of 1886 for their Keishichō Ryū 警視庁流 system.

Kuramadera 鞍馬寺. A Tendai temple located about twelve kilometers north of old Kyōto. According to legend, an enigmatic Daoist magician named Kiichi Hōgen placed a compilation of Chinese texts on military science (see *Genke kin'etsushū*) in Kuramadera during the reign of Emperor Goshirakawa.[46] Stories also state that Minamoto no Yoshitsune (1159–1189), one of Japan's greatest tacticians, secretly copied these texts while imprisoned at Kurama.

Minamoto no Yoshitsune did spend his youth (c.1165–1174) in Kuramadera, and it is very likely that he studied martial arts (*bugei*) in addition to his Buddhist training while ensconced there. After leaving Kurama, Yoshitsune was aided by both Tendai and Shugendō warrior monks (*sōhei*) during his campaigns against the Taira during the Gempei War (1180–1185).

Nen Ryū founder Nen Ami Jion is also said to have spent several years at Kurama during his youth (c.1361–1365), and emerged having obtained great skill with the sword and spear. See also: *Kiichi Hōgan Ryū; Tendai Shū.*

Kurama Hachi Ryū 鞍馬八流. See: *Kiichi Hōgan Ryū.*

Kurama Hōshi 鞍馬法師. Lit. the "Eight Monks of Kurama." A group of eight monks from Kuramadera after whom the Kyō no Hachi Ryū 京の八流 is named. See: *Kiichi Hōgan Ryū.*

Kurama Ryū 鞍馬流. A system of combative swordsmanship (*kenjutsu*) and quick-draw sword art (*iaijutsu*) founded by Ōno Shōgen sometime during the Azuchi-Momoyama period (1568–1600). The curriculum of the Kurama Ryū as it exists today has been greatly influenced by the Japanese Imperial Police. The system has been closely aligned with law enforcement officers since a number of Kurama Ryū techniques were adopted by the police in the Meiji era. Techniques used by law enforcement were likewise absorbed into the tradition.

kuri hanashi 繰放. Lit. "wind around and release." SHINDŌ MŪSŌ RYŪ—A technique in which a medium-length staff (*jō*) is used in a winding movement to throw off the opponent's weapon. *Kuri hanashi* is the eighth of twelve basic techniques (*kihon*) extrapolated from the classical forms of Shindō Musō Ryū by Shimizu Takaji.

Kurikara Fudō 倶利伽羅不動. BUDDHISM—The symbolic form (*sammayagyō*) of Fudō Myōō. It consists of the Black Dragon King (Kurikara Ryūō) coiling around a flaming wisdom-sword (*chikaken*). This symbol is used in Tantric meditation/rituals devoted to Fudō. The flaming sword with coiled dragon is often found engraved on sword blades as a talisman. However, the flaming wisdom-sword (*chikaken*) may also be replaced by the three-point *vajra* wisdom-sword (*sankotsuka no ken*) in these engravings.

Further reading in English:

• de Visser, 1913.

Kurikara Myōō 倶利迦羅明王 <Ch. Julijialuo Mingwang. A symbol form (*sammayagyō*) of Fudō Myōō equivalent to Kurikara Ryūō. A temple/shrine dedicated to Kurikara Myōō is located on Mount Ōyama in Sagami (present-day Kanagawa prefecture). De Visser (1913: 213) notes that there was a temple in the Kurikara mountain range between Etchū and Kaga called Chōrakuji or Kurikara-san, in which the main image (*honzon*) was Fudō Myōō. This same temple was famous for its mysterious lights called *santō-ryūtō* (mountain lanterns–dragon lanterns).

Kurikara Ryūō 倶利迦羅龍王 <Ch. Julijialo Longwang <Skt. Kulikaḥ/Kālakaḥ/Kṛkālaḥ (black snake; black dragon). One of the Eight Dragon Kings. This particular black dragon, wrapped around a flaming wisdom-sword (*chikaken*), is regarded as the "symbol form" (*sammayagyō*) of Fudō Myōō. In India, black dragons or snakes (Skt. *nāga*) were associat-

[46] Goshirakawa Tennō 後白河天皇 (1127–1192; r. 1155–1158).

ed with rain and were considered guardians of water. This tradition was imported into Japan with Buddhism; a sword depicted with the Kurikara Ryūō wrapped around it was considered a "rain sword." See: *Ama Kurikara.*

Further reading in English:

• de Visser, 1913.

KURIKARA FUDŌ
Horimono engraving of Kurikara Ryūō coiled around a three-point *vajra* wisdom sword
(Private collection)

kurikata 栗形. A knob on the side of a scabbard through which the scabbard cord (*sageo*) is threaded. The *kurikata* also prevents the scabbard (*saya*) from slipping down through the sash (*obi*).

kuri tsuke 繰付. Lit. "wind around and adhere." SHINDŌ MŪSŌ RYŪ—A technique in which a medium-length staff (*jō*) is used to wrap and pin the opponent's hands and weapon. *Kuri tsuke* is the seventh of the twelve basic techniques (*kihon*) extrapolated from the classical forms of Shindō Musō Ryū by Shimizu Takaji.

kuroboshi 黒星. Lit. "black star" or "black spot." This term refers to the bull's-eye in a target.

kurobushi 黒節. SHINDŌ MŪSŌ RYŪ—A vital point (*kyūsho*) located on the inside of the leg just above the ankle.

KURODA ICHITARŌ (L)
Shown demonstrating Ikkaku Ryū with Shimizu Takaji (R)
(Photograph courtesy Nishioka Tsuneo)

Kuroda Ichitarō 黒田 一太郎 (1911–2000). One of the most senior Shindō Musō Ryū disciples under Shimizu Takaji. In 1927 Kuroda was one of the first *kendō* champions in Japan; that same year he began training in the Shindō Musō Ryū under Shimizu Takaji. He was Shimizu's first and longest student. In addition holding *menkyo kaiden* in Shindō Musō Ryū he held high ranks in *kendō*, *jōdō*, *iaidō* and *shōdō* (calligraphy), eventually achieving tenth *dan* in all four at the time of his death in January 2000. He was awarded the Emperor's Medal for his Japanese calligraphy in 1978. He served as the chief martial arts instructor to the Tokyo police for most of his life. Kuroda was a major factor in the growth and popularity of Shindō Musō Ryū in the 1970s and 80s.[47]

Kuroda Nagamasa 黒田 長政 (1568–1623). After inheriting a branch of the Kuroda clan at the age of ten, Nagamasa was entrusted into the care of Toyotomi Hideyoshi by Oda Nobunaga. He served under Hideyoshi in Kyushu (1587) and in Korea (1592). However, he ingratiated himself to Tokugawa Ieyasu when he sided with the latter at Sekigahara in 1600. For that service Nagamasa was made suzerain of Najima in Chikuzen. He built a castle there and renamed the area "Fukuoka." During his rule, Musō Gonnosuke, progenitor of Shindō Musō Ryū 神道夢想流, became a retainer of the Kuroda clan.

Kuromi Shōgorō 黒見 勝五郎. Last known

[47] Note: Special thanks to Steve Bellamy for providing additional information on Kuroda Ichitarō.

practitioner of Issa Ryū 一佐流, Kuromi was last mentioned around 1864. The Issa Ryū was a comprehensive martial school (*sōgō bujutsu*) but specialized in espionage (*majutsu*).

kusa 草. Lit. "grass." A variant term for an espionage agent from the mid-1500s through the Edo period. The term *kusa* indicated an agent who used natural terrain, grass, foliage, etc. for cover while scouting near enemy positions. The term is also associated with those used for surprise attack troops (*kamari* and *kishū*) in that those shock troops made use of terrain and foliage for concealment before an attack. See: *ninjutsu.*

kusagama-jutsu 草鎌術. Sickle-and-chain arts (also called *kusarigama-jutsu*) practiced by the Shinkyō Ryū 心鏡流.

Kusaka Isshi Ryū 日下一旨流. A branch tradition of the Itō Ryū (1) 伊東流/Kenkō Ryū 建孝流 founded sometime during the Genroku era (1688–1704) by Makino Kyūbei Shigetoshi. The Kusaka Isshi Ryū concentrated on spear (*sōjutsu*) and sword (*kenjutsu*) systems. For lineage, see: *Itō Ryū (1).*

Kusanagi no Tsurugi 草薙の剣 【草薙劒】. See: *Ame no Murakumo no Tsurugi.*

Kūsankū 公相君 [Also read ***Kusankun***, ***Ku Shanku***, ***Kosokun***, ***Kanku***, etc.] <Ch. Gong Xiang Jun (fl. mid-to late 1700s). OKINAWAN KARATE—Kūsankū is yet another enigmatic combative arts master whose true nature is somewhat obscure. In the world of Okinawan *karate*, he is described as a member of the entourage of a Chinese emissary (*sappōshi* 冊封使) who came to Okinawa in 1762 during the reign of King Shō Boku.[48] Some sources say Kūsankū was an emissary of the Ming dynasty. However, since the Manchurian Qing dynasty replaced the Ming dynasty in 1644, Kūsankū must have arrived with Qing diplomats. In addition, as the Chinese bureaucratic elite were normally disdainful of martial affairs (except, of course, during wartime), it is more likely that Kūsankū was a member of a diplomatic entourage than a diplomat himself. Several Okinawans are known to have trained under Kūsankū in hand-to-hand combat (*kumiai* 組合); notably, Sakukawa Tōdī (Jp. Sakugawa Kanga) and Chatanyara Ridō 北谷屋良 利導.

[48] Ryūkyū King Shō Boku 尚穆 (1739–1794; r. 1756–1794).

Kūsankū (Dai) 公相君 (大). OKINAWAN KARATE—Kūsankū (Dai) is one of two combative forms (*kata*) whose origin is attributed to the eighteenth-century fighting arts master Kūsankū. Along with Kūsankū (Shō), it has been preserved in the Matsubayashi Ryū 松林流, Shōrin Ryū 少林流, and Shōrinji Ryū 少林寺流 schools in Okinawa under a variety of names; e.g., Chatan Yara Kūsankū 北谷屋良公相君, Chibana Kūsankū 知花公相君. See also: *karate kata; Kūsankū.*

Kūsankū (Shō) 公相君(小). See: *Kūsankū (Dai).*

kusari 鎖 【鏁】. 1. A chain. 2. A weighted chain used as a weapon. See: *manrikigusari.* 3. The chain of a composite weapon such as a *kusarigama* or *chigiriki*. 4. Chainmail.

kusari bō 鎖棒 【鏁棒】. A long hardwood staff with two chains attached to one end by means of a hook-like lock (*kagi* 鑰). The chains are about 4.5 inches (11.5 cm) long; each is weighted with a small iron ball resembling a bell clapper (*rindama* 鈴玉) encased in black or purple leather. This weapon was used primarily by the Shiraiwa Ryū 白岩流 and Ikkan Ryū (3) 一貫流 in Owari domain.

kusari fundō 鎖分銅 【鏁分銅】. Lit. "weighted chain." An alternate name for a *manrikigusari.*

kusarigama 鎖鎌 【鏁鎌】. Any of a number of composite weapons combining a chain (*kusari*) and sickle (*kama*). See also: *kusarigama-jutsu.*

Further reading in English:

- Amdur, 2002: 148–176.
- Draeger, 1973A: 86–87.

kusarigama-jutsu 鎖鎌術 【鏁鎌術】. 1. The combative art of the sickle and chain. Fujita (1960: 2) notes eighty *ryū* specializing in *kusarigama-jutsu*. See also: *Araki Ryū; Isshin Ryū; Jiki Shinkage Ryū naginatajutsu; kusagama-jutsu.*

kusarigote 鎖小手 【鏁小手】 [Var. 鎖籠手 【鏁籠手】]. Sleeves (*kote*) covered in chainmail.

K

kusarijutsu 鎖術【鏁術】. Combative arts using a weighted chain. Fujita (1960: 2) notes twenty-six *ryū* specializing in *kusarijutsu*.

kusari tachi 鎖太刀【鏁太刀】. A *tachi* which is hung from a belt or sash by chains attached to the scabbard.

kusazuri 草摺. Skirt armor.

Ku Shanku 公相君. See: *Kūsankū*.

Kusha Shū 倶舎宗 <Ch. Jushe zong. BUDDHISM—One of the early Six Schools of Nara (Nanto Rokushū). The Kusha Shū is often referred to as "scholastic Buddhism," as it concentrates on philosophical discourses found in the Sanskrit text known as the *Abhidharmakośa-śāstra* (Jp. *Kusha-ron*『倶舎論』<Ch. *Jushe lun*).

Further reading in English:
- Matsunaga and Matsunaga, 1974: 28–40 *ff*.

Kushi Iwamado no Mikoto 奇磐間戸命. SHINTŌ—One of the Ya Daijin, the two *kami* that guard the entrance to Shintō shrines. See: *Ya Daijin; zuishin*.

kushimitama 奇魂 [Var. 奇御魂]. SHINTŌ—A miraculous or wondrous spirit. See: *mitama*.

Kūshin Ryū 空真流. OKINAWAN KARATE—A school of *karate* founded in Ōsaka, Japan in 1937 by Ueshima Sannosuke and Kinjō Kensei. Ueshima, a Konshin Ryū *jūjutsu* teacher, began training in *karate* with Kinjō, who was Okinawan. The two men soon decided to combine their knowledge into a new system. To name the new school, they took the character *kū* 空 from *karate* 空手, and *shin* 真 from Konshin Ryū 今真流. Kinjō's most senior student, Yoshizato Shintarō, brought the system to Okinawa in 1960 when he returned to his hometown of Ginowan 宜野湾.

Since before World War II, the Kūshin Ryū was known for practicing freestyle forms (*jiyū kata*) and free sparring (*jiyū kumite*) without protective equipment. In the late 1930s, in fact, Kūshin Ryū teachers and trainees often trained almost naked in all kinds of weather, wearing only a loincloth called a *fundoshi*.

Evidently it was more difficult to disregard the right-wing militarist climate of the late 1930s than the cold Ōsaka winters. Bishop (1999: 104) notes that when giving demonstrations at the Dai Nippon Butokukai in Kyōto, Kūshin Ryū members were required to be fully clothed. They consequently began wearing *jūdōgi* for these events. Local merchants soon began modifying the heavy *jūdōgi* into a lighter version they christened the *karategi*.

Since World War II the school has allowed practitioners to wear protective gear during free sparring. The tradition now includes about twelve formal *kata*:

Kūshin Ryū *kata* 空真流型:
- Gekisai Daiichi (I) 撃砕第一
- Gekisai Daini (II) 撃砕第二
- Sanchin 三戦
- Sēsan 十三
- Seiunchin 制引戦
- Sēpai 十八手
- Sēpārinpē 壱百零八
- Passai (Dai) 抜塞(大)
- Passai (Shō) 抜塞(小)
- Chintō 鎮闘
- Kūsankū 公相君
- Ūsēshī 五十四歩

Further reading in English:
- Bishop, 1999: 103–105.

Kusunagi no Tsurugi 草薙の剣. See: *Ama no Murakumo no Tsurugi*.

kusungobu 九寸五分. An early name for an *aikuchi tantō*; i.e., a dagger without a handguard (*tsuba*). The name *kusungobu* refers to the length of the blade: 9 *sun*, 5 *bu*. As one *sun* was roughly 1.2 inches (3 cm) and one *bu* was approximately .12 inches (3 mm), a *kusungobu* was just under 12 inches (29 cm) long. See: *aikuchi*.

Kusunoki Masashige 楠木 正成 (1294–1336). One of the great tragic figures of Japanese history who epitomized the value of loyalty. In the 1320s, Emperor Go-Daigo[49] intended to challenge the Kamakura *bakufu*—which was under the control of the Hōjō family—in order to restore imperial rule in Japan. In

[49] Go-Daigo Tennō 後醍醐天皇 (1288–1339; r. 1318–1339). Ninety-sixth emperor of Japan.

fact, his chosen imperial name "Go-Daigo," meaning "Second Daigo," harkened back to the first Emperor Daigo of the early tenth century, who in his time had challenged the Fujiwara family for control of the government. Though he had aligned himself with some powerful supporters,[50] Go-Daigo was betrayed by a close advisor and had to flee the capitol in 1331. An attack from the Kamakura *bakufu* was expected at any time, and the emperor had only a few warriors (*bushi*) and warrior monks (*sōhei*) for protection. It was then that Go-Daigo had his famous dream in which he was inspired to call on the services of Kusunoki Masashige. (This is, of course, part of the legend that later arose concerning Kusunoki, for little is known about him other than his actions as a retainer of Go-Daigo from 1331 to 1336. Some of the legends of Kusunoki's origins closely parallel those of Minamoto no Yoshitsune and Nen Ami Jion.)

Whatever his origins, Kusunoki Masashige turned out to be a proficient tactician and a tough guerrilla leader; he and his relatively small band of fighting men are often described as *akutō* (swashbucklers). In the end, however, Kusunoki and his forces were defeated by Go-Daigo's former ally, Ashikaga Takauji, and Kusunoki committed ritual suicide (*seppuku*).

BATTLE STANDARD (*NOBORIBATA*) OF KUSUNOKI MASASHIGE
This banner is emblazoned with Kusunoki's standard "floating chrysanthemum" image (*kikusui*) over the phrase "Ma-Bi Ryō Tennō" 摩毘両天王 ("Two Great Heavenly Guardians"—a reference to Marishiten and Bishamonten)

Much later, several classical martial schools claimed descent from Kusunoki, but there is little or no documentation to support such claims. During the imperial restoration of the late 1860s, Kusunoki's support of Emperor Go-Daigo was held forth as a supreme example of loyalty to the emperor, and Kusunoki became an icon of the new imperial regime.

Further reading in English:

- Draeger, 1978: 113–122.
- Morris, 1975b: 106–142 *ff.*
- Varley, 1994: 181–185 *ff.*

Kusunoki Ryū 1. 楠流. A number of martial schools in Japan have gone by the name Kusunoki Ryū or have used "Kusunoki" as part of their title. Watatani and Yamada (1978: 244–245) list thirteen different Kusunoki Ryū using the ideograms 楠流; several others include those characters as part of their title. Most of these were involved with strategy and tactics (*gumpō*) and espionage (*shinobi no jutsu*) while others concentrated on weapons systems.

Kusunoki Ryū 2. 楠流 [Var. 楠木流]. A system of military strategy (*gumpō*) preserved in transmission scrolls (*densho*) such as the *Kayōheiko no ki* 『河陽兵庫之記』 and the *Kusunoki bukyō* 『楠木武経』. These texts have been reprinted in Ishioka and Arima (1967, vol. 6: 230–369). Other texts attributed to the Kusunoki Ryū indicate an emphasis on espionage tactics (*shinobi no jutsu*) in this school. These include the *Kusunoki Ryū dakkō shinobi no maki* 『楠流奪口忍之巻』 and *Kusunoki Masashige ikkansho* 『楠木正成一巻書』. However, the authenticity of these two texts is in question.

kutsuwa 轡 [Var. 鑣] . A horse's bit.

kuwagata 鍬形. Lit. "hoe-shaped." A helmet crest that supposedly symbolized the leaves of the water plant Sagittarius. The *kuwagata* used on helmets around the beginning of the sixteenth century were sometimes enormous. See also: *tatemono*.

kuzure 崩れ. See: *kuzushi*.

[50] These supporters included some of the powerful Buddhist temples and various members of the warrior class. See, for example, the entry on the *gobukuhō* and the Buddhist monk Monkan.

kuzushi 崩し. Lit. "breaking"; "pulling down"; "demolishing." (The related word *kuzure* 崩れ means "collapse.") 1. To break an opponent's balance. 2. The breaking down of a combative form (*kata*) in order to explain its combative application. See also: *bunkai.*

kuzushi waza 崩技 [Var. 崩業]. Prearranged combative forms (*kata*) which emphasize the application of technique. In *jūjutsu*-type systems, these are simply application techniques that break the opponent's balance. In some weapons systems, the term is used to indicate the "real" combative technique, which required much greater skill and/or control and was considered unsafe for normal training.

kwaiken 懐剣【懷劍】. See: *kaiken.*

kwaitō 懐刀【懷刀】. Archaic romanization for *kaitō* (1). See: *kaiken.*

Kwantō 關刀. See: *Kantō (2).*

Kwan-yu 關羽. See: *Kan'u.*

kwayaku 火薬. See: *kayaku.*

Kyan Chōtoku 喜屋武 長徳 [A.k.a. 朝徳] (1870–1945). OKINAWAN KARATE—Chōtoku's father was an aide to the last Okinawan king, Shō Tai. He followed his ruler into exile in Tōkyō in 1879 when the Ryūkyū kingdom was abolished and became Okinawa prefecture. Chōtoku accompanied his father, and received much of his education in Tōkyō. Upon returning to Okinawa, Chōtoku trained with several different instructors in Shuri *te* and Tomari *te*. Okinawan Shōrinji Ryū 少林寺流 *karate* is essentially the system developed by Kyan Chōtoku.

kyō 香. See: *kyōsha.*

kyōdan 1. 郷談. Lit. "rural talk" or "rural speech." A term for a secret agent. *Kyōdan* (1) indicated agents who were recruited from the local population in enemy territory.

kyōdan 2. 饗談. Lit. "banquet conversation." A term for a secret agent. *Kyōdan* (2) indicated an agent who was recruited from the ranks of high-status enemies who held animosity toward their commander.

kyōge betsuden 教外別伝【教外別傳】. ZEN BUDDHISM—A Zen expression referring to the transmission of doctrine without recourse to written works such as *sūtras*. In some martial systems this term is shortened to *betsuden*; it may indicate highly privileged teaching not written down in a school's transmission scrolls (*densho*).

Kyō Hachi Ryū 京八流. See: *Kiichi Hōgan Ryū.*

kyōi 校尉. TAIHŌ MILITARY SYSTEM—The leader of an assembly of four *tai* (platoons) —a total of about 200 conscript soldiers—in an eighth-century Chinese-style provincial militia unit (*gundan*). The *kyōi* was somewhat equivalent to a major commanding a small battalion in a modern army. In the chain of command he was in charge of two or more *rosochi* (equivalent to captains) and normally under the command of a *daiki* (colonel) or *shōki* (lieutenant colonel). See: *gundan.*

kyojō 居城. A castle which is the residence of a feudal lord.

kyōjo 侠女. A gallant woman; a woman with a chivalrous spirit. This term is often used to refer to gallant women in a martial context.

kyōju dairi「教授代理」【教授代理】[Abbr. for Daitō Ryū *kyōju dairi*「大東流〜」]. DAITŌ RYŪ—The sixth of several Daitō Ryū transmission scrolls (*densho*) awarded in that tradition. This was originally the standard teaching license awarded by Takeda Sōkaku, but later other certificates were added.

kyōkaku 侠客. A "knight of the town"; a chivalrous man.

kyōkan 郷間. See: *gōkan.*

kyōki 侠気【俠氣】[Also read **otokogi**; var. **kyōkotsu** 侠骨]. A chivalrous spirit.

kyōkotsu 侠骨 [Var. **kyōki** 侠気]. See: *kyōki.*

Kyokushinkai Karatedō 極真会空手道. JAPANESE KARATE—Eclectic form of Japanese *karate* founded by Ōyama Masutatsu in 1964. Ōyama, a Korean by birth, mastered Gōjū Ryū under Yamaguchi Gogen. He then combined a number of Chinese and Korean pugilistic arts into a system he called Kyokushinkai Karatedō.

kyōmon 経文【經文】. Buddhist scriptures.

kyōrikisha 強力者. Lit. "strongmen"; one of many terms used over the centuries to describe militant clergy. A term used in the ninth century to describe armed men from the temples of Tōdaiji and Kōfukuji in Nara. In an incident recorded in 850, the *kyōrikisha* were escorted from the temples by armed menial workers (*zōshikinin*). See: *sōhei*.

kyōsha 香車 [Abbr. as ***kyō*** 香]. SHŌGI—Lit. "incense chariot" or "fragrant chariot." In English, this piece from the strategic Japanese game of *shōgi* is usually called the "lance," because it can only move straight forward. The *kyōsha* does not have a direct equivalent in Western chess.

kyōshi 教士 [Var. 教師]. A master teacher of swordsmanship with less seniority than a *hanshi*. Contrast with *shihan* and *renshi*. In modern systems of martial arts and ways (*budō*), *kyōshi* are generally recognized at around the seventh- or eighth-*dan* level, but the title has no direct correspondence to *dan* rank.

Kyōshin Meichi Ryū 鏡新明智流 [Originally written 鏡心明智流]. A school of combative arts founded by Momonoi Hachirōzaemon Naoyoshi sometime during the An'ei era (1772–1781). Having studied Horiuchi Ryū 堀内流, Ittō Ryū 一刀流, Toda Ryū 戸田流, and other systems, Momonoi established the Shigakkan *dōjō* in Edo in 1773, and perfected his system there. The Kyōshin Meichi Ryū was a comprehensive system (*sōgo bujutsu*) which, under Momonoi, included the study of combative swordsmanship (*kenjutsu*), the three polearms used for arresting criminals (*mitsudōgu*), the mid-length staff and chain weapon (*chigiriki*), the mid-sized staff (*jō*), the fighting chain (*kusari*), and throwing blades and darts (*shuriken*).

Kyōto 京都 [A.k.a. ***Heian*** 平安; ***Miyako*** 都; ***Rakuchū*** 洛中]. The capital city of Japan from 794 to 1868. The real political power of the emperor and his imperial court ended with the rise of the warrior class at the end of the Heian period (around 1185), and the center of power shifted geographically to the town of Kamakura. Kyōto's status was restored somewhat during the Muromachi period (1392–1573), when the ruling Ashikaga shogunate resided there. It remained the titular capital until the center of government was officially established in Tōkyō in 1869.

Kyōto no bushi 京都之武士. A twelfth-century term for warrior aristocrats living in Kyōto.

Kyōto Ōbanyaku 京都大番役. A security-guard service for the capital (Kyōto) during the Kamakura and Muromachi periods. The guard service was composed of warrior vassals of the *bakufu*. See also: *kagariya banyaku; Kamakura Ōbanyaku; ōbanyaku; shōgun gosho naibanyaku*.

kyōyū 俠勇. Gallantry, chivalry.

kyū~ 弓. A variant pronunciation for the ideogram for bow; usually used in compounds such as *kyūjutsu* 弓術 (combative archery).

kyū 級. Lit. "class." The term *kyū* is normally used in modern systems of martial arts and ways (*budō*) to designate rank levels below the *dan* grades. See: *dan–kyū*.

kyūba 弓馬. 1. The warrior arts of archery and horsemanship. 2. Mounted bow-and-arrow combat. See: *Daidō Ryū*.

kyūba kojitsu 弓馬故実【弓馬故實】. The combined arts of mounted archery and ancient customs and etiquette. This term was used by the Takeda Ryū (1) 武田流 to describe its curriculum.

kyūba no ie 弓馬家. Lit. "bow-and-horse house." Used in the sense of "warrior house" when referring to a family or clan.

kyūba no michi 弓馬道. Lit. the "way of the bow and horse." This was a term used for warriorship around the late Heian (794–1185) and early Kamakura (1185–1333) periods. *Kyūba no michi* was not a written code, but an aggregation of various cultural elements which evolved from Shintō, Buddhism, Confucianism, and the bonds of loyalty inculcat-

K

ed in the rural martial elite. These ties of loyalty were not grounded so much in kinship as they were based on mutual benefit and a sense of honor. War tales from the Heian and Kamakura periods, such as the *Heike monogatari*, are filled with examples of the *kyūba no michi* warrior ideal.

As times changed during the Muromachi and Azuchi-Momoyama periods (1392–1598), so did the character of the Japanese combatant and his ethical ideals. As war spread across the country, more and more non-*bushi* were incorporated into expanding armies; fewer rural elite horsemen (classical *bushi*) were present in comparison; and new weapons were introduced—most significantly, the firearm—which could be mastered quickly by soldiers who had not spent a lifetime learning the values of the classical warrior elite. Even among the *bushi* themselves the concept of loyalty became passé and treachery was the norm. It was not until the extended peace of the Edo period (1603–1868) that the new "warrior code" of *bushidō* evolved. See also: *bushi no konjō*.

Further reading in English:

- Draeger and Smith, 1969: 85–90.
- Draeger, 1973a.
- Varley, 1994.

kyūba no shi 弓馬士. Lit. "fighting men of the bow and horse." A term for mounted warriors used in the *Mutsuwaki*, an eleventh-century war tale (*gunkimono*).

kyūbi no ita 鳩尾の板. Lit. "pigeon-tail board." An armored board about 8 inches (20 cm) long and 2 inches (5 cm) wide, which hung from the top left of an armored breastplate and shifted to cover the left armpit when the wearer stretched his arms out to use a bow. The *kyūbi no ita* was highly functional on armor of the Heian and Kamakura periods. During the Muromachi period, however, along with its counterpart on the right (the *sendan no ita*), it became ornamental, as the bow was gradually replaced by other weapons and the *ita* were replaced by the *wakibiki* (laced pads worn under the armor to protect the armpits).

kyūdō 弓道. Lit. "bow and arrow way." The practice of Japanese archery with a goal of spiritual development. The evolution of combative archery (*kyūjutsu*) into a spiritual discipline (*kyūdō*) took place over a long period. Like many other combative arts in Japan, archery had roots in Shintō spirituality as well as battlefield combat from the beginning. With the introduction of firearms into Japan in the sixteenth century, however, gunnery quickly began to replace the bow and arrow as the projectile weapons system of choice on the Japanese battlefield. In the early seventeenth century, an archery competition known as the *tōshiya* (or *dōsha*) at a Tendai temple in Kyōto known as Sanjūsangendō led to an archery revival. (Records give various dates for the beginning of the Sanjūsangendō contests.) In 1606, a warrior/archer named Asaoka Heibei is recorded as having won an archery contest by "clearing" fifty-one arrows. The verb "clear" is used in this instance because the arrows had to follow a flat trajectory down a long, narrow corridor with low-hanging beams to a target approximately 400 feet (120 m) distant; this required the archer to fire from a kneeling position. The standing record for this contest is 8,133 hits out of 13,053 arrows fired in a twenty-four hour period. This contest and similar ones soon became popular events. However, even with growing popularity, archery did not regain its central position in battlefield combat. By the late seventeenth century, non-warriors had begun to take up archery target shooting as a spiritual/sportive discipline. Around that time the term *kyūdō* was first used by Morikawa Kozan, founder of the Yamato Ryū 大和流 of *kyūjutsu*. The subsequent two centuries of peace and the gradual importation of more advanced firearms made combat archery obsolete and created the environment in which archery became a primarily spiritual/self-development exercise.

Finally, around the turn of the twentieth century, Honda Toshizane 本多利実, a *kyūdō* instructor at Tokyo Imperial University, created a new, hybrid version of *kyūdō* from traditional ceremonial and warrior styles. His system, which came to be known as Honda

Ryū 本多流, revolutionized *kyūdō* in a way that opened it up as a popular discipline for the general public. Standards for shooting were devised by the Dai Nippon Butokukai in the 1930s. In 1949, the All-Japan Kyudo Federation (Zen Nihon Kyūdō Renmei) was formed; the organization published a new set of standards in 1953.

Further reading in English:

- Hurst, 1998.
- Onuma et al, 2003.
- Sollier and Györbiró, 1969.

kyūdōka 弓道家. A proficient practitioner of *kyūdō*.

kyūgen 弓弦 [Also read ***yunzuru*** or ***yumizuru***]. A bowstring.

kyūguntō 旧軍刀. Lit. "old military swords." *Kyūguntō* are official mountings for swords of the imperial Japanese army and navy which were used from the late 1800s through the late 1930s. The actual swords in these mountings were often cheap, factory-made ceremonial blades. However, some officers and non-commissioned officers carried real swords (*shinken*) in these mountings. See: *guntō*.

kyūjin 弓人. An artisan who makes archery bows.

kyūjutsu 弓術. Combative archery. *Kyūjutsu* has played a prominent role in Japanese history and mythology, especially in its relationship to warriors and warrior status. Since earliest times, the use of the bow and arrow has been closely associated with the spiritual world in Shintō ritual as well as with battlefield combat. A number of terms for "combative archery" may be used, including *kyūba*, *shagei*, *shahō*, *shajutsu*, and others. For centuries the status of warriorship was directly related to *kyūba* (mounted archery). By the late Heian and early Kamakura periods (794–1333), the term *kyūba no michi* (way of the warrior) indicated warrior status, martial capability, and an unwritten code of conduct for the warrior class. Fujita (1960: 2) lists 134 *ryū* specializing in *kyūjutsu*. The use of archery in combat declined after the introduction of firearms into Japan in the mid-sixteenth century. Even so, there are still a number of schools of classical *kyūjutsu* which practice archery for combative application. See also: *ikki-uchi; kyūba no michi; inu i gote; inu i hikime; inu ou mono; kasa kake; kyūdō; ya; yumi; san kasha; yabusame.*

Further reading in English:

- Draeger and Smith, 1969: 105–109.
- Hurst, 1998: 103–143.
- Onuma et al, 2003.

kyūjutsushi 弓術師. An archer.

Kyūkyoku no maki 「究極巻」. One of several original transmission scrolls of the Aisu Kage Ryū 愛洲陰流. This scroll is listed in the Hirasawa family records (*Hirasawa kabunsho* 「平沢家文書」).

JIKI SHINKAGE RYŪ *KYŪRI NO MAKI DENSHO* DATED 1823
(Private collection)

Kyūri no maki 「究理之巻」[Abbr. of ***Jiki Shinkage Ryū Kyūri no maki*** 直心影流究理之巻] (The scroll of the mastery of principles). JIKI SHINKAGE RYŪ—The fourth *densho* (license) awarded in the Jiki Shinkage Ryū. This text was traditionally written in four scrolls, or one long scroll divided into four sections. *Kyūri no maki* is awarded for "understanding deeply" the essence of Jiki Shinkage Ryū by demonstrating mastery of Habiki no Kata.

kyūsen 弓箭. 1. A bow and arrows. 2. Arms. 3. A war; hostilities.

kyūsen no ie 弓箭家. A warrior house (family/clan).

kyūsen no michi 弓箭道. The "way of the warrior"; warrior spirit.

K

kyūshaku e no yari 九尺柄槍. A spear with a shaft measuring about 9 feet (2.7 m). The *kyūshaku e no yari* was commonly used by foot soldiers (*ashigaru*) during the mid to late sixteenth century.

Kyūshin Ryū 汲心流 [A.k.a. ***Inukami Ryū*** 犬上流]. A system of grappling (*jūjutsu*) and quick-draw swordsmanship (*iaijutsu*) founded during the Eroku era (1558–1570) by Inukami Sakon Shōnagakatsu 犬上左近将長勝. The system proliferated in Kyūshū.

kyūsho 急所. Vital points on the human body. A number of these points are simply physically vulnerable points in the anatomy. However, Sino-Japanese medical tradition also mapped out a number of vital points created by combinations of blood flow (*chi*) and vital energy flow (*ki*) along acupuncture meridians. The vital points in this second group are thought to become more or less vulnerable at specific times of day. Texts on these vital points—such as the Okinawan *Bubishi*—often contain illustrations with the symbol for the hour of vulnerability inscribed on the corresponding point. See also: *keiketsu.*

Kyūshū 九州. The southernmost of the four main islands of Japan.

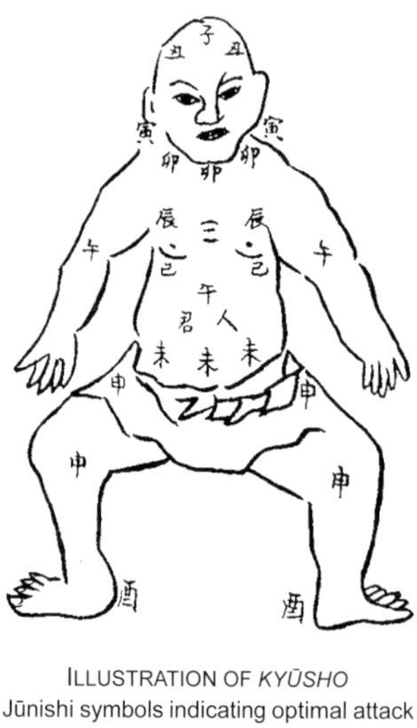

ILLUSTRATION OF *KYŪSHO*
With Jūnishi symbols indicating optimal attack time
(Okinawan Bubishi, anonymous, c. 1895)

M

Ma 1. 摩 [Var. 魔] <Ch. *Mo* <Skt. *Ma* मा. Seed syllable (*shuji*) for the Buddhist goddess Marishiten. This is one of the more common Sanskrit syllables inscribed on Japanese sword blades in *siddhaṁ* script (*shittan*).

MA मा
Sanskrit *siddham* letter representing the Buddhist goddess Marishiten carved into the groove of a Muromachi-period short sword (*kodachi*)
(Private collection)

ma 2. 間. An abbreviation for *maai*. Lit. "interval" (spatial or temporal). ¶ *ma o toru* 間を取る means "to control the combative engagement distance" in combative traditions; in the context of the Japanese tea ceremony (*chadō* 茶道), the phrase means "to control space." See: *maai.*

maai 間合. An interval (spatial and temporal). In a martial context, *maai* refers to a combative engagement distance or interval. In modern *kendō*, for example, the term *maai* simply refers to the distance between opponents. Within the classical martial traditions, a variety of terms may be used to describe a preferred distance when engaging in combat. Most of these lie within three general categories: striking interval (*uchima* 打間), close interval (*chikama* 近間), and distant interval (*tōma* 遠間). The closer the distance, the more dangerous the situation becomes, of course, as there is less time to react.

In classical Japanese combative systems in which hand-held, non-projectile weapons are used, the practitioner attempts to close the distance to a "one-step, one-strike interval" (*issoku ittō no maai* 一足一刀の間合). This is considered an optimum distance for pressing an opponent—neither too near nor too far. This is not, however, a "set" interval, but is flexible depending on reach of weapon, the timing, and other variables. Shimizu Takaji of the Shindō Musō Ryū used to encourage his students to visualize a string running between the foreheads of two partners engaged in *kata* training. The ideal interval would keep the string taut; too close, and it would sag (meaning there was vulnerability); too far and it would break (meaning both parties had to recalibrate their distance). However, depending on an opponent's skill level, a swordsman might choose to approach from a close or distant interval using deceptive postures (*kamae* 構え), movement such as looming (*semari* 迫り), or various types of timing/ rhythm (*hyōshi* 拍子).

Many schools had their own terminology and secrets concerning distance/interval. In the Tenshinshō-den Katori Shintō Ryū the same distance (*maai*) is used for several weapons of different lengths. The Yagyū Shinkage Ryū, on the other hand, does not generally use the term "*maai*" when speaking of optimum striking distance or interval; its proponents prefer the term *suigetsu*.

Regardless of terminology, a mastery of interval (timing/distance) is essential in a martial engagement. See: *chikama; chūma; hyōshi; suigetsu (3); tōma.*

Mabuni Kenwa 摩文仁 賢和 (1889–1952). OKINAWAN KARATE—Founder of Shitō Ryū 糸東流, a system of Okinawan *karate*. Mabuni was also one of the first *karate* masters to teach that combative art in Japan. Mabuni trained initially under Itosu Ankō in what was then called Shuri *te* 首里手. He also trained under Higaonna Kanryō, studying Naha *te* 那覇手/Shōrei Ryū 昭霊流. His Shitō Ryū therefore came to include both the linear techniques of Itosu's Shuri *te* and the short, circular movements of Higaonna's Naha *te*. Mabuni was eclectic in his training; he also studied with other Okinawan and Chinese teachers.

Mabuni made several trips to Japan in the 1920s in order to spread the teachings of *karate*. In 1929 he moved to Ōsaka to teach full-time. Early in this period he called his system "Hankō Ryū" 半剛流 (lit. "half-hard school") to indicate the influences he had incorporated into it. A few years later, however, he changed the name to "Shitō Ryū" 糸東流, apparently in honor of his two main influences: the first character from Itosu Ankō's name is 糸 and the first character from Higaonna Kanryō's name is 東. See: *Shitō Ryū.*

Machi Bugyō 町奉行. A Tokugawa-period term referring to magistrates in the cities of Edo, Kyōto, Ōsaka, and Sumpu (present-day Shizuoka). The samurai who held these positions were of *hatamoto* rank; they were chosen by the Tokugawa government for their judicial abilities. In the city of Edo there were two Machi Bugyō: one in charge of the northern area of the city (modern-day Marunouchi area) who was called the Kita-machi Bugyō; and one in charge of the southern areas of the city (modern-day Yurakucho area) called the Minami-machi Bugyō. These officials oversaw the police and fire departments. To prevent possible corruption, they exercised power by turns in six-month intervals. Assigned under these officials were the police sergeants (*yoriki*) and constables (*dōshin*).[1] See also: *Edo Machikata Jutte Torinawa Atsukaiyō; Machikata.*

Further reading in English:
- Dunn, 1972.
- Nouët, 1990.
- Papinot, 1910.
- Schreiber, 2001.

Machi Bugyōsho 町奉行所. The Office of the Town Magistrate. See: *Machi Bugyō.*

machi dōjō 町道場. Lit. "metropolitan training halls." This is a late Edo-period term used to describe privately owned and operated martial training halls, in contrast to *dōjō* owned and operated by the Tokugawa shogunate, or those located in the various feudal domains. Many who frequented the *machi dōjō* were not of the warrior class. By the late 1700s, the use of training swords made of bamboo (*shinai*) made it possible for non-samurai to practice swordsmanship.

machikata dōshin torimono 町方同心捕者. Equivalent to the term *dōshin* (police constable). See also: *Edo Machikata Jutte Torinawa Atsukaiyō; Machi Bugyō; machikata; yoriki.*

machikata yakunin 町方役人 [Abbr. ***machikata*** 町方]. Edo-period law enforcement officials. A relatively unusual term, this seems to have meant "senior town official," as opposed to the term *machibito* 町人 (also pronounced *chōnin*), which referred to townsmen and the merchant class. Nawa Yumio specifically used the term *machikata* to refer to law-enforcement officials, a group he further subdivided into *machikata yoriki* 町方与力 and *machikata dōshin* 町方同心.[2] See also: *dōshin; Edo Machikata Jutte Torinawa Atsukaiyō; yoriki.*

machikata yoriki 町方与力【町方與力】. Equivalent to the term *yoriki* (police sergeants). See also: *dōshin; Edo Machikata Jutte Torinawa Atsukaiyō; Machi Bugyō; machikata.*

machikata 町方. See: *machikata yakunin.*

machi no sen 待の先. See: go no sen.

machi yakko 町奴. Masterless samurai with a sense of chivalry who championed the underdog and defended the weak against hoodlums, in contrast to *hatamoto yakko* and *kabukimono*, who were gangster-like ruffians. Also called *otokodate*, the *machi yakko* proliferated during the years 1655–1672. See: *hatamoto yakko.*

madō 魔道. 1. BUDDHISM—The path of *māra* (i.e., killing, destroying) as related to the demon Māra. 2. BUDDHISM—The path infested with evil spirits and demons. 3. The path of (evil) magic. 4. The path of evil ways and influences. See: *meifu.*

mae 前. The front.

maedate 前立. Lit. "standing at the front." 1. The *maedate* is a type of ornament (*tatemono*) that was worn on the front of a helmet (*kabuto*). It was usually an image of an animal, mythical creature, deity, or artifact whose nature or character the wearer was

---

[1] Special thanks here to John F. Quinn for providing information from Nawa Yumio.

[2] Special thanks here to John F. Quinn for providing information from Nawa Yumio.

supposed to emulate. Similar objects worn on the back of the helmet were called *ushirodate*; those on the top of the helmet were *kashiradate*; and those on the sides, *wakidate*. See also: *tatemono.*

mae de 前で. Lit. " in front of…," "in the presence of…," "under the tutelage of…" ¶ *Itō Sensei no iru mae de Kage Ryū o uketorimashita.* 伊藤先生のいる前で陰流を受け取りました, I [was privileged] to receive [the teachings of] Kage Ryū directly under the tutelage of Itō Sensei.

magari yari 曲槍. Lit. "curved spear." A spear with three blades in the shape of a cross. The side blades curve forward toward the tip of the main blade. This is an alternate term for *kamayari* (sickle spear). For illustration, see: *jūmonji yari.*

magatama 勾玉. One of the Three Sacred Regalia (Sanshu no Jingi). The *magatama* is a comma-shaped jewel. See: *Sanshu no Jingi; Yasakani no Magatama.*

magoraga 摩睺羅伽 <Ch. *mohouluojia* <Skt. *mahoraga*. BUDDHISM—Title of the twelve divine generals who are considered protectors of Buddhism. See: *Hachibu Shu.*

Mairimashita! 参りました！ See: *Maitta!*

Maitta ! 参った! A term popularly used in fencing (*gekken*) from the Meiji era. It meant "I give up!" "I'm beaten!" More formally, *Mairimashita!* 参りました！

majutsu 魔術. Techniques of invisibility; the art of espionage. See: *Issa Ryū; Marishiten; jujutsu; ninjutsu; ongyōin; ongyōhō; tonkō hōjutsu.*

Makabe An'yaken Ujimoto 真壁 暗夜軒 氏幹. The founder of the Kasumi Shintō Ryū, a comprehensive martial arts school (*sōgō bujutsu*) which centered on swordsmanship (*kenjutsu*) and staff arts. Its signature weapon was a polearm called the *ichiizue*.

make 負け. Defeat. ¶ *Maketa* 負けた!, I've lost! I'm beaten!

makei 麻穴. See: *maketsu.*

maketsu 麻穴 [Also read ***makei***]. An alternate term for *kyūsho* (vital point); a pressure point. (Minouchi, 1982: 6). See also: *kyūsho.*

makimono 巻物. A scroll.

Makino Kyūbei Shigetoshi 槇野 久兵衛 茂俊. The founder of the Kusaka Isshi Ryū 日下一旨流, a school concentrating on swordsmanship (*kenjutsu*) and spear (*sōjutsu*). Makino established this school after mastering the Itō Ryū 伊東流, a school concentrating on pipe spear (*kudayari*) and glaive (*naginata*), under Oda Hikosaburō Kagetoshi. Makino may have also trained with Oda's master, Itō Suketada of the Kenkō Ryū 建孝流 (Itō Ryū [1]), a school which also concentrated on various types of polearms. For lineage, see: Itō Ryū (1).

Makino Entai 牧野 円泰【牧野圓泰】(d. 1729). Founder of the Ichien Ryū 一円流, a branch tradition of the Shin Shinkage Ichien Ryū.

Makiotoshi 巻落. 1. TATSUMI RYŪ—*Makiotoshi* was one of ten classical *kata* adapted from Tatsumi Ryū 立身流 by the Japanese Police Commission of 1886 for their Keishichō Ryū 警視庁流 system. 2. ***maki otoshi*** 巻落. Lit. "wrap and throw down." SHINDŌ MŪSŌ RYŪ—A technique in which a medium-length staff (*jō*) is used to "wrap and throw down" the opponent's sword. *Maki otoshi* is the sixth of twelve basic techniques (*kihon*) extrapolated from the classical forms of Shindō Musō Ryū by Shimizu Takaji.

M

makiwara 巻藁. 1. Lit. "sheaved straw." The *makiwara* was originally used by sword testers for a target in practice cutting (*tameshigiri*). 2. OKINAWAN KARATE—In Okinawa the straw—or straw mat— was wrapped around a wooden post for *karate* (Okinawa *te*) punching practice. It has been speculated that the Okinawan practice was directly influenced by the Jigen Ryū practice known as *tategi uchi*. However, in the practice of *tategi uchi*, the practitioner uses a wooden sword (*bokken*) to strike a standing post which is not covered with a straw mat.

makoto 誠 [Also 真]. CLASSICAL WARRIOR IDEAL—A feeling of absolute sincerity, often seen as the redeeming value for violent actions taken. According to Morris (1975:

472) *makoto* is a key quality of the Japanese hero "…denoting purity of motive, a rejection of self-serving, practical objectives, and complete moral fastidiousness." The character of *makoto* is also associated with a spirit of humility, especially when facing fate or conflict (Draeger, Conversations, 1972–1982).

maku 幕. A curtain or hanging bunting. See: *jimmaku.*

makura dashi 枕出. Lit. "out from the pillow." A term for a "pillow sword," a *katana* mounted on a stand close to a warrior's pillow, where it would be ready for use in an emergency.

makura naginata 枕薙刀. Lit. "pillow glaive." See: *fukuro naginata.*

makura yari 枕槍. Lit. "pillow spear." A lightweight spear with a shaft of about 3 feet (90 cm) in length and a straight head around 2 to 3 inches (5–8 cm) long. It was placed by the bedside for nighttime emergency defense. See also: *teyari.*

mami 1. 魔魅. A demon; an evil spirit.

mami 2. 間見. An espionage agent. See: *mitsumono; ninja.*

mamorigatana 守刀. See: *mamori katana.*

mamori katana 守刀. Lit. "protective sword." A dagger with a blade about a foot (30 cm) in length, worn in place of a short sword (*wakizashi*). The *mamori katana* was typically the first sword worn by samurai boys under the age of five. A "charm sword" or talisman, it was not made for actual use, and was covered in brocade.

mandara 曼荼羅 <Ch. *mantuluo* <Skt. *maṇḍala.* Lit. "mandala." A diagram which illustrates the nature of the cosmos, the human mind, or both; a psycho-cosmigram. Japanese Buddhist *mandara*, like their Indian, Tibetan, and Chinese counterparts, are magic circles which are divided into various squares and circles and inscribed with illustrations of symbols, buddhas, and deities. *Mandara* are normally intended as aids for meditation. In Japan Buddhist and martial training halls (*dōjō*) as well as many Shintō shrines (*jinja/jingu*) and martial exhibition sites (*embujō*) are patterned on *mandara* prototypes. See also: *goma; Kongōkai Mandara; Taizōkai Mandara.*

Further reading in English:

- Matsunaga, 1969: 199–205 ff.
- Snodgrass, 1988.
- Ten Grotenhuis, 1999.
- Tucci, 1973.

Mandokoro 政所. In effect, a "Board of Administration." The Mandokoro handled civilian affairs for the shogunates of the Kamakura and Muromachi periods. (Contrast to Samurai-dokoro.)

Mandokoro Bettō 政所別当【政所別當】. A Kamakura-shogunate term for the "Director of Civil Administration." This was in contrast to the Samurai-dokoro no Bettō. See also: *Samurai-dokoro no Bettō.*

Maniwa Nen Ryū 馬庭念流. One of the oldest existing comprehensive field-combat systems (*sōgo bujutsu*). The Nen Ryū was founded in 1368 by Sōma Shirō Yoshitomo (1351–1408) (better known by his Buddhist name, Nen Ami Jion 念阿弥慈恩). One of Jion's students was a warrior of the Higuchi family, and the Nen system became the martial regimen of the Higuchi clan. However, in the late 1400s the Higuchi family moved to Maniwa and replaced the Nen Ryū system with the local lord's Shintō Ryū 神道流 system.

A century later, clan leader Higuchi Sadatsugu sought out Tomomatsu Gian, the seventh headmaster of the Nen Shuza Ryū 念首座流 (the Akamatsu line of the Nen Ryū) and began replacing the Shintō Ryū system with the Nen Ryū. In 1591, after training in Nen

MANIWA NEN RYŪ
Higuchi Sadahiro (L) and Matsumoto Sadayoshi (R) demonstrate at Kashima Jingu, 1980
(Photograph by author)

Shuza Ryū for several years, Higuchi Sadatsugu received an *inka* (full license) in the Nen Ryū. From that time on, the tradition came to be called the Maniwa Nen Ryū (after the location of the Higuchi clan). The current and twenty-fifth headmaster is Higuchi Sadahito (a.k.a. Tōji Satoru).

Due to these historical events, the Maniwa Nen Ryū's oldest *densho* date back only as far as the late 1500s; that is, from the time of eighth headmaster Higuchi Sadatsugu.

Maniwa Nen Ryū's technical origins lie in the curriculum its founder Nen Ami Jion learned at Kuramadera; its "spiritual" origins are derived from the Marishiten cult. Tomomatsu Gian passed along the importance of Marishiten within the Nen Ryū. In 1796, Higuchi Sadayoshi, the sixteenth-generation headmaster of the Higuchi family tradition, erected a stone monument to Nen Ami Jion on a hill he called Mount Marishiten (Marishitensan 摩利支天山). This monument, which is still standing, has become a place of pilgrimage for Nen Ryū warriors. (Marishitensan is in Nagano prefecture, in a small village called Namiai.) Marishiten rituals are still held in Maniwa each year around 15 February.

The Maniwa Nen Ryū's current curriculum contains several weapons systems including *kenjutsu* (swordsmanship), *naginatajutsu* (long-hafted glaive techniques), *sōjutsu* (spear techniques), and *yadomejutsu* (the art of blocking arrows with a short sword; this was added in the early 1700s).

Current certificates (*menjō*) / licenses (*menkyo*):

Tachigumi Mokuroku	太刀組目録
Mokuroku	目録
Jiri Mokuroku	事理目録
Mokudai	目代
Inka[3]	印可

Sword (*kenjutsu*) curriculum:		**Number of *kata***
Omote—Gohon 表五本		5
• Jōryaku	上略	
• Geryaku	下略	
• Chūryaku	中略	
• Mugamae	無構	
• Gasshō	合掌	
Ura—Sanbon 裏三本		3
• Tsuke Kiriokuri	附切送	
• Jōdan Kiri	上段切	
• Sandan Kiri	三段切	
Kumi (juppon) 組 (十本)		10
• (Section One 其の一)		(5)
• Uchikomi Ranshō	打込乱勝	
• Gyaku Iri	逆入	
• Byōbugaeshi	屏風返	
• Tachi Sabaki	太刀捌	
• Gasshō Kuzushi	合掌崩	
• (Section Two 其の二)		(5)
• Shishi no Mine-kudari	獅子峰下	
• Nakazumi	中墨	
• Chūō Ōzume	中央大ずめ	
• Sumi Iri	澄入	
• Shishi Funjin	獅子奮迅	
		Total —18

Long-hafted glaive (*naginata*):		**Number of *kata***
Naginata (gohon) 薙刀 (五本)		5
—Naginata vs katana—		
• Jōryaku	上略	
• Geryaku	下略	
• Chūryaku	中略	
• Komite	込手	
• Hirakite	開手	

Spear arts (*sōjutsu*):		**Number of *kata***
Yari (gohon) 槍 (五本)		5
—*Suyari vs Kagiyari*—		
• Jōryaku	上略	
• Geryaku	下略	
• Chūryaku	中略	
• Tsuki Harai	付き払い	
• Jōge no Tsuki	上下の付き	

Arrow deflection (*yadomejutsu*)

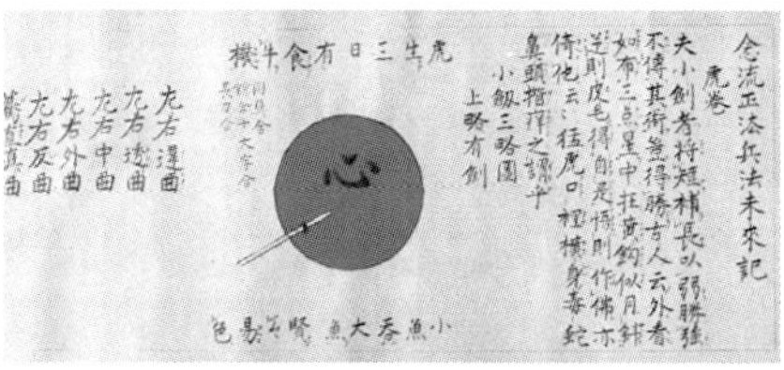

MANIWA NEN RYŪ *DENSHO*
DETAIL FROM *TORA NO MAKI*
(Higuchi family archives)

manji 万字【萬字】[Var 卍字 and 卐字]. BUDDHISM—The Buddhist swastika (<Skt. *sauvastika*—when the arms are bent in a counterclockwise direction 卍; <Skt. *svastika*

[3] It seems that Inka is awarded only to the succeeding headmaster.

—when the arms are bent in a clockwise direction 卐) is a symbol representing the Buddha. An early Buddhist text[4] states that the Buddha directed his disciples to treat his remains as they would the body of a king. This required a great sepulcher, or stupa, to be built at a crossroads with doors facing the four cardinal points in the same manner as the sepulcher of a king. This is symbolized by the *sauvastika*. Additionally, in Hinduism (as in many early religions) the *sauvastika* was considered a solar symbol of good fortune and this interpretation was also adopted by the Buddhists.

In the symbol for "good fortune," the tips of the cross are bent to the left, indicating rotation in a clockwise direction. Devotees visiting such a tomb would thus circumambulate the structure in a clockwise, orthodox direction (Skt. *dakṣiṇācāra*) in contrast to a counterclockwise, sinister, "widdershins" direction (Skt. *vāmācāra*). Ironically, in the infamous Nazi version of the swastika—supposedly selected by Adolf Hitler himself—the arms are bent widdershins. (Some Sanskrit sources refer to this counterclockwise device as a *svastika*, in contrast to the *sauvastika*.) In practice, however, Buddhists and martial traditions in East Asia use the two variants almost interchangeably.

The *manji* often appears in the *densho* of classical martial schools. Depending on the teachings of the *ryū*, it may indicate anything from Buddhist influence or insight to a specific martial technique or weapon. On maps, a *manji* usually indicates the location of a Buddhist temple.

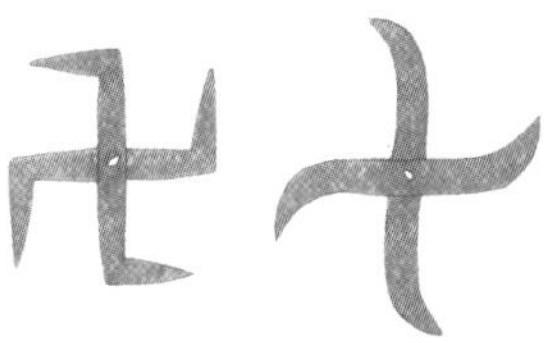

MANJI-SHAPED SHURIKEN

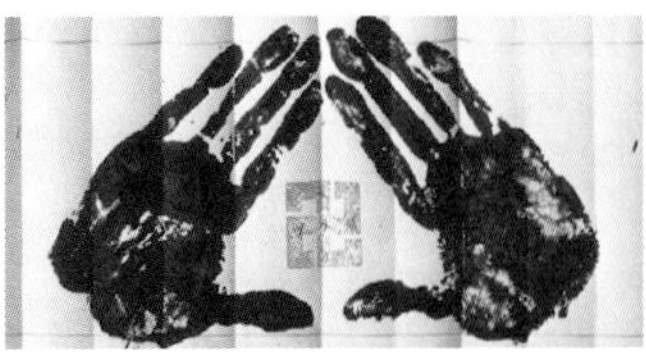

HOKUSHIN ITTŌ RYŪ *DENSHŌ*
Detail showing *manji* stamp
(*Kendō Nihon*, 1978, no. 8, used with permission)

[4] The Pāli *Mahā-parinibbāna-sutta*.

manji kagi 万字鍵【萬字鍵】[Var. 万字鉤【萬字鉤】; 卍字鉤【卍字鉤】; etc.]. A parrying bar (*hadome*) with one "hook" turned forward and one turned rearward.

Ma no Tachi 1. 間ノ太刀. KASHIMA SHINTŌ RYŪ—Third set of combative forms in the Chūgokui *kenjutsu* curriculum of the Kashima Shintō Ryū. See: *Kashima Shintō Ryū*.

ma no tachi 2. 魔之太刀. See: *oni no tachi*.

manriki 万力【萬力】. Lit. "ten-thousand power." 1. A carpenter's vise, so named for its constricting power. 2. An abbreviation for *manrikigusari*.

manrikigusari 万力鎖【萬力鏁】[Also read ***manriki kusari***; a.k.a. ***Masakigusari*** 正木鎖【正木鏁】]. Lit. "ten thousand power chain"; "vise chain." A weapon consisting of a short length of chain with a weight (*fundō*) attached to each end. The *manrikigusari* was developed in the mid-1700s by Masaki Toshimitsu. The chain and weights can be held in the palm of one hand. See also: *Masaki Ryū*.

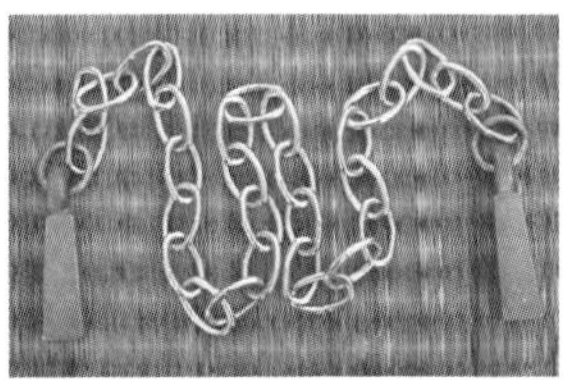

MASAKI RYŪ *MANRIKIGUSARI*
(Private collection)

manriki kusari 万力鎖【萬力鏁】. See: *manrikigusari*.

Mansen shūkai 『万川集海』【萬川集海】[also read ***Bansen shūkai***]. A multi-volume work on espionage tactics and practices. It was reputedly written by Fujibayashi Masatake 藤林正武, headmaster of the Fujibayashi Ryū *ninjutsu* tradition, around 1676. A comprehensive work, the *Mansen shukai* contains sections on weapons, tactics, divination practices, philosophy, and other topics. Along with the *Ninpiden* and *Shōninki*, it is considered one of the "three great books on *ninjutsu*" by those who study that subject. The work is reproduced in Imamura, 1966 (vol. 4): 413–482.

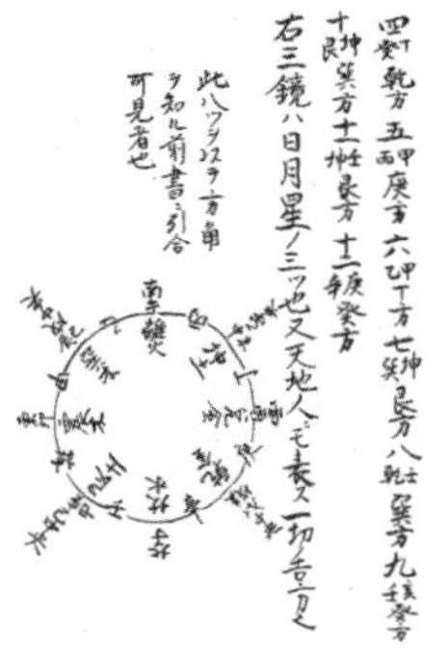

Fengshui-type diagram from the *Mansen shūkai*, used for strategic planning and combat divination

mantara 漫怛羅 <Ch. *mandaluo* <Skt. *mantra*. See: *shingon* 真言.

ma o toru 間を取る. To control the combative distance; to control the space. A term adapted for martial use from the Japanese tea ceremony (*chadō*).

mappō 末法 <Ch. *mofa* <Skt. *saddharma-vipralopa*. BUDDHISM—The last of the three time periods of Buddhism (*shōzōmatsu*). It is thought that during *mappō*, which means the "ending" or "final" law, the doctrine of the Buddha is still accessible, but there is no effective practice or access to enlightenment. The medieval Japanese calculated that *mappō* began in 1052 C.E., partly because an age of political upheaval and social unrest began at that time. At that time the Taira warrior clan was usurping control over the imperial court; Buddhist temples were resorting to armed conflict with each other (see *sōhei*); and a period of pessimism and uneasiness had enveloped the land. War tales (*gunkimono*) of that era, such as the *Heike monogatari*, seem obsessed with the inevitable arrival of *mappō*. See also: *Jōdo*.

Marishisonten 摩利支尊天. See: *Marishiten*.

Marishitembō 「摩利支天法」 [Also read ***Marishitenhō***]. A short ritual text used in various ceremonies devoted to the Buddhist goddess Marishiten. The *Marishtenhō* is essentially an excerpt from the standard Marishiten *darani* texts. See: *Marishiten; Marishiten bempō*.

Marishiten 摩利支天 [Var. 魔利支天; 末利支天; a.k.a. ***Dai Marishi Bosatsu*** 大摩里支菩薩; ***Marishisonten*** 摩利支尊天] <Ch. Molizhitian <Skt. Mārīcī-devī. One of several important Buddhist deities adopted as a protector by the Japanese warrior class. Marishiten, who appears in both female and male forms, is variously known as the Goddess of the Dawn, Goddess of the Dipper,[5] and Goddess of Polaris (the North Star),[6] among others. She is considered a patron goddess of warriors who can bestow upon her followers the power of invisibility and the ability to cloud the mind of enemies.

In medieval Japan, warriors almost always chose boar-mounted images of Marishiten

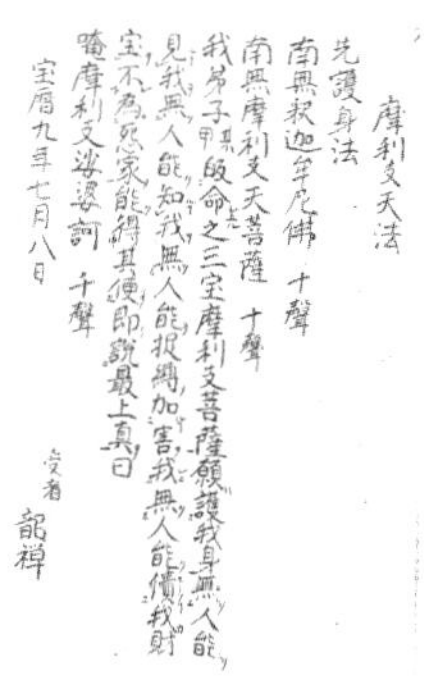

MARISHITEMBŌ
Eighteenth-century manuscript
(Courtesy of the Tendai archives on Mount Hiei)

FEMALE MARISHITEN WITH FAN OF INVISIBILITY
Illustration from twelfth-century Japanese text

5 Tomu 斗母 <Ch. Doumu.
6 Torō 斗姥 <Ch. Doulao.

MARISHITEN
Six-armed Marishiten standing on a charging boar
(Image from Marishiten Zuka temple in Japan)

when the deity was pictured in martial scrolls or on armor. In some cases only the name or seed syllable (*shuji*) of Marishiten appears on a helmet, while other examples feature a boar, or boars, sometimes appearing between images of the sun and moon. In addition, in some Buddhist texts and mandalas devoted to Marishiten, the boar is closely associated with invisibility. (Hall, 1990: 343) As the boar (*inoshishi*) is normally considered a symbol of aggressiveness and volition in warrior cultures, the practitioners of the cult seemed to feel that Marishiten, invisibility, the boar, and, by extension, volition, were all closely connected.

Although Buddhist temples with Marishiten as their main image (*honzon*) are rare in Japan, numerous martial traditions claim Marishiten as their founding inspiration. Among these are the Katori Shintō Ryū, the Nen Ryū, Shinkage Ryū, Shingyōtō Ryū, and many others. See also: *inoshishi; Myōken Bosatsu; ongyōin.*

Further reading in English:

• Hall, 1990; 1997: 87–119.

Marishiten bempō 「摩利支天鞭法」 (Marishiten whipping-rod ritual). A Shūgendō ritual manual aimed at soliciting the power of the goddess Marishiten. It contains many formulae and ritual elements that were also in use by the warrior class during the Muromachi and Edo periods. Manuscripts of this text are common, and early copies are held in libraries such as that of the Tendai school on Mount Hiei. The text begins with the Goshinpō (self-defense ritual) and continues with the Kujihō (ritual method of the nine seals). It includes many elements from a standard Esoteric Buddhist ritual text, the *Jūhachidō shiki*.

Further reading in English:

• Hall, 1990: 225–242.

Marishitenhō 「摩利支天法」. See: *Marishitembō.*

Marishiten hōbyōin 摩利支天宝瓶印【摩利支天寶瓶印】<Ch. Molizhitian *baoping yin*. An abbreviation for Marishiten Hōbyōin. See: *ongyōin (2).*

Marishiten ongyōin 摩利支天穏形印 <Ch. Molizhitian *yinxing yin*. See: *ongyōin (2).*

Marishitenjin 摩利支天神 [Also read ***Marishitenshin***]. An alternate term for Marishiten that appears in various martial documents. An example is the Tenshinshō-den Katori Shintō Ryū transmission scroll (*hidensho*) entitled *Mokuroku*. For illustration, see: *suigetsu.*

Marishiten setsu shōgun kyō 「魔利支天説勝軍経」【魔利支天説勝軍經】[Var. 摩利支天説勝軍經] (The Marishiten discourse on defeating armies). A Nen Ryū text on strategy that has been preserved by the Maniwa Nen Ryū.

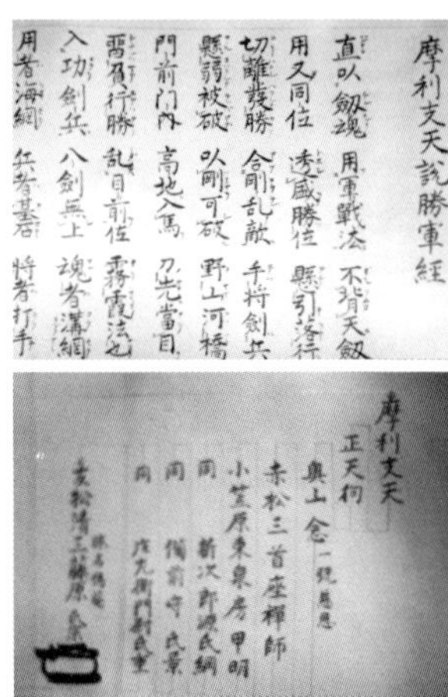

MARISHITEN SETSU SHŌGUN KYŌ
DETAIL FROM NEN RYŪ *DENSHO*, C.1595
(Nen Ryū text from the Higuchi Family Nen Ryū archives)

marobashi 転【轉】. Lit. "to roll," "to turn." SHINKAGE RYŪ—A key principle of the

Shinkage Ryū and its various branches. *Marobashi* indicates the ability to freely shift the sword and the mind at will; that is, to deceptively, fluidly, and explosively switch between offense and defense, rest and movement, all the while dominating the entire combative encounter. Related directly to the concept of the "death-dealing sword, life-giving sword" (*setsunintō katsujinken*), *marobashi* indicates empowerment of the swordsman into a state in which complete freedom of body, breath, and mind is optimized. Kamiizumi Nobutsuna, founder of the Shinkage Ryū, believed that in such a state of freedom or "formlessness," a swordsman could not be fixed or entrapped by an enemy. As a result, he would certainly dominate an encounter and effectively bring the engagement to conclusion. See also: *kamae; kurai; setsunintō katsujinken.*

Marubashi 丸橋. 1. JIKI SHINKAGE RYŪ—The fifth series of *waza* in the Jiki Shinkage Ryū. *Marubashi* consists of *kata*, all performed with *shinken kodachi* (for the *shidachi* role) and *shinken tachi* (for the *uchidachi* role). 2. JIKI SHINKAGE RYŪ—A key principle, akin to *marobashi*, in the Jiki Shinkage Ryū.

maru ki 丸木. 1. A wooden bow with rounded limbs. 2. A stick or staff with a round shaft.

Marume Kurandonosuke 丸目 蔵人佐. See: *Marume Kurandonosuke Tessai.*

Marume Kurandonosuke Tessai 丸目 蔵人佐 徹斎 [A.k.a. ***Nagayoshi*** 長珍] (1540–1629). A famous swordsman of Japan's Warring States period. Marume was one of the best-known disciples of Shinkage Ryū (1) founder Kamiizumi Ise no Kami. After mastering the Shinkage Ryū (1) 新陰流, Marume founded the Taisha Ryū タイ捨流.

Little is known about the training Marume underwent in his early years. At the age of sixteen, he was a combatant in the Battle of Ōhata (Ōhata Kassen 大畑合戦). The following year he trained in Chūjō Ryū with Amakusa Izu no Kami. Two years later, in 1558, the first year of the Eiroku era (1558–1570), he moved to Kyōto. There, he was defeated in a duel by Kamiizumi and became a disciple in the Shinkage Ryū.

MARUME KURANDONOSUKE TESSAI

Marume and his master Kamiizumi performed a martial exhibition for Yoshiteru, the thirteenth Ashikaga *shōgun*, in which Marume acted as *uchidachi* to Kamiizumi's *shidachi*. The *shōgun* sent Marume a letter of commendation that can still be seen today. The year is not specified in the document, but since Yoshiteru's reign ended in the seventh year of Eiroku (1565), the exhibition must have taken place sometime between 1558 and 1565.

There are some discrepancies in the various tales relating to the relationship between Marume and Kamiizumi. It is clear that they trained together in Kyōto; in 1567 Kamiizumi awarded Marume a license in the "secrets" (*gokui*) of the Shinkage Ryū titled *Katsunintō no tachi • Setsuninken no tachi* 「活人刀太刀利人剣太刀」. In the same year, Marume returned to Kyūshū to serve as a retainer for the Sagara clan, but left their service barely two years later, after accepting responsibility for the Sagara defeat at Ōguchi Castle at the hands of the Shimazu clan of Satsuma.

In 1586 Marume again traveled to Kyōto to seek out Kamiizumi for further training, but his master had passed away in 1578.

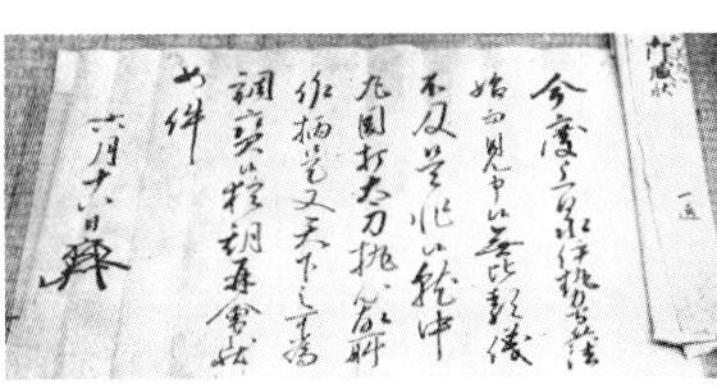

LETTER FROM ASHIKAGA *SHŌGUN* YOSHITERU
This note thanks Kamiizumi and Marume for their demonstration of Shinkage Ryū
(Marume family archives)

Marume then returned to Kyūshū and became the martial arts instructor of the Sagara clan. According to Watatani and Yamada (1978: 512) Marume had, over the years, mastered the secrets (*okugi*) of twenty-one different schools (*ryū*). With this store of combative information he founded the Taisha Ryū, a comprehensive combative school including spear arts (*sōjutsu*), swordsmanship (*kenjutsu*), long-hafted glaive arts (*naginatajutsu*), quick-draw sword arts (*iaijutsu*), and techniques for small throwing blades and darts (*shurikenjutsu*). He also became a well-known calligrapher in later life, and died at the age of ninety. Watatani and Yamada (1978: 513–514) list twenty-nine disciples who studied the Taisha Ryū directly under Marume.

Further reading in English:

- Hurst, 1998: 61–62.

Maruta Kyūzaemon Moritsugu 丸田 九左衛門 盛次. Founder of the Kasumi Ryū (2) 霞流, a school of firearms use. The tradition was established around 1603.

masakari 鉞. A battle-axe. Though these weapons were rarely used in battle by Japanese warriors after the Namboku period, the *masakari* became popular among the *yamabushi* later on. See also: *i no me kizamitaru masakari; ono.*

masakigusari 正木鎖 【正木鏁】. A generic term for the weighted chain weapon (*manrikigusari*) of the Masaki Ryū.

Masaki Ryū[7] 正木流 [A.k.a. ***Shuchin Ryū*** 守愼流 (Lit. "Defensive Chain Tradition")]. Primarily a police-arts system which concentrates on weighted-chain (vise-chain) techniques. Today, Masaki Ryu's weighted-chain system is taught in conjunction with Edomachikata Jutte Torinawa Atsukaiyō 江戸町方十手捕縄扱い様, a curriculum of *hobaku*—techniques and weapons used for restraining, capturing, and arresting. The major weapons systems of this collateral school are *juttejutsu* and *hojōjutsu* (*torinawajutsu*). Under the late Nawa Yumio, the inheritor of both systems, however, Masaki Ryū and Edomachikata Jutte Torinawa Atsukaiyō were actually taught separately.

Masaki Ryū was founded around the mid-1700s[8] by Masaki Tarōdayū Toshimitsu, a low-ranking samurai of the Tōda domain. Masaki had studied numerous systems, including Kotōda Ha Ittō Ryū 古藤田派一刀流 swordsmanship (*kenjutsu*) and spear arts (*sōjutsu*), Sen'i Ryū 先意流 long-hafted glaive (*naginatajutsu*), Heki Ryū 日置流 archery (*kyūjutsu*), and several others. These arts are illustrated in the *Geijutsu bukōron* (Discourses on martial arts exploits) by Kashiwabuchi Yūgi, a student of Masaki Toshimitsu.

Masaki added *manrikigusari* and *kusarigama* to his Masaki Ryū after establishing his original school. By the end of the Edo period, the earlier field-combat arts (*kenjutsu, sōjutsu,* etc.) had been dropped from the school, while the police arts were retained.

Curriculum of the Masaki Ryū

Weapons system		Number of techniques
Manrikigusarijutsu 万力鎖術		
• Kamae no Kata	構方	6
• Omote Iai	表居合	21
• Ura Iai	裏居合	15
Kusarigama-jutsu 鎖鎌術		
• Kamae no Kata	構方	4
• Furikomi Kata	振込方	11
• Uke Kata	受け方	7
• Kirikata (zampō)	切方	7

Nawa Yumio, the tenth-generation headmaster of the Masaki Ryū, established the Masakikai, its training organization in Tōkyō. Along with Masaki Ryū, Nawa also separately taught his students Edo Machikata Jutte Torinawa Atsukaiyō 江戸町方十手捕縄扱い様 as a collateral system (*fuzoku bugei*).

When Nawa retired from active teaching, he decided there would be no single subsequent successor to carry on the Masaki Ryū. Upon his retirement he instituted a *shihanke* system to replace the older headmastership. See also: *Edo Machikata Jutte Torinawa Atsukaiyō; Masaki Ryū Fukuhara Ha Kusarigama-jutsu; Masaki Toshimitsu; Nawa Yumio.*

7 Special thanks to John F. Quinn for providing information on the Masaki Ryū.

8 The actual date is unknown but, according to research by John F. Quinn, falls within the early Hōreki 宝暦 era (1751–1764).

Masaki Ryū Fukuhara Ha Kusarigama-jutsu 正木流福原派鎖鎌術 [A.k.a. ***Heiden Masaki Ryū Kusarigama-jutsu*** 併伝正木流鎖鎌術; abbr. Fukuhara Ha 福原派]. A set of sixteen sickle-and-chain weapon forms (*kata*) taught in the Suiō Ryū 水鴎流. These techniques were incorporated into the Suiō Ryū by ninth headmaster Fukuhara Shinzaemon sometime during the early to mid-1800s. This *kusarigama* system, which was referred to as the Fukuhara Ha, became a collateral art to Suiō Ryū. To indicate this collateral status, however, Suiō Ryū uses the term *heiden* 併伝 instead of *fuzoku bugei* 付属武芸.

Masaki Tarōdayū Toshimitsu 正木太郎太夫利充. See: *Masaki Toshimitsu.*

Masaki Toshimitsu[9] 正木 利充 [Var. Masaki Tarōdayū Toshimitsu 正木 太郎太夫 利充] (1688–1776). Founder of the Masaki Ryū.

MASAKI TARŌDAYŪ TOSHIMITSU
Founder of the Masaki Ryū
(Print from *Tōyūki*; photograph courtesy John F. Quinn)

Masaki, a retainer of the Tōda domain of Ōgaki, was skilled in the martial arts of that feudality. Like many warriors-by-birth of that era, he had begun training at the age of six. He studied a number of systems, including Kotōda Ha Ittō Ryū 古藤田派一刀流 swordsmanship (*kenjutsu*) and spear arts (*sōjutsu*), Sen'i Ryū 先意流 long-hafted glaive (*naginatajutsu*), Heki Ryū 日置流 archery (*kyūjutsu*), and several others. These arts, which were originally part of the Masaki Ryū, are illustrated in the *Geijutsu bukōron* (Discourses on martial arts exploits) by Kashiwabuchi Yūgi, one of Masaki's students.

Masaki added *manrikigusari* and *kusarigama* systems to his school later on, when he was stationed at the castle of the Tokugawa *shōgun* in Edo as chief of the gate guards. In that role, he developed a system based on the *manrikigusari* (weighted chain) with which he could subdue intruders without the use of live blades. See also: *Geijutsu Bukōron; Kotōda Ha Ittō Ryū; Masaki Ryū; Sen'i Ryū.*

Masamune 正宗. See: *Okazaki Masamune.*

mashō 魔障. Evil spirits and the hindrances caused by them.

massugu no kurai 真直の位. YAGYŪ SHINKAGE RYŪ—A middle-level (*chūdan*) sword posture (*kurai*) in which the sword is held directly to the front, with the *tsuka* just above hip level. The right foot is pointing straight forward; the left foot is to the rear at about a 35° angle, and the hips are square. The position is very similar to *seigan* in the Shindō Musō Ryū.

YAGYŪ SHINKAGE RYŪ *MASSUGU NO KURAI*
Swordsman Mutō Masao at Kashima Shrine, 1980
(Photograph by author)

Masuda Yajiemon Masatane 増田 弥次右衛門 正胤【増田彌次右衛門正胤】. A direct disciple of Saitō Denkibō, a well-known warrior who founded the Ten Ryū 天流 in 1582. The Ten Ryū was a comprehensive combat school containing several weapons systems.

Masugi Saburōbei no jō Nyūdō Mitsunobu 真杉 三郎兵衛尉 入道 三設 [A.k.a. ***Masugi Saburōzaemon*** ~三郎左衛門]. The founder of the Shishin Ryū 止心流, a comprehensive school which included a number of combative systems, around 1600.

9 Special thanks to John F. Quinn for providing information on Masaki Toshimitsu.

ma sutemi waza 真捨身技. KŌDŌKAN JŪDŌ—Sacrifice techniques in which the thrower falls onto his back in the execution of the throw. These are a subset of Nage no Kata.

mato 的. KYŪJUTSU/KYŪDŌ—An archery target. The bull's-eye (*kuroboshi*) is normally black.

matoba 的場. KYŪJUTSU/KYŪDŌ—A place for target practice; an archery range.

matoi 纏. See: *umajirushi.*

matoya 的矢. KYŪJUTSU/KYŪDŌ—Blunt, wooden-headed arrows used for target practice. Also referred to as *itatsuki.*

Matsubayashi Ryū 松林流 [Also read ***Shōrin Ryū***]. OKINAWAN KARATE—A system of *karate* founded by Nagamine Shōshin in 1947. See also*: Okinawa Karatedō Renmei.*

Matsuda Hōsaku 松田 豊作【松田豐作】. A student of Takeda Sōkaku who received the license of Daitō Ryū Kyōju Dairi in 1928. Matsuda's most prominent students were Oba Sachiyuki and Okuyama Yoshiji; the latter founded the Hakkō Ryū 八光流. See also: *Sō Dōshin.*

Matsudaira 松平. 1. The name of a village in old Mikawa province (present-day eastern Aichi prefecture). 2. The name of a warrior family established in Matsudaira in 1368 by Minamoto Chikauji. Many later branches descended from Chikauji, including the Tokugawa, Miki, Yoda, Tōjō, and others.

Matsudaira Etchū no Kami Sadatsuna 松平 越中守 定綱. A direct disciple of Yagyū Munenori of the Edo Yagyū Shinkage Ryū. Matsudaira founded the Kōotsu Ryū 甲乙流. He was subsequently appointed to the post of castle commander (*jōshu*) in 1635.

Matsuda Kata Shinkage Ryū 松田方新影流 [A.k.a. ***Shinkage Ryū Matsuda Kata*** 新影流松田方]. A line of the Shinkage Ryū founded by Matsuda Oribenosuke Seiei. The headmasters of the system did not refer to their school as "Matsuda Shinkage Ryū." Instead, their transmission scrolls are entitled "Shinkage Ryū Matsuda Kata 新影流松田方" which

MATSUDA KATA SHINKAGE RYŪ *DENSHO*
(From the archives of Mutō Masao)

means "Shinkage Ryū passed on via Matsuda."

The set of transmission scrolls in the photo above illustrate the integrity of the Shinkage Ryū as passed down in this line. They all date from 1835. Their titles, from right to left, are as follows:

- *Shinkage Ryū Matsuda kata heihō: Empi* 『新影流松田方兵法燕飛』
- *Shinkage Ryū Matsuda kata heihō: Sangaku* 『新影流松田方兵法三學』
- *Shinkage Ryū Matsuda kata heihō: Kuka* 『新影流松田方兵法九箇』
- *Shinkage Ryū Matsuda kata heihō: Tengusho* 『新影流松田方兵法天狗書』
- *Shinkage Ryū Matsuda kata heihō: Goka Daiji* 『新影流松田方兵法五箇大事』
- *Shinkage Ryū Matsuda kata heihō: Kasho* 『新影流松田方兵法歌書』
- *Shinkage Ryū Matsuda kata heihō: Yurushijō* 『新影流松田方兵法許状』

MATSUDA KATA SHINKAGE RYŪ *DENSHO*
Detail from *Shinkage Ryū Matsuda kata heihō: Tengusho*
(From the archives of Mutō Masao)

Yamada (1925: 229–232) notes that Yagyū Muneyoshi and Matsuda Seiei were contemporaries, both being disciples of Kamiizumi Ise no Kami.

Matsuda Oribenosuke Seiei 松田 織部助 清栄. A direct student of Kamiizumi Nobutsuna during the mid-1560s. Matusda's line of Shinkage Ryū is referred to as "Matsuda (Kata) Shinkage Ryū" and "Shinkage Ryū Matsuda Kata."

Matsuda Shinkage Ryū 松田新影流. See: *Matsuda Kata Shinkage Ryū.*

Matsui Kenji 松井 健二 (b. 1935). A student of Shimizu Takaji who received Shindō Musō Ryū *menkyo kaiden* under Otofuji Ichizō. Matsuda has carried out an extensive investigation on the history of the Shindō Musō Ryū and has published several articles, a book, and several videos concerning that tradition. Among his works are the following:

Tenshinshō-den Shindō Musō Ryū jōjutsu (*ōgatahon*)『天真正伝神道夢想流杖術(大型本)』(Tenshinshō-den Shindō Musō Ryū *Jōjutsu*—all forms). Shōshinsha, 1994. [Coauthored with Otofuji Ichizō.]

"Shindō Musō Ryū jōjutsu no zembō"「神道夢想流の全貌(前編)」(The full story of Shindō Musō Ryū *jōjutsu* [Part 1]), in *Hiden koryū bujutsu*『秘伝古流武術』(Issue 6, April, 1991): 32–43; ～(後編) [Part 2], (Issue 7, July, 1991): 78–89.

Matsumora Kōsaku 松茂良 興作 [A.k.a. ***Bushi Matsumora*** 武士松茂良] (1829–1898). OKINAWAN KARATE—Recognized as the central progenitor of Tomari *te*-style *karate.*

Matsumoto Bizen no Kami 松本 備前守 [Var. ***Matsumoto Bizen no Kami Naokatsu*** 松本備前守尚勝] (1468–1524). A famous swordsman of the Kashima area to whom several classical *ryū* trace their ancestry. Notable among these are the Jiki Shinkage Ryu 直心影流, which recognizes Matsumoto as its first headmaster, and the Kashima Shin Ryū.

Matsumoto Nagato Sadayoshi 松本 長門定好 [A.k.a. ***Matsumoto Rizaemon Toshinao*** ～理左衛門利直; ***Matsumoto Isshi*** ～一指] (1585–1660). Founder of the Isshi Ryū 一指流, a school concentrating on polearms such as the pipe spear (*kudayari*) and long-hafted glaive (*naginata*).

Having served several masters, Matsumoto joined Makino Kyūbei Shigetoshi of the Kusaka Isshi Ryū 日下一旨流 in 1605. Fourteen years later, Matsumoto had mastered the system's innermost teachings. He is believed to have trained with the famous Zen priest Takuan Sōhō[10] while the latter was enduring his banishment to Kaminoyama 上ノ山; at the culmination of that training, Matsumoto experienced an awakening (*satori*) to the inner mysteries and hidden purposes (*okugi*) of the art of the spear. He consequently founded his own school, Isshi Ryū, which centered on spear skills (*sōjū* 槍銃). Since Takuan's banishment took place between 1629 and 1632, the Isshi Ryū was likely established around 1630. This spear system became well known and evolved into several branch traditions. See: *Isshi Ryū.*

Matsumura Sōkon 松村 宗棍(～宗昆) [A.k.a. ***Sōho*** 宗秀; ***Bushi Matsumura*** 武士 松村] (1809–1899).[11] OKINAWAN KARATE—Matsumura is considered the progenitor of the various Shōrin styles of *karate* in Okinawa. Some sources state that from the age of fourteen he trained with Sakukawa Tōde. Matsumura was of warrior lineage (*shizoku*) and held the title of mid-level samurai (*pēchin* 親雲上). As an adult he became a "personal attendant" (*osobayaku* 御側役[12])—essentially a bodyguard—for three successive Okinawan kings.[13]

At that time the Ryūkyū archipelago was controlled by the Japanese of Satsuma domain on Kyūshū, who required the Okinawan king to spend half of each year in Kyūshū. As a personal bodyguard, Matsumura evidently accompanied the kings on these visits. While in Kyūshū, he is believed to have learned Jigen Ryu swordsmanship (*kenjutsu*) from Ijuin Yahachirō, and eventually earned a full license (*menkyo kaiden*) in that tradition.[14] He thus came to be called "Bushi Matsumura" (Warrior Matsumura). He also traveled to Fuzhou several times, where he studied Chinese fighting systems. In Okinawa, Matsu-

---

10 Takuan was on close terms both with third Tokugawa *shōgun* Iemitsu and Iemitsu's swordsmanship instructor, Yagyū Munenori. He wrote several treatises on Buddhism and the martial arts.

11 These dates are from Takamiya et al. (2008: 520). Others note c. 1797–1893 and c. 1809–1901.

12 Takamiya notes that this is equivalent to Japanese *kinji* 近侍 (personal samurai attendant) or *kinshin* 近臣 (trusted vassal or personal guard).

13 Shō Kō 尚灝 (r.1804–1834), Shō Iku 尚育 (r. 1835–1847), and Shō Tai 尚泰 (r.1848–1879).

14 See footnote under the Ko Jigen Ryū lineage.

mura taught his *karate* system to Azato Ankō, Itosu Ankō, and others, many of whom resided in Shuri. See also: *Azato Ankō; Funakoshi Gichin; Itosu Ankō; Sakugawa Tōde.*

Matsuno Matsuemon Ienobu 松野 松右衛門 家信 [A.k.a. ***Munenobu*** 宗信]. See: *Yagyū Matsuemon Ienobu.*

Matsuo Iyonosuke Yoshikazu 松尾 伊与亮 喜計【松尾伊與亮 喜計】(c.1750–c.1820). Founder of the Ikkyoku Mubetsu Ryū 一極無別流 sometime during the 1780s. Matsuo espoused the concept of *ken zen itchi* (swordsmanship and Zen are one).

Matsuoka Katsunosuke Hisachika 松岡 克之助 尚周 (1836–1898). Founder of a branch school of Yōshin Ryū 楊心流 *jūjutsu* called the Shindō Yōshin Ryū 神道楊心流. Matsuoka established his system during the Bakumatsu era of the late Tokugawa period.

Matsuoka Shinkage Ryū 松岡神陰流. A branch tradition of the Shinkage Jikishin Ryū 新陰直心流. This line descends from Matsuoka Idayū, a disciple of Kamiya Denshinsai Masamitsu in the mid-1600s. (Kamiya is also recognized by the Jiki Shinkage Ryū as the fifth headmaster of the Shinkage Ryū.)

The system apparently concentrated on swordsmanship (*kenjutsu*). It is not known whether this line survived the end of the feudal period in 1868.

1847 MATSUOKA SHINKAGE RYŪ *DENSHO* TITLED *SHINKAGE RYŪ KIRIGAMI JO I*「神陰流剪紙叙意」
(Private collection)

Matsu Uemon 松 右衛門. See: *Yagyū Matsuemon Ienobu.*

Matsuzaki Kane'emon Shigekatsu 松崎 金右衛門 重勝 (c.1590–c.1660). The third headmaster of the Shindō Musō Ryū. Matsuzaki was probably a direct student of Musō Gonnosuke. He is credited with adding Ikkaku Ryū (1) 一角流 *juttejutsu* and Ittatsu Ryū 一達流 *hojōjutsu* as collateral systems to the Shindō Musō Ryū 神道夢想流 in the Kuroda domain.

Matsuoka Shinkage Ryū[15]
松岡神陰流
(abbreviated lineage)

1. Matsumoto Bizen no Kami 松本 備前守 (c. 1467–c. 1534) **Kashima Shin(kage) Ryū** 鹿島神(影)流
2. Kamiizumi Ise no Kami Nobutsuna 上泉 伊勢守 信綱 (1508–1577) **Shinkage Ryū** 新陰流 / 新影流
3. Okuyama Kyūkasai Kimishige 三代 奥山 休賀斎 公重 (1526–1602) **Shinkage Ryū** 神影流
4. Ogasawara Genshin 四代 小笠原 玄信 (1574–1644) **Shin Shinkage Ryū** 真新陰流
5. Kamiya Denshinsai Masamitsu 五代 神谷 伝心斎 直光 (1582–1663) **Shinkage Jikishin Ryū** 新陰直心流
6. Matsuoka Idayū 松岡 猪太夫 (c. 1620–c. 1700) **(Matsuoka) Shinkage Ryū** (松岡)神陰流
7. Matsuoka Shichirōbei 松岡 七郎兵衛 (c. 1658–c. 1736) **Shinkage Ryū** 神陰流
8. Matsuoka Jirōdayū 松岡 次郎太夫 (c. 1708–c. 1787) **Shinkage Ryū** 神陰流
9. Imabori Kichinosuke 今堀 吉之助 (c. 1722–c. 1792) **Shinkage Ryū** 神陰流
10. Kusumi Junzaburō 久須美 順三朗 (c. 1746–c. 1818) **Shinkage Ryū** 神陰流
11. Nishi Kogōta 西 小號太 (c. 1780–c. 1855) **Shinkage Ryū** 神陰流
12. Yuhi Matatarō 由比 又太郎 (c. 1811–c. 1879) **Shinkage Ryū** 神陰流

Mawarigake 廻り掛. TAMIYA RYŪ—One of a number of classical prearranged quick-draw sword forms (*battō kata*) developed by the Tamiya Ryū. *Mawarigake* was also one of five classical *battō kata* adapted by the Japanese Police Commission of 1886 for their Keishichō Ryū 警視庁流 system.

15 Watatani and Yamada (1978: 333) refer to this as a branch of Kamiya's "Jikishin Ryū" 直心流. The line they list also varies slightly from the one given here.

mawashi mono 回し者. A variant term for an espionage agent. See: *ninjutsu.*

ma wo toru 間を取る. See: *ma o toru.*

meido 冥途 [Also read ***yomiji***; var. ***meidō*** 冥道]. BUDDHISM—Lit. the "dark path"; the underworld; realm of the dead. According to popular belief, it is the place where the souls of the dead reside. See also: *madō; meifu; meikai.*

Meidōkan 明道館. Lit. "Hall of the Shining Path." A martial arts *dōjō* in Fukuoka belonging to the Gen'yōsha organization in the late 1800s. The primary system taught at the Meidōkan was Jigō Tenshin Ryū 自剛天真流 *jūjutsu*. At the Meidōkan, potential Gen'yōsha members were tested and observed for "...their composure, mental alertness and ability to withstand physical strain and crisis..." (Sabey, 1973: 76). It was by this method that Uchida Ryōhei was selected as a protégé of Tōyama Mitsuru.

meifu 冥府. Hell, Hades; the realm of the dead. ¶ *meifu madō ni ochi* 冥府魔道に落ち, "to fall into the demon-infested road to hell," "to fall into the pit of hell." See also: *madō; meido; meikai.*

Meifu Shinkage Ryū 明府真影流. A modern (late twentieth century) school concentrating on small throwing blades and darts (*shurikenjutsu*). The tradition was founded by Someya Chikatoshi, who evidently trained in Katori Shinto Ryu under Hayashi Yazaemon Iekiyo and nineteenth Katori headmaster Iizasa Shurinosuke Kinjirō prior to World War II. Being most attracted to the *shuriikenjutsu* of that system, Someya subsequently experimented with a variety of throwing weapons and founded his own school in the 1950s. Upon his death in 1999, Someya was succeeded by current headmaster Ōtsuka Yasuyuki.

meigen 鳴弦. The practice of plucking a bowstring to disperse evil spirits (*mashō*) in a formal, ritual method of propitiation to the gods of a shrine. *Meigen* is considered part of the secret teachings (*gokui*) of combative archery (*shajutsu*).

meigo 明悟. An awakening or enlightening experience. The word may also refer to an oracle or vision, much like *musō* 夢想.

NAMIKI YASUSHI PERFORMS *MEIGEN*
Kashima Jingu—1978
(Photograph by author)

meijin 名人. A master; an expert.

meikai 冥界. BUDDHISM—1. Hades, hell. 2. The lower three realms of reincarnation into which one may be born: hell realm (*jigoku*), hungry ghost realm (*gaki*), and animal realm (*chikushō*). See also: *meido; meifu.*

Meishidō 名士道. Lit. "the spiritual path of the master warrior." Meishidō was an early (c.1938) name for Okuyama Yoshiji's *jūjutsu* system. Okuyama changed the name to Hakkō Ryū 八光流 in 1941.

meiyo 名誉 【名譽】. CLASSICAL WARRIOR IDEAL—The term *meiyo* refers to "honor," an essential characteristic of the Japanese warrior class. See: *bushi no konjō.*

mekiki 目利き. 1. A judge (of things); an expert. 2. An expert who judges and evaluates swords and other bladed weapons.

mekugi 目釘. The peg securing the tang of a sword in the hilt.

memboku 面目 [Also read ***menboku***]. "Face"; pride, honor, self-interest. This tenth-century term, found in the *Shōmonki*, is roughly equivalent to the term *na* (name) used in the same period.

mempō 面頬 [Also read ***menpō***]. A face guard; an armored facemask. The *mempō*

M

is essentially a metal or leather mask which covers some or all of the face. Unlike a European helmet visor, it is not attached to the helmet and cannot be raised. Different types of *mempō* have different names, depending on how much of the face is covered. A *hoate,* for example, covers only the face below the nose. Some *mempō* were artistically designed to have the appearance of a demon; these were referred to as *akuryō* (evil demon).

menboku 面目. See: *memboku.*

menjō 免状. A certificate of proficiency or a license in a martial school. See: *densho.*

menkyo 免許. 1. A license. 2. A license of proficiency or a document authorizing a person to teach in a martial school.

Menkyoden 免許伝 【免許傳】. Abbreviation for *Jiki Shinkage Ryū Menkyoden.* See: *menkyo kaiden.*

menkyo kaiden 免許皆伝 【免許皆傳】. Lit. "complete transmission license." The content of a *menkyo kaiden* license varies greatly depending on the school it is issued by. A Shindō Musō Ryū *menkyo kaiden,* for example, is the final, full license in Shindō Musō Ryū *jōdō/jōjutsu.* This document, written in *densho* form, contains narrative information as well as a list of the *hiden gokui* (the most privileged secret teachings of the school). In contrast, the Jiki Shinkage Ryū *menkyoden,* while also written in *densho* form, originally consisted simply of an illustration of a circle and transmission data such as the name of the master, the successor, and the date. Later editions of this *densho* contained additional text.

MATCHED PAIR OF *MENUKI* DEPICTING THE SUN (GOLD JEWEL AT TOP) AND MOON (SILVER JEWEL AT BOTTOM)
Taken together, these represent the Buddhist deity Marishiten
(Private collection)

menpō 面頬. See: *mempō.*

menuki 目貫. Ornaments on the sides of the hilt of a sword or knife.

metezashi 右手差し [Var. 馬手差]. Lit. "worn on the right." A sword worn on the right, rather than on the left. This short sword or dagger, generally around 9 inches (23 cm) long, was used for armored grappling. In the illustration below, note that the *kurikata* and *soritsuno* are placed on the right side of the scabbard (*saya*). See: *yoroidōshi.*

METEZASHI

metsubushi 目潰. 1. JŪJUTSU—A strike to the eyes, intended to blind an opponent. See also: *kasumi.* 2. Any of a variety of weapons or weapon-usable objects used to blind an opponent. See also: *gantsubushi.*

metsuke 目付け. Lit. "sticking to the eyes"; a look; an expression. 1. To point a weapon right between the enemy's eyes; to focus on the enemy's eyes. 2. 目付. An abbreviation for *metsukeyaku.* 3. 目付. An espionage agent. See: *mitsumono; ninja.*

metsukeyaku 目付役. During the Edo period, a *metsukeyaku* (also simply *metsuke*) was a superintendent police officer who functioned as a public censor or "watchdog." In addition, covert *metsukeyaku* were used somewhat like a branch of secret police by the Tokugawa to keep an eye on the various great lords (*daimyō*), minor lords (*shōmyō*), and other personages holding political, financial, and military power. These secret police were variously referred to as *shinobi metsuke, kakushi metsuke,* etc. See also: *ninjutsu.*

mi 1. 巳. a. The sixth duodenary hour of the Chinese Twelve Branches (Jūnishi). *Mi,* which symbolizes the Serpent, indicates the hours from 9 to 11 a.m. b. KYŪSHO—In certain Sino-Japanese boxing texts, this symbol (corresponding to the Hour of the Serpent) in dicates the optimal time of day for striking a specific vital point (*kyūsho*). See also: Appendix 1.

mi 2. 未. Symbol for Ram. See: *hitsuji.*

michi 道 [also read **~dō** in compound words]. The "way," the "path." See: *dō (3).*

michidassha 道達者 [Also read ***michidatsu-sha***. See: *hayagake.*

Mifune Kyūzō 三船 久蔵 (1883–1965). One of the most famous practitioners of Kōdōkan Jūdō. Mifune was born only one year after the founding of Kōdōkan Jūdō. He had only trained for about a year as a high-school student when, in 1896, he defeated nine opponents in a single *jūdō* contest. After graduating from high school he moved to Tōkyō, where he was supposed to enroll in a preparatory school for Waseda University. The Kōdōkan at that time required new students to have an interview with its founder, Kanō Jigorō, and a letter of recommendation. Knowing no one attached to the Kōdōkan, Mifune sought out Yokoyama Sakujirō, whose powerful *jūdō* had given him the reputation as one of the "four stalwarts" (Shitennō) of the early Kōdōkan. Mifune's tenacity finally won him a recommendation from Yokoyama, and he joined the Kōdōkan in 1903. He progressed rapidly, remaining undefeated in tournaments. By 1912 he was already a *rokudan* (sixth-degree black belt) and had been nicknamed the "Judō no Kami-sama" (god of Jūdō). In 1945 he was promoted to *jūdan*, or tenth-degree black belt.

MIFUNE KYŪZŌ (L) GRAPPLES WITH KANŌ JIGORŌ (R) c. 1920

Mifune had an enormous influence on post-WWII *jūdō* due to his status at the Kōdōkan and his fluid, seemingly effortless, technique. In a video from the 1950s titled *Judo's Greatest Master! Kyuzo Mifune, 10th Dan*, Mifune, then in his 70s, easily handles judoists who are twice his weight. In 1960 Mifune published the *Canon of Judo*, still considered a classic today, which covers most of the techniques in Kōdōkan Jūdō.

migi 右 [Also read ***u*** or ***yū***]. Right. ¶ *migi ni* 右に, to the right.

Migi no Teki 右の敵. KYŌSHIN MEICHI RYŪ—One of a number of classical prearranged quick-draw sword forms (*battō kata*) developed by the Kyōshin Meiichi Ryu 鏡新明智流. It was also one of five classical *battō kata* adapted by the Japanese Police Commission of 1886 for their Keishichō Ryū 警視庁流 system.

migi seigan no kamae 右青眼の構. A combative engagement posture (*kamae*, *kurai*) found in a number of *ryū* in which the proponent's sword is pointed directly at the opponent's eyes; the right foot is placed slightly in front of the left.

MIGI SEIGAN NO KAMAE
Miyauchi Akira of the Jiki Shinkage Ryū during a 1980 training session
(Photograph by author)

Migumo Ryū 三雲流. A system of strategy and tactics (*gunkai*) including espionage (*shinobi no jutsu*) founded by Migumo Shin'emon, a retainer of Katō Kiyomasa. (Katō was a general and *daimyō* who became famous for his successful strategy in Korea in the early 1590s.) Migumo's *gunkai* appears to have been a significant element in Katō's rise to fame and his successes in Korea. Later, when

M

Migumo Ryū
三雲流
(abbreviated lineage)

1. Migumo Shin'emon
初代 三雲 新右衛門
Migumo Ryū (*gunkai*)
三雲流(軍貝)

- Hattori Buzaemon Masanobu
  服部 武左衛門 正信
  Iga Ryū (2) (*ninjutsu*)
  伊賀流(忍術)
- 2. Takano Ryūhei Masatane
  二代 高野 留平 正種
  Migumo Ryū (*gunkai*)
  三雲流(軍貝)

Katō was aligned with Tokugawa Ieyasu, Migumo passed on one line of the Migumo Ryū to Hattori Buzaemon Masanobu. Hattori established a family-transmitted line of the system concentrating on espionage, which he christened Iga Ryū.

After the downfall of the Katō family in 1611, Migumo was invited to teach Migumo Ryū in Tosa domain by a landed samurai (*goshi*) named Takano Ryūhei Masatane. There he transmitted Migumo Ryū *gunkai.*

Migumo Shin'emon 三雲 新右衛門 [A.k.a. ***Tameemon*** 為右衛門]. Founder of the Migumo Ryū tradition of strategy and tactics (*gunkai*). Early in his career, Migumo was a retainer of Katō Kiyomasa, who was aligned first with Toyotomi Hideyoshi and later Tokugawa Ieyasu. During his association with the Tokugawa (c.1590–1611), Migumo passed on the Migumo Ryū to Hattori Buzaemon Masanobu. After the fall from favor and assassination of his master, Katō Kiyomasa, Migumo was invited to Tosa domain in 1611. There he instructed the clan of Takano Ryūhei Masatane in the strategies (*heigaku*) of Ōe Ryū 大江流 *gumpō* and Kusunoki Ryū 楠流 as well as his own Migumo Ryū *gunkai.*

Miidera 三井寺 [A.k.a. Onjōji 園城寺]. BUDDHISM—The main temple of the Tendai Jimon branch. It is located in Shiga prefecture.

Mikado 御門 [Var. 帝]. The emperor of Japan. It is speculated that the characters 御門, which literally mean "exalted gate" (or "palace gate"), may have originally referred to the imperial court. It should be noted that the Japanese people do not normally use the term "Mikado" for the emperor; rather, the title Tennō 天皇 is preferred.

mikata 見方. An espionage agent. See: *mitsumono; ninja.*

mikire 三切. Lit. "three cuts." An expression indicating that in a duel, the third of three cuts is bound to cut flesh.

Miki Ryū 三木流. A school teaching the use of firearms (*bōbiya*). It was founded by Miki Shigedayū Anmon.

Miki Shigedayū Yasukado 三木 茂太夫 安門. Founder of the Miki Ryū, a school of firearms use.

mikkyō 密教 <Ch. *mizong* 密宗. BUDDHISM—Lit. "esoteric teachings." *Mikkyō* refers to the Tantric Buddhist doctrines, practices, and rituals of several Japanese Buddhist schools. They are found primarily in the Shingon school (where these teachings, called *tōmitsu*, make up most of the system) and the Tendai school (where they are called *taimitsu*, and are on an equal footing with four other categories of teaching). Other Buddhist schools in Japan, such as the Rinzai Zen Shū 臨済禅宗, Jōdo [Pure Land] Shū 浄土宗, and Nichiren Shū 日蓮宗, also contain a smattering of *mikkyō.*

Further reading in English:
- Chou, 1945.
- Hall, 1977; 1978; 1990.
- Payne, 2005.
- Sawa, 1972.

miko 巫女. SHINTŌ—1. Young female attendants at Shintō shrines. These maidens are normally seen wearing white *kimono* with scarlet *hakama.* 2. A virgin who has been consecrated to a deity. 3. A sorceress, also known as an *ichiko* 市子.

Mikogami Tenzen 神子上 典膳. See: *Ono Jirōemon Tadaaki.*

mikoshi 神輿 [Var. 御輿]. SHINTŌ—A portable shrine or sacred palanquin of a Shintō god (*kami*). Often carried today in festivals, the *mikoshi* was commonly used by warrior monks (*sōhei*) in medieval times in order to intimidate the imperial court and other enemies.

Mikusa no Kandakara 三種神器【三種神器】. See: *Sanshu no Jingi.*

Mima Yoichizaemon Kagenobu 三間与一左衛門 景延【三間與一左衛門景延】(1577–1665). A retainer of the Satake clan (Satake Shi 佐竹氏) who founded the Suiō Ryū 水鴎流 around 1600. Mima was born the son of a shrine attendant/retainer (*hafuribe*) of the Jūnisō Gongen[16] shrine. As a young man, he trained in Bokuden Ryū 卜伝流 swordsmanship (*kempō* [1]) with his father, as well as in the quick-draw swordsmanship (*iaijutsu*) of the Hayashizaki Ryū 林崎流 with Sakurai Gorōzaemon Naomitsu.[17] At the Jūnisō Gongen shrine, Mima performed austerities and prayers (*sanrō*), propitiating the Buddhist deity Fudō Myōō (of whom Jūnisō Gongen is a manifestation). While engaged in this *shugyō*, he is said to have trained tirelessly before the sacred tree (*shimboku* 神木) of the shrine, concentrating on his quick-draw swordsmanship. Documents of the school refer to this training as *battō shugyō.* Mima also periodically engaged in warrior pilgrimage (*musha shugyō*), traveling around Japan to improve his skills. According to some sources, he engaged in *battō shugyō* for twenty years before founding his own system. Mima was finally rewarded with a dream of a seagull rising from under the surface and floating on the water (*suiō* 水鴎). This vision awakened him to the secrets of a new sword system he christened Suiō Ryū 水鴎流. From this awakening experience, he devised twenty-eight combative forms (*kata*) based on the constellations of the Nijūhasshuku (the twenty-eight constellations through which the moon is seen to pass). These combative forms formed the core of the Suiō Ryū. See: *Suiō Ryū.*

Minami Machi Bugyō 南町奉行. Title of an Edo-period magistrate who presided over the southern areas of the city of Edo (modern-day Yūrakuchō). The samurai who held this position was normally of *hatamoto* rank. See: *Miachi Bugyō; Kita Machi Bugyō.*

Minamoto 源 [A.k.a. ***Genji*** 源氏]. A family name given to many sons and grandsons of various emperors. The most prominent warrior (*bushi*) line, which traced its origin to Emperor Seiwa,[18] was called the Seiwa Genji 清和源氏. Many *bushi* families, such as the Ogasawara, are descended from the Minamoto. See: *Seiwa Genji.*

Further reading in English:

- Papinot, 1910: 373–386.

Minamoto Tokushū 源 徳修. An itinerant master swordsman who traveled the country for over a decade visiting a large variety of combative schools. He collected his notes into a volume called the *Gekken sōdan*『撃劍叢談』, which he published in 1843.

Minamoto no Yoritomo 源 頼朝 (1147–1199). Chief of the Minamoto clan in the 1180s. With the help of his brother Yoshitsune, Yoritomo led the Minamoto to a victory over the Taira clan in the Gempei War. In 1192 he established the first permanent shogunate in Kamakura.

Further readings in English:

- Draeger, 1973a.
- Kitagawa and Tsuchida (trans.), 1975.

PORTRAIT THOUGHT TO BE THAT OF MINAMOTO NO YORITOMO

(In 1995 scholar Yonekura Michio suggested that this is actually a portrait of Ashikaga Tadayoshi)

Minamoto no Yoshiie 源 義家 [A.k.a. ***Hachiman Tarō*** 八幡 太郎] (1041–1108). One of

---

16 Jūnisō Gongen 十二社権現 (also read "Jūnisha Gongen") is a Ryōbu Shintō manifestation of the Shintō *kami* Fudō Myōō. For many years there was a shrine and waterfall in Edo which bore this name.

17 Sakurai Gorōzaemon Naomitsu 桜井 五郎左衛門直光【櫻井五郎左衛門直光】.

18 Seiwa Tennō 清和天皇 (850–880; r. 858–876). The fifty-sixth emperor of Japan.

the most renowned warriors of Japan's medieval period. Records of Yoshiie's numerous combative exploits have been supplemented by many legends. The Ōe Ryū 大江流, a school of strategy and tactics which flourished from the fifteenth century through the end of the pre-modern period (c.1868), recognized Yoshiie as the formulator of Minamoto family battle strategy. These strategies (*gumpō*) were later transmitted via the Ogasawara (a Minamoto branch family) to the Ōe Ryū. See also: *Genke kin'etsushū; Ōe no Koretoki; Ōe Ryū; Seiwa Genji.*

Minamoto no Yoshimitsu 源 義光 [A.k.a. ***Shinra Saburō Minamoto no Yoshimitsu*** 新羅 三郎 源 義光] (1056–1127). Brother of Minamoto no Yoshiie. Yoshimitsu is considered the progenitor of several warrior families via his son, Minamoto Yoshikiyo, and grandson, Minamoto Kiyomitsu. From his line of the Seiwa Genji descend the Henmi 逸見, Takeda 武田, Ogasawara 小笠原, Yasuda 安田, and Takenouchi 竹内. Yoshimitsu was an accomplished warrior who is best known for aiding his brother Yoshiie in putting down the revolt of the Kiyowara 清原 clan of Dewa in 1087. See: *Seiwa Genji.*

Minamoto no Yoshitsune 源 義経 [A.k.a. ***Ushiwakamaru*** 牛若丸; ***Hōgan*** 判官; ***Kurō***] (1159–1189). A legendary tactician and tragic figure of Japan. According to the *Azuma kagami*, Yoshitsune was about a month old when his father, Minamoto no Yoshitomo, was killed soon after the Heiji War. In 1171, when he was eleven years old (some sources say this was 1165, when he was six), Yoshitsune's stepfather Ichijō no Naganori arranged for him to enter Kuramadera, a Tendai temple north of Kyōto. However, around 1174 Yoshitsune left Kurama and proceeded to Mutsu, where he was taken in by Fujiwara no Hidehira. There is some question as to the authenticity of this sequence of events as found in the *Azuma kagami*, but historians generally accept it for the most part.

In 1180, just after the start of the Gempei War, Yoshitsune left Hidehira to join his half-brother Yoritomo. Yoshitsune made no significant contribution to the war against the Taira until 1184, however, when he and another half-brother, Noriyori, took a Minamoto force and drove Minamoto no Yoshinaka out of Kyōto.

CLASSICAL DEPICTION OF MINAMOTO NO YOSHITSUNE
(Illustration by Kikuchi Yosai, 1781–1878)

In that same year, the almost-unknown Yoshitsune became the star general of the Minamoto, crushing the Taira forces at Ichinotani. In 1185 Yoshitsune was again sent against the Taira, destroying the remaining Taira stronghold on the island of Yashima. He dealt them a final blow at Dan-no-ura a short time later. However, when Yoshitsune ran afoul of his commander brother Yoritomo he became discredited and had to flee for his life. With a relatively small band of loyal followers, he was able to avoid capture by his brother's forces for several years, but they caught up with him in 1189. Yoshitsune committed ritual suicide (*seppuku*) while his retainers held off the enemy.

There are many legends concerning the life of Minamoto no Yoshitsune, and it is difficult to separate fact from fiction. One legend concerns a number of Chinese texts on military strategy that were brought to Kuramadera by an enigmatic Daoist magician named Ki'ichi Hōgan during the reign of Emperor Go-Shirakawa.[19] Yoshitsune is supposed to have secretly studied these works while imprisoned at Kurama. According to another legend, while ensconced at Kuramadera, Yoshitsune made secret visits to a small ravine called Sōjōgatani, located above the temple com-

[19] Go-Shirakawa Tennō 後白河天皇 (1127–1192; r.1155–1158), seventy-seventh emperor of Japan.

plex. There he was instructed in strategy and swordsmanship by a powerful *tengu* (mountain demon) named Sōjōbō.

Legends aside, Yoshitsune did become a highly effective general; further, he was in fact imprisoned at Kuramadera during his youth, and was supported by both Tendai and Shugendō warrior monks (*sōhei*) during his campaigns against the Taira during the Gempei War, 1180–1185. *Tengu* are often depicted dressed in the garb of Shugendō priests/monks, which may be the basis for the story that Yoshitsune learned swordsmanship from a *tengu*. See also: *Genji no heihō; Genke Kin'etsushū; Kuramadera; Seiwa Genji.*

Further reading in English:

- McCullough, 1966.
- Kitagawa and Tsuchida, 1975.
- Morris, 1975: 67–105.

Mino 美濃. An ancient province in what is now Gifu prefecture.

Mino den 美濃伝【美濃傳】[A.k.a. ***Seki den*** 関伝【關傳】]. See: *Gokaden.*

mi no maedate 魅の前立. An ornament or figure worn on the front of a helmet (*maedate*) meant to place a bewildering enchantment (*mi*) on an enemy.

Such ornaments, which proliferated during the Warring States period, may have been influenced by the Buddhist cult of Marishiten. In the texts (*sutras*) dedicated to that warrior goddess, the practitioner is directed to create an image of Marishiten and affix it to the front of a helmet or other head garment in order to provide protection for the wearer. There are numerous examples of helmets from that period featuring figures of Marishiten, and the use of a talismanic charm to bewilder enemies soon spread to other devices as well.

MI NO MAEDATE
FESTIVAL AT KATORI JINGU, 1978
(Photograph by Pat Lineberger)

Miroku Bosatsu 弥勒菩薩【彌勒菩薩】<Ch. Mile Pusa <Skt. Maitreya-bodhisattva). A being considered to be the next Buddha. Now residing in Tosotsuten,[20] Miroku is scheduled to appear on the earth some 5,000 years after the passing (*nirvāṇa*) of *Śākyamuni*, the previous earthly Buddha. (However, according to some sources, the amount of time is 4,000 heavenly years, which is roughly equivalent to 5,670,000,000 earthly years.) Numerous cults centering on the anticipation of Miroku's appearance have arisen in East Asia.

Miru 弥楼【彌樓】. See: *Shumi-sen.*

misogi 禊. 1. A purification ceremony. 2. A *yamabushi* purification rite which includes the practices of meditation, *mudra*, and mantra recitation under waterfalls. These practices, which date back centuries, are intended to develop spiritual power for performing exorcism and healing and to achieve heightened states of consciousness.

Misshaku 密迹. See: *Niō.*

Misshaku Kongō Rikishi 密迹金剛力士. See: *Niō.*

mitama 御魂 [Var. 御霊【御靈】]. SHINTŌ—1. A spirit which is part of all humans, and which also acts as a vehicle for humans to commune with the *kami*. There are thought to be four types of *mitama*, two of which were of primary importance to the warrior. The four are:

nigimitama	和魂	gentle spirit
aramitama	荒魂	rough spirit
sakimitama	幸魂	luck spirit
kushimitama	奇魂	wondrous spirit

According to Draeger (1995: 2.21), it was considered best for a commander of troops to

[20] Tosotsuten 兜率天 <Ch. Doushuaitian <Skt. Tuṣita. One of several Buddhist heavens, the Tuṣita is where a *bodhisattva* (*bosatsu*) resides before being born in the human universe as a buddha.

be more influenced by *nigimitama*, causing his nature to be mild, but with strength, adaptability, and flexibility.[21] In contrast, front-line troops should be of a type more influenced by *aramitama*; i.e., a "rough, charging, hard group of men."

The influence of the *kami* of a Shintō shrine via the *mitama* is thought to be especially powerful and beneficial on shrine grounds. For this reason, most classical martial traditions in Japan prefer to hold exhibitions of their skills at shrines. 2. Spirits of the dead.

mitama shiro 霊代【靈代】. An object of worship within a Shintō shrine. The spirit of the enshrined deity (*kami*) is thought to inhabit the object. Also called *shintai*.

mitsudōgu 三道具 [Var. ***torimono mitsudōgu*** 捕者三道具]. Lit. the "three tools." This refers to the three polearms carried by arresting officials (*torimono*), which were used to apprehend violent swordsmen during the Edo period (1603–1867). These included the *sodegarami* (sleeve entangler), the *sasumata* (thorned fork), and the *tsukubō* (T-shaped, barbed polearm). Fujita (1960: 2) notes approximately thirty-four *ryū* specializing in the *mitsudōgu*. (See illustration entitled "Hobaku from the early 1800s" at the end of Section "H.")

mitsumono 三ツ者. Lit. "three agents." A term used by the warlord (*sengoku daimyō*) Takeda Shingen to designate three types of espionage agents: *mami* 間見, *mikata* 見方, and *metsuke* 目付. There are also variant lists which include alternate terms such as *kagi* 嗅, *monogiki* 物聞, *kenmi* 検見, *onkō* 遠候, etc.

Mitsutachi 三太刀. JIGEN RYŪ—The fourth set of primary sword forms (*kata*) used by the Jigen Ryū.

miuchi 御内. A special term used to designate direct vassals of the Hōjō family.

---

[21] A manifestation of this "spirit" is found in an eleventh-century war tale (*gunkimono*), the *Mutsu waki*. In that account, the warrior chieftain Minamoto Yoshiyori was able to collect a large following of warrior vassals due to his "…kindness and generosity, from his loving, personal care of them." (Varley, 1994: 37).

Miura Anjin 三浦 按針 (1564–1620). Lit. "the pilot (or navigator) Miura." The Japanese name for British sailor William Adams. Adams became an advisor to *shōgun* Tokugawa Ieyasu, and was instrumental in establishing trade factories in Japan for England and the Netherlands. He was given the status of samurai by Ieyasu. His life is chronicled in *The Needle-Watcher: The Will Adams Story, British Samurai* by Richard Blaker. Later, his life was fictionalized as the character John Blackthorn in the novel *Shogun* by James Clavell.

Miyagi Chōjun 宮城 長順 (1888–1953). Okinawan *karate* master who established the Gōjū Ryū. Miyagi began training with Higaonna Kanryo in 1902, and had become one of his top students by the time of Higaonna's death in 1915. Just before Higaonna passed away, Miyagi and a friend named Nakamoto Eishō traveled to Fuzhou, hoping to study with Higaonna's teacher, Rū-rū Kō. Although they did not meet this master, they evidently trained in some type of southern Shaolin at that time. In 1917 Miyagi again journeyed to Fuzhou, this time with a Chinese colleague named Go Kenki, in order to continue his training. He stayed for a full year, training in southern Shaolin white crane boxing and—according to some sources—Chinese internal systems.

Miyagi introduced his system of *karate* to Japan via the Kyōto Imperial University Club in 1928. He brought it to Hawaii in 1934, and in the same year registered the name of Gōjū Ryū Karate 剛柔流唐手 with the Dai Nippon Butokukai Hombu in Japan (Higaonna *et al.*, 2008: 532).

Miyake Gempachirō Shigehide 三宅 源八郎 重栄 (c.1680–c.1740). Founder of the Miyake Ha Shinkage Ryū in Hagi domain.

Miyake Ha Shinkage Ryū 三宅派新陰流. A branch line of the Yagyū Shinkage Ryū established in the Hagi domain (the present-day town of Hagi, in Yamaguchi prefecture) via the Arichi Shinkage Ryū 有地真陰流. The school was founded by Miyake Gempachirō Shigehide around 1710.

Miyako 都. A term for the imperial palace and court in the Heian and Kamakura periods. By

Miyake Ha Shinkage Ryū
三宅派新陰流
(abbreviated lineage)

the Ashikaga period it had come to refer to the capital city of Kyōto.

miyako no musha 都の武者. Lit. "warriors of the capital." An eleventh- and twelfth-century term for the warriors and nobles who made up the group from which provincial governors were drawn. Normally they were selected from the fourth or fifth court rank. Contrast to "warriors of the provinces" (*shokoku no musha*). See also: *samurai; kuni no musha; shokoku no bushi.*

Miyamoto Iori 宮本 伊織 (1612–1678). The second adopted son of Miyamoto Musashi. Iori met Musashi in 1624. He was later employed by Ogasawara Tadazane[22] and eventually rose to the position of chief retainer (*karō*) of that warrior house. Iori figures prominently in Yoshikawa Eiji's novelization of Musashi's life.

Miyamoto Mikinosuke 宮本 三木之助 (c.1600–1626). The first adopted son of Miyamoto Musashi. Mikinosuke met Musashi some time between 1617 and 1619. According to the *Hyoho senshi denki* 『兵法先師伝記』, when Musashi stopped at an inn in Nishinomiya he met a young stable boy who took his horse. Musashi was so impressed by the boy's demeanor that he offered to adopt him on the spot. Tokitsu (2004: 95–96) provides additional information on Mikinosuke from the Shinmen family genealogy provided by Harada Mukashi:

Through Musashi's connections, Mikinosuke was hired as a page (*warawa*) by Honda Tadatoki.[23] Upon Tadatoki's death (from tuberculosis?) in 1626, Mikinosuke followed his lord into death via suicide (*junshi*).

Miyamoto Munisai 宮本 無二斎【宮本無二齋】 [A.k.a. ***Hirata Munisai*** 平田 無二斎【平田無二齋】; ***Shinmen Munisai*** 新免無二斎【新免無二齋】]. Father of Miyamoto Musashi. Munisai was an expert in several of the combative weapons systems of his time, including the sword, single-tined truncheon (*jutte*), and throwing darts (*shuriken*). He is recognized as the founder of several schools, including the Shinmen Ryū 新免流 and the Tōri Ryū 当理流. According to a text known as the *Kenjutsu kizu* 『剣術系図』, Munisai was asked by the thirteenth Ashikaga *shōgun*, Yoshiteru, to duel with the *shōgun*'s sword master, Yoshioka Kempō Naomitsu, and defeated him. This incident took place between 1546 and 1565. Munisai, whose family name was originally Hirata, eventually adopted the Shinmen name, as he was a retainer of that clan.

Miyamoto Musashi Genshin 宮本 武蔵 玄信 [A.k.a. ***Shinmen*** 新免; ***Takezō*** 武蔵; ***Genshin*** 玄信 (also read ***Harunobu***); ***Shinmen Musashi no Kami*** 新免武蔵守; ***Fujiwara Genshin*** 藤原玄信] (1584–1645). Japan's most famous swordsman. Several martial schools (*bujutsuryū*) stem from Musashi's teachings, the most notable of which are the Nitenichi Ryū 二天一流 and the Emmei Ryū (1) 円明流. Although Musashi survived more than sixty individual duels and can certainly be considered a master swordsman, he may have suffered two or three defeats. Due to his quest for

[22] Ogasawara Tadazane 小笠原忠真 (1596–1667), a lord (*daimyō*) in the early Edo period.

[23] Honda Tadatoki 本多忠刻 (1596–1626), was a lord (*daimyō*) during the early Edo period. He sponsored Miyamoto Musashi for a period when Musashi was instructing his retainers in swordsmanship.

spiritual perfection through swordsmanship (*ken no michi* 剣の道) and his text entitled *Gorin no sho*『五輪書』, however, his ideas exerted significant influence on the development of early *kendō* during the Edo period (1603–1867). See also: *Dokkōdō; Gorin no sho; Hyōdōkyō; Hyōhō sanjūgo ka jō; Hyōhō shijūni ka jō; Musō Gonnosuke; Sasaki Kojirō; Terao Kumenosuke Nobuyuki; Terao Magonojo Nobumasa.*

Further reading in English:

- Draeger, 2000.
- Hurst, 1998: 57–58.
- Sugawara, 1985: 32–86.
- Terry (translation), 1981.
- Tokitsu, 2004.
- Wilson, 2004a.

miyatsuko 造. Abbreviation for *kuni no miyatsuko* 国造 and *shima no miyatsuko* 島造.

Mizoguchi Shūta 溝口 周太. Co-founder of Seigan Jiki Shinkage Ryū. Mizoguchi was a samurai from the Shibata domain in Echigo province. Both he and another warrior, Kubota Ryōzaburō, trained with Odani Seiichirō in the Jiki Shinkage Ryū from 1843 through 1847. Both were awarded the title of "caretaker of swordsmanship training" (*kenjutsu keiko seiwayaku*) by the domain. Their lines came to be called Seigan Jiki Shinkage Ryū.

Mizugami 水神. The patron goddess of Isshin Ryū (3) 一心流 *karatedō*, who was seen in a vision by its founder, Shimabukurō Tatsuo. Mizugami is half goddess and half sea snake, symbolizing the gentleness of a woman and the strength of a sea snake. See: *Isshin Ryū (3).*

mizu gumo 水蜘蛛. Lit. "water spider." A flotation device that was supposedly used by espionage agents.

Mizuhaya Nobumasa 水早 信正 [Also read ***Isahaya***[24]] [Var. ***Mizuhaya Chōzaemon Nobumasa*** 水早 長左衛門 信正] (c. 1568–c. 1630). Founder of the Seigō Ryū. Mizuhaya established this system after studying *jūjutsu* with the enigmatic monk Seigō (Seigō Sō). He is also credited with the founding of Namban Ippon Ryū 南蛮一品流, a system of police arts, which he developed after extensive study and research in China.

Mizuno Sakubei Tadakatsu 水野 作兵衛 正勝 [A.k.a. ***Mizuno Yazaemon*** ～弥左衛門【～彌左衛門】]. An early eighteenth-century warrior in Bishū domain who founded the Yawara Shinshin Ryū 柔新心流 (a combative school concentrating on grappling and quick-draw swordsmanship) and the Ko Sekiguchi Ryū 小関口流 (a combative school concentrating on quick-draw swordsmanship). Mizuno first mastered the Sekiguchi Ryū 関口流 under Suzuki Kozaemon Masashige, who was a headmaster in the line from Sekiguchi Yazaemon Yorinobu. Due to his preference for a small sword over a large one, his line came to be called the Ko 小 (small) Sekiguchi Ryū. Mizuno's Yawara Shinshin Ryū concentrated on both quick-draw sword arts (*iaijutsu*) and grappling (*jūjutsu*).

Mizuno Shingozaemon Shigeji 水野 新五左衛門 重治 (?–c. 1659). The founder of the Mizuno Ryū 水野流, a system of quick-draw swordsmanship (*iaijutsu*), grappling (*jūjutsu*), and arresting rope (*hojōjutsu*). Mizuno, who established this school sometime during the first half of the seventeenth century, had been a student of Yagyū Munenori in the Edo Yagyū Shinkage Ryū 江戸柳生新陰流. One of Mizuno's most prominent students was Wada Heisuke Masakatsu, founder of the Shin Tamiya Ryū 新田宮流.

Mizuno Shinpō Ichiden Ryū 水野真法一伝流【水野真法一傳流】. Originally called the Ishō Ryū 猪嘯流 (Wild Boar's Roar School), this tradition was founded by Mizuno Tomojūrō Toshitada sometime during the Tempō era (1830–1844). Mizuno's system, which he referred to as *geppo* or *getsuho* ("crunching maw"), specialized in swordsmanship with long sword (*ōdachi*), short sword (*kodachi*), a combination of both (*nitō*), and grappling (*kumiuchi*).

Mizuno Tomojūrō Toshitada 水野 伴十郎 利忠. Founder of Mizuno Shinpō Ichiden Ryū

[24] The Yagyushinkage-ryū Heihou official site (http://www.yagyu-shinkage-ryu.jp/rekisi_e.html) reads 水早 as "Isahaya." However, this is an unusual reading. Watatani and Yamada (1978: 930) and other sources give it the standard reading of "Mizuhaya."

during the Tempō era (1830–1844).

Mochida Moriji 持田 盛二 [A.k.a. ***Kuniyoshi*** 邦良] (1885–1974). A tenth-degree *kendō* master (*hanshi*), one of only five swordsmen to ever be awarded that rank. Along with Nakayama Hakudō and Takano Sasaburō, Mochida is considered one of the few real "sword saints" (*kensei*) of the twentieth century.

Mochida began training in the swordsmanship of the Hōshin Ryū 法神流 under his father in 1891, at the age of six. (His father, the fourth-generation headmaster of the school, ran a *dōjō* attached to his own home.) Sixteen years later, in 1907, Mochida entered a class for swordsmanship instructors with the Dai Nippon Butokukai. At that time he began training in the classical swordsmanship of the Hokushin Ittō Ryū 北辰一刀流 with Naitō Takaji. In 1927 he was made a *kendō hanshi*, the highest title awarded, by the Butokukai. During the decades before the Second World War, Takano Sasaburō's Meishinkan *dōjō* and Nakayama Hakudō's Yūshinkan were considered the two major forces in the world of *kendō*. However, Mochida did not align himself with either. In 1930 he became the official *kendō* master of the Noma Dōjō at the Kodansha publishing company, and also became an employee there. During that same era he instructed at the Tōkyō Metropolitan Police Department, the Imperial Police Department, and several university clubs. In 1957, he was awarded the rank of tenth *dan* by the All-Japan Kendō Federation (Zen Nihon Kendō Renmei).

Mochigakari 持掛. JIGEN RYŪ—The fifth set of primary swordsmanship forms (*kata*) in the Jigen Ryū 示現流.

mochi tate 持楯. A hand-held shield made of wood that appears in some depictions of Kamakura-period battles. It was apparently a rarity at that time, and its use was never generally adopted by the warrior class (*bushi*). See also: *tate (1).*

mochi yari 持槍. A spear carried by an attendant of a high-status individual. The spear and spear-bearer (*yarimochi*) were indicators of the person's status. See: *yarimochi.*

Mochizuki Minoru 望月 稔 (1907–2003). Founder of Yōseikan Budō 養正館武道. Licensed in Daitō Ryū by Ueshiba Morihei in 1932, Mochizuki went on to create his own system (c. 1935). Yōseikan Budō contains elements of *aikidō*, *kenjutsu*, *karate*, *jūdō*, and *jūjutsu*.

Mochizuki Sagami no Kami Sadatomo 望月 相模守 定朝 (?–1575). Founder of the Shōtoku Taishi Ryū 聖徳太子流 in the mid-sixteenth century. Sadatomo, a warrior attached to the Takeda clan, performed austerities (*shugyō*) which resulted in his "awakening" to the essence of military strategy. His insight was facilitated by the spirit of sixth-century imperial regent and cultural hero, Shōtoku Taishi. Although Sadatomo was frequently successful in applying these strategies, he was killed in battle in 1575.

Mochizuki Shinbei Yasukatsu 望月 新兵衛 安勝 (1642–1718). Founder of the Yasumitsu Ryū 安光流 school of swordsmanship in Aizu.

Mochizuki Sōichirō 望月 庄一朗. A direct disciple of Okuyama Yoshiji, founder of the Hakkō Ryū 八光流. Mochizuki subsequently established a school he called Goshindō 護身道.

Mō Gengi 茅 元儀. See: *Bō Gengi.*

mogitō 模擬刀. An imitation sword; a practice sword. See also: *iaitō.*

Mō ichido! もう一度！ A command meaning "Do it once more!" "Repeat!" or "Again!"

Mō ippen! もう一遍！ A command meaning "Do it once more!" "Repeat!"

mojiri 錑 [Var. 捩利]. A sleeve-tangling polearm. See: *sodegarami.*

Mōko Shurai Ekotoba 『蒙古襲来絵詞』【蒙古襲來繪詞】(The Mongol picture scroll), c. 1293. A famous picture scroll depicting the Mongol invasion of Japan.

Further reading in English:

- Conlan et al., 2012.

mokuba 木馬. A wooden horse used for training in *yabusame* (horse-mounted archery contests). See also: *Ogasawara Ryū.*

mokudai 目代. A twelfth-century term for a

M

MŌKO SHURAI EKOTOBA
Detail depicting the anti-Mongol wall around Hakata Bay in Kyūshū
(Picture scroll c. 1293)

proxy or deputy of an absentee provincial governor. Provincial governors at that time often resided in Kyōto, leaving the actual duties of administration to a *mokudai*. 2. NEN RYŪ—Abbreviation for *Nen Ryū Mokudai* 『念流目代』, the fourth of five licenses awarded by the Maniwa Nen Ryū.

mokujū 木銃. A wooden training rifle with a padded tip used in bayonet training systems such as *jūkendō*.

mokuroku 目録. Lit. "catalog" or "list." 1. An index of a systems techniques. 2. A transmission scroll (*densho*) or license (*menkyo*; *menjō*) containing a list of a system's techniques. 3. ***Mokuroku*** 目録. NEN RYŪ—Abbreviation for ***Nen Ryū Mokuroku*** 「念流目録」, the second of five licenses awarded by the Maniwa Nen Ryū.

Mokuroku jōden 「目録上傳」 [Abbr. for ***Jiki Shinkage Ryū mokuroku jōden*** 鹿島神傳直心影流～]. Lit. "upper transmission list." JIKI SHINKAGE RYŪ—The second transmission scroll of the Jiki Shinkage Ryū. This license is awarded for showing proficiency in the system's Tō no Kata section.

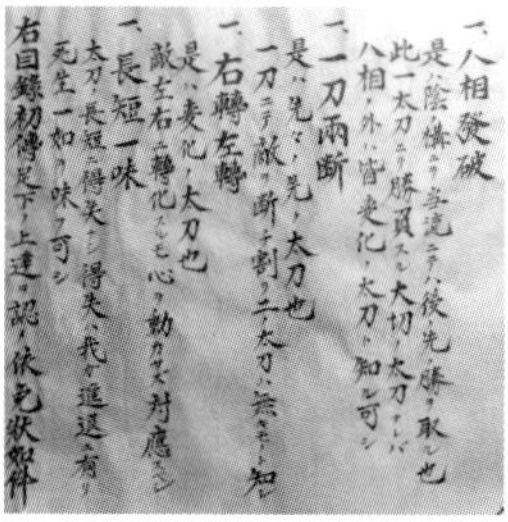
一、八相発破
一、一刀両断
一、右轉左轉
一、長短一味

DETAIL FROM A JIKI SHINKAGE RYŪ
MOKUROKU SHODEN
(Densho from private collection)

Mokuroku shoden 「目録初傳」 [Abbr. for ***Jiki Shinkage Ryū mokuroku shoden*** 鹿島神傳直心影流～]. Lit. "first transmission list." JIKI SHINKAGE RYŪ—The first transmission scroll of the Jiki Shinkage Ryū. This license is awarded for showing proficiency in the system's Hōjō section.

mokushi 木士. A swordsman who is an expert with a wooden sword (*bokutō*; *bokken*), in contrast to a live blade (*shinken*) or bamboo training sword (*shinai*; *chikutō*). See also: *chikushi, kenshi*.

mokusō 黙想. Meditation; contemplation. ¶ *Mokusō yoi!* 黙想用意!, Begin meditation! (Command used in various modern *budō*.)

momen tabi 木綿足袋. Cotton socks (*tabi*).

Momonoi Hachirōzaemon Naoyoshi 桃井八郎左衛門 直由. Founder of the Kyōshin Meichi Ryū 鏡心明智流. Momonoi established this system sometime during the An'ei era (1772–1781) after training in Horiuchi Ryū 堀内流, Ittō Ryū 一刀流, Toda Ryū 戸田流, and others. In 1773 he established the Shigakkan *dōjō* in Edo, where he both perfected his own style of *kenjutsu* and developed one of the strongest training halls in the city.

mon 紋. Heraldry; a family crest. An abbreviation for *kamon* 家紋.

monjin 門人. Lit. a "person at the gate." A martial disciple; a group member. See also: *deshi.*

Monju Bosatsu 文殊菩薩 [Var. ***Monjushiri Bosatsu*** 文殊師利菩薩] <Ch. Wenshushili Pusa < Skt. Mañjuśrī-bodhisattva. The *bodhisattva* (*bosatsu*) who meditates on Supreme Wisdom. Monju Bosatsu is normally depicted sitting on a lion with a wisdom sword (*riken*) in his right hand and a scroll of the *Perfection of Wisdom* (*Daihannya-haramita-kyō*) in his left. Monju is also relevant in a martial-arts context. According to a text called the *Jie Daishiden*, the Tendai priest Ryōgen created the organization of Tendai warrior monks (*sōhei*) in 975 based on the precedent that "…Monju Bosatsu holds a *sūtra* container in one hand and a *riken* in the other." While this statement by Ryōgen may be apocryphal, the martial aspect of this and other Buddhist deities is very clear.

monogiki 物聞. An espionage agent. See: *mitsumono; ninja.*

monokiri 物切. Lit. "cutting area." The cutting edge of a sword.

monomi 物見. Lit. "viewing the armed opponent." 1. A watchtower, scout, or patrol. 2. TATSUMI RYŪ—Special reconnaissance techniques of the Tatsumi Ryū. 3. The name of a prearranged combative form (*kata*) in several traditions. 4. KYŪDŌ—The third of three processes included in *yugamae* (readying the bow). *Monomi* is the process of viewing the target. See: *hassetsu; yugamae.*

mono no aware ものの哀れ. 1. Sadness; melancholy. 2. Yet another key trait of the Japanese "failed hero." Morris (1975: 474) notes *mono no aware* is "…a central theme in traditional Japanese sensibility and aesthetics...," especially where there is confrontation with "…adversity, suffering, defeat, and death."

mononobe 物部. In ancient times the *mononobe* were a group of fighting men whose chief had the title of Mononobe no Muraji. They originally carried out Shintō, judicial, and police functions for the emperor and were in charge of palace guards at the Yamato court. By the seventh and eighth centuries, most provincial governors and strongmen (*kuni no miyatsuko* and *shima no miyatsuko*) had an entourage of twenty or more *mononobe* as a guard unit. (Papinot, 1910: 401.) In 807 the *mononobe* palace guards were folded into the Eijifu guard units. See also: *Efu.*

Mononobe no Moriya 物部守屋. Chief (Ōmuraji) of the Monobe, Moriya was killed in battle against Soga in 587. See: *Mononbe no Uji.*

Mononobe no Muraji 物部連. Chief of the Mononobe. One of several titles created in 682 by Emperor Temmu,[25] it was given to the nobleman—a leader of the Mononobe clan—who was in charge of the palace guard units. See: *muraji; Ōmuraji.*

Mononobe no Uji 物部氏. The Mononobe clan. Evidently the actual family which held the title of Mononobe no Muraji at the Yamato court kept "Mononobe" as a family name in later times. They opposed the Soga family (and the new Buddhist religion imported by the Soga), but were defeated in 587 in battle at Mount Shigi (Shigisan 信貴山).

mononofu 武士. A warrior. The term *mononofu* is often found in the *Man'yōshū* (a collection of poems). The characters 武士 can also be read as *bushi.*

mononogu 物の具. Arms and armor.

monouchi 物打. Lit. "striking area." The last 8 inches (20 cm) or so of a weapon; i.e., the most usable area for striking or cutting. See: *monokiri.*

montei 門弟. Disciples; pupils.

monto 門徒. BUDDHISM—1. Disciple; student. 2. A Buddhist disciple. 3. A supporter of a Jōdo Shinshū temple. 4. An abbreviation for Montoshū.

Montoshū 門徒宗. BUDDHISM—A popular term used to indicate the Jōdo Shinshū, a Japanese school of Buddhism.

monzenbarai 門前払【門前拂】. Lit. "to drive away from the group." *Monzenbarai* was a

---

[25] Temmu Tennō 天武天皇 (631–686; r.672–686), fortieth emperor of Japan.

M

Tokugawa-period punishment inflicted upon delinquent samurai; it was essentially disenfranchisement. The convicted man was deprived of his stipend and the privilege of wearing two swords (*daishō*) and was "driven from the gate" (*monzenbarai*) of his lord (*daimyō*) or the city police magistrate (*bugyō*). From that point he no longer had the privilege—or protection—of samurai status. See also: *kaieki; seppuku; shikei.*

mori 銛. A harpoon; a gaff.

Mori Injuken Toshikatsu 森 員寿軒 利勝. Founder of Ichiden Ryū 一伝流, a branch tradition of the Asayama Ichiden Ryū 浅山一伝流, a comprehensive combative school.

Mori Kambei 森 勘兵衛 [Var. 轟 勘兵衛]. A master of the Torao line (虎尾流) of Itō Ryu 伊東流. He taught the pipe spear (*kudayari*) to Tsuda Nobuyuki, who founded the Kan Ryū 貫流, a system whose primary weapon was the *kudayari*, in 1671.

Morikawa Buhei Takamasa 森川 武兵衛 高政. Founder of the Kashin Ryū 霞新流, a school of combative grappling, sometime during the mid-1600s.

Morikawa Kozan 森川 香山. Founder of the Yamato Ryū 大和流, a school of archery (*kyūjutsu*) in the late seventeenth century. Morikawa may have been the first archer to use the term *kyūdō*. See: *kyūdō.*

Morishige Ryū 森重流. A classical system of matchlock musketry (*hinawaju*) founded in 1803 by Morishige Yukie Tsuyoshi.

Further reading in English:

• Skoss, 1997: 73.

Mori Kazuma 森 一馬. A samurai in Nagaoka domain. Mori was a *menkyo kaiden* practitioner of Takashima Ryū 高島流 gunnery (*hōjutsu*) and infantry training (*gunpō chōren*) under Shimosone Kanesaburō Nobuatsu. He changed the name of the system to Seiyō Ryū 西洋流 in 1854 after Takashima Shūhan was pardoned from prison. Mori transmitted the system in Nagaoka domain. See: *Ien Ryū.*

Morito Sandayū Kanesada 森戸 三太夫 金制. Thirteenth lineal successor of the Asayama Ichiden Ryū 浅山一伝流 school of *jūjutsu*. One of Morito's best-known students was Kobayashi Tōjūrō Tadahide, who founded a branch tradition known as the Sakura Ichiden Ryū 佐倉一伝流.

Moriyama Shimizuemon Motoshige 森山 清水右衛門 元重. Founder of Asayama Ichiden Shin Ryū 浅山一伝新流, a branch tradition of Asayama Ichiden Ryū 浅山一伝流 in Mito domain. As a Mito-domain retainer, Moriyama was a direct retainer of the Tokugawa family. The system he modified from Asayama Ichiden Ryū specialized in *jūjutsu.* Apparently Moriyama designated it "Shinryū" 新流 (revised tradition) in contrast to Kobayashi Moemon's Asayama Ichiden "Koryū" 古流 (classical tradition) to emphasize his support for techniques modified from the original system. Both lines were transmitted in Mito domain. See also: *Asayama Ichiden Koryū; Asayama Ichiden Shinryū.*

moroha 諸刃. A blade with a double cutting edge (i.e., sharpened on both edges).

Moro Kobudō Araki Ryū Kempō 茂呂古武道荒木流拳法. See: *Araki Ryū Kempo Kogusoku.*

mosa 猛者. 1. A twelfth-century term for a warrior. 2. A man of valor.

Motobu Chōki 本部 朝基 <Oki. Motobu Chokki [A.k.a. ***Motobu no Saru*** 本部の猿] (1870–1944). Motobu Chōki hailed from the area of Shuri. He was of a noble family which had its own combative tradition known as Motobu Udundī 本部御殿手, but Chōki's status as third son excluded him from formal training in the family system. As a result, his *karate* training was eclectic: he began with Itosu Ankō, and also trained with Tokumine Pēchin Matsumora Kosaku, perhaps Matsumura Sōkon, and several others. Motobu's agility was such that he was nicknamed "Motobu no Saru" (Monkey of the Motobu). Bishop (1999: 68) classifies Motobu as a Tomari *te* 泊手 stylist, but acknowledges that his system was a mixture of various *karate* influences and earlier Okinawan *tī* (*te*). Motobu Chōki was succeeded by his third son, Chōsei, who teaches his father's system

under the rubric of Motobu Ryū (2) 本部流.

Further reading in English:

- Bishop, 1999: 68–71.
- McCarthy and McCarthy, 2002.

Motobu Chōyū 本部 朝勇 (1857–1927). As a descendant of the Ryūkyū king Shō Shitsu,[26] Motobu Chōyū was the last family head of noble status to hold the title of *anji*.[27] Chōyū formulated his family-transmitted combative system, which was known as Motobu Udundī 本部御殿手, into the Motobu Ryū (1) 本部流. See: *Motobu Udundī*.

Motobu Gotente 本部御殿手 <Oki. Motobu Udundī. See: *Motobu Udundī*.

Motobu Ryū 1. 本部流. OKINAWAN KARATE—A modern (twentieth century) term for Motobu Udundī 本部御殿手. 2. OKINAWAN KARATE—A system of *karate* founded by Motobu Chōki around 1923. The secret Motobu family system (Motobu Udundī) was passed to Motobu Chōyū and from Chōyū to Uehara Seikichi. However, only the first and second sons of the family were privy to the secrets of Udun; Chōyū's younger brother Chōki, being the third son, received only incomplete training in the system. Chōki spent much of his youth training with other masters and developing his own style, which reputedly looked like street fighting with a smattering of *karate* technique. Chōki later became known for his victories over a "Western" boxer and Japanese *jūdō* expert, after which he was able to become a full-time *karate* teacher. According to anecdotal information, however, Chōki later attempted to match his tough fighting style against his older brother's Udundī, and Chōyū supposedly toyed with Chōki as if he were dancing with him. Chōki is subsequently thought to have modified his system by adding more flexible Udundī elements. Although there are only a small number of followers, Chōki's son Chōsei continues to preserve the system.

Further reading in English:

- Bishop, 1999: 68–71.
- Noble, 2003.

Motobu Udundī 本部御殿手 [Abbr. ***Motobu Udun***] (Oki.) [Read in Jp. as ***Motobu Gotente***]. OKINAWAN KARATE—Motobu Udundī refers to a fighting system (Oki. *tī*) passed down in the Motobu Udun family for eleven generations. The Okinawan term *udundī* (Jp. *gotente*) means the "hand-to-hand fighting arts of the palace." Motobu Chōyū, last of the family line of inheritors of Udundī, was also the last to teach this fighting system to the last Okinawan king, Shō Tai.[28] Chōyū's sons were either unable or unwilling to carry on the family system and, upon his death in 1927, the school passed to a non-family member, Uehara Seikichi. Uehara named the system Motobu Ryū 本部流 in 1961, but in 1970 re-christened it Motobu Udundī.[29]

Evidently Motobu Udundī has retained its original nature as a true *tī* system. Bishop (1999: 132) notes:

> ...it combines the finer points of the three most acclaimed internal Chinese boxing styles and more, having within its various guises the swift, straight-lined attack of Hsing-I, the softness of T'ai-chi and the everchanging circular defense of Pa Kua...

Perhaps this native Okinawan art, passed down in a noble family for over ten generations, finds is ultimate origins in the Wu-tang internal boxing systems of the Chinese mainland. The system certainly relies on dance-like forms and careful use of vital points (*kyūsho*) to "gently goad the opponent into a submissive state." (Bishop, 1999: 133). The original core form (*kata*) of Udundī was known as "Anjikata no Mekata," which translates as the "Combative Dance Form of the Nobility." This original *kata* was not passed on to Uehara from Motobu Chōyū. However, some practitioners believe that similar forms are still extant in women's dances (*onna odori* 女踊り).

---

26 Shō Shitsu Ō 尚質王 (r.1648–1668).

27 *Anji* 按司 (also read *aji* or *azu*). A title of nobility indicating a descendant of an Okinawan prince. See Kerr, 1958: 188–189 ff.

28 Shō Tai Ō 尚泰王 (1843–1901, r.1848–1879). Last Okinawan king.

29 Takamiyagi et al. (2008: 187). However, Bishop (1999:131) notes that in 1947 Uehara named the system Motobu Ryū, and changed the name to Motobu Ryū Kobujutsukai in 1969.

Motobu Udundī Curriculum:

Original combative form (lost)

- Anjikata no Mekata 按司方の舞方

Weapons systems

- *Kenjutsu* 剣術 swordsmanship
- *Sōjutsu* 槍術 spear arts
- *Kyūjutsu* 弓術 archery
- *Bōjutsu* 棒術 staff arts
- *Sai* サイ trident arts
- *Bajutsu* 馬術 horsemanship

Motobu Udundī Kobujutsu 本部御殿手古武術. See: *Motobu Udundī.*

Moto no nawa 本縄【本繩】. See: *Honnawa.*

Motsugai Ryū 物外流. A variant name for the Fusen Ryū 不遷流 founded around 1820 by Takeda Motsugai 武田物外. The martial system he established was therefore named Motsugai Ryū. The actual fighting art developed by Takeda was referred to as *genkotsu oshō* (Buddhist-priest fist). Although classified as a type of *jūjutsu*, it appears to have been a pugilistic system.

mubyōshi 無拍子. Lit. "rhythm-less." A timing concept introduced in the mid-1600s into the grappling arts of the Kitō Ryū 起倒流 by Terada Kanemon, a practitioner of Teishin Ryū 貞心流.

muchi 鞭. A riding crop or whip. Like a Western crop, it is essentially a flexible stick or switch and has no lash. As the *muchi* is a weapon-usable object (as opposed to an actual weapon), there was no formal system for its use in combat. See: *shikigu.*

mudansha 無段者. A modern *budō* term referring to a practitioner who has not achieved *dan* rank (black belt in most systems).

muga 無我 <Ch. *wuwo* <Skt. *anātman*. Lit. "no self," "self-less." BUDDHISM—Non-ego or realization of the emptiness of a self or soul. In the Buddhist sense, *muga* can also mean the non-substantiality of the elements of existence. In a martial context, *muga* indicates selflessness or egolessness. See also: *muga mushin; mushin.*

Mugai Ryū 無外流 [A.k.a. ***Mugai Ryū Iai Heidō*** ~居合兵道]. Mugai Ryū is a system of combative swordsmanship (*kenjutsu*) and quick-draw sword arts (*iaijutsu*) founded by Tsuji Gettan Sukemochi. See also: *Tsuji Gettan Sukemochi.*

Mugai Ryu Curriculum:

Set	Number of *kata*
Seiza 正座 (seated techniques)	
Goyō 五用	5
Goka 五箇	5
Tachiwaza 立業 (standing techniques)	
Goō 五応	5
Hashiriwaza 走業 (running techniques)	
Hashirigakari 走り懸り	5
Hogyō 歩業 (walking techniques)	
Naiden 内伝	3
Kumi-iai 組居合 (partner training)	
Kodachi 小太刀 [*seiza* 正座 (seated)]	5
Daitō 大刀 [*tachiwaza* 立業 (standing)]	5

mugamae no jutsu 無構の術. See: *mugae no ri.*

mugamae no ri 無構の理. In his analysis of combative behavior, hoplologist Richard Hayes has classified *mugamae no ri* as the "combative omnipoise trait," equivalent to a "natural stance" (*shizen hontai*). This natural stance incorporates "potential or latent possibilities which are infinite in number." Significantly, many classical traditions emphasize the concept of *shizen hontai*, and many prearranged combative forms (*kata*) begin and end in the posture of *mugame.* See: *bu no ri.*

Further reading in English:

- Hayes, 1989: 29–31.

muga mushin 無我無心. An egoless (*muga*), non-intellect (*mushin*) state. In the Zen school of Buddhism—and in the case of the warrior—this indicates a state of freedom from discriminative thinking; a state akin to enlightenment; an awakened state. See also: *muga; mushin.*

Muhi Muteki Ryū 無比無敵流 [A.k.a. Muhi Ryū 無比流]. A school concentrating on long hardwood staff arts (*bōjutsu*) and medium-length hardwood staff arts (*jōjutsu*). Muhi Muteki Ryū is a very aggressive system. According to the history of this school, a warrior named Sasaki Tessai Tokuhisa, a veteran of the battle of Sekigahara in 1600, founded the school during the first two de-

PRACTITIONER OF MUHI MUTEKI RYŪ *JŌJUTSU*
Kashima Jingu, 1978
(Photograph by Jon Driscol)

cades of the seventeenth century. Sasaki was known for his skill with the nine-foot spear. At Sekigahara, Sasaki's spearhead was broken from the shaft, but he continued to fight using the shaft alone in the intense combat that took place that day. After the battle he drifted around the country for a number of years perfecting his skills and visiting many shrines and temples. He practiced religious austerities at many of these, seeking guidance from the Buddhist deity Marishisonten in particular. He eventually received an oracle (*reiken* 霊験) which awakened him to the truth of "no beginning, no end" (*mushi mushū* 無始無終) from which he subsequently developed his system of long hardwood staff arts (*bōjutsu*) around 1625. He originally called his school Muhi Ryū Heijō 無比流兵杖 (lit. the Peerless School of the Combat Staff).[30] While many of the combative forms (*kata*) in the system also involve a sword, the sword mainly seems to be a target for the staff techniques.

Mugai Ryu Curriculum:

Set		Number of *kata*
Omote no Kō	表の格	4
Chūi Go-ka-jō	中位五ヶ条	5
Gokui Jū-ka-jō	極意十ヶ条	10

mujō 無常 <Ch. *wuchang* <Skt. *anitya*. BUDDHISM—Impermanence; the concept that all things arise, change, and pass away; nothing remains constant.

mujūshin 無住心. Lit. "non-abiding mind." A term coined by Harigaya Sekiun when he founded his Mujū Shinken Ryū. The term, which is taken from Buddhism, indicates a state of mind that has transcended concerns of birth and death (*seishi o chōetsu*). It is somewhat equivalent to *fudōshin*.

Mujū Shinken Ryū 無住心剣流【無住心劍流】[A.k.a. ***Sekiun Ryū*** 夕雲流; ***Hasō Ryū*** 破想流]. The "School of the Sword of Non-abiding Mind." A school founded by Harigaya Sekiun in the early seventeenth century, primarily dealing with combative swordsmanship (*kenjutsu*). The system was based on the philosophy of "mutual escape" (*ainuke*), a style of swordsmanship that was promoted in later years by Sekiun's disciple, the swordsman Odagiri Ichiun.

Sekiun's choice of name for his school is significant. The term *mujū* 無住 (lit. "non-abiding") is derived from the Hossō School of Buddhism, which postulated four kinds of *nirvāṇa* (enlightenment). The fourth and "highest" type was called *mujūsho nehan* 無住處 涅槃 or "non-abiding *nirvāṇa*." This refers to the *nirvāṇa* of one who has eliminated both illusion- and knowledge-based hindrances and has become aware that there is no distinction between the realms of *nirvāṇa* (bliss) and *saṁsāra* (transmigration and suffering). Like a bodhisattva (*bosatsu*), an awakened person such as this does not dwell in tranquility, but actively works in the world for the benefit of all sentient beings. In incorporating this word in the name of his school, Sekiun may have been implying that a master of this school of swordsmanship has attained this state of awakening and is actively engaged in transmitting its benefits to others.

Sekiun's successor Odagiri Ichiun notes that Sekiun had been a disciple of Ogasawara Genshin Nagaharu (1574–1644), founder of the Shin Shinkage Ryū 真新陰流, and says that Sekiun defeated Ogasawara in duel. Odagiri records this duel along with a treatise on the essence of the philosophy of the Mujū Shinken Ryū that was composed around 1700. An abbreviated version of this manuscript was translated by D. T. Suzuki in *Zen and Japanese Culture* (Suzuki, 1958: 170–180).

The curriculum of the Mujū Shinken Ryū

[30] The term *heijō* 兵杖 is also a homophone for *heijō* 平常, which indicates the Buddhist term *heijōshin*, the awakened mind.

has not survived, but as it was a branch system of the Shinkage Ryū as passed on by Ogasawara Genshin Nagaharu, it likely resembled that school. See also: *ainuke; aiuchi.*

mujūsho nehan 無住處涅槃. BUDDHISM—A term used by the Hossō school of Buddhism to indicate the highest type of enlightenment. Harigaya Sekiun used the first two characters for the name of his school of swordsmanship, the Mujū Shinken Ryū.

mukade 百足. A centipede. The *mukade* is often found decorating sword fittings and armor. The use of this motif harkens back to legends of the warrior Tawara no Tōda Hidesato (whose name translates literally as "My Lord Bag of Rice"). Legend has it that the Dragon King of Lake Biwa was plagued by a huge centipede that would kidnap and devour one of his children or servants every night. Hidesato defeated and killed the *mukade*, and in return for this deed he was given a bag or rice which could never be emptied. See also: *Fujiwara Hidesato.*

Mukaijima 向島 (also read ***Mukōjima***). See: *Ganryūjima.*

mukei bunkazai 無形文化財. An official term meaning "intangible cultural asset." Many classical martial schools (*koryū bujutsu*) and their headmasters have been officially classified by the Japanese government as intangible cultural assets; these include Tenshinshō-den Katori Shintō Ryū, Tatsumi Ryū, and others.

mukei no kurai 無形の位. YAGYŪ SHINKAGE RYŪ—Lit. "no-form posture." This is considered a neutral posture. The sword is held pointing straight forward at the lower level (*gedan*), and the feet are together. Also referred to as *mu no kurai.*

Mukōjima 向島 (also read ***Mukaijima***). See: *Ganryūjima.*

mune 棟. The back ridge of a sword; the "spine" of a blade.

munenbara 無念腹. Suicide (*seppuku*) performed to show vexation or resentment due to one's superior; *seppuku* performed as an act of mortification. See: *funshi; seppuku.*

munen musō 無念無想. BUDDHISM—Without discriminative thought; formless. In a martial-arts context, *munen musō* indicates an ideal state of mind for the warrior in combat.

Munen Ryū 無念流. See: *Shindō Munen Ryū.*

mune uchi 棟打. A strike made with the back (*mune*) of the sword, in contrast to using the cutting edge.

Muni 無二【無二】. See: *Miyamoto Munisai.*

Munisai 無二斎【無二齋】. See: *Miyamoto Munisai.*

mu no kurai 無の位. YAGYŪ SHINKAGE RYŪ—See: *mukei no kurai.*

muraji 連. One of several titles created in 682 by Emperor Temmu.[31] This title was given to the nobleman who was in charge of the palace guard units. Since this was always a leader of the Mononobe clan, he was also referred to as "Mononobe no muraji." See also: *Ōmuraji.*

mura kamari 村かまり. 1. Covert assault troops who hid in villages until a signal was given for them to join together and make a surprise attack on enemy forces. 2. A surprise attack mounted from a village. See also: *kamari (1), ninjutsu.*

Murakami Ha Niten Ichi Ryū 村上派二天一流 [A.k.a. ***Murakami Ryū*** 村上流]. A branch line of the Hyōhō Niten Ichi Ryū 兵法二天一流 founded by Murakami Hirauchi Masao around 1710. It survived over ten generations into the twentieth century. For partial lineage, see: *Hyōhō Niten Ichi Ryū.*

Murakami Heinai Masao 村上 平内 正雄. Founder of the Murakami Ha Niten Ichi Ryū 村上派二天一流. Murakami established the system around 1720 after mastering the Shinmen Nitō Ryū 新免二刀流, a branch line of Miyamoto Musashi's Niten Ichi Ryū 二天一流.

Murakami Ryū 村上流. See: *Murakami Ha Niten Ichi Ryū.*

Murakumo no tsurugi 叢雲剣【叢雲劍】. Lit. "pile-of-clouds sword." An abbreviation for

31 Temmu Tennō 天武天皇 (631–686; r.672–686), fortieth emperor of Japan.

the mythical sword named *Ame no Murakumo no Tsurugi*. This weapon was pulled from the tail of the eight-headed dragon, Yamata no Orochi, after which a large cloud arose. See: *Ame no Murakumo no Tsurugi.*

Muraku Ryū 無楽流【無樂流】. A school of quick-draw swordsmanship (*iaijutsu*) established by Nagano Murakusai Kinro around 1620. Nagano, also recognized as third headmaster of the Shin Musō Hayashizaki Ryū 神夢想林崎流, had previously trained in *iaijutsu* with Hayashizaki Jinsuke (founder of the Shin Musō Hayashizaki Ryū) and Tamiya Heibei, one of Hayashizaki's direct successors. For lineage, see: *Shin Musō Hayashizaki Ryū.*

Muramasa 村正 [A.k.a. ***Sengo Muramasa*** 千子村正]. One of the most celebrated Japanese sword makers, second only to Okazaki Masamune. Muramasa's blades were supposed to be so sharp that if the end of the sword were placed in a stream, leaves floating against it on the current would be cut in two. His blades were also supposed to be unlucky and bloodthirsty, and would not stay in their scabbards. They impelled their owners to use them to kill others or commit suicide. As they were considered particularly unlucky for the Tokugawa family, for a while blades made by Muramasa were banned from the *shōgun's* court.

Murata Shukō 村田 珠光 [Also read ***Murata Jukō***] (1423–1502). Former Zen monk who initiated the practice of the Japanese tea ceremony (*chadō*) in the fifteenth century. See: *cha no yu.*

Musashi 武蔵【武藏】. 1. An old province on the Tōkaidō (the primary route from Edo to Kyoto during the Edo period). The Chinese name for the area was Bushū. In modern times, this area includes parts of Saitama prefecture, Kanagawa prefecture, and Tōkyō. 2. An abbreviation for the name of Miyamoto Musashi.

Musashibō Denkei 武蔵坊 弁慶【武藏坊辯慶】. See: *Benkei.*

Musashi Emmei Ryū 武蔵円明流【武藏圓明流】[A.k.a. ***Emmei Ryū Taijutsu*** 円明流体術]. A school of combative swordsmanship (*kenjutsu*) and grappling (*taijutsu*) founded between 1736 and 1744. The system was not derived from Miyamoto Musashi Genshin's tradition.

musha 武者. A term meaning "warrior" that dates from at least the mid-fourteenth century. See also: *bushi; ikusa (1); kondei; kuni no miyatsuko; tsuwamono.*

mushadokoro 武者所. A mid-fourteenth century term for barracks for troops, such as those built by Emperor Go-Daigo[32] for his military support units during the Kemmu Restoration (1333).

mushae 武者絵【武者繪】. Lit. "warrior prints." Depictions of battles and warriors both historical and mythical. War tales (*gunki monogatari*) chronicling various battles became an important part of Japanese culture with the rise of the warrior class from the tenth century. A number of the scrolls in which these stories were written also had illustrations. However, the subcategory of woodblock prints (*ukiyoe*) known as *mushae* which proliferated during the eighteenth and nineteenth centuries are, perhaps, the most outstanding of the warrior illustration genre. Whereas artists prior to this period tended to draw their inspiration from the early war tales only, in the mid-1800s Kuniyoshi began using the battles of the sixteenth and seventeenth centuries for his prints. Other artists soon followed this trend and a golden age of the *mushae* began. See also: *Tsukioka Yoshitoshi; Utagawa Kuniyoshi.*

Further reading in English:

- King and Iwakiri, 2007.
- Robinson, 1982.

Mushakōjisenke 武者小路千家. A school of Japanese tea ceremony (*chadō*) descended from tea master Sen no Rikyū. See: *Sen no Rikyū.*

musha shugyō 武者修行. [Var. ***musha shūgyō*** 武者修業]. Itinerant warrior training/austerities. *Musha shugyō* was a martial pilgrimage

---

32 Go-Daigo Tennō 後醍醐天皇 (1288–1339; r.1318–1339), ninety-sixth emperor of Japan.

M

in which a warrior would travel about Japan testing his skill in battle and in duels with other warriors. Some of Japan's most famous warriors gained their reputations during *musha shugyō*; among them were Kamiizumi Ise no Kami, Tsukahara Bokuden, Miyamoto Musashi, Musō Gonnosuke, and others.

mushi mushū 無始無終. Lit. "without beginning or end"; "eternal." A revelation experienced by Sasaki Tessai Tokuhisa, founder of the Muhi Muteki Ryū 無比無敵流. See: *Muhi Muteki Ryū.*

mushin 無心. An egoless state of mind. In the case of the warrior in combat, this term refers to acting without conscious thought, without fear or thought of victory; acting intuitively. *Mushin* is also somewhat akin to the psychological "flow state" postulated by Mihály Csikszentmihályi in his groundbreaking work on the topic.

Further reading in English:

- Csikszentmihályi, 2008.
- Jackson and Csikszentmihályi, 1999.

musō 1. 夢想. BUDDHISM/SHINTŌ—A vision seen in, or as if in, a dream; an oracle or inspiration which appears in a dream. This is often an intuitive, mystic vision seen in a dream or in a moment of awakening. In Japan this was a relatively unusual phenomenon outside of warrior culture. In fact, anthropologist Carmen Blacker (1989) noted to this author that she only encountered the term *musō* as "a healing oracle (incubatory) at Hasedera and Ishiyamadera in the Kyōto–Nara area." However, founders of several of the early warrior traditions in the fourteenth through seventeenth centuries claimed to have received a divine oracle (*musō*) from Shintō *kami* or Buddhist spirits—or both—that provided them with the inspiration for a new combative systems. Consequently, the martial concept of this term is closely related with intuition (*kan*). Martial-arts masters during the Edo period frequently claimed to have had such revelations as well. See also: *Anryakuji; gonyū; Heki Danjō Masatsugu; Hokushin Musō Ryū; Ichi no Tachi; Itō Suketada; kan (1); Kashima no Tachi; Kasumi no Tachi; Katayama Hōki no Kami Fujiwara no Hisayasu; Kuninazu no Mahito; meigo; Musō Gonnosuke Katsuyoshi; musō no kura; musō shinden; Nen Ami Jion; Ōtsubō Ryū; Ōtsubō Ryū; Shindō Musō Ryū; Shintō (1); Tendō Ryū; Ten Ryū; Tose Yosazaemon Osamune.*

Further reading in English:

- Hall, 1990: 344–351; 1997: 102–108.
- Knutsen, 2004, *passim.*

musō 2. 無双 【無雙】. Peerless; unequaled. The term *musō* written with these ideograms is found in the names of several martial schools such as the Musō Jūen Ryū 無双柔円流, a classical martial school concentrating on arresting arts (*torite*).

musō 3. 無想 <Ch. *wuxiang*. BUDDHISM—Without discursive thought; without thinking; a state of awakening or enlightenment. *Musō* written with these ideograms is found in the names of a number of martial schools such as the Musō Ten Ryū 無想天流, a classical martial school concentrating on swordsmanship (*kenjutsu*), long hardwood staff arts (*bōjutsu*), and quick-draw swordsmanship (*iaijutsu*).

musō 4. 無相 <Ch. *wuxiang* <Skt. (trans. of) *animitta* or *nirābhāsa*. BUDDHISM—without form; non-differentiated; absolute truth. The term *musō* written with these ideograms is sometimes found in the names of classical martial traditions such as the Musō Isshin Ryū 無相一心流, a classical martial school concentrating on swordsmanship (*kenjutsu*).

Musōgaeshi 夢相返し. SHINDŌ MUNEN RYŪ—One of a number of classical prearranged quick-draw sword forms (*battō kata*) developed by the Shindō Munen Ryū. Musōgaeshi was also one of five classical *battō kata* adapted by the Japanese Police Commission of 1886 for their Keishichō Ryū 警視庁流 system.

Musō Gonnosuke Katsuyoshi 夢想 権之助勝吉【夢想權之助勝吉】[A.k.a. Hirano Gonbei 平野権兵] (c.1575–c.1645). A master of the medium length staff who founded the Shindō Musō Ryū 神道夢想流 sometime around 1610. Recognized as a master of the Kasumi Shintō Ryū 霞神道流—a tradition with origins in both the Tenshinshō-den Katori Shintō Ryū 天真正伝香取神道流 and Kashima Shinkage Ryū—Gonnosuke is said to have undergone

MUSŌ GONNOSUKE
From the *Honchō bugei shōden*, c.1716

musha shūgyō and remained undefeated in battle and in duels until he met Miyamoto Musashi. According to legend, Musashi won by trapping Gonnosuke's long staff[33] between two swords with a technique called *jūjidome*. This duel is thought to have taken place in 1606 or 1607, although the earliest record of it is found in the *Kaijo monogatari*, published around 1629.

Chagrined by his defeat (and survival), Gonnosuke entered a period of self-training on Mount Homan in Kyūshū. There, after many days of physical and spiritual austerities, he was awarded a vision (*musō*) by the *kami* of Mount Homan. Part of this "vision" was the admonition *Maruki o motte, suigetsu o shire*—"Take a round stick and 'know' the *suigetsu*." Due to this vision Gonnosuke was able to create a new weapon—the *jō*—and a system for its use. According to Shindō Musō Ryū tradition, Gonnosuke sought out and defeated Musashi in a rematch in 1607. From this inspiration, Gonnosuke founded the Shindō Musō Ryū. In 1607 he became a retainer in Kuroda domain in Kyūshū, and his system was only taught to Kuroda retainers.

Musō Jikiden Eishin Ryū 無双直伝英信流【無雙直傳英信流】[Also read ***Musō Jikiden Hidenobu Ryū***; a.k.a. ***Hasegawa Eishin Ryū*** 長谷川英信流 (also read ***Hasegawa Hidenobu Ryū***); ***Eishin Ryū*** 英信流 (also read ***Hidenobu Ryū***); ***Musō Jikiden Eishin Ryū Iaijutsu*** 〜居合術]. A martial school originally specializing in quick-draw swordsmanship (*iaijutsu*), long hardwood staff techniques (*bōjutsu*), and arresting arts (*torinawa*). This school is essentially the Shin Musō Hayashizaki Ryū 神夢想林崎流 as reformulated by its seventh headmaster, Hasegawa Chikaranosuke Eishin, around 1736. The transmission line split into two branches after the death of eleventh headmaster Ōguro Motoemon Kiyokatsu; one branch became the Shinomura Ha and the other the Tanimura Ha. The current curriculum, which consists primarily of quick-draw swordsmanship (*iaidō*), was reformulated by Gotō Magobei Masasuke (d. 1898) and Ōe Masamichi Shikei (1852–1927), the respective sixteenth and seventeenth headmasters of the Tanimura Ha. During the Taishō era (1912–1926), Ōe began formally referring to his branch as the Musō Jikiden Eishin Ryū. In contrast, Nakayama Hakudō, the sixteenth headmaster of the Shinomura Ha, reformulated his curriculum in a slightly different way and gradually began using the term "Musō Shinden Ryū" 夢想神伝流 for his line. See: *Shin Musō Hayashizaki Ryū lineage*.

Further reading in English:

- Warner and Draeger, 1982: 85–86; 90–94.

MUSŌ GONNOSUKE SHRINE IN KYŪSHŪ
(Photograph courtesy John Quinn)

Musō Jikiden Ryū 無双直伝流【無雙直傳流】. A famous but enigmatic school of *heijutsu*

[33] It is commonly believed that the weapon used by Gonnosuke was a standard six-foot staff (*rokushaku bō*). However, Watatani and Yamada note that the signature weapon of the Kasumi Shintō Ryū was the *ichiizue*, a much larger, heavier weapon suited for armored combat, and suggest this may have been the weapon with which Gonnosuke originally faced Musashi.

(martial strategy) and *yawara* (*jūjutsu*-like combative arts). This school's founding is attributed to a Buddhist priest by the name of Inkeibō Chōhen. Following standard, accepted genealogies, Watatani and Yamada (1978: 823) list Katori Shintō Ryū founder Iizasa Ienao as seventh headmaster of this system. In fact, the term *jikiden* 直伝 can both be interpreted as "correct transmission" or as an abbreviation for the term "Ienao-den" 家直伝, meaning "transmission from (Iizasa) Ienao." However, Warner and Draeger (1982: 86) are skeptical of this claim, since Musō Jikiden Ryū is no longer extant and nothing is known of its curriculum or its relationship (if any) to Katori Shintō Ryū. According to Draeger, there is no record of this connection within Iizasa family archives.

A direct connection with Shin Musō Hayashizaki Ryū, however, may be better substantiated. Momo Gumbei Mitsushige, Banno Dan'emon Nobusada, and Hasegawa Chikaranosuke Eishin —the fourth, sixth, and seventh headmasters respectively of the Shin Musō Hayashizaki Ryū—are also listed as the respective sixteenth, seventeenth, and nineteenth headmasters of the Musō Jikiden Ryū. Whether or not this connection is factual, Hasegawa Eishin was certainly influenced by the Musō Jikiden Ryū enough to change the name of his line from Shin Musō Hayashizaki Ryū to Musō Jikiden Eishin Ryū 無双直伝英信流.

See: *Shin Musō Hayashizaki Ryū.*

Further reading in English:

• Warner and Draeger, 1982: 85–86; 90–92.

musō no kura 夢想の鞍. An oracle received by Ōtsubō Yoshihide Dōzen from the Shintō deity Kashima Myōjin. This oracle, which was concerned with saddle and stirrup design, became a core element in the teachings of the Ōtsubō Ryū of combative horsemanship (*bajutsu*).

Musō Ryū. Watatani and Yamada (1978: 825–828 list more than thirty martial schools known by the name "Musō Ryū." These systems use a variety of ideograms which can all be read this way. They are 夢想流 (18 schools); 無想流 (1 school); 夢相流 (3 schools); 無相流 (3 schools); 無双流 (9 schools); 無総流 (1 school); 武宗流 (1 school); and 無左右流 (1 school). Some of these are abbreviations for other systems, but a number of them are the names of unique schools. Their diverse curricula include grappling (*jūjutsu/yawara*) medium-length staff arts (*jōjutsu*); long-hafted glaive (*naginatajutsu*); quick-draw swordsmanship (*iai/battō*), combative swordsmanship (*kenjutsu*); cross-piece spear (*kagiyari*); arresting rope arts (*torinawa*); arresting arts (*torite*); long hardwood staff techniques (*bōjutsu*); gunnery (*hōjutsu*); matchlock pistol techniques (*tanzutsujutsu*); military encampment sickle (*jingamajutsu*); grappling in armor with small weapons (*kogusoku/koshi no mawari*); military strategy (*gumpō*); and others.

Musō Ryū 夢想流. 1. An abbreviation for Shindō Musō Ryū. 2. An alternate name for the Nen Ryū. 3. An alternate name for the Hayashizaki Musō Ryū.

musō shinden 夢想神伝【夢想神傳】. An oracle, revelation, or inspiration transmitted to a warrior by a deity.

Musō Shinden Ryū 夢想神伝流【夢想神傳流】. A derivative branch of the Hasegawa Eishin Ryū (i.e., the Musō Jikiden Eishin Ryū). The Musō Shinden Ryū was founded by Nakayama Hiromichi (Hakudō) in 1932. However, the name "Musō Shinden Ryū" did not come into general use until after Nakayama's death in 1958. This system as currently practiced consists primarily of quick-draw swordsmanship (*iaidō*).

Today Musō Shinden Ryū is one of the most popular schools of *iaidō* practiced in Japan. Its curriculum is divided into three levels as follows:

Musō Shinden Ryū Curriculum

Level	Source		Posture
Shōden 初伝	Omori Ryū 大森流		*seiza* 正座
Chūden 中伝	Hasegawa Eishin Ryū 長谷川英信流		*tatehiza* 立膝
Okuden 奥伝	(Oku Iai) 奥居合	*suwariwaza* 座業	*tatehiza* 立膝
Okuden 奥伝	(Oku Iai) 奥居合	*tachiwaza* (standing) 立業	

See also: *Hasegawa Eishin Ryū.*

Further reading in English:

- Warner and Draeger, 1982: 85–86.
- Yamatsuta, 2005.

Musō Shinden Ryū battōjutsu 夢想真伝流抜刀術【夢想真傳流拔刀術】. See: *Musō Jikiden Ryū; Musō Jikiden Eishin Ryū; Musō Shinden Ryū; Shin Musō Hayashizaki Ryū.*

Mutei Taishin Ryū 無停滞心流 [Var. 無滞体心流【無滞躰心流・無滞體心流】]. A derivative tradition of Edo Yagyu Shinkage Ryū founded by Natsumi Takanosuke Yoshitane around 1760. This school, which concentrated on combative swordmanship, survived until the Meiji era (1868–1912).

mutekatsu 無手勝. Lit. "no-hands victory." This term recalls a story about Tsukahara Bokuden, the founder of the Kashima Shintō Ryū 鹿島新当流, in which Bokuden defeated a ruffian without fighting while on a ferry crossing Lake Biwa. Bokuden talked the ruffian into dueling on a small island rather than on the ferry. Once the ruffian had alighted on the island, Bokuden pushed off, leaving the ruffian stranded on the island. In this way he defeated the opponent without resorting to arms; such a no-hands victory is what is meant by *mutekatsu.* While there was in fact a Mutekatsu school, it was not founded by Bokuden. This tale, in a modified form, appeared in the 1973 Bruce Lee film *Enter the Dragon*. See: *Mutekatsu Ryū; Shin Shin Mutekatsu Ryū.*

Mutekatsu Yasudayū 無手勝 安太夫. Founder of the Mutekatsu Ryū. He established the school around 1620 after mastering Yamamoto Sakondayū Akimune's Shin Shin Mutekatsu Ryū 新心無手勝流.

Mutekatsu Ryū 無手勝流. Lit. "No-Hands Victory School." A system of combative swordsmanship (*kenjutsu*) and quick-draw swordsmanship (*iaijutsu*) founded around 1620 by Mutekatsu Yasudayū. Yasudayū had mastered a system of combative and quick-draw swordsmanship called Shin Shin Mutekatsu Ryū 新心無手勝流 under the tutelage of a warrior named Yamamoto Sakondayū Akimune. See also: *mutekatsu; Shin Shin Mutekatsu Ryū.*

Mutī nu hō 無手ヌ法. OKINAWAN KARATE—A general term for empty-handed combative forms used in the Ryūei Ryū (2) 劉衛流.

mutō 無刀. An abbreviation for *mutōdori.*

mutōdori 無刀取り. KAGE RYŪ/SHINKAGE RYŪ—Methods for disarming an enemy swordsman without using one's own sword. These empty-handed tactics were originally created by Aisu Ikōsai (Kage Ryū), further developed by his student Kamiizumi Nobutsuna (Shinkage Ryū), and later elaborated upon by Kamiizumi's students in the various lines of Shinkage Ryū, including Hikita Bungorō (Hikita Kage Ryū), Yagyū Muneyoshi (Yagyū Shinkage Ryū), Marume Kurandonosuke (Taisha [Shinkage] Ryū), etc.

Mutō Masao 武藤 正雄 (1924–2001). Successor to Ōtsubō Shihō in the Ōtsubō line of the Owari Yagyū Shinkage Ryū. (This made him a twenty-second-generation successor of the Owari Yagyū Shinkage Ryū.) Additionally, Mutō was a tenth-generation headmaster of the Yagyū Shingan Ryū. Continuing in Ōtsubō's footsteps, Mutō made an extensive investigation of the Edo Yagyū Shin kage Ryū and incorporated his findings into his understanding and performance of the

MUTŌ MASAO
Twenty-second-generation successor, Yagyū Shinkage Ryū; second headmaster, Ōtsubo line of the Shinkage Ryū; tenth headmaster, Yagyū Shingan Ryū
(Photograph courtesy Lynne Riggs)

M

Shinkage Ryū. He was also an avid collector of *densho* and a martial historian.

Mutsu waki 『陸奥話記』. The *Mutsu waki* (Tale of Mutsu) is an eleventh-century chronicle of the Former Nine Years War (1055 to 1063). It records a conflict between the Abe clan, led by Abe no Yoritoki, and Minamoto no Yoriyoshi. The Abe were crushed by Yoriyoshi.

Further reading in English:

- Varley, 1994: 35–40.

Muun Ryū 無雲流. See: *Gan Ryū (3).*

muyoku 無欲. CLASSICAL WARRIOR IDEAL—The quality of being unselfish, not covetous. *Muyoku* was considered one of the essential characteristics of the classical warrior (*bushi*). See: *bushi no konjō.*

Myōan Eisai 明庵 栄西【明菴榮西】. See: *Eisai.*

myōbu 名簿. A written oath of allegiance.

myōden 名田. Lit. "name fields." During the medieval period, a family that cleared land and turned it into cultivated fields became the proprietor of that land In contrast to government rice fields (*kōden* 功田), these holdings received a special name, which was often then adopted by the proprietors. Such fields were given the general designation of *myōden*; their proprietors were generally referred to as *myōju*. If their holdings were considerable, they came to be called *daimyō*, lit. "large name [field holdings]." If the holdings were small, the proprietors were called *shōmyō*, lit. "small name [field holdings]." Over time these terms became specific to warrior families (*buke*) with greater or lesser fief holdings. See: *bushi dan; daimyō; shōmyō; shugo.*

myōgō honzon 名号本尊【名號本尊】. A scroll inscribed with the invocation spell for Amida Buddha: "Namu Amida Butsu!" Such scrolls were venerated by followers of True Pure Land Buddhism. During the Warring States period, the Ikkō Ikki 一向一揆, a powerful militant force made up of peasants, warriors, and Buddhist monks, carried battle standards (*noboribata*) in the form of a *myōgō honzon.*

myōji taitō 苗字帯刀. An Edo-period term indicating that one had the right to a surname and a sword. Although this was a privilege normally restricted to the warrior class, throughout the Edo period certain individuals from the peasant and merchant classes won the right of *myōji taitō.*

Myōken Bosatsu 妙見菩薩 <Ch. Miaojian Pusa <Skt. Sudriṣṭiḥ, ("Bodhisattva of the Beautiful Sight [Ursa Major]") [A.k.a. ***Myōken Daishi*** 妙見大士 <Ch. Miaojian Dashi ("Great Warrior of the Beautiful Sight"); ***Hokushin Bosatsu*** 北辰菩薩 <Ch. Beichen Pusa ("Bodhisattva of the Great Bear"); ***Sonjyōō*** 尊星王 ("Exhaulted Star Lord")]. BUDDHISM—This *bosatsu* has also been referred to as Hokuto Myōken Bosatsu 北斗妙見菩薩 (Bodhisattva of the Beautiful Sight of the Northern Dipper) and, in a Ryōbu Shintō form, as Myōken-shin 妙見神 (the *kami* of Ursa Major).

As the various pseudonyms for this deity indicate, the cult of Myōken Bosatsu is closely aligned with Chinese Daoist cosmology, the constellation of the Great Bear (Hokuto), the star Polaris (Hokushin), and, by extension, the militant Daoist Pole Star Sect[34] and Daoist thunder magic. In the Buddhist canon, a text called the *Discourse on the Magical Spells of the Seven Buddhas and Eight Bodhisattvas* contains the protective spell (*darani*) associated with Myōken Bosatsu.[35] Although a festival was dedicated to this *bodhisattva* during the Nara period, it was officially abandoned in the late eighth century, and there are few temples or images of Myōken Bosatsu remaining today. Some sources note that the elements of the cult were transmitted in secret during medieval times by the Tendai branch in Miidera. During the Edo period, a Tendai temple dedicated to this *bodhisattva* located in Sōma (modern-day Chiba prefecture) was important in the development of the combative swordsmanship (*kenjutsu*) of the Hokushin Musō Ryū and the Hokushin Ittō Ryū. See also: *Hokuto; Hokuto Daishin; Marishiten; Myōken-shin.*

---

34 Jp. Hokkyoku Ha 北極派 <Ch. Beiji pai. See Saso, 1978.

35 Ch. *Qi fo ba pusa shenzhou jing* 『七佛八菩薩神呪經』, Taishō, v. 21, no. 1332, p. 546c–547a. Myōken Bosatsu is also called Hokushin Bosatsu (Pole-star Bodhisattva) in this text, p. 546c.

Myōken Daishi 妙見大士. See: *Myōken Bosatsu.*

Myōken-shin 妙見神 (lit. "*Kami* of the Beautiful Sight" [i.e., Ursa Major]). A Ryōbu Shintō name for Myōken Bosatsu.

Myōkō 妙光. See: *Shumi-sen.*

Myōkō (San Ō) 妙高 (山王). See: *Shumi-sen.*

myōō 明王 <Skt. *vidyārāja* (masc.) or *vidyārājñī* (fem.). BUDDHISM—A class of tantric Buddhist deities. The title *myōō* literally means "king/queen of wisdom." Tantric Buddhism, however, gave a dual meaning to the term *vidyā*—that is, it indicated both "knowledge" and "magical skill." Tantric Buddhism produced many types of "spells" which were chanted for a variety of reasons. (Hall, 1990: 30–44; Bharati, 1965: 101–163.)

As early as the first half of the fifth century C.E. in India, certain of these spells called *vidyā* became personified as *vidyārāja* (king of magical skill) and *vidyārājñī* (queen of magical skill). In Buddhist art these were usually represented with an angry or fierce countenance, and personified spells were considered masters of miraculous powers (*shijji* or *jōju*). See also: *Aizen Myōō; Fudō Myōō; Niō.*

myōjutsu 妙術. BUDDHISM—An art or skill that is, depending on the context, wonderful, profound, excellent, miraculous, and/or mysterious.

Myōshi 妙翅. See: *Kinshichōō.*

N

na 名. Lit. "name." In the tenth-century war tale known as the *Shōmonki*, the term *na* is used to refer to a warrior's name, fame, honor, or pride. It is roughly equivalent to the term *memboku*, which was used during the same period.

Nabeshima Goryūgi 鍋島御流儀. A school of combative arts derived from the Edo Yagyū Shinkage Ryū 江戸柳生新陰流. Founded by Nabeshima Katsushige, it was passed down in the Saga domain (Saga *han* 佐賀藩) by his family.

Nabeshima Shinano no Kami Katsushige 鍋島 信濃守 勝茂 (1601–1654). As a disciple (*deshi*) of Yagyū Munenori, Nabeshima acted as a senior swordsmanship training partner for the third Tokugawa *shōgun* Iemitsu. He subsequently founded his own school, the Nabeshima Goryūgi, which was transmitted in the Saga domain.

Nāfa tī 那覇手 (Oki.). See: *Naha te*.

nafuda kake 名札掛け. A wooden rack (*kake*) containing wooden name-plates (*nafuda*) found in both traditional and modern martial training halls (*dōjō*). The *nafuda* are normally arranged in hierarchal order according to seniority and rank or license.

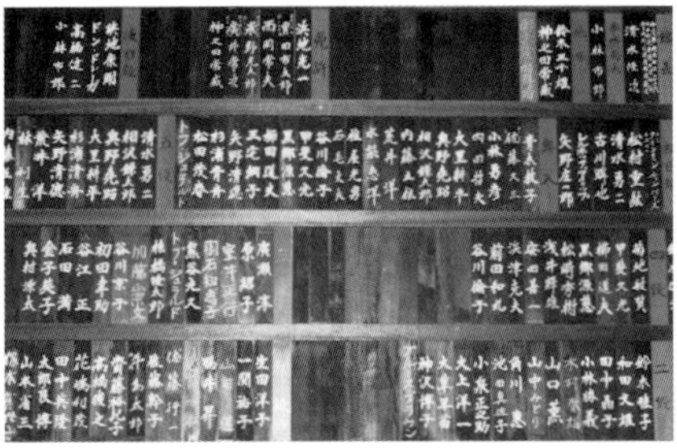

REMBUKAN *NAFUDA KAKE* C.1977
(Photograph by author)

nagabakama 長袴. Formal dress pants for samurai. *Nagabakama* were intended for indoor use only; the legs of the garment covered the feet and trailed behind.

NAGABAKAMA

Nagabokutō 長木刀. The seventh set of primary sword forms (*kata*) in the Jigen Ryū. A wooden sword around 5 to 6 feet (1.5–1.8 m) in length is used in these *kata* to simulate a *nodachi*.

nagadōgu 長道具. An Edo-period term indicating spears and other polearms.

nagae 長柄 [Also read ***nagatsuka***]. Lit. "long haft." The shaft of a polearm.

nagae no kama 長柄鎌 [Also read ***chōegama*** and ***nagatsuka no kama***]. 1. ISSHIN RYŪ—A long-hafted sickle and chain; a polearm sickle. 2. ***Nagae no Kama*** 長柄鎌. ISSHIN RYŪ—The eight long-hafted sickle-and-chain techniques forming the most inner or secret teachings (*gokui*) of the Isshin Ryū.

NAGAE NO KAMA (TOP) AND *YARI* (BOTTOM)
(Kaminoda, © 2002; used with permission)

Nagai Sakunoemon no jō Kōken 長井 作野右衛門 尉弘賢. Founder of the Shin Ryū (1) 神流. Nagai's tradition specialized in quick-draw swordsmanship (*iaijutsu*). See: *Shin Ryū (1)*.

nagamaki 長巻. A Japanese polearm which approximates, in size and shape, the European glaive. In its early forms (around the ninth century) it is essentially a blade around 25 or 30 inches (60–75 cm) long mounted on a haft of approximately 3 feet (1 m) in length.

KNEELING *ASHIGARU* WITH *NAGAMAKI*
Detail of an engraving by Roald Knutsen
(Knutsen, © 1980; used with permission)

Further reading in English:

- Bieri, 1984b.
- Knutsen, 1963.
- Knutsen and Knutsen, 2004.

Nagamine Dōjō 長嶺道場. OKINAWAN KARATE—The central training hall (*hombu dōjō*) of Matsubayashi Ryū 松林流 *karatedō* under Nagamine Shōshin. In 1956 the headmasters of four central *karate* schools met at the Nagamine Dōjō to form the Okinawa Karatedō Renmei (Okinawa Karatedō Federation).

Nagamine Shōshin 長嶺 将真【長嶺將真】(1907–1997). A student of Motobu Chōki (Motobu Ryū 本部流 *karate*) and Arakaki Ankichi (Arakaki Ryū 新垣流 *karate*) who established his own system, the Matsubayashi Ryū 松林流, around 1947. See also: *Okinawa Karatedō Renmei.*

nagamiyari 長身槍 [Also called ***ōmi no yari*** 大身の槍 or ***honagayari*** 穂長槍【穗長槍】]. A spear with a long straight blade 24 inches (30 cm) or more in length. See also: *suyari.*

Nagano jūrokunin yari 長野十六人槍. The "Sixteen Spearmen of Nagano." A formidable assault team of sixteen spearmen led by Kamiizumi Ise no Kami Hidetsuna. This group became famous at the siege of Minowa Castle (1561) for their valiant fight against the surrounding forces of Takeda Shingen.

Nagano Murakusai Kinro 長野 無楽斎 槿露【長野無樂齋槿露】. Third headmaster of the Shin Musō Hayashizaki Ryū 神夢想林崎流. Nagano is also credited with having established the Muraku Ryū 無楽流, a system of quick-draw swordsmanship (*iaijutsu*), around 1620. Nagano had previously trained in *iaijutsu* with Hayashizaki Jinsuke (founder of the Shin Musō Hayashizaki Ryū) and Tamiya Heibei, one of Hayashizaki's direct successors. For lineage, see: *Shin Musō Hayashizaki Ryū.*

Naganuma Geki Tansai 長沼 外記 澹斎【長沼外記澹齋】(1634–1690). Founder of the Naganuma Ryū (2), a school concentrating on battle strategy and military drill, around 1668.

Naganuma Ryū 1. 長沼流. A branch tradition of the Jiki Shinkage Ryū descended from Naganuma Shōbei Masato; in Kōzuke prefecture it came to be called Shinkage Ryū. (See Shinkage Ryu [8] 悳影流). This branch spread widely; Watatani and Yamada (1978: 330) list

Naganuma Ryū (1)
長沼流
(abbreviated lineage)

7. Yamada Ippūsai
七代 山田 一風斎
(1638–1716)
Jiki Shinkage Ryū
直心影流

8. Naganuma Shirōzaemon Kunisato
八代 長沼 四郎左衛門 国郷
(1688–1767)

9. Naganuma Shōbei Tsunasato Katsuzensai
九代 長沼 正兵衛 綱郷 活然斎
(1702–1772)

10. Fujikawa Chikayoshi
十代 藤川 近義
(1726–1798)
Jiki Shinkage Ryū & Fujikawa Ha
直心影流・藤川派

10. Naganuma Shōbei Tadasato
十代 長沼 正兵衛 忠郷
(c. 1730–c. 1800)
Jiki Shinkage Ryū Naganuma Ha
直心影流長沼派

11. Naganuma Shōbei Masato
十一代 長沼 正兵衛 真郷
(c. 1755–c. 1820)
Naganuma Ryū
長沼流
The Naganuma line survived for about nine generations, until Bakumatsu times.

at least forty-five well-known swordsmen who mastered it over a period of two or three generations. Several important traditions descend from the Naganuma Ryū, including the Shin Reiken Ryū and the Sekigawa Ittō Ryū. See also: *Jiki Shinkage Ryū.*

Naganuma Ryū 2. 長沼流. A school of battle strategy/tactics (*gumpō*) and military drill (*chōren*) founded by Naganuma Geki Tansai around 1668.

Naganuma Shōbei Masato 長沼 正兵衛 真郷 (c.1755–c.1820). Progenitor of the Naganuma Ryū (1) 長沼流, a branch tradition of the Jiki Shinkage Ryū 直心影流.

Nagao Ichizaemon Katsushi 中尾 市左衛門 勝之 (c.1600–1669). The founder of a school of combative spear arts (*sōjutsu*) known as Ayō Hikita Ryū 阿陽疋田流. This was a branch tradition of the Hikita Kage Ryū 疋田陰流.

Nagao was a retainer of Awa domain (modern-day Tokushima prefecture). Though his original surname was Murakami 村上, at some point he was adopted by the Nagao family. Having trained extensively in Hikita Kage Ryū *sōjutsu* with Inoda Iori Shigekichi, Nagao modified the tradition and renamed it "Ayō Hikita Ryū." He then taught that system in the Awa domain.

Nagaoka Jūrōemon Fusahide 長岡 重郎右衛門 房英 (c.1644–1713). A retainer from Bishū, one of a group of fifty Yagyū Ryū 柳生流 swordsmen who served as master advisors in the tradition. While in this role, Nagaoka studied the Seigō Ryū 制剛流 under that tradition's fifth headmaster, Ōhashi Kinosuke Masanaga, and combined the two systems into the Yagyū Seigō Ryū 柳生制剛流.

Nagasawa Narishige 長沢 成繁 [A.k.a. ***Nagasawa Sawatoshi*** 長沢 兌翁]. A direct disciple of Hakkō Ryū 八光流 founder Okuyama Yoshiji. Nagasawa subsequently created his own martial school concentrating on *aiki*-type grappling that he called Sōshindō 双真道.

Nagasawa Sawatoshi 長沢 兌翁. See: *Nagasawa Narishige.*

nagashi 流し. YAGYŪ SHINKAGE RYŪ—Lit. "flowing"; moving like a water wheel. *Nagashi* is usually affected as a large movement in which the sword rotates around the practitioner's head; normally completed with a *jun*, *gyaku*, or *massugu* strike to the enemy's wrist (*kote*) or forehead (*men*). Contrast to *kaeshi*, *oni no tachi*, and *kaitō*.

nagatachi 長太刀. A longsword similar to an *ōdachi*. See: *Anazawa Ryū; ōdachi (3).*

nagatsuka 長柄. See: *nagae.*

nagatsuka no kama 長柄の鎌. See: *nagae no kama.*

nagaye 長柄. Archaic romanization for *nagae.*

nage 投げ. Lit. "the thrower." In some grappling/throwing systems, the person executing the technique is referred to as *nage.* Contrast to *uke*.

nagegama 投鎌. Lit. "throwing sickle." A sickle weapon with a very short (2 inches/5 cm) blade that is forged in one piece with the shaft. A chain or cord is attached at the distal end. The sickle (*kama*) was evidently thrown and drawn back by the chain.

NAGEGAMA

Nage no Kata 投の形. Lit. "throwing forms." KŌDŌKAN JŪDŌ—A subcategory of Kōdōkan Jūdō Randori no Kata. See: *Kōdōkan Jūdō.*

nageyari 投槍. Lit. "throwing spear." A short spear about 18 inches (45 cm) long, including the shaft; it was thrown like a javelin.

NAGEYARI

nage waza 投技. Lit. "throwing techniques" (in contrast to striking or grappling techniques). See also: *atemi; Kanō Jigorō; Kitō Ryū; Kōdōkan Jūdō.*

naginata 薙刀 [Var. 長刀]. A long-hafted glaive. Contrast to *nagamaki.* There are many types and designs of *naginata*.

NAGINATA

Further reading in English:

- Bieri, 1984b.
- Knutsen, 1963: 31–41; 2004a.

naginatadō 薙刀道 [Var. 長刀道]. Modern, spiritual/sportive glaive systems which find their roots in *naginatajutsu.*

naginatajutsu 薙刀術 [Var. 長刀術]. Combative long-hafted glaive/halberd arts. Over the approximately seven hundred-year span of the classical warrior period, approximately 425 *ryū* included this weapon system in their curriculum. Some of the earliest comprehensive systems (*sōgōbujutsu*) to include *naginatajutsu* were the Nen Ryū, the Katori and Kashima Shintō Ryū, and the Kage Ryū.

naginata no saki 長刀の先. A *naginata* blade with a socket for the shaft (as opposed to a blade with a tang). See also: *tsukushi naginata.*

Naha-shi 那覇市. The capital city of Okinawa.

Naha te 那覇手 <Oki. *Nāfa tī.* OKINAWAN KARATE—A *karate* school founded by Higaonna Kanryō around 1890.[1] Originally called the Shōrei Ryū 昭霊流 (Bright spirit tradition) by Higaonna, it commonly came to be called Naha *te* due to the location of its training center.

Naifanchi 内歩進 (Oki.). See: *Naihanchi.*

Naihanchi 内歩進 <Oki. *Naifanchi.* OKINAWAN KARATE—One of a number of prearranged combative forms (*kata*) taught within Okinawan Shōrin Ryū 少林流 and Shitō Ryū 糸東流 systems. It is normally divided into three levels: *shodan*, *nidan*, and *sandan*. See also: *karate kata.*

naikan 内間<Ch. *neijian.* The second of the five types of secret agents (*ninja*; *shinobi*) mentioned in Sun Tzu's *Art of War* (*Sonshi no heihō*). The term *naikan* refers to inside agents who are employed from the enemy's governmental officials. See: *kanja; kyōdan (1); ninjutsu; Sonshi no heihō.*

Naikū 内宮. The "Inner Shrine" at Ise, which is dedicated to the Sun Goddess, Amaterasu Ōmikami.

nakadachi 中太刀. An alternate, but uncommon, reading for *chūdachi*, a mid-length sword.

Nakada Shichizaemon Masatsune 中田七左衛門 政経. The seventh lineal successor of the Asayama Ichiden Ryū 浅山一伝流. Nakada's student Kobayashi Moemon founded the Asayama Ichiden Koryū 浅山一伝古流.

nakago 中子. The tang of a blade. Also referred to as the *kuki.*

nakago ana 中子穴. The opening in a handguard (*tsuba*) through which the tang of the sword (*nakago*) passes.

Nakaima Chikudon Pēchin Kenri (Norisato) 仲井間 筑登之 親雲上 憲里. See: *Nakaima Norisato.*

Nakaima Kenchū 仲井間 憲忠. The son of Nakaima Norisato. Kenchū is recognized as second headmaster of the family-transmitted *karate* system that became known as Ryūei Ryū (2) 劉衛流.

Nakaima Kenji 仲井間 憲児 (b.1934). The great-grandson of Nakaima Norisato; current (2008) headmaster of the Ryūei Ryū (2) 劉衛流.

Nakaima Kenkō 仲井間 憲孝 (1911–1988). The grandson of Nakaima Norisato. Kenkō is recognized as third headmaster of the family-transmitted *karate* system that became known as Ryūei Ryū (2) 劉衛流. It was Kenkō who shifted the system from a secret, family-transmitted system to one open to the public.

Nakaima Norisato 仲井間 憲里 [A.k.a. ***Nakaima Chikudon Pēchin Kenri*** 仲井間 筑登之 親雲上 憲里] (c.1850–1927). First headmaster of what became known as the Ryūei Ryū school of Okinawan *karate*. Around 1870, when he was a young man, Nakaima journeyed to Fuzhou, where he became the first known Okinawan student of the boxing master Rū-rū Kō. After six years of training under Rū-rū Kō, Nakaima travelled around China collecting

[1] According to some sources, systems similar to Higaonna's—perhaps from the same Chinese sources in Fuzhou—were being taught in Naha as early as the 1820s.

weapons and weapons techniques. Upon returning to Okinawa he secretly taught what he had learned to his son Nakaima Kenchū. Kenchū secretly passed the system on to his own son Nakaima Kenkō, who opened it up to non-family members as the Ryūei Ryū (2) 劉衛流.

Nakajima Asayoshi 中島 浅吉 (1917–1976). A student of the Shindō Musō Ryū who received *menkyo kaiden* under Shimizu Takaji. Nakajima was the police *jōjutsu* instructor for the Ōsaka Kidōtai (riot police).

In the mid-1970s, under Shimizu Takaji's editorial direction, Nakajima co-authored a large work on Shindō Musō Ryū with Kaminoda Tsunemori. Published by the Japan Publications Trading Company in 1976, it was titled *Shindō Musō Ryū jōdō kyōhan* 『神道夢想流杖道教範』 (Shindō Musō Ryū stick arts—the master text).

NAKAJIMA ASAYOSHI (STANDING)
Demonstrating Oku with Shimizu Takaji, c. 1965
(Photograph courtesy of Nishioka Tsuneo)

Nakajima Shōhitsu 中島 将弼 (1910–1981) [A.k.a. ***Tsugio*** 次男]. Nakajima Shōhitsu is often listed as the twenty-fourth-generation successor of the Shinkage Ryū (6) 神影流; however, it is uncertain whether any documents such as *densho* confirming this claim exist. In any case, after mastering the Shinkage Ryū taught to him by his father, Nakajima Katsu 中島 勝, Shōhitsu studied a variety of other arts which he added to his own system. (He was a direct disciple of Ueshiba Morihei during the mid to late 1940s.) In 1942 he founded his own system called the Shin Shin Musō Ryū 神心無想流. By 1953 he had established the Ryūshinkan Dōjō, where he taught a comprehensive mix of martial disciplines he called Ryūshinkan Budō 柳心館武道.

Nakamura battōjutsu 中村抜刀術. See: *Nakamura Ryū.*

Nakamura Senjūrō 中村 泉十郎. A direct disciple of Kamiizumi Ise no Kami in the Shinkage Ryū (1) 新陰流. Nakamura founded a branch tradition of that school in the late 1500s.

Nakamura Naomasa 中村 尚政 (fl. late 1500s–early 1600s). Founder of the Nakamura Ha 中村派 (Nakamura branch) of the Hōzōin Ryū 宝蔵院流. See Hōzōin Ryū for lineage.

Nakamura Ryū 中村流. A system of quick-draw swordsmanship (*iaidō/battōdō*) founded by Nakamura Taisaburō in the postwar years. Nakamura was a master of the Toyama Ryū 戸山流, a system of swordsmanship called *guntō sohō* which had been formulated at the Rikugun Toyama Gakkō Bujutsu Kyōkan (also called the Toyama Gakkō) by 1925. Nakamura was also skilled in the military use of the bayonet (*jūkenjutsu*), a short-sword art which makes use of the detached bayonet (*tankenjutsu*), modern *kendō*, archery (*kyūdō*), and *jūdō*.

Nakamura Shigeru 中村 茂 (1891–1969). Founded Okinawa Kempō 沖縄拳法 in 1960. Nakamura's school reflects his extensive training in traditional Okinawa *te*, and various Chinese-influenced styles of pugilism.

Nakamura Taisaburō 中村 泰三郎 (1911–2003). Founder of the Nakamura Ryū. See also: *guntō sohō; Toyama Gakkō.*

Nakanishi Chūbei Tsugumasa 中西 忠兵衛子正. Fourth-generation successor of Nakanishi Ha Ittō Ryū. Nakanishi's most famous disciple was Chiba Shūsaku.

Nakanishi Chūta 中西 忠太. After receiving a license in Ono Ha Ittō Ryū, around 1750 Nakanishi founded his own branch school which he christened Nakanishi Ha Ittō Ryū 中西派一刀流. Following the example of the Jiki Shinkage Ryū, Nakanishi modified the standard training by adding a torso protector (*mune-ate*), gloves (*kote*), and the bamboo sword (*shinai*). These modifications greatly facilitated the safety of training matches; Nakanishi was able to attract a large number of students interested in match sparring (*shinaigeiko*) as a result.

Nakanishi Ha Ittō Ryū 中西派一刀流. An offshoot of the Ono Ha Ittō Ryū 小野派一刀流 established by Nakanishi Chūta. It is very similar in practice to its parent system, and its prearranged combative forms (*kata*) are essentially the same. The main difference is that the training gear has been modified to facilitate practice matches with bamboo swords (*shinaigeiko*). See: *Ono Ha Ittō Ryū.*

Nakano Gakkō 中野学校【中野學校】[A.k.a. ***Rikugun Nakano Gakkō*** 陸軍中野学校【陸軍中野學校】]. A school in Tōkyō that was supported by the Japanese Imperial Army and Navy during Japan's World War II years (1938–1945). Its main thrust was covert operations training, including military intelligence and counterintelligence, foreign-language training, and associated espionage skills. Students were also trained in various Japanese martial arts, including *aikibudō* under Ueshiba Morihei (Pranin, 1992), and *ninjutsu* under Fujita Seiko (Saitō, interviews, 1986).

Further reading in English:

- Mercado, 2002.

Nakano Michiomi 中野 道臣. See: *Sō Dōshin.*

Nakayama Hiromichi (Hakudō) 中山 博道 (1873–1958). Founder of the Musō Shinden Ryū[2] 夢想神伝流 quick-draw sword arts (*iaidō, battō*) in the 1930s. Nakayama was expert at several sword traditions: he held a full license in the Shindō Munen Ryū, and was headmaster of Shimomura Ha Musō Jikiden Eishin Ryū *iaijutsu*. He also held a license (Shindō Musō Ryū *shomokuroku*) in combative staff arts (*jōjutsu*). Nakayama headed the committee of swordsmen who formulated the sword system called *guntō sohō* for the military at the Toyama Gakkō in 1925, and generally popularized the art of the quick-draw sword in the 1920s and 1930s. He was probably the first swordsman to make widespread use of the term *iaidō* for this art.

Nakayama Masatoshi 中山 正敏 (1913–1987). Japanese *karate* master who is largely responsible for the spread of Shōtōkan *karate* in Japan and around the world. Nakayama began his *karate* training under Funakoshi Gichin at Takushoku University in 1931. In 1955, he became the chief instructor of the Japan Karate Association (JKA) (Nihon Karate Kyōkai). Nakayama. He produced a number of books on *karate*, many of which, notably his *Best Karate* series, have appeared in English.

namakura gatana 鈍ら刀. An alternate (and rarely used) reading for *dontō* 鈍刀, a dull-bladed sword.

***Namba Heiji* Mitsunobu** 難波 平次 光閑. Founder of both the Namba Ryū 難波流—a system concentrating on long-hafted glaive (*naginata*)—and the Chikubujima Ryū 竹生島流, which used a long hardwood staff (*bōjutsu*).

Namba Ippo Ryū 難波一甫流 [A.k.a. ***Namba Ippo Ryū Koshi no Mawari*** 〜腰廻]. A branch tradition of the Takenouchi Ryū founded sometime around the Genna era (1615–1624) by Namba Ipposai Hisanaga. Much like its antecedent system, it was a comprehensive field-combat system (*sōgo bujutsu*) which included a small-weapon grappling system (*dōmawari* or *koshi no mawari*), combative swordsmanship (*kenjutsu*), medium-length hardwood staff techniques (*jōjutsu*), arresting techniques using small weapons and a rope (*torite*), and arresting/capturing tying-cord arts (*torinawa*). Several branch traditions later sprung from this school.

Namba Ipposai Hisanaga 難波 一甫斎 久永 (c.1590–c.1660). Founder of the Namba Ippo Ryū. Namba established this school sometime around the Genna era (1615–1624).

Namba Ippo Shintoku Ichi Ryū 難波一甫真得一流. A branch tradition stemming from the Namba Ippo Ryū. Founded by Kodama Tokuzaemon around 1670, this school focused on combative grappling (*jūjutsu*). See: *Namba Ippo Ryū.*

[2] The name "Musō Shinden Ryū" was not applied to Nakayama's system until around 1955, only a few years before his death. (Yamatsuta, 2005: 15).

N

namban 南蛮【南蠻】[Also read ***nanban***] <Ch. *nanman*. 1. Lit. "southern barbarian." This term, coined by the Chinese, referred to Europeans who came to Japan during the sixteenth and seventeenth centuries. As Europeans usually came to Japan via the Southern China / Canton sea route, the Japanese called them "southern barbarians" (*namban*) as well. 2. A popular style of sword fittings based on southern Chinese or Canton style. Stone (1934: 464) believed this style was most likely derived from Portuguese influence. 3. A prefix referring to Japanese armor of European design or of European import. Thus, a *nambandō* was a cuirass of European origin or design; a *namban kabuto* was a helmet of European design, etc.

nambanbō 南蛮頬【南蠻頬】[Also read ***nanbanbō***]. Lit. "southern barbarian face." A type of armored face guard (*menpō*) made to look like a European/Caucasian face.

nambandō 南蛮胴【南蠻胴】[Also read ***nanbandō***]. A European-style cuirass, some versions of which look much like those worn by the Spanish and Portuguese in the sixteenth century.

Namban Ippon Ryū 南蛮一品流【南蠻一品流】[A.k.a. 一品流 ***Ippō Ryū*** or ***Ippon Ryū***]. A parallel tradition of the Seigō Ryū 制剛流 founded by Mizuhaya Chōzaemon Nobumasa. (Mizuhaya is also credited with establishing Seigō Ryū). Namban Ippon Ryū concentrated on capturing arts for police (*hobakujutsu*), a tying-cord system (*torinawa*), and the police baton (*hananeji*). According to Watatani and Yamada (1978: 662), Mizuhaya created this system after returning from a period of research and training in China.

namban kabuto 南蛮兜【南蠻兜】[Also read ***nanban kabuto***]. A European-style helmet that looks much like those worn by the Spanish and Portuguese in the sixteenth century.

namban tetsu 南蛮鉄【南蠻鐵】. 1. Lit. "southern barbarian iron." Foreign iron from Europe was highly valued by the Japanese in the sixteenth and seventeenth centuries. It was used for making armor.

Namba Ryū 難波流. A combative glaive system (*naginatajutsu*) founded by Namba Heiji Mitsunori.

Nambokuchō 南北朝. The period of the Northern and Southern courts (1336–1392) when Japan had two contending imperial lines.

Namiki Yasushi 並木 靖 (1926–1999). JIKI SHINKAGE RYŪ—Recognized as eighteenth-generation headmaster of the Jiki Shinkage Ryū through Yamada Jirokichi's line. Namiki published *Ken no kokoro: Katsu Kaishū to Jiki Shinkage Ryū*「剣のこころ：勝海舟と直心影流」(The spirit of swordsmanship: Katsu Kaishū and the Jiki Shinkage Ryū) in 1979.

NAMIKI YASUSHI (1979)
Late eighteenth headmaster of the Jiki Shinkage Ryū
(Photograph courtesy Namiki Yasushi)

Nanajō no Tachi 七条ノ太刀. KASHIMA SHINTŌ RYŪ—The first set of combative forms in the Kashima Shintō Ryū's Chūgokui *kenjutsu* curriculum. See: *Kashima Shintō Ryū*.

Nana ka Jō 七箇條. YAGYŪ SEIGŌ RYŪ—The fifth series of *battō waza* in the Yagyū Seigō Ryū, consisting of seven *kata* plus one addition. These combative forms (*kata*) are all executed from a standing posture (*tachiai*).

Nana Tachi 七太刀. Lit. "Seven sword techniques." 1. YAGYŪ SHINKAGE RYŪ—A set of seven (*nana*) combative forms referred to in the Yagyū scroll entitled *Shinkage Ryū Nana Tachi*. These *waza*, which were transmitted to Yagyū Muneyoshi by Kamiizumi Ise no Kami Nobutsuna, stand as counters to the Shintō Ryū's Nanatsu no Tachi 七津之太刀. Although no longer practiced in the main Owari Yagyū Shinkage Ryū line, they are preserved in other branch lines of the Owari Yagyū and Hikita Kage Ryū lines. See also: *Shinkage Ryū Nana Tachi (no maki)*. 2. ***Nana Tachi*** 七太刀. Abbreviation for *Shinkage Ryū Nana Tachi*.

Nanatsu no Tachi 七津之太刀. 1. KATORI SHINTŌ RYŪ—The second armored *kata* in Katori Shintō Ryu's Omote no Tachi section. 2. HIKITA KAGE RYŪ—See: *Nana Tachi; Tenshinshō-den Katori Shintō Ryū.*

nanban 南蛮. See: *namban.*

nanbanbō 南蛮頰. See: *nambanbō.*

nanbandō 南蛮胴. See: *nambandō.*

nanban kabuto 南蛮兜. See: *namban kabuto.*

Nanba Ryū 難波流. See: *Namba Ryū.*

nanori 名乗【名乗】. *Nanori* was the practice of name-announcing in battle. First mentioned in the tenth century *Shōmonki* period, it became a common practice in subsequent centuries. The actual announcing had become very elaborate by the twelfth-century *Heike monogatari* period; it might include a warrior's lineage, victories, charges led, etc. The purpose of *nanori* was both to intimidate opponents and to find someone among the enemy of equal or higher status with whom to engage in personal combat (*ikki uchi*). There was little honor or gain in fighting and defeating an enemy too far below one's own status. The custom of *nanori* began to fall out of use around the time of the Mongol invasions in the thirteenth century.

Nara 1. 奈良. The capital of Japan from 710 to 794. It lent its name to the Nara period (Narachō, 710–794).

nara 2. 那羅 <Ch. *naluo* <Skt. *nārā* = Pāli *nara.* A term found in Sanskrit, Buddhist Hybrid Sanskrit, and Pāli indicating a "proverbially powerful personage" (Edgerton, 1953: vol. 2, 293). Haines (1995: 24) references the *Lotus Sutra*, where the term *nara* is interpreted as a "manly character, a dancer or performer." Haines also references Konishi Yasuhiro's *Karate nyūmon* (1958: 216) where the term *nara* is associated with "a fighting style akin to *karate* or *quanfa.*" While Konishi's interpretation may be stretching the point, the association between *nara* and the martial arts has some credibility, as one of the two Buddhist temple guardian deities (Niō) is known as Naraen Kengoō 那羅延堅固王, and is typically shown in an empty-hand fighting stance. The prefix *nara* also appears as part of the name of a variety of powerful deities found in a number of Buddhist tantric texts. Many of these are normally depicted in combative stances. See: *Niō.*

narabinaki tsuwamono 並び無き兵. An accolade used in the war tales (*gunkimono*) of the tenth and eleventh centuries, meaning a "warrior without equal" or "warrior without peer." Its meaning was somewhat equivalent to a similar term of that period, *ichinin tōsan no tsuwamono*.

Narachō 奈良朝. The Nara period; the era when the city of Nara was capital of Japan (710–794).

Naraen Kengoō 那羅延堅固王 <Ch. Naluoyan Jianguwang. Lit. "the powerful king Nārāyaṇa." See: *nara (2); Niō.*

Nara hōshi 奈良法師. A term for Japanese Buddhist warrior monks who hailed from the temples of Nara. See also: *sōhei.*

narigin 成銀 [Abbr. as ***zen*** 全]. Lit. "promoted silver." SHŌGI—In the Japanese strategic game of *shōgi*, this piece is a promoted "silver general" (*ginshō* 銀将) which gives it additional movement characteristics.The *narigin* does not have a direct equivalent in Western chess.

narikei 成桂 [Abbr. as ***kei*** 圭 or ***kin*** 今]. Lit. "promoted laurel." SHŌGI—In the Japanese strategic game of *shōgi*, the *narikei* is a promoted knight (*keima* 桂馬). This piece does not have a direct equivalent in Western chess.

narikyō 成香 [Abbr. as ***kyō*** 杏 or ***zen***全]. Lit. "promoted lance." SHŌGI—In the Japanese strategic game of *shōgi*, the *narikei* is a promoted lance (*kyōsha* 香車). This piece does not have a direct equivalent in Western chess.

nasake 情け. Sympathy; compassion. CLASSICAL WARRIOR IDEAL—Morris (1975: 475) notes that *nasake* was considered to be a special character of the warrior (*bushi*). *Nasake* indicated the ability to perceive the suffering inherent in the human condition as well as to "sympathize with the weak and helpless." (Growald and Luks, 1988: 51–53). See also: *jihi.*

N

Natori Ryū 名取流 [A.k.a. ***Shinnan Ryū*** 新楠流]. A school of military strategy and tactics (*gumpō*) and espionage (*shinobi no jutsu*) founded around 1560 by Natori Yoichinojō Masatoshi. The third headmaster of this tradition, Natori Sanjūrō Masazumi, also studied the strategy and tactics of Kusunoki Ryū 楠木流 and several other systems. Combining all these teachings, Masazumi created the Shinnan Ryū 新楠流 in 1654.[3] In the domain of Echigo, the Natori/Shinnan Ryū became closely associated with the Echigo Ryū 越後流 [A.k.a. Kenshin Ryū 謙信流]. See: *Echigo Ryū.*

Natori Sanjūrō Masazumi 名取 三十郎 正澄 [A.k.a. Fuji Masatake 藤 正武] (d. 1708). Third lineal headmaster of the Natori Ryū 名取流. He renamed the school Shinnan Ryū 新楠流 in 1654.

Natori Yoichinojō Masatoshi 名取 与市 之丞 正俊【名取與市之丞正俊】(d. 1619). Founder of the Natori Ryū.

Natsumi Zokunosuke Yoshitane 夏見 族之助 義種 (c.1730–1799). Founder of the Mutei Taishin Ryū 無停滞心流, a derivative school of Edo Yagyū Shinkage Ryū 江戸柳生新陰流. Natsumi established his system around 1760.

nawa 縄【繩】. 1. Lit. "rope" or "cord." 2. An abbreviation for *torinawa* 捕縄 (arresting/capturing tying-cord arts). See: *Ittatsu Ryū; Oguri Ryū.*

Nawa Yumio 名和 弓雄 (1912–2006).[4] The tenth-generation headmaster of Masaki Ryū and eighth-generation headmaster of Edo Machikata Jutte Torinawa Atsukaiyō martial and police arts as follows:

- Masaki Ryū 正木流:
  manrikigusari 万力鎖 (weighted chain)
  kusarigama 鎖鎌 (sickle and chain)
- Edo Machikata Jutte Torinawa Atsukaiyō 江戸町方十手捕縄扱い様:
  Edo Police *jutte* (single-tined truncheon) and *torinawa* (tying-cord) arts

NAWA YUMIO
The late tenth headmaster of the Masaki Ryū
(Photo courtesy John F. Quinn)

Nawa was long recognized as a martial/police arts historian, writer, advisor to the Japanese government's NHK television network, and martial artist. He also founded the Masakikai 正木会, a martial arts training organization in Tōkyō, in the early 1970s. Over the years he trained many students and disciples—both Japanese and non-Japanese—including Hatsumi Masaaki, Charles V. Gruzanski (author of *Spike and Chain*; Tuttle 1968), and John F. Quinn (author of the forthcoming *Kusari Bujutsu*).

Nawa wrote a number of well-researched works over the years, including, but not limited to:

Gōmon keibatsushi『拷問刑罰史』
(A history of torture and punishment). Yūzankaku, 1966.

Jutte Hojō no Kenkyū『十手捕縄研究』
(A study of truncheon and arresting-rope arts). Yūzankaku, 1964.

Jutte・Hojō jiten: Edo machi bugyōshō no sōbi to taihojutsu『十手・捕縄事典:江戸町奉行所の装備と逮捕術』
(A guide to the truncheon and arresting-rope: Gear and arresting techniques of the Edo magistrate). Yūzankaku, 1996.

Kakushi buki soran『隠し武器総覧』
(An overview of concealed weapons). Sojinsha, 1998.

Nagashino, Shidaragahara Gassen no Shinjitsu『長篠・設楽原合戦の真実一甲斐武田軍団はなぜ壊滅したか』(The truth behind the Nagashino and Shidaragahara battles—

[3] These characters (新楠流) can also be read as "Shin Kusunoki Ryū," meaning "Revised Kusunoki School."

[4] Special thanks to John F. Quinn for providing additional information on Nawa Yumio.

Why were the Takeda forces defeated?). Yuzankaku Shuppan, 1998.

Ninjutsu no kenkyū: Hisshō no heihō 『忍術の研究：必勝の兵法』 (Studies on *ninjutsu*: Winning strategies). Japan Publications, Inc., 1972.

Ninjutsu tejina no himitsu 『忍術手品の秘密』 (The secrets of *ninjutsu* sleight-of-hand). Gakken, 1982.

Shinobi no buki 『忍びの武器』 (Espionage agent weapons). Jinbutsu Oraisha, 1967.

Zukai kakushi buki hyakka 『図解隠し武器百科』 (Illustrated encyclopedia of concealed weapons). Shin Jinbutsu Oraisha, 1977.

ne 子 [Also read ***shi***]. The symbol corresponding to the Rat in the Chinese "twelve branches" or Jūnishi zodiac. The Hour of the Rat is the first duodenary hour, lasting from 11 p.m. to 1 a.m. In certain Sino-Japanese boxing texts, the symbol for Rat indicates the optimal time of day for striking the corresponding vital point (*kyūsho*). See also: Appendix 1.

Negishi Ryū 根岸流. A martial school founded by Negishi Shōrei around 1870. The system centers on throwing darts and blades (*shurikenjutsu*) and swordsmanship (*kenjutsu*). According to M. Skoss (1999: 84), Negishi created his system after mastering the teachings of the Gan Ryū, which included swordsmanship (*tachi uchi*) with long and short swords, quick-draw swordsmanship (*iai*), long-hafted glaive techniques (*naginatajutsu*), medium-length staff arts (*jōjutsu*), and grappling (*kumiuchi*). Watatani and Yamada (1978: 191, 682), however, do not mention the Gan Ryū connection; they associate Negishi with Kaiho Hanpei Yoshisato 海保 帆平 芳郷, a practitioner of Kadono Ryū 上遠野流 *shurikenjutsu*. Kadono was also a master of Hokushin Ittō Ryū 北辰一刀流 swordsmanship. The fifth and current headmaster of the Negishi Ryū is Saitō Satoshi.

nehan 涅槃 <Ch. *niepan* <Skt. *nirvāṇa*. BUDDHISM—Liberation from existence; a blown-out flame; extinction; eternal bliss; joy. The ultimate goal of Buddhist practice.

nehan mon 涅槃門. Lit. "nirvana gate." The *nehan mon* was a term used for the south gate or entrance into an area set aside for ritual suicide (*seppuku*). The *nehan mon* was the entrance used by the "second" (*kaishakunin*). (Seward, 1966: 44–45). See also: *seppuku; shugyō mon.*

Neko no myōjutsu 『猫の妙術』 (The cat's miraculous skill). A fascinating anecdote or parable on the nature of the ultimate level in swordsmanship, written by the samurai/scholar Issai Chozan. The story was originally published in 1727 in a larger work by the same author entitled *Inka Sōshi* 『田舎荘子』 (The rustic Zhuangzi), a text written in a humorous, satirical style with the purpose of educating the common man. According to the late martial-arts scholar Watanabe Ichirō, the story was passed down as a transmission scroll (*densho*) of the Ittō Ryū. (Watanabe, 1979: 7) The text has been translated into English several times.

Translations in English:

- Friday, 2002: 17–33.
- Suzuki, 1958: 428–435.

Nembutsu 念仏【念佛】<Ch. *nianfo*. An invocation of the name of Amida Buddha: *Namu Amida Butsu*. Believers in Pure Land Buddhism (Jōdo Shū 浄土宗 and Jōdo Shinshū 浄土真宗) recite the *nembutsu* in order to be reborn in the Pure Land (Jōdo). See: *Jōdo; mappō.*

Nen Daioshō 念大和尚. See: *Nen Ami Jion.*

Nen Ami Jion 念 阿弥 慈恩 (c.1350–c.1408) [A.k.a. ***Okuyama*** 奥山 ***Nen Ami Jion; Nen Daioshō*** 念大和尚; and ***Sōma Shirō Yoshitomo Nyūdō Jion*** 相馬 四郎 義元 入道 慈恩]. Founder of the Nen Ryū 念流 and son of a renowned warrior, Sōma Shirō Tadashige.

According to Higuchi family archives (Higuchi, 1985–1989), Jion had a history similar to that of Minamoto no Yoshitsune. Jion was born in Sōma 相馬in Ōshu 奥州, and given the name Yoshitomo. When he was about five years old his father was assassinated. Held in hiding by his wet nurse until the age of seven, the young Yoshitomo is said to have been passed over into the care of a Buddhist priest at Yugyōji temple in Sōma. At that time he was given the Buddhist name Nen Ami Jion.

NEN RYŪ MARISHITEN ASTRIDE A WILD BOAR
(Higuchi family Nen Ryū archives)

This indicates that Yugyōji was a Pure Land temple—probably of the Jishū branch—and that Yoshitomo had taken the vows of a lay priest (*tonseisha*). Around the age of ten or eleven, he was placed in Kuramadera (the famous temple in which Minamoto no Yoshitsune had spent his youth), where he began learning martial arts (*bugei*) in addition to whatever Buddhist training he may have had. On his move to Kuramadera, he became known as Okuyama Nen Ami Jion. By the age of sixteen he had become exceptionally proficient in the martial curriculum at Kuramadera, which included archery (*shagei*), swordsmanship (*kenjutsu*), long-hafted glaive arts (*naginatajutsu*), spearmanship (*sōjutsu*), long staff techniques (*bōjutsu*), and grappling (*yoroi kumiuchi*).

Jion then moved to Jufukuji in Kamakura and received the *hiden* (secret teachings of swordsmanship) from a priest named Eiyū. By his eighteenth year (1368) he was teaching swordsmanship and the use of the spear at Jufukuji. In that same year he traveled to Kyūshū, where, at a temple in Tsukushi known as Anryakuji, he performed austerities. There in an altered psychic state, he received an oracle (*musō*) from the Buddhist goddess Marishiten. From this oracle he derived the secrets of what would later be called the Nen Ryū.

In other versions of the story, Yoshitomo went through martial training at Kuramadera north of Kyōto, Jufukuji in Kamakura, and Anryakuji in Kyūshū. He then avenged his father, after which he took Buddhist vows and the name Jion. He is then said to have built Chōfukuji temple 長福寺 in Nagano prefecture, where he became known by the Buddhist name Nen Daioshō 念大和尚.

Nen Ryū texts such as the *Marishiten setsu shōgun kyō* reveal that Nen Ami Jion derived his Nen tradition from an inspiration received from Marishiten. The lineage given in that text begins: "Marishiten—Shōtengu—Okuyama Nen…" The inclusion of the Shōtengu here is also interesting, as it indicates a *tengu* is the intermediary between Marishiten and Jion. This harkens back to legends of the young Yoshitsune learning swordsmanship from the *tengu* Sōjōbō in Sōjōgatani, a ravine on Mount Kurama. It may also indicate Shugendō influences, for the *tengu* are often depicted in the clothing of *yamabushi* (the mountain ascetics of Shugendō). In any case, there are a number of parallels in the respective legends of Minamoto no Yoshitsune and Nen Ami Jion.

Jion had at least fourteen known disciples (see entry on Nen Ryū). See also: *Maniwa Nen Ryū; Kuramadera; Jufukuji.*

Nen Ami Ryū 念阿弥流. See: *Nen Ryū.*

Nen Daioshō 念大和尚. See: *Nen Ami Jion.*

nenju 念珠. A rosary of the type carried by Buddhist priests and Shugendō *yamabushi*. See also: *irataka no juzu.*

Nen Ryū 念流 [A.k.a. ***Nen Ami Ryū*** 念阿弥流, ***Jion Ryū*** 慈恩流, ***Okuyama Nen Ryū*** 奥山念流, and ***Kamakura Nen Ryū*** 鎌倉念流]. The early Nen Ryū was a comprehensive field-combat system (*sōgo bujutsu*). Like many early classical *ryū*, the name of this school varies depending on the location where it was taught. Additionally, over the years founders sometimes changed their own terminology for a school/style. Nen Ryū tends to be referred to as *Okuyama Nen Ryū* when Nen Ami Jion (its founder) was located at Kuramadera (a Tendai Buddhist temple north of Kyōto) and *Kamakura Nen Ryū* when he was teaching at Jufukuji, a Zen temple in Kamakura. The only currently known extant branch is the Maniwa Nen Ryū 馬庭念流. This is one of the oldest existing warrior traditions in Japan; its formalization by Nen Ami Jion (c.1368) predates Tenshinshō-den Katori Shintō Ryū 天真正伝香取神道流 by almost eighty years. Several other *ryū* are derived from or are technically indebted to the Nen Ryū, including the Chūjō Ryū 中条流 and Kamiizumi's Shinkage Ryū (1) 新陰流.

Nen Ami Jion had at least fourteen disciples who mastered his Nen Ryu. Eight of these were from eastern Japan, when Jion was teaching in Kamakura; six were from the area of Kyōto when he was located there. Watatani (1967: 80) lists eight of them.

Disciples of Nen Ami Jion:

1. Nikaidō Umanosuke 二階堂右馬助 of the Nikaidō Ryū 二階堂流
2. Akamatsu Mishuza 赤松三首座, founder of the Nen Shuza Ryū 念首座流 (Shōbō Nen Ryū 正法念流)
3. Tsutsumi Hōzan 堤法参 (a.k.a. Hōzan 法讃), credited with the founding of the Isshin Ryū 一心流 and the Hōzan Ryū 宝山流
4. Chūjō (Hōgan) Nagahide 中条(判官)長秀 of the Chūjō Ryū 中条流
5. Kai Chikuzen no Kami 甲斐筑前守 (a.k.a. Toyozen no Kami 豊前守) of the Chūjō Ryū 中条流 and/or the Fuda Ryū 富田流
6. Sarugozen 猿御前[5]
7. Numata Hōin 沼田法印 of the Tanseki Ryū 丹石流
8. Higuchi Tarō Kaneshige 樋口太郎兼重, founder of the Higuchi Nen Ryū 樋口念流

Two of these disciples, Akamatsu Jisan and Higuchi Tarō Kaneshige, directly influenced the Nen Ryū line that survives today, making them especially significant. Both Akamatsu and Higuchi received the full teachings of Nen Ami and carried on separate lines of Nen Ryū. In later generations, Akamatsu Jisan's line was referred to as the Nen Shuza Ryū 念首座流, while Higuchi Kaneshige's descendents followed the Higuchi Nen Ryū 樋口念流.

In 1500, two generations after Higuchi Kaneshige, his grandson, Higuchi Takashige (1425–1513), moved the family from Higuchi village to Maniwa village (in present-day Gunma prefecture). Soon after that, Takashige gave up the Higuchi Nen Ryū which had been passed down in his family and took up the Shintō Ryū 神道流.

For three generations the Higuchi family continued the Shintō Ryū. Then, in the late 1500s, Higuchi Sadatsugu, having mastered the Shintō Ryū, sought out Tomomatsu Gian, the seventh headmaster of the Akamatsu line of the Nen Ryū. In 1591 Higuchi Sadatsugu received an *inka* (full license) in the Nen Shuza Ryū. From that time on, the tradition came to be called the Maniwa Nen Ryū due to the location of the home of the Higuchi clan. See: *Akamatsu Jisan; Arakawa Nen Ryū; Higuchi Matashichirōgen Sadatsugu; Maniwa Nen Ryū; Nen Shuza Ryū.*

Nen Shuza Ryū 念首座流 [A.k.a. ***Shōbō Nen Ryū*** 正法念流]. This term refers to the Akamatsu line of the Nen Ryū beginning with Akamatsu Jisan (c.1394). Some two hundred later (c.1585), the seventh headmaster of this line, Tomomatsu Seizo Fujiwara no Ujimune (Gian), was sought out by Higuchi Sadatsugu. After several years of arduous training, Higuchi succeeded Tomomatsu, becoming the eighth-generation headmaster of the Nen Shuza Ryū. Since Higuchi and his descendants lived in Maniwa, the tradition has been called Maniwa Nen Ryū since that time. See: *Akamatsu Jisan; Higuchi Matashichiro Minamoto no Sadatsugu; Maniwa Nen Ryū.*

nichō kama 二丁鎌. OKINAWAN KOBUDŌ—Dual hand-held farmer's sickles used in some schools of Okinawan *kobudō*. See: *icchō kama; ōkama; Okinawa kobudō; Ryūei Ryū (2).*

Nidan 二段. 1. The second section of prearranged combative forms (*kata*) in Jigen Ryū's advanced-level swordsmanship (Dan no Kata). There are three scenarios in this set referred to as Sun Man Sen 寸満煎. 2. ***nidan*** 二段. Lit. "second grade." A modern *budō* term derived from Kōdōkan Jūdō indicating that a practitioner is the second degree in

[5] Watatani (1967: 80) indicates Sarugozen was associated with Kage no Ryū 陰の流. As the Kage tradition was not formulated until 1488, this association is unclear.

Nen Shuza Ryū
念首座流
(abbreviated lineage)

Nen Ami Jion
念 阿弥 慈恩
Nen Ryū
念流

2. Akamatsu Mishuza Jisan
二代　赤松 三首座 慈三
Nen Shuza Ryū
念首座流

3. Ogasawara Tōsenbō Kōmyō
三代　小笠原 東泉坊 甲明

4. Ogasawara Shinjiro Ujitsuna
四代　小笠原 新次郎 氏綱

5. Ogasawara Bizen no Kami Ujikage
五代　小笠原 備前守 氏景

6. Ogasawara Saemon Jō Ujishige
六代　小笠原 左衛門 尉氏重

7. Tomomatsu Hyōgo no Kami Ujimune
(Seiza Nyūdō Gian)
七代　友松 兵庫頭 氏宗
(清三 入道 偽庵)

Higuchi Matashichirō
Minamoto no Sadatsugu
樋口 又七郎 源定次
Maniwa Nen Ryū
馬庭念流

Arakawa Magosaburō
Tokimune
荒川 孫三郎 時宗
Arakawa Nen Ryū
荒川念流

Arakawa
Hachizaemon no Jō
荒川 八左衛門尉
Arakawa Nen Ryū
荒川念流

Atsumi Heihachirō
渥美 平八郎
Arakawa Nen Ryū
渥美念流

rank. In most modern systems, this indicates a "second-degree black belt."

nigimitama 和魂 [Var. 和御魂]. SHINTŌ—A gentle spirit. See: *mitama.*

Nihon Budōkan 日本武道館. See: *Budōkan.*

Nihon Jōdōkai 日本杖道会. A modern *jōdō* organization founded by Kaminoda Tsunemori in 1978 upon the death of Shimizu Takaji.

Nihon Karatedō Shōtōkai 日本空手道松涛会【日本空手道松濤會】. JAPANESE KARATE—The *karate* organization out of which the Nihon Karate Kyōkai (Japanese Karate Association, or JKA) was formed. It was founded by Funakoshi Yoshitaka, Funakoshi Gichin's son, in 1936.

Nihon Karate Kyōkai 日本空手協会. JAPANESE KARATE—The Japan Karate Association (JKA). Gichin Funakoshi established the JKA in 1948 and was the executive chief instructor. Several years later, in 1955, Masatoshi Nakayama became the chief instructor. The JKA was primarily responsible for making *karate* into a sport. However, this trend had begun taking root as early as 1936, when Funakoshi's Shōtōkan initiated free sparring (*jiyū kumite*). After Funakoshi's death in 1957, this emphasis led to the development of competitions and championships. As this sports-oriented move began in the mid-1930s, many of Funakoshi Gichin's self-defense tactics were dropped by his son Yoshitaka. In addition, both the use of weapons and throwing techniques were de-emphasized, limiting the combative applications of JKA *karate*. The JKA's influence is such that all styles of Japanese *karate* were affected by this shift.

After Nakayama's death in 1986, there was a split in the organization. One group was headed by Nakahara Nobuyuki (with chief instructor Sugiura Motokuni); the other, by Asai Tetsuhiko. Both groups continued to use the Nihon Karate Kyōkai name until 1999, when Sugiura's group obtained rights to the name and Asai's group became the Nippon Karate Shōtōkai (Japan Karate Shōtōkai).

Nihon Kempō 日本拳法 [originally known as Dai Nippon Kempō 大日本拳法]. A pugilistic fighting system established by Sawayama Sōkai 沢山宗海 in 1932. Nihon Kempō was one of several systems studied by Sō Dōshin before he founded his Nippon Shōrinji Kempō in the late 1940s.

Nihon Kendō Kata 日本剣道形【日本劍道形】. During the Meiji era (1868–1912), the Japanese police were the first organization to develop a standardized set of *kata* for *kendō* practitioners. The police commission of 1886 drew these *kata* from ten different schools to formulate the Keishichō Ryū 警視庁流. Many skillful swordsmen had been hired as police instructors in the 1870s, and this first standard was an attempt to accommodate some of the most important *ryū* incorporated in their training program. According to Yamada (1925:

360), the police commission also selected five *iai kata* (see entry on *iaijutsu*).

In 1906, the Butokukai created a commission to form its own system of *kata*. By 1912 they had created a set of ten *kata*—seven with the long sword (*katana* or *ōdachi*) and three with the short sword (*kodachi*)—which they called the Dai Nippon Teikoku Kendō Kata 大日本帝国剣道形 (Imperial Japanese *kendō* forms). The establishment of these forms provided a benchmark set to which many schools, colleges, and universities matched their forms. As these forms were "created," they did not retain terminology from the classical systems (*koryū*) and are simply numbered:

Kata name	Ideogram	Meaning
1. Ipponme	一本目	Number 1
2. Nihonme	二本目	Number 2
3. Sanbonme	三本目	Number 3
4. Yonhonme	四本目	Number 4
5. Gohonme	五本目	Number 5
6. Ropponme	六本目	Number 6
7. Nanahonme	七本目	Number 7
8. Kodachi Ipponme	小太刀一本目	Short sword #1
9. Kodachi Nihonme	小太刀二本目	Short sword #2
10. Kodachi Sanbonme	小太刀三本目	Short sword #3

These forms have been significantly modified, especially since World War II. A comparison video is available, as of this writing, on the Internet (Stroud and Honda, 2007; http://www.yorku.ca/kendo/KendoForms.htm).

CREATORS OF THE DAI NIPPON TEIKOKU KENDŌ KATA, 1912
Front row, left to right: Tsujima Osamu 辻真 平, Negishi Shingorō 根岸 信五郎; back row, left to right: Takano Saburō 高野 佐三郎, Naitō Takaji 内藤 高治, Kadona Masao 門奈 正

The practice of *kendō* and its associated *kata* forms was banned by Occupation authorities in the postwar years (1945–1952). With the end of the occupation and the formation of the Zen Nihon Kendō Renmei in 1952, these forms were again revised and renamed the Nihon Kendō Kata. See also: *Keishichō Ryū.*

Nihon Kendō Renmei 日本剣道連盟. See: *Zen Nippon Kendō Renmei.*

Nihon Kobudō Kyōkai 日本古武道協会 (the Japanese Classical Martial Arts Society). One of several organizations formed for the purpose of preserving classical Japanese martial arts. Formed in 1979 in association with the Nippon Budōkan, the Nihon Kobudō Kyōkai is a relatively new organization. It should be noted that not all classical schools (*ryū*) belong to "preservation organizations." See also: *Nihon Kobudō Shinkōkai.*

Nihon Kobudō Shinkōkai 日本古武道振興会【日本古武道振興會】(the Society for the Promotion of Classical Japanese Martial Arts). One of several organizations formed for the purpose of preserving classical Japanese martial arts. Formed in 1935, the Nihon Kobudō Shinkōkai is one of the older organizations of this type. It should be noted that not all classical schools (*ryū*) belong to preservation organizations. See also. *Nihon Kobudō Kyōkai.*

Nihon Sōtsuibushi 日本総追捕使【日本總追捕使】. Lit. "National Arresting Officer." This title was sometimes used in reference to Minamoto no Yoritomo. See: *Minamoto no Yoritomo; sōtsuibushi.*

Nihontō 日本刀 [Also read ***Nippontō***]. Japanese swords. See: *gendaitō; guntō; kaiguntō; kotō; kyūguntō; shinguntō; shinshintō; shintō (2); Shōwatō; Yasukunitō.*

Further reading in English:

- Inami, 1948.
- Joly and Inada, 1979.
- Kishida, 2004.
- Nagayama, 1997.
- Robinson, 1971.
- Yumoto, 1958.

N

Nijūhasshuku 二十八宿 <Ch. Ershiba su <Skt. Aṣṭā-viṃśati Nakṣatrāṇi [A.k.a. ***Ten no Nijūhasshuku*** 天の二十八宿]. The Twenty-eight Lunar Mansions. This is a series of twenty-eight constellations through which the moon is seen to pass. They were first cataloged by the ancient Chinese and later modified in the first or second century C.E. under the influence of Indian culture and Buddhism. The twenty-eight constellations, which are divided into four groups of seven, have directional significance both as individuals and in groups. They are found in psycho-cosmigrams (mandala), and have mystical import. See also: *Mima Yoichizaemon Kagenobu; Suiō Ryū*

Further reading in English:

- Schumacher, Mark. (2012).
- Williams, 1974: 351–358.

Nikaidō Heihō 二階堂平法. See: *Nikaidō Ryū (1).*

Nikaidō Ryū 1. 二階堂流 [A.k.a. ***Nikaidō Heihō*** 二階堂兵法]. A comprehensive field-combat system (*sōgo bujutsu*) founded by Nikaidō Umanosuke around the year 1380. The Nikaidō Ryū was derived from the Nen Ryū; its curriculum was primarily that of Nen Ami Jion's Nen Ryū.

Nikaidō Ryū 2. 二階道流. A comprehensive martial system (*sōgo bujutsu*) consisting of grappling in light armor (*kogusoku*), swordsmanship (*kenjutsu*), quick-draw sword arts (*iaijutsu*), and long hardwood staff arts (*bōjutsu*). The tradition was founded by Fujita Shichizaemonjō Mitsushige, whose best-known student was Tesaki Minamoto no Kura.

Nikaidō Umanosuke 二階堂 右馬助. A disciple of Nen Ami Jion who founded the Nikaidō Ryū (1) around the year 1380.

ningen 人間. BUDDHISM—The "human realm." One of the six realms (Rokudō) into which beings are subject to rebirth. One is considered very fortunate to be reborn as a human being, for this is the easiest realm in which to attain enlightenment.

ningengaku o osameru shugyō 人間学を修める修行. Lit. "austere training in which one masters the study of humanity." Striving toward this goal is a key concept of the archery system founded by Awa Kenzō in the early 1900s.

ningu 忍具. Special tools used by espionage agents (*shinobi no mono*). These are quite diverse, as they vary with the agent's organization, operational parameters, the school/tradition in which the agent was trained, and so on.

ninja 忍者 [Also read *shinobi no mono*]. A term for a feudal-era spy, espionage agent, or mole that became popular in the Meiji era (1868–1912). During the medieval and early modern centuries when these agents were actually performing their craft, the term *shinobi no mono* was generally used. (Nawa, 1972: 47.) See: *ninjutsu.*

ninjō 1. 人情. Human feelings; empathy.

ninjō 2. 刃傷. Bloodshed.

ninjōzata 刃傷沙汰. An affair involving bloodshed.

ninjutsu 忍術 [Also read ***shinobijutsu; shinobi no jutsu***]. A generic modern term for the practice of espionage during the medieval (1185–1558) and premodern eras (1558–1867). The Chinese characters for this term were most often read *shinobijutsu* or *shinobi no jutsu* during those times. However, since 1868 the reading *ninjutsu* has become popular (Nawa, 1972: 47). As a generic term, many historians and scholars now apply the designation "*ninjutsu*" to everything from intelligence collection and covert operations to non-conventional warfare. In popular media and the modern combative arts world, the term *ninjutsu* is also applied to a number of systems in which the connection with authentic, classical traditions of espionage is suspect at best, and often approaches the absurd.

During the medieval and premodern eras, there were dozens of terms used for espionage operations and operatives, counterintelligence activities, and covert and guerrilla-type military actions. Many of those terms were more descriptive in their context than the generic terms used today, while others were, of necessity, used to obscure those same activities. The term *shinobijutsu* (as *ninjutsu* was then called) was generally used to refer to espionage practices similar to those defined in Sun Tzu's *Art of War* (*Sonshi no heihō*).[6] However, this generic term needs to be qualified in that the wide-ranging espionage activities it is associated with were practiced by divergent groups: warriors of the classical martial traditions (*koryū*), warriors who were not members of the *koryū*, and specific, non-warrior lines of clan-based espionage organizations.

Some Japanese historians have postulated that any type of non-conventional warfare should be classified as *ninjutsu*. Okabe Shūzō (1975), for example, notes that the guerrilla warfare practices used by Kusunoki Masashige in the fourteenth century indicated that he was a student of *ninjutsu* training. Indeed, the methods of Kusunoki—a warrior who hailed from central Japan—were certainly non-conventional when compared to the contemporary style of warfare carried out by the eastern warriors (Bandō *musha*) of his time. However, Kusunoki's tactics appear to have been more in line with those of the rowdy warrior bands (*akutō*) and the non-conventional methods of the "warriors who hid in the fields" (*nobushi*) of central and western Japan. Those battlefield tactics, which had developed subsequent to the Mongol invasions of 1274 and 1281, were already commonly used by warriors of all classes in western and central Japan during Kusunoki's lifetime. Although Kusunoki's guerrilla tactics had nothing to do with espionage, they might rightly be considered *shinobi no jutsu* in the later definition of the term. However, there is no indication that they were referred to as such at the time.

During the Sengoku period (c. 1482–c. 1600), an era in which intrigue, espionage, and double-dealing reached a pinnacle of development, *shinobi no jutsu* as a practice independent of the warrior traditions also began to develop broadly and deeply. Depending on clan alignments, some of those schools of *shinobi no jutsu* were directly influenced by warrior-tradition espionage and operational tactics, while others were much more independent. The non-warrior traditions quickly came to include both intelligence gathering techniques and, of necessity, operational skills including combative arts. This development took place in various locations around Japan. However, due to historical and geographical factors, *ninjutsu* development appears to have been more concentrated in the Iga and Kōga areas of central Japan. Consequently, it is very likely that many of the non-conventional warfare techniques mentioned above were included by various clans involved in its development. Fujita (1960: 2) notes seventeen *koryū* specializing in *ninjutsu*; however, Nawa (1972: 98) seems to think there were about forty prior to 1868. Neither author makes a distinction between *bushi* and non-*bushi* traditions.

The multiplicity of terms used for espionage agents was due to the number of clans practicing *ninjutsu* during the Sengoku period and the variety of services *shinobi no mono* might perform in military and civilian operations; the agents also used different terms in order to obscure the nature of their profession. Imamura (1974: 8), in his discussion of the Yagyū family's involvement with espionage and its practitioners, gives a representative list: *ninja* 忍者, *shinobi no mono* 忍びの者, *rappa* 乱破, *suppa* 透波, *o-niwaban* お庭番, *kakushi metsuke* 隠し目付, *kanchō* 間諜, *kanja* 間者, *saisaku* 細作, Igamono 伊賀者, Kōgamono 甲賀者, *kusa* 草, *nokizaru* 簷猿, and so on. Over the centuries many other tasks were sometimes taken up by espionage agents, including the duties of military scouts (*teisatsusha* 偵察者), covert assault troops (*kamari* [1] かまり or *kishū* 奇襲), agitators (*kōran* 攪乱), and, of course, the "female" ninja (*kunoichi* くノ一), etc. Imamura goes on to say that several of these terms—*onmitsu* 隠密, *kanja*, *kanchō*, *saisaku*, etc.—mean essentially the same thing. However, some of them carry a definite "*ninja*" image for the Japanese, such as *shinobi no mono*, *ninja*, Igamono (indicating the Iga clan), and Kōgamono (indicating the Kōga clan). Others, such as *kamari* (3) 奸, carry a connotation of wartime villainy and are still associated with groups such as the *nobushi* mentioned above.

N

[6] See, for example, the entry on *kanja* .

Due to the popular image of *ninjutsu* which was promoted in movies, plays, and comic books (*manga*) in Japan during the first half of the twentieth century, the international popularity of some so-called *ninjutsu* martial-arts systems in the latter half of the century, and the subsequent proliferation of books on *ninjutsu* in various languages, it is often difficult to discern the grain from the chaff in the available literature on this topic. One should remember that the best espionage agents were never uncovered. Their techniques were kept a well-guarded secret and many were lost to history. Consequently, what is today called *ninjutsu* may or may not be that which was most effective during the medieval and premodern periods. With due respect to many scholarly historians in Japan, this author finds Nawa (1972) and Miyazaki (1974) to be the best-researched works in the field in Japanese. None of the English works available are completely reliable.

Ninpiden 『忍秘伝』【忍秘傳】 [also read *Shinobi hiden*]. Text on espionage (*shinobi no jutsu*) attributed to Hattori Hanzō. Legend states that a descendant of Hanzō named Hattori Mino no Kami Yasukiyo compiled this work in 1653 from the teachings of Iga Ryū *nimpō* which had been passed down within that family. Along with the *Shōninki* and *Mansen shūkai*, it is considered one of the "three great books on *ninjutsu*" by aficionados of those studies.

Niō 仁王 [Var. 二王]. The Niō represent Vajradhāra, a tantric deity based on the Indian Vedic god Indra, whose image is usually found in a dual form. In Japan, this dual form often takes shape as the two fierce guardians at the gates of temples.

The guardians are known by various names (sometimes mixed together), the most common being Misshaku 密迹 and Kongō 金剛. Mishaku Kongō Rikishi 密迹金剛力士 and Naraen Kengoō 那羅延堅固王 are also common.

Normally these two temple guards are pictured intoning the sacred syllables "*a*" and "*un*" (<Skt. "*a*" and "*hūṁ*"). These two syllables also represent the Taizōkai 胎蔵界 (the Womb World) and Kongōkai 金剛界 (the Thunderbolt or Diamond World), which are the two great *maṇḍala* of East Asian tantric Buddhism. The Taizōkai symbolizes the material realm of the five elements: earth, water, fire, air, and emptiness (*śunyatā*). The Kongōkai symbolizes the spiritual realm of one element: the mind.

When the Two Guardian Kings are associated with these tantric realms, they are equated with the powerful *myōō*, Aizen and Fudō. Thus, the King intoning the sound *a* is equated with Aizen and the Womb Mandala, and the King intoning the sound *hūṁ* is equated with Fudō and the Diamond World Mandala. See: *a-un (1); myōō.*

niō dachi 仁王立. JIKI SHINKAGE RYŪ—A centered, balanced stance used in the Hōjō *kata* of the Jiki Shinkage Ryū 直心影流. This stance, based on the posture used by the Niō temple guards, is used throughout the four *kata* of Hōjō and is directly equated with the adamantine determination of Kongō Rikishi (<Skt. Vajradhāra) and the Imperturbable Mind of Fudō Myōō. See also: *fudōshin.*

NIŌ DACHI DEMONSTRATED BY MIYAUCHI AKIRA
Jiki Shinkage Ryū Hombu Dōjō,
Chūō-ku, Taikukan, Tōkyō, 1978
(Photograph by author)

Nippon Budōkan 日本武道館. See: *Budōkan.*

Nipponden Echigo Ryū 日本伝越後流【日本傳越後流】. A branch school of combative strategy (*gungaku*) founded around 1560 by Uesugi Minbu Daisuke Yoshiharu, a direct disciple of Uesugi Kenshin. See: *Echigo Ryū.*

Nipponden Jūjutsu Kōrindō Aikidō 日本伝柔術光輪洞合気道. See: *Kōrindō.*

Nippon Kakuten Ryū 日本覚天流【日本覺天流】. See: *Kakuten Ryū.*

Nippon Kendō Kata 日本剣道形【日本劍道形】. See: *Nihon Kendō Kata.*

Nippon Kobudō Shinkōkai 日本古武道振興会【日本古武道振興會】. See: *Nihon Kobudō Shinkōkai.*

Nippon Shōrinji Kempō 日本少林寺拳法 [A.k.a. ***Shōrinji Kempō*** 少林寺拳法]. This modern pugilistic and grappling-based system was founded in Japan in 1947 by Nakano Michiomi (a.k.a. Sō Dōshin). Although supposedly based on the combative boxing techniques of northern Chinese Shaolin *quanfa*, Shōrinji Kempō is not a combative system that was transported unchanged from China to Japan. If fact, it was greatly influenced by Japanese systems such as Hakkō Ryū 八光流 and Daitō Ryū 大東流 *jūjutsu*, as well as Nihon Kempō 日本拳法 pugilism. Due to a Japanese court decision in 1972, Nippon Shōrinji Kempō is legally considered a religious system which combines civilian self-defense, combative practices, and the philosophy of Kongō Zen.

Further reading in English:

- Draeger, 1974: 163–172.
- So, 1970a; 1970b.

Nippontō 日本刀 [Also read ***Nihontō***]. A Japanese sword. See: *gendaitō, guntō, kaiguntō, kotō, kyūguntō; shinguntō; shinshintō; shintō (2); Shōwatō; Yasukunitō.*

Nippon tōken 日本刀剣【日本刀劍】 [A.k.a. ***tōken*** 刀剣【刀劍】]. Japanese swords. See also: *gendaitō; guntō; kotō; shinshintō; shintō (2); Shōwatō.*

DETAIL FROM *TENGUSHŌ DENSHO*, C. 1598
Nishi Itton Shinkage Ryū
(From the archives of the late Mutō Masao)

Nishi Itton Minamoto no Takanori 西一頓源高乘【西一頓源高乘】 (c.1535–c.1605). A direct disciple of Kamiizumi Nobutsuna. Nishi is known only from the original *densho* that have been passed down. The *densho* closely parallel those of the Yagyū Shinkage Ryū.

Nishioka Tsuneo 西岡常夫 (b.1925). One of Shimizu Takaji's most senior disciples in the Shindō Musō Ryū神道夢想流. Nishioka received *menkyo kaiden* under Shimizu in 1975. He began training in Shindō Musō Ryū in 1939, while still in high school. Since around 1990 Nishioka has served as technical advisor to the International Jodo Federation. As one of Shimizu's earliest students, Nishioka has a unique style which reflects Shimizu Takaji's *jōjutsu* in the prewar era.

SHIMIZU TAKAJI (L) AND NISHIOKA TSUNEO (R)
demonstrating Shindō Musō Ryū—Kage (c. 1950)
(Photograph courtesy Nishioka Tsuneo)

Niten Ichi Ryū 二天一流. A variant name for Hyōhō Niten Ichi Ryū. This is one of several martial traditions that trace their origins to Miyamoto Musashi. See: *Hyōhō Niten Ichi Ryū.*

Nitenki 『二天記』. Anecdotal collection of stories about Miyamoto Musashi and his disciples compiled by Toyoda Matashiro. It was published in 1755. The text has been reprinted and published many times. See, for example, Imamura (1966, vol. 1: 411–429).

nitō 二刀. Lit. "dual swords." Techniques in which two swords are used in tandem by the same exponent.

Nitobe Inazo 新渡戸稲造【新渡戸稻造】(1862–1933). Author, educator, and politician of the Meiji and Taishō eras. Nitobe is best known

N

in the martial arts world as the author of *Bushido: The Soul of Japan.*

Nitō Seihō 二刀勢法. The third set of combative scenarios (*kata*) listed by the Hyōhō Niten Ichi Ryū 兵法二天一流 under the general category of Tachi Seihō. This set is made up of five scenarios involving long and short sword. See: *Hyōhō Niten Ichi Ryū.*

Nitten 日天 <Ch. Ritian <Skt. Sūrya/Āditya. [A.k.a. Nittenson 日天尊]. In Indian mythology, Sūrya/Āditya is the sun god. Nitten is one of a group of twelve guardian deities adopted from Brahmanism by Buddhism. See: *Jūniten; suigetsu.*

Nittenson 日天尊 <Ch. Ritianzun. See: *Nitten.*

niwaban 庭番. See: *o-niwaban.*

Niwa Jūrōzaemon Tadaaki 丹羽 十郎左衛門 忠明. See: *Issai Chozanshi.*

Niwa Tadaaki 丹羽 忠明. See: *Issai Chozanshi.*

nō 能. See: *nōgaku.*

nobori 幟. See: *hatajirushi; noboribata.*

noboribata 幟旗. During the Warring States period (Sengoku Jidai), *noboribata* were flags or banners attached to the back of a warrior's armor. Their creation is attributed to the famous warrior general Hatakeyama Masanaga, who first used them in 1456. At that time a *noboribata* was called a *chitsuke hata* 乳付旗 (banner with loops). Although generally used to identify the bearer, they were occasionally emblazoned with a commander's standard, a family crest (*kamon*), the names of protective deities, or spells.

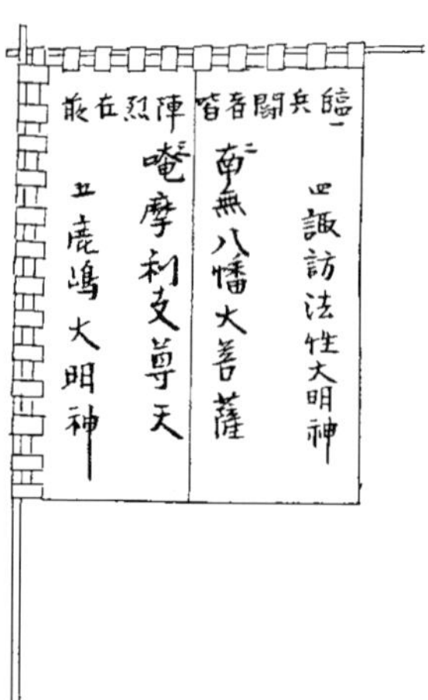

NOBORIBATA
(Illustration from a scroll dated 1646)

The standard shown on this page (an illustration from a 1646 *densho*) has the spell of the nine mystic letters (*kuji*) written across the top horizontally from right to left. The illustration itself contains numbers to indicate which phrase is read first and from which direction. For the convenience of the Western reader, these are transcribed below:

1. ren	pyō	tō	sha	kai	jin	retsu	zai	zen
臨	兵	闘	者	皆	陣	列	在	前

The vertical text, from right to left, is as follows:

4. Suwa Hōsshō Daimyōjin
   四 諏訪法性大明神
2. Namu Hachiman Daibosatsu
   二 南無八幡大菩薩
3. On Marishisonten
   三 唵摩利支尊天
5. Kashima Daimyōjin
   五 鹿島大明神

See also: *sashimono hata.*

nobuseri 野伏. 1. A wandering samurai; a soldier of fortune. 2. A *nobushi.*

nobushi 野武士 [Var. 野伏]. Lit. "warriors who hide in the fields." This term began to appear in the late Kamakura period in reference to armed bands of brigands and guerrilla fighters. The term is thus related to *akutō* (rowdy or evil bands). *Nobushi* are also mentioned as guerrilla fighters in the *Taiheiki*. Historian Kuroda Toshio (1975: 482) has postulated that this nontraditional style of fighting may have evolved after the warriors of western Japan had to deal with the Mongol invasions of 1274 and 1281. Kuroda goes on to say that the "western warriors" had been sorely tested during the Mongol invasions. Whereas the Japanese had been used to name-announcing (*nanori*) in preparation for one-on-one combat, the Mongols and their subservient troops, such as groups of Chinese spearmen—who of course did not speak Japanese or have such customs—

fought in disciplined groups. Consequently, the surviving western warriors developed new tactics during the post-Mongol invasion period. This is the same period and geographical location in which most *akutō* incidents occurred. Thus, by the time period covered by the *Taiheiki* (early to mid-1300s) these new methods were familiar to the warriors of western Japan. The tactics used by these guerrilla-type combatants who "hid in the fields" stood in contrast to the more formal name-announcing customs of the eastern warriors (Bandō *musha*). The western warriors of the *Taiheiki* often acted in the manner of guerrilla fighters. Varley (1994: 174) notes:

> ...(they) are guerrillas...they specialize particularly in erecting and defending fortresses...but they are also adept in hit and run tactics of harassment. They recognize no rules in warfare and employ unorthodox and wily stratagems. Many are organized as units of foot soldiers and use spears (*yari*), as well as bows and swords.

Nobushi can also simply refer to brigands. See also: *jisamurai*.

Nochi no Raitō Jūsan Seihō 後雷刀 十三勢法. YAGYŪ SHINKAGE RYŪ—The fourth series of Shiai Seihō *waza*, consisting of thirteen *kata*. See: *shiai seihō*.

Nochi no Raitō Nana Seihō 後雷刀 七勢法. YAGYŪ SHINKAGE RYŪ—The fifth series of Shiai Seihō *waza*, consisting of seven *kata*. See: *shiai seihō*.

nodachi 野太刀. 1. Lit. "field sword." A longsword measuring around 60 inches (1.5 meters) or more in length. Like the *ōdachi*, this type of sword first appears around the fourteenth century. Its use is preserved in very few of the classical martial traditions (*koryū*) today. See: *Jigen Ryū; Nodachi Jigen Ryū*.

Nodachi Jigen Ryū 野太刀示現流 [A.k.a. ***Nodachi Ryū*** 野太刀流; ***Yakumaru Jigen Ryū*** 薬丸示現流【藥丸示現流】; ***Yakuma Jigen Ryū*** 薬丸示現流【藥丸示現流】; ***Yakuma Ryū*** 薬丸流【藥丸流】]. The Nodachi Jigen Ryū was founded by Yakumaru Gyōbuzaemon Kanenobu (1607–1689). Having learned martial arts from Tōgō Shigetaka (founder of the Jigen Ryū), Kanenobu carried on a separate line of the school. As practiced by this Yakumaru line, the system concentrates on swordsmanship (*kenjutsu*) and combative staff arts (*bōjutsu*). Due to his emphasis on the *nodachi*, Kanenobu appended that term to the tradition's name in order to distinguish it from that of the Tōgō family line. See also: *Ko Jigen Ryū*.

Nodachi Ryū 野太刀流. See: *Nodachi Jigen Ryū*.

nodowa 咽喉輪. Throat-protecting armor.

nōgaku 能楽【能樂】[A.k.a. *nō* 能]. A Noh play. These musical plays, favored by the warrior class and Japanese nobility, have been performed since the fourteenth century. Much more restrained in character than the later *kabuki*, *nōgaku* was very influential on the ruling class as well as other facets of Japanese society. See: *kabuki*.

nokizaru 簷猿 [Also read ***tan'en***] [Var. ***nokizaru*** 軒猿]. Lit. a "monkey (hidden) in the eaves (of a house)." This was a variant term for espionage agent. According to Miyazaki (1974: 239), the Uesugi Ryū 上杉流 used an alternate term, *ken'en* 軒轅 (also read *nokizaru*), which means the same thing. See: *ninjutsu*.

N

nokogiribiki 鋸引. Lit. "sawing the throat." *Nokogiribiki* was one of the four prescribed forms of execution for Tokugawa-period commoners. See: *shikei*.

Noma Kyūroku Masateru 野間 久六 正照. A master of Chikurin Ryū combative archery (*kyūjutsu*). One of Noma's best-known students was Ōguchi Gonkurō Shiseki, who subsequently founded the Ōguchi Ryū 大口流 (also a school of combative archery).

Nomi Hamao Minamoto no Yasuchika 野見 浜雄 源安親 (1854–1932). The fifteenth-generation successor to the Jiki Shinkage Ryū and progenitor of the Jiki Shinkage Ryū Nomi Ha. Nomi was a direct student of Sakakibara Kenkichi. See also: *Ishigaki Yasuzō*.

Nonaka Shinzō Naritsune 野中 新蔵 成常 (c.1540–c.1600). A direct disciple of Kamiizumi Ise no Kami in the Shinkage Ryū (1) 新陰流. Nonaka founded a branch tradition known as the Shin Shinkage Ichien Ryū 新神陰一円流 in the late 1500s.

norito 祝詞 [Also read **shukushi**]. SHINTŌ—A ritual prayer. *Norito* begin to appear around 900 C.E. They are spoken with a cadence much like esoteric Buddhist spells (*shingon* 真言 and *darani* 陀羅尼). As Draeger notes (1995: 3.4), *norito* are "intimately tied to Japanese martial arts." In fact, *norito* are, to this day, recited by practitioners of many classical warrior traditions (*koryū bujutsu*) at the beginning of martial exhibitions (*hōnō embu*) held at Shintō shrines. See also: *gohei; harai (2); shimenawa.*

noroshi 狼火. 1. A signal fire. 2. Abbreviation for *noroshijutsu.*

noroshijutsu 狼火術. The battlefield art of creating and using signal fires.

nōtō 納刀. The last of the four stages executed in the combative forms (*kata*) of quick-draw sword arts (*iaidō*, *iaijutsu*, *battōjutsu*, etc.). *Nōtō* is the action of replacing the blade in its scabbard (*saya*). See: *iaijutsu.*

nuguigami 拭紙. Lit. "wiping paper." The tear-resistant, highly absorbent paper (*washi* [2]) with multi-directional fibers, used for cleaning Japanese swords. See also: *washi; uchiko.*

nukiai 抜合【拔合】. Lit. "simultaneous strike." One of several alternate terms for combative quick-draw sword arts (*iaijutsu*). See: *iaijutsu.*

nukiashi 抜足【拔足】. Stealthy walking with a pulled, sliding step; sneaking up on someone.

nuki-tsuke 抜付【拔付】. In most combative forms of the quick-draw sword arts (*iaijutsu*, *iaidō*, *battō*, etc.), *nuki-tsuke* is the act of drawing the sword out of the scabbard (*saya*). See: *iaijutsu.*

nuki-uchi 抜打【拔打】. Essentially the same in meaning as *battō*. *Nuki-uchi* involves quickly drawing out a sword and slashing at an opponent in one movement. See: *iaijutsu.*

Numazawa Jingozaemon 沼沢 甚五左衛門【沼澤甚五左衛門】(c.? –1647). Founder of the Shin Ryū (2) 神流, a school specializing in quick-draw swordsmanship (*iaijutsu*) and police tying-cord skills (*torinawa*), during the first half of the 1600s. Numazawa was a student of Nagano Murakusai Kinro in the Muraku Ryū 無楽流, a branch line of the Shin Musō Hayashizaki Ryū 神夢想林崎流.

nunchaku 双節棍【雙節棍】(Oki.) [Read **sō-setsukon** in Japanese; normally written phonetically as ヌンチャク]. OKINAWAN KARATE/KOBUDŌ—Lit. "two-section staff." A flail-type weapon most commonly used in Okinawan *karate* systems. Each flail is about 16 inches (40 cm) long—sufficient to protect the forearm when the weapon is held in a reversed grip. There are various types. See: *Okinawa kobudō.*

nyoi 如意 <Ch. *ruyi*. 1. BUDDHISM—A priest's scepter, normally held in one hand when giving a lecture or while officiating at a votive service. The *nyoi* was sometimes used by Buddhist teachers to "encourage" their trainees. Isshū Miura noted in his "Kōan Study in Rinzai Zen":

> Nanshinken, the late Roshi of the Nanzen-ji Sodo, in his day had the reputation of being the most severe of all the *sodo roshis* in Japan. Whenever he found any of us negligent in our practice, he would wield his *nyoi* ruthlessly, and, every O Sesshin, many of us would bear the resultant bumps on our heads. I am still deeply grateful for Nanshinken's *nyoi*.
>
> Miura and Sasaki, 1965: 40.

2. SHŌRINJI KEMPŌ—A short stick. The *nyoi* is one of the three weapons taught in Shōrinji Kempō.

nyoi hōju 如意宝珠【如意寶珠】. BUDDHISM—A jewel which grants all desires.

nyūdō 入道. One who has "entered the path [of the Buddha]." This is a title given to a person who has become a lay Buddhist priest (*zaike hōshi*). Many Japanese *bushi*, such as Iizasa Chōisai Nyūdō Ienao, founder of the Tenshinshō-den Katori Shintō Ryū, took this step. Lay priests shaved their heads and "entered the way" by taking some—but not all—of a priest's vows and practicing Buddhist rituals. The *nyūdō* often lived in their homes, though some took up residence in a temple. See also: *sōhei (1); tonseisha; zaike hōshi.*

nyūdō sanzen 入道参禅【入道參禪】. A Kamakura-period term used to indicate the Zen *kōan* practice of Kamakura warriors. See also: *Kamakura Zen; kien Zen; shikin Zen.*

Nyūdō sanzenki 『入道参禅記』【入道參禪記】 (Accounts of lay [warrior] Zen). This document consists of records of warrior training in Zen *kōan* practice at the five temples (*gozan*) of Kamakura. A number of similar texts were compiled on this topic, many of which were summarized in Imai Fukuzan's *Shōnan Kattōroku* 『湘南葛藤録』 in 1925. This text by Fukuzan, including 100 of the *kōan*, was translated in Trevor Leggett's *The Warrior Koans: Early Zen in Japan* (Leggett, 1985). See: *Kamakura Zen; nyūdō sanzen.*

NAGINATAJUTSU OF THE TENSHINSHŌ-DEN KATORI SHINTŌ RYŪ
Donn F. Draeger, with *ōnaginata*, invites a swordsman's attack in a 1978 demonstration at Katori Jingu
(Photography courtesy Pat Lineberger)

O

ō 王. See: *ōshō* 王将.

ōbanyaku 大番役. The security-guard service for the capital (Kyōto) during the Kamakura and Muromachi periods. The guard service was manned by warrior vassals of the *bakufu*. See also: *kagariya banyaku*; *Kamakura Ōbanyaku*; *Kyōto Ōbanyaku*; *shōgun gosho naibanyaku*.

Obata Kagenori 小幡 景憲 (1572–1662). Author of the *Kōyō gunkan* (Military chronicles of the Takeda clan of Kai), one of the most influential works on the Edo-period samurai. Obata, the son of a military strategist in the Takeda clan, was a warrior and Confucian scholar who grew up as a retainer of the Tokugawa after the destruction of the Takeda in 1582.

obi 帯【帶】. A belt; a sash.

obigane 帯金【帶金】[Also read ***obikane***]. A type of hook (*soritsuno*) on the outside of a scabbard (*saya*) which prevents the *saya* from being pulled through the sash (*obi*) when the sword is drawn.

obikane 帯金. See: *obigane*.

ōbyōshi 大拍子. A large beat; a large, relatively slow attack. See: *hyōshi*.

ōdachi 大太刀. 1. A variant name for a *katana*. 2. A *katana*-type *bokken* used in training. 3. A long sword—longer than a *tachi* but shorter than a *nodachi*—measuring 3 to 5 feet (1–1.5 m) in length. In some cases the cutting edge of the blade was not sharpened close to the guard (*tsuba*), so that the weapon could be drawn directly from its carrying location on the back. Like the *nodachi*, this type of sword appeared around the fourteenth century. Its use is preserved in very few of the classical martial traditions (*koryū*) today. (See the end of section "O" for photograph.) See also: *seoidachi*.

Odagiri Ichiun 小田切 一雲 (1630–1706). A swordsman of the Mujū Shinken Ryū 無住心剣流 and a disciple of its founder, Harigaya Sekiun. What is known today about Odagiri's master, Harigaya, and Harigaya's relationship to Ogasawara Genshin Nagaharu, is known through Odagiri's writing. See: *Mujū Shinken Ryū*.

Odani Ha Jiki Shinkage Ryū 男谷派直心影流. The main lineage of the Jiki Shinkage Ryū descended from Odani Nobutomo, its thirteenth headmaster. Watatani and Yamada list forty-eight swordsmen who were direct disciples of Odani and fully licensed in the Jiki Shinkage Ryū.

Odani Nobutomo 男谷 信友 [A.k.a. ***Seiichirō*** 精一郎; ***Shimōsa no Kami*** 下総守【下總守】] (1789–1864). Recognized thirteenth headmaster of the Jiki Shinkage Ryū 直心影流. Known as a *chōichiryū kenshi* (super swordsman), Odani was one of the most famous swordsmen of mid-1800s Japan. As a young man he began training with Dannō Yoshitaka, twelfth headmaster of the Jiki Shinkage Ryū, and mastered that school's teachings in only three years. Odani was an avid martial artist; he trained in strategy (*gumpō*) with Hirayama Kōzō, in the combative spearmanship (*sōjutsu*) of the Hōzōin Ryū, and in the archery (*kyūjutsu*) of the Yoshida Ryū. In addition to being a "super swordsman," he was also well respected as a refined, educated gentleman.

Odani was a passionate advocate of competitive matches between different schools of swordsmanship (*taryūjiai*). In fact, he and his students often engaged in this practice using the special protective gear (*bōgu*) developed by earlier Jiki Shinkage Ryū masters. According to some sources, he would accept challenge matches from anyone. He would allow any challenger to score at least one out of the first two points in a match, but would then seal his victory with the third point. This allowed opponents to think they had just been barely defeated. However, in any return matches Odani would soundly defeat them. In this way he gained many disciples; he is said to have had as many as 20,000 trainees.

Odani was made chief of the guards of Edo Castle by Mizuno Tadakuni, the latter a member of the *shogun*'s Council of Elders. Odani also headed the Kōbusho, a government training institute which taught various martial arts, gunnery, and military strategy (*heihō*), including fighting strategies from Europe. According to Sakai (2010: 190–191) Odani was chosen over other prominent swordsmen of the day to direct the Kōbusho because the purpose of that organization was to teach practical combative swordsmanship. As head of the Kōbusho, Odani was also instrumental in setting the length of the bamboo practice sword (*shinai*) used in training there at 46 inches (117 cm). This created a "blade" length approximating that of a real sword (*shinken*) but with an extended handgrip (*tsuka*) to facilitate the use of protective gloves (*kote*).

ODANI NOBUTOMO
Thirteenth-generation headmaster of the Jiki Shinkage Ryū, pictured here with his special short sword
(Picture courtesy Namiki Yasushi)

Odani taught the Jiki Shinkage Ryū to a number of young men and government officials including Sakakibara Kenkichi, Yokokawa Shichirō, and Katsu Kokichi and his son, Katsu Kaishū. (Kaishū, a principle retainer of the shogunate, also learned about Western science and navigation from Odani). Kaishū later became an important figure in the turbulent days when the shogunate collapsed and Japan entered the modern age with the Meiji Restoration in 1868.

According to Namiki Yasushi, eighteenth headmaster of the Jiki Shinkage Ryū, in place of a sword Odani wore a mock *kodachi* made of a solid piece of iron that was lacquered to look like a short-sword scabbard, complemented by a handguard (*tsuba*) and wrapped hilt (*tsuka*). This bludgeon could be drawn and used within the *shōgun*'s palace without breaking the ban on drawing a blade. This special short sword is currently in the hands of the Namiki family in Tōkyō.

Among Odani's best-known disciples were Shimada Toranosuke, Sakakibara Kenkichi (who succeeded Odani as fourteenth headmaster of the *ryū*), and Katsu Kaishū. See: *Jiki Shinkage Ryū*.

Further reading in English:

- Craig, 1988.
- Cundy, 2002.
- Hall, 1983.
- Hurst, 1998: 91.
- Sakai, 2010: *passim*.

Oda Nobunaga 織田 信長 (1534–1582). One of the most famous and important warlords of Japan's Warring States period. Oda was the first of the three great unifiers of Japan in the latter half of the sixteenth century. He conquered a good portion of the country and broke the power of the great warrior-monk (*sōhei*) armies of Mount Hiei and other temples. During his heyday Yagyū Sekishūsai Muneyoshi was one of his retainers.

ODA NOBUNAGA
(Sixteenth-century painting by Kano Motohide)

Further reading in English:

- Jansen, 2000, *passim*.
- Lamers, 2001.

Oda Taisha Ryū 小田タイ捨流. A branch tradition of the Taisha Ryū founded around 1690 by Oda Shichirōemon Sadanori. Oda was a sixth-generation headmaster of the Taisha Ryū. The school exists today under the name of Taisha Ryū Kempō タイ捨流剣法. See: *Taisha Ryū*.

odoshi 縅 [Var. 威]. Lit. "lacing." The decorative lacing on Japanese armor. *Odoshi* comes in several types and many colors. In fact, like Scottish tartans, various colors of *odoshi* were associated with specific warrior clans (*buke*) in the early classical period, around the time of Emperor Seiwa,[1] the progenitor of the Seiwa Genji.

Ōe no Koretoki 大江 維時 (888–963). Koretoki was a tenth-century figure who, according to the *Honchō bugei shōden* (*Biographical sketches in Japanese martial arts*, published c.1716), returned from Tang China with forty-two volumes of text, several of which were concerned with military science. Among these were the *Liutao*『六韜』(Jp. *Rikutō*), *Sanlue*『三略』(Jp. *Sanryaku*), *Junshengtu*『軍勝図』(Jp. *Gunshōzu*), and others (Watatani, 1967: 39). These texts, along with a mixture of Buddhist and Daoist esoterica, became the family-transmitted martial tradition of the powerful Seiwa Genji warrior clan (also known as the Minamoto). Legend has it that one of Koretoki's descendants passed a translated compendium of these texts to either Minamoto Yoriyoshi (995–1082) or Minamoto Yoshiie (1041–1108). A variant legend claims these texts were stored at Kuramadera, and were secretly copied by Minamoto no Yoshitsune (1159–1189).

As this family-transmitted compendium on military strategy was a well-guarded secret, the Minamoto family strategy in its entirety did not materialize in written form until the late 1500s, when it appeared within the Ogasawara family under the title of *Genke kin'etsushū*. See also: *Genji no heihō; Genke kin'etsushū; Kiichi Hōgan; Kiichi Hōgan Ryū; Rikutō; Sanryaku; Seiwa Genji.*

Ōe Ryū 大江流. A system of military strategy, tactics, and divination (*gumpō*) attributed to the eleventh-century warrior Minamoto no Yoshiie, who according to legend learned Sun Tzu's *Art of War* (*Sonshi no heihō*) from Ōe no Masafusa. However, the actual lineage available in current sources lists the first verifiable transmission of the Ōe Ryū to Ogasawara Takeo Nyūdō Yoriuji 小笠原武勇入道頼氏 (c.1450–?). These mythical beginnings parallel the history of the *Ginke kin'etsushū*. See also: *Genji no heihō; Genke kin'etsushū.*

Ōe no Masafusa 大江 匡房 (1040–1111). Sixth-generation descendant of Ōe no Koretoki. Masafusa was renowned for his poetry and scholarship, and served as governor of Dazaifu (1098–1102). He taught Sun Tzu's *Art of War* (*Sonshi no heihō*) and other Chinese texts on military strategy to Minamoto Yoshiie. The Ōe Ryū, a school of strategy and tactics which flourished from the fifteenth century through the end of the premodern period (c.1868), recognized Masafusa's teachings as the source from which the Minamoto family designed its battle strategies. See also: *Genke kin'etsushū; Ōe no Koretoki; Ōe Ryū.*

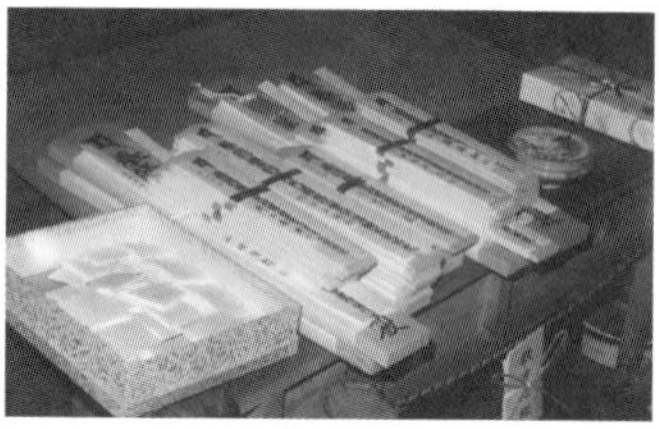

OFUDA
A stack of *ofuda* awaiting presentation to participants in a *goma* ritual at the Marishitenzuka temple, 1988
(Photograph by author)

ofuda お札 [A.k.a. ***gofu*** 護符]. SHINTŌ—Wooden tablets inscribed with the name of the Shintō shrine where they are produced. Used as talismans, these devices are often placed alongside the *kamidana* in martial training halls (*dōjō*).

Ogasawara Shi 小笠原氏. A branch family of the Seiwa Genji. The Ogasawara descended from Takeda Yoshikiyo. See: *Seiwa Genji.*

Ogasawara Genshin Nagaharu 小笠原 玄信 長治 [A.k.a. ***Genshinsai*** 玄信斎【玄信齋】] (c.1545–c.1630). Founder of the Shin no Shinkage Ryū 真新陰流; recognized as fourth headmaster by the Jiki Shinkage Ryū 直心影流. According to transmission documents of the Jiki Shinkage Ryū,[2] Ogasawara was a successor to Okuyama Kyūgasai Kimishige in the Shinkage Ryū (4) 神影流. Some sources state he also trained directly with Kamiizumi Ise no Kami in the Shinkage Ryū (1) 新陰流. After several changes of sides in the incessant wars of the late 1500s (fighting with Imagawa

[1] Seiwa Tennō 清和天皇 (850–880; r.859–876). Fifty-sixth emperor of Japan.

[2] Various editions of the Kashima Shinden Jiki Shinkage Ryū *Kyūri no maki*『窮理の巻』.

Yoshimoto until the latter's death in 1560; then with Tokugawa Ieyasu for a period; then with Takeda Shingen's heir, Katsuyori, until 1582; and then with Hōjō Ujimasa until 1590), Genshin's family earned the wrath of Ieyasu when the latter came to power after Sekigahara in 1600. Genshin fled to China (probably the Beijing area) where he taught the Shinkage Ryū, and supposedly studied Chinese boxing and spear systems.[3] Upon Ieyasu's death in 1616, Genshin returned to Japan, traveling to Edo and teaching an again renamed version of the *ryū* which he called Shin no Shinkage Ryū, which means the "True Shinkage Ryū." He may have changed the name to distinguish his tradition from the Yagyū Shinkage Ryū 柳生新陰流, which was the official school of the Tokugawa. Genshin's lineal successor was Kamiya Denshinsai. See also: *Harigaya Sekiun; Jiki Shinkage Ryū; Kamiizumi Ise no Kami Nobutsuna.*

Ogasawara Jōnosuke Nagamasa 小笠原 城之助 長政. Founder of the Shintō Seibu Ryū 神道精武流. Ogasawara established this school in the late 1700s, after training extensively in Tenshinshō-den Katori Shintō Ryū 天真正伝香取神道流. See lineage under: *Itō Ryū (1).*

Ogasawara Nagahide 小笠原 長秀 (1366–1424). Grandson of Ogasawara Sadamune and founder of the Ogasawara Ryū. Nagahide was a master martial artist, well known for his ability in combative horsemanship (*kisha* [1]) and mounted bow and arrow combat (*kyūba*). He was a close advisor to the third Ashikaga *shōgun*, Yoshimitsu,[4] in matters of warrior etiquette as well as other subjects. Alongside Ise Noritada and Imagawa Ujiyori, Nagahide was charged with creating a code of etiquette and ceremonies for the warrior class. This set of rules, which was set down in a work called the *Sangi ittō*, came to be one of the three central teachings of the Ogasawara Ryū. (The other two were horsemanship and mounted archery.)

Ogasawara Nagakiyo 小笠原 長清 (fl. early thirteenth century). Nagakiyo, the great-grandson of Minamoto Yoshikiyo, was the first Minamoto to take the name Ogasawara. He was a warrior of note, and came to be known as one of the "Big Four" (Shitennō) champion archers of the middle ages, along with contemporaries Takeda Nobumitsu, Unno Yukiuji 海野 幸氏, and Mochizuki Shigetaka 望月 重隆.

Ogasawara Ryū 小笠原流 [A.k.a. ***Ogasawara Ryū Kyūba*** ~弓馬; ***Ogasawara Ryū Kisha*** ~騎射]. The oldest extant classical combative school with a focus on *kyūjutsu* and *yabusame*. Founded by Ogasawara Nagahide, the Ogasawara Ryū originally contained a number of war arts, including strategy and battlefield divination (*gumbai heihō*), warrior etiquette and ceremonies (*reihō*), mounted archery (*kyūba*), combative horsemanship (*kasha*), "pipe archery" (*kanya* 管矢), and "heavy arrow" (*uchine*). See also: *yabusame.*

Ogasawara Ryū Sahō 小笠原流作法. The formal etiquette of the Ogasawara Ryū.

OGASAWARA KIYONOBU
The late headmaster of Ogasawara Ryū *kyūjutsu* prepares to loose an arrow at a Meiji Jingū exhibition in 1977
(Photograph by author)

---

3 In his early Edo-period work entitled *Sekiun Ryū kenjutsusho zenshū* 『夕雲流剣術書全集』, Kawamura Hideharu quotes Odagiri Ichiun concerning Ogasawara's years in China. He notes that Ogasawara trained in Chinese spear systems with one Chō Ryō 張良(<Ch. Zhang Liang), and brought his system, called *nobegane* 延金 (<Ch. *yanjin*), back to Japan. However, Jiki Shinkage Ryū documents do not specifically name this Chinese martial artist or his system of spearmanship.

4 Ashikaga Yoshimitsu 足利 義満 (1358–1408, r.1368–1394).

Ogasawara Sadamune 小笠原 貞宗 (1294–1350). Fourteenth-century figure who formalized *yabusame*—a type of mounted archery contest—into its present form.

Sadamune lived during Japan's trouble-filled Nambokuchō period. Governor of Shinano while administering two other provinces under the Kamakura *bakufu*, he sided at first with Hōjō Takatoki, the ninth and last Kamakura *shikken* (shogunal regent). With the fall of the Kamakura shogunate (1333), Sadamune then sided with the imperial forces (*kangun*) of Emperor Go-Daigo,[5] supporting Nitta Yoshisada. However, in 1336 Sadamune joined forces with Ashikaga Takauji and fought against Go-Daigo's Southern Court. Sadamune's relationship with Ashikaga Takauji evidently pivoted on the former's support of the elevation to emperor of Ashikaga's cousin, Emperor Kōmyō.[6] Takauji later placed Sadamune in charge of matters of etiquette among the new *shōgun's* retainers. See: *Ogasawara Nagahide.*

Ogasawara Takeo Nyūdō Yoriuji 小笠原 武勇 入道 頼氏 (c.1450–?). Fifteenth-century warrior who codified the combative strategies of the Minamoto family into Ōe Ryū 大江流 *gumpō*.

ōgi 1. 奥義 [Also read **okugi**]. Secret teachings. See: *okugi; okuden.*

ōgi 2. 扇. A folding fan. See: *tessen.*

ōgisaki 扇先. Lit. "fan-shaped point." A round-pointed blade.

Ōguchi Gonkurō Shiseki 大口 権九郎 子積. Founder of Ōguchi Ryū, a school of combative archery (*kyūjutsu*). Ōguchi was a warrior of the Tottori domain. He had trained in Chikurin Ha 竹林派 (a variant name for Chikurin Ryū 竹林流, a widespread school of combative archery [*kyūjutsu*]), under Noma Kyūroku Masateru. However, Ōguchi's swordsmanship was derived from the Tōgun Ryū 東軍流.

Ōguchi Ryū 大口流. A system of combative archery founded by Ōguchi Gonkurō Shiseki around 1730.

Oguri Niuemon Masanobu 小栗 仁右衛門 正信 (1582–1661). Founder of the Oguri Ryū. Niuemon was a veteran warrior of Sekigahara (1600), as well as the Winter (1614) and Summer (1615) battles in Ōsaka. This combat experience, and his years of training with both Yagyū Muneyoshi and Yagyū Munenori, enabled him to found his own system in 1616.

Oguri Ryū 小栗流. A system founded around 1616 by Oguri Niuemon. The Oguri Ryū was a true comprehensive martial school (*sōgo bujutsu*) which included a variety of combative weapons arts: swordsmanship (*kenjutsu* with *tachi* and *kodachi*), quick-draw sword arts (*iaijutsu*), spear arts (*sōjutsu*), long-hafted glaive arts (*naginatajutsu*), and long hardwood staff arts (*bōjutsu*). Various combinations of armed and unarmed, armored and unarmored grappling and capturing arts such as *wajutsu*, *kumiuchi*, *suieijutsu*, and *nawa* were taught as well, along with a number of horse-mounted fighting arts including aquatic horsemanship (*suibajutsu*) and mounted combat (*kisha* [1]).

Further reading in English:

- Mol, 2001: 44–46.

Ōhashi Kinosuke Masanaga 大橋 喜之助 政長 (c.1620–c.1700). Sixth headmaster of the Seigō Ryū. One of his disciples was Nagaoka Jūrōemon Fusahide, founder of the Yagyū Seigō Ryū branch tradition.

Ōhen Ryū 応変流【應變流】. A *jūjutsu* system founded by Daitō Sonbei Hidesada sometime during the Kyōhō era (1716–1736). Daitō christened it the "quick response" (*ōhen*) tradition. His school was based on the Asayama Ichiden Ryū 一伝流, which he had mastered.

ōhō 王法. Imperial law; imperial rule.

oibara 追い腹. A Warring States–period term referring to suicide (*seppuku*) performed in order to accompany one's lord into death; i.e., *seppuku* performed as an act of loyalty. Equivalent to *junshi*. See: *seppuku.*

Ōishi Shinkage Ryū 大石神影流. A school of *kendō* founded in Kyūshū by Ōishi Susumu

[5] Go-Daigo Tennō 後醍醐天皇 (1288–1339; r.1318–1339). Ninety-sixth emperor of Japan.

[6] Kōmyō Tennō 光明天皇 (1322–1380, r.1337–1348). Second emperor of the "Brief Northern dynasty."

of the Aisu Shinkage Ryū 愛洲神陰流. Ōishi and his students used a very long *shinai*—often wielded with one hand for greater reach—and wore a *men* (face protector) designed to deflect blows from a *shinai*.

Further reading in English:

• Draeger, 1974: 98–99.

Ōishi Susumu Tanetsugu 大石 進 種次 (1798–1865). According to tradition, Ōishi founded the Ōishi Shinkage Ryū after inheriting the Aisu Shinkage Ryū 愛洲神陰流 from his father. Ōishi became famous for his *dōjō*-storming (*dōjō arashi*) with an extremely long (around 5 feet/1.5 m) bamboo training sword (*shinai*). He evidently turned this into a money-making enterprise by blackmailing heads of *dōjō* in Kyūshū. Ōishi's reign of terror was ended after he was soundly defeated in a match (*shinai shiai*) with Odani Nobutomo, thirteenth headmaster of the Jiki Shinkage Ryū.

ōka 桜花【櫻花】. Lit. "cherry blossom." This term was also used for manned suicide bombs in World War II.

Further reading in English:

• Morris, 1975: 276–281.

okachi 御徒士 [A.k.a. ***kachizamurai*** 徒侍]. An Edo-period term for an official shogunal foot-soldier.

ōkama 大鎌. OKINAWAN KOBUDŌ—A long-hafted hand-held farmer's sickle used in some schools of Okinawan *kobudō*. The *ōkama* is essentially a long hardwood staff with a sickle blade attached to one end. See: *icchō kama; nichō kama; Okinawa kobudō.*

ōkamari 大かまり. 1. Members of a large group of covert assault troops who hid in various locations—reed fields, forests, mountain valleys, and even in villages—until a signal was given for them to form up and make a surprise attack on enemy forces. 2. A large surprise attack. See also: *kamari (1), ninjutsu.*

ōkamayari 大鎌槍. A larger or longer version of the *kamayari*.

Okamoto Seigō 岡本 正剛 (b.1925). Founder of the Daitō Ryū Aikijūjutsu Roppōkai. Okamoto became a student of Daitō Ryū instructor Horikawa Kodō in 1963. He received the rank of master teacher (Daitō Ryū Kyōju Dairi) in 1978, and founded after the Roppōkai after Horikawa's death in 1980.

Further reading in English:

• Pranin, 1996: 178–189.

okashi gusoku お貸し具足. Lit. "loan armor." Light armor worn by light infantry or "light foot soldiers" (*ashigaru*). See also: *ichiryō gusoku.*

Okazaki Masamune 岡崎 正宗 [Also known as ***Okazaki Gorō Nyūdō Shōsō*** 岡崎 五郎 入道 正宗 or simply ***Masamune***] (1264–1344). Japan's most celebrated swordsmith. Masamune traveled extensively and trained under many famous sword makers (*katana kaji*). His blades were renowned for their strength and cutting ability.

During the Mongol invasions of Japan in 1274 and 1281 many Japanese swords had been broken or were so severely damaged that they became useless. Masamune and his father were able to develop a forging process that fixed the defects. Masamune forged blades for renowned swordsmen such as Kusunoki Masashige. Many of Masamune's blades were unsigned, as he evidently assumed no one would mistake his superior blades for someone else's.

According to legend, Masamune's blades were of superior character—it was said that while they were extremely durable and sharp, they were filled with compassion. Consequently, if the end of the sword were placed in a stream, leaves floating against it on the current would pass around the blade and not be cut. This is in contrast to the legends surrounding Muramasa, another famous sword maker of the medieval period. Muramasa's blades were also thought to be extremely sharp, but bloodthirsty and imbued with violence. Leaves that drifted against Muramasa's blades were instantly cut in two.

okina men 翁面. Lit. "old man's face." A common type of armored mask (*menpō*). It was normally decorated with a long, gray moustache.

Okinawa 沖縄【沖繩】<Oki. Uchinā. The largest island of the Ryūkyū archipelago, which

lies between the southernmost island of the Japanese homeland (Kyūshū) and Taiwan. Okinawa has long been a crossroads of East Asian, Southeast Asian, and Pacific traffic, and cultural elements from all of these areas can still be found there. The islands were under weak Chinese control when the Japanese Satsuma clan from Kyūshū took military and political control in the seventeenth century. It was on Okinawa that *karate* developed from a mix of local fighting arts and heavy Chinese influence, primarily from Fujian province.

OKINAWADEN BUBISHI DETAIL
Nineteenth century

Okinawaden Bubishi 沖縄伝『武備志』【沖縄傳武備志】[A.k.a. ***Bubishi*** 『武備志』]. OKINAWAN KARATE—A text concerned with White Crane boxing[7] and Chinese medicine. The author is unknown, but the text was written or collated from earlier texts in Fujian province. A variety of editions have been imported into Okinawa by various practitioners of fighting arts. One of the best-known editions is that brought from Fuzhou by Miyagi and Nakamoto in 1915. (Higaonna *et al.*, 2008: 531). Since that time the text has been passed down within Miyagi's Gōjū Ryū in Okinawa.

Further readings in English:

- McCarthy, 1995 (Trans.); 2008 (Trans.).

Okinawa Karatedō Renmei 沖縄空手道連盟 (Okinawa Karatedō Federation). OKINAWAN KARATE—With the internationalization of *karate* in the 1950s, it became apparent to Okinawan *karate* leaders that an umbrella organization for setting standards was needed. Prior to and just after World War II, most Okinawan *karate* schools (*ryū*) had, like their Japanese martial counterparts, gone their own way as small, private schools. However, with the explosion of the popularity of *karate* among U.S. servicemen in postwar Okinawa and their exportation of various *karate ryū* abroad, those small schools were no longer able to handle the number of teachers and students in Okinawa and abroad looking to them for guidance. Consequently, in 1956 the headmasters of four important *karate* schools met at the Nagamine Dōjō in the city of Naha and founded the Okinawa Karatedō Renmei. Representatives at that meeting were: Uechi Kan'ei (Uechi Ryū上地流), Yagi Meitoku (Gōjū Ryū 剛柔流), Chibana Chōshin (Kobayashi Ryū 小林流), and Nagamine Shōshin (Matsubayashi Ryū 松林流).

Okinawa Kempō 沖縄拳法【沖縄拳法】. OKINAWAN KARATE—Originally referred to as *Okinawa no tī* 沖縄の手. Founder Nakamura Shigeru renamed this system *Okinawa Kempō* in 1960. In formulating his school, Nakamura aimed for a system incorporating relatively free sparring based in traditional *kata*. This emphasis on competition places the school within the modern *budō*/sportive systems.

Nakamura began his training in *te* (<Oki. *tī*) with his father, who passed away when Shigeru was only ten years old. Nakamura subsequently learned various *te* styles from a variety of instructors. Most influential were those based in Chinese boxing (*kempō* 拳法 <Ch. *quanfa*). He later opened a training hall (*dōjō*) in the town of Nago, where he called his style *Okinawa no tī* 沖縄の手. That first *dōjō* was destroyed during the Allied attack on Okinawa during World War II; many of his students were killed during the conflict. After the war Nakamura opened a new *dōjō* and, in 1960, renamed his system *Okinawa Kempō* 沖縄拳法, a term which more accurately reflected his school's orientation toward Chinese boxing. The system today contains many *kata* and Okinawa *kobudō* weapons arts.

Okinawa kobudō 沖縄古武道【沖縄古武道】[A.k.a. ***Okinawa kobujutsu*** 沖縄古武術; ***Ryūkyū kobudō*** 琉球古武道; ***Ryūkyū kobujutsu*** 琉球古武術]. Generic term for Okinawan weapons arts. Over the past 250 years a number of weapons arts have been brought to Okinawa from the Chinese mainland, both by Chinese

[7] Jp. *hakkakuken* or *hakutsuruken* 白鶴拳 <Ch. *bai hao quan*.

visiting the island or immigrating to Okinawa, and by Okinawans visiting the mainland. A number of schools in Okinawa today teach these weapons arts under the general rubric of Okinawa *kobudō*. However, no single school of *karate* or *te* has a monopoly on the use of weaponry. Some of the better-known weapons in the Okinawa *kobudō* category include the long staff (*bō* or *kon*); the single-handed trident (*sai*); flail (*nunchaku*); "handled truncheon" (*tonfā*); knuckle-dusters (*tekkō*); ladies' ornamental hairpin (*jīfā*); single sickle (*icchō kama* 一丁鎌); dual sickles (*nichō kama* 二丁鎌); polearm sickle (*ōkama* 大鎌); shield (*tate* 楯) and spear (*hoko* 鉾) in a system called *tinbē* テインベー; boat paddle/oar (*ēku* 櫂); weighted chain (*suruchin* スルチン); and a number of others, depending on the specific school.

Further reading in English:

• Bishop, 1996: 92–171.

Okinawa kobujutsu 沖縄古武術 【沖縄古武術】. See: *Okinawa kobudō.*

Okinawa no sandai kensei 沖縄の三大拳聖. Lit. the "Three Okinawan boxing saints." Three boxing masters who were seminal in the development of *karate* in Okinawa in the late 1800s: Matsumura Sōkon (formulator of Shuri *te* 首里手), Higaonna Kanryō (formulator of Naha *te* 那覇手), and Matsumora Kōsaku (formulator of Tomari *te* 泊手).

Okita Sōji 沖田 総司. A Tennen Rishin Ryū 天然理心流 swordsman and member of the Shinsengumi. Okita was a young prodigy and instructor of the Tennen Rishin Ryū in the 1860s.

oku 奥. 1. The innermost area; the place furthest from the entrance. 2. Abbreviation for *okuden* (innermost teachings).

Ōkubo Toshimichi 大久保 利通 (1830–1878). A Jigen Ryū–trained Satsuma samurai. Ōkubo was one of the "Three Heros of the [Meiji] Restoration" (Ishin no Sanketsu) who led the revolution of 1867. That conflict overthrew the Tokugawa shogunate and restored the Japanese imperial line to power with Emperor Meiji.[8]

[8] Meiji Tennō 明治天皇 (1852–1912; r.1867–1912). The 122nd emperor of Japan.

Ōkubo Yamato 大久保 大和. See: *Kondō Isami Masayoshi.*

okuden 奥伝【奥傳】. Lit. "inner-transmission" or "secret-transmission"; secret teachings. 1. A term used in several *ryū* indicating a set of high-level, often subtle, combative forms. 2. ***Okuden.*** SHINDŌ MŪSŌ RYŪ—The seventh series of Shindō Mūsō Ryū *waza* consisting of twelve *kata*. Also referred to as *shiai kuchi* 試合口.

okugi 奥義 [Also read ***ōgi***]. "Inner" or "secret" teachings. See: *okuden.*

Okugi Tachi Seihō 奥義太刀勢法. The fourth set of combative scenarios (*kata*) listed by the Hyōhō Niten Ichi Ryū under the general category of Tachi Seihō. This set is made up of four advanced sword scenarios, and is therefore considered a privileged or "secret" transmission. See: *Hyōhō Niten Ichi Ryū.*

Okuirishō 「奥入証」. See: *Shindō Musō Ryū Okuirishō.*

okuriashi 送り足. A sliding step in which the right foot springs forward as the left foot pushes the body forward. The right foot always stays in front of the left foot. This type of step, which is common in the practice of *kendō*, usually ends with the right foot stamping down, a step known as *fumikomiashi*. See also: *ayumiashi; fumikomiashi; suriashi.*

Oku Yahei Takemasa 奥 弥兵衛 猛雅 【奥彌兵衛猛雅】. Founder of Ikkan Ryū (4) 一貫流 gunnery (*hōjutsu*). Oku first mastered the Inatomi Ryū 稲富流 under founder Inatomi Ichimusai.

Okuyama Kyūgasai 奥山 休賀斎 [A.k.a. ***Kimishige*** 公重; ***Magojirō*** 孫次郎] (1526–1602). JIKI SHINKAGE RYŪ—Progenitor of the Shinkage Ryū (4) 神影流 as inherited from Kamiizumi Nobutsuna; founder of the Okuyama Ryū 奥山流; recognized as third headmaster by the Jiki Shinkage Ryū直心影流.

While still a young man, Okuyama traveled to Kōzuke to study with Kamiizumi Hidetsuna, founder of the Shinkage Ryū. After training with Kamiizumi and enduring religious austerities at Kashima Jingū, Okuyama changed the name of Kamiizumi's tradition from Shin-

O

kage Ryū 新陰流 ("New" or "Revised" Kage Ryū) to Shinkage Ryū 神影流 ("Under the influence of the *kami* of Kashima Shrine"). It is from this line that the Jiki Shinkage Ryū evolved. Okuyama later returned from the east to Okuyama in Mikawa, hence the name Okuyama. His lineal successor was Ogasawara Genshin Nagaharu. See also: *Jiki Shinkage Ryū; Shinnuki Ryū.*

Okuyama Magojirō 奥山 孫次郎. See: *Okuyama Kyūgasai.*

Okuyama Nen Ami Jion 奥山 念 阿弥 慈恩. See: *Nen Ami Jion; Nen Ryū.*

Okuyama Nen Ryū 奥山念流. See: *Nen Ryū.*

Okuyama Ryū 奥山流. See: *Okuyama Kyūgasai; Shinkage Ryū (4).*

Okuyama Ryūhō 奥山 龍峰. See: *Okuyama Yoshiji.*

Okuyama Saemon Dayū Tadanobu 奥山 左衛門 大夫 忠信 (c.1600–c.1680). The Shinnuki Ryū 信抜流 recognizes Okuyama as the progenitor of their system of combative swordsmanship (*kempō* [1]) and lists him as a disciple of Marume Kurandonosuke, founder of the Taisha Ryū タイ捨流 (Nihon Kobudō Kyōkai, 1989: 102). However, according to Watatani and Yamada (1978: 450) some sources list Kamiizumi Nobutsuna as Okuyama's teacher, while others list Kamiizumi as Okuyama's disciple. Okuyama's dates are estimated here based on the Taisha Ryū lineage.

Okuyama Toshio 奥山 俊夫 [A.k.a. ***Ryūhō*** 龍峰]. Second headmaster of the Hakkō Ryū 八光流. Toshio assumed leadership of the organization upon the death of his father in 1987.

Okuyama Yoshiharu 奥山 吉治. See: *Okuyama Yoshiji.*

Okuyama Yoshiji 奥山 吉治 [Also read ***Okuyama Yoshiharu***; a.k.a. ***Okuyama Ryūhō*** 奥山 龍峰] (1901–1987). Founder of the Hakkō Ryū 八光流. Okuyama trained extensively in the Daitō Ryū 大東流 under Matsuda Hosaku, and for a short time under Daitō Ryū formulator Takeda Sōkaku. According to the Hakkō Ryū official history, Okuyama also trained in Seigō Ryū 制剛流 grappling arts (*jūjutsu*), Hasegawa Ryū 長谷川流 and Nitō Ryū 二刀流 swordsmanship (*kenjutsu*), and several unnamed combative schools of spear (*sōjutsu*), medium-length staff arts (*jōjutsu*), archery (*kyūjutsu*), small throwing blades and darts (*shurikenjutsu*), and "other lesser-known systems." Interestingly, none of these seem to have been passed on to his Hakkō Ryū disciples. Okuyama also studied Japanese medicine, including circulation theory (meridian-*in*/*yo*), finger pressure medicine (*shiatsu*), and acupuncture. In 1939 he broke with the Daitō Ryū and began teaching what he at first called Meishidō 名士道, which combined what he had learned in the various *jūjutsu* schools with circulation theory. In 1941 he renamed his system Hakkō Ryū. He was succeeded by his son, Okuyama Toshio.

Further reading in English:

- http://www.hakkoryu.com/
- Palumbo, 1987; 1988; 1993.

Okuzōin 奥蔵院. See: *Ōzōin.*

Okuzōin Ihei 奥蔵院 猪兵衛. See: *Ōzōin Ihei.*

o-kyō 御経 【御經】<Ch. *jing* 經 <Skt. *sūtra.* BUDDHISM—A sacred Buddhist text; a Buddhist *sūtra.*

ōmarobashi 大転 【大轉】. YAGYŪ SHINKAGE RYŪ—The *marobashi* technique performed with a large sword and/or a large movement.

ōmetsuke 大目付. The five chief censors appointed by the Tokugawa *bakufu*. Early in the Tokugawa period (1632), this title was awarded to the Yagyū family by *shōgun* Tokugawa Iemitsu, giving the Yagyū the authority and responsibility of surveillance of the *daimyō*.

omi 臣. A retainer; a vassal.

ōmi no yari 大身の槍 [Also called ***honagayari*** 穂長槍 or ***nagamiyari*** 長身槍]. A spear with a straight blade about 1 foot (30 cm) or more in length. See also: *sōjutsu; suyari; yari.*

Ōmori Rokurōzaemon Masamitsu 大森 六郎左衛門 正光 (c.1710–c.1785). Founder of the Ōmori Ryū system of quick-draw swordsmanship (*iaijutsu*). Ōmori trained under Hasegawa Eishin, seventh headmaster of Shimmei Musō Ryū 神明夢想流 (Shin Musō Hayashizaki Ryū 神夢想林崎流) and founder of Hasegawa Eishin Ryū 長谷英信流, but was expelled by his master around 1735. After his expulsion he modified a number of the system's combative forms (*kata*) and created his own tradition known as the Ōmori Ryū 大森流. Prior to Ōmori, the quick-draw swordsmanship of the Shimmei Musō Ryū/Hasegawa Eishin Ryū tradition was performed from the postures of *tatehiza* and *tachiai*. However, Ōmori had trained in the etiquette of Ogasawara Ryū Sahō 小笠原流作法, in which the kneeling *seiza* posture was common, as well as in the five sword-drawing techniques used in the Owari Yagyū Shinkage Ryū (*saya-no-uchi battō gohon*); he incorporated these elements into the quick-draw swordsmanship he received from Hasegawa Eishin. Eventually Ōmori became a teacher of Hayashi Rokudayū Morimasa (ninth headmaster of the Shimmei Musō Ryū and third-generation successor to Hasegawa Eishin Ryū). As a result, twelve of the "modified" techniques making up Ōmori Ryū were incorporated into the Shimmei Musō Ryū/Hasegawa Eishin Ryū lineage.

Ōmori Ryū 大森流. A school of quick-draw swordsmanship (*iaijutsu*) and combative swordsmanship (*shiken*) founded by Ōmori Rokurōzaemon Masamitsu. As Ōmori was originally a student of Hasegawa Eishin (seventh headmaster of Shimmei Musō Ryū 神明夢想流), and also taught Hayashi Rokudayū Morimasa (who subsequently became ninth headmaster of that same school), the Ōmori Ryū had great influence on the development of the Shimmei Musō Ryū.

Ōmori Sōgen 大森 曹玄 (1904–1994). A Zen priest, Jiki Shinkage Ryū swordsman, and founder of the International Zen Dojo. Early in his life Ōmori Sōgen was a student of both Buddhism and swordsmanship: Zen and *ken*. At the age of twenty-one, he began *zen* practice as a lay disciple of Seki Seisetsu, who was then abbot of Tenryūji. A passionate student of Zen, Ōmori notes that he experienced awakening (*satori*) at the age of twenty-nine.

During this same period, at around the age of twenty or twenty-one, Ōmori also became a student of Yamada Jirokichi, fifteenth-generation headmaster of the Jiki Shinkage Ryū. He trained so diligently that, at age twenty-five, he was able to engage in a special Jiki Shikage Ryū ordeal (*shugyō*) with Ōnishi Hidetaka, a senior disciple of Yamada. This ordeal, known as *hyakuhongeiko*, requires the practitioners to perform Hōjō (the Jiki Shinkage Ryū's *omote kata* forms) one hundred times a day for seven days. One repetition of these *kata* takes approximately ten minutes, and requires great concentration, breath control, and display of volition.

Not long after Yamada's death in 1931, Ōmori founded his own line of the Jiki Shinkage Ryū, establishing the Jiki Shin Dōjō in 1934. Interestingly, Ōmori's patrons in this venture were Tōyama Mitsuru and his son Tōyama Ryūsuke, both of whom were important figures in two ultra-right wing secret societies: the Kokuryūkai and the Gen'yōsha. At the Jiki Shin Dōjō, Ōmori taught several traditional disciplines, including sitting in *zen* meditation (*zazen*), *jūdō*, Jiki Shinkage Ryū *kenjutsu*, and calligraphy (*shodō* 書道). However, in combining these other systems in a package with Jiki Shinkage Ryū, he set out on his own path and broke away from the orthodox line headed by his seniors (*sempai*) Kawashima Takashi and Ōnishi Hidetaka. In fact, according to Arahara Bokusui, a right-wing historian of the period, the Jiki Shin Dōjō gave the "impression of having been the inner citadel of the Imperial Way Faction among all the patriotic organizations of the day." (Victoria, 2003: 50)

Ōmori subsequently published *Ken to zen* 『剣と禅』 (Zen and the sword) in 1958, a book which was praised by Zen priest D. T. Suzuki. In spite of this, Ōmori's understanding of the inner secrets of Jiki Shinkage Ryū is controversial, and his expertise with the sword in that system was later questioned by senior practitioners in the orthodox line. In 1972 he established Chozen-ji, the International Zen Dojo in Hawaii. That organization has since become an international enterprise.

Further reading in English:

- Hosokawa, 1999.
- Victoria, 2003: 39–65.

O

omote 表. 1. The "front"; the outer layer of clothing; the obvious; the "face." In this sense *omote* is akin to the term *tatemae*, which indicates an official position or stance on a matter in contrast to what may be the real intent. Simple on the surface, the term *omote*—along with *ura*, *tatemae*, and *honne*—are key, critical concepts in understanding any facet of Japanese culture—including martial culture. (See "Further Reading in English" below.) 2. In a martial-arts context, *omote* was used in many classical traditions (*ryū*) to indicate the first, and often most important, set of technical forms (*kata*). However, as an "entry-level" set, these *kata* are often named and performed in a way that obscures their real intent. In addition, *omote* forms could also be demonstrated in public without fear of compromise. 3. ***Omote*** 表. SHINDŌ MŪSŌ RYŪ—The first series of Shindō Mūsō Ryū *waza*, consisting of twelve *kata*. 4. The side of the tang of a sword that faces outward when the sword is worn. Consequently, the *omote* side of a *tachi* is normally opposite to that of a *katana.* 5. The direction from which an enemy is more easily attacked. For example, if a swordsman stands in a right-foot-forward stance with the sword held pointing forward in a posture such as *seigan no kamae*, the area to the left of his sword and body are considered his *omote*; by contrast, the area to the right side of his posture and weapon are considered his *ura*. See also: *honne; tatemae; ura.*

Further reading in English:

- Doi, 1985.
- Hall, Edward, 1973; 1976; 1983
- Lebra, 1976.

Omote no Bō 表之棒. KATORI SHINTŌ RYŪ—First set of long hardwood staff forms taught in the Tenshinshō-den Katori Shintō Ryū 天真正伝香取神道流. There are six forms (*kata*) included in this set.

Omote no Iai 表居合. KATORI SHINTŌ RYŪ—First set of combative quick-draw swordsmanship forms taught in the Tenshinshō-den Katori Shintō Ryū 天真正伝香取神道流. There are six forms (*kata*) included in this set.

Omote no Tachi 面の太刀 [Var. 表之太刀]. 1. 面の太刀. KASHIMA SHINTŌ RYŪ—Primary combative swordsmanship forms (*kenjutsu kata*). 2. 表之太刀. KATORI SHINTŌ RYŪ—Primary combative swordsmanship forms (*kenjutsu kata*). There are four forms (*kata*) included in this set.

Omote no Naginata 表之薙刀. KATORI SHINTŌ RYŪ—First set of combative halberd forms taught in the Tenshinshō-den Katori Shintō Ryū 天真正伝香取神道流. There are four forms (*kata*) included in this set.

Omote no Shuriken 表之手裏剣. KATORI SHINTŌ RYŪ—First set of combative throwing blades/darts forms taught in the Tenshinshō-den Katori Shintō Ryū 天真正伝香取神道流. There are seven forms (*kata*) included in this set.

Omotesenke 表千家. A school of Japanese tea ceremony (*sadō*) descended from tea master Sen no Rikyū. See: *Sen no Rikyū.*

Ōmoto Kyō 大本教. A religious movement founded in the late 1800s by a Japanese woman named Deguchi Nao. Nao's adopted son-in-law, Onisaburō, enthusiastically promoted the new religion in the early 1900s. Ueshiba Morihei, who became an adherent in 1919, was strongly influenced by the movement's pacifist philosophy in his development of *aikidō*. Morihei's involvement with Ōmoto Kyō was an important factor in his gradual alienation from his Daitō Ryū mentor, Takeda Sōkaku.

Ōmuraji 大連. A minister-level title, the creation of which was attributed to Emperor Suinin.[9] It was apparently held by such families as the Mononobe. See also: *muraji.*

on 1. 唵 <Ch. *an* <Skt. *oṁ* ॐ. BUDDHISM—A pivotal mystic syllable in esoteric Buddhism found at the beginning of a number of spells (Skt. *dhāraṇī* and *mantra*). Traditionally *oṁ* is said to be made up of the syllables *a*, *u*, and *m* which themselves represent the threefold nature of the Buddha: first, the Buddha-nature itself; second, the nature of bliss; and third, the nature of transformation via which the Bud-

---

9 Suinin Tennō 垂仁天皇. (c.29 B.C.E.–c.70 C.E.; r. 31–70). Legendary eleventh emperor of Japan; his actual dates are unknown.

dha nature can appear in any form. Outside the esoteric traditions, the syllable *on* is often used as a focus of meditation. In addition, it appears as a talisman on a number of martial accoutrements at the beginning of particular spells. In many cases, *on* is found written as a stand-alone seed syllable (*shuji*).

on 2. 恩. CLASSICAL WARRIOR IDEAL—Obligation. The concept of obligation and related warrior ideals such as honor (*gi* 義) were emphasized early on in the Japanese war tales (*gunkimono*). Although idealized in those tales, they are clearly elements of reciprocal obligation and respect. As Varley (1994: 37–38) notes in his analysis of the *Mutsu waki* tale, the commander Minamoto no Yoriyoshi is successful in attracting vassals and inspiring their loyalty (*gi*) by "his kindness and generosity, from his loving, personal care of them." Varley goes on to note how those characteristics are related to the self-sacrifice (*kenshin*) ideal espoused in the war tales. It should be noted that such ideals were seldom manifested in reality. See: *bushi no konjō.*

ongyōhō 隠形法 【隱形法】 <Ch. *yinxingfa.* BUDDHISM—Lit. "methods of form-hiding," "methods of invisibility," "methods of concealment." A Buddhist ritual most often associated with the goddess Marishiten. See also: *ongyōin.*

Further reading in English:
• Hall, 1990: 163; 1997: 22.

ongyōin 隠形印 【隱形印】 <Ch. *yinxing yin* [A.k.a. ***hōbyōin*** 宝瓶印; ***Marishiten hōbyōin*** 摩利支天宝瓶印]. 1. Lit. "form-hiding seal" or "invisibility seal." This hand seal/gesture (Skt. *mudrā*) first appears in a section of a seventh-century Chinese Buddhist text[10] devoted to Marishiten. The text describes certain mantras (spells) that, used along with the seal, are supposed to make the devotee invisible.

The mudra (hand gesture/seal) is effected by making a fist with the left hand and either encircling the left fist with the right hand or placing the right hand, palm open and down, over the space made in the center of the fist.

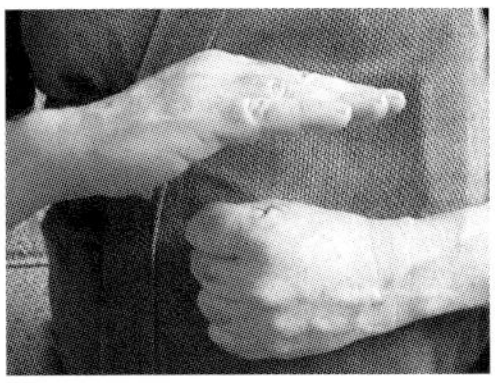

ONGYŌIN
Buddhist tradition

There are several variations of this mudra, some making a fist of the right hand, some the left.

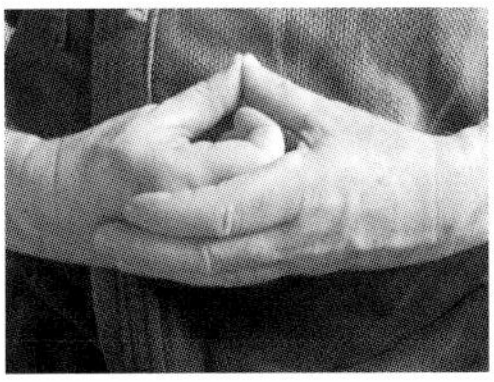

ONGYŌIN
Tenshinshō-den Katori Shintō Ryū

Followers of the martial cult of Marishiten in Japan often depicted Marishiten (or a symbol for the deity) bracketed by the characters

MARISHITEN
Shown between the sun (R) and moon (L) in an old Musō Jūen Ryū 無双柔円流 *densho*

MARISHITEN
Name of the goddess interposed between the sun and moon and two wild boars on a Japanese helmet
(Illustration courtesy Sasama Yoshiko, 1989)

[10] One of the largest texts devoted to Marishiten, this appeared in mid-seventh century China. It is included as the first half of section 10 of the *Collected Dhāraṇī-sūtras* (Ch. *Fo Shuo Tuoluoniji jing* 『佛說陀羅尼集經』, T. 901, XVIII: 869b–874b). See Hall, 1990: 105–147.

for sun and moon. According to Sasama Yoshihiko, a recognized expert on Japanese arms, armor, and the esoteric art that adorns them, Marishiten was often represented on helmets and other pieces of armor simply by the application of a sun and moon motif; no actual depiction of the goddess herself was needed. (Sasama, interviews, 1985–1990).

This also corresponds to the *ongyōin*: if the left hand is curved around the right fist, the hands take on the shape of the Chinese characters for sun 日 and moon 月. When placed together, they form the compound character *myō* 明 (Ch. *ming*).

In some Buddhist combative traditions in China—such as Shaolin—practitioners associated this sun-and-moon Ming seal with the Ming dynasty. Perhaps coincidentally, the character "Ming" literally means "bright" or "shining" and the root of the Sanskrit term for Marishiten (Mārīcī-devī) means "shining mote."

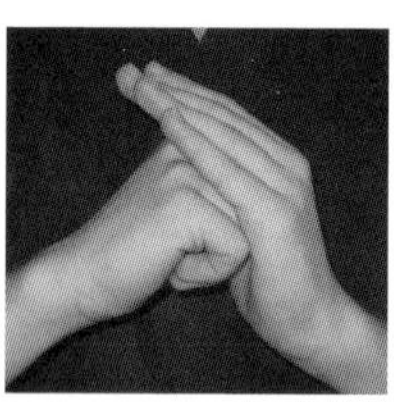

SHAOLIN *QUANFA* SALUTE
Illustration of the character for Ming (dynasty) and its comparison with the *ongyōin* or "Shaolin salute."

The fact that secret Daoist and Buddhist martial societies were often instrumental in the creation of Chinese dynasties such as the Ming may also relate to this. 2. The *ongyōin* is also referred to as the *hōbyōin* 宝瓶印 or Marishiten *hōbyōin* 摩利支天宝瓶印, lit. "Seal of the Precious Receptacle of Marishiten." Early development of the Marishiten cult took place in northwest India, where a wide variety of cultures—from western, central, southern, and eastern Asia—came together. Because of this, elements of several religious traditions and cultures, including Zoroastrianism, can be found within the cult. In addition to parallels with the Persian cult of Mithraism, it is also apparent that the form of this seal—a bottle or receptacle with a goddess ensconced inside—may have been influenced by the cult of the genie-in-a-bottle in Mideastern Semitic cultures.

SHAOLIN SALUTE (*REIHAISHIKI*)[11]
(Photograph from an old Chinese boxing manual)

3. The ninth seal (mudra) of the Kujihō. This seal corresponds with *zen* 前, the ninth character of the Kuji, and the Buddhist deity Marishiten.

ongyōjutsu 隠形術【隠形術】. Lit. "form-hiding skills," "concealment skills." Also called ***onshinjutsu*** 隠身術【隠身術】; lit. "body-hiding skills" or, more subtly, "skills for hiding one's soul/mind/self." This term encompasses a number of arts and skills for "disappearing" used by traditional espionage agents. These skills were generally divided into two categories: methods of disappearing by melting away (*inpō*); and methods of disappearing by escape (*tonpō*). Each of these categories contained a dozen or more tactics. See also: *ninjutsu; ongyōhō; ongyōin.*

Ongyō no ju 隠形の呪【隠形の呪】. A spell of invisibility taken from a Tantric Buddhist text devoted to Marishiten.[12] In the eighth-century

[11] *Reihaishiki* 令牌式 <Ch. *lingpaishi.*

[12] This ritual manual is one of the shortest texts devoted to Marishiten and covers only twenty-two lines in the Taishō Canon. Its title is the *Single Seal Ritual of Marishiten* (Ch. *Molizhitian yiyinfa* 『摩利支天一印法』, T. 1259, XXI: 285c). See Hall, 1990: 171–173.

Chinese text this spell is associated with the Invisibility Seal of Marishiten. The Ongyō no ju was later used in both Buddhist and Shugendō ritual manuals in Japan. There are several variant renderings in Japanese, but the one closest to the Chinese text is *on ajichā marishi sowaka*.[13] The spell is said to have been used with various rituals such as the Quail Obscuration Ritual (Uzura *kakure* 鶉隠れ) and the Kannon Obscuration Ritual (Kannon *gakure* 観音隠れ), which are martial rituals for making oneself invisible.

oni 鬼. A demon; a goblin.

onikote 鬼小手 [Var. ***uchikote*** 打小手; also pronounced ***onigote***]. Padded gloves (*kote*) used by various branches of the Ittō Ryū (1).

Ōnin no Ran 応仁乱【應仁亂】. A civil war which began during the Ōnin era. It lasted approximately ten years (1467–1477), ushering in the Warring States period (Sengoku Jidai). The Ōnin no Ran was chronicled in the *Sandaiki*.

Further reading in English:

- Varley (translation), 1967.

oni no tachi 魔之太刀 [Also read ***ma no tachi***]. Lit. "demon sword," "magic sword," "invisible sword." YAGYŪ SHINKAGE RYŪ—Technique in which the sword is quickly rotated around in a vertical circle with the right hand. In contrast to *nagashi*—a large movement in which the sword rotates around the head—the sword inscribes a vertical circle pivoting on the right wrist.

Ōnishi Hidetaka 大西 英隆 (1906–1966). JIKI SHINKAGE RYŪ—Recognized as seventeenth headmaster by the Jiki Shinkage Ryū 直心影流. Ōnishi was one of Yamada Jirokichi's most senior students at the time of the latter's death in 1931. Ōnishi published *Kensei: Yamada Jirokichi Sensei no shōgai*『剣聖 山田次郎吉先生の生涯』(Sword saint: The life of Yamada Jirokichi sensei) in 1956. See also: *Jiki Shinkage Ryū*.

ŌNISHI HIDETAKA
Seventeenth-generation headmaster of the Jiki Shinkage Ryū
(Photograph courtesy Namiki Yasushi)

o-niwaban お庭番 [Var. ***niwaban*** 庭番]. 1. A guard of the inner garden or inner courtyard. 2. Variant term for an espionage agent. However, according to Nawa (1972: 47), the term *o-niwaban* was specifically applied to *bakufu* operatives engaged in secret missions, spying, etc. See: *ninjutsu*.

Onjōji 園城寺. See: *Miidera*.

onkitōsho 御祈祷所. A Kamakura-period term referring to temples throughout Japan that received special patronage and protection from the Kamakura *bakufu*. The term literally means "prayer centers."

onkō 遠候. An espionage agent. See: *mitsumono*; *ninja*.

onmitsu 隠密【隱密】[Also read ***immitsu***]. This term refers to both espionage and espionage agents used by the Tokugawa shogunate. Many groups of Japanese espionage agents were active during the Warring States period (Sengoku Jidai). At the beginning of the Edo period, *shōgun* Tokugawa Ieyasu organized these groups into agents of his shogunate. As this organization was called the Kōgi Onmitsu, the agents were known as *onmitsu*. See: *ninjutsu*.

onmitsu kōdō 隠密行動【隱密行動】. Espionage operations.

onmyō 陰陽. See: *in'yō*.

Onmyōdō 陰陽道. [Also read ***On'yōdō, In'yōdō***]. Daoism; Daoist divination.

13 As noted, a number of variations of this spell are found in Japan. Some even add a proper Sanskrit grammatical ending to the term; e.g., *marishiei* <Skt. *mārīcyai*. However, while this spell associates Marishiten with the Hindu solar deity Āditya, it is not found in any original Sanskrit texts devoted to Marishiten. See Hall, 1990: 50, 172, 228.

onna men 女面. Lit. "woman's face." A common type of armored mask (*mempō*) designed to look like a woman's face.

on-ninjutsu 陰忍術. See: *innin no jutsu.*

onnin no jutsu 陰忍術. See: *innin no jutsu.*

ono 斧. 1. A war axe. As this weapon was used primarily in historical eras predating the rise of the classical martial schools, few classical *ryū* included it in their curriculum. 2. A pole-arm axe used by the *yamabushi* as one of their mountain tools. For illustration, see: *i no me kizamitaru masakari.*

Onodera Kōhō 小野寺 光峰. Onodera Kōhō was a direct disciple of Hakkō Ryū 八光流 founder Okuyama Yoshiji. Onodera subsequently founded a branch school he called the Ōshin Ryū 大心流.

Ono Ha Ittō Ryū 小野派一刀流. A branch tradition of Itō Ittōsai Kagehisa's Ittō Ryū founded by Ono Jirōemon Tadaaki. The Ono Ha is the oldest recognized line of Ittō Ryū, as its founder was a direct disciple of Itō Ittōsai.

The following is a representative example of the Ono Ha Ittō Ryū curriculum. For a full list see Sasamori, 1986:

Ono Ha Ittō Ryū Curriculum

Set	Number of *kata*
Kumitachi 組太刀 **(sword forms)**	
Ōdachi 大太刀 (Longsword vs. longsword techniques)	60
Kodachi 小太刀 (Short sword vs. longsword techniques)	9
Ai Kodachi 合小太刀 (Short sword vs. short sword techniques)	8
Sanjū 三重 (Longsword vs. longsword techniques)	3
Habiki 刃引 (Techniques practiced with dull-edged swords)	11
Hichū no Hi Gokui 秘中の秘極意 **(secret transmission)**	
Hoshatō 払捨刀 ("Throwing off" sword techniques)	10
Kōjō Gokui 高上極意 **(Highest secret transmission)**	
Goten 五点 (The five)	5
Hakiri Ai ハキリ合 (Dull-edged sword techniques)	12
Kuka no Tachi 九個之太刀 (The nine)	9
Ta Ryū Kachi no Tachi 他流勝之太刀 (Techniques to defeat other schools)	12
Battō 抜刀 **(Quick-draw swordsmanship)**	
Tsumeza Battō 詰座抜刀 (Seated quick-draw sword techniques)	12
Tsumeza Battō･Ai Kodachi 詰座抜刀･合小太刀 (Seated quick-draw sword techniques—*kodachi* vs. *kodachi*)	12
Tachiai Battō 立会抜刀 Standing quick-draw sword techniques	5

See also: *Goten no Shidai; Hokushin Ittō Ryū; Ittō Ryū; Ittō Shōden Mutō Ryū; Ittō Ryū; Kinshichōō Ken; Kogen Ittō Ryū; Nakanishi Ha Ittō Ryū; and Ono Jirōemon Tadaaki.*

Further reading in English:

- Skoss (2002): 109–127.

Ono Jirōemon Tadaaki 小野 次郎右衛門 忠明 [A.k.a. ***Mikogami Tenzen*** 神子上 典膳] (?–1628). Progenitor of the Ono Ha Ittō Ryū. Ono was originally a retainer of Satomi Awa no Kami; his birth name was Mikogami Tenzen. He was challenged to a duel by Itō Ittōsai and soundly defeated, subsequently becoming Itō's student. After succeeding his master as head of the Ittō Ryū, he changed his name to Ono Tadaaki. He went on to become *kenjutsu shinanyaku* (instructor of swordsmanship) to Tokugawa Hidetada, the second Tokugawa *shōgun*, and also served the third Tokugawa *shōgun* Iemitsu. Ono's swordsmanship is said to have rivaled that of the other shogunal instructor, Yagyū Munenori of the Shinkage Ryū, but the two men never met in a duel.

Further reading in English:

- Hurst, 1998: 60–61.
- Skoss, 2002: 109–127
- Sugawara, 1985: 183–200.

Ōno Matabei Ikkan 大野 又兵衛 一貫 [A.k.a. ***Chūdayū*** 忠大夫] (1753–1816). Founder of the Ikkan Ryū (2) 一貫流, a comprehensive martial school. Ōno, who hailed from the Tottori domain, trained in the combative archery system of Ōguchi Gonkurō Shiseki, founder of Ōguchi Ryū 大口流 *kyūjutsu*; and the spearmanship (*sōjutsu*) of Ijiri Buzaemon Harutsune of the Hikita Kage Ryū 疋田陰流. Ōno was also a student of the combative

Ono Ha Ittō Ryū
小野派一刀流
(abbreviated lineage)

Ono Jirōemon Tadaaki
小野 次郎右衛門 忠明
(Mikogami Tenzen 神子上 典膳)
Ittō Ryū
一刀流
(Tadaaki had at least twelve direct disciples who mastered his system.)

Ono Jirōemon Tadatsune
小野 次郎右衛門 忠常
(Itō Jirōzaemon no jō 伊藤 次郎左衛門尉)
Ono Ha Ittō Ryū
小野派一刀流
(Tadatsune had at least seven disciples who mastered his system.)

Ono Tadao
小野 忠於
(1657–1715)

Ono Tadaichi
小野 忠一
(c.1680–c.1720)

Ono Sukekurō Tadahisa
小野 助九郎 忠久
(1689–1738)
Ono Ha Ittō Ryū
小野派一刀流

Nakanishi Chūta Tanesada
中西 忠太 子定
Nakanishi Ha Ittō Ryū
中西派一刀流

Ono Jirōemon Tadakata
小野 次郎右衛門 忠方
(1712–1749)
Ono Ha Ittō Ryū

Ono Jiroemon Tadayoshi
小野 次郎右衛門 忠喜
(1732–1798)
Ono Ha Ittō Ryū

Nakanishi Chūzō Tanetake
中西 忠蔵 子武
Nakanishi Ha Ittō Ryū

Ono Jirōemon Tadataka
小野 次郎右衛門 忠孝
Ono Ha Ittō Ryū
(Continues in several lines)

Nakanishi Chūta (Itarō) Tsuguhiro
中西 忠太(伊太郎)子啓
Nakanishi Ha Ittō Ryū

Takayanagi Matashirō Yoshimasa
高柳 又四郎 義正
Toda Ryū
戸田流

Nakanishi Chūbei Tsugumasa
中西 忠兵衛 子正
(At least 8 disciples are known.)
Nakanishi Ha Ittō Ryū

Terada Goemon Muneari
寺田 五右衛門 宗有
Tenshin Ittō Ryū
天真一刀流

Nakanishi Chūbei Tsuguuke
中西 忠兵衛 子受
Nakanishi Ha Ittō Ryū

Asari Matashichirō Yoshinobu
浅利 又七郎 義信
Asari Ryū
浅利流

Chiba Shūsaku Narimasa
千葉 周作 成政
(1794–1855)
Hokushin Ittō Ryū
北辰一刀流

Nakanishi Itarō Tsugumichi
中西 猪太郎 子路
Nakanishi Ha Ittō Ryū

Asari Matashichirō Yoshiaki
浅利 又七郎 義明
(c.1790–c.1850)
Asari Ryū

(Nakanishi Ha continues for many generations in several lines)

Yamaoka Tesshū
山岡 鉄舟
(1836–1888)
Ittō Shōden Mutō Ryū
一刀正伝無刀流

swordsmanship of the Musashi Emmei Ryū 武蔵円明流 under Takasaka Kagetsuna.

Ōno Matsuemon 大野 松右衛門. See: *Yagyū Matsuemon Munenobu.*

Ōno Ryū 大野流. A system of gunnery (*hōjutsu*) founded by a masterless samurai from Bishū named Torii. During the early to mid-1700s, one of the fifth-generation inheritors of the tradition, Chikamatsu Hikonoshin Shigenori, integrated this school with Imagawa Ryū gunnery (*hōjutsu*) into a revised school of firearms called Jitoku Ryū 自得流. Around the same time, in a show of respect to the fourth headmaster, another fifth-generation inheritor of the tradition, Hara Kiuemon Masanori, began calling the tradition "Ōno Ryū" so that it stood in contrast to Chikamatsu's reformed school.

Ōno Ryū
大野流
(abbreviated lineage)

1. Torii
初代　鳥居
(masterless samurai [*rōnin*])

2. Ban Kaemon Yoshitomo
二代　伴 嘉右衛門 資友
(Retainer [*kashin*] of the Kuroda clan)

3. Ōno Sagouemon Yoshiki
三代　大野 左五右衛門 吉規
(Retainer [*kashin*] of the Hotta clan)

4. Ōno Uemon Takenori
四代　大野 宇右衛門 武範

5. Hara Kiuemon Masanori 五代　原 喜右衛門 政軌 **Ōno Ryū** 大野流	5. Chikamatsu Hikonoshin Shigenori 五代　近松 彦之進 茂矩 **Jitoku Ryū** 自得流

Ōno Shōgen 大野 将監. Founded the Kurama Ryū 鞍馬流, a system of combative swordsmanship (*kenjutsu*) and quick-draw sword arts (*iaijutsu*), during the late 1500s.

Ono Tetsutarō 小野 鉄太郎【小野鐵太郎】. See: *Yamaoka Tesshū.*

onshinjutsu 隠身術【隱身術】. See: *ongyōjutsu.*

onteki 怨敵. A malicious, hateful, or bitter enemy; a sworn enemy.

on'yōji 陰陽師. A master of divination; a fortuneteller.

oō 経鷲【經鷲】. See: *heō.*

origane 折金. See: *soritsuno.*

ōryōshi 押領使. A tenth- and eleventh-century provincial military post. *Ōryōshi* translates as "territory-suppressing envoy"; the title indicated a provincial sheriff. Provincial governors sometimes awarded this post to local warrior leaders in order to bring in rural support troops. In that case it was called "provincial territory-suppressing envoy" (*shokoku ōryōshi*). See also: *tsuibushi.*

Os'! おす! [Var. ***Ōs'!*** おおす!]. See: *Ossu!*

osaekomi waza 押込技 [Var. 抑込技]. KŌDŌKAN JŪDŌ—A set of five hold-down/pinning techniques. The *osaekomi waza* are a sub-category of the Katame no Kata in Kōdōkan Jūdō.

osame 収め【收め】. The process of returning a weapon to a "ready" or "normal" position, usually at the end of a prearranged combative form (*kata*) or drill.

Ō Sekiguchi Ryū 大関口流【大關口流】. See: *Ko Sekiguchi Ryū.*

ōsensei 1. 大先生. Lit. "great teacher" or "honored master." A term of respect for an older or most senior teacher (*sensei*) when other teachers in a tradition are present.

ōsensei 2. 翁先生 [Often Romanized as ***O-sensei***]. Lit. "venerable teacher" or "elder master." This term is used in reference to the founder of *aikidō*, Ueshiba Morihei.

Ose Yosazaemon Osamune 小瀬 与三左衛門 長宗. See: *Tose Yosazaemon Osamune.*

oshikiiuchi 御敷居内. See: *oshikiuchi.*

oshikiuchi 御式内 [Var. ***oshikiiuchi*** 御敷居内]. A family-based martial system of the Takeda clan. There is some controversy over what this art actually entailed. *Oshikiuchi* was apparently a system of formal etiquette and *jūjutsu*-type arts developed for, and used exclusively by, the upper-class samurai of Aizu domain. In this way it may have been somewhat like the Ogasawara Ryū or Tatsumi Ryū, both of which contain extensive training in etiquette as well as combative systems. The context of the art indicates that it was used inside the precincts of the Aizu lord's court and residence, where warriors would be in more formal dress and wearing restrictive clothing such as *nagabakama*.

Around the time of the dissolution of the Aizu domain in 1871, the headmastership of this art was in the hands of a warrior-*cum*-Shintō priest of the Nikkō Tōshōgu shrine named Saigō Tanomo Chikanori (a.k.a. Hoshina Chikanori). In 1877 Chikanori began teaching *oshikiuchi* to a nine-year-old prodigy named Shida Shirō. Shida mastered *oshikiuchi* and, later moving to Tōkyō for his education, joined Kanō's Kōdōkan, where he quickly mastered *jūdō* also. However, due to the pressures of loyalty placed on Shirō by Chikanori, Shirō left Tōkyō, Kanō's *jūdō*, and Chikanori's *oshikiuchi*, and moved to far-away Kyūshū. This left Saigō Chikanori without an inheritor for *oshikiuchi*. So, in 1898 Chikanori began teaching this art to Takeda Sōkaku, a former samurai (*shizoku*) who hailed from Aizu. Sōkaku quickly mastered *oshikiuchi* and began modifying it in combination with other combative arts he had mastered for use by police and military units. By 1908 he was instructing police units in Hokkaidō in this reformed art, which he called "Daitō Ryū *jūjutsu*." Sōkaku apparently did not pass on *oshikiuchi* as a separate system to anyone, but instead incorporated it into his Daitō Ryū system as *aikijūjutsu*. In reviewing the Daitō Ryū curriculum as it exists today, it appears that the fifty-three techniques of Takeda's *Aiki no jutsu* were probably derived from *oshikiuchi*, while the thirty-six techniques of the *Hiden ōgi mokuroku* are a synthesis of Takeda-clan *jūjutsu* and *oshikiuchi*. See also: *aiki*.

Further reading in English:

- Pranin, 1996: 22.
- Draeger, 1974: 137–140.

Ōshin Ryū 応心流【應心流】. Branch tradition of Anazawa Ryū taught in Owari domain (present-day Aichi prefecture). This line,which specialized in combative long-hafted glaive arts (*naginatajutsu*), attributed its origin during the mid-1500s to Anazawa Tonomonosuke Moriyoshi and his direct disciple (*deshi*) Aoki Owari no Kami Nobutatsu.

oshō 和尚 [Also read ***wajō*** and ***kashō*** (see below)] <Ch. *heshang* <Skt. *upādhyāya*. BUDDHISM—Originally used as a title for a precepts master, *oshō* later became a title of respect for a virtuous monk or teacher. The pronunciation varied among the sects in Japan: *oshō* in Zen Shū and Jōdo Shū; *wajō* in Hossō Shū, Ritsu Shū, and Shingon Shū; and *kashō* in Tendai Shū.

ōshō 王将【王將】[Abbr. as ***ō*** 王]. SHŌGI—Lit. "ruling general" or "royal general." In the Japanese strategic game of *shōgi*, the *ōshō* is equivalent to the "white" king in chess; however, there are no black or white colored pieces in *shōgi*.

Ōshū gosannen ki 『奥州後三年記』(Chronicle of the Later Three Years' War in Mutsu province). A semi-historical account of the Later Three Years' War (Gosannen no Eki) which took place from 1086 to 1089. The chronicle is made even more interesting in that it provides the source for the legend of one of the great Japanese war heroes, Minamoto no Yoshiie.

ōsode 大袖. Lit. "great sleeve." The armored shield/sleeves found on early medieval period "great armor" (*ōyoroi*). For photo see: *ōyoroi*.

Osu! おす! See: *Ossu!*

Ossu! おっす! (Also written 押忍) [Var. ***Ōsu!*** おおす!; ***Osu!*** おす!]. Lit. "Hi!"; "Yes, sir!"; "Please train with me!" The exclamation *Ossu!* is most often used as a greeting by young men engaged in athletic activities, specifically those of an agonistic nature. Women rarely use the term, even when engaged in the same activities. Outside training situations, the use of *Ossu!* is considered vulgar and boorish.

The origins of the expression are obscure, but there are several theories. One proposes that *Ossu!* is a contraction of the common Japanese greeting, *ohayō gozaimasu* (lit. "it's early"; "good morning") (Mizutani, 2003). In support of this, *Ossu!* is used as a greeting among many practitioners of modern martial/sportive/spiritual arts (*budō*), especially those practiced in collegiate or military environments. A second theory (Drossoulakis, 2003) analyzes the Chinese characters most often used to write *Ossu!*: 押忍.[14] The first (押), read *osu*, literally means "to push," while the second (忍), read *shinobu*, literally means "to endure." Drossoulakis, a Shōtōkan *karate* practitioner, notes the term was first used in the Imperial Japanese Navy Officers' Academy in the early twentieth century, but provides no reference in support of this. He also points out that the use of the term became widespread among college *karate* organizations which developed in the militaristic climate of 1930s Japan. A third commonly proposed theory is that the term was derived from the expression *onegai shimasu* お願いします, "I beg your favor." This common Japanese request is often used in martial training situations when a junior requests a lesson or assistance from a senior. Yet another proposed origin notes the relationship of *Ossu!* to the term *ōse*仰せ, which literally means, "As you say!" "As you wish!" or "Yes, sir!" in Japanese military jargon. ¶ *Ōse ni shitagaimashō* 仰せに従いましょう, "I shall obey your order! ¶ *Nandemo ōse no mama ni itashimasu* 何でも仰せのままにいたします, "I am at you service!"

Ōsu! おおす. See: *Ōssu !*

Otagai ni rei! お互いに礼! "Bow to each other!" A command often used in modern martial training halls (*dōjō*).

Ōtake Risuke 大竹 利典. Current (2009) chief instructor (*shihan*) of Tenshinshō-den Katori Shintō Ryū.

Otani Seiichirō 男谷 精一郎. See: *Odani Nobutomo.*

Otani Shimōsa no Kami Seiichirō 男谷 下總守 精一郎. See: *Odani Nobutomo.*

otera 御寺 [Var. お寺]. A Buddhist temple. See: *tera.*

otokodate 男伊達 [Var. 男立]. Chivalrous, vagrant samurai (*rōnin*). See: *machi yakko.*

otokogi 侠気【俠氣】[Also read: ***kyōki***]. Var. ***kyōkotsu*** 侠骨]. A chivalrous spirit.

otomeryū 御留流. A martial tradition which became the official system of a clan or feudal domain (*han*).

Ōtomo 大伴. An ancient Yamato-period noble family that specialized in martial arts. They were thought to have been brothers-in-arms with the first emperor, Jimmu Tennō.[15] During the Yamato Court period (fifth and sixth centuries) the Ōtomo were in charge of the archery guard at the imperial palace. Their leader was given the title Ōtomo no Muraji (Chief of the Ōtomo).

Ōtomo no Muraji 大伴連. Chief of the Ōtomo. See: *Ōtomo.*

ōtoneri 大舎人. An imperial bodyguard or retainer. See: *toneri.*

otoya 乙矢 [Var. 兄矢; 弟矢]. The second of two arrows fired in the practice of Japanese archery (*kyūdō*). (The first arrow is called the *haya.*) Japanese arrows use fletching taken from both wings of a bird, so the feathers curve left or right. The *otoya* has fletching which curves to the right, so the arrow rotates counter clockwise in flight.

Ōtsubō Ryū 大坪流. The first classical martial school (*ryū*) to systematize combative horsemanship (*bajutsu*). This organization was established in the early 1400s by Ōtsubō Yoshihide Dōzen, a retainer attached to *shōgun* Ashikaga Yoshimitsu[16] and Ashikaga Yoshimochi.[17] Before founding his own system, Ōtsubō studied Ogasawara Ryū mounted archery under Ogasawara Shinano no Kami Masanaga 小笠原 信濃守 政長. Subsequently, after a period of religious austerities at Kashima Jingū, he experienced a vision concerning the

[14] The character compound 押忍 was originally used as a female personal name pronounced "Oshino." Only since the early twentieth century has this compound been read "*ossu*" and used in a *budō* context. The Japanese often assign unusual readings to Chinese characters which have meanings to which they are emotionally attached.

[15] Jimmu Tennō (c.660–c.585 B.C.E.). The legendary first emperor of Japan; his actual dates are not known.

[16] Ashikaga Yoshimitsu 足利義満 (1358–1408; r.1368–1394). Third Ashikaga *shōgun*.

[17] Ashikaga Yoshimochi 足利義持 (1386–1428; r.1394–1423). Fourth Ashikaga *shōgun*.

design of a saddle and stirrup (*musō no kura*); this became a core element of his school.

Ōtsubō Shihō 大坪 指方 (1906–1992). A twenty-first-generation successor of the Owari Yagyū Shinkage Ryū 尾張柳生新陰流, and progenitor of the Ōtsubō line of the Yagyū Shinkage Ryū. Ōtsubō became a student of Yagyū Genshū in 1920, and trained in the Owari Yagyū Shinkage Ryū most of his life. He was privy to the most intimate secrets of the *ryū* through his teachers—nineteenth headmaster Yagyū Toshichika (Genshū) and twentieth headmaster Yagyū Toshinaga (Genchō) of the Owari Yagyū Shinkage Ryū. Ōtsubō also investigated the writings and teachings of the Edo Yagyū Shinkage Ryū 江戸柳生新陰流. He was awarded the Yagyū Shinkage Ryū *inka* for full mastery of the *ryū*, which made him a twenty-first-generation successor.

ŌTSUBŌ SHIHŌ, TWENTY-FIRST-GENERATION SUCCESSOR OF THE SHINKAGE RYŪ; PROGENITOR OF THE ŌTSUBO LINE OF THE SHINKAGE RYŪ
Demonstrating Sangakuen no Tachi at Kashima Jingū, 1979
(Photograph courtesy Lynn Riggs)

Ōtsubō Yoshihide Dōzen 大坪 慶秀 道禅【大坪慶秀道禪】. Founder of the Ōtsubō Ryū, a school of combative horsemanship (*bajutsu*) in the early fifteenth century.

otsukai お使. See: *kami no otsukai.*

Ōtsuka Hironori 大塚 博紀 (1892–1982). Founder of Wadō Ryū 和道流 *karate* around 1933. Ōtsuka had already received a full license (*menkyo kaiden*) in Yōshin Ryū 楊心流 *jūjutsu* in 1922 when he began training in *karate* with Funakoshi Gichin. By 1929 he had become one of Funakoshi's assistant instructors. However, Ōtsuka also began training with another Okinawan *karate* expert, Motobu Chōki. This evidently led to a rift between Funakoshi and Ōtsuka, and the latter left to found his own style. He continued to modify his system over the next ten years, but did not name it Wadō Ryū until 1940.

Ōtsuka Yasuyuki 大塚 保之. Current (2009) headmaster of the Meifu Shinkage Ryū 明府真影流, a school specializing in small throwing blades and darts (*shurikenjutsu*). Ōtsuka has recently published a book on this school titled *Meifu Shinkage Ryū shurikenjutsu no susume* 『明府真影流手裏剣術のススメ』 (The art of Meifu Shinkage Ryū throwing darts).

Ōuma jirushi 『大馬印』. 1. A compendium of the heraldry of the Warring States period written by the Buddhist monk Kyūan in 1650. It contains text and illustrations of the family crests, and the devices on which they were displayed, from most of the battles of that period. 2. ***ōumajirushi*** 大馬印. A large battle standard. See: *umajirushi.*

o-umamawarishū 御馬廻衆. See: *umamawari.*

owari 終り. Finished; ended.

Owari Han 尾張藩. The feudal domain of Owari (present-day Aichi prefecture) during the reign of the Tokugawa shogunate.

Owari Kan Ryū 尾張貫流 [A.k.a. ***Ikkei Ryū*** 一分流; ***Itō Ryū Kan Ryū*** 伊東流管流; ***Kan Ryū*** 管流; ***Owari Kan Ryū Sōjutsu*** ~槍術]. The Kan Ryū was founded in 1671 by Tsuda Gonnojō Nobuyuki (1654–1698). Tsuda was an outstanding warrior who, at the age of sixteen, had mastered and received a license (*menkyo*) in the spear arts of Saburi Enuemon Tadamura's Itō Ryū 伊東流. Though he called his system Itō Ryū Kan Ryū 伊東流管流 at first, Tsuda later shortened the name to Kan Ryū 貫流, although it was sometimes referred to as Ikkei Ryū 一分流 (Ikkei being one of Tsuda's names).

This system was originally a comprehensive field-combat system (*sōgo bujutsu*) which included combative application of the sword (*kenjutsu* with *tachi, kodachi,* and *katana*), small throwing blades and darts (*shurikenjutsu*), iron fan (*tessen*), pipe spear (*kudayari*), and combative quick-draw swordsmanship (*iaijutsu*). Kan Ryū today concentrates on combative spearmanship (*sōjutsu*).

As a positive combative system, the Kan Ryū emphasizes *sen no sen*; that is, overwhelming attacks so that the opponent is unable to gain the initiative. In order to instill this attitude in its practitioners—and in contrast to many classical traditions—Kan Ryū *sōjutsu* requires trainees begin with mock combat (*shiai*) and only later begin learning prearranged combative forms (*kata*). In *shiai*, opponents are armed with *kudayari* (pipe spear) held in the forward hand. The spear may be powered by either the left or right arm, depending on the stance.

From 1913 through 1955, seventh-generation headmaster Kambe Takeyasu trained extensively in the Yagyū Shinkage Ryū under both Yagyū Genshū and his successor Yagyū Genchō. In this way Kambe was able to incorporate the complete teachings of both the Yagyū Shinkage Ryū and the Hikita Kage Ryū into this tradition. This also included several original Shinkage Ryū spear *kata*.

Owari Yagyū Shinkage Ryū 尾張柳生新陰流 [A.k.a. ***Yagyū Shinkage Ryū Heihō*** 柳生新陰流; ***Yagyū Ryū*** 柳生流]. Descending from Yagyū Hyōgonosuke Toshiyoshi (Yagyū Muneyoshi's grandson), this branch of the Yagyū Shinkage Ryū has stood in contrast to the Edo Yagyū Shinkage Ryū since the early 1600s. The Owari line (based in Owari, present-day Nagoya) continues down to the present, and is currently under the direction of twenty-second headmaster Yagyū Kōichi.

Owari Yagyū Shinkage Ryū *densho*

Certificate (*menjō*) / license (*menkyo*):

- Omote「表」
- Ōmarobashi「大転」
- Komarobashi「小転」
- Tengushō「天狗抄」
- Tengushō-oku「天狗抄奥」
- Mokuroku「目録」
- Inka「印可」

The early Owari line appears to have consisted of approximately thirteen sets of *kata* involving longsword (*katana*) and short sword (*kodachi*):

Sword curriculum	**Number of *kata***
• Empi no Tachi 燕飛之太刀	6 (+2 oku)
• Nana Tachi 七太刀	7
• Sangakuen no Tachi 三学圓之太	5
• Kuka no Tachi 九箇之太刀	9
• Tengushō 天狗抄	8
• Okugi no Tachi 奥義之太刀	6
• Gokui no Tachi 極意之太刀 (Hakka no Hisshō 八箇必勝)	8
• Ōmarobashi 大轉	3
• Komarobashi 小轉	3
• Mutōdori 無刀取	3
• Zamutōdori 座無刀取	3
• Mutōdori 無刀取	5

ORIGINAL *DENSHO* OF THE SHINKAGE RYŪ
Passed from Kamiizumi Ise no Kami Nobutsuna to Yagyū Sekishūsai Muneyoshi in 1565 and 1566
(Yagyū family archives)

oyakata 親方. A house lord; the head of a clan; a boss or chief.

Ōyama Masutatsu 大山 倍達 [A.k.a. Mas' Ōyama] (1923–1994). Founder of Kyokushin *karatedō*. Ōyama was born Choi Yeong-eui in Korea (under Japanese occupation in 1923) but spent most of his life in Japan. He began his martial-arts journey on his sister's farm in Manchuria at the age of nine. There he trained in Chinese boxing (Ch. *quanfa*) with Li Xiangzhi 李相志, a seasonal worker. In 1938 Ōyama moved to Japan to train at the Imperial Army Aviation School in Yamanashi. After the war in 1946 he entered Waseda University, where he studied sports education. Around the same time, he also became a student of Shōtōkan 松涛館 *karate* under Funakoshi Gichin. Later he moved on to Gōjū Ryū *karatedō*, first with Sō Neichū 曹寧柱, a Korean student of Yamaguchi Gōgen, and with later Yamaguchi himself. In 1957 Ōyama founded his own eclectic system of *karatedō* which he called Kyokushin 極真 (lit. "ultimate truth"),

Owari Yagyū Shinkage Ryū

尾張柳生新陰流

(abbreviated lineage)

Kamiizumi Ise no Kami Nobutsuna
上泉 伊勢守 信綱
Shinkage Ryū
新陰流

↓

Yagyū Sekishūsai Tajima no Kami Muneyoshi
柳生 石舟斎 但馬守 宗厳
(1529–1606)
Yagyū Shinkage Ryū
柳生新陰流

↓ (students of Muneyoshi)

- Yagyū Shinjirō Yoshikatsu
  柳生 新次郎 厳勝
  (1552–1617)
  (Muneyoshi's eldest son; severely wounded in battle in Tatsuichi in 1571)
- 3. Yagyū Hyōgonosuke Toshitoshi
  柳生 兵庫助 利厳
  (1579–1650)
  (Yoshikatsu's second son, recognized as founder of the Owari line; became retainer to Tokugawa Yoshinao, lord of Owari, in1615)
  Owari Yagyū Shinkage Ryū
  尾張柳生新陰流
- Yagyū Tajima no Kami Munenori
  柳生 但馬守 宗矩
  (1571–1646)
  (Muneyoshi's youngest son; became a retainer to Tokugawa Ieyasu in 1594)
  Edo Yagyū Shinkage Ryū
  江戸柳生新陰流
- Yagyū Matsuemon Munenobu
  柳生 松右衛門 宗信
  (Matsuno Uemon Munenobu)
  (松野 右衛門 宗信)
  Yagyū Shinkage Ryū
  柳生新陰流

↓ (from 3. Yagyū Hyōgonosuke Toshitoshi)

4. Tokugawa Yoshitada
徳川 義直
(c. 1601–c. 1670)

5. Yagyū Shichirō Hyōgo Toshikane
柳生 七郎 兵庫 厳包
(1625–1694)

6. Tokugawa Mitsutomo
徳川 光友
(c. 1630–c. 1700)

7. Tokugawa Tsunanari
徳川 綱誠
(c. 1660–c. 1715)

8. Yagyū Hyōgo Toshinobu
柳生 兵庫 厳延
(1663–1720)

9. Tokugawa Yoshimichi
徳川 吉通
(c. 1690–c. 1760)

10. Yagyū Rokurobei Toshitomo
柳生 六郎兵衛 厳儔
(1699–1756)

11. Yagyū Hyōsuke Toshiharu
柳生 兵助 厳春
(1741–1808)

12. Tokugawa Haruyuki Chūjō Haruyuki
徳川 宰相 中将 治行
(17??–1812)

13. Yagyū Matauemon Toshiyuki
柳生 又右衛門 厳之
(17??–1812)

14. Yagyū Heisuke Toshihisa
柳生 平助 厳久
(1792–1821)

15. Tokugawa Naritomo
徳川 斎朝
(1793–1850)

16. Yagyū Yoshimasa Toshimasa
柳生 新六 厳政
(?–1870)

17. Yagyū Chūjirō Toshishige
柳生 忠次郎 厳蕃
(?–1887)

18. Tokugawa Yoshikumi
徳川 慶恕
(?–c. 1900)

19. Yagyū Sangorō Toshichika (Genshū)
柳生 三五郎 厳周
(1845–1932)

↓ (students of 19. Yagyū Sangorō Toshichika)

- Shimojō Kosaburō
  下條 小三郎
  (1867–?)
- 20. Yagyū Hyōgo Toshinaga (Genchō)
  柳生 兵庫 厳長
  (1892–1966)
- Kambe Takeyasu
  神戸武保
  Kambe Line Shinkage Ryū and Hikita Kage Ryū
  (1894–1980)
  - Katō Isao
    加藤 伊三男
    Shumpūkan
    春風館

↓ (students of 20. Yagyū Hyōgo Toshinaga)

- 21. Yagyū Nobuharu Toshimichi
  柳生 延春 厳道
  (1919–2007)
  - 22. Yagyū (Ishida) Koichi
    柳生(石田)幸一
    (c. 1952–)
- Watanabe Tadatoshi
  渡辺 忠敏
  (1894–1972)
  Watanabe Line
  - Watanabe Tadashige
    渡辺 忠成
    (1941–)
- Ōtsubo Shihō
  大坪 指方
  (1906–1992)
  Ōtsubo Line
  - Mutō Masao
    武藤 正雄
    (1924–2001)
    - Kajitsuka Yasushi
      梶塚靖司

establishing the Kyokushinkai 極真会 *dōjō* in 1964. Finally, in 1965 Ōyama established the International Kyokushinkai Karatedo Organization (Kokusai Karatedō Renmei 国際空手道連盟). He has written a number of books on *karate*, many of which have been published in English.

Oyamada Shōgen Sadamasa 小山田 将監 貞政. Direct disciple of Anazawa Tonomonosuke Morihide in the Anazawa Ryū. Oyamada is somemes credited with founding the Shinten Ryū 真天流. He was also instrumental in the development of the Isshin Ryū (2) 一心流 long hardwood staff system (*bōjutsu*) as transmitted to him by Anazawa. Oyamada was succeeded by his son, Oyamada Tamon Sadashige.

Oyamada Tamon Sadashige 小山田 多門 貞重 [A.k.a. ***Hyōei*** 兵衛尉; ***Nyūdō Dōzon*** 入道 道存] (?–1653). Founder of the Shinten Ryū 真天流, a comprehensive combative system. His father was Oyamada Shōgen Sadamasa. Sadashige succeeded his father in the Isshin Ryū 一心流 long hardwood staff system (*bōjutsu*); he also trained in the Ten Ryū 天流 under founder Saitō Denkibō, and later under Saitō's disciple, Masuda Yajiemon Masatane. He is also thought to have trained extensively in Bokuden Ryū 卜伝流 and Shintō Ryū 神刀流. Having mastered these traditions, Oyamada devised his own school, the Shinten Ryū, which centered on a revelation he referred to as the "sword technique of the spider-legged swastika" (*kumoashi manji ken* 蜘蛛足万字剣).

Ōyashi 欧冶子【歐冶子】 <Ch. Ou Yezi. A legendary Chinese swordsmith of the Spring and Autumn period (c.771—c.403 B.C.E.) who is credited with forging five treasured swords. He is also said to have forged three marvelous swords with another smith known as Kanshō. See also: *Fūkoshi; Kōfu no ken; Ryūen no ken; Taiaki; Taia no ken.*

Ōyōmeigaku 王陽明学 【王陽明學】. CONFUCIANISM—One of three major schools of Neo-Confucianism. Ōyōmeigaku was developed by the Chinese philosopher Wang Yangming 王陽明 (Jp. Ō Yōmei) (1472–1529). It spread across China during the sixteenth century and moved into Japan during the Tokugawa period (1603–1867). The philosophy, which stresses a unity of thought and action and emphasizes intuition (*kan* 勘), became popular among the warrior class.

ōyoroi 大鎧. Lit. "great armor." Full armor worn by high-status mounted warriors (*tsuwamono* or *bushi*) during the late Heian and Kamakura periods. *Ōyoroi* was relatively light—about 65 or 70 lbs. (30–32 kg)—and flexible. Even so, it did restrict the warrior's movements when he dismounted.

The trunk-protecting section (*dō*) was made of four lamellar plates laced together. The lacing cords were usually of silk or leather and often brightly colored. (Japanese war tales of the Kamakura period such as the *Heike*

ŌYOROI
Festival at Katori Jingū, 1978
(Photograph courtesy Pat Lineberger)

ŌYOROI (BACK)
Festival at Katori Jingū, 1978
(Photograph courtesy Pat Lineberger)

monogatari spend a significant amount of time discussing the color and lacings of armor.) As combative archery (*shagei*) was a required skill for the early *bushi,* a leather cover (*tsurubashiri*) was attached to the front of the *dō* to prevent the bowstring from catching. This cover was often decorated.

Hanging from the top of the *dō* were two shields or sleeve-guards (*sode*). These were attached to the *dō* with straps (*watagami*) and tied at the back, often with a silk brocade cord called an *agemaki*. Two smaller boards of armor were hung at the top front of the *dō*: the *sendan no ita* (on the warrior's right) and the *kyūbi no ita* (on the warrior's left).

These were mounted so that they would shift to protect the armpits when the warrior drew his bow.

Hanging from the bottom of the *dō* were four skirt-like attachments, also made of lamellar iron or leather and tied together with highly colored silk or leather cords.

Ōyoroi began to fall out of popularity in the thirteenth century, as it could be pierced by Mongol crossbows. Later, in the Muromachi and Sengoku periods, the horse became less of an element on the battlefield, infantry engagements proliferated, and the use of *ōyoroi* generally disappeared. Its replacement was a lighter type of armor called *dōmaru.*

During the Tokugawa period the *daimyō* sometimes wore *ōyoroi* on their biannual required visits to the *shōgun*'s court in Edo. Some tried to outdo each other by wearing the most elaborate sets of *ōyoroi* they could have made. These suits of armor, however, were for show; they were not practical for battlefield use.

ōyōwaza 応用技【應用技】. 1. Applied techniques; advanced techniques. 2. Advanced or applied arresting techniques. These are a subdivision of a variety of arresting techniques taught by the modern Japanese police force under the rubric *taihojutsu.*

ōyumi 1. 弩. A large siege crossbow.

ōyumi 2. 大弓. See: *daikyū.*

ōzeki 大関【大關】. Lit. "great barrier" or "great checkpoint." SUMŌ—The rank of *ōzeki* is the second highest in modern sport *sumō*. The term is usually translated as "champion."

Ōzōin 奥蔵院【奧藏院】[Var. 興蔵院【興藏院】] [Also read ***Ōkuzōin***]. A Nichiren temple built close to the Hōzōin temple in Nara c.1600.

Ōzōin Ihei 奥蔵院 猪兵衛 【奧藏院 猪兵衞】 [Also read ***Okuzōin Ihei***] (c.1580–c.1650). A Nichiren priest from the Ōzōin (a temple located close to the Hōzōin temple in Nara). Ihei is listed by Watatani and Yamada (1978: 751) as a direct disciple of Hōzōin Inei, founder of the Hōzōin Ryū. Ihei taught Hōzōin Ryū spear arts (*sōjutsu*) to Hōzōin Inshu after Inei's death in 1607. Inshu then became the second headmaster of the Hōzōin Ryū.

Ihei is probably the "Nichiren Ōzōin" priest mentioned in the *Nitenki* who, in 1604, dueled with Miyamoto Musashi, matching his *kamayari* against Musashi's sword. The *Nitenki* notes that Musashi beat Ihei in two matches. The Hōzōin monks evidently felt no animosity toward Musashi, and even invited him to dinner. They are said to have engaged in a discussion of martial concerns which lasted all night; Musashi departed the next day. See also: *sōhei.*

ō-zutsu 大筒 [Var. ***taihō*** 大砲]. A cannon; a piece of artillery.

TRAINING WEAPONS USED IN THE SHINKAGE RYŪ
Naginata—8 feet (2.44 m) *Ōdachi*—4.5 feet (1.36 m)
Jūbei no jō—4.5 feet (1.36 m) *Katana* (*bokken*)—3 feet 4 inches (1.02 m)
Katana (*fukuro shinai*)—3 feet 4 inches (1.02 m) *Kodachi*—22.5 inches (57 cm)

P

Pangainūn Ryū 半硬軟流 [Also read ***Hankōnan Ryū***] [Var. ***Pangainū Ryū*** パンガキヌー流]. See: *Uechi Ryū.*

Pangainun Ryū Karatejutsu Kenkyūjō 半硬軟流空手術研究場. See: *Uechi Ryū.*

Passai 抜塞【拔塞】(Oki.) [Jp. ***Bassai***]. OKINAWAN KARATE—The term *Passai* refers to two Shōrin Ryū 少林流 *karate kata*. Their origins are attributed to Matsumura Sōkon and Itosu Ankō. See also: *karate kata.*

pēchin 親雲上 (Oki.). A term used to denote a member of the middle to upper aristocratic class in premodern Okinawa.

Further reading in English:

- Kerr, 1958, *passim*.

Pinan Kata 平安型 (Oki.) [Jp. ***Heian Kata***]. OKINAWAN KARATE—Several prearranged combative forms (*kata*) taught primarily in the Shōrin Ryū 少林流, Shitō Ryū 糸東流, and derivative traditions. There are five numbered sets of these forms: Pinan Shodan, Pinan Nidan, Pinan Sandan, Pinan Yondan, and Pinan Godan. Their origin is generally attributed to *karate* master Itosu Ankō, who is said to have developed them from an earlier form called Kūsankū (Dai). See also: *karate kata.*

Further reading in English:

- Funakoshi, (trans.) 2001: 58–72.

pyō 兵 [Normally read *hyō*, this character is read *pyō* when preceded by a labial consonant such as (*p*) or (*m*)]. Lit. "troops"; "military forces." The fifth seal/character of the nine mystic letters (*kuji*) found in the Kujihō (Ritual Method of the Nine Seals). *Pyō* is the pronunciation for *hyō* when the preceding syllable ends in a sibilant (in the case of the Kujihō, the preceding syllable is "*rem*"). See: *Kujihō.*

R

Raigakuin 莱岳院. SHUGENDŌ—A Shugendō temple located on Mount Horai (Hōraisan 蓬莱山) during the Tokugawa period. Among its members (known as *shugenja* or *yamabushi*) in the early 1600s was Hiki Yoshio, founder of the Jikishin Ryū (4) 直心流, a school concentrating on combative swordsmanship (*kenjutsu*) and long hardwood staff arts (*bōjutsu*).

raise 来世【來世】. The life to come; the next world; the next life; the hereafter; the afterlife.

raitō 雷刀 Abbrev. for *raitō no kurai*.

raitō no kurai 雷刀位 [Abbrev. as ***raitō*** 雷刀]. Lit. "lightning-sword posture." YAGYŪ SHINKAGE RYŪ—An upper level (*jōdan*) sword posture (*kurai*) in which the sword is held above the head with the hilt (*tsuka*) pointed at the center line of the enemy, and the sword tip (*kissaki*) pointing toward the rear. *Raitō no kurai* is equivalent to *jōdan no kamae* in most other systems.

Rakuchū 洛中. An alternate name for the city of Kyōto during the Kamakura and Muromachi periods.

rakusho 落書 [Also written 楽書【樂書】]. Satirical verse. According to Varley (1994: 188) this was a form of propaganda mentioned in the *Taiheiki* in which warrior leaders were mocked for incompetence. Okabe (1975: 242) considers this a "ninja practice" (*ninjutsu tejina*). However, Okabe tends to consider almost any type of non-conventional warfare to be a "ninja practice." The use of satirical verses in this manner is more akin to a guerrilla-warfare propaganda ploy.

rambō 乱暴【亂暴】. Lawlessness; violence.

rambōmono 乱暴者【亂暴者】. A vandal; a rascal.

ran 乱【亂】. 1. War, riot, rebellion; discord, chaos. 2. KITŌ RYŪ—Freestyle training.

Ran'ai 乱合【亂合】. SHINDŌ MŪSŌ RYŪ—The third series of *waza*, consisting of two *kata*. Ran'ai is not an "original" Shindō Musō Ryū series; it dates from the Bakumatsu period during the closing days of the Tokugawa shogunate, c. 1853–1867.

randori 乱取【亂取】. KŌDŌKAN JŪDŌ—A term for freestyle sparring in modern *jūdō. Randori* is a practice that was borrowed and modified by Kanō Jigorō, founder of Kōdōkan Jūdō. Prior to forming his own system, Kanō had studied Kitō Ryū *jūjutsu* with a teacher named Iikubō Tsunetoshi. Although the Kitō Ryū had evolved into a civilian self-defense system by the 1800s, Kanō was interested in the system's emphasis on *ran* 乱, which under Iikubō was "freestyle training" in contrast to reliance on prearranged *kata*. From the *ran* of the Kitō Ryū, Kanō created *randori*.

randorihō 乱取法【亂取法】. Lit. "freestyle sparring method." See: *randori*.

Randori no Kata 乱取の形【亂取の形】. KŌDŌKAN JŪDŌ—Lit. "Free Exercise Forms." A category of Kōdōkan Jūdō *kata* which is divided into two subsets: Nage no Kata 投の形 (throwing techniques); and Katame no Kata 固の形 (grappling forms).

Nage no Kata, developed by Kanō Jigorō around 1887, contains fifteen techniques (*waza*)—three each from the five categories of throwing techniques:

1. *te waza* (hand-throwing techniques)
2. *koshi waza* (hip-throwing techniques)
3. *ashi waza* (leg-throwing techniques)
4. *ma suteme waza* (rear-sacrifice techniques)
5. *yoko suteme waza* (side-sacrifice techniques).

Katame no Kata also contains fifteen *waza*—five each from the three categories of grappling techniques:

1. *osaekomi waza* (holding techniques)
2. *shime waza* (choking techniques)
3. *kansetsu waza* (joint-locking techniques)

Further reading in English:

- Draeger, 1974: 112–123.
- Kano, 1986.
- Mifune, 2004.
- Otaki and Draeger, 1982.

rangaku 蘭学【蘭學】. An Edo-period term referring to the study of Western sciences

P

R

(including military science) via the Dutch language.[1] See: *gumpō chōren; Seiyō Ryū; Takashima Ryū; Takashima Shūhan.*

rangeki 乱撃【亂擊】. A melee; a confused battle.

ransen 乱戦【亂戰】. A melee or free-for-all battle.

ransō 濫僧. A ninth-century term found in the *Nihon sandai jitsuroku.*[2] It means "rowdy monks." See: *sōhei (1).*

rantō 乱闘【亂鬪】. A melee or free-for-all battle.

rantōgeki 乱闘劇【亂鬪劇】. A melee drama; a swordplay movie. See: *chambara; jidaigeki.*

rappa 乱破【亂破】[Var. 乱波【亂波】]. A variant term for an espionage operative. *Rappa* is apparently an abbreviation for *tekijin o kōrappakai suru mono* 敵陣を撹乱破壊するもの—"one who disrupts or sabotages enemy encampments." See: *ninjutsu.*

rasetsuten 羅刹天 <Ch. *luochatian* <Skt. masc. *rākṣasa*, fem. *rākṣasī*. 1. One of several types of demon found in both Buddhist and Hindu cosmology. The *rākṣasa* were thought to be demons that devoured men. 2. ***Rasetsuten*** 羅殺天. One of a group of twelve guardian deities adopted from Brahmanism by Buddhism. See: *Jūniten.*

rei 礼【禮】. A bow performed as a show of respect. There are a variety of *rei* performed from standing, kneeling, or seated positions.

Irie (2005: 161) delineates three types of *rei* which, with Tokugawa-period origins, have been passed down to modern *budō* and in many classical systems (*koryū*) as they are practiced today. The first type is *rei* based on Confucianism, aimed at maintaining harmonious relationships between individuals and preventing martial training from degenerating into uncontrolled violence. The second type of *rei* finds its origins in Buddhist discipline (*shugyō*) for tempering body and mind. Thirdly, *rei* based in Shintō ritual purification are considered necessary when transitioning the boundary between the mundane and the sacred. In all three of these aspects, *rei* is an external / internal activity in which practitioners pursue a deeper understanding of themselves through hard training. See: *reihō, reigi sahō, and illustrations under Fujisan and sonkyo no shisei.*

reigen 霊験【靈驗】. See: *reiken.*

reigi sahō 礼儀作法【禮儀作法】[Abbr. ***reigi*** 礼儀【禮儀】]. An etiquette ritual often performed at the beginning and end of a martial demonstration, training sessions, etc. Equivalent to *reihō*. See: *Ogasawara Ryū.*

reihō 礼法【禮法】. 1. An etiquette ritual often performed at the beginning and end of a martial demonstration. 2. SHINDŌ MŪSŌ RYŪ—See: *kazari, Fujisan.*

reiken 霊験【靈驗】[Also read ***reigen***]. SHINTŌ—A miracle, magical in its effect; an oracle.

Reikenden 「霊剣伝」【霊劍傳】. JIKI SHINKAGE RYŪ—Abbreviation of *Kashima Shinden Jiki Shinkage Ryū Reikenden* 「鹿島神伝直心影流霊剣伝」【鹿島神傳霊劍傳】. The title of the third Jiki Shinkage Ryū transmission scroll. In the main line (Seitō Ha) of the Jiki Shinkage Ryū, Reikenden is awarded to a trainee who has shown mastery of the curriculum through the school's Kodachi no Kata. The Nomi Ha, however, awarded Reikenden as their first *densho*, once the trainee had shown sufficient competency in Hōjō.

Reirōshū 『玲瓏集』(Collected sounds of jewels). One of three essays written for warriors by the Zen priest Takuan. In contrast to the *Fudōchi shinmyōroku* and the *Taiaki*, the *Reirōshū* does not deal directly with swordsmanship. Instead, this third essay is focused more on the basic question of what it is to be human, desire, life itself, and right-mindedness. See also: *Takuan Sōhō.*

Further reading in English:

• Wilson (trans.), 2003.

reishakei 礼射型【禮射型】. Ceremonial shooting style used in modern archery (*kyūdō*). This style, which was developed for and by foot

[1] *Ran* 蘭 is an abbreviation of Oranda 和蘭陀, the characters used to transliterate the term "Holland."

[2] *Nihon sandai jitsuroku* 『日本三代実録』, a late ninth-century historical work.

soldiers, was later influenced by Ogasawara Ryū formalized archery. (Onuma et al, 1993: 65). This method is essentially that found in *hassetsu*, the eight stages of shooting in modern *kyūdō*. Contrast to *bushakei*. See also: *kishakei*.

reishiki 礼式【禮式】. An etiquette ritual often performed at the beginning and end of a martial demonstration. Equivalent to *reihō*.

Rembukan 練武館. Shimizu Takaji's last *dōjō*, located in the Shibuya area of Tōkyō. It was constructed from the wood of the old Imperial Police Dōjō, where Shimizu had also taught the Shindō Musō Ryū 神道夢想流. After Shimizu passed away in 1978, training continued there under his senior students/successors until 1982, when the building was demolished.

REMBUKAN *DŌJŌ*
Shibuya, Tokyo, 1977

REMBUKAN *DŌJŌ* ENTRANCE
The sign reads
"SHINDŌ MUSŌ RYŪ JŌDŌ HOMBU DŌJŌ"
(Photographs by author)

rempeihō 練兵法. Methods of military drill; military parade. See: *Ichizen Ryū*.

Rempeikan 練兵館. A training hall (*dōjō*) founded in Edo in 1826 by Saitō Yakurō Yoshimichi, fourth-generation successor of the Shindō Munen Ryū 神道無念流. The Rempeikan was one of the most popular *dōjō* in Edo during the Bakumatsu period (1853–1867), and is considered one of the three great *dōjō* of Edo at the end of the Tokugawa period (the other two being the Gembukan and the Shigakkan). The popularity of the Rempeikan was in part due to Saitō's skill with the sword, but the common political/philosophical bent of Saitō's students was also a factor. The Rempeikan was, in fact, a hotbed of the anti-*bakufu* teachings of Mito scholars which were popular among the trainees. Two of Saitō's well-known disciples were Kido Kōin and Takasugi Shūsaku of Chōshū domain, one of the core groups that would topple the *bakufu* in 1867. See: *Bakumatsu Edo Sandai Dōjō; Gembukan; Saitō Yakurō Yoshimichi; Shigkkan; Shindō Munen Ryū.*

Rendaino 蓮台野【蓮臺野】. The name of a field adjacent to Rendaiji 蓮台寺【蓮臺寺】, a Buddhist temple just outside of Kyōto. Rendaino became a well-known location due to a duel which took place there in 1604, in which the young and relatively unknown itinerant swordsman Miyamoto Musashi defeated Yoshioka Seijūrō (Kenpō), head of one of the premier martial arts schools of the times, the Yoshioka Ryū 吉岡流. This audacious victory was arguably the first in which Musashi defeated a swordsman of such stature that he became considered a duelist of note.

renge 蓮華. A lotus flower, a lotus blossom. BUDDHISM—This plant is often depicted in the hands of various Buddhist deities or shown as the platform/seat on which they sit. The lotus is an important symbol in Buddhism, as it represents the process of awakening. Beginning as a seed, it becomes rooted in the muck of a pond, and grows out of that environment to produce a beautiful, pure blossom. As a metaphor it represents the purity of the awakened spirit, which, in order to manifest itself, has to spring from the "muck" of normal existence.

Rengeōin 蓮華王院. An alternate name for Sanjūsangendō, a Tendai temple in Kyōto where an annual archery contest called the Tōshiya is held.

rengeza 蓮華座. BUDDHISM—A term for the lotus sitting posture in Esoteric Buddhism. Outside the Tantric schools it is called *kekka fuza*.

rensabō 連鎖棒. A medium-length staff with a chain attached to one end. See: *Shingetsu Musō Yanagi Ryū.*

rensa sankaku bō 連鎖三角棒【連鏁三角棒】. Chain-linked, three-section staff used by the Takagi Ryū高木流. Each section is about 28 inches (70 cm) long.

renshi 錬士 [Var. 錬師]. A junior swordsmanship teacher; an assistant trainer. Contrast with *shihan, hanshi,* and *kyōshi*. In modern martial arts and ways systems (*budō*), a *renshi* is about equivalent to a fifth- or sixth-*dan* ranked exponent.

retsu 列. The seventh seal/character of the nine mystic letters (*kuji*) found in the Kujihō (Ritual Method of the Nine Seals). The literal meaning is a "line-up," "procession," or "array." See: *Kujihō.*

ri 離. See: *shu-ha-ri.*

riai 理合い. 1. Reason; coherence. 2. In a martial-arts context, *riai* is the fundamental principle or theory underlying prearranged combative forms (*kata*) or techniques (*waza*).

riken 利剣【利劒】. 1. A "wisdom sword" of the type held by Monju Bosatsu in depictions of that deity. 2. A Chinese-style straight sword with a double cutting edge.

Rikugun Nakano Gakkō 陸軍中野学校. See: *Nakano Gakkō.*

Rikugun Toyama Gakkō Bujutsu Kyōkan 陸軍戸山学校陸武術教官. See: *Toyama Gakkō.*

Rikutō 『六韜』 <Ch. *Liutao* (Six strategies) [A.k.a. ***Taikō rikutō***『太公六韜』<Ch. *Tai Gong Liutao* (Tai Gong's six strategies); ***Taikō rikutō gokan***『太公六韜五巻』<Ch. *Tai Gong Liutao Wu Juan* (Tai Gong's six strategies in five volumes)]. The *Rikutō* is one of several texts on Chinese military strategy that was first imported to Japan during the early tenth century. According to Okada (1979: 7), the Chinese term *tao* 韜 (Jp. *tō*) originally meant a "quiver for arrows." As a euphemism, the *rikutō* (a storage receptacle for six arrows) is a text which stores six military strategies. Sawyer (1993: 19) translates the original Chinese term (*liutao*) as "six secret teachings."

As the title states, the work comprises six sections:

Jp.	Ch.		
1. Buntō	Wentao	文韜	Civil strategies
2. Butō	Wutao	武韜	Military strategies
3. Ryūtō	Longtao	龍韜	Dragon strategies
4. Kotō	Hutao	虎韜	Tiger strategies
5. Hyōtō	Baotao	豹韜	Leopard strategies
6. Kentō	Quantao	犬韜	Dog strategies

Many later Japanese traditions of strategy (*heihō*) are supposedly based on the *Rikutō* and related works. However, the Japanese texts are filled with divination techniques and magical spells not found in the *Rikutō*. On the other hand, two of the chapter titles found in the *Rikutō*—Dragon Strategies and Tiger Strategies—are commonly used in Japanese traditions.

At least one version of this text has been published in English under the title *Tai Gong Liutao Wujuan* (Tai Gong's Six Strategies in Five Volumes) (see below). See also: *Buryaku shichi sho; Genji no heihō; Genke Kin'etsushū; Kiichi Hōgan; Kiichi Hōgan Ryū; Ōe no Koretoki; Rikutō; Sanryaku; Taikō rikutō.*

Further reading in English:

• Sawyer, 1993: 19–105.

rin 臨 [Also read ***rin*** or ***rim***]. The first seal/character of the nine mystic letters (*kuji*) found in the Kujihō (Ritual Method of the Nine Seals). See: *Kujihō.*

Rinpō Hiden 麟凰秘伝【麟凰秘傳】. Lit. "Secret Transmission of the *kirin* and the *hōō*." A combative system specializing in small throwing blades and darts (*shurikenjutsu*), grappling arts (*taijutsu*), and long hardwood staff techniques (*bōjutsu*). Its founding is attributed to the enigmatic Buddhist monk Sō Unryū, c.1570. This system evolved into the Takagi Ryū under the next two successors, Itō Kiinokami Sukesada and Takagi Oriemon Shigetoshi.

Why Unryū gave his system this name is unclear now. However, the fabled *kirin* (a four-legged mythical beast) and the *hōō* (phoenix or firebird) are categorized along with the tortoise (*kame*) and dragon (*ryū*) as the four marvelous, mythical beasts in the term "Rinpō Kiryū" 麟鳳亀竜【麟鳳龜龍】.

Rinzai Shū 臨済宗【臨濟宗】<Ch. Linji zong [A.k.a. Rinzai Zen 臨済禅【臨濟禪】]. In Japan, the Rinzai school of Zen Buddhism (Rinzai Shū) was founded by the priest Eisai in 1191. By mixing Chinese Linji *zong* (the Chinese antecedent of Rinzai Shū) with tantric elements from the Japanese Tendai and Shingon schools, Eisai was able to create an eclectic form of Zen Buddhism which appealed to the warriors of Kamakura. See: *Kamakura Zen; Eisai.*

Further reading in English:

• Collcutt, 1981.

Rinzai Zen 臨済禅【臨濟禪】. See: *Rinzai Shū.*

risshi 律師 <Ch. *lüshi*. BUDDHISM—A *vinaya* master; a master of the rules of monastic discipline.

ritsurei 立礼【立禮】. A standing bow. See: *rei.*

Ritsuryō Kyakushiki 律令格式. A system of legal codes adopted from the Chinese by the Japanese imperial court during the seventh and eighth centuries. There were several of these codes; the ones that most affected the Japanese military system were the Taihō Codes of 702.

ritsuzen 立禅【立禪】. *Zen* meditation performed while standing (in contrast to sitting *zazen*).

rōdō 郎党【郎黨】. A general term for military retainers and civil servants in the medieval and premodern eras. See also: *rōtō.*

Rokkō hijū 六甲秘祝 <Ch. Liujia Mizhu [Also written as ***Rokkō hiju*** 六甲秘呪 in Japan]. The "Secret Spell of the Six Protecting Martial Spirits." This incantation first appears in a fourth-century Chinese Daoist text called the *Baopuzi* (*Hōbokushi*『抱朴子』). It is thought that the *Rokkō hijū* is the origin of the Kujihō.

Roku Buten 六武天. BUDDHISM—Lit. the "Six Martial Celestial Beings" or "Six Heavenly Warriors"; sometimes translated as the "Six Gods of War." Six Buddhist *deva* (*ten* 天) popularly associated with warriors and warfare. They include the Four Deva Kings (Shitennō)—Jikokuten, Zōchōten, Kōmokuten, and Tamonten—in addition to Bonten and Taishakuten.

Rokudō 六道. BUDDHISM—The Six Realms of Transmigration through which beings pass, each depending on one's *karma*. The realms are as follows:

- The hells (Jigoku 地獄)
- The realm of hungry ghosts (Gakidō 餓鬼道)
- The realm of animals (Chikushō 畜生)
- The realm of *asuras* (Ashura 阿修羅)
- The realm of humans (Ningen 人間)
- The realm of gods and goddesses [devas] (Ten 天 or Daiba 提婆).

Roku Efu 六衛府. This term referred to the "Six-section imperial guard" extant during the reign of Emperor Shōmu.[3] When originally created by the Taihō Codes in 702, the imperial guards only consisted of five divisions; the sixth was added in 728. At that time they were divided into six units: Emon, Chūe, Sa Eji, U Eji, Sa Hyōe, and U Hyōe. See: *Efu.*

rokushaku bō 六尺棒. Lit. "six-*shaku* staff" or "six-foot staff." A long hardwood staff around 6 feet (1.8 m) in length. See also: *bō; bōjutsu; tetsubō; yoribō.*

rōnin 浪人. Lit. "wave man," or "a man adrift." [Var. 牢人]. A masterless samurai. Many *rōnin* were created during the Warring States period (Sengoku Jidai) when their patron families were destroyed in the incessant wars of the time. During the Edo period many warriors became *rōnin* due to the dissolution of their *han* (domain), because of misbehavior, or other reasons. Due to the strictures of the Neo-Confucian society in which they lived, the samurai were prohibited from working as anything but warriors. Since there were few opportunities for that after the mid-1600s, many became "hired guns" or outlaws.

Roppōkai 六法会. See: *Daitō Ryū Aikijūjutsu Roppōkai.*

3 Shōmu Tennō 聖武天皇 (701–756; r.724–749). Forty-fifth emperor of Japan.

Roshana 盧遮那. See: *Rushana.*

rōshi 1. 老師. A senior Zen teacher; a Zen master.

rōshi 2. 浪士. A Tokugawa-period term for a "masterless samurai." Equivalent to *rōnin.*

rosochi 旅帥 [Also read ***ryosochi***]. TAIHŌ MILITARY SYSTEM—A *rosochi* was the leader of an assembly called a *ryo*, which comprised about 100 conscript soldiers in the Chinese-style eighth-century provincial militia unit (*gundan*). As a commander of 100 men, the *rosochi* was somewhat equivalent to a modern army captain in command of a company. In the chain of command, the *rosochi* was in charge of two or more *taisei* (=lieutenants), and normally under the command of a *kyōi* (=major). See: *gundan*; Appendix 2.

Rō-Sō no Gaku 老荘の学【老莊の學】. DAOISM—The study of philosophical Daoism, in contrast to religious Daoism; the study of the *Laozi*『老子』and the *Zhuangzi*『莊子』.

rōtō 郎等. A vassal or retainer. A term commonly used for non-kin vassals in the tenth and eleventh centuries; it is found in the *Konjaku monogatari*. See also: *kenzoku; rōdō; ruiban.*

Further reading in English:

- Varley, 1994: 30–31.

ruiban 類伴. A vassal or retainer. This term was commonly used in the tenth and eleventh centuries; it is found in the *Konjaku monogatari*. See also: *kenzoku; rōdō.*

Rū-rū Kō 如如哥 <Ch. Ruru Ge [Var. ***Rū-rū Kō*** 魯六哥 <Ch. Luliu Ge, and ***Ryū-ryū Kō*** 劉龍公 <Ch. Liulong Gong (1852–1930). An additional alternate is given in Takamiyagi *et al.* (2008: 187): ***Sha Sū-shō*** 謝崇祥 <Ch. Xie Chongxiang].[4] A Chinese combative arts master who resided in Fuzhou during the 1870s and 1880s. Several progenitors of seminal Okinawan *karate* schools traveled to Fuzhou and trained with Rū-rū Kō. These included Nakaima Norisato (Kenri) and Sakiyama Kitoku (Ryūei Ryū 劉衛流), Higaonna Kanryō (Shōrei Ryū 昭霊流), and others.[5] Several students of Higaonna also journeyed to Fuzhou during the years 1915–1917 seeking instruction. These were Miyagi Chōjun, Nakamoto Eishō, and Go Kenki (all Shōrei Ryū, later called Gōjū Ryū 剛柔流) but the venerable master Rū seems to have been unavailable to visiting Okinawan students during the first two decades of the twentieth century. Due to the chaotic situation on the Chinese mainland at the time—the Boxer Rebellion of 1899–1901; the Nationalist Revolution and the fall of the Qing dynasty in 1911; and the usurpation of political and military control of the country by foreign expeditionary forces and Chinese warlords—his low profile is understandable.

Takamiyagi *et al* (2008: 187) and McCarthy (1995: 35; 59, note 8) indicate that "Rū-rū Kō 如如哥" was a nickname for Xie Chongxiang 謝崇祥, a famous combative arts master in the Fuzhou area in the late nineteenth and early twentieth centuries. McCarthy (1995: 35) further notes that Rū-rū Kō founded the Whooping Crane system,[6] a variant of southern Shaolin White Crane boxing.

Rushana 盧遮那 [Also read ***Roshana***]. Abbreviation for Birushana. See also: *Dainichi Nyorai.*

ryo 旅. TAIHŌ MILITARY SYSTEM—A company of 100 men; that is, two platoons (*tai*) as was implemented in the Chinese-style eighth-century provincial militia unit (*gundan*). A *ryo* was commanded by a *rosochi* (equivalent of a captain) who was normally drawn from the provincial warrior class.

ryō 1. 両【兩】. During the Tokugawa period a *ryō* was a gold piece weighing approximately 16.5 g.

ryō~ 2. 両〜【兩〜】. A prefix meaning a pair; both of a set; e.g., ¶ *ryōte* 両手, both hands. ¶ *ryōtedōri* 両手取り, an *aikidō* attack in which the opponent holds both hands of the person

---

4 An additional complication in transliterating these names to standard Mandarin Chinese is that the dialect spoken in Fuzhou around the turn of the twentieth century was not Mandarin.

5 There are various lists of Okinawan students who trained with Rū-rū Kō and his colleague, Wai Hsin-hsien. Among others listed were Sakiyama Kitoku, Kojō Taitei, and Aragaki Seisho.

6 Ch. *minghe quan* 鳴鶴拳 (Jp. *meikaku ken*).

executing the technique.

ryō 3. 竜【龍】. A dragon. See: *ryū (2).*

ryōba 両刃【兩刃】. A blade with a double cutting edge.

Ryōbu Mandara 両部曼荼羅【兩部曼荼羅】[A.k.a. ***Ryōkai Mandara*** 両界曼荼羅【兩界曼荼羅】]. BUDDHISM—The two great mandala which are the central ritual focus of the Japanese Tendai and Shingon Tantric Buddhist schools. These two devices are, at the same time, representations of the cosmos and the human psyche. (See Tucci, 1973, and Govinda, 1976 for good introductory texts on the use of mandala as psycho-cosmigrams in Tantric Buddhism.) In Japanese, the two mandala are known as the Taizōkai and the Kongōkai; the Taizōkai represents the material world, while the Kongōkai represents the spiritual world. See also: *Taizōkai Mandara; Kongōkai Mandara.*

Further reading in English:

- Govinda, 1976.
- Ten Grotenhuis, 1999.
- Tucci, 1973.

Ryōbu Shintō 両部神道【兩部神道】. Lit. "Dual-aspect Shintō." A doctrine developed by the Tendai and Shingon Esoteric Buddhist schools around the early ninth century. It stated that the Shintō tutelary deities of Japan were actually temporary manifestations (*gongen*) of Buddhist deities and that their true home (*honji*) was India, but that they had left "traces" (*suijaku*) of their manifestation in Japan. This theory—also known as *Shim-Butsu konkō*—enabled a smooth fusion of the two religions in Japan, and after its emergence most Shintō shrines and Buddhist temples gradually fused into one. Exceptions were shrines at Ise and Izumo, which remained purely Shintō.

This union remained in place until the Meiji Restoration of 1868, when Shintō was declared a state religion; Buddhist temples and organizations were forced to return all Shintō sites. The extreme nationalism which accompanied this resulted in the defrocking of a number of Buddhist monks and nuns and the destruction of many Buddhist temples and graveyards. With the elimination of State Shintoism at the end of World War II, many Buddhist and Shintō sites have once again become reunified.

Further reading in English:

- Matsunaga, 1969.
- Victoria, 2006.

ryōfundōgusari 両分銅鎖【兩分銅鏁】. A chain with weights on both ends, much like the *manrikigusari* of the Masaki Ryū.

Ryōgen 良源 (912–985). Famous Tendai monk who was chief of the temple on Mount Hiei in 966. A favorite at the imperial court in Kyōto, Ryōgen was also famous—or infamous—for his involvement with the warrior monks (*sōhei*) on Mount Hiei.

Further reading in English:

- Adolphson, 2007.

Ryōi Shintō Ryū 良移心当流. A *jūjutsu* school popular in the 1800s. One of its branches, located in the Kuroda domain, was the Isei Jitoku Tenshin Ryū 為勢自得天真流. See: *Ise Jitoku Tenshin Ryū; Jigō Tenshin Ryū; Kitō Ryū.*

Ryōkai Mandara 両界曼荼羅【兩界曼荼羅】. See: *Ryōbu Mandara.*

Ryōrin Sōshin Ryū 両輪相心流【兩輪相心流】. A system of quick-draw sword arts (*iaijutsu*) that became incorporated into the Ikkan Ryū (3) 一貫流. According to Watatani and Yamada (1978: 917), the meaning of *ryōrin* 両輪 is as follows: If an enemy is too close, the practitioner does not draw the sword, but instead uses the sword in the scabbard to entrap and capture the opponent; if the enemy is at a distance, the sword is drawn to defeat him. Thus, the system teaches winning both by capturing and by drawing and cutting.

ryōshinogi yari 両鎬槍【兩鎬槍】. Lit. "dual-ridge spear." A spearhead with a diamond-shaped cross-section. Two of the ridges were unsharpened *shinogi*, while the other two were sharpened edges. See also: *sōjutsu; yari.*

ryōshu 領主. Prior to the Tokugawa period, the *ryōshu* were commanders of territories smaller than a province. According to Papinot (1910: 66), just prior to the Tokugawa era, there were thirty-two *ryōshu*. See also: *daimyō.*

ryosochi 旅帥. See: *rosochi.*

R

ryōtan shikaku bō 両端四角棒【兩端四角棒】. Lit. "staff with a square shape on both ends." Normally about 5 feet (1.5 m) in length, the *ryōtan shikaku bō* is a staff with a square-ended metal "glove" covering each end.

ryōtō 両刀【兩刀】. Two swords; dual swords. ¶ *ryōtō o sasu* 両刀を差す, to wear two swords. During the Tokugawa period this indicated samurai status. 2. ***Ryōtō***. KATORI SHINTŌ RYŪ—The third set of *kenjutsu kata* traditionally taught in the Tenshinshō-den Katori Shintō Ryū. In these forms the trainee learning the Katori techniques (*shidachi*) is trained in using dual sword tactics against an opponent (*uchidachi*) armed with a single sword.

ryū 1. 流. Lit. "flow." A martial tradition or school. Also referred to as *ryūgi* and *ryūha*. See also: *koryū*.

ryū 2. 竜【龍】[Also read ***ryō***]. <Ch. *long* <Skt. *nāga*. A dragon. BUDDHISM—The dragon is one of the eight types of beings who are considered protectors of Buddhism. See: *Hachibu Shū*.

As an artistic motif, the dragon normally symbolizes "spirit" in contrast to "flesh" (symbolized by the tiger). When the two are illustrated together in harmony, it symbolizes dominion over all. When illustrated in conflict it indicates the struggle between spirit and flesh. In East Asia and Japan, the number of claws on the dragon indicated the status of the bearer: three claws for commoners, four claws for nobility, five claws for the emperor or crown prince. The dragon is a common motif on Japanese arms and armor.

Further reading in English:

- de Visser, 1913.

ryū 3. 【龍】. See: *ryūō*.

Ryūbi Ryū 柳彼流 <Ko. *Ryupee Ryu*. An obscure school of Japanese swordsmanship described and illustrated in an eighteenth-century Korean text known as the *Bugei zufu tōshi*『武藝圖譜通志』<Ko. *Muye dobo tongji*. See: *Bugei zufu tōshi*.

Further reading in English:

- Kim, (trans.) 2001: 185–189, 195.

Ryūei Ryū 1. 柳影流 [Also read ***Yanagi Kage Ryū***]. An early name for a sword (*ken*) and glaive (*naginata*) system founded sometime after the Meiji Restoration (1868) by Satake Kanryūsai Yoshinori. Satake later changed the name to Jikishin Ryūei Ryū.

Ryūei Ryū 2. 劉衛流. OKINAWAN KARATE—The earliest Gōjū-type system of hand-to-hand combat taught by the Chinese combative arts master Rū-rū Kō to an Okinawan student. Sometime between 1870 and 1880, the Okinawan Nakaima Chikudon Pēchin Kenri (Norisato) journeyed to Fuzhou. There he was introduced to Rū-rū Kō, with whom he trained for about six years.[7] After that time Nakaima evidently travelled extensively around Fujian, Beijing, and Guangdong, where he collected a number of Chinese weapons. Upon returning to Okinawa he secretly trained his son Kenchū, who, in turn, trained only his own son Kenkō. Nakaima Kenkō subsequently founded the Ryūei Ryū in 1971 based on this family tradition. The current headmaster is Nakaima Kenji.

The curriculum of Ryūei Ryū echoes other systems derived from Rū-rū Kō and includes the following combative forms (*kata*):

Empty-hand forms (*Mutī nu hō* 無手ヌ法)

1. Basic forms (Kihon 基本):

- Sanchin 三戦
- Nīsēshī 二十四歩
- Sansērū 三十六
- Sēsan 十三
- Sēyunchin 制引戦
- Pēcchurin[8] 壱百零八

2. Mid-level forms (Chūdan 中段):

- Pāchū 巴球
- Ōhan オーハン
- Heikū 黒虎
- Paikū 白虎

3. Upper-level forms (Jōdan 上段):

- Ānan 安南 I
- Ānan 安南 II

4. Transmission from father to son (*Sōden* 相伝):

[7] As noted elsewhere, Rū-rū Kō would later train a number of students from Okinawa, including Higaonna Kanryō and others.

[8] This *kata* is now referred to under the standard term Sūpārinpē 壱百零八手.

- Paihō 白鶴 (Ryūei Ryū Paihō 劉衛流白鶴)
- Hakkaku 白鶴 (Ryūei Ryū Hakkaku 劉衛流白鶴)

Chinese weapon forms (*Karawaza* 唐技)

1. Staff (Kon no bu 棍の部)

- Kubō no kon クボーの棍
- Kātin no kon 柯娓の棍
- Ryū-ryū no kon 劉龍の棍
- Tankon 短棍
- Saku gusan 錫杖

2. Trident (*Sai no bu* 釵の部)

- Sai I no dan 釵 I の段
- Sai II no dan 釵 II の段

3. Dual Sickles (Nichō Kama 二丁鎌)

4. Short Spear and Shield (Tinbē 団牌−藤牌)

According to Nakaima Kenji, (2008: 192) *tinbē* is the combined use of a shield and short spear or short, thrusting sword. The shield is held in the right hand, the sword in the left.

1. Chinese Glaive (Bisentō 眉尖刀)

2. Oar (Kai no hō 櫂の法)

3. Spear (Hoko 鉾)

- Sōjutsu I 槍術 I
- Sōjutsu II 槍術 II

Further reading in English:

- Bishop, 1999: 19–24.

Ryūen no ken 竜淵の剣【龍淵劍】<Ch. Longyuan *jian*. The "Sword of Ryūen." "Ryūen" is the Japanese pronunciation for "Longyuan," the name of one of the three legendary Chinese swords commissioned by Feng Huzi (Fūkoshi). See also: *Fūkoshi; Kōfu no ken; Ōyashi; Taiaki; Taia no ken.*

ryūgi 1. 流技. The techniques of a *ryū*.

ryūgi 2. 流儀. A martial tradition or school. See: *ryū (1).*

ryūha 流派. A martial tradition or school. While often used synonymously with the terms *ryū* (1) and *ryūgi* (2), the suffix *ha* 派 here is derived from the term *habatsu* 派閥 meaning "to branch off" or "break away." Thus, the term *ryūha* originally referred to a branch tradition of a classical school (*koryū*); i.e., a line not different enough from the parent tradition to completely change the name, but one that may have added or subtracted a portion of the curriculum. In addition, a *ryūha* might have been formed—especially during the Edo period—due to political conflicts over succession. See also: *koryū, ryū (1).*

ryūha daihyō 流派代表. A representative of a martial tradition or school; a successor to the leadership of a martial school.

ryū-ko-kaku no ken 龍虎鶴の拳. Lit. "dragon-tiger-crane boxing." A term sometimes used to describe the boxing methods of Uechi Ryū 上地流 *karate*.

Ryūkyū kobudō 琉球古武道. See: *Okinawa kobudō.*

Ryūkyū Kobudō Hozon Shinkokai 琉球古武道保存振興会 (The Society for the Promotion and Preservation of the Classical Martial Arts of the Ryūkyūs). OKINAWAN KOBUDŌ—Organization founded in 1955 by Taira Shinken for the preservations of classical Ryūkyūan weapons systems.

Ryūkyū Kobujutsu Kenkyūkai 琉球古武術研究会 (Ryūkyū Classical Martial Arts Research Society). Okinawan *kobudo* research organization founded in 1911 by Yabiku Mōden.

Ryūkyū kobujutsu 琉球古武術. See: *Okinawa kobudō.*

Ryūkyū Rettō 琉球列島 <Ch. Liuqiu Liedao. The Ryūkyū archipelago. A chain of islands extending from just south of the Japanese island of Kyushū to just northeast of Taiwan. The largest island of the chain is Okinawa.

ryūma 龍馬 [Abbr. as ***uma*** 馬]. SHŌGI—Lit. "dragon-like horse," a "big and powerful horse." In the Japanese strategic game of *shōgi*, this piece is a "promoted angle-mover" (*kakugyō* 角行=bishop) which gives it additional movement characteristics. The *ryūma* does not have a direct equivalent in Western chess. See also: *ryū no gotoki uma.*

ryūme 龍馬. See: *ryūma.*

ryū no gotoki uma 竜の如き馬【龍如馬】. Lit. a "dragon-like horse." A description used in the war tales (*gunkimono*) of the medieval period for big and powerful horses. See: *uma.*

R

Ryū no maki 「竜の巻」【龍之巻】(Dragon scroll on strategy). Variant name for *Heihō Ryū-no-maki*. See: *Genke Kin'etsushū; Heihō Ryū no maki.*

ryūō 龍王. [Abbr. as ***ryū*** 竜【龍】]. SHŌGI—Lit. "dragon king." In the Japanese strategic game of *shōgi*, this piece is a promoted "flying chariot" (*hisha* 飛車=rook), which gives it additional movement characteristics. The *ryū-ō* does not have a direct equivalent in Western chess.

Ryūshinkan Budō 柳心館武道. Current name for a martial school founded by Nakajima Shōhitsu. In 1953, Nakajima opened the Ryūshinkan Dōjō, where he taught his arts as a comprehensive system under the term Ryūshinkan Budō.

A fourteenth-generation successor to the Shinkage Ryū 神影流 (6), Nakajima added techniques from Ueshiba *aikidō* and a variety of other arts, including *karate*, *taijutsu*, and archery (*kyūdō*). A primary portion of the system is a regimen of quick-draw sword arts (*iaidō*) and test-cutting techniques (*tameshigri*) which Nakajima christened Shin Shin Musō Ryū in 1942. The system also encompasses prearranged combative forms (*kata*) dealing simultaneously with one and two opponents (*futari iai* and *sannin iai* respectively). To supplement these kata, Ryūshinkan Budō also includes an unusual type of training called bokutō kendō. Bokutō kendō is an intense practice, much like a kendō match, but in which hardwood swords (*bokutō*) are used and the participants wear no armor.

The distinctions between what is "Shinkage Ryū" and what is "Shin Shin Musō Ryū" under the Ryūshinkan Budō rubric seem to have become blurred over the years. However, a program for an exhibition of Ryūshinkan Budō published in 1979 listed the following systems:

School	Systems
• Shinkage Ryū 神影流	*kendō*
	naginatadō
	jōdō
• Shin Shin Musō Ryū 神影流	*iaidō*
	futari iaidō
	sannin iaidō
	tameshigiri
• [Non-specific]	*kendō*
	bokutō kendō
• [Non-specific]	*karatedō*
• [Non-specific]	*taijutsu*

According to Jeff Acopian, a longtime practitioner in the tradition, Nakajima Shōhitsu, along with his successor (now third lineal headmaster) Toyoshima Kazutora and one other senior practitioner, a Mr. Koide, appeared in martial demonstrations at the 1964 New York World's Fair. Both Toyoshima and Koide demonstrated Shin Shin Musō Ryū *iaidō* in the 1967 James Bond film *You Only Live Twice*. The system is also prominently displayed in the 1980s film *Budo: The Art of Killing*. See also: *Dai Nippon Teikoku Kai.*

Ryūshin Ryū 柳心流. A system of grappling and striking techniques (*taijutsu*) subsumed under Ryūshinkan Budō.

Ryū Sō Etsu 立双越【立雙越】. Shodan level combative forms taught by the Jigen Ryū. See: *Jigen Ryū; Shodan (1).*

Ryūtō 龍韜. See: *Rikutō.*

S

sabi 1. 寂び. An aesthetic quality of rusticity, elegant simplicity, or patina. In traditional Japanese culture, items of good quality and age were greatly appreciated by those with a sense of *sabi*. See also: *cha no yu; Sen no Rikyū; wabi; wabi-sabi.*

Further reading in English:

• Leonard, 2008.

sabi 2. 錆 [Var. 銹【鏽】]. Rust, tarnish, or patina.

Saburi Inosuke Shigetaka 佐分利 猪之助 重隆. Founder of the Saburi Ryū 佐分利流, one of the best known, most widespread schools of combative spear arts. Inosuke began his career as a student of the spear under Toda Gosei in the Toda Ryū 富田流 school of spearmanship. Later, in 1600, he took part in the battle of Sekigahara on the (winning) side of Tokugawa Ieyasu.

Saburi Ryū 佐分利流 [A.k.a. ***Saburi Ryū Sōjutsu*** 佐分利法槍術]. A school of combative spear arts (*sōjutsu*) founded by Saburi Inosuke Shigetaka in the late 1500s. The school is extant today. See: *Saburi Inosuke Shigetaka.*

sadō 茶道 [Also read ***chadō***]. The Japanese tea ceremony. See: *cha no yu.*

Sa Ejifu 左衛士府. The Imperial Gate Guard Unit of the Left, a section of the eighth-century imperial guards. See: *Ejifu.*

Sagawa Kai no Kami Sukenao 狭川 甲斐守 助直. Direct disciple of Kamiizumi Ise no Kami in the Shinkage Ryū (1) 新陰流. Sakugawa founded a branch tradition known as the Sakugawa Ha Shinkage Ryū 狭川派新陰流 in the late 1500s.

Sagawa Yukiyoshi 佐川 幸義 (1902–1998). A disciple of Takeda Sōkaku in the Daitō Ryū. Sagawa began training at the age of eleven in 1913, and received the teaching license of Kyōju Dairi in 1932.[1] Sagawa often traveled around Japan with Sōkaku, functioning as an assistant instructor. He remained active in Daitō Ryū into his eighties, teaching at a small *dōjō* attached to his home in Kodaira, a suburb of Tōkyō.

Further reading in English:

• Pranin, 1996: 79–86.

sageo 下緒. A cord used for securing the scabbard of a sword to the sash (*obi*) and/or for other utilitarian purposes. The *sageo* is normally threaded through the eye of the *kurikata.*

sagetō shisei 堤刀姿勢 [Var. 下刀姿勢]. A sword-carrying posture—very similar to *teitō shisei*—in which the sword (*katana*) is held in the left hand, with the arm relaxed and extended so that the left hand is positioned at about mid-thigh. See also: *teitō shisei.*

saguru mono 探る者. A variant term for an espionage agent. See: *ninjutsu.*

Sa Hyōefu 左兵衛府. The "Left Guard Unit" responsible in ancient times for guarding the imperial palace gate. See: *Hyōefu.*

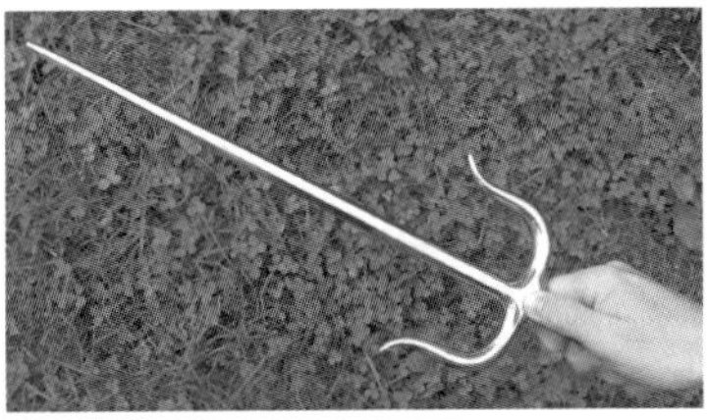

SAI

Typical *sai* used in Okinawan *karate*

(Private collection)

sai 釵. OKINAWAN KARATE/KOBUDŌ—A trident-shaped weapon around 15 to 20 inches (40–50 cm) long. (As with similar hand-held weapons, this length is generally sufficient to protect the forearm when the weapon is held in a reverse-hand grip.) The use of the *sai* is retained in several Okinawan *karate* and Okinawan *kobudō* systems. This single-handed trident (normally used in tandem with a second *sai*)[2] probably originated in India; it

---

1 Pranin (1996: 79) is given this date in an interview with Sagawa in 1996. Watatani and Yamada (1978: 521) give the date as 1924.

2 "Single-handed" in contrast to a polearm trident held in both hands.

is also commonplace throughout Southeast Asia. There are a number of varieties. See: *Okinawa kobudō*.

Saichō 最澄 [posthumous title "Dengyō Daishi" 伝教大師 【傳教大師】] (767–822). The monk who founded the Tendai school, one of the primary denominations of Tantric Buddhism (*mikkyō*) in Japan. Saichō was one of several monks who journeyed to Tang China in the early ninth century. Much like his contemporary, Kūkai, Saichō had begun studying *mikkyō* prior to visiting China. However, Saichō was more eclectic in his approach to Buddhism, and did not restrict himself to Tantricism. While on Mount Tiantai near the Chinese coast, he perfected his understanding of that school's doctrine (essentially *Fahua*/Lotus Sutra teachings) under the monks Daosui and Xingman, and mastered meditation (*shikan*) with Xiaoran. He also received *bodhisattva* ordination from Daosui, esoteric initiation from Weixiang,[3] and collected both Tiantai texts and esoteric scriptures, along with several mandala. The following year, planning to return to Japan, he stayed in Yuezhou, where he also trained in Esoteric/Tantric Buddhism (*mantrayāna*) with the monk Shunxiao[4] of the Longxing temple. From this and other elements he founded the Tendai school on Mount Hiei (Hieizan) near Kyōto.

Further reading in English:

- Groner, 2000.
- Matsunaga, 1974: 139–149 *ff.*
- Tsunoda *et al*, 1958: 116–120 *ff.*
- Weinstein, 1974: 177–191.

Saigō Shirō 西郷 四郎 [A.k.a. ***Shida Shirō*** 志田四郎] (1867–1922). One of the Shitennō (four stalwarts) of early Kōdōkan Jūdō. Shirō was a student of both Kōdōkan founder Kanō Jigorō and *oshikiuchi* master Saigō Tanomo Chikanori.

Born the son of a samurai of the Aizu domain, Shirō became a *shizoku* (an individual of samurai lineage) at the time of the dissolution of the samurai class. Although relatively small in stature, Shirō was very agile, and was a brilliant martial artist. In 1880 he moved to Tōkyō to continue his education. In 1881 he joined the Inoue Dōjō, where Tenshin Shin'yō Ryū 天神真楊流 was taught; in 1883 he first met Kanō Jigorō, who was also studying the Tenshin Shin'yō Ryū, at this *dōjō*. Kanō was very impressed by Shirō's technical skills, and invited him to become an instructor at the nascent Kōdōkan. Shirō accepted, moving quickly through Kanō's curriculum to become one of the first two *shodan* (first-degree black belt rank) in 1883. In 1888 he became the first Kōdōkan *godan* (fifth-degree black belt).

SAIGŌ SHIRŌ AROUND THE AGE OF TWENTY

In 1886 the famous Metropolitan Police *jūjutsu* match was held under the auspices of then-chief of police Mishima. Ostensibly held to decide which grappling system was superior in an actual fight, in reality the meet was held because several traditional *jūjutsu* schools wanted to embarrass the upstart Kanō and put his Kōdōkan Jūdō in its place. However, of the fifteen matches held, the Kōdōkan won twelve, lost two, and tied one. In the most famous of these, the small, agile Saigō Shirō used a technique derived from *oshikiuchi* called *yama arashi* ("mountain storm") to defeat a larger, heavier opponent. From that point Kōdōkan Jūdō became famous, and Shirō became established as one of the pillars of early *jūdō*.

Shirō's reign was not to last long, however. According to anecdotal information, in a match in 1889 he dealt Ara-umi, a *sumō* wrestler, a blow to the chest that proved to

---

3 Jp. Ishō 惟象 <Ch. Weixiang. See Weinstein, 1974.

4 Jp. Jungyō 順暁 <Ch. Shunxiao. See Weinstein, 1974.

be fatal. In addition, Shirō was having an increasingly difficult time with conflicting loyalties between his *oshikiuchi* teacher Saigō Tanomu Chikanori and Kanō. Around 1885 Shirō had married into Chikanori's family and was adopted, changing his family name from Shida to Saigō. Kanō, meanwhile, had made him director of the Kōdōkan in 1888. The burden of reconciling his obligations, combined with the fatal incident in 1889, resulted in Shirō's departure from Tōkyō in 1891. He moved to Nagasaki, where he became a journalist and gave up both *oshikuchi* and *jūdō*. For the next thirty years he trained only in archery (*kyūjutsu*), eventually obtaining the rank of *hanshi* (master instructor).

Saigō Takamori 西郷 隆盛 (1827–1877). A Jigen Ryū–trained samurai of the Satsuma domain. Takamori played an important role in the alliance between Satsuma and Chōshu against the Tokugawa during the Boshin War (Boshin no Eki) in 1868. Because of this he is considered one of the "Three Heroes of the [Meiji] Restoration" (Ishin no Sanketsu). In 1872 he was made commander of the imperial Japanese armed forces, but due to disagreements with other governmental factions over how to deal with Korea, he retired to Kagoshima in 1873. There he opened a school called the Shigakkō, which was dedicated to the teaching of traditional samurai values. Many young disenfranchised samurai (*shizoku*) flocked to this school, and it soon became a center of dissent against the Meiji government's policies. In 1877 Takamori led an army of nine thousand samurai against the government, but they were ultimately defeated by imperial troops. Takamori perished in the final battle at Shiroyama on 24 September 1877.

Further reading in English:

- Buck, 1973.
- Morris, 1975c.
- Ravina, 2004.

Saigō Tanomo Chikanori 西郷 頼母 近徳 [A.k.a. ***Hoshina Chikanori*** 保科 近徳] (1830–1903). Last master of the Takeda *oshikiuchi*. Speculation has it that Chikanori, a Shintō priest of the Nikkō Toshogu shrine, became the headmaster of a grappling art called *oshikiuchi* around the time of the dissolution of Aizu domain in 1871. His first well-known student was Saigō Shirō (a.k.a. Shida Shirō), whom he began training in 1877. Shirō, a prodigy, made a name for himself as a champion at Kanō Jigorō's Kōdōkan, where he used *oshikiuchi* techniques such as *yama arashi* to defeat all comers. However, not long after that Shirō gave up both *oshikiuchi* and *jūdō* due to conflicting loyalties to both Chikanori and Kanō Jigorō.

Left without a successor in *oshikiuchi*, Chikanori began to teach the system to a well-known swordsman named Takeda Sōkaku. Sōkaku quickly mastered *oshikiuchi* after becoming Chikanori's student in 1898, and began modifying it for use by police and military units. By 1908, Sōkaku was instructing police units in Hokkaido in this reformed art, which he referred to as Daitō Ryū *jūjutsu*/*aikijūjutsu*.

Other sources speculate that Chikanori's *oshikiuchi* was not a martial art, but a system of samurai etiquette, and that Sōkaku actually learned his grappling arts from his father, Takeda Sōkichi 武田惣吉. In the Daitō Ryū transmission scrolls (*densho*) produced by Takeda Sōkaku, both Saigō Chikanori and Takeda Sōkichi are absent from the lineage, while *densho* produced by his son, Takeda Tokimune, include Chikanori. (Pranin, 1996: ??)

SAIGŌ TANOMO CHIKANORI (c.1890)
Oshikiuchi instructor of Takeda Sōkaku

saiha 再刃. A re-tempered sword. A sword was often given a new edge if was damaged in a fire or its original differential hardening had otherwise been destroyed. However,

S

sword connoisseurs usually consider a *saiha* blade to be badly flawed.

saihai 采配. 1. A baton with a tassel of paper or leather attached to one end. This device was often used by commanders on the battlefield for signaling. A similar baton with a yak's-tail fly whisk on one end is used in Buddhism. 2. A tasseled fan used by commanders to signal troop movement orders.

SAIHAI (1)

Saiki 再起. JIGEN RYŪ—The third set of primary swordsmanship forms (*kata*) in the Jigen Ryū 示現流.

Saimen no Bushi 西面の武士. Lit. "Warriors of the Western Sector." Much like the earlier Hokumen no Bushi, the Saimen no Bushi were established in 1206 by the retired emperor Go-Toba.[5] The Saimen were a personal military guard unit. They were dissolved at the end of the Jōkyū War (Shōkyū no Ran) when Go-Toba was exiled to the island of Nakanoshima in 1221.

Sai no Bu 釵の部. A term used by the Ryūei Ryū (2) 劉衛流 to categorize imported Chinese hand-trident (*sai*) combative forms.

saisaku 細作. A variant term for an espionage agent. *Saisaku* indicated someone who carried out detective work (*tantei* 探偵) or espionage. The term is related to *hosori* and *mawashimono*. See: *hosori; ninjutsu*.

Saitō Akinobu 斎藤 明信【齋藤明信】(c.1835–c.1910). A fifteenth-generation successor of the Jiki Shinkage Ryū 心影流 in the line of the Fujikawa Ha 藤川派. Akenobu published a work entitled *Jiki Shinkage Ryū kenjutsu* in 1901. See also: *Jiki Shinkage Ryū; Jiki Shinkage Ryū Fujikawa Ha*.

[5] Go-Toba Tennō 後鳥羽天皇 (1180–1239; r.1183–1198), eighty-second emperor of Japan.

SAITŌ AKINOBU
Fifteenth-generation successor of the Jiki Shinkage Ryū Fujikawa Ha
(Photograph from Saitō's *Jiki Shinkage Ryū*, c. 1900)

Saitō Denkibō Katsuhide 斎藤 伝鬼房 勝秀【齋藤傳鬼房勝秀】[A.k.a. ***Saitō*** 首藤; ***Kanehira*** 金平; ***Tadahide*** 忠秀; ***Denkibō*** 伝輝坊; ***Denkibō*** 伝鬼坊; ***Denki Nyūdō*** 伝記入道 (c.1550–1588). Founder of the Ten Ryū 天流/Tendō Ryū 天道流, a comprehensive combative school, in 1582.

saitō goma 柴燈護摩 [Var. 採燈護摩]. SHUGENDŌ—The esoteric fire ritual as performed by followers of Shugendō. See also: *gobukuhō; goma*.

Further reading in English:

- Earheart, 1970, *passim*.

Saitō Jisaburō 斉藤 治三郎【齊藤治三郎】. See: *Edo Yagyū Shinkage Ryū Yamane Ha*.

Saitō Morihiro 斉藤 守弘【齊藤守弘】(1928–2002). A disciple of Ueshiba Morihei who specialized in *aiki* weaponry. Saitō attained the rank of ninth-degree black belt (*kyūdan*) in *aikidō* under the Aikikai.

Saitō began training in *aikidō* under Ueshiba Morihei at the Iwama *dōjō* in 1946. He is considered by some to have been the most competent exponent of *aikijō* and *aikiken* as taught by Ueshiba Morihei. Saitō produced several volumes on *aiki* weaponry and advanced techniques in the 1970s (text both in English and Japanese) in a series called *Traditional Aikido*. These volumes covered a good deal of the curriculum on the medium-length staff (*aikijō*) and sword (*aikiken*). Saitō began awarding certification in *aikiken* and *aikijō* as distinct from *aikidō dan* ranks in 1989.

His English-language publications are:

Aikido: Its Heart and Appearance. Minato Research & Publishing Company, 1975.

Traditional Aikido: Sword·Stick·Body Arts, Volume 1: Basic Techniques『合気道:剣·杖·体術の理合 第一巻』. Minato Research & Publishing Company, 1973.

Traditional Aikido: Sword·Stick·Body Arts, Volume 2: Advanced Techniques『合気道:剣·杖·体術の理合 第二巻』. Minato Research & Publishing Company, 1973.

Traditional Aikido: Sword·Stick·Body Arts, Volume 3: Applied Techniques『合気道:剣·杖·体術の理合 第三巻』. Minato Research & Publishing Company, 1974.

Traditional Aikido: Sword·Stick·Body Arts, Volume 4: Vital Techniques『合気道:剣·杖·体術の理合 第四巻』. Minato Research & Publishing Company, 1974.

Traditional Aikido: Sword·Stick·Body Arts, Volume 5: Training Works Wonders『合気道:剣·杖·体術の理合 第五巻』. Minato Research & Publishing Company, 1974.

Saitō Musashibō Benkei 西塔 武蔵坊 弁慶【西塔武藏坊辨慶】. See: *Benkei.*

Saitō Satoshi 斉藤 聡. Fifth and current headmaster of the Negishi Ryū 根岸流, a martial school focusing on throwing darts and blades (*shurikenjutsu*).

Saitō Yakurō Yoshimichi 斎藤 弥九郎 善道【齋藤彌九郎善道】 (1799–1872). A fourth-generation successor of the Shindō Munen Ryū 神道無念流 who founded the Rempeikan *dōjō* in Edo in 1829.

Saiyūki『西遊記』<Ch. *Xiyouji* (Journey to the West). The *Saiyūki* is a Ming-dynasty novel published anonymously in the 1590s. Also referred to as *Monkey*, the *Saiyūki* is loosely based on the seventh-century journey to India made by the Tang-dynasty Buddhist monk Xuanzang.[6] This text was partially translated into English by Arthur Waley. A metaphorical journey toward enlightenment, the *Saiyūki* is an adventure tale filled with action scenes and hosts of supernatural characters. It became a popular story in Japan's Edo period, and illustrations of some of the characters from this tale are frequently seen as art motifs among the Japanese warrior class. See: *Shi Daikisho.*

sakaishi 堺仕. A variant term for an espionage agent, used during the late Warring States period (Sengoku Jidai). See: *ninjutsu.*

sakaki 榊. A flowering evergreen, *Cleyera japonica*, considered sacred in the Shintō tradition. Branches of *sakaki* were sometimes carried by monks of Kōfukuji temple in protest marches during the early medieval period. In modern *dōjō* a *sakaki* branch may be placed in the altar area (*kamidana*).

Sakakibara Kenkichi 榊原 鍵吉 (1830–1894). Recognized as fourteenth headmaster by the Jiki Shinkage Ryū 直心影流. Sakakibara Kenkichi began his swordsmanship career with a leaning toward Jiki Shinkage Ryū, as his father Sakakibara Masutaro was a member of Inoue Denbei's Jiki Shinkage Ryū *dōjō*. However, the Inoue *dōjō* closed when young Sakakibara was thirteen, and Kenkichi moved to the Odani *dōjō*. By the age of nineteen he had mastered the system.

Seven years later, in 1856, Sakakibara joined his teacher Odani Nobutomo, thirteenth headmaster of the Jiki Shinkage Ryū, at the Kōbusho, where he instructed in *kenjutsu* until the establishment closed in 1866. Sakakibara, a close associate of *shōgun* Tokugawa Iemochi,[7] was deeply affected when young Iemochi died at the age of twenty-one. This apparently influenced his view of the increasing pace of Westernization which was overtaking Japan in the late 1860s and early 1870s. Even his beloved martial culture was on the wane as a new Western-style military system was adopted and the citizenry began rejecting classical traditions such as swordsmanship. Kenkichi's response to this trend was to organize a society called the Gekikenkai, which promoted matches with bamboo swords (*shinai*), wooden glaives (*naginata*), and wooden-bladed sickle-and-chain composite weapons (*kusarigama*). The first of these demonstrations—which were called "public

S

6 Genjō 玄奘 <Ch. Xuanzang (600–664).

7 Tokugawa Iemochi 徳川 家茂 (1846–1866, r.1858–1866). Fourteenth Tokugawa *shōgun*.

SAKAKIBARA KENKICHI
Fourteenth headmaster of the Jiki Shinkage Ryū
(pictured here wearing *a yamatozue* in lieu of a *wakizashi*)
(Photograph courtesy Namiki Yasushi)

entertainments" (*kōgyō*)—was held in 1873. The events were almost immediately a big hit, and dozens of locations quickly began catering to these popular matches.

Kenkichi himself was known as quite a showman. He became well known for his cutting abilities when, in front of Emperor Meiji, he alone was able to split a traditional helmet (*kabuto*) with the power of his "terrible sword." Even foreign visitors to Japan were attracted to Kenkichi's *dōjō*. According to a recent article on Jiki Shinkage Ryū (Cundy, 2002: 55–61) these included Tōkyō University Professor Dr. Erwin von Baelz, Austrian fencer Henry Sieboldt, British consulate official Thomal McClatchie, and French instructors Vilare and Kiele at the Toyama Military Academy, among others.

In similar fashion to his Jiki Shinkage Ryū master Odani, Sakakibara is often pictured wearing a heavy truncheon called a *yamatozue* in lieu of a sword (*katana*). Like previous masters of the Jiki Shinkage Ryū, Sakakibara was a believer in "positive" swordsmanship. Watatani and Yamada (1978: 155–156) list twenty *menkyo kaiden* successors under Sakakibara. Some of his best-known students include Yamada Jirokichi (fifteenth-generation successor and main line headmaster of the Jiki Shinkage Ryū), Nomi Hamao (progenitor of the Nomi Ha Jiki Shinkage Ryū), Takeda Sōkaku (founder of Daitō Ryū *aikijūjutsu*), and Satake Kanryūsai Yoshifumi (founder of the Jikishin Ryūei Ryū).

sakamogi 逆茂木. Wooden spikes often used in temporary field fortifications.

Sakamoto Ryōma 坂本 龍馬 [A.k.a. ***Saitani Umetarō*** 才谷梅太郎] (1836–1867). An expert swordsman who trained in Hokushin Ittō Ryū under Chiba Shūsaku. Ryōma was drawn to the Sonnō Jōi 尊王攘夷 (lit. "Revere the emperor and expel the barbarians") movement, and led a faction planning to overthrow the Tokugawa *shogunate* in the 1860s. Ryōma had planned to assassinate Katsu Kaishū, a Jiki Shinkage Ryū swordsman who was a high official of the shogunate at the time. However, Kaishū convinced Ryōma that fighting the Western powers was futile and that a long-term plan was needed to establish Japan as a world power. Ryōma became Kaishū's protégé and later played a key part in the peaceful resignation of the last Tokugawa *shōgun*. However, on the eve of the Emperor Meiji's ascent to power, Ryōma was assassinated.

Further reading in English:
- Hillsborough, 1999.
- Jansen, 1995.

Sakanoue no Tamuramaro 坂上 田村麻呂 (758–811). The first warrior to be awarded the title of *seii taishōgun* (barbarian-quelling general). Sakanoe received this title from Emperor Kammu[8] in 801, when he was sent against the Ebisu. Sakanoue pushed them out of Suruga to Mutsu, where he then built a fort which later became Izawa castle. He also funded the construction of a temple called Kiyomizudera in Kyōto, and was the progenitor of the Tamura *daimyō* family of Mutsu.
See also: *Shōgun Jizōhō.*

Sakata Shigemichi 坂田 成道. A direct disciple of Hakkō Ryū 八光流 founder Okuyama Yoshiji. In the mid-twentieth century, Sakata subsequently founded a school he called Sodō Ryū 祖道流 which concentrated on grappling (*jūjutsu*).

saki 先. The second of three categories of initiative (*sen*) recognized in modern Japanese police tactics (*taihōjutsu*). *Saki* is akin to the

8 Kammu Tennō 桓武天皇 (737–806; r.781–806). Fiftieth emperor of Japan.

older concept of *nori hyōshi*; that is, an arresting officer is able to join with an assailant's attack and still gain the advantage over his opponent. The other two categories are *sensen no saki* and *ato no saki*. See also: *bu no ri; go no saki; go no sen; sen; sen no sen; sensen no saki; sensen no sen.*

sakigake 先駆 [Var. 魁; a.k.a. ***senjin*** 先陣]. Lit. "first in battle." This term and concept, somewhat equivalent to *senjin*, is often found in the medieval war tales (*gunkimono*). Warriors in those stories seemed to be constantly vying with each other to be first on the battlefield, as they derived great status, fame, and reward from this achievement. See, for example, the race between the warriors Shigetada and Shigechika to cross the Uji River in the *Heike monogatari* (Kitagawa and Tsuchida, 1975: 511–514). This custom appears to have been in place at least as early as the battle of Paekch'ŏn River in Korea in 663. The meaning of the term later changed; during the Warring States period (Sengoku Jidai) it came to refer to combatants who were in the vanguard, leading troops into battle.

Further reading in English:

- Varley, 1994: 93–98.
- Yonekura, 1975: 22.

sakimitama 幸魂 [Var. 幸御魂]. SHINTŌ—A lucky spirit. See: *mitama.*

sakimori 防人. Border guard units established as part of the Taika Reform Edict of 646. The *sakimori* were required to provide their own weaponry, including "...a sword, armor, bow and arrows, a flag, and a drum..." (Farris, 1992: 37). The *sakimori* often had to travel great distances—from the Kantō plain to northern Kyūshū—to protect Japan from continental invaders. In 737 there were about 2,300 *sakimori* posted in northern Kyūshū. Most were mounted archers. The use of Kantō border guards on the islands of Iki and Tsushima was abandoned in 835.

Further reading in English:

- Farris, 1992: 106–107.

sakkatsu tsubo 殺活穴所. TAKENOUCHI RYŪ—An alternate term for a vital point; a pressure point. (Minouchi, 1982: 11). See also: *kyūsho.*

sakoku 鎖国【鎖國】. Lit. "chaining the country." A general term for the policy of closing up Japan which was instituted by the third Tokugawa *shōgun* Iemitsu. (The original term used by the shogunate was *kaikin* 海禁, which means "maritime restrictions.") This policy of national isolation prevented anyone from entering or leaving the country on penalty of death. It was accomplished through several edicts during the period 1633–1639. *Sakoku* remained in effect until 1853, when Commodore Perry forced the shogunate to open the country to foreign trade and diplomatic relations.

The policy of *sakoku* was an important factor in the preservation of classical martial systems (*koryū bujutsu*) in Japan. Due to national isolation, the Japanese were able to maintain the status quo of their hierarchical social system and restrict the development of firearms technology. Under the more than 250 years of Edo-period peace, the Tokugawa shogunate and the classical warrior traditions modified battlefield systems (*bujutsu*) into martial arts (*bugei*) and martial/spiritual ways (*budō*). Without *sakoku*, pressure from abroad in the form of trade—along with religious evangelism and technological advances—might have forced the Japanese to adopt new military technologies and strategies, displacing the classical warrior traditions at a much earlier date. This did in fact happen in just a few short years after the1868 Meiji Restoration.

Further reading in English:

- Perrin, 1980.

saku 柵. A stockade or fenced-in area. This term is found in the early medieval war tales such as the *Mutsu waki* and *Ōshū gosannenki*, where it refers to temporary fortifications.

Sakugawa Kanga 佐久川 寛賀 [Also read ***Sakugawa Satunushi***; a.k.a. ***Sakukawa Tōde*** 佐久川 唐手 <Oki. *Sakugawa Tōdī*] (1786–1867).[9] According to Okinawan oral tradition, Sakugawa was the progenitor of the Okinawan fighting system called *tōde* 唐手 (China hand). His first venture into the martial arts is said

9 Note: Some sources give Sakugawa's dates as 1733–1815 but the dates above are those established by Takamiyagi et al (2008: 434).

S

to have been under a local teacher named Takahara. He subsequently trained in Chinese pugilistic arts (Ch. *quanfa*) with a military attaché to the Okinawan royal court whose name was Gong Xiang Jun 公相君 (pronounced "Kūshankū" in Okinawan dialect).

No documents remain to clarify the status of Gong Xiang Jun, but, as Martin (2007: 4) points out, the oral history of the Shōtōkan school is unclear as to whether the term "Gong Xiang Jun" was a person's name or the rank held by the military attaché. In an alternate version of the story, Sakugawa journeyed to China in order to study martial arts (Ch. *wushu* 武術)—specifically staff fighting and boxing—from a Chinese master named Kūsankū or Kushanku. In either case, Sakugawa later began teaching an art he called "Sakugawa's Chinese boxing system" in the city of Shuri in Okinawa. The ideograms for this term—佐久川唐手—can be read as either "Sakugawa Tōde" or "Sakugawa no Karate." Tradition states that this was the earliest use of the term *tōde* in Okinawa, although the story is undocumented.

Caution is needed here, for several lineages of *karate* in Okinawa, such as the Shōrin Ryū, claim that their own progenitor made the first use of the term *tōde*/*karate* 唐手. According to Shōtōkan oral tradition, Sakugawa created a prearranged combative form (*kata*) he called Kushanku in honor of his Chinese teacher. The Kushanku *kata* was the basis for two later *kata* known as Kanku Dai and Kanku Shō—Kanku Dai being the "master Shōtōkan *kata*" from which the later Pinan (Heian) *kata* was derived. See also: *Azato Ankō; Funakoshi Gichin; Itosu Ankō; Matsumura Sōkon.*

Further reading in English:

- Bishop, 1999: 120–121 *ff.*
- Nagamine, 2000: 11–16.

Sakugawa Tōde 佐久川 唐手 <Oki. *Sakugawa Tōdī* [Also read ***Sakukawa Tōde***]. See: *Sakugawa Kanga.*

sakura 桜 【櫻】. Flowering cherry; cherry blossoms. Throughout history the Japanese have used the symbol of falling cherry blossoms when alluding to the special beauty arising from the impermanence of the human condition and the "pathos of things" (*mono no aware*). This theme extended into the era of the modern Japanese military, as indicated in this *haiku* by a twenty-two year old *kamikaze* pilot who sacrificed himself in battle in 1945:

> If only we might fall
> Like cherry blossoms in the Spring—
> So pure and radiant ![10]

Ivan Morris (1975) devoted a masterly work to this topic titled *The Nobility of Failure: Tragic Heroes in the History of Japan*. See also: *mono no aware.*

Sakurada Jirōzaemon Sadakuni 桜田 次郎左衛門 貞国 【櫻田次郎左衛門貞國】. An avid martial artist who roamed around the country on a warrior pilgrimage from the age of twenty-two to forty-two. After mastering the Komagawa Kaishin Ryū 駒川改心流 under founder Kamagawa Kuniyoshi, he modified the school and renamed it Sakurada Ryū 桜田流 sometime around the early 1600s. See: *Komagawa Kaishin Ryū.*

Sakurada Ryū 桜田流 【櫻田流】. See: *Komagawa Kaishin Ryū.*

Sakura Ichiden Ryū 佐倉一伝流 【佐倉一傳流】. A branch tradition of the Asayama Ichiden Ryū founded by Kobayashi Tōjūrō Tadahide and transmitted in Sakura domain (present-day city of Sakura in Chiba prefecture). The system concentrated on swordsmanship (*kenjutsu*), quick-draw sword arts (*iaijutsu*), capturing arts (*torite*), and long hardwood staff arts (*bōjutsu*).

sama 様. An honorific used when addressing superiors.

samayagyō 三摩耶形 <Ch. *sanmoye xing*. See: *sammayagyō.*

sambagarasu 三羽烏. Lit. "three crow feathers." Somewhat equivalent to "three birds of a feather." The term normally refers to a trio; in a martial context, it means three famous retainers.

same 鮫. Abbreviation for *samegawa.*

samegawa 鮫皮. Skin of a giant stingray;

---

[10] Translation by Ivan Morris (1975: 276).

sharkskin. Because of its toughness, rayskin or sharkskin is often used for covering the hilts of swords and short bladed weapons.

Further reading in English:

- Joly and Inada, 1913.

samidare 五月雨 [Also read ***satsukiame***]. 1. A poetic term for a monsoon. *Samidare* turns up as a *kata* name or *kata* series name in several martial traditions. There are various interpretations of the term. One of these alludes to the rainy season and its blinding rain, rain which is blowing in several directions at once and makes seeing difficult. In this sense it is akin to the terms *kagerō* and *kasumi*. In the twentieth-century Imperial Japanese Navy, the name "Samidare" was given to a Shiratsuyu-class destroyer. This was certainly apropos as one of the main tasks of destroyers was to create smoke screens to hide larger craft—aircraft carriers, cruisers, battleships, troop carriers, etc.—from enemy vessels. See also: *kagerō, kasumi*. 2. ***Samidare*** 五月雨. SHINDŌ MUSŌ RYŪ—The fifth series of combative forms in the Shindō Musō Ryū, consisting of six *kata*.

sammai 三昧 <Ch. *sanmei* <Skt. *samādhi*. See: *sammaiji*.

sammaiji 三摩地. <Ch. *sanmodi* <Skt. *samādhi*. [Also read ***sanmaji***] [Var. 三昧地 <Ch. *sanmeidi*; also read ***sanmaiji, sammaji***]. 1. BUDDHISM—The practice of concentrating the mind on a particular object. There are many methods of for achieving *sammaiji*; dozens of ritual texts and manuals with recipes for performing practices devoted to specific deities. 2. BUDDHISM—one of the three types of learning (*sangaku*). See also: *sammayagyō*.

sammaiyagyō 三昧耶形. See: *sammayagyō*.

sammaji 三摩地. See: *sammaiji*.

sammayagyō 三昧耶形 [Also read ***sanmaiyagyō, sammayagyō***] <Ch. *sanmeiye xing* [Var. ***samayagyō*** 三摩耶形]. BUDDHISM—In the Esoteric Buddhist schools, *sammayagyō* refers to a distinguishing symbol of a buddha, *bodhisattva*, or other spiritual being used in meditative ritual (*sammaiji*). The symbol is usually pictured held in the hand of an image of the particular being. For example, the *sammayagyō* for Kannon Bosatsu is a lotus blossom (*renge*), while that for Fudō Myōō is the Black Dragon King (Kurikara Ryūō) wrapped around a flaming, *vajra*-hilted sword (*sankotsuka no ken*).

During *sammaiji*, the practitioner meditates on a painting or image of the symbol (*sammayagyō*) of the deity particular to the chosen ritual. Slowly the practitioner causes the visualized image of the symbol to morph into a visualization of the image of the deity itself. Next the practitioner meditates upon his/her own self merging with the spirit of the deity. This is normally accomplished by a combination of visualization (mind focus), chanting of spells (speech focus), and assumption of postures and hand gestures (body focus), imitating the target deity. The merging complete, the practitioner is thought to obtain the characteristics and magical powers (*shijji* or *jōju*) of the heavenly being. See also: *sammaiji*.

sampei 散兵. Skirmishers.

samurai 侍. The title "samurai," which originally meant "servant" or "those who serve," came into use during the twelfth century. In the late Heian and Kamakura periods, certain high-status warriors who were servants of the imperial court were accorded the sixth (lowest) court rank and the title of samurai.

Court rank and samurai status gave the warrior a number of privileges not held by commoners (*bonge*). Farris (1992: 339) elaborates on these privileges:

> ...freedom from interrogation when suspected of a crime, the prerogative to become a retainer of the Shogunate, and the right to use surnames and to wear certain clothes.

Warrior-followers who held no rank or office were not called samurai in the early medieval period.

In the Edo period (1603–1867) and modern era (post-1867), the term "samurai" came into generic use for members of the Japanese warrior class in the Edo period. See: *kuge; Yōrō Ryōritsu*.

Further reading in English:

- McCullough and McCullough, 1980a.

S

Samurai-dokoro 侍所. In effect a "Board of Retainers," the Samurai-dokoro was a government bureau that handled all affairs concerning the warrior class (*bushi*) during the Kamakura and Muromachi periods.

Samurai-dokoro no Bettō 侍所別当【侍所別當】. A Kamakura-shogunate term for "Director of the Samurai-dokoro." See also: *Mandokoro Bettō.*

san さん. An honorific used when addressing someone of roughly equal rank.

Sanada Nobushige 真田 信繁 [A.k.a. ***Sanada Saemon no Suke Yukimura*** 真田 左衛門佐 幸村] (1567–1615). A well-known commander who fought under Takeda Shingen and later the Toyotomi clan; he is famous partly due to his use of chemical warfare.

Sanada was a samurai and son of a Sengoku-period *daimyō* named Sanada Masayuki. Popularly known since the Tokugawa period as Sanada Yukimura, he was never referred to as Yukimura during his lifetime. His personal name, Nobushige, was taken from Takeda Shingen's younger brother, Takeda Nobushige.

Throughout his life Sanada appears to have been a courageous fighter and commander. Although he first sided with Takeda Shingen, after Shingen's death he drifted between alliances with the Uesugi, Tokugawa, and Hōjō clans, ending up serving Toyotomi Hideyoshi. He sided with the Toyotomi clan through the battles at Ōsaka Castle in 1614 and 1615.

Sanada is thought to have been one of the first Japanese commanders to use chemical warfare on a large scale. It has been recorded that in 1615, during the siege of Ōsaka Castle, Sanada gathered a large number of red jellyfish (*kurage*) and had them dried and crushed into powder. (Although the toxin of the red *kurage* is not deadly, exposure to it is very painful, even when the jellyfish is dead and dried out.) As the wind blew toward the enemy, Sanada had his men scatter the poisonous powder in the breeze. When it reached the enemy, its painful effect completely disrupted their formation.

***Sanada Saemon no Suke* Yukimura** 真田 左衛門佐 幸村. See: *Sanada Nobushige.*

sanchin 三戦【三戰】(Oki.) [Read ***sansen*** or sanchin in Japanese]. OKINAWAN KARATE—An Okinawan term for several *karate* combative forms (*kata*) emphasizing breath control and movement. The term *sanchin*, which literally means "three battles," refers to the battles of unifying and stabilizing body, breath, and mind. Several versions of *sanchin* were introduced to Okinawa at several different times.

sanchindachi 三戦立【三戰立】(Oki.). OKINAWAN KARATE—The stance taken in *sanchin.*

sanchin kokyūhō 三戦呼吸法【三戰呼吸法】(Oki.). OKINAWAN KARATE—Lit. the "breathing method of *sanchin.*" The breath control used in the practice of *sanchin kata.* This respiratory technique enables the practitioner to learn how to stabilize his body, breath, and mind for combat. This stabilized mental state—a basis for imperturbability—is referred to in Japanese as *heijōshin.*

sandai kensei 三大拳聖. See: *Okinawa no sandai kensei.*

Sandaiki 『三代記』(Chronicle of the three periods). This work, the title of which is usually translated as the *Chronicle of Ōnin*, is a record of the events of the Ōnin War (Ōnin no Ran) which lasted from 1467 to 1477.

Further reading in English:

- Varley (translation), 1967.

Sandan 三段. 1. JIGEN RYŪ—The third section of prearranged combative forms (*kata*) in Jigen Ryū's advanced level swordsmanship (Dan no Kata). The three scenarios in this set are referred to as Hei An Kō 平安行. 2. ***sandan*** 三段. Lit. "third grade." A modern *budō* term derived from Kōdōkan Jūdō which indicates the rank of a practitioner as third degree. In most modern systems, this indicates a "third-degree black belt."

Sangaku 「三学」【三學】[also written「参学」【參學】] <Ch. *sanxue* <Skt. *tisraḥ śikṣāḥ*. 1. BUDDHISM—Three types of learning: moral conduct (*kai*), meditation/concentration of the mind on a single object (*sammaiji*), and wisdom (*chi-e*). 2. YAGYŪ SHINKAGE RYŪ—

The name of the third picture scroll (*emaki*) presented to Yagyū Muneyoshi by Kamiizumi Ise no Kami Nobutsuna (founder of the Shinkage Ryū) in 1566. This scroll illustrates the set of combative scenarios (*kata*) now called Sangaku En no Tachi 三学円之太刀.

EXCERPT FROM SANGAKU *DENSHO*
Yagyū Shinkage Ryū *densho* (*emaki*) presented to Yagyū Muneyoshi by Kamiizumi Ise no Kami Nobutsuna in 1566
(From the archives of Yagyū Nobuharu)

SANGAKU EN NO TACHI
Yagyū Nobuharu (L) and Ikenaga Kōichirō (R) demonstrating at Meiji Jingu, 1981
(Photograph by author)

Sangaku En no Tachi 三学円之太刀【三學圓之太刀】. YAGYŪ SHINKAGE RYŪ—The first set of combative *kata* currently taught to trainees in the Yagyū Shinkage Ryū. The emphasis in these first *kata* places the mind in *ken* 懸 (attack mode) and the body in *tai* 待 (waiting mode). The Shinkage Ryū exponent then waits for the enemy to approach instead of advancing to attack. Transmitted to Yagyū Muneyoshi by Kamiizumi Nobutsuna, these *kata* stood as counters to Shintō Ryū's Itsutsu no Tachi. See also: *ken (2)*; *Kuka no Tachi*; *Empi no Tachi*; *tai (1)*.

sangaku shinkō 山嶽信仰. Lit. "mountain beliefs" or "mountain faiths." A generic scholastic term referring to religious phenomena associated with mountains in Japan. According to Earhart (1970: 169) the term encompasses "beliefs, myths, special *kami* (*yama no kami*), shrines, and festivals, all of which are religiously related to mountains." These phenomena are closely related to Shugendō and its mountain ascetics (*yamabushi*), though not exclusively so.

Sangi ittō 『三議一統』. At the order of the third Ashikaga *shōgun*, Yoshimitsu,[11] Ogasawara Nagahida, Ise Noritada and Imagawa Ujiyori, were charged with creating a code of etiquette and ceremonies for the warrior class. The results of their efforts were set down in this work called the *Sangi ittō*. See: *Ogasawara Nagahide*.

Sangoku shi engi 『三国志演義』【三國志演義】 <Ch. *Sanguo yanyi* 『三國演義』 (Romance of the three kingdoms). A fourteenth-century Chinese historical novel dealing with the end of the Han dynasty and the succeeding Three Kingdoms period, c.169–280 C.E. Classified as one of the four great classical novels (Shi Daikisho) of China, it was well known by the Japanese. Illustrations of some of the characters from this tale, such as the general Guanyu (Kan'u), became popular art motifs among the Japanese warrior class. See: *Kan'u*; *Shi Daikisho*.

Sanjūsangendō 三十三間堂 [A.k.a. ***Rengeō-in*** 蓮華王院]. Tendai temple located in the Higashiyama section of Kyōto. Since the Edo period, an archery tournament known as the Tōshiya has been held at Sanjūsangendō every January. See: *Tōshiya*.

sankaku yari 三角槍. A spearhead with a triangular cross-section. See also: *sōjutsu*; *yari*.

Sanka Muteki Ryū 三化無敵流 [Also written 三花無敵流 and 山河無敵流]. An Edo-period branch of the Shinkage Ryū (1) 新陰流 which concentrated on combative swordsmanship (*kenjutsu*) and spearmanship (*sōjutsu*). See also: *Kiraku Ryū*.

sanke 三家. This term referred to the three branches of the Tokugawa family that descended from the first Tokugawa *shōgun*, Ieyasu:

---

[11] Ashikaga Yoshimitsu 足利 義満 (1358–1408, r.1368–1394).

Son		Branch	
9th–Yoshinao	義直	Owari	尾張
10th–Yorinobu	頼宣	Kii	紀伊
11th–Yorifusa	頼房	Mito	水戸

If a *shōgun* did not leave an heir, the successor could be chosen from one of these three family branches.

It is worth noting that the headmastership of the Owari Yagyū Shinkage Ryū is intertwined with the Owari Tokugawa branch family.

sankin kōdai 参勤交代. See: *sankin kōtai.*

sankin kōtai 参勤交代【參勤交代】. The alternating Edo residence of the *daimyō*. Enacted as a law in 1632 by the *shōgun* Tokugawa Iemitsu,[12] this system required all *daimyō* to divide their residence between their home domain and Edo. The actual periods were not set, but most *daimyō* stayed one year in Edo and one year in their domains. While the *daimyō* were in their domains, their wives and children were essentially held hostage in Edo to ensure fealty.

san kisha 三騎射. The "three equestrian archery (contests)." During Japan's medieval period (c.1185–1558), the *san kisha* were competitive archery "sports" practiced by the warrior class. These included dog hunting (*inu ou mono*), hat shooting (*kasagake*), and target shooting (*yabusame*). All three were executed from horseback.

sanko 三鈷. See: *sankosho.*

sankosho 三鈷杵. A three-point Buddhist *vajra* scepter. The *sankosho*—or simply *sanko*—is a ritual instrument generally made of brass; it is anywhere from 5 to 10 inches (12–25 cm) long. It is used in various rituals performed by Esoteric Buddhist schools (Tendai and Shingon) and Shugendō.

The *sankosho* is often found engraved on sword blades and various other weapons as a talisman. It is also found in Buddhist art and statuary forming the hilt of a sword held by such deities as Fudō Myōō, in which case it is called a *sankotsuka no ken.* See also: *gokosho, kongō; kongōsho; sankotsuka no ken; tokkosho.*

sankotsuka no ken 三鈷柄剣【三鈷柄劍】. Lit. "three point *vajra*-hilted straight sword." A votive sword about 2 feet (60 cm) in length with a hilt made of a three-point *vajra* (*sankosho*). The *sankotsuka no ken* is often found held in the hand of Buddhist deities such as Fudō Myōō, in which case it is most often designed with the Black Dragon King (Kurikara) coiled around the blade. In those instances the sword itself is called the Kurikara Fudō, a symbolic, meditational object (*sammayagyō*) of Fudō Myōō. This version is often found engraved into sword blades as a talisman.

During the Heian and Kamakura periods the *sankotsuka no ken* was carried by the *yamabushi* in the mountains. Originally used somewhat like a machete, its main purpose was to clear away dense vegetation. Later it came to be employed in a more ceremonial fashion with the performance of the *goma* fire ritual. In those cases it was used to exorcise evils or demons from the four directions. Currently the *yamabushi* carry a "wood-cutter" sword (*shiba-uchi*) primarily used to cut wood for the *saitō goma* fire ritual.

sanmai 三昧. See: *sammaiji.*

sanmaji 三摩地. See: *sammaiji.*

sanmayagyō 三昧耶形. See: *sammayagyō.*

sanninbari 三人張. A "three-man bow." A bow which required three men working in a team to string it.

sannin iaidō 三人居合道. A practice found in Shin Shin Musō Ryū 神心無想流 in which quick-draw sword arts are practiced against two live partners (in contrast to standard *iaidō*, in which the proponent practices solo *kata*). See also: *futari iaidō; kumi iai; Ryūshinkan Budō.*

sanpei 散兵. See: *sampei.*

sanrō 参籠【參籠】. A retreat; the act of retiring to a Buddhist temple, Shintō shrine, or other sacred location for prayer and the practice of austerities. This is normally done for a fixed number of days.

sanrō kaigan 参籠開眼【參籠開眼】[Also read ***sanrō kaigen***]. Lit. "a religious retreat for

[12] Tokugawa Iemitsu 徳川家光 (1604–1651; r.1623–1651). Third Tokugawa *shōgun*.

opening the eyes." A religious retreat taken for the purpose of achieving an awakening experience or receiving an oracle.

In a martial context, the term *sanrō kaigan* is sometimes used to indicate a spiritual retreat made by exceptional warriors in order to reach a deeper understanding of their art and themselves. Typically warriors who engaged in this practice were successful in battle and/or duel but had reached a psychological and spiritual impasse in their lives. They would retreat to a solitary location known for its spiritual power (a remote Shintō shrine or temple) and engage in religious practices and austerities for a specific number of days. Their hope was to achieve a spiritually enlightening experience during this retreat. Many warriors engaged in this practice; although not all were successful, those who were include founders of new traditions such as Iizasa Ienao of the Tenshinshō-den Katori Shintō Ryū, Tsukahara Bokuden of the Kashima Shintō Ryū, Aisu Ikōsai of the Kage Ryū, and Kamiizumi Ise no Kami of the Shinkage Ryū, to name only a few.

Sanryaku 『三略』 <Ch. *Sanlue* (The three briefs [on strategy]) [A.k.a. ***Kōsekikō sanryaku*** 『黄石公三略』 <Ch. *Huang Shigong sanlue*]. One of several Chinese texts on military strategy that were supposedly imported into Japan by Ōe no Koretoki during the reign of Emperor Daigo.[13] The title *Sanryaku* is a reference to a three-section explanation of the secret inner workings of military strategy (*senryaku* 戦略).

This and other texts were translated into Japanese during the tenth century, and were included, along with a mixture of Buddhist and Daoist esoterica, into the family-transmitted martial traditions of the Minamoto clan. This compendium was kept a well-guarded secret until it appeared in written form centuries later as the *Genke Kin'etsushū.*

At least one version of the *Sanryaku* entitled *Huang Shigong sanlue* 『黄石公三略』 (Huang Shigong's three briefs on strategy) has been published in English (see below). See also: *Buryaku shichi sho; Genji no heihō; Genke kin'etsushū; Kiichi Hōgan; Kiichi Hōgan Ryū; Ōe no Koretoki; Rikutō.*

Further reading in English:

- Sawyer, 1993: 277–306.

sansen 三戦 【三戰】 <Oki. *sanchin*. See: *sanchin.*

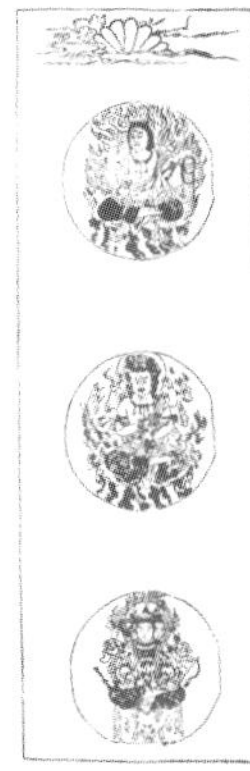

THE SANSENJIN (THREE WAR GODS)
The Sansenjin depicted on Uesugi Kenshin's battle banner (*noboribata*)
(Illustration from an old untitled manuscript in the collection of Sasama Yoshihiko)

Sansenjin 三戦神 【三戰神】. The "Three War Gods." Membership in this group varies; the depiction above includes Fudō Myōō, Aizen Myōō, and Marishiten.

- Fudō Myōō—A Buddhist deity manifesting *fudōshin* (steadfast or imperturbable mind).
- Aizen Myōō—A Buddhist deity manifesting battle passion.
- Marishiten—A Buddhist tutelary goddess of warriors manifesting the ability to make oneself invisible and confuse the minds of one's enemies. Marishiten also represents several combative traits: *fudōshin* (imperturbability), *kan* (intuition), *sen* (volition), and *jihi* (compassion).

COMMANDER'S WAR FAN (*GUNSEN*) EMBLAZONED WITH THE SANSENJIN
(Left to right): Bishamonten, Marishiten, Benzaiten
(Illustration from a *densho* dated 1646)

---

13 Daigo Tennō 醍醐天皇 (885–930; r.897–930). Sixtieth emperor of Japan.

In other depictions, the Sansenjin might include, for example, Bishamonten, Marishiten, and Benzaiten; Daikokuten, Marishiten, and Bishamonten; and so on.

Sanshin Ryū 三心流. A classical school of sickle-and-chain arts (*kusarigama-jutsu*) attributed to Kanemaki Jisai Michiie, c.1595.

Sanshū 三舟. See: *Bakumatsu no Sanshū.*

Sanshu no Jingi 三種神器【三種神器】[Also read ***Sanshu no Shinki*** and ***Mikusa no Kandakara***]. SHINTŌ—The three sacred treasures given to the Shintō deity (*kami*) Ninigi no Mikoto by Amaterasu Ōmikami. These treasures, which include the sacred sword (Ame no Murakumo no Tsurugi), mirror (Yata no Kagami), and jewel (Yasakani no Magatama), are considered the three sacred regalia of the Japanese imperial throne.

Sanshu no Shinki 三種神器【三種神器】. See: *Sanshu no Jingi.*

sansō 山僧. A Buddhist priest.

Santoku Tō Ryū 三徳当流【三德當流】. A combative school which flourished in Sendai domain during the Edo period. The Santoku Tō Ryū specialized in the "three arresting weapons" (*mitsudōgu*).

sanzen 参禅【參禪】. 1. Zen meditation. 2. Practicing meditation under the care of a master. 3. A Zen *kōan* interview between a master and a student.

Further reading in English:

• Miura and Sasaki, 1965: 29–30.

sanzoku 山賊. A brigand; a mountain bandit.

Sanzu no Kawa 三途の川. Lit. the "River of Three Crossings." An article of Japanese folk Buddhist belief somewhat equivalent to the river Styx of Greek mythology. All dead souls must pass over one of the crossings on the seventh day after death. One is shallow, the second deep, and the third fathomless. A soul's crossing place depends on how that person's life was lived; the worse the soul, the deeper the crossing.

Saraba ja! 然らばじゃ! [Var. 薩囀喏!]. Farewell! Goodbye! The term *Saraba ja!* was a traditional "farewell" used by members of the warrior class in during the Edo period. The term appears to be a colloquialization of *sabba' j'na* 薩囀喏那 [Var. 薩婆若(那)] <Ch. *saforena* <Skt. *sarvajñā*. Lit. "all wisdom" (a Buddhist term meaning universal wisdom, the mental state of the Buddha), originally transliterated into Japanese as *sarubajana* or *sabba'j'na* and later "creoled" into *saraba ja*.

saru 申. The ninth duodenary hour of the Chinese Twelve Branches (Jūnishi). *Saru*, which symbolizes the Monkey, indicates the hours from 3 to 5 p.m. In certain Sino-Japanese boxing texts, this symbol (corresponding to the Hour of the Monkey) indicates the optimal time of day for striking a specific vital point (*kyūsho*). See also: Appendix 1.

sarubō 猿頰. Lit. "monkey face." A type of face guard (*mempō*) that covered only the cheeks and chin.

Sasaki Ganryū 佐々木 巌流. See: *Sasaki Kojirō.*

Sasaki Kojirō 佐々木 小次郎 [A.k.a. ***Sasaki Ganryū*** 佐々木 巌流; ***Sasaki Kojirō Ganryū*** 佐々木 小次郎 巌流] (1572–1612). Founder of the Gan Ryū school of swordsmanship (*kenjutsu*). In addition to founding the Gan Ryū, Kojirō was a famous duelist in the early years of the seventeenth century. After receiving a full license in the Chūjō Ryū, he set out on *musha shugyō* to perfect his own Gan Ryū. Through his travels he became known as the best swordsman in western Japan. According to legend, he became famous for creating a sword technique called *tsubamegaeshi* with which he was able to move his sword so deftly that he could cut a swallow in flight. Counter to author Yoshikawa Eiji's fictional story about the life of Miyamoto Musashi, Kojirō was revered for both his swordsmanship and his personal demeanor—he was seen as a man of integrity, culture, and compassion. Though he was famous for his dueling skills with an outsized sword (*ōdachi*), he was killed in a contest with Miyamoto Musashi in 1612. In that duel Musashi is said to have used an extra-long *bokken* carved from an oar against Kojirō's famed *ōdachi.*

Further reading in English:

- Sugawara, 1985: 48–51, 83.
- Tokitsu, 2004: 70–89 *ff.*

Sasaki Saburōbei Moritsuna 佐々木 三郎兵衛 盛綱 (c. 1698–c. 1770). Founder of Issa Ryū 一佐流, a comprehensive martial school (*sōgō bujutsu*) sometime during the Gembun era (1736–1741).

Sasaki Tessai Tokuhisa 佐々木 哲斎 徳久【佐々木哲齋德久】. Founder of the Muhi Muteki Ryū 無比無敵流, a combative school concentrating on staff arts, c. 1625.

sashichigae 刺し違え. A type of mutual suicide mentioned in the war tales of the early medieval period. The term means "mutual stabbing"; warriors carried it out by simultaneously falling on the swords of their comrades.

sashimono 差物 [Var. 指物]. See: *sashimono hata.*

sashimono hata 差物旗 [Var. 指物旗]. A small pennant, flag, banner, or other device, usually attached to a long pole and used as a standard. *Sashimono* were evidently first used in 1456 by the warrior Hatakeyama Masanaga. See: *hatajirushi*; *noboribata.*

SENGOKU-PERIOD USE OF *SASHIMONO HATA*
(Sixteenth-century painting)

sashizoe 差添え. The assisting or auxiliary sword; the "side sword" (*wakizashi*) or "small sword" (*kodachi*).

sasumata 刺叉 [Var. 挟朕/指叉]. A forked polearm approximately 6.5 feet (2 m) in length, used to trap opponents. A number of variations were developed. This weapon found wide use during the Azuchi-Momoyama and early Edo periods as one of the three primary weapons (*mitsudōgu*) for used in concert for trapping and restraining swordsmen. See also: *sodegarami*; *tsukubō.*

SASUMATA

sasumatajutsu 刺股術 [Var. 挟股術; 刺叉術]. 1. Techniques using the forked polearm (*sasumata*) to entrap opponents. 2. A general term for arresting techniques and systems which make use of the *mitusdōgu.* (Kaminoda, 2006: 94).

EDO-PERIOD POLICEMAN (*DŌSHIN*) THREATENING A SWORDSMAN WITH A *SASUMATA*
Detail from the nineteenth-century *Tokugawa Bakufu keiji zufu honpen*
(Used with permission of the Meiji University Museum)

Satake Kanryūsai Yoshifumi 佐竹 鑑柳斎 義文【佐竹鑒柳齋義文】(fl. early to late 1800s). A direct student of Sakakibara Kenkichi who founded the Jikishin Ryūei Ryū 直心柳影流, a system of sword (*kenjutsu*) and glaive (*naginata*). Satake apparently founded the Ryūei Ryū (1) 柳影流; later, after training extensively with Sakakibara Kenkichi in the Jiki Shinkage Ryū 直心影流, he combined the two systems and renamed his tradition the Jikishin Ryūei Ryū. One of Satake's most prominent students was his wife, Satake Shigeo, who was the progenitor of Jiki Shinkage Ryū Naginatajutsu 直心影流薙刀術.

Satake Shigeo 佐竹 茂雄 (fl. early to late 1800s). Wife of Satake Kanryūsai. Shigeo apparently founded Jiki Shinkage Ryū Naginatajutsu 直心影流薙刀術 in the late 1800s. Her successor in the system was Sonobe Hideo (1895).

Satō Ikkaku 佐藤 一覚【佐藤 一覺】. Founder of the Ikkaku Ryū (2) 一覚流, a comprehensive martial arts school (*sōgō bujutsu*), in 1585.

sato kamari 里かまり. 1. Covert assault troops who hid in hamlets until a signal was given for them to form up and make a surprise attack on enemy forces. 2. A surprise attack mounted from a hamlet. See also: *kamari (1), ninjutsu.*

Satō Kinbei 佐藤 金兵衛. A direct disciple of Hakkō Ryū founder Okuyama Yoshiji. In 1966 Satō founded a martial school he called the Daiwadō 大和道, which was a mixture of grappling techniques (*aikijutsu* and *jūjutsu*), fist attacks (*kempo* [2]), and several weapon arts including swordsmanship (*kenjutsu*), long hardwood staff arts (*bōjutsu*), and medium-length hardwood staff arts (*jōjutsu*). In appearance, Daiwadō is very similar to the *aiki* systems Satō studied: Daitō Ryū 大東流, Hakkō Ryū 八光流, and Ueshiba Ryū Aikidō 植芝流合気道, among others.

Satomura Zuishinsai Masauji 里村 随心斎正氏【里村隨心齋正氏】. Founder of the Zuishin Ryū 随心流, a system of swordsmanship (*kenjutsu*) based on the Seigō Ryū, c.1640.

satori 悟り [Var. 覚り【覺り】]. BUDDHISM—enlightenment; awakening. See also: *gonyū.*

Satsuma Han 薩摩藩. A feudal domain located on the southwestern corner of the island of Kyūshū, now part of Kagoshima prefecture. Satsuma was controlled by the Shimazu 島津 family from the twelfth century until 1871 when, like all other remaining *daimyō*, they were suppressed and pensioned out by the Meiji government. From the seventeenth century, Satsuma also controlled the Ryukyu archipelago, including Okinawa.

A number of martial *ryū* were developed or took up residence in Satsuma, including the Jigen Ryū 示現流, the Ko Jigen Ryū 小示現流, the Nodachi Jigen Ryū 野太刀示現流, the Taisha Ryū タイ捨流, and others.

satsu ya 殺矢. A hunting arrow.

satsu yumi 殺弓. A hunting bow.

Sawara Minamoto no Nisaburō Sukemitsu 佐原 源二三郎 祐光. Sawara was the ninth-generation headmaster of the Gassan Ryū 月山流, a school concentrating on three polearms: long-hafted glaive (*naginata*), spear (*yari*), and pole sickle (*nagae no kama*). One of his successors was Hiki Yoshio, who founded the Jikishin Ryū (4) 直心流.

Sawayama Sōkai 沢山 宗海【澤山宗海】. Founder of a pugilism-based fighting system known as Nihon Kempō 日本拳法 in 1932.

saya 鞘. A scabbard for a Japanese sword.

saya ate 鞘当て【鞘當】. 1. The act of striking another warrior's scabbard (*saya*) with one's own scabbard (either intentionally or accidentally). This often provoked a combative engagement. 2. A challenge.

se 施. See: *hodokoshi.*

Seia Ryū 雖井蛙流 [Also written 井蛙流]. Originally a martial school concentrating on combative swordsmanship (*kenjutsu*) with either the longsword (*katana*) or short sword (*kodachi*); spearmanship (*sōjutsu*); and armored grappling (*kumiuchi*). The Seia Ryū today refers to its swordsmanship as *heihō* (2) 平法 ("methods of peace" or "methods of quelling conflict").

The school was founded around 1670 by a landed warrior (*goshi*) of Tottori domain named Fukao Kakuma Shigeyoshi. (Fukao was also known by the name Seia 井蛙.) An eclectic martial artist, Seia learned Tanseki Ryū 丹石流 from his father and went on to train in a number of diverse combative schools. With this experience he proceeded to modify the armored swordsmanship of the Tanseki Ryū into an efficient system adaptable to unarmored situations. He categorized these revised, unarmored forms as *heihō*, but used the characters 平法 (methods of peace) in lieu of 兵法 (combative strategies). Due to some misfortune, Seia was ordered to commit *seppuku* in 1682. He was fifty-two years old. His school divided into several lines, at least one of which has been passed down to the present.

Seia Ryū
雖井蛙流
(abbreviated lineage)

Kawada Riemon
河田 理右衛門
Tanseki Ryū
丹石流
(fifth-generation successor)
Father of Fukao Kakuma Shigeyoshi

Fukao Kakuma Shigeyoshi (Seia)
初代　深尾 角馬 重義(井蛙)
Seia Ryū
雖井蛙流

Shirai Gendayū Masashige
白井 源太夫 正林
Shirai Ha
白井派

Ichihara Sōbei
市原 惣兵衛
Ichihara Ha
市原派

The Ichihara Ha subdivides into several branches over the succeeding years of the Edo period.

Ishiko Yomozaemon Masakata
石河 四方左衛門 正方
Ishiko Ha
石河派

Ishiko Yomozaemon Masao
石河 四方左衛門 正直
Ishiko Ha

The Ishiko Ha subdivides into several branches over the succeeding years of the Edo period. At least one of these, the Yokoo Ha 横尾派, is still practiced today.

Seia Ryū Ichihara Ha 雖井蛙流市原派. See: *Seia Ryū lineage.*

Seia Ryū Ishiko Ha 雖井蛙流石河派 [Also written 井蛙流石河派] [A.k.a. ***Ishiko Ha*** 石河派]. See: *Seia Ryū lineage.*

Seia Ryū Shirai Ha 雖井蛙流白井派. See: *Seia Ryū lineage.*

Seia Ryū Yokoo Ha 雖井蛙流横尾派. See: *Seia Ryū lineage.*

seii shi 征夷使. See: *seii taishōgun.*

seii taishōgun 征夷大将軍【征夷大將軍】[Var. ***seii shi*** 征夷使]. Lit. "commanding general sent against the barbarians" or "barbarian-quelling general." This title, which was used as early as 720, originally referred to a temporary post for various generals who were sent out on expeditions to quell the barbarians (the Ebisu 夷) in the eastern and northern areas of the Japanese islands. This title was given permanent status, becoming a hereditary lifetime post, when it was bestowed upon Minamoto no Yoritomo in 1192. It was under this title (abbreviated as *shōgun* [general]) that the Minamoto (1192–1219), the Fujiwara (1220–1244), several imperial princes (1245–1334), the Minamoto branch family called the Ashikaga (1336–1573), and the Minamoto branch family called the Tokugawa (1603–1868) ruled Japan under unrestricted military control. From the time of Minamoto no Yoritomo the title was generally reserved for members of the Minamoto family (that is, the Seiwa Genji).[14] Consequently some of the great conqueror-rulers of later years, such as Oda Nobunaga (a descendant of the Taira) and Toyotomi Hideyoshi (who was of commoner origins), were never awarded the title. See also: *chinjufu shōgun.*

Sei Ezo Shōgun 征蝦夷将軍【征蝦夷將軍】. See: *chinjufu shōgun.*

seigan 1. 誓願 <Ch. *shiyuan* <Skt. *praṇidhāna.* Vows taken by buddhas and *bodhisattvas* when they aspire to buddhahood. See also: *tachigiri seigan.*

seigan 2. 青眼. An abbreviation for *seigan no kamae.*

Seigan Jiki Shinkage Ryū 青眼直心影流. A branch tradition of the Jiki Shinkage Ryū which descended from thirteenth headmaster Odani Seiichirō through several of his disciples. According to official documents (*hanmyō*) from Shibata domain in Echigo, two samurai, Kubota Ryōzaburō and Mizoguchi Shūta, became disciples of Odani in 1843. (Watatani and Yamada, 1978: 480). Both men received the complete system from Odani and, in 1847, each was appointed "caretaker of swordsmanship training" (*kenjutsu keiko seiwayaku*) by Shibata domain. The two lines of this school descend from that time.

seigan no kamae 青眼の構. A variety of combative engagement postures in which one's weapon is pointed right between the opponent's eyes. See also: *chokuritsu seigan (no kamae); jun seigan (no kamae);* and *migi seigan (no kamae).*

[14] An exception was the so-called Fujiwara *bakufu*, in which the Hōjō regents appointed members of the Fujiwara family as *shōgun*.

S

Seigō Ryū 制剛流. The founding of this important *jūjutsu* tradition is attributed to Mizuhaya Chōzaemon Nobumasa (c.1568–c.1630). Little is known about Nobumasa, and even less is known about the monk named Seigō (Sō Seigō) who, according to legend, introduced Nobumasa to *jūjutsu*, and for whom the system is named.

The Seigō Ryū originally centered on various types of grappling, and also included other arts, as indicated by *densho* dating from the seventeenth century. Those documents contain titles indicating the following combat systems: grappling in light armor (*kogusoku*), arresting arts (*torite*), unarmored grappling (*yawara*), and quick-draw sword arts (*iaijutsu*). Many martial schools specializing in one or more of the combative arts found in the original system were later derived from the Seigō Ryū, such as the Jigan Ryū 慈眼流, the Yagyū Seigō Ryū 柳生制剛流, the Kashin Ryū 霞新流, and the Araki Kashin Ryū 荒木霞新流, to name only a few. Because of this, the Seigō Ryū made a major contribution to the wide development of *jūjutsu* in later years. Watatani Kiyoshi categorized it as one of the "Big Four" schools of grappling which, because of their technical acumen and wide base of practitioners, most influenced Japanese *jūjutsu*. The other three were the Kitō Ryū, the Sekiguchi Ryū, and the Takenouchi Ryū. (See lineage chart below.)

See also: *Zuishin Ryū*.

Further reading in English:

- Mol, 2001: 172–176.

Seigō Sō 制剛 僧. See: *Sō Seigō*.

Seigō Ryū
制剛流
(abbreviated lineage)

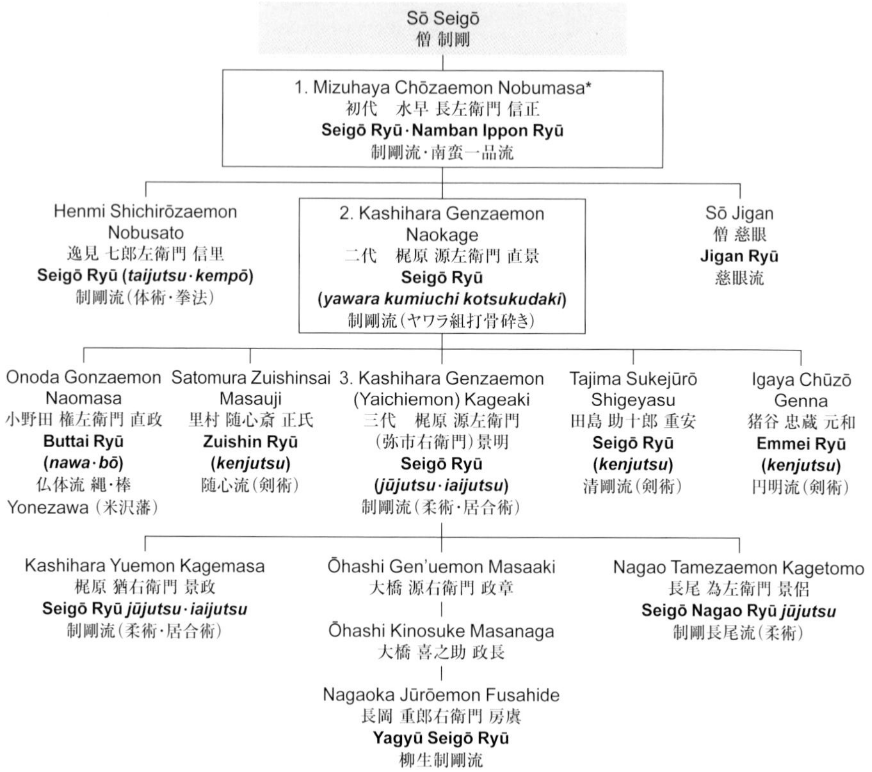

* The Yagyu Shinkage Ryū Heihou Official Site (http://www.yagyu-shinkage-ryu.jp/rekisi_e.html) reads 水早 as "Isahaya." However, this is an unusual reading. Watatani and Yamada (1978: 930) and other sources give it the standard reading of "Mizuhaya."

seihei 精兵. A term used in a tenth-century chronicle, the *Shōyūki*,[15] to mean a "soldier of good quality," a "fine soldier"; or elite troops. The term probably refers to the rising professional warrior class in contrast to part-time soldiers or armed civilians. Farris, who uses the reading ***jōhei*** (1992: 64), speculates that in the eighth century this term may have referred to mounted archers from eastern Japan.

seihō 勢法. YAGYŪ SHINKAGE RYŪ—Lit. "mighty methods" or "methods of energy." The Yagyū Shinkage Ryū uses *seihō* to refer to prearranged fighting forms (*kata*). This term was inherited from Kamiizumi Nobutsuna's Shinkage Ryū. See: *Shiai Seihō.*

seikan 生間 <Ch. *shengjian.* The fifth of the five types of secret agents (*ninja*; *shinobi*) mentioned in Sun Tzu's *Art of War* (*Sonshi no heihō*). The term *seikan* refers to "living agents" or "surviving agents"; i.e., spies who return with information. See: *kanja; kyōdan (1); ninjutsu; Sonshi no heihō.*

seika tanden 臍下丹田 <Ch. *qixiz dantian*]. See: *tanden.*

seikotsu 整骨. Bone-setting. This healing art was practiced by several traditions, especially those with an emphasis on grappling and joint-locking techniques.

Seinan Sensō 西南戦争【西南戰爭】. Lit. the "Southwestern War." The Satsuma Rebellion of 1877. This conflict, led by Saigo Takamori, was a revolt against the Meiji government spurred by the dissolution of the samurai class and the 1876 edict banning of the carrying of swords (Haitōrei). See: *Saigō Takamori.*

Further reading in English:

- Buck, 1973.
- Morris, 1975c.
- Ravina, 2004.

Seininki 『正忍記』. See: *Shōninki.*

seiōken 星王剣【星王劍】[Also read *shōōken*]. Lit. "star-lord sword." A term used in both Hokushin Musō Ryū and Hokushin Ittō Ryū to define the concepts and techniques which are the core of those schools of swordsmanship. The term *seiō* 星王 refers to Polaris, the North Star, and is related to the term Sonjōō 尊星王, a pseudonym for Myōken Bosatsu, the deity from whom Chiba Kichinosuke Tsuneshige received the oracle of the secrets of the Hokushin Musō Ryū. See also: *Hokushin Ittō Ryū; Hokushin Musō Ryū; Myōken Bosatsu.*

seirei 蜻蛉 [Also read ***akitsu***]. A dragonfly. See: *akitsu.*

seiryōken 青竜剣【青龍劍】<Ch. *qinglong yanyue dao* 青龍偃月刀. The Japanese term *seiryōken* literally means "green dragon sword." The word is derived from the Chinese term *qinglong yanyue dao* meaning "green dragon crescent-moon-shaped glaive." The weapon, which is traditionally shown in pictures with the Chinese hero (and later god of war) Guanyu (Jp. Kan'u), was a type of heavy glaive (Ch. *guandao* 闕刀 or *yanyue dao* 偃月刀) with a curved blade that appeared to be emanating from a dragon's mouth. Many Japanese sword fittings are decorated with a depiction of Guanyu with his *seiryōken.*

seiryoku saizen katsuyō 精力最善活用. A concept articulated by the Kōdōkan Culture Council (Kōdōkan Bunkakai 講道館文化会) in 1922. The phrase essentially means "effective use of the power of body and mind is the key to self-perfection."

seiryoku zenyō 精力善用. KŌDŌKAN JŪDŌ—The term *seiryoku zenyō,* which means "maximum, efficient use of energy," is often found pared with *jita kyōei*, "mutual prosperity for self and others." These two maxims, first proposed by Kōdōkan Jūdō founder Kanō Jigorō, officially became the central guiding philosophy of the Kōdōkan in 1922. As articulated in Kōdōkan (2000: 114), this dual concept means that the purpose of *jūdō* is to cultivate the self so that one may then contribute fully to the prosperity of others and society in general.

Seiryoku Zen'yo Kokumin Taiiku no Kata 精力善用国民体育の形. KŌDŌKAN JŪDŌ—The "Maximum-Efficiency National Physical Education Forms" of Kōdōkan Jūdō. These *kata* are designed for warm-up before, and

[15] *Shōyūki* 『小右記』.

S

cool-down after, performing *randori* or other *kata* sets. Kanō Jigorō considered them an essential part of *jūdō* training, and particularly recommended them to "beginners, women, and children under the age of fifteen." The set includes solo strikes and excerpts from paired forms taken from the Kime no Kata and Jū no Kata:

- Tandoku Renshū 単独練習 (solo exercises)
  - 29 standing exercises
- Kime Shiki 極式 (partnered checking forms)
  - 5 Idori 居取 (kneeling forms)
  - 5 Tachiai 立会 (standing forms)
- Jū Shiki 柔式 (partnered flexible forms)
  - 5 forms (set 1)
  - 5 forms (set 2)

seishin no mono 精神の物. Lit. a "spiritual endeavor." A term used by Yamaguchi Gōgen of the Gōjūkai *karate* organization to indicate his shift in emphasis toward spiritual perfection through *karate* training.

seishinryoku 精神力. The power of the mind; power of the spirit. In some modern systems, *seishinryoku* is thought to be a mental power akin to hypnotism (*saiminjutsu*) or domination via the emission of energy (*kiryoku*); that is, *kiai*. (Sasaki, 1991: 98). See also: *aiki; kiai; kiaijutsu.*

seishin shūyō 精神修養. "Development of a healthy mind." This is one of the primary aims espoused by practitioners of Nippon Shōrenji Kempō.

seishin tanren 精神鍛練. Spiritual forging; forging a pure spirit through training.

seishi o chōetsu 生死を超越. Lit. "transcending life and death." A state of mind in which the exponent transcends concerns over life and death. *Seishi o chōetsu*, an important concept within the classical martial arts (*bujutsu*), was considered a keystone of the samurai "mindset," and was in accordance with the tenets of what later became referred to as *bushidō*. See also: *fudōshin.*

seishi wo chōetsu 生死を超越. See: *seishi o chōetsu.*

seiteigata 制定形. Common abbreviation used for a variety of standardized combative form sets (*kata*) created by and for the Nihon Kendō Renmei.

seitō ha 正統派. Lit. "legitimate line" or "orthodox lineage." JIKI SHINKAGE RYŪ—The term *Seitō Ha* is sometimes used to describe the lineage of Jiki Shinkage Ryū passed down from tenth headmaster Fujikawa Chikayoshi through twentieth headmaster Yoshida Hajime. See: *Jiki Shinkage Ryū.*

Seiwa Genji 清和源氏. A warrior branch of the Minamoto family which traces its noble origins to Sadazumi Shinnō (874–916), the son of the emperor Seiwa (r. 858–876). A number of Minamoto warrior families make up the Seiwa Genji. Taking names from the places in which they came to reside, they include the Ashikaga 足利, Hosokawa 細川, Nitta 新田, Ogasawara 小笠原, Sakakibara 榊原, Takeda 武田, Takenouchi 竹内, Tokugawa 徳川, and others.

Further reading in English:
- Papinot, 1910: 552–553.

Seiyō Ryū 西洋流 Lit. "Western School." Also referred to as the Takashima Ryū 高島流. A school of gunnery (*hōjutsu*) founded in the mid-1800s by Takashima Shūhan. Well-trained in both Japanese and Dutch firearms and methods, Takashima developed a system of gunnery exercises and infantry drill he christened *gumpō chōren.* He greatly impressed the Tokugawa shogunate with a demonstration in 1841, and subsequently took his Seiyō Ryū on the road, instructing many of the feudal lords and their retainers.

Partly in response to ever-increasing attempts by foreign powers to "open" Japan in the early nineteenth century, politics and suspicion against anything Western soon came to the fore at the *shōgun*'s court, and in 1846 Takashima was imprisoned.[16] Many of his disciples in the Seiyō Ryū changed the name of the system in order to avoid political fallout. As a result, many branch systems with different names appeared in the first generation

---

[16] Even Western scholarship (*rangaku*) had been suppressed in 1839 as the result of an order called the Bansha no Goku 蛮社の獄.

The Seiwa Genji
清和源氏
(abbreviated lineage)

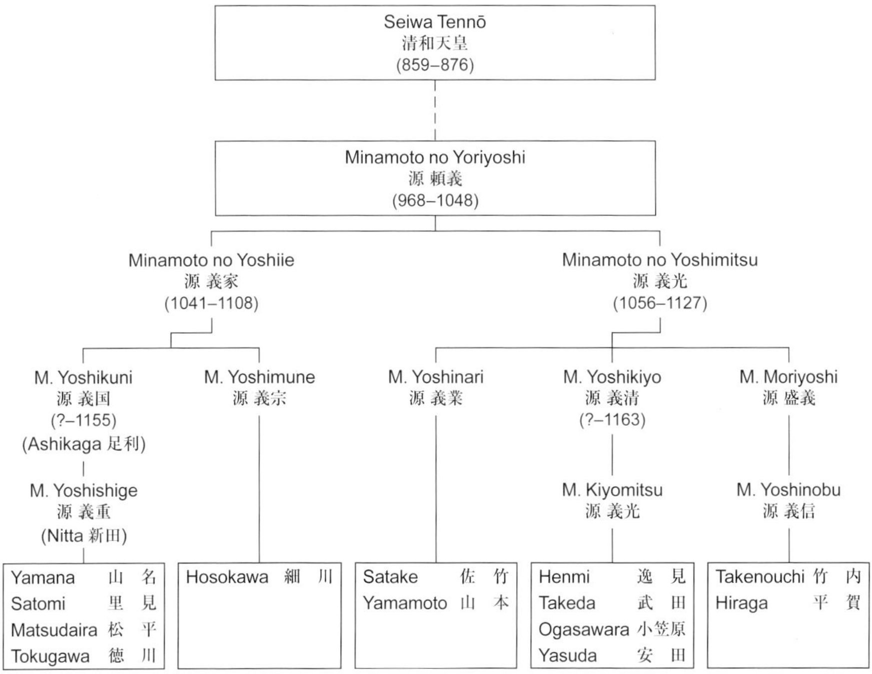

after Takashima. Around the time of Commodore Perry's "opening" of Japan in 1853, Takashima was pardoned; the term "Seiyō Ryū" again became politically correct, and its teachings were again permitted to proliferate.

seiza 正座【正坐】. Traditional sitting posture. In *seiza*, both legs are folded under the body, buttocks resting on the soles of the feet, and the tops of the feet are flat on the floor or a cushion. For the classical warrior, *seiza* was considered a "dead" posture, intended for sitting at rest and for certain ritual procedures such as the tea ceremony. It is difficult to initiate a combative response from this posture. See also: *agura*; *iaidō*; *iaigoshi*; *iaijutsu*, *rengeza*, *tatehiza*.

Seiza Nyūdō Gian 清三 入道 偽庵. Alternate name for Tomomatsu Hyōgo no Kami Ujimune, seventh headmaster of the Nen Shuza Ryū 念首座流.

seki 関【關】. See: *sekisho*.

sekibō 石棒. A type of stone club or staff used in pre-Yamato Japan.

Seki den 関伝【關傳】[A.k.a. ***Mino den*** 美濃伝]. See: *Gokaden*.

Sekigahara no tatakai 関ヶ原の戦い. The battle of Sekigahara. This conflict, which took place on October 21, 1600, established the Tokugawa family as the rulers of Japan for the next 267 years.

Sekigawa Ittō Ryū 積川一刀流. A branch tradition of the Naganuma Ryū (1) 長沼流 (=Jiki Shinkage Ryū 直心影流).

Sekiguchi Jūshin 関口 柔心 [A.k.a. ***Yaroku-emon*** 弥六右衛門【彌六右衛門】] (1598–1670). Founder of the Sekiguchi Ryū 関口流.

Sekiguchi Ryū 関口流【關口流】[A.k.a. ***Shinshin Ryū*** 新心流; ***Sekiguchi Shinshin Ryū*** 関口新心流【關口流新心流】; Sekiguchi Ryū Iaijutsu 関口流抜刀術【關口流拔刀術】]. Originally a comprehensive field-combat system (*sōgo bujutsu*) founded in the early Edo period by

Sekiguchi Jūshin. Sekiguchi had studied quick-draw sword arts (*iai*) under Hayashizaki Jinsuke, founder of Shin Musō Hayashizaki Ryū; grappling arts (*kumiuchi*) under Miura Yojiuemon; and possibly, while traveling on *musha shugyō*, *kempō hobaku* (arresting arts relying on pugilistic striking techniques). Sekiguchi's original system included unarmored grappling (*yawara*), combative swordsmanship (*kenjutsu*), combative spear arts (*sōjutsu*), quick-draw sword arts (*iaijutsu*), horsemanship (*bajutsu*), capturing arts (*torinawa*), and combative staff arts (*bōjutsu*). However, the core of the original system was grappling. Today, few of the battlefield weaponry systems of this school seem to have survived.

Many *jūjutsu* systems were later derived from, or heavily influenced by, the Sekiguchi Ryū. These included Shibukawa Ryū 渋川流, Daitō Ryū 大東流, and Shinkage Ryū (9) 真蔭流 (a *jūjutsu* school not related to the famous sword tradition), to name only a few. Because of this, the Sekiguchi Ryū made a major contribution to the wide development of *jūjutsu* during the Tokugawa period. Watatani Kiyoshi (1974: 4–5) includes it as one of the "Big Four" schools of grappling which, because of their technical acumen and wide base of practitioners, most influenced Japanese *jūjutsu*. The other three are the Kitō Ryū, the Seigō Ryū, and the Takenouchi Ryū.

Further reading in English:

• Mol, 2001: 179–190.

Sekiguchi Yarokuemon Jūshin 関口 弥六右衛門 柔心【關口彌六右衛門柔心】. See: *Sekiguchi Jūshin*.

Sekine Gentarō Masateru 関根 源太郎 正光【關根源太郎正光】. Founder of the Shintō Goshin Ryū 神道五心流, a comprehensive combative school, during the mid to late seventeenth century. Sekine, an eclectic martial artist, received a full license in several traditions, including the Ishikawa Ryū 石川流, the Kiraku Ryū 気楽流, the Yōshin Ryū 楊心流, the Shin Shintō Ryū 新神道流, and others.

Seki Ryū 関流【關流】[A.k.a. ***Seki Ryū Hōjutsu*** ～炮術]. A classical system of matchlock musketry (*hinawaju*) founded in 1803 by Morishige Yukie Tsuyoshi.

Further reading in English:

• Skoss, 1997: 73.

sekisho 関所【關所】[Abbr. ***seki***]. A checkpoint; a barrier station. *Sekisho*, or *seki*, were barrier stations between domains during the premodern periods. They were used to control travel between the territories of the various lords.

Sekiun Ryū 夕雲流. See: *Mujū Shinken Ryū*.

sekiwake 関脇【關脇】. SUMŌ—Lit. "to the side of the barrier" or "beside the checkpoint." The third-highest rank in the modern sport of *sumō*. *Sekiwake* can be translated as "supporting champion" or "contender."

semari 迫り. To press or loom in. ¶ *teki ni semaru* 敵に迫る, to press an opponent; to loom over an enemy.

seme 攻め. 1. An assailant. 2. An attacking military force. 3. Offense or aggression. ¶ *semekakomu* 攻め囲む, to besiege. ¶ *semetatakau* 攻め戦う, to assault.

semedaiko 攻太鼓. A drum signal used to order a charge.

semete 攻手. 1. An assailant. 2. An attacking military force. 3. Offense or aggression.

sempai 先輩. A senior; one who entered training before oneself. (Compare *dōhai*, *kohai*.)

sempō 1. 先鋒. The van or vanguard; the spearhead.

sempō 2. 戦法【戰法】. Tactics; strategy.

sen 先. Lit. "first," "initiative," or, by extension, "volition." In the Japanese combative context, volition is described variously as *sen*, *go no sen*, *sen no sen*, and *sensen no sen*. All of these terms indicate a type of action taken (or, in some cases, withheld) in relation to a combative situation, i.e., the interval (*ma*) of space and time separating opponents. For example, in Japanese the phrase *sen o toru* literally means "to take the initiative."

The ability of a warrior to take the initiative—especially in the early *ryū*—was often associated with the Buddhist goddess Marishiten and the spirit of the *inoshishi* (wild boar) on which she is often pictured.

In the area of combative behavior and performance, the Japanese martial concept of *sen*, or volition, is one of the three key psychological combative adaptive traits; the other two are steadfast/imperturbable mind (*fudōshin*) and intuition (*kan*). See also: *ato no saki; bu no ri; go no sen; saki; sen no sen; sensen no saki; sensen no sen.*

sendan no ita 栴檀の板. An armored board about 8 inches (20 cm) long and 2 inches (5 cm) wide which hung from the top right of an armored breastplate. The *sendan no ita* was designed to shift to cover the right armpit when the wearer stretched his arms out to draw a bow. The *sendan no ita*, along with its counterpart on the left, the *kyūbi no ita*, was a very functional part of the armor of the Heian and Kamakura periods. They became nonfunctional ornaments during the Muromachi period, however, when the bow was gradually replaced by other weapons and the *ita* were replaced by the *wakibiki*.

(Photograph courtesy Pat Lineberger)

sengoku daimyō 戦国大名【戰國大名】. A term characteristically used for local warlords in the Warring States period (Sengoku Jidai). During the fourteenth and fifteenth centuries, the *daimyō*, in general, evolved from hereditary land-holding stewards to local warlords intent on the military domination of whatever territories they could conquer and hold.

Further reading in English:

- Davis, 1974.
- Miyagawa and Kiley, 1977.
- Nagahara, 1977.

Sengoku Jidai 戦国時代【戰國時代】. The Warring States period, an age in which Japan was completely torn by civil war. Various beginning and ending dates are given for this era, such as 1490–1600; 1482–1588; 1467–1568, etc. The Sengoku Jidai was a period of approximately 100 years, beginning after the Ōnin War (1467–1477) and lasting through the end of the sixteenth century. The actual dates depend on which battles are used to identify the beginning and end of the period.

Sengo Muramasa 千子 村正. See: *Muramasa.*

sengun 船軍. See: *funa-ikusa; funa-ikusa no hō.*

sengunhō 船軍法. Naval strategy and tactics. See: *funaikusa no hō.*

ILLUSTRATION OF SEN'I RYŪ *NAGINATAJUTSU*
Geijutsu Bukoron, 1768

Sen'i Ryū 先意流. A system of long-hafted glaive arts (*naginatajutsu*) practiced in the Tōda domain during the eighteenth and nineteenth centuries. Kashiwabuchi Yūgi, a student of Masaki Toshimitsu, illustrated a number of the techniques of this *ryū* in his late eighteenth-century work *Geijutsu bukoron* 『芸術武功論』 (Discourses on martial arts exploits). See also: *Kotōda Ha Ittō Ryū; Masaki Ryū.*

senjin 先陣. See: *sakigake.*

senjōjutsu 戦場術【戰場術】. Tactics of warrior deployment on the battlefield; battlefield tactics.

senjutsu 戦術【戰術】. Battle skills/arts; tactics. See: *heihō.*

senkimono 戦記物【戰記物】[Var. ***senki monogatari*** 戦記物語【戰記物語】]. Classical war tales. See: *gunkimono.*

Senmoto Akiteru 宣本 英照. A direct disciple of Hakkō Ryū founder Okuyama Yoshiji. Along with Watanabe Akiteru, Senmoto subsequently founded a school called Uchūdō 宇宙道, which concentrated on self-defense (*goshin* 護身).

Sen no Rikyū 千 利休 (1522–1591). The tea master for two important warlord unifiers of Japan: Oda Nobunaga and Toyotomi Hideyoshi. Sen no Rikyū was the progenitor of the Senke Ryū 千家流, a school of tea ceremony emphasizing simplicity and rusticity (*wabi-sabi*). This aesthetic appealed to both the semi-noble warrior class and commoners. Through Sen no Rikyū's descendants, the school divided into three main lines of tea ceremony: Urasenke, Omotesenke, and Mushakōjisenke.

Further reading in English:
- Anderson, 1991.
- Okakura, 1964.

sen no sen 先の先 [Var. ***sen no tai*** 先の対【先の對】; ***tai no tai*** 対の対 【對の對】]. One of three categories of initiative (*sen*) recognized by most classical *ryū*. In this case it is preemptive action; using initiative to prevent the enemy's taking initiative; attack initiative. This is also seen as an aspect of *kōbō ichi*, which means attack and defense are simply different aspects of the same combative matrix. See also: *ato no saki; bu no ri; go no sen; saki; sen; sensen no saki; sensen no sen.*

sen o toru 先を取る [Also written ***sen wo toru***]. To take the initiative (in a combative situation). See: *sen.*

senpai 先輩. See: *sempai.*

senpō 1. 先鋒. See: *sempō (1).*

senpō 2. 戦法【戰法】. See: *sempō (2).*

senryaku 戦略【戰略】<Ch. *zhanlue*. Military strategy; battle tactics. See: *heihō; Sanryaku.*

senryū 川柳. A short satirical poem similar to a *haiku*. This style of humorous verse became popular during the Edo period. According to Seward (1968: 88), it was often used by the *chonin* (townsmen or merchant class) as an indirect, and thus relatively safe, way to criticize the samurai.

Senryū Ryū 千柳流 <Ko. *Ryupee Ryu*. An obscure school of Japanese swordsmanship described and illustrated in an eighteenth-century Korean text known as the *Bugei zufu tōshi*『武藝圖譜通志』<Ko. *Muye dobo tongji*. See: *Bugei zufu tōshi.*

Further reading in English:
- Kim, (Trans.) 2001: 175–184, 194–195.

sensei 先生. Teacher; professor. In the context of modern martial arts and ways, the term *sensei* is used when addressing one's teacher or recognized teachers of other traditions, or in referring to a person of that status in the third person. It is never used to refer to oneself or listed as a title on one's calling card (*meishi* 名刺). Use of this term varies somewhat by tradition. See: *osensei; ōsensei.*

sen sen 先先. See: *sen no sen.*

sensen no saki 先々の先. One of three categories of initiative (*sen* 先) recognized by modern Japanese police combative systems (*taihōjutsu*). *Sensen no saki* is akin to the older concept of *sensen no sen*; that is, an arresting officer is able to control an assailant before the latter can contemplate an attack. In *taihōjutsu* this is considered the most advantageous of three types of initiative (*sen*). The other two are *saki* and *ato no saki*. See also: *ato no saki; bu no ri; go no sen; saki; sen; sen no sen; sensen no sen.*

sensen no sen 先々の先 [Var. ***kakari no sen*** 懸の先]. Pre-active/pre-emptive action; using initiative to suppress or defeat an enemy before he has a chance to contemplate an attack. See also: *ato no saki; bu no ri; go no sen; saki; sen; sen no sen; sensen no saki.*

senshi 撰士. Lit. "select warriors." A late eighth-century term from Kyūshū for "mounted warriors."

sensō 戦争【戰爭】. War.

sentōhō 戦闘法【戰闘法】. Battle strategy; combat strategy.

seoidachi 背負い太刀. Any long sword worn slung over the shoulder; an *ōdachi*. See: *ōdachi (3).*

seppa 切羽. On Japanese bladed weapons, *seppa* are metal spacers—essentially washers—

placed between the blade collar (*habaki*) and the handguard (*tsuba*), and between the handguard and the hilt (*tsuka*) of the weapon.

seppuku 切腹. 1. Lit. "belly cutting." Ceremonial suicide via self-disembowelment. By reversing the ideograms, the pronunciation of the term is changed to *hara-kiri* 腹切, a vulgar term for the same act. In this method of self-immolation, the warrior would cut open his lower abdomen from left to right. This was a very painful process, and by the Edo period it had become customary for a "second" (*kaishakunin*) to stand by with a drawn sword in order to behead the performer once the cut was completed. In reality the beheading was often executed almost immediately after the incision was begun.

Over the centuries several types of *seppuku* evolved for various purposes, such as *chūgibara* (to show support and loyalty to a superior), *kanshi* (as a statement of non-support for a superior), *munenbara* (to show vexation or chagrin due to one's superior), *sokotsushi* 粗忽死 (as atonement for a blunder), etc. Over the course of the peaceful Edo period, various methods of *seppuku* evolved which did not actually require the condemned to cut himself. Descriptions of these less painful methods and criticism of them can be found in Seward (1968: 68–71).

Seppuku is mentioned on occasion in documents and tales from the early medieval period during the Hōgen Conflict (Hōgen no Ran, 1156), but does not appear to have been a common custom at that time. When it does appear it is usually performed by "eastern warriors" (Bandō *musha*) in order to remove a stain on one's honor. However, in the fourteenth-century *Taiheiki* the act of *seppuku* appears quite often and is performed by warriors from all regions of Japan, sometimes in explicit and graphic detail. As Nitobe (1969: 116) points out, by the Edo period *seppuku* had become "an institution, legal and ceremonial...by which warriors could expiate their crimes, apologize for errors, escape from disgrace, redeem their friends, or prove their sincerity."

Other methods of warrior suicide—at least in the early medieval period—included falling on one's own sword, as well as mutual stabbing (*sashi-chigaete*) with warrior comrades. In the *Taiheiki* a new reason for performing suicide emerged, as well: to follow one's lord into death (*junshi* or *oibara*). See, for example, McCullough, (1959): 310–311. See also: *kanshi; junshi; monzenbarai; shikei.*

2. ***seppuku*** 切腹. The order for self-immolation was the most severe of the five grades of penalties applied to the samurai during the Tokugawa period. See also: *chikkyo; heimon; hissoku; kaieki.*

Further reading in English:

- Brinkley and Kikuchi, 1915: 641–642 *ff.*
- Draeger, 1995: 6.26–28.
- Dürckheim, 1962: *passim.*
- Nitobe, 1969: 111–130.
- Schreiber, 2001.
- Seward, 1968.
- Varley, 1994: *passim.*

seppuku mono 切腹者. An idiom indicating a situation in which the appropriate solution is suicide (*seppuku*).

setsunintō katsujinken 殺人刀活人剣【殺人刀活人劍】[Also read ***setsunintō katsuninken***]. Lit. "death-dealing sword—life-giving sword." 1. A term used in several places in the classical Chinese work on Zen called the *Blue Cliff Records* (*Hekiganroku*). 2. SHINKAGE RYŪ—*Setsunintō katsujinken* is one of the most profound concepts within the Shinkage Ryū 新陰流; naturally, it has many nuances. The *Heihō kadensho* by Yagyū Munenori contains three sections: The Shoe-presenting Bridge (*Shinrikyō* 進履橋); Death-dealing Sword (*Setsunintō*); and Life-giving Sword (*Katsujinken*). Munenori notes that *setsunintō katsujinken* means the killing of one evil person allows many others to live in peace; i.e., in this way, the sword that kills (*setsunintō*) is the sword that gives life (*katsujinken*). The priest Takuan, who was a close associate and friend of Munenori, elaborates further on this concept. He notes in his *Taiaki*:

> ...the accomplished man uses the sword but does not kill others. He uses the sword and gives others life. When it is necessary to kill, he kills. When it is necessary to give life, he gives life. When killing, he kills in complete

S

> concentration; when giving life, he gives life in complete concentration…

Takuan then comments on these lines:

> *…the accomplished man* means the man accomplished in the martial arts.
>
> *He uses the sword, but not to kill others* means that even though he does not use the sword to cut others down, when others are confronted by this principle, they cower and become as dead men of their own accord. There is no need to kill them.
>
> *He uses the sword and gives others life* means that while he deals with his opponent with a sword, he leaves everything to the movements of the other man, and is able to observe him just as he pleases.
>
> *When it is necessary to kill, he kills; when it is necessary to give life, he gives life. When killing, he kills with complete concentration; when giving life, he gives life with complete concentration* means that in either giving life or taking life, he does so with freedom in a meditative state that is total absorption, and the meditator becomes one with the object of meditation.
>
> Wilson, 2002: 116

Thus, this phrase can also refer to defeating an enemy without killing him (*katsujinken*) and defeating an enemy by killing him (*setsunintō*). This principle, according to Yagyū Nobuharu, facilitated the evolution of the Yagyū Shinkage Ryū from, as he put it, "swordsmanship which conquered the country" into "swordsmanship which ruled the country" under the ensuing protracted peace of the Edo period.[17] This attitude also helped facilitate the transition of the Shinkage Ryū and other combative systems (*bujutsu ryū*) during that period from systems primarily aimed at destroying an enemy in battle into systems focused on dealing with suppression of lawlessness (policing), the preservation of a peacetime social hierarchy in which the warrior class held the top tier, and spiritual introspection. 3. SHINKAGE RYŪ—According to the late Mutō Masao[18] of the Ōtsubo Line of the Yagyū Shinkage Ryū, the concept of *setsunintō katsujinken* is directly related to the tactical practice of swordsmanship (*heihō*) in the Shinkage Ryū. The Shinkage Ryū refrains from using the term/concept of *kamae* (fixed postures) when referring to combative postures and positioning, as it is considered "static"—hence the term *setsunintō*—lit. "dead-person sword," meaning "static swordsmanship." Mutō noted that *kamae* in static swordsmanship was intended to dominate a combative situation in such a way that the enemy would be forced into an action that would result in his death, a double-entendre for *setsunintō*: the swordsman executing the technique was himself locked into the situation; the opponent, also locked in, would surely die.

The Shinkage Ryū under Kamiizumi came to cultivate *katsujinken*—lit. "living-person sword" meaning "dynamic swordsmanship." While the Shinkage Ryū swordsman uses what appears to be *kamae*, they are referred to as *kurai* (lit. "thereabouts"; "almost"). Thus Kamiizumi's Shinkage Ryū emphasized a dynamic flexibility of body, breath, movement, and mind in its swordsmanship. By extension, this does not limit the swordsman to killing an opponent in a contest with lethal weapons. *Katsujinken* is thus seen as freedom from static postures, freedom of movement, freedom of mind, freedom from the single choice of killing an adversary. In this way it is very close to the Shinkage Ryū concept of *marobashi*. 4. SHINKAGE RYŪ—A *gokui* transmission scroll passed from Kamiizumi Ise no Kami Nobutsuna to various disciples such as Marume Kurandonosuke Tessai and Nishi Itton. 5. ITTŌ RYŪ—A high-level privileged (*gokui*) transmission of the Ittō Ryū.

Further reading in English:

- Wilson, 2004b.
- Sato, 1986.

settō 節刀. A ceremonial sword prescribed in official legislation of the eighth century as being assigned to commanders on campaign.

sha 1. 者. The fourth seal/character of the nine mystic letters (*kuji*) found in the Kujihō (Ritual Method of the Nine Seals). See: *Kujihō*.

sha 2. 車. An engagement posture in which the body is in left (*hidari*) *hanmi* and sword is held low with the *kensaki* toward the rear. In many traditions, *sha* is identical to *wakigamae*.

---

[17] From conversations with Yagyū Nobuharu during the period 1985–1995.

[18] From conversations with Mutō Masao during the period 1985–1990.

shadō 射道. Lit. "way of shooting." Heki Ryū 日置流 archer Awa Kenzō (1880–1939) began using this term from about 1915 to indicate his modification of classical Japanese archery (*kyūjutsu*) into a more "spiritual" path.

shagei 射芸【射藝】[A.k.a. **shajutsu** 射術]. A term used for combative archery in the Heian, Kamakura, and Muromachi periods. See also: *shahō*.

shahō 射法. 1. A term for archery in the Heian, Kamakura, and Muromachi periods. 2. The "rules for shooting" used in the combative archery of the Heian, Kamakura, and Muromachi periods.

shirogashi 白樫. White evergreen oak. This wood is often used for weapons (especially training weapons). See also: *kashi; akagashi*.

shajutsu 射術. See: *shagei*.

shaken 車剣【車劍】. A variety of *shuriken* (throwing dart). The *shaken* is normally a small, rounded, multipointed or cross-shaped blade, hidden in the hand, which could either be thrown at an enemy or held for close combat. This type of *shuriken* is thrown so that it spins horizontally on its axis in flight. Contrast to *shuriken* 手裏剣.

shaku 尺. A measurement equivalent to just under a foot (30.3 cm).

shakuhachi 尺八. 1. A measurement of "one *shaku* eight *sun*" (around 20 inches [50 cm]). 2. A Japanese bamboo flute of about one *shaku* in length. As the *shakuhachi* was a weapon-useable-object, it was a prominent accoutrement of the Komusō mendicant monks (and the espionage agents who impersonated them). See also: *Fuke Shū; Komusō*.

shakujō 錫杖 <Ch. *xizhang*; transliterated as **gekkira** 隙棄羅 <Ch. *qiqiluo* <Skt. *khakkhara*. 1. BUDDHISM—A Buddhist priest's ringed staff; a mendicant monk's staff. Most forms of this priest's staff have decorative metalwork attached at the top of a staff. From the metalwork are suspended six metal rings which represent the six states of rebirth (Rokudō). The rings are arranged so as to make noise and thus warn small animals and insects to get out of the way so they will not be inadvertently stepped upon by the mendicant. The noise of the rings is also used for demon exorcisms.

The *shakujō* can be short (for use in chanting and ritual) or long (for use as a walking staff). It may also be wielded as a weapon.

PRIEST'S *SHAKUJŌ*

Although there are many Chinese stories in which a mendicant Shaolin monk defends himself with a *shakujō*, this type of story is not so common in Japan. In legend and literature, Japanese warrior monks (*sōhei*) tended to prefer the glaive (*naginata*) or spear (*yari*). 2. SHUGENDŌ—As one of the "sixteen accoutrements of the *yamabushi*" (*yamabushi juroku dogu*), the *shakujo* is a weapon-usable object which can be utilized as a magical staff for exorcism or, in a more mundane fashion, for defense against animals or bandits. 3. Abbr. for *shakujō yari*. 4. SHŌRINJI KEMPŌ—The *shakujō* was one of three original weapons taught to advanced practitioners of Nippon Shōrinji Kempō by their founder, Sō Dōshin. The use of these weapons seems rarely to be taught today. See also: *shakujō yari; yamabushi; yamabushi jūroku dōgu*.

shakujō yari 錫杖槍. A mendicant monk's staff with a removable head which covered a straight-bladed spear. This type of concealed weapon was evidently used by samurai, espionage agents, and similar types while traveling incognito.

sharei 射礼【射禮】. Ceremonial archery; formal etiquette used in *kyūjutsu* and *kyūdō*.

shari kenshō 射裡見性. Lit. "see true nature in the shot." This maxim is one of two key concepts used in the archery system founded by Awa Kenzō in the early twentieth century.

shashu 射手 [Also read ***ite***]. An archer; a bowman; a shooter.

shateki 射的. 1. An archery target. 2. Archery target practice.

shatekijō 射的場. An archery training range.

shi 1. 士. Fighting men, warriors, soldiers.

shi 2. 巳. See: *mi*.

shi 3. 使. An abbreviation for *shidachi*.

shi 4. 子. See: *ne*.

shiai 試合. A match; a contest; a bout or duel. See also: *tameshiai*.

shiaijō 試合場. A location where a duel (*shiai*) is held. In the realm of modern *budō* (*jūdō*, *karate*, etc.), a *shiaijō* is a location where a competition is held.

shiai kuchi 試合口. SHINDŌ MUSŌ RYŪ—See: *Okuden (2)*.

shiai naginata 試合薙刀 [A.k.a. ***keiko naginata***]. A training glaive composed of a wooden shaft and split bamboo blade for use in the practice of *atarashii naginata*. See: *atarashii naginata*.

Shiai Seihō 試合勢法. YAGYŪ SHINKAGE RYŪ—Sets of *kata* officially known as the Shinkage Ryū *heihō gaiden tōhō shiai seihō* 新陰流兵法外伝刀法試合勢法, these are most commonly referred to simply as Shiai Seihō. They consist of twenty-one sets encompassing 108 *kata*, all of which are variations on the original Shinkage Ryū curriculum (in contrast to the *kata* referred to as the *honden*, "original tradition"). Although developed and practiced by the Owari line of Yagyū Shinkage Ryū, many of these *kata* are rarely seen today. The Shiai Seihō techniques are also referred to as the *gaiden* 外伝, "outside tradition." They are, for the most part, variations based on original Shinkage Ryū *kata* as formulated by the Owari Yagyū Shinkage Ryū.

Curriculum	Number of *kata*
1. Sō Raitō[19] 相雷刀 (Hasseihō 八勢法)	8
2. Chūdan 中段 (Jūyon seihō 十四勢法)	14
3. Gedan 下段 (Hasseihō 八勢法)	8
4. Nochi no Raitō (Ōmarobashi Hen) 後雷刀(大転変) (Jūsan seihō 十三勢法)	13
5. Nochi no Raitō (Raitō Uchi Chū-/Gedan) 後雷刀 (雷刀打中下段) (Nana seihō 七勢法)	7
6. Komarobashi Gedan Hen 小転下段変 (Nana seihō 七勢法)	7
7. Komarobashi Raitō Hen 小転雷刀変 (Roku seihō 六勢法)	6
8. Nochi no Raitō (Osae-tekii) 後雷刀 (抑敵位) (Hasseihō 八勢法)	8
9. Nochi no Raitō (Ohigoshi Sakii) 後相雷 (應被越先位) (San seihō 三勢法)	3
10. Soto Raitō (Sō Raitōgata Chūdan Osae) 外雷刀 (相雷刀形中段抑) (Go seihō 五勢法)	5
11. Sō Raitō Sōsō Raisha 相雷刀操躁来者 (Ni seihō 二勢法)	2
12. Sō Jōkakusei 相城郭勢 (Ni seihō 二勢法)	3
13. Sō Gedansei 相下段勢 (Go seihō 五勢法)	5
14. Hassō Uchi Raitōsei 撥草打雷刀勢 (Ni seihō 二勢法)	2
15. Tōdachi Hensei 十太刀変勢 (Ni seihō 二勢法)	2
16. Enkai Hensei 猿廻変勢 (Ni seihō 二勢法)	2
17. Ittō Hensei 一刀変勢 (Ni seihō 二勢法)	2
18. Sō Raitō Hen Tōbōsei 相雷刀 変刀棒勢 (San seihō 三勢法)	3
19. Raitō Uchi Hassōsei 雷刀打撥草勢 (Ni seihō 二勢法)	2
20. Raitō Uchi Tōdachi/Shasei 雷刀打十太刀·車勢 (San seihō 三勢法)	3
21. Sō Raitō Aiyokui 相雷刀 合抑位 (San seihō 三勢法)	3

Further reading in English:

- Watanabe, 1993a; 1993b.

[19] In some derivative lines of Yagyū Shinkage Ryū, the term *sō* 相 is given the alternate pronunciation of *ai*; e.g., Watanabe (1993). However, the meaning is the same.

Shibahō 『司馬法』 <Ch. *Sima fa*. One of the seven military classics of China. See: *Buryaku shichi sho*.

shibami 芝見. A variant term for an espionage agent. *Shibami* indicates a bush scout; one who often worked on field operations requiring concealment close to enemy positions or encampments. See: *kamari (1)*; *ninjutsu*.

shiba-uchi 柴打. SHUGENDŌ—A heavy sword used by Shugendō practitioners (*yamabushi*) to cut wood for a ritual fire ceremony (*saitō goma*). As one of the "sixteen accoutrements of the *yamabushi*" (*yamabushi jūroku dōgu*) during the medieval period, a *sankotsuka no ken* was traditionally used for this purpose; that weapon was much closer in shape and use to a warrior's sword than the modern-day *shiba-uchi*. See: *yamabushi*; *yamabushi jūroku dōgu*.

shibu dōjō 支部道場. An authorized branch training hall (*dōjō*). Contrast to *hombu dōjō*.

shibui 渋い. The term *shibui* refers to a quality of subtle beauty which is quiet and sober, perhaps even astringent or bitter.

Shibukawa Bangorō Yoshikata 渋川 伴五郎 義方 (c.1656–1704). Founder of Shibukawa Ryū c.1686. Although some sources say his father was a retainer of *hatamoto* rank for the Ashikaga shogunate, this information is suspect.[20]

At the age of sixteen, Shibukawa began training in Sekiguchi Ryū with its second-generation headmaster, Sekiguchi Hachirō. Fourteen years later in 1686 he received a full license in that school. It is thought that he opened a training hall (*dōjō*) known as the Dōgikan 道凝館 around that time, but this is unclear. (The term *dōgi* essentially means "devotion to the 'way' "). According to other sources, in the 1680s he moved to Edo where he opened a *dōjō* called the Mugidō (or Bugidō) 武義堂 (Hall of warrior honor and integrity). He passed away in 1704.

Shibukawa Ryū 渋川流. A comprehensive combative school (*sōgō bujutsu*) founded by Shibukawa Bangorō Yoshikata in 1686. At that time it included grappling (*jūjutsu*), swordsmanship (*kenjutsu*), quick-draw sword arts (*iaijutsu*), spearmanship (*sōjutsu*), and long hardwood staff arts (*bōjutsu*) in its curriculum. While it still includes many of these combative systems, the Shibukawa Ryū is best known today for its *jūjutsu*.

shibumi 渋味. Severity, refinement, elegant simplicity. Trevanian, in his 1979 novel entitled *Shibumi*, provides an eloquent description:

> *Shibumi* is understanding, rather than knowledge. Eloquent silence. In demeanor, it is modesty without prudency. In art, where the spirit of *shibumi* takes the form of *sabi*, it is elegant simplicity, articulate brevity. In philosophy, where *shibumi* emerges as *wabi*, it is spiritual tranquility that is not passive; it is being without the angst of becoming. And in the personality of a man, it is…authority without domination.
>
> Trevanian, 1979: 62–63

shichishō hōkoku 七生報国【七生報國】. Lit. "reborn seven times to serve the nation." This famous quote by Kusunoki Masashige became the slogan of several *kamikaze* units in World War II. (Morris, 1975: *passim*.)

shidachi 使太刀. Written with various characters and depending on the combative school (*ryū*) and weapon, this term usually indicates the person who executes the school's technique against an opponent. As written here, the *shidachi* is the "employer" (*shi* 使) of the "sword techniques" (*tachi* 太刀) of the *ryū*. The techniques employed by his opponent—the *uchidachi*—are sometimes derived from other schools. For training purposes in most classical weapons systems, the proponent in the position of the *shidachi* is the junior participant. Contrast with *uchidachi*.

Shi Daikisho 四大奇書 [Also read ***Yon Daikisho***] <Ch. Si Da Ming Zhu 四大名著. Lit. the "four great stories." A set of four Chinese sagas which include: *Sangoku shi engi* 『三国志演義』 (Romance of the Three Kingdoms); *Suikoden* 『水滸伝』 (The Water Margin); *Saiyūki* 『西遊記』 (Journey to the West); and *Korōmu* 『紅楼夢』 (Dream of the Red Chamber). In Japan, *Kōrōmu* is sometimes replaced with

20 The Ashikaga shogunate ended in 1573, and Bangorō was born around 1656; there is a span of eighty-three years between these dates.

Kinbeibai『金瓶梅』(The Plum in the Golden Vase).

The first three tales in this list are filled with scenes of combat, and have often been the subject of Japanese artists such as Kuniyoshi. The *Shi Daikisho* were very popular with Japanese of all social levels.

Further reading in English:

• Klompmakers, 2003.

Shi Daitennō 四大天王. See: *Shitennō.*

Shida Shirō 志田 四郎. See: *Saigō Shirō.*

shidō 士道. Sometimes used as an abbreviation for *bushidō*, the term evolved from Tokugawa-period Confucian ideals relating to the warrior/gentlemen (*shi* 士) and the path (*dō* 道) of martial virtue (*butoku* 武徳). Martial scholar and classical Japanese archery expert Irie Kōhei notes that this was a popular Tokugawa-period warrior ethos "used to justify the *bushi*'s position at the top of the said pyramid as moral leaders." (Irie, 2005: 166.) See also: *Yamaga Sokō.*

shidōin 指導員. 1. An instructor or supervisor. 2. A title awarded in some martial arts (including some classical and modern martial systems) to confer teaching responsibility.

Shido kegyō 四度加行. BUDDHISM—A set of four basic tantric rituals all practitioners of Japanese Esoteric Buddhism (*mikkyō*) must master. They include the *jūhachidō*, *kongōkai*, *taizōkai*, and *goma*. These four rituals are also initiations into the secrets of various mandala and practices. The actual sequence of the four varies, depending on the tradition practicing them. See: *Goma shiki; Jūhachidō shiki; Kongōkai shiki; Taizōkai shiki.*

shieiden ryōshu 私営田領主【私營田領主】. A private landlord with large holdings. This tenth-century term was used in reference to warrior-landlords like Taira no Masakado. Farris (1992: 155) notes that this term is similar—although not exactly the same—in meaning to the twelfth-century term *zaichi ryōshu* 在地領主, which means "country lord." The country lords were also landed warriors.

Shigakkan 士学館【士學館】. A training hall (*dōjō*) established in Edo (in current day Chūō ward) in 1773 by Momonoi Hachirōzaemon Naoyoshi. Momonoi also founded his own school of swordsmanship, the Kyōshin Meichi Ryū 鏡新明智流, around the same period. In 1849 the second-generation *dōjō* proprietor, Momonoi Shunzō 桃井春蔵 (1826–1886), moved the training hall to a new location in the Minami Hatchōbori area of Edo; there it became known as one of the three great *dōjō* of Edo at the end of the Tokugawa period (the other two being the Gembukan and the Rempeikan). See also: *Bakumatsu Edo Sandai Dōjō; Gembukan; Rempeikan.*

Shigakkō 私学校【私學校】. A system of private schools established in Kyūshū in 1874 under the auspices of Saigō Takamori. The schools were aimed at teaching traditional samurai values and skills to the young soldiers who remained loyal to Saigō when he resigned from the Meiji government in 1874. According to Ravina (2004: 193), there were two divisions within the school system: infantry and artillery. However, in addition to military skills, the Shigakkō also taught the Chinese classics.

shihan 師範. A senior instructor of swordsmanship; a senior combative arts instructor. See: *hanshi.*

shihan dai 師範代. 1. A proxy instructor; an assistant master swordsmanship instructor; an assistant chief swordsmanship instructor. 2. JIKI SHINKAGE RYŪ—A master swordsman who has not been officially named as a successor to the current headmaster.

shihanke 師範家. A group or "family" of senior teachers who run a classical school such as a martial tradition (*ryū*). The senior member of the *shihanke* may or may not be considered the lineal headmaster of the school. See: *shihan.*

shihi 鯔飛 [Also read ***inatobi***; ***shibi***]. Lit. "jumping like a mullet." A practice found in combative swimming (*suieijutsu*) in which the proponent leaps from the water.

Shihō 四方. TATSUMI RYŪ—One of a number of classical prearranged quick-draw sword forms (*battō kata*) developed by the Tatsumi Ryū. It was also one of five classical *battō kata* adapted by the Japanese Police Commission of 1886 for their Keishichō Ryū 警視庁流 system.

shijji 悉地 [Var. 悉底] <Ch. *xidi* <Skt. *siddhi*. Magical or miraculous powers obtained via meditative concentration (*sammaiji*) of the mind on a particular deity or object. Often translated into Japanese as *jōju*.

shijin 資人. An eighth-century term referring to aristocratic, quasi-military attendants.

shikan 1. 死間<Ch. *sijian*. The fourth of the five types of secret agents (*ninja*; *shinobi*) mentioned in Sun Tzu's *Art of War* (*Sonshi no heihō*). The term *shikan* refers to expendable agents (lit. "death-agents" or "dead-agents") who are employed to spread false information among the enemy. See: *kanja; kyōdan (1); ninjutsu; Sonshi no heihō*.

shikan 2. 止観 【止觀】<Ch. *zhiguan*. BUDDHISM—Sitting meditation as practiced by the Tendai school (Tendai Shū) of Buddhism in Japan. *Shikan* is similar to *zazen*.

shikatsuhō 死活法. A system of techniques encompassing both killing and healing arts via use of vital points (*kyūsho*). This particular system was created by Akiyama Shirobei Yoshitoki, who founded the Yōshin Ryū 楊心流 around 1650.

shikei 死刑. Execution; capital punishment. During the Tokugawa period, execution of members of the warrior class was generally restricted to disembowelment (*seppuku*) with decapitation by a "second" (*kaishakunin*).[21] However, depending on the type and severity of the crime, commoners might face one of several prescribed methods: decapitation (*zanzai*); crucifixion (*haritsuke*); burning at the stake (*hi aburi*); or death by sawing the neck (*nokogiribiki*).

Further reading in English:

- Schriber, (2001): 46–56.

shikeijo 死刑所. Execution grounds. Many cities had these areas during the Tokugawa period. Two of the most infamous were Kozukappara in the northern section of Edo, and Suzagamori in the southern section of Edo.

shiken 試剣. Term used for combative swordsmanship in several Edo-period schools such as the Enshin Ryū, Ōmori Ryū, and others.

shiki 士気 【士氣】. Martial heart or spirit. See: *gunki (1)*.

shikigu 指揮具 [A.k.a. ***jin'eigu*** 陣営具 【陣營具】]. During the medieval and premodern periods, the *shikigu* were a battlefield commander's accoutrements; a commander's tools for signaling; the symbols of command. A group of articles which might include a riding crop or horse whip (*muchi*), folding war fan (*gunsen*), baton with tassel (*saihai*), and rigid, non-folding fans for battlefield divination (*gunbai uchiwa*). In addition, all of these items could be used for visual signaling. A commander of a force large enough to have a headquarters unit might also use auditory signaling devices such as a large gong (*kane*), small hand-held gongs (*kane* or *dora*), wooden clappers (*hyōshigi*), conch shells (*kai*) for bugling, and large war drums (*taiko*).

shikin Zen 即今禅 【即今禪】 [Also read ***sokkon Zen***]. "Instant Zen"; "on-the-spot Zen." An early Kamakura-period practice during which Zen masters made up riddles (*kōan*) on the spot for warrior disciples. This practice was developed by the monk Daikaku, who came to Japan from China in 1246. See also: *Daikaku; Kamakura Zen; kien Zen; kōan*.

Further reading in English:

- Leggett, 1978; 1985.

shikken 執権 【執權】. The official title of the regent to the Kamakura *shōgun*. In 1203 Minamoto no Yoriie handed over the shogunate to his younger brother Sanetomo, who was only twelve years old at the time. Due to Sanetomo's youth, his maternal grandfather Hōjō Tokimasa received the title of *shikken* and began directing the affairs of the shogunate in Sanetomo's stead.

In 1205 Tokimasa handed the duties and title

S

---

21 A samurai might also be punished by disenfranchisement (*monzenbarai*) or other, less severe penalties.

of *shikken* over to his own son Hōjō Yoshitoki. After defeating Wada Yoshimori, who revolted against the Hōjō in 1213, Yoshitoki also assumed the title of Samurai-dokoro no Bettō. Since he was already Mandokoro Bettō, this act centered both military and civil power with the *shikken*. The Hōjō then held these powers within the Kamakura shogunate until 1333, when the last *shikken*, Hōjō Takatoki, was defeated in battle by Nitta Yoshisada, and committed suicide along with hundreds of Hōjō retainers.

shiko 四股. SUMŌ—A ritual exercise in which *sumō* wrestlers lift each leg in succession and stomp on the ground. This is performed by practitioners before each bout. While in training, wrestlers may perform *shiko* hundreds of times in succession. It is also a ritual performance by *yokozuna*-ranked practitioners, intended to drive away demons at the beginning of matches.

Shikoku 四国【四國】. Smallest of the four main islands of Japan. Shikoku is located east of Kyūshū.

shikomizue 仕込み杖. A sword cane.

shikoro 錏. Neck-protecting flap armor which hang from the sides and back of a helmet bowl (*hachi*). The ends of the *shikoro* on medieval period helmets flared out to deflect cuts that might damage the lacings of the flap.

Shimabukuro Tatsuo 島袋 龍夫. Founder of Isshin Ryū (3) 一心流 *karate*. Shimabukuro established the school in 1956.

Shimada Toranosuke 島田 虎之助(寅之助) [A.k.a. ***Naochika*** 直親] (1814–1852). Jiki Shinkage Ryū swordsman, student of Odani Nobutomo, and samurai from Nakatsu domain (Buzen province). Shimada began his *kenjutsu* training in Kyūshū when he was thirteen. By the age of sixteen he had become very proficient in matches with bamboo swords (*shinai shiai*) and was essentially unbeatable in his home area. He subsequently set out on a warrior's pilgrimage (*musha shugyō*). At first he lost many matches, but quickly learned from his defeats. He then entered into a two-year period of prayer and self-training at a Buddhist temple in Kyūshū. Around the age of twenty-one in 1834, he set out for Edo and began *dōjō*-storming (*dōjō arashi*), challenging the heads of the *dōjō* he visited. He soon became famous in both western Japan (Kansai) and eastern Japan (Kantō)—as much for his arrogance as his skill in swordsmanship.

At that time Odani Seiichirō, thirteenth headmaster of the Jiki Shinkage Ryū, had a training hall in Edo. Inevitably, Shimada appeared there and challenged Odani, and was soundly defeated. Namiki Yasushi noted in his *Ken no kokoro*:

> ...Facing Shimada with a straight-forward, controlled mind, the small Odani stood in *seigan no kamae* and looked quite like a little mound. Before long, however, the mound moved.
>
> "Is he slowly but steadily pressing in on me?" worried Shimada as he felt himself being pressed and entangled by an invisible wall of *kiai*. "Strange, I don't know why but I'm slowly retreating." Shimada then noticed his back had come up against the *dōjō's* rear wall.
>
> "I must act now!" he decided and his will returned in a rush. He began to concentrate the energy of his whole being and started to force back his opponent, but pushing Odani's *kiai* wall was like pushing a cloud which offered no resistance; the small mound, inhaling, retreated.
>
> Odani backed up to the center of the hall and stopped abruptly. Again an invisible wall seemed to push against Shimada. Slowly but steadily it forced him back and he soon arrived at the rear of the building once more....
>
> Not once being able to strike, being pushed and pushing back, over and over, Shimada's breathing became distorted. He began to puff and sweat and became dizzy. He soon lost free movement in his arms and legs. Just before losing consciousness he conceded the match and fell prostrate on the floor! Soon after, Shimada begged to become a member of the *dōjō*.
>
> Namiki, 1979: 18–22

As a student of Odani, Shimada matured and became a highly skilled swordsman. He mastered Jiki Shinkage Ryū within a year and founded his own branch, the Jiki Shinkage Ryū Shimada Ha. Later in his career Shimada taught *kenjutsu* to Katsu Kaishū, mentored the young man, and encouraged him to engage in *zazen* and "Western studies." In his memoir, Katsu Kokichi notes that Shimada was also a member of his (Katsu's) son's *jūjutsu* class, and that he was a strong swordsman "feared as much for his quick temper as for his skills." (Craig, 1988: 111). Though he was beaten by Odani, Shimada is rumored to have defeated all the students in Odani Nobutomo's *dōjō*. He later opened his own training hall, but died of an illness in 1852, at the age of thirty-nine.

Shimada Toranosuke was represented in the movie *Sword of Doom* (1966) where he was played by Mifune Toshiro.

shima no miyatsuko 島造. Governors of island provinces during the late Yamato period. See: *kuni no miyatsuko*.

Shimazu 島津. A *daimyō* family which ruled the Satsuma feudal domain from the twelfth century through 1871 when, like all other *daimyō* families, they were pensioned out by the Meiji government. The family descends from Tadahisa 忠久, the illegitimate son of Minamoto no Yoritomo, who married the sister of Hiki Yoshikazu. Tadahisa accompanied his father Yoritomo on a military expedition to Mutsu in 1189, and subdued southwestern Kyūshū in 1196. He built a castle in the area of Shimazu (Hyūga) and, like many of the Minamoto, adopted the name of the local domain.

It was the Shimazu who, as the ruling *daimyō* family of Satsuma domain, took control of Okinawa in 1609 and placed a ban on the use of weapons by the local populace.

Shimazu Kenji 島津 兼治 (1938–). Current headmaster of Yagyū Shingan Ryū (3) Katchū Kempō 柳生心眼流甲冑拳法.

shimban 審判. See: *shimpan*.

Shim-Butsu konkō 神仏混淆 【神佛混淆】 [Also read ***Shim-Butsu kongō***]. RYŌBU SHINTŌ—A Shintō-Buddhist amalgamation which began in the early ninth century. See: Ryōbu Shintō.

shime 1. 絞め. Lit. "to strangle." An abbreviation for *shimeru* or *shime waza*.

shime 2. 注連. SHINTŌ—A sacred Shintō rope. See: *shimenawa*.

shimenawa 注連縄 【注連繩】. SHINTŌ—A straw rope from which are usually hung narrow strips of zigzag-shaped white paper (*gohei*). These ropes are seen at Shintō shrines and other hallowed grounds and serve to indicate the boundary of sacred places. Apparently this function of the *shimenawa* has been influenced by esoteric Buddhism over the centuries, in that the zigzag *gohei* echo the placement of *vajra* (thunderbolts) at the border areas of Buddhist mandala. This evolution of the *shimenawa* into a thunderbolt-encrusted barrier is apparently only one aspect of the Buddhist-Shintō syncretic mandalization of space which occurred in Japan over many hundreds of years beginning around the ninth century. (See Grapard, 1995: 38–42.)

Shimenawa are often used to surround martial exhibition sites (*embujō*) located on the grounds of shrines such as Kashima Jingu. Their purpose is to purify the site of the votive martial exhibition (*hōnō embu*) and protect the participants. See also: *gohei*.

SHIMENAWA BOUNDARY
Young members of the Kashima Shintō Ryū demonstrate *kenjutsu* within the *shimenawa* boundary of an *embujō* at Kashima Jingu, 1978
(Photograph courtesy Jon Driscoll)

shimeru 絞める. Strangulation; to strangle. See: *shime waza*.

shimeshi-awasu mono 諜し合す者. A variant term for an espionage agent. See: *ninjutsu*.

shime waza 絞技. Lit. "strangulation techniques." 1. A generic term for techniques in which an opponent is strangled by use of one's hands, arms, legs, or weaponry. 2. KŌDŌKAN JŪDŌ—The formal term used in *jūdō* for strangulation techniques, one of the three subcategories of Katame no Kata.

Shimizu Takaji 清水 隆次 (1896–1978). Recognized as twenty-fifth headmaster[22] of the Shindō Musō Ryū, Shimizu modified its *jōjutsu* into *jōdō* in the mid-twentieth century. He began training in Shindō Musō Ryū in 1913, at the age of seventeen. He obtained *menkyo kaiden* from Shiraishi Hanjirō in 1920, and later became chief instructor for the Tōkyō Riot Police (Kidōtai).

Shimizu had a number of prominent senior students, including the following:

1. Kuroda Ichitarō	黒田 一太郎
2. Nakajima Asakichi	中島 浅吉
3. Nishioka Tsuneo	西岡 常夫
4. Yoneno Kōtarō	米野 光太郎
5. Hiroi Tsunetsugu	広井 常次
6. Kaminoda Tsunemori	神之田 常盛

With the assistance of his first and most prominent foreign student, Donn F. Draeger, Shimizu founded the International Jodo Federation (IJF) in order to give *jōdō* an international scope.

Shimizu Takaji wrote several books over the years, among which are:

Jōdō kyōhan—kihon rengi kaisetsu 『杖道教範—基本錬技解説』 (*Jōdō* textbook: An explanation of basic training methods), 1940 (reprint, Shimazu Shobō, 1988).

Shindō Musō Ryū jōdō kyōhan 『神道夢想流杖道教範』 (Shindō Musō Ryū *Jōdō*—The master text). Japan Publications Trading Company, 1976. [Co-authored by Nakajima Asakichi and Kaminoda Tsunemori; the text was published under Shimizu Takaji's name.]

SHIMIZU TAKAJI
Twenty-fifth headmaster of the Shindō Musō Ryū
(Shown here in *nitō no kamae*)
(Photograph courtesy Nishioka Tsuneo)

[22] See entry on Shindō Musō Ryū.

Shimmei Musō Ryū 神明夢想流. See: *Shin Musō Hayashizaki Ryū.*

Shimojō Kosaburō 下條 小三郎 (1867–?). The most senior disciple of Yagyū Genshū in the Yagyū Shinkage Ryū.

Shimomura Ha Musō Jikiden Eishin Ryū 下村派無双直伝英信流 【下村派無雙直傳英信流】. See: *Musō Jikiden Eishin Ryū; Shin Musō Hayashizaki Ryū.*

shimoseki 下席. Lit. "lower seat." In a martial training hall (*dōjō*) the *shimoseki* is the place where the most junior person sits. This seat is normally farthermost from the "upper seat" (*jōseki*) where the most senior person sits. Its actual location in any training hall depends on the physical layout of the structure and the location of the altar area (*shinden*/*shōmen*). *Shimoseki* is equivalent to *shimoza.*

Shimosone Kanesaburō Nobuatsu 下曽根金三郎 信敦 [A.k.a. **Kai no Kami** 甲斐守; **Keien** 桂園]. Founder of the Ien Ryū, a school of gunnery (*hōjutsu*), and tactical training (*gumpō chōren*), around 1842. Shimosone was a direct disciple of the renowned Takashima Shūhan.

shimoza 下座 【下坐】. Lit. "lower seat." The position at the end of a table or the end of the line where the most junior participant sits, in contrast to the "upper seat" (*kamiza*). *Shimoza* is equivalent to *shimoseki.*

shimpan 審判 [Also read **shinpan, shimban**]. 1. A referee, umpire, or judge. 2. SUMŌ—A ringside judge who makes a decision on disputed matches. There are five *shimpan* for each match.

shimpan daimyō 親藩大名. During the Edo period (1603–1867), the *shimpan daimyō* were feudal lords directly related to the Tokugawa family. There were twenty-three of these. See: *daimyō.*

shimpō 心法 [Also read *shinpō* or *shimbō*] <Ch. *xinfa* <Skt. *cittadharma.* 1. BUDDHISM—

Mental "elements"; those elements which are not physical; essentially, that which is related to the mind. In some Buddhist schools—e.g., Yogācāra (Hossō Shū)—these mental elements (mind) are seen as the origin of all phenomena. 2. In a martial-arts context, *shimpō* are religio-psychological methods used in various sword schools aimed at intuitive, awakening experiences and higher states of consciousness.

shimpū 神風. See: *kamikaze.*

Shimpūren 神風連. A right-wing society of former samurai (*shizoku*) in Kyūshū formed in the early to mid-1870s. The Shimpūren was strongly anti-Western, and in 1876 fomented an uprising called the Shimpūren no Ran in Kumamoto. The participants were wiped out by government forces.

Further reading in English:

• Hardacre and Kern, 1997: 144–167.

shin 辰. Symbol for dragon. See: *tatsu.*

shinai 竹刀. Any of a variety of training swords made of bamboo tied together with leather. Some modern *kendō* versions of the *shinai* have replaced the bamboo with carbon fiber. See also: *chikutō; fukuro shinai.*

shinaigeiko 竹刀稽古. Training with *shinai* in lieu of wooden swords (*bokken*) or live blades (*shinken*).

Shin Aikidō 新合気道 [Var. ***Tomiki Aikidō*** 富木合気道; ***Tomiki Ryū*** 富木流]. A branch tradition of Ueshiba Ryū Aikidō founded by Tomiki Kenji.

shinai kyōgi 竹刀競技. A match or bout with bamboo swords (*shinai*).

shinai shiai 竹刀試合. A match or contest using *shinai* in lieu of the much more dangerous *shinken* (live swords) or *bokken* (hardwood swords). *Shinai shiai* became the most common method for testing one's combative skills during the Edo period, as bouts with live blades or wooden swords were forbidden by the Tokugawa *bakufu*. During the early to mid-1800s, swordsmen such as Ōishi Susumu and Katōda Heihachirō 加藤田平八郎 started a trend in Edo with their use of extra-long *shinai*, modified footwork, and quick tap/touch strikes and thrusts. This gave them an advantage in *shinai shiai*, although it caused an accelerated drift away from combative swordsmanship. This drift was due to the very different requirements pertaining to target, timing, and distance found in combative *kenjutsu* in contrast to *shinai shiai*. This trend greatly influenced the development of *shinai shiai* into the more sportive *kendō* seen today. See also: *fumikomiashi; gekken; gekken kōgyō; okuriashi; shiai; shinai.*

shinai uchi 竹刀打. A match with bamboo swords (*shinai*). See: *shinai shiai.*

shinanban 指南番 [A.k.a. ***shinanyaku*** 指南役]. An instructor or official teacher. A *kenjutsu shinanban*, for example, would be a master teacher of combative swordsmanship.

shinanyaku 指南役. See: *shinanban.*

shin budō 新武道. Modern agonistic/sportive/spiritual-way systems created after the end of the Japanese feudal period (post-1868). These systems can be further subdivided depending on whether they were created before or after WWII.

Shinbu Ryū 神捕流 [A.k.a. ***Kajima Shinbu Ryū*** 加島神捕流]. A martial school concentrating on combative spear tactics (*sōjutsu*) with the straight spear (*suyari*) and half-spear (*hansō*). It was established by Torao Jō around 1651.

shinden 神殿. A shrine or sanctuary. See: *kamidana; shinzen; shōmen.*

Shinden Fudō Ryū 神伝不動流【神傳不動流】. According to Watatani and Yamada (1978: 414–415), this is a system concentrating on *daken taijutsu,* a boxing/striking system which claims Chinese origins. It is currently one of several systems passed down via Hatsumi Masaaki in the Bujinkan.

Further reading in English:

• Hatsumi, 2008: 144–167.

Shinden Ryū 心伝流 【心傳流】. A branch school of the Hakkō Ryū 八光流 founded by Akumi Kohō. The Shinden Ryū specializes in grappling.

S

shindō 1. 臣道. The practice of loyalty.

Shindō~ 2. 神道~. A variant pronunciation for *Shintō* (1) 神道 used in some compound terms. See, for example, *Shindō Munen Ryū* below.

Shindō Munen Ryū 神道無念流. A school of combative swordsmanship (*kenjutsu*) which traces its origins to Kamiizumi's Shinkage Ryū via the Shin Shinkage Ichien Ryū. The Shindō Munen Ryū was founded by Fukui Hachiemon Nagayuki. Fukui was born in 1702 and opened a training hall (*dōjō*) in the Yotsuya neighborhood of Edo sometime during the 1720s. At first he called his school Munen Ryū 無念流, but according to Watatani and Yamada (1978: 428), he changed the name to Shindō Munen Ryū after receiving a revelation sometime during the Hōreki era (1751–1764) at the Izuna Gongen 飯縄権現 shrine (located in present-day Nagano prefecture). The school spread far and wide after Fukui's time and is still practiced today.

In 1826 one of the fourth-generation successors of the school, Saitō Yakurō Yoshimichi, founded the Rempeikan *dōjō* in Edo, as well as his own branch system which he called the Saitō Ha Munen Ryū 斎藤派無念流. During the Bakumatsu period (1853–1867) the Rempeikan was one of the most popular training halls in the city of Edo.

Shindō Munen Ryū
神道無念流
(abbreviated lineage)

Kamiizumi Ise no Kami Nobutsuna
上泉 伊勢守 信綱
Shinkage Ryū
新陰流

|

Nonaka Shinzō Naritsune
野中 新蔵 成常
Shin Shinkage Ichien Ryū
新神陰一円流

Nonaka Hachiemon Nagayuki
野中 八右衛門 長行
Shin Shinkage Ichien Ryū
新神陰一円流

|

Makino Kazuhiro
牧野 円泰
Ichien Ryū
一円派

Fukui Heiuemon Kahei
福井 平右衛門 嘉平
Shindō Munen Ryū
神道無念流

TALISMAN FROM THE IZUNA GONGEN SHRINE

Shindō Musō Ryū [Also read **Shintō Musō Ryū**] 神道夢想流; var. 真道夢想流; 新当夢想流【新當夢想流】]. As a derivative of the Kashima Shin Ryū and Katori Shintō Ryū schools, Shindō Musō Ryū may have originally included many of the weapons systems of those traditions. Watatani and Yamada (1978: 426) ascribe to it long hardwood staff arts (*rokushaku bō*), medium-length staff arts (*jōjutsu*), swordsmanship (*kenjutsu*) and arresting-cord arts (*torinawa*). However, as practiced today the school is restricted to staff (*jōjutsu*) and sword arts (*kenjutsu*). Additionally, as part of the "men's arts" (*dangyō*) used by the warriors of the Kuroda domain in Kyūshū, it became aligned with several collateral traditions (*fuzoku bugei*) such as Ikkaku Ryū 一角流 truncheon arts (*juttejutsu*) and Ittatsu Ryū 一達流 arresting-cord arts (*hojōjutsu*).

Shindō Musō Ryū was founded during the first decade of the seventeenth century by Musō Gonnosuke. The tradition falls into the category of "positive" weapons arts in that it emphasizes taking the initiative and closing with the enemy.

The founding legend of this tradition relates how Gonnosuke had mastered the Kasumi Shintō Ryū 霞神道流—a system with roots in both Kashima Shin Ryū 鹿島神流 and Tenshinshō-den Katori Shintō Ryū 天真正伝香取神道流—at the end of the sixteenth century. Travelling around Japan on a warrior pilgrimage (*musha shūgyō*), he apparently defeated all comers until he dueled with

Miyamoto Musashi.[23] Gonnosuke, using a long staff,[24] is said to have been defeated by Musashi, who locked his opponent's weapon by using two swords in a technique called *jūjidome*. (*Jūjidome* means "[numeral] 10 block"; Musashi's swords crossed in an x-block resembling the Chinese character for the number ten [十]). As the legend has it, Musashi spared Gonnosuke's life, which is apparently true or there would be no Shindō Musō Ryū today!

Gonnosuke, irked by the defeat, retired to Mount Hōman (Hōmanzan 宝満山) in Kyūshū, where he began a period of martial/religious *shūgyō* (physical and spiritual austerities). The details of this *shūgyō* are not available, but in later years his successors would spend about a month in Esoteric Buddhist training in the mountains before being awarded the full license of *menkyo kaiden*. This training evidently concentrated on the Kujihō (Ritual Method of the Nine Seals) and was known as *kuji mippō*「九字密法」(Matsui, 1991b: 84). After many days (the number varies in disparate versions of the tale), Gonnosuke was awarded a vision or oracle (*musō* 夢想) by the *kami* of Mount Homan, who gave him the cryptic instructions: *Maruki o motte, suigetsu o shire!* (Take a round stick and know the *suigetsu*!) It was probably from this point that Gonnosuke became *Musō* Gonnosuke. Supposedly it was from this instruction/inspiration Gonnosuke retooled his weapon into a shorter staff with a smaller diameter.

This new weapon—the *jō*—had several advantages over the longer *bō* and similar polearms. Primarily, it was better adapted to unarmored combat/duel than was the *bō*. Although the long staff was effective against an armored swordsman, the duels faced by warriors on *musha shūgyō* in the early 1600s were rarely fought in armor. Consequently a lighter, faster-moving weapon had an advantage over a heavier, slower weapon. And, as the armor was off, many more *kyūsho* (vital points) on an opponent's body became available for attack. The *jō* was also a more versatile weapon than the *bō*. This fact is itself touted in the *densho* that have been passed down, which note that the stick can be used like a staff, spear, sword, or glaive. In addition, the *jō* can be used effectively against an armored or unarmored enemy.

After receiving his oracle and revising his fighting system, Musō Gonnosuke is supposed to have sought out and faced Musashi once again, this time defeating the famous swordsman and sparing the latter's life. This second duel is not mentioned in the standard legends and hagiographies of famous warriors collected during the ensuing Edo period. However, the legend persists within Shindō Musō Ryū. In fact, certain *kata* within the tradition's Okuden forms establish scenarios in which a practitioner armed with a *jō* defeats a swordsman armed with two swords, much as in the Gonnosuke/Musashi tale. Today there appears to be only one, slightly suspect, source mentioning this second duel; that is a single scroll preserved in Tsukuba Shrine in Ibaragi prefecture.

Donn F. Draeger[25] noted that he had asked Shimizu Takaji about the second duel. Shimizu replied that the information had come from the school's *densho*. When Draeger asked if he could see the documents, Shimizu replied, "The birds had gotten them." Seeing Draeger's confused expression, he explained that they had been destroyed by American aircraft participating in the Tōkyō fire-bombing raids during World War II. Not to be deterred, Draeger contacted Miyakawa Yasukō 宮川泰孝, who was then the headmaster of Nitenichi Ryū (one of several traditions which trace their descent from Miyamoto Musashi). Unfortunately Miyakawa would neither confirm nor deny that Nitenichi Ryū documents contain any information about a second duel between Gonnosuke and Musashi.

In any case, Gonnosuke soon became a retainer of the Kuroda *han* (feudal domain) in Kyūshū, where the tradition was kept secret until the late 1800s. There it became one of

23 This duel is thought to have taken place prior to 1609.

24 The actual weapon type is unknown. It may have been a six-foot staff (*rokushaku bō*), a larger polearm such as an *ichiizue*, or some other staff-type weapon.

25 See Bibliography.

S

the men's arts (*dangyō*) practiced by the lower-level samurai who handled domain police and military duties. Collateral *dangyō* included several Edo-period police disciplines, such as Ikkaku Ryū *jutte* and *tessen*, Ittatsu Ryū arresting cord, and others. After the dissolution of the feudal domains in the 1870s, Shiraishi Hanjirō (1842–1927) became the headmaster of the Shindō Musō Ryū. The *jō* system and some of the other men's arts were taught in Shiraishi's training hall (known as the Shiraishi *dōjō*) in Kyūshū. After Shiraishi's death in 1927, training was moved to the Fukuoka *dōjō*.

The Kuroda-domain samurai who practiced Shindō Musō Ryū became *shizoku* (disenfranchised warriors) upon the dissolution of the feudal system in 1871. During that difficult transition period many found themselves in dire economic straights and drifted into ultra-rightist organizations such as the Gen'yōsha. Because of this connection, and also also due to the fact that the honored patriot Hirano Kuniomi had been a member of the Shindō Musō Ryū, the Gen'yōsha (founded in 1879) consistently supported the Shindō Musō Ryū during the Meiji, Taishō, and pre–WWII Shōwa eras.

Shindō Musō Ryū was popularized internationally in the mid-twentieth century by Shimizu Takaji (twenty-fifth headmaster of the *ryū*) and Donn F. Draeger.

Note regarding Shindo Muso Ryu lineage:

It should be noted that like many martial systems—including those traditionally passed down in only one domain—the Shindō Musō Ryū has historically had several parallel lines of transmission. (Matsui: 1991a, 1991b, 1993.) Consequently, the actual designation of a headmaster can be interpreted in several ways. In the case of the Shindō Musō Ryū, Shimizu Takaji is usually referred to in English publications as the twenty-fifth headmaster. This is understandable, since his name is twenty-fifth in the list of successors copied at the end of various transmission documents (*densho*). However, this is complicated by the fact that when two major lines of Shindō Musō Ryū united after the end of the feudal era in 1868, they combined their lineage lists into that found today. Consequently the number of successors in the list almost doubled. Nishioka Tsuneo, in his work entitled *Jōdō jikai* 『杖道自戒』 (Nishioka, 1989), places this list of headmasters in a clear historical perspective. Using this method, Shimizu Takaji and his contemporaries were all tenth-generation successors, and his students were all eleventh-generation successors.

The primary weapons are the 4-foot (1.2 m) staff (*jō*) and the long and short swords (*katana* and *kodachi*). Collateral traditions incorporated into the Shindō Musō Ryū today are Ikkaku Ryū *juttejutsu*, Ittatsu Ryū *hojōjutsu*, Isshin Ryū *kusarigama-jutsu* and Uchida Ryū *sutteki jutsu*.

Certificate (*menjō*) / license (*menkyo*)

Okuirishō	「奥入証」
Shomokuroku	「初目録」
Gomokuroku	「後目録」
Menkyo kaiden	「免許皆伝」

Stick (*jō*) curriculum		Number of *kata*
Omote	表	12
Chūdan	中段	12+1
Ran'ai (later addition)[26]	乱会	2
Kage	影	12+2
Samidare	五月雨	6
Gohon no Midare (recent)[27]	五本ノ乱	5
Okuden (Shiai Kuchi)	奥伝 (試合口)	12
Hiden Gokui (Gomusō no Jō)	秘伝極意 (五夢想ノ杖)	5

Sword (*tachi*) curriculum		Number of *kata*
Oku no Tachi	奥ノ太刀	8
Oku no Kodachi	奥ノ小太刀	4

See also: *Shimizu Takaji; Uchida Ryōgorō; Uchida Ryōhei.*

Further reading in English:

- Draeger, 1973a.
- Draeger and Smith, 1969: 118–119.
- Krieger, 1989.
- Matsui, 1993.

[26] Added during the Bakumatsu (1853–1867) or early Meiji era (1868–c.1890).

[27] Added by Shimizu Takaji during the mid-twentieth century.

Shindō Musō Ryū
神道夢想流
(abbreviated lineage)

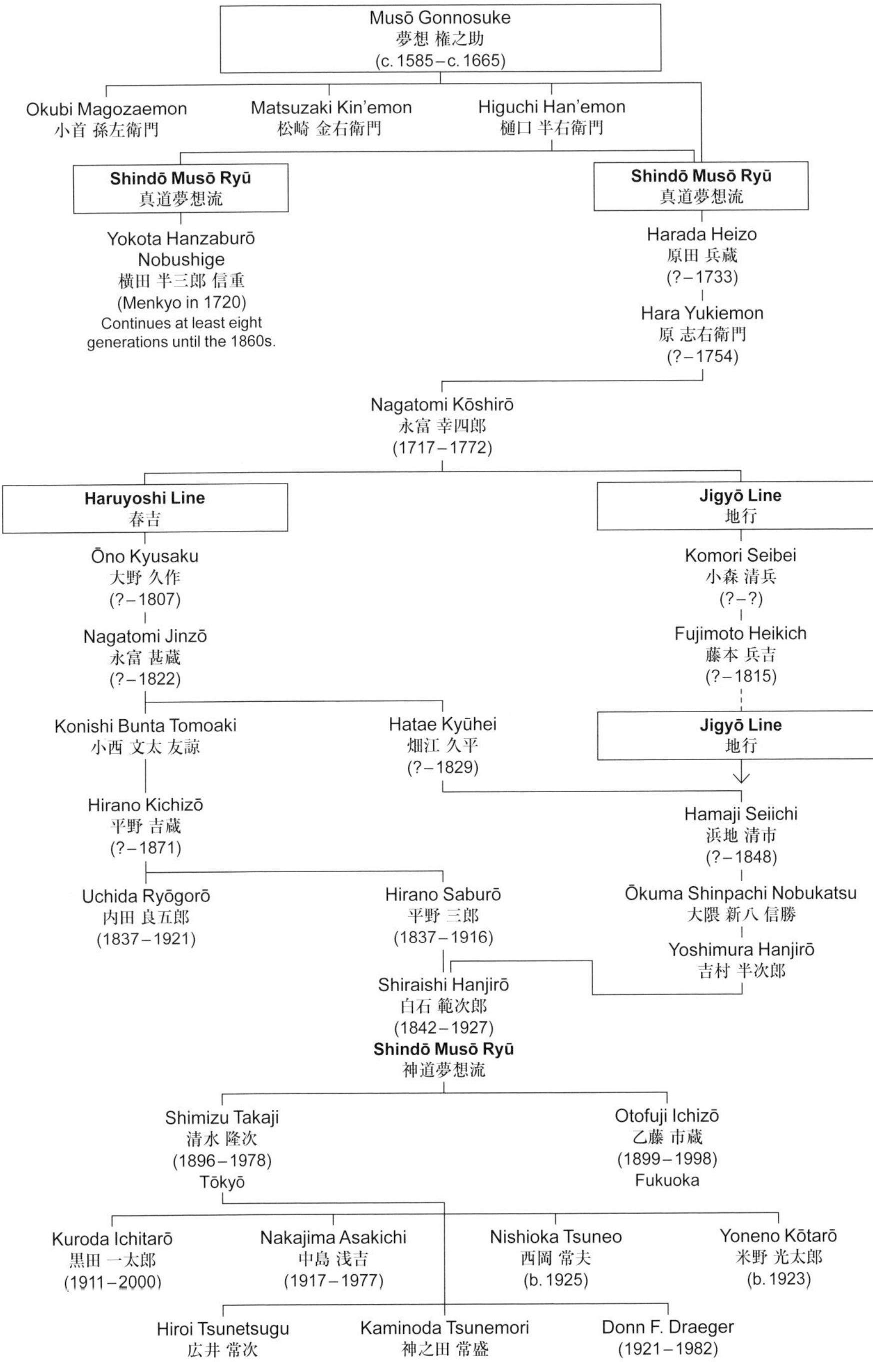

S

Shindō Musō Ryū Jōdō gomokuroku 「神道夢想流杖道後目録」 [Var. **Shindō Musō Ryū Jōjutsu gomokuroku** 神道夢想流杖術初目録] ("latter list"). SHINDŌ MUSŌ RYŪ—The third teaching license (*densho*) in the Shindō Musō Ryū.

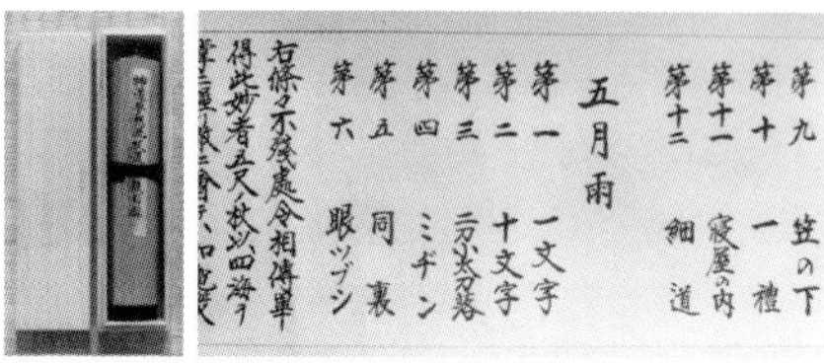

SHINDŌ MUSŌ RYŪ *GOMOKUROKU*
Detail from the *gomokuroku* presented to Donn F. Draeger by Shimizu Takaji in 1973

Shindō Musō Ryū Jōdō menkyo kaiden 「神道夢想流杖道免許皆伝」【神道夢想流杖道免許皆傳】 [Var. **Shindō Musō Ryū Jōjutsu menkyo kaiden** 神道夢想流杖術免許皆伝」【神道夢想流杖術免許皆傳】] (full license). SHINDŌ MUSŌ RYŪ—Originally the only license/scroll awarded in the Shindō Musō Ryū, *menkyo kaiden* is now the last of four licenses awarded to practitioners of the school.

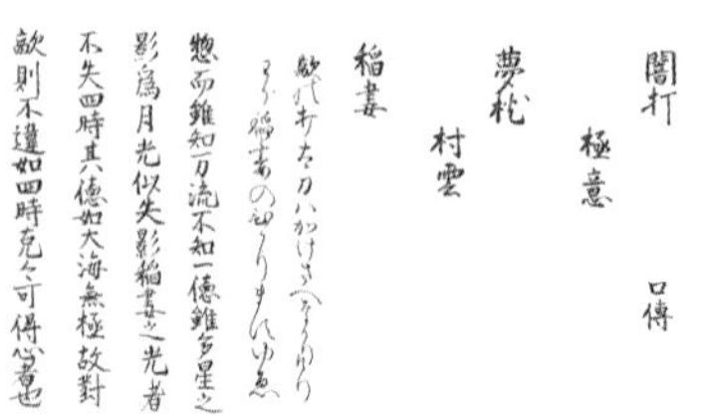

SHINDŌ MUSŌ RYŪ *MENKYO*
Detail from *menkyo kaiden* license dated 1720

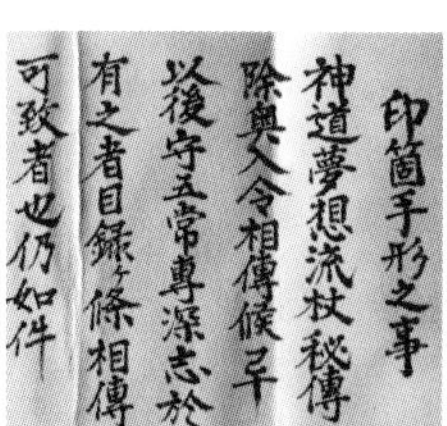

SHINDŌ MUSŌ RYŪ *OKUIRISHŌ*
(Detail)

Shindō Musō Ryū okuirishō 神道夢想流「奥入証」【神道夢想流「奥入證」】 ("certification of entering *Oku*"). SHINDŌ MUSŌ RYŪ—The first, or entry-level, certificate in Shindō Musō Ryū. A student at the Rembukan during the 1960s and 1970s was normally expected to have a minimum of eight years of training before being awarded *okuirishō*.

Shindō Musō Ryū Jōdō shomokuroku 「神道夢想流初目録」 [Var. **Shindō Musō Ryū Jōjutsu shomokuroku** 神道夢想流杖道初目録]. SHINDŌ MUSŌ RYŪ—The second teaching certificate awarded in traditional Shindō Musō Ryū. Issuance of this license evidently dates from the Bakumatsu period, prior to which the only Shindō Musō Ryū license was the *menkyo*.

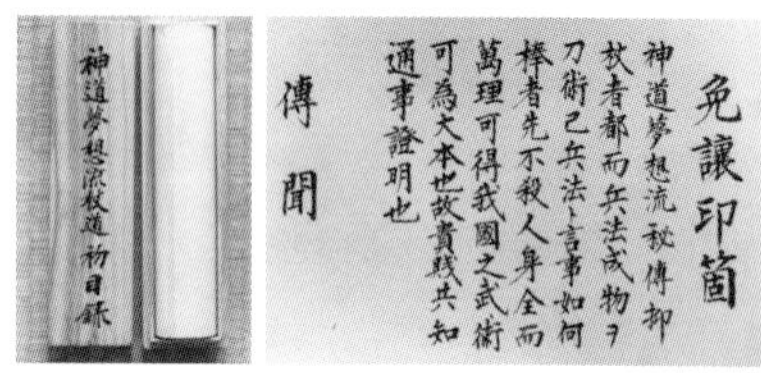

SHINDŌ MUSŌ RYŪ *SHOMOKUROKU*
Detail from the *shomokuroku* presented to Donn F. Draeger by Shimizu Takaji in 1967

Shindō Ryū 心働流. A branch tradition of Katayama Hōki Ryū 片山伯耆流. This system of swordsmanship (*kenjutsu*) and quick-draw sword arts (*iaijutsu*) was founded by Katayama Hōki no Kami Hisayasu. There are many variant names. See: *Katayama Hōki Ryū*.

Shindō Yōshin Ryū 神道楊心流. A Bakumatsu-era (1853–1867) *jūjutsu* tradition founded by Matsuoka Katsunosuke Hisachika. Having mastered the *jūjutsu* of Hirotsuka Totsuka's Yōshin Ryū 楊心流, Matsuoka incorporated those teachings into his own system. Matsuoka was also greatly influenced by his training in the powerful sword systems (*kenjutsu*) of the Jiki Shinkage Ryū 直心影流 and the Hokushin Ittō Ryū 北辰一刀流, as well as the eclectic *jūjutsu* of Tenshin Shin'yō Ryū 天神真楊流. Matsuoka evidently emphasized graceful, natural movement in his own system.

Ōtsuka Hironori, founder of Wadō Ryū 和道流 *karate* in the twentieth century, mastered Shindō Yōshin Ryū 神道楊心流 *jūjutsu* before training in *karate* under Funakoshi Gichin and establishing his own eclectic *karate* system. According to Draeger (1974: 132), Ōtsuka began training in the Shindō Yōshin Ryū in 1898, when he was about six years old.

Shin'ei Taidō 親英体道. See: *Shinwa Taidō.*

shingan 心眼. Mental vision; the eyes of the mind; the eyes of the spirit.

Shingan Ryū 1. 心眼流. See: *Yagyū Shingan Ryū.*

Shingan Ryū 2. 震感流. A branch of the Ien Ryū 威遠流 school of gunnery (*hōjutsu*) and tactical training (*gumpō chōren*) transmitted in Tosa domain in the mid-1850s.

Shingan Ryū 3. 心厳流【心嚴流】. A branch line of the Yagyū Shingan Ryū 柳生心眼流 concentrating on swordsmanship (*kenjutsu*). The Shingan Ryū (3) proliferated in Sendai domain.

Shingetsu Musō Yanagi Ryū 心月無想柳流. A combative school founded by Iwanaga Gennojō Masamitsu in 1753. This school encompassed a number of combative arts mastered by Iwanaga, including grappling (*jūjutsu*), swordsmanship (*kenjutsu*), spear arts (*sōjutsu*), long-hafted glaive techniques (*naginatajutsu*), chain-staff (*rensabō*), sickle-and-chain techniques (*kusarigama-jutsu*), police truncheon techniques (*juttejutsu*), and other related systems. See: *Iwanaga Gennojō Masamitsu; Yanagi Ryū.*

shingi 信義. CLASSICAL WARRIOR IDEAL—Fidelity, trust. *Shingi* as fidelity was considered one of the essential characteristics of the classical warrior (*bushi*). See: *bushi no konjō.*

shingi ittai 心技一体【心技一躰】. Lit. "mind and technique are one." This term was evidently coined by Yamaoka Tesshū, founder of the Ittō Shōden Mutō Ryū 一刀正伝無刀流. For Yamaoka, the ultimate goal of swordsmanship was spiritual forging.

The concept of *shingi ittai* was seen by Yamada Jirōkichi, fifteenth headmaster of the Jiki Shinkage Ryū 直心影流, as the pinnacle of spiritual maturity obtainable via swordsmanship. In his view, the term indicates that the spiritual development and technical skill with the sword go hand in hand. Yamada himself was an outstanding example of *shingi ittai*, and devoted much of his life in the quest for spiritual perfection via the sword. See also: *isshin ittō; Yamaoka Tesshū.*

shingon 真言 <Ch. *zhenyan* <Skt. *mantra* [Var. ***mantara*** 漫怛羅 <Ch. *mandaluo* <Skt. *mantra*]. Sacred sounds or spells. 1. In India, among both Hindus and Buddhists, a *mantra* was a sacred syllable or word or phrase revealed to a religious practitioner during meditation. These sacred sounds were then passed on to disciples in a prescribed manner during initiation rituals. *Shingon* are often seen as a verbal embodiment of a deity. 2. BUDDHISM—An incantation or magical spell; a verbal tool for obtaining union with an object of meditation. *Shingon* (*mantra*) played such an important part in the development of Esoteric or "Tantric" Buddhism that the early stage of its development is referred to as Mantrayāna, the "Vehicle of Spells." 3. BUDDHISM—Abbreviation for Shingon Shū. See also: *darani; shuji.*

Further reading in English:

- Bharati, 1965: 101–163.
- Hall, 1990: 30–44.
- Winternitz, 1933.

Shingon Shū 真言宗. One of the two major schools of Esoteric (Tantric) Buddhism in Japan. Shingon Shū was founded by the monk Kūkai (Kōbō Daishi) in the early ninth century.

Further reading in English:

- Kiyota, 1978.
- Matsunaga, 1974: 171–201 *ff.*
- Hakeda, 1972.
- Payne, 2005.

Shingun Ryū 神軍流. A system of military strategy (*gumpō*) preserved in two transmission scrolls (*densho*) known as the *Tachibana ke shingunden* and the *Taishi ryū shingun shimpi no maki*. These documents have been published in Ishioka and Arima (1967, Vol. 6: 370–406).

shinguntō 新軍刀. Lit. "new military swords." Official mountings for Imperial Japanese Army swords which were used from 1937 to 1945. The actual swords in these mountings were often cheap, factory-made ceremonial swords. However, some officers and non-commissioned officers carried traditionally forged swords (*shinken*) in these mountings. See: *guntō.*

Shingyōtō Ryū 心形刀流 [Also read ***Shinkeitō Ryū***]. An early Edo-period comprehensive

S

field-combat system (*sōgo bujutsu*). This system contains somewhat less weaponry than earlier *ryū* founded in the Warring States period (Sengoku Jidai).

Shingyōtō Ryū was founded in 1682 by Iba Josuiken Hideaki. This school falls into the category of "positive" weapons arts, in that it emphasizes taking the initiative and closing with the enemy. According to this school's current headmaster, Kobayashi Masao, the school's name refers to its core philosophy: Shingyōtō literally means *Mind* (*shin* 心) *Form* (*gyō* 形) *Sword* (*tō* 刀). This indicates that *swordsmanship is a manifestation of the mind.* Consequently, a correct mind gives rise to correct form (or expression) which is manifested via the sword.

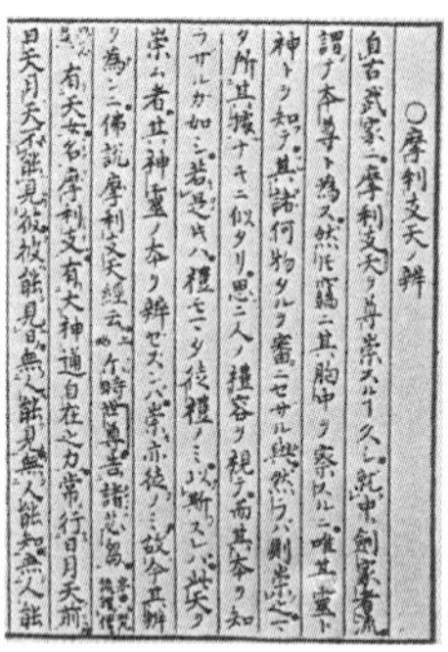

TEXT ENTITLED *MARISHITEN NO BEN*
Copy of the *Marishiten no ben* incorporated as part of the transmission scrolls (*densho*) of the Shingyōtō Ryū, c. 1800
(Matsura Historical Records Collection)

What, then is correct mind? The fact that one of the core *densho* of the Shingyōtō Ryū is actually a verbatim copy of a Buddhist text entitled *Marishiten no ben* 『摩利支天ノ辨』 would seem indicate that that, at least in part, a correct mind is one in which imperturbable mind, intuition, and volition have been fully cultivated.

Weapons systems included in the Shingyōtō Ryū are swordsmanship (*kenjutsu*) with great sword (*ōdachi*), short sword (*kodachi*), and dual swords (*nitō*); quick-draw sword arts (*iaijutsu*); and glaive arts (*naginatajutsu*).

It should be noted here that the *naginatajutsu* of this tradition makes use of the *kagitsuki naginata*, a glaive with an iron crossbar. According to Skoss (1997: 77), this is one of only two schools to preserve this particular weapon system.

Shinjin Ryū 神人流. A branch tradition of the Anazawa Ryū 穴沢流 taught in Satsuma domain (present-day Kagoshima prefecture). The origin of this line, which specialized in long-hafted glaive combative arts (*naginatajutsu*), is attributed to Anazawa Tonomonosuke Moriyoshi and his direct disciple (*deshi*) Honda Hyōsuke, c. 1590.

shinju 神呪. A magic spell; a Buddhist *mantra* (*shingon/mantara*) or *dhāraṇī* (*darani*).

shinjū 1. 臣従. Service as a retainer; a retainer.

shinjū 2. 心中. Lit. "to reveal the heart." A double suicide; a lover's suicide. This type of suicide, which began to appear during the Edo period, was usually carried out due to unrequited or illicit love. See Seward (1968: 73–89) for a comparison with *seppuku*.

shinka 臣下. A retainer; a vassal.

Shinkage Jikishin Ryū 新陰直心流. JIKI SHINKAGE RYŪ—The name and characters used by Kamiya Denshinsai Naomitsu (1582–c. 1645) to denote the Shinkage Ryū. See also: *Jiki Shinkage Ryū*.

Shinkage Ryū. There have been, over the centuries, dozens of "Shinkage Ryū," many of which are completely unrelated. Several have used identical *kanji* (Chinese characters) in their name, but are not related; others have very different characters in their name and are related. Watatani and Yamada (1978: 385–393) list twenty-nine schools using this name, many with variant Chinese characters and encompassing different weapons and/or grappling systems.

Those simply referred to as Shinkage Ryū are: 新陰流 (3 schools); 新影流 (1 school); 新蔭流 (1 school); 神陰流 (2 schools); 神景流 (1 school); 神影流 (4 schools); 真陰流 (4 schools); 真影流 (5 schools); 悳影流 (1 school); 心陰流 (2 schools); 心蔭流 (2 schools); 心影流 (2 schools); 心景流 (1 school). There are many more which include some form of the term *shinkage* in their name.

Shinkage Ryū 1. 新陰流. Lit. "New Kage Tradition" or "Revised Kage Tradition." The original "Shinkage Ryū," this school was founded by Kamiizumi Ise no Kami Nobutsuna (a.k.a. Hidetsuna).

According to Yagyū Genchō in his *Shōden Shinkage Ryū*『正傳新陰流』published in 1956, Kamiizumi Hidetsuna studied the Nen Ryū 念流 of Nen Ami Jion in Kamakura during his youth. After that he journeyed to the Katori Shrine area, where he learned Iizasa's branch of the Shintō Ryū (Tenshinshō-den Katori Shintō Ryū 天真正伝香取神道流) as well as Bokuden's Kashima Shintō Ryū 鹿島新当流. He then began his study of the Aisu Kage Ryū 愛洲陰流 under its founder, Aisu Ikōsai Hisatada. In 1530, at the age of twenty-two, Kamiizumi received the title Ise no Kami (protector/lord of Ise) and began his military career.

According to the *densho* passed down in the various lines of Shinkage Ryū, sometime between 1530 and 1560, Kamiizumi spent time performing religious austerities concentrating on the Buddhist goddess Marishiten. During that time he attained an awakening—both to the essence of combative success and, in a Buddhist sense, the nature of reality. Kamiizumi comments upon this in one of his key *densho*, the *Empi no maki*, which has been handed down in several derivative traditions:

> After practicing the secret methods of Marishisonten day after day for an extended period, and training day and night, I received an inspiration from the deity. Suddenly, from my own heart, the Shinkage Ryū gushed out!

Kamiizumi had evidently conceived of and begun to develop his own style of strategy (*heihō* or *hyōhō*) as early as the 1540s, and was teaching and modifying it with his closest students at that time. Those early students are unknown, but it is almost certain that one of the earliest was Okuyama Kyūgasai, who trained with Kamiizumi as a young man, and from whom the Jiki Shinkage Ryū ultimately descended.

Shinkage Ryū weapons systems under Kamiizumi reflected the times, especially as he had developed counter-techniques to the most prominent systems of his day, including the Shintō Ryū, the Nen Ryū/Chūjō Ryū, and possibly others. Weapons systems included spear (*yari*), long-hafted glaive (*naginata*), great sword (*ōdachi*—a long, curved sword around 5 feet [1.5 m] or more in length), standard-length sword (*tachi*), mid-length sword (*chūdachi*), short sword (*kōdachi*), and several empty-handed grappling techniques (*mutōdori*).

As in the Shintō Ryū, the core combative forms (*kata*) of the Shinkage Ryū can be performed with a variety of hand-held weapons. Consequently, the principle of "one mind, any weapon" is prominent in this school. In Kamiizumi's time, training in the system was conducted through several sets of *kata*. These sets included Empi, Nanatachi, Sangaku, Kuka, Tengushō, Okugi, etc., totaling around forty-five *kata*. The names and contents of these forms varied, however, as Kamiizumi developed his school. While this may seem to be a large number of forms for a combative school, it must be remembered that when it comes to combative technique, warriors in most cultures—ancient, classical, or modern—are very pragmatic. Their lives depend on their effectiveness. Consequently, a closer look at Kamiizumi's Shinkage Ryū *kata* reveals that Empi, the core set, actually contains most, if not all, of the Shinkage Ryū curriculum. Successive sets during Kamiizumi's time were meant to refine, polish, and fortify the trainee's skills in movement, breathing, and psychological/physical dominance of the opponent. Later, during the more than 200 years of relative peace provided by the Tokugawa period, the sequence of these original *kata* was changed in some lines and some scenarios were dropped altogether in others. Today, however, most of these original *kata* survive in one form or another in the several lines that have come down to us.

The real innovation of Kamiizumi's Shinkage Ryū, however, was in its emphasis on spiritual/psychological training. This is evident in the evolution of the term most central to his school; that is, *kage*. One authority on the Shinkage Ryū, Imamura Yoshio, noted in his *Yagyū ibun* (Imamura, 1974: 66–69) that,[28]

[28] Here Imamura paraphrases from an earlier work by the noted martial-arts historian Shimokawa Ushio called *Kendō no hattatsu* (1925: 163).

S

In all human behavior—martial arts, performing arts, etc.—postures and physical movement follow the movement of the mind. In other words, the movement of the mind is manifest in postures and body movement. The term *kage* 陰 (reflection, shadow, *yin* in contrast to *yang*) in the Shinkage Ryū indicates that one's mind is invisible (to the enemy). This lies in contrast to postures and movement which are *yang* 陽. Consequently, in the Shinkage Ryū the swordsman reads the enemy's mind via his postures and movement. Because of this the Shinkage Ryū places more emphasis on piercing the enemy's mind than on technique.

Imamura then asks,

What kind of mind can penetrate an enemy's mind? It is a mind that has been trained to be detached and free. It is clear, like a mirror, and thus can reflect the movement of an enemy's mind. Only someone with a clear, mirror-like mind can correctly respond to the movements of an enemy's mind and body. So, in swordsmanship a mind that moves with victory is called a *kage* (*yin* 陰) mind and the motion of that swordsman's body is called *hi* (*yang* 陽).

In addition, when a swordsman faces an enemy, the warrior who understands *kage* will not reveal his mind with his movement or postures. His mind will only reflect his enemy's mind like *suigetsu* 水月 (water reflecting the moon). This is how victory is achieved.

As can be seen here, the meaning of *kage* is closely parallel to—if not directly derived from—the powers said to be bestowed on the devotees of Marishiten.

This psychological aspect—the "edge" that Kamiizumi had over all the opponents he faced—was made possible by his mastery of Kage Ryū and immersion in the practice of the Marishiten *hihō*. In that area, Kamiizumi had certainly outdistanced his predecessors and moved into new territory by the time he left Minowa castle with his new name, Nobutsuna, in 1561.

The Shinkage style manifested by Kamiizumi and his close disciples enabled them to successfully take on all comers in duel—they sought out and faced the best swordsmen in the land. Primarily using *fukuro shinai* in duels, even when facing hardwood *bokken*, Kamiizumi and his entourage succeeded in "converting" powerful warriors such as Yagyū Muneyoshi and Hōzōin Inei to the Shinkage Ryū. This was truly compassionate swordsmanship in action.

Kamiizumi's Shinkage Ryū brought together a unique combination of several critical elements. For one, it united high-level combative skills, techniques, and strategies derived from the Shintō Ryū, the Nen Ryū, and the Kage Ryū. It also involved a powerful mix of psychological elements from Esoteric Buddhism, in particular the combative adaptive traits cultivated within the cult of Marishiten. Kamiizumi's mastery of the multi-layered meanings of *kage* as taught by his teacher, Aisu, also contributed; as did a deep realization of certain principles which became the linchpin of his new school—*katsujinken satsujintō, marobashi, shūji shuriken,* and others.

Eventually, over twenty warriors received certificates of mastery in the Shinkage Ryū from Kamiizumi; several of their descendant lines are extant today.

As Kamiizumi traveled around, he constantly tweaked and modified his regimen. This is evident in the changes he made in its *kata* and the name of the school; he occasionally changed the characters used for the term "*kage*," sometimes within a single document. In the *densho* he presented to Yagyū Muneyoshi in 1566, the term Shinkage Ryū is first written as 新陰流, and then marked out and changed to 新影流.

(From the archives of Yagyū Nobuharu)

There are subtle differences in meaning between the characters 陰 and 影. Kamiizumi's own conception of the term was obviously evolving, as was its application to combat. Other lines of the school sometimes display additional alternate versions of the original term "Shinkage Ryū," such as 神陰流.

Shinkage Ryū curriculum:

As noted, Kamiizumi Nobutsuna continually adjusted the weaponry and curriculum of his Shinkage Ryū. Consequently, while there is much similarity in the descending lineages of his disciples, few sets of *kata* are identical in every line. The following list basically includes those sets passed on to Yagyū Muneyori around 1565. These *kata* can be performed with a variety of weaponry.

Curriculum		Number of *kata*
Empi 燕飛		6
• Empi	燕飛	
• Enkai	猿廻	
• Yamakage	山陰	
• Tsukikage	月影	
• Uranami	浦波	
• Ukifune	浮舟	
(Empi no oku)		2
• Shishi Funjin	獅子奮迅	
• Yamagasumi	山霞	
Nanatachi 七太刀		7
• Kyochi no Shishi	踞地獅子	
• Tenkan	天関【天關】	
• Yōhatsu	容髪	
• Kotegiri	籠手切	
• Chijiku	地軸	
• Meigetsu no Kaze	明月風	
• Engan	燕雁	
Sangaku 三学【参學】		5
• Ittō Ryōdan	一刀両断	
• Zantei Settetsu	斬釘截鉄	
• Hankai Hanko	半開半向	
• Usen Saten/Sasen Uten	右旋左転·左旋右転	
• Chōtan Ichimi	長短一味	
Kuka 九箇		9
• Hisshō	必勝	
• Gyakufū	逆風	
• Tōdachi	十太刀	
• Kaboku	華卜（和卜）	
• Shōkei	捷径【捷徑】	
• Kozume	小詰	
• Ōzume	大詰	
• Yaegaki	八重垣	
• Murakumo	村雲	
Tengushō 天狗抄 (Alternate Tengu names)		8
• Kasha 花車	(Kōrinbō 高林坊)	
• Akemi 明身	(Fūgenbō 風眼房)	
• Zentai 善待	(Tarōbō 太郎房)	
• Tebiki 手引	(Eiibō 栄意坊【榮意坊】)	
• Nitō 二刀	(Chiraten 智羅天)	
• Uchimono 打物	(Karanbō 火乱房【火亂房】)	
• Ranken 乱剣【亂劍】	(Shutokubo 修德房)	
(Tengushō oku 天狗抄奥)		
• Ninin Gakkari 二人懸	(Konpirabō 金比羅房)	

Other (Note: Some of the following "sets" and individual *kata* are found within the Yagyū school, others are found in diverse lines.)

Okugi 奥義
There is much variation between diverse Shinkage Ryū lines. The Owari Yagyū line includes:
- Tensetsu Ransetsu 添截乱截【添截亂截】
- Muniken 無二剣【無二劍】
- Katsujintō 活人刀
- Kōjō 高上
- Gokui 極意
- Shinmyōken 神妙剣【神妙劍】

Marobashi 転【轉】—Ōmarobashi 大転【大轉】/ Komarobashi 小転【小轉】(There is much variation between diverse Shinkage Ryū lines.)

Kogusoku 小具足

Mutōdori 無刀取 (There is much variation between diverse Shinkage Ryū lines.)

Yari 槍 (Shinkage Ryū spear techniques)
Most of these seem to have been preserved in the Hikita Kage Ryū and, possibly, the Hōzōin Ryū. Only a few appear in other lines. Miscellaneous *kata* attributed to Kamiizumi are found in various branches of the Shinkage Ryū:
- Matsukaze 松風
- Reiken 霊剣

Shinkage Ryū *densho*:

Kamiizumi Nobutsuna passed on a variety of *densho* to his disciples. There was no "set," and each recipient evidently received something a little different. The contents of the *densho* also varied. The most common—reflecting the names of *kata* included—are:
- Empi
- Sangaku
- Kuka
- Tengusho

Shinkage Ryū 2. 新影流. SHINKAGE RYŪ—Alternate characters used by Kamiizumi Nobutsuna for indicating the name of his "Revised *Kage* Tradition." See also: *Shinkage Ryū (1).*

Shinkage Ryū 3. 神陰流. JIKI SHINKAGE RYŪ—According to *densho* of the Jiki Shinkage Ryū, these characters were used by Matsumoto Bizen no Kami to name his sword style after a period of meditation at Kashima Jingu. Prior to that, he had referred to his tradition as the Kashima Shin Ryū.

S

Shinkage Ryū Heihō
新陰流兵法
(abbreviated lineage)

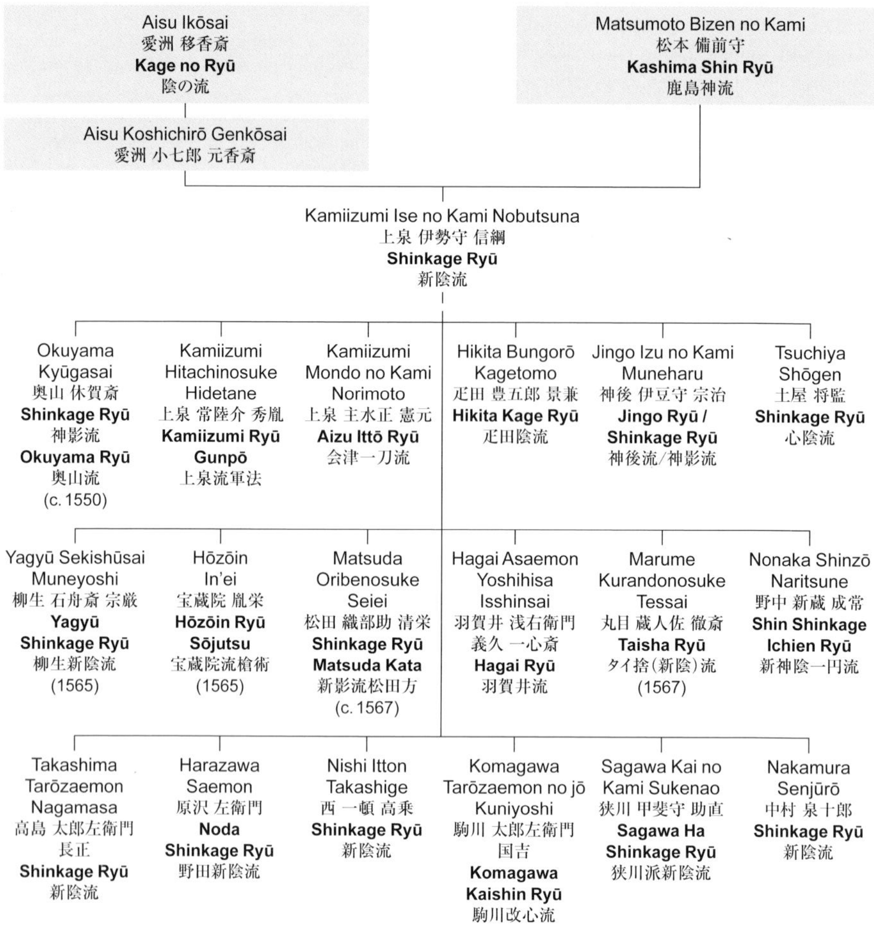

Shinkage Ryū 4. 神影流. JIKI SHINKAGE RYŪ—Characters/name used for Shinkage Ryū by Okuyama Kyūgasai Kimishige (1526–1602). Also referred to as Okuyama Ryū 奥山流. See also: *Jiki Shinkage Ryū.*

Shinkage Ryū 5. 真影流. A branch tradition of Kamiizumi's Shinkage Ryū (1) passed down in Okuyama via samurai Katayama Tomotarō and Takeshita Taizō. Weapons systems included swordsmanship (*kenjutsu*) with *katana* and *tachi*, long-hafted glaive arts (*naginatajutsu*), and a spear system (*sōjutsu*) using the cross-blade spear (*jūmonji yari*). A specialty of the school appears to have been the ability to disarm an opponent and use his own weapon against him (*shinken shirahadōri*).

Shinkage Ryū 6. 神影流. A branch tradition of Kamiizumi Ise no Kami Nobutsuna's Shinkage Ryū created by Jingo Izu no Kami Muneharu. See: *Jingo Ryū.*

Shinkage Ryū 7. 陰流. A branch line of the Shinkage Ryū descended from Kamiya Denshinsai's Shinkage Jikishin Ryū via Matsuoka Sonae Tayū in the mid-1600s. See: *Matsuoka Shinkage Ryū.*

Shinkage Ryu 8. 悳影流. A branch tradition of the Jiki Shinkage Ryū 直心影流 passed down in Jōshū (Kōzuke prov.). This line of the Jiki Shinkage Ryū descended from Naganuma Shōbee Masato, who is also credited with founding the Naganuma Ryū (1) 長沼流. At some point it became the custom of this tradition to combine the characters "*jiki*" 直 and "*shin*" 心 into one character read as "shin" 悳. See also: *Naganuma Ryū (1)*.

Shinkage Ryū 9. 真蔭流 [Var. ***Shinkage Ryū Jūjutsu*** 真蔭流柔術]. A system of *jūjutsu* dating from the late Edo period, founded by Imaizumi Hachirō Tomoaki. Its central curriculum is comprised of forty-eight combative scenarios (*kata*) divided into five sections:

Curriculum		Number of *kata*
Shodan Tehodoki	初段手解	6
Shodan Idori	初段居捕	10
Chūdan Tachiai	中段立居	10
Chūdan Nagesute	中段投捨	12
Gokui Jōdan	極意上段	10

Shinkage Ryū heihō 新陰流兵法. 1. A variant name for Shinkage Ryū (1). 2. The combative strategies and martial techniques of the Shinkage Ryū. See also: *Kōizumi Ryū Hyōhō; Shinkage Ryū (1)*.

Shinkage Ryū heihō gaiden tōhō shiai seihō 新陰流兵法外伝刀法試合勢法. See: *Shiai Seihō*.

Shinkage Ryū Jujutsu 真蔭流柔術. [Var. ***Shinkage Ryū*** 真蔭流]. See: *Shinkage Ryū (9)*.

Shinkage Ryū Matsuda Kata 新影流松田方. See: *Matsuda Kata Shinkage Ryū*.

Shinkage Ryū nana tachi 「新陰流七太刀」 [A.k.a. ***Shinkage Ryū nana tachi no maki*** 「新陰流七太刀」の巻]. Name of the second picture scroll (*emaki*) presented to Yagyū Muneyoshi by Shinkage Ryū founder Kamiizumi Ise no Kami Nobutsuna in 1566. This scroll depicts the set of *kata* known as Nana Tachi 七太刀.

These forms are listed as follows:

- Kyochi no Shishi 踞地獅子
- Tenkan 天関
- Yōhatsu 容髪
- Kotegiri 籠手切
- Chijiku 地軸
- Meigetsu no Kaze 明月風
- Engan 燕雁

DETAIL FROM THE SHINKAGE RYŪ
NANA TACHI NO MAKI
(From the archives of the late Yagyū Nobuharu)

Shinkage Taisha Ryū 新陰タイ捨流. See: *Taisha Ryū*.

Shinkeitō Ryū 心形刀流. See: *Shingyōtō Ryū*.

shinken 真剣【真劍】. 1. A real sword; a sword with a sharpened cutting edge. Contrast to a metal practice sword with no cutting edge (*iaitō*), a rebated-edge *shinken* (*habiki*), or a wooden sword (*bokken; bokutō*).

shinken shirahadori 真剣白刃取【真劍白刃取】. The martial skill of taking (*~dori*) a live blade (*shinken shiraha*) from an enemy, usually in bare-handed form. The enemy can also be subdued, or the confiscated blade can be used to dispatch him. Usually referred to as *mutōdori* in Kamiizumi's Shinkage Ryū and derivative traditions, it is also commonly referred to as *shinken shirahadori*.

shinken shōbu 真剣勝負【真劍勝負】. 1. Lethal combat. 2. A duel to the death. 3. A duel with live swords. Prior to the Edo period, swordsmen who followed the "positive styles" of swordsmanship considered *shinken shōbu* to be the only realistic test of a swordsman's skill. See also: *shinai shiai; taryūjiai*.

Shinken Shōbu no Kata 真剣勝負の形【真劍勝負の形】. KŌDŌKAN JŪDŌ—Lit. "forms for actual combat." See: *Kime no Kata*.

Shinki Ien Ryū 神奇威遠流. A branch of the Ien Ryū 一円流, a school of gunnery (*hōjutsu*) and tactical training (*gumpō chōren*). The Shinki Ien Ryū was transmitted in Uwajima domain.

Shinkoku 神国【神國】. Divine land, land of the gods. A term for Japan.

Shinkyoku Ryū. Watatani and Yamada (1978: 397) list nine different traditions that used the name "Shinkyoku Ryū" using the characters 心極流, 新極流, and 真極流. Specializations of the traditions varied; they included striking systems (*kempō* [2] 拳法), grappling (*jūjutsu*), swordsmanship (*kenjutsu*), arresting arts (*torite*), restraining cord (*hojōjutsu*), quick-draw sword arts (*iaijutsu*), gunnery (*hōjutsu*), spear arts (*sōjutsu*), long hardwood staff techniques (*bōjutsu*), and the use of small throwing blades and darts (*shuriken-jutsu*).

Shinkyō Ryū 心鏡流. A martial school founded by Yamane Sagoemon Yoshifusa in 1684. The school at that time had a comprehensive curriculum (*sōgō bujutsu*), including combative swordsmanship (*kenjutsu*), spear tactics (*sōjutsu*), long-hafted glaive techniques (*naginatajutsu*), and sickle-and-chain arts (*kusagamajutsu*). At least one branch of this system is extant today.

Shinmei Musō Ryū 神明夢想流 [Also read ***Shimmei Musō Ryū***]. See: *Shin Musō Hayashizaki Ryū*.

Shinmen Munisai 新免 無二斎. See: *Miyamoto Munisai*.

Shinmen Musashi no Kami 新免武蔵守. See: *Miyamoto Musashi*.

Shin Musō Hayashizaki Ryū 神夢想林崎流 [A.k.a. ***Battōjutsu Shinmei Musō Ryū*** 抜刀術神明夢想流; ***Hayashizaki Ryū*** 林崎流; ***Jūshin Ryū*** 重信流; ***Hayashizaki Shigenobu Ryū*** 林崎重信流; ***Hayashizaki Jinsuke Shigenobu Ryū*** 林崎甚助重信流; ***Shigenobu Ryū*** 重信流; ***Shimmei Musō Ryū*** 神明夢想流]. An early *ryū* specializing in quick-draw sword arts (*iaijutsu*) founded by Hayashizaki Jinsuke Shigenobu around 1600. During the Edo period, almost 200 schools specializing in *iaijutsu* descended from this school. See also: *Hasegawa Chikaranosuke Eishin (Hidenobu)*.

Shinmyōken 神妙剣 【神妙劍】. An alternate term for Ichi no Tachi, a sword system "revealed" to Kuninazu no Mahito in the seventh century. See: *Ichi no Tachi; Kasumi no Tachi; Kuninazu no Mahito*.

Shinnan Ryū 新楠流. See: *Natori Ryū*.

Shinnen Ryū 心念流. A school of long hardwood staff arts (*bōjutsu*) founded by Chikamatsu Hikonoshin Shigenori. It flourished in Bishū domain, and was closely related to the Ichizen Ryū (1) 一全流, also founded by Chikamatsu.

Shin no Goten 真之五点. See: *Goten no Shidai*.

Shin no Shin Ishikawa Ryū 真之真石川流 [A.k.a. ***Ishikawa Ryū*** 石川流; ***Shin Ryū*** 真流]. A branch system of the Edo Yagyū Shinkage Ryū founded by Ishikawa Kurando Masaharu sometime during the Kan'ei era (1624–1644). Ishikawa was a direct disciple of school founder Yagyū Muneyori. This branch line concentrated on swordsmanship (*kenjutsu*). For lineage, see: *Edo Yagyū Shinkage Ryū*.

Shin no Shintō Ryū 真之神道流. A classical school of *jūjutsu* created in the sixteenth century by Yamamoto Minzaemon.

Shinnuki Ryū 信抜流 【信拔流】 [Also written 心抜流] [A.k.a. ***Shinnuki Ryū Kempō/ Iaijutsu*** ~剣法·居合術]. A school of combative swordsmanship (*kempō* [1] 剣法) and quick-draw sword tactics (*iaijutsu*) which traces its origins to Okuyama Saemon Dayū Tadanobu. Okuyama was an early disciple of Taisha Ryū founder Marume Kurandonosuke Tessai.[29] Although originally a comprehensive combative system (*sōgō bujutsu*), the school today concentrates on swordsmanship.

shinobi 忍. 1. Espionage; stealing into; endurance. The term *shinobi*, meaning espionage, was used throughout the classical period from at least the fourteenth century through the nineteenth century. With the beginning of the modern era (Gendai) in 1868, the variant reading of "*ninja*" became more popular. 2. A spy. See: *ninjutsu*.

shinobi metsuke 忍目付 [Var. 忍び目付]. A variant term for a member of the Tokugawa-period secret police. See: *metsukeyaku*.

shinobi monomi 忍び物見. A variant term for an espionage agent. *Shinobi monomi* indicates

[29] There is some controversy over this connection.

*Shin Musō Hayashizaki Ryū·Shimmei Musō Ryū**

神夢想林崎流·神明夢想流

(abbreviated lineage)

1. Hayashizaki Jinsuke Shigenobu
初代　林崎 甚助 重信
(c. 1550–c. 1620)

- Takamatsu Kanbei Nobukatsu
高松 勘兵衛 信勝
Ichinomiya Ryū
一宮流
  - Takamatsu Heihachirō Nobushige
  高松 平八郎 信重
- Azuma Shimotsuke no Kami Motoharu
東 下野守 元治
Shimmei Musō Azuma Ryū
神明夢想東流
- Katayama Hōki no Kami Hisayasu
片山 伯耆守 久安
Battō Hōki Ryū·Ikkan Ryū
抜刀伯耆流·一貫流
- Honma Zenzaemon Takakatsu
本間 善左衛門 高勝

- Sekiguchi Jūshin
関口 柔心
Sekiguchi Ryū
関口流
- 2. Tamiya Heibei Shigemasa
二代　田宮 平兵衛 重正
Shin Musō Hayashizaki Ryū·Tamiya Ryū
神夢想林崎流·田宮流
- 3. Nagano Murakusai Kinro
三代　長野 無楽斎 槿露
Shin Musō Hayashizaki Ryū·Muraku Ryū
神夢想林崎流·無楽流

4. Momo Gumbei Mitsushige
四代　百々 軍兵衛 光重
Shin Musō Hayashizaki Ryū

5. Arikawa Shōzaemon Munetsugu
五代　蟻川 正左衛門 宗続

6. Banno Dan'emon Nobusada
六代　万野 団右衛門 信定

7. Hasegawa Chikaranosuke Eishin
七代　長谷川 主税助 英信
Hasegawa Eishin Ryū
長谷川英信流
(c. 1736)

8. Arai Seitetsu Kiyonobu
八代　荒井 勢哲 清信

9. Hayashi Rokudayū Morimasa†
九代　林 六太夫 守政

10. Hayashi Yasudayū Masatomo
十代　林 安太夫 政朝
(1662–c. 1740)

11. Ōguro Motoemon Kiyokatsu
十一代　大黒 元右衛門 清勝

(later called) Tanimura Ha
谷村派

12. Hayashi Masunojō Masanari
十二代　林 益之丞 政誠

13. Yoda Manzō Norikatsu
十三代　依田 万蔵 敬勝

14. Hayashi Yadayū Masataka
十四代　林 弥太夫 政敬

15. Tanimura Kamenojō Takakatsu
十五代　谷村 亀之丞 自雄
(d. 1862)

16. Gotō Magobei Masasuke
十六代　五藤 孫兵衛 正亮
(d. 1898)

17. Ōe Masamichi
十七代　大江 正路
(1852–1927)

(lineage divided and in dispute)

(later called) Shimomura Ha
下村派

12. Matsuyoshi Sadasuke Hisamori
十二代　松吉 貞助 久盛

13. Yamagawa Kyūzō Yukio
十三代　山川 久蔵 幸雄
(d. 1848)

14. Shimomura Shigeichi Sadamasa
十四代　下村 城市 定正

15. Hosokawa Yoshimasa Yoshiuma
十五代　細川 義昌 義馬
(d. 1923)

16. Nakayama Hakudō
十六代　中山 博道
(1873–1958)
Musō Shinden Ryū
夢想神伝流

(lineage divided and in dispute)

* Various other names are used for this tradition, such as Hayashizaki Ryū 林崎流 and others.

† Ninth headmaster Hayashi Morimasa trained under Ōmori Musturō Zaemon Masamitsu, and added Ōmori Ryū techniques to the Hasegawa Eishin Ryū around 1740.

S

a concealed lookout. See: *kamari; ninjutsu.*

shinobi no jutsu 忍術 [Var. 忍びの術]. See: *ninjutsu.*

shinobi no mono 忍者 [Var. 忍びの者]. A term used for espionage agents of various types during the Muromachi, Sengoku, Azuchi-Momoyama, and Tokugawa periods. This reading has been replaced by the pronunciation *ninja* since the early Meiji era (post-1868). See: *ninja; ninjutsu.*

shinogi 鎬. The raised ridge on the side of the sword; the highest point of the side of the blade.

shi nō kō shō 士農工商. The four social classes as recognized under the Tokugawa shogunate. The Japanese term was a modification of the original Chinese Confucian categories of government official (官吏), peasant farmer (百姓), artisan (職人), and merchant (商人). With the warrior (*bushi*) holding both military and civil power, the Japanese replaced the civil servant with the warrior:

Jp. abbr.	Class
1. shi 士	warriors
2. nō 農	farmers
3. kō 工	artisans
4. shō 商	merchants

Other categories which were extant during the Tokugawa period but were not part of the main four included:

• *kuge* 公家	court nobles
• *burakumin* 部落民	outcasts
• *hinin* 非人	ex-convicts, drifters, vagrants, and entertainers
• *onmitsu* 隠密	espionage agents

Shi no maki 「私之巻」. One of several extant Aisu Kage Ryū 愛洲陰流 transmission documents (*densho*). See: *Aisu Kage Ryū.*

shinpan 審判. See: *shimpan.*

shinpō 心法. See: *shimpō.*

Shinra Saburō Minamoto no Yoshimitsu 新羅 三郎 源 義光 (1056–1127). See: *Minamoto no Yoshimitsu.*

Shin Reiken Ryū 神霊剣流 【神靈劍流】. A branch tradition of the Naganuma Ryū (1) 長沼流 (=Jiki Shinkage Ryū 直心影流).

shinryoku 心力. Mental or spiritual power.

Shin Ryū 1. 神流 [Var. 真流]. A branch tradition of the Katayama Hōki Ryū 片山伯耆流. This system of swordsmanship (*kenjutsu*) and quick-draw sword arts (*iaijutsu*) was founded by Nagai Sakunoemon no jō Kōken. There are many variant names. See: *Katayama Hōki Ryū.*

Shin Ryū 2. 神流. A system specializing in quick-draw swordsmanship (*iaijutsu*) and police tying-cord skills (*torinawa*), which flourished during the first half of the 1600s. It was founded by Numazawa Jingozaemon.

Shinsengumi 新撰組. The "Newly Selected Corps" (*Shinsengumi*) was a name given to several units made up of *rōnin* and armed peasants sent to Kyōto by the Tokugawa shogunate in the early 1860s. Their official purpose was to expel foreigners and protect the *shōgun*.

Due to pressure by foreign powers and the weakness of the Tokugawa *bakufu*, Kyōto—the imperial capital—had become a lawless city plagued by battles between rival political factions. Most prominent were several clans and a miscellaneous assortment of *rōnin* who were plotting to overthrow the *shōgun* and restore the emperor to power. These samurai created a wave of terror in the capital. To counter this, the Tokugawa shogunate recruited expert swordsmen of low status from eastern provinces such as Aizu to restore law and order to Kyōto. Unfortunately, this "most dreaded security force," which the shogunate designated the "Shinsengumi," created its own reign of terror for the next several years.

Further reading in English:

• Hillsborough, 2005.

shinsetsu 臣節. CLASSICAL WARRIOR IDEAL—*Shinsetsu* indicates loyalty. As such, it was considered one of the essential characteristics of the classical warrior (*bushi*). See: *bushi no konjō.*

shinshi 臣子. A retainer; a vassal.

Shin Shinkage Ichien Ryū 新神陰一円流 【新神陰一圓流】 [Var. ***Ichien Ryū*** 一円流 【一圓

流】]. A school of swordsmanship (*kenjutsu*) derived from Kamiizumi Nobutsuna's original Shinkage Ryū (1) 新陰流, c. 1570. Its founder, Nonaka Shinzō Naritsune, was a direct disciple of Kamiizumi.

Shin no Shinkage Ryū 真新陰流. JIKI SHINKAGE RYŪ—Name used by Ogasawara Genshin Nagaharu for the Shinkage Ryū. The prefix *shin* 真 means "true" or "correct." It is thought that Ogasawara may have chosen this character to establish his "Shinkage Ryū" in the city of Edo as the "true" line from Kamiizumi, in contrast to the Edo Yagyū who were aligned with the Tokugawa family. See: Ogasawara Genshin Nagaharu.

Shin Shinkansō Ryū 新心貫相流. A variant name for the Amō Ryū.

Shin Shin Musō Ryū 神心無想流. A modern *budō* combative system founded in 1942 by Nakajima Shōhitsu, who had inherited the Shinkage Ryū (6) 神影流. Prior to World War II, Nakajima's group was called the Dai Nippon Teikoku Kai (Great Imperial Japan Society). After the post–World War II ban on martial arts practice was lifted in 1952, Nakajima changed the name to Ryūshinkan Budō 柳心館武道 (Martial Ways of the Willow Heart Hall).

Primarily based on quick-draw sword techniques (*iaijutsu*) and test-cutting practice (*tameshigiri*), the school includes a variety of empty-hand techniques (*taijutsu*) and weaponry including warrior sickle (*kama*), long-hafted glaive (*naginata*), and others.

The second headmaster of this tradition, Toyoshima Kazutora, appeared as the florid *iai* practitioner in the 1968 James Bond film *You Only Live Twice*. See also: *Ryūshinkan Budō.*

Shin Shin Mutekatsu Ryū 新心無手勝流. A school of combative swordsmanship (*kenjutsu*) and quick-draw sword (*iaijutsu*) founded by Yamamoto Sakondayū Akimune around 1600. Inspired by the legend of Tsukahara Bokuden's *mutekatsu* (no-hands victory), Yamamoto trained vigorously in several of the combative schools of his day. Then, beginning in 1596, he began four years of austere training and religious practices at Mount Atago (Atagosan) close to Kyōto, after which he emerged with his new system. See also: *Atagosan Daigongen; mutekatsu; Mutekatsu Ryū.*

Shin Shin Sekiguchi Ryū 新心関口流【新心關口流】. A combative system founded by Yoshida Sakubee Tadafusa c. 1685. It concentrated on grappling (*jūjutsu*) and quick-sword draw (*iai* 居相). See also: *Ikkan Ryū (3); Yawara Shinshin Ryū.*

shinshintō 新々刀. A classification term for Japanese blades made generally from the late 1700s (c. 1781) through 1868, the year of the Meiji Restoration. During this period, swordsmiths looked back to the golden age of swordmaking in the fourteenth century for their models. See also: *gendaitō; guntō; kaiguntō; kotō; kyūguntō; Nippontō; shinguntō; shintō (2); Shōwatō; Yasukunitō.*

Shinshin Tōitsu Aikidō 心身統一合気道 (Unity of Body and Mind Aikidō) [Var. ***Ki Aikidō*** 気合気道]. Aikidō organization founded by Tōhei Kōichi in the 1970s, also known as the Ki Society. Tōhei's system emphasizes soft, flowing technique.

Further reading in English:

- Official Ki Society Website (Japan): http://www.ki-society.com/english/
- Official Ki Society Website (US): http://ki-aikido.net/

shintai 1. 神体【神體】[A.k.a. ***go-shintai*** 御神体]. SHINTŌ—An object of worship within a Shintō shrine. The spirit of the enshrined deity (*kami*) is thought to inhabit the object. Also called *mitama shiro*.

shintai 2. 身体【身體】. The human body; the system.

shintai 3. 進退. Advance and retreat; movement.

Shin Tamiya Ryū 新田宮流 [A.k.a. ***Shin Tamiya Ryū Battōjutsu*** ～抜刀術]. A school of quick-draw swordsmanship (*battōjutsu*) founded by Wada Heisuke Masakatsu sometime during the Kambun era (1661–1673). Wada first mastered the quick-draw swordsmanship (*iaijutsu*) of the Tamiya Ryū 田宮流 under Ahina Mudō Tōrudai. Later, after also training in the Mizuno Ryū 水野流—a school of grappling (*jūjutsu*), quick-draw swordsmanship, and tying-cord arts (*hojōjutsu*)—under

S

founder Mizuno Shingozaemon Shigeji, Wada founded his own school. The Shin Tamiya Ryū is extant today.

shinte 死手 [A.k.a. ***mete*** 雌手; ***inte*** 陰手]. OKINAWAN KARATE—Lit. "dead hand" or "dying hand." According to Funakoshi (2001: 36), this term indicates the hand that has already been used for blocking. The equivalent terms *mete* 雌手 (female hand) and *inte* 陰手 (*yin* hand) both relate to Chinese *yin-yang* theory in which energy waxes and wanes in a cyclical fashion. Funakoshi (2001: 36–37) elaborates on this, noting that the relative movements and principles of *yin* and *yang* are the "cardinal principles of our *karatejutsu*." See also: *kisei; ikite*.

Shinten Ryū 真天流. Lit. the "Straight/Correct Ten Ryū." A comprehensive combative system (*sōgō bujutsu*) which concentrated on swordsmanship (*kenjutsu*). The Shinten Ryū was founded by Oyamada Tamon Sadashige in the early 1600s. Oyamada had previously trained in the Ten Ryū 天流 *sōgō bujutsu* of Saitō Denkibō; the Isshin Ryū 一心流 staff arts (*bōjutsu*) of his own father; and the swordsmanship (*kenjutsu*) of the Bokuden Ryū 卜伝流 and the Shintō Ryū 神刀流. Having mastered these traditions, Oyamada devised his own school, the Shinten Ryū. The Shinten Ryū later divided into several lines, of which the main one was preserved in Yonezawa domain.

Shintō 1. 神道. The native religion of Japan. Although Shintō is classified as a "religion," it is unlike Western religions in that it has no dogma, moral code, or sacred book.[30] The term "Shintō," in fact, was not used by the Japanese until the importation of continental religious systems—Buddhism, Daoism, and Confucianism—necessitated some sort of designator for native shamanistic practices and beliefs. Under the powerful influence of Buddhism, certain elements of Shintō were amalgamated into a new form referred to as Ryōbu Shintō. In the early Meiji era this amalgamation was disrupted as the xenophobic Japanese government attempted to separate Shintō shrines and practices from non-native Buddhist influences. At the same time the government tried to create a new, pure Shintō religion that was based on nationalism and focused on the cult of the Japanese emperor. This religion—later referred to as State Shintō (Kokka Shintō 国家神道)—was dismantled at the end of World War II.

Traditional Shintō as a belief system has been oriented toward animism, nature worship, ritual purity, and agricultural harvests. Of major concern in Shintō are *kami*. Although this term is often translated as "god" or "deity," it is more akin to the concept of "spiritual power" or "spiritual essence."[31] According to Shintō belief, almost everything contains *kami*: humans, spirits of departed ancestors, animals, intriguingly shaped rocks, large trees, mountains, the wind, weapons, etc. There are so many of these that the Japanese refer to them as the *yaoyorozu no kami* 八百万の神. Sometimes translated as the "Eight Million Gods," the term actually means the "myriad spirits."

As the native belief system of Japan, Shintō has had a relationship with the country's martial arts since earliest times. Japanese mythology, detailing the prehistoric creation of the Japanese islands and people, is filled with weaponry and martial symbolism. Wrestling matches (*sumō* or *sumai*) were performed as part of Shintō ritual as early as the Tumulus period (c.250–645); during the Yamato period (c.300–c.550), Shintō priests and priestesses took part in military campaigns where they "offered prayers for victory and blessed weapons before battle" (Farris, 1992: 25).

Also during the Yamato period, the hereditary local warrior leaders (*kuni no miyatsuko*) sanctioned by the Yamato emperors were required to fulfill both military and Shintō religious duties. Later, during the Heian period (794–1185), one way for a provincial governor to enlist personal support from local rural warriors was to have them perform in provincial religious rites. Farris (1992: 185) notes that, "Warrior participation in Shintō rites originated in the tenth century or thereabouts..."

30 See Fritz Staal's informative article on the differences between Western Asian religions and East and South Asian religions. (Staal, 1982)

31 See the entry on *kami* in this *Encyclopedia*.

At that time they took part in *sumō*, dancing, and mounted archery contests. It also became customary for medieval governors to designate one Shintō site as the main one for their province (*ichi no miya* 一の宮). The purpose of this was to consolidate religious and military power under the governor. By the thirteenth century, however, service in Shintō rites at such famous shrines became a privilege, and distinguished a person as being of martial lineage.

In the area of weapon production, the proper forging of swords and other martial implements was traditionally carried out in coordination with specific Shintō rites. In addition, Shintō has also been closely allied with the spiritual foundations of Japanese swordsmanship. There are records of Japanese swordsmen receiving spiritual revelations of combative strategy at Shintō shrines as early as the seventh century. (See: *Kashima no Tachi.*) By the mid-fourteenth century this practice had become widespread, with the founders of numerous martial schools (*koryū*) engaged in retreats and pilgrimages to Shintō shrines and Buddhist temples.[32] There, after a period of austere training and religious practice, they expected to experience an oracle (*musō*) or some similar type of empowerment experience in which the *kami* of the shrine would reveal to them the secrets that would become the core of a new martial school.

This relationship between Shintō and things martial has lasted throughout Japanese history. Even today, martial exhibitions (*hono embu*) are performed periodically at numerous shrines around Japan. These exhibitions, while normally open to the public, are not intended to entertain. They are meant to reaffirm the connection between the practitioners, the martial tradition (*koryū*), and the shrine, which in many cases may have been the spiritual power center from which the school's founder received his inspiration. Consequently, as martial historian and hoplologist Donn F. Draeger[33] often noted, "All native martial arts in Japan have Shintō as their aesthetic and ethical base." See also: *kami, mitama.*

[32] Due to Ryobu Shintō, by that time most Buddhist temples included at least a small Shintō shrine.

[33] See Bibliography: Interviews, Conversations, Correspondence.

Further reading in English:

- Draeger, 1995.
- Farris, 1992.
- Kitagawa, 1966.

shintō 2. 新刀. A classification term for Japanese blades made between 1596 (or 1603, depending on the source used) and around 1781. See also: *gendaitō; guntō; kaiguntō; kotō; kyūguntō; Nippontō; shinguntō; shinshintō; Shōwatō; Yasukunitō.*

Shintō Goshin Ryū 神道五心流. Considered a branch tradition of the Ishikawa Ryū (2) 石川流, the Shintō Goshin Ryū was founded in the seventeenth century by Sekine Gentarō Masateru. This tradition was a comprehensive combative school (*sōgo bujutsu*) which included grappling (*jūjutsu*), long hardwood staff techniques (*bōjutsu*), quick-draw sword arts (*iaijutsu*), police truncheon (*jutte*), sickle-and-chain techniques (*kusarigama-jutsu*), and tying cord (*torinawa*).

Shintō Katori Ryū 真当揖取流【真當揖取流】. A system of combative swordsmanship practiced in Bishu domain during the early to mid-1600s. See also: *Hiki Yoshio.*

Shintō Munen Ryū 神道無念流. See: *Shindō Munen Ryū.*

Shintō Musō Ryū 神道夢想流. See: *Shindō Musō Ryū.*

Shintō Ryū. A number of martial schools in Japan have gone by the name Shintō Ryū (or Shindō Ryū). Watatani and Yamada (1978: 433–449) list approximately fifty traditions named Shintō Ryū, using a variety of ideograms. There are dozens more that use the term "Shintō Ryū" as part of their name. Those simply referred to as "Shintō Ryū" are: 神道流 (12 schools); 新当流 (8 schools); 神当流 (2 schools); 神統流 (4 schools); 神東流 (1 school); 神刀流 (2 schools); 新刀流 (3 schools); 心当流 (3 schools); 心倒流 (1 school); 心刀流 (2 schools); 真刀流 (1 school); 真到流 (1 school); 真当流 (3 schools); 新道流 (1 school); 新堂流 (1 school); 心道流 (2 schools); 心働流 (1 school); 真道流 (3 schools); 進藤流 (1 school); 真藤流 (1 school).

These many schools cover diverse curricula,

S

including swordsmanship (*kenjutsu*), spear arts (*sōjutsu*), long-hafted glaive arts (*naginata-jutsu*); longsword (*nagadachi*), grappling (*jūjutsu*), gunnery (*hōjutsu*), horsemanship (*bajutsu*), combat swimming (*suieijutsu*), sword dance (*kenbu*), quick-draw swordsmanship (*iaijutsu*), grappling in armor (*kumiuchi*), composite sickle-and-chain techniques (*kusarigama-jutsu*), and others.

Shintō Ryū 1. 神道流. a. An abbreviation for the Tenshinshō-den Katori Shintō Ryū 天真正伝香取神道流. b. An abbreviation for various branch systems of the Tenshinshō-den Katori Shintō Ryū.

Shintō Ryū 2. 神道流. SHINDŌ MUSŌ RYŪ—An alternate term used for the *kenjutsu* sets of the Shindō Musō Ryū. These *kata* (referred to in the Shindō Musō Ryū *densho* as Oku no Tachi and Oku no Kodachi) are thought to be originally derived from Tenshinshō-den Katori Shintō Ryū 天真正伝香取神道流 via a line referred to as Kasumi Shintō Ryū 霞神道流. As they exist today, however, any technical relationship seems to be tenuous at best.

Shintō Ryū 3. 神道流. A branch tradition of the Anazawa Ryū 穴沢流 taught in Takata domain (present day Echigo City). This line—a comprehensive combative school (*sōgō bugei*)—attributed its origin to Anazawa Tonomu Nobuyuki and his direct disciple (*deshi*) Anazawa Ichimi Shinobu.

Shintō Ryū 4. 新当流【新當流】. a. An abbreviation for Kashima Shintō Ryū 鹿島新当流. b. An alternate term for Tenshinshō-den Katori Shintō Ryū 天真正伝香取神道流.

Shintō Ryū 5. 新当流【新當流】. A term used by Anazawa Tonomonosuke Moriyoshi for the variant of Katori Shintō Ryū longsword (*nagadachi*) system he transmitted in both Fukuoka domain (present-day Fukuoka prefecture) via his direct disciple (*deshi*), Yagyū Matsuemon Ienobu; and in Satsuma domain (present-day Kagoshima prefecture) via his son, Anazawa Sachika Genshin. See: *Anazawa Ryū.*

Shintō Ryū 6. 新当流【新當流】. A term used by Anazawa Tonomonosuke Moriyoshi for the variant of Tenshinshō-den Katori Shintō Ryū 天真正伝香取神道流 he transmitted in Takata domain. See: *Anazawa Ryū.*

Shintō Ryū 7. 新当流【新當流】. A branch tradition of the Anazawa Ryū transmitted in Satsuma domain (present-day Kagoshima prefecture). This line, which specialized in the longsword (*nagadachi*), attributed its origin to Anazawa Tonomonosuke Moriyoshi and his direct disciple (*deshi*) Anazawa Sachika Genshin.

Shintō Ryū 8. 新刀流. A variant name for Tenshinshō-den Katori Shintō Ryū 天真正伝香取神道流.

Shintō Ryū Naginata no Empi 神道流薙刀之猿飛. See: *Empi no Naginata.*

Shintō Seibu Ryū 神道精武流. A combative school founded in the late 1700s by Ogasawara Jōnosuke Nagamasa. Ogasawara trained in Tenshinshō-den Katori Shintō Ryū 天真正伝香取神道流 with Iizasa Naoyoshi 飯篠 直可, after which he founded his own system. The Shintō Seibu Ryū concentrates on combative swordsmanship (*kenjutsu*), grappling (*jūjutsu*), and small throwing blades (*shurikenjutsu*).

Shintō Tenshin Ryū 神道天心流. A school of pugilistic combat (*kempō* [2] 拳法), medium-length staff (*jō*), and a variety of other combative arts founded by Ueno Shin'emon Takayuki sometime during the Keichō era (1596–1615). Like many of his day, Ueno was an eclectic warrior; he trained in Ichiden Ryū 一伝流 arresting arts (*torite*), the Katori Shintō Ryū 香取神道流 comprehensive combative curriculum (*sōgō bujutsu*), the Takagi Ryū 高木流, and others. In the mid-twentieth century, several ninth-generation Shintō Tenshin Ryū successors trained in Hakkō Ryū 八光流 under that system's founder, Okuyama Yoshiji. At least one of those, Anegawa Katsuyoshi, founded a branch system; Anegawa's is named Tenshin Koryū 天心古流.

Shinwa Taidō 親和体道. A branch system of Ueshiba Ryū Aikidō founded by Inoue Noriaki, nephew and disciple of Ueshiba Morihei. Inoue originally called his system Aiki Budō 合気武道; he changed the name to Shinwa Taidō in 1956, and later renamed it Shin'ei Taidō 親英体道.

shinza 神座【神坐】[Also read ***kamiza***]. Lit. "seat of the *kami*." SHINTŌ—The *shinza* is also defined as the "seat or locus of divine power (*shinrei* 神霊)." In traditional Shintō shrines the term indicates the location in the inner sanctuary where the *kami* (and its symbol) reside. In a *dōjō*, this term refers to the central location at the head of the room. According to Krieger (1989: 137), the *shinza* should contain an "engraving of the Founding Master or photograph of the actual Headmaster"; in practice, however, this is not always the case. The *shinza* can simply be the center area at the front of the *dōjō* where the participants assume or, perhaps visualize, the presence of the presiding *kami*. This area is equivalent to the *shinzen* or *shōmen*. To the left side (weapon side) of the *shinza* is the seat of the senior participant, the *kamiza* (2).
See also: *kamidana; shinden; shōmen.*

shinzen 神前. Lit. "before the *kami* (deity)"; "in front of the shrine." The *shinzen* is the space in front of the special shelf (*kamidana*) on which is placed a small Shintō altar (*shinden*). The *kamidana* and *shinden* are normally situated high over the central area of the front wall of a *dōjō*. The *shinzen* is equivalent to the *shōmen*. ¶ *Shinzen ni rei!* 神前に礼!, a command: Bow to the altar in front!

Further reading in English:
- Draeger, 1995:
- Krieger, 1989: 135–137.
- Lowry, 2006: 95–112.

Shioda Gōzo 塩田剛三 (1915–1994). An *aikidō* master who achieved the rank of ninth degree (*kyūdan*) under Ueshiba Morihei. Shioda began his practice of Kōbukai Aikijutsu 皇武会合気術 under Ueshiba Morihei at the Kōbukan Dōjō in 1932, and trained vigorously until 1941. After graduating from Takushoku University, he was posted abroad in Borneo, China, and Taiwan during World War II. During this period, he was placed in a situation where he had to use the *aikijutsu* that he had learned from Ueshiba in a life-and-death situation. After World War II, Shioda again trained for a time in Iwama with Ueshiba, but soon had to leave to make a living in the difficult postwar years. By 1950 he was able to begin teaching *aikidō*, and in 1954 he was awarded a prize for giving the best demonstration at an All-Japan Kobudō event. This led to some notoriety and, with a sponsor's help, he founded Yōshinkan Aikidō 養神館合気道 in 1955. In 1990, he and his son founded the International Yōshinkan Aikidō Federation. Throughout his postwar career Shioda maintained what he believed to be the spirit and style of the *aikidō* taught by Ueshiba as Aiki Budō 合気武道 in the 1930s; that is, when Ueshiba was at his technical peak. Shioda authored many books on *aikidō*, several of which are available in English:

Aikido: The Complete Basic Techniques
(with Shioda Yasuhisa).
Kodansha International, 2006.
Dynamic Aikido.
Kodansha International, 1977.
Total Aikido: The Master Course
(with Shioda Yasuhisa).
Kodansha International, 1997.

Further reading in English:
- Pranin, 1992: 10–16; 1993: 170–197.

shiraha 白刃 [Also read ***hakujin***]. A naked blade; a drawn sword.

Shirai Ryū 白井流 [A.k.a. ***Tenshin Shirai Ryū*** 天真白井流]. A system founded by Shirai Tōru Yoshikane sometime during the late 1700s that was transmitted primarily in Aizu domain. The Shirai Ryū came to be known for its use of small throwing blades and darts (*shuriken-jutsu*), stick techniques (*tebōjutsu*), and sickle-and-chain arts (*kusarigama-jutsu*). However, its founder was an expert in many martial arts, several of which he passed on to his students. Its *shuriken* system was a branch of the Kadono Ryū 上遠野流. However, Watatani and Yamada (1978: 379) note that in Shirai Ryū the straight throw of the *shuriken* in Kadono Ryū was changed to a method which causes the dart to tumble in flight. In later years, successive headmasters of the tradition also included Shin Musō Muraku Ryū 神夢想無楽流 quick-draw sword arts (*iaijutsu*), Inatome Shinmyō Ryū 稲止心妙流 *jūjutsu*, Shizuka Ryū 静流 and Anazawa Ryū 穴沢流 glaive arts (*naginata-jutsu*), and Tenshindō Ittō Ryū 天真道一刀流 short staff (*tebōjutsu*) and throwing blade

S

(*shurikenjutsu*) systems. The art of blowing needles from the mouth (*fukibarijutsu*) was also taught in this tradition. The school used needles of about 1 inch (2.5 cm) in length; practitioners were able to "shoot" one or two needles at time while holding ten of them in the mouth at one time. The quick-draw sword system of this tradition became incorporated into the Ikkan Ryū (3) 一貫流.

Shiraishi Hanjirō 白石 範次郎 (1842–1927). Recognized as twenty-fourth headmaster of the Shindō Musō Ryū. Shiraishi was born to a minor *bushi* family, and presumably gained a low-ranking official position. After the Meiji Restoration he worked for the Akaike coal mine. Shiraishi began his martial arts study under Hirano Kichizō Yoshinobu, a leader of the Haruyoshi branch of Shindō Musō Ryū, and Hirano's assistant Sada Teisuke. Shortly after the Meiji Restoration in 1868, Shiraishi received a mid-level license (*mokuroku*) from Ōkuma Shinmpachi of the Jigyō branch. Shiraishi later received a full teaching license (*menkyo*) from Yoshimura Hanjirō. His most prominent students were Hidari Keiichirō, Takayama Kiroku, Shimizu Takaji, and Otofuji Ichizō.

Further reading in English:

• Matsui, 1993.

SHIRAISHI HANJIRŌ (SEATED RIGHT) C.1921
Shimizu Takaji (seated left), Otofuji Ichizo (center)
(Photograph courtesy Nishioka Tsuneo)

Shirai Tōru Yoshikane 白井 亨 義謙. Founder of the Shirai Ryū sometime during the late 1700s.

Shiraiwa Ryū 白岩流. A system of fighting-staff arts which centered on a weapon called a *kusari bō* (a hardwood staff with two chains attached). The founder is unknown. In Bishū, the Shiraiwa Ryū became incorporated into the Ikkan Ryū (3) 一貫流.

shirasaya 白鞘. Lit. "white scabbard." A plain wooden scabbard and hilt, used to hold a blade with no guard (*tsuba*). *Shirasaya* are used for storing and transporting blades when they are not expected to be needed for immediate use.

SHIRASAYA
Muromachi-period *kodachi* in *shirasaya*
(Private collection)

shirikarage 尻紮. Tucking up one's *kimono* or *hakama*. This was commonly done in Japan's hot months for relief from the heat. In a martial context, *shirikarage* indicates tucking up the *kimono* or *hakama* in preparation for impromptu combat, training, or martial exhibition (*embu*). This is often done in coordination with tying back one's kimono sleeves (*udemakuri* or *tasuki-gake*).

shiro 城 [Also read as ***jō*** in some compounds]. A stronghold, fortress, or castle. The actual meaning of the term varied depending on the time period and location. (See Varley, 1994: 185–189). Stone-walled fortifications did not appear until the Warring States period; the fantastic castles of that era were probably influenced by European architecture.

shīsā 獅子 (Oki.) [Also read ***shīshi***]. See: *karajishi; shishi (1)*.

shisei 姿勢. Posture; attitude.

shishi 1. 獅子 [Equivalent to ***karajishi*** 唐獅子]. A Chinese representation of a lion often used to decorate arms and armor. Like many non-Asian animals depicted by the Chinese and Japanese, the shape of the *shishi* is somewhat odd when compared to the actual animal. See: *karajishi*.

shishi 2. 志士. Lit. "loyalist samurai," "patriot,"

Shishin Ryū
止心流
(abbreviated lineage in Bishū domain)

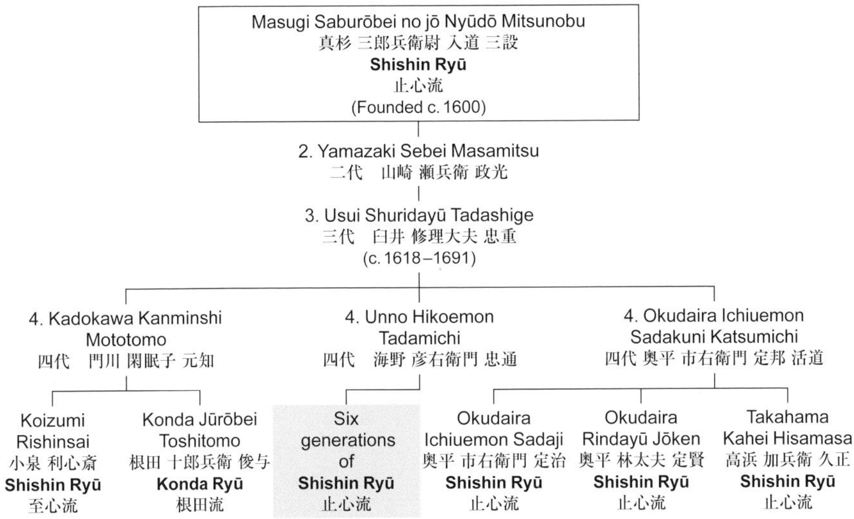

"public-spirited person." During the Meiji era, many young men from disenfranchised warrior families (*shizoku* 士族) in Kyūshū joined ultra-rightist organizations such as the Gen'yōsha and Kokuryūkai. These young warrior-types preferred being called *shishi* (loyalist samurai) to being labeled *shizoku*. The fact that *shishi* is a homophone for "lion" was probably an added attraction.

Shishido Baiken 宍戸 梅軒.[34] A master of the sickle-and-chain composite weapon (*kusari-gama*) who was defeated in a lethal duel with Miyamoto Musashi in 1607.

Shishi Funjin 獅子奮迅. NEN RYŪ 1. The final combative form of the Kumi (Sono Ni) set of *kata* of the Nen Ryū 念流. 2. SHINKAGE RYŪ—In the Shinkage Ryū 新陰流 as passed from Kamiizumi Nobutsuna to Yagyū Muneyoshi, Shishi Funjin is the name of the first combative form (*kata*) of the set known as Nanatachi. Kamiizumi probably borrowed this term/*kata* from the Nen Ryū, which he had mastered. The term's Buddhist origins would indicate that domination over the opponent is a key factor in its application. See: *shishi funjin zammai.*

shishi funjin zammai 獅子奮迅三昧 <Ch. *shizi fenxun sanmei* <Skt. *siṃhavikrīḍita-samādhi*. BUDDHISM—Lit. "lion-like severe *samādhi*." From the viewpoint of Tantric Buddhism, the power of this concentrated meditative state is like that of the power and dignity of a lion. A person in this state can keep all opponents in awe and is empowered to have control over them.

Shishin Ryū 止心流. A martial school founded around 1600 by Masugi Saburobei no jo Nyūdō Mitsunobu. This was a comprehensive martial tradition (*sōgō bujutsu*) which included quick-draw sword arts (*iai no jutsu*), arresting techniques (*torite*), battlefield armored grappling (*kumiuchi*), long hardwood staff arts (*bōjutsu*), grappling in light armor (*koshi no mawari*), and the use of small throwing blades and darts (*shurikenjutsu*). Some of the later derivative traditions in Bishū domain retained only the grappling systems (*jūjutsu*). One line of Shishin Ryū was incorporated into the Ikkan Ryū (3). See. *Ikkan Ryū (3).*

shishi ya 獅子矢. A hunting arrow. See also: *satsu ya; satsu yumi.*

---

34 The *Nitenki* (published in 1755) only gives the surname "Shishido." In the twentieth century, Yoshikawa Eiji's novel *Musashi* adds the personal name Baiken.

shisho 私書. A document of authorization to pass on a tradition. In the Aisu Kage Ryū, for example, this document is referred to as the *Shi no maki*『私之巻』.

Shitennō 四天王 <Ch. Sitianwang <Skt. Caturmahārājā or Lokapāla [A.k.a. ***Shi Daitennō*** 四大天王, ***Gose Shiō*** 護世四王]. Lit. the "Four Deva Kings"; also, the "Four Heavenly Guardians." 1. BUDDHISM—Well known as guardians of the four directions, the Four Deva Kings are Indra's generals who dwell on the four sides of Mount Sumeru. They protect the Buddha's teachings (*buppō*), as well as all fully enlightened buddhas (*nyorai*) and benevolent, enlightened beings (*bosatsu*). Commanded by Taishakuten (Skt. Indra), the Shitennō are normally illustrated standing guard at the four cardinal directions of altars, temples, and mandala. They are assigned as follows:

Direction	Deva King	Accoutrement
East	Jikokuten 持国天	Spear/sword
South	Zōchōten 増長天	Spear
West	Kōmokuten 広目天	Writing brush
North	Tamonten 多聞天	Spear/treasure
[Center]	[Taishakuten 帝釈天]	

The Shitennō are of Indian origin, and the original texts describing them are in Sanskrit. As Buddhism moved through China and Korea to Japan, however, those texts were translated into Chinese. Over the centuries, Chinese cultural elements were added; by the time they reached Japan, a variety of weaponry—more often Chinese or Japanese than Indian—could be depicted in the hands of each Deva King. Additionally, the Four Deva Kings became associated with Chinese cosmological ideas concerning the makeup of the universe. Consequently they are also associated with the animals the Chinese assign to the four directions: a green dragon (east), a red phoenix (south), a yellow tiger (west), and a black tortoise (north). Images of these Buddhist divinities are sometimes used in decorating arms and armor. 2. The "Big Four"; the Four Stalwarts; the Four Champions. The term "Shitennō" may be used to indicate, for example, the four most skilled students in a martial arts *dōjō* or the four most important generals or retainers in a combat force. In *jūdō*, for example, the Shitennō were Saigō Shirō, Tomita Tsunejirō, Yamashita Yoshitsugu, and Yokoyama Sakujirō, as these early *jūdōka* as they were the stalwarts who defended the early Kōdōkan's reputation against all comers. Other "Shitennō" groups may be found in various warrior clans, martial traditions, etc.

Shiten Ryū 四天流. A particular branch tradition of quick-draw swordsmanship (*iaijutsu*) related to Kashima no Tachi which is preserved in the town of Shiga. Knutsen (correspondence, 2009) notes that while the combative form practiced by this tradition is a sword dance, it is not typical Japanese *kenbu*. Its purpose is to "drive away minor disobedient spirits…, who might interfere and spoil felicitous ceremonies." The dance is composed of eight cuts and one final "seal" using the sword as a mudra. It appears that the dance is actually a practical, combative form adapted to the Kujihō ritual.

Also according to Knutsen, the late Prof. Carmen Blacker was of the opinion that this unusual sword dance was an element of the ancient Kashima no Tachi which had been preserved outside the line of swordsmanship derived from Tsukahara Bokuden. Blacker also noted that the sword dance may be connected to the earliest period of swordsmanship practiced in the Kashima Shrine area.

shitō 刺刀. An early term for a dagger (*tantō*).

Shitō Ryū 糸東流. OKINAWAN KARATE—A style of *karatedō* founded by Mabuni Kenwa and based on Okinawan Shuri *te* and Naha *te*. Mabuni was an eclectic practitioner who combined teachings from a number of instructors into his system. He travelled to Japan several times in the 1920s in order to spread *karate*, and in 1929 finally moved to Ōsaka to teach full-time. At first he called his system "Hankō Ryū" 半剛流 (lit. "half-hard school") which reflected its incorporation of both linear, power techniques from Itosu Ankō's Shuri *te* and short, circular movements from the Naha *te* of Higaonna Kanryō. Mabuni later changed the name to Shitō Ryū, borrowing ideograms from the names of his two most influential instructors: Itosu 糸洲 and Higaonna 東恩納.

See also: *Gōjū karatedō; Gōjū Ryū; Shōtōkan.*

Further reading in English:

- Bishop, 1999: 105–108.

shittan 悉曇 <Ch. *xitan* <Skt. *siddhaṁ* (*siddhāṁ*). A type of script used for writing Sanskrit. *Shittan* disappeared from use in South Asia, and is now found only in East Asia. In Japan it was primarily used in Esoteric Buddhism for writing spells (*shingon* and *darani*). *Shittan* characters are often inscribed on weapons and various martial accoutrements as a talisman. See also: *bonji; shuji.*

Further reading in English:

- van Gulik (1956).
- Stevens (1981): 1–69.

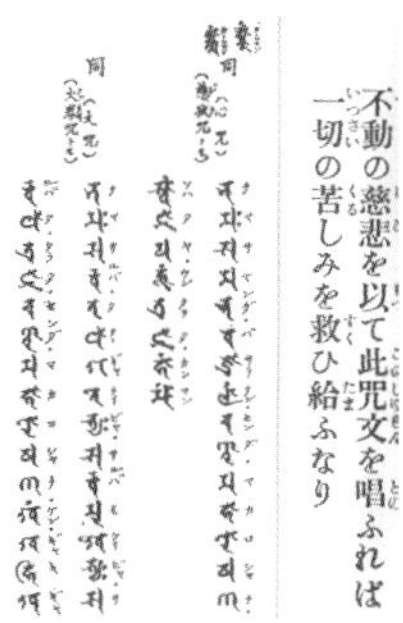

SHITTAN SCRIPT (LEFT) AND EQUIVALENT CHINESE CHARACTERS (RIGHT) IN FUDŌ MYŌŌ RITUAL TEXT
Both Chinese text and Shittan text contain *kana* syllabary to indicate Japanese pronunciation
(Detail from *Shō Fudō-kyō*『聖不動経』)

Shi uchi kōtai! 使打交替! A command given by an instructor during practice: "*Shidachi* and *uchidachi* exchange roles!"

shiyū o kessuru 雌雄を決する. Battle; conflict. *Shiyū o kessuru* is a late Heian-period (twelfth century) term for battle. It literally means "to determine who is male and who is female."

shizen hontai 自然本体. A basic, natural stance.

shizen no kamae 自然構. HOPLOLOGY—A "natural stance" combative posture.

shizentai 自然体. A natural posture.

shizoku 士族. Lit. "samurai family." A Meiji-era term denoting citizens who were descendents of samurai, in contrast to commoners (*heimin*). Use of the term *shizoku* was part of an effort to restructure society away from the feudal Tokugawa-era designations of warrior (*shi*), farmer (*nō*), artisan (*kō*), and merchant (*shō*).

Shizuka Ryū 静流【靜流】. This is a name used by at least five martial schools centering on the long-hafted glaive (*naginata*). Most claimed origins going back to the well-known seventh-century imperial regent Shōtoku Taishi 聖徳太子. However, these claims of ancient ancestry are without documentation.

Shōbayashi Fujiwara no Michikazu 庄林藤原 道一. Credited with founding the Jigō Tenshin Ryū 自剛天真流 sometime during the first half of the nineteenth century in the Kuroda domain in Kyūshū.

Shōbayashi Matashichirō 庄林 又七郎. Successor to Shōbayashi Fujiwara no Michikazu. Matashichirō may have been the actual formulator of Jigō Tenshin Ryū 自剛天真流.

Shōbō Nen Ryū 正法念流. See: *Nen Shuza Ryū.*

shōbu 勝負 (Abbr. of ***shinken shōbu*** 真剣勝負). 1. A match; a contest. 2. A real fight. See: *shinken shōbu.*

shochūgeiko 暑中稽古. Lit. "training in the heat of the summer." A special summer training held in many modern martial arts and ways *dōjō*. *Shochūgeiko*, held during the mid to late summer months, may last for several weeks. The trainees strive to achieve easy facility of movement in the heat and push themselves to the limit of their ability to resist heat and fatigue. Contrast to *kangeiko.* See also: *gasshuku.*

Shōda Kazaemon Noritaka 荘田 嘉左衛門教高. Student of Yagyū Munenori and founder of the Shōda Shin Ryū 荘田心流, a school of combative swordsmanship, sometime during the first half of the seventeenth century.

Shodan 初段. 1. JIGEN RYŪ—The first level of prearranged combative forms (*kata*) in Jigen Ryū's advanced-level swordsmanship (Dan no Kata). There are three scenarios in this set, which is referred to as Ryū Sō Etsu 立双越. 2. ***shodan*** 初段. Lit. "first grade." A modern *budō* term derived from Kōdōkan Jūdō which indicates a practitioner of the first degree in rank. In most modern systems, this indicates a "first-degree black belt."

Shōda Shin Ryū 荘田心流. A branch tradition of the Edo Yagyū Shinkage Ryū 江戸柳生新陰流 founded by Shōda Noritaka, a student of Yagyū Munenori during the first half of the seventeenth century. This school centered on swordsmanship (*kenjutsu*).

shodō 書道. Sino-Japanese calligraphy; brush writing.

Shōdōkan Aikidō 昭道館合気道. A school of *aikidō* founded by Tomiki Kenji. See: *Tomiki Kenji; Tomiki Ryū.*

Shōdōkan Hombu Dōjō 昭道館本部道場. Home training hall of Tomiki Aikidō (a.k.a. Shōdōkan Aikidō) built in Ōsaka, Japan, in 1967.

shōen 荘園【莊園】. A manor or estate. With the decline of the Chinese-style Ritsuryō government in ninth-century Japan, a system of tax-free estates (*shōen*) evolved. Under this system, holders of large amounts of land (both private families and temples) redirected part of the income of their estates to powerful members of the imperial court in order to avoid paying the heavy taxes demanded by the Ritsuryō government. This practice also helped estate-holders avoid the Chinese-style "equal fields" systems which required periodic land redistribution. Under the Kamakura shogunate, a wealthy landed hierarchy evolved from this practice; this included estate holders (*jitō*), provincial military governors (*shugo*), and the shogunate itself. In addition to tax exemption, the estates were relatively independent from any government interference. This situation persisted until the Warring States period, when the financially destitute government (i.e., the court) had no power to speak of and the weakened Ashikaga shogunate had lost much of its military power; the whole country fell into a period of chaos lasting almost a century.

shōgi 将棋【將棊】. Lit. "commander's chess," "general's chess." A Japanese board game closely related to Western chess. *Shōgi* is very similar to its Indo-European counterpart; in *shōgi*, however, as in Sengoku-period conflicts, a player (or general) can take a captured piece (or enemy warrior) and use it against his opponent. According to several masters of classical martial schools today, many generals and lords (*daimyō*) played the game of *go*, but the best generals were expert at *shōgi*. See also: *go (2).*

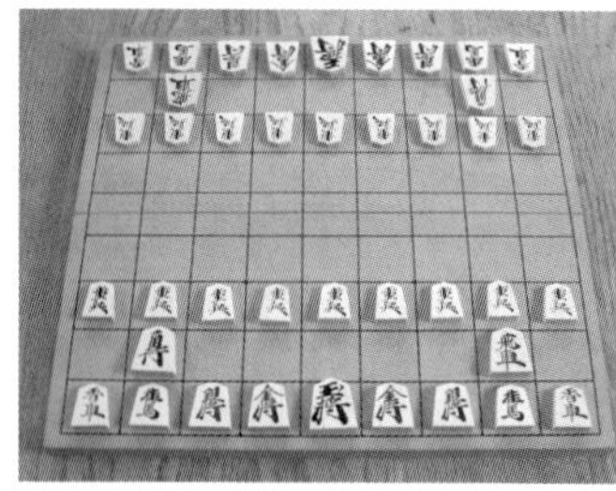

SHŌGI BOARD
Shōgi board with playing pieces set up in beginning formation
(Photograph by author)

shōgun 将軍【將軍】. 1. A commander; a general. 2. TAIHŌ MILITARY SYSTEM—Under the eighth-century Chinese-style military system defined in the Taihō Codes (Taihō Ritsuryō), a *shōgun* commanded an army corps (*gun*). 3. An abbreviation for *seii taishōgun*. During the period from 1192 to 1868, this title was given to the military rulers of Japan if they were descendents of the Minamoto family or their deputies. See: *seii taishōgun.*

Shōgun Gosho Naibanyaku 将軍御所内番役【將軍御所內番役】. Muromachi-period term for the security guard service for the shogunal palace. The guard service was composed of warrior vassals of the *bakufu*. See also: *kagariya banyaku; Kamakura Ōbanyaku; Kyōto Ōbanyaku; ōbanyaku.*

Shōgun Jizō 勝軍地蔵【勝軍地藏】. See: *Shōgun Jizō Bosatsu.*

Shōgun Jizō Bosatsu 勝軍地蔵菩薩【勝軍地藏菩薩】. Lit. the "Army-conquering Kṣitigarbha-bodhisattva." Shōgun Jizō is a martial form of Jizō Bosatsu used as the focal point of the Shōgun Jizōhō ritual, a meditation and ritual aimed at subjugating enemy armies and driving out demons. This martial Buddhist form of Jizō Bosatsu evidently does not appear in standard Buddhist canonical texts.

Rather, Shōgun Jizō is an early Ryōbu Shintō amalgamation of the cult of Atagosan Daigongen and the Buddhist Jizō Bosatsu. See: *Atagosan Daigongen; Shōgun Jizōhō.*

Further reading in English:

- Bays, 2003: 29–32.
- Hackin, 1932: 434.
- de Visser, 1915: 98–105; 1935: 225.

Shōgun Jizōhō 勝軍地蔵法【勝軍地藏法】. Lit. the "Army-conquering Jizō Ritual." An aggressive ritual performed with a *sammaiji* focused on Shōgun Jizō Bosatsu.

In the early ninth century (around 801 C.E.) the Hossō Shū *bonze* Enchin 延鎮 (founder of Kiyomizudera temple) received a request from the warrior Sakanoue no Tamuramaro to perform a powerful ritual in support of his mission against the Ebisu. (Sakanoe had been commissioned with the title of *seii taishōgun* in order to perform this task.) As Sakanoe had been Enchin's patron in funding Kiyomizudera, Enchin complied with the request, performing both the Shōgun Jizōhō and Shōteki Bishamonhō rituals. A medieval biography[35] of Enchin notes that the campaign was going badly when a small Buddhist priest, accompanied by a boy, appeared on the battlefield. They began to pick up spent arrows from the field, and presented them to Sakanoe. Using those arrows, Sakanoe was able to kill the Ebisu leader (Takamaru 高丸), and defeated the enemy forces. See: *Atagosan Daigongen; Shōgun Jizō Bosatsu.*

shōgunshoku 将軍職【將軍職】. The "shogunate"; the office of the *shōgun*.

shōhei 荘兵【莊兵】. Lit. "estate warriors." A medieval term referring to retainers and low-status warriors who were employed to defend private tax-exempt estates (*shōen*).

Shōhō Nen Ryū 正法念流. See: *Akamatsu Jisan; Nen Shuza Ryū; shōzōmatsu.*

shōji ketsujō 生死決定 [Also read ***shōji kechijō***]. Lit. "to determine life and death." This phrase is commonly used to indicate combative skills. See also: *seishi o chōetsu.*

[35] De Visser (1915: 98) cites the *Genkō Shakusho*, a text composed prior to 1364.

shojū 所従. A twelfth-century term for a groom or attendant; equivalent to *genin* (1). Many of the warriors in the twelfth-century war tales (*gunkimono*) travel with an entourage of *shojū* or *genin*. Much like the European squire, the *shojū* attended to the horses of the warriors, took care of equipment, sometimes participated in "mopping up" toward the end of a battle—but rarely participated in one-on-one combat (*ikki uchi*) with the higher-ranking mounted warriors. If their master was killed in battle, however, they sometimes participated in name-announcing (*nanori*). In paintings and picture scrolls of the era, such as the famous *Heiji Monogatari Emaki*, these attendants are depicted in light armor—*haramakidō* and *kusazuri*—armed with glaive-like polearms such as the *naginata* and *nagamaki*.

shoka no heishi 諸家の兵士. A tenth- and eleventh-century term for "warriors of all the noble houses." *Shoka no heishi* referred to troops of the new military, the noble aristocrats of the capital (Kyōto). The court saw them and their leaders as the second tier of the military system. (At that time the first tier was still made up of government troops—the Efu and *kebiishi*—controlled by provincial officials.)

shōki 小毅. TAIHŌ MILITARY SYSTEM—The *shōki* was the leader of an assembly of six *tai* (platoons) [=three *ryo* (companies)] for a total of about 600 conscript soldiers in the eighth-century Chinese-style provincial militia unit (*gundan*). As a commander (or assistant commander) of 600 men, the *shōki* was somewhat equivalent to a modern army lieutenant colonel who leads a small battalion or acts as its executive officer. In the chain of command the *shōki* was in charge of two or three *kyōi* (majors) and normally under the command of a *daiki* (colonel). See: *gundan.*

shokoku no bushi 諸国の武士【諸國の武士】. A twelfth-century term for "warriors of the provinces." Contrast to "warriors of the capital" (*miyako no musha*). See also: *kuni no musha; miyako no musha.*

shokoku no gumpei 諸国の軍兵【諸國の軍兵】. A twelfth-century term for "troops of the provinces"; "fighting men of the provinces."

S

This term may have referred to both horse-mounted *bushi* and those of lower status. See also: *shokoku no bushi*; *kuni no musha*.

shokoku ōryōshi 諸国押領使【諸國押領使】. A "provincial territory-suppressing envoy," i.e., a provincial arresting officer. This was an eleventh-century provincial military post which governors sometimes awarded to local warrior leaders in order to bring in rural support troops. See: *shokoku tuibushi*.

shokoku tsuibushi 諸国追捕使【諸國追捕使】. A provincial arresting officer. This was an eleventh-century provincial military post which governors sometimes awarded to local warrior leaders in order to bring in rural support troops.

The function of this post appears to have been very similar to the *shokoku ōryōshi*. Requirements for both titles included status as a martial adept and being of proper martial lineage according to provincial lineage charts (*fudaizu*). The major difference in the two posts was the geographical location of the appointment. Farris (1992: 186) notes that the provincial arresting officers (*shokoku tsuibushi*) were appointed mostly in the Kinai and Inland Sea areas, whereas the provincial overseers (*shokoku ōryōshi*) tended to be appointed in Kyūshū and eastern Honshū.

Shōkyūki 『承久記』 [Also read ***Jōkyūki***] (A chronicle of the Shōkyū (Jōkyū) Era, 1219–1222). A thirteenth-century war tale (*gunki-mono*) describing the revolt of Emperor Go-Toba[36] against the Hōjō family–controlled Kamakura *bakufu* in 1221. See: *Shōkyū no Ran*.

Shōkyū no Ran 承久乱【承久亂】[Also read ***Jōkyū no Ran***]. A thirteenth-century war chronicled in the *Shōkyūki*. This conflict revolved around the revolt of Emperor Go-Toba against the Hōjō family–controlled Kamakura *bakufu* in 1221. Go-Toba's revolt failed, and he was exiled; as a result, Kyōto and the imperial court came more directly under warrior rule, and the Kamakura *bakufu* was enriched by estate lands confiscated from Go-Toba. The *bakufu* then appointed its own vassals as stewards (*jitō*), a policy first begun by Minamoto no Yoritomo when he consolidated power in eastern Japan (Kantō) during the Gempei War (Gempei Gassen). The stewards and *bakufu*-appointed constables (*shugo*) acted as policing agents of the *bakufu*. However, many estates in central and western Japan had no *bakufu* steward, and remained autonomous.

Further reading in English:

- Farris, 1992: 320–328.

REMBUKAN DŌJŌ *KAMIDANA/SHOMEN*, C. 1977
(Photograph by author)

shōmen 1. 正面. SHINTŌ—The central area at the inside front of a martial training hall (*dōjō*). A Shintō altar (*shinden*) is normally located on a shelf (*kamidana*) placed high on the wall of the *shōmen* area. In some training halls, especially those located in public sports facilities, the *shōmen* may have a Japanese flag or a temporary altar or *dōjō* identifier for the group. All *dōjō* members normally face the *shōmen* in order to offer a respectful bow when entering or leaving, as well as at the beginning or ending of training sessions. See also: *kamidana; kamiza (2), shinden*.

shōmen 2. 正面. The front of the head or face.

shōmen uchi 正面打. A cut or strike (*uchi* 打) directly to the front of the head or face (*shōmen* 正面). Compare to *yokomen uchi*.

shomokuroku 「初目録」. Lit. "first list." 1. A term commonly used to designate the first of several "list" licenses. 2. Abbreviation for "Shindō Musō Ryū *shomokuroku*," one of several teaching licenses in that tradition. See: *Shindō Musō Ryū shomokuroku*.

Shōmonki 『将門記』【將門記】(The chronicle of Masakado). The earliest known Japanese

---

[35] Go-Toba Tennō 後鳥羽天皇 (1180–1239; r.1183–1198). Eighty-second emperor of Japan.

war tale, the *Shōmonki* is the story of the rebellion of Taira no Masakado (Tengyō no Ran), which took place during the period 935–940. The text dates from 1099.

The rebellion evidently began over a domestic squabble. In the tenth century it was customary in aristocratic warrior families for a husband to go live with his wife's family. In this case, however, Taira no Masakado refused to move to his uncle's (Taira no Yoshikane) residence upon marrying Yoshikane's daughter. Farris (1992: 132–133) posits that the Tengyō no Ran was Japan's first "samurai conflict." See: *Tengyō no ran.* See also other war tales: *Heiji monogatari*; *Heike monogatari*; *Hōgen monogatari*; *Taiheiki*; *Yoshitsune monogatari*.

Further reading in English:

- Friday, 2007.
- Farris, 1992: 133–142.
- Rabinovitch, 1986, for a translation of the tale.
- Varley, 1994: 9–12.

shōmyō 小名. As a term used to indicate a "minor lord," *shōmyō* is an abbreviation for *shōmyōden* (small [holdings in] name fields). This is a medieval term referring to mounted warriors who had relatively little income-producing land (see *myōden*) and thus could not afford to support vassals. Consequently, they had to win a name for themselves by being successful combatants. *Shōmyō* normally had only one or two family members in their battle entourage. Compare to *daimyō*. See: *daimyō*; *shugo*.

shōmyōden 小名田. See: *shōmyō*.

shōnin 証人【證人】. A witness. In the context of medieval warfare, a *shōnin* was a witness to a warrior's exploits in battle who could later attest to his bravery, confidence, prowess, etc.

Shōninki 『正忍記』 [Also read ***Seininki***]. Title of a restricted text (*hidensho*) on the espionage practices (*shinobi no jutsu*) of the Kishū Ryū 紀州流. The *Shōninki* is attributed to Fuji Masatake (or Fujibayashi Masatake), a strategist (*heihōsha*) attached to the Tokugawa family, c. 1681. However, Watatani and Yamada (1978: 215) and various other historians consider this document and others related to Kishū Ryū to be unreliable. Along with the *Ninpiden* and *Mansen shūkai*, the *Shōninki* is considered one of the "three great books on *ninjutsu*" by aficionados of those studies. See: *Kishū Ryū.*

Further reading in English:

- Cummins and Minami, trans., 2011.
- Graham, trans., 2009.
- Natori, 2010.

shorei 諸礼【諸禮】. Warrior etiquette and ceremony as taught by such classical warrior schools as the Ogasawara Ryū 小笠原流 and the Ise Ryū 伊勢流.

Shōrei Ryū 昭霊流 【昭靈流】. OKINAWAN KARATE—A *karate* school founded by Higaonna Kanryō around 1890. The school was originally referred to as Naha *te* 那覇手, but became the Gōjū Ryū 剛柔流 under Miyagi Chōjun.

Shōrinji 少林寺 <Ch. Shaolinsi. The famous temple where the legendary Indian monk Bodhi Dharma (Daruma) is supposed to have founded Chinese Chan (Zen) Buddhism. See also: *Daruma.*

Shōrinji Ryū 少林寺流 [A.k.a. ***Renshinkan Karatedō*** 錬心館空手道]. JAPANESE KARATE/ OKINAWAN KARATE—An eclectic system of *karate* founded by Tamotsu Isamu in 1955. Tamotsu's system claims to be a mix of *karate*, Okinawan *kobudō*, and Hakkō Ryū *aikijūjutsu.* See: *Tamotsu Isamu.*

Shōrinji Kempō 少林寺拳法. See: *Nippon Shōrinji Kempō.*

Shōrin Ryū 小林流·少林流·松林流. OKINAWAN KARATE—Terms used for a variety of Okinawan *karate* schools. Most, but not all, are related through the teachings of Matsumura Sōkon. See: *Azato Ankō; Azato Ha karate; karate kata; Matsubayashi Ryū; Matsumura Sōkon.*

Further reading in English:

- Bishop, 1999: 53–64.

Shōrin Samanosuke 松林 左馬之助 [A.k.a. ***Ganryū*** 願立; ***Muun*** 無雲; ***Henyasai*** 蝙也斎【蝙也齋】] (1593–1667). After studying a number of systems, Samanosuke founded the Gan Ryū (3) around 1625. One of his instructors may have been Musō Gonnosuke of the Shindō Musō Ryū 神道夢想流.

S

Shōteki Bishamonten 勝敵毘沙門天. A variant form of Bishamonten. This worthy is the center of a tantric ritual referred to as the Shōteki Bishamonhō.

Shōteki Bishamonhō 勝敵毘沙門法. Lit. the "Enemy-conquering Vaiśravaṇa (Bishamon) Ritual." See: *Shōgun Jizōhō.*

Shōtōkan 松涛館【松濤館】. JAPANESE KARATE —The Shōtōkan was a *karate dōjō* founded in Tōkyō by Funakoshi Gichin in 1935. As Funakoshi's home *dōjō*, it gave its name to the *karate* style that would develop there. Funakoshi used a variant pronunciation for the characters of his pen name, "Shōtō 松濤," which literally means "pine waves." (The characters for *shōtō* can also be pronounced *matsunami*). To this he added the character for hall (*kan* 館).

The style of *karate* practiced at the Shōtōkan, now known as "Shōtōkan Karate," was essentially Funakoshi's version of Shuri *te*, the Okinawan *karate* style he learned from Itosu Ankō. See also: *Azato Ha karate; Gōjū Ryū; Shitō Ryū.*

Shōtoku Taishi Ryū 聖徳太子流 [A.k.a. ***Taishi Ryū*** 太子流]. Considered one of the Five Traditions of Aizu domain (Aizu Go Ryū 会津五流), this school was known for its emphasis on strategy and tactics (*gunyō*). It apparently did not survive past 1868, the end of the feudal period.

The Shōtoku Taishi Ryū was founded in the mid-sixteenth century by Mochizuki Sagami no Kami Sadatomo. In addition to focusing on battle strategy and tactics, it was a comprehensive combative school (*sōgō bujutsu*). Its curriculum included swordsmanship (*kenjutsu*), long-hafted glaive arts (*naginatajutsu*), long sword (*nagadachi*) techniques, and a grappling art called *irimi* 入身.

Shōwatō 昭和刀. A classification term for Japanese sword blades made during the Shōwa era (1925–1989), especially during the military build-up preceding and during World War II (1925–1945). The term "Shōwatō" generally, but not always, refers to the cheap, mass-produced swords made by the Japanese military during the 1930s and 1940s. These stand in contrast to the traditionally forged swords made during that same period, such as the Yasukunitō. See also: *gendaitō; guntō; kaiguntō; kotō; kyūguntō; Nippontō; shinguntō; shinshintō; shintō (2); Yasukunitō.*

shōzōmatsu 正像末. BUDDHISM—An abbreviation of the terms for the three periods of the Buddha's teachings after his passing. The first is the period of the righteous law (*shōbō* 正法); the second, the period of the imitative law (*zōbō* 像法); the third, the period of the last or "ending" law (*mappō* 末法). During the period of the righteous law, the Buddha's doctrines, effective practices, and access to enlightenment (awakening) all exist. During the period of the imitative law, doctrine and correct practices exist but enlightenment is no longer accessible. During the last period, the doctrine is still accessible but there is no effective practice or access to enlightenment. It is thought that after the three periods, even the doctrine will disappear.

There are several opinions as to how long each of these periods last:

1.	*shōbō*	500 years
	zōbō	1,000 years
	mappō	10,000 years
2.	*shōbō*	1,000 years
	zōbō	500 years
	mappō	10,000 years
3.	*shōbō*	500 years
	zōbō	500 years
	mappō	10,000 years
4.	*shōbō*	1,000 years
	zōbō	1,000 years
	mappō	10,000 years

The Japanese of the early medieval period (c.1185–1568) were particularly obsessed with the concept of *mappō*. See also: *Miroku Bosatsu.*

shu 守. See: *shu-ha-ri.*

shubaku 手搏. A variant term for *jūjutsu*.

Shuchin Ryū 守慎流. See: *Masaki Ryū.*

shuchō 主帳. TAIHŌ MILITARY SYSTEM—In the eighth-century Chinese-style provincial militia unit (*gundan*), the *shuchō* was a "clerk"; a military rank above squad leader. The position may have been something like a sergeant master-at-arms. See: *gundan*.

shūdan sentōhō 集团戦闘法【集團戰鬪法】. Group combat tactics used by the Tatsumi Ryū.

Shugendō 修験道. A native Japanese religious movement dating from the seventh century. The name can be translated as "the way of practice to master beneficial, magical power." Its legendary founder was En no Gyōja 役の行者. Shugendō is an interesting combination of native Japanese shamanism and Shintoism, Daoism, and the Esoteric (Tantric) Buddhism of the Tendai and Shingon schools. Its practitioners are referred to as *shugenja* 修験者or *yamabushi* 山伏. See also: *tengu*.

Further reading in English:

- Earhart, 1970.

shugenja 修験者. SHUGENDŌ—A practitioner of Shugendō; a *yamabushi*.

shugo 守護. During the Kamakura period, this term referred to a provincial-level constable who acted as a liaison between the Kamakura *bakufu* and its provincial vassals. The post replaced that of the former provincial governors. At that time the *shugo* also led local retainers of the Kamakura shogunate in military and police operations. The title for this office was originally *sōtsuibushi*. See: *sōtsuibushi*.

During the Muromachi period, *shugo* came to indicate a provincial *bakufu*-appointed military governor. These governors were eventually called *shugo daimyō*. See also: *daimyō*.

Further reading in English:

- Mass, 1990: 80–87.

shugo daimyō 守護大名. Early Muromachi-period provincial lords. See: *daimyō; shugo*.

shugyō 修行 [Also read ***shūgyō***; var. 修業]. Training; practice; ordeal; ascetic practices. This term is borrowed from Buddhism (a translation of the Sanskrit word *caryā*, which means "to cultivate oneself in right practice"), and may or may not indicate actual martial practices depending on the context in which it is used. See also: *gyō; gyōsha*.

shugyō mon 修行門. Lit. "ascetic gate." The north gate entrance into an area set aside for formal self-immolation (*seppuku*). The *shugyō mon* was the entrance used by the person committing *seppuku* (Seward, 1966: 44–45). See also: *seppuku; nehan mon*.

shugyōsha 修行者. A practitioner of (Buddhist or martial) austerities. See also: *gyō; shugyō*.

shu-ha-ri 守破離. A metaphorical equation describing the three stages of development through which exponents of classical martial disciplines may pass on the way to attaining expertise. Kuroda Ichitarō, in a private communication, summed up his understanding of *shu-ha-ri* along the following lines:

Shu 守 (Also read ***mamoru***). Lit. "protect." This refers to the trainee's dedication to study in a chosen martial *ryū*. Here the trainee must concentrate on only one *ryū*. This inculcates in him the techniques and underlying principles of the *ryū*. Another aspect of *shu* that is equally, if not more, important than mastering the physical and technical aspects of training is the "spiritual"—or psychological—factor. This requires the trainee to develop and apply *kan* (intuition) in his training. *Shu* is meant to be experienced and intuited as explanations are often non-verbal.

Ha 破 (Also read ***yaburu*** and ***yabureru***). Lit. "break," "to be torn." Traditionally, upon completion of *shu*, a trainee was permitted by his original headmaster to examine and train in other *ryū*. In a martial sense, *ha* indicates the conclusion of *shu* and recognizes the trainee's having obtained a "solid technical basis" in the *ryū* he has been studying. At this point it is assumed that the trainee has become an efficient technician and is able to perform "naturally and automatically." Thus, he may "break" (*ha*) with his original *ryū* and seek training in other schools. Here the concept of *giri* applies, and the trainee should naturally feel an obligation to maintain his skill in the original *ryū*.

Ri 離 (Also read ***hanareru***). Lit. "to separate from," "to be dispersed." *Ri* relates to the natural evolution of seasoned martial artists aspiring to create their own systems or schools (*ryū*). Assuming the practitioner has mastered several classical *ryū*, he may be allowed to leave his original tradition and concentrate on this endeavor. If properly approached, the

S

expert practitioner may accomplish this without being accused of disloyalty or betraying his former school. This may be manifested in several ways. He may create an entirely new *ryū*, or he may become headmaster of one or more of the schools he has studied over the years, or he may create a branch tradition of his former *ryū*. In all three of these scenarios the exponent has separated himself from his original relationship with his primary tradition and has become a leader in creating a new—or renewed—tradition.

It should also be noted that not all *koryū* follow this paradigm.

Further reading in English:

• Kuroda, (1974a, 1974b, 1974c).

shuji 種字 <Ch. *zhongzi* <Skt. *bīja*. Lit. "seed letters"; "seed syllables." BUDDHISM—In Esoteric Buddhism the *shuji* are letters or syllables which symbolize various tantric deities. Intoning and visualizing *shuji* in a ritual facilitates the unification of the practitioner with that particular deity and its power. Various *shuji,* written in *siddhaṁ* (*shittan*) script, are often placed or inscribed on weapons and martial accoutrements as protective talismans.

SHUJI SYLLABLE *TRĀK* (SKT. *trāḥ*)
Meditational seed syllable for Kokūzō Bosatsu
(*Siddhaṁ* script by Daishin, 1983)

SHUJI SYLLABLE *Sa* स ON *DŌMARU* ARMOR
Festival at Katori Jingu—1978
(Photograph by Pat Lineberger)

shuji shuriken 手字手裏剣. 1. YAGYŪ SHINKAGE RYŪ—Like other subtle concepts of the Yagyū Shinkage Ryū, this has several layers of meaning. According to Yagyū Nobuharu, late twenty-first headmaster of the Yagyū Shinkage Ryū, *shūji shuriken* refers to a Shinkage Ryū combative principle: that a straight vertical cut defeats any angled cut. This interpretation dates back at least to the time of Yagyū Munenori's *Heihō kadensho*, and is also explained in Yagyū Jūbei's *Tsuki no sho*. Yagyū Nobuharu often illustrated the concept of *shuji shuriken* by inscribing a Chinese "numeral 10" (*jūji* 十字) with his hands indicating how a straight cut (丨)would defeat any other cut, such as a horizontal cut (一). 2. Homophone for "*shuriken* in the shape of the numeral 10" (*jūji shuriken* 十字手裏剣).

shujū 主従. Master and servant; the lord/vassal relationship.

shukke 出家 <Ch. *chujia*. BUDDHISM—Lit. "leave home"; "out from the family." This is a term for a Buddhist monk, one who has left his home and family for the priesthood. Contrast to *zaike*.

Shumi-sen 須弥山【須彌山】<Ch. Xumishan <Skt. Sumeru; [Var. ***Miru*** 弥楼【彌樓】<Ch. Milou <Skt. (Su) meru; ***Shumi*** 須弥【須彌】<Ch. Xumi; ***Shumiru*** 須彌樓、蘇彌樓、修迷楼 <Ch. Xumilou <Skt. Sumeru; and ***Suru*** 蘇盧 <Ch. Sulu. Trans. as ***Myōkō*** (***San Ō***) 妙高 (山王) and ***Myōkō*** 妙光]. Mount Sumeru. The central mountain in the Hindu and Buddhist universe; the point at the center of the cosmos. The central mountain of all universes.

Shunpūkan 1. 春風館. The name of Yamaoka Tesshū's *dōjō*. Yamaoka founded it as a place to teach his Ittō Shōden Mutō Ryū 一刀正伝無刀流. The name is derived from a poem by the Chinese Rinzai Zen priest Bukkō Kokushi, who taught Kamakura Zen to warriors in the early fourteenth century. See also: *Bukkō Kokushi.*

Shunpūkan 2. 春風館. The home *dōjō* of the Owari Kan Ryū and the Kambe line of Owari Yagyū Shinkage Ryū, located in Nagoya.

shura 修羅. 1. A medieval-period term for "warrior ghost." *Shura* is derived from the Buddhist term *ashura*. 2. A scene of carnage. 3. ***Shura***

修羅. SHUGENDŌ—The fourth (of six) ascetic ritual performance engaged in by Shugendō followers (*yamabushi*) during mountain retreats. Shura was traditionally the practice of *sumai*, an early, combative form of *sumō*. In a lecture series presented at the University of Hawaii in 1981, Draeger (1995: 6.13) noted that the Shugendō practice of Shura (*sumai*) has always been a "no-holds-barred" form of grappling, with lethal consequences. This was necessary for the *yamabushi* because of the chance of running into bandits and wild animals in the mountains. See also: *Jikkai; Shugendo; yamabushi.*

shuraba 修羅場 [Also read ***shurajō***]. A place in which a battle or scene of carnage is reenacted. See also: *chambara; jidaigeki; tate.*

shuriken 手裏剣【手裏劍】[Many variations: 手利剣; 修裏剣 ; etc.]. A small blade, knife, or dart, hidden in the hand, which could either be thrown at an enemy or held in the hand for close combat. There are many types; the designs are often *ryū*-dependent. Contrast to *shaken*. See also: *Araki Ryū.*

Further reading in English:

- Gruzanski, 1968: 89–102.
- Mol, 2001: 155–184.

shurikenjutsu 手裏剣術【手裏劍術】. The art of throwing or utilizing small blades or darts held in the hand. Fujita (1960: 2) notes forty *ryū* specializing in *shurikenjutsu.*

Further reading in English:

- Gruzanski, 1968: 89–102.
- Mol, 2001: 155–184.

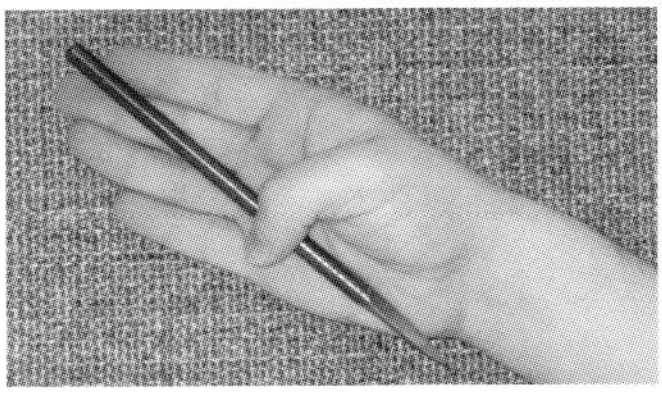

PROPER GRIP FOR THROWING *SHURIKEN* OF THE SHIRAI RYŪ 白井流 TYPE
(Private collection)

Shuri te 首里手 <Oki. *Sui dī.* OKINAWAN KARATE—A *karate* system taught in the area of Shuri. Its development is generally attributed to Matsumura Sōkon.

Shū Shi-wa 周子和<Ch. *Zhou Zihe* (1874–1926). OKINAWAN KARATE—A Chinese fighting-arts master who taught tiger boxing[37] at a Buddhist temple[38] in Fujian province in the late 1800s and early 1900s. His best-known student in Japan was Uechi Kanbun from Okinawa. See: *Uechi Ryū.*

shūsokugarami 収束搦. A fundamental aspect of combative swimming arts (*suieijutsu*). 1. A leg-entanglement technique used against an enemy while swimming. 2. A technique for swimming even when one's arms and legs are bound.

shuto 衆徒 [Also read ***shūto***]. Lit. "gang," "clique," or "entourage." The term *shuto* is often used in medieval literature when referring to warrior monks (*sōhei*). It appears to be related to the contemporary term *dōshu* (1), which was used at Enryakuji and other temples to indicate low-level priests who performed miscellaneous duties at the temple. However, the connotation here is that of "security detail" or "armed entourage."

sode 袖. 1. Japanese armored shoulder guards. The *sode* were usually made up of small armored scales fastened together in strips with silk cords. 2. A sleeve, whether armored or unarmored.

sodegarami 袖搦. Lit. "*sode* tangler." 1. In this compound term, *sode* can refer to an armored shoulder guard or the sleeve of an opponent's garments. The *sodegarami* was a barbed polearm approximately 6.5 feet (2 m) long used to ensnare opponents. This weapon found wide use during the Sengoku and early Edo periods as one of the three primary weapons (*mitsudōgu*) for used in concert for trapping and restraining swordsmen. See also: *sasumata; tsukubō.* 2. The term *sodegarami* is also used as a *kata* name in several *ryū*. In this context, it indicates techniques for binding or entan-

[37] McCarthy (2008: 73) specifies "tiger fist" (*koken* 虎拳 <Ch. *hu quan*). However, Momohara (2008: 161) simply refers to the system studied by Uechi as a variety of "southern Shaolin boxing" (*namba* Shōrinken 南派少林拳 <Ch. *nanpai* Shaolin Quan).

[38] The name of the temple was recorded as Chūō Bukkyōji 中央佛教寺 <Ch. Zhongyang Fojiaosi.

gling an enemy's sleeves (*sode*) with a chain, rope, or other device.

SODEGARAMI

Edo-period policeman (*dōshin*) threatening a swordsman with a *sodegarami*
Detail of illustration from the nineteenth-century *Tokugawa Bakufu keiji zufu honpen*
(Used with permission of the Meiji University Museum)

sodegaramijutsu 袖搦術. Techniques using a barbed polearm (*sodegarami*) to ensnare opponents.

Further reading:

• Kaminoda, 2006: 93–100. (Japanese)

Sōden 1.『総伝』【総傳】. Alternate title for the *Daitō ryū aiki budō densho zen jūikkan mokuroku*, a Daitō Ryū text composed by Hisa Takuma. See: *Daitō Ryū; Daitō ryū aiki budō densho zen jūikkan mokuroku; Hisa Takuma.*

sōden 2. 相伝【相傳】. a. Inheritance; heirship. The term *sōden* indicates a transmission or tradition passed directly from father to son. See: *Ryūei Ryū (2).* b. The conference of priestly orders.

Sō Dōshin 宗 道臣 [A.k.a. ***Nakano Michiomi*** 中野道臣] (1911–1980). Espionage agent for the infamous Kokuryūkai (Amur River Society, a.k.a. Black Dragon Society); founder of Nippon Shōrinji Kempō. Sō notes that, in order to facilitate his covert activities for the Kokuryūkai in China, he became a disciple of a Daoist priest named Chen Liang,[39] who was a leader in a Chinese secret society known as the Zaijiali.[40] Chen was also a master of a school of martial arts called the Bailianmen *quan*[41]. According to Sō, this school was a Shaolin derivative but the techniques were few and unorganized.

Later Sō went to Beijing and trained with Wen Taizong,[42] whom he states was the "twentieth headmaster of Giwamonken," a secret society with ties to the Boxers.[43] Sō claims that in 1936 Wen made him the twenty-first successor of the Chinese system and "the only true successor to the Shorinji (Ch. Shaolinsi) tradition."

Repatriated to Japan in 1946, Sō amalgamated the Chinese boxing (*quanfa*) he had learned in China with Japanese systems such as the *jūjutsu* of the Hakkō Ryū 八光流 and Daitō Ryū 大東流, and Nihon Kempō 日本拳法 pugilism, to found his own school of "Shōrinji Kempō" in 1947.

Further reading in English:

• Draeger, 1974a: *passim.*

• So, 1970a; 1970b: 155–184.

Soga 蘇我. A warrior family descended from Takeshiuchi no Sukune 武内宿禰. Under the leadership of Soga no Umako, the Soga introduced Buddhism along with other Sino-Korean establishments into Japan in the late sixth century. In the process, they ran into opposition from the Mononobe family, which was under the leadership of clan chief (Ōmuraji) Mononobe no Moriya. Though this was traditionally seen as a clash between Buddhism and the native religions of Japan (Shintō), historians have pointed out that the real conflict was between forces in favor of a more centralized, Chinese-style government and political system

---

39 J. Chin Ryō 陳良 <Ch. Chen Liang.

40 J. Zaijari <Ch. Zaijiali.

41 J. Byakurenmon *ken* 白蓮門拳 <Ch. Bailianmen *quan*, lit. "White Lotus Sect boxing." However, in Chinese this term is usually rendered as "Bailian quan 白蓮拳."

42 J. Mon Daishū <Ch. Wen Taizong 文太宗.

43 Ch. Yihemen quan 義和門拳 [Note: Sō (1970: 13) romanized this term as "Ihermen-thuen."] "Giwamonken" is an unusual term for the Boxers. The normal term in Japanese is Giwaken 義和拳 <Ch. Yihe *quan*. Biographies of Sō state that Wen's system was a branch derived from the original Shaolin temple of Mount Song 嵩山少林寺 (Ch. Songshan Shaolinsi).

(of which Buddhism was an integral, state-supporting entity) and those favoring the decentralized independence of local strongmen (*kuni no miyatsuko*). In 587 this dispute flamed into a short war in which the Mononobe were crushed in a famous battle at Mount Shigi (Shigisan 信貴山).

sōga 爪牙. Lit. "teeth and claws." A Heian-period term sometimes used to refer to the Capital Police (*kebiishi*). *Sōga* can also refer to a person or organization that is a cat's-paw or tool used by someone else.

Soga monogatari 『曽我物語』. Sometimes considered a war tale (*gunkimono*), the *Soga monogatari* is the story of two Soga brothers, Jūrō and Gorō, who spent seventeen years in the late twelfth century tracking down their father's killer. The two brothers are often lauded for their vendetta (*katakiuchi*), and a number of plays have been based on their story.

Soga no Umako 蘇我 馬子 (c.550–626). Warrior leader of the Soga clan who aligned himself closely with Prince Shōtoku[44] and Empress Suiko.[45] Umako was a strong supporter of importing Chinese technology, learning, and political, philosophical, and cultural systems (such as Buddhism). However, his support and promotion of a more Chinese-style centralized government under the imperial throne brought him and his family into direct conflict with clans such as the Mononobe, who favored the longstanding decentralized type of government. A war ensued in 587. The Soga crushed the Mononobe at Mount Shigi and the importation of Chinese systems continued.

sōgō budō 綜合武道. A modern, comprehensive system of martial ways that encompasses a number of fighting arts.

sōgō bugei 綜合武芸【綜合武藝】. A classical comprehensive martial system/school.

sōgō bujutsu 綜合武術. A classical comprehensive martial system/school.

44 Shōtoku Taishi 聖徳太子 (572–621)

45 Suiko Tennō 推古天皇 (554–628; r.593–628). Empress Suiko was the thirty-third imperial ruler of Japan.

sōhei 1. 僧兵. A generic term for Japanese warrior monks; warrior priests; militant clergy; or any combatant associated with religious organizations.

The use of force by militant Buddhist clergy is a phenomenon not restricted to Japan. Warrior monks have also appeared at various times and places in such areas as Central Asia,[46] Tibet,[47] China,[48] Korea, and other locations. However, in all of these geographical areas the phenomenon of the "warrior monk" is a complex one; Japan is no different.[49] Most of what is considered significant "warrior monk" activity took place in Japan prior to the seventeenth century. However, according to Japanese scholar Kuroda Toshio, the term *sōhei* does not appear in Japanese documents until 1715.

Similar in fashion to the romanticization of the espionage agent (*ninja*) in twentieth-century Japan, Japanese scholarship and popular culture images have resulted in a "*sōhei*-ification" of the warrior monk phenomenon. Consequently, the term *sōhei* and the image of the warrior-like cowled monk have become fused into a generic stereotype which is now applied to any use of force associated with Buddhist institutions. The period during which these incidents occurred was a

46 Buddhists established "fortified monasteries defended by martial monks" as the religion moved along trade routes from India through Central Asia (Staal, 1982: 40).

47 In the thirteenth century, the Tibetan Sa-sky and 'Bri-khug sects waged war for political power and territory with the assistance of Mongol supporters (Snellgrove and Richardson, 1968: 149).

48 Paul Demiéville has also written of numerous accounts of warrior monk activity in China during the period from the Sui Dynasty (581–618) through the Sino-Japanese war in the 1930s (Demiéville, 1957).

49 The trend among twentieth-century Japanese scholars investigating the nature of the *sōhei* has often been to regard militant acts by clergy as a somewhat purely "religious phenomenon" outside the context of the evolution of Japanese political, economic, and military institutions. However, more recent scholarship (e.g., Adolphson, 2007) has pointed out that the evolution of religious institutions (including the use of force for political and economic gain) cannot be divorced from the larger cultural context.

long one—generally from the eighth century until the sixteenth century—and the incidents are of a large variety: everything from unarmed peaceful protests to armed conflict. The dominant popular view, both among Japanese scholars and writers of fiction, is that almost all confrontational incidents involving Buddhist temples were of a combative nature; that most were due to some sort of decline in Buddhism; and that the main participants were ordained clergy in the guise of warrior monks (*sōhei*).

However, over the hundreds of years in which these incidents took place, and depending on the specific event and the Buddhist institutions involved, the participants may have actually included a large variety of players: temple residents of an unspecified nature (*bōjin*); menial temple workers who were not ordained (*zōshikinin*); Buddhist laymen (*dōbōshū* or *tonseisha*); and warriors of many varieties, such as armed strongmen (*kyōrikisha*) employed as a security force by a temple, secular warriors who supported a temple (*zokuhei*), general clergy (*daishu*), ordained monks (*hosshi*), and a large cast of unknown participants who may or may not have been costumed in the traditional *sōhei* garb.

In brief, the warrior-monk phenomenon can be divided into three general types:

Type One—*The Great Monasteries*:

From its earliest introduction to Japan in the sixth century, Buddhism was seen by the Japanese as a superior form of magic, long practiced by the advanced civilization in China, a culture the Japanese respected and sought to emulate. Consequently Buddhism has always had many faces in Japan: spiritual, magical, and closely intertwined with political, economic, and military power.

By the eighth century, the Japanese had adopted a form of government based on that used by the Tang-dynasty Chinese. This system, called the Ritsuryō government (Taihō Ritsuryō), was a religio-political system which revered the emperor as the central ruling figure of both the mundane and spiritual realms. Thus, in addition to his position as head of the court and a descendent of the native Shintō *kami*, the Japanese emperor was also seen as a manifestation of the Universal Buddha, Vairocana (Birushana). This buddha was the central buddha of the then-popular *Avataṁsaka-sūtra* (*Kegonkyō* 華厳経). It was during the eighth century that Tōdaiji temple in Nara—which houses a huge statue of the Buddha Vairocana—was built. Tōdaiji and its Great Buddha image (Daibutsu 大佛), which were funded through government support, represented both the mundane and spiritual power of the Japanese emperor. Tōdaiji quickly became the leading temple of the Buddhist Kegon school. Because of these ties, many of the monks who came to populate Tōdaiji were members of the imperial family. In contrast, the Kōfukuji—also in Nara—was a family temple of the Fujiwara clan, a center of the Buddhist Hossō school, and soon came to rival Tōdaiji in prestige, wealth, and political power.

In the eighth century, reports of martial monks involved in armed conflict with opposing forces began to appear. By the late tenth century, a number of Buddhist schools—Tendai being the best known—had become known for employing detachments of "warrior monks," which were used to pressure the government and other opposing political forces, as well as defend the school's own large, tax-free land holdings (*shōen*).

As a result, by the eleventh century a number of temples were becoming known as much for their military forces and martial training as for their spiritual accomplishments. Several temples mentioned in this *Encyclopedia* certainly fit into this category, including Kuramadera (just north of Kyōto), Enryakuji (on Mount Hiei just northeast of Kyōto), Miidera (on the coast of Lake Biwa), Kongōbuji (on Mount Kōya), Negoroji (in Wakayama), Tōdaiji and Kōfukuji in Nara, etc.

A variety of terms such as *hōshi musha* (priest warrior) have been used for the military clergy of the great monasteries. Warrior monks from the old capital city of Nara were referred to as *Nara hōshi* (Nara priests), while Tendai monks from Enryakuji on Mount Hiei were called *yama hōshi* (mountain monks); those from Onjōji/Miidera were referred to as *tera hōshi* ([Mii]dera monks). In many records, these warrior monks are referred to as *akusō* (evil monks) or *shuto* (security details).

The power of the Buddhist and Shintō centers relying on military forces waxed during the period from the tenth through the sixteenth centuries, with representatives from almost every denomination joining in the fray at one time or another. However, with the rise of powerful warlords during the Warring States period, the influence of the monasteries and their monk armies began to weaken. Oda Nobunaga, one of those warlords, began destroying the power of the great monasteries once and for all when, in 1573, he razed Mount Hiei, burning many of the temples and putting thousands of monks to the sword. Although there were militant clergy who survived the late 1500s, the military power of the great monasteries came to an end.

Type Two—*The Ikkō Ikki* (single-minded military groups):

Although composed partially of militant clergy, the Ikkō Ikki were rather different from the powerful, organized military monk armies attributed to the great monasteries. They were, in fact, a variant of armed provincial groups (*kuni ikki*) made up of peasant farmers, low-level warriors, and monks associated with the Honganji, a sub-sect of the Buddhist Jōdo Shinshū school. However, when the Ikkō Ikki entered into the fray of the Warring States period in the fifteenth and sixteenth centuries, they caused great havoc. The Ikkō Ikki uprisings—sometimes referred to as the Ikkōto no Ran—occurred in several locations and were of diverse character. In fact, Japanese historians today still argue whether their origins and motivations were of a religious, political, or economic nature.

Type Three—*The nyūdō*:

As noted above, the term *nyūdō* (meaning one who has "entered the path" of the Buddha) was a title given to a person who had become a lay Buddhist priest (*zaike hōshi*). Members of the warrior class did this for various reasons: some were setting out on a spiritual path, while others may have been attempting to hide from enemies. Some were young house-arrest hostages while others made spiritual vows as adults due to the oracular revelations they had received at sacred sites (spiritual power centers). Some later returned to a completely secular life; others did not. Throughout the period when the classical martial systems (*koryū*) flourished (that is, the fourteenth through nineteenth centuries) there arose numerous accounts of martial schools being founded by Buddhist monks, Shintō priests, and Shugendō *yamabushi*. Most founders of martial schools who were known as Buddhist monks were probably actually warriors by birth or circumstance who had taken some of the Buddhist vows; they did not spend their entire lives as professional priests. Numerous temples and shrines are associated with this phenomenon, both as centers of martial/spiritual revelations and combative training. A few of these are mentioned in this *Encyclopedia*, such as Anryakuji in Kyūshū, Atagosan Daigongen north of Kyōto, Hōzōin in Nara, Jufukuji in Kamakura, and Kuramadera just north of Kyōto, etc. See also: *akusō, Benkei; dōbōshū; dōshu (1); gosō; hafuribe; Hōzōin Inei; Hōzōin Inshu; Ikkō Ikki; kyōrikisha; Minamoto no Yoshitsune; Nen Ami Jion; Ōzōin Ihei; zokuhei; zōshikinin.*

Further reading:

- Adolphson, 2007. (English)
- Demiéville, 1957. (French)
- McMullin, 1985. (English)
- Renondeau, 1957. (French)
- Tsang, 2008. (English)
- Turnbull, 2005: 202–267. (English)

sōhei 2. 槍兵. A spearman; a lanceman.

sōhō 槍法. The combative use of the spear; spearmanship; drilling with spears.

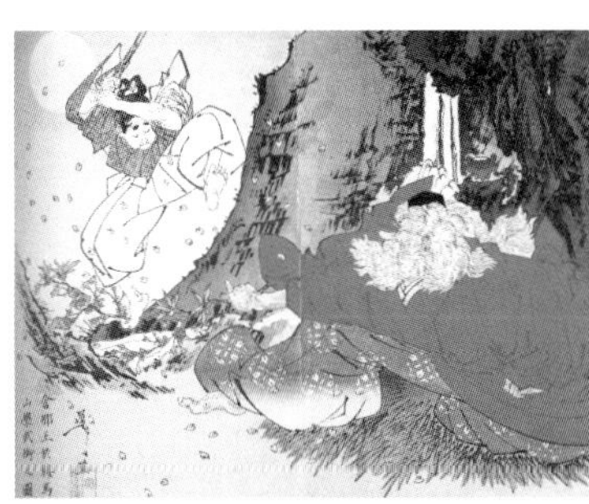

USHIWAKAMARU (YOSHITSUNE) LEARNS SWORDSMANSHIP FROM THE *TENGU* SŌJŌBŌ

Woodblock print by Yoshitoshi (1839–1892)

S

Sōjōbō 僧正坊. The king of the mountain demons (*tengu*) from whom Minamoto no Yoshitsune is supposed to have learned swordsmanship. This training is said to have taken place on Mount Kurama, in a ravine called Sōjōgatani.

Further reading in English:

- de Visser, 1908: 70.
- McCullough, 1966: 37–38.

Sōjōgatani 僧正ヶ谷. A small valley on Mount Kurama located above the Tendai temple of Kuramadera. It was here that the young Minamoto no Yoshitsune (called Ushiwakamaru at that time) is supposed to have learned swordsmanship from Sōjōbō, the king of the mountain demons (*tengu*).

sōjōsōchi 早乗早馳【早乘早馳】[Var. ***sōjō*** 早乗【早乘】; also read ***hayanori*** or ***hayagake***]. According to Watatani and Yamada (1978: 56), *sōjōsōchi*, an art included under the rubric of military horsemanship (*gumba*), was the ability to cover a distance of 60 *ri* (146.4 miles or 235.8 kilometers) in one day on horseback. See: *Ichizen Ryū.*

sōjū 槍銃. A term used for spearmanship by Matsumoto Nagato Sadayoshi in the school he founded, the Isshi Ryū 一指流. *Sōjū*, which literally means "spear-gun," was chosen by Matsumoto because the movements of his technique were so fast that they resembled the firing of a bullet from a matchlock musket.

sōjutsu 槍術 [Var. 鎗術]. Combative spear arts. Over 450 *ryū* containing *sōjutsu* have been cataloged, the earliest being the Nen Ryū and the Katori Shintō Ryū.

In addition to its combative aspects, the use of the Japanese spear (*hoko* or *yari*) plays an important role in Japanese mythology. The formation of the Japanese islands is thought to have been brought about by two Shintō *kami* using a spear. See also: *Hōzōin Ryū; Katori Shintō Ryū; Nen Ryū; Hikita Kage Ryū; yari.*

Further reading in English:

- Knutsen, 1963; 2004a.

Sōkaku Ryū 惣角流. A variant name for the line of the Daitō Ryū founded by Takeda Sōkaku. Watatani and Yamada (1978: 505) note that the Sōkaku Ryū included spear techniques (*sōjutsu*), dual sword techniques (*nitō ryū*), long hardwood staff techniques (*bōjutsu*), and the use of small throwing blades and darts (*shurikenjutsu*), in addition to a grappling system referred to as *aikijūjutsu*. See: *Daitō Ryū; Takeda Sōkaku.*

sōke 宗家. The head family, or head man (or woman) of a school. *Sōke* is a much-misunderstood and misused term—especially among Western practitioners of Japanese "martial arts"—and the application of this title has changed over the centuries in Japan. During the Tokugawa period the term *sōke* came to refer to the family head of non-martial artistic lineages such as tea ceremony (*chadō*), flower arranging (*kadō*), etc.—which, like commercial guilds, held exclusive rights regarding techniques, instruction, licensing, etc. in those arts. The *sōke* (or *iemoto* 家元) system developed in such a way that any instructors anywhere in Japan in a specific tradition paid fees to, and issued diplomas in the name of, the *sōke*.

During the incessant warfare of the sixteenth century the *bushi* did not develop a *sōke* system, as it would have been impractical for a master teacher to withhold secret or essential techniques for years from students who might be engaged in battle at any time. In addition, the martial *ryū* of that period did not have hundreds of techniques and concepts to teach. (Many of those systems greatly expanded their repertoire during the more than 250 years of Tokugawa peace.) An example of this is the complete transmission of the Shinkage Ryū from Kamiizumi Nobutsuna to Yagyū Muneyoshi in a period of two and a half years or less. At that time (c. 1565) the Shinkage Ryū consisted of approximately forty-five *kata* and a number of tactical, strategic, psychological, and philosophical concepts. Over the Tokugawa period more than a hundred *kata* were added, as well as variations and many additional concepts.

Furthermore, unlike the non-martial *sōke*-style traditions, the martial traditions and branches (*ryū-ha*) that proliferated during the Tokugawa period did so in many locations around Japan; each local lineage was independent of other lineages in the same *ryū*. Consequently, the martial *ryū* of the Tokugawa period never developed an exclusive *sōke* system.

In his fine article on the topic (Bodiford, 2002), William M. Bodiford points out that the closest thing to a *sōke/iemoto* system to develop in the world of Japanese *budō* was Kano's Kōdōkan Jūdō, which was not established until the Meiji era (1882). However, because of Kano's emphasis on modernity and Western pedagogy, no one ever refers to the Kōdōkan or its head as a *sōke*. In an odd turn of events, however, a number of systems—especially *jūjutsu*-type systems—began using the term *sōke* in the early twentieth century. This trend may have emerged due to the rising popularity of classical martial systems (especially grappling systems) and in an attempt to give the image of legitimacy and exclusivity. It is also related to the phenomenon in which disenfranchised samurai during the Meiji era—such as Takeda Sōkaku of the Daitō Ryū—found themselves without any means of support except to teach their *jūjutsu* skills to the public, police, and military. In order to compete in the *budō* marketplace, having exclusive rights to an in-demand system meant financial stability. Consequently, a default *iemoto/sōke* system evolved (even if the term *sōke* was not used).

As a final note, the suffix of the term *sōke*—that is, *ke* 家—has a specific significance in Japan. Since Tokugawa times, all Japanese families (*ke* 家) have had to maintain official registers (*koseki tohon*) and their abbreviated abstract (*koseki shohon*) with the local governments. Consequently, non-Japanese do not have an official, registered *ke*, so the idea of a non-Japanese *sō-ke* is alien to the Japanese system.

Further reading in English:
- Bodiford, 2002.

sokkon Zen 即今禅【即今禪】. Variant pronunciation for *shikin* Zen. See: *kōan*; *shikin Zen*.

sokotsushi 粗忽死. Expiatory *seppuku*; suicide performed as atonement for a blunder or misdeed. See: *seppuku*.

Sōma Shirō Tadashige 相馬 四郎 忠重. A well-known and feared warrior who fought in many battles alongside Nitta Yoshisada (1301–1338) and Kusunoki Masashige in support of Emperor Go-Daigo.[50] Sōma was the father of Sōma Shirō Yoshitomo (Nen Ami Jion), who founded the Nen Ryū.

Sōma Shirō Yoshitomo Nyūdō Jion 相馬 四郎 義元 入道 慈恩. Founder of the Nen Ryū 念流. Sōma took Buddhist vows and assumed the Buddhist name "Nen Ami Jion." See: *Nen Ami Jion*.

Someya Chikatoshi 染谷 親俊. The founder of a modern *budō* system called Meifu Shinkage Ryū 明府真影流 in 1960. The school concentrates on small throwing blades and darts (*shurikenjutsu*).

Sonjōō 尊星王. See: *seiōken*.

sonkyo no shisei 蹲踞の姿勢. Lit. "crouching posture." A posture in which the practitioner squats on the balls of his feet, heels close together with the knees deeply bent and the buttocks lowered over the heels. This posture is used in many classical *ryū*; it also appears in *sumō* as part of a match's opening etiquette.

SONKYO NO SHISEI
Jiki Shinkage Ryū swordsman Watanabe Tokiji in *sonkyo no shisei* posture at a Meiji Jingu exhibition, 1977
(Photograph by author)

Sonobe Asano 園部 朝野. Recognized as sixteenth headmaster of Jiki Shinkage Ryū Naginatajutsu. See also: *kiaijutsu*.

Sonobe Hideo 園部 秀雄. Direct disciple of

[50] Go-Daigo Tennō 後醍醐天皇 (1288–1339; r.1318–1339).

naginatajutsu master Satake Shigeo. Hideo may have also trained with Shigeo's husband, Satake Kanryūsai, in the late 1800s. Hideo is recognized as fifteenth headmaster by Jiki Shinkage Ryū Naginatajutsu. According to the current website sponsored by Jiki Shinkage Ryū Naginatajutsu, Hideo became fifteenth headmaster in 1895.

In reality it is now unclear whether Hideo trained in the late 1800s in the use of the sword and glaive with Satake Yoshifumi, his wife Satake Shigeo, or both. Certainly Hideo trained in the popular *budō* of the times, and evidently established a training hall (*dōjō*) for *naginatajutsu* practice in Tōkyō by 1936. However, in 1973 this author spoke with a woman in Ōsaka who had been a student of Sonobe Hideo as a young girl in the late 1920s. She said that Hideo had not used the term "Jiki Shinkage Ryū *naginatajutsu*" during that early period, raising the possibility that the name and auspicious lineage may have been added later. Sonobe Hideo should probably be regarded as the second or third headmaster of a combined system that began with Satake Kanryūsai. See also: *Jiki Shinkage Ryū Naginatajutsu; Satake Kanryūsai Yoshifumi.*

sonnō jōi 尊皇攘夷. Lit., "revere the emperor and expel the barbarians." *Sonnō jōi* was a political philosophy which can be traced, in its Japanese form, to two seventeenth-century Mito school political philosophers.[51] During the Bakumatsu period (1853–1867), *sonnō jōi* became a political slogan and rallying cry for the forces attempting to overthrow the Tokugawa shogunate. Samurai of the Satsuma and Chōshū domains—feudatories which had been at odds with the shogunate since the early 1600s—united behind this cry and, in 1868, overthrew the shogunate in a short civil war known as the Bōshin no Eki. After the fall of the Tokugawa shogunate and the "restoration" of the emperor in the person of Emperor Meiji, the slogan was dropped for a new one: *fukoku kyōhei* 富国強兵, meaning "rich nation, strong military."

[51] These were Neo-Confucian scholars Yamazaki Ansai 山崎闇斎 (1619–1682) and Yamaga Sokō 山鹿素行 (1622–1685).

Sono mama! 其のまま! Lit. "[Stop] just like that!" A command meaning "Cease movement!"

Sono Seigō 曽野 正鴻. Current (2008) headmaster of the Yamato Yagyū Kai.

Sonshi no heihō 『孫子兵法』<Ch. *Sunzi bingfa* (The art of war). One of the seven Chinese classics on military strategy. the *Sonshi no heihō* was written by Sunzi in the fourth century B.C.E. This text is often quoted in Japanese martial transmission documents (*densho*). There have been several translations into English.

Further reading:

- Griffith. trans. 1963.
- Sawyer. trans. 1993: 145–186.

Sōraitō Hasseihō 相雷刀 八勢法. See: *shiai seihō.*

sōren 繰練. 1. Military strategy and tactics. 2. Synonym for *heihō* 兵法 and related terms.

sori 反り. The concave curve of a sword along the back (non-cutting-edge) side.

SORI

soritsuno 反角 [Var. ***kaerizuno*** 逆角; ***origane*** 折金]. A small hook on a scabbard (*saya*) below the *kurikata* which prevents the scabbard from being pulled through the sash (*obi*) when the sword is drawn. The *soritsuno* is usually made of lacquered wood or horn to match the scabbard (*saya*), but may be made of metal matching other sword fittings. See also: *kurikata.*

soroimono 揃い物 [Var. ***sorimono*** 揃物]. Lit. "uniform set." A set of sword fittings; sword furniture. *Sorimono* can indicate a uniform set of almost anything except the *kogai, kozuka*, and pair of *menuki* (these items are referred to as *midokoromono*). A complete set of *sorimono* fittings for the two swords typically worn by samurai was called a *daishō no soroimono.*

Sō Seigō 僧 制剛 [A.k.a. ***Seigō Sō*** 制剛 僧; abbr. as ***Seigō*** 制剛]. An enigmatic Buddhist monk who, according to legend, taught *jūjutsu* to Mizuhaya Nobumasa (c.1568–c.1630). Mizuhaya subsequently founded the Seigō Ryū 制剛流.

sōsenhō 繰船法. Naval strategy and tactics.

sōsetsukon 双節棍【雙節棍】[Also read ***nunchaku***]. See: *nunchaku.*

sōshi 壮士【壯士】. As a term meaning "swashbucklers," *sōshi* was used during the Meiji era to refer to young ultra-nationalist disenfranchised samurai (*shizoku*) who gathered around such political radicals as Tōyama Mitsuru.

Soshijjikara-kyō 『蘇悉地羯羅経』【蘇悉地羯羅經】<Ch. *Suxidi jieluo jing* <Skt. *Susiddhikara-sūtra*). BUDDHISM—One of three central texts in the tantric practices of the Tendai and Shingon schools of Buddhism in Japan. This text is closely associated with the *Jūhachidō* and its rituals for propitiating warrior deities such as Marishiten and Bishamonten. See also: *Jūhachidō; Shido kegyō.*

Sōshindō 双真道. A martial school founded in the mid to late twentieth century by Nagasawa Narishige. Nagasawa was a direct disciple of Hakkō Ryū 八光流 founder Okuyama Yoshiji. The system concentrates on *aiki*-type grappling.

Sōshū den 相模伝【相模傳】. See: *Gokaden.*

Sōsuishi Ryū 双水執流【雙水執流】. See: *Sōsuishitsu Ryū.*

Sōsuishitsu Ryū 双水執流【雙水執流】[Also read ***Sōsuishi Ryū***; A.k.a. ***Sōsuishitsu Ryū Kumiuchi Koshi no Mawari*** 双水執流組討腰の廻【雙水執流組討腰廻】]. A school of *taijutsu* which at first concentrated on grappling in light armor (*kumiuchi koshi no mawari*). It was created in 1650 by the samurai Futagami Hannosuke of the Takeda domain (*han*) in Bungo (present-day northeastern Kyūshū).

Futagami mastered the *koshi no mawari* of the Takenouchi Ryū 竹内流 and had formed his own school, which he called the Futagami Ryū 二神流. However, feeling his system was not perfected, he set out on a martial pilgrimage (*musha shugyō*). Tradition tells us that upon reaching the Yoshino River in Yamato (modern-day Nara prefecture), he retreated into a remote valley on Mount Yoshino where he meditated and trained for thirty-seven days. One day while viewing the Yoshino River, he awakened to a unique insight, and from that revelation devised a distinctive way to meld grappling techniques (*taijutsu*) with swordsmanship (*kenjutsu*). He subsequently renamed the system "Sōsuishitsu," meaning "to grasp/take hold of the two waters"—an allusion to the dual swirling/mixing waters of the river.

Today the main line of the Sōsuishitsu Ryū continues in Fukuoka (southwestern Kyūshū) at the Fukuoka Sekiryūkan Dōjō. In addition, since 1888 there has been a branch tradition in

Sōsuishitsu Ryū
双水執流
(abbreviated lineage)

1. Futagami Hannosuke Masasato
初代　二神 半之助 正聡
Founded 1650

2. Tashiro Seijirō Noritada
田代 清次郎 則忠
Headmaster in 1666

3. Shitama Shinjirō Muneyoshi
舌間 新次郎 宗督
Headmaster in 1683

4. Shitama Kihei Munekazu
舌間 喜兵衛 宗一
Headmaster in 1697

5. Ōno Yahei Munekatsu
大野 弥兵衛 宗勝
Headmaster in 1718

6. Shitama Sakugorō Munekado
舌間 作五郎 宗廉
Headmaster in 1725

7. Enomoto Kyūemon Tadana
榎本 久右衛門 忠直
Headmaster in 1730

8. Shitama Shichirō Munemasu
舌間 七郎 宗益
Headmaster in 1739

9. Usuki Kujurō Munenao
臼木 九十郎 宗直
Headmaster in 1774

10. Shitama Shinjirō Muneaki
舌間 真次郎 宗章
Headmaster in 1818

11. Shitama Yagorō Munetsuna
舌間 真次郎 宗章
Headmaster in 1834

12. Shitama Shingo Munetsugu
舌間 真吾 宗継
Headmaster in 1861
1843–1877

13. Shitama Bota Munetsuna
舌間 忘多 宗綱
Headmaster in 1877
(same man as #11)

14. Aoyagi Kihei Masatoshi
青柳 喜平 正聡
Headmaster in 1895
1871–1929

15. Shitama Shuzo Muneaki
舌間 修三 宗聽
Headmaster in 1929
c.1900–1966

16. Shitama Manzō Munetoshi
舌間 萬三 宗利
Headmaster in 1966
1947–present

Tōkyō known as the Sōsuishitsu Ryū Matsui Ha. The current curriculum of the school includes grappling (*kumiuchi*) and quick-draw swordsmanship (*koshi no mawari*). Evidently *tameshigiri* is also practiced, but is not considered to be a part of the original system.

Sōsuishitsu Ryū Kumiuchi Koshi no Mawari 双水執流組討腰之廻【雙水執流組討腰廻】. See: *Sōsuishitsu Ryū.*

Sōsuishitsu Ryū Matsui Ha 双水執流松井派【雙水執流松井派】. A line of the Sōsuishitsu Ryū that has operated as a separate entity in Tōkyō since 1888. In recent years this branch tradition has reestablished ties with the Fukuoka main line, but continues to operate separately.

sōtai renshū 相対練習. Combative exercises with a partner acting as an adversary. Contrast to *tandoku renshū.*

sōto 僧徒. Buddhist clergy.

Sōtō Shū 曹洞宗 <Ch. Caodong zong. The Sōtō school of Zen Buddhism brought to Japan by the monk Dōgen Kigen in the thirteenth century.

sōtsuibushi 総追捕使【總追捕使】. A "general arresting officer." This title was used by Minamoto no Yoritomo in 1185 for the officials he sent out to the provinces to replace the governors. The term itself is a continuation of the established tradition of the "arresting officer" (*tsuibushi*) and "provincial arresting officer" (*shokoku tsuibushi*), who were military men sent out by the court to exert military control over the provinces. (Yoritomo was, in fact, sometimes known by the title of "Nihon Sōtsuibushi.") The title *sōtsuibushi* was later changed to *shugo* 守護.

Sō Unryū 僧 雲竜【僧雲龍】. See: *Unryū.*

soya 征矢. A plain arrow for use in battle.

suburi 素振り. A drill in which a sword (or other weapon such as a *naginata*) is swung in a repetitive cutting motion targeting a visualized opponent.

suburi tō 素振刀. A heavy wooden sword (*bokutō*) used for *suburi* practice.

Sūden 崇伝【崇傳】[A.k.a. ***Ishin Sūden*** 以心崇伝【以心崇傳】; ***Konchiin Sūden*** 金地院崇伝【金地院崇傳】] (1569–1633). Rinzai Zen priest who served as an advisor to retired *shōgun* Tokugawa Ieyasu, and later Tokugawa Hidetada and Tokugawa Iemitsu. Sūden acted as a consultant on religious and political matters, and was instrumental in the compilation of the *Buke shohatto.*

suemono 据物. See: *suemonogiri.*

suemonogiri 据物切 [Abbr. ***suemono*** 据物]. Synonym for *tameshigiri* (test cutting).

Sugano Taketomi 菅野 武臣. Current (twentieth) headmaster of the Takeda Ryū (3) 武田流, a school of military strategy and tactics (*gunryaku*) and military signaling with the conch shell (*jingaijutsu*).

Sugita Shūhō Kiyoichi 杉田 修峰 清一. A direct disciple of Hakkō Ryū 八光流 founder Okuyama Yoshiji who subsequently founded a school called Shintō Ryū Heishujutsu 神道流 平手術. Sugita's school concentrated on grappling (*heishujutsu*).

suibajutsu 水馬術. Aquatic, combative horsemanship. See: *Oguri Ryū.*

Sui dī 首里手 (Oki.). See: *Shuri te.*

suieijutsu 水泳術. Combative swimming arts. These included a variety of skills: treading water (*fumiashi*), leaping from the water (*shihi*), grappling in water (*ashigarami*), swimming with arms and legs bound (*shusokugarami*), etc. While in use during the entire 700-year reign of the *bushi*, *suieijutsu* was not formalized into a particular school until the sixteenth century, when the Shinden Ryū 心伝流 set up a formal curriculum. Fujita (1960: 2) lists ninety-two *ryū* specializing in *suieijutsu*.

suigaku 水学【水學】. Naval strategy and tactics. The term *suigaku* was used interchangeably with the terms *funa-ikusa no hō* (*sengunhō*) 船軍法, *sōsenhō* 繰船法, and *suigun* 水軍.

suigetsu 水月 <Ch. *shuiyue* <Skt. *udaka-candra.* The enigmatic term *suigetsu* has a variety of meanings within various aspects of East Asian culture. Within the classical martial traditions

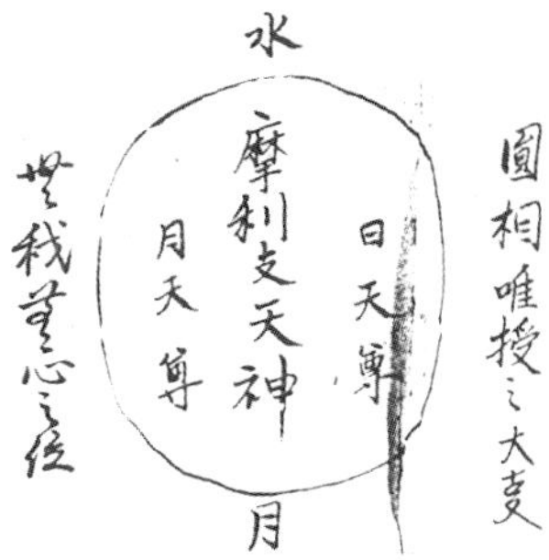

SUIGETSU ILLUSTRATION
From a Tenshinshō-den Katori Shintō Ryū *mokuroku* dated 1864
(Private collection)

(*koryū*), each school seems to have added its own shades of meaning. 1. BUDDHISM—The reflection of the moon's disk on water. This symbol indicates that the appearance of all phenomena is illusory and temporary. 2. SHINDŌ MUSŌ RYŪ— *Suigetsu* has several meanings in this tradition. It may refer to a vital-point target at the solar plexus; vital points in general; or more subtle concepts that are revealed only to highly-advanced disciples. 3. YAGYŪ SHINKAGE RYŪ—*Suigetsu* has several meanings in this tradition. Basically it is the "event horizon" around a combatant at which a decision must be made regarding an attack. 4. KATORI SHINTŌ RYŪ—The term *suigetsu* is illustrated within the Tenshinshō-den Katori Shintō Ryū's license *densho* known as *mokuroku*, where it is depicted as a circle (moon disk) encompassing the names of three deities: Nittenson 日大尊, Marishitenjin 摩利支天神, and Gattenson 月天尊 (that is, the Sun, Marishiten, and the Moon). In this respect, *suigetsu* appears to be related to *ongyōin* and *uto*.

suigun 水軍. Naval strategy and tactics. See: *suigaku* 水学.

suijōhokōjutsu 水上歩行術. Techniques for crossing water. Watatani (1967: 30) notes that this skill is also called *ukigutsu* 浮沓.

Suikoden 『水滸伝』【水滸傳】<Ch. *Shuihuzhuan* (The Water Margin). A Yuan-dynasty novel loosely based on the actions and adventures of a twelfth-century Chinese bandit by the name of Sō Kō (Ch. Song Jiang 宋江) and his thirty-six associates. This novel was popular in Japan, especially during the Tokugawa period. Utagawa Kuniyoshi, a Japanese artist famous for his prints of warriors, created a series of seventy-four prints illustrating the story during the nineteenth century. See: *Shi Daikisho.*

Suiō Ryū 水隝流【水鷗流】[A.k.a. ***Suiō Ryū Kenpō Iai*** ～剣法居合【劍法居合】]. A comprehensive combative school (*sōgō bujutsu*) founded by Mima Yoichizaemon Kagenobu around the year 1600. Kagenobu included a variety of weapon systems: swordsmanship (*kenjutsu*) with longsword (*katana*) and short sword (*wakizashi*); quick-draw sword skills (*iai kempō*); medium-length staff (*jōhō*), long-hafted glaive (*naginatajutsu*); sickle and chain (*kusarigama-jutsu*); and grappling in light armor (*kogusoku*).

Curriculum		**Number of *kata***
Iai Kempō	居合剣法	
Goyō	五陽	5
Goin	五陰	5
Kuyō	九曜	9
Tachi Iai	立居合	9
Kage	影	18
Kumi Iai	組居合	9
Jōhō	杖法	
Tachiai (Omote)	立合(表)	16
Tachiai (Ura)	立合(裏)	16
Oku	奥	10
Betsuden Tantō-tori	別伝短刀取	3
Tanjō	短杖	5
Aijō	相杖	10
Betsuden Musōgaeshi	別伝無想返	6
Masaki Ryū Fukuhara Ha Kusarigama-jutsu 正木流福原派鎖鎌術		16
Naginata	薙刀	
Omote	表	9
Ura	裏	9
Ai-Naginata 相薙刀		
Omote	表	9
Ura	裏	9
Okuhi	奥秘	
Kogusoku	小具足	10
Wakizashi	脇差	13

Licenses:

Shoden	初伝
Chūden	中伝
Shōmokuroku	小目録
Chūmokuroku	中目録

S

Daimokuroku 大目録
Shōmenkyo 小免許
Menkyo kaiden 免許皆伝

See also: *Fukuhara Shinzaemon; Masaki Ryū Fukuhara Ha Kusarigama-jutsu.*

Suiten 水天 <Ch. Shuitian <Skt. Varuṇa. In Indian mythology, Varuṇa (Jp. Suiten) is the god of water, an "elemental" spirit. Suiten is one of a group of twelve guardian deities adopted from Brahmanism by Buddhism. See: *Jūniten.*

sujibachi 筋鉢. See: *sujikabutobachi.*

sujikabutobachi 筋兜鉢. A type of multi-plate helmet which began to appear around the Nambokuchō period.

suki 隙. 1. Opportunity, a chink, discord; a weak ness in physical posture or mental focus. 2. A crack or opening in a defense.

sumai 相撲 [Also written 捔力]. See: *sumō.*

sumai no sechie 相撲の節会【相撲の節會】. A ritual performance of Japanese *sumō.*

Sumen Ryū 素面流. Lit. "No-mask Tradition." See: *Ichien Ryū.*

sumō 相撲 [Also read **sumai**]. When the characters 相撲 are read *sumō*, they refer to the sportive grappling art that is still a favorite of Japanese spectators today. When the characters 相撲 are read *sumai* the term indicates an antecedent of modern sport *sumō.*

Sumai (originally written as 捔力) was a no-holds-barred form of combative wrestling in which an opponent could be killed. It was not a sport. *Sumai* was practiced by warriors and Shugendō priests (*shugenja* or *yamabushi*). Draeger and Smith (1969: 131) note that ancient *sumai* was "fully effective in combat" and was restricted to chosen fighters who might represent opposing parties in a dispute. As *sumai* included striking, butting, and kicking techniques, similar to earlier Han Chinese martial contests, it has been speculated that in addition to Korean and Central Asian elements, Chinese wrestling antecedents such as *jiaodi*[52] may have influenced early *sumai.* (Matsuda, 1972: 12).

Among the warrior class, *sumai* influenced and became adapted to various forms of battlefield grappling (*kumiuchi*). Shugendō practitioners (*yamabushi*) found it useful because they often wandered alone in the mountains, where they sometimes ran into bandits or dangerous animals. For the *yamabushi*, *sumai* was (and is) both a religious ritual[53] and a self-defense system.

It is probable that religious ritual elements (primarily those which later came to be called Shintō) were an integral part of *sumai/sumō* from the early first millennium C.E. During the Yamato period (c.300–c.550) matches were staged to propitiate the gods (*kami*), and even today a number of amateur *sumō* events are held for various religious festivals at Shintō shrines.

During the Nara (646–794) and Heian (794–1185) periods *sumai/sumō* became patronized by the imperial court. In imitation of the elaborate Chinese Sui and Tang dynasty festival practices, a somewhat less lethal version of *sumai* became a popular spectator sport. With the rise of the warrior class (*bushi*) in the late Heian and early Kamakura (1185–1333) periods, many of the more combatively effective techniques were adopted and adapted by the warrior class in such arts as *kumiuchi.*

Later, during the peaceful Edo period (1603–1867), sport *sumō* gained the great popularity which continues down to this day. As a modern, agonistic sport, *sumō* encompasses seventy techniques, including pulls, slaps, shoves, throws, thrusts, and trips. Forty-eight of these are considered classical techniques. However, unlike its predecessor *sumai*, *sumō* does not allow kicks, punches, or trampling a downed opponent. Rank in modern sport *sumō* is based purely on success in matches. This determines the wrestler's pay, how he will dress, and how he will be treated. There are several divisions in the ranking hierarchy, the uppermost being *yokozuna* (grand champion), *ōzeki* (champion), and *sekiwake* (contender). See also: *ōzeki; sekiwake; shiko; shimpan;*

[52] J. *kakutei* 角抵 (var. 角觝) <Ch. *jiaodi.*

[53] *Sumai* is practiced as part of Shura, the fourth (of six) ascetic ritual performance engaged in by Shugendō followers (*yamabushi*) during mountain retreats.

Shugendō; shura; yokozuna.

Further reading in English:

- Adams and Hatano, 1979.
- Cuyler, 1979.
- Draeger and Smith, 1969: 131–133 *ff.*
- Sergeant, 1959.

sumpō musha 寸法武者 [Also read ***sunpō musha***]. According to Watatani and Yamada (1978: 476), a *sumpō musha* was a warrior who wore no ornamentation or flag on his armor, and was therefore of low rank.

Sumpō Ryū 寸法流 [Also read ***Sunpō Ryū***]. A martial tradition concentrating on a sickle-and-chain weapon (*kusarigama*) and polearm sickle (*tegama* 手鎌). The founder is apparently unknown; Watatani and Yamada (1978: 476) do not list one. They do, however, give the dimensions of the weapons used in this school: the *kusarigama* had a shaft approximately 20 inches (50 cm) long, to which a 7.4-foot (2.25 m) leather-wrapped chain was attached. The sickle blade was approximately 5 inches (13 cm) long with a 3-inch (7.6 cm) cutting edge. A crossbar (*kagi* 鍵) was also attached to the blade end of the shaft. The polearm sickle had a shaft of approximately *ichi jō* 一杖 (nearly 10 feet, or 3 m) in length; the blade end was the same as the *kusarigama*. The polearm sickle also sported a crossbar, and worked much like a *kamayari* or *kagiyari*.

The Sumpō Ryū flourished in the Bishū and Sendai domains during the Edo period. The *tegama* techniques of this school were adopted by the Ikkan Ryū (3) 一貫流.

Watatani and Yamada (1978: 476) speculate that the name of this tradition comes from the term *sumpō musha* 寸法武者, a warrior who wore no ornamentation or flag on his armor, and was therefore low in status. Such low-ranking warriors used weapons like the *tegama* and *kusarigama*, giving the Sumpō Ryū its name.

sun 寸. Measurement of about 1.2 inches (3.03 cm).

suneate 脛当【脛當】. 1. Greaves; shin guards; shin-protecting armor. 2. Bamboo shin-protectors used in modern sport *naginata* practice (*atarashii naginata*).

SUNEATE (SHIN-PROTECTING ARMOR)
Festival at Katori Jingu, 1978
(Photograph courtesy Pat Lineberger)

Sun Man Sen 寸滿煎. Nidan-level 二段 combative forms taught by the Jigen Ryū. See: *Jigen Ryū; nidan (1).*

sunpō musha 寸法武者. See: *sumpō musha.*

Sunpō Ryū 寸法流. See: *Sumpō Ryū.*

suppa 素破 [Var. 透波]. 1. A Warring States–period term referring to low-ranking retainers. *Suppa* included everything from part-time combatants (*nobushi*) to brigands (*gōtō*). 2. A variant term for *ninja/shinobi no mono.* See: *ninjutsu.*

suriashi 摺り足. A sliding step. See also: *ayumiashi; fumikomiashi; okuriashi.*

Suru 蘇盧. See: *Shumi-sen.*

suruchin スルチン. OKINAWAN KOBUDŌ—A weighted chain weapon around 6 to 7 feet (1.8–2.15 m) long. Its use is retained in several Okinawan *kobudō* systems. See: *Okinawa kobudō.*

Susano-o no Mikoto 素戔鳴尊 [Var. 須佐之男尊, etc.]. SHINTŌ—A Shintō deity born of the god Izanagi, brother of Amaterasu. Always troublesome, Susano-o was banished to Izumo, where he fought and triumphed over the eight-headed serpent Yamata no Orochi.

The founder of the Kageyama Ryū 影山流, a warrior named Kageyama Zenga Nyūdō Kiyoshige, claimed direct descent from Susano-o no Mikoto.

sute kamari 捨かまり. 1. Members of a group of expendable, covert assault troops who hid in various locations—reed fields, forests, mountain valleys, and even in villages—until a signal was given for them to form up and make a surprise attack on enemy forces. 2. A surprise attack by covert, expendable troops. See also: *kamari (1), ninjutsu.*

sutteki ステッキ <Eng. *stick*. Variant name for the short staff (*tanjō*) used in Uchida Ryū 内田流 *suttekijutsu*. The *sutteki* is a short staff weapon—essentially a baton—about 2 to 2.5 feet (75–90 cm) in length.

sutteki jutsu ステッキ術. SHINDŌ MUSŌ RYŪ—A variant name for *tanjōjutsu* 短杖術 in the Uchida Ryū 内田流.

suwari waza 座り技【坐技】. Seated techniques.

Suyama Ichiemon 陶山 市右衛門. The only known practitioner of Azuma Ryū (2) 東流.

suyari 直槍 [Also read **chokusō**], [Var. 素槍; 直鎗; 徒鎗]. A spear with a straight blade. See also: *ōmi no* yari; *sōjutsu*; *yari.*

Suzagamori 鈴ヶ森. One of two infamous execution grounds during the Tokugawa period. The Suzagamori was located in the southern section of Edo. See also: *Kozukappara*; *shikei*; *shikeijjo*.

Suzuki Kozaemon Masashige 鈴木 小左衛門 正重. A fifth-generation successor of the Sekiguchi Ryū 関口流, a comprehensive field-combat system. Suzuki's best-known student was Mizuno Sakubee Tadakatsu, who founded the Kosekiguchi Ryū 小関口流 and the Yawara Shinshin Ryū 柔新心流.

Suzuki Saburōemon no Jō Kagemasa 鈴木 三郎右衛門尉 陰政. Founder of the Kagemasa Ryū 陰政流, a combative school known for its dual sword techniques, sometime during the late seventeenth or early eighteenth century.

NAWA YUMIO WEARING A *SASHIMONO HATA* IN THE STYLE OF THE SENGOKU PERIOD c. 1990
(Photograph courtesy John F. Quinn)

T

tabi 足袋. Split-toed socks having a gap between the big toe and other toes in order to facilitate the wearing of Japanese wooden clogs (*geta*) or sandals (*zori*).

tachi 1. 太刀. a. A long curved sword with a single cutting edge. Normally worn with the cutting edge down, the *tachi* is generally associated with the classical Japanese warrior (*bushi*). While the blade is very similar to that of the later *katana*, the *tachi* has more curvature (*sori*). Further, a *tachi* is signed on the opposite side of the tang to a *katana*; thus in both cases the signature of the swordsmith faces outward when the sword is worn.

TACHI WORN WITH ARMOR
Ōtake Shigetoshi of the Katori Shintō Ryū, 1978
(Photograph by Pat Lineberger)

Historically, *tachi* began to appear with the rise of the *bushi*, who constituted a martially proficient, horse-mounted, elite fighting force. The date of the first *tachi* is not known, but the earliest examples appear at the time of the rebellion of Taira no Masakado (935–940 C.E.).[1] This type of blade was primarily wielded with one hand from horseback in a similar manner to the Middle Eastern *scimitar* and Indian *talwar*. Although tactics used in tenth-century Japan relied heavily on archery, the modification of the sword from the straight, dual-cutting-edge type used in the Nara period and earlier indicates a rise in the importance of horse-mounted swordsmanship. (See Conroy, 1980 and 1981, for the mechanical implications of this change.) Both *tachi* and *katana* were normally in the range of 24 to 30 inches (60–76 cm) long. b. SHINDŌ MUSŌ RYŪ—a *bokken*. c. SHINDŌ MUSŌ RYŪ—The practitioner executing the *uchidachi* side of a *kata*. d. A sword technique or *kata*. e. A counting word for sword techniques; e.g., *jūyon tachi* 十四太刀 (fourteen sword techniques). See also: *kodachi, nodachi, ōdachi.*

tachi 2. 立. Standing; stance.

tachiai 1. 立合. The practice of quick-draw sword arts (*battō* or *iai*) from a standing position (in contrast to the kneeling position normally associated with the term *iai*).

tachiai 2. 立会【立會】. a. During the Tokugawa period, *tachiai* referred to a combative encounter or match. Today this term is used to indicate a modern *budō*/competitive sports match. b. KŌDŌKAN JŪDŌ—A standard term for a competitive match.

Tachiai Battōjutsu 立合抜刀術. KATORI SHINTŌ RYŪ—The second series of quick-draw sword forms (*battō waza*) in the Tenshinshō-den Katori Shintō Ryū 天真正伝香取神道流. See also: *tachiai (1).*

Tachiai Kiai Nage no Bu 立合気合投之部. KATORI SHINTŌ RYŪ—The third set of *jūjutsu* forms taught in the Tenshinshō-den Katori Shintō Ryū 天真正伝香取神道流. There are six throwing forms (*kata*) included in this set, all of which begin from a standing posture.

Tachiai no Bu 立合之部. KATORI SHINTŌ RYŪ—The second set of *jūjutsu* forms taught in the Tenshinshō-den Katori Shintō Ryū 天真正伝香取神道流. There are seventeen forms (*kata*) included in this set; all begin from a standing posture.

Tachiai Omote 立合表. YAGYŪ SEIGŌ RYŪ—The third series of quick-draw sword forms (*battō waza*) in the Yagyū Seigō Ryū. See also: *tachiai (1).*

[1] See Rabinovitch, 1986.

S
T

Tachiai Ura 立合裏. YAGYŪ SEIGŌ RYŪ—The fourth series of quick-draw sword forms (*battō waza*) in Yagyū Seigō Ryū. See also: *tachiai (1).*

Tachiawase Bō Seihō 太刀合棒勢法. First set of combative scenarios (*kata*) listed by the Hyōhō Niten Ichi Ryū 兵法二天一流 under the category titled Bōjutsu. This set is made up of seven longsword-vs.-staff techniques. See: *Hyōhō Niten Ichi Ryū.*

Tachibanake shingunden 『橘家神軍伝』【橘家神軍傳】. See: *Kitsuke shingunden.*

tachigiri seigan 立ち切り誓願 [A.k.a. ***tachigiri seigan shiai*** 立ち切り誓願試合]. A practice instituted by Yamaoka Tesshū in which, after an extended period of training, the trainee was required to face 200 sequential opponents in a match (*shiai*). If successful, the trainees could attempt the second *seigan*, which was 600 matches in three days. A third followed—seven days and 1400 matches. Yamaoka evidently required completion of these *seigan* in order to be awarded a full license (*menkyo kaiden*) in his Ittō Shōden Mutō Ryū 一刀正伝無刀流. See also: *Ittō Shōden Mutō Ryū; seigan (1); Yamaoka Tesshū.*

Further reading in English:

- Stevens, 1981: 22–27.

Tachigumi Mokuroku 「太刀組目録」(Abbreviation for ***Nen Ryū Tachigumi Mokuroku*** 「念流-」. The first of five licenses awarded by the Maniwa Nen Ryū 馬庭念流.

Tachihaki no Jin 授刀陣 [Var. 帯刀陣; also read ***Tachiwaki no Jin***]. The Unit of Mounted Body Guards; the Office of the Tachihaki. See: *Tachihaki no Toneri.*

Tachihaki no Toneri 授刀舎人 [Var. 帯刀舎人; also read ***Tachiwaki no Toneri***]. A special body guard of mounted soldiers. This type of unit was assigned to Empress Kōken[2] upon her ascent to the throne in 749. They were primarily armed with swords. Later, in the eighth century, similar small forces were used to guard the heir apparent.

tachi kake 太刀掛. A sword stand; a sword rack. A stand for a *tachi* has a broad base and an upright stand with a notch on the top that holds the sword. A *tachi* placed in the stand stands with the point (*kensaki*) upward and the pommel (*kashira*) on the base. This method prevents the weight of the hilt and hand-guard from causing the blade to cut through the scabbard (*saya*). See also: *kake.*

tachi no monodomo 館の者共. An eleventh-century term for a governor's personal residential retainers. Contrast to rural warriors (*kuni no tsuwamono*).

Tachi Seihō 太刀勢法. 1. One of two major categories of combative scenarios (*kata*) taught in the Hyōhō Niten Ichi Ryū 兵法二天一流. The second category is called Bōjutsu. 2. The first set of combative scenarios listed by the Hyōhō Niten Ichi Ryū under the general category of Tachi Seihō. This set is made up of twelve scenarios involving a single longsword. See: *Hyōhō Niten Ichi Ryū.*

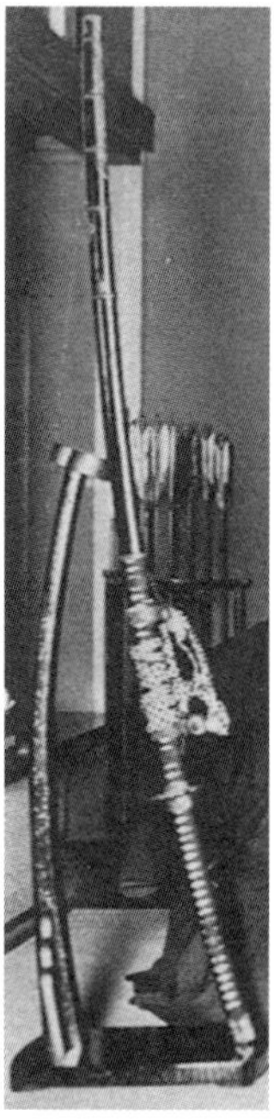

TACHI KAKE MOUNTING WITH *ŌDACHI*
(Photograph courtesy Nishioka Tsuneo)

---

[2] Kōken Tennō 孝謙天皇 (718–770, r.749–758). Empress Kōken was both the forty-sixth and forty-eighth imperial ruler of Japan. She reigned as Kōken Tennō, 749–758, and Shōtoku Tennō 称徳天皇, 764–770.

tachi uchi 太刀打. Combat using *tachi*. This is a late Heian to early Kamakura-period term found in the *Gempei seisuiki*, a large historical work written in the twelfth century which dealt with the period 1160 to 1185. Several more recent systems have retained this term.

Tachiwaki no Jin 帯刀陣. See: *Tachihaki no Jin.*

tachiwaki no toneri 授刀舎人 [Var. 帯刀舎人]. See: *Tachihaki no Toneri.*

tachi waza 立ち技. A general term for techniques performed from a standing posture. Contrast to *suwari waza*.

tadashii 正しい. CLASSICAL WARRIOR IDEAL—Honest, just, correct, straightforward. See also: *jikishin (2).*

tai 1. 待. Lit. "waiting." a. YAGYŪ SHINKAGE RYŪ—A mental state in which one's mind is in "waiting mode"; i.e., calm and relaxed, although one may be moving to attack. b. YAGYŪ SHINKAGE RYŪ—A physical state in which the proponent waits for the enemy to attack; still, unmoving. Contrast to *ken* (2). See: *Sangakuen no Tachi; Kuka no Tachi.*

tai 2. 隊. TAIHŌ MILITARY SYSTEM—A platoon of fifty men, or five squads (*ka*), as implemented in the eighth-century Chinese-style provincial militia unit (*gundan*). The *tai* was commanded by a *taishō.* See: *gundan.*

Taia no ken 太阿の剣【太阿劍】<Ch. Taia *jian* [Ch. var. Taia *jian* 泰阿的劍]. The "Sword of Taia." One of three ancient Chinese swords said to have been commissioned by Feng Huzi (Fūkoshi). The *Taia no ken* was so finely made that in later times it was referred to as the ideal sword, and became the benchmark to which all other swords were compared. See also: *Fūkoshi; Kōfu no ken; Ōyashi; Ryūen no ken; Taiaki.*

Taiaki 「太阿記」. A treatise on swordsmanship written to the swordsman Yagyū Munenori in the early 1600s by Rinzai Zen priest Takuan. Referring to Chinese history and the famously idealized Sword of Taia (*Taia no ken*), Takuan wrote this treatise essentially comparing the perfect swordsman to the *Taia no ken*. See also: *Fūkoshi; Kōfu no ken; Ōyashi; Ryūen no ken; Taia no ken; Takuan Sōhō.*

Further reading in English:

- Suzuki, (translation) 1958: 161, 166–168.
- Wilson, (translation) 2003.

tai atari 体当【躰當·體當】. Lit. "body striking," "body checking." 1. SHINDŌ MUSŌ RYŪ—A technique in which a medium-length staff (*jō*) is used to move the opponent's weapon above his head while using the fists to strike his body. This is the ninth of the twelve basic techniques (*kihon*) extrapolated from the classical forms of Shindō Musō Ryū by Shimizu Takaji. 2. JIKI SHINKAGE RYŪ—A body-checking technique taught in Hōjō (3).

taifu 大夫. A holder of the fifth or fourth court rank. This term means "gentleman" or "high steward." Warriors who had some official capacity or post with the court were usually accorded the (lower) sixth court rank and the status of "servant" (*samurai*). See also: *kuge; kugyō; samurai.*

taigun 大軍. A great army; a large military force.

tai hazushi uchi 体外打【躰外打·體外打】. Lit. "body evasion and strike." SHINDŌ MUSŌ RYŪ—A technique in which the body is used to evade the opponent's weapon while a medium-length staff (*jō*) is used to strike his weapon or body. This is the twelfth of the twelve basic techniques (*kihon*) extrapolated from the classical forms of Shindō Musō Ryū by Shimizu Takaji.

Taiheiki 『太平記』. A Japanese war tale (*gunkimono*) in forty volumes. It relates the events from 1318 to 1368, a turbulent time that saw the end of the Kamakura *bakufu* and the beginning of the Muromachi *bakufu.* The text is attributed to a Tendai monk from Mount Hiei named Kojima. See also other war tales: *Heike monogatari; Heiji monogatari; Hōgen monogatari; Shōmonki; Yoshitsune monogatari.*

Further reading in English:

- McCullough (translation), 1959.
- Varley, 1994: 159–213.

taihō 大砲 [A.k.a. ***ō-zutsu*** 大筒]. A cannon; a piece of artillery.

T

taihojutsu 逮捕術. A modern police arresting system dating from 1947. Its antecedents draw heavily on the classical Japanese martial systems (*koryū*), especially those dealing with arresting arts such as *hobakujutsu*. However, neither the severe techniques of the *koryū* nor the derivative spiritually focused systems of modern *budō* (e.g., *jūdō*, *kendō*, etc.) proved to be entirely suitable for modern police work. In 1924, a special committee was established to create a system of arresting procedures and techniques for the Japanese police. This system was closely aligned with classical martial techniques. After World War II, when Occupation forces placed a ban on martial arts, the Japanese again revised police techniques into a new system christened *taihojutsu*. A manual on the system entitled *Taihojutsu kihon kōzō* 『逮捕術基本構造』 was published in 1947 and has been revised several times since then.

Taihōjutsu is practiced in both unarmed fashion (*toshu*) and armed with a police baton (*keibō*). Training relies heavily on proper postures (*kamae*) and prearranged combative scenarios (*waza*). There are fourteen basic scenarios (*kihon waza*) and sixteen application scenarios (*ōyō waza*). Police trainees also practice six handcuffing techniques (*seijō*), search techniques (*soken*), and control methods for bringing a resisting detainee to his feet (*hikitate oyobi*).

Other non-firearm systems practiced by the police are:

Weapon	System
baton (*keibō*警棒)	*keibō sōhō* 警棒操法
telescoping baton (*tokushu keibō* 特殊警棒)	*tokushu keibō sōhō* 特殊警棒操法
medium-length staff (*keijō*警杖)	*keijōjutsu* 警杖術
restraining cord (*nawa*縄)	*hōjōjutsu* 捕縄術

See also: *hobaku; torite.*

Further reading in English:

• Draeger, 1974a: 70–72 ff.

Taihojutsu kihon kōzō 『逮捕術基本構造』. A manual on modern police arresting techniques. First published in 1947, it has been revised many times since. See: *taihojutsu.*

Taihō Ritsuryō 大宝律令 【大寶律令】. The Taihō Codes; a code of laws created in the first year of the Taihō era (701) and implemented the following year.These codes were responsible for the adoption of the Chinese military system, which influenced Japanese combative culture for several hundred years. Chinese-style conscription of soldiers into provincial military garrisons called *gundan* had begun with the Taika Reforms (Taika no Kaishin) in 645. However, the Taihō Ritsuryō refined and expanded this policy by reorganizing the *gundan* in a fashion similar to the Chinese military system. The codes themselves eventually proved unwieldy, almost bankrupting the central government, and were abandoned in 792.

An additional purpose of the adoption of a conscription military system had been to disarm the provincial warrior elite (*kuni no miyatsuko*). However, as several scholars have pointed out, the revolt of Fujiwara no Hirotsugu in 740—almost 100 years after the initiation of the Chinese conscript system—indicates that the local strongmen were still powerful and had not given up their weaponry. See: *gundan; Taika no Kaishin.*

Further reading in English:

• Tsunoda, de Bary, and Keene, 1958: 81–87 ff.

taijutsu 体術 【躰術; 體術】. Lit. "body techniques." A generic term for unarmored grappling and throwing techniques.

taikai 大会【大會】. A mass meeting; a convention. In a martial-arts context, a *taikai* usually denotes a major demonstration of classical martial arts (*koryū*) or modern martial/sportive/spiritual ways (*budō*), or a tournament held by practitioners of modern martial/spiritual/sportive disciplines.

Taika no Kaishin 大化改新. The Taika Reforms. First promulgated in 645, the Taika no Kaishin were political and military reforms predominantly based on Tang Chinese models. These reforms lasted until 701, when they were modified and/or replaced by the Taihō Codes (Taihō Ritsuryō), also based on Chinese models. The Taika Reforms revolutionized distribution and control of agricultural lands and established provincial military units called *gundan*.

Further reading in English:

- Tsunoda, de Bary, and Keene, 1958: 54–55, 70–90.

taiken 帯剣【帶劍】. The sword in one's sash (*obi*). ¶ *taiken suru* 帯剣する, to carry a sword in one's belt (*obi*).

taiko 太鼓. A large battle drum used for signaling. See: *shikigu*.

TAIKO
Signaling the beginning of a martial demonstration at the Budōkan in 1978
(Photograph by author)

taikō 太閤. A retired regent. *Taikō* was an imperial court title taken by an imperial regent (*kampaku*), if and when the title of regent was passed to his son. The best-known person to hold this title was Toyotomi Hideyoshi, when his adopted son Hidetsugu took the title of *kampaku* in 1592.

Taikō katanagari 太閤刀狩 [Also read ***Taikō no katanagari***]. See: *katanagari*.

Taikō rikutō 『太公六韜』 <Ch. *Tai Gong Liutao* (Tao Gong's six strategies) [A.k.a. ***Taikō rikutō gokan*** 『太公六韜五巻』<Ch. *Tai Gong Liutao Wu Juan* (Tai Gong's six strategies in five volumes)]. One of the seven Chinese classics on military strategy. See: *Rikutō*.

Taikō rikutō gokan 『太公六韜五巻』<Ch. *Tai Gong Liutao Wu Juan*]. See: *Rikutō; Taikō rikutō*.

taikoyaku 太鼓役. A *taiko* drummer.

taimitsu 台密【臺密】. The term *taimitsu* refers specifically to the Tantric (Esoteric) teachings (*mikkyō*) practiced within the Japanese Tendai Buddhist school (Tendai Shū). Contrast to *tōmitsu*.

Taira 平 (A.k.a. ***Heishi*** 平氏; ***Heike*** 平家). A warrior family descended from Prince Katsurahara Shinnō (786–853), son of Emperor Kammu.[3] A number of the Taira in the Kantō area became vassals of the Minamoto clan. Others in the family line, however, were not content to be subservient to the Minamoto and moved to the islands of Kyūshū and Shikoku. One branch which became known as the Ise Taira proliferated and extended into the area of Ise in the eleventh century, and from there extended their power base into Iga.

The Taira also extended their political connections with several successive retired emperors, namely Shirakawa, Toba, and Go-Shirakawa.[4] From the twelfth century they also developed their skills in naval warfare and seafaring.

In extending their power in central and western Japan, the Taira eventually came into conflict with the Minamoto (Seiwa Genji), who had developed a power base among the warriors in the east (Bandō *musha*). Their long struggle with the rival Minamoto family covers some of the most interesting periods of Japanese history. Many *bushi* families—such as the Chiba, Iizasa, and Yagyū—are descended from the Taira.

Further reading in English:

- Papinot, 1910: 617–625.
- Varley, 1994: 46–50 ff.

Taira no Korehira 平 維衡 (fl. eleventh century). The fourth son of *chinjufu shogun* Taira no Sadamori, Korehira was the progenitor of the Ise Taira. He moved into the area of Ise when he was appointed governor there in 1006. (Varley, 1994: 221, note 65).

Taira no Sadamori 平 貞盛 (fl. tenth century). Son of Taira Kunika. Sadamori joined forces with Fujiwara Hidesato in battling Taira no Masakado. They defeated Masakado in 940,

---

3 Kammu Tennō 桓武天皇 (737–806; r.781–806), fiftieth emperor of Japan.

4 Shirakawa Tennō 白河天皇 (1053–1129; r.1073–1129), seventy-second emperor of Japan; Toba Tennō 鳥羽天皇 (1103–1156; r.1107–1123), seventy-fourth emperor of Japan; Go-Shirakawa Tennō 後白河天皇 (1127–1192; r.1155–1158), seventy-seventh emperor of Japan.

and Sadamori was named *chinjufu shōgun*. Sadamori's son was Taira no Korehira 平維衡.

Taira Shinken 平 信賢 (1897–1970). A well-known *karate* and Ryūkyū *kobudō* practitioner who founded the Society for the Promotion and Preservation of the Classical Martial Arts of the Ryukyus[5] in 1955. Taira began training in *karate* with Funakoshi Gichin in Japan in 1922, and later trained with Mabuni Kenwa. He went on to train with Yabiku Mōden in Ryūkyū *kobudō*, and began to teach both disciplines in Okinawa around 1940. See: *Itosu Ryū karate*.

tairiku rōnin 大陸浪人. Lit. "continental *rōnin*." An adventurer; a soldier of fortune. The term *rōnin* was used during the Tokugawa period to refer to masterless samurai. Under the Tokugawa shogunate, if a lord was deposed his samurai retainers were cast adrift, becoming masterless. *Tairiku rōnin* is a post-Tokugawa term for Japanese adventurers who went to China, Korea, Manchuria, and Mongolia for whatever type of aggrandizement might be available. Some could be characterized as drifters and thugs, but a significant portion were men of samurai lineage (*shizoku*) who had found themselves without position or means of support after the Meiji government abolished the Tokugawa-period social classes. A number of these *shizoku* became members of ultra-rightist organizations. Two such groups, the Gen'yōsha and the Kokuryūkai, sent members to the Asian mainland as spies, sometimes in cooperation with the Japanese Imperial Army (Sabey, 1973: 105–106, note 12).

Several men who could be called *tairiku rōnin* also played a significant role in the twentieth-century martial-arts world in Japan: Uchida Ryōhei (Shindō Musō Ryū *jōjutsu*), Morihei Ueshiba (*aikidō*), Deguchi Onisaburō (Ōmoto Kyō), and Sō Dōshin (Nippon Shōrinji Kempō), among others.

taisabaki 体捌【躰捌; 體捌】. Lit. "body manipulation." A type of body movement/displacement in which the practitioner avoids an enemy's attack and places himself in a position to mobilize a counterattack.

taisei 隊正. TAIHŌ MILITARY SYSTEM—Commander of a fifty-man unit (*tai*) in the eighth-century provincial militia (*gundan*). The *taisei* was somewhat equivalent to a modern Army lieutenant who commands a platoon, and was under the command of a *rosochi* (captain). See: *gundan*.

Taiseigai Ryū 大星外流. A school of martial divination (*gumbai*) devised by Chikamatsu Hikonoshin Shigenori during the Kyōhō era (1716–1735). The school, according to Watatani and Yamada (1978: 516), was a derivative of an earlier system of martial divination (*gungaku*) known as the Hōjō Ryū 北条流.

Taisha Kage Ryū タイ捨陰流. See: *Taisha Ryū*.

Taishakuten 帝釈天【帝釋天】<Ch. Dishitian <Skt. Indra [A.k.a. ***Shaka Daiba Indara*** 釋迦提婆因陀羅 <Ch. Shijia Tipo Yintoluo <Skt. Śakra-devānām-indra]. The Hindu god Indra. Taishakuten (Indra) commands the Four Heavenly Guardians (Shitennō). Taishakuten is also one of a group of twelve guardian deities adopted from Brahmanism by Buddhism. See: *Jūniten*.

Taisha Ryū タイ捨流 [Var. ***Shinkage Taisha Ryū*** 新陰タイ捨流; ***Taisha Kage Ryū*** タイ捨陰流; ***Taisha Shinkage Ryū*** タイ捨新陰流]. A variety of characters have been used for the term *taisha* over the years; e.g., 大捨, 体捨【躰捨; 體捨】, 体棄【躰棄; 體棄】, 待捨, etc.]. Founded by Marume Kurandonosuke Tessai (c. 1567), the Taisha Ryū was one of the more influential traditions derived from Kamiizumi's Shinkage Ryū (1) 新陰流.

Combative arts training in the Taisha Ryū has traditionally included swordsmanship (*kenjutsu*), spear arts (*sōjutsu*), long-hafted glaive arts (*naginatajutsu*), quick-draw sword arts (*iaijutsu*), and the combative art of small throwing blades and darts (*shurikenjutsu*). This tradition is still practiced today in Kumamoto prefecture in Kyūshū. The current headmaster is Yamakita Takenori. See: *Marume Kurandonosuke Tessai*.

Taisha Ryū Kenpō タイ捨流剣法. See: *Oda Taisha Ryū*.

5 Ryūkyū Kobudō Hozon Shinkōkai 琉球古武道保存振興会.

Taisha Ryū
タイ捨流
(abbreviated lineage and derivatives)

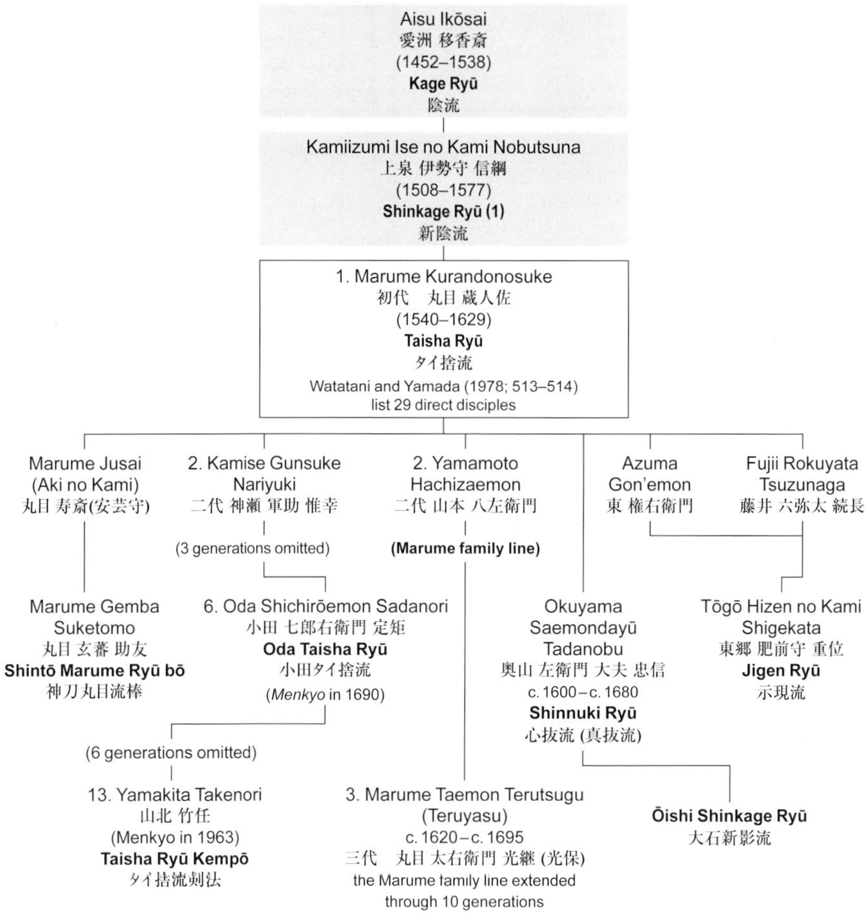

Taishiden Yasumitsu Ryū 太子伝安光流【太子傳安光流】. See: *Yasumitsu Ryū.*

Taishi Ryū 太子流. See: *Shōtoku Taishi Ryū.*

Taishi ryū shingun shimpi no maki 『太子流神軍神秘巻』. One of several transmission scrolls (*densho*) which preserve the martial strategies of the Shingun Ryū and the Taishi Ryū. The text has been published in Ishioka and Arima, 1967 (Vol. 6): 383–406.

taishōgun 大将軍【大將軍】. TAIHŌ MILITARY SYSTEM—A title given to the commander of three combined army corps (*gun*) under the eighth-century Chinese-style military system defined in the Taihō Codes (Taihō Ritsuryō). As a commander of 1800+ men, the *taishōgun* was somewhat equivalent to an early twentieth-century army senior colonel or a brigadier general commanding a brigade. See: *gundan; seii taishōgun; shōgun.*

taisuisō 袋穗槍 [Also read **_taisui yari_**]. See: *fukuro yari.*

taisui yari 袋穗槍 [Also read **_taisuisō_**]. See: *fukuro yari.*

taitō 帯刀. The sword in one's belt (*obi*). ¶ *taitō suru* 帯刀する, to carry a sword in one's belt (*obi*). See also: *taiken.*

Taizōkai Mandara 胎蔵界曼荼羅 【胎藏界曼荼羅】 <Ch. Taicangjie Mantuluo <Skt. Garbhadhātu-maṇḍāla. BUDDHISM—The Womb Matrix (mandala). The Taizōkai is one of the two great mandala which are the central ritual focus of the Japanese Tendai and Shingon Tantric Buddhist schools. The Taizōkai, which represents the material world, is filled with a pantheon of buddhas, *bodhisattvas*, *devas*, and other beings. The mandala and its ritual text are based on the *Dainichi-kyō*, a major Tantric Buddhist text; its ritual is an integral part of the training series all Tendai and Shingon monks must master. Many of the Buddhist deities which became popular in Japanese culture are found in the Taizōkai. See also: *Shido kegyō; Kongōkai Mandara; Taizōkai shiki.*

TAIZŌKAI MANDARA
Heian-period painting (c. 1000 CE) in the Tōji temple (Shingon sect) in Kyōto

CENTER DETAIL OF THE *TAIZŌKAI MANDARA*
(Collection of the Tōji temple [Shingon sect] in Kyōto)

Taizōkai shiki 『胎蔵界私記』. BUDDHISM—A text composed in Japan which contains directions for performing the ritual associated with the *Taizōkai Mandara*. It is one of four basic exoteric/tantric rituals (*Shido kegyō*) that must be mastered by members of the Tendai and Shingon schools of Japanese Buddhism. The text was originally derived from ritual instructions included in the *Dainichikyō* and associated Chinese manuals. Several variations are found in both the Tendai and Shingon schools. See also: *Dainichi-kyō; Jūhachidō shiki; Kongōkai shiki; Shido kegyō; Taizōkai mandara.*

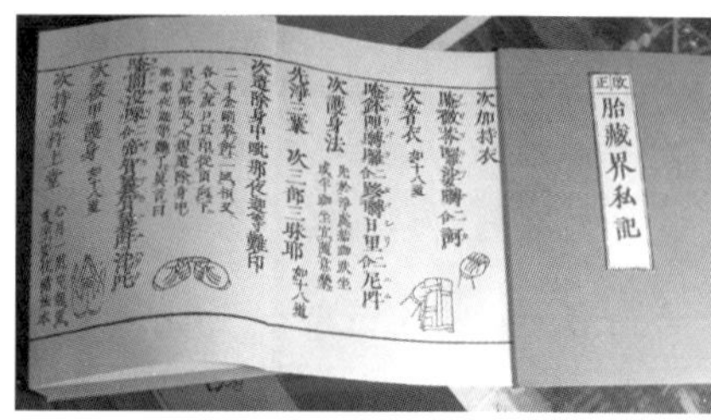

TAIZŌKAI SHIKI
Ritual formula text for use with the *Taizōkai Mandara*
(Private collection)

taka 鷹. A falcon; a hawk.

Takada Matabei Yoshitsugu 高田 又兵衛 吉次 (fl. mid-1500s–early 1600s). A student of Kakuzenbō Hōzōin Inei, as well as of Inei's direct disciple Nakamura Naomasa. Takada founded his own branch line of spearmanship (*sōjutsu*) called the Hōzōin Ryū Takada Ha around 1610. See also: *Hōzōin Ryū.*

takagari 鷹狩. Falconry. According to the *Nihon shoki*,[6] this practice was introduced from Korea during the fourth-century reign of Emperor Nintoku[7]. Over the centuries, the practice of *takagari* was viewed as a status symbol; it was occasionally used by land owners to resolve disputes over property. See also: *heō; washi (1).*

---

6 *Nihon shoki* 『日本書紀』, 720 C.E.

7 Nintoku Tennō 仁徳天皇 (c.313–c.399 C.E.), legendary sixteenth emperor of Japan. His actual dates are unknown.

Takagi Ryū 高木流 [A.k.a. ***Hontai Takagi Ryū*** 本体高木流; ***Takagi Ryū Jūjutsu*** 高木流柔術; ***Takagi Yōshin Ryū*** 高木揚心流]. A comprehensive martial system (*sōgō bujutsu*) which traces its origins to the Buddhist monk Unryū, c.1570. Unryū, one of those enigmatic figures of legend, was said to have been an expert at concealed weapons arts such as small throwing blades and darts (*shurikenjutsu*), grappling arts (*taijutsu*), and the long hardwood staff (*bōjutsu*). He referred to his system as Rinpō Hiden 麟鳳秘伝 ("Secret transmission of the *kirin* and the *hōō*"). The actual formulation and naming of the Takagi Ryū was accomplished in 1645 by a samurai named Takagi Oriemon Shigetoshi. The original school concentrated on grappling (*jūjutsu*), and also covered a variety of weapons systems: staff arts (*bōjutsu*), including a three-section linked staff (*rensa sankaku bō*); spear arts (*sōjutsu*); long-hafted glaive techniques (*naginatajutsu*); and *teppan tōjutsu*, a system using a type of *shaken* (round *shuriken*).

Takagi Ryū
高木流
(abbreviated lineage)

Sō Unryū
僧 雲竜
Rinpō Hiden
(麟鳳秘伝)

Itō Kiinokami Suketada
伊東 紀伊守 佐忠
Itō Ryū · Kenkō Ryū
伊東流·建孝流

1. Takagi Oriemon Shigetoshi
初代　高木 折右衛門 重俊
(c. 1625–1711)
Takagi Ryū
高木流

2. Takage Umanosuke Shigesada
二代　高木 馬之輔 重貞
(c.1655–c.1746)

3. Takagi Gennoshin Hideshige
三代　高木 源之進 英重

3. Fujii Shōbei Shigeji
三代 藤井 庄兵衛
(勝兵衛) 重次
(Fujii family line)

3. Kagawa Rokurōzaemon Masashige
香川 六郎左衛門 正重

Takagi Ryū Jūjutsu 高木流柔術. See: *Takagi Ryū.*

Takagi Yōshin Ryū 高木揚心流. See: *Takagi Ryū.*

Takahashi Danjōzaemon Shigeharu 高橋弾正左衛門 重治【高橋彈正左衛門重治】(1610–1690). Recognized as sixth headmaster by the Jiki Shinkage Ryū 直心影流. Takahashi began training in Kamiya Denshinsai's Shinkage Jikishin Ryū 新陰直心流 along with his master Abe Shirōgorō, who was a retainer of the Tokugawa shogunate. In order to distinguish his authentic line from those of many Shinkage Ryū variants and imitators, Takahashi renamed it Jikishin Seitōichi Ryū 直心正統一流 (the "One True Lineage of the Jikishin Ryū"). His lineal successor was Yamada Heizaemon Mitsunori (Ippūsai). See also: *Jiki Shinkage Ryū.*

Takahashi Deishū 高橋 泥舟 [A.k.a. ***Ise no Kami Masaaki*** 伊勢守政晃; nickname ***Shitamō*** 寛猛 (lit. "composed ferocity"); ***Kenzaburō*** 謙三郎; ***Seiichirō*** 精一郎] (1835–1903). One of the "Bakumatsu no Sanshū," three prominent swordsmen/statesmen of the Bakumatsu whose names all ended with the character "*shū*." Deishū was also the brother-in-law of swordsman Yamaoka Tesshū.

Born into the Yamaoka clan, he studied Jinshin Ryū 刃心流 spearmanship under his maternal grandfather, Takahashi Gizaemon 高橋義左衛門. Jishin Ryū was a martial school specializing in spearmanship (*sōjutsu*), swordsmanship (*kenjutsu*) and long hafted glave arts (*naginatajutsu*). Deishū was adopted at the time of his marriage and changed his surname to that of his wife's family, Takahashi. He then became a spearmanship instructor at the government's martial training school, the Kōbusho, and founded his own school of "pipe spear" (*kudayari*) known as the Jitokuin Ryū 自得院流. Deishū taught spearmanship to the last Tokugawa *shōgun*, Yoshinobu,[8] and at Yoshinobu's request demonstrated his skills in a match with Sakakibara Kenkichi of the Jiki Shinkage Ryū in 1860.

Due to his positions as instructor in the Kōbusho and confidant to Tokugawa Yoshi-

8 Tokugawa Yoshinobu 徳川慶喜 (1837–1913; r.1866–1867), fifteenth Tokugawa *shōgun.*

nobu, Deishū became an important political figure in the last days of the Tokugawa shogunate. In 1868 he followed Tokugawa Yoshinobu into retirement, and spent most of his remaining years composing poetry and brushing calligraphy. He is considered to be the best calligrapher of the Bakumatsu no Sanshū.

Takahashi Ryū 高橋流. A branch tradition of Seigō Ryū / Zuishin Ryū system of combative swordsmanship (*kenjutsu*) and grappling arts (*jūjutsu*). It was founded by Takahashi Zuietsu Shoshi. For lineage, see: *Zuishin Ryū*.

Takahashi Zuietsu Shoshi 高橋 随悦 諸氏. Founded the Takashi Ryū sometime during the mid to late seventeenth century. For lineage chart, see: *Zuishin Ryū*.

taka hassō 高撥草. Lit. "high/raised *hassō* posture." YAGYŪ SHINKAGE RYŪ—An upper-level (*jōdan*) sword posture (*kurai*) in which the sword is held to the right of the head with the hilt (*tsuka*) at face level or higher. Often abbreviated as *hassō*. Some contemporary Yagyū Shinkage Ryū lines do not append the term *taka*.

TAKA HASSŌ
Yagyū Shinkage Ryū *taka hassō* demonstrated by Ikenaga Kōichirō, Meiji Jingū, 1981
(Photograph by author)

Takaki Ryū 高木流. See: *Takagi Ryū*.

Takamagahara 高天原 (Also read ***Taka Ama Hara; Taka no Amahara; Takama no Hara; Takama-ga-hara***). Takamagahara literally means "high heavenly plane." According to Japanese mythology, this is the dwelling place of the Shintō *kami*. In various Shintō rituals, such as clapping hands before a shrine, the *kami* are invited to leave Takamagahara and enter the shrine. They are thought to make this journey by crossing the heavenly floating bridge called Ama no Ukihashi 天浮橋.

Takamatsu Toshitsugu 高松 寿嗣 (1887–1972). Martial artist who popularized the Kuki Shin Ryū 九鬼神流 (a comprehensive combative system) and the Togakure Ryū 戸隠流 (primarily a school of espionage) in the 1930s by opening them up to the public. His best-known students were Hatsumi Masaaki, founder of the Bujinkan; and Kiba Kōshirō, who published a book entitled *Kuki Shin Ryū bujutsu*『九鬼神流武術』in the 1930s.

Takanao Ryū 貫直流. A comprehensive school of martial arts (*sōgō bujutsu*) encompassing military strategy (*gungaku*), combative swordsmanship (*kenjutsu*), long-hafted glaive arts (*naginatajutsu*), and long hardwood staff (*bōjutsu*). The system was founded by Inagaki Jūrōbei Takanao, a warrior from Kii. Inagaki spread the system in the domains of Bishū and Toyooka.

Takano Kurōzaemon Yasunaga 高野 九郎左衛門 安長. Founded the Yō Ryū 陽流, a school of combative musketry (*hōjutsu*), in the late sixteenth century.

Takano Sasaburō 高野 佐三郎 (1862–1950). A sword master of the Ono Ha Ittō Ryū 小野派一刀流 and *kendō* practitioner with the rank of *hanshi* (master swordsman) who played a significant role in the development of modern *kendō*. Takano was considered one of the top three competitors in *gekken* (a form of dueling with protective gear and bamboo swords) of the Meiji era (1868–1912); during the Taishō and early Shōwa eras (1912–1989), he was considered the foremost practitioner of *kendō* in Japan.

In 1867, Takano began receiving instruction in the classical swordsmanship (*kenjutsu*) of the Nakanishi Ha Ittō Ryū 中西派一刀流 from his grandfather, Takano Sakichirō, at the age of five. In 1879, Takano began training with master swordsman Yamaoka Tesshū. Tesshū had studied the Jiki Shinkage Ryū 直心影流 and two lines of the Ittō Ryū: Ono Ha Ittō Ryū and Nakanishi Ha Ittō Ryū. At the time Takano entered his training hall, Tesshū was creating his own school, the Ittō Shōden Mutō Ryū 一刀正伝無刀流, from this experience. Consequently, Takano was in the vanguard of the severe training regimen Tesshū was developing. Sixteen years later, in 1886, Takano was appointed as a *gekken* instructor at the Honjo police station in Tōkyō. Around 1888 he moved to Saitama to instruct the police there, and opened a training hall (*dōjō*) he called the Meishinkan 明信館. By 1896 Takano had become the chief martial arts (*bujutsu*) instructor of the Saitama police, and continued to promote *kendō*, establishing the Tōkyō Meishinkan in the Kudanshita area in 1899. Anecdotal information indicates he was involved in the teaching of around 10,000 trainees in over forty training halls at that time. By 1907 Takano had begun working with *kendō* clubs at a number of universities in the Kantō area; he became one of the key members selected by the Dai Nippon Butokukai to establish a formal set of training forms known as Dai Nippon Teikoku Kendō Kata in 1912. In 1913, he was awarded the title of "master swordsman" (*hanshi*).

Takasaka Kagetsuna 高坂 景綱. Practitioner of the Musashi Emmei Ryū 武蔵円明流, a school of combative swordsmanship (*kenjutsu*) and grappling (*taijutsu*). Takasaka instructed Ōno Matabei Ikkan in the *kenjutsu* of this tradition before Ōno created Ikkan Ryū (2) 一貫流 in 1785.

Takashima Ryū 高島流 [A.k.a. ***Seiyō Ryū*** 西洋流; ***Shindo Seiyō Ryū*** 新渡西洋流; ***Ien Ryū*** 威遠流; ***Ranshiki*** 蘭式]. A school of Western gunnery and drill (*gumpō chōren*) founded by Takashima Shūan in the 1830s. See: *Takashima Shūhan.*

Takashima Shūhan 高島 秋帆 [A.k.a. ***Takashima Shirōdayū Shūhan*** 高島四郎太夫秋帆; ***Shigeatsu*** 子厚; ***Shigeatsu*** 茂敦; ***Shunshin*** 舜臣; ***Yoshihira*** 喜平] (1798–1866). Founder of the Seiyō Ryū 西洋流 (lit. "Western School"), a martial system that focused on Western gunnery.

Born in Nagasaki, Takashima had inherited the position of town councilor (*machidoshiyori* 町年寄)[9] from his father, who was also his first gunnery teacher. With the approval of the Tokugawa shogunate and the use of his own funds, Takashima imported a variety of firearms from Holland—everything from small arms to field guns. Then, with the assistance of the Dutch in Deshima, he became an expert in the operation, maintenance, and use of those weapons. He also studied intently with Reserve Colonel Jan Willem de Sturler, who was stationed in Deshima by the Dutch during the years 1823–1827. De Sturler taught him the intricacies of the weapons and tactics that had been used in Europe during the Napoleonic Wars.

From this knowledge Takashima developed a system of gunnery exercises and infantry drill he christened *gumpō chōren*. He demonstrated this system to the Tokugawa shogunate at Tokumarugahara (a parade ground in Edo) in 1841. This was well received, and Takashima subsequently taught his system to many of the feudal lords (*daimyō*). However, when anti-Western factions at the *shōgun*'s court made accusations against him, he was recalled to Edo and imprisoned in 1842. He remained in disgrace and incarcerated until 1853, at which time he was pardoned.

Further reading in English:

- Goodman, 2000. 155.

Takashima Tarōzaemon Nagamasa 高島太郎左衛門 長正. A direct disciple of Kamiizumi Ise no Kami in the Shinkage Ryū 新陰流. Takashima founded a branch tradition of that school in the late 1500s.

Takeda 武田. A warrior family descended from Minamoto Yoshimitsu (1156–1127) via Yoshimitsu's son, Minamoto Yoshikiyo, and grandson, Minamoto Kiyomitsu. See: *Seiwa Genji.*

Takeda heihō 『武田兵法』. See: *Genji no heihō.*

Takeda Motsugai 武田 物外 (1794–1867).

[9] The *machidoshiyori* evidently ranked under the *machibugyō*, but had more direct control over local administration and commerce on a day-to-day basis.

T

Founder of the Fusen Ryū 不遷流 who was a ninth-generation descendant of the famous Warring States warlord Takeda Shingen. In 1830, when he was about thirty-five years old, Motsugai became the chief priest (*jūshoku*) of a Buddhist temple known as Zaihōji 済法寺 in the town of Onomichi in Bingo (present-day eastern Hiroshima).

An accomplished martial artist, Motsugai was intimately familiar with several contemporary schools, including Ippo Ryū 一甫流 *jūjutsu*, Ōtsubo Ryū 大坪流 horsemanship (*bajutsu*), Hōzōin Ryū 宝蔵院流 spearmanship (*sōjutsu*), Yamada Ryū 山田流 sickle-and-chain arts (*kusarigama-jutsu*), and others. He was a powerful man known for his ability in a pugilistic art known as *genkotsu oshō* (Buddhist-priest fist). His own system was referred to as Motsugai Ryū 物外流, but his *jūjutsu* was called Fusen Ryū 不遷流. After his death in 1867, he was buried at Zenrinji temple in Ōsaka. See: *Fusen Ryū; Motsugai Ryū.*

Takeda Nobumitsu 武田 信光 (1152–1248). Attributed with the founding of Takeda Ryu (1), a school of mounted archery, ancient customs, and etiquette (*kyūba kojitsu*).

Takeda Ryū 武田流. Several different martial arts schools in Japan have gone by the name "Takeda Ryū." Watatani and Yamada (1978: 533–536) list eighteen known to have existed. These schools cover diverse curricula, including gunnery and explosives (*kajutsu, hōjutsu*); the combined arts of mounted archery, ancient customs and warrior etiquette (*kyūba kojitsu*); ritual archery (*meigen*); military strategy and tactics (*gumpō, gunkai, gunra*, etc.); combative horsemanship (*gumba*); grappling (*jūjutsu, aikijūjutsu*, etc.); combative stick/short-staff arts (*jōjutsu*); iron fan techniques (*tessenjutsu*); bugling with a conch shell (*gunra*); combative swimming (*suieijutsu*); espionage (*shinobi no jutsu*); swordsmanship (*kenjutsu*); spear (*sōjutsu*); signaling with large war drums (*jindaiko*); the art of throwing or utilizing small blades or darts (*shurikenjutsu*); techniques for using rockets and fireworks for signaling (*gunyō enka*); and others.

Takeda Ryū 1. 武田流 [A.k.a. ***Takeda Ryū Kisha Yabusame*** –騎射流鏑馬]. A medieval-period school founded by Takeda Nobumitsu which concentrated on mounted archery and ancient customs and rules for archers (*kyūba kojitsu*). Nobumitsu is said to have been highly skilled in the "three equestrian archery contests" (*san kisha*) of the medieval period: dog hunting (*inu ou mono*), hat shooting (*kasa kake*), and mounted target shooting (*yabusame*). For this reason, he is numbered among the "Big Four" (Shitennō) champion archers of the middle ages, along with contemporaries Ogasawara Nagakiyo, Unno Yukiuji 海野幸氏, and Mochizuki Shigetaka 望月重隆. Various classical sources attribute the formal rules for archers transmitted in the Henmi Ryū 逸見流, along with the archery techniques of Heki Ryū, 日置流 to the Takeda Ryu (1).

Takeda Ryū 2. 武田流. An alternate name for the Daitō Ryū.

TAKEDA RYŪ (3) *JINGAIJUTSU*
Kashima Jingū, 1980
(Photograph by author)

Takeda Ryū 3. 武田流. A school of military strategy and tactics (*gunkai*) and military signaling with the conch shell (*jingaijutsu*) founded in 1665 by Ushiwatashi Hachirōemon. The school exists today under the leadership of twentieth headmaster Sugano Taketomi.

Takeda Ryū aikijūjutsu 武田流合気柔術. DAITŌ RYŪ—Daitō Ryū grappling techniques derived from *oshikiuchi*.

Takeda Ryū jūjutsu 武田流柔術. DAITŌ RYŪ—Daitō Ryū combative grappling techniques derived from earlier Takeda-clan *jūjutsu.*

Takeda Ryū Kisha Yabusame 武田流騎射流鏑馬. See: *Takeda Ryū (1).*

Takeda Shingen 武田 信玄 (1521–1573). A warlord (Sengoku Daimyō) of Kai province who was one of the preeminent contenders for unifying Japan during the late Warring States period. At the age of twenty, Shingen deposed his father in order to prevent him from making Shingen's younger brother the family heir. Shortly after unifying Kai, Shingen faced his greatest rival, Uesugi Kenshin of Echigo. The two were closely matched in military power and cunning, and contended with each other for over twenty-five years, but neither was able to gain sufficient advantage over the other. In 1573 Shingen was apparently wounded by a musket ball and died soon after. (Kurosawa Akira presented a fanciful depiction of these events in his 1980 film *Kage Musha.*)

Takeda Sōkaku 武田 惣角 (1859–1943) [A.k.a. ***Takeda Sōkaku Minamoto no Masayoshi*** 武田 惣角 源正義]. Founder of Daitō Ryū *jūjutsu* and *aikijūjutsu.* Takeda was skilled in the Ono Ha Ittō Ryū, having received *menkyo* from Shibuya Tōma in 1876 (Watatani and Yamada, 1978: 505); as well as the Jiki Shinkage Ryū, in which he served as *uchideshi* to Sakakibara Kenkichi in 1873 (Watatani and Yamada, 1978: 505). He was a well-known swordsman of the late 1800s who excelled at *gekken* in public matches in which the opponents wielded *fukuro shinai.* Though of small stature—he was only about 5 feet (1.5 m) tall—his prowess as a combatant was proven so many times over the years that he was nicknamed Aizu Kotengu 会津小天狗 ("Little Mountain Demon from Aizu"). Stanley Pranin (1996: 15) relates one incident that occurred in 1875 while Takeda was traveling. Takeda was about to cross a bridge at twilight when he was set upon by several brigands. In order to escape an attack from both sides, he cut off the legs of four or five attackers before jumping into the river. Evidently he had wandered into a turf battle between two local gangs.

According to Watatani and Yamada (1978: 505), Takeda received a *menkyo* in *aikijūjutsu* from Saigō Chikanori on 20 May 1898, thereafter founding a branch of Daitō Ryū which included spearmanship (*sōjutsu*), dual sword techniques (*nitō ryū*), long hardwood staff techniques (*bōjutsu*), and small throwing blades and darts (*shurikenjutsu*), in addition to *aikijūjutsu.* Takeda had many disciples, and his school and its offshoots are known by a variety of names, such as Daitō Ryū, Takeda Ryū, and Sōkaku Ryū. He had many excellent students who started their own lines of *aikijūjutsu.* His most famous student was, of course, Ueshiba Morihei, who subsequently created *aikidō* and founded the Aikikai. Most of Sōkaku's top students received a teaching license known as Daitō Ryū Kyōju Dairi, but later in his life he awarded two "full licenses" (Daitō Ryū *menkyo kaiden*). One of these was to Hisa Takuma, who subsequently founded Nipponden Aikijūjutsu.

Further reading in English:

- Draeger, 1974, passim.
- Pranin, 1996: 35–39 ff.

Takeda Tokimune 武田 時宗 (1916–1993). Succeeded his father Takeda Sōkaku, becoming the second headmaster of Sōkaku's line of Daitō Ryū. Tokimune founded the Daitōkan Dōjō in Abashiri, Hokkaido, in 1953, and reorganized the many techniques passed down from his father. In addition, he further incorporated certain aspects of Ono Ha Ittō Ryū 小野派一刀流 *kenjutsu* into the system, evolving it into what he termed Daitō Ryū *aikibudō.* He also instituted a *kyūdan* ranking system which supplemented the classical *mokuroku-menkyo* system. Tokimune named Kondo Katsuyuki his successor in 1988 with the presentation of a unique license: Daitō Ryū Sōke Dairi.

Further reading in English:

- Pranin, 1996: 40–77.

take gusoku 竹具足. Light armor made of bamboo slats. *Take gusoku,* which dates from the mid-Edo period, was the antecedent of modern *kendō* armor. For illustration, see: *Kotoda Ha Ittō Ryū sōjutsu.*

T

take hoko 竹矛【竹鉾】[A.k.a. ***take yari***]. A bamboo spear. See: *take yari.*

Takemikazuchi no Kami 建御雷神. SHINTŌ—A variant name for the main Shintō deity enshrined at Kashima Jingū. See: *Takemikazuchi no Mikoto.*

Takemikazuchi no Mikoto 武甕槌命 [Var. 武甕槌大神; ***Takemikazuchi no Kami*** 武甕槌神 (var. 建御雷神); ***Kashima Ōkami*** 鹿島大神 (Also read ***Kashima Daijin***)]. SHINTŌ—The main *kami* enshrined at Kashima Jingū in Ibaraki Prefecture. Takemikazuchi no Mikoto is a deity of the bow. According to Japanese mythology, Takemikazuchi was one of two warrior deities called upon by the sun goddess, Amaterasu Ōmikami, to subdue a number of trouble-causing spirits (*kami*) and thus pacify the earth.

Takemikazuchi has been a tutelary deity of the Fujiwara regents, an avatar of several Buddhist divinities, and one of many patron deities of warriors and warrior arts. Furthermore, the most secret teachings of combative tactics and strategy (*heihō*) passed to warriors such as Tsukahara Bokuden (Kashima Shintō Ryū 鹿島新当流), Matsumoto Bizen no Kami (Kashima Shin Ryū 鹿島神流), Yamada Heizaemon Mitsunori (Jiki Shinkage Ryū 直心影流), and others, are attributed to the warrior *kami* Takemikazuchi. See also: *Futsunushi no Ōkami.*

Takemikazuchi no Ōkami 武甕槌主大神. See: *Takemikazuchi no Mikoto.*

Takemusu Aiki Budō 武産合気武道【武産合氣武道】. One of the early terms (c.1944) used by Ueshiba Morihei for the grappling system he modified from Daitō Ryū *aikijūjutsu* into *aikidō*. According to Pranin (1992: 11), this term refers to *aikidō*'s "highest level of mastery"; it was developed by Ueshiba during his Iwama years (c.1942–c.1954).

Takenouchi Hisamori 竹内 久盛 (1469–1535) [A.k.a. ***Takenouchi Nakatsukasa Dayū Hisamori*** 竹内 中務 大夫 久盛]. Founded the Takenouchi Ryū in 1532. Watatani Kiyoshi notes that Takenouchi was known for his primary weapon—an extremely long *ōdachi*—partly because of his height. Although he had great martial prowess, he was short in stature; his colleagues referred to him as "a long sword walking along with a short man attached" (Watatani: 1974: 5).

Takenouchi became aware that that the long *ōdachi* was at a disadvantage in the rough terrain and dense undergrowth in the area surrounding his castle. Consequently he began developing techniques that made use of a shorter sword, the *kodachi*, and a length of rope he wound around his hips. He called this small-weapon grappling system *koshi no mawari* which literally means "around the hips." Successive headmasters elaborated on this system, creating a number of related fighting arts.

Further reading in English:

- Watatani (March 1974): 4–6.

Takenouchi Ryū 竹内流 [Var. ***Takenouchi Ryū Jūjutsu/Torite; Koshi no Mawari*** —柔術・捕手・腰廻]. A comprehensive field-combat system (*sōgo bujutsu*) founded around 1532 by Takenouchi Hisamori, a landowner and warrior of Mimasaku (present-day Okayama prefecture). The Takenouchi Ryū is a very aggressive system which emphasizes taking the initiative and closing with the enemy.

A line of successive headmasters developed a number of small-weapon and empty-handed grappling arts from *koshi no mawari*, a fight-

TAKENOUCHI RYŪ
Eleventh headmaster Takenouchi Tōichirō shows the use of the *kodachi* in *koshi no mawari*
(© Martial Arts International, March 1974), used with permission.

Takenouchi Ryū
竹内流
(abbreviated lineage)

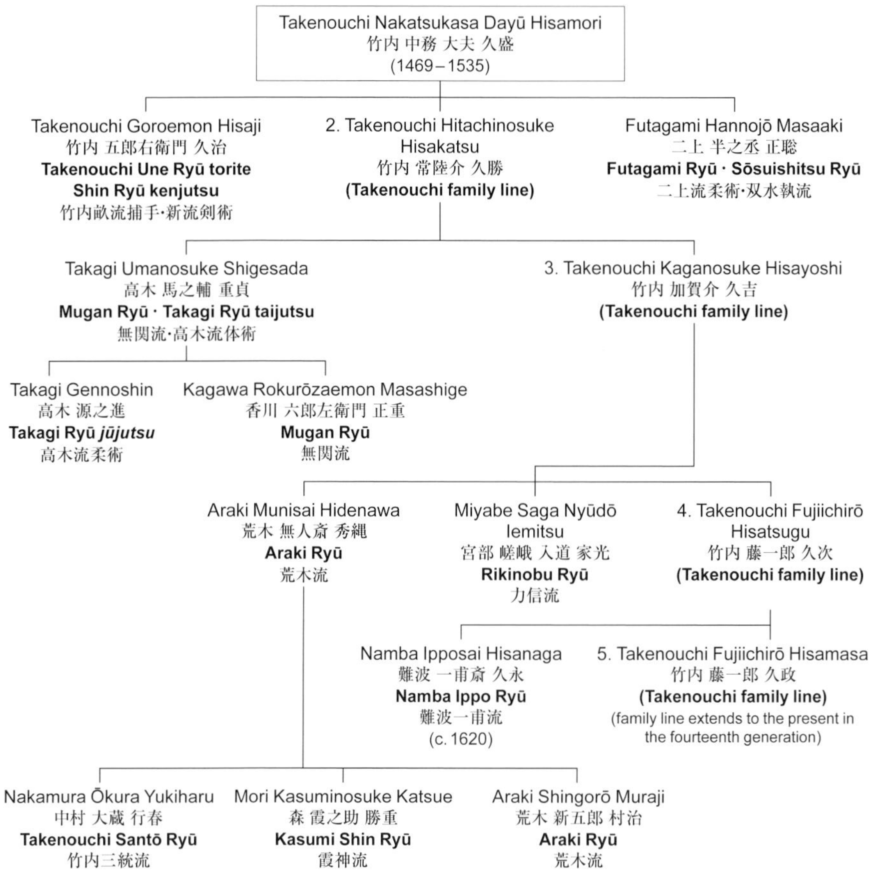

ing art developed by Takenouchi Hisamori. Early in the tradition's history, these included *yawara* (a form of unarmored combat), *torite* (arresting techniques using small weapons and a rope), *kogusoku* (minimally armed grappling in light armor), and *kempō* (2) (a striking art in which fists, elbows, knees, etc. are used to strike vital points on the enemy's body). The Takenouchi family also retained earlier field-combat arts,including *bōjutsu* (long hardwood staff techniques), *jōjutsu* (medium-length hardwood staff techniques), *iaijutsu* (quick-draw sword arts), *naginata-jutsu* (combative glaive arts), *tanken* (short sword combat), and others.

The Takenouchi Ryū was extremely important in the wide development of *jūjutsu* in later years. In fact, Watatani Kiyoshi includes it as one of the "Big Four" schools which, because of their technical acumen and wide base of practitioners, most influenced Japanese *jūjutsu*. The other three are Kitō Ryū, Sekiguchi Ryū, and Seigō Ryū.

Further reading in English:

- Mol, 2001, pp. 99–121.
- Watatani (March 1974). 4–6.

Takeshita Taizō 竹下 大造. See: *Shinkage Ryū (5).*

take yari 竹槍 [A.k.a. ***take hoko*** 竹矛【竹鉾】]. A bamboo spear. The *take yari* is a simple rod of bamboo with one end cut off at a sharp angle; the sharp end may be hardened over a fire. The *take yari* was an inexpensive weapon for spearmen, could be used as a substitute for broken weapons.

takezutsu hajikidama 竹筒弾き玉. A bamboo tube used as a pellet-throwing weapon. It consists of a hollow bamboo tube around 8 inches (20 cm) long which was used to throw a variety of pellets. As the projectile was powered by the throwing arm of the user, it was not a very powerful weapon. Osano (2007: 39) suggests it was used in police/civilian situations to distract or confuse a perpetrator while some other weapons system—sword, arresting rope, etc.—was brought into play.

takiguchi 滝口【瀧口】. An eleventh-century term for a palace guard.

Takino Yūken 滝野 遊軒【瀧野遊軒】[A.k.a. ***Takino Sen'emon Sadataka Yūken*** 滝野 専右衛門 貞高 遊軒] (c.1670–c.1740). A warrior from Matsue domain (present-day Shimane prefecture) who founded the Jikishin Ryū (3) 直心流, a school specializing in combative spear arts (*sōjutsu*). Takino, a well-known warrior in his time, was also the inheritor of Kitō Midare Ryū 起倒乱流 *jūjutsu* from Hotta Sagoemon Yoriyasu.

takkei 磔刑. See: *Haritsuke kei.*

Takuan Sōhō 沢庵宗彭【澤庵宗彭】[A.k.a. ***Takuan Zenji*** –禅師【禪師】(Zen-master Takuan); ***Takuan Oshō*** –和尚 (Buddhist-priest Takuan)] (1573–1645). Famous Rinzai Zen monk who greatly influenced the Edo Yagyū Shinkage Ryū under Yagyū Munenori. Takuan wrote three essays addressing the warrior, two of which were on swordsmanship and strategy: the *Taiaki*『太阿記』(Annals of the Sword of Taia) and the *Fudōchi shinmyōroku*『不動智神妙録』(Record of the miraculous wisdom of imperturbability). The third, entitled the *Reirōshū*『玲瓏集』(Collected sounds of jewels), deals more with the basic question of what it is to be human, desire, life itself, and right-mindedness.

A prolific writer, Takuan was also well known for his sharp wit and artistic abilities (particularly in painting and calligraphy). He began Rinzai Zen training at age fourteen, and by the age of thirty-seven had become abbot of Daitokuji in Kyōto. In 1629, at age fifty-six, he was banished to Kaminoyama by Hidetada, the second Tokugawa *shōgun*,[10] but later returned to Edo under a general amnesty to be a close advisor to the third Tokugawa *shōgun*, Iemitsu.[11] Takuan had a long relationship with Yagyū Munenori, who was Iemitsu's swordsmanship instructor, and proved an important influence in Munenori's life.

Although the story is not supported by documentation, Takuan is credited with the creation of the yellow-brown, brine-pickled Japanese radish that bears his name. He supposedly developed *takuan* so that warriors could carry it as part of their rations on long journeys. See also: *Miyamoto Musashi; Kamakura Zen; Yagyū Munenori.*

Further reading in English:

- Suzuki, 1958: passim.
- Wilson (trans.), 2003.

Takuma Kai 琢磨会. A group of Daitō Ryū schools formed in 1975 around the teachings of Hisa Takuma.

tama 1. 魂. See: *tamashii.*

tama 2. 玉. a. A jewel. b. A bullet. c. A weight.

tamagusari 玉鎖【玉鏁】. An alternate, generic term for the weighted-chain weapon (*manrikigusari*) used by the Masaki Ryū.

tamagusuri 玉薬【玉藥】. Bullets and gunpowder; ammunition.

tamahagane 玉鋼. Lit. "jewel steel." Steel made in a traditional Japanese smelter called a *tatara*. The most common source of ore is iron sand from certain locations in Japan; the carbon is supplied from specially selected charcoal. *Tamahagane* is considered the best steel for making traditionally forged Japanese swords (*nihonto*).

tamashii 魂 [Also read ***tama***]. Soul, spirit. When read *tamashii*, this character can indi-

[10] Tokugawa Hidetada 徳川秀忠 (1579–1632, r. 1605–1623). Second Tokugawa *shōgun*.

[11] Tokugawa Iemitsu 徳川家光 (1604–1651, r. 1623–1651). Third Tokugawa *shōgun*.

cate *Yamato damashii*, the spirit of the Japanese fighting man: brave, resourceful, etc.

tameshi 様. Abbreviation for *tameshigiri.*

tameshi no mono 様者. A practitioner of *tameshigiri.*

tameshiai 試合. Competitive matches. According to Sawada Hanae of the Tendō Ryū, competitive matches (*shiai*) should be *tameshiai* —"a mutual testing or trial. You are testing each other." (M. Skoss, 1997: 49).

tameshigiri 試切 [Var. ***tameshi*** 様, ***suemono*** 据物]. Lit. "test-cutting." [Originally 試斬, "test beheading"]. The practice of testing a blade by cutting through bamboo, bundles of soaked straw, rolled-up straw mats soaked in water, or human bodies. The practice of testing swords dates back at least to the introduction of metal swords into Japan. However, the use of the term *tameshigiri* 試斬 seems to have become prominent during the Edo period. During the early 1600s in particular, when many battle-hardened warriors were available to perform the cutting, the practice was primarily aimed at testing a particular sword for sharpness, strength, and durability. After the end of the Edo period, when the sword was no longer carried, much less used as a primary weapon in battle, the quality and experience of swordsmen were in general decline; in the post-feudal world, the practice of *tameshigiri* became a test of the aspiring swordsman himself.

TATSUMI RYŪ *TAMESHIGIRI* DEMONSTRATION
Swordsman Katō Hisashi demonstrating at Sakura City Middle School in 1937
(Photograph courtesy Liam Keeley)

As mentioned above, the primary items used in these test cuttings were water-soaked straw and fresh bamboo, formed into a bundle approximately the thicknesses and density that of certain parts of the human anatomy such as an arm, a leg, the trunk, etc. In fact, condemned criminals—male and female, alive or recently deceased—were also used as targets for *tameshigiri.* Some swords from the Edo period bear inscriptions on the tang stating the type of testing cut used, the targets on the cadaver, and occasionally the number of cadavers through which the sword cut. Several schools (*ryū*) of *tameshigiri* evolved during that period, each with their own set of anatomic drawings by which targets were selected. Throughout that period, however, the purpose of *tameshigiri* was to test the sword. After the end of the feudal period in 1868, in an effort to popularize "traditional swordsmanship," a number of swordsmen began traveling around Japan giving demonstrations of *kenjutsu*, *kendō*, *iaidō*, and *tameshigiri.* The evolution of *tameshigiri* as a "show" for an audience started its rise in popularity at that time.

Today the practice of *tameshigiri* (using straw mats or bamboo) has become a popular exercise in some postwar schools of swordsmanship.[12] In these modern schools, *tameshigiri* is seen as an important exercise when balanced with a good system of *kenjutsu.* With the exception of the Tatsumi Ryū 立身流 and a few others, classical *ryū* generally do not include it as a normal discipline; they historically considered their *kenjutsu* training sufficient to teach a swordsman how to cut combatively. In fact, the practice of *tameshigiri* is generally disdained by the classical *ryū.* This bias has historical roots, as *tameshigiri* was seen as the purview of low-class executioners during the feudal period.

Many modern schools of *iaidō* have slowly but surely drifted away from their martial origins by focusing only on the aesthetics of *iaidō kata* while de-emphasizing the practice

[12] This trend was spearheaded by swordsmen such as Nakamura Taisaburō, who had been involved with similar training at the Toyama Gakkō before and during World War II.

T

of solid, partnered *kenjutsu* training and actual cutting ability. In order to correct this drift, a number of modern *ryū* focusing on *iaidō* or *battō*, such as the Toyama Ryū 戸山流 and the Nakamura Ryū 中村流, include *tameshigiri* as a major part of their training regimen. Some swordsmen from these traditions are able to cut through several mats in one strike. Such feats, while impressive, are not unlike the breaking of boards or blocks of ice in various schools of *karatedō*: while such exercises allow the *karate* practitioner or swordsman to test his basic capability in punching or cutting, it is done in a vacuum, removed from any combative reality. As *tameshigiri* is practiced against a static target, on its own it does not develop other characteristics essential to a competent, battle-ready swordsman, such as psychological readiness; the combative capabilities of targeting a moving object; the ability to adjust timing and rhythm (*hyōshi*); the skill of distancing (*ma-ai*) in a flexible environment; the taking of initiative (*sen*); and dominance, among others.

Further reading in English:

- Joly and Inada, 1913: 117–127.

Tamiya Heibei Shigemasa 田宮 平兵衛 重正 (c.1600–c.1670). Recognized as the second-generation headmaster of the Shin Musō Hayashizaki Ryū 神夢想林崎流. Tamiya also founded the Tamiya Ryū in the early seventeenth century. One of his best-known students was Izawa Genta Zaemon Ryōeki, an eclectic martial artist who founded the Izawa Ryū 伊沢流.

Tamiya Ryū 田宮流 [A.k.a. ***Tamiya Ryū Iaijutsu*** – 居合術]. System of *iaijutsu* founded around 1620 by Tamiya Heibei Shigemasa. Many branches of Tamiya Ryū appeared during the Edo period; the school is still extant today.

Tamonten 多聞天 <Ch. Duowentian <Skt. Vaiśravaṇa (or Dhanada). BUDDHISM—One of the Shitennō (Four Deva Kings), Tamonten guards the northern slope of Mount Sumeru (Shumi-sen). His name means "the *deva* who hears much (and is, consequently, knowledgeable)"; his color is yellow. He is a variant form of Kubeira,[13] the "god of wealth." His accoutrement is the writing brush. See also: *Bishamonten*.

Tamotsu Isamu 保勇 (1919–2000). A direct disciple of Hakkō Ryū 八光流 founder Okuyama Yoshiji. Having studied the Chinese boxing (*kempō* [2] <Ch. *quanfa*) of Taiwan and Manchuria, Okinawan *karate* under Shimabukuro Zenryō (Shōrin Ryū 少林流), and Hakkō Ryū, Tamotsu founded a new school he called Shōrinji Karatejutsu 少林寺空手術. This system includes both Shōrin Ryū-style *karate* and Okinawan *kobudō* weaponry.

tampei 短兵. A short sword akin to a *kodachi*.

tampei sen 短兵戦 【短兵戰】. Close-quarter combat; hand-to-hand fighting.

tampyō no jutsu 短兵術. Tactics depending on short weapons.

tanden 丹田 <Ch. *dantian* [Var. ***seika tanden*** 臍下丹田 <Ch. *qixiz dantian*]. Lit. "cinnabar field." In general use, this term refers to the lower abdomen. Martial and alchemical traditions from both China and Japan emphasize the importance of the *tanden*, both as a physical center of gravity and a center of the spirit. Martially, the concepts surrounding the *tanden* are closely related to *haragei*.

Further reading in English:

- Dürckheim, 1962, passim.
- Harrison, c.1956, passim.
- Saso, 1972; 1978.

tandoku renshū 単独練習. Combative exercises without a partner/adversary; a solo combative exercise. Contrast with *sōtai renshū*.

tanegashima 種子島 [Abbr. of ***tanegashima teppō*** 種子が島鉄砲]. A matchlock musket; an arquebus. The earliest ones were imported into Japan by the Portuguese in 1543.[14] As these weapons entered Japan via an island known as Tanegashima, the weapon came to be called by that name.

---

13 Kubeira 倶吠羅 <Ch. Jufeilo <Skt. Kuvera. Often equated to Bishamonten.

14 Yamamoto Kansuke 山本勘助 (1501–1561), one of Takeda Shingen's generals, suggested that firearms were first imported from China in 1501. (Knutsen and Knutsen, 2004: 122).

Tanegashima Jirōuemon Tokisada 種子島次郎右衛門 時貞 (c.1650–c.1720). Founder of the Ko Jigen Ryū (2) 古示現流. Tanegashima was the grandson of Tōgō Shigekata, founder of the Jigen Ryū; he was also a disciple of Tōgō Shigemasa, the third headmaster of the Jigen Ryū.

tanegashima teppō 種子島鉄砲【種子島鐵砲】. A matchlock musket. See: *tanegashima*.

Tanemura Shōtō 種村匠刀. Founder of Genbukan Ninpō Bugei 玄武館忍法武芸, a modern combatives organization with much the same focus as the Bujinkan, in 1984.

tanen 簷猿. See: *nokizaru*.

Tanimura Ha Musō Jikiden Eishin Ryū 谷村派無双直伝英信流【谷村派無雙直傳英信流】. See: *Musō Jikiden Eishin Ryū; Shin Musō Hayashizaki Ryū*.

Tan Isshin 丹 一心. According to Watatani and Yamada (1978: 66), Tan was the probable founder of Isshin Ryū (1) 一心流 *kusarigamajutsu*.

tanjō 短杖. A short stick or cane around 2 to 3 feet (60–90 cm) in length. A number of classical and modern schools such as the Kuki Shin Ryū 九鬼神流, the Tatsumi Ryū 立身流, the Uchida Ryū 内田流, and others employ the *tanjō*. See also: *hanbō (1)*.

tanjōjutsu 短杖術. 1. The combative art of the short stick. 2. UCHIDA RYŪ—A variant name for *sutteki-jutsu* ステッキ術.

tanjū 短銃. A matchlock handgun.

tanken 短剣【短劍】. 1. An Edo-period term for short swords of various types. 2. A bayonet.

tankendō 短剣道. A short-sword art taught as an adjunct to the modern martial way of bayonet combat (*jūkendō*). *Tankendō* is essentially a system of techniques employing the bayonet when it is detached from the rifle.

tankenjutsu 短剣術【短劍術】. The antecedent of *tankendō*. See: *tankendō*.

tankō 短甲. Lit. "short armor." A solid breastplate armor worn by the combatants of the early first millennium. This type of armor is depicted on the *haniwa* statues of the Kōfun period. By the fifth century, however, it had fallen out of use.

tanpei 短兵. See: *tampei*.

tanpo たんぽ. A leather cover placed over a spear tip for training purposes. Training spears (*tanpo yari*) made more recently use a rubber tip.

tanpo yari たんぽ槍. A spear with a padded tip for use in training.

tanren 鍛錬. The forging process in swordmaking. Over time, the word for "forging" or "tempering" metal also came to refer to martial training or drilling. See also: *seishin tanren*.

tanren-geiko 鍛錬稽古. Martial training for the purpose of spiritual forging. See: *tanren*.

tantei 探偵. Detective work, espionage; a spy or espionage agent. See: *saisaku; ninjutsu*.

tantō 短刀. A dagger approximately 12 to 16 inches (30–40 cm) in length. Strictly speaking, a *tantō* has a small handguard (*tsuba*); the otherwise similar *aikuchi* has none.

tantōjutsu 短刀術. Combative techniques using a dagger.

tanzutsu 短筒. A matchlock pistol.

tanzutsujutsu 短筒術. A variant term for combative techniques using a matchlock pistol.

tare 垂. Waist-protecting armor worn in *kendō*.

tariki 他力. BUDDHISM—Lit. "other-power." Practices which require the practitioner to seek enlightenment by calling on help from specific buddhas or *bodhisattvas* such as Amida Buddha. Prayers and/or spells—e.g., *Namu amida butsu!* —are often used in this process. Contrast to: *jiriki*.

taryūjiai 他流試合 [Also read ***taryū shiai***]. A match between different martial schools (*ryū*), usually carried out with bamboo training swords (*shinai*). Though this practice was common during the Edo period, it is no longer in vogue.[15]

[15] In recent years (c.2008) some groups associated with classical *ryū*—e.g., the Takenouchi Ryū and the Jiki Shinkage Ryū—have again begun to engage in *taryūjiai*, but it is still a rare occurrence.

T

However, competitions and an occasional case of "*dōjō* storming" (*dōjō arashi*) still take place among many of the modern empty-hand arts.

tasuki-gake 襷掛. To tie up or roll up one's sleeves. In a martial context, *tasuki-gake* indicates tying up the sleeves of one's *kimono* with a cord (*tasuki*) in preparations for impromptu combat, training, or martial exhibition (*embu*). This was often done in coordination with tucking up one's *hakama* (*shirikarage*). The restraining of the sleeves is also called *ude-makuri*.

tate 1. 楯 [Var. 盾; 干]. a. A standing shield supported by a leg, prominent in the tenth-century conflict known as the Tengyō no Ran. The *tate* was apparently more commonly used by foot soldiers (*banrui*) during the customary opening of battle in which both sides fired volleys of arrows (*yariawase*) at each other. As these shields were large, man-height wooden doors which leaned upon one leg, they were not used by mounted warriors (*tsuwamono*). A similar, derivative shield is used by the Japanese police today in riot control. b. A hand-held shield used in the Okinawan *kobudō* system called *tinbē*. See: *Okinawa kobudō; tinbē.*

tate 2. 殺陣. a. Staged combat; a fight scene in a stage play. b. A reenactment of a scene of carnage. See also: *chambara; jidaigeki; shuraba.*

JIGEN RYŪ DEMONSTRATION OF *TATEGI UCHI*
(Budōkan, 1978)
(Photograph courtesy Jeff Acopian)

tategi uchi 立木打ち. JIGEN RYŪ—A basic practice in the Jigen Ryū 示現流 in which the trainee makes diagonal strikes to a standing post or tree. During the Tokugawa period, a trainee was expected to make 3,000 cuts in the morning and 8,000 cuts in the evening for a period of about three years. This practice developed powerful *kiai* and correct movement and attitude. After this three-year initiation period, the trainee moved on to a range of *kata* with various weapons. According to Tōgō Shigemasa, the late eleventh headmaster of the Jigen Ryū, today's trainees move on to *kata* practice after two or three months of *tategi uchi*.

tatehiza 立膝. A seated posture in which the left heel is under the buttocks and the right knee is drawn up; the right foot is next to the left knee.

tate hoko 楯鉾. A fourteenth-century term from the *Taiheiki* which means "shield and spear."

tate ichimonji no kamae 立一文字の構え. 1. Any of a variety of postures in which a straight weapon is held vertically. *Ichimonji* refers to the Chinese character for the number "1" which is written as a single horizontal stroke (一). However, *tate* means this character (一) is rotated to a vertical position (|). 2. SHINDŌ MUSŌ RYŪ—A posture in which the medium-length staff (*jō*) is held vertically. See also: *ichimonji no kamae.*

tatemae 建前. The principles or rules of a system; more importantly, the official stance or policy. Simple on the surface, the concept of *tatemae*—along with *omote*, *ura*, and *honne*—is critical to understanding any facet of Japanese culture—including martial culture. Contrast to *honne*. See also: *omote; ura.*

Further reading in English:

- Doi, 1985.
- Hall, Edward, 1973; 1976; 1983.
- Lebra, 1976.

tatemono 立物. A helmet crest. There are several types of *tatemono*, named according to their location. For example, there is a crest on the front of a helmet (*maedate* 前立), one on the sides of a helmet (*wakidate* 脇立), one on the rear of a helmet (*ushirodate* 後立) and a crest on the crown of a helmet (*zudate* 頭立). As the ideogram for *tate* is usually read ~ *date* when it is a suffix in compound terms, the crest is often mislabeled a "*date*" in Western literature.

tatsu 辰 [Also read ***shin***]. Dragon. 1. The hour of the Dragon is the fifth duodenary hour of the Chinese Twelve Branches (Jūnishi): 7 to 9 a.m. 2. KYŪSHO—In certain Sino-Japanese boxing texts, the Dragon character indicates the optimal time of day for striking the corresponding vital point (*kyūsho*). See also: *kyūsho; Appendix 1.*

tatsujin 達人. A master; an adept. ¶ *kenjutsu no tatsujin* 剣術の達人, a master swordsman. ¶ *heihō no tatsujin* 兵法の達人, a master strategist or master swordsman.

Tatsumi Ryū 立身流. A comprehensive combative school (*sōgō bujutsu*) founded c.1525 by Tatsumi Sankyō. Combative systems found in the curriculum of the school include swordsmanship (*kenjutsu* with long, short, or dual swords), quick-draw sword arts (*iaijutsu*), spear (*sōjutsu*), long-hafted glaive techniques (*naginatajutsu*), long hardwood staff arts (*bōjutsu*), armed and unarmed grappling (*yawara*), arresting-cord skills (*hojōjutsu*), throwing-blade arts (*shurikenjutsu*), group strategy and tactics (*shūdan sentōhō*), and reconnaissance (*monomi*), among others.

Further reading in English:

- Keely, 1997: 143–153; 1999: 111–149.
- Skoss, 1999: 70–72.

TATSUMI RYŪ SWORDSMAN HENMI SŌSUKE MINAMOTO NO NOBUTAKA
c. 1853–1868
(Photograph courtesy Liam Keeley)

Tatsumi Sankyō 立身 三京 (c.1485–c.1550). Founder of the Tatsumi Ryū, a comprehensive combative school (*sōgō bujutsu*). Tatsumi established this system around 1525[16] after making an extensive study of swordsmanship, grappling, and other combative systems.

Tawara (no) Tōta (Hidesato) 田原 藤太 秀郷. See: *Fujiwara Hidesato.*

te 手. 1. The hand. 2. An empty-handed technique. 3. A counter for empty-handed techniques; e.g., *jūyon te* 十四手 (fourteen hand techniques). 4. ***te*** < Oki. *tī* 手. OKINAWAN KARATE—An early name for Okinawan fighting arts.

tebōjutsu 手棒術. A combative art apparently using a short stick as a weapon. Developed by the Shirai Ryū 白井流.

tedate 手楯 [Var. 手盾]. A buckler or hand-held shield; rarely used in Japan. See: *mochi tate; tate.*

tegusari 手鎖 【手鏁】. A chain with weights on both ends (*ryōfundōgusari*), much like the Masaki Ryū *manrikigusari.*

tehen no ana 天辺の孔. See: *tehen no za.*

tehen no za 天辺の座【天辺の坐】[Var. 頂辺の座【頂辺の坐】]. A hole in the top of a helmet (*kabuto*) surrounded by an ornamental ring. This opening could vary in diameter. Different names were used depending on the historical period: it was also called a *tehen no ana*, a *tenkū ikidashi*, or a *hachimanza no ana.* (Sasama, 1982: 488). The opening and decorative ring were evidently larger on early helmets of the Heian period, allowing room for a stiff pigtail to protrude. The *tehen no za* later became smaller and more decorative.

teisatsu 偵察. Scouting; reconnaissance.

teisatsusha 偵察者. 1. A military scout. 2. An espionage and operations agent.

Teishin Ryū 貞心流. A system of grappling (*yawarajutsu* 和術) founded around 1650 by

[16] According to Liam Keeley, a longtime practitioner of this school, Tatsumi Ryū documents indicate Tatsumi Sankyō was an "active *bushi* during the Eishō period" (1504–1520).

T

Terada Heizaemon Sadayasu.

teitō shisei 堤刀姿勢. A sword-carrying posture in which the sword (*katana*) is held in the left hand, at waist height. See also: *sagetō shisei.*

teki 1. 敵. An enemy.

teki 2. 狄 [Also read ***ebisu***]. A barbarian.

tekkan 1. 鉄貫【鐵貫】[Var. 鉄環【鐵環】]. A concealable metal ring weapon—much like brass knuckles—used in *jūjutsu*-type arts. See also: *bankokuchōki.*

tekkan 2. 鉄簡【鐵簡】[Var. 鉄幹【鐵幹】]. An alternate term for *jutte.*

tekkanjutsu 鉄貫術【鐵貫術】. The art of using the *tekkan* (1). Also called *tetsurinjutsu.*

tekkō 鉄甲【鐵甲】. OKINAWAN KOBUDŌ—Metal knuckle-dusters used in some schools of Okinawan *kobudō*. See: *Okinawa kobudō.*

tekkō kagi 鉄甲鉤【鐵甲鉤】. Metal claws worn on the hands.

tekubi 手首. Wrist.

temoto 手元. The part of a Japanese sword blade that is covered by the blade collar (*habaki*). Also called the *habakimoto*.

ten 天 <Ch. *tian* <Skt. *deva* (masc.) and *devī* (fem.)]. BUDDHISM—A classification of deities from other religions that were incorporated into Buddhism as it moved across Asia. Many of the *ten* have a warlike appearance, and were popular among the Japanese warrior class (*bushi*); e.g., Bishamonten, Marishiten, etc.

tenarashigata 手慣らし型. A solid piece of metal (for combative use) or wood (for training) that has been made into the shape of a folded fan. It does not unfold. See: *tessen.*

Ten Bu 天部. The "Section of Divine Beings" as categorized by East Asian Tantric Buddhism. Members of the Ten Bu are considered "protectors" of the Buddha; they were generally incorporated into Buddhism from Hinduism. In India they were given the title "celestial being" in Sanskrit: *deva* (male) and *devī* (female). Both these terms were translated into Chinese with the character 天 (*tian* in Chinese; *ten* in Japanese). There are dozens of *ten* in Japanese Buddhism. A number of other beings that were not originally *deva* or *devī* in the Hindu pantheon are also included in the Ten Bu. These include dragons, bird-like beings called *garuda*, heavenly nymphs and musicians, and other miscellaneous characters.

TENARASHIGATA-TYPE *TESSEN* (IRON FAN)
Inscribed with a three-point *vajra* sword
(*sankotsuka no ken*)
(Photograph of author by Bruce Brown)

tenchi 天地. Lit. "heaven and earth." This term is often found used to indicate high and low postures, actions that move from high to low positions (or vice versa), or weapons or hands held high and low.

Tendai Shū 天台宗【天臺宗】<Ch. *Tiantai zong*. The Tendai Shū (Tendai school) is a major school of East Asian Mahāyāna Buddhism which descended from the Chinese Tiantai or Lotus school (Hokke <Ch. *Fahua zong* 法華宗). Tendai became one of the two major sects of Esoteric (Tantric) Buddhism in Japan, Shingon Shū being the other. Unlike Shingon, which is primarily Esoteric, Tendai could be called the "Catholic Church" of East Asian Buddhism, in that it includes almost all Mahāyāna teachings: everything from Zen-like meditative practices (*shikan* 止観) to monastic discipline (*binaya* 毘奈耶 or *ritsu* 律). It

was from Tendai that most of the Kamakura-period Buddhist schools emerged, including Hōnen's Pure Land school (Jōdo Shū 浄土宗), Shinran's True Pure Land school (Jōdo Shin Shū 浄土真宗), Nichiren's Lotus school (Nichiren Shū 日蓮宗), and both early branches of Zen (Eisai's Rinzai Shū 臨済宗 and Dōgen's Sōtō Shū 曹洞宗). All of those monks—Hōnen, Shinran, Nichiren, Eisai, and Dōgen—trained in Tendai on Mount Hiei before founding their own schools.

The Chinese term "Tientai," from which the Japanese term "Tendai" is derived, is the name of a mountain in southeastern China. The Buddhist philosopher Zhiyi 智顗 (531–597), third patriarch of the Lotus school, lived and taught on that mountain. Over time, the school derived from his teachings came to be called by the name of the mountain. However, the teachings of Zhiyi are more correctly referred to as Fahua, a term taken from the title of the Lotus Sutra (Ch. Fahua jing『法華經』). Much of the Buddhist literature which flowed into China from the beginning of the first millennium through the sixth century C.E. was collected and organized by the Tientai school.

Tendai was first imported into Japan in the mid-eighth century, but it did not obtain popular support until the Japanese monk Saichō 最澄 (767–822)—posthumously known as Dengyō Daishi 傳教大師—mastered it in China and brought its full teachings, along with a number of Tantric/Esoteric rituals, to Japan in 805 C.E. Later, in the ninth century, a number of Japanese Tendai monks traveled to China to bring additional Esoteric texts and teachings back to Japan.[17]

As Tendai received a good deal of imperial support, the school on Mount Hiei became wealthy and expansive. By the tenth century, Saicho's school was becoming a rival of the older Nara sects. Tendai monks[18] began to get involved in external combative incidents with the Nara schools, as well as in intramural conflicts between Tendai branch schools . The military power of the Tendai monks was finally destroyed by Oda Nobunaga's armies in 1573, but the Tendai school continues to this day, and now has an international following. See also: *Shingon Shū; sōhei; Zen Shū.*

Further reading in English:

- Harrelson, 1993.
- Ichishima and Chappell, 1983.
- Matsunaga and Matsunaga, 1974: 139–171.
- Swanson, 1989.
- Tamura, 1993.
- Weinstein, 1974.

Tendō Ryū 天道流 [A.k.a. ***Tendō Ryū Naginatajutsu*** –薙刀術; ***Ten Ryū*** 天流; ***Denkibō Ryū*** 伝鬼坊流【傳鬼坊流】]. A comprehensive combative school (*sōgō bujutsu*) founded by Saitō Denkibō Katsuhide in 1582. Denkibō's school included swordsmanship (*kenjutsu*), a spear system (*sōjutsu*), long-hafted glaive arts (*naginatajutsu*), and sickle-and chain-arts (*kusarigama-jutsu*).

Denkibō originally trained in the Kashima Shintō Ryū 鹿島新当流 with founder Tsukahara Bokuden. After mastering that tradition he entered a period of meditation, training, and religious austerities at the Hachiman shrine in Kamakura.[19] There, it is said, he was rewarded with an oracle (*musō*) which inspired him to form his own system. The year was 1582;[20] Denkibō was thirty-one years old. He subsequently set out on a warrior pilgrimage (*musha shugyō*) during which he visited Kyōto and the imperial palace, where he received the title of *hōgan.*[21]

Although he was an accomplished martial artist who had many disciples in his Ten Ryū, Denkibō is remembered as an aggressive, rowdy troublemaker. A duel with a swordsman named Sakurai Kasuminosuke ended in the death of the latter and a vendetta against Denkibō. As a result of that vendetta, Denkibō was killed at the age of thirty-eight.

17 See, for example, Reischauer, 1955a; 1955b.

18 These monks are often referred to as "militant clergy" (*sōhei*), "evil monks" (*akusō*), and a variety of other terms.

19 Tsurugaoka Hachimangū 鶴岡八幡宮.

20 Many dates for events such as this are speculative and unreliable. One work, the *Kenjutsu keizu*『剣術系図』, gives the year as 1582; another, the *Nippon bujutsu shoryu shū*『日本武術諸流集』, gives the year 1556.

21 The title of *hōgan* 判官 (also read as *hangan*) indicates a lieutenancy in the Kebiishi Chō. By Denkibō's time, however, it was a ceremonial title.

Today Denkibō's *naginata* system is preserved as the Tendō Ryū, while his *kenjutsu* system is still practiced under the name of Ten Ryū.

TENDŌ RYŪ *NAGINATAJUTSU*
Sawada Hanae (R) and an unknown training partner demonstrating the Tendō Ryū in 1986
(Photograph by author)

Ten'en Ryū 天淵流. A branch school of the Kenkō Ryū 建孝流 (=Itō Ryū [1] 伊東流) which specialized in the pipe spear (*kudayari*).

tengu 天狗. 1. Long-nosed goblins or demons usually depicted as part human, part bird (usually a crow), which were thought to reside in the mountainous areas of Japan. There are two general categories of *tengu:* human-shaped *tengu* (*konoha tengu*) with wings and a very long nose; and bird-shaped *tengu* resembling a crow, called *karasu tengu*. *Tengu* are often associated with marvelous feats of swordsmanship, and legend has it that the young warrior Minamoto no Yoshitsune learned swordsmanship from a *tengu* named Sōjōbō in Sōjōgatani, a ravine on Mount Kurama.

ILLUSTRATION FROM THE *TENGU GEIJUTSU RON*
A nameless samurai eavesdrops on a *tengu* who is lecturing on the art of swordsmanship
(Woodcut c. 1729)

By the late Heian/early Kamakura period (c.1150–1250) the *tengu* had become associated with the *yamabushi.* The *yamabushi* at that time were mountain ascetics who practiced Shugendō, which was a mixture of native shamanism, Shintō, Daoism, and Tendai and Shingon Esoteric Buddhism. A number of the *yamabushi* participated in combative actions (see *sōhei*) and were known for their martial prowess and military involvement in the conflicts of the time. The Japanese populace thought that the *yamabushi* were sometimes possessed by *tengu*, or that a *tengu* could actually take the form of a *yamabushi*—the *yamabushi* certainly encouraged this association. By the late Muromachi period (mid-1500s) the identification of the *yamabushi* with the martial *tengu* image was very common.

Throughout the Japanese medieval period (c.1100–c.1600), *tengu* were often depicted as *yamabushi* or *sōhei* (warrior monks) and the close association of the *bushi* (warrior class) and the *tengu/yamabushi/sōhei* for military purposes was commonplace. In fact, a well-known text from that era, the *Tengu zōshi* (Tengu storybook), is filled with illustrations of monks-as-*tengu*. During that same period, a number of founders of martial traditions alluded to having been instructed by *tengu* during spiritual retreats. Traditions related to Nen Ami Jion, Tsukahara Bokuden, and others refer to *tengu* as spiritual messengers (*kami no otsukai*) who instructed them in swordsmanship. Because of the frequent association of *tengu* with the teaching of swordsmanship,[22] they are often found on armor and sword ornaments as talismans. See: *kami no otsukai; Tengushō; Tengu geijutsu ron.*

Further reading in English:

- Knutsen, 2004: 190–229; 2011.
- de Visser, 1908: 25–99.

Tengu geijutsu ron 『天狗芸術論』【天狗藝術論】(The Tengu's discourse on the martial arts). The *Tengu geijutsu ron* is a classic text on

[22] See, for example, entries in this *Encyclopedia* on Minamoto no Yoshitsune, Sōjōbō, Nen Ami Jion, the *Tengu geijutsu ron*, the *Tengushō* (transmission document from the Shinkage Ryū), and the *Marishiten setsu shōgun kyō* (transmission document of the Nen Ryū 念流).

swordsmanship written by Issai Chozanshi. In this tale, a "nameless samurai" journeys to a small valley on Mount Kurama, the location where centuries earlier Minamoto no Yoshitsune and later Nen Ami Jion were supposed to have been taught swordsmanship by *tengu*. There the warrior encounters a multitude of these beings, and engages them in a series of dialogues on the principles of swordsmanship.

Further reading in English:

- Kammer, 1978.
- Wilson, 2006.

Tengu Kurama Ryū 天狗鞍馬流. A system of swordsmanship which, according to Watatani and Yamada (1978: 596), is said to have originated with Minamoto no Yoshitsune. See: *hōgan; Kiichi Hōgan Ryū.*

tengu mempō 天狗面頬. An armored mask (*mempō*) shaped like the face of a *tengu*. There are two varieties: the human-faced *tengu*, which has a long nose; and a crow-faced *tengu*, which has a crow's beak.

Tengushō 「天狗抄」. The fifth picture scroll (*emaki*) presented to Yagyū Muneyoshi by Kamiizumi Ise no Kami Nobutsuna, founder of the Shinkage Ryū, in 1566. This scroll illustrated the set of *kata* now called Tengushō 天狗抄. The original *densho* is apparently no longer extant, but a copy of it is included in a long scroll brushed by Yagyū Munenori in 1601.

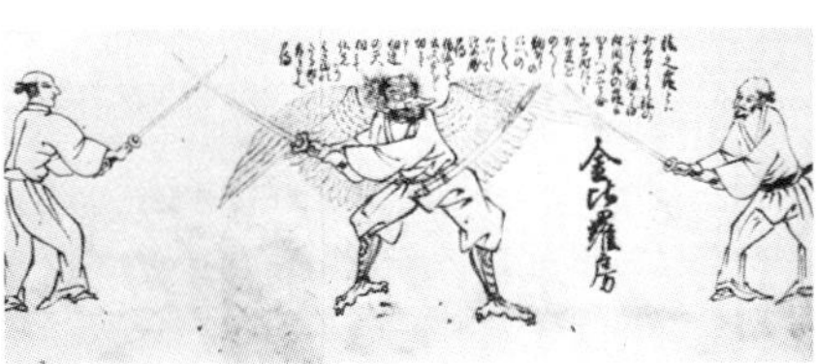

TENGUSHŌ
Detail from the Tengushō section of the *Shinkage ryū heihō mokuroku* signed by Yagyū Munenori, dated 1601
(*Densho* from the archives of Hōzanji temple in Nara)

Tengu zōshi (emaki) 「天狗草紙(絵巻)」 (The demon storybook [picture scroll]). A text dating from 1296 which criticized arrogant Bud dhist priests who end up becoming *tengu*.This document is significant for its criticism of the great monasteries and their habit of mobilizing militant clergy in pursuit of mundane goals.

Tengyō no Ran 天慶乱【天慶亂】. A rebellion begun by Taira no Masakado during the Tengyō era (938). The conflict is chronicled in the *Shōmonki*. Up until that point the Japanese had had a strong central government which had directed troops against "outgroups"—that is, Koreans and the *emishi* in Tōhoku. Anthropologists tell us that this type of conflict tends to be "predatory."

Farris (1992: 132–133) believes the Tengyō no Ran "is the beginning of a shift from predatory to intraspecies warfare" With this in mind, he posits that the Tengyō no Ran was Japan's first real "samurai conflict."

Further reading in English:

- Farris, 1992: 131–149.
- Friday, 2007.

Tenjiku 天竺. See: *Jikuten.*

Tenjin Shin'yō Ryū 天神真楊流. See: *Tenshin Shin'yō Ryū.*

Tenkai 天海 [A.k.a. ***Zuifū*** 随風【隨風】; ***Nankōbō*** 南光坊; posthumous title, ***Jigen Daishi*** 慈眼大師] (c.1536–1643). A Tendai Buddhist monk who entered the priesthood at the age of ten (c.1547) and trained at several Tendai monasteries around Mount Hiei (Hieizan). By 1571 Tenkai had become involved in the tumult of the Warring States period (Sengoku Jidai), and at the request of Takeda Shingen journeyed to that warlord's stronghold in Kōfu. It is unclear what his exact status was with Shingen, but he probably acted as a *kigan sō* 祈願僧 (a monk who prayed and performed rituals especially for the benefit of the sponsor). By 1573 Shingen had been assassinated; Kōfu subsequently fell under the control first of Oda Nobunaga, then Toyotomi Hideyoshi, and finally Tokugawa Ieyasu.

The next information on Tenkai places him in an audience with Tokugawa Ieyasu in 1589. Ieyasu was greatly impressed by the Tendai monk and Tenkai became a trusted member of Ieyasu's staff, acting as a liaison between the Tokugawa, the imperial court in Kyōto, and the Tendai school on Mount Hiei. In fact, one of his projects became the rebuilding of Enryakuji temple on Mount Hiei, which had been destroyed by the warlord Oda Nobunaga in 1571. Tenkai assisted in selecting a posthumous name for Tokugawa Ieyasu (which became Tōshō Daigongen). After Ieyasu's death in 1616, Tenkai remained as a consultant for the next two Tokugawa *shōgun*, Hidetada and Iemitsu. In 1624, at the age of eighty-seven, he founded Kan'ei-ji temple in Edo; in 1636, at the ripe old age of 101, he founded a printing establishment at that temple which published the "Tenkai" edition of the Buddhist canon.

Tenkan 天干 [A.k.a. ***Jikkan*** 十干]. Lit. the "Heavenly Stems." A base-ten numbering system used in East Asia. This is in contrast to the Jūnishi, a base-twelve system also used in East Asia. See: Appendix 1.

tenkū ikidashi 天空息出. The hole in the top of a Japanese helmet (*kabuto*). See: *tehen no za*.

Tenneiji 天寧寺. A Buddhist temple (Sōtō Zen school) near Kuramadera in Kyōto. At this site in 1588–1589, the monk Zenkitsu taught the Tenshinshō Jigen Ryū 天真正自顕流 to Tōgō Shigekata, founder of the Jigen Ryū 示現流.

Tennen Rishin Ryū 天然理心流. A school of combative arts founded by Kondō Kuranosuke Nagahiro sometime during the Kansei era (1789–1801). The tradition included combative swordsmanship (*kenjutsu*), empty-handed and small weapons grappling arts (*jūjutsu*), field combat-oriented grappling (*kumiuchi*), and combative tying-cord arts (*hojōjutsu*). The Tennen Rishin Ryū is considered to be a branch tradition of the Tenshinshōden Katori Shintō Ryū 天真正伝香取神道流. However, a close look at its curriculum indicates it contains elements and influences from many contemporary schools of the late 1700s. The fourth headmaster was Kondō Isami Masayoshi. When Kondō Isami was commissioned as one of the commanders of the Shinsengumi in Kyōto, he took a number of Tennen Rishin Ryū swordsmen with him to Kyōto, including Okita Sōji (a young prodigy and instructor of the school), Inoue Genzaburō, Hijikata Toshizō, and others. The system is still practiced today.

Watatani and Yamada (1978: 607–608) list a number of combative forms (*kata*) found in this system (romanized pronunciations of Japanese terms may vary from these):

Swordsmanship (*kenjutsu*)
- Hiryū-ken 飛竜剣
- Inyū-ken 陰勇剣
- Kobi-ken 虎尾剣
- Samidare-ken 五月雨剣

Field-combat grappling (*kumiuchi*)
- Tsuba-gaeshi 鍔返
- Yoko-tsuke 横附
- Tori-kaeshi 取返
- Gorin-gaeshi 五輪返
- Sutemi-gaeshi 捨身返
- Shishi-gaeshi 獅子返
- Teppu 錣俯

Secrets (Okuden)
- Ichigyōshin 一行心

Empty-handed and small-weapon grappling arts (*jūjutsu*) — left and right variations for the following:
- Hijimaki 臂巻
- Ura-otoshi 裏落
- Gyaku-kaeshi 逆返
- Aya-otoshi 綾落
- Sakomi 差込
- Hishi-wari 菱割
- Kamo-nuki 鴨抜
- Gankō 巌向
- Sentō 沈当
- Tani-otoshi 谷落
- Hiza-guruma 膝車
- Sune-kujiki 脛挫
- Tsuruha 鶴羽
- Ha-otoshi 羽落
- Hazu-kiri 筈切
- Tomo-kara 朋搦
- Iwanami 岩波
- Tsubamegaeshi 燕返
- Hagaeshi 羽返
- Jukaku 鷲摑
- Tetsubiki 錣引
- Maki-age 巻揚
- Jasai 蛇殺
- Yoku-shime 翼締
- Unjō 雲上
- Mijintō 微塵倒
- Gorin-kudaki 五輪砕

The list goes on to include more than thirty-five additional grappling techniques.

tennin 天人<Ch. *tianren* <Skt. *deva* or *apsaras*. Lit. "heavenly beings." This translation of the Sanskrit term *deva* refers to the many gods of

Brahmanism. They were imported into Chinese culture along with Buddhism and from there to Japan. Images of *tennin* are often found as talismans decorating Japanese arms and armor.

TENNIN

tennō 天皇. 1. An emperor. 2. The emperor of Japan; ¶ *Meiji Tennō* 明治天皇 = Emperor Meiji. See also: *Mikado.*

Ten no Maki 「天乃巻」. KASHIMA SHINTŌ RYŪ—A list of twenty-one primary quick-draw sword forms (*battōjutsu*). See: *Kashima Shintō Ryū.*

Ten no Nijūhasshuku 天の二十八宿. See: *Nijūhasshuku.*

tennyo 天女 <Ch. *tiannü* <Skt. *devī* or *devatā.* Lit. "heavenly ladies." The *tennyo* are the female equivalent of the *tennin.* They were imported into Chinese culture along with Buddhism, and from there they entered Japan. Like the *tennin*, the *tennyo* are often found used as talismans decorating Japanese arms and armor.

te no uchi 手内 1. Grip; skill; one's ability. 2. KYŪDŌ—The second of three processes included in *yugamae* (readying the bow). *Te no uchi* is the process of gripping the bow properly. See: *hassetsu; yugamae.* 3. A small pestle-type weapon such as a *tokkosho*, which can be concealed in the hand.

Ten Ryū 天流 [A.k.a. ***Tendō Ryū*** 天道流]. A comprehensive combative school (*sōgō bujutsu*) founded by Saitō Denkibō Katsuhide in 1582. See: *Tendō Ryū.*

Tenshin Aikibudo 大真合気武道 【大真合氣武道】. One of the early terms (c.1944) used by Ueshiba Morihei for the grappling system he modified from Daitō Ryū *aikijūjutsu* into *aikidō.*

Tenshin Koryū 天心古流. A branch system of Shintō Tenshin Ryū 神道天心流 founded by Anegawa Katsuyoshi. However, the extensive curriculum of the parent tradition was somewhat reduced in Tenshin Koryū to include only pugilistic combat (*kempō* [2] 拳法), medium-length staff (*jō*), and self-defense techniques (*goshinjutsu*) after Anegawa became a disciple of Hakkō Ryū founder Okuyama Yoshiji.

Tenshin Ryū 天心流. A branch school of the Edo Yagyū Shinkage Ryū 江戸柳生新陰流, the Tenshin Ryū specialized in combative swordsmanship (*kenjutsu*). The school was founded during the first half of the seventeenth century by Tokizawa Yahei, a direct disciple (*deshi*) of Yagyū Munenori.

Tenshin Shin'yō Ryū 天神真楊流 [Also written 天神心揚流; also read ***Tenjin Shin'yō Ryū***]. A late Tokugawa-period (Bakumatsu-era) *jūjutsu ryū* founded sometime between 1825 and 1830 by Iso Mataemon. Based on Yōshin Ryū 楊心流 and Shin no Shintō Ryū 真之神道流, it focused on choking and joint locks. This school was studied extensively by Kanō Jigorō, and was very influential on the development of modern *jūdō.*

Tenshin Shirai Ryū 天真白井流. See: *Shirai Ryū.*

Tenshinshō-den Katori Shintō Ryū 天真正伝香取神道流 [Several variations: ***Katori Shintō Ryū*** 香取神道流; ***Shintō Ryū*** 神刀流; etc.]. One of the oldest existing warrior traditions in Japan. Many other *ryū* are derived from the Katori Shintō Ryū, or are technically indebted to it. Founded in 1447 by Iizasa Chōisai Ienao (1387–1488), it is a comprehensive field-combat system (*sōgo bujutsu*) containing several combative weapons systems, including swordsmanship (*kenjutsu*), long hardwood staff arts (*bōjutsu*), long-hafted glaive arts (*naginatajutsu*), quick-draw sword arts (*iaijutsu*), spearmanship (*sojutsu*), and the use of small throwing blades and darts (*shurikenjutsu*), among others.

T

TENSHINSHŌ-DEN KATORI SHINTŌ RYŪ
Demonstrated by Donn F. Draeger (L) and Ōtake Risuke (R) in 1978
(Photo by Pat Lineberger)

The Katori Shintō Ryū falls into the category of "positive" swordsmanship in that it emphasizes taking the initiative and closing with the enemy.

Curriculum		**Number of *kata***
Iaijutsu 居合術		
• Omote no Iai	表居合	6
• Tachiai Battōjutsu	立合抜刀術	5
• Gokui no Iai	極意之居合	5
Bōjutsu 棒術		
• Omote no Bō	表之棒	6
• Gogyō no Bō	五行之棒	6
Kenjutsu 剣術		
• Omote no Tachi	表之太刀	4
○ Itsutsu no Tachi	五津之太刀	
○ Nanatsu no Tachi	七津之太刀	
○ Kasumi no Tachi	神集之太刀	
○ Hakka no Tachi	八神之太刀	
• Gogyō no Tachi	五行之太刀	5
○ Mitsu no Tachi	三津之太刀	
○ Yotsu no Tachi	四津之太刀	
○ In no Tachi	陰之太刀	
○ Sha no Tachi	捨之太刀	
○ Hotsu no Tachi	発之太刀	
• Ryōtō 両刀		4
○ Eigetsu no Tachi	永月之太刀	
○ Suigetsu no Tachi	水月之太刀	
○ Isonami no Tachi	磯浪之太刀	
○ Murakumo no Tachi	村雲之太刀	
• Gokui no Kodachi	極意之小太刀	3
○ Hangetsu no Kodachi	半月之小太刀	
○ Suigetsu no Kodachi	水月之小太刀	
○ Seigan no Kodachi	清眼之小太刀	
Naginatajutsu 薙刀術		
• Omote no Naginata	表之長刀	4
○ Itsutsu no Naginata	五津之長刀	
○ Nanatsu no Naginata	七津之長刀	
○ Kasumi no Naginata	霞之長刀	
○ Hakka no Naginata	八箇之長刀	
• Gokui Shichijo no Naginata	極意七条之長刀	3
• Sōjutsu	鎗術	6
○ Hiryū no Yari	飛龍之鎗	
○ Koryū no Yari	去龍之鎗	
○ Tsukidome no Yari	突留之鎗	
○ Anya no Yari	揚矢之鎗	
○ Denkō no Yari	電光之鎗	
○ Yoru no Yayari	夜之矢鎗	
Shurikenjutsu 手裏剣術		
• Omote no Shuriken	表之手裏剣	7
• Gogyō no Shuriken	五行之手裏剣	8
• Gokui no Shuriken	極意之手裏剣	9
Jūjutsu 柔術		
• Idori no Bu	居取之部	13
• Tachiai no Bu	立合之部	17
• Tachiai Kiainage no Bu	立合気合投之部	6
Ninjutsu 忍術		
Chikujōjutsu 築城術		
Gumbai Heihō 軍配兵法		
In-Yō Kigaku 陰陽気学		

Today there are at least four lines of the Katori Shintō Ryū in Japan. The main family line is that of the Iizasa family, who still live in close proximity to Katori Jingū. Another line is that of the late Sugino Yoshio (1904–1998); and yet another recently split when Sugawara Tetsutaka defected from the family line of Iizasa Yasusada. There is also one separate line not transmitted through the Iizasa family; this one dates from about the same time as Sugino's line. Interestingly, all four lines owe their technical origins to the previous chief instructor of the *ryū*, Hayashi Yazaemon Iekiyo (1882–1964).

Further reading in English:

• Ōtake, 1977a; 1977b; 1978; 2007.

Tenshinshō Jigen Ryū 天真正自顕流. A branch tradition of the Tenshinshō-den Katori Shintō Ryū. The founder of Tenshinshō Jigen Ryū was a warrior named Tose Yosazaemon Osamune, from Kasama domain in Hitachi. According to tradition, Osamune received a license of mastery (*inka*) in the Tenshinshō-den Katori Shintō Ryū from Iizasa Wakasa no Kami Morichika (second-generation head-

Tenshinshō-den Katori Shintō Ryū
天真正伝香取神道流
(abbreviated lineage)

1. Iizasa Wakasa no Kami Morichika
初代 飯篠 長威斉 家直

2. Iizasa Wakasa no Kami Morichika
二代 飯篠 若狭守 盛近

3. Iizasa Wakasa no Kami Morinobu
三代 飯篠 若狭守 盛信

4. Iizasa Yamashiro no Kami Moritsuna
四代 飯篠 山城守 盛綱

5. Iizasa Saemon-no-jō Morichika
五代 飯篠 左衛門尉 盛秀

6. Iizasa Ōi no Kami Morishige
六代 飯篠 大炊守 盛繁

7. Iizasa Shurinosuke Morinobu
七代 飯篠 修理亮 盛信

8. Iizasa Shurinosuke Morinaga
八代 飯篠修理亮 盛長

9. Iizasa Shurinosuke Morihisa
九代 飯篠 修理亮 盛久

10. Iizasa Shurinosuke Morisada
十代 飯篠 修理亮 盛定

11. Iizasa Shurinosuke Morishige
十一代 飯篠 修理亮 盛重

12. Iizasa Shurinosuke Moritsugu
十二代 飯篠 修理亮 盛次

13. Iizasa Shurinosuke Morikiyo
十三代 飯篠 修理亮 盛清

14. Iizasa Shurinosuke Nagateru
十四代 飯篠 修理亮 長照

15. Iizasa Shurinosuke Moriteru
十五代 飯篠 修理亮 盛照

16. Iizasa Shurinosuke Morishige (Kanrokusai)
十六代 飯篠 修理亮 盛重(寛陸斉)

17. Iizasa Shurinosuke Morifusa
十七代 飯篠 修理亮 盛房

18. Iizasa Shurinosuke Morisada
十八代 飯篠 修理亮 盛貞

19. Iizasa Shurinosuke Kinjirō
十九代 飯篠 修理亮 金次郎

20. Iizasa Shurinosuke Yasusada
二十代 飯篠 修理亮 快貞

master). However, a variant tradition names Iizasa Morinobu (third-generation headmaster) as Osamune's teacher. Yet another tradition lists Kaneko Moritada as Osamune's teacher in Katori Shintō Ryū. (Kaneko is normally listed as Osamune's student, not his teacher.) The only established date available for this school appears to be when it was transmitted to Tōgō Tōbei Shigekata in 1588–1589.

Sometime after mastering Katori Shintō Ryū, Osamune underwent a spiritual ordeal at Kashima Jingū. The culmination of this *shugyō* was a revelation and new insight into the spiritual core of combat. Basing his new school on this insight, Osamune named his system Tenshinshō Jigen Ryū 天真正自顕流. In doing this he took the term "Tenshinshō" 天真正, meaning "true and correct transmission from the deity of Katori Jingū," from Tenshinshō-den Katori Shintō Ryū and added the term "self-[powered] awakening" (*jigen* 自顕) which had come to him after his spiritual ordeal at Kashima Shrine.

Although Kasama's license of mastery from Tenshinshō-den Katori Shintō Ryū—a comprehensive martial system (*sōgō bujutsu*)—indicates competence in a variety of weaponry, little is known about the combative arts of Tenshinshō Jigen Ryū other than its emphasis on swordsmanship.

Tenshinshō Jigen Ryū
天真正自顕流
(abbreviated lineage)

3. Iizasa Wakasa no Kami Morinobu
三代 飯篠 若狭守 盛信
Tenshinshō-den Katori Shintō Ryū
天真正伝香取神道流

1. Tose Yosazaemon Osamune
初代 十瀬 与三左衛門 長宗
Tenshinshō Jigen Ryū
天真正自顕流

2. Kaneko Shinkurō Morisada
二代 金子 新九郎 盛貞

3. Terasaka Yakurō Masatsune (Zenkitsu)
三代 寺坂 弥九郎 政雅(善吉)

tentō 店頭. The vital point at the crown of the head.

Tentō Ryū 天道流. See: *Tendō Ryū.*

teppō 鉄砲【鐵砲】. Guns, firearms.

teppan tōjutsu 鉄板投術【鐵板投術】. A type of *shuriken jutsu* making use of round, flat metal *shuriken* (or *shaken*). Several classical traditions (*ryū*) including the Takagi Ryū 高木流 and Kuki Shin Ryū 九鬼神流 provided training in *teppan tōjutsu* systems.

tera 寺 [Also read ***~dera*** in some compounds]. A Buddhist temple; a Buddhist temple compound. [Note: In conversational Japanese the term for a Buddhist temple is normally preceded by an honorific "*o*"; thus, *o-tera* 御寺 (Var. お寺).] See: *in (3).*

Terada Heizaemon Sadayasu 寺田 平左衛門 定安 (c.1580–c.1650). Founded Teishin Ryū 貞心流, a system of grappling (*yawara-jutsu* 和術), sometime during the Kan'ei era (1624–1644).

Terada Kan'emon 寺田 勘右衛門 (A.k.a. ***Terada Kan'emon Masashige*** 寺田 勘右衛門 正重) (1616–1674). Kan'emon was an important figure in the development of *jūjutsu* in the mid-seventeenth century. He was a low-ranking *bushi* of the Matsue feudal domain who learned the Teishin Ryū 貞心流 founded by his grandfather, and also studied the Kitō Midare Ryū 起倒乱流 and Ryōi Shintō Ryū 良移心当流 with his father. Due to his broad understanding of combative grappling, Kan'emon became a pivotal figure in the development of *jūjutsu* and *jūdō*. Both the Kitō Midare Ryū and the Jikishin Ryū 直心流 descend from him. For lineage, see: *Kitō Ryū.*

Terada Kan'emon Masashige 寺田 勘右衛門 正成. See: *Terada Kan'emon.*

tera hōshi 寺法師. A term for Japanese Tendai Buddhist warrior monks who hailed from the temple of Onjōji (Miidera). See: *sōhei.*

terakoya 寺子屋. Temple schools that proliferated during the Edo period. Although formal schooling had been directed toward the children of the warrior class prior to the Edo period, the *terakoya* of the Edo period also catered to the children of the rising merchant class.

Terao Kumenosuke Nobuyuki 寺尾 求馬助 信行. Younger brother of Terao Magonojo. Nobuyuki is thought to have been the original recipient of Miyamoto Musashi's famous *Hyōhō sanjūgo ka jō* (Thirty-five articles on strategy). Nobuyuki continued Musashi's teachings of swordsmanship under the school name Musashi no Ryū 武蔵流.

Terao Magonojo Nobumasa [Shinshō] 寺尾 孫之丞 信正 [A.k.a. ***Katsunobu*** 勝信]. A favorite disciple of Miyamoto Musashi. Magonojo is thought to have been the original recipient of the famous *Gorin no sho* (Book of Five Rings) text. Magonojo continued his master's teachings of swordsmanship under the school name Niten Ichi Ryū 二天一流.

Terasaka Yakurō Masatsune 寺阪 弥九郎 政雅【寺阪彌九郎政雅】. See: *Zenkitsu.*

tessen 鉄扇【鐵扇】[Also read ***tetsu-sen***]. Lit. "iron fan." A hand-held iron fan. There are various types; some are one solid piece of metal (*tenarashigata*) while others are functional folding fans with iron or steel ribs. A number of classical *ryū* favored this weapon, and it is often used with the police truncheon (*jutte*). *Tessen* were normally carried by samurai of lower rank, in contrast to commanders whose sign of office was the *uchiwa* (non-folding fan). Even lower on the Tokugawa totem pole were the police constables (*dōshin*) who carried a horse baton (*hananeji*) in lieu of a *tessen*, along with the ubiquitous *jutte*. See also: *tenarashigata.*

tessenjutsu 鉄扇術【鐵扇術】. Techniques which concentrate on the use of the hand-held iron fan. Many *ryū* specializing in *jūjutsu* or *hobaku*—especially during the Edo period—included *tessenjutsu*. Fujita (1960: 2) notes twenty-one *ryū* specializing in *tessenjutsu*. See also: *Edo Machikata Jutte Torinawa Atsukaiyō; Ikkaku Ryū.*

Tesshū 鉄舟【鐵舟】. See: *Yamaoka Tesshū.*

tetsu 鉄【鐵】. Iron; metal.

tetsubō 鉄棒【鐵棒】. A staff or rod of iron,

generally 4 to 6 feet (120–180 cm) in length. Sometimes used by ground troops against horses or other warriors, it was apparently most effective when used from horseback in "polo" fashion. The *tetsubō* was one of the earliest weapons to be brought to Japan from the Asian continent. See also: *bō; konsaibō; rokushaku bō; yoribō.*

tetsubōjutsu 鉄棒術 【鐵棒術】. Techniques using an iron staff.

tetsubyō 鉄鋲 【鐵鋲】. Iron (or steel) rivets which were sometimes affixed to staff weapons to increase the focus of a strike. For example, see: *ichiizue.*

tetsurin 鉄輪 【鐵輪】. A concealable metal ring weapon used much like brass knuckles. See: *tekkan (1).*

tetsurinjutsu 鉄輪術 【鐵輪術】. The art of using a *tetsurin*; also called *tekkanjutsu*. Fujita (1960: 2) notes only two *ryū* that specialized in *tetsurinjutsu*. See also: *tekkanjutsu.*

tetsu sen 鉄扇 【鐵扇】. See: *tessen.*

te waza 手技. 1. KŌDŌKAN JŪDŌ—Hand techniques that are a subset of Nage no Kata. 2. A generic term for *jūjutsu*-type hand-throwing techniques.

te yari 手槍. A short spear. The *te yari* was designed for use in enclosed spaces.

te yumi 手弓. A small bow.

teyumijutsu 手弓術. Combative art of the short bow. Fujita (1960: 2) notes only one *ryū* specializing in *teyumijutsu*.

tinbē ティンベー. OKINAWAN KOBUDŌ—A combative system which makes use of a shield (*tate*) and spear (*hoko*). It is preserved in some schools of Okinawan *kobudō*. See: *Okinawa kobudō; Ryūei Ryū (2).*

to 斗 <Ch. *dou*. 1. A measure, peck, or bushel; a ladle. 2. ***To*** 斗. Abbreviation for Hokuto 北斗, the Big Dipper constellation.

tō 闘 【鬪】. The third seal/character of the recitation found in the Kujihō (Ritual Method of the Nine Seals). *Tō* 闘 literally means "combat." See: *Kujihō.*

tōate no jutsu 遠当術 【遠當術】. Lit. the "art of striking at a distance." Harrison (1956: 137) mentions *tōate no jutsu* as a combative art using *kiai*. See: *kiai no jutsu.*

tobi dōgu 飛び道具. Bows and firearms; projectile weapons.

tobikiri no jutsu 飛切りの術. See: *karumijutsu.*

tōbōsei 刀棒勢. YAGYŪ SHINKAGE RYŪ—A left-foot-forward posture in which the sword covers the head, with the left hand holding the back of the sword and the right hand holding the hilt (*tsuka*). Right-foot-forward versions are also used.

YAGYŪ SHINKAGE RYŪ *TŌBŌSEI* (LEFT)
Demonstration at Meiji Jingū, 1989
(Photograph by author)

tobuhi 烽 [Var. 烽燧]. TAIHŌ MILITARY SYSTEM—A complicated system of beacons set up under the Chinese-style military organization of the eighth century. Farris (1992: 56) speculates that it was so complex that it was "doubtful such a system of communication would have worked." However, the Japanese did have a working system of signal fires that formed a link between northern Kyūshū, the Inland Sea, and the capital.

Toda Gyūshō 富田 牛生 [Also read ***Toda Gosei***]. Founder of the Toda Ryū (2) school of spearmanship. Toda was a retainer of the Asakura clan (Asakura Ke 朝倉家), a *daimyō* family that controlled Echizen. [Note: Some sources list the reading of this name as "Tomita." However, Watatani and Yamada (1978: 635) list it as "Toda."]

Toda Ha Bukō Ryū 戸田派武甲流 [A.k.a. ***Toda Ryū*** 戸田流]. A comprehensive combative school (*sōgō bujutsu*) which includes in its

T

curriculum swordsmanship (*kenjutsu*); glaive skills (*naginatajutsu*) with straight glaive (*su naginata*), crosspiece glaive (*kagitsuki naginata*), and short glaive (*nagamaki*); spearmanship (*sōjutsu*); sickle-and-chain arts (*kusarigamajutsu*); and long hardwood staff techniques (*bōjutsu*).

The school was founded around 1560 by Toda Seigen, an expert swordsman of the Chūjō Ryū. Later, under the thirteenth headmaster, the name was modified to Toda Ha Bukō Ryū; the reason for this change is unknown. The system has survived into the present.

Toda Ha Bukō Ryū naginatajutsu 戸田派武甲流薙刀術. See: *Toda Ha Bukō Ryū.*

Toda Ryū 1. 戸田流. An early name for Toda Ha Bukō Ryū. See also: *Chūjō Ryū.*

Toda Ryū 2. 富田流. A school of combative spearmanship founded by Toda Gyūshō.

tōde 唐手 <Oki. *tōdī* [Also read ***karate***]. OKINAWAN KARATE—Lit. "Tang hand" or "China hand." The term *tō* in this compound refers to the Tang dynasty (618–907) in China. The term *tōde*—usually abbreviated as *te* (<Okinawan *tī*)—may have been in use in Okinawa as early as the first decade of the nineteenth century to indicate the fighting arts that later came to be called *karate* 唐手. According to one Okinawan oral tradition, a young man whose family name was Sakugawa was the progenitor of the Okinawan system of *tōde*. He therefore came to be called Sakugawa Tōde.

Tōde Sakugawa 唐手 佐久川 <Oki. *Tōdī Sakugawa*. See: *Sakugawa Kanga.*

tōdī 唐手 (Oki.). See: *tōde.*

Tōdī Sakugawa 唐手策川 (Oki.). See: *Sakugawa Kanga.*

Togakure Ryū 戸隠流【戸隱流】. A school of espionage. Today Togakure Ryū is taught as part of the curriculum of the Bujinkan and the Gembukan. According to Watatani and Yamada (1978: 626), the organization of this school and its lineage was pieced together by Takamatsu Toshitsugu in the early twentieth century. Takamatsu accomplished this using the oral teachings of his grandfather, Toda Shinryūken 戸田真竜軒,[23] who passed away in 1908 at the age of 90. According to Toda's teachings, Togakure Ryū traces its history to an eleventh-century personage named Ikai 異勾. This lineage eventually passes through the enigmatic Daoist Haku-un (credited with the founding of Haku-un Ryū 白雲流, also a school of espionage). Haku-un supposedly flourished sometime around the Yōwa era, 1181–1182. Unfortunately, no documentation remains from that era which corroborates these lineages.

toga riya 尖矢. A wide, sometimes heart-shaped arrowhead which tapers to a point. See also: *ya no ne.*

togimonoshi 研物師 [Abbr. ***togishi***; also ***togiya*** 研屋]. A (sword) polisher.

togishi 研師. See: *togimonoshi.*

togiya 研屋. See: *togimonoshi.*

Tōgō Jigen Ryū 東郷示現流.See: *Jigen Ryū.*

Tōgō Jūi 東郷 重位. See: *Tōgō Shigekata.*

Tōgō Shigemasa 東郷 重政. The late eleventh headmaster of the Jigen Ryū.

Tōgō Shigekata 東郷 重位 [A.k.a. ***Tōgō Jūi; Tōgō Tōbei Shigekata*** 東郷 藤兵衛 重位; ***Tōgō Hizen no Kami Shigekata*** 東郷 肥前守 重位] (1560–1643). A samurai from Satsuma (present-day Kagoshima prefecture on the island of Kyūshū) who founded the Jigen Ryū

JIGEN RYŪ EMPI *KATA*
Demonstration at the Tōkyō Budōkan in 1979.
(Photograph courtesy Tōgo Shigemasa)

[23] Some sources say Toda was Takamatsu's uncle.

示現流 around 1591. Shigekata was about ten years older than Yagyū Munenori, and fifteen years older than Miyamoto Musashi.

At the age of seventeen, Shigekata first experienced field combat at the battle of Mimigawa in 1577.[24] By the age of twenty he had mastered Marume Kurandonosuke Tessai's Taisha Ryū タイ捨流 and been initiated into the *gokui* (secrets) of that tradition. (Marume had settled in Kyūshū's Kagoshima area after parting with Kamiizumi Ise no Kami.) In 1588, at the age of twenty-eight, Shigekata traveled to the capital (Kyōto) with Shimazu Yoshihiro 島津義弘, the lord of Satsuma domain. While in Kyōto, Shigekata was introduced to a Buddhist priest who went by the name of Zenkitsu. At that time Zenkitsu was chief priest of the Tenneiji temple (not far from Kuramadera) and third-generation successor of a school of martial arts called the Tenshinshō Jigen Ryū 天真正自顕流. Shigekata began training diligently with Zenkitsu, and in less than a year had mastered Tenshinshō Jigen Ryū.

Returning to Satsuma, Shigekata faithfully preserved the teachings he had learned from Zenkitsu. At his home he used posts and live trees as training aids and, within the premises of his residence, pounded all of the trees to death. (This practice is retained today in Jigen Ryū as *tategi uchi*). After working for three years, he synthesized and combined the Taisha Ryū and the Tenshinshō Jigen Ryū into a new school he renamed the Jigen Ryū 示現流. At the age of forty-four he became the chief swordsmanship instructor for Satsuma domain.

Shigekata's renaming of his school was based on an insight he gained by performing religious austerities (*shugyō*). While meditating on a section of the Lotus Sutra,[25] Shigekata became inspired by the phrase "*jigen jintsūriki*" 示現神通力 (a sudden revelation of divine power). He therefore changed the characters of Jigen Ryū from *jigen* 自顕 (self-power revelation) to a set of characters from the Buddhist text—*jigen* 示現 (sudden revelation). In this sense, *jigen* indicates the use by a buddha of a "manifest form" in order to teach sentient beings.[26] Interestingly, in his new Jigen Ryū Shigekata retained the Empi *kata* he had learned from the Taisha Ryū. Empi remains to this day a core element of the Jigen Ryū.

Shigekata also trained in a variety of combative systems, including archery (*kyūjutsu*), horsemanship (*bajutsu*), arresting arts (*hobaku*), glaive arts (*naginatajutsu*), and others. In addition, he was a cultured Renaissance man well known for his expertise in *kadō* 歌道 (*tanka* poetry) and *chadō* 茶道 (the tea ceremony). See also: *Ko Jigen Ryū; Nodachi Jigen Ryū; Taisha Ryū.*

Further reading in English:

• Hurst, 1998: 62–63.

Tōgō Tōbei Shigekata 東郷 藤兵衛 重位. See: *Tōgō Shigekata.*

Tōgun Gon Sōjō 東軍 権 僧正【東軍權僧正】. Founder of the Tōgun Ryū.

Tōgū no Toneri 東宮の舎人. Bodyguards who protected the imperial prince. See: *toneri.*

Tōgun Ryū 東軍流. A comprehensive combative school (*sōgō bujutsu*) founded by Tōgun Gon Sōjō. In its curriculum, it included swordsmanship (*kenjutsu*), long-hafted glaive arts (*naginatajutsu*), strategy and tactics (*gumpō*), horsemanship (*bajutsu*), and gunnery (*hōjutsu*).

Tōgun Ryū Hirai Ha 東軍流平井派. A branch tradition of the Tōgun Ryū in Tōkyō led by Hirai Minoru. Hirai's line specialized in swordsmanship (*kenjutsu*). See also: *Kōrindō.*

Tōhei Kōichi 藤平 光一 (1920–2011). A famous *aikidō* practitioner who attained the rank of tenth degree (*jūdan*) under Ueshiba Morihei. Tōhei was one of the senior *aikidō* disciples of Ueshiba Morihei who established his own style; he founded Shin Shin Toitsu Aikidō.

He began his practice of *aikibudō* at the Kōbukan Dōjō in 1939, and went on to pop-

24 Mimigawa no Tatakai 耳川の戦い (See Imagawa *et al*., 1988: 133–135).

25 I.e., *Myōho renge kyō*『妙法蓮華經』<Ch. *Miaofa-lianhua jing* <Skt. *Saddharma-puṇḍrīka-sūtra*; T. 262, IX: 1–62. Several editions of this text were translated into Chinese. It is unknown which version was used by Shigekata.

26 Compare with *jiriki* and *tariki*.

ularize *aikidō* in Hawaii in the early 1960s. By the 1970s he had became one of the best-known international figures in *aikidō*; several of his books were translated into English and other languages. Tōhei achieved the position of chief instructor (*shihan buchō* 師範部長) of the World Aikido Headquarters (Aikidō Hombu Dōjō) in Tōkyō, and was awarded tenth *dan* by Ueshiba Morihei in the late 1960s.

Although Tōhei held the highest rank in *aikidō* and was chief instructor of the system, he was not the inheritor of the school. That role fell to Ueshiba Kisshomaru, son of the founder. Kisshomaru felt that Tōhei's interpretation of *aikidō* and his emphasis on *ki* were not in line with the teachings of his father, and in 1971, he restricted what Tōhei could teach at the Aikidō Hombu Dōjō. Tōhei retained his position at the Aikikai and formed a new separate organization he christened the Ki no Kenkyūkai (Ki Research Society). Tension increased, and in 1974 Tōhei finally broke with the Aikidō Hombu Dōjō. This caused ripples all through international *aikidō*, with instructors and organizations all over the world forced to choose between the Aikikai headed by Ueshiba Kisshomaru and the Ki no Kenkyūkai under Tōhei.

Tōhei's interpretation of *aikidō*, his emphasis on cultivation of *ki*, and his association with Nakamura Tempū, founder of Shinshin Tōitsudō,[27] led him, in the mid-1970s, to found his own style/organization called Shin Shin Tōitsu Aikidō.

Several works by Tōhei have been published in English. Among these are:

Aikido: The Arts of Self-Defense. Rikugei Pub. House, 1961.

Ki in Daily Life. Japan Publications Trading (revised edition), 2001.

This is Aikido. Japan Publications, Inc., 1968.

What is Aikido? Rikugei Pub. House, 1962.

tōhō 刀法. A Muromachi- and Edo-period term for swordsmanship.

[27] Shinshin Tōitsudō 心身統一道 is a system of yoga founded by Nakamura Tempū. Nakamura founded his system after an extensive study of both Rama Yoga and Karma Yoga. It is not a martial system; its goal is to free one's mind and body so one's true nature as a human being can be realized.

tohohei 徒歩兵. A footsoldier.

tohosen 徒歩戦【徒歩戰】. Lit. "warfare on foot." Battle engaged in by footsoldiers, in contrast to that conducted by cavalry (*kibasen*). See: *kibasen.*

tōjō 刀杖. Lit. "swords and staffs." A generic term for arms in the medieval period.

tōjutsu 刀術. Swordsmanship; an alternate term for *kenjutsu.* See: *Daidō Ryū.*

Tōkaidō 東海道. The principal highway between Kyōto and Edo during the Edo period.

Tokashiki Iken 渡嘉敷 唯賢. The second headmaster of the Gōhaku Ryū 剛泊流. Tokashiki founded Gohakukai Karatedō 剛泊会空手道 in 1982. He was a direct disciple of founder Fukuji Seikō.

tōken 刀剣【刀劍】[A.k.a. ***Nippon tōken*** 日本刀剣【日本刀劍】]. Swords. See also: *gendaitō; guntō; kotō; shinshintō; shintō (2); Shōwatō.*

tokin 1. 兜巾 [Var. 頭巾; 頭襟; also read ***zukin***]. Originally a hood (*zukin*), this traditional *yamabushi* accoutrement is usually a very small black cap (*tokin*) which is worn on the forehead and tied in place with a strap under the chin. It is also seen on most depictions of *tengu.*

tokin 2. と金 [Abbr. as と or 个]. SHŌGI—Lit. "reaches gold." In the Japanese strategic game of *shōgi*, this piece is a promoted pawn (*fuhyō* 歩兵). The *tokin* does not have a direct equivalent in Western chess.

Toki Yamashiro no Kami Yoriyuki 土岐山城守 頼行. Founder of the Jitokuki Ryū 自得記流, a school concentrating on the pipe spear, sometime during the Edo period.

Tokizawa Yahei 時沢 弥平【時澤彌平】. Founder of the Tenshin Ryū 天心流 sometime during the 1630s. Tokizawa was a direct disciple of Edo Yagyū Shinkage Ryū founder Yagyū Munenori.

tokko 独鈷【獨鈷】. See: *tokkosho.*

tokkosho 独鈷杵【獨鈷杵】. 1. A single-point *vajra* (Buddhist thunderbolt scepter; Buddhist diamond scepter). The *tokkosho*, a ritual instrument usually about 4 to 8 inches (10–25

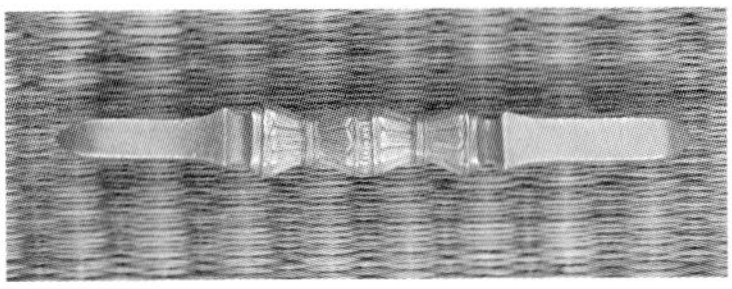

TOKKOSHO
Brass single-point *vajra* scepter (Japanese)
(Private collection)

cm) long and made of brass, is used in various rituals performed by Shugendō practitioners and Buddhist esoteric schools (Tendai Shū and Shingon Shū). *Tokkosho* also make up the spokes of the Buddhist Wheel of the Law (*hōrin*).

While the *tokkosho* is primarily a votive accoutrement used in Buddhist ritual, its shape enhances its utility as a "weapon-usable object" for self-defense. 2. SHŌRINJI KEMPŌ—A version of the *tokkosho* is also used for self-defense training within the curriculum of Nippon Shōrinji Kempō. This object, written with the same ideograms (独鈷) but pronounced *dokko*, is a short cylinder of wood similar to a *yawara*. Its use is evidently now rarely taught.

Tokugawa 徳川. A family descended from early thirteenth-century samurai Nitta Yoshishige, the grandson of Minamoto Yoshiie. One descendant branch came to be called the Matsudaira (after the village in which the line lived in 1369). Under Ieyasu (1542–1616), who came from this line, the name Tokugawa was renewed. The descendants of Ieyasu ruled Japan during the Edo period (1603–1867).

Tokugawa bakufu 徳川幕府. The government of the Tokugawa shogunate, which ruled from 1603 to 1867.

Tokugawa Ieyasu 徳川 家康 (1542–1616). The first Tokugawa *shōgun*. Ieyasu ruled as *seii taishōgun* from 1603 to 1605. Even after his retirement from that post, he held the real reins of power until his death in 1616.

Ieyasu was one of many contending warlords of the late Warring States period. He allied with Oda Nobunaga in 1561, and found it convenient to support Oda until the latter was assassinated in 1582. After some sparring with Toyotomi Hideyoshi, Ieyasu signed a truce with him, and they became distrustful allies until 1590. Under his alliance with Hideyoshi, Ieyasu moved his army into the Kantō area in the early 1590s and took up residence in a backwater castle town called Edo. After the battle of Sekigahara in 1600, Ieyasu essentially controlled the whole nation.

There is at least one story about Ieyasu that relates to historic martial arts. Having heard of the fame of the Yagyū swordsmen, Ieyasu invited Yagyū Muneyoshi to his villa in Kyōto in 1594. Yagyū Munenori accompanied his father to this meeting. Ieyasu was so impressed by the Yagyū Shinkage Ryū skills known as *mutōdori* that he asked Muneyoshi to become his swordsmanship instructor. Muneyoshi, then sixty-six years old, declined, offering his twenty-three-year-old son Munenori as a retainer and sword instructor in his stead. Ieyasu accepted, and Munenori began to establish his Edo Yagyū Shinkage Ryū.

Tokukgawa Jidai 徳川時代. The historical period (1603–1867) when the Tokugawa family ruled Japan via the Tokugawa shogunate (Tokugawa *bakufu*).

Tokugawa Yoshimune 徳川 吉宗 (1684–1751). The eighth Tokugawa *shōgun*. It was Yoshimune, who reigned from 1716 to 1745, who ordered Kamei Magoroku Shigemura to develop an effective system of police tactics. See: *Edo Machikata Jutte Torinawa Atsukaiyō.*

Tokugawa Yoshinao 徳川 義直 (1600–1650). Ninth son of Tokugawa Ieyasu. Yoshinao was the progenitor of the Owari Tokugawa. He is also considered the fourth headmaster of the Yagyū Shinkage Ryū in Owari, and is listed after Yagyū Hyōgonosuke Toshitoshi. Interestingly, the fact that both Yoshinao and Toshitoshi died in 1650 indicates that the practice of naming the Tokugawa lords as head of the Owari Yagyū Shinkage Ryū owed as much to politics as it did to technical expertise. Apparently the close family relationship between the Tokugawa and Yagyū families engendered this policy.

Yoshinao also had a close relationship with another legendary martial artist (and architect), Chin Gempin.

tokushu keibō 特殊警棒. A telescoping police baton adopted for use in 1966.

TOKUSHU KEIBŌ
(Private collection)

tokushu keibō sōhō 特殊警棒操法. A police combative system based on the use of the telescoping police baton (*tokushu*). See also: *hobaku; hōjōjutsu; keibō sōhō; keijōjutsu; taihojutsu; torite.*

tōma 遠間. Abbreviated from *tōmaai*, this term indicates a "distant" combative-engagement interval (with respect to either space or time) between opponents. If using a projectile weapon such as a bow and arrow or throwing blade, various ranges of *tōma* might be required depending on the weapon type. With a sword or other handheld weapon, *tōma* might require closing with the enemy before an attack can be made. According to some classical systems, *tōma* is any combative engagement distance or interval greater than one step. See: *maai.*

tōmaai 遠間合. See: *tōma.*

Tōmai dī 泊手 (Oki.). See: *Tomari te.*

Tomari Hyōbu Shōyū Fujiwara no Ikka 泊兵部 少輔 藤原一火 (c.1550–c.1610). Founded the Ikka Ryū 一火流, a school of gunnery (*hōjutsu*), around 1585.

Tomari te 泊手 <Oki. *Tōmai dī.* OKINAWAN KARATE—A *karate* system taught in the area of Tomari. Its development is generally attributed to Matsumora Kōsaku.

Tomiki Aikidō 富木合気道. A variant name for the Tomiki Ryū. See also: *Tomiki Kenji.*

Tomiki Kenji 富木 謙治 (1900–1979). Founder of the Tomiki Ryū. Tomiki began training in Kōdōkan Jūdō at the age of ten, in 1910. By 1928, he had obtained the rank of fifth degree (*godan*). Tomiki began training with Ueshiba Morihei in 1926. Later, in 1936, he moved to Manchukuo (Japanese-occupied Manchuria), where he began teaching *aikibujutsu* to students from the Manchukuo government and military police at Daido Gakuin. In 1938 he took charge of the *aikibudō* program at Kenkoku University.[28]

Tomiki was stranded in Manchuria in a prison camp with thousands of other Japanese nationals at the end of World War II, and was not repatriated to Japan until 1948. In 1958 he started the Waseda University Aikidō Club. Interestingly, he kept up his *jūdō* training, and was awarded an eighth *dan* in Kōdōkan Jūdō in 1964. (He had been the first student of Ueshiba to receive an eighth *dan* in *aikibudō* in 1940). Due to the influence of his *jūdō* training, Tomiki added similar competitions to his version of *aikidō*. In 1967, he established his home training hall, the Shōdōkan Hombu Dōjō, in Ōsaka.

Further reading in English:

- Pranin, 1981a; 1981b; 1982; 2009.

Tomiki Ryū 富木流 [Var. ***Shin Aikidō*** 新合気道; ***Tomiki Aikidō*** 富木合気道; ***Shōdōkan Aikidō*** 昭道館合気道, etc.]. A branch tradition of Ueshiba Ryū Aikidō founded by Tomiki Kenji.

Tomita Gyūshō 富田 牛生. See: *Toda Gyūshō.*

Tomita Ryū 富田流. See: *Toda Ryū.*

tōmitsu 東密. ESOTERIC BUDDHISM—Refers specifically to the Tantric (Esoteric) teachings (*mikkyō*) practiced within the Japanese Shingon Buddhist denomination (Shingon Shū). Contrast to *taimitsu.*

Tomoe Gozen 巴 御前. Lady Tomoe. Thought to be a daughter of Nakahara Kanetō, Tomoe appears in the *Heike monogatari* as a beautiful, powerful, and courageous combatant who

---

[28] Kenkoku University (Kenkoku Daigaku 建国大学) was evidently pan-Asian in its student body and, for the times, international in scope. It had several Japanese martial arts clubs, including a *jūdō* club, a *kendō* club, an *aikibudō* club, a *kyūdō* club, and a *sumō* club (Shishida, 1992).

rides an untamed horse (*arauma*), a wild animal much prized by the early medieval warriors. In the *Heike* she is described as Kiso Yoshinaka's mistress, but her historical existence is unclear. Even the *Heike* is confused, as she is described in one place as a servant (*binjo*) and in another as a warrior commander (*ippō no taishō*). Upon Kiso's death in 1184, she "retired" to Echigo province (present-day Niigata prefecture).

Further reading in English:

- Amdur, 2002a: 181–182.
- Kitagawa and Tsuchida, 1975: 519–521.
- Varley, 1994: 104.

toneri 舎人. An imperial bodyguard or royal retainer. Emperor Yūryaku[29] is credited with the creation of this post in the fifth century. The post of *toneri* (which was at first referred to as *ōtoneri* 大舎人) included security duty for the imperial palace and the houses of the Yamato nobility. The *toneri* served under the auspices of noble martial families such as the Ōtomo and the Seki. Under Emperor Ninken[30] the *toneri* were divided into two sections, the Sa Toneri 左舎人 (Security Detail of the Left) and the U Toneri 右舎人 (Security Detail of the Right). There was a third category of guards known as the Uchi Toneri 内舎人 (Inner Security Detail) who carried swords and protected the emperor's carriage. A fourth category known as Tōgū no Toneri 東宮の舎人 protected the imperial prince. (See also: *yugei*.)

During the eighth century the title *toneri* still meant "royal retainer," but it was sometimes honorific, and did not necessarily indicate someone who was a warrior or had any combat experience or training. The number of *toneri* was set at 600 during the eighth century by the Taihō Code of 701.

During the medieval period, the term *toneri* came to refer to a groom or warrior attendant. Although they were often armed with polearms such as *naginata*, they rarely participated in one-on-one combat. They did, however, occasionally take part in mopping-up operations.

tonfā トンファー [A.k.a. ***tonkwā*** トンクァー; ***toifā*** トイファー; ***tunfā*** トゥンファー] (Oki.). OKINAWAN KOBUDŌ—A truncheon-type weapon made of wood with a handle placed at a right angle to the shaft about one-quarter of the distance from one end of the shaft. The length of the shaft is generally around 18 inches (45 cm) or more. As with similar hand-held weapons, this length is generally sufficient to protect the forearm. The *tonfa* is one of the characteristic weapons of Okinawa; there are several varieties. See: *Okinawa kobudō*.

tonkō hōjutsu 遁甲方術. The "arts of concealment" or "arts of invisibility." This term dates back at least as early as the *Nihongi* (720 C.E.). That text contains a reference to a Buddhist monk importing various Chinese arts into Japan from Korea during the reign of Empress Suiko:[31]

> A Paekche priest named Kwalluk (Sō Karoku 僧 觀勒) arrived and presented by way of tribute books of calendar making, of astronomy and of geomancy, and also books on the art of invisibility (*tonkō hōjutsu*) and magic.
>
> Aston, 1896: 126.

According to the *Nihon koten bungaku taikei,* vol. 68, this manual on concealment was a work existing in the late Han dynasty (25–220 C.E.). It is noted as such in the *Houhanshu* 『後漢書』, an eleventh-century Chinese work. Later Japanese reference works refer to *tonkō hōjutsu* as the art of stealth or espionage, using the terms *shinobijutsu* and *ninjutsu*.

tono 殿. Form of address: Mr.–, Sir–; Sire. See: *dono; Tono sama*.

Tō no Kata 韜之形 [Also read *Fukuro Shinai no Kata*]. JIKI SHINKAGE RYŪ—The second series of Jiki Shinkage Ryū *waza*, consisting of fourteen *kata*. All are performed with *fukuro shinai*. According to the oral tradition of the Jiki Shinkage Ryū, these *kata* were created by Ogasawara Genshin Nagaharu in the early seventeenth century. (Namiki, interviews,

29 Yūryaku Tennō 雄略天皇 (c.418–c.479; r.c.456–c.479). Legendary twenty-first emperor of Japan. His actual dates are unknown.

30 Ninken Tennō 仁賢天皇 (c.448–c.498; r.c.488–c.498). Legendary twenty-fourth emperor of Japan. His actual dates are unknown.

31 Suiko Tennō 推古天皇 (554–628; r.593–628). The thirty-third imperial ruler of Japan.

T

1978–1981). For photograph, see: *Jiki Shinkage Ryū*.

To no Mono Tachi 外之物太刀. KASHIMA SHINTŌ RYŪ—Additional combative swordsmanship forms (*kenjutsu kata*) taught only after the trainee has mastered the high-level forms of the Kashima Shintō Ryū 鹿島新当流. See: *Kashima Shintō Ryū*.

Tono sama! 殿様！A form of address: "Lord!" "Sire!"

tō no ya 当の矢【當の矢】. An "answering arrow." *Tō no ya* were often fired in single, one-on-one combat after an initial arrow had been loosed at a warrior. However, one of a volley of arrows in response to a volley was also considered a *tō no ya*.

tonpō 遁法【遯法】. A method used by espionage agents (*ninja/shinobi*) for disappearing by escape. This is in contrast to disappearing by "melting away" (*inpō*). See also: *ninjutsu; ongyōjutsu*.

tonseisha 遁世者. A Muromachi-period term for an individual who has taken Buddhist vows, usually under the auspices of the Jishū branch of the Pure Land School (Jōdo Shū). Most of these *tonseisha* followed the practice of adding the term *ami* 阿弥 to their Buddhist names. (*Ami* is an abbreviation of Amida Butsu 阿弥陀佛.) A number of *tonseisha* lived in the residences of feudal lords, where they acted as advisors on artistic matters. See: *dōbōshū; Nen Ami Jion; nyūdō*.

toppa 突破. A variant term for an espionage agent. *Toppa* literally means to strike (突) through an enemy's weak point and destroy (破) his physical infrastructure. According to Miyazaki (1974: 236), this term was used by agents in the geographical area of Shinshū 信州 (present-day Nagano prefecture).

tora 寅 [Also read ***in***]. Tiger. 1. The hour of the Tiger is the third duodenary hour of the Chinese Twelve Branches (Jūnishi): 3 to 5 a.m. 2. KYŪSHO—In certain Sino-Japanese boxing texts, the Tiger character indicates the optimal time of day for striking the corresponding vital point (*kyūsho*). See also: *Appendix 1*.

tora hashiru 虎走る. Lit. "to walk like a tiger." To move like a stalking tiger; to move in a predatory manner; to move with stealth.

***Tora no mak*i** 「虎之巻」(Tiger scroll on strategy). Variant name for *Heihō tora no maki*. See also: *Genke kin'etsushū; Heihō Tora no maki*.

Torao Jō 虎尾 尉 (c.1620–c.1700). Founded the Shinbu Ryū 神捕流, a martial school concentrating on combative spear tactics (*sōjutsu*), around 1651.

Torao Ryū 虎尾流. One of many branch schools of the Kenkō Ryū 建孝流 (=Itō Ryū [1] 伊東流) which specialized in the pipe spear (*kudayari*). See Itō Ryū (1) 伊東流 for abbreviated lineage.

tori 1. 酉. Cock. a. The hour of the Cock is the tenth duodenary hour of the Chinese Twelve Branches (Jūnishi): 5 to 7 p.m. b. KYŪSHO—In certain Sino-Japanese boxing texts, the Cock character indicates the optimal time of day for striking the indicated *kyūsho*. See also: Appendix 1.

tori 2. 取. Lit. "taker." In many empty-hand grappling systems, *tori* refers to the person who executes a technique; the "thrower."

torii 鳥居. SHINTŌ—The archway ("gate") of a Shintō shrine.

Torii Ryū 鳥居流. A school of gunnery (*hōjutsu*) founded by Torii Jinzaemon Masanori. The Torii Ryū proliferated in Fukuoka domain in Kyūshū in the late 1500s and early 1600s. In the 1700s it split into several branch traditions, including the Jitoku Ryū 自得流 and the Ōno Ryū 大野流.

Torii Jinzaemon Masanori 鳥居 甚左衛門正教. Founder of the Torii Ryū, a system of gunnery (*hōjutsu*). Torii had initially trained in the use of the firearms (*bōbiya*) of the Miki Ryū 三木流 under Miki Shigedayū Yasukado.

torikake 取り掛け. KYŪDŌ—The first of three processes included in readying the bow (*yugamae*). *Torikake* is the process of fixing the archer's glove and nocking the arrow. See: *hassetsu; yugamae*.

torimi 取身. TENSHIN SHIN'YŌ RYŪ—The

proponent who executes a technique. See: *shidachi; tori (2); uchidachi.*

torimono 1. 捕物. Arresting arts.

torimono 2. 捕者. An arresting official.

torimono mitsudōgu 捕者三道具. Lit. the "three tools of arresting officials." See: *mitsudōgu.*

torinawa 捕縄【捕繩】[Also read ***hojō***; Var. ***hojōjutsu*** 捕縄術【捕繩術】]. Restraining-cord arts. These systems were used by many of the classical *ryū.* Although restraining was not a primary combat activity, there were often times on the battlefield when it was necessary to take an enemy alive. Consequently, restraining cord techniques evolved along with grappling in armor (*yoroi kumiuchi*). These arts continued to develop along with police techniques during the Edo period, and many schools specializing in arresting arts (*hobaku*) and *jūjutsu* included *torinawa.* One of the earliest traditions to formalize a curriculum in *torinawa* was the Takenouchi Ryū 竹内流. See also: *Edo Machikata Jutte Torinawa Atsukaiyō; hashiri nawa; hojōjutsu; Ikkaku Ryū: Ittatsu Ryū; Masaki Ryū.*

torite 捕手 [Also read ***tode***; a.k.a. 取手]. Lit. "seizing with the hands." 1. Arresting arts. See also: *Araki Ryū; Edo Machikata Jutte Torinawa Atsukaiyō; Masaki Ryū.* 2. An Edo-period policeman. See: *torimono (2).*

toritejutsu 捕手術. See: *torite.*

tōryaku 韜略 <Ch. *taolue.* Strategy; tactics.

tōryō 棟梁. Lit. "pillar." This term came to mean a warrior chief, leader, or overlord.

Tōryū gumpō kōshasho 『当流軍法功者書』【當流軍法功者書】(Text on the outstanding military strategies of this tradition). An Ogasawara Ryū 小笠原流 text on military strategy. It has been published in Ishioka and Arima, 1967 (vol. 6): 177–229.

tōsatsu 遠殺. Lit. "distant kill." One of several combative systems used by the Issa Ryū 一佐流. The purpose of *tōsatsu* was to kill an opponent in close combat without resorting to grappling. This was in contrast to restraint-oriented systems such as *jūjutsu* and *torite.*

tōseigusoku 当世具足【當世具足】. Lit. "current-period armor" or "modern armor." A relatively light and very flexible type of armor which was in use from the late Muromachi period (c.1500s) through the 1800s.

Tōsenkyō genkai 『闘戦経諺解』【闘戰經諺解】(Colloquial commentary on the [Minamoto] discourse on war strategy). This text is listed by Ishioka and Arima as part of a collection called the *Genke kohō densho* 源家古法伝書 (Transmission scrolls on the ancient methods of Minamoto war strategy). The text itself is subtitled *Genke kohō gungaku nijūgosei* 『源家古法軍学二十五世』 (Twenty-five sections on the ancient methods of military strategy of the Minamoto clan). It has been published in Ishioka and Arima, 1967 (vol. 6): 145–176.

Tose Yosazaemon Osamune 十瀬 与三左衛門 長宗 [Variant readings for 十瀬 are "Kose" and "Ose"] (c.1540–c.1600). A contemporary of Yagyū Muneyoshi who founded the Tenshinshō Jigen Ryū 天真正自顕流.

Tose was a rural land-holding warrior (*gōshi*) from the Kasama domain in Hitachi. During the Eiroku era (1558–1570), he sought out Iizasa Wakasa no Kami Morinobu,[32] the third headmaster of Katori Shintō Ryū. After training for five years, he received a full license in the tradition.

Later, Tose returned to Hitachi (present-day Ibaraki prefecture). After performing religious austerities at Kashima Jingū he received via an oracle (*musō*) a catalog of martial techniques in a divine inspiration from the *kami* of the shrine. In addition, he received a vision of a technique so swift that with it he could cut a flying swallow out of the air. From this inspiration he named his new system Tenshinshō Jigen Ryū 天真正自顕流, taking the "Tenshinshō" 天真正 (true and correct transmission from the deity of the shrine) from the Tenshinshō-den Katori Shintō Ryū, and adding the term "self-power revelation" (*jigen* 自

[32] Some sources list second headmaster Iizasa Wakasa no Kami Morichika as Osamune's teacher. However, the timeline for Morichika and Tose does not match.

顯) which had come to him after his spiritual ordeal at Kashima Shrine.

Tōshiya 通し矢 [A.k.a. ***dōsha*** 堂射]. A famous archery tournament held annually at Sanjūsangendō temple in Kyōto. Archers fire arrows the length of a long veranda (nearly 400 feet, or 120.7 m.) over a period of 24 hours. Since the ceiling is low (16 feet/4.9 m.), the trajectory of the arrows must be relatively flat, and a powerful bow is required. The record, set in 1686, was by a warrior named Wada Daihachi who made 8,133 hits.

Further reading in English:

- Hurst, 1998: 136–141.
- Onuma, 1993: 18–19.

tōshō 刀傷. A sword wound; a sword cut. See also: *katana kizu.*

Tōshō Daigongen 東照大権現【東照大權現】. RYŌBU SHINTŌ—A posthumous Ryōbu Shintō title used in reference to Tokugawa Ieyasu.

toshu 徒手. Empty-hand arresting techniques. These techniques are a subdivision of a variety of arresting techniques taught by the modern Japanese police force under the rubric of *taihojutsu*.

toshu kakutō 徒手格闘. A system of empty-hand combat developed for Japan's Self-Defense Force (Jieitai 自衛隊) by Captain Chiba Sanshu in 1952.

Further reading in English:

- Draeger, 1974a: 75–76.

tōsō 闘争. A struggle, a combat.

tōsō honnō 闘争本能. Fighting instinct.

tōsōsei 闘争性. Combative nature.

tōsu 刀子. A very small dagger carried by nobles (*kuge*) for self-defense. In the fifteenth century, the blade length was restricted to 4.9 inches (12.5 cm) by imperial order, although longer—and shorter—examples exist. This small dagger was normally kept in a scabbard (*saya*) which had a *kurikata* and *soritsuno* for stabilizing it in the sash (*obi*). However, there are examples which have a hole in the chape (*kojiri*) of the scabbard so that a cord could be used to secure it to the *obi*.

Tō Taisō Ri Eikō montai 『唐太宗李衛公問對』<Ch. *Tang Taizong · Li Weigong wendui* [A.k.a. ***Ri Eikō montai*** 『李衛公問對』<Ch. *Li Weigong wendui*]. One of the seven Chinese classics on military strategy. See: *Buryaku shichi sho.*

Toyama Gakkō 戸山学校 [Var. ***Rikugun Toyama Gakkō Bujutsu Kyōkan*** 陸軍戸山学校陸武術教官]. A school for training army (*rikugun*) personnel—commissioned and non-commissioned officers—in Western military skills. Part of the curriculum of the academy included some of the more traditional Japanese martial/military arts, such as quick-draw sword arts (*iaijutsu*). At the Toyama Gakkō this art was referred to as *guntō sohō.* Several famous swordsmen in the 1920s, such as Nakayama Hakudō, contributed to the development of an army style of swordsmanship at the academy. This system was formalized in 1925. Consequently, the quick-draw sword system which developed for the army at the Toyama Gakkō was heavily influenced by Nakayama's line of Musō Jikiden Eishin Ryū 無双直伝英信流. See: *guntō sohō; Nakamura Ryū; Nakamura Taisaburō; Nakayama Hiromichi (Hakudō); Toyama Ryū.*

Tōyama Kanken 遠山 寛賢 (1888–1966). An Okinawan *karate* master who laid the foundations for the Shūdōkan style of *karate*. Born in Shuri, Okinawa, Tōyama first began training under Itarashiki Chōiku 板良敷朝郁 in 1897. Subsequently he also trained under Itosu Ankō and Higaonna Kanryō. (Evidently Tōyama and Funakoshi Gichin were the only two students to receive the title of master instructor [*shihanshi*] from Itosu.) Tōyama also learned long hardwood staff arts (*bōjutsu*), trident arts (*saijutsu*), and other Okinawan *kobudō* weapon systems from Ōshiro Chōjo 大城朝恕, Tana Soregashi 田名某, and Chibana Chōshō 知花朝章.

In 1924, Tōyama moved to Taiwan, where he taught school and began learning Chinese combatives. In 1930 he moved to the Tōkyō area and opened a training hall (*dōjō*) called the Shūdōkan 修道館. After the war he created an organization for the purpose of unifying the various schools of *karate* in Okinawa and Japan under one governing entity. In order to do this, he registered the Shūdōkan as the headquarters of the All-Japan Karatedo Federation (AJKF)[33] throughout Japan.

Tōyama Mitsuru 頭山 満 [A.k.a. (pen name) ***Ritsuun*** 立雲] (1855–1944). A powerful right-wing leader and promoter of classical martial arts in the Meiji, Taishō, and Shōwa eras.

Born into a poor samurai family in Fukuoka and trained in the swordsmanship of the Jigen Ryū,[34] Tōyama rose to become one of the most feared men in Japan during the first half of the twentieth century. He accomplished this as a right-wing activist, co-founding the Gen'yōsha (Black Ocean Society; Dark Ocean Society) with Hiraoka Kotarō in 1879.

Tōyama attracted a number of *sōshi* (swashbucklers, nationalists) to his cause, and encouraged them to train in the classical martial arts (*bugei*). However, most of them seem to have preferred the more modern disciplines of *jūdō* and *kendō*. With the support of the Kokuryūkai, a similar ultra-rightist organization founded in 1901, Tōyama and his Gen'yōsha patronized a number of classical martial arts figures during the Meiji, Taishō, and Shōwa eras including Ōmori Sōgen (Jiki Shinkage Ryū), Nakano Michiomi (Shōrinji Kempō), Uchida Ryōhei and Shimizu Takaji (both of the Shindō Musō Ryū), and others.

Although historian David Bergamini, in his work *Japan's Imperial Conspiracy*, described Tōyama as "Lord High Assassin" of the Gen'yōsha, there is no proof of this, and other scholars in the field have a somewhat more benign interpretation of the role played by Tōyama and the Gen'yōsha.

Further reading in English:

- Bergamini, 1971.
- Sabey, 1972.

L to R: Deguchi Onisaburo, Tōyama Mitsuru, and Uchida Ryōhei, c.1923

Toyama Ryū 戸山流. An early term used by Nakamura Taisaburō for the system of quick-draw swordsmanship (*iaidō, battōdō*) he practiced at the Toyama Gakkō in the late 1920's and 1930s. The system at Toyama Gakkō, called *guntō sohō*, was formulated for the military by a group of swordsmen headed by Nakayama Hakudō.[35] As Nakayama was a master of the Musō Jikiden Eishin Ryū 無双直伝英信流, that system heavily influenced the techniques of the Toyama Ryū. However, since the Toyama Gakkō was a school for the military, the system was simplified, with an emphasis on cutting practice. Later, after World War II, Nakamura Taisaburō further modified Toyama Ryū into Nakamura Ryū 中村流. See: *guntō sohō; Nakamura Taisaburō; Toyama Gakkō.*

Toyo Iwamado no Mikoto 豊磐間戸命【豐磐間戶命】. SHINTŌ—One of the two Ya Daijin, the two Shintō *kami* found guarding the entrance to Shintō shrines. See: *Ya Daijin; zuishin.*

Toyoshima Kazutora 豊島 一虎. Second (current) headmaster of Ryūshinkan Budō, and twenty-fifth headmaster of the Nakajima line of the Shinkage Ryū (6).

Toyotomi Hidetsugu 豊臣 秀次【豐臣秀次】(1568–1595). Nephew of Toyotomi Hideyoshi. Hidetsugu was made Kampaku (imperial regent) by Hideyoshi in 1591. However, their relationship deteriorated after the birth of Hideyoshi's heir, Hideyori, in 1593; Hidetsugu was ordered to commit suicide (*seppuku*) in 1595.

---

33 Zen Nihon Karatedō Sōhombu Shūdōkan 全日本空手道連盟総本部修道館.

34 This according to Shimizu Takaji c. 1973.

35 Nakayama was the sixteenth-generation headmaster of the Shimomura Ha Musō Jikiden Eishin Ryū 下村派無双直伝英信流. However, by 1932 he had moved in his own direction, formatting a new system which eventually came to be called the Musō Shinden Ryū 夢想神伝流.

Toyotomi Hideyoshi 豊臣 秀吉【豐臣秀吉】(1536–1598). Hideyoshi is one of the most remarkable men in Japanese history. He was the son of a peasant who was possibly a foot-soldier (*ashigaru*). From his poor origins, he moved from having servant status under Oda Nobunaga to commanding some of Oda's forces, and eventually became Oda's successor as the most powerful warlord in Japan. A detailed treatment of his life can be found in Elizabeth Berry's *Hideyoshi* (1982).

Hideyoshi was such an important figure in Japanese history that legends about his life abound and several novels have been written about him. Japanese author Yoshikawa Eiji produced a swashbuckling story about Hideyoshi entitled *Taikōki*『太閤記』, which has been translated into English as *Taiko* by William Scott Wilson.

Further reading in English:

- Berry, 1982; 1983.
- Wilson, (trans.), 2000.

Toyu Ryū 土由流 [Also read ***Toyū Ryū***] <Ko. Toyu Ryu. An obscure school of Japanese swordsmanship described and illustrated in an eighteenth-century Korean text known as the *Bugei zufu tōshi*『武藝圖譜通志』<Ko. *Muye dobo tongji*. See: *Bugei zufu tōshi*.

Further reading in English:

- Kim, (trans.) 2001: 161–168; 193.

tozama daimyō 外様大名. Lit. "outsider *daimyō*." This term originally referred to warlords who were not shogunal vassals. After the battle of Sekigahara in 1600, Tokugawa Ieyasu gave this title to the eighty-six lords who finally submitted to him. The 176 *daimyō* who had submitted to Ieyasu prior to Sekigahara were called *fudai daimyō*.

Tozan Ryū 渡山流. OKINAWAN KARATE—A system of *karate* founded by Kaneshima Shinsuke. Kaneshima began training at the age of fourteen with Motobu Chōyū in a traditional Okinawan combative system known as Motobu Udundī 本部御殿手. Furthermore, as a young man Kaneshima spent time in Taiwan training with Tokuyama Chōgi 渡久山 朝義 in Shuri Te. He also trained with several other Okinawan *karate* masters. However, in naming his own system "Tozan Ryū" he used the characters from the name of his Shuri Te instructor, Tokuyama 渡久山 (these characters can also be read "Tozan").

There are eleven kata in the Tozan Ryū:

- Sēsan 十三
- Naihanchi 内半進
- Pinan 平安
- Passai 抜塞
- Chintō 鎮闘
- Jitte 十手
- Jion 慈思
- Ūsēshī 五十四歩
- Kūsankū 公相君
- Rushan (from Taiwan)
- Dōchin (from Taiwan)

Further reading in English:

- Bishop, 1999: 109–113.

Tozawa Tokusanrō 戸沢 徳三郎. Instructed Morihei Ueshiba in Tenshin Shin'yō Ryū 天神真楊流 *jūjutsu*, c.1901.

tsuba 鍔. 1. The handguard on a sword. There are many varieties of *tsuba*; those used on metal swords are normally made of metal, while those used on wooden swords are usually made of cured cowhide, boar hide, wood, or plastic. The handguards on bamboo swords (*shinai*) are usually made of cured cowhide, boar hide, or plastic. 2. SHINDŌ MUSŌ RYŪ—A specific *kyūsho* (vital point on the body).

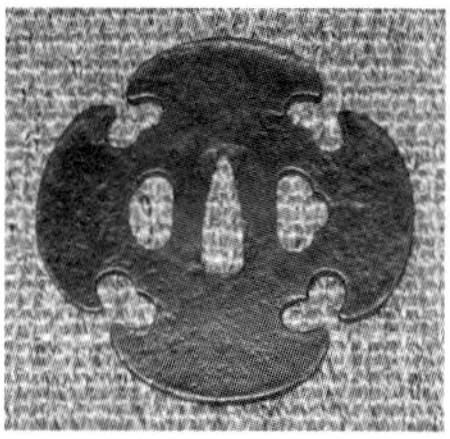

TSUBA WITH PERIPHERAL *I NO ME* DESIGN
(Private collection)

tsubadome 鍔留. A flexible ring, usually made of rubber, which is used to secure a *tsuba* on a *bokken*.

Tsubamegaeshi 燕返. Lit. "Returning Swallow" or "Swallow Counter." A special sword technique for which Sasaki Kojirō became famous in the early seventeenth century. The name can mean "[sword technique fast enough to] cut a swallow" or "[sword technique which] moves in the manner of as a swallow." Although the actual technique is unknown, there are references here and there to its similarity to an Ittō Ryū technique called Kinshichōō Ken. See also: *Gan Ryū (1); Ittō Ryū (1); Kinshichōō Ken; Sasaki Kojirō.*

tsuba yari 鍔槍. A spear (*yari*) with a handguard (*tsuba*). See: *Iki Tōtōmi no Kami Ryū.*

tsuba-zeriai 鍔迫合 [Var. 鍔競合]. 1. To lock handguards (*tsuba*) and press the opponent. 2. Close-in fighting.

tsubo ツボ [Also a non-standard reading for 経穴【經穴】]. An alternate term for a vital point; a pressure point; an acupuncture point. (Minouchi, 1982). See also: *kyūsho.*

tsuchi ikki 土一揆 [Also read ***doikki***]. Organizations formed by peasants in the fourteenth century. The *tsuchi ikki* were originally aimed at protesting and rebelling against the economic demands of regional authorities and the proprietors of private estates (*shōen*). These "protests" often turned violent. See: *ikki; Ikkō Ikki; kuni ikki.*

Further reading in English:

- Davis, 1974: 226–233.
- Tsang, 2008.

Tsuchiya Shōgen 土屋 将監. Tsuchiya trained under Kamiizumi Ise no Kami's student Jingo Izu no Kami Muneharu in the Shinkage Ryū 新陰流. He subsequently founded a branch tradition known as the Shinkage Ryū 心陰流 in the late 1500s.

Tsuda Gonnojō Taira no Nobuyuki 津田 権之丞 信之【津田權之丞信之】. See: *Tsuda Nobuyuki.*

Tsuda Ichiden Ryū 津田一伝流【津田一傳流】. A branch tradition of the Asayama Ichiden Ryū 浅山一伝流 founded by Tsuda Ichizaemon Masayuki in the mid-nineteenth century. The system concentrated on swordsmanship (*kenjutsu*).

Tsuda Ichizaemon Masayuki 津田 一左衛門 正之 (1821–1871). Founder of the Tsuda Ichiden Ryū. Having mastered the Asayama Ichiden Ryū 浅山一伝流 taught by his father, Tsuda traveled to Nakatsu, Edo, and Kyōto in order to train with master swordsmen in those areas. He subsequently revised the Asayama Ichiden Ryū of his father and renamed this branch tradition the Tsuda Ichiden Ryū. Following the dissolution of the warrior class in 1871, Tsuda committed suicide (*seppuku*).

Tsuda Kenmotsu Kazunaga 津田 監物算長. Founder of the Tsuda Ryū, a school of gunnery (*hōjutsu*).

Tsuda Nobuyuki 津田 信之 [A.k.a. ***Tsuda Gonnojō Taira no Nobuyuki Ikkei*** 津田 権之丞 平 信之 一兮] (1654–1698). An outstanding warrior of the late seventeenth century who founded the Kan Ryū 貫流 in 1671. Tsuda was a martial genius who, at the age of sixteen, had mastered and received licenses (*menkyo*) in the spear arts of Saburi En'uemon Tadamura's Saburi Ryū 佐分利流 and Mori Kambee's line of Itō Ryū 伊東流.

Tsuda Ryū 津田流. A school of gunnery (*hōjutsu*) founded by Tsuda Kenmotsu Kazunaga. The third headmaster was Tsuda Jiyūsai Masakatsu 津田自由斎正勝.

tsue 杖 [Normally read ***zue*** in compounds; also read ***jō***]. Japanese term for a medium-length staff.

tsugi ashi 継足【繼足】. 1. A sliding step. 2. A foot movement specific to the martial arts, in which one foot takes a step and the other foot is then drawn toward it via a sliding step.

tsuibatsushi 追罸使. A twelfth-century term for an arresting officer; this title took the place of the earlier *tsuibushi*. These officers were assigned by the court and sent to provincial posts.

tsuibushi 追捕使. Lit. "pursue-and-capture envoy." This tenth-century title was conferred for the first time on the warrior Ono Yoshifuru in 939, when he was charged with leading a search-and-destroy mission (*tsuitō*) against the rebel pirate Fujiwara Sumitomo on the island of Shikoku.

In the eleventh century, *tsuibushi* was a provincial military post; the title meant "arresting officer." When provincial governors awarded this post to local warrior leaders in order to bring in rural support troops, it carried the title "provincial arresting officer" (*shokoku tsuibushi*). See also: *ōryōshi; sōtsuibushi; tsuibatsushi.*

tsuitō 追討. To pursue and subjugate; to strike down. This term referred to search-and-destroy missions sent against Fujiwara Sumitomo's pirates during the mid-tenth century.

tsuitōshi 追討使. Lit. "pursue-and-strike-down envoy." A tenth- and eleventh-century title meaning "search-and-destroy officer."

Tsuji Gettan Sukemochi 辻 月旦 資茂 (1648–1728). Founder of the Mugai Ryū 無外流, a school of combative swordsmanship (*kenjutsu*) and quick-draw sword arts (*iaijutsu*). At the age of thirteen, Tsuji journeyed to the capitol city of Kyōto and became a student of Yamaguchi Bokushinsai 山口卜真斎 of the Yamaguchi Ryū 山口流 school of combative swordsmanship. After training under Yamaguchi for thirteen years, Tsuji made a pilgrimage to Aburahi Peak (Aburahi Take 油日嶽) in Kōka,[36] and to Mount Atago just outside Kyōto, where he performed religious austerities (*shugyō*). He subsequently proceeded on a warrior's pilgrimage (*musha shugyō*) to northern Japan in the area of Echigo (modern-day Niigata prefecture). He then entered training again in the Yamaguchi Ryū under Itō Shōgen 伊藤将監. In 1674, at the age of twenty-six, he received a full license (*menkyo kaiden*) in Yamaguchi Ryū from Yamaguchi Bokushinsai and opened a training hall (*dōjō*) in Edo. While residing in Edo, Tsuji began studying Zen Buddhism with the monk Sekitan 石潭. The teachings of the Zen school deeply impressed him, and one Zen text passage he learned from Sekitan struck him in such a way that he took it for the name of his new martial arts tradition. The phrase began, *Ippō jitsu mugai…* (一法実無外) "There is truly nothing other than the one way…" meaning that Zen was the one path to enlightenment. Tsuji applied this to his swordsmanship, and came to a realization that "Zen and swordsmanship are one" (*ken zen itchi* 剣禅一致). Later, Tsuji also trained in the quick-draw swordsmanship of Jikyō Ryū 自鏡流 with Taga Jikyōsai Morimasa, and added Taga's teachings to his own Mugai Ryū. Tsuji's school flourished during the succeeding centuries and became very widespread, with many sub-branches.

tsujigiri 辻斬. Lit. "street killing." 1. The practice of testing one's newly acquired sword on a chance passerby. See also: *kirisute gomen.* 2. A samurai who engages in *tsujigiri.* 3. A Meiji-era term for "street fighting with live blades" or "assassination." 4. A Meiji-era term meaning "street fighter" or "assassin."

tsuka 柄. The haft or hilt of a dagger, knife, or sword.

tsukagashira 柄頭. [Also read ***heitō***; var. ***kashiragane*** 頭金]. The cap covering the pommel of a sword or knife. Its design often matched that of the metal ring (*fuchi*) on the opposite end of the hilt; both were usually made by the same artist.

Tsukahara Bokuden 塚原 卜伝 【塚原卜傳】 (1489–1571). One of the most famous swordsmen of the early sixteenth century; founder of the Kashima Shintō Ryū 鹿島新当流.

TSUKAHARA BOKUDEN
(Yoshikawa family archives)

[36] 甲賀 is also read "Kōga."

Bokuden was born a member of the Yoshikawa family, who served as the shrine guards and diviners of Kashima Jingū. He took the new family name of Tsukahara upon being adopted into that clan. In addition to the martial arts of his birth family (Kashima no Tachi), he later learned the Tenshinshō-den Katori Shintō Ryū 天真正伝香取神道流 from his adopted father.[37] While engaging in *musha shugyō* (warrior pilgrimage and ascetic training), Bokuden received a vision or spiritual revelation. From this, he systematized the teaching of the Kashima area's local martial arts into a new system he christened the Kashima Shintō Ryū.

Ichi no Tachi (Hitotsu no Tachi), a pivotal sword strategy attributed to Bokuden, was a key element in the Kashima Shintō Ryū; it is thought to have been transmitted to other, later descendant traditions such as the Jiki Shinkage Ryū 直心影流. It is the first technique in the curriculum of both traditions.

Further reading in English:

- Knutsen, 2004: 221–229.
- Sugawara, 1985: 15–31.

tsukaiban 使番 [A.k.a. ***gunshi*** 軍使]. Messengers whose job it was to transport messages between commanding generals and troops during battle. Turnbull (2005: 273) refers to them as a "high-ranking elite messenger corps."

tsukai sute 使捨. Lit. "use and discard." A cheap sword issued to low-ranking warriors during the Warring States period (Sengoku Jidai).

tsuka ito 柄糸. The cord wound around the hilt of a sword or knife.

tsuki 1. 突き. A thrust.

tsuki 2. 月. The moon.

tsukigata jūmonji yari 月型十文字槍. A variant of the *jūmonji yari* or *kamayari* in which the side blades curve forward in a crescent-moon shape.

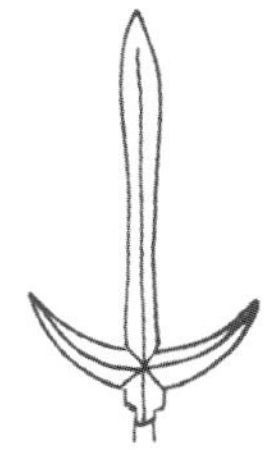

TSUKIGATA JŪMONJI YARI

tsuki hazushi uchi 突外打. Lit. "evade a thrust and strike." SHINDŌ MUSŌ RYŪ—A technique in which the medium-length staff (*jō*) is used to help direct the opponent's weapon away as the body simultaneously pivots (*taisabaki*) to evade the attack. This is the tenth of the twelve basic techniques (*kihon*) extrapolated from the classical forms of Shindō Musō Ryū by Shimizu Takaji.

tsuki kage 1. 月影. Lit. "moonbeams" or "moonlight," the term *tsuki kage* is often used as a poetic reference in Japanese swordsmanship. See: *tsuki kage (2)*.

tsuki kage 2. 月陰 [Also read ***getsu kage*** in some traditions]. As this term is a homophone for *tsuki kage* (1), it is often used as a poetic reference in Japanese swordsmanship. Its earliest use is attributed to Aisu Ikōsai of the Aisu Kage Ryū 愛洲陰流 in the late fifteenth century. As the name of a key *kata* in the Empi series, it was passed down to Kamiizumi Nobutsuna, where it was incorporated in most branches of his Shinkage Ryū (1) 新陰流.

tsukinari yari 月形槍. Lit. "moon-shaped spear." A polearm with a crescent-shaped spearhead. **See also:** *sōjutsu; yari*.

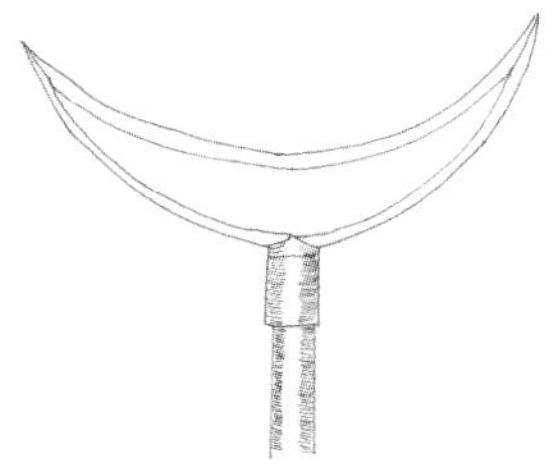

TSUKINARI YARI

[37] Knutsen (2004: 28) notes that Bokuden learned Kashima no Tachi 鹿島之太刀 and Kashima Chūko Ryū 鹿島中古流 from his father-in-law, and studied *kenjutsu* under Matsumoto Bizen no Kami (recognized founder of Kashima Shin Ryū 鹿島神流 and chief counselor of the Kashima clan until his death in battle in 1525).

T

Tsuki no sho 『月之抄』. Text on Shinkage Ryū 新陰流 swordsmanship written in 1637 by Yagyū Jūbei Mitsuyoshi.

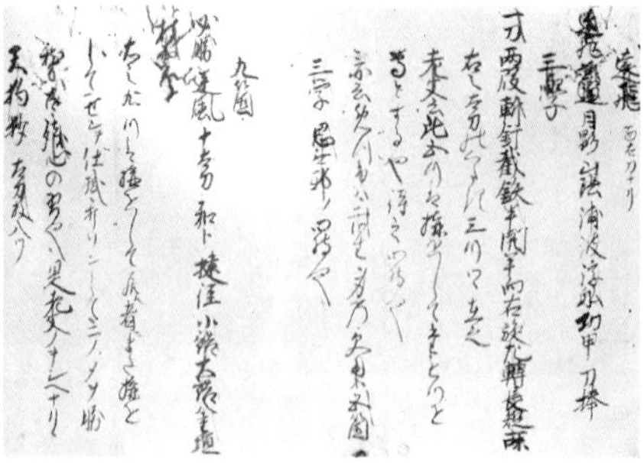

DETAIL OF *TSUKI NO SHO* BY YAGYŪ JŪBEI
Shown are Jūbei's comments on several sets of Shinkage Ryū *kata*: Empi, Sangaku, and Kuka
(Tōkaiji temple archive—Tōkyō)
(Reprinted in Imamura, vol. 1, ©1966)

Tsukioka Yoshitoshi 月岡 芳年 [A.k.a. ***Taiso Yoshitoshi*** 大蘇芳年] (1839–1892). Japan's latest, and to some, greatest master of the woodblock print. Tsukioka lived at a time of great change, through the end of Japan's premodern era and the beginning of the modern era. He was extremely prolific (especially in *mushae*, images of warriors) and created many woodblock prints depicting the violent times of Japan's 1860s when the country was in the throes of moving from a feudal to a modern society. Many of his collections may be seen today. See also: *mushae; Utagawa Kuniyoshi.*

Edo period policeman (*dōshin*) threatening a swordsman with a *tsukubō*
Detail of illustration from the nineteenth-century *Tokugawa bakufu keiji zufu honpen*
(Used with permission from Meiji University Museum)

TSUKUBŌ

tsukubō 突棒. Lit. "thrusting staff." A T-shaped polearm used to ensnare opponents. A number of varieties were developed. This weapon found wide use during the Sengoku and early Edo periods as one of the three primary weapons (*mitsudōgu*) for use in concert for trapping and restraining swordsmen. See also: *sodegarami; sasumata.*

tsukushi naginata 筑紫薙刀 [Also called ***naginata no saki*** 長刀の先]. A *naginata* with a socketed head. This was an early type of the weapon.

Tsukushi naginata

tsumeru 詰める. A dueling and training technique in which the proponent would stop a strike a centimeter or so away from the target. Yagyū Muneyoshi was evidently regarded as the swordsman with the best *tsumeru* in his time (mid-sixteenth century), while a generation later, Miyamoto Musashi was said to be able to cut halfway through a rice grain on a person's forehead. See also: *yakusoku.*

tsumi 罪. Vice, wickedness, blame, or fault. *Tsumi* is seen as the natural counterpart of virtue; the two were seen to be in a *yin/yang* relationship. *Tsumi* could also be washed off or wiped away via austere religious practices (*shugyō/gyō*) or, in severe cases, suicide in the form of *seppuku*. See also: *gyō; bushi no konjō; shugyō.*

tsune no kamae 常の構. Lit. the "normal posture." SHINDŌ MUSŌ RYŪ—A posture in which the body is positioned with hips/trunk/shoulders facing forward toward the opponent. The staff (*jō*) is held in the right hand at the balance point. The front end of the *jō* is raised slightly and is angled toward the opponent's center line. At *awase* distance (one at which the ends of the partners' weapons touch or cross for several inches), the front tip of the *jō* would follow a line toward the point between the opponent's eyes. At contact distance, the tip of the *jō* would be aimed approximately at the opponent's solar plexus.

tsura 弦. See: *tsuru.*

tsurao 弦. See: *tsuru.*

tsurebyōshi 連拍子. Lit. "to follow or shadow the opponent's beat." YAGYŪ SHINKAGE RYŪ—An attack in which the proponent strikes the enemy just as the latter prepares to strike (Mutō, 1985–1990). See: *hyōshi.*

tsuru 弦 [Also read ***tsura; tsurao***]. A bowstring.

tsurubashiri 弦走. A leather cover used on the front of the trunk-protecting armor (*dō*) in Japanese "great armor" (*ōyoroi*). The *tsurubashiri* provided a smooth surface over the scaled or laced armor so a bowstring would not become entangled. This smooth leather cover was often elaborately decorated with symbols or pictures of mythical beings.

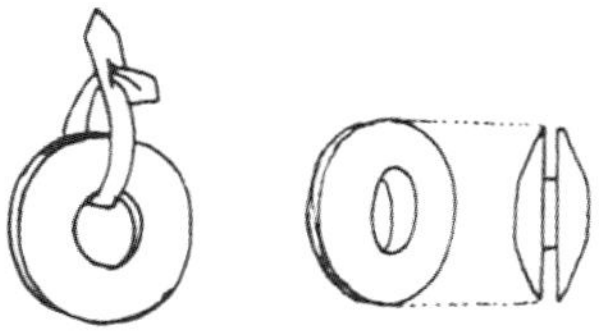

TSURUBUKURO
Illustrations from the *Buyō benryaku*, an Edo-period work

tsurubukuro 弦袋 [Also read ***tsurufukuro***; a.k.a.: ***tsurumaki*** 弦巻]. A bowstring holder; a bowstring spindle. Early descriptions of the *tsurubukuro/tsurumaki* are found in two Edo-period works, the *Teijō zakki*『貞丈雑記』and the *Buyō benryaku*『武用弁略』. Scrolls and screens of the Heian and Kamakura periods often show his device being worn by *bushi* archers.

tsurufukuro 弦袋. See: *tsurubukuro.*

Tsurugaoka Hachimangū 鶴岡八幡宮 [Abbrev. ***Hachimangū*** 八幡宮]. A shrine in the city of Kamakura dedicated to Hachiman, the god of war (whose name literally means "Eight Banners"). All Hachimangū shrines are dedicated to the fifteenth emperor, Ojin,[38] who came to be identified with the god Hachiman. Hachiman later became a tutelary deity of the Minamoto clan under Minamoto no Yoritomo, founder of the Kamakura shogunate. The Tsurugaoka Hachimangū shrine in Kamakura is one of the most prestigious shrines in Japan, and martial exhibitions are held there on special occasions. See also: *Kashima Jingū; Katori Jingū; Yasukuni Jinja.*

tsurugi 剣【劍; 劒】. A straight sword, sometimes widening toward the point, often used for votive purposes. *Tsurugi* are often found held in the hands of Buddhist statues. Early straight swords imported from China and Korea were of two types: *tsurugi* and *tachi*. The *tsurugi* had a double cutting edge, and the *tachi* had a single cutting edge.

tsurumaki 弦巻. See: *tsurubukuro.*

tsuru oto 弦音. The sound of a vibrating bowstring.

tsurushi 弦師. A bowstring maker; a stringer.

Tsutsumi Hōzan Ryū 堤宝山流【堤寶山流】[Var. 堤法参流]. A comprehensive combative tradition (*sōgō bujutsu*) founded by Tsutsumi Yamashiro no Kami Hōzan c.1390. The school included swordsmanship (*kenjutsu*), unarmored grappling (*jūjutsu*), armored grappling (*kogusoku*), sickle-and-chain arts (*kusarigama-jutsu*), long hardwood staff techniques (*bōjutsu*), long-hafted glaive techniques (*naginatajutsu*), spear (*sōjutsu*), archery (*yumi*), horsemanship (*bajutsu*), a heavy medium-length staff sometimes affixed with a weighted chain (*furijō*), and the tying-cord (*torinawa*).

Caution should be used in evaluating secondary sources on this system. Although the *kusarigama-jutsu* techniques of Isshin Ryū (1) 一心流 are attributed to the Nen Ryū 念流 via the Tsutsumi Hōzan Ryū, the sickle-and-chain art that has been passed down in that system does not appear practical in the context of the armored warfare of the late fourteenth through sixteenth centuries. It is possible, however, that the original sickle-and-chain composite weapon of the Tsutsumi Hōzan Ryū was the *nagae no kama*, a polearm. The *kusarigama*, a shorter weapon, may have been developed later for use outside a battlefield context.

[38] Ōjin Tennō 応神天皇 (c.201–c.312). A legendary emperor; his actual dates are unknown.

T

Tsutsumi Yamashiro no Kami Hōzan 堤山城守宝山【堤山城守寶山】[Var. **Hōzan** 法讃; 法参【法參】] (c.1350–c.1425). Founder of the Tsutsumi Hōzan Ryū. Tsutsumi is included in the list of fourteen direct disciples of Nen Ami Jion's Nen Ryū, and is supposed to have mastered swordsmanship (*kenjutsu*), spear arts (*sōjutsu*), and armored grappling (*yoroi kumi*) under Jion. According to Nen Ryū documents, Tsutsumi excelled at armored grappling. Legends also indicate he was also an expert in the use of the *jutte* and *kusarigama*, but these are probably apocryphal.

tsuwamono 兵. A word meaning "warrior" used around the time of the tenth-century conflict known as the Tengyō no Ran. This term most likely refers to mounted archers, in contrast to foot soldiers (*banrui*). However, the *tsuwamono* of the tenth century were unlike the ruling warrior class (*bushi*) of later years in that they were often only part-time warriors. Because they did not have a monopoly on the profession of arms, they made extensive use of peasant foot soldiers (*banrui*), and their armies were ad-hoc, temporary affairs—quickly put together and just as quickly dispersed. See also: *hyōe; ikusa; bushi; kondei; musha.*

tsuwamono no ie 兵の家. Lit. "warrior house," "warrior clan." 1. This term refers to hereditary warrior families that began to appear in Japan at least as early as the eighth century. They specialized in warrior arts (*bugei*), especially mounted archery, and, in the eighth century, included such families as the Ōtomo 大友, Saeki 佐伯, and Sakanoe 坂上. By the ninth century the list had expanded to include the Ono 小野 and Ōkura 大倉. There were many others including the Ise Taira 伊勢平, Montoku Genji 文徳源氏, Nagara Fujiwara 長良藤原, Tachibana 立花, Hidesato Fujiwara 秀郷藤原, etc. In the tenth century the court curtailed social mobility by fixing official warrior society into heredity houses with official court ranks of the sixth, fifth, and sometimes fourth level. (A fifth-level court rank gave the warrior the status of a noble or aristocrat.) These hereditary "martial aristocrats" were usually aligned with one court noble or another, and birth into a warrior house gave the warrior a strong sense of elite status. However, according to some sources many of the military aristocrats of the eleventh century were nothing more than "hired assassins." 2. A tenth- and eleventh-century term denoting a warrior's residence. *Tsuwamono no ie* tended to be large and complex. In addition, a substantial amount of wealth was required to support even one horse-mounted, armored warrior and his assistants. Living with the *tsuwamono* would most likely be warrior-followers (*jūrui*) who were economically dependent on the warrior and fought alongside him as mounted archers.

A typical *tsuwamono no ie* would contain barns and stables, storage buildings, a forge, and other necessary industries. There would be a main residence for the *tsuwamono* and several homes for support personnel, both civil and martial. The whole thing would be enclosed by a wall which included security posts. According to Farris (1992: 150–151), entry or search of a *tsuwamono no ie* was illegal.

tsuwamono no michi 兵の道. A tenth-century term for the "way of the warrior." At the time, it apparently referred to proficiency in martial arts. The word is found in the war tale called the *Shōmonki*. See also: *bushidō; kyūba no michi.*

Tsuwamono no Tsukasa 兵部省. An ancient term for the Hyōbushō, a seventh-century office equivalent to a Ministry of War.

tsuyoyumi 強弓. To be powerful with a bow (and arrow). An accolade used in the *Heike monogatari* to describe the "eastern" warriors (Bandō *musha*). It is somewhat equivalent to the term *yunzei* (powerful with the bow).

tsuzumi 鼓. A hand drum with a body shaped like an hourglass.

MINAMOTO NO YOSHITSUNE (USHIWAKAMARU)
LEARNING SWORDSMANSHIP FROM A *TENGU*
(Woodblock print by Sadahide, c. 1835)

T

U

u 卯 [Also read ***bō***]. Hare. 1. The Hour of the Hare is the fourth duodenary hour of the Chinese Twelve Branches (Jūnishi): 5 to 7 a.m. 2. KYŪSHO—In certain Sino-Japanese boxing texts, the Hare character indicates the optimal time of day for striking the corresponding vital point (*kyūsho*). See also: Appendix 1.

u~ 右~. The term for "right" (in contrast to "left") used in compounds such as *ukan* 右貫 ("piercing the right").

ubai 優婆夷 <Ch. *youpoyi* <Skt. *upāsikā*. A female lay Buddhist who has received the five precepts (*gokai*) for laymen and laywomen. See also: *dōbōshū; nyūdō; tonseisha; ubasoku.*

ubasoku 優婆塞 <Ch. *youpose* <Skt. *upāsaka*. 1. A male lay Buddhist who has received the five precepts (*gokai*) for laymen and laywomen. 2. A religious ascetic; a religious hermit; a practitioner of a variety of spiritual/magical arts and mysticism such as In'yōdō. See also: *dōbōshū; nyūdō; tonseisha; ubai.*

ubusuna no kami 産土の神. SHINTŌ—The tutelary deity of one's birthplace. An infant is normally taken to a family's home shrine, and the deity of the shrine is supposed to protect the person throughout their life. Even if the person moves away from the original home area, they may return periodically to that shrine during festival times to propitiate its deity. Contrast to *ujigami.*

uchi 打. 1. An abbreviation for *uchidachi*. 2. ***~uchi*** ~打ち. This is a term used in a compound to indicate a strike; i.e., *shōmen-uchi* indicates a strike (*uchi*) to the front of the head (*shōmen*).

uchidachi 打太刀. Lit. "striking sword" or "struck sword." Written with various characters, depending on the particular school (*ryū*), this term indicates the person against whom the school's technique is executed. In most classical weapons systems, the proponent in this position is the senior. The *uchidachi*'s technique is sometimes derived from another *ryū*. Contrast to *shidachi.*

Uchida Ryōgorō 内田 良五郎 (1837–1921). Creator of the Uchida Ryū 内田流. Uchida, who received Shindō Musō Ryū 神道夢想流 *menkyo kaiden* from Hirano Kichizō 平野吉蔵, was the son of Hiraoka Nisaburō 平岡仁三郎, a *menkyo kaiden* holder in Shindō Musō Ryū. Ryōgorō's younger brother, Hiraoka Kōtarō 平岡浩太郎, became the family inheritor; Ryōgorō took another family name upon being adopted at the age of fourteen.

Ryōgorō, his brother Kōtarō, and other Shindō Musō Ryū *shizoku* (disenfranchised samurai), along with Tōyama Mitsuru, were among the founding members of the Gen'yōsha (Black Ocean Society; Dark Ocean Society) in 1879. Kōtarō became the first official head of the society.

Ryōgorō was a passionate martial artist. He began training at an early age and mastered Ono Ha Ittō Ryū 小野派一刀流 swordsmanship (*heihō*), Hōzōin Ryū Takada Ha 宝蔵院流高田派 spearmanship (*sōjutsu*), Kyūshin Ryū 汲心流 grappling arts (*jūjutsu*), Shindō Musō Ryū 神道夢想流 medium-length staff (*jō*), and Ikkaku Ryū 一角流 arresting techniques (*torite*). He also studied horsemanship (*bajutsu*), archery (*kyūjutsu*), gunnery (*hōjutsu*), and other arts. In addition, he excelled in the study of literature. He personally taught classical martial arts to his children during the 1870s and had them train in Jigō Tenshin Ryū 自剛天真流 *jūjutsu* at the Meidōkan, the Gen'yōsha *dōjō*.

By 1902 Ryōgorō was living in Tōkyō, where he was teaching Shindō Musō Ryū to naval officers at the Dai Nippon Butokukai near Shiba Park. The famous *kendō* practitioner Nakayama Hiromichi (Hakudō) came to the Butokukai to learn Shindō Musō Ryū. Around that same time, Ryōgorō developed his system of short stick-fighting with a cane, calling it *sutekkijutsu* (stick art). Although living in Tōkyō, Ryōgorō often visited the Shiraishi Dōjō 白石道場 in Fukuoka, which had become the "home" training hall for the Shindō Musō Ryū. On those visits he also transmitted his *sutekkijutsu* to the members there, so that it proliferated in both Fukuoka and Tōkyō.

Further reading in English:

• Matsui (trans.), 1993: 18–19.

Uchida Ryōhei 内田 良平 (1873–1936). A *menkyo kaiden* practitioner of the Haruyoshi branch of the Shindō Musō Ryū 神道夢想流. Ryōhei, an ultra-nationalist, founded the Kokuryūkai (Amur River Society). He was also well known for his expertise in *jūdō* (Sabey, 1973: 83, note 40).

Prior to becoming the founding head of the Kokuryūkai, Ryōhei was handpicked for a right-wing activist group intended to stir up trouble in Korea. This group, the Tenyūkō, was a subordinate organization of the Gen'yōsha. Ryōhei had been selected for his expertise in "the manufacture and use of dynamite," and acted as the group's demolition man (Sabey, 1973: 142). He had been introduced to the group via his training in the Gen'yōsha's *dōjō*, the Meidōkan. His prowess in grappling greatly impressed Gen'yōsha leader Tōyama Mitsuru, and despite his young age (twenty-one) Ryōhei quickly became the default leader of the Tenyūkō organization. In 1894 these disenfranchised samurai-cum-soldiers of fortune journeyed to Korea, where they engaged in guerrilla-like activities to destabilize the peninsula.

In 1901 Ryōhei was primarily responsible for the conversion of the Tenyūkō into the Kokuryūkai. Under the new name, Ryōhei's organization worked to increase Japanese awareness of the "Russian Threat" just across the Amur River from Manchuria, and to promote *Dai Ajia shugi* (Greater "Asian-ism"), Ryōhei's concept of an East Asia under Japanese tutelage. For photo, see: *Tōyama Mitsuru.*

Uchida Ryū 内田流. A system of stick-fighting arts which originated with Uchida Ryōgorō, a *menkyō kaiden*-ranked practitioner of the Haruyoshi branch of Shindō Musō Ryū 神道夢想流. Some do not consider the Uchida Ryū to be a separate school (*ryū*) from the Shindō Musō Ryū; in any event, the system became a collateral tradition (*fuzoku bugei*) within Shindō Musō Ryū. The "system" consists of a set of twelve baton/walking-stick scenarios referred to as *suttekijutsu* (alternately, *tanjōjutsu*). These combative forms are derived from Ikkaku Ryū 一角流 *toritejutsu* and Shindō Musō Ryū *jōjutsu*.

uchi deshi 内弟子. A live-in disciple; an apprentice.

uchigane 打金 [Var. 撃鉄【撃鐵】]. The serpentine (match holder) of a matchlock; the hammer of a gun.

uchigatana 打刀. A sword type which began to appear during the early to mid-Muromachi period. Due to the change in the methods for manipulating a sword during the Muromachi period, there was a shift away from the use of the *tachi* (a long, curved sword with a single cutting edge, most efficiently used for one-handed slashing attacks from horseback) to a new, less-curved sword with a single cutting edge, most efficiently used for slash-and-thrust attacks while on foot. This new sword type was called the *uchigatana*, a term which was soon shortened to "*katana*." The *uchigatana* was typically worn cutting-edge upwards and thrust through the sash (*obi*). See also: *tachi; katana; warabite tō.*

uchikagi 内鉤【内鈎】. A grappling hook used for holding two ships together during battle.

uchiko 打ち粉. A slightly abrasive, finely powdered limestone—much like talcum powder—used for cleaning sword blades. The powder is normally kept in a small "pom-pom" made of a layer of silk and a layer of cotton. In the process of sword cleaning, the pom-pom is tapped lightly against the blade so that some of the fine powder adheres to the blade. This powder absorbs the oil which has previously been placed on a stored blade or the oil and perspiration which may have collected on the blade during use. As the *uchiko* is slightly abrasive, it will also remove very light rust stains (*sabi*). The *uchiko* is then wiped from the blade with a special type of absorbent paper. See also: *nuguigami; washi (2).*

uchikomi 打込み. 1. A strike or thrust. ¶ *uchikomu* 打込む, to attack. See also: *fumikomi.* 2. A catching device used by Edo-period police. 3. A training method (most often found in grappling systems such as *jūdō*) in which a technique is repeated several times in order

U

to facilitate learning. 4. ITTŌ SHŌDEN MUTŌ RYŪ—A training practice in which the proponent makes repeated straight strikes with a bamboo sword (*shinai*) to the opponent's forehead (*men*). Often referred to as "attack training" (*kakarigeiko*). Ittō Shōden Mutō Ryū founder Yamaoka Tesshū required his trainees to make repeated strikes until they collapsed.

UCHIKOMI
Edo-period police capturing device
Detail of illustration from the nineteenth-century *Tokugawa bakufu keiji zufu honpen*
(Used with permission from Meiji University Museum)

uchikomigeiko 打込み稽古. A type of competitive fencing match between opponents using protective gear and bamboo swords (*shinai*). *Uchikomigeiko* became popular during the 1700s.

uchikomi no ikusa 打込みの軍 [Var. 打込みの戦]. A mass attack; an assault group.

uchikote 打小手 [A.k.a. ***onikote*** 鬼小手]. Term for protective padded gloves (*kote*) used by various branches of the Ittō Ryū.

uchima 打間. Lit. "striking distance." This term indicates the distance from which a strike or cut can be made effectively. Compare with *suigetsu (3)* and *maai (2)*.

uchimono 打ち物. A weapon.

Uchinā 沖縄【沖繩】(Oki.). See: *Okinawa*.

uchine 打根. A short, heavy, feathered javelin (or heavy arrow) which was thrown by hand or used as a stabbing weapon. According to Knutsen and Knutsen (2004: 123), this weapon was carried by passengers for self-defense while riding in a palanquin.

uchinejutsu 打根術. The art of throwing *uchine* by hand (without the use of a bow). Fujita (1960: 2) notes only one school (*ryū*) specializing in *uchinejutsu*.

uchiokoshi 打起こし. KYŪDŌ—The fourth of the eight formal stages (*hassetsu*) in firing an arrow in the modern martial way of archery (*kyūdō*). *Uchiokoshi*, the process of addressing the target, occurs in two steps: first, the archer turns his head to the left and looks at the target (*monomi*); second, he twists his body to the left toward the target as he raises the bow and arrow above and to the front of his head (*daisan* 大三). See also: *hassetsu*.

Uchiotoshi 打落. 1. A name for a variety of classical combative forms (*kata*) developed by various martial schools. 2. SHINDŌ MUNEN RYŪ—*Uchiotoshi* is one of a number of classical prearranged combative forms (*kata*) developed by this school. It was also one of ten classical *kata* adapted by the Japanese Police Commission of 1886 for their Keishichō Ryū 警視庁流 system.

Uchi Toneri 内舎人. An imperial bodyguard or retainer. See: *toneri*.

uchiwa 団扇【團扇】[A.k.a. ***gunsen*** 軍扇]. A flat, non-folding war fan carried by upper-level officers as a sign of command. *Uchiwa* may be made of embossed or inlaid iron, or wood covered with lacquered leather. They are often decorated with family crests (*mon*), religious symbolism, or patterns used for combative divination. In the latter case, they are often called *gumbai uchiwa*. See also: *gumbai; gumbaisha; gumbai uchiwa*.

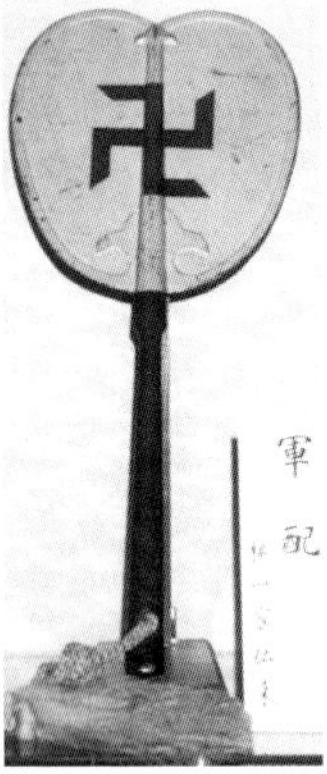

GUMBAI UCHIWA
Designed to look like Marishiten's fan of invisibility
(Fan in the collection of the Kyōto Arashiyama Museum)

uchō no jutsu 雨鳥の術. A system employing tactics involving the use of inclement weather—wind, rain, etc.—to perform covert operations. See: *ninjutsu*.

Uchūdō 宇宙道. A system of self-defense (*goshin* 護身) developed by Senmoto Akiteru and Watanabe Akiteru in the mid-twentieth century. Both were disciples of Hakkō Ryū 八光流 founder Okuyama Yoshiji.

udaishō 右大将 [Also read ***utaishō***]. Although it had become a sinecure in the Kamakura period, the title *udaishō* indicated a commander's position in the palace guards. This was the highest official imperial title received by Minamoto no Yoritomo.

ude 腕. The arm.

ude makuri 腕捲. To roll up one's sleeves. In a martial context, the term *ude makuri* indicates rolling up the sleeves of one's *kimono* in preparation for impromptu combat, training, or martial exhibition (*embu*). This was often done in coordination with tucking up the *hakama* (*shirikarage*). If the sleeves are retained with a cord kept for that purpose, the style is called *tasugigake*.

udenuki 腕貫. A cord attached to or through the hilt (*tsuka*) of a sword; it goes around the user's wrist to prevent the weapon from being dropped.

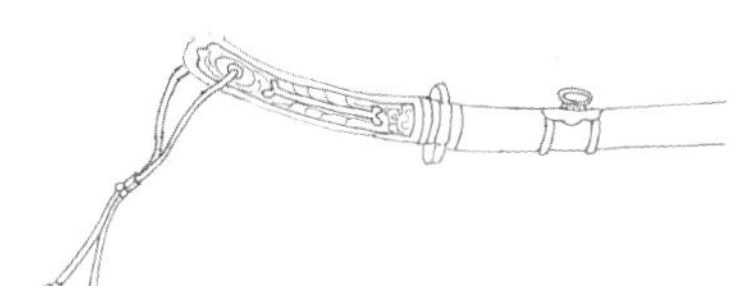

UDENUKI

Udo Daigongen 鵜戸大権現. RYŌBU SHINTŌ—A Ryōbu Shintō deity enshrined in the Udo Jingū in Kyūshū. According to tradition, Kage Ryū founder Aisu Ikōsai was washed ashore on the rocky beach below Udo Jingū after a shipwreck in 1487.

Udoneri 右舎人 [Also read ***U Toneri***]. An imperial bodyguard or retainer. See: *toneri*.

udundī 御殿手 (Oki.). See: *Motobu Udundī*.

Uechi Kambun 上地 完文 (1877–1948). The founder of Uechi Ryū *karatedō*. In 1897, at the age of twenty, Kanbun left Okinawa for the city of Fuzhou in Fujian province in order to learn Chinese fighting arts. At a Buddhist temple in Fujian[1] he trained in "tiger fist"[2] with a Chinese boxing master named Shū Shi-wa (Ch. Zhou Zihe). However, much like other Okinawan foreign students in Fujian, Kanbun did not train with only one instructor, nor did he simply bring back one boxing system to Okinawa. Consequently, the boxing techniques of Uechi Ryū are described as "dragon-tiger-crane boxing" by Momohara (2008: 161).[3]

UECHI KANBUN
Founder of Uechi Ryū *karatedō*
(Photograph courtesy Donald J. McHoul)

For thirteen years Uechi devoted himself to various boxing methods, which he later called Pangainūn Ryū パンガイヌーン流 (Jp. Hankōnan 半硬軟). *Pangainūn* means "half-hard and half-flexible," but this term is not found as such in the Chinese language of Fujian. Its use by Uechi seem to echo the term *gōjū* (hard/soft or force/yield). Additionally, as the combative forms (*kata*) brought back by Uechi are similar in name and execution to some of the Gōjū Ryū *kata* imported by Higaonna Kanryō, a common origin is apparent.

Uechi returned to Okinawa in 1909 due to

1 Chūō Bukkyōji 中央佛教寺 <Ch. Zhongyang Fojiaosi.

2 *Koken* 虎拳 <Ch. *hu quan*. McCarthy (1995: 38) specifies "tiger fist"; however, Momohara (2008: 161) simply refers to the system studied by Uechi as a variety of "southern Shaolin boxing" (*namba* Shōrinken 南派少林拳 <Ch. *nanpai* Shaolin *quan*).

3 *Ryū-ko-kaku no ken* 龍虎鶴の拳 <Ch. *longhuhe quan*.

an incident in Fujian. Apparently one of his students had had a lethal altercation with a local farmer; this may have been the reason he was reluctant to teach combative arts openly for the next seventeen years. In addition, as Higaonna's similar Shōrei Ryū system was already established in Naha, there also may have been some political problem with setting up a similar school in the same area. According to an interview with McHoul (2008), locals in Okinawa knew that Uechi was a combative expert, although he did not teach anyone. Then, in 1925 or 1926, he was asked by the mayor of his local village to demonstrate his art at a town festival. Uechi complied, and it was evident from his demonstration that he was a boxing master. In 1926 he moved his family to Wakayama, Japan, in order to find work. There he finally opened a *karate* training hall (*dōjō*) in 1932 and founded the Pangainūn Ryū Karatejutsu Research Center (Pangainūn Ryū Karatejutsu Kenkyūjō). He returned to Okinawa in 1946, and passed away there at the age of seventy-one in 1948. In 1949 his students renamed the school "Uechi Ryū."[4]

Uechi brought three[5] important forms (*kata*) from China:

- Sanchin 三戦
- Sēsan 十三
- Sansēryū 三十三

See: *Uechi Ryū*.

Uechi Kan'ei 上地 完英 <Oki. Uechi Kanyei (1911–1991). Second headmaster of Uechi Ryū *karatedō* and son of the founder. See: *Uechi Ryū*.

Further readings in English:

- Bishop, 1999: 38–43.

Uechi Ryū 上地流. OKINAWAN KARATE—A school of *karate* founded by Uechi Kambun in 1932. The Uechi Ryū originally encompassed only three primary *kata* which Kambun had learned in China:

- Sanchin 三戦
- Sēsan 十三
- Sansēryū 三十三

Since its founding, however, five additional *kata* have been added to Uechi Ryū by Kambun's son Kan'ei and other students. These are:

Uechi Kan'ei 上地完英
- Kanshiwa 完子和
- Sēryū 十六
- Kanchin 完戦

Itokazu Seiki 糸数盛喜
- Kanshū 完周 (Dai Ni Sēsan 第二セーサン)

Uehara Saburō 上原三郎
- Sēchin 十戦

Since the death of Uechi Kan'ei in 1991, the school has split into several branch factions.

Further readings in English:

- Bishop, 1999: 38–43.

UECHI KAN'EI
Tenth *dan* and second headmaster of Uechi Ryū *karatedō*
(Photograph courtesy Donald J. McHoul)

Uehara Seikichi 上原 清吉 (1904–2004). OKINAWAN KARATE—The first person to head the combative system known as Motobu Udundī 本部御殿手 who was not a Motobu family member. Uehara became the default leader of the system in 1927, and remained at its head for more than seventy-five years. In 1961[6] he renamed the system "Motobu Ryū" in honor of his teacher, Motobu Chōyū. In addition, due to an increasing demand with an influx of foreign students, he formed the Motobu Ryū Kobujutsu Association in 1969. See: *Motobu Udundī*.

[4] According to Donald J. McHoul, a student of Uechi Kan'ei, the students of Uechi Kanbun changed the name of the school to "Uechi Ryū" in 1949 in honor of Uechi Kanbun, who had passed away in 1948. (McHoul, 2008). However, Momohara (2008: 163) says the renaming took place in 1940.

[5] Evidently Uechi Kanbun was not taught a fourth *kata* called Sūpārinpē 壱百零八手, even though he remained with Zhou for ten years.

[6] Bishop (1999: 131) gives this date as 1947; Miyagi (2008: 187) suggests 1961.

U Ejifu 右衛士府. The Imperial Gate Guard Unit of the Right during the eighth century. See: *Ejifu*.

Ueki Yasuyuki 植木 康行. Current (2010) headmaster of the Dai Nippon Yamato Yagyū Kai. See: *Edo Yagyū Shinkage Ryū Yamane Ha*.

Ueno Takashi 上野 貴. Ueno was a direct disciple of Hakkō Ryū 八光流 founder Okuyama Yoshiji. He subsequently founded a school he called Shindō Tenshin Ryū 神道天心流, which concentrated on grappling.

Ueno Shin'emon Takayuki 上野 辰右衛門 隆幸. Ueno founded Shintō Tenshin Ryū 神道天心流 during the Keichō era (1596–1615). He was an eclectic warrior who had mastered Ichiden Ryū 一伝流 arresting arts (*torite*), the Tenshinshō-den Katori Shintō Ryū 天真正伝香取神道流 comprehensive combative curriculum (*sōgō bujutsu*), the Takagi Ryū 高木流, and others.

Ueshiba Aikidō 植芝合気道. See: *Ueshiba Ryū Aikidō*.

Ueshiba Kisshōmaru 植芝 吉祥丸 (1921–1999). Son of *aikidō* founder Ueshiba Morihei. Kisshōmaru became the second Aikidō Dōshu upon the death of his father in 1969.

UESHIBA KISSHŌMARU
Aikidō demonstration in Osaka, 1974
(Photograph by author)

Kisshōmaru began training in *aikidō* as a teenager around 1937. In 1942 he became director of the Kōbukan Dōjō upon his father's retirement to Iwama. Over the next fifty years he published more than twenty books on *aikidō*, several of which were translated into English. Upon his death in 1999, he was succeeded by his son Moriteru.

Ueshiba Morihei 植芝 盛平 (1883–1969). Without doubt the best-known student of Takeda Sōkaku, Ueshiba was the creator of *aikidō*. At the age of eighteen (c. 1901), Ueshiba began training in Tenshin Shin'yō Ryū *jūjutsu* under Tozawa Tokusaburō 戸沢徳三郎.[7] Several sources note that Ueshiba also trained in Yagyū Shingan Ryū *jūjutsu* with Nakai Masakatsu, receiving *menkyo* in 1908.[8] Ueshiba was subsequently introduced to Takeda Sōkaku's Daitō Ryū 大東流 (via Yoshida Kōtarō) in 1916, and received two licenses in that school in the late 1920s and the early 1930s.

UESHIBA MORIHEI
Founder of *aikidō*
(Photograph ©Aikikai Foundation)

From that point Ueshiba began moving more in his own direction and, increasingly under the influence of Deguchi Onisaburō and the Ōmoto Kyō religious movement, he began modifying the Daitō Ryū *aikijūjutsu* system into what became *aikidō*. This was a gradual process, as is reflected in the different names that Ueshiba assigned to his evolving system:

1928 Aioi Ryū 相生流
1932 Kōbukai Aikijutsu 皇武会合気術
1933 Asahi Ryū 朝日流
1937 Dai Nippon Budō 大日本武道

7 Pranin (On-line: http://www.aikidojournal.com/encyclopedia?entryID=692) notes that this was only for a few months and had little influence on Ueshiba's later development of *aikidō*.

8 Some sources give this instructor's name as Nakai Masakatsu 中井 正勝 while Watatani and Yamada (1978: 851) say it was Nakai Kazusaburō 中井 和三郎.

Ueshiba Ryū Aikidō
植芝流 合気道
(abbreviated lineage)

Takeda Sōkaku
武田 惣角
Daitō Ryū *jūjutsu · aikijūjutsu*
大東流(柔術·合気柔術)

Ueshiba Morihei
植芝 盛平

Aioi Ryū period 相生流時代
1928–1932

- Inoue Hōken (Noriaki) 井上 方軒(鑑昭) — **Shinwa Taidō** 親和体道
- Nishimura Shūtarō 西村 秀太郎
- Ōtsuki Yutaka 大槻 豊 — **Ōtsuki Ryū Aiki** 大槻流 合気
- Oshikawa Gunzō 押川 郡三

Kōbukai Aikijutsu period 皇武会合気術時代
1932–1937

- Mochizuki Minoru 望月 稔 — **Yōseikan Budō** 養正館武道
- Tomiki Kenji 富木 謙治 — **Tomiki Ryū** 富木流
- Shirata Rinjiroō 白田 林二郎
- Hashimoto Masahiro 橋本 正博

Dai Nippon Budō period 大日本武道時代
1932–1937

- Shioda Gōzō 塩田 剛三 — **Yōshinkan** 養神館
- Hoshi Tetsuomi 星 哲臣 — **Kōbujutsu** 皇武術

Aiki Budō period 合気武道時代
1937–1944

- Hirai Minoru 平井 稔 — **Dai Nippon Kōrindō** 大日本光輪洞
- Nakajima Shōhitsu 中島 将弼 — **Ryūshinkan Budō** 柳心館武道
- Tanaka Seitarō 田中 清太郎 — **Shinryaku Heihō** 神略兵法
- Ōtsuyama Eiko 大津山 栄子 — **Fujin Kōbujutsu** 婦人皇武術
- Fukui Harunosuke 福井 治之助 — **Yaei Ryū** 弥栄流
- Tōhei Kōichi 藤平 光一 — **Shinshin Tōitsu Aikidō** 心身統一合気道
- Sunadomari Kanehira 砂泊 兼平 — **Banseikan** 万世館
- Saitō Morihiro 斉藤 守弘

Aikidō period 合気道時代
1949–present

Ueshiba Kisshōmaru
植芝 吉祥丸
Aikidō Dōshu
1969

Ueshiba Moriteru
植芝 守央
Aikidō Dōshu
1999

1944 Tenshin Aiki Budō 天真合気武道 / Takemusu Aiki Budō 武産合気武道
1949 Zaidanhōjin Aikikai and Aikidō 財団法人合気会, 合気道

Ueshiba's own combative capabilities were highly respected by his contemporaries, and from all reports his own art was a cut above most others. In a 1985 interview in *Aiki News*, Sugino Yoshi remarked on Ueshiba's grappling techniques as follows:

> ...Tenryu (the famous Sumo wrestler) thought that O-Sensei's (Ueshiba's) demonstration was all prearranged when he saw it. Then O-Sensei said to Tenryu, "You really have a strong physique. Why don't you grab hold of my arm?" When Tenryu grabbed him he realized that O-Sensei's art was the real thing...

Concerning Ueshiba's weapons technique, Sugino (1985: 13) further commented:

> ...His jo was alive. When his opponent came to strike him like this, he didn't react in a flashy way but only moved his jo a little. The tip of his jo was alive. That was the difference. His way of using the jo was what we call "natural" or "pure." when you use the sword or bo, the tip must be alive. His movements were really wonderful.

See also: *Ueshiba Ryū Aikidō.*

Ueshiba Ryū Aikidō 植芝流合気道. A term used by Watatani and Yamada (1978: 94) for the *aikidō* tradition founded by Ueshiba Morihei.

Ueshima Sannosuke 上島 三之助 [A.k.a. ***Kiyotada*** 清忠]. Founded Kūshin Ryū *karate* with the help of Kinjō Kensei in 1937.

Uesugi Minbu Dayū Yoshiharu 上杉 民部大輔 義春. Warrior and disciple of *daimyō* Uesugi Kenshin. Yoshiharu is credited with founding a major branch of the Echigo Ryū 越後流 known as Nipponden Echigo Ryū 日本伝越後流 around 1560. This was a school of combative strategy (*gungaku*) and espionage (*shinobijutsu*). See: *Echigo Ryū.*

Uesugi Ryū 上杉流. A family tradition concentrating on military strategy and tactics (*gumpō*), warrior etiquette and ceremonies (*reihō*), and espionage (*shinobijutsu*). It flourished within the Uesugi clan of Echigo province during the Sengoku and Tokugawa periods. See also: *Echigo Ryū.*

uguisubari 鶯張【鶯張】. A "nightingale floor"; a "singing floor." A type of flooring designed to "sing" (squeak) when walked upon. It was installed in important residences to provide an alarm if an intruder entered the premises. Such floors can still be viewed and experienced today in such places as Nijō palace (Nijōjō 二条城) in Kyōto.

U Hyōefu 右兵衛府. The "Guard Unit of the Right," responsible in ancient times for guarding the imperial palace gate. See: *Hyōefu.*

uji 氏. 1. A clan. 2. A family or patronymic name.

ujidera 氏寺. A temple erected to house a clan's tutelary deity. See: *ujigami.*

ujigami 氏神. SHINTŌ—The chief tutelary deity of a clan, usually found in the principle aristocratic and warrior lineages. The *ujigami* may be a Shintō deity which has been attached to the clan since "time immemorial," or it may be the first ancestor of a lineage. (It should be noted here that in some instances these may be one and the same. See, for example, the case of the war god Hachiman.) During Japan's middle ages, these clans erected temples (*ujidera*) dedicated to their respective *ujigami.*

ujiko 氏子. SHINTŌ—This term has shifted in meaning over time. During the premodern era, all members of a clan who venerated the same *ujigami* were referred to as *ujiko*. Today, *ujiko* may refer to anyone who lives in the geographical area considered under the protection of a specific shrine.

uji no chōja 氏長者. See: *uji no kami.*

uji no kami 氏上 [A.k.a. ***uji no chōja*** 氏長者]. Lit. "chief of a clan." Sometime around the tenth century, this title was used by the chiefs of the principal families whose responsibility it was to verify who had the right to use a patronymic name. These families were mainly the Fujiwara, Minamoto, Tachibana, and Taira. A similar term—*uji no chōja*—was also used. Papinot (1910: 721) notes that one of the titles used by the Tokugawa *shōgun* was "Genji no Chōja" (Chief of the Minamoto Clan). See also: *ubusuna no kami.*

ukagau-mono 窺う者. Lit. "someone who spies"

U

or "someone who reconnoiters." A variant term for an espionage agent. See: *ninjutsu.*

uke 受. Lit. "receiver." A term used in various grappling arts to refer to the person who receives a technique; the person on whom the technique is executed. See also: *nage; tori (2); ukemi.*

ukebari 受張. A padded liner for a helmet (*kabuto*).

ukegusari 受鎖【受鏁】. See: *kusarigama.*

ukemi 受身. Lit. "receiving body." A term used in various grappling arts such as *aikidō, jūdō* and some of the classical martial schools containing grappling systems to refer to controlled methods of falling in order to soften the impact. Like the term *uke, ukemi* can also indicate the person who receives a grappling technique and, consequently, must dissipate the effect of the technique by falling safely. See: *uke.*

ukigutsu 浮沓. See: *suijōhokōjutsu.*

U Konoefu 右近衛府. A ninth-century term for the Imperial Attendants of the Right. See: *hyōefu.*

uma 1. 馬. a. A horse. Especially during the late ancient and early medieval periods (c. 700–c. 1400) the horse was a critical element in both actual warfare and as a symbol of warrior status. Only a warrior/archer of means could afford a horse. Big and powerful horses were especially prized and were referred to in the war tales (*gunkimono*) as "big and powerful" (*kiwamete futō takumashii*), "dragon-like" (*ryū no gotoki uma*), and "untamed" (*arauma*). Varley (1994: 16) notes that the *arauma* were valued in battle because of the "damage they could inflict with their hooves, especially upon foot soldiers." In fact, using horses to trample foot soldiers or dismounted warriors was a common battlefield tactic of those times and was referred to as *uma ate.*

In the medieval war tales such as the *Heike monogatari* a significant portion of battle preparation was devoted to construction of antihorse impediments including spikes, ropes for tripping horses, and other implements. Varley (1994: 95) notes that in some of the *gunkimono*, such as the *Gempei seisui ki*, "greater attention appears to be given to the caliber of the horses than to their warrior riders."

The use of the horse in battle was an identifying trait of the semi-aristocratic warrior class through the ages in Japan. Whether referring to the *tsuwamono* of the ancient period or the *bushi* of the medieval period, horse-mounted archery was the defining characteristic of this class. In fact, a number of twelfth-century warrior families (*buke*) still maintained pasture land established under the Taihō Codes (Taihō Ritsuryō) of the eighth century. Some of the well-known "pastured" *buke* were the Shida 志田, Chichibu 秩父, Mochizuki 望月, Sara 沙羅, and Kodama 児玉. With the rise of the classical *ryū* in the fourteenth century, combative horsemanship began to become codified as *bajutsu* in a variety of traditions beginning with the Ōtsubo Ryū 大坪流. b. SHŌGI—An abbreviation or notation for *ryūma* 龍馬.

Further readings in English:

- Farris, 1992: 57–60.
- Varley, 1994: *passim.*

uma 2. 午. The hour of the Horse. a. This is the seventh duodenary hour of the Chinese Twelve Branches (Jūnishi): 11 a.m. to 1 p.m. b. KYŪSHO—In certain Sino-Japanese boxing texts, the Horse character indicates the optimal time of day for striking the corresponding vital point (*kyūsho*). See also: Appendix 1.

uma ate 馬当【馬當】. A practice of horse-mounted archers in which their mount was used to strike and trample foot soldiers.

umabari 馬針. A variant pronunciation of *bashin*, lit. "horse needle." See: *bashin.*

umagoya sangu 馬小屋三具. Lit. "the three tools of the stable." These included the baton (*hananejiri bō*), horse needle (*bashin*), and the camp sickle (*jingama*). Although such items were used to deal with horses, they could also, in a pinch, be used as weapons against armored or unarmored opponents. Several *ryū* included training in these weapon-usable tools.

umajirushi 馬印 [Also written 馬標, 馬験, 千旄; a.k.a. ***matoi*** 纏; ***umanobori*** 馬幟]. Lit. "horse insignia." Large standards—battle flags, gongs, kites, etc.—used by generals and lords (*dai-*

myō). There were two sizes: larger ones were referred to as "great insignia" (*ō umajirushi*) and the smaller as "small insignia" (*ko umajirushi*). In 1645 the Tokugawa shogunate created guidelines designating which *daimyō* were allowed to use which standard.

umamawari 馬廻 [A.k.a. ***umamawarishū*** 馬廻衆; ***on-umamawarishū*** 御馬廻衆]. Lit. "surrounding horsemen." *Umamawari* 馬廻 is a homophone derived from *umamawari* 馬周囲 (perimeter horsemen); it means "perimeter horse guardsmen" or "mounted guards." During the Warring States period this term was used by generals such as Oda Nobunaga to refer to their closest retainers. Later, during the Edo period, it came to be a formalized position under some of the *daimyō*.

umamawarishū 馬廻衆. Horse-guard cadre. See: *umawari*.

uma sashimono 馬指物. Lit. "horse standard." A pole-mounted banner or other standard that was so large it normally had to be carried by a rider. *Uma sashimono* featured a great variety of designs, including religious symbols such as *vajra* (*kongō*), or Sanskrit spells written in *siddhaṁ* script (*shittan*); martial accoutrements such as war fans (*uchiwa*); family crests (*mon*); and so on.

uma yoroi 馬鎧. Horse armor.

uma yumi 馬弓. A bow normally used from horseback.

Unchū Ryū 1. 運籌流. A variant name for the Itō Ryū (1) 伊東流. This system is also referred to as the Echizen Unchū Ryū 越前運籌流, as it was passed down in Echizen province. As a branch tradition of Itō Ryū (1) 伊東流 in Echizen, the school included spear arts (*sōjutsu*) with pipe spear (*kudayari*), straight-bladed spear (*suyari*), and cross-bladed spear (*jūmonji-yari*); long-hafted glaive techniques (*naginatajutsu*); and swordsmanship (*kenjutsu*) with *tachi*. This system was not related to Unchū Ryū (2), which was derived from the Yagyū school.

Unchū Ryū 2. 運籌流. A school of combative swordsmanship (*kenjutsu*) that was a branch tradition of the Edo Yagyū Shinkage Ryū. Kimura Sukekurō Noriyasu, a student of Yagyū Munenori, is credited with its founding. However, the name Unchū Ryū was given to the branch founded by Kimura's disciple, Izubuchi Heibei. Its curriculum was identical with that of Edo Yagyū Shinkage Ryū.

Unchū Ryū (2)
運籌流
(abbreviated lineage)

Unkō Ryū 運羌流 <Ko. Woonkwang Ryu. An obscure school of Japanese swordsmanship described and illustrated in an eighteenth-century Korean text known as the *Bugei zufu tōshi*『武藝圖譜通志』<Ko. *Muye dobo tongji*. See: *Bugei zufu tōshi*.

Further reading in English:
- Kim (Trans.), 2001: 169–174; 193–194.

unmei 運命. Fate, destiny. See: *mappō*.

unpō 運法. Footwork; methods of walking. JIKI SHINKAGE RYŪ—A basic walking method which is the first practice a new trainee learns in Jiki Shinkage Ryū 直心影流.

Unryū 雲竜【雲龍】[A.k.a. ***Sō Unryū*** 僧 雲竜【僧雲龍】]. A Buddhist monk thought to have created the combative system that became the Takagi Ryū 高木流.

ura 裏. Lit. "the inside"; "the inner layer of clothing"; "the obscure" or "that which is hidden." 1. The word *ura* is akin to the term *honne*, which means "the motive" or "real intent" concerning a matter, as opposed to what may be *tatemae*—the "public stance," "façade" or "formality." Simple on the surface, the term *ura*—along with *omote*, *honne*, and *tatemae*—is a key, critical concept in understanding any facet of Japanese culture, including martial culture. (See reference below.) 2. In martial systems, while the term *omote* generally refers to the first set of combative forms (*kata*) taught to a new trainee, *ura* usually indicates a second or even later set of technical forms (*kata*). The combative forms of an *ura* set may have identical names to those in a system's *omote* set. However, the *ura* forms are executed differently in order to help the trainee understand the real combative meaning/application of the comparable *omote* technique. The differences, which may be gross or subtle, are manifested in a number of ways: through movement pattern, targeting, breathing, timing, etc. In sum, the *omote* techniques are taught in a way that obscures their real intent so that the *ryū* will not be compromised if a new trainee turns out to be disloyal. The *ura* techniques are often intended to impart the real combative meaning to the trainee. 3. SHINDŌ MUSŌ RYŪ—In Ikkaku Ryū *juttejutsu*, *ura* is the second series of *waza*, consisting of twelve *kata*. 4. SHINDŌ MUSŌ RYŪ—In Isshin Ryū *kusarigama-jutsu*, *ura* is the second series of *waza*, consisting of twelve *kata* (and one variation). 5. The side of the tang of a sword that faces inward when the sword is worn. Consequently, the *ura* side of a *tachi* is on the opposite side of the tang compared to that of a *katana*. See also: *honne; tatemae; omote.*

Further reading in English:

- Doi, 1985.
- Hall, Edward, 1973; 1976; 1983.
- Lebra, 1976.

Urasenke 裏千家. School of Japanese tea ceremony (*chadō*) descended from tea master Sen no Rikyū. See: *Sen no Rikyū.*

urawaza 裏技. Sets of *kata* that provide "inner" meaning or insight into more obvious technique. See: *ura.*

urushi 漆. Lacquer made from the Japanese sumac tree; this substance is poisonous. Among other purposes, *urushi* is used to finish scabbards (*saya*), and is also used to coat the leather coverings of bamboo practice swords used by the Yagyū Shinkage Ryū.

Usamiden Echigo Ryū 宇佐美伝越後流【宇佐美傳越後流】[A.k.a. ***Echigo Ryū*** 越後流; ***Kenshin Ryū*** 謙信流]. One of three major branch traditions of the Echigo Ryū. Usamiden Echigo Ryū was a school of combative strategy (*gungaku*) founded by a warrior named Usami Echigo no Kami Sadayuki. (Under the name "Kenshin Ryū," the school is attributed to the *daimyō* of Echigo province, Uesugi Kenshin.) See: *Echigo Ryū.*

Usami Echigo no Kami Sadayuki 宇佐美越後守 定行 (1488–1564). Founder of the Usamiden Echigo Ryū, a classical tradition centering on battlefield strategy and tactics (*gungaku*).

Usami Ryū 宇佐美流. See: *Usamiden Echigo Ryū.*

ushi 丑 [Also read ***chū***]. Ox. 1. The Hour of the Ox is the second duodenary hour of the Chinese Twelve Branches (Jūnishi): 1 to 3 a.m. 2. KYŪSHO—In certain Sino-Japanese boxing texts, the Ox character indicates the optimal time of day for striking the corresponding vital point (*kyūsho*). See also: Appendix 1.

ushiro 後. Back; rear; second; the latter.

ushirodate 後立. An ornament on the back of a helmet. See: *tatemono.*

Ushiwakamaru 牛若丸. The "youth name" of Minamoto no Yoshitsune.

Ushiwatari Hachirōuemon 牛渡 八郎右衛門. Founder of the Takeda Ryū (3) 武田流, a school of military strategy and tactics (*gunryaku*) and military signaling with the conch shell (*jingaijutsu*). Ushiwatari established the system in 1665.

Utagawa Kuniyoshi 歌川 国芳【歌川國芳】[A.k.a. ***Yoshisasburō*** 芳三郎] (1798–1861). A Japanese artist known as one of the last great masters of the *ukiyoe* woodblock print (pictures of the "floating world"). Utagawa painted a wide variety of subjects: fantastic and sometimes mythical animals, actors, beautiful women, and especially warriors and heroes. He had a number of fine students in his branch of the Utagawa school, including such notables as Yoshitoshi, an artist renowned for his *mushae* (pictures of heroes and warriors). Utagawa's students often began their training by working on *mushae* and then progressing to other topics. See also: *mushae; Tsukioka Yoshitoshi.*

Further reading in English:

- King and Iwakiri, 2007.
- Robinson, 1982.

utaishō 右大将. See: *udaishō.*

uto 烏兎【烏兔】<Ch. *wutu*. Lit. crow and hare; sun and moon. 1. The first character—烏 *u* or *karasu*—refers to a three-legged crow usually depicted in a circle symbolizing the sun. The second character—兎 *to* or *usagi*—refers to a hare usually depicted in a circle symbolizing the moon. 2. In various classical and modern traditions the term *uto* refers to the vital point between the eyes. See: *ongyōin.*

U Toneri 右舎人 [Also read ***udoneri***]. An imperial bodyguard or retainer. See: *toneri.*

utsubo 靫. An arrow case. See: *yazutsu.*

Utsuryōshi 『尉繚子』<Ch. *Wei Liaozi*. One of the seven Chinese classics on military strategy. See: *Buryaku shichi sho.*

uwagi 上着. See: *dōgi, karategi, keikogi, jūdōgi, uwagi.*

Uyeshiba Morihei 植芝 盛平. An archaic romanization for Ueshiba Morihei.

U

W

wa 和. CLASSICAL WARRIOR IDEAL—Peace, harmony. Although a seeming contradiction, many warriors, soldiers, and fighting men of various cultures and eras have seen peace, not war, as their *raison d'être*. The classical Japanese warrior included this concept as part of his ethical makeup. Draeger (1995: Part 2, 28) quotes the chief priest of Katori Jingu (a Shintō shrine closely aligned with the Tenshinshō-den Katori Shintō Ryū 天真正伝香取神道流):

> To beget an enemy is evidence of self-failure. Not appeasing somebody inflicts upon ourselves an external enemy status. When our enemy or opponent commits a fault we are always responsible for it. He would not have done so if we had sufficiently appeased him.

Draeger commented that appeasement here means to walk away before confrontation. However, it does not indicate passivity. It is more akin to what the Buddhists refer to as "skillful means," resolving an issue without resort to combat. It is also reflected in one of the principles espoused by the Tenshinshō-den Katori Shintō Ryū: *Heihō wa heihō nari* 兵法は平法也 (The arts of war are identical to the arts of peace). See: *bushi no konjō.*

wabi 侘. A subdued taste; a minimalist aesthetic style, often referred to in combination with *sabi* (1). See: *wabi-sabi.*

wabi-sabi 侘寂. A Japanese aesthetic emphasizing appreciation of beauty in the natural, imperfect, and impermanent. Emphasized in the tea ceremony of Sen no Rikyū during the sixteenth century, *wabi-sabi*, along with *zen*, became an important Japanese artistic and philosophical element in Japanese warrior culture during the succeeding Edo period. See also: *cha no yu; Sen no Rikyū.*

Further reading in English:

- Leonard, 2008.

Wada Heisuke Masakatsu 和田 平助 正勝 (1624–1683). Founded the Shin Tamiya Ryū 新田宮流 sometime during the Kambun era (1661–1673).

Wada Jūrōzaemon Masashige 和田 十郎左衛門 正重 [A.k.a. ***Zuishin*** 随心; ***Zuika*** 随加 (c.1620–1680). Founder of the Kankyoku Ryū 鑑極流, a branch tradition of the Zuishin Ryū 随心流, a school which concentrated on combative swordsmanship (*kenjutsu*) and grappling arts (*jūjutsu*).

Wada, who hailed from Buzen, mastered the Gan Ryū (3) 願立 of Abe Shichizaemon Michikore. Later he formulated this into his own system, Kankyoku Ryū. According to Watatani and Yamada (1978: 204), one of the characteristics of this system was that practitioners usually trained with wooden swords (*bokutō*); if the student could not win six out of ten matches with him, Wada would not award them a full license (*menkyo*) in the system.

Wada subsequently became a student of Satomura Zuishinsai, a third-generation successor of the Seigō Ryū 制剛流, and learned both Seigō Ryū and Tsutsumi Hōzan Ryū 堤宝山流 from him. However, he apparently completed his training in the Seigō Ryū under Satomura's disciple, Takahashi Zuietsu Shoshi.

Watatani and Yamada (1978: 204) list several *kata* found in the transmission scrolls left by Wada:

Shabenken	車遍剣
Suishaken	水車剣
Muniken	無二剣
Suiminken	睡眠剣
Shinmyōken	神明剣
Shin'i	真位
Torikake	取掛
Ken	捲
Midare	乱
Suigetsu no Gohō	水月の五法

Wada Ryū 和田流. Variant name for Kōga Ryū Wada Ha 甲賀流和田派.

Wadō Ryū 和道流 [A.k.a. ***Wadō Ryū Karate-dō·Jūjutsu Kempō*** ～空手道·柔術拳法]. JAPANESE KARATE—A Japanese school of *karate* created by Ōtsuka Hironori in 1939. Ōtsuka, who had received a full license (*menkyo*) in the Yōshin Ryū 楊心流 school of *jūjutsu* in 1921, began studying *karate* under Funakoshi Gichin in 1922, and by 1939 had created a synthesis of *jūjutsu* and *karate*.

wajō 和尚. See: oshō.

wajutsu 和術. A variant term for *jūjutsu*-type arts. See: *Oguri Ryū.*

Wakisaka Genzaemon 脇坂 源左衛門 (c.1710–c.1780). Founder of the Zuihen Ryū 随変流, a branch tradition of the Zuishin Ryū 随心流. The Zuishin Ryū focused on combative swordsmanship (*kenjutsu*) and grappling arts (*jūjutsu*). However, Wakisaka had studied a variety of martial traditions, and he founded a more eclectic system. His Zuihen Ryū included swordsmanship (*kenjutsu*), quick-draw sword arts (*iaijutsu*), long hardwood staff (*bōjutsu*), warrior sickle (*kama*), and combative grappling (*jūjutsu*). Apparently his most influential mentor was Wada Jūrōzaemon of the Kankyoku Ryū 鑑極流. For lineage chart, see: *Zuishin Ryū.*

Waken sōfu 「倭劍總譜」<Ko. *Wae Gum Chong Bo* (A complete manual of Japanese swordsmanship). The "Waken sofu" is a chapter of a larger eighteenth-century Korean text known as the *Muye dobo tongji* 『武藝圖譜通志』(*Bugei zufu tōshi*). See Kim, 2001: 158–199 for an English translation. See also: *Bugei zufu tōshi.*

wakibiki 脇引. Laced pads worn under the armor to protect the armpits. Not to be confused with the *kyūbi no ita* or *sendan no ita*, which hung over the armor. There were a number of types of *wakibiki*.

wakidate 脇立. Ornaments located on the sides of a helmet. See: *tatemono.*

wakigamae 脇構. An engagement posture with the body in left (*hidari*) *hanmi*; the sword is held low, with the *kensaki* pointed toward the rear.

wakizashi 脇差. A short sword around 16 to 20 inches (40–50 cm) in length. *Wakizashi* were often more highly decorated than the standard longsword (*daitō*), as they were normally carried inside and were thus more likely to be observed closely. When a samurai entered someone's home he would remove his longsword at the door, sometimes leaving it at the entrance, while the *wakizashi* would remain in his sash (*obi*).

wakō 倭寇 <Ch. *wokou*. Japanese pirates, bandits, robbers, or smugglers. *Wakō* is a generic term used for Japanese pirates who raided ships and coastal towns from as far north as the Korean peninsula to as far south as the coast of Kwangtung province and Hainan island. The term, which literally means "Japanese brigands," came into common use in the thirteenth century, when this type of activity proliferated. However, the earliest use of the word is found on fifth-century stone inscriptions from Korea.

Piracy became a problem for the Japanese Court government as early as the ninth century (Amino, 1982: 77–82). At that time, incidents occurred in the Inland Sea trade area, which actually stretched from Lake Biwa to Dazaifu in northern Kyūshū. In the early years pirates often aligned themselves with merchants and officials from the country of Silla in Korea. According to Farris (1992: 143), these pirates were usually small-scale "fishermen or traders, often in league with aristocratic retainers, state officials, or 'rich vagrants.'" (The pirate Fujiwara Sumitomo was of a different caliber, as he was rumored to command as many as 1000 ships.) The Japanese term for pirates at that time was *kaizoku*.

Pirates referred to as *wakō* became active in the thirteenth century (Kamakura period), persisting until the end of the sixteenth century (late Azuchi-Momoyama period). During this time they were active from Japan and Korea as far south as Southeast Asia. In their heyday, the *wakō* included not only Japanese pirates, masterless samurai (*rōnin*), and smugglers; but also Chinese militia and bandits, samurai clans, Portuguese sailors, and missionaries. Several Japanese martial traditions have roots springing from the *wakō*. For examples, see: *Aisu Ikōsai; Kage ryū no mokuroku.*

Further reading in English:

- So Kwan-wai, 1975.

warabide katana 蕨手刀. See: *warabite tō.*

warabite tō 蕨手刀 [Also read ***warabide katana***]. An early, slightly angled sword, normally with a single cutting edge. The *warabite tō* appeared around the eighth century. Some experts believe that it was the direct predecessor of the curved sword (*tachi*) preferred by the Japanese warriors of later eras. As can be seen in the illustration below, the *warabite tō* appears to be constructed for single-hand use. In addition, the angle of the handle/grip is such that the cutting edge of the blade will strike the target with the effect of a "slice" rather than a "chop," much like a blade with more curvature. See Conroy (1980; 1981) for a discussion of this effect.

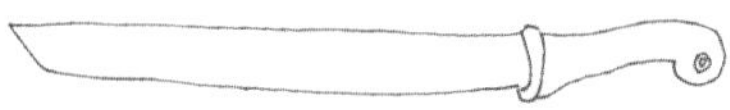

ROUGH APPROXIMATION OF A *WARABITE TŌ*
Early (eighth-century) one-handed slashing sword
(After Joly & Inada, 1913: 11)

waraji 草鞋. Straw sandals normally worn with split-toed cotton socks (*momen tabi*) or split-toed tanned-leather socks (*kawa tabi*).

warawa 童. A medieval term for a page; a young assistant.

wari kōgai 割笄 [Also called ***hashi*** 箸]. 1. Lit. "dividable *kōgai*." A tool that was part of a sword mounting. *Wari kōgai* are skewers (*kōgai*) that are split lengthwise, looking like chopsticks (*hashi*, in fact, means "chopsticks"). There is some disagreement as to whether *wari kōgai* were used as ceremonial tweezers to handle incense and ashes, or simply as chopsticks for eating during a campaign.

washi 1. 鷲 [Also read ***ju***; ***shū***]. a. An eagle; a raptor. Falconry was popular among certain upper-level warriors during the medieval period. Falcons or eagles were sometimes awarded "ranks" of proficiency indicated by colored leashes. See: *heō*. b. The term *washi* or *ju* was sometimes used as a name for a prearranged combative scenario (*kata*). See: *takagari*.

washi 2. 和紙. Lit. "Japanese paper." There are many types of *washi*. The variety made from the paper mulberry is especially prized for use as *nuguigami*, the paper used when cleaning a Japanese sword. See also: *nuguigami; uchiko*.

watakuri 腸繰. Lit. "eviscerate." A barbed, flesh-tearing arrowhead. See also: *ya no ne*.

Watanabe Tadashige 渡辺 忠成 (b. 1941). Successor to Watanabe Tadatoshi as second headmaster of the Watanabe line of the Shinkage Ryū (and thus a twenty-second-generation successor of the Owari Yagyū Shinkage Ryū). Watanabe is the author of several books in Japanese, and two in English, on the Yagyū Shinkage Ryū:

Shinkage-ryu Sword Techniques, Vol. 1 & 2. Sugawara Martial Arts/Japan Publications, 1993.

Shinkage Ryū nyūmon 『新陰流入門』 (An introduction to Shinkage Ryū), 1979.

Shinkage Ryū heihō tachiden 『新陰流兵法太刀伝』(Traditional sword techniques and strategy of the Shinkage Ryū), 1969 (co-authored by Watanabe Tadatoshi.)

Watanabe Tadatoshi 渡辺 忠敏 (1894–1972). A disciple of both Yagyū Toshichika (Genshū) and Yagyū Genchō (Toshinaga). Watanabe Tadatoshi was awarded a license of full mastery (*inka*), making him a twenty-first generation successor of the Owari Yagyū Shinkage Ryū. He authored several books in Japanese on the Yagyū Shinkage Ryū:

Yagyū Ryū heihō kuden kikigaki 『柳生流兵法口伝聞書』(Verbatim notes on the oral transmissions of Yagyū Ryū strategy), 1974 (pub. posthumously).

Shinkage Ryū heihō tachiden 『新陰流兵法太刀伝』(Traditional sword techniques and strategy of the Shinkage Ryū), 1969. (co-authored by Watanabe Tadashige).

IWASA KATSU (L) AND WATANABE TOKIJI (R)
Demonstrating Hōjō at Meiji Shrine, 1985
(Photograph by author)

Watanabe Tokiji 渡辺 時次 (b.1945). JIKI SHINKAGE RYŪ—A disciple of Ōnishi Eiryū and Hayakawa Kōichi (founder of the Jiki Shinkage Ryū Hyakurenkai). Watanabe is the nineteenth-generation *shihan dai* of the Jiki Shinkage Ryū through Yamada Jirokichi's line.

Watanabe Tsunaki 渡辺 綱紀. A direct disciple of Hakkō Ryū 八光流 founder Okuyama Yoshiji. Along with Senmoto Akiteru, Watanabe subsequently founded a school he called Uchūdō 宇宙道 which concentrated on self-defense (*goshin* 護身).

Watatani Kiyoshi 綿谷 雪 (1903–1983). A journalist, novelist, and martial-arts historian. Watatani wrote and edited more than forty books in a variety of fields, twenty-five of them dealing with the history of martial arts and traditions. He is best known in the West for his works on classical martial traditions, especially the several editions of his martial schools encyclopedia (*Bugei ryū-ha daijiten*) which he co-authored with Yamada Tadashi.

Donn F. Draeger[1] noted on several occasions that Watatani was also a skillful swordsman who was trained in the Ono Ha Ittō Ryū.

A short bibliography of Watatani Kiyoshi:

Bugei ryū-ha jiten『武芸流派事典』(Dictionary of martial traditions) with Yamada Tadashi. Jimbun ōraisha, 1963.

Bugei ryū-ha daijiten『武芸流派大事典』(Great dictionary of martial traditions) with Yamada Tadashi. Shin-jimbun ōraisha, 1969.

Bugei ryū-ha daijiten『武芸流派大辞典』(Great dictionary of martial traditions) with Yamada Tadashi. Revised edition. Tōkyō kopii, 1978.

Jutsu『術』[The (esoteric) arts:]. Sei'abō, 1964.

Nippon bugei shōden『日本武芸小傳』(Biographies from Japanese martial arts) [This is Watatani's edited/annotated/indexed edition of the *Honcho bugei koden*『本朝武芸小傳』published in 1716 along with several other historical texts on Japanese martial arts.] Jimbun ōraisha, 1961.

Nippon kengō 100 sen『日本剣豪100選』(One hundred Japanese master swordsmen). Akita shoten, 1971.

Zusetsu kobudō-shi『図説・古武道史』(An illustrated history of classical martial arts). Sei'abō, 1967.

waza 技 [Var. 業]. Technique; prearranged combative form.

[1] See Bibliography: Interviews, Conversations, Correspondence.

W

Y

ya 矢. An arrow.

ya awase 矢合. A volley-exchange of arrows. According to several war tales (*gunkimono*) of the early medieval period, the *ya awase* followed the firing of a humming-bulb arrow (*kabura ya*) and indicated the beginning of hostilities in battle.

yaba 矢場. An archery range. Equivalent to *yumiba*.

yabako 矢箱. An arrow case.

yabane 矢羽. Arrow fletching.

Yabiku Mōden 屋比久 孟伝 【屋比久孟傳】 (1878–1941). A *karate* student of Itosu Ankō; Yabiku also studied Okinawan *kobudō* weapons arts with Chinen Pēchin Masanra[1] (Yamannī Ryū 山根流), Tawada Shinpoku,[2] and Kinjō Ufuchiku.[3] In 1911 he founded the Ryūkyū Kobujutsu Kenkyūkai 琉球古武術研究会 (Ryūkyū Classical Martial Arts Research Society). When Yabiku died in World War II, the organization dissolved. See: *Itosu Ryū karate.*

yaburi dōjō 破道場. See: *dōjō arashi.*

yabusame 流鏑馬. A systematized training method and sportive contest involving mounted archery. In this competition, a horseman rides down a dirt track at full gallop and attempts to shoot three arrows into three separate targets. During Japan's middle ages, *yabusame* was one of the "three equestrian archery contests" (*san kisha*) which had both a training and a sportive purpose. *Yabusame* was formalized into its present form by Ogasawara Sadamune in the fourteenth century. See also: *san kisha.*

YABUSAME ARCHER IN KAMAKURA, 1979
(Photo courtesy Jon Driscoll)

yabusuma 矢衾 [Var. 矢襖]. A barrage, volley, or shower of arrows.

Ya Daijin 矢大臣. SHINTŌ—Lit. "arrow minister of state," the term indicates the "official who is armed with bow and arrows." The Ya Daijin are two Shintō *kami* often represented by statues of bow-and-arrow–armed warriors guarding the entrance to Shintō shrines. While representations vary from place to place, the two *kami* represented are usually Toyo Iwamado no Mikoto and Kushi Iwamado no Mikoto. The Ya Daijin are also referred to as Zuishin. See also: *Zuishin.*

yadane 矢種. A supply of arrows (as in a quiver).

yadomejutsu 矢留術. The combative art of arrow deflection using a short sword. See also: *Maniwa Nen Ryū.* For photograph, see: *Higuchi Sadahiro.*

yadzutsu 矢筒. Archaic romanization for *yazutsu.*

yae kamari 八重かまり. 1. Covert assault troops who hid in various locations—reed fields, forests, mountain valleys, and even in villages—until the signal was given for them to form up and make a deceptive dual (or even multi-directional) surprise attack on enemy forces. 2. A deceptive, convoluted surprise attack. See also: *kamari (1), ninjutsu.*

Yae Ryū 弥栄流. See: *Iyasaka Ryū.*

yagara 矢柄. An arrow shaft.

Yagi Ikugorō Hisayoshi 八木 幾五郎 久善 (c.1810–c.1844). Thirteenth headmaster of the Takagi Yōshin Ryū 高木揚心流. Watatani and Yamada (1978: 46) note that Yagi was a masterless samurai of Akō (*Akō rōnin*).

---

1 Chinen Pēchin Masanra 知念親雲上真三良.

2 Tawada Shinpoku 多和田真睦. Bishop (1996: 127) renders this name as "Tawata Pechin" (多和田親雲上?).

3 Kinjō Ufuchiku 金城大筑. Bishop (1996: 127) renders this name as "Kanagusuki Sanda" (金城三良?).

Yagi Sadanosuke 八木 貞之助. A master of Tenshin Shin'yō Ryū 天神真楊流 who was sought out by Kanō Jigorō in his early *jūjutsu* training years. Yagi turned down Kanō and recommended him to Fukuda Hachinosuke.

yagoro 矢頃. A bowshot.

yagura 矢倉. A watchtower of a fort; an elevated archery platform.

Yagyū Genchō (Toshinaga) 柳生 厳長【柳生嚴長】[A.k.a. ***~Taira no Toshinaga*** 平厳長【平嚴長】] (1892–1966). Twentieth headmaster of the Owari Yagyū Shinkage Ryū. Continuing in the footsteps of his father Genshū, Yagyū Genchō (Toshinaga) taught Yagyū Shinkage Ryū in both Nagoya and Tōkyō. During the 1930s he acted as the swordsmanship instructor for the Imperial Guards Officers Group (Konoe Gubu Shōkōdan 近衛供奉将校団) and frequently taught seminars for the Dai Nippon Butokukai in various branch *dōjō* around the country.

During World War II the city of Nagoya was a primary target for Allied bombing due to its industrial infrastructure. Most of the city was razed, including the Yagyū home *dōjō*, which had been built during the Tokugawa period. Although the *dōjō* was lost, Genchō was able to preserve the original *densho* passed to Yagyū Muneyoshi by Kamiizumi Nobutsuna in 1565–1566 by securing them in the shaft of a well on the property (Yagyū Nobuharu, 1985–1990). Consequently, these original documents are preserved today in the Yagyū family archives. (For photo, see: *Yagyū Shinkage Ryū*.)

YAGYŪ GENCHŌ (TOSHINAGA)
Twentieth headmaster of the Owari Yagyū Shinkage Ryū
Photograph courtesy Yagyū Nobuharu

Due to the razing of Nagoya and Tōkyō, the general destruction of the country, the death of Genchō's two eldest sons who had been groomed to be the next generation of the family tradition, and the general Allied ban on martial arts training during the post–World War II occupation,[4] there was little chance to expand the Yagyū Shinkage Ryū during those years. However, after his return from China at the end of the war, Genchō's youngest son Nobuharu began concentrating his efforts on mastering the Shinkage Ryū.

The Allied occupation of Japan ended in 1952; soon after, in 1955, Genchō founded the Tōkyō Yagyūkai in order to again begin spreading the Yagyū Shinkage Ryū. In 1957 he published a definitive work on the school entitled *Shōden Shinkage Ryū*『正傳新陰流』(The authentic record of Yagyū Shinkage Ryū).

His most notable students were Kanbe Takeyori and Ōtsubō Shihō (both of whom also trained with Genchō's father, Genshū); Watanabe Tadatoshi; and Genchō's son, Yagyū Nobuharu.

YAGYŪ TADAMITSU (L) AND YAGYŪ GENSHŪ (R) C. 1913
Demonstrating Sangakuen no Tachi at Nagoya Toshogu

Yagyū Genshū (Toshichika) 柳生 厳周【柳生嚴周】[A.k.a. ***~Taira no Toshichika*** 平厳周

[4] This ban was enacted by the Supreme Commander of Allied Powers (SCAP) under General McArthur, SCAP Directives 548 and 550. It was not lifted until 1950.

【平嚴周】] (1845–1932). In 1864, at the age of nineteen, Genshū became the nineteenth headmaster of the Owari Yagyū Shinkage Ryū.[5] That same year Genshū was made the official strategist (*heihō shihan*) for the Owari line of the Tokugawa family, and joined the samurai participating in the subjugation of Chōshū domain (Chōshū Seibatsu).

Toward the end of his reign, Emperor Meiji[6] (r. 1867–1912) issued a proclamation in support of preserving traditional Japanese arts. Because of this, in 1913, the second year of the reign of the Taishō emperor, Yagyū Genshū traveled to Tōkyō with his oldest son in order to demonstrate Yagyū Shinkage Ryū at the Saineikan,[7] a martial *dōjō* run by the Imperial Household Department (Kunaishō).[8] Genshū subsequently taught Yagyū Shinkage Ryū at the Saineikan. This continued until a reorganization of the Kunaishō in 1922, when the training was discontinued. Genshū officially retired in 1923 at the age of seventy-eight; however, he continued to be active in teaching Yagyū Shinkage Ryū until his death in 1932.

According to Akabane (2007: 12–13), at the time of his official retirement in 1923, Genshū's most senior disciples were Shimojō Kosaburō (age fifty-six), Yagyū Genchō (age thirty-one), and Kambe Takeyasu (age twenty-nine). Other notable students of Genshū at that time were Watanabe Tadatoshi (age twenty-nine) and Ōtsubō Shihō (age seventeen).

***Yagyū Hyōgonosuke Taira no Toshiyoshi* (*Toshitoshi*)** 柳生 兵庫助 平利厳. See: *Yagyū Toshiyoshi.*

Yagyū Hyōsuke 柳生 兵助 (c.1580–c.1640). Son of Yagyū Matsuemon Ienobu. Hyōsuke passed on the Yagyū Shinkage Ryū in Fukuoka domain.

Yagyū Jūbei 柳生 十兵衛 (1606–1650). [A.k.a. ***~Taira no Mitsuyoshi*** 平三厳【平三嚴】]. Son of Yagyū Munenori. Jūbei is recognized as the second headmaster of the Edo Yagyū Shinkage Ryū 江戸柳生新陰流. He composed a famous work on swordsmanship known as the *Tsuki no shō*『月之抄』which, to date, has not yet been translated into English.

In legend and popular literature, Jūbei is probably the most famous of all the Yagyū swordsmen. Ironically, we know very little about him. Jūbei was noted for his peerless swordsmanship, his preference for "positive" *kenjutsu*, his development of specialized weapons such as the *Jūbei no jō*, and his presumed work as an espionage organizer for the Tokugawa shogunate.

YAGYŪ JŪBEI MITSUYOSHI
Second headmaster of
the Edo Yagyū Shinkage Ryū

One of the most famous legends concerning Jūbei was that of the loss of his eye. As the story goes, he tended toward mischievousness when he was young. After he had played some prank, his father threw a rock at him, and the stone hit him in the eye. Jūbei, instead of covering the damaged eye, immediately covered his other eye to keep it from being injured. As there is no corroboration for this story, it is probably apocryphal. However, the story displays Jūbei's well-known quick reflexes and boar-like determination.

At the age of thirteen (in 1619) Jūbei entered service with the Tokugawa shogunate as a page (*warawa* 童) to the shogunal heir apparent, Tokugawa Takechiyo. Takechiyo was sixteen years old at the time; he and Jūbei had been childhood companions. The young Jūbei's duties as a page may have included such tasks as being Takechiyo's opponent in swordsmanship practice (*kenjutsu*). However, this is unclear. The two young men evidently had an amicable relationship continuing into

---

[5] Tenth headmaster by some reckoning. See lineage chart under Owari Yagyū Shinkage Ryū.

[6] Meiji Tennō 明治天皇 (1852–1912; r.1867–1912), 122nd emperor of Japan.

[7] Saineikan 済寧館【濟寧館】.

[8] Kunaishō 宮内省.

Takechiyo's sudden ascent as third Tokugawa *shōgun* Iemitsu in 1623. Iemitsu was nineteen years old at the time; Jūbei was sixteen.

In 1626, when Jūbei was twenty years old, he was suddenly removed from public life for twelve years by Tokugawa Iemitsu. This is a strange incident, especially since Jūbei and Iemitsu had been boyhood friends for many years. Years later, at the age of thirty-one, Jūbei glosses over this incident, writing that it occurred "for certain reasons." Early in his period of exile Jūbei is thought to have returned to his birthplace in Yagyū village, where he devoted himself to training in Shinkage Ryū. Upon his return to Edo twelve years later, he was an accomplished swordsman. Just prior to returning to official public life, he wrote his well-known treatise on swordsmanship, the *Tsuki no shō*. Obviously he had become very experienced in exile.

Writers over the years have made much of this episode, and assume Tokugawa Iemitsu sent his childhood friend on secret missions to set up spy networks to watch over the feudal lords under his rule. There are no documents which corroborate this. However, the most effective espionage agent is the one who is never discovered.

Jūbei succeded his father Munenori as head of the Edo Yagyū Shinkage Ryū in 1646. He had several students, including his sons, who carried on the tradition. However, after Jūbei there do not seem to have been any swordsmen of particular note in the Edo Yagyū line.

Further reading in English:

• Sugawara, 1985: 146–160.

Yagyū Kōichi 柳生 耕一 (1952–). Twenty-second headmaster of the Owari Yagyū Shinkage Ryū. A cousin of twenty-first headmaster Yagyū Nobuharu Toshimichi, Yagyū Kōichi was among the first rank of disciples in the Yagyū Kai *dōjō* in Tōkyō. Upon Nobuharu's retirement in 2006, Kōichi was adopted into the Yagyū family and formally assumed the headmastership of the *ryū*.

Yagyū Matsuemon Munenobu 柳生 松右衛門 宗信 [A.k.a. ***Matsu Uemon*** 松右衛門; ***~Ienobu*** ～家信] (c.1560–c.1620). Originally using the surname of Matsuno 松野 or Ōno 大

YAGYŪ KŌICHI
Twenty-second headmaster of
the Yagyū Shinkage Ryū, 1989
(Photograph by author)

野, Ienobu (or Munenobu) was evidently adopted by Yagyū Muneyoshi and subsequently changed his surname to Yagyū. It appears he transmitted several traditions in Fukuoka. Firstly, according to some documents, he was a direct disciple (*deshi*) of Anazawa Kiyomi Hidetaka. In that capacity, Ienobu transmitted Shintō Ryū longsword (*nagadachi*), a branch tradition of the Anazawa Ryū, in Fukuoka domain (present-day Fukuoka prefecture). In addition, in several *densho* examined by Watatani and Yamada (1978: 859), Ienobu is listed as a successor of Yagyū Muneyoshi in the Shinkage Ryū 新陰流. From Ienobu descend two major lines of Yagyū Shinkage Ryū 柳生新陰流 in Fukuoka domain: the Yagyū Shinkage Ryū passed on by Ienobu's son, Yagyū Hyōsuke 柳生 兵助, and the Arichi Shinkage Ryū 有地真陰流 passed on by Ienobu's disciple, Arichi Kuranosuke Motokatsu 有地内蔵丞元勝. Finally, a third account states that Ienobu was also founder of a system known as Gan Ryū (2) 眼流 swordsmanship (*kenjutsu*).

Yagyū Munenori 柳生 宗矩 (1571–1646). [A.k.a. ***~Tajima no Kami*** 但馬守, ***Shinzaemon*** 新左衛門, ***Mataemon*** 又右衛門]. The youngest son of Yagyū Muneyoshi. Munenori became one of the inheritors of the Yagyū Shinkage Ryū; he is the progenitor of the Edo Yagyū line.

After learning of Yagyū Muneyoshi's accomplishments, Tokugawa Ieyasu invited him to his villa in Kyōto in 1594. Munenori accompanied his father to this meeting. Ieyasu was so impressed by the Yagyū Shinkage Ryū

Y

technique known as *mutō* 無刀 that he asked Muneyoshi to become his swordsmanship teacher. Muneyoshi (then sixty-six years old) declined and offered his twenty-three-year-old son Munenori to be Ieyasu's retainer and sword instructor. After the battle of Sekigahara in 1600, Ieyasu became *shōgun*, and ruled from the city of Edo from 1603. Munenori accompanied him; the Edo Yagyū Shinkage Ryū 江戸柳生新陰流 dates from that time. Munenori was greatly influenced by the Zen priest Takuan, and composed a famous work on swordsmanship known as the *Heihō kadensho*『兵法家伝書』.

Further reading in English:
- Sato, 1986.
- Sugawara, 1985: 112–145.
- Wilson, 2004.

Yagyū Muneyoshi (Munetoshi) 柳生 宗厳【柳生宗嚴】[A.k.a. ***~Sekishūsai*** 石舟斎【石舟齋】, ***~Shinzaemon*** 新左衛門] (1529–1606). Inheritor of the Shinkage Ryū from Kamiizumi Nobutsuna; progenitor of the Yagyū Shinkage Ryū 柳生新陰流. Muneyoshi, well known as the best swordsman in Japan's Kinki district in the early 1560s, was defeated in a duel with Hikita Bungorō, and then by Hikita's master and uncle, Kamiizumi Ise no Kami Nobutsuna, in 1563. Muneyoshi became Kamiizumi's disciple and mastered the most subtle concepts of the Shinkage Ryū; after two years, in 1565, he was awarded an *inka* (full license) in the Shinkage Ryū. It is from this point that the Yagyū line of the Shinkage Ryū began.

MARISHITEN ILLUSTRATION BY YAGYŪ MUNEYOSHI
(Yagyū family archives)

Attesting to the ties between the Yagyū Shinkage Ryū founder Muneyoshi and the cult of Marishiten is the avove brushing of the goddess attributed to him.

Further reading in English:
- Hurst, 1998: 58–60.
- de Lang, 2006, *passim*.
- Sugawara, 1985: 100–111.

Yagyū Nobuharu 柳生 延春 [A.k.a. ***~Taira no Toshimichi (Gendō)*** 平厳道] (1919–2007). Twenty-first headmaster of the Owari Yagyū Shinkage Ryū 尾張柳生新陰流. Yagyū Nobuharu began training in Yagyū Shinkage Ryū at the age of six. He recalled once that on first being whacked with a bamboo sword (*shinai*), he ran crying out of his father's *dōjō*. However, he continued to train sporadically until he was stationed abroad in China during World War II. His two older brothers, who had been groomed to lead the tradition, were killed during the war.

YAGYŪ NOBUHARU, C. 1988
Twenty-first headmaster of the Owari Yagyū Shinkage Ryū
(Photograph by author)

Consequently, after his return from China at the end of the war, Nobuharu concentrated his efforts on mastering the Shinkage Ryū. At the urging of his father Genchō, he often tested his skills against *kendō* practitioners. The postwar period was an especially difficult time for classical martial arts groups in Japan, as their practice was banned under the 1946

SCAP directives 548 and 550.[9] This ban was not lifted until 1950. It was around this time that Nobuharu earned a degree in Japanese literature from Waseda University. He subsequently worked as a junior high school teacher, becoming the first Yagyū to be employed in any occupation other than that of a professional swordsman.

A few years later, in 1955, his father opened the Yagyūkai in Tōkyō. In 1966, upon the death of his father Yagyū Genchō, Nobuharu became headmaster of the Owari line of the Yagyū Shinkage Ryū. At that time he left the teaching profession and devoted himself to promoting and spreading the Yagyū Shinkage Ryū. Having no son to inherit the Owari line, he adopted his cousin, Yagyū (Ishida) Kōichi in order to pass on the inner teachings of the Shinkage Ryū to the next generation. In addition, Nobuharu was the first headmaster to welcome non-Japanese into the Yagyū Shinkage Ryū.

Yagyū Ryū 柳生流. A term generally applied to the Yagyū Shinkage Ryū and its collateral weapons arts which were not necessarily part of the Shinkage Ryū tradition, such as the use of small throwing blades and darts (*shuriken-jutsu*), grappling in armor (*yoroi kogusoku*), etc. However, the term Yagyū Ryū is sometimes used in popular literature to refer to any Yagyū-family martial arts.

Yagyū Seigō Ryū
柳生制剛流
(abbreviated lineage)

Seigō Sō
制剛僧

1. Mizuhaya Chōzaemon Nobumasa
初代 水早 長左衛門 信正
Seigō Ryū · Namban Ippon Ryū
制剛流·南蛮一品流

[Headmasters 2–4]
[see Seigō Ryū]

5. Ōhashi Kinosuke Masanaga
五代 大橋 喜之助 政長

6. Nagaoka Jūrōemon Fusahide
六代 長岡 重郎右衛門 房廣
Yagyū Seigō Ryū
柳生制剛流

[Headmasters 7–10]
(All were Nagaoka family members)

11. Yagyū Sangorō Genshū (Toshichika)
十一代 柳生 三五郎 厳周

12. Yagyū Kanaji Genchō (Toshinaga)
十二代 柳生 金治 厳長

13. Yagyū Nobuharu Gendō (Toshimichi)
十三代 柳生 延春 厳道

14. Yagyū Kōichi
十四代 柳生 耕一

Ban Yasuyuki
坂 保行

Yagyū Seigō Ryū 柳生制剛流. A branch line of the Seigō Ryū which became a collateral system (*fuzoku bugei*) to the Yagyū Shinkage Ryū during the late Tokugawa period. Its quick-draw sword techniques are referred to as *battō no tachi*.

The Yagyū Seigō Ryū branch tradition is believed to have been founded by Nagaoka Jūrōemon Fusahide (c.1644–1713), a retainer from Bishū who was one of a group of fifty Yagyū Ryū master advisors. While in that position, he learned Seigō Ryū from the sixth headmaster, Ōhashi Kinosuke Masanaga. Nagaoka combined the teachings of the Yagyū Ryū with Seigō Ryū, creating the Yagyū Seigō Ryū.

The curriculum of the Yagyū Seigō Ryū was revised extensively by Yagyū Genshū and his son/successor Yagyū Genchō during the early to middle twentieth century. This was done in an era when the shift from *bugei* to *budō* was at its height; *kendō*, *jūdō*, and other martial disciplines were becoming nationwide—even international—sports, and disciplines such as quick-draw swordsmanship (*iai*) were being influenced by such imposing national figures as Nakayama Hakudō. Consequently the combative effectiveness of the revised Seigō Ryū may have been compromised as its practice was reoriented toward new goals.

[9] These directives were apparently aimed at purging fascists and ending the martial arts training practiced in the public schools at the end of the war in 1945. That "martial arts" regimen had come to concentrate on "bayonet training and grenade throwing" by that time. (Svinth, 2002). See also: *Dai Nippon Butokukai*.

Curriculum		Number of *kata*
Battōjutsu 抜刀術		
• Iai Omote	居合表	7+2
• Iai Ura	居合裏	7
• Tachiai Omote	立合表	2
• Tachiai Ura	立合裏	8
• Nanakajō	七箇條	7+1
• Gokajō	五箇條	5+1
• Gokui	極意	3

See also: *Seigō Ryū*.

Further reading in English:

- Mol, 2001: 172–176.
- Mori, 2004.

Yagyū Sekishūsai Muneyoshi (Munetoshi) 柳生 石舟斎 宗厳. See: *Yagyū Muneyoshi*.

Yagyū Shingan Ryū. Several schools have referred to themselves as "Yagyū Shingan Ryū" or "Shingan Ryū" using various characters to write the name. There are at least three lines of this tradition existing today. In various publications in Japanese, they have differentiated themselves by adding a combative arts description to their titles as follows: 1) Yagyū Shingan Ryū Taijutsu; 2) Yagyū Shingan Ryū Katchū Heihō; and 3) Yagyū Shingan Ryū Katchū Kempō.

All three trace their origins to Yagyū Munenori and have permission to use the Yagyū name; but their lines come down through different disciples. One group names Araki Mataemon 荒木 又右衛門 (1584–1637) as its founder, while the other two groups name Takenaga Hayato 竹永隼人.

In either case, the early Yagyū Shingan Ryū was a truly comprehensive combative system. While its *kenjutsu* was likely influenced by Munenori's Yagyū Shinkage Ryū, the Yagyū Shingan Ryū included many systems that reflect the combative needs of the early seventeenth century. These included martial techniques practiced in full and light armor (*katchū bujutsu*); socketed spear (*hoko*); grappling in light armor (*kogusoku*); arresting arts (*torite*); arresting-cord arts (*torinawa*); police-truncheon techniques (*jitte* [1] 実手); iron-fan techniques (*tessen*); combative swordsmanship (*kenjutsu*) with longsword (*ōdachi*), middle-length sword (*chūdachi*), and short sword (*kodachi*); quick-draw swordsmanship (*iai*); short spear (*tansō*); long glaive techniques (*naginatajutsu*); long hardwood staff arts (*bōjutsu*); and composite sickle-and-chain arts (*kusarigama-jutsu*).

Yagyū Shingan Ryū (1) Taijutsu 柳生心眼流 (体術【躰術】). This line of the Yagyū Shingan Ryū attributes its founding in the early 1600s to Araki Mataemon (1584–1637). (Several schools, in fact, attribute their origins to Mataemon, but the lineage is often unclear.) The school was best known for its *taijutsu* (=*jūjutsu*)—often performed as armored grappling —but the curriculum also includes swordsmanship (*kenjutsu*), quick-draw swordsmanship (*iaijutsu*), long-hafted glaive techniques (*naginatajutsu*), and long hardwood staff arts (*bōjutsu*).

Araki Mataemon initially trained in the Edo Yagyū Shinkage Ryū 江戸柳生新陰流 with Yagyū Munenori. He also trained in a variety of combative arts and traditions, including the Musō Jikiden Ryū 無双直伝流. Later, under Yagyū Jūbei Mitsuyoshi, Araki obtained permission to create a new school, borrowing the name "Yagyū" from his affiliation with Yagyū Shinkage Ryū.

YAGYŪ SHINGAN RYŪ (1) TAIJUTSU
Kajitsuka Yasukazu (L) and Mutō Masao (R) demonstrate *kenjutsu* at Kashima Grand Shrine, 1980
(Photograph by author)

Yagyū Shingan Ryū (2) Katchū Heihō 柳生心眼流 (甲冑兵法) [A.k.a. ***Yagyū Shingan Ryū Heihō*** ～兵法]. A system founded in the early 1600s by Takenaga Hayato. The school is best known for its armored *taijutsu* (=*jūjutsu*), often performed in armor or for armored grappling. The curriculum also includes various weapons systems practiced while in armor. Takenaga was apparently a contemporary of Araki Mataemon. See: *Yagyū Shingan Ryū (1) Taijutsu*.

Yagyū Shingan Ryū (3) Katchū Kempō
柳生心眼流（甲冑拳法）[A.k.a. ***Yagyū Shingan Ryū Heihōjutsu*** ～兵法術]. This system has the same lineage as the Yagyū Shingan Ryū (2) Katchū Heihō. However, current head-

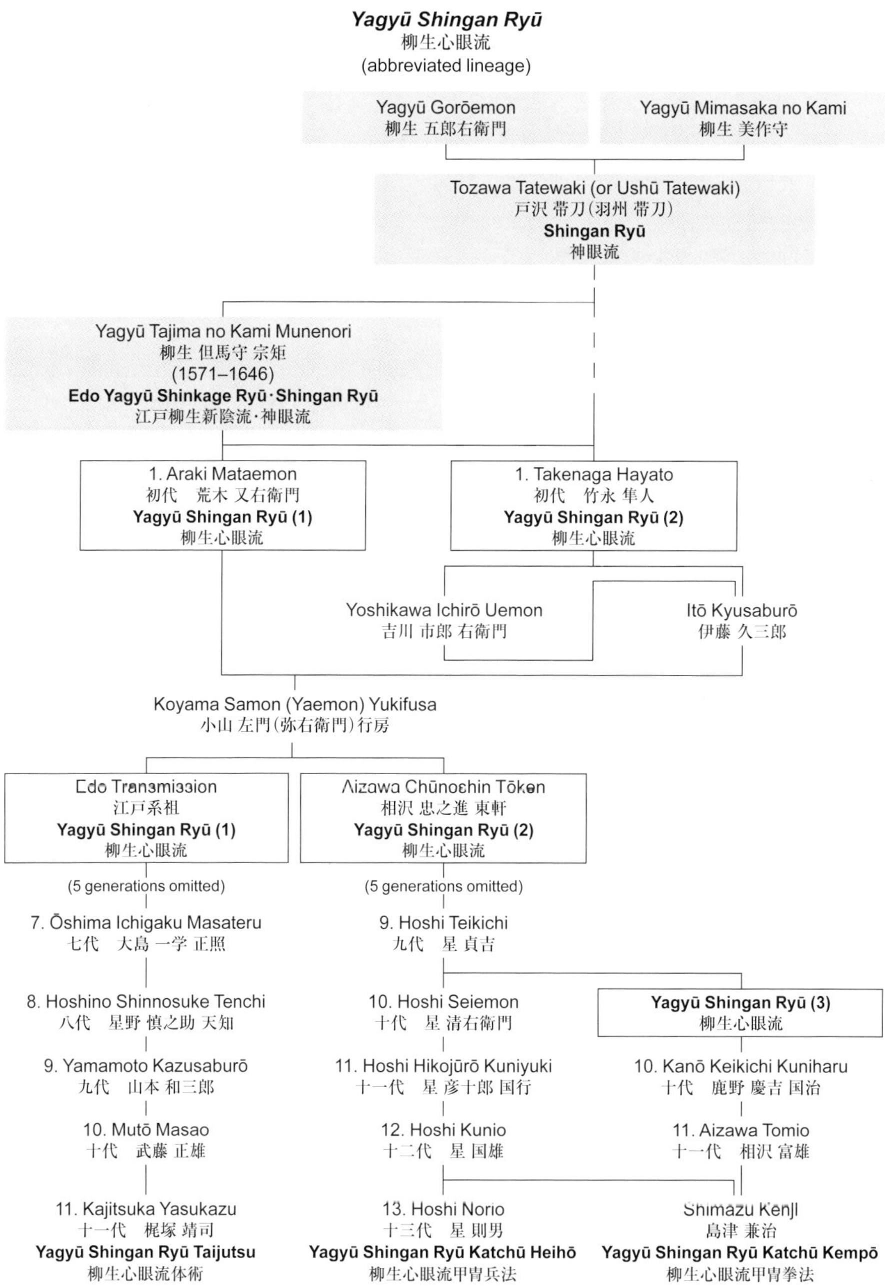

Y

Yagyū Shingan Ryū Katchū Heihō
Demonstration of *katchū heihō* at the Budōkan in 1979
(Photograph courtesy Jeff Acopian)

master Shimazu Kenji trained in several sublines before striking out on his own.

Yagyū Shinjirō Yoshikatsu 柳生 新次郎 厳勝. See: *Yagyū Yoshikatsu.*

Yagyū Shinkage Ryū 柳生新陰流 [A.k.a. ***Shinkage Ryū hyōhō (heihō)*** 新陰流(兵法)]. The original tradition established by Yagyū Sekishūsai Muneyoshi in 1565, from which all branches of Yagyū Shinkage Ryū are derived. The Yagyū tradition preserves the Shinkage Ryū as it was taught by Kamiizumi in the early 1560s; it has also added and dropped various elements over the succeeding 450 years. Like Kamiizumi's Shinkage Ryū (1) 新陰流, the Yagyū Shinkage Ryū falls into the category of "positive" swordsmanship in that it emphasizes *sen o toru* (winning by taking the initiative). In addition to rigorous training of the body in the techniques of the *ryū*, there is great emphasis on developing the mind. Yagyū Shinkage Ryū exponents must master a number of subtle concepts, including *kage, marobashi, shūji shuriken, setsunintō/katsujinken*, and others.

Over the years variations on the original Shinkage Ryū system were developed and added by the Yagyū, who at the same time continued to preserve the original tradition. The core tradition split into two Yagyū family lines—the Edo and Owari—by the time of founder Muneyoshi's death in 1606. Muneyoshi arranged for his son Munenori to become a retainer of Tokugawa Ieyasu in 1594. After prevailing at Sekigahara in 1600, Ieyasu established the Tokugawa shogunate in Edo in 1603. From this time the Edo Yagyū line became a separate tradition, begun by Munenori. Prior to his death in 1606, Muneyoshi also passed on the Yagyū Shinkage Ryū to his grandson, Yagyū Hyōgonosuke Toshiyoshi (Toshitoshi), giving him several of the *densho* he had originally received from Kamiizumi. The Edo Yagyū produced many competent swordsmen both within and outside the Yagyū family. However, the Edo line as a separate system declined during the years of Tokugawa-period peace (c.1650–1850) and had completely disappeared as a sword tradition by the end of the Edo period in 1867.[10] The Owari line remains extant today.

The Owari Yagyū Shinkage Ryū also produced many fine swordsmen. Some of these who were non-Yagyū family members founded lines of their own. Several of these separated from the Yagyū family tradition during the twentieth century and are currently strong non-family traditions. These include the lines founded by Kambe Takeyasu, Ōtsubo Shihō, and Watanabe Tadatoshi. There are other minor lines claiming a relationship, but they are neither so well known nor as well documented.

According to Katō Isao (conversations, 1986), the Owari line under Yagyū Genshū had faithfully preserved not only the Owari Yagyū Shinkage Ryū tradition, but also the complete

Original *Densho* of the Shinkage Ryū
Passed from Kamiizumi Ise no Kami Nobutsuna to Yagyū Sekishūsai Muneyoshi in 1565 and 1566
Left to right: *Inka, Kuka, Sangaku, Nanatachi,* and *Empi*
(Yagyū family archives)

[10] It now appears that a group in Ōsaka, Japan, calling itself the Yamato Yagyū-Kai claims to preserve a line of Yagyū Shinkage Ryū directly descendant from the Edo Yagyū line. Although their technique distantly resembles that of the Owari Yagyū line, it diverges from the Edo Yagyū technique preserved by the Owari line. This author has seen no documentation to establish their claim.

teachings of both the Edo Yagyū Shinkage Ryū line and the Hikita Kage Ryū. Today each of the extant lines contains variant amounts of these curricula; none apparently retained the complete syllabus.

As for documentation, Kamiizumi was constantly changing the number and content of the various *densho* he passed on to his disciples; however, they usually included *inka* (full mastery) and several *emaki* depicting postures from the various sets of *kata* such as Sangaku and Kuka. The list below approximates what the several current lines of Owari Yagyū Shinkage Ryū award their students; however, not all lines are the same. In fact, Yagyū Nobuharu of the Owari Yagyū family tradition did not award any Shinkage Ryū *densho* to his students. In 2006 he passed on the original Shinkage Ryū *densho* to his successor, Yagyū Kōichi.

Certificate (*menjō*)/license (*menkyo*):	
• Omote	「表」
• Ō-marobashi	「大転」
• Ko-marobashi	「小転」
• Tengusho	「天狗抄」
• Tengusho-oku	「天狗抄奥」
• Mokuroku	「目録」
• Inka	「印可」

The early Yagyū Shinkage Ryū appears to have consisted of approximately thirteen sets of *kata:*

Curriculum		**Number of *kata***
Sword (*katana/kodachi*) forms:		
• Empi no Tachi	燕飛之太刀	6 (+2 oku)
• Nana Tachi	七太刀	7
• Sangakuen no Tachi	三学円之太	5
• Kuka no Tachi	九箇之太刀	9
• Tengushō	天狗抄	8
• Okugi no Tachi	奥義之太刀	6
• Gokui no Tachi (Hakka no Hisshō	極意之太刀 八箇必勝)	8
• Ōmarobashi	大轉	3
• Komarobashi	小轉	3
• Mutōdori	無刀取	3
• Zamutōdori	座無刀取	3
• Mutōdori	無刀取	5

Yagyū Shinkage Ryū heihō 柳生新陰流 兵法 [Also read: ***Yagyū Shinkage Ryū hyōhō***]. See: *Yagyū Shinkage Ryū.*

Yagyū Shinkage Ryū hyōhō 柳生新陰流 兵法 [Also read: ***Yagyū Shinkage Ryū heihō***]. See: *Yagyū Shinkage Ryū.*

Yagyū Tajima no Kami Munenori 柳生 但馬守 宗矩. See: *Yagyū Munenori.*

Yagyū Toshichika 柳生 厳周. See: *Yagyū Genshū (Toshinaga).*

Yagyū Toshinaga 柳生 厳長. See: *Yagyū Genchō (Toshinaga).*

Yagyū Toshiyoshi* (*Toshitoshi*)** 柳生 利厳【柳生利嚴】[A.k.a. ***Yagyū Hyōgonosuke Taira no Toshiyoshi (Toshitoshi) 柳生 兵庫助 平利厳【柳生兵庫助平利嚴】] (1579–1650). Son of Yagyū Shinjiro Yoshikatsu; progenitor of the Owari Yagyū Ryū. According to Yagyū family history, Toshiyoshi was the most beloved of Yagyū Muneyoshi's grandchildren. Perhaps this was because Toshiyoshi's father (Muneyoshi's eldest son, Yoshikatsu) had been so severely injured in 1571 during a battle in Tatsuichi that he could no longer practice swordsmanship, and that his older brother, Kyūsaburō, had been killed in the Korean campaign. Toshiyoshi was therefore the eldest surviving son of the eldest surviving (but incapacitated) son.

YAGYŪ HYŌGONOSUKE TOSHIYOSHI (TOSHITOSHI)
Founder of the Owari Yagyū Shinkage Ryū
(From the archives of Yagyū Nobuharu)

In 1606 Toshiyoshi was named third headmaster of the Shinkage Ryū by his grandfather, Yagyū Muneyoshi. At that time Toshiyoshi also inherited most of the original Shinkage Ryū *densho* which Kamiizumi Nobutsuna had awarded to his grandfather in 1565 and 1566. In 1615 he became the official instructor of *heihō* (martial strategy/fencing) to Tokugawa Yoshinao, the lord of Owari (an area that included present day Nagoya; it was one of several areas directly governed by members of the Tokugawa family). Toshiyoshi is recognized as the progenitor of the Owari Yagyū Shinkage Ryū.

Yagyū Yoshikatsu* (*Toshikatsu*)** 柳生 厳勝【柳生嚴勝】[A.k.a. ***Shinjiro 新次郎] (1552–1617). The eldest son of Yagyū Muneyoshi. Along with his younger brother, Yagyū Munenori, Yoshikatsu co-inherited the Yagyū Shinkage Ryū from his father. Unfortunately, he was severely wounded in 1571 during a battle in Tatsuichi in Yamato Province. Yoshikatsu received the original *densho* Kamiizumi Ise no Kami Nobutsuna had written for his father; they were passed on to Yoshikatsu's son Toshiyoshi in 1606.

yahagi 矢矧. 1. Making arrows. 2. An arrow maker.

yahagishi 矢矧師. An arrow maker; a fletcher.

yahaki 矢矧. See: *yahagi*.

yahazu 矢筈. The nock of an arrow.

yajiku 矢軸. An arrow shaft.

yajiri 鏃 [Var. 矢尻]. An arrowhead; the barb on an arrow.

yakiba 焼刃【燒刃】. The tempered area along the cutting edge of a blade. See: *hamon (1)*.

yakizu 矢傷. A wound made by an arrow.

Yakuma Jigen Ryū 薬丸示現流【藥丸示現流】[Usually read ***Yakumaru Jigen Ryū***]. See: *Nodachi Jigen Ryū*.

Yakumaru Gyōbuzaemon Kanenobu 薬丸刑部左衛門 兼陳【藥丸刑部左衛門兼陳】(1607–1689). Founder of Nodachi Jigen Ryū. See also: *Jigen Ryū; Nodachi Jigen Ryū; Tōgō Tōbei Shigekaka*.

Yakumaru Jigen Ryū 薬丸示現流【藥丸示現流】[A.k.a. 薬丸自顕流【藥丸自顯流】] See: *Nodachi Jigen Ryū*.

Yakuma Ryū 薬丸流【藥丸流】[Usually read ***Yakumaru Ryū***]. See: *Nodachi Jigen Ryū*.

yakusoku 約束. 1. A promise, stipulation, or agreement. 2. During the performance of prearranged combative forms (*kata*) in classical martial traditions (*koryū*), there are many occasions when the participants restrain their blows so as not to harm their training partner. The use of restrained techniques is sometimes referred to as *yakusoku*, indicating that an agreement is in place in which the participants have "promised" not to injure each other. See also: *tsumeru*.

yama arashi 山嵐. Lit. "mountain storm." DAITŌ RYŪ—A devastating Daitō Ryū *jūjutsu* technique, evidently derived from *oshikiuchi*, which enabled Saigō Shirō to defend Kōdōkan Jūdō against all challengers in 1886. Today there are several contending versions of what this technique actually entailed. See: *oshikuchi*.

yamabushi 山伏 [Orig. 山臥] [A.k.a. ***shugenja*** 修験者]. Lit. "prostrating (or humbling) oneself in the mountains." This term refers to mountain ascetics who are followers of Shugendō. The religion appeared in Japan around the seventh century; its antecedents lie in native Japanese shamanism, Shintō, Daoism, and Esoteric (Tantric) Buddhism of the Tendai and Shingon sects. Shugendō practitioners were called *yamabushi* because their ascetic practices, aimed at obtaining spiritual power, were held in remote mountain areas.

These practices closely resemble some of the harsher Tendai austerities carried out on Mount Hiei. They include the tantric fire ritual (*goma* 護摩, referred to as *saito goma* 柴燈護摩 in Shugendō); fasting (*danjiki* 断食) from food and water; recitation of Buddhist *sūtras*; and tantric meditation. Sometimes fire walking (*hiwatari* 火渡) and purification rites (*misogi* 禊) such as meditation/*mudrā*/*mantra*-recitation under waterfalls were also practiced. The aim of such austerities is to develop spiritual power for performing exorcism and healing, and to achieve heightened states of consciousness.

Over time these spiritually empowered *yamabushi* became associated in the popular mind with the *tengu*—long-nosed mountain goblins. Probably due to Shugendō's incorporation of Tantric Buddhism in its practices, a natural association evolved between the various groups of *yamabushi* and the temples of the Tendai and Shingon sects. This apparently pulled a number of *yamabushi* into the political and military upheavals of the times. As early as the tenth century, Shugendō and its *yamabushi* were becoming involved as combatants in the great political/military struggles of the Heian, Kamakura, Muromachi, and Sengoku periods. The many Shugendō texts devoted to Marishiten and the manipulation of the Kujihō make it clear that some of the ascetic practices of the *yamabushi* were also aimed at gaining magical powers that would aid them in battle.

Although the warrior-monk phenomenon declined in the late 1500s and the professional warrior class (*bushi*) was disenfranchised in the 1870s, Shugendō is still practiced by *yamabushi* today in Japan. These mountain ascetics are still seen as persons who are able to cross the gap between the mundane and spiritual world. They are adept in ritual, purification, magical charms, and other esoterica. They are believed to be able to obtain power from the spiritual world which can affect their community for good or evil. Furthermore, all of their power is obtained through religious austerities.

As for any remaining combative capability, Draeger (1995: 6.14–15) noted in a lecture series at the University of Hawaii in 1981 that several items among the *yamabushi's* traditional sixteen pieces of equipment (*yamabushi jūroku dōgu*) have a martial purpose. *Yamabushi* carry a bone-strung rosary (*irataka no juzu* or *nenju*) which can be used like a whip; a conch shell (*hora*) may be used for signaling; a staff (*shakujō*) is used for self-defense and exorcism; a *vajra*-topped cane (*kongōzue*) is used as an aid in climbing and as a weapon against wild animals; a fan (*hiōgi*) can be used like a warrior's iron fan (*tessen*); a short sword (*shiba-uchi*)[11] for cutting wood, sometimes referred to as a "sword that gives life" (*katsujinken*); and a rope (*hashiri nawa*) used for ritual, climbing, and tying and subduing. Draeger also noted that when *yamabushi* were asked about the use of these implements in a fighting system, a response was not forthcoming. See also: *tengu; Shugendō; shura; sumai; Tendai Shū; Shingon Shū.*

Further reading in English:

- Earhart, 1970.

yamabushi jūroku dōgu 山伏十六道具. The "sixteen tools and dress of the *yamabushi.*" The dress and tools of the *yamabushi* were probably organized into an official "set" by the Kamakura period. However, there are two versions, a set of twelve and a set of sixteen. (See: Earhart, 1970: 25). The sixteen items are:

1. *tōhatsu*	頭髪	long hair
2. *tokin*	頭巾	small black cap
3. *ayaigasa*	綾笠	straw hat
4. *suzukake*	鈴掛	*yamabushi* robe
5. *yuigesa*	結袈裟	surplice
6. *nenju*	念珠	rosary
7. *hora*	法螺	conch
8. *shakujō*	錫杖	priest's staff
9. *oi*	笈	portable altar
10. *katabako*	肩箱	portable altar cover
11. *kongōzue*	金剛杖	diamond staff
12. *hisshiki*	引敷	sitting mat
13. *hiōgi*	檜扇	cypress fan (or "fire fan")
14. *shiba-uchi*	柴打	"wood-cutter" sword
15. *hashiri nawa*	走縄	rope
16. *waraji*	草鞋	straw sandals

Several of these items have combative uses in addition to their "normal" function. See: *yamabushi.*

Further reading in English:

- Draeger, 1995: 6.14–15.
- Earhart, 1970: 25–27.

Yamada Asaemon 山田 朝衛門. Commonly referred to as Kubikiri Asaemon 首切り 朝衛門 (Asaemon the Decapitator), the first "Yamada Asaemon" became the *shōgun's* official sword-tester and executioner of commoners (non-samurai class criminals) in 1736. During the Edo period, samurai sentenced to death were normally required to commit *seppuku* and were able to choose their own second (*kaishakunin*) to perform the *coup de grace*. However, people of non-samurai status who were convicted of capital crimes were sent to the execution grounds (*shikeijo*). It should be noted here that

[11] In the medieval period the *yamabushi* carried a *sankotsuka no ken*, which was closer in form—and use—to a warrior's sword.

decapitation was considered the most humane form of execution, less severe than crucifixion (*haritsuke kei*), burning at the stake (*hi-aburi*), or sawing off a criminal's head (*nokogiribiki*).

There were a number of official executioners in the Edo of the 1600s. However, by 1736 there were relatively fewer heads to remove; somewhat by default, the exclusive right to the job of decapitator at the *shikeijo* in Edo fell to a man named Yamada Asaemon. (Executions continued to be carried out in Edo prisons by police sergeants called *yoriki*.) Yamada's position became hereditary (along with the name) and was passed down through eight generations. The last Yamada Asaemon performed his final beheading in 1881.

In his memoirs, Yamada Yoshifusa, the eighth Yamada Asaemon, revealed the Yamada family secret to the mental focus required for the many executions. He would recite four passages from a Buddhist scripture, the *Nirvana Sutra*.[12] Each of the four short passages would be synchronized with one of the four stages of mental and physical preparation for the execution. With the recitation of the final line he would perform the *coup de grace*.

Shogyō mujō 諸行無常
All things are impermanent
Zeshō meppō 是生滅法
This is the law of birth and death.
Shōmetsu metsui 生滅滅已
Both birth and death
having been extinguished,
Jyakumetsu iraku 寂滅爲樂
This quiescence (*nirvāṇa*) is bliss.

In addition to beheading criminals, Yamada was also an official sword tester, and much of his income came from this service. These test cuttings (*tameshigiri*) were often made on the corpses of criminals which he had recently executed.

The stories of the third Yamada's exploits in the mid to late Edo period—partly based in legend and partly from historical records—were published in Japan in graphic novel (*manga*) form by Koike Kazuo and Kojima Goseki. They are currently available in English under the title *Samurai Executioner*.

YAMADA ASAEMON
Execution scene from
Koike and Kojima's *manga*
titled *Kubikiri Asaemon*
(© 1980, Futabasha, used with permission)

Further reading in English:
• Schreiber, 2001: 46–52.

Yamada Heizaemon Mitsunori 山田 平左衛門 光徳 [A.k.a. ***Yamada Ippūsai*** 山田 一風斎【山田 一風齋】] (1638–1716). Master swordsman of both the Edo Yagyū Shinkage Ryū 江戸柳生新陰流 and the Jikishin Seitō Ichi Ryū 直心正統一流; recognized as the seventh headmaster by the Jiki Shinkage Ryū 直心影流.

Yamada was a practitioner of Edo Yagyū Shinkage Ryū when, around 1670, he met Takahashi Shigeharu, sixth headmaster of the Okuyama line of the Shinkage Ryū. (Under Takahashi the system had been renamed as the Jikishin Seitō-ichi Ryū.) Yamada appears to have switched between the Edo Yagyū Shinkage Ryū and Jikishin Seitō-ichi Ryū several times. After he succeeded Takashi around 1680, Yamada restored the term *shinkage* to the *ryū*, but used new characters (心影) for *shinkage*, renaming it the (Kashima Shinden) Jiki Shinkage Ryū (鹿島真伝) 直心影流 (the correct Shinkage Ryū as transmitted from the deity of Kashima Shrine), commonly abbreviated as Jiki Shinkage Ryū 直心影流. The name of the tradition has remained the same since his time.

Yamada—a proponent of the positive style of swordsmanship—lamented the "general lack of martial ardor" in the swordsmen of

[12] *Daihatsu nehan-gyō* 『大般涅槃經』 <Ch. *Da bo niepan jing* <Skt. *Mahā-parinirvāṇa-sūtra*; T. XII:374. Several editions of this text were translated into Chinese. It is not known which version was used by Yamada.

his day. He was concerned that *kata*-centered training alone would be insufficient for training swordsmen. Consequently, although his own method of training began with *kata*-based training (*kahō*), he supplemented it with vigorous training in *shinai-geiko* (matches with *shinai*). As the *shinai* used by the Jiki Shinkage Ryū were hefty, Yamada experimented with protective equipment for the head and arms which would reduce injuries to trainees. Because of this, many young men were attracted to Yamada's *dōjō*, where they could engage in vigorous, and relatively safe, mock combat. See also: *Jiki Shinkage Ryū.*

Yamada Ippūsai 山田 一風斎 【山田一風齋】 (1638–1716). See: *Yamada Heizaemon Mitsunori.*

Yamada Jirokichi 山田 次朗吉 (1863–1931). JIKI SHINKAGE RYŪ—Recognized as fifteenth headmaster by the main line (Seitō Ha 正統派) of the Jiki Shinkage Ryū 直心影流. In 1885, at the age of twenty-two, Jirokichi moved from Chiba prefecture to Tōkyō in order to train in the Jiki Shinkage Ryū under Sakakibara Kenkichi. Tough training with extensive use of a *furibō* was required by Sakakibara, and Jirokichi went at it with a passion. However, he soon realized that there were many branch factions of the Jiki Shinkage Ryū in Tōkyō. Some, such as the Odani and Naganuma branches, emphasized matches using bamboo swords (*shinai*) and protective equipment (*bōgu*). Other branches, such as the Fujikawa Ha, emphasized training in the traditional *kata* of the *ryū*. Jirokichi was attracted to the latter, and obtained permission from Sakakibara to train with Yamada Hachirō of the Fujikawa-ha. Learning these methods in depth, Yamada united both approaches into what became the combined line called the Seitō Ha 正統派 (legitimate/orthodox line).

YAMADA JIROKICHI, c. 1900
Fifteenth headmaster of the Jiki Shinkage Ryū
(Photograph courtesy Itō Masayuki)

Yamada published a number of works on swordsmanship, including *Nippon kendōshi* 『日本劍道史』 (A history of Japanese swordsmanship) in 1925; *Kashima Shinden Jiki Shinkage Ryū* 『鹿島神傳直心影流』 in 1927; and several others.

Yamaga Ryū 山鹿流 [Also called ***Sekitokudō***]. A school of martial theory and ethics. Sometimes referred to as Yamaga Ryū *heigaku* and Yamaga Ryū *gumpō*. See: *Yamaga Sokō.*

Yamaga Sokō 山鹿 素行 (1622–1685). A warrior of Aizu domain who founded Yamaga Ryū *gumpō* (military strategy and tactics). He was also a strong proponent of *kogaku*, a school of thought that was then challenging the Neo-Confucianism of the Tokugawa shogunate. In support of this doctrine he wrote the *Seikyō Yōroku* 『聖教要録』 (1665) criticizing the conduct of Tokugawa government functionaries in Edo. For this he was imprisoned for twelve years.

Yamaga came up with his own interpretation of *bushidō* and incorporated this into his own martial system, which came to be referred to as the Yamaga Ryū. He wrote several works dealing with the "ideal" samurai and the dual concepts of gallantry/heroism (*bukyō* 武侠) and the way of the gentlemanly warrior (*shidō* 士道). Yamaga was concerned with the inactivity of the warrior (*bushi*) in the shift from a state of incessant war to one of prolonged peace under Tokugawa rule. Consequently, he emphasized the study of peaceful arts, letters, and history. These, he felt, were key elements in the development of the samurai into the Confucian ideal of the "superior man." He was also a proponent of the study of Western military weapons and tactics. Perhaps his most important student was Daidōji Yūzan, the samurai author of *Budō shoshinshu.* See also: *bushidō; bushi no konjō; Hagakure.*

Y

Yamagishi Ichirōemon Nagasada 山岸 市郎右衛門 長定. The founder of the Yamagishi Ryū, a school focusing on swordsmanship (*kenjutsu*) and quick-draw sword arts (*iaijutsu*).

Yamagishi Ryū 山岸流. As a branch tradition of Katayama Hōki Ryū 片山伯耆流, this system of swordsmanship (*kenjutsu*) and quick-draw sword arts (*iaijutsu*) was founded by Yamagishi Ichirōemon Nagasada. See: *Katayama Hōki Ryū.*

Yamaguchi Gōgen 山口 剛玄 [A.k.a. "The Cat"] (1909–1989). Founder of the main Japanese line of Gōjū Ryū *karate.* Yamaguchi was a student of Miyagi Chōjun around 1929, and co-founded the Ritsumeikan Daigaku Karate Kenkyūkai 立命館大学空手研究会 in 1930.

yama hōshi 山法師. A term for Japanese Tendai Buddhist warrior monks who hailed from the temple of Enryakuji on Mount Hiei. See also: *sōhei.*

Yamakita Takenori 山北 竹任. Current (2009) headmaster of the Taisha Ryū タイ捨流, a comprehensive combative school.

Yamakumo Enshin 山雲 円信【山雲圓信】[Var. ～円心【～圓心】] (c.1650–c.1710). Founder of the Issei Ryū 一勢流 (also called Aji Ittō Ryū 阿字一刀流) sometime during the Jōkyō era (1684–1688). Yamakumo was a masterful practitioner of quick-draw sword arts (*iaijutsu*), long hardwood staff techniques (*bōjutsu*), and arresting-cord arts (*torinawajutsu*). He was from Edo, but the main line of his Issei Ryū was transmitted in Komezawa domain. It apparently disappeared with the end of the feudal period in 1867.

Yamamoto Kyūya Masakatsu 山本 久弥 正勝【山本久彌正勝】. Founded Kage no Ryū (2) 景之流, a combative school focusing on swordsmanship (*kenjutsu*) and quick-draw sword arts (*iaijutsu*), sometime during the period 1600–1630. See: *Katayama Hōki Ryū.*

Yamamoto Minzaemon 山本 民左衛門. Founder of the Shin no Shintō Ryū 真之神道流 school of *jūjutsu.*

Yamamoto Sakondayū Akimune 山本 左近大夫 秋宗. Founded the Shin Shin Mutekatsu Ryū 新心無手勝流, a system of combative and quick-draw swordsmanship, c.1600.

Yamane Muneichirō 山根 宗一郎. See: *Edo Yagyū Shinkage Ryū Yamane Ha.*

Yamane Sagoemon Yoshifusa 山根 左五右衛門 由房. Founder of the Shinkyō Ryū 心鏡流, a school of combative swordsmanship (*kenjutsu*), spear tactics (*sōjutsu*), long-hafted glaive (*naginatajutsu*), and sickle-and-chain arts (*kusagamajutsu*). Yamane established the system in 1684.

Yamannī Ryū [Also read **Yamani Ryū; Yamane Ryū**] 山根流. OKINAWAN KOBUDŌ—A system of Okinawan long-staff arts (*bōjutsu*) preserved by the Chinen family from the time of Chinen Masanra (1842–1925) through the time of Chinen Masami (1898–1976). It is no longer extant, but some of its combative forms (*kata*) are preserved in other systems.

Yamaoka Tesshū 山岡 鉄舟【山岡鐵舟】[A.k.a. **Ono Tetsutarō** 小野鉄太郎 【小野鐵太郎】] (1836–1888). Founder of Ittō Shōden Mutō Ryū 一刀正伝無刀流 in 1880. Born Ono Tetsutarō, Tesshū became a famous samurai who reached his maturity during the turbulent period when Japan was making the transition from the feudal Tokugawa period to the Imperial Restoration and the Meiji era. Originally trained in Jiki Shinkage Ryū 直心影流, he later polished his swordsmanship in the Ono Ha Ittō Ryū 小野派一刀流 and Nakanishi Ha Ittō Ryū 中西派一刀流. Tesshū was the most skilled of the *sanshū*—the three top statesmen/swordsmen—of his era (the other two being Katsu Kaishū and Takahashi Deishū). He later trained in the spear (*sōjutsu*) under Yamaoka Seizan 山岡静山. When Seizan died, Tesshū married his teacher's sister and was adopted into the Yamaoka family in order to carry on the family name.

Tesshū, much like superlative swordsmen of earlier eras, believed that spiritual perfection was the ultimate goal of swordsmanship. He realized that, ironically, in order to "preserve peace and maintain life," the superior warrior had to first learn how to draw and wield the sword. Through intense practice (*shūgyō*) of this "outside skill," one could perfect one's inner self to the point at which "mind and technique are one." Yamaoka referred to this as *shingi ittai*. This same state had been referred to in various ways by previous masters: Miyamoto Musashi's "rock body" (*iwao no mi*); Kamiizumi Nobutsuna's "life-giving sword" (*katsujin ken*) and *marobashi*; and Itō Ittōsai's "one mind, one sword" (*isshin ittō*) all refer to this state. Tesshū's insight empowered him as a key figure in the Meiji Restoration. Draeger (1974: 102) notes:

> Yamaoka had many chances to fight when his great skill certainly would have prevailed; but because he believed in the classical concept of bushido he never drew his blade in actual combat.

See also: *Ittō Shōden Mutō Ryū; tachigiri seigan.*

Further reading in English:

- Draeger, 1974: 101–103.
- Stevens, 1989.
- Sugawara, 1985: 209–213

Yamashiro den 山城伝【山城傳】. See: *Gokaden.*

Yamashita Yoshitsugu 山下 義韶 [A.k.a. ***Yamashita Yoshiaki***] (1865–1935). The first practitioner to receive the rank of tenth *dan* in Kōdōkan Jūdō. Yamashita was the *jūdō* instructor of Theodore Roosevelt. He was considered one of the Four Heavenly Guardians (Shitennō) of the early Kōdōkan, along with Saigō Shirō, Tomita Tsunejirō, and Yokoyama Sakujirō.

Yamata no Orochi 八岐大蛇. The fabulous serpent with eight heads and eight tails. It is from this serpent's tail that the sword named Ame no Murakumo no Tsurugi was drawn by the Shintō *kami* Susano-o no Mikoto.

Yamato 大和. Early (native) name for Japan.

Yamato damashii 大和魂. Japanese spirit; the soul of Japan.

Yamato den 大和伝【大和傳】. See: *Gokaden.*

Yamato Jidai 大和時代. A historical period lasting from roughly 300 to 550 C.E.

Yamato Yagyū Kai 大和柳生会. See: *Edo Yagyū Shinkage Ryū Yamane Ha.*

yamato-zue 倭杖. Lit. "Japanese rod." This single-tined, truncheon-like stick was worn by such Jiki Shinkage Ryū 直心影流 swordsmen as Sakakibara Kenkichi and Takeda Sōkaku in the post-feudal Meiji era, probably because of the edict prohibiting the wearing of swords.

Yame! 止め! A command meaning "Stop!"

yami no metsuke 闇の目付. Lit. "hidden (or eclipse) targeting." A method of sighting the target in Japanese archery (*kyūjutsu* and *kyūdō*) in which the bull's-eye of the target is completely hidden by the bow. See also: *ariake no metsuke; hangetsu no metsuke.*

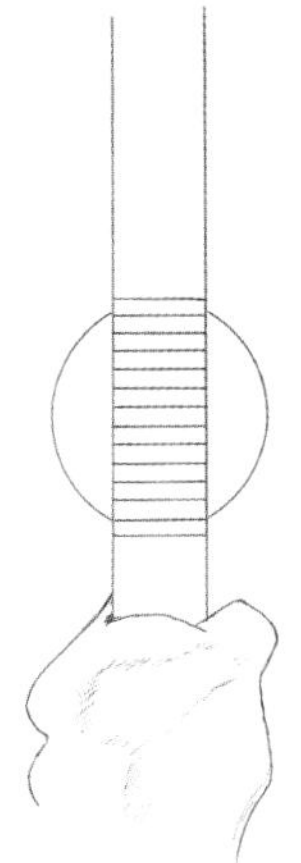

YAMI NO METSUKE

yanagiha 柳葉. Lit. "willow leaf." A straight, pointed arrowhead shaped like a willow leaf. See also: *ya no ne.*

yanagiho no yari 柳穂の槍. See: *suyari.*

Yanagi Kage Ryū 柳影流. See: *Ryūei Ryū* (1).

Yanagi Ryū 柳流. A school concentrating on grappling (*jūjutsu*) founded around 1768 by Iwanaga Gennojō Masamitsu, a provincial samurai (*gōshi*) from the old province of Hizen. See: *Iwanaga Gennojō Masamitsu; Shingetsu Musō Yanagi Ryū.*

yaniwa 矢庭. An archery range.

ya no ne 矢の根. An arrowhead. The variety of Japanese arrowheads seems infinite. However, they are generally divided into four categories:

Y

Type		Description
yanagiha	柳葉	Willow-leaf shaped; straight, pointed
togari ya	尖矢	Wider, tapering to a point
karimata	雁股	Forked
watakuri	腸繰	Flesh-tearing, barbed

yaoto 矢音. The humming sound an arrow makes in flight.

yari 槍 [Var. 鎗; 鑓]. A spear with a tang-type head which fits into the spear shaft. (An exception is the *fukuro yari*.) This is in contrast to a spear with a *hoko*-type head, which fits like a glove over the end of the spear shaft. The *yari* was monopolized by Buddhist warrior monks (*sōhei*) until the Muromachi period, when many warriors—both classical *bushi* and those of lower rank such as *ashigaru*—began using it in the incessant battles of the Warring States period. See also: *fukuro yari; jūmonji yari; kagi yari; kama yari; katakama yari; Kikuchi yari; kuda yari; ōmi no yari; ryōshinogi yari; sankaku yari; sōjutsu; suyari; tsukinari yari.*

Yari Bugyō 槍奉行. A Tokugawa-period shogunal office which was responsible for the management of spears and other polearms. It was incorporated, along with several other similar agencies, into the Bugu Bugyō in 1863.

yaribusuma 槍衾. A line of spearmen with spears held ready to attack or defend.

Yaridome 鎗留. Advanced techniques involving spear-deflection, practiced by the Jigen Ryū.

yarigusoku 槍具足. Spear-training armor. Similar to light bamboo armor (*take gusoku*), and from the same period, *yarigusoku* was sometimes made of padded leather.

yarikake 槍掛 [Var. 槍懸]. A spear rack.

yarimochi 槍持. Lit. a "spear carrier." 1. A spearman. 2. A warrior bearing a spear who accompanied personages of high status when travelling. See: *mochi yari.*

yarisaki 槍先. A spearhead. ¶ *yarisaki no kōmyō* 槍先の功名, a distinguished exploit (in battle).

Yasakani no Magatama 八坂瓊勾玉. A comma- or claw-shaped jewel which was one of the three sacred regalia of the imperial house. Some anthropologists believe the shape is originally derived from a bear claw. See: *magatama; Sanshu no Jingi.*

Yasaka Ryū 弥栄流. See: Iyasaka Ryū.

yasaki 矢先. An arrowhead.

yasha 夜叉 <Ch. *yecha* <Skt. *yakṣa* [often romanized as *yaksha*]. A nature spirit, usually benevolent; sometimes a devil or demon in Hindu mythology. The *yasha* was sometimes regarded as a protector in Buddhism. The *yasha* comprise one of the eight categories of beings that protect Buddhism (Hachibu Shū).

Yasukuni Jinja 靖国神社【靖國神社】. A shrine in Tōkyō dedicated to Japanese war dead. Kamikaze pilots in World War II, when setting off for their final suicide flights, were said to have promised to "meet each other at Yasukuni." Due to its easy accessibility in the city of Tōkyō, its association with twentieth-century militarism, and its selection as a rallying place for right-wing extremists groups, Yasukuni remains a controversial place. Nevertheless, classical martial arts demonstrations (*hōnō embu*) are held there several times each year.

Yasukunitō 靖国刀【靖國刀】. Lit. "Yasukuni swords." This term refers to a number of swords made at a special forge located in Yasukuni Shrine during the years 1933–1945. Created in a forge on the grounds of the shrine especially constructed for this purpose, the Yasukunitō were an attempt to both supply the huge demands of the imperial army and preserve the techniques and spirit of time-tested sword-forging methods developed in Japan's premodern era. Although these swords chronologically fall under the category of *gendaitō* (modern swords), they stand in contrast to the cheaply-made, mass-produced "Shōwatō" created during the era. See also: *gendaitō; guntō; kaiguntō; kotō; kyūguntō; Nippontō; shinguntō; shinshintō; shintō (2); Shōwatō.*

Further reading in English:

• Kishida, 2004.

Yasumitsu Ryū 安光流 [Var. 安密流; more formally, ***Taishiden Yasumitsu Ryū*** 太子伝安光流【太子傳安光流】]. Considered one of the Five Traditions of Aizu domain (Aizu

Goryū), this school of swordsmanship (*kenjutsu*) claimed Shōtoku Taishi (imperial regent in 593) as its founder; it was supposedly transmitted via the enigmatic Ki'ichi Hōgen and Minamoto no Yoshitsune (twelfth century). However, Watatani and Yamada (1978: 868) ascribe the system's founding to an Aizu retainer named Mochizuki Shinbei Yasukatsu (1642–1718). Yasukatsu was the son of Mochizuki Sansei Nyūdō Ankō (Yasumitsu), a warrior who had taken Buddhist vows. Yasukatsu learned Taishi Ryū strategy (*gunyō*) and swordsmanship (*kenjutsu*) from his father, and subsequently developed a system to which he gave his father's Buddhist name, Yasumitsu.

Yata-garasu 八咫烏. A sacred three-legged crow. This symbol, which finds its origins in the pan-Asian symbol of a three-legged sunbird, has had a long relationship with the Japanese imperial family, Shintō, Shugendō, and various martial traditions. As a sun symbol it is often found contrasted with the moon and the hare in a matrix with esoteric implications. In this form, the Yata-garasu is often equated with the Buddhist goddess Marishiten. See also: *uto.*

Further reading in English:

- Earhart, 1970: 44–45.
- Knutsen, 2006: 17–18.

YATA-GARASU PERCHED ON A WILD BOAR
Marishiten symbol painted
by Sesshū Tōyō 雪舟等楊 in 1499

Yata no Kagami 八咫鏡. The sacred mirror. This was one of the three sacred regalia of the Japanese imperial house. See: *Sanshu no Jingi.*

yatsugibaya 矢継ぎ早. Firing arrows in rapid succession.

yawara 1. 柔 [Var. 和]. a. One of several terms for *jūjutsu*-type arts. Though the interpretation varies from *ryū* to *ryū*, this term generally refers to unarmored, empty-hand techniques. See also: *Jikishin Ryū.* b. An abbreviation for *yawara bō*.

yawara 2. 軟. This unusual ideogram for *yawara* (1a) was used by one of the several branches of the Yagyū Shingan Ryū 柳生心眼流.

yawara 3. 倻. This unusual ideogram for the term *yawara* (1a) was used by one of the several branches of the Seigō Ryū 制剛流. Some later schools teaching *yawara* also used this character.

yawara bō 柔棒. A small pestle-type weapon, such as a *tokkosho* or *te no uchi*, which can be concealed in the hand.

yawaragei 柔芸【柔藝】. A variant term for *jūjutsu.*

yawaragi 和儀. A variant term for *jūjutsu.*

Yawara Shinshin Ryū 柔新心流. A combative system founded by Mizuno Sakubei Tadakatsu that flourished in Bishū domain. It concentrated on grappling (*jūjutsu*) and quick-draw sword techniques (*iaijutsu*). In the late 1600s Yoshida Sakubei Tadafusa, an eclectic martial artist of those times, combined it with other combative arts to form the Shin Shin Sekiguchi Ryū 新心関口流.

yazutsu 矢筒 [Var. ***utsubo*** 靫]. An arrow case used for protecting arrows in storage. The cases are sometimes elaborately decorated and may be arranged for display in a frame between two bows.

Yōi! 用意! A command meaning "Get ready!"; "Prepare!" ¶ *Mokusō yōi!* 黙想用意! Prepare to engage in meditation! ¶ *Gyakute-uchi yōi!* 逆手打用意! Prepare to execute a reverse-hand strike!

yōjimbō 用心棒. 1. A bodyguard or protector. 2. A rod or cudgel.

Y

yoki kataki 良き敵. A "worthy foe." This term was used generally during the eleventh through thirteenth centuries to indicate enemies whose status made them worthy of engaging in single combat (*ikki uchi*). Criteria varied, and might include family lineage, rank, prior accomplishments and victories, or crimes. Contrast with *awanu kataki* (unworthy foe).

Further reading in English:

• Varley, 1994: 62–63.

yokomen 横面. The side of the head or face. ¶ *yokomen uchi* 横面打ち, a cut or strike (*uchi* 打ち) to either side of the head or face (*yokomen* 横面). Compare to *shōmen uchi.*

Yokoo Ha 横尾派. See: *Seia Ryū lineage.*

yoko raitō 横雷刀. YAGYŪ SHINKAGE RYŪ—An upper-level (*jōdan*) sword posture (*kurai*) in which the sword is held above the head with the hilt (*tsuka*) pointed to the left and the sword tip (*kissaki*) pointing toward the right. For illustration, see: *Bugei zufu tōshi.*

yoko suteme waza 横捨身技. KŌDŌKAN JŪDŌ—Side-sacrifice techniques in which the thrower falls to the side (right or left) in the execution of the throw. These are a subset of Kōdōkan Jūdō's Nage no Kata.

yokozuna 横綱. SUMŌ—Lit. "horizontal rope." The highest rank in modern sport *sumō*; *yokozuna* indicates a grand champion. The term refers to the sacred rope that is worn by the grand champion as he enters the ring at the beginning of a tournament. See also: *dohyō-iri.*

yōkyū 揚弓. Lit. "bow for offering or praise"; a "votive bow." A type of bow that was generally smaller than the standard Japanese war bow (*daikyū*). The *yōkyū* was normally used for ritual purposes.

Yomi 黄泉 [A.k.a. ***Yomi no Kuni*** 黄泉国【黄泉國】]. The realm of the dead; Hades; the land of shades.

yondan 四段. 1. Lit. "fourth grade." A modern *budō* term derived from Kōdōkan Jūdō which indicates the rank of a practitioner as fourth degree. In most modern systems, this indicates a "fourth degree black belt." 2. ***Yondan*** 四段. The fourth section of prearranged combative forms (*kata*) in the advanced-level swordsmanship (Dan no Kata) of the Jigen Ryū. There are three scenarios in this set, referred to as Kei Dō Shin 軽道真.

Yoneno Kōtarō 米野 光太郎 (1923–?). Shindō Musō Ryū practitioner who received *menkyō kaiden* under Shimizu Takaji. One of Shimizu Takaji's most senior students, Yoneno was a *jō* teacher for the Tōkyō Kidōtai (riot police).

YONENO KŌTARŌ (R)
Demonstrating Oku with Shimizu Takaji (L)
(Photograph courtesy Nishioka Tsuneo)

Yō no Ryū 陽ノ流. See: *Yō Ryū.*

yoribō 縒棒. A club, generally cone-shaped with a design much like a *furibō*, approximately 4 to 6 feet (1.2–1.8 m) in length. Due to its weight and balance, this weapon was used much like a *tetsubō* from horseback. See also: *bō; bōjutsu; rokushaku bō; tetsubō.*

yoriki 与力【與力】. Lit. "to give power." 1. In the eleventh-century war tale (*gunkimono*) the *Shōmonki*, which chronicles the tenth-century Tengyō no Ran, the term *yoriki* appears to mean a low-level retainer or warrior follower. 2. *Yoriki* was originally a title rank given to

TYPICAL EDO-PERIOD *YORIKI* COSTUME
Nawa Yumio c. 1990
(Photograph courtesy John Quinn)

Hattori Hanzō by Tokugawa Ieyasu in 1590; it included command of 200 troops. Under Hanzō's son Masanari, who inherited the rank of *yoriki*, the 200 troops became *shōgun* Tokugawa Ieyasu's Edo-castle guard after Ieyasu moved his residence there in 1603. The title of *yoriki* later became the equivalent of "police sergeant" in Edo. This was in contrast to the *dōshin*, who were the constables on the beat. The *yoriki* were members of the samurai class. They often inherited their jobs, and, in the city of Edo, lived in a communal neighborhood with the *dōshin* along the Hatchōbori canal. However, the *yoriki* were a step higher socially, and were considered equal in rank to the retainers (*hatamoto*) of provincial lords. In addition to police work, the *yoriki* and *dōshin* had additional responsibilities involving fire watch and local administration. They were also responsible for a number of ceremonial duties. See also: *dōshin; Edo Machikata Jutte Torinawa Atsukaiyō; machi bugyō; machikata.*

Further reading in English:

• Schreiber, 2001: 27–33.

yoroi 甲 [Also 冑; 鎧]. Armor.

yoroidōshi 鎧通し [Also read ***yoroi tōshi***]. A short-bladed, thick dagger, about 9 to 12 inches (23–30 cm) in length, which came into popular use during the Muromachi period. A *yoroidōshi* had little or no curvature (*sori*), and was used in combative grappling against an armored opponent. The thick blade was ideal for sliding in between the slats of Japanese armor. Early on, it was worn thrust through the back of the sash (*obi*). During the Warring States period, it was carried in the *obi* on the right side, with the hilt toward the front and the cutting edge up, like a small sword. At that time it came to be called a *metezashi* (lit. "worn on the right,") meaning "right-handed sword." For illustration, see: *metezashi.*

yoroigumi 鎧組. See: *yoroi kumi.*

yoroi kumi 鎧組 [Also read ***yoroigumi***]. Abbreviation for *yoroi kumiuchi*.

yoroi kumiuchi 鎧組打. Techniques for grappling in full armor.

yoroisei 鎧製. An armor maker.

yoroi tōshi 鎧通し. See: *yoroidōshi.*

Yōrō Ritsuryō 養老律令. The legal codes promulgated during the Yōrō era (717–723). These codes were an extension of the large code of Chinese-derived laws (the Taihō Ritsuryō) promulgated in 701. The Yōrō revisions made in 718 included establishment of the imperial court ranks which persisted until the Meiji Restoration in 1868. Many of these are referred to in such classic works as the *Genji monogatari*, the *Eiga monogatari*, and the ancient and medieval war tales (*gunkimono*). As McCullough and McCullough (1980: 790) point out in "Appendix A: Some Notes on Rank and Office" in their translation of the *Eiga Monogatari*:

> Court rank entitled the holder to present himself at the Imperial Palace, to occupy a specific seat at public and private functions, and to participate in ceremonies and other official events…it determined eligibility for office…(and) conferred valuable economic prerequisites…

Consequently, during the late Heian through the Nambokuchō period, obtaining court rank became an important pursuit for warrior leaders. See: *samurai.*

Yō Ryū 陽流 [A.k.a. ***Yō Ryū Hōjutsu*** ～砲術; ***Yō no Ryū*** 陽ノ流]. A school of matchlock musketry (*hōjutsu*; also referred to as *hōtō* [2] within this school) founded by Takano Kurōzaemon Yasunaga in the late 1500s. The school has been passed down to the present in Kyūshū through the Onoe family (Onoe Ke 尾上家).

Yōseikan Budō 養正館武道. An eclectic school of modern spiritual/sportive combatives (*shin budō*) concentrating on *aikidō*, *karatedō*, *jūdō* and *jūjutsu* systems. The school also includes swordsmanship (*kenjutsu*). Founder Mochizuki Minoru was a direct disciple of *aikidō* founder Ueshiba Morihei, with whom he began training in the 1930s.

Yoshida Izumo no Kami Shigemasa 吉田 出雲守 重政. Founder of the Izumo Ha 出雲派, a branch school of the Heki Ryū 日置流 system of combative archery (*kyūjutsu*), c.1520. See also: *Heki Ryū.*

Yoshida Kōtarō 吉田 幸太郎 (1883–1966). A direct disciple of Takeda Sōkaku. Yoshida introduced Ueshiba Morihei to Sōkaku. According to Watatani and Yamada (1978), Yoshida received the Daitō Ryū license of Kyōju Dairi in 1915.[13] Starting around 1964, Kondo Katsuyuki, who received the Daitō Ryū title of Sōke Dairi from Takeda Tokimune, also trained under Yoshida for about two years.

Yoshida Sakubei Tadafusa 吉田 作兵衛 正房 [A.k.a. ***Yoshida Zensuke Masanao*** ~善助 正直] (1655–1736). Founder of the Shin Shin Sekiguchi Ryū 新心関口流. Yoshida first trained with Mizuno Sakubei Tadakatsu in the grappling arts (*jūjutsu*) and quick-draw sword system (*iaijutsu*) of the Yawara Shin Shin Ryū 柔新心流. An eclectic martial artist, Yoshida also excelled in Shinkage Ryū (1) 新陰流 swordsmanship (*tōhō*), Shinbu Ryū 神捕流 half-spear (*hansō*), and Inatomi Ichimu Ryū 稲富一夢流 firearms (*hōjutsu*).

Yōshinkan Aikidō 養神館合気道. An *aikidō* organization founded by Shioda Gōzo in 1955. See: *Shioda Gōzo.*

Yōshin Ryū 楊心流 [A.k.a. ***Yōshin Ryū Naginatajutsu*** ~薙刀術]. Originally a comprehensive martial system (*sōgō bujutsu*), this school is generally considered to have been founded around 1660 by Akiyama Shirobei Yoshitoki. Its original curriculum evidently included swordsmanship (*kenjutsu*) with an emphasis on the short sword (*kodachi*), quick-draw sword arts (*iaijutsu*), long hardwood staff arts (*bōjutsu*), glaive arts (*naginatajutsu*), composite sickle-and-chain arts (*kusarigama-jutsu*), spearmanship (*sōjutsu*), and grappling (*yawara; jūjutsu*) centered on vital points for killing and healing (*shikatsuhō* 死活法). Akiyama also included a curriculum of Chinese medicine which he had learned on the continent.

During the Tokugawa period, the glaive arts of the school were used to train female household members of the feudal lords in Yanagawa domain. Consequently, female members of the tradition train to this day in restrictive *kimono.* Since the end of the premodern period in 1868, the curriculum has been reduced somewhat to include only glaive, short staff, composite sickle-and-chain, and spear. The current (thirteenth) headmaster of the tradition is Koyama Takako 小山孝子.

The grappling art of the Yōshin Ryū was one of the systems studied by Kanō Jigorō in his development of Kōdōkan Jūdō.

Further reading in English:

- Mol, 2001: 131–147.
- Skoss, 1999: 61–63.

Yōshin Ryū jūjutsu 楊心流 柔術. The grappling arts of the Yōshin Ryū.

Yoshioka Kempō 吉岡憲法. See: *Yoshioka Ryū.*

Yoshioka Kenpō 吉岡 憲法 [The name ***Kenpō*** is also written as 拳法; 兼房; 建法; 剣峰, etc.; also read ***Yoshioka Kempō***]. As with a number of family-centered combative schools, the name of the founder of the Yoshioka Ryū was inherited by the successor when he assumed leadership of the school. Thus, several successive members of the Yoshioka family were known as "Yoshioka Kenpō." See: *Yoshioka Kenpō Naomoto.*

Yoshioka Kenpō Naokata 吉岡 憲法 直賢 [A.k.a. ***Matasaburō*** 又三郎]. The third headmaster of the Yoshioka Ryū. Naokata served the fifteenth Ashikaga *shōgun*, Yoshiaki.[14] The *Yoshioka-den*『吉岡傳』recounts that Naokata, at the request of the *shōgun*, engaged in a match with swordsman Shinmen Munisai, future father of Miyamoto Musashi. See: *Yoshioka Ryū.*

Yoshioka Kenpō Naomitsu 吉岡 憲法 直光. Second headmaster of the Yoshioka Ryū. Naomitsu was the younger brother of Yoshioka Naomoto. He served the thirteenth Ashikaga *shōgun*, Yoshiteru, who reigned from c.1546 to 1565. Ashikaga Yoshiteru was very interested in martial arts and hosted the best swordsmen of the day, including Tsukahara Bokuden, founder of Kashima Shintō Ryū; Kamiizumi Ise no Kami, founder of the Shinkage Ryū; and others. See: *Yoshioka Ryū.*

Yoshioka Kenpō Naomoto 吉岡 憲法 直元. A sixteenth-century swordsman who established

[13] According to Pranin (http://www.aikidojournal.com/encyclopedia? entryID=783), Yoshida began training in 1915.

[14] Ashikaga Yoshiaki 足利義昭 (1537–1597; r.1568 to 1573).

a school of combative arts known in later years as the Yoshioka Ryū. Naomoto developed a close relationship with the twelfth Ashikaga *shōgun* Yoshiharu,[15] and performed combative duties for the Ashikaga during the years 1532–1546. Yoshioka was succeeded by his son, Yoshioka Kenpō Naomitsu.

Yoshioka Ryū 吉岡流 [A.k.a. ***Kenpō Ryū*** 憲法流]. A system of swordsmanship founded by a sixteenth-century swordsman named Yoshioka Kenpō Naomoto. This school was generally thought to be a derivative of the Kyōhachi Ryū 京八流 (see Kiichi Hōgan Ryū 鬼一法眼流), which traced its origins to the Kyōto area. In fact, according to Watatani and Yamada (1978: 900), a third-generation successor of the Yoshioka Ryū named his branch tradition "Kiichi Ryū" 鬼一流, indicating a direct connection to the Kyōhachi Ryū founded by Kiichi Hōgan. However, various sources such as the eighteenth-century *Honchō bugei shōden* associate this tradition with the Shintō Ryū (神道流/新当流), a school which developed in eastern Japan.

Yoshioka Naomoto performed combative services for the twelfth Ashikaga *shōgun* Yoshiharu from 1532 to 1546; he is believed to have formed his school during that period. Naomoto's son Naomitsu (also known as Kenpō) also acted as a sword master for the Ashikaga. The leader of the system customarily took the name of "Kenpō."

Some sources, such as the *Yoshioka-den*, indicate that the third headmaster of the system, Yoshioka Naokata, fought several non-lethal duals with a young samurai named Shinmen Munisai (father of Miyamoto Musashi). This is unconfirmed, but years later, in 1604, Miyamoto Musashi sought out the Yoshioka family as a target in his quest to become a famous swordsman. The duels Musashi had with the Yoshioka family were disastrous, leaving all the family's best swordsmen either dead or maimed; their school of swordsmanship ceased to exist. The family continued, but not as warriors. They instead took up the textile industry and became master dyers.

Further reading in English:

- Tokitsu, 2004: 50–60.

Yoshioka Seijūrō 吉岡 清十郎 [A.k.a. ***Genzaemon*** 源左衛門; ***Naotsuna*** 直綱; ***Kenpō*** 憲法]: The eldest son of Yoshioka Naokata. Seijūrō succeeded his father as fourth head-

Yoshioka Ryū
吉岡流
(abbreviated lineage)

1 Yoshioka Kenpō Naomoto
吉岡 憲法 直元
Kenpō Ryū
憲法流

2. Yoshioka Kenpō Naomitsu
吉岡 憲法 直光

3. Yoshioka Kenpō Matasaburō Naokata
吉岡 憲法 又三郎 直賢
Kenpō Ryū
憲法流

Gion Fujitsugu
祇園 藤次
Kiichi Ryū
鬼一流

4. Yoshioka Genzaemon Naotsuna (Seijūrō) (Kenpō)
吉岡 源左衛門 直綱(清十郎)(憲法)
Yoshioka Ryū
吉岡流

Yoshioka Matashichirō
吉岡 又七郎
(c.1592–1604)

Yoshioka Mataichi Naoshige (Denshichirō)
吉岡 又市 直重(伝七郎)
Yoshioka Ryū
吉岡流

Yoshioka Seijirō Shigekata
吉岡 清次郎 重堅
Yoshioka Ryū
吉岡流

15 Ashikaga Yoshiharu 足利義晴 (1511–1550; r.1521 to 1546).

master of the Kenpō Ryū 憲法流, which, under his tenure, came to be called the Yoshioka Ryū 吉岡流. Seijūrō was known as one of the top swordsmen of his day. In addition to rigorous training in swordsmanship (*kenjutsu*), he also practiced a Tendai Buddhist meditational system known as *shikan*. However, Seijūrō was defeated and maimed in a duel with Miyamoto Musashi in 1604 in a field just outside of Kyōto. Because of his defeat, Seijūrō subsequently withdrew from the practice of swordsmanship and became a Buddhist priest.

Yoshitsune 義経. See: *Minamoto no Yoshitsune*.

Yoshitsune gunka 『義経軍歌』【義經軍歌】 [The Yoshitsune war song (poem)]. A text on military strategy produced by the Yoshitsune Ryū. This text has been published in Ishioka and Arima, 1967 (vol. 6): 129–144.

Yoshitsune monogatari 『義経物語』【義經物語】. One of several texts dealing with the important events in the life of Minamoto no Yoshitsune. Most of these texts are similar. See: *Gikeiki*. In addition, see other war tales: *Heiji monogatari*; *Heike monogatari*; *Hōgen monogatari*; *Shōmonki*; *Taiheiki*.

Further reading in English:

• McCullough (translation), 1966.

Yoshitsune Ryū 義経流【義經流】[Also read ***Gikei Ryū***]. A system of military strategy (*gumpō*). Its teachings are preserved in a transmission scroll (*densho*) called the *Yoshitsune gunka* 義経軍歌 (The Yoshitsune war song). See: *Yoshitsune gunka*.

Yoshizato Shintarō 吉里 真太郎. See: *Kūshin Ryū*.

yo-uchi 夜討. A night attack. This strategy was a favorite of many commanders, especially during the tenth through twelfth centuries. An enemy stronghold would be set afire in the night; those escaping the flames were easily targeted by archers.

yuba 弓場 [Also read ***yumiba***]. An archery range. Equivalent to *yaba*.

yūbu 勇武. Bravery, martial prowess.

yūdansha 有段者. A modern *budō* term referring to a practitioner who has achieved *dan* rank (black belt in most systems). Compare to *mudansha*.

yūga 優雅. CLASSICAL WARRIOR IDEAL—Elegance or refinement. *Yūga* was considered one of the essential characteristics of the classical warrior (*bushi*). See: *bushi no konjō*.

yugaeri 弓返り. KYŪDŌ—At the execution of *hanare,* the seventh of the formal stages of firing an arrow (*hassetsu*), the bow (*yumi*) will spin in the archer's left hand so that the bowstring touches the outside of the left arm. This is called *yugaeri*. Onuma (1993: 84) speculates that this affectation developed in ceremonial archery.

yugake 韘 [Var. 弓懸]. An archer's glove.

yugamae 弓構え. 1. KYŪJUTSU—A combative engagement posture for shooting the bow in *kyūjutsu*. 2. KYŪDŌ—The third of the eight formal stages (*hassetsu*) in firing an arrow in the modern martial way of archery (*kyūdō*). There are two types of *yugamae*: in one, called *shōmen no kamae*, the bow is held in front of the practitioner's body; in the second, *shamen no kamae*, the bow is held angled forward by the practitoner's left side. *Yugamae*, the process of readying the bow, is divided into three stages: *torikake* (fixing the glove and nocking the arrow); *tenouchi* (gripping the bow correctly); and *monomi* (viewing the target). See also: *hassetsu*.

yugei 靫負. 1. An ancient term meaning "quiver bearer." The *yugei* made up a guard unit for the Yamato leaders during the sixth century. According to Farris (1992: 27), they hailed from western Japan and were under the command of the Ōtomo family. 2. Military status. See also: *toneri*.

yūgen 幽玄. Lit. "mystery," "occult"; "mysterious skills"; also, subtle elegance. An aesthetic term indicating an aura of mysteriousness. In the classical martial systems (*koryū*), the term *yūgen* indicates an emphasis on cultivating intuition as both a result of training in prearranged combative forms (*kata*) and as a basis for action in combative situations. This emphasis was reinforced in the seventeenth century with the rise in Japan of a school of thought known as the *yomeigaku* 陽明学 (school of intuition).

Interestingly, this type of traditional education/training emphasis was rejected by such modern *budō* reformers as Kanō Jigorō, who founded Kōdōkan Jūdō based on Western pedagogical methods.

yugi 靫. An archer's quiver.

yugote 弓籠手. See: *yumigote*.

Yugyōji 遊行寺. A Pure Land Buddhist temple which was located in the area of Sōma in Shimōsa province (present-day Chiba and Ibaraki prefectures). According to tradition, it was in Yugyōji that the young Sōma Shirō Yoshitomo was hidden after the assassination of his father in 1357. At that time, the young boy was given the Buddhist name of Nen Ami Jion. Nen Ami later went on to found the Nen Ryū 念流 in 1368.

yūki 勇気【勇氣】. Courage, valor, nerve.

yumi 弓 [Usually read as ***kyū*** in compounds]. 1. A bow. 2. Japanese archery. The spiritual significance and combative effectiveness of the bow is not well understood by most modern practitioners of classical martial schools (*koryū*), much less by practitioners of modern martial spiritual/sport ways (*budō*) in Japan and abroad. As Irie (2005: 157) points out, although all weapons were viewed by the warrior as being imbued with spiritual power or significance (*kami*), the bow was most "empowered." Combatively, it was a superior weapon, and research has shown most battle casualties from the mid-fifteenth to mid-sixteenth centuries were due to the bow.[16] In a spiritual context, the bow is still used in a ritual fashion in traditional martial ceremonies for expelling demons. See: *meigen*.

yumiba 弓場 [Also read ***yuba***]. An archery range. Equivalent to *yaba*.

yumibukuro 弓袋. A bow bag; a cover for a bow.

yumigote 弓籠手 [Also read ***yugote***; var. ***igote*** 射籠手]. A pair of archer's gloves/sleeves.

yumigumi 弓組. A company of archers.

yumi mato 弓的. An archery target.

yumi no tsuru 弓の弦. A bowstring.

yumishi 弓師. A bow maker.

yumitori 弓取. 1. An archer; a famous archer. 2. An early term for a warrior. 3. Archery. 4. SUMŌ—The designated wrestler who performs the *yumitori shiki* ceremony at the end of each day of wrestling competition.

yumitori shiki 弓取り式. SUMŌ—A ritual in which an archer's bow is twirled in a prescribed manner at the end of each day of a wrestling tournament. The wrestler who twirls the bow is called the *yumitori*.

yumi-ya 弓矢. Bow and arrow. ¶ *Yumi-ya ni kakete chikau*, 弓矢にかけて誓う To make a pledge of honor on one's bow and arrow; to swear by one's weapons.

Yumi-ya Bugyō 弓矢奉行. A Tokugawa-period shogunal office which was responsible for the management of combative archery equipment. It was incorporated, along with several other similar agencies, into the Bugu Bugyō in 1863.

Yumi-ya Hachiman 弓矢八幡. An alternate name for Hachiman, the god of war.

yumi-ya no ie 弓矢の家. A house of the bow and arrow; a warrior house. This eleventh- and twelfth-century term is somewhat equivalent to *tsuwamono no ie* (warrior house) and *bubi no ie* (military house) in that it indicates a sense of elite status and duty.

yumi-ya no michi 弓矢の道. Archery; martial arts.

yumi-yari 弓槍. A spearhead which fits on the

[16] Irie (2005: 168, note 6), referring to research by Suzuki Masaya (2000), notes that "…in battles from the mid-fourteenth to the mid-fifteenth centuries, out of 554 examples, the percentage of casualties caused by arrows was 86%, sword cuts 8.3%, rocks 2.7%, spears and stab wounds 1.1%. From the mid-fifteenth to the mid-sixteenth centuries, 1461 examples are analyzed, with arrow wounds at 41.3%, guns 19.6%, spears and stab wounds 17.9%, rocks 10.3%, and 3% for swords."

end of a bow. See also: *hazuyari*.

Yumi-ya Santen 弓矢三天. Lit. the "Three Deities of the Bow and Arrow." A grouping of three Buddhist deities (*san ten* 三天) who protect warriors: Marishiten, Benzaiten, and Daikokuten.

Yumi-ya Yari Bugyō 弓矢槍奉行. A title created in 1637 for officials acting as chief master-at-arms dealing with bows, arrows and spears for the Tokugawa *shōgun*'s army. The office was folded into the Bugu Bugyō in 1863.

yumizuru 弓弦 [Also read ***yunzuru*** or ***kyūgen***]. A bowstring.

yunde 弓手. 1. The bow hand; an archer's hand. 2. The left hand.

yunzei 弓勢. 1. To be powerful with a bow and arrow. This type of accolade is used in the *Heike monogatari* to describe the "eastern" warriors (Bandō *musha*). Somewhat equivalent to *tsuyoyumi* (powerful with the bow). 2. The power of the bow. 3. The archer's strength.

yunzuru 弓弦 [Also read ***yūzuru***; ***yumizuru*** or ***kyūgen***]. A bowstring.

yūryoku 勇力. Courage, bravery.

yūshi 勇士. A brave warrior, a brave man.

yūshō 勇将【勇將】. A great general, a brave commander.

yūzuru 弓弦. See: *yunzuru*.

Z

zahō 座法【坐法】. Sitting posture; methods of sitting.

zai 1. 采 [Also read ***sai***] [abbreviation for ***saihai*** 采配]. A commander's staff or baton. See: *saihai; shikigu.*

zai 2. 在. The eighth seal/character of the nine mystic letters (*kuji*) of the Ritual Method of the Nine Seals (Kujihō).

zaichi ryōshu 在地領主. Lit. "lords who live on the land." This is a twelfth-century term for landed warriors meaning "country lord." These new landholders resided on their holdings, in contrast to the *zaikyō ryōshu*, who were absentee landlords living in the capital. Compare to *shieiden ryōshu.* See also: *kaihatsu ryōshu.*

Zaidanhōjin Aikikai & Aikidō 財団法人 合気会 & 合気道. Relatively late (c.1949) term used by Ueshiba Morihei for the grappling system he modified from Daitō Ryū *aikijūjutsu* into *aikidō*.

zaike 在家 <Ch. *zaijia* [abbreviation for ***zaike bosatsudō*** and ***zaike hōshi***]. BUDDHISM—A Buddhist lay priest.

zaike bosatsudō 在家菩薩道 <Ch. *zaijia pusa dao*. BUDDHISM—The path of the lay priest (*zaike hōshi*), often pursued by warriors at certain times in their lives. According to Ōtake (interviews, 1989), Iizasa Chōisai, the founder of Tenshinshō-den Katori Shintō Ryū 天真正伝香取神道流, followed the path of the Shingon *zaike bosatsudō*. Other warriors, such as Uesugi Kenshin and Takeda Shingen, also pursued this path. See also: *zaike hōshi.*

zaike hōshi 在家法師 [Normally read ***zaike hosshi*** in Buddhist texts and sources.] <Ch. *zaijia fashi*. BUDDHISM—Lit. "priests who live at home." A Buddhist lay priest. Someone who has taken several, but not all, of the Buddhist vows. A number of warriors took these vows but did not enter the official priesthood. This permitted them to add the term *nyūdō* 入道 (one who has entered the way) to their name. See also: *kaihatsu ryōshu; zaike; zaike bosatsudō.*

zaike hosshi 在家法師. See: *zaike hōshi.*

zaikyō ryōshu 在京領主. Lit. "lords who live in the capital." A twelfth-century term for absentee lords who resided in Heian (Kyōto). Compare to *zaichi ryōshu.*

zankanjō 斬奸状. A written statement of the reason for an assassination; an assassin's written vindication.

zanshin 残心【殘心】. 1. Combative awareness; a state of focused, extended vigilance before, during, and after execution of a technique or combative form (*kata*). 2. Physical and mental domination of an opponent. See also: *kiai* (2). 3. KYŪDŌ—The eighth of the eight formal stages (*hassetsu*) in firing an arrow in the modern martial way of archery (*kyūdō*). *Zanshin* is the process of maintaining awareness. In the *zanshin* stage the archer watches the arrow flying to the target and waits for the bow string to stop twanging. He then lowers the bow and brings his feet together in the same stance that he assumed in the first stage (*ashibumi*). See also: *hassetsu.*

Further reading in English:
• Hayes, 1994: 20–27.

ZANSHIN
Ōtake Risuke (R) and his training partner display unwavering *zanshin* during a demonstration at the Budōkan in Tōkyō in 1979
(*Kendō Nihon*, 4:1979, used with permission)

zanzai 斬罪. Decapitation; beheading; execution via a sword. This was the only one of the four prescribed forms of execution for Tokugawa-period commoners that continued into the Meiji era. The practice was stopped in 1881. See: *Yamada Asaemon; shikei.*

zappei 雑兵【雜兵】. See: *zōhyō.*

zappyō 雑兵【雜兵】. See: *zōhyō.*

zarei 座礼【坐禮】<Ch. *zuoli*. A respectful bow made from sitting (*seiza*) posture.

zasu 座主【坐主】. Title of the chief priest of the Tendai school of Buddhism.

zazen 座禅【坐禪】<Ch. *zuochan*. *Zen* meditation practiced in sitting postures, namely *seiza* or *renge*. See also: *zen (2); Zen Shū.*

zen 1. 前. Lit. "the front." a. SHINDŌ MUSŌ RYŪ—*Zen* (in contrast to *go*) designates the first of two combative scenarios (*kata*) when they have identical names; i.e., Ushirozue (*zen*) and Ushirozue (*go*). Contrast with *go* 後 which designates the second of two. 2. The ninth of the nine mystic letters (*kuji*) of the Ritual Method of the Nine Seals (Kujihō). As a talisman indicating the Kujihō, this character is sometimes found decorating armor, armor cases, and other accoutrements. See also: *ongyō-in*; *Kujihō.*

zen 2. 禅【禪】<Ch. *chan* <Ch. *channa* 禪那 <Skt. *dhyāna*. a. The act of meditation as practiced by the Zen school of Buddhism. This term is often found as a compound with other characters, as in *zazen* 座禅 (sitting meditation), or *gyōzen* 行禅 (moving meditation). b. The philosophy or worldview of the Zen school of Buddhism, as in the phrase *ken zen itchi* 剣禅一致: the practice of swordsmanship (*ken*) and the practice of *zen* are one and the same (*itchi*). See also: *Zen Shū.*

zen 3. 善. CLASSICAL WARRIOR IDEAL—*Zen*, connoting "moral good," was seen as one of the bases of classical warriorship. A moral person, or ethical warrior, was called a *zennin* 善人; a moral consciousness was *zenshin* 善心. ¶*zensen suru* 善戦する, to fight a moral battle; to carry out battle in an ethical fashion.

Zen'eibō Inshun 禅栄房 胤舜. See: *Hōzōin Inshun.*

Zen'etsu 前越. ASAYAMA ICHIDEN RYŪ—One of a number of classical prearranged quick-draw sword forms (*battō kata*) developed by the Asayama Ichiden Ryū. Zen'etsu was one of five classical *battō kata* adapted by the Japanese Police Commission of 1886 for their Keishichō Ryū 警視庁流 system.

zenji 禅師【禪師】<Ch. *chanshi*. A Zen master; a patriarch.

THE MONK ZENKITSU
(From the Jigen Ryū Archives of Tōgō Shigemasa)

Zenkichi 善吉. See: *Zenkitsu.*

Zenkitsu 善吉 [Var. ***Zenkichi***] (1567–1594). The Buddhist *dharma* name for the samurai Terasaka Yakurō Masatsune. Zenkitsu was chief priest of the Sōtō Zen temple called Tenneiji, located not far from Kuramadera in Kyōto; he was also the third-generation successor of a school of martial arts called Tenshinshō Jigen Ryū 天真正自顕流.

Tōgō Shigekata, a warrior from Satsuma domain in Kyūshū, began training diligently with Zenkichi and in less than a year had mastered Tenshinshō Jigen Ryū. Shigekata later founded the Jigen Ryū 示現流, which was a synthesis of Zenkitsu's Tenshinshō Jigen Ryū and the Taisha Ryū タイ捨流. See also: *sōhei*; *Tenshinshō-den Katori Shintō Ryū.*

Zen Nihon Karatedō Sōhombu Shūdōkan 全日本空手道連盟総本部修道館 (All-Japan Karatedo Federation, or AJKF). An umbrella *karate* organization founded by Tōyama Kanken in 1946. Tōyama established the organization in order to place the *karate* styles of Okinawa and Japan under one governing organization. The purpose of the AJKF was also to facilitate and provide a medium for the exchange of techniques and ideas.

zennin 善人. A moral person or a moral warrior. See: *zen (3)*.

Zen Nippon Iaidō Renmei 全日本居合道連盟 [Also read ***Zen Nihon Iaidō Renmei***]. The All-Japan Iaidō Federation, founded in 1948. This organization is responsible for setting national standards for *iaidō* technique.

Zen Nippon Jōdō Renmei 全日本杖道連盟 [Also read ***Zen Nihon Jōdō Renmei***]. The All-Japan Jōdō Federation, founded in 1955. This organization is responsible for setting national standards for *jōdō* technique.

Zen Nippon Kendō Renmei 全日本剣道連盟 [Also read: ***Zen Nihon Kendō Renmei***; abbreviated as Zen-ken-ren 全剣盟]. The All-Japan Kendō Federation, founded in 1928 (re-established in 1952). This organization is responsible for standardizing *kendō* on a national basis in Japan. The current organization also promotes and manages a quick-draw sword system (*iaidō*) and a medium-length staff system (*jōdō*).

Zen Nippon Kendō Renmei jōdō seiteigata 全日本剣道連盟杖道制定形 [Also read ***Zen Nihon Kendō Renmei jōdō seiteigata***]. The official *jōdō kata* of the All-Japan Kendō Federation. There are currently twelve kata in this set.

Further reading in English:

- Zen Nippon Kendō Renmei, 2006.

Zen Nippon Kyūdō Renmei 全日本弓道連盟 [Also read ***Zen Nihon Kyūdō Renmei***]. The All-Japan Kyūdō Federation, founded in 1949. This organization began publishing guidelines in 1953 detailing how archers from different schools (*ryū*) can shoot together in competition.

Zen Nippon Naginata Renmei 全日本なぎなた連盟 [Also read ***Zen Nihon Naginata Renmei***]. The All-Japan Naginatadō Federation, founded in 1953. This organization is responsible for setting national standards for *naginatadō* technique.

zenpō 1. 鋒. The vanguard. See: *senpō (1)*.

zenpō 2. 戦法【戰法】. Tactics. See: *senpō (2)*.

Zenryū Rempeiden 全流練兵伝【全流練兵傳】. Lit. "military drills transmitting all the martial schools." This was a term used for the collective combative arts taught by Chikamatsu Hikonoshin Shigenori in the early to mid-1700s. See: *Ichizen Ryū*.

zensen suru 善戦する【善戰する】. To fight well in battle; to put up a good fight. See: *zen (3)*.

zenshin 善心. A moral or ethical consciousness. See: *zen (3)*.

Zen Shū 禅宗 【禪宗】<Ch. Chan zong. The Zen school of Buddhism. The origins of this tradition may be traced to back to sixth-century China. There, according to legend, Bodhidharma, the twenty-eighth patriarch of Buddhism in India, brought Buddhism and its meditation practices (Ch. *channa* <Skt. *dhyāna*) to the Shaolin Temple in Honan province. After the fifth Chinese patriarch, Hongren 弘忍, the school split into five divisions with seven schools. Three of these were later transmitted to Japan: Rinzai by Eisai in 1191, Sōtō by Dōgen in 1227, and Ōbaku by Ingen in 1654.

In order to appeal to the needs of the warrior class (*bushi*) in Japan, Eisai promoted a blend of Rinzai Zen and tantric Buddhist esotericism. See also: *zen (2)*.

Further reading in English:

- Collcutt (1981).

Zōchōten 増長天 <Ch. Zengzhangtian <Skt. Virūḍhaka. One of the Shitennō (Four Deva Kings). Zōchōten guards the southern slope of Mount Sumeru (Jp. Shumi-sen). His name means "the *deva* of increasing growth," and his color is blue; his martial accoutrement is the spear.

zōhyō 雑兵 【雜兵】 [Also read ***zappei*** and

Z

zappyō]. An average soldier; a low-status soldier somewhat equivalent to an *ashigaru*.

zoku 賊. A rebel. Taira no Masakado, for example, was eventually considered a *zoku* due to his rebellion in the tenth century.

zokuhei 俗兵 [A.k.a. **zokuheishi**]. Lit. "secular warriors." This term is sometimes used to indicate the bulk of the armed forces mobilized by Buddhist temples during the *insei* age (1086–1156).[1] This period was also a time when the Japanese warrior class (*bushi*) was evolving into a powerful socio-political class in early medieval Japan. See: *sōhei.*

zokuheishi 俗兵士. See: *zokuhei.*

zōshikinin 雑職人. A Heian-period term for menial workers at Buddhist temples. This term was used in the ninth century to describe armed men from the temples of Tōdaiji and Kōfukuji in Nara. In a combative incident recorded in 850, the *zōshikinin* were accompanied by armed "strongmen" (*kyōrikisha*) from those temples. See: *sōhei.*

Zōshūkan 蔵脩館. Shindō Musō Ryū *dōjō* located on the precincts of the Toyosaka Inari Jinja 豊栄稲荷神社 in Shibuya ward, Tōkyō. It was constructed as a new *dōjō* for Shimizu Takaji in the mid-1970s, and passed into the hands of Kaminoda Tsunemore and the Nihon Jōdō Kai upon Shimizu's death in 1978.

zuboshi 図星【圖星】. A bull's-eye in a target. The *zuboshi* normally appears as a black dot. See also: *kurobushi; mato.*

zudate 頭立. Ornaments located on the sides of a helmet. See: *tatemono.*

zuichō 瑞鳥. See: *hōō.*

Zuihen Ryū 1. 随変流【隨變流】. A branch tradition of the Kankyoku Ryū 鑑極流 that was founded by a samurai named Wakisaka Genzaemon. The Zuihen Ryū concentrated on swordsmanship (*kenjutsu*), quick-draw sword arts (*iaijutsu*), long hardwood staff arts (*bōjutsu*), warrior sickle (*kama*), and combative grappling (*jūjutsu*). Prior to forming his own school, Wakisaka trained in a variety of systems. However, he was most heavily influenced by Wada Jūrōzaemon, founder of the Kankyoku Ryū. Wakisaka's Zuihen Ryū was passed down for a number of generations and spawned several branch traditions. The most prominent of those was the Zuihen Tō Ryū 随変当流 founded by Fuji Zuio Kiyonobu. For lineage, see: *Zuishin Ryū.*

Zuihen Ryū 2. 随変流【隨變流】. A branch tradition of the Zuihen Ryū (1). This line was evidently only taught at the Jishūkan 時習館 training hall (*dōjō*) in Kasama domain (present-day Ibaraki prefecture). Interestingly, the system included long-hafted glaive arts (*naginatajutsu*) in addition to the typical Seigō Ryū 制剛流–lineage weapons systems: long hardwood staff arts (*bōjutsu*), arresting arts (*torite*), and police tying-cord arts (*hojōjutsu*). For lineage, see: *Zuishin Ryū.*

Zuihen Tō Ryū 随変当流【隨變當流】. A branch tradition of Seigō Ryū 制剛流 via the Zuihen Ryū line. This system concentrated on combative swordsmanship (*kenjutsu*) and grappling (*jūjutsu*). It was founded by a samurai named Fuji Zuio Kiyonobu, a shogunal retainer who trained in the Zuihen Ryū under Yokochi Nuidonosuke. For lineage, see: *Zuishin Ryū.*

zuihyō 随兵【隨兵】. A "warrior follower." This tenth- and eleventh-century term is found in the *Konjaku monogatari*.

Zuishin 随身【隨身】. 1. SHINTŌ—Two Shintō *kami* who guard the main entrances to Shintō shrines. The Zuishin are often represented by two statues, one on each side of the entrance. These two shrine guardians are also referred to as the Ya Daijin: Toyo Iwamado no Mikoto and Kushi Iwamado no Mikoto. See: *Ya Daijin.* 2. **zuishin** 随身【隨身】. A term used from the Heian through Muromachi periods indicating palace bodyguards or warrior attendants who accompanied people of high rank when they traveled about. There were two types of *zuishin*: the *hompu no zuishin*, who guarded

1 The *insei* 院政 age (1086–1156) was a period in which the power of the noble Fujiwara family waned as the political influence of a succession of retired emperors (*in* 院) increased. This age ended in 1156, with the rise of the warrior class in a short war known as the Hōgen no Ran.

the emperor; and the *shōzuishin*, who attended the higher officers of the imperial guard. Both types carried a bow (*yumi*), arrows (*ya*), and a sword (*tachi*).

Zuishin Ryū 随心流【隨心流】. A major branch tradition of the Seigō Ryū 制剛流 founded by Satomura Zuishinsai Masauji. Satomura's line, which concentrated on combative swordsmanship (*kenjutsu*) and grappling arts, (*jūjutsu*), spawned a number of branch lines.

Zuishin Ryū
随心流
(abbreviated lineage and derivatives)

Seigō Sō
制剛僧

1. Mizuhaya Chōzaemon Nobumasa
初代　水早 長左衛門 信正
Seigō Ryū·Namban Ippin Ryū
制剛流·南蛮一品流

2. Kashihara Genzaemon Naokage
二代　梶原 源左衛門 直景
Seigō Yawara Kumiuchi Kotsukudaki
制剛ヤワラ組打骨砕き

Satomura Zuishinsai Masauji
里村 随心斎 正氏
Zuishin Ryū
随心流

Takahashi Zuietsu Shoshi
高橋 随悦 諸氏
Takahashi Ryū
高橋流

Nakaegawa Kiyōemonsuke
中江川 清右衛門亮
Zuishin Ryū
随心流

Wada Jūrōzaemon Masashige Zuishin Zuika
和田 十郎左衛門 正重 随心 隋加
Kankyoku Ryū
鑑極流

Morikawa Buhei Takamasa
森川 武兵衛 高政
Kashin Ryū
霞新流

Wakasaka Genzaemon
脇坂 源左衛門
Zuihen Ryū
随変流

Wakasaka Genzō
脇坂 源蔵

Yokochi Nuidonosuke
横地 縫殿助

Fuji Zuio Kiyonobu
富士 隋翁 清信
Zuihen Tō Ryū
随変当流

zuryō 受領. Provincial government officials drawn from courtiers and imperial family members. The *zuryō* often maintained a provincial home as well as a separate residence in Kyōto, even after leaving office. In this way they were able to both exploit their formal, official land incomes and maintain their political influence in the capital.

Z

APPENDICES

APPENDIX 1: TRADITIONAL EAST ASIAN NUMBERING SYSTEMS

***Jūnishi* 十二支 (The Twelve Branches)/*Chishi* 地支 (The Earthly Branches)**

	Branch	Japanese* *on/kun*	Chinese	Animal	Direction	Season	Month (lunar)	Duodenary hour
1	子	*shi/ne*	*zi*	Rat	north	winter	11	11 p.m.–1 a.m.
2	丑	*chu/ushi*	*chou*	Ox	north-northeast		12	1 a.m.–3 a.m.
3	寅	*in/tora*	*yin*	Tiger	east-northeast	spring	1	3 a.m.–5 a.m.
4	卯	*bō/u*	*mao*	Hare	east		2	5 a.m.–7 a.m.
5	辰	*shin/tatsu*	*chen*	Dragon	east-southeast		3	7 a.m.–9 a.m.
6	巳	*mi*	*si*	Serpent	south-southeast	summer	4	9 a.m.–11 a.m.
7	午	*uma*	*wu*	Horse	south		5	11 a.m.–1 p.m.
8	未	*mi/hitsuji*	*wei*	Ram	south-southwest		6	1 p.m.–3 p.m.
9	申	*saru*	*shen*	Monkey	west-southwest	autumn	7	3 p.m.–5 p.m.
10	酉	*tori*	*you*	Cock	west		8	5 p.m.–7 p.m.
11	戌	*jutsu/inu*	*xu*	Dog	west-northwest		9	7 p.m.–9 p.m.
12	亥	*gai/i*	*hai*	Boar	north-northwest	winter	10	9 p.m.–11 p.m.

*Japanese often uses two pronunciations for each character, a "Chinese" reading (*on*) and a "Japanese" reading (*kun*).

***Jikkan* 十干 (The Ten Stems)/*Tenkan* 天干 (Heavenly Stems)**

	Stem	Japanese	Chinese	Yin / Yang	Element
1	甲	*kinoe*	*jia*	yang	wood
2	乙	*kinoto*	*yi*	yin	
3	丙	*hinoe*	*bing*	yang	fire
4	丁	*hinoto*	*ding*	yin	
5	戊	*tsuchinoe*	*wu*	yang	earth
6	己	*tsuchinoto*	*ji*	yin	
7	庚	*kanoe*	*geng*	yang	metal
8	辛	*kanoto*	*xin*	yin	
9	壬	*mizunoe*	*ren*	yang	water
10	癸	*mizunoto*	*gui*	yin	

The Stems and Branches (天干地支) can also be combined in sequence to designate years in a sixty-year cycle. For example:

甲子 = 1924—1984—2044	甲戌 = 1934—1994—2054
乙丑 = 1925—1985—2045	乙亥 = 1935—1995—2055
丙寅 = 1926—1986—2046	丙子 = 1936—1996—2056
- -	- -
癸酉 = 1933—1993—2053	癸未 = 1943—2003—2063

Appendix 2: Ancient Period Military Organization

Ritsuryō Provincial Regiment (Gundan 軍団)			
Military rank	**Unit of command**	**Number of troops**	**Approx. Western military equivalent**
Gunki (Ki) 軍毅 (毅)	***Gundan*** **軍団** (provincial regiment)		General
Daiki 大毅	Commander of a large regiment	Units of 600 men or more	Colonel
Shōki 小毅	Executive officer of a large regiment or commander of a small regiment	Units of 600 men or more, assisting a *daiki*	Lieutenant colonel
Kyōi 校尉	**Two *ryo* 旅** (Two companies)	200 men	Major
Rosochi 旅帥	***Ryo*** **旅** (company)	100 men	Captain
Taisei 隊正	***Tai*** **隊** (platoon)	50 men A fundamental tactical unit of the *gundan*, the *tai* were of two types: infantry (*hōtai*) or cavalry (*kitai*)	Lieutenant
Shuchō 主帳	-NA-	None. Worked directly under a *daiki* or *shōki*.	Master sergeant; master-at-arms (clerk)
Kachō 火長	***Ka*** **火** (combat squad)	10-man squad	Sergeant
Gochō 伍長	***Go*** **伍** (combat team)	5-man team	Corporal
Heishi 兵士	-NA- (conscript soldier)	-NA-	Private (conscript soldier)

Selected Bibliography

Selected Bibliography (Western Sources)

Acopian, Jeff, Hall, David A. and Meik Skoss. (1982). *The Martial Arts and Ways of Japan.* Video, privately published.

Adams, Andy. (1970). *Ninja: The Invisible Assassins*. Los Angeles: Ohara Publications.

Adams, Andy and Ryo Hatano (1979). *Sumo History and Yokozuna Profiles.* Vol. 1 of *The Wonderful World of Sumō*. Tokyo: Bat Publications.

Adolphson, Mikael S. (2007). *The Teeth and Claws of the Buddha: Monastic Warriors and Sohei in Japanese History.* Honolulu: University of Hawaii Press.

All-Japan Kendo Federation. (2006). *JODO: Zen Nihon Kendo Renmei Jodo—English Version Manual*. Tokyo: Satou-Inshokan Inc.

Alphen, J. van. (1999). *Enku, 1632–1695: Timeless images from 17th century Japan: Etnografisch Museum Antwerpen, 5 May–29 August 1999*. Antwerpen: Etnografisch Museum.

Amdur, Ellis. (2002a). *Old School: Essays on Japanese Martial Traditions.* Seattle: Edgework.

______. (2002b). "Renovation and Innovation in Tradition." In *Keiko Shokon: Classical Warrior Traditions of Japan, Vol. 3*, edited by Diane Skoss. Berkeley Heights: Koryu Books.

Armstrong, Hunter. (1992). "The Two Faces of Combatives (Part I of II)." *Hoplos: The Journal of the International Hoplology Society* 7, no. 2 (Winter 1992).

______. (1994). "The Two Faces of Combatives (Part II of II)." *Hoplos: The Journal of the International Hoplology Society* 7, no. 3 (Winter 1994).

______. (1997). "The Koryū Bujutsu Experience." In *Koryu Bujutsu: Classical Warrior Traditions of Japan*, edited by Diane Skoss. Berkeley Heights: Koryu Books.

Anderson, Jennifer L. (1991). *An Introduction to the Japanese Tea Ritual*. Albany: State University of New York.

Aston, W. G ., trans. (1896). *Nihongi: Chronicles of Japan from the Earliest Times to A.D. 697*. 2 vols. The Transactions and Proceedings of the Japan Society, London, Supplement I. London: Kegan Paul, Trench and Trübner.

Ball, Katherine M. (1927). *Animal Motifs in Asian Art: An Illustrated Guide to Their Meanings and Aesthetics.* Reprinted by Dover Publications, 2004.

Bays, Jan Chozen. (2003). *Jizo Bodhisattva: Guardian of Children, Travelers, and Other Voyagers*. Boston: Shambhala.

Bennett, Alexander C. (1999). "Neglected Treasure: The Koyo Gunkan." In *Sword & Spirit: Classical Warrior Traditions of Japan, Vol. 2*, edited by Diane Skoss. Berkeley Heights: Koryu Books.

______, ed. (2005). *Budō Perspectives*. Auckland: Kendō World Publications Ltd.

Bergamini, David. (1971). *Japan's Imperial Conspiracy.* 2 vols. New York: William Morrow and Company, Inc.

Berry, Mary Elizabeth. (1982). *Hideyoshi*. Harvard East Asian Series 97. Cambridge: Harvard University Press.

______. (1983). "Restoring the Past: The Documents of Hideyoshi's Magistrate in Kyoto." *Harvard Journal of Asiatic Studies* 43, no. 1 (June 1983).

______. (1994). *The Culture of Civil War in Kyōto*. Berkeley: University of California Press.

Bharati, Agehananda. (1965). *The Tantric Tradition*. London: Rider and Company.

Bieri, Larry E. (1984b). "*Naginata*: The Japanese Halberd (Part II)." *Hoplos* 4, no. 3 (December 1984).

Bishop, Mark. (1996). *Zen Kobudo* 禅古武道: *Mysteries of Okinawan Weaponry and Te*. Tokyo: Charles E. Tuttle.

______. (1999). *Okinawan Karate: Teachers, Styles and Secret Techniques*. 2nd ed. Tokyo: Charles E. Tuttle.

Bodiford, William M. (2002). "Soke: Historical Incarnations of a Title and Its Entitlements." In *Keiko Shokon: Classical Warrior Traditions of Japan, Vol. 3*, edited by Diane Skoss, 129–143. Berkeley Heights: Koryu Books.

Bouchy, Anne-Marie. (1987). "The Cult of Mount Atago and the Atago Confraternities." *Journal of Asian Studies* 46, no. 2 (May 1987).

Brousse, Michel and David Matsumoto. (2005). *Judo in the U.S.: A Century of Dedication*. Berkeley: North Atlantic Books.

Brinkley, Capt. Frank and Baron Dairoku Kikuchi. (1915). *History of the Japanese People: From the Earliest Times to the End of the Meiji Era*. New York: Encyclopedia Britannica Company.

Buck, J. H. (1973). "The Satsuma Rebellion of 1877." *Monumenta Nipponica,* 28, no. 4.

Chappelear, Kei Kaneda. (1987). *Japanese Armor Makers for the Samurai*. Tokyo: Miyoshi Printing Co., Ltd.

Chen, Jim, M.D. and Theodore Chen. (2004). "Judo Greats: Past and Present." JudoInfo OnLine Dojo. http://www.judoinfo.com/greats.htm (accessed 10 November 2009).

Chesneaux, Jean. (1971). *Secret Societies in China in the Nineteenth and Twentieth Centuries*. Ann Arbor: University of Michigan Press.

______. (1973). *Peasant Revolts in China: 1840–1949*. London: Thames and Hudson Ltd.

Chito-Ryu Karate (Sohonbu Office), http://www.chitoryu.co.jp/en/what01.html (accessed 5 February 2012).

Chou Yi-liang. (1945). "Tantrism in China." *Harvard Journal of Asiatic Studies* 8, nos. 3–4 (March).

Clayton, Bruce D. (2004). *Shotokan's Secret: The Hidden Truth Behind Karate's Fighting Origins*. Black Belt Books. Los Angeles: Ohara Publications, Inc.

Clery, Thomas, trans. (2002). *Secrets of the Blue Cliff Record: Zen Comments by Hakuin and Tenkei*. Boston: Shambhala.

Clery, Thomas and J. C. Clery, trans. (1977). *The Blue Cliff Record*. [Trans. of the *Biyan Lu* (*Hekiganroku*) 『碧巌録』] Boston: Shambhala.

Collcutt, Martin. (1981). *Five Mountains: The Rinzai Zen Monastic Institution in Medieval Japan*. Cambridge: Harvard University Press.

Conlan, Thomas Donald. (2001). *In Little Need of Divine Intervention: Takezaki Suenaga's Scrolls of the Mongol Invasions of Japan.* Cornell East Asia, No. 113. Ithaca: Cornell East Asia Series.

Conroy, Tom. (1980). "Preliminary Case Study: The Military Sabre." *Hoplos* 2, no. 1 (February).

______. (1981). "Chop, Slice, and Slanted Chop." *Hoplos* 3, no. 5 (October).

Conze, Edward. (1951). *Buddhism: Its Essence and Development*. New York: Philosophical Library.

______. (1975). *The Large Sutra on Perfect Wisdom with the Divisions of the Abhisamayalankara*. Berkeley: University of California Press.

______. (2001). *Buddhist Wisdom: The Diamond Sutra and the Heart Sutra.* New York: Vintage.

Craig, Teruko, trans. (1988). *Musui's Story: The Autobiography of a Tokugawa Samurai.* [Translation of Katsu Kokichi's *Musui dokugen*『夢酔独言』(A Monologue by Musui).] Tucson: University of Arizona Press.

Csikszentmihalyi, Mihaly. (2008). *Flow: The Psychology of Optimal Experience.* New York: Harper Perennial Modern Classics.

Cumins, Antony and Yoshie Minami, trans. (2011). *True Path of the Ninja: The Definitive Translation of the* Shoninki. [Translation of Natori Masatake's *Shōninki*『正忍記』]. Rutland: Tuttle Publishing.

Cundy, Antony. (1999). "The Go no Kata: An Introduction to the Forgotten Form of Kodokan Judo." *Hoplite*. International Hoplology Society. (Fall 1999).

______. (2002). Photos by Ron Beaubien. "Tradition & Transmission: Kashima Shinden Jikishinkage-ryu." *Kendo World: Crossing Swords & Borders* 1, no. 4.

Cuyler, Patricia Lee. (1979). *Sumo: From Rite to Sport.* Tokyo: Charles E. Tuttle.

Dann, Jeffrey Lewis. (1978). "'Kendō' in Japanese Martial Culture: Swordsmanship as Self-Cultivation." Ph.D. diss., University of Washington.

Davis, David L. (1974). "*Ikki* in Late Medieval Japan." In *Medieval Japan: Essays in Institutional History*, edited by John W. Hall and Jeffrey P. Mass. New Haven: Yale University Press.

Davis, Fei-Ling. (1971). *Primitive Revolutionaries of China: A study of secret societies in the late ninteenth century*. Honolulu: University of Hawaii Press.

Demiéville, Paul. (1957). "Le Bouddhisme et la guerre." *Melanges publies par l'instituit des hautes études Chinoises* 1.

Doi, Takeo, M.D. (1985). *The Anatomy of Self: The Individual Versus Society*. Translated by Mark A. Harbison. Tokyo: Kodansha International.

Draeger, Donn F. (1960a). "Weight Training for Jūdō." *Strength and Health*, April 1960.

______. (1960b). "Weight Training for Jūdō: Exercise Principles." *Strength and Health*, May 1960.

______. (1960c). "Weight Training for Jūdō." *Strength and Health*, June 1960.

______. (1960d). "Abbreviated Weight Training." *Strength and Health*, September 1960.

______. (1960e). "Weight Training for Jūdō: Power Training." *Strength and Health*, October 1960.

______. (1961). "Weight Training at Kodokan." *Strength and Health*, August 1961.

______. (1971). *Ninjutsu: The Art of Invisibility—Japan's Feudal-Age Espionage Methods*. Tokyo: Simpson-Doyle and Company.

______. (1973a). *Classical Bujutsu*. Vol. 1 of *The Martial Arts and Ways of Japan*. Tokyo: Weatherhill.

______. (1973b). *Classical Budo*. Vol. 2 of *The Martial Arts and Ways of Japan*. Tokyo: Weatherhill.

______. (1974a). *Modern Bujutsu and Budo*. Vol. 3 of *The Martial Arts and Ways of Japan*. Tokyo: Weatherhill.

______. (1974b). "The Japanese Martial Arts are Different from the Japanese Martial Ways." *Martial Arts International* 1, no. 1 (January).

______. (1974c). "The Japanese Martial Arts and Ways are Composed of Classical and Modern-Cognate Disciplines." *Martial Arts International* 1, no. 2 (March).

______. (1974d). "The Classical Japanese Martial Arts are Not Sports." *Martial Arts International* 1, no. 3 (May/June).

______. (1978). "Brigand or Patriot? Kusunoki Masashige." In *Great Historical Figures of Japan*, edited by Murakami Hyoe and Thomas J. Harper. Japan Culture Institute. Tokyo: Japan Publications Trading Company.

______. (1981). "Miyamoto Musashi." Reprint, *Journal of Asian Martial Arts* 8, no. 3 (1999). Reprint, *Journal of Combative Sports*. Electronic Journals of Martial Arts and Sciences. (10 Nov. 2009). http://ejmas.com/jcs/jcsdraeger_musashi.htm

______. (1995). "Belief Systems in Japanese Martial Culture." Lecture series, University of Hawaii, Honolulu, HI, 1981. Transcribed by Patrick H. Lineberger, edited by Hunter B. Armstrong. Sedona, AZ: International Hoplology Society.

Draeger, Donn F. and Robert W. Smith. (1969). *Asian Fighting Arts*. Tokyo: Kodansha International.

Drossoulakis, Spiros G., (2003). "'Osu!' Its meaning and use." Newsletter, Kase Ha Shōtōkan Ryu Karate-dō, March 2003. http://www.shotokanryukaseha.com/other_languages/budo_themes/themes_2003/3_osu.htm (accessed 22 Sept. 2009).

Dunn, Charles J. (1972). *Everyday Life in Traditional Japan (1600–1850)*. Tokyo: Charles E. Tuttle.

Dürckheim, Karlfried. (1962). *Hara: The Vital Centre of Man*. Translated by Sylvia-Monica von Kospoth in collaboration with Estelle R. Healey. London: George Allen & Unwin Ltd.

Earhart, H. Byron. (1970). *A Religious Study of the Mount Haguro Sect of Shugendō*. Tokyo: Sophia University Press.

Ernst, Earle. (1974). *The Kabuki Theater*. Honolulu: University of Hawaii Press.

Esherick, Joseph W. (1987). *The Origins of the Boxer Uprising*. Berkeley: University of California Press.

Farris, William Wayne. (1992). *Heavenly Warriors: The Evolution of Japan's Military, 500–1300*. Cambridge: Harvard University Press.

Fisher, Aaron. (2010). *The Way of Tea: Reflections on a Life with Tea*. North Clarendon, VT: Tuttle Publishing.

Friday, Karl F. (1988). "Teeth and Claws: Provincial Warriors and the Heian Court." *Monumenta Nipponica* 43, no. 2 (Summer 1988).

______. (1992). *Hired Swords: The Rise of Private Warrior Power in Early Japan*. Stanford: Stanford University Press.

______. (2002). "The Cat's Eerie Skill: A Translation of Issai Chozan's 'Neko no Myojutsu.'" In *Keiko Shokon: Classical Warrior Traditions of Japan, Vol. 3*, edited by Diane Skoss. Berkeley Heights: Koryu Books.

______. (2007). *The First Samurai: The Life and Legend of the Warrior Rebel, Taira Masakado*. Hoboken, NJ: Wiley.

Friday, Karl, and Seki Humitake. (1997). *Legacies of the Sword: The Kashima-Shinryu and Samurai Martial Culture*. Honolulu: University of Hawaii Press.

Fukuda, Keiko. (2004). *Ju No Kata: A Kodokan Judo Textbook*. Berkeley: North Atlantic Books.

Funakoshi, Gichin. (1973). *Karate-dō Kyōhan: The Master Text*. Translated by Tsutomu Ohshima. Tokyo: Kodansha International.

______. (1975). *Karate-dō: My Way of Life*. Translator unknown. Tokyo: Kodansha International.

______. (2001). *Karate Jutsu: The Original Teachings of Master Funakoshi*. Translated by John Teramoto.『錬膽護身「唐手術」』 Tokyo: Kodansha International.

Fung Yu-lan. (1953). *A History of Chinese Philosophy, Volume II: The Period of Classical Learning*. Translated by Derk Bodde. Princeton: Princeton University Press.

Getty, Alice. (1914). *The Gods of Northern Buddhism*. Oxford: Oxford University Press. Reprint, Charles E. Tuttle, 1962

Goodman, Grant K. (2000). *Japan and the Dutch: 1600–1853*. Richmond, VA: Curzon Press.

Goodrich, Luther Carrington. (1976). *Dictionary of Ming Biography, 1368–1644*. New York: Columbia University Press.

Graham, Jon E., trans. (2009). *Shōninki: The Secret Teachings of the Ninja; The 17th-Century Manual on the Art of Concealment*. [Translation of Natori Masazumi's *Shōninki*『正忍記』]. With commentaries by Axel Mazuer. Rochester: Destiny Books.

Grapard, Allan G. (1995). "Flying Mountains & Walkers of Emptiness: Sacred Space in Japanese Religion." In *The Sacred Mountains of Asia*, edited by John Einarsen. Boston: Shambhala. (Reprint from *Seminar on Time and Space in Japanese Culture* in Maui, Hawaii, January 1977, sponsored by the Social Science Research Council and the American Council of Learned Societies.)

Griffith, Samuel B., trans. (1963). *Sun Tzu: The Art of War*. Oxford: Oxford University Press.

Groner, Paul. (2000). *Saicho: The Establishment of the Japanese Tendai School*. Honolulu: University of Hawaii Press.

Grossberg, Kenneth Alan. (1981). *Japan's Renaissance: The Politics of the Muromachi Bakufu*. Council on East Asian Studies. Cambridge: Harvard University Press.

Growald, Eileen Rockefeller and Allan Luks. (1988). "Beyond Self: The Immunity of Samaritans." *American Health*. (March 1988).

Gruzanski, Charles V. (1968). *Spike and Chain: Japanese Fighting Arts*. Tokyo: Charles E. Tuttle.

van Gulik, R. H. (1935). *Hayagrīva: The Mantrayanic Aspect of Horse Cult in China and Japan*. Leiden: International Archiv fur Ethnographie. Reprinted as *Hayagrīva: Horse Cult in Asia*. Bangkok: Orchid Press, 2005.

______. (1956). *Siddham: An Essay on the History of Sanskrit Studies in China and Japan*. Vol. 36 of the Sarasvati-Vihara Series. New Delhi: International Academy of Indian Culture. Reprint, 2001.

______. (1961). "Appendix 1: Indian and Chinese Sexual Mysticism." In *Sexual Life in Ancient China*, 339–359. Leiden: E. J. Brill. Reprint, 1974.

Hackin, J., Clément Huart, Raymonde Linossier, H. de Wilman-Grabowska, Charles-Henri Marchal, Henri Maspero, and Serge Eliseev. (1932). *Asiatic Mythology: A Detailed Description and Explanation of the Mythologies of All the Great Nations of Asia*. Reprint, New York: Crescent Books, 1963.

Haines, Bruce A. (1962). "Karate and Its Development in Hawaii to 1959." Master's thesis, University of Hawaii.

______. (1968). *Karate's History and Traditions*. Tokyo: Charles E. Tuttle.

______. (1995). *Karate's History and Traditions*. Revised edition. Tokyo: Charles E. Tuttle.

Hakeda, Yoshito S. (1972). *Kūkai: Major Works—Translated, with an Account of His Life and a Study of His Thought*. New York: Columbia University Press.

Hakko Ryu Jujutsu. (2006). http://www.hakkoryu.com/ (accessed 10 November 2009).

Hall, David A. (1977). "A Study of the Development of Esoteric Buddhism." Master's thesis, University of Hawaii, Honolulu.

______. (1978). "The Question of the 'Left Hand' Path in China and Japan." *Young East—New Series: A Quarterly on Buddhism and Japanese Culture* 4, no. 1. (Winter 1978).

______. (1979a). "Bujutsu and the Esoteric Tradition (Part I of II)." *Hoplos* 1, no. 5 (November 1979).

______. (1979b). "Bujutsu and the Esoteric Tradition (Part II of II)." *Hoplos* 1, no. 6. (December 1979).

______. (1982). "The Apocryphal Texts of the Tachikawa-ryū." Paper presented for publication in a special graduate seminar on Buddhist Apocryphal Texts, Buddhist Studies Program, University of California, Berkeley, CA.

______. (1983). "Martial Scrolls of the Jiki Shinkage Ryū—With special reference to religious symbolism." Paper presented to a special graduate seminar on premodern warfare, History Department, University of California, Berkeley, CA, May. Rev. ed. privately published, 2005.

______. (1987). "Neglecting the Hoplological Data: A Review Article on *Lives of Master Swordsmen* by Makoto Sugawara. *Hoplos: Journal of the International Hoplology Society* 5, nos. 3 & 4. (Spring 1987).

______. (1988). "The Yagyū Shinkage Ryū (Part 1)." *Hoplos: Journal of the International Hoplology Society* 6, no. 3. (Fall 1988).

______. (1989). "The Yagyū Shinkage Ryū (Part 2)." *Hoplos: Journal of the International Hoplology Society* 6, no. 4. (Winter 1989).

______. (1990). "Marishiten: Buddhism and the Warrior Goddess." Ph.D. dissertation, University of California.

______. (1991a). "Martial Aspects of the Buddhist Mārīcī in Sixth-century China." *Annual of the Institute for Comprehensive Studies of Buddhism—Taisho University* 13 (March 1991).

______. (1991b). "The Rise of the *Bushi* (Japanese Warrior)." Paper prepared for the Santa Clara County Office of Education, Central Office, San Jose, CA.

______. (1992). "*Sen* and *Hyōshi*: Initiative and Rhythm in Shindō Musō Ryū (Part 1)." *IJF Newsletter*. (Fall).

______. (1993). "Beat and Rhythm (*Hyōshi*): Second part of David A. Hall's article." *IJF Newsletter*. (Spring).

______. (1997). "Marishiten: Buddhist Influences on Combative Behavior." In *Koryu Bujutsu: Classical Warrior Traditions of Japan,* edited by Diane Skoss. Berkeley Heights: Koryu Books.

Hall, Edward T. (1973). *The Silent Language*. New York: Anchor Press/Doubleday & Company, Inc.

______. (1976). *Beyond Culture*. New York: Anchor Press/Doubleday & Company, Inc.

______. (1983). *The Dance of Life: The Other Dimension of Time*. New York: Anchor Press/Doubleday & Company, Inc.

Hall, John W. and Jeffrey P. Mass, eds. (1974). *Medieval Japan: Essays in Institutional History*. New Haven: Yale University Press.

Hall, John W. and Takeshi Toyoda, eds. (1977). *Japan in the Muromachi Age*. Berkeley: University of California Press.

Hardacre, Helen and Adam Kern, eds. (1997). *New Directions in the Study of Meiji Japan*. Brill's Japanese Studies Library. Conference on Meiji Studies, Harvard University, 1994. Leiden: Brill Academic Publishers.

Harrelson, Walter. (1993). "T'ien-t'ai." In *Encyclopedia of Religion,* vol.14, edited by Mircea Eliade. New York: Macmillan Publishing Company.

Harrington, Lorraine F. (1982). "Social Control and the Significance of *Akutō*." In *Court and Bakufu in Japan*, edited by Jeffrey P. Mass, 221–250. New Haven: Yale University Press.

Harrison, E. J. (1912). *The Fighting Spirit of Japan: A Study of the Esoteric Basis of Judo and Martial Arts in Relation to Japanese Culture and Way of Life.* Revised edtion, London: W. Foulsham & Co. Ltd., 1956.

Hatsumi, Masaaki. (2008). *Unarmed Fighting Techniques of the Samurai*. Tokyo: Kodansha International.

Hatsumi, Masaaki and Quintin Chambers. (1971). *Stick Fighting; Techniques of Self-Defense*. Kodansha International.

Hayes, Richard. (1984a). "Paleolithic Adaptive Traits and the Fighting Man." *Hoplos* 4, no. 2 (June 1984).

______. (1984b). "Conceptual Tools for the Hoplologist: The IAT/MAT Continued." *Hoplos* 4, no. 3 (December 1984).

______. (1985). "Conceptual Tools for the Hoplologist: The IAT/MAT Continued." *Hoplos* 4, no. 4 (August 1985).

______.(1986). "Conceptual Tools for the Hoplologist: The IAT/MAT Continued." *Hoplos* 5, nos. 1 & 2. (Spring 1986).

______. (1987a): "Hoplology Theoretics, an Overview: Part 1–The IAT/MAT." *Hoplos: The Journal of the International Hoplology Society* 5, nos. 3 & 4 (Spring 1987).

______. (1987b): "Hoplology Theoretics, an Overview: Part 2–The Innate/Manifest Volitional Trait." *IHS Newsletter* (December 1987).

______. (1988a): "Hoplology Theoretics, an Overview: Part 3–The Innate/Manifest Cognitive/Intuitive Trait." *Hoplos: The Journal of the International Hoplology Society* 6, nos. 1 & 2 (Winter 1988).

______. (1988b): "Hoplology Theoretics, an Overview: Part 4–The Innate/Manifest Imperturbable-mind/Steadfast-mind Trait." *Hoplos: The Journal of the International Hoplology Society* 6, no. 3 (Fall 1988).

______. (1989): "Hoplology Theoretics, an Overview: Part 5–The Innate/Manifest Omnipoise Trait." *Hoplos: The Journal of the International Hoplology Society* 6, no. 4 (Winter 1989).

______. (1990). "Hoplology Theoretics, an Overview: Part 6–Innate/Manifest Abdominal Trait and Innate/Manifest Respiratory-Vocality Trait. *Hoplos: The Journal of the International Hoplology Society* 7, no.1 (Summer 1990).

______. (1992). "Hoplology Theoretics, an Overview: Part 7–Innate/Manifest Force/Yield Trait and Innate/Manifest Synchronous Trait." *Hoplos: The Journal of the International Hoplology Society* 7, no. 2 (Winter 1992).

______. (1994). "Hoplology Theoretics, an Overview: Part 8–Transcendent Synergy of the Manifest Adaptive Traits; Part 9–Practical Application." *Hoplos. The Journal of the International Hoplology Society* 7, no. 3 (Winter 1994).

Herrigel, Eugen. (1953). *Zen in the Art of Archery*. New York: Pantheon Books, Inc.

Hevener, Phillip T. (2008). *Fujita Seiko: The Last Koga Ninja*. Bloomington, IN: Xlibris Corporation.

Hillsborough, Romulus. (1999). *Ryoma: Life of a Renaissance Samurai.* San Francisco: Ridgeback Press.

______. (2001). *Samurai Sketches: From the Bloody Final Years of the Shōgun*. San Francisco: Ridgeback Press.

______. (2005). *Shinsengumi: The Shōgun's Last Samurai Corps*. Tokyo: Charles E. Tuttle.

Hosokawa, Dogen. (1999). *Omori Sogen: The Art of a Zen Master*. London: Kegan Paul International.

Hurst III, G. Cameron. (1998). *Armed Martial Arts of Japan: Swordsmanship and Archery.* New Haven: Yale University Press.

Ichishima, Shōshin (Masao), trans. (1995). *Juhachi-dō*『十八道』. Caanan, NY: Tendai Overseas Charitable Foundation.

______, trans. (2007). *Tendai-shu Juhachi-do*. Caanan, NY: Tendai-shu New York Betsuin.

Ichishima, Masao and David W. Chappell. (1983). *T'ien-t'ai Buddhism: An Outline of the Fourfold Teachings*. Tokyo: Daiichi-Shobō.

Ihara, Saikaku. (1981). *Tales of Samurai Honor*. Translated by Caryl Ann Callahan. [Translation of Ihara Saikaku's 井原西鶴 *Buke giri monogatari*『武家義理物語』.] *Monumenta Nipponica* Monograph 57. Sophia University, Tokyo.

Inada, Kenneth K., trans. (1970). *Nāgārjuna: A Translation of his Mūlamadhyamakakārikā with an Introductory Essay*. Tokyo: Hokuseido Press.

Inami, Hakusui. (1948). *Nippon-tō: The Japanese Sword*. Tokyo: Japan Sword Co., Ltd.

Irie Kōhei. (2005). "*Budō* as a Concept: An Analysis of *Budō*'s Characteristics." In *Budo Perspectives,* edited by Alexander Bennett. Auckland: Kendō World Publications Ltd.

Jackson, Susan and Mihaly Csikszentmihalyi. (1999). *Flow in Sports: The Keys to Optimal Experiences and Performances*. Champaign, IL: Human Kinetics.

Jansen, Marius B. (1995). *Sakamoto Ryoma and the Meiji Restoration.* New York: Columbia University Press.

______. (2000). *The Making of Modern Japan.* Cambridge: Belknap Press.

Joly, Henri L. and Hogitaro Inada. (1913). *The Sword and Samé*. Reprint, London: The Holland Press, 1979.

Joya, Mock. (1985). *Things Japanese*. Tokyo: The Japan Times, Ltd.

Kammer, Reinhard. (1978). *Zen and Confucius in the Art of Swordsmanship: The Tengu-geijutsu-ron of Chozan Shissai*. Translated by Betty J. Fitzgerald. London: Routledge & Kegan Paul.

Kanemoto, Sunadomari. (1990). "Morihei Ueshiba Founder of Aikido." *Aiki News*, no. 85 (Summer 1990).

Kano, Jigoro. (1986). *Kodokan Judo.* Tokyo: Kodansha International.

Kato, Genchi. (1971). *A Study of Shinto: The Religion of the Japanese Nation.* 2nd ed. London: Curzon Press.

Keeley, Liam. (1997). "Kato Takashi: Reflections of the Tatsumi-ryu Headmaster." In *Koryu Bujutsu: Classical Warrior Traditions of Japan,* edited by Diane Skoss. Berkeley Heights: Koryu Books.

______. (1999). "The Tojutsu of the Tatsumi-ryu: Murphy's Law, and the K.i.s.s. Principle." In *Sword and Spirit: Classical Warrior Traditions of Japan, Vol. 2*, edited by Diane Skoss. Berkeley Heights: Koryu Books.

Keene, Donald, trans. (1967). *Essays in Idleness*. (Translation of Yoshida Kenkō's *Tsurezuregusa*). New York: Columbia University Press.

Kerr, George H. (1958). *Okinawa: The History of an Island People*. Tokyo: Charles E. Tuttle.

Kiba, Kōshirō. (2002). *Kuki Shin Ryū Bujutsu: Bōjutsu, Hanbōjutsu, Tachiai*. Buyu Books & Publishing. [Translation of the original Japanese text published in 1937.]

Kim, Sang H., trans. (2001). *The Comprehensive Illustrated Manual of Martial Arts of Ancient Korea.* [Translation of *Muye dobo tongji* 『武藝圖譜通志』.] Hartford: Turtle Press.

King, James and Yuriko Iwakiri. (2007). *Japanese Warrior Prints, 1646–1905*. Hotei Publishing. Leiden: Brill.

Kishida, Tom. (2004). *The Yasukuni Swords: Rare Weapons of Japan 1933–1945*. Tokyo: Kodansha International.

Kitagawa Hiroshi and Bruce T. Tsuchida, trans. (1975). *Tale of the Heike: Heike Monogatari.* Foreword by Edward Seidensticker. Tokyo: University of Tokyo Press.

Kitagawa, Joseph M. (1966). *Religion in Japanese History*. New York: Columbia University Press.

Kiyota, Minoru. (1978). *Shingon Buddhism: Theory and Practice.* Los Angeles: Buddhist Books International.

Klompmakers, Inge. (2003). *Of Brigands and Bravery: Kuniyoshi's Heroes of the Suikoden.* Amsterdam: Hotei Publishing.

Knutsen, Roald M. (1963). *Japanese Polearms*. London: The Holland Press.

______. (2004). *Rediscovering BUDŌ: From a Swordsman's Perspective.* Kent: Global Oriental.

______. (2006). *Sun Tzu and the Art of Medieval Japanese Warfare.* Kent: Global Oriental.

______. (2011). *Tengu: The Shamanic and Esoteric Origins of the Japanese Martial Arts.* Kent: Global Oriental.

Knutsen, Roald and Patricia Knutsen. (2004). *Japanese Spears: Polearms and Their Use in Old Japan.* Kent: Global Oriental.

Kodokan Judo Institute. (2000). *Kōdōkan New Japanese-English Dictionary of Judo* 『和英対照柔道用語小辞典』. Tokyo: Kodokan Judo Institute.

Koren, Leonard. (2008). *Wabi-Sabi: for Artists, Designers, Poets & Philosophers.* San Francisco: Imperfect Publishing.

Krieger, Pascal. (1989). *La voie du bâton / the way of the stick.* Switzerland: Sophia Diffusion, S.A.

Kuroda, Ichitaro. (1974a). "Shu-Ha-Ri," Part 1. *Martial Arts International: The Fine Quality Martial Culture Journal* 1, no. 1 (January 1974).

______. (1974b). "Shu-Ha-Ri," Part 2. *Martial Arts International: The Fine Quality Martial Culture Journal* 1, no. 2 (March 1974).

______. (1974c). "Shu-Ha-Ri," Part 3. *Martial Arts International: The Fine Quality Martial Culture Journal* 1, no. 3 (May–June 1974).

Lamers, Jeroen P. (2001). *Japonius Tyrannus: The Japanese Warlord Oda Nobunaga Reconsidered.* Amsterdam: Hotei Publishing.

Lang, Tom. (1977). "The Kyusho of Ate Mi: A Review of the Literature." Privately prepared report.

de Lange, William. (2006). *Famous Japanese Swordsmen: The Warring States Period.* Warren, CT: Floating World Editions.

______. (2007). *Famous Japanese Swordsmen: The Two Courts Period.* Warren, CT: Floating World Editions.

______. (2008). *Famous Japanese Swordsmen: The Period of Unification.* Warren, CT: Floating World Editions.

Lebra, Takie Sugiyama. (1976). *Japanese Patterns of Behavior*. Honolulu: University of Hawaii Press.

Leggett, Trevor. (1978). *Zen and the Ways.* London: Routledge and Kegan Paul, Inc.

______. (1985). *Warrior Koans: Early Zen in Japan*. Arkana. London: Routledge and Kegan Paul, Inc.

Lowry, Dave. (2006). *In the Dojo: A Guide to the Rituals and Etiquette of the Japanese Martial Arts*. Boston: Weatherhill.

Martin, Ashley P. (2007). *The Shotokan Karate Bible: Beginner to Black Belt*. Firefly Books.

Mass, Jeffrey P. (1979). *The Development of Kamakura Rule, 1180–1250: A History with Documents*. Stanford: Stanford University Press.

______, ed. (1982). *Court and Bakufu in Japan: Essays in Kamakura History*. New Haven: Yale University Press.

______. (1990). "The Kamakura Bakufu." In *Medieval Japan.* Vol. 3 of *Cambridge History of Japan*, edited by Kozo Yamamura, 80–87. Cambridge: Cambridge University Press.

Matsui, Kenji. (1993). *The History of Shindō Musō Ryū.* IHS Monograph Series. Translated by Hunter B. Armstrong, edited by David A. Hall. Kamuela: International Hoplology Society.

Matsunaga, Alicia. (1969). *The Buddhist Philosophy of Assimilation: The Historical Development of the Honji-Suijaku Theory*. Tokyo: Charles E. Tuttle and Sophia University.

Matsunaga, Daigan M. and Alicia Matsunaga. (1974). *Foundations of Japanese Buddhism, Vol. I: The Aristocratic Age*. Tokyo: Buddhist Books International.

______. (1976). *Foundations of Japanese Buddhism, Vol. II: The Mass Movement.* Tokyo: Buddhist Books International.

McCarthy, Patrick, trans. (1995). *The Bible of Karate: Bubishi*. Tokyo: Charles E. Tuttle.

______, trans. (2008). *Bubishi: The Classic Manual of Combat*. Tokyo: Charles E. Tuttle.

McCarthy, Patrick and Yuriko McCarthy, trans., eds. (2002). *Motobu Chōki: Karate, My Art.* [Translation of Motobu Chōki's *Watashi no karatejutsu*『私の唐手術』and *Okinawa kempō karatejutsu*『沖縄拳法唐手術』.] Australia: International Ryukyu Karatejutsu Research Society.

McCullough, Helen Craig, trans. (1959). *Taiheiki: A Chronicle of Medieval Japan.* New York: Columbia University Press.

______, trans. (1966). *Yoshitsune: A Fifteenth-century Japanese Chronicle.* Tokyo: University of Tokyo Press.

______, trans. (1988). *Tale of the Heike.* Stanford: Stanford University Press.

McCullough, William H. and Helen Craig McCullough. (1980a). "Appendix A: Some Notes on Rank and Office." In *A Tale of Flowering Fortunes—Annals of Japanese Aristocratic Life in the Heian Period* [translation of the *Eiga monogatari*]. Stanford: Stanford University Press.

______. (1980b). "Appendix B: The Greater Imperial Palace." In *A Tale of Flowering Fortunes—Annals of Japanese Aristocratic Life in the Heian Period* [translation of the *Eiga monogatari*]. Stanford University Press.

McMullin, Neil. (1985). *Buddhism and the State in Sixteenth-century Japan*. Princeton: Princeton University Press.

Mercado, Stephen C. (2002). *The Shadow Warriors of Nakano: A History of the Imperial Japanese Army's Elite Intelligence School*. Washington, DC: Brassey's Inc.

Mifune, Kyuzo. (2004). *The Canon of Judo: Classic Teachings on Principles and Techniques*. Translated by Francoise White. 2nd ed. Tokyo: Kodansha International.

Miura, Isshū and Ruth Fuller Sasaki. (1965). *The Zen Koan: Its History and Use in Rinzai Zen*. New York: Harcourt, Brace & World, Inc.

Miyagawa, Mitsuru and Cornelius J. Kiley. (1977). "From Shōen to Chigyō: Proprietary Lordship and the Structure of Local Power." In *Japan in the Muromachi Age*, edited by John W. Hall and Takeshi Toyoda. Berkeley: University of California Press.

Miyake, Hitoshi. (2001). *Shugendo: Essays on the Structure of Japanese Folk Religion*. Edited by H. Byron Earhart. Michigan Monograph Series in Japanese Studies. Ann Arbor: University of Michigan.

Miyamoto, Musashi. (2002) *The Book of Five Rings*. Translated by William Scott Wilson. [Translation of *Gorin-no-sho*.] Tokyo: Kodansha International.

Mizutani, Osamu. (1990). *Japanese: The Spoken Language in Japanese Life*. Tokyo: The Japan Times, Ltd.

Mol, Serge. (2001). *Classical Fighting Arts of Japan: A Complete Guide to Koryū Jūjutsu*. Tokyo: Kodansha International.

______. (2003). *Classical Weaponry of Japan: Special Weapons and Tactics of the Martial Arts*. Tokyo: Kodansha International.

Monumenta Nipponica. (1984). "A Tale of Two Swords." *Monumenta Nipponica* 39, no. 2 (Summer 1984).

Morris, Ivan. (1975). *The Nobility of Failure: Tragic Heroes in the History of Japan*. New York: Holt, Rinehart and Winston. [Note: Morris includes several essays in this work, which are cited separately.]

______. (1975a). "Victory Through Defeat: Minamoto no Yoshitsune, 12th Century." In *The Nobility of Failure: Tragic Heroes in the History of Japan*. New York: Holt, Rinehart and Winston.

______. (1975b). "Seven Lives for the Nation: Kusunoki Masashige, 14th Century." In *The Nobility of Failure: Tragic Heroes in the History of Japan*. New York: Holt, Rinehart and Winston.

______. (1975c). "The Apotheosis of Saigō the Great." In *The Nobility of Failure: Tragic Heroes in the History of Japan*. New York: Holt, Rinehart and Winston.

Nagahara, Keiji and Yamamura Kozo. (1977). "Village Communities and Daimyo Power." In *Japan in the Muromachi Age*, edited by John W. Hall and Takeshi Toyoda. Berkeley: University of California Press.

Nagamine, Shoshin. (2000). *Tales of Okinawa's Great Masters*. Translated by Patrick McCarthy. Tokyo: Charles E. Tuttle.

Nagayama, Kokan. (1997). *The Connoisseur's Book of Japanese Swords*. Translated by Kenji Mishina. Tokyo: Kodansha International.

Needham, Joseph. (1983). *Gunpowder as the Fourth Power, East and West: First East Asian History of Science Foundation Lecture Presented at the University of Hong Kong, 20 October 1983.* Occasional Papers Series No. 3. Hong Kong: Hong Kong University Press.

Nitobe, Inazo. (1969). *Bushido: The Soul of Japan: An Exposition of Japanese Thought with an Introduction by William Elliot Griffis*. Tokyo: Charles E. Tuttle.

Nouët, Noël. (1990). *The Shogun's City—A History of Tokyo*. Paul Norbury Publications.

Noble, Graham. (2003). "A Meeting with Chosei Motobu." *Classical Fighting Arts*, no. 1.

Oda, Jishū. (1963). "Acalāgra Vidyārāja." In *Encyclopaedia of Buddhism*, Fascicle: *Acala-Ākaṅ*, edited by G.P. Malalasekera. Ceylon: The Government Press of Sri Lanka.

Ogawa, Morihiro, ed. (2009). *Art of the Samurai: Japanese Arms and Armor, 1156–1868*. New York: Metropolitan Museum of Art.

Ohlenkamp, Neil. (2006). "Go no Kata: Forms of Hardness/Strength." JudoInfo OnLine Dojo. http://www.judoinfo.com/gonokata.htm (accessed 12 November 2009).

Okakura, Kakuzo. (1964). *The Book of Tea.* Toronto: Dover Publications.

Onuma, Hideharu H., Dan de Prospero, and Jackie de Prospero. (1993). *Kyudo: The Essence and Practice of Japanese Archery*. Tokyo: Kodansha International.

Ōtake Risuke. (1977a). *The Deity and the Sword: Katori Shinto Ryu.* (無形文化財 香取神道流). Vol. 1. Translated by Donn F. Draeger. Tokyo: Minato Research & Publishing Co., Ltd.

______. (1977b). *The Deity and the Sword: Katori Shinto Ryu.* (無形文化財 香取神道流). Vol. 2. Translated by Donn F. Draeger. Tokyo: Minato Research & Publishing Co., Ltd.

______. (1978). *The Deity and the Sword: Katori Shinto Ryu.* (無形文化財 香取神道流). Vol. 3. Translated by Donn F. Draeger. Tokyo: Minato Research & Publishing Co., Ltd.

______. (2007). *Katori Shintō-ryū Warrior Tradition* (香取神道流). Berkeley Heights: Koryu Books.

Otaki, Tadao and Donn F. Draeger. (1983). *Judo Formal Techniques: A Complete Guide to Kodokan Randori No Kata.* Tokyo: Charles E. Tuttle.

Palumbo, Dennis G. (1987). *Secrets of Hakkoryu Jujutsu: Shodan Tactics*. Boulder, CO: Paladin Press.

______. (1988). *Secret Nidan Techniques of Hakkoryu Jūjutsu.* Boulder, CO: Paladin Press.

______. (1993).*Techniques of Sandan GI: The Essence of Hakkoryu Jūjutsu*. Boulder, CO: Paladin Press.

Papenfuss, Tony. (1997). "Mikonosuke Kawaishi." Edited by Neil Ohlenkamp, copyright 2004, JudoInfo.com, USA. http://www.judoinfo.com/kawaishi.htm. (accessed 12 November 2009).

Papinot, E. (1910). *Historical and Geographical Dictionary of Japan*. 2 vols. Reprint, New York: Frederick Ungar Publishing Co., 1968.

Payne, Richard, ed. (2005). *Tantric Buddhism in East Asia.* Somerville, MA: Wisdom Publications.

______. (2006). *Discourse and Ideology in Medieval Japanese Buddhism. Routledge Critical Studies in Buddhism.* London: Routledge.

Perrin, Noel. (1980). *Giving Up the Gun: Japan's Reversion to the Sword, 1543–1879.* Boulder, CO: Shambhala.

Pranin, Stanley A. (1981a). "Editorial (Regarding Tomiki Kenji)." *Aiki News* no. 43. (December 1981).

______. (1981b). "Interview with Kenji Tomiki Sensei (1)." *Aiki News* no. 43. (December 1981).

______. (1982). "Interview with Kenji Tomiki Sensei (2)." *Aiki News* no. 44. (January 1982).

______. (1992). "Interview with Gozo Shioda." *Aiki News* no. 93. (Fall 1992).

______. (1993). *Aikido Masters Volume 1: Prewar Students of Morihei Ueshiba*. Tokyo: Aiki News.

______. (1994). "Interview with Minoru Hirai." *Aiki News* no. 100. Vol. 21, no. 3 (Fall 1994).

______. (1996). *Daito-ryu Aikijujutsu: Conversations with Daito-ryu Masters*. Tokyo: Aiki News.

_____. (2009). "Tomiki, Kenji 富木謙治." *The Encyclopedia of Aikidō*. http://www.aikidojournal.com/encyclopedia?entryID=704 (accessed October 9, 2009).

Purcell, Victor. (1963). *The Boxer Uprising: A Background Study*. Cambridge: Cambridge University Press.

Rabinovitch, Judith N., trans. and ed. (1986). *Shōmonki: The Story of Masakado's Rebellion*. Tokyo: Monumenta Nipponica, Sophia University.

Rambelli, Fabio. "Texts, talismans, and jewels: The *Reikiki* and the performativity of sacred texts in medieval Japan." In *Discourse and Ideology in Medieval Japanese Buddhism*, edited by Richard Payne. Routledge Critical Studies in Buddhism. New York: Routledge.

Rankin, Andrew. (2011). *Seppuku: A History of Samurai Suicide*. New York: Kodansha USA.

Ravina, Mark. (2004). *The Last Samurai: The Life and Battles of Saigō Takamori.* Hoboken, NJ: John Wiley & Sons.

Reischauer, Edwin O. (1955a). *Ennin's Diary: The Record of a Pilgrimage to China in Search of the Law.* New York: The Ronald Press Company.

______. (1955b). *Ennin's Travels in T'ang China*. New York: The Ronald Press Company.

Renondeau, R. (1957). "Histore des moines guerriers du Japon," *Melanges publies par l'instituit des hautes études Chinoises.* 1 (1957).

Robinson, B.W. (1971). *The Arts of the Japanese Sword.* 2nd ed. Tokyo: Charles E. Tuttle.

______. (1982). *Kuniyoshi: The Warrior-Prints*. Ithaca, NY: Cornell University Press.

Robinson, Richard H. (1976). *Early Mādhyamika in India and China*. Delhi: Motilal Banarsidass.

Rogers, John M. (1990a). "Arts of War in Times of Peace: Archery in *Honchō bugei shōden*, Chapter 3." *Monumenta Nipponica* 45, no. 3 (Autumn 1990).

______. (1990b). "Arts of War in Times of Peace: Archery in *Honchō bugei shōden,* Chapter 5." *Monumenta Nipponica* 45, no. 4 (Winter 1990).

______. (1991). "Arts of War in Times of Peace: Archery in *Honchō bugei shōden,* Chapter 6." *Monumenta Nipponica* 46, no. 2 (Summer 1991).

Rosenbaum, Michael. (2005). *Kata and the Transmission of Knowledge in Traditional Martial Arts*. Boston: YMAA Publication Center.

Sabey, John Wayne. (1972). "The Gen'yōsha, The Kokuryūkai, and Japanese Expansionism." Ph.D. dissertation, University of Michigan.

Saitō, Morihiro. (1973a). *Traditional Aikido: Sword·Stick·Body Arts, Volume 1: Basic Techniques*『合気道：剣·杖·体術の理合 第一巻』. Tokyo: Minato Research & Publishing Company, 1973.

______. (1973b). *Traditional Aikido: Sword·Stick·Body Arts, Volume 2: Advanced Techniques*『合気道：剣·杖·体術の理合 第二巻』. Tokyo: Minato Research & Publishing Company, 1973.

______. (1974a). *Traditional Aikido: Sword·Stick·Body Arts, Volume 3: Applied Techniques*『合気道：剣·杖·体術の理合 第三巻』. Tokyo: Minato Research & Publishing Company, 1974.

______. (1974b). *Traditional Aikido: Sword·Stick·Body Arts, Volume 4: Vital Techniques*『合気道：剣·杖·体術の理合 第四巻』. Tokyo: Minato Research & Publishing Company, 1974.

______. (1974c). *Traditional Aikido: Sword·Stick·Body Arts, Volume 5: Training Works Wonders*『合気道：剣·杖·体術の理合 第五巻』. Tokyo: Minato Research & Publishing Company, 1974.

Sakai, Toshinobu 酒井利信. (2010.) *A Bilingual Guide to the History of Kendō*『英訳付け日本剣道の歴史』. Translated by Alexander Bennett. Tokyo: Skijournal.

Sakudō, Masao. (2005). "The Culture of '*Bu*'." In *Budo Perspectives*, edited by Alexander Bennett, 185–192. Auckland: Kendō World Publications Ltd.

Sandesara, Bhogilal Jayachandbhai and Ramanlal Nagarji Mehta, eds. (1964). *Mallapurāṇa: A Rare Sanskrit Text on Indian Wrestling especially as practiced by the Jyeṣṭhimallas*. Gaekwad's Oriental Series no. 144. Baroda: Oriental Institute.

Sanford, James H. (1977). "Shakuhachi Zen: The *Fukeshū* and *Komusō*." *Monumenta Nipponica* 32, no. 4 (Winter 1977).

______. (1991). "The Abominable Tachikawa Skull Ritual." *Monumenta Nipponica* 46, no. 1 (Spring 1991).

Sansom, George. (1958). *A History of Japan to 1334.* Stanford: Stanford University Press.

______. (1961). *A History of Japan: 1334–1615.* Stanford: Stanford University Press.

______. (1963). *A History of Japan: 1615–1867*. Stanford: Stanford University Press.

Sasamori, Junzo and Gordon Warner. (1964). *This is Kendo: The Art of Japanese Fencing.* Tokyo: Charles E. Tuttle.

Saso, Michael R. (1972). *Taoism and the Rite of Cosmic Renewal*. Pullman: Washington State University Press.

______. (1978). *The Teachings of Taoist Master Chuang*. New Haven: Yale University Press.

Satō, Elizabeth. (1974). "Early Development of the *Shōen.*" In *Medieval Japan: Essays in Institutional History*, edited by John W. Hall and Jeffrey P. Mass. New Haven: Yale University Press.

Sato, Hiroaki, trans. (1986). *The Sword and the Mind.* (Translation of Yagyū Munenori's *Heihō kadensho*.) Woodstock, NY: Overlook Press.

Sawa, Takaaki. (1972). *Art in Japanese Esoteric Buddhism*. The Heibonsha Survey of Japanese Art. Translated by Richard L. Gage. Tokyo: Weatherhill/Heibonsha.

Sawyer, Ralph D. and Mei-chün Sawyer. (1993). *The Seven Military Classics of Ancient China* 武經七書. Boulder: Westview Press.

Schreiber, Mark. (2001). *The Dark Side: Infamous Japanese Crimes and Criminals.* Tokyo: Kodansha International.

Seidensticker, Edward G., trans. (1976). *The Tale of Genji* by Murasaki Shikibu. New York: Alfred A. Knopf.

Seigle, Cecilia Segawa. (2003). *Yoshiwara: The Glittering World of the Japanese Courtesan*. Honolulu: University of Hawaii Press.

Sergeant, J.A. (1959). *Sumō: The Sport and the Tradition*. Tokyo: Charles E. Tuttle.

Seward, Jack. (1968). *Hara-kiri*. Tokyo: Charles E. Tuttle.

Shimabukuro, Masayuki and Leonard J. Pellman. (1995). *Flashing Steel: Mastering Eishin-Ryu Swordsmanship.* Berkeley: Frog Books.

Shine, Jerry. (1994). "Honcho Bugei Shoden: The Original Martial Arts Survey," *Journal of Asian Martial Arts* 3, no. 4.

Skoss, Diane, ed. (1997). *Koryu Bujutsu: Classical Warrior Traditions of Japan.* Berkeley Heights: Koryu Books.

______. (1999). *Sword & Spirit: Classical Warrior Traditions of Japan, Vol.2*. Berkeley Heights: Koryu Books.

______. (2002). *Keiko Shokon: Classical Warrior Traditions of Japan, Vol. 3.* Berkeley Heights: Koryu Books.

Skoss, Meik. (1997). "The Meaning of Martial Arts Training: A Conversation with Sawada Hanae." In *Koryu Bujutsu: Classical Warrior Traditions of Japan,* edited by Diane Skoss. Berkeley Heights: Koryu Books.

______. (2002). "Itto-ryu Kenjutsu: An Overview." In *Keiko Shokon: Classical Warrior Traditions of Japan, Vol. 3*, edited by Diane Skoss. Berkeley Heights: Koryu Books.

Smith, Robert W. (1958). *A Complete Guide to Jūdō: Its Story and Practice*. Tokyo: Charles E. Tuttle.

Snellgrove, David and Hugh Richardson. (1968). *A Cultural History of Tibet*. New York: Frederick A. Praeger.

Snodgrass, Adrian. (1988). *The Matrix and Diamond World Mandalas in Shingon Buddhism.* 2 vols. Sata-Pitaka Series, Indo-Asian Literaturen, volumes 354–355. New Delhi: Rakesh Goel.

So, Doshin. (1970a). *Shorinji Kempo: Philosophy and Techniques*. Tokyo: Japan Publications Trading Company.

______. (1970b). *What is Shorinji Kempo?* Tokyo: Japan Publications Trading Company.

So, Kwan-wai. (1975). *Japanese Piracy in Ming China during the 16th Century*. East Lansing, MI: Michigan State University Press.

Sollier, André and Zsolt Györbiró. (1969). *Japanese Archery: Zen in Action*. Tokyo: John Weatherhill, Inc.

Staal, Fritz. (1982). "The Himalayas and the Fall of Religion." In *The Silk Route and the Diamond Path*, edited by Deborah E. Klimburg-Salter. Los Angeles: UCLA Art Council.

Stevens, John. (1981). *Sacred Calligraphy of the East*. Boulder, CO: Shambhala.

______. (1984). *The Sword of No Sword: Life of the Master Warrior Tesshu*. Boulder, CO: Shambhala.

______. (2007). *Zen Bow, Zen Arrow: The Life and Teachings of Awa Kenzo, the Archery Master from "Zen in the Art of Archery."* Boulder, CO: Shambhala, 2007.

Stone, George Cameron. (1934). *Glossary of the Construction, Decoration and Use of Arms and Armor in All Countries and in All Times Together with Some Closely Related Subjects*. The Southworth Press. Reprint, New York: Jack Brussel, 1961.

Strickmann, Michel. (1981). "Homa in East Asia." In *Tantric and Taoist Studies in Honor of R.A. Stein.* Bruxelles: Institut belge des hautes études chinoises.

______. (1983). "Homa in East Asia." In *Agni: The Vedic Ritual of the Fire Altar,* vol. 2. Edited by Frits Staal. Fremont: Asian Humanities Press.

Stroud, Robert and Tasuke Honda. (2007). http://www.yorku.ca/kendo/KendoForms.htm (accessed 12 November 2009).

Stutley, Margaret. (1980). "Battle Charms." In *Ancient Indian Magic and Folklore: An Introduction*. Boulder: Great Eastern.

Sugawara, Makoto. (1985). *Lives of Master Swordsmen.* Tokyo: East Publications.

Sugino, Yoshio. (1985). "Yoshio Sugino Interview," *Aiki News*, no. 69 (November 1985).

Suino, Nicklaus. (1994). *The Art of Japanese Swordsmanship: A Manual of Eishin-Ryu Iaido.* Tokyo: Weatherhill.

Suzuki, D. T. (1958). *Zen and Japanese Culture*. Bollingen Foundation. Princeton: Princeton University Press.

Svinth, Joseph, ed. (2002). "Documentation Regarding the Budo Ban in Japan, 1945–1950." *Journal of Combative Sport.* Electronic Journals of Martial Arts and Sciences. (13 November 2009). http://ejmas.com/jcs/jcsart_svinth_1202.htm (accessed 10 November 2009).

Swanson, Paul L. (1989). *Foundations of T'ien-t'ai Philosophy: Flowering of the Two Truths Theory in Chinese Buddhism.* Berkeley: Asian Humanities Press.

Takaiwa, Setsuo, Yoshindo Yoshihara, Leon Kapp, and Hiroko Kapp. (2006). *The Art of Japanese Sword Polishing.* Tokyo: Kodansha International.

Takakusu, Junjirō. (1947). *Essentials of Buddhist Philosophy.* Honolulu: University of Hawaii Press. Reprint, second Indian edition, New Delhi: Oriental Books Reprint Corporation, 1975.

Tamura, Yoshirō. (1993). "Tendaishū." In *Encyclopedia of Religion,* vol.14. Edited by Mircea Eliade. New York: Macmillan Publishing Company.

Ten Grotenhuis, Elizabeth. (1999). *Japanese Mandalas: Representations of Sacred Geography.* Honolulu: University of Hawaii Press.

Terry, Charles S., trans. (1981). *Musashi.* [Translation of Yoshikawa Eiji's *Musashi* 『武蔵』.] Tokyo: Kodansha International.

Tokitsu, Kenji. (2004). *Miyamoto Musashi: His Life and Writings.* Boston: Shambhala.

Trevanian. (1979). *Shibumi.* New York: Crown Publishers.

Tsang, Carol Richmond. (2007). *War and Faith: Ikko Ikki in Late Muromachi Japan.* Harvard East Asian Monographs 288. Cambridge: Harvard University Asia Center.

Tsunoda, Ryusaku, Wm. Theodore de Bary, and Donald Keene. (1958). *Sources of Japanese Tradition.* Vol. LIV of *Records of Civilization, Sources and Studies: Introduction to Oriental Civilizations.* New York: Columbia University Press.

Tucci, Giuseppe. (1973). *The Theory and Practice of Mandala: With Special Reference to the modern psychology of the subsconscious.* New York: Samuel Weiser.

Turnbull, Stephen. (1977). *The Samurai: A Military History.* New York: Macmillan Publishing Co., Inc.

______. (1991). *Ninja: the True Story of Japan's Secret Warrior Cult.* New York: Firebird Books Ltd.

______.(2005). *Warriors of Medieval Japan.* Oxford: Osprey Publishing.

Tyler, Royall, trans. (2001). *The Tale of Genji* by Murasaki Shikibu. New York: Penguin Classics.

Varley, H. Paul. (1967). *The Ōnin War: History of Its Origin and Background—With Selective Translation of the Chronicle of Ōnin.* Studies in Oriental Culture no 1. New York: Columbia University Press.

______. (1977). "Ashikaga Yoshimitsu and the World of Kitayama: Social Change and Shogunal Patronage in Early Muromachi Japan." In *Japan in the Muromachi Age,* edited by John W. Hall and Takeshi Toyoda. Berkeley: University of California Press.

______. (1994). *Warriors of Japan: As Portrayed in the War Tales.* Honolulu: University of Hawaii Press.

Victoria, Brian Daizen. (2003). *Zen War Stories*. New York: Routledge Curzon.

______. (2006). *Zen at War.* 2nd ed. Oxford: Rowman & Littlefield Publishers, Inc.

de Visser, M.W. (1908). "The Tengu." *Transactions of the Asiatic Society of Japan* 36 (1908).

______. (1913). *The Dragon in China and Japan*. Amsterdam. Reprint, Whitefish, MT: Kessinger Publishing, 2003.

______. (1915). *The Bodhisattva Ti-tsang (Jizō) in China and Japan.* Erst Sonderveröffentlichung der Ostasiatischen Zeitschrift. Berlin: Oesterheld & Co.

______. (1935). *Ancient Buddhism in Japan: Sūtras and Ceremonies in Use in the Seventh and Eighth Centuries A.D. and Their History in Later Times*. 2 vols. Leiden: E. J. Brill.

Wagner, Eduard. (1967). "Amulets, the Exorcizing and Charming of Weapons." In *Cut and Thrust Weapons.* Translated by Jean Layton. London: Spring Books.

Warner, Gordon and Donn F. Draeger. (1982). *Japanese Swordsmanship: Technique and Practice*. Tokyo: Weatherhill.

Watanabe Tadashige. (1993). *Shinkage-ryu Sword Techniques*. 2 vols. Tokyo: Sugawara Martial Arts/Japan Publications.

Watatani Kiyoshi. (1974). "The Takenouchi Ryu." *Martial Arts International* 1, no. 2. (March 1974).

Weinstein, Stanley. (1974). "The Beginnings of Esoteric Buddhism in Japan: The Neglected Tendai Tradition." *The Journal of Asian Studies.* 34, no. 1 (November, 1974).

Whitehead, Lt. Col. J.G.O. (ret.). (1961). "An Ancient Military System." *Journal of the United Service Institution on India* 91, no. 383 (April–June, 1961).

Wilder, Kris. (2007). *The Way of Sanchin Kata: The Application of Power*. Boston: YMAA Publication Center.

Williams, C.A.S. (1974). *Chinese Symbolism and Art Motifs*. 4th ed. Tokyo: Charles E. Tuttle.

Wilson, William R., trans. (1971). *Hōgen monogatari: Tale of the Disorder in Hōgen*. Tokyo: Monumenta Nipponica, Sophia University.

______. (1973). "The Way of the Bow and Arrow: The Japanese Warrior in *Konjaku Monogatari*." *Monumenta Nipponica*: 28, no. 2 (1973).

Wilson, William Scott, trans. (1982). *Ideals of the Samurai: Writings of Japanese Warriors*. Los Angeles: Ohara Publications, Inc.

______, trans. (1984). *Budoshoshinshu: The Warrior's Primer of Daidōji Yūzan.* Santa Clarita: Los Angeles: Ohara Publications.

______, trans. (2000). *Taiko: An Epic Novel of War and Glory in Feudal Japan.* (Translation of Yoshikawa Eiji's *Taikō*.) Tokyo: Kodansha International.

______, trans. (2002). *Hagakure: The Book of the Samurai.* (Translation of Yamamoto Tsunetomo's *Hagakure*.) Tokyo: Kodansha International.

______, trans. (2003). *The Unfettered Mind: Writings from a Zen Master to a Master Swordsman.* Tokyo: Kodansha International.

______. (2004a). *The Lone Samurai: The Life of Miyamoto Musashi*. Tokyo: Kodansha International.

______, trans. (2004b). *The Life-Giving Sword: Secret Teachings from the House of the Shogun.* (Translation of Yagyu Munenori's *Heihō kadensho*『兵法家伝書』). Tokyo: Kodansha International.

______, trans. (2006). *The Demon's Sermon on the Martial Arts*. (Translation of Issai Chozanshi's *Tengu geijutsu ron*『天狗芸術論』). Tokyo: Kodansha International.

Winternitz, Maurice. (1933). *Buddhist and Jain Literature*. Vol. 3 of *A History of Indian Literature*. Calcutta.

Yamada Shōji. (2001). "The Myth of Zen in the Art of Archery." *Japanese Journal of Religious Studies* 28, 1–2. Trans. by Earl Hartman.

Yamamura, Kozo. (1990). *Medieval Japan.* Vol. 3 of *Cambridge History of Japan*. Cambridge: Cambridge University Press.

Yamatsuta, Shigeyoshi 山蔦重義. (2005). *Iaido Hongi: Muso Shinden Ryū with English Translation & Photo Technical Book*.『居合道本義：夢想神伝流』. Trans. by Sheryl Hogg. Tokyko: Airyudo.

Yonekura, Isamu. (1975). "The Ethos of Samurai of Kamakura." *The East* 11, no. 5 (June 1975): 17–27.

Yumoto, John M. (1958). *The Samurai Sword: A Handbook*. Tokyo: Charles E. Tuttle.

Selected Japanese/Chinese Bibliography

Akabane Tatsuo 赤羽根龍夫. (2007). *Yagyū shinkage ryū o manabu: Edo bushi no shintai sōsa*『柳生新陰流を学ぶ：江戸武士の身体操作』(Yagyū Shinkage Ryū: The Edo-period warrior class and body movement dynamics). Tokyo: Ski Journal.

Amino Yoshihiko 網野善彦. (1982). *Higashi to nishi no kataru Nihon no rekishi*『東と西の語る日本の歴史』(Japanese History, East and West). Tokyo: Soshite bunko.

Arakawa Takenori 荒川武仙. (1973). *Shin Ryūkyū budō nunchaku*『新琉球武道双節棍』(Modern Ryūkyū Budō Nunchaku). Tokyo: Fuji insatsu shuppansha.

Besson zakki『別尊雑記』(Miscellaneous Texts on Other Heavenly Worthies). (1924–1935). Compiled by the monk Shinkaku, c.1180. In *Taishō shinshū daizōkyō zuzō*, edited by Takakusu Junjirō and Watanabe Kaikyoku, vol. 3 (T. 88). Tokyo: Taishō shinshū daizōkyō kankōkai.

Chiba Satoshi and Satō Yasuji 千葉仁・佐藤安治. (1999). "Keishi Ryū: Kidachi kata" 警視流: 木太刀形 (Keishi Ryū: Combative scenarios executed with wooden swords). *Kendo Nippon* 剣道日本 no. 283 (September 1999).

Chigiri Kōsai 知切光歳. (1977). *Zushū tengu retsuden*『圖聚天狗列伝』(Collected biographies of mountain demons). 2 vols. Tokyo: Miki shobō.

Fujita Seiko 藤田西湖. (1953). *Shindō Musō Ryū jōjutsu zukai*『神道夢想流杖術図解』(The illustrated Shindō Musō Ryū). Tokyo: Bujutsu kenkyūjo.

______. (1958). *Saigo no ninja doronron: Kōga Ryū ninjutsu jūyon sei*『最後の忍者どろんろん：甲賀流忍術十四世』(The last *ninja doronron*: Fourteenth headmaster of the Kōga School). Reprint, Tokyo: Shinpūsha, 2004.

______. (c.1960). *Bujutsu kenkyū shōbō*『武術研究所報』(Research report on martial arts).

______. (1985a). *Kempō gokui: Atemi setsu-kappō meikai*『拳法極意當身殺活法明解』(Secrets of boxing methods: A clear explanation of body strikes for killing and healing). Tokyo: Meicho Kankōkai.

______. (1985b). *Zukai Hojōjutsu*『図解捕縄術』(Illustrated combative arresting-rope technique). Tokyo: Meicho Kankōkai.

______. (1985c). *Zukai Shurikenjutsu*『図解手裏剣術』(Illustrated throwing-dart technique). Tokyo: Meicho Kankōkai.

Gomi Yasuhiro 五味康祐. (1985). *Kempō okugi*『剣法奥儀』(The inner secrets of swordsmanship). Tokyo: Bungei Shunjū.

Higaonna Morio 東恩納盛男, Kate Karitōru 嘉手苅徹, and Takamiyagi Shigeru 高宮城繁. (2008). "Miyagi Chōjun"「宮城長順」. In *Okinawa karate kobudō jiten*, edited by Takamiyagi *et al*. Tokyo: Hakushobō.

Hioki Shōichi 日置昌一. (1934). *Nihon sōhei kenkyū*『日本僧兵研究』(An investigation of the Japanese "warrior monk" phenomenon). Tokyo: Heibonsha. Reprint, Tokyo: Kokusho kankōkai, 1972.

Hirata Toshiharu 平田俊春. (1965). *Sōhei to bushi*『僧兵と武士』(Warriors and warrior monks). Tokyo: Nihon Kyōbunsha.

Iijima Fumio 飯嶌文夫. (1985). “Kiraku ryū jūjutsu”「気楽流柔術」. Private document.

Imagawa Tokuzō 今川徳三, Takahashi Kō 高橋貢, Shimura Kunihiro 志村有弘, Matsumoto Yasushi 松本寧至, Takahashi Masaaki 高橋政清, and Yashiro Kazuo 矢代和夫. (1988). *Nihon kassen jiten*『日本合戦事典』(A dictionary of Japanese battles). Tokyo: Sōbunshakan.

Imamura Yoshio 今村嘉雄, ed. (1966). *Nihon budō zenshū*『日本武道全集』(Complete works on Japanese martial arts). 7 vols. Tokyo: Jimbutsu ōraisha.

- Volume 1: *Kenjutsu 1: Yagyū Shinkage Ryū, Taisha Ryū, Shingyōtō Ryū, Niten-ichi Ryū*『剣術：柳生新陰流、タイ舎流、心形刀流、二天一流』.
- Volume 2: *Kenjutsu 2: Ittō Ryū, Shintō Ryū, Jigen Ryū, Maniwa Nen Ryu*『剣術：一刀流、神道流、示現流、馬庭念流』.
- Volume 3: *Kyūjutsu, bajutsu*『弓術、馬術』(Combative archery and combative horsemanship).
- Volume 4: *Hōjutsu*『砲術・水術・忍術』(Combative gunnery, combative swimming, and espionage).
- Volume 5: *Jūjutsu, kempō, karate, aikidō*『柔術、拳法、空手、合気道』(*Jūjutsu* grappling methods, Chinese boxing systems, Okinawan boxing systems, *aiki* grappling methods).
- Volume 6: *Sōjutsu, naginatajutsu, bōjutsu, tashojutsu*『槍術、薙刀術、棒術、他諸術』(Combative spearmanship, combative glaive systems, combative staff systems, etc.).
- Volume 7: *Kenjutsu 3: Shindō Munen Ryū, Jiki Shinkage Ryū, Ta* (and others)『剣術：神道無念流、直心影流、他』.

______, ed. (1967). *Shiryō Yagyū Shinkage Ryū*『史料柳生新陰流』(Historical records of the Yagyū Shinkage Ryū). 2 vols. Tokyo: Jimbutsu ōraisha.

______. (1974). *Yagyū ibun*『柳生遺聞』(Remnants of Yagyū writings). Tokyo: Erumu.

______. (1979). *Nihon kengō shi*『日本剣豪史』(A history of Japanese master swordsmen). Tokyo: Shin-jimbutsu ōraisha.

______, ed. (1982). *Nihon budō taikei*『日本武道大系』(A survey of Japanese martial arts). 10 vols. and 1 supplement. Tokyo: Dōbōsha 同朋舎.

- Volume 1: *Kenjutsu*『剣術』(Combative swordsmanship).
- Volume 2: *Kenjutsu*『剣術』(Combative swordsmanship).
- Volume 3: *Kenjutsu*『剣術』(Combative swordsmanship).
- Volume 4: *Kyūjutsu*『弓術』(Combative archery).
- Volume 5: *Hōjutsu, suijutsu, ninjutsu, and bajutsu*『砲術・水術・忍術・馬術』(Combative firearms, swimming, espionage and guerrilla warfare, and horsemanship).
- Volume 6: *Jūjutsu and aikijutsu*『柔術・合気術』(Combative grappling).
- Volume 7: *Sōjutsu, naginatajutsu, bōjutsu, kusarigama-jutsu, and shurikenjutsu*『槍術・薙刀術・棒術・鎖鎌術・手裏剣術』(Combative spear arts, long-hafted glaive arts, long hardwood staff arts, composite sickle-and-chain arts, and throwing blades).
- Volume 8: *Karatedō, aikidō, shōrinji kempō, taikyokuken*『空手道・合気道・小林寺拳法・太極拳』(Modern martial/spiritual/sportive fighting arts: *karate*, *aiki*, Shōrinji Kempō, and *t'ai-chi ch'üan*).

- Volume 9: *Bugei zuihitsu*『武芸随筆』(Miscellaneous writings on martial arts).
- Volume 10: *Budō no rekishi*『武道の歴史』(A history of martial arts).
- Supplement Volume: *Heihō kadensho*『兵法家伝書』(The Yagyū family treatise on strategy).

Imai Masayuki 今井正之. (1987). *Miyamoto Musashi: Dokkōdō Niten Ichi Ryū*『宮本武蔵独行道・二天一流』(Miyamoto Musashi: Niten Ichi Ryū—The path of self-reliance). Usashi: Gentei shuppan.

Inagaki Moto-o 稲垣史生. (1982). *Kengō meishōbu hyaku-wa*『剣豪名勝負100話』(100 tales of famous duels between master swordsmen). Tokyo: Rippū shobō.

Inoue Kiyoshi 井上清. (c.1986). *Nen Ryū nijū wa*『念流二十話』(Twenty stories about Nen Ryū). Edited by Ōsawa Matsuo 大澤末男. Tokyo: Yoshīmachi Bunka Kyōkai.

Irie Kōhei 入江康平, ed. (1988a). *Tamiya Ryū heihō iai*『田宮流兵法居合』(Tamiya Ryū quick-draw swordsmanship strategy and tactics). Vol. 1 of *Budō densho shūsei* 武道傳書集成. Tsukuba: Tsukuba Daigaku Budō Bunka Kenkyūkai.

______. (1988b). *Kenjutsu shoryū shimpō ronshū*『剣術諸流心法論集』(Collected treatises on the psychological teachings of various schools of swordsmanship), vol. 1. In vol. 2 of *Budō densho shūsei* 武道傳書集成. Tsukuba: Tsukuba Daigaku Budō Bunka Kenkyūkai.

______. (1988c). *Kenjutsu shoryū shimpō ronshū*『剣術諸流心法論集』(Collected treatises on the psychological teachings of various schools of swordsmanship), vol. 2. In vol. 3 of *Budō densho shūsei* 武道傳書集成. Tsukuba: Tsukuba Daigaku Budō Bunka Kenkyūkai.

______. (1989). *Kinsei budō bunken mokuroku*『近世武道文献目録』(A catalog of latter-day martial arts literary works). Tokyo: Daiichi shobō.

______. (1990a). *Shinkage Ryū kankei shiryō*『新陰流関係史料』(Shinkage Ryū archives), vol. 1. In vol. 4 of *Budō densho shūsei* 武道傳書集成. Tsukuba: Tsukuba Daigaku Budō Bunka Kenkyūkai.

______. (1990b). *Shinkage Ryū kankei shiryō*『新陰流関係史料』(Shinkage Ryū archives), vol. 2. In vol. 5 of *Budō densho shūsei* 武道傳書集成. Tsukuba: Tsukuba Daigaku Budō Bunka Kenkyūkai.

______. (1990c). *Shinkage Ryū kankei shiryō*『新陰流関係史料』(Shinkage Ryū archives), vol. 3. In vol. 6 of *Budō densho shūsei* 武道傳書集成. Tsukuba: Tsukuba Daigaku Budō Bunka Kenkyūkai.

______ and Sugie Masatoshi 入江康平・杉江正敏, eds. (1989). *Nihon budōgaku kenkyū: Watanabe Ichirō kyōju taikan kinen ronshū*『日本武道学研究：渡辺一郎教授退官記念論集』(Studies in Japanese martial arts: Collected works commemorating the faculty retirement of Watanabe Ichirō). Tokyo: Shimazu shōbō.

Ishigaki Yasuzō 石垣安造. (1992). *Kashima Shinden Jiki Shinkage Ryū Gokui Denkai*『鹿島神伝直心影流極意伝開』(Opening up the secret transmissions of the Kashima Shinden Jiki Shinkage Ryū). Tokyo: Shinjusha.

Ishioka Hisao 石岡久夫. (1972). *Nihon heihō shi*.『日本兵法史』(A history of Japanese strategy and tactics). 2 vols. Tokyo: Yūzankaku.

______. (1981). *Heihōsha-no-seikatsu* (Lives of [famous] strategists).『兵法者の生活』. Tokyo: Yūzankaku.

______ and Arima Shigeyoshi 有馬成甫, eds. (1967). *Nihon heihō zenshū.*『日本兵法全集』(Complete works on Japanese strategy and tactics). Tokyo: Jimbutsu ōraisha.

- Volume 1: *Kōshū Ryū heihō*『甲州流兵法』(Strategy of the Kōshū school).
- Volume 2: *Echigo Ryū heihō*『越後流兵法』(Strategy of the Echigo school).
- Volume 3: *Hōjō Ryū heihō*『北条流兵法』(Strategy of the Hōjō school).
- Volume 4: *Naganuma Ryū heihō*『長沼流兵法』(Strategy of the Naganuma school).
- Volume 5: *Yamaga Ryū heihō*『山鹿流兵法』(Strategy of the Yamaga school).
- Volume 6: *Sho-ryū heihō*『諸流兵法』(Part 1) (Strategies of various other schools).
- Volume 7: *Sho-ryū heihō*『諸流兵法』(Part 2) (Strategies of various other schools).

______. (1969). *Echigo Ryū heihō—Kenshin Ryū heihō*『越後流兵法—謙信流兵法』. Tokyo: Shinjinbutsu ōraisha, 1969.

______, Okada Kazuo 岡田一男, and Katō Hiroshi 加藤寛. (1980). *Nihon no kobugei.*『日本古武芸』(Classical Japanese martial arts). Tokyo: Shinjinbutsu Orisha.

Iwasa Masaru 岩佐 勝. (2002). *Kashima Shinden Jiki Shinkage Ryū*『鹿島神傳直心影流』: *The Origin of Samuraihood—Swordsmanship from Kashima Shrine, the god of Bushido Kashima—A Symbol of Justice by the Sword*. Tokyo: Budō shinkōkai.

Jinen Jiseki Kenshōkai 慈念事蹟顕彰会. (1965). *Jinen to sono iseki: Nihon kendō no shiso*『慈念とその遺蹟: 日本剣道の始祖』(Jinen [Nen Ami Jion] and the historical evidence: founders of Japanese swordsmanship). Tokyo: Jinen Jiseki Kenshōkai.

Kaminoda Tsunemori 神之田常盛. (2002). *Isshin Ryū kusarigama-jutsu*『一心流鎖鎌術』(Isshin Ryū sickle-and-chain arts). Tokyo: Privately published.

______. (2005). *Ikkaku Ryū jutte-jutsu, Ittatsu Ryū hojō jutsu, Tobidashi juttejutsu*『一角流十手術 一達流捕縄術 飛び出し十手術』(Ikkaku Ryū single-tined truncheon arts, Ittatsu Ryū tying-cord arts, and police telescoping-truncheon arts). Tokyo: Privately published.

______. (2006). *Kenjutsu—Shintō Kasumi Ryū; Heiki—Uchida Ryū tanjōjutsu, mitsu dōgu (tsūshō) sasumatajutsu*『剣術 神道霞流 併記 内田流短杖術 三道具(通称)刺服術』(Swordsmanship Shintō Kasumi Ryū; including Uchida Ryū short staff arts and polearm arresting weapons [a.k.a. *sasumatajutsu*]). Tokyo: Privately published, 2006.

______ and Nakajima Asakichi 中島浅吉. (1976). *Shindō Musō Ryū jōdō kyōhan*『神道夢想流杖道教範』(Shindō Musō Ryū stick arts—the master text). Editorial supervision by Shimizu Takaji 清水隆次. Tokyo: Japan Publications Trading Company.

Katsuno Ryūshin 勝野隆信. (1959). *Sōhei*『僧兵』(Warrior monks). Tokyo: Nihon Rekishi Shinsho.

Kawaguchi Itsukō 川口厳孝. (1893). *Tokugawa Bakufu keiji zufu*『徳川幕府刑事図譜』(Illustrations of criminal cases under the Tokugawa military government). Republished in 1977 as *Edo keibatsu jitsuroku*『江戸刑罰実録』(Authentic records of crime and punishment during the Edo period). Tokyo: Misaki Shobō.

Kawamura Hideharu 川村秀東. (n.d.). *Sekiun Ryū kenjutsusho zenshū*『夕雲流剣術書全集』(The complete collected works of the swordsmanship of the Sekiun Ryū).

Kawazoe Takeru 川添猛. (1985). "Fujita Seiko bunkoten kaisai ni ate"「藤田西湖文庫展開催にあって」(Reports from the colloquium on the Fujita Seiko Archive). *Fujita Seiko bunkoten: Nihon kobudō kenkyū no hōko*『藤田西湖文庫展：日本古武道研究の宝庫』(The Fujita Seiko Archive: Treasures of classical Japanese martial arts) vol. 3, (November 11–17, 1985).

Kitamura Kaitsu 北村佳逸.(1933). *Heihō Rikutō Sanryaku*『兵法六韜三略』(Strategies of the *Liutao* and the *Sanlue*). Kyoto: Ritsumeikan shuppanbu.

Kinen jigyō jikkōi-in i-inkai 記念事業実行員委員会 (Executive commemorative ceremony committee). (1989). *Kensei Tsukahara Bokuden seitan gohyaku nen matsuri kinen-shi*『剣聖塚原卜伝生誕五百年祭記念誌』(Record of the commemorative festival of the 500th anniversary of the birth of sword saint Tsukahara Bokuden). Kashima, Japan.

Kuroda Toshio 黒田俊雄. (1965). *Mōko shūrai*『蒙古襲来』(The Mongol invasion [of Japan]). Tokyo: Chūō Kōronsha.

Manabe Takejirō 眞鍋竹治郎, editor. (1938). *Genke kin'etsushū*『源家訓閲集』(The Minamoto family collected examinations [of military matters]). Ōsaka: Tanaka Genshōten.

Mao Yuanyi 茅元儀. (1621). *Wu-pei-chih* (Records of armaments), Section 92『武備志九十之九十貳』.

Matsuda Masashi. (1972). *Chūgoku Bujutsu: Shorin ken to taikyoku ken*『中国武術：少林拳と太極拳』(Chinese martial arts: Shaolin boxing and *taiji* boxing.) Tokyo: Shinjinbutsu ōraisha.

Matsui Kenji 松井健二. (1991a). "Shindō Musō Ryū jōjutsu no zembō"「神道夢想流の全貌(前編)」(The full story on Shindō Musō Ryū *jōjutsu* [Part 1]), *Hiden koryū bujutsu*〔秘伝古流武術〕(The magazine of secret transmissions of classical martial arts schools) no. 6 (April 1991).

______. (1991b). "Shindō Musō Ryū jōjutsu no zembō"「神道夢想流の全貌(前編)」(The full story on Shindō Musō Ryū *jōjutsu* (後編) [Part 2]), *Hiden koryū bujutsu*〔秘伝古流武術〕(The magazine of secret transmissions of classical martial arts schools) no. 7 (July 1991)

Matsumoto Kenichi 松本建一. (1996). *Bakumatsu no sanshū: Kaishū·Tesshu·Deishū no ikikata*『幕末の三舟：海舟・鉄舟・泥舟の生きかた』(The three *Shū* of the Bakumatsu: The lives of Kaishū, Tesshū, and Deishū). Tokyo: Kodansha.

Minouchi Sōichi 簑内宗一. (1982). *Tsubo to Nihonjin*『ツボと日本人』([The art of attacking] pressure points and the Japanese). Tokyo: Inaho Shobō.

______. (c.1982). "Hyōhōka no Kōdō Igaku"「兵法家の行動医学」(Behavioral medicine and martial strategists). Publisher unknown.

Miyagi Takao 宮城鷹夫. (2008). "Motobu Ryū (Motobu Udundī)"「本部流(本部御殿手)」. In *Okinawa karate kobudō jiten*, edited by Takamiyagi *et al*. Tokyo: Hakushobō.

Miyake Hitoshi 宮家準. (1985). *Shugendō shisō no kenkyū*『修験道思想の研究』(Research on Shugendō thought). Tokyo: Shunjūsha.

Miyazaki Osamu 宮崎惇. (1974). *Hiroku sengoku ninjaden*『秘録戦国忍者伝』(Warring States–period *ninja* traditions: secret documents). Tokyo: Momozono Shobō.

Momohara Keichō 桃原慶長. (2008). "Uechi Ryū"「上地流」. In *Okinawa karate kobudō jiten*, edited by Takamiyagi *et al*. Tokyo: Hakushobō.

Mori Jūrō 森十郎. (2004). *Yagyū shinkage ryū kyōhon*『柳生新陰流教本』(Textbook on Yagyū Shinkage Ryū).

Murayama Makoto 村山孚. (1965). *Sonshi·Goshi: Chūgoku no shisō* 10『孫子・呉子：中国の思想 10』(Sunzi, Wuzi: Chinese thought, vol. 10). Tokyo: Tokkan shoten.

Mutō Masao 武藤正雄. (1985). "Nihon kobudō"「日本古武道」(Classical Japanese martial arts). In *Fujita Seiko bunkoten: Nihon kobudō kenkyū no hōko*『藤田西湖文庫展：日本古武道研究の宝庫』(The Fujita Seiko Archive: Treasures of classical Japanese martial arts) vol. 3 (November 11–17, 1985).

Nagazumi Yasuaki and Shimada Isao, eds. (1961). *Hōgen monogatari, Heiji monogatari*『保元物語・平治物語』(Tale of the disorder in the Hōgen era, & tale of the disorder in the Heiji era). In *Nihon koten bungaku taikei*『日本古典文学大系』(An outline of classical Japanese literature), vol. 31. Tokyo: Iwanami Shoten.

Nakamura Akira 中村晃. (2004). *Shinkage Ryū: Kamiizumi Nobutsuna.*『新陰流 上泉信綱』. Tokyo: Bensey shuppan.

Nakamura Taisaburō 中村泰三郎. (1973). *Iai kendō: Seiteigata·tōken no chishiki·tameshigiri*『居合剣道：制定形・刀剣の知識・試し切り』(Quick-draw swordsmanship: Established forms; understanding the sword; test cutting). Tokyo: Seitōsha.

Namiki Yasushi 並木靖. (1979). *Ken-no kokoro: Katsu Kaishū to Jiki Shinkage Ryū*『剣のこころ：勝海舟と直心影流』(The spirit of swordsmanship: Katsu Kaishū and the Jiki Shinkage Ryū). Tokyo: Suzuran shobō.

______. (1979). "Gendai ni okeru budō no katsuyō." 現代に置ける武道の活用 (The practical use of martial ways in the modern age). *J & A —Jyaji ando Apiru.* (December 1979).

Natori Masatake 名取正武. (2010). Shoninki: The Ninja Manual in the Original Japanese Text『正忍記』. Bloomington: Wordclay.

Nawa Yumio 名和弓雄. (1964). *Jutte Hojō-no Kenkyū*『十手捕縄研究』(A study of truncheon and arresting-rope Arts). Tokyo: Yūzankaku, 1964.

______. (1966). *Gōmon keibatsushi*『拷問刑罰史』(A history of torture and punishment). Tokyo: Yūzankaku.

______. (1967). *Shinobi no buki*『忍びの武器』(*Ninja* weapons). Tokyo: Jinbutsu ōraisha.

______. (1972). *Ninjutsu no kenkyū: Hisshō no heihō*『忍術の研究：必勝の兵法』(Studies on *ninjutsu*: winning strategies). Tokyo: Japan Publications, Inc., 1972.

______. (1977). *Zukai kakushi buki hyakka*『図解隠し武器百科』(Illustrated encyclopedia of concealed weapons). Tokyo: Shinjinbutsu ōraisha.

______. (1982). *Ninjutsu tejina no himitsu*『忍術手品の秘密』(The secrets of *ninjutsu* sleight-of-hand methods). Tokyo: Gakken.

______. (1996). *Jutte·Hojō jiten: Edo machi bugyōshō no sōbi to taihojutsu*『十手・捕縄事典：江戸町奉行所の装備と逮捕術』(A guide to the truncheon and arresting rope: gear and arresting techniques of the Edo magistrate). Tokyo: Yūzankaku.

______. (1998a). *Kakushi buki soran*『隠し武器総覧』(An overview of concealed weapons). Tokyo: Sojinsha.

______. (1998b). *Nagashino, Shidaragahara Gassen no Shinjitsu*『長篠・設楽原合戦の真実—甲斐武田軍団はなぜ壊滅したか』(The truth behind the Nagashino and Shidaragahara battles—why were the Takeda forces defeated?). Tokyo: Yūzankaku Shuppan.

Nihon Budōkan 日本武道館. (1978). *Dai ikkai zen Nihon kobudō embu taikai* 『第一回全日本古武道演武大会』(First all-Japan classical martial arts exhibition). Tokyo: Nihon Budokan.

______. (1979). *Dai nikai zen Nihon kobudō embu taikai* 『第二回全日本古武道演武大会』(Second all-Japan classical martial arts exhibition). Tokyo: Nihon Budokan.

______. (1980). *Dai sankai zen Nihon kobudō embu taikai* 『第三回全日本古武道演武大会』(Third all-Japan classical martial arts exhibition). Tokyo: Nihon Budokan.

______. (1981). *Dai yonkai zen Nihon kobudō embu taikai* 『第四回全日本古武道演武大会』(Fourth all-Japan classical martial arts exhibition). Tokyo: Nihon Budokan.

______. (1988). *Dai jūikkai zen Nihon kobudō embu taikai* 『第十一回全日本古武道演武大会』(Eleventh all-Japan classical martial arts exhibition). Tokyo: Nihon Budokan.

______. (1991). *Dai jūyonkai zen Nihon kobudō embu taikai* 『第十四回全日本古武道演武大会』(Fourteenth all-Japan classical martial arts exhibition). Tokyo: Nihon Budokan.

Nihon Kobudō Kyōkai 日本古武道協会. (1989). *Nihon Kobudō sōran* 『日本古武道総覧：日本古武道協会十周年記念編集』(A comprehensive view of classical Japanese martial arts: Nihon Kobudō Kyōkai tenth anniversary commemorative collection). Tokyo: Shimaza shobō.

Nihon Kobudō Shinkōkai 日本古武道振興會. (1980). *Shin-ei.* 『真鋭』(The cutting edge). Supplement. Tokyo: Nihon kobudō shinkōkai.

______.(1985). *Nihon kobudō taikai: Nihon Kobudō Shinkōkai sōritsu gojūnen kinen* 『日本古武道大会：日本古武道振興会創立五十年記念』(Japanese classical martial arts convention commemorating the fiftieth anniversary of the Nihon Kobudō Shinkōkai). Tokyo: Nihon *Kobudō Shinkōkai.*

______.(1990). *Nihon kobudō taikai: Nihon Kobudō shinkōkai sōritsu gojūgonen kinen* 『日本古武道大会：日本古武道振興会創立五十五年記念』(Japanese classical martial arts convention commemorating the fifty-fifth anniversary of the Nihon Kobudō Shinkōkai). Tokyo: Nihon *Kobudō Shinkōkai*.

Nishioka Tsuneo 西岡常夫. (1984). *Shimizu Takaji Katsuyasu Sensei o omou: Shindō Musō Ryū jōdō shihan* 『清水隆次克泰先生を想う：神道夢想流杖道師範』(Remembering Shimizu Takaji Katsuyasu Sensei: Master of Shindō Musō Ryū *jōdō*). Tokyo. Privately published.

______. (1989). *Budō shiron: jōdō jikai* 『武道試論 杖道自戒』(Preliminary essays on martial arts: *Jōdō* self-discipline). Tokyo: Shimazu shobō.

Odagiri Ichiun 小田切一雲. (c. late seventeenth century). *Sekiun sensei heijutsu dempōshu* 『夕雲先生兵術伝法書』(Traditional combative methods of my teacher, Sekiun).

Odawara Shiritsu Toshokan 小田原市立図書館. (1985). "Fujita Seiko bunko tenjimokuroku" 「藤田西湖文庫展示目録 特別集書」(Special collection: A catalog of the Fujita Seiko Archive). *Fujita Seiko bunkoten: Nihon kobudō kenkyū no hōko* 『藤田西湖文庫展: 日本古武道研究の宝庫』(The Fujita Seiko Archive: Treasures of classical Japanese martial arts) Vol. 3 (November 11–17, 1985).

Okabe Shūzō 岡部周三. (1975). *Namboku-chō no kyozō to jitsuzō: Taiheiki no rekishigaku-teki kōsatsu.* 『南北朝の虚像と実像—太平記の歴史学的考察』(Image and reality during the Northern and Southern Courts period: An historical investigation of the *Taiheiki*). Tokyo: Yūzankaku, 1975.

Okada Osamu 岡田脩. (1979). *Rikutō & Sanryaku*『六韜・三略』(The *Liu-t'ao* [Six Strategies] and The *San-lüeh* [Three Briefs]). Translation of the texts into Japanese alongside the original Chinese. Chūgoku koten shinsho. Tokyo: Meitoku shuppansha.

Ōnishi Hidetaka大西英隆. (1956). *Yamada Jirokichi Sensei no shōgai*『山田次朗吉先生の生涯』(The life of Sensei Yamada Jirokichi). Tokyo: Tōbunsha.

Ōno, Kazuaki 大野一英. (1975). *Kokoro no heihō*『こころの兵法』(The essence of martial strategy). Tokyo: Roppō shuppansha.

Osano Jun 小佐野淳. (2001). *Koryū bugei chō*『古流武芸帖』(A notebook on classical Japanese martial arts). Tokyo: Airyūdō.

______. (2006). [*Gaisetsu*] *Bugeisha*『概説武芸者』(Martial artists—an outline). Tokyo: Shinkigensha.

______. (2007). [*Zusetsu*] *Bukijutsu*『図説武器術』(Weapons arts—illustrated). Tokyo: Shinkigensha.

Otofuji Ichizō and Matsui Kenji 乙藤市蔵·松井健二. (1994). *Tenshinshō-den Shindō Musō Ryū*『天真正伝神道夢想流』. Hatagaya: Shōshinsha.

Ozawa Ichio 小沢 一雄. (1985). *Iaidō hikkei—kiso chishiki kara shōdan shinsa made*『居合道必携—基礎知識から昇段審査まで』 (Iaidō manual—from basic knowledge to promotion examinations). Tokyo: Taiikku to Supōtsu Shuppansha.

Saitō Satoshi 斎藤聰. (1982). "Shurikenjutsu"「手裏剣術」(The combative art of throwing darts and small blades). In *Nihon budō taikei*, edited by Imamura Yoshio, vol. 7. Tokyo: Dōbōsha.

______. (1985). "Saigo no ninja: Fujita Seiko Sensei"「最後の忍者 藤田西湖先生」(Fujita Seiko: The last *ninja*). *Fujita Seiko bunkoten: Nihon kobudō kenkyū no hōko*『藤田西湖文庫展：日本古武道研究の宝庫』(The Fujita Seiko Archive: Treasures of classical Japanese martial arts) vol. 3 (November 11–17, 1985).

______. (1986). A unique binder of documents compiled by Saitō Satoshi and presented to David and Margie Hall in 1986 including:

- "Shurikenjutsu"「手裏剣術」(The combative art of throwing darts and small blades). (1982). In *Nihon budō taikei*『日本武道大系』(An outline of Japanese martial arts) vol. 7. Dōbōsha Shuppan Hakkō 同朋舎出版発行. (Personally annotated by Saitō Satoshi.)
- "Shurikenjutsu"「手裏剣術」. (Undated). Short article with illustrations from *Chigen Imagawa Ryū Densho*「智元今川流伝書」.
- "Uchihō"「打法」(Throwing methods). (Undated). Short article with illustrations.
- Annotated photographs.

Sasaki Kazusuke 佐々木一介. (1991). "Kiaijutsu to chōikihō"「気合術と調息法」(The combative art of *kiai* and breath control methods). *Hiden koryū bujutsu*『秘伝古流武術』(The magazine of secret transmissions of classical martial arts schools) no. 6 (April 1991).

Sasama Yoshihiko 笹間良彦. (1987). *Nihon katchū daikan*『日本甲冑大鑑』(The great illustrated dictionary of Japanese arms and armor). Tokyo: Gogatsu Shobō.

______. (1982). *Zusetsu nihon budō jiten.*『図説日本武道辞典』(Illustrated dictionary of Japanese martial arts and ways). Tokyo: Kashiwa Shobō.

______. (1970). *Zukan nihon no gunsō.*『図鑑日本の軍装』(The illustrated picture book of Japanese martial dress and equipment), 2 vols. Tokyo: Yūzankaku.

Sasamori Junzō 笹森順造. (1986). *Ittō Ryū Gokui*『一刀流極意』(The secrets of the Ittō Ryū). Tokyo: Taiiku to Supōtsu Shuppansha.

Satō Yoshiki 佐藤良樹 and Nakamiya Yoshio 中宮好郎. (1970). *Nihontō no horimono*『日本刀の彫物』(Japanese sword engraving). Tokyo: Kōgei Shuppan.

Sennohara Yasukata 千原靖方. (2007). *Ittōryū kaidenshi*『一刀流皆伝史』(A history of the Ittō Ryū *kaiden*). Nagareyama City: Ronshobō Shuppan.

Shimizu Takaji 清水隆次. (1940). *Jōdō kyōhan—kihon rengi kaisetsu*『杖道教範—基本錬技解説』(*Jōdō* textbook: An explanation of basic training methods). Reprint, Tokyo: Shimazu shobō, 1988.

Shimokawa Ushio 下川潮. (1925). *Kendō no hattatsu*『劍道の發達』(The development of *kendō*). Reprint, Dai Ichi Shobō, 1985.

Shinzato Katsuhiko 新里勝彦. (2008). "Kojō Ryū・Kugusuku Ryū"「湖城流(こじょうりゅう・クグスクりゅう)」. In *Okinawa karate kobudō jiten*, edited by Takamiyagi *et al*. Tokyo: Hakushobō.

Shioda Gōzo 塩田剛三. (1967). *Aikidō nyūmon*『合気道入門』(Introduction to *aikidō*). Sports Graphic [series]. Tokyo: Tsuru Shobō.

Shishida Fumiaki 志々田文明. (1992). *Kenkoku Daigaku ni okeru budō: kagai katsudō*「建国大学における武道・課外活動」(Extracurricular *budo* activities at Kenkoku University: Budo education at Kenkoku University in Manchuria, Part II). In *Waseda Daigaku ningen kagaku kenkyū*〔早稲田大学人間科学研究〕, vol.5, no.1 (1992 0325).

Shoda Seiji 諸田政治. (1983). *Kensei Kamiizumi Nobutsuna shōden*『剣聖上泉信綱詳伝』(A detailed biography of the sword-saint Kamiizumi Nobutsuna). Vol. 2 of *Kamitsuke kenjutsu shi* 上毛剣術史 (History of the combative swordsmanship of Kamitsuke [Kōzuke]). Maebashi: Kankodō.

Suzuki Masaya 鈴木眞哉. (2000). *Katana to kubitori: Sengoku kassen isetsu*『刀と首取り—戦国合戦異説』(Swords and head-taking: Another view of Sengoku-period battles). Tokyo: Heibonsha.

Takahashi Ken'ichi 高橋賢一. (1973). *Buke no kamon to hatajirushi*『武家の家紋と旗印』(Family crests and battle standards of the warrior families). Tokyo: Akita shoten.

Takagi Ichinosuke 高木市之助, *et al*. (1932–1957). *Nihon koten bungaku taikei*『日本古典文学大系』(An outline of classical Japanese literature). Tokyo: Iwanami shoten.

Takamiyagi Shigeru 高宮城繁, Shinzato Katsuhiko 新里勝彦, and Nakamoto Masahiro 仲本政博. (2008). *Okinawa karate kobudō jiten*『沖縄空手古武道事典』(A dictionary of Okinawan *karate* and classical weapons arts). Tokyo: Hakushobō.

Tominaga Yoshimatsu 富永好松. (1986). *Hiradohan no bugei kyōiku: Matasuura Seizan o chūshin to shite*『平戸藩の武芸教育：松浦静山を中心として』(Martial-arts education in Hirado domain: Focus on Matsuura Seizan). Nagasaki: Nagasaki shuppan bunka kyōkai.

Tsukamoto Zenryū 塚本善隆. (1942). *Shina bukkyōshi kenkyū, Hoku-Gi hen*『支那佛教史研究・北魏篇』(An investigation of Chinese Buddhist history: The Northern Wei). Reprint, Shimizu Kōbundō, 1969.

Tsuruyama Terumizu 鶴山晃瑞. (1975). *Zukai Kōchi: Aikidō*『図解コーチ合気道』(Illustrated coach [series]: *Aikidō*). Tokyo: Seibidō Publications.

Watanabe Akira 渡辺誠 and Kikuchi Tōta 菊池東太. (1978). "Ten Ryū 天流." *Kendō Nihon*『剣道日本』, (October 1978).

Watanabe Ichirō 渡辺一郎, ed. (1979). *Budō no meicho*『武道の名著』(Masterpieces of Japanese martial arts). Tokyo: Tōkyō Kopii Shuppanbu.

______, ed. (1990). *Budō densho shūei*『武道伝書聚英』, vols. 1 & 2. Utsunomiya: Utsunomiya Daigaku Kyōiku-bu 宇都宮大学教育部.

______. (1990). Nihon kobudō taikai: Nihon Kobudō shinkōkai sōritsu gojūgonen kinen『日本古武道大会：日本古武道振興会創立五十五年記念』(Japanese classical martial arts convention commemorating the fifty-fifth anniversary of the Nihon Kobudō Shinkōkai). Tokyo: Nihon Kobudō Shinkōkai.

Watanabe Tadashige 渡辺忠成. (1979). *Shinkage Ryū nyūmon*『新陰流入門』(An introduction to the Shinkage Ryū). Tokyo: Shinkage ryū heihōkai.

Watanabe Tadatoshi 渡辺忠敏. (1974). *Yagyū Ryū heihō kuden kikigaki*『柳生流兵法口伝聞書』(Verbatim notes on the oral transmissions of Yagyū Ryū strategy). Kawagoe: Shinkage Ryū heihō marobashikai shuppanbu.

Watanabe Tadatoshi 渡辺忠敏 and Watanabe Tadashige 渡辺忠成. (1969). *Shinkage Ryū heihō tachiden*『新陰流兵法太刀伝』(Traditional sword techniques and strategy of the Shinkage Ryū). Kawagoe: Shinkage Ryū heihō marobashikai shuppanbu.

Watatani Kiyoshi 綿谷雪. (1961). *Nihon bugei shōden*『日本武藝小傳』(Short biographies from Japanese martial arts). Edited and translated by Watatani Kiyoshi. Tokyo: Jinbutsu ōraisha.

______. (1964). *Jutsu*『術』(The [esoteric] arts). Tokyo: Sei'abō.

______. (1967). *[Zusetsu] Kobudōshi*『図説古武道史』(A History of Japanese Martial Arts—Illustrated). Tokyo: Sei'abō.

______. (1971). *Nihon kengō 100 sen*『日本剣豪100選』(One hundred Japanese master swordsmen). Tokyo: Akita shoten.

______. (1985). "Kengōjiten"『剣豪辞典』(Dictionary of master swordsmen). In *Rekishi to tabi: Nihon kengō sōran*『歴史と旅：日本剣豪総覧』(History and travels: Japanese master swordsmen), edited by Suzuki Akira 鈴木亨. Tokyo: Akita shoten.

Watatani Kiyoshi and Yamada Tadashi. (1969). *Bugei ryū-ha daijiten*『武芸流派大事典』(Dictionary of [Japanese] martial traditions). Tokyo: Shinjinbutsu ōraisha.

______. (1978). *Bugei ryū-ha daijiten*『武芸流派大事典』(Dictionary of [Japanese] martial traditions). Tokyo: Tōkyō kopī.

Yagyū Genchō 柳生厳長. (1957). *Shōden Shinkage Ryū* 正傳新陰流 (The authentic record of the Yagyū Shinkage Ryū). Tokyo: Dainihon yūbenkai kōdansha. Reprint, Tokyo: Shimazu shobō, 1989.

Yagyū Munenori 柳生宗矩. (1985). *Heihō kadensho* 兵法家伝書 (The family transmission on strategy). Edited by Watanabe Ichirō 渡辺一郎. Tokyo: Iwanami bunko.

Yamada Jirokichi 山田次朗吉. (1927). *Kashima Shinden Jiki Shinkage Ryū*『鹿島神傳直心影流』. Tokyo: Hitotsubashi kenyūkai. Reprint, Tokyo: Tōkyō kopī, 1976.

______. (1925). *Nippon kendōshi*『日本劍道史』(A history of Japanese swordsmanship). Tokyo: Hitotsubashi kenyūkai. Reprint,Tokyo: Tōkyō kopī, 1976.

Yamashita Yajūrō 山下 弥十郎. (1972). *Komusō: Fukeshū Reihōji no kenkyū*『虚無僧:普化宗鈴法寺の研究』(Monks of emptiness: An investigation of the Fuke sect and the Reihō temple). Tokyo: Tamakyōdo no Kenkyūkai.

■ Reference Works

Kokusho sōmokuroku『國書總目録』(Catalog of national [Japanese] works [published prior to the Meiji era]). (1963). 9 vols. Tokyo: Iwanami shoten.

Mikkyō daijiten『密教大辭典』(Encyclopedia of [East Asian] Tantrism [Esoteric Buddhism]). (1969). 6 vols. Kyoto: Hōzōkan.

Miyaji Naokazu･Saiki Ariyoshi 宮地直一・佐伯有義. *Shintō diajiten*『神道大辞典』(Large dictionary of Shintō). (1937). Tokyo: Heibonsha. Reprint, Tokyo: Rinsen shoten, 1986.

Mochizuki Shinkō 望月信享. (1936). *Mochizuki Bukkyō daijiten*『望月佛教大辭典』(Mochizuki encyclopedia of Buddhism). 10 vols. Tokyo: Sekai seiten. Reprint, 1988.

Morohashi Tetsuji 諸橋轍次. (1958). *Dai Kan-Wa jiten*『大漢和辭典』(Great Sino-Japanese character dictionary). 13 vols. Tokyo: Taishukan shoten. Reprint, 1984.

Nakamura Hajime 中村元. *Bukkyōgo daijiten*『佛教語大辭典』(Great dictionary of Buddhist terminology). (1975). 3 vols. Tokyo: Tōkyō shoseki.

Sawa Ryūkei 佐和隆研. *Mikkyō jiten*『密教辭典』(Dictionary of [East Asian] Tantrism [Esoteric Buddhism]). (1975). Kyoto: Hōzōkan.

Shinmura Izuru 新村出, ed. (1981). *Kōjien*『広辞苑』(A broad garden of words). Revised second edition. Tokyo: Iwanami shoten.

Ui Hakuju 宇井伯寿. (1938). *Bukkyō jiten*『佛教辭典』(Dictionary of Buddhism). Eighth printing, Daitō shuppansha, 1974.

■ Buddhist and Taoist Canonical Works

Taishō shinshu daizōkyō『大正新修大藏經』(The new Taishō-era compilation of the Buddhist canon). (1924–1934). Edited by Takakusu Junjiro and Watanabe Kaigyoku. 100 vols. Tokyo: Taishō issaikyō kankōkai.

Zhengtong daozang『正統道藏』(The Daoist canon). (1924–1926). Shanghai: Commercial Press.

■ Bilingual Reference Works

Davids, T.W. Rhys and William Stede. (1925). *The Pali Text Society's Pali-English Dictionary*. Chipstead, Surrey: The Pali Text Society.

Edgerton, Franklin, editor. (1953). *Buddhist Hybrid Sanskrit Grammar and Dictionary*. 2 vols. Yale University Press. Reprint, Delhi: Motilal Banarsidass, 1977.

Malalasekera, G.P., editor. (1961). *Encyclopaedia of Buddhism*. Ceylon: The Government Press of Sri Lanka..

■ Reference and Canonical Works

Nelson, Andrew N. (1966). *The Modern Reader's Japanese-English Character Dictionary.* Revised Edition. Tokyo: Charles E. Tuttle.

Soothill, William Edward and Lewis Hodous. (1935). *A Dictionary of Chinese Buddhist Terms—with Sanskrit and English Equivalents and a Sanskrit-Pali Index.* London: Kegan Paul, Trench, Trubner & Co., Ltd. Reprint, Taipei: Ch'eng Wen Publishing Co., 1975.

Torao, Toshiya and Delmer M. Brown, editors. (1987). *Chronology of Japan.* 『日本の歴史』. Tokyo: Business Intercommunications Inc. BII.

Informants
Interview, Conversations, Correspondence

Amdur, Ellis. Licensed in both Araki Ryū and Toda Ha Bukō Ryū.
(1977–2009). Conversations and correspondence.

Armstrong, Hunter. Director, International Hoplology Society.
(1980–2009). Conversations and correspondence.
(1983–1993). Extensive collaboration, International Hoplology Society.

Blacker, Professor Carmen (1924–1909). Japan scholar at the University of Cambridge.
(1989). Personal correspondence and telephone interviews, Tokyo, Japan.

Chambers, Quintin. Shintō Musō Ryū Shomokuroku under Shimizu Takaji; Shintō Musō Ryū Menkyo Kaiden under Nishioka Tsuneo; Katori Shintō Mokuroku under Ōtake Risuke Shihan.
(1974–2009). Personal correspondence, conversations, interviews, training sessions.

Draeger, Donn F. (1922–1982). Career Marine; long-time judoist (over 50 years of experience); Shindō Musō Ryū Gomokuroku under Shimizu Takaji/Shindō Musō Ryū Menkyo under Kaminoda Tsunemori/Katori Shintō Ryū Menkyo Kyōshi under Iizasa Yasusada; martial arts researcher, historian and prolific writer; founder of the International Hoplological Research Center (IHRC). Author Robert W. Smith referred to him as "...one of the great samurai of the last half of the twentieth century." (Smith, 1999: 85). Draeger's impact on Japanese classical martial arts systems during the 1960s and 1970s—both in his explanation of these systems to the world outside of Japan and his mastery of the systems in Japan—was powerful in that he opened doors for non-Japanese into many of the classical systems mentioned in this *Encyclopedia*.
(1972–1982). Personal correspondence, conversations, interviews, training sessions.

Hayes, Richard. Field hoplologist.
(1983–1997). Extensive personal correspondence regarding the nature of combative behavior and performance.

Higuchi Sadahiro. Twenty-fourth generation headmaster, Maniwa Nen Ryū.
(1980–1981). Various correspondence with author.
(1985–1990). Occasional interviews and discussions.

Ichishima, Rev. Masao. Professor, Taishō University.
(1975–2009). Personal correspondence, conversations, interviews, training sessions.

Irie Kōhei. Professor, Tsukuba University. Member of the Kinyōbikai.
(1985–1990). Occasional interviews and discussions.

Itō Masayuki. Nineteenth-generation headmaster, Jiki Shinkage Ryū.
(1978–1981; 1985–1988.) Weekly discussions with author. Various lectures.

Karunakaran s/o R. Chindan. Shindō Musō Ryū *Okuirisho* under Shimizu Takaji; recipient of the charter for the Malaysian Jōdō Federation from Shimizu Takaji; personal disciple and recipient of the Shindō Musō Ryū tradition from Donn F. Draeger.
(1978; 1989). Personal conversations and direct training.
(1978–2009). Correspondence.

Katō Isao. Eighth-generation headmaster of the Owari Kan Ryū; twenty-first-generation successor of the Shinkage Ryū through Kambe Kinshichi.
(1986). Interview.

Knutsen, Roald M. Seventh *dan* in *kendō* and 30+ years practitioner of Kashima Shintō Ryū. Author of several books on Japanese martial culture.
(1979–1982; 2009). Personal correspondence.

McHoul, Donald J. Long time *karate* student of Uechi Kanei.
(2008–2009). Interviews and conversations.

Mutō, Masao (1924–2001). Tenth-generation headmaster of the Yagyū Shingan Ryū; generation successor of the Yagyū Shinkage Ryū. Member of the Kinyōbikai.
(1985–1990). Weekly interviews and discussions.
(1987). Monthly interviews.
(1991–1995, 1998). Yearly phone interviews.

Namiki Yasushi (1926–1999). Eighteenth-generation headmaster, Jiki Shinkage Ryū.
(1978–1981; 1985-1988.) Weekly discussions. Various lectures.
(1981–1985). Various correspondence.

Nitta Suzuyo (1923–2009). Nineteenth-generation headmaster, Toda Ha Bukō Ryū.
(1986–1990). Interviews and conversations in Japan.

Ōtake, Risuke. Chief instructor, Tenshinshō-den Katori Shintō Ryū.
(1976). Lectures and conversations at University of Hawaii.
(1978–1981). Conversations in Japan.
(1986–1990). Interviews and conversations in Japan.

Ōtsubo Shihō, progenitor of the Ōtsubo line of the Yagyū Shinkage Ryū; twentieth-generation successor of the Yagyū Shinkage Ryū.
(1980–1981). Interviews in Japan.

Relnick, Phil. Trained in Kōdōkan Jūdō (4th dan) from 1957 to 1980; Shintō Musō Ryū Shomokuroku under Shimizu Takaji; Shintō Musō Ryū Menkyo Kaiden under Nishioka Tsuneo; Katori Shintō Ryū Shidōsha Menkyo under Ōtake Risuke Shihan. Relnick was active in the early International Hoplology Research Center with Donn F. Draeger in the late 1970s and early 1980s. He left the organization upon Draeger's death in 1982 and formed JMAS (the Japan Martial Arts Society) in 1983. From 1982 until 1993 he was president of the International Jodo Federation. He currently teaches Shintō Musō Ryū at his Shintōkan *dōjō* (神稲館道場) in Seattle, and is the only person in Tenshinshō-den Katori Shintō Ryū to obtain permission from headmaster Iizasa Sensei to teach that combative school in the United States.
(1977–2009). Personal correspondence, conversations, interviews, training sessions.

Saitō, Satoshi, Fifth headmaster, Nigishi Ryū.
(1986–1990). Conversations and interviews.

Sasama Yoshihiko.
(1986–1990). Conversations and interviews in Japan.

Saso, Michael. Professor, University of Hawaii at Manoa, Honolulu.
(1974–1985). Conversations and lectures, phone conversations.

Shimizu Takaji. Twenty-fifth headmaster, Shindō Musō Ryū.
(1977–1978). Conversations and interviews in Japan.

Skoss, Meik. Licensed practitioner of Toda Ha Bukō Ryū, Tendo Ryū, Shintō Musō Ryū. (1977–2009). Conversations and correspondence.

Strickmann, Michel. Professor. University of California, Berkeley. (1981–1994). Conversations and lectures, phone conversations, correspondence.

Tōgō Shigemasa. Eleventh headmaster of the Jigen Ryū. (1981–1983). Correspondence.

Watanabe Ichirō. Professor, Tsukuba University. Member of Kinyōbikai. (1985–1990). Interviews and discussions.

Yagyū Nobuharu. (1979–1981). Twenty-first headmaster, Owari Yagyū Shinkage Ryū. Various correspondence.
(1985–1990). Monthly interviews, Tokyo, Japan.
(1991–1996). Yearly phone interviews.

INDICES

Chinese Character (Kanji 漢字) Stroke-Order Index/Kana Index

一画

二画

三　画

四　画

五　画

六　画

八　画

九　画

十一画

十二画

十三画

十五画

十六画

十七画

十八画

十九画

二十画

二十一画

二十二画

二十三画

二十四画

二十五画

KANA ONLY AND KANA PREFIX

ひらがな

カタカナ

Chinese Reference Index
Pinyin (Wade-Giles) {Postal Map} Romanization

G

H

J

K

L

M

N

O

P

Q

R

S

T

W

X

Y

Z

Chinese Reference Index
Wade-Giles (Pinyin) {Postal Map} Romanization

H

I

J

K

L

M

N

O

P

S

T

W

Y

Sanskrit Reference Index

General Reference Index

A

B

C

H

I

J

K

L

M

N

O

P

Q

R

S

T

U

V

W

X

Y

Z